THIRD EDITION

Johnson & Stoskopf's

COMPARATIVE HEALTH SYSTEMS

A Global Perspective

Leiyu Shi, DrPH, MBA, MPA
Professor
Bloomberg School of Public Health, Johns Hopkins University
Director
Johns Hopkins Primary Care Policy Center
Johns Hopkins Asia-Pacific Center for Hospital Management and Leadership Research
Baltimore, Maryland

Richard G. Greenhill, DHA, HACP-CMS, CPHQ, PMP, FACHE
Chief Transformation Officer
Quality Insights
Charleston, West Virginia

JONES & BARTLETT
LEARNING

World Headquarters
Jones & Bartlett Learning
25 Mall Road
Burlington, MA 01803
978-443-5000
info@jblearning.com
www.jblearning.com

Jones & Bartlett Learning books and products are available through most bookstores and online booksellers. To contact Jones & Bartlett Learning directly, call 800-832-0034, fax 978-443-8000, or visit our website, www.jblearning.com.

Substantial discounts on bulk quantities of Jones & Bartlett Learning publications are available to corporations, professional associations, and other qualified organizations. For details and specific discount information, contact the special sales department at Jones & Bartlett Learning via the above contact information or send an email to specialsales@jblearning.com.

28943-5

Production Credits
Vice President, Innovative Learning and Assessment Solutions: Ada Woo
Senior Director, Content Production and Delivery: Christine Emerton
Director, Product: Melissa Kleeman-Moy
Product Manager: Sophie Fleck Teague
Senior Outsourcing Specialist: Carol Brewer Guerrero
Content Manager: Jennifer Lynn
Content Coordinator: Samantha Gillespie
Manager, Intellectual Properties and Content Production: Kristen Rogers
Content Production Manager: John Fuller
Senior Digital Project Specialist: Angela Dooley
Senior Marketing Manager: Susanne Walker
Director, Product Fulfillment: Aaron McKinzie
Purchasing Manager: Wendy Kilborn
Composition: Exela Technologies
Cover Design: MPS Limited
Text Design: MPS Limited
Media Development Editor: Faith Brosnan
Rights Specialist: James Fortney
Cover Image (Title Page, Part Opener, Chapter Opener): © Sean Gladwell/Moment/Getty Images
Printing and Binding: Lakeside Book Company

Library of Congress Cataloging-in-Publication Data
Names: Shi, Leiyu, editor. | Greenhill, Richard G., editor.
Title: Johnson & Stoskopf's comparative health systems : a global perspective / [edited by] Leiyu Shi, Richard G. Greenhill.
Other titles: Comparative health systems (Johnson) | Comparative health systems
Description: Third edition. | Burlington, MA : Jones & Bartlett Learning, [2026] | Preceded by Comparative health systems : a global perspective / [edited by] James Johnson, Carleen Stoskopf, Leiyu Shi. Second edition. [2018] | Includes bibliographical references and index.
Identifiers: LCCN 2024033474 | ISBN 9781284289268 (paperback)
Subjects: MESH: Delivery of Health Care–organization & administration | Health Policy | Internationality | Cross-Cultural Comparison | BISAC: BUSINESS & ECONOMICS / Accounting / Financial
Classification: LCC RA418 | NLM W 84.1 | DDC 362.1–dc23/eng/20241209
LC record available at https://lccn.loc.gov/2024033474

6048

Printed in the United States of America
29 28 27 26 25 10 9 8 7 6 5 4 3 2 1

Brief Contents

European Region

Middle East and African Region

Asia and Pacific Region

Bonus eBook Chapters

The bonus chapters are available in the Navigate eBook that accompanies this text.

Contents

Bonus eBook Chapters

The bonus chapters are available in the Navigate eBook that accompanies this text.

Foreword

By James A. Johnson, PhD, MPA, MSc

Students in the United States, and in many other countries as well, too often have a somewhat limited view of health care, health systems, and population health, many times failing to see beyond their own borders. This is especially so when we consider the myriad health systems that have emerged in the widest range of cultures and social contexts imaginable. Each of the countries of the world has a responsibility to its citizens and residents to provide for health and well-being. Some take this responsibility seriously and others do not. Some have severe resource constraints and others do not. Given the diversity of socio-political circumstances and variations in culture and history, we now see many variations and differences around the globe.

The World Health Organization (WHO), with its nearly 200 member countries, has stated that a well-functioning health system working in harmony is built on having trained and motivated health workers and leaders, a well-maintained infrastructure, and a reliable supply of medicines and technologies, backed by adequate funding, strong health plans, and evidence-based policies.

Students in health administration, public health, and health policy programs, at all levels, would be wise to broaden their perspectives by undertaking study of the health systems around the world. By studying comparative health systems, students can expect to gain a better understanding of the global context of health, along with valuable knowledge and insights into various health systems that function in disparate social, political, and economic conditions across countries.

More specifically students can expect to accomplish the following in such a course or program of study:

Learning from others—the health systems of the world can all serve as laboratories of learning. Each one is a social experiment attempting to accomplish certain goals. In the United States, for example, these goals are articulated in *Healthy People 2030*. We learned about primary care centers from South Africa and national health insurance from Germany. Likewise, there are many health systems in the world today that are more efficient and have better outcomes than that in the United States. We only have to look to our neighbor, Canada, to see such an example.

The way of knowledge—we see comparative studies in other fields such as science and medicine. For example, an experiment, tested procedure, or new technology developed in one country can be utilized or imported by another country. It is no surprise that many Nobel Prizes are won by people working in international teams.

Our shared global village—we live in an increasingly interdependent world that "shrinks" in the face of rapid developments in connective technologies such as telemedicine, social media, and distance education. This also includes the ability to cross borders and span oceans in real time for meetings, diagnostic consultations, or disease surveillance. As is often stated, "disease respects no borders" and I suggest that our minds not create walls, but vistas instead.

Urgency of systems thinking—the future belongs to systems thinkers. By studying comparative health systems, students take a big step toward inculcating this valuable skill and perspective into their own future careers. They enhance their own capabilities in the widest range of domains, including management, leadership, and policy, by better understanding interconnections and the potential impact of unintended consequences.

The future is now—whether one looks at climate change, pandemics, the aging global population, or any number of other challenges heretofore relegated as "the future," we are facing all of these now and will continue to do so in the coming decades. There is a certain urgency for students and faculty to better know the world they occupy. Health challenges are real and present. Health systems are part of the solution, and the ability for these systems to effectively adapt can be a matter of life and death.

Innovation is unexpected—the next most salient innovation in health care, medical science, public health, or health policy can occur anywhere at any time. Health systems need to innovate in order to survive, thrive, and assure their nation's health. The innovations can be small or large, but when taken from a system's thinking perspective, the ripple effect can actually be global in scope. We certainly saw this with vaccinations in the last century and will likely see many innovations that improve health outcomes in the years (or perhaps days) ahead.

It's enjoyable—studying comparative health systems is enjoyable for almost all students. I have taught this subject for more than 25 years and consistently have students tell me it was their favorite course. Many went on to extend their comparative study with courses in global health, international affairs, and study abroad experiences. The current generations in college and graduate school are eager to learn about other cultures and are predisposed to learning from divergent perspectives. There seems to be an embrace of diversity and the valuing of differences. A course in comparative health systems provides just such an enriched learning opportunity.

Keeping with the tradition of the first edition of this book, conceptualized by James Johnson and Carleen Stoskopf two decades ago, the third edition of this book, *Johnson & Stoskopf's Comparative Health Systems,* now edited by Leiyu Shi and Richard Greenhill, analyzes 30 health systems around the world, providing a very current and information-rich text for just such a meaningful learning adventure. To further underscore the timeliness of this subject matter, Columbia University professor, Jeffery Sachs, in his recent book, *Building the New American Economy: Smart, Fair, and Sustainable*, states that "Sooner or later the United States will have to learn from the better performance of Canada, Japan, and Europe, where health care coverage, affordability, and outcomes are far better than those enjoyed by Americans."

The time to learn is now and the clear path forward is through the study of comparative health systems. Enjoy!

New to the *Third Edition*

Johnson & Stoskopf's Comparative Health Systems: A Global Perspective, Third Edition addresses emerging events, advances, reforms, and challenges in the delivery of health care around the world.

- **Section Dividers:** The book is divided into two parts. Part I introduces foundational concepts of healthcare delivery systems, including health and disease, and policy and economics. In Part II, the health systems of 30 unique countries are each examined in individual chapters.

PART I

Global Health and Health Systems

CHAPTER 1	Introduction to Health Systems	2
CHAPTER 2	Global and International Health Frameworks	14
CHAPTER 3	Global Health and Disease	20
CHAPTER 4	Global Health Systems Politics, Economics, and Policy	49
CHAPTER 5	Role of International Organizations in Health Systems	66

1

- **New Chapters:** Thirteen new chapters have been included in this edition.

Chapter 3, Global Health and Disease, emphasizes the importance of integration of the healthcare system with the public health system for effective intervention in the cycles of diseases.

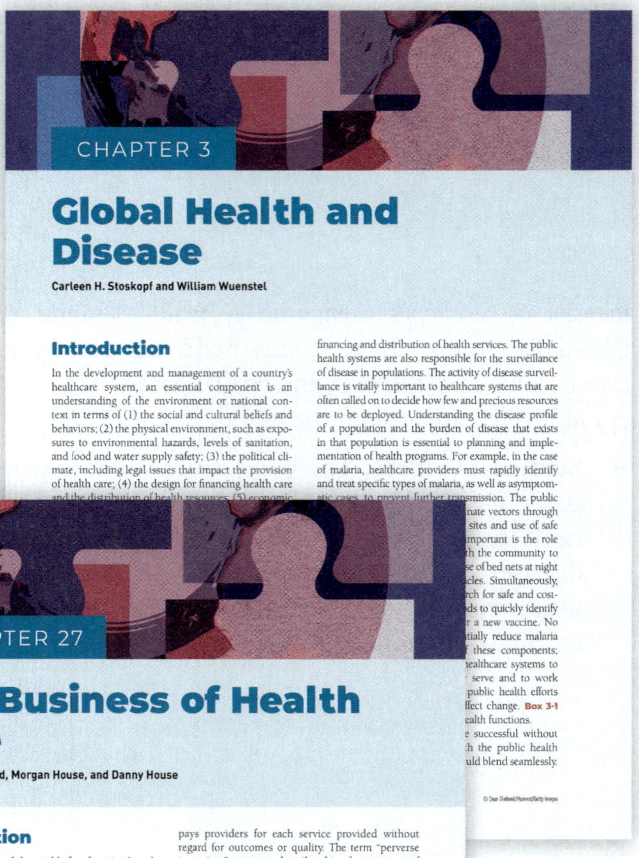

CHAPTER 3

Global Health and Disease

Carleen H. Stoskopf and William Wuenstel

Introduction

In the development and management of a country's healthcare system, an essential component is an understanding of the environment or national context in terms of (1) the social and cultural beliefs and behaviors; (2) the physical environment, such as exposures to environmental hazards, levels of sanitation, and food and water supply safety; (3) the political climate, including legal issues that impact the provision of health care; (4) the design for financing health care and the distribution of health resources; (5) economic ...

financing and distribution of health services. The public health systems are also responsible for the surveillance of disease in populations. The activity of disease surveillance is vitally important to healthcare systems that are often called on to decide how few and precious resources are to be deployed. Understanding the disease profile of a population and the burden of disease that exists in that population is essential to planning and implementation of health programs. For example, in the case of malaria, healthcare providers must rapidly identify and treat specific types of malaria, as well as asymptomatic cases, to prevent further transmission. The public ...

Chapter 27, The Business of Health Care, discusses value-based care and long-term care as it relates to the business of health care.

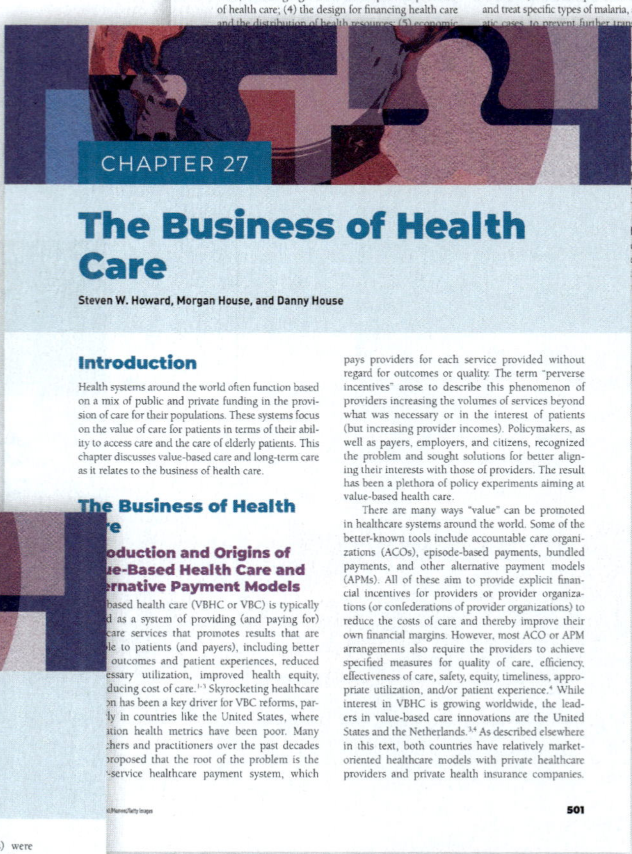

CHAPTER 27

The Business of Health Care

Steven W. Howard, Morgan House, and Danny House

Introduction

Health systems around the world often function based on a mix of public and private funding in the provision of care for their populations. These systems focus on the value of care for patients in terms of their ability to access care and the care of elderly patients. This chapter discusses value-based care and long-term care as it relates to the business of health care.

The Business of Health Care

Introduction and Origins of Value-Based Health Care and Alternative Payment Models

pays providers for each service provided without regard for outcomes or quality. The term "perverse incentives" arose to describe this phenomenon of providers increasing the volumes of services beyond what was necessary or in the interest of patients (but increasing provider incomes). Policymakers, as well as payers, employers, and citizens, recognized the problem and sought solutions for better aligning their interests with those of providers. The result has been a plethora of policy experiments aiming at value-based health care.

There are many ways "value" can be promoted in healthcare systems around the world. Some of the better-known tools include accountable care organizations (ACOs), episode-based payments, bundled payments, and other alternative payment models (APMs). All of these aim to provide explicit financial incentives for providers or provider organizations (or confederations of provider organizations) to reduce the costs of care and thereby improve their own financial margins. However, most ACO or APM arrangements also require the providers to achieve specified measures for quality of care, efficiency, effectiveness of care, safety, equity, timeliness, appropriate utilization, and/or patient experience.[4] While interest in VBHC is growing worldwide, the leaders in value-based care innovations are the United States and the Netherlands.[3,4] As described elsewhere in this text, both countries have relatively market-oriented healthcare models with private healthcare providers and private health insurance companies.

501

Chapter 29 (available in the eBook only), The Sustainable Development Goals, focuses on how the SDGs demonstrate a new understanding of the complexity and interconnection of current health and development challenges. It expands on the targets under SDGs employed in monitoring health.

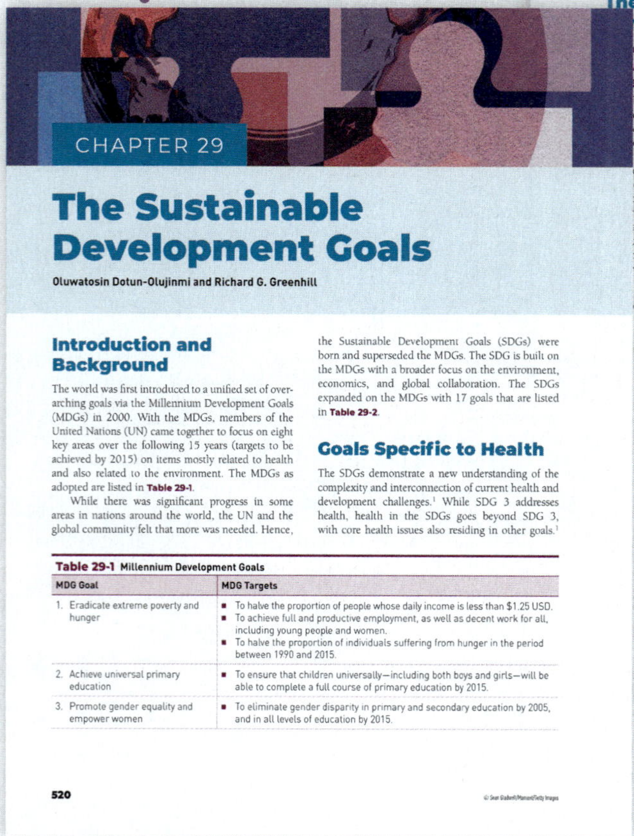

CHAPTER 29

The Sustainable Development Goals

Oluwatosin Dotun-Olujinmi and Richard G. Greenhill

Introduction and Background

The world was first introduced to a unified set of overarching goals via the Millennium Development Goals (MDGs) in 2000. With the MDGs, members of the United Nations (UN) came together to focus on eight key areas over the following 15 years (targets to be achieved by 2015) on items mostly related to health and also related to the environment. The MDGs as adopted are listed in **Table 29-1**.

While there was significant progress in some areas in nations around the world, the UN and the global community felt that more was needed. Hence, the Sustainable Development Goals (SDGs) were born and superseded the MDGs. The SDG is built on the MDGs with a broader focus on the environment, economics, and global collaboration. The SDGs expanded on the MDGs with 17 goals that are listed in **Table 29-2**.

Goals Specific to Health

The SDGs demonstrate a new understanding of the complexity and interconnection of current health and development challenges.[1] While SDG 3 addresses health, health in the SDGs goes beyond SDG 3, with core health issues also residing in other goals.[1]

Table 29-1 Millennium Development Goals

MDG Goal	MDG Targets
1. Eradicate extreme poverty and hunger	▪ To halve the proportion of people whose daily income is less than $1.25 USD. ▪ To achieve full and productive employment, as well as decent work for all, including young people and women. ▪ To halve the proportion of individuals suffering from hunger in the period between 1990 and 2015.
2. Achieve universal primary education	▪ To ensure that children universally—including both boys and girls—will be able to complete a full course of primary education by 2015.
3. Promote gender equality and empower women	▪ To eliminate gender disparity in primary and secondary education by 2005, and in all levels of education by 2015.

520

- **Ten new countries**—Cuba, Norway, Finland, Poland, Slovakia, Czech Republic, Egypt, South Africa, Taiwan, and Singapore—have been added in this third edition of the book in its endeavor to offer students an understanding of the global health systems, outcomes, and practices through comparative study.

CHAPTER 17

South Africa

Immaculate Sabelile Tenza and Yandisa Ngqangashe

CHAPTER 18

Ghana

Umar Haruna, Anthony Mwinilanaa Tampah-Naah, and Musah A. Sugri

CHAPTER 19

India

Sudha Xirasagar, Puneet Misra, and Roy Daniel

Country Description

India is the world's second most populous country with an estimated 1.39 billion people in 2023, over four times the U.S. population, and a third of the U.S. land area.[1] Viewed from a global perspective, India has 17% of the world's population, 2.45% of the global land area, and 4% of fresh-water resources.[2] It has 22 officially recognized languages, spoken in 844 different dialects rooted in two ancient indigenous languages, Sanskrit and Tamil.[3] Elements of Persian, Arabic, and English were imbibed over the course of trade relations and armed conquests. **Table 19-1** presents some key descriptive information.

Table 19-1 Country Profile—India

Nationality	India, since independence on August 15, 1947 (Adjective: Indian)
Ethnic groups	Indo-Aryan 72%, Dravidian 25%, Mongoloid/other 3% (2007)[a]
Languages[b]	Official language of the Union: Hindi Official languages for governance communications: Central government: English and Hindi State governments: English and each state's official language (22 recognized languages)
Religion	Hindu 79%, Muslim 14%, Christian 2.3%, Sikh 1.7%, Buddhist 0.7%, Jain 0.4%, other 0.8%, unspecified 0.2%[c]
Government	Parliamentary democracy, constitutional republic, union of states
Natural hazards	Severe heat waves; droughts; catastrophic rainfall and flash flooding; drought prone (68% of cultivable area); monsoon flooding (12% of land area at risk); occasional moderate- to high-intensity earthquakes (58.6% of land area at risk); cyclones and tsunami (5,700 km at risk, out of total 7,516 km of coastline); and landslides in the north/northeastern mountainous/hilly areas[d]
Environmental challenges	Deforestation, soil erosion; overgrazing; air and ground water pollution from industrial effluents and vehicle emissions; scarcity of potable water in many areas of the country
Macroeconomic Indicators	
Gross domestic product (GDP)	3.39 trillion in 2022 (current USD)[e]
Per capita GDP	International PPP* 8,379 USD in 2022 versus 5,187 USD in 2014[f]

332

CHAPTER 20

China

Ning Lu, Kuo-Cherh Huang, and Ruiling Guo

Country Description

Table 20-1 China

Nationality	Noun: Chinese (singular and plural) Adjective: Chinese
Ethnic groups	Han Chinese 91.1%, ethnic minorities 8.9% (includes Zhang, Hui, Manchu, Uighur, Miao, Yi, Tujia, Tibetan, Mongol, Dong, Buyei, Yao, Bai, Korean, Hani, Li, Kazakh, Dai, and other nationalities) (2021 est.)*
Religions	China is officially atheist. Folk religion 21.9%, Buddhist 18.2%, Christian 5.1%, Muslim 1.8%, Hindu <0.1%, Jewish <0.1%, others 0.7% (include Daoist (Taoist)), unaffiliated 52.1% (2021 est.)
Language	Standard Chinese or Mandarin (Putonghua; based on the Beijing dialect), Yue (Cantonese), Wu (Shanghainese), Minbei (Fuzhou), Minnan (Hokkien–Taiwanese), Xiang, Gan, Hakka dialects, minority languages (see "Ethnic groups" row)**
Literacy	Definition: Age 15 and over and can read and write. Total population: 99.83% Male: 98% Female: 95% (2021 est.)
Government type	Communist state
Date of independence	January 1, 1912 (Qing Dynasty replaced by the Republic of China); October 1, 1949 (People's Republic of China established)
Gross domestic product (GDP) per capita	17,600 USD (2021 est.)
Unemployment rate	4.82% (2021 est.)***
Natural hazards	Frequent typhoons (approximately five per year along southern and eastern coasts); damaging floods; tsunamis; earthquakes; droughts; land subsidence; volcanism****
Environment: current issues	Air pollution (greenhouse gases, sulfur dioxide particulates), from reliance on coal, producing acid rain; water shortages, particularly in the north; water pollution from untreated wastes; deforestation; estimated loss of one-fifth of agricultural land since 1949 to soil erosion and economic development; desertification; trade in endangered species

366

- **Country Description Table:** In Part II, all chapters begin with a table, which gives the history, size and geography, government and political system, macroeconomics (GDP, OECD), and demographics (including religion, gender, and poverty) of that country.

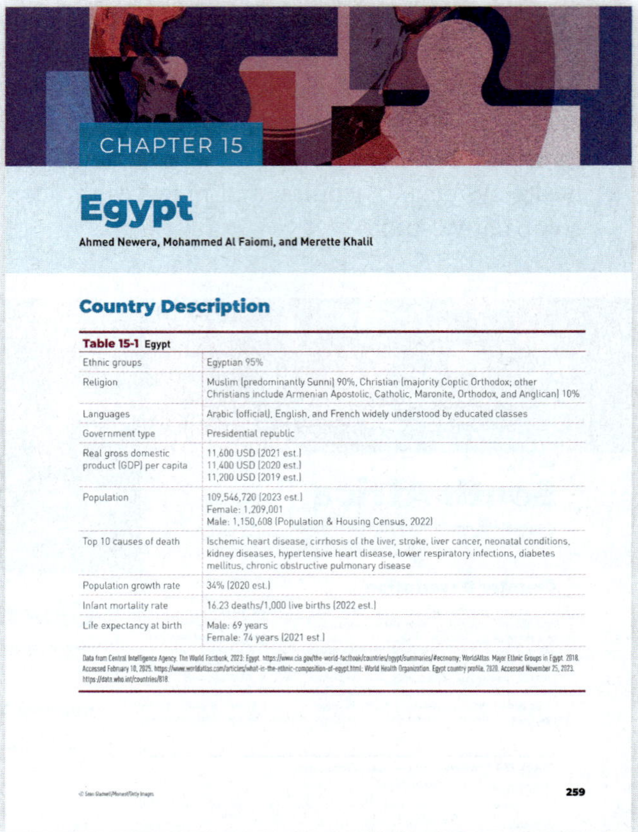

CHAPTER 15

Egypt

Ahmed Newera, Mohammed Al Faiomi, and Merette Khalil

Country Description

Table 15-1 Egypt

Ethnic groups	Egyptian 95%
Religion	Muslim [predominantly Sunni] 90%, Christian [majority Coptic Orthodox; other Christians include Armenian Apostolic, Catholic, Maronite, Orthodox, and Anglican] 10%
Languages	Arabic [official], English, and French widely understood by educated classes
Government type	Presidential republic
Real gross domestic product [GDP] per capita	11,600 USD [2021 est.] 11,400 USD [2020 est.] 11,200 USD [2019 est.]
Population	109,546,720 [2023 est.] Female: 1,209,001 Male: 1,150,608 [Population & Housing Census, 2022]
Top 10 causes of death	Ischemic heart disease, cirrhosis of the liver, stroke, liver cancer, neonatal conditions, kidney diseases, hypertensive heart disease, lower respiratory infections, diabetes mellitus, chronic obstructive pulmonary disease
Population growth rate	34% [2020 est.]
Infant mortality rate	16.23 deaths/1,000 live births [2022 est.]
Life expectancy at birth	Male: 69 years Female: 74 years [2021 est.]

Data from Central Intelligence Agency. The World Factbook, 2023: Egypt. https://www.cia.gov/the-world-factbook/countries/egypt/summaries/#economy; WorldAtlas. Major Ethnic Groups in Egypt. 2018. Accessed February 10, 2025. https://www.worldatlas.com/articles/what-is-the-ethnic-composition-of-egypt.html; World Health Organization. Egypt country profile. 2020. Accessed November 25, 2023. https://data.who.int/countries/818.

259

- *Use of Figures* to help depict complex ideas, and *Tables* to make difficult material and data more manageable and easily understood.

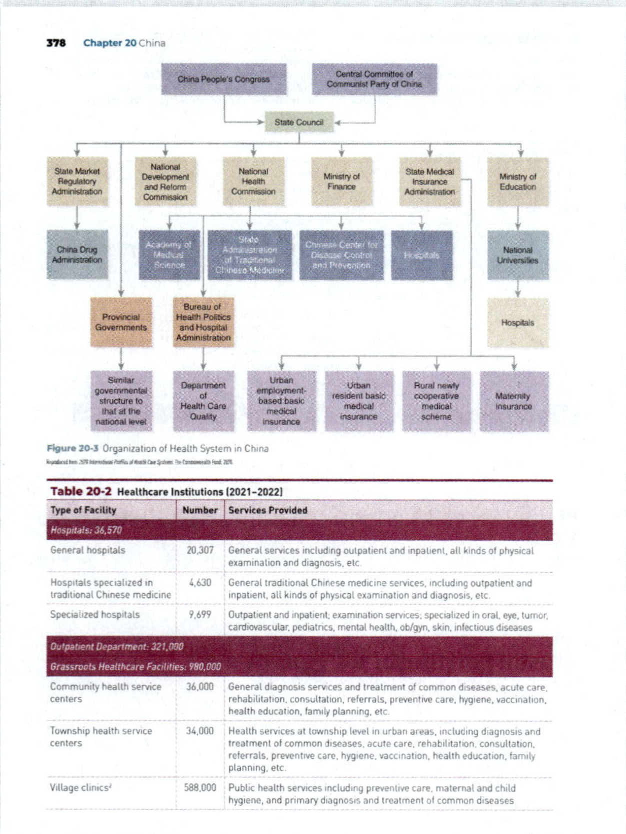

378 Chapter 20 China

Figure 20-3 Organization of Health System in China

Table 20-2 Healthcare Institutions (2021–2022)

Type of Facility	Number	Services Provided
Hospitals: 36,570		
General hospitals	20,307	General services including outpatient and inpatient, all kinds of physical examination and diagnosis, etc.
Hospitals specialized in traditional Chinese medicine	4,630	General traditional Chinese medicine services, including outpatient and inpatient, all kinds of physical examination and diagnosis, etc.
Specialized hospitals	9,699	Outpatient and inpatient; examination services; specialized in oral, eye, tumor, cardiovascular, pediatrics, mental health, ob/gyn, skin, infectious diseases
Outpatient Department: 321,000		
Grassroots Healthcare Facilities: 980,000		
Community health service centers	36,000	General diagnosis services and treatment of common diseases, acute care, rehabilitation, consultation, referrals, preventive care, hygiene, vaccination, health education, family planning, etc.
Township health service centers	34,000	Health services at township level in urban areas, including diagnosis and treatment of common diseases, acute care, rehabilitation, consultation, referrals, preventive care, hygiene, vaccination, health education, family planning, etc.
Village clinics[2]	588,000	Public health services including preventive care, maternal and child hygiene, and primary diagnosis and treatment of common diseases

- **Section on COVID-19 Pandemic:** A dedicated section examines the impact of and response to the global COVID-19 pandemic on and by the various countries' healthcare systems.

COVID-19 Pandemic **167**

care, including widespread testing and counseling, condom distribution, harm reduction programs for people who inject drugs, and the provision of antiretroviral therapy (ART) to all those who need it. As a result, Cuba has achieved an HIV prevalence rate of 0.1%, one of the lowest in the world.

Another important aspect of Cuba's HIV/AIDS response has been its focus on community-based approaches. The country has established a network of HIV/AIDS support groups, which provide education, counseling, and other services to people living with HIV/AIDS and their families. These groups are also involved in the development of policies and programs related to HIV/AIDS, ensuring that the perspectives and needs of people living with HIV/AIDS are taken into account.

Cuba's HIV/AIDS response has also been characterized by a strong commitment to research and innovation. The country has been a leader in the development of new HIV prevention technologies, including the use of pre-exposure prophylaxis (PrEP) and the development of a therapeutic vaccine for HIV. Cuba has also been actively involved in international collaborations to share its expertise and contribute to the global effort to end the HIV/AIDS epidemic.

Cuba has the lowest incidence rate of HIV/AIDS in the Caribbean, and indeed one of the lowest rates in the world. The country's commitment to universal access to prevention, care, and treatment services, community-based approaches, research and innovation, and the empowerment of people living with HIV/AIDS has enabled it to achieve low HIV prevalence rates and high treatment coverage. While challenges remain, Cuba's success in addressing the HIV/AIDS epidemic offers important lessons for the global effort to end the epidemic.[12,61,62]

COVID-19 Pandemic

The one nation in Latin America and the Caribbean that might have been expected to have had the least negative experience with the COVID-19 pandemic would be Cuba, long the leader in public health measurements. But after initially very low numbers of cases and deaths, Cuba lamentably moved back to join the rest of the world in COVID-19 miseries.

Cuba certainly benefited, at least at the start of the pandemic, from the isolation afforded by its island geography. When the pandemic first emerged, Cuba quarantined anyone arriving who showed the symptoms of viral infections. Within days, Cuba had halted all incoming flights.[63] But measures like this could only work in the short term. Although Cuba managed comparatively well during the first part of the pandemic, this success did not continue with each follow-on wave and iteration of coronavirus.

Cuba's overall situation during the pandemic was shaped by the strength of its public healthcare system. As the virus appeared, Cuban medical professionals, organized into doctor/nurse/public health worker teams from the over 11,000 *consultorios*, went door to door in their designated catchment zones.[64] With the additional assistance of 28,000 medical students, Cuban healthcare professionals scouted for any possible COVID-19 case, tested, and then isolated those identified with the virus.[63,65] Testing in Cuba kept up with the challenge of the pandemic, with 27 laboratories operating on the island.[64,66,67] At first, those with a confirmed case of COVID-19, as well as those exposed to the virus, were sent to one of the 200 quarantine facilities set up to deal with the crisis.[68] This imposition was eventually relaxed, with a home quarantining system taking its place. By monitoring and isolating the situation in each household, the Cuban healthcare system allowed the country to effectively beat back the first wave of the pandemic.[69,70]

The strength of the biotechnical industries in Cuba offered some victories against the coronavirus. Alone in Latin America and the Caribbean, Cuba created its own COVID-19 vaccines. Cuba's biotechnology industry, BioCubaFarma, developed several coronavirus vaccines.[70,71] Based on older vaccine technologies, both Cuban vaccines require only normal refrigeration, not the super-low temperatures necessary for mRNA vaccines like those developed by Pfizer and Moderna.[72] The Cuban vaccines come in a series of three doses, a requirement that complicates matters: It necessitates tracking of those who got just one shot or two, following up, and making sure everyone gets all three. It eases things somewhat that mixing Abdala and Soberana 02 shots is acceptable, but it is clear that some Cubans who were vaccinated did not complete the three-shot regimen. Established social connection organizations, the Committees for the Defense of the Revolution and the Women's Federation, greatly facilitated the efficiency of the COVID-19 vaccination rollouts.[70] These groups provided information and mobilized neighbors to get the vaccine.

A key issue for Cuba was the continuing U.S. economic embargo, making medicines and medical supplies often impossible to obtain. As the Delta and Omicron variants swept the world, with 43,000 confirmed cases in Cuba just 2 weeks

- **References:** *References* and *Suggested Readings* provide a list of additional resources to help students gain a deeper understanding of the material. New references have been included to reflect the current research in the field.

References **135**

Worst off are the regions of Mexico that are home to the nation's Indigenous populations. Health disparities and inequities continue to impact these communities. They face a range of challenges, including poverty, lack of access to healthcare services, and language barriers. Mexico's healthcare system must address these disparities if it is to meet the needs of its diverse populations. While Mexico's healthcare system has made progress in recent years, there is still much work to be done. The country's relative wealth should enable it to achieve better health outcomes.

References

1. Mexico. BIOFIN. Updated 2021. Accessed April 29, 2023. https://www.biofin.org/mexico#:~:text=Mexico%20is%20a%20mega%20diverse,be%20found%20in%20its%20territory.
2. Pico de Orizaba, Mexico. NASA Earth Observatory. Updated February 10, 2011. Accessed April 29, 2023. https://earthobservatory.nasa.gov/images/49462/pico-de-orizaba-mexico#:~:text=The%20snow%2D%20and%20ice%2Dclad,tallest%20volcano%20in%20North%20America.
3. Central Intelligence Agency. Explore all countries—Mexico. In: *The World Factbook*. Updated April 26, 2023. Accessed April 29, 2023. https://www.cia.gov/the-world-factbook/countries/mexico/.
4. Mexico: country commercial guide. U.S. Department of Commerce International Trade Administration. Updated September 9, 2022. Accessed April 29, 2023. https://www.trade.gov/country-commercial-guides/mexico-oil-and-gas.
5. Byrd Simpson L. *Many Mexicos*. University of California Press; 1960.
6. Beaubien J. Border-town factories give manufacturers edge. *NPR*. November, 2011. https://www.npr.org/2011/11/20/142536024/border-town-factories-give-manufacturers-an-edge.
7. Sanchez J. Share of population living in poverty in Mexico in 2022, by state. Statista. July 5, 2024. Accessed January 25, 2025. https://www.statista.com/statistics/1036147/poverty-rate-mexico-state/.
8. Aceves B, Ingram M, Nieto C, et al. Non-communicable disease prevention in Mexico: policies, programs and regulations. *Health Promot Int*. 2020;35(2):409-421. doi: 10.1093/heapro/daz029.
9. Manzanares-Rivera JL. Expenditure patterns and social determinants of type II diabetes epidemic in the Coahuila–Texas border. *Papeles de Población*. 2016;22(89). http://www.scielo.org.mx/scielo.php?pid=S1405-74252016000300255&script=sci_arttext&tlng=en.
10. Aburto JM, Riffe T, Canudas-Romo V. Trends in avoidable mortality over the life course in Mexico, 1990–2015: a cross-sectional demographic analysis. *BMJ*. 2018;8(7):1-11.
11. Diamond M, Testa L, Novak C, et al. *A Population in Peril: A Health Crisis Among Asylum Seekers on the Northern Border of Mexico 2020*. Harvard Global Health Institute; 2020.
12. Barquera S, Rivera JA. Obesity in Mexico: rapid epidemiological transition and food industry interference in health policies. *Lancet Diabetes Endocrinol*. 2020;8(9):746-747. doi: 10.1016/S2213-8587(20)30269-2.
13. Bartley P, Monterrosas E, Ruiz PP. Resisting a hostile and insecure environment for defending rights in Mexico. In: *Protecting Human Rights Defenders at Risk*. Routledge; 2020:104-129.
14. Barrow LK. Party on? Politicians and party switching in Mexico. *Politics*. 2007;27(3):165-173.
15. Greene KF, Sánchez-Talanquer M. Latin America's shifting politics: Mexico's party system under stress. *J Democracy*. 2018;29(4):31-42. doi: 10.1353/jod.2018.0060.
16. Berg NM, Welsh P, Ford K, Romero HM. AMLO 2021: is the Mexican administration's fight against corruption all rhetoric? Ropes & Gray. June 2021. https://www.ropesgray.com/en/newsroom/alerts/2021/june/amlo-2021-is-the-mexican-administrations-fight-against-corruption-all-rhetoric.
17. Morris SD. Corruption and the Mexican political system: continuity and change. *Third World Quarterly*. 1999;20(3):623-643.
18. Palifka BJ. Corruption, organized crime and the public sector in Mexico. In: *Handbook on Corruption, Ethics and Integrity in Public Administration*. Edward Elgar Publishing; 2020:274-288.
19. Craske N. Mexican women's inclusion into political life: a Latin American perspective. In: *Women's Participation in Mexican Political Life*. Routledge; 2019:41-62.
20. Yörük E, Öker I, Şarlak L. Indigenous unrest and the contentious politics of social assistance in Mexico. *World Development*. 2019;104618.
21. World Bank. Mexico overview. Accessed April 30, 2023. https://www.worldbank.org/en/country/Mexico/overview#:~:text=Its%20economic%20growth%20averaged%20just,to%20the%20COVID%2D19%20pandemic.
22. MacLeod D. *Downsizing the State: Privatization and the Limits of Neoliberal Reform in Mexico*. Penn State Press; 2004.
23. Silva V. A new dawn or a false hope for Mexico's left? Overcoming neoliberal legacies in an uncertain world. *Latin Am Perspect*. 2023; 0094582X231164127.
24. U.S. Department of State. 2022 investment climate statements: Mexico. 2022. https://www.state.gov/reports/2022-investment-climate-statements/Mexico/.
25. Agarwal R, Kimball M. Will inflation remain high? International Monetary Fund. 2002. https://www.imf.org/en/Publications/fandd/issues/2022/03/Future-of-inflation-part1-Agarwal-kimball.
26. Instituto Nacional de Estadistica y Geografía (INEGI) [National Institute of Statistics and Geography]. *Índice Nacional de Precios al Consumidor* [National Consumer Price Index]. https://www.inegi.org.mx/temas/inpc/.
27. Villarreal V. How do Mexicans get healthcare? Wilson Center. 2022. Accessed April 16, 2023. https://www.wilsoncenter.org/article/infographic-how-do-mexicans-get-healthcare.

Instructor Resources

Qualified instructors can receive the following Instructor Resources:

- Test Bank in LMS-compatible formats
- Slides in PowerPoint format

Student Resources

Each new purchase of the print textbook or Navigate Advantage course includes an eBook containing:

- Chapter Review Slides
- Flashcards
- Interactive glossary

We Value Your Feedback

Do you love this text? Spot an error you'd like to report? Follow this QR code to give us your observations and suggestions for improvement.

Acknowledgments

Contributors

Takuya Aoki, MD, PhD, MMA
Division of Clinical Epidemiology
Research Center for Medical Sciences
Jikei University School of Medicine
Tokyo, Japan

Stephanie J. S. Baiyasi, DVM, MPH, HSAC
Saginaw Valley State University
University Center, Michigan

Antonio Pires Barbosa, PhD, MD
Universidade Nove de Julho
São Paulo, Brazil

Merritt Brockman, DHA, FACHE
Texas Tech University Health Science Center
Lubbock, Texas

Vivienne Byers, BA (Mod), MA, MSc, PhD
Technological University Dublin
Grangegorman, Ireland

Robin Choo, MMedPhys, MBA, MSc
Singapore

Raul Chuquiyauri, MD, MPH, PhD
Universidad Peruana Cayetano Heredia
Lima, Peru

Omur Cinar Elci, MD, PhD
Western Atlantic University
School of Medicine
Freeport, The Bahamas

Maria B. Creavin, RD, SM, MAS
Faculty
Healthcare Systems and Informatics
University of Denver
Denver, Colorado

Kelcie R. Creel, MPH
Albuquerque, New Mexico

Roy Arokiam Daniel, MD, DNB
Senior Resident
AIIMS
New Delhi, India

Kimberly S. Davey, PhD, MBA
Samford University
Birmingham, Alabama

Gary E. Day, RN, EM, DipAppSc, BNurs, MHM, DHSM
Professor
College of Health Sciences
Education Centre of Australia
Brisbane, Queensland, Australia

Oluwatosin Dotun-Olujinmi, DHA
IDEY Public Health Consulting Inc.
Ontario, Canada

R. Paul Duncan, PhD
Professor Emeritus
Department of Health Services Research
University of Florida
Gainesville, Florida

Samir Wahid EL-Dmiry, TQM, MBA, PhD
Ministry of Health and Population
Cairo, Egypt

Rachel Ellison, PhD
Associate Professor
Health Services Administration Program Coordinator
College of Nursing & Health Sciences
University of Louisiana at Lafayette
Lafayette, Louisiana

Lesego Gabaitiri, PhD
Botswana International University of Science and Technology
Palapye, Botswana

Tony Garthwaite, PhD, MSc
Visiting Professor
University of South Wales
Pontypridd, South Wales

Mariusz Gujski, MD, PhD
Professor
Department of Public Health
Medical University of Warsaw
Warsaw, Poland

Ruiling Guo, DHA
Professor
Idaho State University
Pocatello, Idaho

Eunkyung Han, MD (DKM), Dr. PH, MPH
Ho-Young Institute of Community Health
Goyang, Korea

Umar Haruna, PhD, Mphil, BA
School of Public Health
University for Development Studies
Tamale, Ghana

Danny D. House, MBA, LNHA
Texas Tech University Health Sciences Center
Levelland, Texas

Morgan House, PhD, MBA, LNHA
Texas Tech University Health Sciences Center
Lubbock, Texas

Steven Howard, PhD, MBA
University of Alabama at Birmingham
Birmingham, Alabama

Kuo-Cherh Huang, Dr.PH
School of Health Care Administration
Taipei Medical University
Taipei, Taiwan

Styn M. Jamu, DHA, PhD (c), MPA
Department of Population Studies
University of Botswana
Gaborone, Botswana

Mateusz Jankowski, MD, PhD
Department of Public Health
School of Public Health
Centre of Postgraduate Medical Education
Warsaw, Poland

Allen Johnson, Dr. PH, MPH
Department of Health Professions
Rollins College
Winter Park, Florida

James A. Johnson, PhD, MSc, MPA
School of Health Sciences
Central Michigan University
Mount Pleasant, Michigan

Joseph Adam Johnson, MLA, BS Ed
Asker International School
Asker, Norway

Walter J. Jones, PhD
Professor Emeritus
Department of Healthcare Leadership and Management
Medical University of South Carolina
Charleston, South Carolina

Diluma Madushani Kariyawasam, MPH
Texas Tech University Health Sciences Center El Paso
El Paso, Texas

Mpho Keetile, PhD
University of Botswana
Gaborone, Botswana

Michael H. Kennedy, PhD, MHA, FACHE
University of Texas at Tyler Health Science Center
Tyler, Texas

Sophie Kobouloff, DHA, MBA, EDHEC MBA
Saddle Implant Technologies
Geneva, Switzerland

Zigmond A. Kozicki, DHA, MSA, MA, LLP
University of Detroit Mercy
Detroit, Michigan

Veronica Leary, MLS, MPhil, MPH (c)
Rollins College
Winter Park, Florida
University of Pennsylvania
Philadelphia, Pennsylvania

Gerald (Jerry) R. Ledlow, PhD, MHA, FACHE
University of Texas at Tyler Health Science Center
Tyler, Texas

Jehoshua R. Lopez, MD, MPH
Seguro Social de Salud
Iquitos, Peru

Ning Lu, PhD, MPH
Governors State University
University Park, Illinois

Wesam Mansour, PhD
Public Health Consultant
London, United Kingdom

Thomas Maryon, DHA, MA, BSN, RN
University of Texas at Tyler Health Science Center
Tyler, Texas

Linda A. McCarey, MS, BSN, RN
Haliburton, Kawartha, Pine Ridge Health Unit
Haliburton, Ontario, Canada

Puneet Misra, MD, MPH
Professor
AIIMS
New Delhi, India

Raheleh Mohammadi, PhD (c), MPH
Health Professions Department
Rollins College
Winter Park, Florida

Michael E. Morris, PhD, MPH, MPA
University of Florida
Gainesville, Florida

Paulina Mularczyk-Tomczewska, PhD
Public Health Department
Medical University of Warsaw
Warsaw, Poland

Jannatul Nayeem, MBBS, MPH
Central Michigan University
Mount Pleasant, Michigan

Ahmed Newera, MBBCH, MPH, CPHQ, FISQua
Ministry of Defense Health Services
Taif, Saudi Arabia

Marcia Cristina Zago Novaretti, PhD, MD
Universidade Nove de Julho
São Paulo, Brazil

Ronn Pineo, PhD
Professor Emeritus
Towson University
Towson, Maryland

Chelsea Pritchard, MPH
Sherwood, Oregon

Ahmed Qabeel, MSc, MBA, DBA Candidate
Cleopatra Hospitals Group
Sahafeyeen, Giza, Egypt

Sophie Randall, MSc, BSc
Research Assistant
University of South Wales
Pontypridd, South Wales

Percy A. Rojas, MD, MP
Gerencia Regional de Salud de Loreto
Iquitos, Peru

Caren Rossow, DHA, MSA, RN, FACHE
Indiana University
South Bend, Indiana

Carrie Shaver, DHA, IHC, FACHE
Texas Tech University Health Sciences Center
Lubbock, Texas

Carmen Stein

Carleen H. Stoskopf, ScD, MS
Professor and Chair
Health Management and Policy
San Diego State University
San Diego, California

Musah A. Sugri, MSA, MBA, DrPH (c)
Social Services Case Manager
Georgia Department of Health and Human Services
Lawrenceville, Georgia
Georgia Southern University
Statesboro, Georgia

Anthony Mwinilanaa Tampah-Naah, DR, PhD
SD Dombo University of Business and Integrated Development Studies
WA, Upper West Region, Ghana

Immaculate Sabelile Tenza, BSc, MSc, PhD
School of Nursing Science
North-West University
Potchefstroom, South Africa
Centre for Health Policy & South African Research Chairs Initiative
School of Public Health
University of Witwatersrand
Johannesburg, South Africa

Sion Tetlow, PhD, MSc
Researcher
University of South Wales
Pontypridd, South Wales

Cheryl Nelson Theuninck, DHA, MS
Central Michigan University
Mount Pleasant, Michigan

Shin-Yi Tsai, Dr. PH
Department of Health Policy and Management
Johns Hopkins Bloomberg School of Public Health
Johns Hopkins University
Baltimore, Maryland

Reyhan Ucku, MD
Specialist in Public Health
Professor
Dokuz Eylül University
Izmir, Türkiye

Dan J. Vick, MD, DHA, MBA, CPE
Maine General Medical Center
Augusta, Maine
Herbert H. & Grace A. Dow College of Health Professions
Central Michigan University
Mount Pleasant, Michigan

Stalin Vilcarromero, MD, DTM&H
Hospital Nacional Edgardo Rebagliati Martins
Lima, Peru

Victor Weeden, DHA, MA
College of Public Health
University of South Florida
Tampa, Florida

Jiebing Wen, PhD
Division of Health Policy and Economics
Department of Population Health Sciences
Weill Cornell Medical College
Cornell University
New York, New York

Jaroslaw Wierzbicki, PhD
Chair of Administrative and Corporate Financial Law
Warsaw School of Economics (SGH)
Warsaw, Poland

William Wuenstel

Sudha Xirasagar, MBBS, PhD
Professor
Department of Health Services Policy and Management
University of South Carolina
Columbia, South Carolina

Gaia Zori, PhD, MPH, CHES
University of Florida
Gainesville, Florida

Reviewers

The authors and publisher also wish to thank the reviewers, whose valuable feedback contributed greatly to the preparation of this new edition.

John A. Brennan
Professor
Cambridge College
Cambridge, Massachusetts
MA Licensed Nursing Home Administrator
Chairman of the Board of Trustees, Taunton State Hospital
Department of Mental Health of Trustees, Taunton State Hospital
Taunton, Massachusetts

Susan Enfield, BSN, MSN, PEL-CSN
RNBSN Program Director; Director of Assessment; Assistant Professor
Olivet Nazarene University
Bourbonnais, Illinois

Elizabeth Fischer
University of Denver
Denver, Colorado

Marzell I. Gray, Dr. PH, MBA
Assistant Professor
University of Minnesota Duluth
Duluth, Minnesota

Ismael Hoare, PhD, MPH
Assistant Professor
College of Public Health
University of South Florida
Tampa, Florida

Sherry Lawrence
University of South Alabama
Mobile, Alabama

Samantha Marocco, PT, DPT, MS, EdD, GCS Emeritus
Utica University
Utica, New York

Susan Mintz, PT, DPT
Utica University
Utica, New York

Patti R. Rose, MPH, EdD
President and CEO
Rose Consulting
Miami, Florida

Alan Rowan, Dr. PH
Public Health Program
Florida State University
Tallahassee, Florida

David M. Scott, BPharm, MPH, PhD
Professor Emeritus
North Dakota State University
Fargo, North Dakota

Rishi Sood, MPH
Adjunct Faculty, CUNY School of Public Health
CUNY School of Public Health
New York, New York

Ron Watson, MA, PhD
Associate Professor, Political Science and Health & Society
Beloit College
Beloit, Wisconsin

About the Editors

Dr. Leiyu Shi is Professor of Health Policy and Management at Johns Hopkins University, Bloomberg School of Public Health, Department of Health Policy and Management. He received his doctoral education from University of California Berkeley, majoring in health policy and services research. He also has a master's degree in business administration, focusing on finance. Academically, he serves as Director of the Johns Hopkins-Tsinghua DrPH Program for Healthcare Management and Leadership and Director of the Asia-Pacific Rim DrPH Program. In terms of research, he serves as Director of Johns Hopkins Primary Care Policy Center and Director of Johns Hopkins Asia-Pacific Center for Hospital Management and Leadership Research. Dr. Shi's research and practice focus on primary care, hospitals, healthcare systems, community health centers, health disparities, and vulnerable populations. Dr. Shi is also one of the developers of the Johns Hopkins Primary Care Assessment Tools, which have been widely used internationally to measure primary healthcare performance at the individual, practice, and system levels. Dr. Shi is the author of 13 textbooks and over 300 scientific journal articles. He was named by Thomson Reuters in 2014 as among the top cited (and therefore most influential) scientists in the world in the area of social science in general.

Dr. Richard G. Greenhill serves as the chief transformation officer (CTO) at Quality Insights and Editor-in-Chief of the *International Journal for Quality in Healthcare, Communications* (IJCOMS), an Oxford University Press and International Society for Quality in Healthcare (ISQua) peer-reviewed publication. In his CTO role, he spearheads transformative initiatives focused on efficiency, productivity, and competitiveness. His career spans more than 30 years, with vast experience across the continuum. He is a sought-after international and national speaker on topics related to AI use in healthcare delivery, quality, and patient safety. Dr. Greenhill serves nationally on the American College of Healthcare Executives faculty.

He is a subject matter expert for the International Society for Quality in Healthcare (ISQua), the World Health Organization (WHO), and the National Association for Healthcare Quality (NAHQ). Dr. Greenhill was elected to the prestigious International Academy for Quality in Healthcare (IAQS), joining such luminaries in the universe of quality improvement and patient safety as Sir Liam Donaldson, Donald Berwick, and Jeffrey Braithwaite. Membership in the IAQS is lifelong and one of the highest honors that someone in healthcare quality can achieve.

Dr. Greenhill is Board Certified in Healthcare Management and a ACHE Fellow (FACHE), a Project Management Professional (PMP), a Six Sigma Master Black Belt (SSMBB), a Certified Professional in Healthcare Quality (CPHQ), and a Healthcare Accreditation Certified Professional (HACP-CMS).

PART I

Global Health and Health Systems

CHAPTER 1

Introduction to Health Systems

James A. Johnson

Introduction

A health system, as described by the World Health Organization (WHO), is the sum total of all of the organizations, institutions, and resources whose primary purpose is to improve health. A health system needs staff, funds, information, supplies, transport, communications, and overall guidance and direction. Furthermore, it needs to provide services that are responsive and financially fair, while treating people decently.[1]

Within this definition, there are several concepts that must be understood before one embarks on the task of studying health systems. First and foremost, an agreed-upon definition of health is paramount. Health is too often seen as a concept that applies only to physical well-being or the absence of disease; however, the most widely accepted definition of health is the one first published by the WHO in 1948:

> Health is a state of complete physical, mental, and social well-being and not merely the absence of disease and infirmity.[2]

This comprehensive concept of health is the one used in this book and serves to inform discussions on health systems worldwide.

The other key word that needs to be explored here is the word "system." As an example, the human body is a system composed of many physiologic subsystems that are interconnected in a holistic way. The subsystems, including the respiratory, circulatory, neurological, endocrine, and musculoskeletal systems, communicate and are interdependent. They work together for the purposes of survival, adaptation, growth, and development. They also interact with the environment and respond to feedback from within and outside of the system. In many ways, the interconnectivity of the various subsystems and their extension as a whole into the environment form the building blocks of larger systems such as family, community, and nation. Thus, a natural (biologic) system such as a human being is also a participant in and creator of larger social systems. The human-created systems have many of the same attributes as biologic systems. Additionally, it can be said that these larger systems are characterized by:

- A structure that is defined by its parts and processes.
- Generalizations of reality.
- A tendency to function in the same way. This involves the inputs (material, human resources, finances, etc.) and outputs (products and services) that are then processed, causing them to change in some way.
- The various parts of a system, which have functional as well as structural relationships with one another.

Human-created systems can be small, as in a three-person family, or quite large, as in a nation state such as India with its population of 1 billion people. The most widely dispersed human-created systems are organizations. As with the other examples described previously, organizations share the same attributes and adapt accordingly to their environments. In their book *Health*

Organizations, Johnson and Rossow describe organizations as complex human systems that have evolved over time and continue to do so.[3] The natural emergence of human-created systems, such as organizations and communities, probably grew out of the struggle for survival. In the hostile world of early humankind, food, shelter, and safety needs usually required cooperative efforts. In turn, cooperative efforts typically require some form of organization. This is no less true in the case of providing health services. In order to meet the criteria of health as a state of complete physical, mental, and social well-being, individuals, communities, organizations, and nation states have worked together to form elaborate and diverse health systems throughout the world.[4]

While there are about 200 countries on the planet, only 40 have adopted a formal health system. The four most prevalent models of health systems as identified by the Comparative Health Policy Library at Columbia University are described next.[5]

Beveridge Model

- Named after William Beveridge, the U.K. social reformer who helped create the National Health Service (NHS)
- Health care both paid for and provided by the government
- Free at the point of service
- Financed through taxation—sometimes dedicated taxation, sometimes general tax revenues, and sometimes both
- Examples: United Kingdom, New Zealand, Spain, U.S. Veterans Health Administration

Bismarck Model

- Named after Prussian Chancellor Bismarck
- Health care paid for by nonprofit insurance firms and provided by the public and private sectors
- Financed by employees and employers, generally through payroll deductions; often complemented by general tax revenues
- Examples: Germany, France, Switzerland, Japan

Single-Payer Model (National Health Insurance)

- Health care paid for by government-run insurance programs and provided by public and private actors
- Financed through taxation—sometimes dedicated taxation, sometimes general revenues, and sometimes both
- Examples: Canada, Norway, Spain, U.S. Medicare

Out-of-Pocket

- Health care paid for by consumers to public and private care providers
- Little to no insurance coverage
- The model most often used by most low- and middle-income countries
- Examples: India, Rwanda, some segments of the U.S. "system"

All of these models differ in both how they are funded and how health care is delivered.[5] Publicly funded systems are paid for with taxation, while privately funded systems are paid for with individual contributions to a collective fund, like an insurance company. Facilities that deliver health care can be either owned by the government or privately owned by an organization, like a corporation or a nonprofit.

In the Beveridge model, funding and delivery are primarily provided by the government, whereas both are provided privately in the Bismarck model. In the national health insurance model, funding is public but facilities are private. And in the uninsured model, only those who are able to pay out of pocket receive care. As described by Johnson, Davey, and Greenhill in their recent book *Health Care USA*, the United States uses all four of these models for different segments of its population.[6]

Regardless of which model a country embraces, the WHO identifies the qualities of a good healthcare system as follows[7]:

- **Safe and effective:** The care that is delivered takes into account individuals' unique needs, preferences, and values.
- **Timely:** Wait times have been minimized to avoid potentially harmful delays in care.
- **Equitable:** All residents and citizens are able to access the care they need.
- **Integrated:** The full range of healthcare services are available throughout a person's life.
- **Efficient:** Benefits have been maximized and waste has been minimized.

Health System Characteristics

As with all systems, a health system has inputs. These include financial, material, and human resources that differentiate one health system from another. The data in **Table 1-1** demonstrate some of these differences.

Table 1-1 Selected Health Input and Financial Data 2019–2022

Total global expenditure for health	9 trillion USD (approximately 11% of global GDP)
Total global expenditure for health per person per year	1,129 USD (2019)
Country with highest total spending per person per year on health	United States (12,318 USD) (2021)
Country with lowest total spending per person per year on health	Democratic Republic of the Congo (19 USD per person annually) (2020)
Country with highest government spending per person per year on health	United States (12,318 USD) (2021)
Country with lowest government spending per person per year on health	Croatia (1,448 PPS per inhabitant) and Romania (1,428 PPS per inhabitant)—2020
Country with highest annual out-of-pocket household spending on health	Switzerland (1,577 USD)/(22.0%)—2021
Country with lowest annual out-of-pocket household spending on health	Kiribati (0.18)—2019
Average amount spent per person per year on health in countries belonging to the Organization for Economic Co-operation and Development (OECD)	More than 4,000 USD (2019)
WHO estimate of minimum spending per person per year needed to provide basic, life-saving services	$44
Countries where health spending was lower than 20 USD per person per year	Somalia and the Democratic Republic of the Congo

Updated by Jannatul Nayeeem, MD, MPH, from the following sources:
Data from Increased out-of-pocket spending threatens universal health coverage in "missing middle" countries: Institute for Health Metrics and Evaluation (healthdata.org); Out-of-pocket expenditure per capita (current US$)—Kiribati: Data (worldbank.org); Healthcare expenditure statistics: Statistics Explained (europa.eu); CHARTS: How much rich and poor countries spend per person on health: Goats and soda: NPR; Per capita health expenditure by country 2021: Statista; Health spending per capita globally 2019 and 2050: Statista; Global health: Statistics & facts: Statista; Global expenditure on health: Rising to the pandemic's challenges—world: ReliefWeb; Out-of-pocket expenditure per capita (current US$)—Kiribati: Data (worldbank.org).[8]

One of the major "inputs" into any healthcare system is patients. Patients present with a variety of symptoms/diseases/injuries; however, they also come with a myriad of characteristics such as personality, life experiences, knowledge, attitudes, age, gender, race, ethnicity, socioeconomic status, education level, income level, intellect, prejudice, religious and other belief systems, emotions, biologic strengths and weaknesses, and genetic makeup. In addition, patients may or may not be plugged into society's infrastructure, such as having access to transportation, childcare, or health insurance. The complexity that these factors create cannot be overlooked by health systems, nor should they be overlooked by health policymakers. It has been well established that income is a generally reliable predictor of health. The income gradient within a population is highly associated with the health status of individuals or groups in that population, and the per capita incomes and the gross domestic product (GDP) of nations are also highly correlated with the health status of that country's population. Viewed from this perspective, health policy is also concerned with poverty and lifting populations out of poverty through social policies designed to improve education, housing, infrastructure, job creation, and the environment.

As described by Johnson, Anderson, and Rossow in their book *Health Systems Thinking*, health systems arise within a social context: historical, cultural, political, and economic.[9] Within all human constructed systems, there is considerable diversity in size, scope, and form. As a result, health systems have structure, processes, and outcomes that vary considerably. **Table 1-2** shows the variation along some of these dimensions for the group of countries profiled in this book. As you can see, financial and

Table 1-2 Financial Healthcare Resources for Selected Countries: The Building Blocks of Health Systems

	% of GDP	US$	PPP$	Government	Private	Out-of-Pocket	% of Total Government Expenditures Spent on Health
Australia	10.6	5,901	152,223	165,281	54,835	13.8	46.6
Bangladesh	2.6	51	22,240	129,918	551,060	74	15.4
Botswana	6.2	363	2,229	79.05	20.77	4.6	38.5
Brazil	10.3	701	326,071	344,642	424,367	22.4	42.9
Canada	11.7	6,086	229,223	217,036	74,132	12.4	53
China	5.6	583	1,371,194	3,139,485	2,597,453	34.8	36.4
DR Congo	4.1	21	26	586,768	1,697,177	69.8	10.4
France	12.2	4,769	386,444	215,631	65,435	8.9	61.6
Germany	12.8	5,930	584,823	338,708	93,097	12.5	50.8
Ghana	4	85	7,123	7,610	6,286	30.8	29
India	3	57	266,344	2,147,407	3,654,189	50.6	32.7
Ireland (2021)	6.7	6,700	36,572	22,234	6,127	10.3	24.9
Israel	8.3	3,867	30,274	82,581	32,654	17.1	45.4
Japan	10.9	4,388	579,629	49,435,344	9,246,473	12.6	44.5
Jordan	7.5	299	761	1,152	1,056	69.1	13.5
Korea	8.4	2,642	196,083	98,652,685	63,038,024	27.7	37.6
Mexico	6.2	539	1,061	770,943	686,758	38.8	28.7
Nigeria	3.4	70	150,266	780,484	3,934,478	95.8	12
Peru	6.3	389	25,089	30,715	14,413	22.8	26.2
Russia	7.6	774	331,750	5,732,327	2,393,182	27.8	39.4
Turkiye	4.6	395	106,075	183,759	49,303	16.4	34
United Kingdom	12	4,927	373,829	215,568	41,961	13.6	51.5
United States	18.8	11,702	3,931,331	2,231,783	1,699,548	9.9	47.8

Updated 2023 by Nayeem Jannatul, MD, MPH. Data from WHO Global Health Expenditure Database 2022; Global Health Expenditure Database (who.int).

human resource inputs are interrelated with health outcomes.

Even though every health system is unique in its given social and cultural environment, it has common elements that are necessary to function. These building blocks not only help us in understanding health systems better, but also provide opportunities for system improvement. The WHO, the World Bank, and various governments around the world have a common understanding of these key elements. Johnson refers to them as critical success factors, emphasizing how essential they are to a health system's survival (**Table 1-3**).

One widely accepted way of measuring the building blocks or the overall functioning of a health system is through the lenses of cost, quality,

Table 1-3 Health Systems Building Blocks (Critical Success Factors)[6,10]

Service Delivery	Medical Technology
Good health services are those that deliver effective, safe, quality personal and non-personal health interventions to those who need them, when and where needed, with minimum waste of resources.	A well-functioning health system ensures equitable access to essential medical products, drugs, vaccines, and technologies of assured quality, safety, efficacy, and cost-effectiveness, and their scientifically sound and cost-effective use.
Health Workforce	**Health Financing**
A well-performing health workforce is one that works in ways that are responsive, fair, and efficient to achieve the best health outcomes possible, given available resources and circumstances (i.e., there are sufficient staff, fairly distributed; they are competent, responsive, and productive).	A good health financing system raises adequate funds for health, in ways that ensure people can use needed services and are protected from financial catastrophe or impoverishment associated with having to pay for them. It provides incentives for providers and users to be efficient.
Health Information	**Leadership and Governance**
A well-functioning health information system is one that ensures the production, analysis, dissemination, and use of reliable and timely information on health determinants, health system performance, and health status.	Leadership and governance involves ensuring that strategic policy frameworks exist and are combined with effective oversight, coalition building, regulation, attention to system design, and accountability.

Data from World Health Organization. The WHO Health Systems Framework 2016. www.wpro.who.int/health_services/health_systems_framework/en/

and access. The cost, quality, access triangle is shown in **Figure 1-1**.

In the era of rapid globalization and change, it is becoming increasingly prudent to add a fourth dimension, "innovation." The result can be depicted as a cost, quality, access, innovation diamond, as shown in **Figure 1-2**.

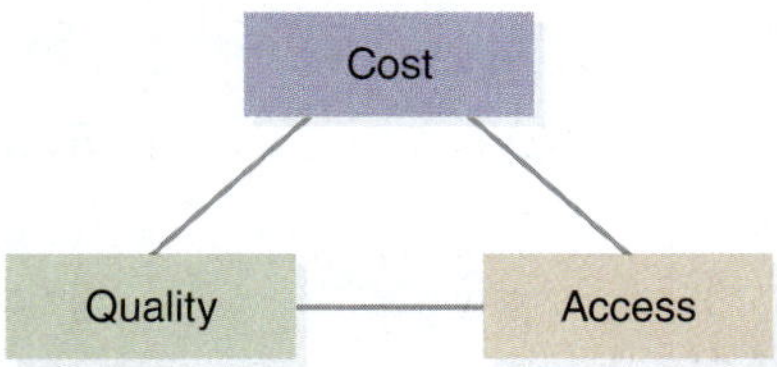

Figure 1-1 The Cost, Quality, Access Triangle[4]

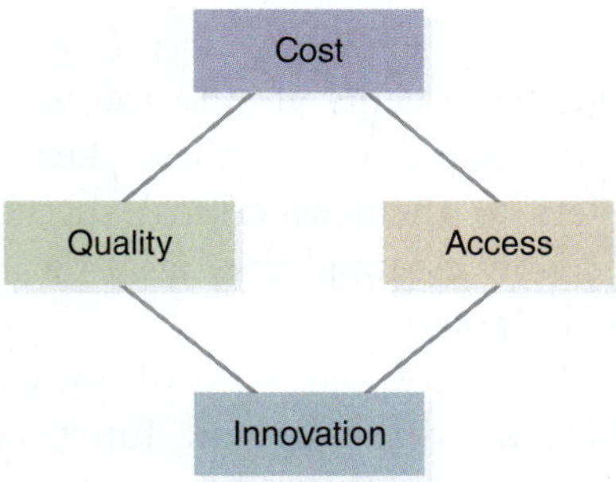

Figure 1-2 The Cost, Quality, Access, Innovation Diamond[4]

Health Systems Within Larger Social Systems

Starting with the Ottawa Charter for Health in 1986 and subsequently embraced in Finland at the 2013 Helsinki Conference, the WHO adopted and began to promulgate a "health in all policies" paradigm to help guide health systems globally to an essential understanding that all sectors of a society must work together to promote health and support health systems. This approach is profiled in **Box 1-1**.

UCLA medical sociologist Ron Andersen identified some of the factors that influence whether a

Box 1-1 Health in All Policies[4]

Health in All Policies is an approach to public policies across sectors that systematically takes into account the health implications of decisions, seeks synergies, and avoids harmful health impacts in order to improve population health and health equity. It improves accountability of policymakers for health impacts at all levels of policymaking. It includes an emphasis on the consequences of public policies on health systems, determinants of health, and well-being.

Reproduced from World Health Organization. *Health in all policies: Training manual.* Geneva: Author; 2015.

person even accesses health services. This model has three main components: *predisposing factors*, *enabling factors*, and *need factors*. Predisposing factors include family characteristics, social structure, and health beliefs. Enabling factors include family resources and community resources. The "need" factors include illness and the response to illness. This work was later expanded into the "Behavioral Model of Health Services," as it pertains to vulnerable populations. This model applies to many people around the world, and perhaps within every health system. Understanding the characteristics of the population a health system serves is key to designing the system processes, providing adequate and appropriate resources, and having clear expectations for desired outcomes.

The notion that one's social circumstances, or socioeconomic status, can influence one's health is now well established. In recent decades, social science researchers have laid the groundwork for further exploration of this relationship. It is thought that social circumstances lead to disease in individuals and populations via three pathways: behavioral, material, and psychological. The premise is that social circumstances such as socioeconomic status based on income and education influences behaviors. For example, smoking is a behavior often found in persons with low socioeconomic status.[11,a]

> The only exceptions were for Asian and Hispanic women, where low educational attainment was not associated with a high prevalence of cigarette smoking, and among Hispanic men and Asian women, where there was no association between poverty status and smoking. (CDC, 2019)

Smoking has a direct impact on health status, as the incidences of lung cancer, emphysema, asthma, and other respiratory illnesses are higher among smokers. Other behaviors that are believed to be associated with lower socioeconomic status are under study and include such behaviors as alcohol use, risky sexual behavior, drug use, and violence.

A second pathway is material circumstances associated with deprivation from many causes, both local and global. Persons living with a substantially lower income are unable to provide for their most basic needs, such as adequate food, shelter, and safety. As a result, some segments of the population suffer from malnutrition, inadequate home heating and warm clothing, and environmental exposures and are more exposed to community violence. These factors in turn result in lower health status through increased infectious diseases due to overcrowding, malnutrition, limited access to appropriate medical care, exposure to pollutants both in the community and in substandard housing, and an increased risk of being a victim of violence.

The third pathway, the psychosocial pathway, is more complex. This pathway requires a connection between social structure and health. Extensive research has established mechanisms that make the connection between social structures, stress, and biology, or the "biopsychosocial stress response." World health trends and health systems implications related to these three pathways are summarized in **Box 1-2**.

Box 1-2 Commentary from the Field: Rising Health Systems Challenges

Population Aging

A demographic revolution is under way throughout the world. Today, there are around 600 million people in the world aged 60 years and older. This number will likely double by 2025, and by 2050, it will reach 2 billion, with the vast majority of these people living in the developing world. Such accelerated global population aging will increase economic and social demands on all countries.[12]

Although the consequences of population aging in the areas of health and income security are already at the center of discussions by policymakers and planners in the developed world, the speed and impact of population aging in the less-developed regions are yet to be fully appreciated. In 2025, in countries such as Brazil, China, and Thailand, the proportion of older people is more than 15% of the population, whereas in Colombia, Indonesia, and Kenya, the absolute numbers will increase by up to 400% over the next 25 years. This rate is as much as eight times higher than the increases in already aged societies in Western Europe, where population aging occurred over a much longer period of time.

Population aging is related to two factors: a decline in the proportion of children, reflecting declines in fertility rates in the overall population, and an increase in the proportion of adults 60 years of age and older as mortality rates decline. This demographic transition will bring with it a number of major challenges for health and social policy planners.

Improving health systems and their responses to population aging makes economic sense. With old-age dependency ratios increasing in virtually all countries of the world, the economic contributions and productive roles of

(continues)

[a]Centers for Disease and Prevention (CDC). Preventing chronic disease. 2019. https://www.cdc.gov/pcd/issues/2019/18_0553.htm

Box 1-2 Commentary from the Field: Rising Health Systems Challenges *(continued)*

older people will assume greater importance. Supporting people to remain healthy and ensure a good quality of life in their later years is one of the greatest challenges for the health sector in both developed and developing countries.

The Burden of Mental Illness

A large proportion of individuals with mental illness do not receive any health care for their condition because (1) the mental health infrastructure and services in most countries are grossly insufficient for the large and growing needs and (2) widely prevalent stigma and discrimination prevent them from seeking help. A policy for mental health care is lacking in 40% of countries, and 25% of those with such a policy assign no budget to implement it. Even where a budget exists, it is very small: 36% of countries devote less than 1% of their total health resources to mental health care. Although community-based services are recognized as the most effective approach, 65% of all psychiatric beds are still in mental hospitals—cutting into the already-meager budgets while providing largely custodial care in an environment that may infringe patients' basic human rights.

Cost-effective healthcare interventions are available. Recent research clearly demonstrates that disorders such as depression, schizophrenia, alcohol problems, and epilepsy can be treated within primary health care. Such treatment is well within the reach of even low-income countries and will substantially reduce the overall burden imposed by these disorders. Interventions rely on inexpensive medicines that are commonly available and, for the most part, free of patent restrictions; prescribing them also requires only basic training of health professionals.

Contributed by Dr. DaNita Weddle; https://www.who.int/news-room/fact-sheets/detail/ageing-and-health

Although stress can be an important factor in survival in a "fight or flight" scenario, if prolonged stress occurs and the body no longer can return to homeostasis quickly, long-term effects on health can occur, including cardiovascular disease, cancer, infection, and cognitive decline.[13]

A number of social determinants and social conditions have been studied to better understand the association between these factors and health status of both individuals and populations. **Table 1-4** identifies many of the commonly known social and political determinants. **Box 1-3** provides a more detailed example.

Table 1-4 Social Determinants of Health Status

Social Determinant	Mediating Factor(s)	Health Status: Increased (>) or Decreased (<)
Unemployment		< Health status
Employment		> Health status
Unemployment	Financial stress	< Health status
Unemployment	Psychological stress	< Health status
Unemployment	Health-damaging behavior	< Health status
Poor work environment		Ill health Poor health status
Psychosocial work environment	Job demand/control (low efficacy)	< Health status
Psychosocial work environment	Effort–reward imbalance (low self-esteem)	< Health status
Psychosocial work environment		Social gradient of ill health
Transportation	Traffic-related accidents	< Health status
Transportation	Air pollution	> Respiratory illnesses
Transportation	Noise	< Health status
Social support		> Health status < Health status

Social Determinant	Mediating Factor(s)	Health Status: Increased (>) or Decreased (<)
Social support	Moderating effects	> Health status
Social injustice	Reduced economic opportunity	< Impaired healthcare access
Inadequate nutrition		< Health status
Proper nutrition		> Health status
Poor nutrition		> Obesity
Poverty		< Health status > Mortality
Poverty	Material deprivation	< Health status
Poverty	Social deprivation	< Health status
Poverty	Unemployment	< Health status
Poverty	Inequity	< Health status
Poverty	Social exclusion	< Health status
Poverty	Minorities and/or refugees	< Health status
Poverty	Homelessness	< Health status < Mental health status
Ethnic and racial groupings		< Health status > Health status Social support > Mortality < Mortality
Ethnicity	Income	> Health status < Health status
Ethnicity	Maternal education	> Health status < Health status
Ethnicity	Education level	> Health status < Health status
Ethnicity	Experience of racial harassment and discrimination	< Health status
Neighborhood environment		> Health status < Health status
Neighborhood environment	Physical environment	> Health status < Health status
Social environment		> Health status < Health status
Neighborhood environment	Amenities	> Health status < Health status
Sexual behavior		< Health status > Health status
Sexual behavior	Increased rate of partner change	< Health status
Sexual behavior	Increased variation in sexual behavior	< Health status
Sexual behavior	Demography	Demography
Sexual behavior	Social disruption (war)	Social disruption (war)

Box 1-3 Social Determinants of Health: Birth and Infancy as an Example

Research has shown that early life circumstances are one of the most important predictors of health status. In the 1970s, it was established that malnutrition in a pregnant woman has a direct impact on the health and well-being of her fetus and hence its susceptibility to low birth weight. Further research has demonstrated that undernutrition for a fetus results in long-term changes in physiology, metabolism, and structure.[14] Research has shown that poor nutrition, smoking, alcohol consumption, atmospheric pollution, and infections associated with a pregnant mother are also associated with low birth weight. Low birth weight in turn is related to poor growth in children and is eventually associated with poor adult health. The accumulation of risk occurs when both poor growth and poor socioeconomic status interact to create a lifetime of poor social and health status or when adverse circumstances and health in early life, coupled with a negative health event at an older age, result in poor adult health.

Some studies have found that although poor growth in early childhood is associated with poor health in adulthood, mitigating circumstances can overcome some of these effects. Improvement in social conditions can result in better health and performance later in life. When parents improve their social condition, and attain higher levels of education, their low-birth-weight children have less of an association with poor health and other types of attainment as adults and achieve higher levels of cognitive development. These results may be due to improved nutrition or parental stimulation.

The phenomenon of "social accumulation" is also important in understanding the complexity of inputs into the health system. Social accumulation reflects the fact that both disadvantage and advantage tend to accumulate throughout a lifetime and can even be transgenerational. For example, a mother of lower socioeconomic status is more likely to have a low-birth-weight baby who in turn is more likely to be exposed to more environmental hazards, have poorer nutrition and less education, attain less in school, and emerge as an adult with poorer health status and the same disadvantages as those that they experienced in childhood. This disadvantage is then experienced by their children. The same is true for those who are advantaged. It has also been found that when a person crosses social economic boundaries, their health status changes in accordance with the direction of change.

Data from Torche, F. Early-life circumstances and their effects over the life course. *Popul Res Policy Rev.* 2019;38:771–782. doi: 10.1007/s11113-019-09555-w

Sustainable Development and Health Systems

The sustainable development goals (SDGs) are a relatively new, universal set of goals, targets, and indicators that United Nations (UN) member states are expected to use to frame their agendas and political policies through 2030.[15]

The eight health-related goals of the 17 SDGs are as follows:

- Goal 1: No poverty
- Goal 2: Zero hunger
- Goal 3: Good health and well-being
- Goal 4: Quality education
- Goal 5: Gender equality
- Goal 6: Clean water and sanitation
- Goal 7: Affordable and clean energy
- Goal 8: Decent work and economic growth

As described by Johnson, Anderson, and Rossow, these goals build on the successes of the Millennium Development Goals, while integrating new areas such as climate change, economic inequality, innovation, sustainable consumption, peace, and justice, among other priorities.[16] In keeping with the systems thinking perspective, the goals are *interconnected*—often, the key to success on one will involve tackling issues more commonly associated with another. They serve to identify and address *root causes* while uniting people for positive change. The UNDP provides support to governments to integrate the SDGs into their national development plans and policies, including health systems and public health. A track record of *working across multiple goals* to achieve systemwide improvements increases the likelihood of reaching the targets set out in the SDGs by 2030. Partnerships among all stakeholders—governments, private sector, civil society/nongovernmental organizations (NGOs), and citizens—will continue to be a critical success factor. The area of health is multisectoral, highly interconnected, and has challenges with many root causes (see **Table 1-5** for information on global health and disease).[16] SDG 3, Health and Well-Being, provides a good example of how health systems can be utilized and can serve to integrate action across the 17 goals. This is illustrated in **Figure 1-3**.[10]

Table 1-5 Global Health and Disease

Indicator	Adult HIV Prevalence Rate (%)	Obesity—Adult Prevalence Rate	Underweight Children <5 Years Old (%)	Infectious Disease Risk	Adult Smoking Rate (%)	Literacy Rate (% of Adult Population)	Unemployment Rate (% Age 15–24) (Data Year)	BCG, ≤1 Year Old	DPT, ≤1	Hep B	Hib (3)	MEV	PAB	Pol (3)
Australia	0.10%	29%	—	—	13.60%	—	10.80%	—	95	95	95	93	—	95
Bangladesh	<0.1%	3.60%	22.60%	High	34.70%	74.90%	14.70%	99	98	98	98	97	98	98
Botswana	18.60%	18.90%	—	High	19.40%	88.50%	41.20%	98	95	95	95	97	91	96
Brazil	0.60%	22.10%	—	Very high	12.80%	93.20%	31.90%	63	68	68	68	73	96	68
Canada	—	29.40%	—	High	13%	—	14%	—	92	84	92	90	—	92
China	—	6.20%	2.4% (2013)	High	25.60%	96.80%	11.40%	99	99	99	—	99	—	99
DR Congo	0.70%	6.70%	23.1% (2017/18)	Very high	12.80%	77%	10.10%	67	65	65	65	55	85	65
France	0.30%	21.60%	—	—	33.40%	—	20.10%	—	96	91	95	92	—	96
Germany	—	—	0.5% (2014/17)	—	22%	—	7%	—	91	87	90	97	—	91
Ghana	1.70%	10.90%	12.6% (2017/18)	Very high	3.50%	79%	9.60%	99	98	98	98	94	90	98
India	0.20%	3.90%	33.4% (2016/18)	Very high	27.20%	74.40%	28.30%	84	85	85	85	89	90	85
Ireland	0.30%	25.30%	—	—	20.80%	—	17.40%	0	94	93	93	90	—	94
Israel	—	26.10%	—	High	21.20%	97.80%	8.80%	—	98	96	98	99	—	98

(continues)

Table 1-5 Global Health and Disease *(continued)*

Indicator	Adult HIV Prevalence Rate (%)	Obesity—Adult Prevalence Rate	Underweight Children <5 Years Old (%)	Infectious Disease Risk	Adult Smoking Rate (%)	Literacy Rate (% of Adult Population)	Unemployment Rate (% Age 15–24) (Data Year)	BCG, ≤1 Year Old	DPT, ≤1	Hep B	Hib (3)	MEV	PAB	Pol (3)
Japan	—	4.30%	—	—	20.10%	—	4.40%	95	96	92	95	98	—	96
Jordan	—	35.50%	3% (2012)	—	34.80%	98.20%	40.50%	76	77	77	77	76	92	76
Korea	—	4.70%	—	NA	20.80%	—	7.80%	98	98	98	98	98	—	98
Mexico	0.40%	28.90%	4.7% (2018/19)	Inter-mediate	13.10%	95.20%	8.10%	98	78	80	78	99	96	78
Nigeria	1.30%	8.90%	18.4% (2019/20)	Very high	3.70%	62%	19.60%	75	56	56	56	59	65	53
Peru	0.40%	19.70%	2.4% (2019)	Very high	8.10%	94.50%	11.20%	87	82	82	82	78	85	79
Russia	—	23.10%	—	Inter-mediate	26.80%	99.70%	16.90%	95	97	97	—	97	—	97
Turkiye	—	32.10%	1.5% (2018/19)	—	30.70%	96.70%	24.30%	95	95	96	95	96	95	95
United Kingdom	—	27.80%	—	High	15.40%	—	13.20%	—	93	93	93	91	—	93
United States	—	36.20%	0.4% (2017/18)	—	23%	—	9.60%	—	93	91	90	91	—	92

Data from Nayeem Jannatul, MD, MPH. Source: CIA World Factbook 2023. Accessed May 1, 2023. https://www.cia.gov/the-world-factbook/

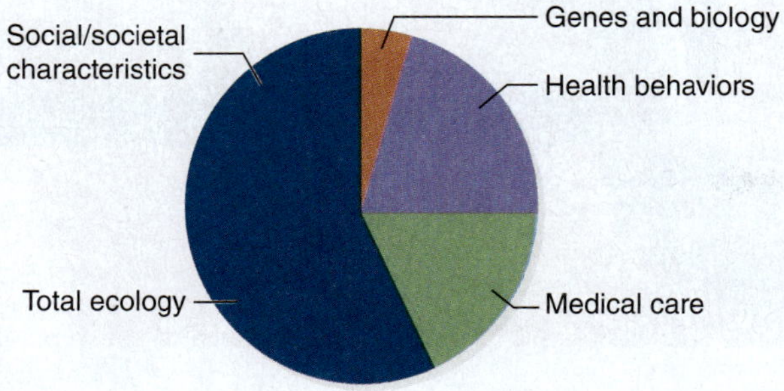

Figure 1-3 Major Determinants of Health

Reproduced from Shi L, Johnson J, eds. *Public Health Administration: Principles for Population-Based Management*. 4th ed. Burlington, MA: Jones & Bartlett; 2020.

Conclusion

As health systems continue to evolve in every country in the world, we will see many variations. Some will follow predictable pathways that reflect local government structure, and others will follow a unique pathway shaped by racial, ethnic, national, and cultural forces. All systems, regardless of locale, will be challenged by changes in economics and pressures to provide services based on measures of cost, quality, and access. Health systems do not exist in a vacuum; instead, they are profoundly influenced by a range of social and political determinants of health. These determinants shape demand for services and the range of options that need to be provided within the system. They also influence the kinds of medical practitioners needed, as well as appropriate levels of education. Finally, in the context of growing populations and diverse demands, health systems will need to find ways to adapt to a global community and meet the push for greater sustainability and responsiveness.

References

1. Marmot M. Social determinants of health inequalities. *Lancet*. 2005;365:1099–1104.
2. International Health Conference. Constitution of the World Health Organization. 1946. *Bull World Health Organ*. 2002;80(12):983–984.
3. Johnson JA, Rossow C. *Health Organizations: Theory, Behavior, and Development*. Burlington, MA: Jones & Bartlett Learning; 2020.
4. Johnson JA, Stoskopf C, Shi L. *Comparative Health Systems: A Global Perspective*, 2nd ed. Burlington, MA: Jones & Bartlett Learning; 2019.
5. *Types of Health Systems*. Comparative Health Policy Library, Columbia University. https://www.publichealth.columbia.edu/research/comparative-health-policy-library/types-health-systems. Accessed May 1, 2023.
6. Johnson JA, Davey KS, Greenhill RG. *Health Care USA: Understanding Its Organization and Delivery*. 10th ed. Burlington, MA: Jones & Bartlett Learning; 2023.
7. *Quality of Care*. World Health Organization. https://www.who.int/health-topics/quality-of-care#tab=tab_1. Accessed May 1, 2023.
8. IHME. *Global Burden of Disease (GBD)*. 2021.
9. Johnson JA, Anderson DE, Rossow C. *Health Systems Thinking: A Primer*. Burlington, MA: Jones & Bartlett Learning; 2020.
10. Shi L, Johnson JA. *Public Health Administration: Principles of Population-Based Management*, 4th ed. Burlington, MA: Jones & Bartlett Learning; 2021.
11. Garrett BE, Martell BN, Caraballo RS, King BA. Socioeconomic differences in cigarette smoking among sociodemographic groups. *Prev Chronic Dis*. 2019;16:180553. doi: 10.5888/pcd16.180553.
12. World Health Organization. *Ageing and Health: Key Facts*. 2022.
13. Chu B, Marwaha K, Sanvictores T, Awosika AO, Ayers D. Physiology, stress reaction. In: *StatPearls [Internet]*. Treasure Island, FL: StatPearls Publishing; 2024.
14. Torche F. Early-life circumstances and their effects over the life course. *Popul Res Policy Rev*. 2019;38:771–782. https://doi.org/10.1007/s11113-019-09555-w.
15. Andersen RM. *Families' Use of Health Services: A Behavioral Model of Predisposing, Enabling, and Need Components*. Purdue, IN: Purdue University; 1968.
16. Johnson JA, Anderson DE, Rossow C. Systems thinking for public health practice and administration. In: Shi L, Johnson JA. *Public Health Administration: Principles of Population-Based Management*, 4th ed. Burlington, MA: Jones & Bartlett Learning; 2021.

CHAPTER 2

Global and International Health Frameworks

Richard G. Greenhill and Merritt Brockman

Introduction to Global Coordination of Health and Frameworks

The international community has long been concerned about disease outbreaks and their impact on population health and the global economy. While this type of planning had long been in the works, it was the Spanish flu and other outbreaks that pushed global leaders to conceptualize and plan for future incidents. In fact, Sanitary Conferences in the years before the Spanish flu of 1918 showed opportunities for greater global coordination at a time when the world was less connected. The mass deaths and suffering laid the foundation for many of the international frameworks that are seen today. This chapter focuses on types of frameworks as well as some of the main frameworks and processes used today to reduce the impact of public health emergencies of international concern.

Types of Frameworks

Before going further, it is helpful to understand some basics about frameworks. Frameworks are guides that countries can use to create processes at the health ministry level and that cascade through their public health and personal healthcare systems. Frameworks are not meant to be overly prescriptive in their implementation, but rather allow flexibility based on country needs, resources, and geopolitics. There are four main categories of frameworks: disease, preparedness and response, disaster prevention, and monitoring and evaluation. Next, we will explore them from a U.S. perspective.

Disease

Frameworks focused on disease include those that are associated with detection, notification, coordination, and responding. For example, in the United States, the coordinating agency is the U.S. Centers for Disease Control and Prevention (CDC). The CDC defines its Infectious Disease Framework as "developed to provide a roadmap for improving our ability to prevent known infectious diseases and to recognize and control rare, highly dangerous, and newly emerging threats through a strengthened, adaptable, and multi-purpose U.S. public health system." The CDC framework is broadly described in **Figure 2-1**.

Preparedness and Response

"The Federal Emergency Management Agency (FEMA) defines the National Response Framework (NRF) as a guide to how the nation responds to all types of disasters and emergencies. It is built on scalable, flexible, and adaptable concepts identified in the National Incident Management System to align key roles and responsibilities."[1]

Element 1: Strengthen infrastructure

- To strengthen public health fundamentals including infectious disease surveillance, laboratory detection, and epidemiologic investigation

Element 2: Identify and mitigate

- To identify and implement high-impact public health interventions to reduce infectious diseases

Element 3: Policy strengthening

- Develop and advance policies to prevent, detect, and control infectious diseases

Figure 2-1 CDC Infectious Disease Framework

Data from CDC's Infectious Disease Framework. Accessed June 2023. https://www.cdc.gov/ddid/framework.html

Disaster Prevention

"The Federal Emergency Management Agency (FEMA) defines the National Disaster Recovery Framework (NDRF) as a system that enables effective recovery support to disaster-impacted states, tribes, territorial and local jurisdictions. It provides a flexible structure that enables disaster recovery managers to operate in a unified and collaborative manner. The NDRF focuses on how best to restore, redevelop and revitalize the health, social, economic, natural and environmental fabric of the community and build a more resilient nation."[2]

Monitoring and Evaluation

"The World Health Organization's main objective of the Monitoring and Evaluation Framework is to establish and maintain a set of global and country indicators to support: strategic thinking, operational tracking, real-time evidence-based decision-making, and to ensure advocacy and transparency between donors, UN agencies, and partners involved in response."[3]

Global Health Preparedness, Security, and Resilience

The COVID-19 outbreak once again reminded global leaders of our connectedness when a viral contagion starts in one country and quickly spreads around the world. The international community had conceptualized plans for this type of event in the form of various frameworks and initiatives as shown in **Figure 2-2**. Each of these was poised to push nations to think about planning, detection, mitigation, response, and prevention of outbreaks and other disasters as they relate to health.

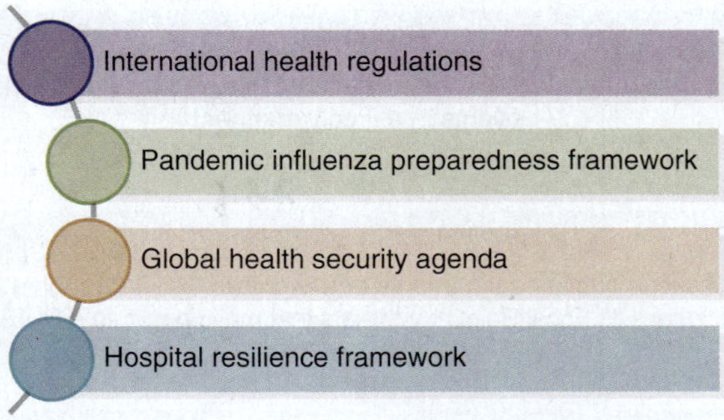

Figure 2-2 Key global health preparedness frameworks and initiatives

Key Frameworks and Systems of Significance

International Health Regulations (IHR)

The IHR is a legal framework that was adopted by the international community and that defines each ratifying nation's rights and responsibilities in dealing with public health emergencies.[4] The rules under which the IHR was created contain a host of provisions for everything from designation of outbreaks [e.g., a Public Health Emergency of International Concern (PHEIC)] as well as guidelines for implementation and preparedness activities. The IHR set forth specific guidelines as noted in **Figure 2-3**.

Pandemic Influenza Preparedness (PIP) Framework

The PIP Framework represents a global collaboration between national health ministries and the WHO to facilitate pandemic influenza preparedness and response.[5] The overarching goals of the framework are improvements in sharing data on viruses with potential to cause global pandemics, as well as increasing the vaccine supply and access to developing nations in the world. The framework came into effect in May 2011, as it was adopted by members of the World Health Assembly (WHA) with a unanimous vote. Currently, there are continued iterations of implementation, with the most recent being called Partnership Contribution High-Level Implementation Plan III 2024–2030. This plan includes a strategy for strengthening pandemic influenza preparedness activities from 2024 to 2030.

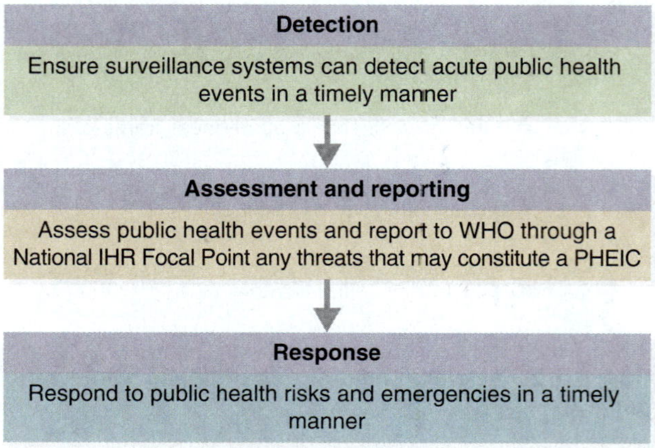

Figure 2-3 Key capacities of the IHR

Data from *International Health Regulations*. World Health Organization. Accessed July 6, 2023. https://www.who.int/health-topics/international-health-regulations#tab=tab_1

Global Health Security Agenda (GSHA)

The GSHA was created in the United States to focus on infectious disease spread, particularly for new bacteria, viruses, and pathogens becoming resistant to treatment.[6] This effort established an ecosystem of partnerships between international organizations, nongovernment entities, and more than 50 countries to expand the core capacities found in the IHR. The Office of Global Affairs' Office of Pandemics and Emerging Threats (PET) is the key coordinator of this multilateral effort representing the United States.

Hospital Resilience Framework

Hospital resilience is defined as the ability of a hospital facility or healthcare system to respond appropriately during an emergency or disaster and to minimize or reduce the risk associated with such events. The Hospital Resilience Framework[7] has three main components:

- **Absorb:** The facility or system's ability to absorb the shocks of a disaster or emergency.
- **Adapt:** The facility or system's ability to respond to the needs of its community and continue essential healthcare services.
- **Transform:** The facility or system's ability to learn from, recover, and improve responsiveness for future events.

Resilience in hospitals (or health systems) does not just happen; rather, it is a deliberate and coordinated effort to address seven key functions to strengthen preparedness and ultimately the building of a resilient entity. These seven key functions are:

1. Build capacity for leadership and coordinate information about roles, responsibilities, and overall disaster response plans.
2. Create contingency plans with detailed operating procedures to improve operations, capacity, and recovery from events. Additionally, ensure flexible financing mechanisms to address shortages in staffing and supplies (to include disruptions to the supply chain). These funding mechanisms can include collaborations between departments or sectors, or even the establishment of public–private partnerships.
3. Invest in infrastructure, logistics, and supplies to ensure the organizational culture, transportation system, and supply chain are all poised to maintain core operations in spite of the shocks and supply disruptions experienced as a result of a disaster.
4. Focus on building adequate, multidisciplinary teams to address the needs for surge staffing, task-shifting, and critical shortages. These efforts should include timely communication about preparedness and response protocols, distribution of adequate supplies for staff, and consistent and appropriate compensation.
5. Identify and continue critical clinical services in a safe manner and successfully enable the ability to surge.
6. Engage with communities and communicate to reduce fear, combat rumors, increase surveillance, and protective measures.
7. Adopt and maintain functional information systems that act as the central hub of operationality, preparedness, and subsequent resilience.

Introduction to OneHealth

OneHealth is defined as "a collaborative, multisectoral, and transdisciplinary approach—working at the local, regional, national, and global levels—with the goal of achieving optimal health outcomes recognizing the interconnection between people, animals, plants, and their shared environment."[8]

With the increase in global population and people living in new geographic areas, it is only natural that human settlement puts us in areas where we live in closer proximity to animals (wild and domestic). Coupled with the changes that humans bring to these new areas, this disruption leads to the perfect environment

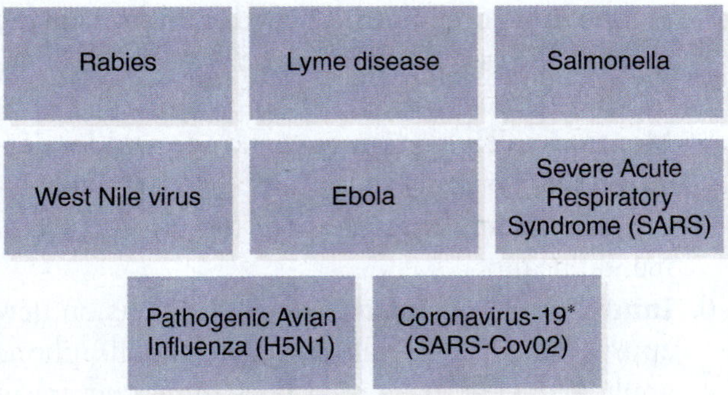

*At the time of publilcation, there were several emerging theories as to the origins of the COVID-19 pandemic. One of the dominant theories points to COVID-19 being a zoonotic disease that passed from animals to humans.[9]

Figure 2-4 Zoonose diseases[8]

Data from Goodman B. Scientists parse another clue to possible origins of COVID-19 as WHO says all possibilities "remain on the table." CNN. March 17, 2023. https://www.cnn.com/2023/03/17/health/covid-origins-raccoon-dogs/index.html

for disease to pass from animals to humans. Diseases that pass from animals to humans are called zoonotic diseases. Examples of zoonotic diseases, listed in **Figure 2-4**, are well known and some have had a significant impact on humans in recent years.

OneHealth's approach is to involve experts in a variety of disciplines (physicians, nurses, epidemiologists, veterinarians, etc.) to monitor and control emerging public health threats posed by diseases that have the potential (or do) spread among humans, animals, and the environment.[10]

National Incident Management System (NIMS)[11]

The National Incident Management System is a Federal Emergency Management Agency (FEMA) framework that guides government and nongovernment agencies on how to work together to plan, respond, and recover from incidents. This framework emphasizes shared vocabulary, processes, and systems.

The precursor to NIMS was developed in the 1970s with the creation of a system known as the Firefighting Resources of California Organized for Potential Emergencies (FIRESCOPE). In the aftermath of the September 11, 2001, terrorist attacks, the need for a more integrated nationwide incident management system with shared terminology, processes, and resources became even clearer.

In 2004, FEMA published the first NIMS document, with further revisions occurring in 2008 and ultimately in 2017. The revisions reflect progress made through lessons learned, best practices, and changes in policy.

Regardless of the scope, size, or nature of the incident, the NIMS framework can be used to ensure a coordinated response and recovery effort. NIMS incorporates three components in order to facilitate response and recovery within and among agencies: flexibility, standardization, and unity of effort.

NIMS includes six major functional areas:

- **Command Function:** Provides unity of effort and functional responsibility for the incident to manage and direct activities.
- **Operations Function:** Plans and performs tactical activities that could focus on saving lives, reducing hazards, protection, or restoration.
- **Planning Function:** Collects, evaluates, and disseminates information to both the command function and other incident personnel.
- **Logistics Function:** Provides support to include facilities, security, transportation, supplies, equipment, food, communication, information technology, equipment maintenance, and medical services (for incident personnel).
- **Finance/Administration Function:** Established when the incident calls for specific finance and administrative support services. These include recording personnel time, negotiating or maintaining leases and contracts, tracking and analyzing costs, and administering claims.
- **Intelligence/Investigations Function:** Collects, analyzes, and shares incident information. Typically, this base function is performed by the planning function; however, for incidents that involve criminal or terrorist acts, or epidemiologic investigations, this function will be initiated to perform intensive intelligence gathering and investigative activity.

Mental Health Framework 2022

Mental health is defined by the Organization for Economic Cooperation and Development (OECD) as "a state of well-being in which every individual realizes his or her own potential, can cope with the normal stresses of life, can work productively and fruitfully, and is able to make a contribution to his or her community." The need to address mental health is not only a social responsibility but an economic one. In fact, the costs associated with ill mental health average 3.5% to 4% of countries' gross domestic product.

In 2017, the health ministers (or equivalent) from several OECD countries highlighted the deficiencies many countries face regarding mental health care.

These ministers charged the OECD with benchmarking mental health performance and looking for policies and best practices across countries that have well-established, effective mental healthcare systems. The next year (2018), the OECD convened a 6-day conference of 40 mental health experts (e.g., policymakers, clinicians, academics, and advocates) to determine the key principles of mental health performance. Together, they agreed on six principles that define a high-performing mental health sector:

1. Focuses on the individual who is experiencing mental ill-health
2. Has accessible, high-quality mental health services
3. Takes an integrated, multisectoral approach to mental health
4. Prevents mental illness and promotes mental well-being
5. Has strong leadership and good governance
6. Is future-focused and innovative[12]

These principles serve as the basis for benchmarking mental health measures across OECD countries. In 2021, the OECD published *A New Benchmark for Mental Health Systems*, which outlined steps to improve mental health care and examples of what has been implemented and been successful. Examples ranged from peer-delivered services in Australia and New Zealand to Canada's Wellness Together, which provides remote self-assessment, tracking, and self-guided courses.

OECD's benchmark principles are:

1. **Patient-centered care:** Collect information about people's experiences and outcomes of their mental health care.
2. **Accessibility:** Ability for individuals who want to access mental health care and their ability to access that care.
3. **Integrated/multisectoral:** Systematic integration across health, education, and employment for individuals who are in mental health distress.
4. **Promoting good mental health and preventing mental illness:** Programs to educate the population about social-emotional skills.
5. **Mental health system governance and leadership:** Leaders and health ministers acknowledging and communicating about the importance of mental health.
6. **Innovation and future-focused:** Focus on new approaches such as telemedicine, mobile phone applications, and a strong data infrastructure to track and ultimately improve performance.[13]

Risk Assessment

Risk Identification and Site Criticality Toolkit

One of the core agencies within the U.S. Department of Health and Human Services is the Administration for Strategic Preparedness and Response (ASPR). This agency acts as the lead for all medical and public health responses in the event of a disaster or public health emergency, whether naturally occurring or human-made. A critical resource provided by ASPR is the Risk Identification and Site Criticality (RISC) Toolkit. This toolkit provides data-driven hazard risk assessment, which can be used to inform emergency preparedness planning, risk management, and resource investments.[14]

The RISC Toolkit is a three-module platform that can be downloaded for free. The three modules allow users to self-assess to identify external threats and internal hazards, determine vulnerability, and predict consequences to a site in the event of an incident.[15]

Toolkits are updated by the ASPR. The new toolkit is projected to contain multiple dashboards that allow multiple users to interact concurrently, aggregate data across multiple sites, and store data in a central repository.

References

1. National disaster recovery framework. Federal Emergency Management Agency. https://www.fema.gov/emergency-managers/national-preparedness/frameworks/recovery.
2. National disaster recovery framework. Federal Emergency Management Agency. https://www.fema.gov/emergency-managers/national-preparedness/frameworks/recovery#:~:text=The%20National%20Disaster%20Recovery%20Framework,a%20unified%20and%20collaborative%20manner.
3. Monitoring and evaluation framework. World Health Organization. https://www.who.int/publications-detail-redirect/monitoring-and-evaluation-framework.
4. *International Health Regulations*. World Health Organization. Accessed July 6, 2023. https://www.who.int/health-topics/international-health-regulations#tab=tab_1.
5. Pandemic Influenza Preparedness (PIP) framework. World Health Organization. Accessed July 6, 2023. https://www

.who.int/initiatives/pandemic-influenza-preparedness-framework.

6. Global Health Security Agenda. U.S. Department of Health and Human Services. January 18, 2023. Accessed July 6, 2023. https://www.hhs.gov/about/agencies/oga/global-health-security/agenda/index.html.
7. *Strengthening Hospital Resilience in the Eastern Mediterranean Region*. https://applications.emro.who.int/docs/9789290229582-eng.pdf.
8. Mackenzie JS, Jeggo M. The OneHealth approach: why is it so important? *Trop Med Infect Dis*. 2019. https://www.ncbi.nlm.nih.gov/pmc/articles/PMC6630404/.
9. Goodman B. Scientists parse another clue to possible origins of COVID-19 as WHO says all possibilities "remain on the table." CNN. 2023. https://www.cnn.com/2023/03/17/health/covid-origins-raccoon-dogs/index.html.
10. Centers for Disease Control and Prevention. OneHealth basics. 2022. https://www.cdc.gov/onehealth/basics/index.html.
11. National Incident Management System. Federal Emergency Management Agency. https://www.fema.gov/sites/default/files/2020-07/fema_nims_doctrine-2017.pdf.
12. Organization for Economic Cooperation and Development. Mental Health Performance Framework. https://www.oecd.org/health/OECD-Mental-Health-Performance-Framework-2019.pdf.
13. Organization for Economic Cooperation and Development. *A New Benchmark for Mental Health Systems: Tackling the Social and Economic Costs of Mental Ill-Health*. OECD Health Policy Studies. Paris: OECD Publishing; 2023. https://doi.org/10.1787/4ed890f6-en.
14. RISC toolkit 2.0. Administration for Strategic Preparedness and Response. https://www.phe.gov/Preparedness/planning/RISC-Toolkit-2.0/Pages/default.aspx.
15. West J. Risk Identification and Site Criticality (RISC) toolkit. *Homeland Security Digital Library*. 2023. https://www.hsdl.org/c/risc-toolkit/.

CHAPTER 3

Global Health and Disease

Carleen H. Stoskopf and William Wuenstel

Introduction

In the development and management of a country's healthcare system, an essential component is an understanding of the environment or national context in terms of (1) the social and cultural beliefs and behaviors; (2) the physical environment, such as exposures to environmental hazards, levels of sanitation, and food and water supply safety; (3) the political climate, including legal issues that impact the provision of health care; (4) the design for financing health care and the distribution of health resources; (5) economic development, including poverty levels, distribution of wealth, types of industry, and agriculture; (6) other social structures, such as the education and judicial systems; and finally, (7) the types of diseases that are present in the population (morbidity) and rates of mortality, the disease burden. Assessment of the population's health needs in light of the national profile should drive how medical resources are distributed and health services are provided. Healthcare systems are called on to do disease prevention, primary treatment, secondary treatment, and tertiary treatment. Integration of the healthcare system with the public health system is essential for effective intervention in the cycles of disease that plague many populations.

Public health systems can provide a variety of nonmedical services, such as sanitation improvements, environmental hazard control, vector control, health promotion, community interventions to improve health and well-being, and setting health policy for the financing and distribution of health services. The public health systems are also responsible for the surveillance of disease in populations. The activity of disease surveillance is vitally important to healthcare systems that are often called on to decide how few and precious resources are to be deployed. Understanding the disease profile of a population and the burden of disease that exists in that population is essential to planning and implementation of health programs. For example, in the case of malaria, healthcare providers must rapidly identify and treat specific types of malaria, as well as asymptomatic cases, to prevent further transmission. The public health system must work to eliminate vectors through destruction of mosquito breeding sites and use of safe and effective pesticides. Equally important is the role of health educators who work with the community to change behavior by encouraging use of bed nets at night and emptying local water receptacles. Simultaneously, researchers must continue the search for safe and cost-effective new treatments, for methods to quickly identify asymptomatic individuals, and for a new vaccine. No campaign to eliminate or substantially reduce malaria will be successful without all of these components; therefore, it is incumbent upon healthcare systems to understand the populations they serve and to work with their communities through public health efforts and other social institutions to effect change. **Box 3-1** identifies the 10 essential public health functions.

No healthcare system can be successful without a close working relationship with the public health system. In an ideal world, they would blend seamlessly.

Box 3-1 Ten Essential Public Health Functions

Monitor health statuses to identify and solve community health problems.
Diagnose and investigate health problems and health hazards in the community.
Inform, educate, and empower people about health issues.
Mobilize community partnerships to identify and solve health problems.
Develop policies and plans that support individual and community health efforts
Enforce laws and regulations that protect health and ensure safety.
Link people to needed personal health services and assure the provision of health care when otherwise unavailable.
Assure a competent public and personal healthcare workforce.
Evaluate effectiveness, accessibility, and quality of personal and population-based services.
Research for new insights and innovative solutions to health problems.

Reproduced from Centers for Disease Control and Prevention. The public health system and the 10 essential public health services. March 2014. http://www.cdc.gov/nphpsp/essentialServices.html

Burden of Disease

Disease is measured in many ways. In public health, the term *prevalence* is used to measure the number of individuals with a disease in a specific population at a discrete point in time. *Incidence* is the number of new cases of a disease in a population over a specified period of time.[1] A vast amount of data are available on the incidence and prevalence of diseases (morbidity data) by country, states, regions, and cities and by population demographics, such as age, gender, and race/ethnicity. Disease severity is commonly measured by disease-specific mortality for that disease. Disease-specific mortality is the number of deaths due to a given disease per time, usually expressed per 1,000 or 100,000 people per year. An example is the mortality from prostate cancer (25 per 100,000 in 2000 in Germany).

To communicate the magnitude of a disease in different populations, it can also be reported as a case fatality rate—that is, the rate of death among those who have the disease reported per 1,000 or 100,000 people with the disease. For example, 720 out of 1,000 men with prostate cancer that has spread to other areas of the body will die within 5 years. Mortality rates are often reported based on age groups or other demographic variables.[1] A list of commonly used health indicators can be found in **Table 3-1**.[2]

The burden of disease is expressed by statistics that attempt to determine the impact of disease on a population through measuring disability and healthy-life years lost. The World Health Organization (WHO) initiated the Global Burden of Disease study in 1992 that continues to the present. The study selected disability-adjusted life years for its measurement.[3,4] Other measures include quality-adjusted life years, health expectancies, and healthy-life years.[1] Implicit in these measures is the idea that one can apply cost-benefit analyses in terms of the cost to a population to prevent and treat diseases versus the cost that population pays for years lived with disability and/or early mortality from those same diseases. Healthcare providers who avail themselves of these types of measures as applied to their populations can make better decisions when appropriating scarce resources. National health policymakers can use the economic data applied to loss of healthy-life years to better understand the impact of diseases upon their nation's population and, therefore, its productivity as measured in gross domestic product (GDP). An understanding of the burden of disease results in better decision making in terms of allocation of resources for specific programs for prevention, treatment, eradication, and control of specific diseases that severely impact their populations and ultimately the economic viability of the country. A good example of this is the burden that malaria places on populations where it is endemic.

The collection of health statistics is difficult and complicated, even in countries with well-developed health systems like the United States. Collection of these statistics requires standardized definitions of diseases, consistent standards for diagnosis of these diseases, and a well-defined population at risk for these diseases. For developing countries struggling to meet the most basic healthcare needs of their communities, the collection of useful statistics can be a daunting but nevertheless vital task. **Table 3-2** illustrates the burden of disease, both communicable and noncommunicable, for the countries presented in this book, allowing a comparison across countries.

Noncommunicable diseases (NCDs) are of immense in scope and growing in importance worldwide. The global boom in premature mortality and morbidity from NCDs may share similarities with the pandemics of infectious diseases. Like communicable diseases, NCDs create disabilities and impairments that affect people with day-to-day activities. One could argue that there is a growing association between communicable and noncommunicable

Table 3-1 Commonly Used Population Health Indicators

Indicator[a]	Definition[b]
Crude birth rate	Number of live births per 1,000 people in a population during a specific period of time
Crude death rate per 100,000 people	Number of deaths per 100,000 people in a population during a specific period of time
Specific death rate per 100,000 people (age, gender, cause)	Deaths by age, gender, or per 100,000 people in a population during a specific period of time
Infant mortality rate per 1,000 live births	Deaths under 1 year of age per 1,000 live births in a population
Neonatal mortality rate per 1,000 live births	Deaths under 28 days of age per 1,000 live births in a population
Maternal mortality rate per 100,000 women	Deaths from maternal causes per 100,000 women of childbearing age
Proportionate mortality	Percentage of deaths that can be attributed to a particular disease, calculated out of all deaths within that population
Incidence rate	New cases for a condition per 1,000 or 100,000 people in a population during a specific period of time
Prevalence (point in time)	Number of cases of a condition at a specific point in time per 100,000 people in a population
Disease-specific mortality rate	Number of deaths from a specific condition in a defined population group per 1,000 or 100,000 people during a specified period of time
Case fatality rate	Number of deaths among those with a specific condition per 1,000 people with that condition

[a]All indicators are per year.
[b]All definitions are per a defined population.

Data from Basch PF. *Textbook of International Health.* 2nd ed. Oxford University Press; 1999, pp. 80, 81; World Health Organization. WHO global health observatory data. Accessed June 8, 2016. https://www.cia.gov/library/publications/resources/the-world-factbook/CIA.

Table 3-2 Major Causes of Death per 100,000 Population, 2016, in Selected Countries

Country	All Causes of Death	Communicable Diseases	Noncommunicable Diseases	Injuries
Australia	345	14	303	28
Bangladesh	847	235	549	64
Botswana	1,255	555	612	88
Brazil	687	93	514	80
Canada	372	23	318	31
China	668	41	576	50
DR Congo	1,782	920	724	137
France	369	21	313	35
Germany	410	22	365	23
Ghana	1,222	476	670	76

Country	All Causes of Death	Communicable Diseases	Noncommunicable Diseases	Injuries
India	1,051	253	682	116
Ireland	397	22	344	32
Israel	363	31	311	21
Japan	319	34	244	41
Jordan	746	53	640	54
Mexico	589	57	468	63
Nigeria	1,685	866	674	146
Peru	533	121	453	58
Korea	389	34	302	53
Russia	967	74	790	103
Turkiye	638	44	555	39
United Kingdom	409	29	359	22
United States	488	31	413	44

Data from World Health Organization. Global Health Observatory Data Repository. Accessed July 5, 2016. http://www.who.int/gho/en/

diseases. Recent discussion has centered on this topic as low- and middle-income countries (LMICs) continue to be plagued by communicable diseases such as the human immunodeficiency virus/acquired immune deficiency syndrome (HIV/AIDS) and tuberculosis (TB), while at the same time being increasingly threatened with NCDs such as cardiovascular disease (CVD) and diabetes.

As both communicable diseases and NCDs occur within the same population, it is vital to understand the importance of establishing effective programs to combat their threats. The following section discusses NCDs; the subsequent section focuses on communicable infectious diseases. Both types pose similar challenges in LMICs.

Noncommunicable/ Chronic Diseases

The epidemic of NCDs has emerged as one of the major health challenges of the 21st century, especially in terms of mortality, disability, and the socioeconomic status of countries. NCDs, also known as chronic diseases, are nontransmissible diseases of often long duration. Examples of NCDs and chronic diseases include cardiac, cardiovascular (ischemic heart disease), cerebrovascular (stroke), and lung diseases, such as emphysema and chronic bronchitis (including chronic obstructive pulmonary disease [COPD]), as well as cancer, diabetes, obesity, and mental disorders. Globally, NCDs are the leading cause of death, killing more people yearly than all other causes combined. Individually, cardiovascular disease, which includes ischemic heart disease, is the leading cause of death. Available data indicate that 80% of NCD deaths occur in LMICs. Sub-Saharan Africa is the only exception; the burden of communicable diseases in this region is currently higher than that of NCDs. However, in African nations, NCDs are rapidly trending upward and are projected to exceed communicable, maternal, perinatal, and nutritional diseases as the most common causes of death by 2030.[1]

The burden of NCDs in developing countries has led to a double burden as LMICs continue to deal with infective communicable diseases, such as malaria, HIV/AIDs, and diarrheal disease, as well as NCDs, with ill-equipped healthcare systems that are characterized as having limited financial and human resources. In its predictions, the World Health Organization (WHO) echoes the growing threat posed by NCDs/chronic diseases. According to WHO, 17 million people will die prematurely or before age 70 due to NCDs and mortality from NCDs has increased in more than 20 LMICs.

The worldwide threat from NCDs is also growing. One burden of disease report summarized the

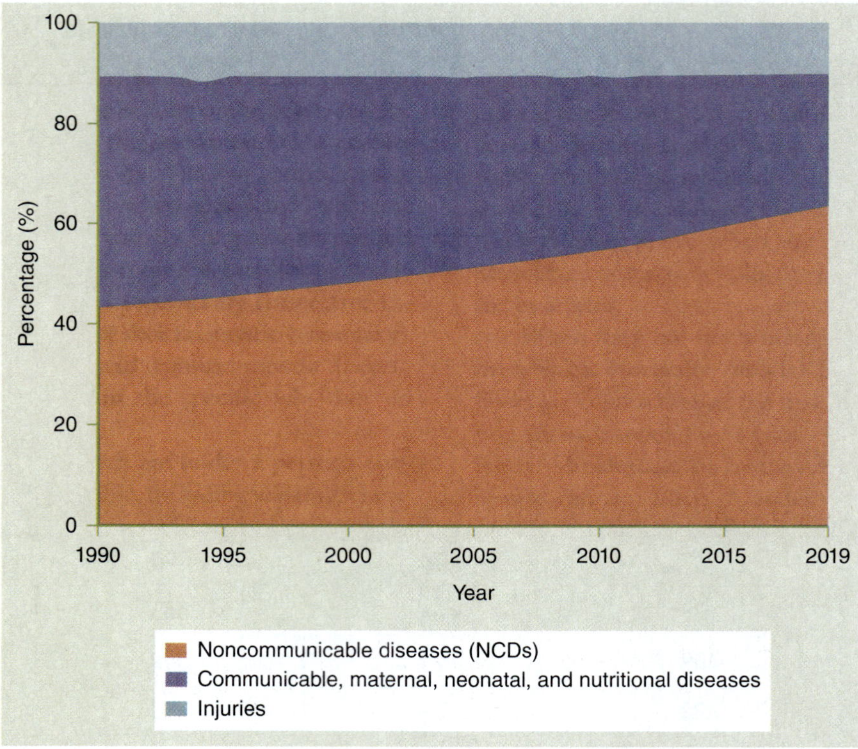

Figure 3-1 Total disease burden by cause, world, 1990 to 2019

Reproduced from Roser M, Ritchie H, Spooner F. Burden of disease. OurWorldInData.org. 2021. Accessed April 15, 2023. https://ourworldindata.org/burden-of-disease.

total disease burden by cause globally from 1990 to 2019. As shown in **Figure 3-1**, a notable shift in this burden has occurred since 1990, when communicable disease held the highest share at 46%. The shift in burden toward NCDs/chronic diseases resulted from significant reductions in communicable and preventable diseases as incomes rise and overall health and living standards improve. In high-income countries, NCDs typically account for over 80% of the disease burden. This contrasts with communicable diseases representing less than 5% of the burden. The opposite is true in LMICs, where communicable disease still accounts for more than 60% of the disease burden across many countries.

To understand NCDs/chronic disease, one must understand the multicausation disease model of chronic diseases. The complexity of various causes, known as etiologies, that result in the development of chronic disease is illustrated in **Figure 3-2**. In this model, the human host is pictured in the center of the environment in which they live. Within the host, there exists a unique genetic endowment that is inalterable. These genes are what a person inherits from their parents and affect physical and physiologic characteristics such as body build, cardiovascular traits, the likelihood of getting specific diseases, and mental abilities. The host exists in a complex environment that includes exposure to many risk factors that can contribute to

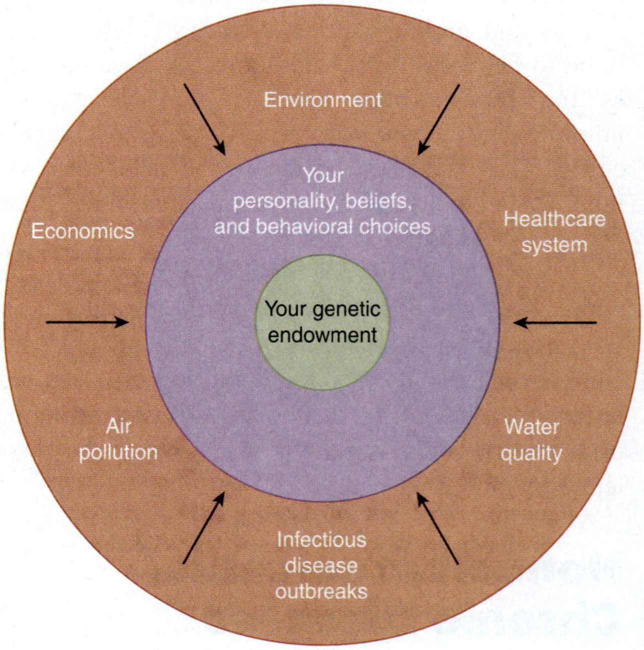

Figure 3-2 Multicausation disease model

Data from Bocos Benedict/Shutterstock. Copyright 2018 by Jones & Bartlett Learning LLC an Ascend Learning Company WWW.jblearning.com.

disease development. These environmental risk factors may be physical, chemical, biologic, or social, depending on geography, environmental pollutants, exposure to communicable diseases, and social factors such as occupation, income, and recreational activities.

The multicausation model clearly demonstrates the connection of an individual's health to their lifestyle behaviors and the environment. The WHO asserts that some modifiable risk factors are driving the rapid growth of chronic diseases—specifically, modifiable behavioral risk factors and metabolic risk factors.

Modifiable behaviors, such as tobacco use, physical inactivity, unhealthy diet, and the harmful use of alcohol, all increase the risk of NCDs. Here are the facts on these behaviors:

- Tobacco accounts for over 8 million deaths every year (including from the effects of exposure to secondhand smoke).
- 1.8 million annual deaths have been attributed to excess salt/sodium intake.
- More than half of the 3 million annual deaths attributable to alcohol use are from NCDs, including cancer.
- 830,000 deaths annually can be attributed to insufficient physical activity.

The following metabolic risk factors contribute to four vital metabolic changes that increase the risk of NCDs:

- Raised blood pressure
- Overweight/obesity
- Hyperglycemia (elevated glucose in the blood)
- Hyperlipidemia (elevated levels of fat in the blood)

In terms of attributable deaths, the leading metabolic risk factor globally is elevated blood pressure (to which 19% of global deaths are attributed), followed by elevated blood glucose, overweight, and obesity. Poor choices in one's life can increase the severity of these risk factors and lead to the development of chronic disease.

Other risk factors can also lead to the development of chronic diseases. Psychosocial determinants of chronic disease include lack of meaning or purpose in life, alienation, and the loss of culture or identity. Likewise, several bio-psycho-social factors influence health-related quality of life (HRQoL) and can result in poor health outcomes. Also, several infectious pathogens are considered risk factors, including human papillomavirus, which may lead to cervical cancer, and hepatitis, which can cause liver cancer. Moreover, the environment affects the risk of developing chronic diseases, including air pollution, water pollution, heavy metals, and toxic elements such as arsenic, cadmium, lead, and mercury (see **Table 3-3** and **Figure 3-3**). These toxic elements are typically found in drinking water, foods, dust, fish, dental amalgams, consumer products, and old pesticides. Many have

Table 3-3 Examples of Sources and Pathways of Human Exposure to Selected Chemicals

Exposure Media	Example Sources of Exposure and Exposure Pathways	Examples of Chemicals
Outdoor air	Inhalation of toxic gases and particles from vehicle and industrial emissions, or naturally occurring sources such as volcanic emissions or forest fires	Sulfur dioxide, nitrogen oxides, ozone, suspended particulate matter, lead, benzene, dioxins, and dioxin-like compounds
Indoor air	Inhalation of pollutants released during indoor combustion of solid fuels, from tobacco smoking, or from construction materials and furnishings, contaminants in indoor air, and dust	Suspended particulate matter, nitrous oxides, sulfur oxides, carbon monoxide, formaldehyde, polyaromatic hydrocarbons (PAH), mercury, lead dust from lead-based paints, benzene, asbestos, mycotoxins, phthalates, polybrominated diphenyl ether fire retardants (PBDEs)
Drinking water	Ingestion of drinking water contaminated with toxic chemicals from industrial effluents, human dwellings, agricultural runoff, oil and mining wastes, or natural sources	Pesticides, herbicides, fertilizers, metals (copper, lead, mercury, selenium, chromium), arsenic, fluoride, nitrate, cyanide, industrial solvents, petroleum products, disinfection by-products
Food	Consumption of food contaminated with chemicals at toxic levels through agricultural practices, industrial processes, environmental contamination, and natural toxins	Pesticides, methylmercury, lead, cadmium, dioxins, aflatoxin

(continues)

Table 3-3 Examples of Sources and Pathways of Human Exposure to Selected Chemicals *(continued)*

Exposure Media	Example Sources of Exposure and Exposure Pathways	Examples of Chemicals
Nonfood consumer products	Exposure by ingestion, inhalation, or dermal exposure to toxic chemicals contained in toys, jewelry and decoration items, textiles, food containers, or consumer chemical products	Lead, mercury, cadmium, phthalates, formaldehyde, dyes, fungicides, or pesticides
Soil	Ingestion (particularly for children) or inhalation of soil contaminated through industrial processes, agricultural processes, or inadequate household and industrial waste management	Heavy metals, pesticides, and persistent organic pollutants
Occupational exposure	Chronic or acute exposures through inhalation, dermal absorption, or secondary ingestion of toxic chemicals or by-products of industrial processes such as agriculture, mining, or manufacturing	Pesticides, benzene, heavy metals, solvents, suspended particulate matter
Human to human	Fetal exposure to toxic chemicals during pregnancy (through placental barrier) or through consumption of contaminated breast milk	Heavy metals, pesticides, benzene, etc.

Reproduced from Prüss-Ustün A, Vickers C, Haefliger P, Bertollini R. Knowns and unknowns on burden of disease due to chemicals: a systematic review. *Environ Health.* 2011;10:9. doi: 10.1186/1476-069X-10-9.

been classified as carcinogenic, and exposure to them can result in neurologic and organ dysfunction.

According to WHO, the top 10 leading causes of death worldwide in 2019 were as follows:

1. Ischemic heart disease
2. Stroke
3. Chronic obstructive pulmonary disease
4. Lower respiratory infections
5. Neonatal conditions
6. Lung cancer
7. Alzheimer's disease and other dementias
8. Diarrheal diseases
9. Diabetes mellitus
10. Kidney disease

These top 10 causes of death accounted for 55% of the 55.4 million deaths worldwide. From a global perspective, 7 of the 10 leading causes of death were NCDs; they accounted for 44% of all deaths, or 80% of the top 10 (see **Figure 3-4**).

The world's biggest killer is ischemic heart disease, responsible for 16% of worldwide deaths. Since 2000, the largest increase in deaths has been from for this disease, rising by more than 2 million deaths to 8.9 million deaths in 2019. Stroke and chronic

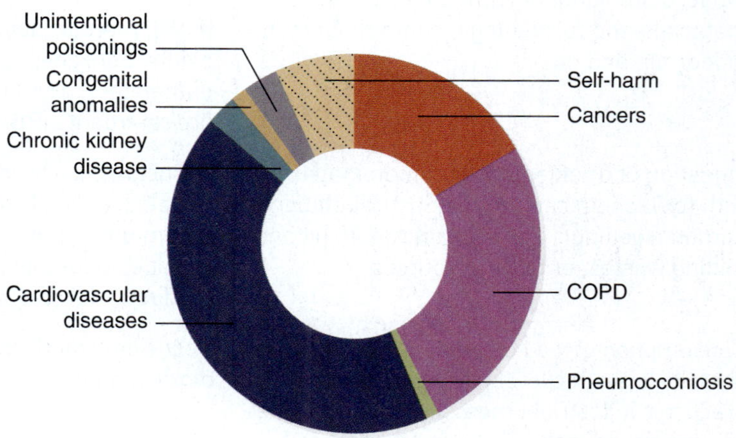

Figure 3-3 Public health impact of chemicals: knowns and unknowns

Reproduced from World Health Organization. The public health impact of chemicals: knowns and unknowns—data addendum for 2019. Published July 6, 2021. Accessed April 16, 2023. https://www.who.int/publications/i/item/WHO-HEP-ECH-EHD-21.01.

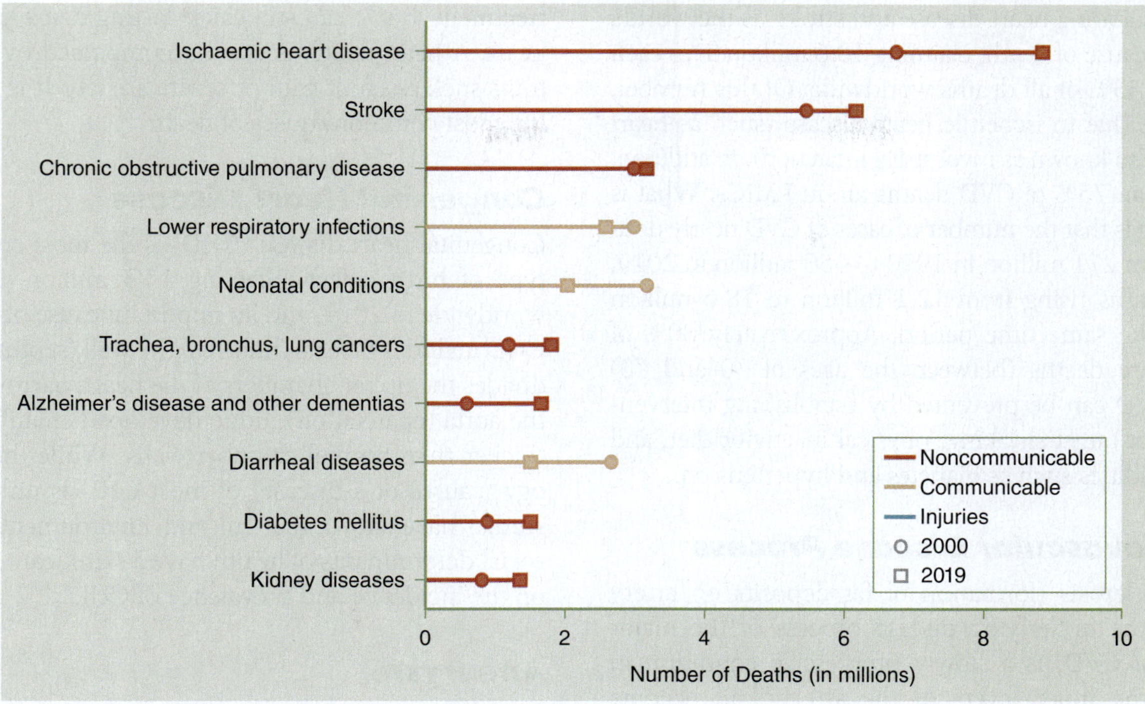

Figure 3-4 Leading causes of death globally

Reproduced from World Health Organization. The top 10 causes of death. Published December 9, 2020. Accessed April 18, 2023. https://www.who.int/news-room/fact-sheets/detail/the-top-10-causes-of-death.

obstructive pulmonary disease are the second and third leading causes of death, responsible for approximately 11% and 6% of total deaths, respectively.

Lower respiratory infections remained the world's most deadly communicable disease, ranking as the fourth leading cause of death. However, the number of deaths has decreased substantially: In 2019, this cause claimed 2.6 million lives, 460,000 fewer than in 2000.

Neonatal conditions are ranked fifth. However, deaths from neonatal conditions are one of the categories for which the global decrease in deaths in absolute numbers over the past two decades has been the greatest. These conditions killed 2 million newborns and young children in 2019, 1.2 million fewer than in 2000.

Deaths from NCDs are on the rise. Trachea, bronchus, and lung cancer deaths have risen from 1.2 million to 1.8 million and are now ranked sixth among leading causes of death.

In 2019, Alzheimer's disease and other forms of dementia ranked as the seventh leading cause of death. Women are disproportionately affected. Globally, 65% of deaths from Alzheimer's and other forms of dementia occur in women.

One of the largest declines in the number of deaths is from diarrheal diseases, with global deaths falling from 2.6 million in 2000 to 1.5 million in 2019.

Diabetes has entered the top 10 causes of death, following a significant percentage increase of 70% since 2000. Diabetes is also responsible for the largest rise in male deaths among the top 10 causes of death, with an 80% increase since 2000.

Other diseases that were among the top 10 causes of death in 2000 are no longer on the list. HIV is one of them. Deaths from HIV and AIDS have fallen by 51% during the last 20 years, moving HIV/AIDS from the world's eighth leading cause of death in 2000 to the 19th in 2019.

Lastly, kidney diseases have risen from the world's 13th leading cause of death to the 10th. Mortality has increased from 813,000 in 2000 to 1.3 million in 2019.

We cannot underestimate the impact NCDs/chronic diseases have on the global population, as most chronic illnesses lead to poor health outcomes. The increasing burden of NCDs, which falls disproportionately on LMICs, has made the prevention and management of NCDs a global priority. However, limited human and financial resources have hampered many countries from achieving significant gains in the battle against NCDs.

Cardiovascular Disease

Cardiovascular disease (CVD) refers to a wide variety or class of heart and blood vessel diseases (veins and arteries), including coronary heart disease (CHD), cerebrovascular disease (also referred to as stroke), heart failure, and peripheral arterial disease (PAD).

CVD, including heart disease and stroke, is the world's leading cause of death, claiming 18.6 million lives each year, or 33% of all deaths worldwide. Of this number, 85% are due to ischemic heart disease (such as heart attack, also known as myocardial infarction). In addition, more than 75% of CVD deaths are in LMICs. What is alarming is that the number of cases of CVD nearly doubled from 271 million in 1990 to 550 million in 2019, with deaths rising from 12.1 million to 18.6 million across the same time period. Approximately 80% of premature deaths (between the ages of 30 and 70) from CVD can be prevented by establishing interventions that target smoking, physical inactivity, diet, and comorbidities such as diabetes and hypertension.

Cardiovascular Disease Process

Atherosclerosis (formation of fat deposits on artery walls), the underlying disease process of the major forms of CVD, is a slowly progressive condition in which the inner layers of the artery wall become thick, irregular, and rigid. The process is complex, with contributing factors including deposition of fat and cholesterol, inflammation, migration and proliferation of smooth muscle cells, formation of raised fibrous legions, and calcification. With the progression of atherosclerosis, the arteries narrow, the blood flow is decreased, and there is a greater likelihood that the build-up of materials, known as plaque, will be disrupted, creating a traveling blood clot (embolism).

Ischemic Heart Disease

Coronary heart disease, also called ischemic heart disease or coronary artery disease, is a term used to identify several disorders that reduce the blood supply to the heart muscle. This impairment of circulation to the heart is most frequently the result of the narrowing of the coronary arteries by atherosclerosis. The onset and much of the progression of ischemic heart disease is caused by narrowed coronary arteries that supply blood to the heart muscle. When arteries are narrowed, less blood and oxygen reach the heart muscle, which can cause a heart attack. For many people, a heart attack will be the first time they realize they are living with ischemic heart disease.

Heart Attack

A heart attack, or myocardial infarction, is a medical emergency that occurs when something, usually a blood clot, cuts off the flow of blood to the heart. Without oxygen and nutrients, the heart muscle begins to die. A heart attack may not be fatal, especially if the individual receives immediate medical attention and treatment, but it can still cause lasting damage to the heart. A heart attack is often accompanied by symptoms such as chest pain or severe anxiety. It is among the most common causes of death.

Congenital Heart Disease

Congenital heart disease (CHD) is the most common type of birth defect, affecting 13.3 million patients worldwide in 2019, and an important cause of NCDs. CHD includes defects (holes) in the wall (septum) that divides the upper chambers of the heart, narrowing of the aorta (coarctation), underdeveloped chambers, or thicker than normal chamber walls. While the etiology (causes of a disease) of most CHD is unknown, studies have shown that cultural, environmental, and social determinants of health have a significant impact on the incidence and prevalence of CHD.

Aneurysm

Aneurysm is a balloon-like bulge that occurs when part of an artery wall weakens, allowing it to balloon out or widen abnormally. The etiology is sometimes unknown, but aneurysms can be either congenital (born with them) or hereditary. They can also be caused by high blood pressure, high cholesterol, atherosclerosis, chest injuries, smoking, and stress. Most commonly, aneurysms are located in the aorta, abdominal aorta, and brain arteries.

Heart Failure (Congestive Heart Failure)

Congestive heart failure (CHF) is a serious condition in which the heart does not pump blood as efficiently as it should. The heart has not stopped working; rather, it does not contract as strongly as needed, leading to a backup of blood traveling through the body at a slower rate, so that the pressure within the heart increases. As a result, the heart cannot pump enough oxygen and nutrients to meet the body's needs. With increased pressure in the heart, the muscle walls weaken and become stiff and thickened, leading to decreased organ perfusion. Lung congestion, fluid and water retention, fatigue and weakness, irregular heartbeats, weight gain, and persistent coughing are the typical body responses to CHF.

High Blood Pressure (Hypertension)

Hypertension is the leading modifiable cause of premature death and one of WHO's global targets for preventing NCDs. The number of people with hypertension globally in 2019 was over 1 billion, and has doubled since 1990. Elevated blood pressure is a common condition that affects the body's arteries. It is measured in millimeters of mercury (mm Hg), categorized as normal with a reading of 120/80 mm Hg and elevated with a reading of 130/80 mm Hg or higher. Higher than normal blood pressure increases the force of the blood pushing against the artery walls, which causes the heart to work harder to pump blood. Atherosclerosis (plaque buildup in the arteries) increases pressure as the heart pumps blood through narrowed arteries. If undiagnosed and untreated, hypertension increases the risk of heart attack, stroke, and other serious health problems. In many cases, people with high blood pressure have no symptoms, and the condition usually develops over time. Unhealthy lifestyle choices that contribute to hypertension include physical inactivity, high-sodium diet, alcohol consumption, smoking, obesity, family history, increased age, and certain chronic conditions such as kidney disease and diabetes.

Stroke (Cerebrovascular Disease)

Cerebrovascular disease refers to a group of conditions that affect blood flow to the brain. Problems with blood flow may occur from blood vessel narrowing (stenosis), clot formation (thrombosis), artery blockage (embolism), or blood vessel rupture (hemorrhage). The resulting conditions can include stroke, brain aneurysm, brain bleeding, and other vascular conditions. Interruptions in blood flow to the brain for any reason result in decreased oxygen supply to the brain. If the cells in the brain go too long without oxygen, they will die. The affected area of the brain loses the ability to function, resulting in paralysis, aphasia (difficulty with or loss of speaking ability), loss of muscle control on one side of the face, sudden loss (either partial or total) of one or more senses (vision, hearing, smell, taste, and touch), blurred or double vision, loss of coordination, vertigo, nausea and vomiting, confusion or agitation, seizures, memory loss, headaches, fainting, and coma.

The major modifiable risk factors for stroke include high blood pressure, tobacco use, physical inactivity, diabetes, obesity, cardiac arrhythmias (such as atrial fibrillation), and peripheral artery disease (PAD; atherosclerosis of the arteries in the lower extremities).

Arrhythmias

Arrhythmias occur when the heart conducts electrical impulses that are too fast, too slow, or erratic, causing an irregular heartbeat. Regular impulses are necessary to coordinate the heart's beat and promote blood flow throughout the body. Risk factors that may increase the development of arrhythmias include coronary artery disease, high blood pressure, congenital heart disease, excessive alcohol, caffeine, and tobacco use (nicotine). The cardiovascular disease burden of NCDs is associated with a wide range of risk factors and causes. The diverse list includes high blood pressure, high cholesterol, diabetes, obesity, and kidney disease, as well as physical inactivity, an unhealthy diet, air pollution, tobacco use, alcohol use, and stress. Millions of people worldwide struggle to control the risk factors that lead to cardiovascular disease, while many others are unaware that they are at high risk.

At least 75% of the world's deaths from CVDs occur in LMICs, which often do not have strong and widely accessible primary healthcare programs for early detection of CVD and key risk factors such as hypertension and diabetes. As a result, for many people in these countries, detection comes late in the course of the disease, when complications have already developed. This results in higher treatment costs, which often must be paid out of pocket and can be catastrophic to households, preventing people from pursuing or adhering to treatment. At the macroeconomic level, CVDs place a heavy burden on the economies of all countries, but especially LMICs.

It is estimated that 80% of CVDs can be prevented. Stopping smoking, eating less salt and more fruits and vegetables, getting regular physical exercise, and avoiding alcohol have been shown to reduce the risk of cardiovascular disease. However, while individual choices play a part in these behaviors, health policies also have an important role in ensuring people have what they need to live a healthy life, including clean air, affordable healthy food, and urban spaces that encourage an active lifestyle.

Cancer

Cancer is a term used to define diseases that affect any part of the body. The terms malignant tumor (cancer tumor that is likely to spread) and neoplasm (abnormal growth of tissue) are used interchangeably in defining cancer. Cancer is not a single disease, but rather a group of more than 200 different diseases. It is characterized by rapid, abnormal cell growth that then spreads to other parts of the body (metastasis). A major cause of cancer death is when these abnormal cells form lumps in the vital organs. According to WHO, cancer kills 10 million people every year. While there are regional and sex differences, globally the main types of cancer are:

- Breast cancer (2.26 million cases and 685,000 deaths in 2020)

- Lung cancer (2.21 million cases and 1.8 million deaths)
- Colon and rectum cancer, including bowel cancer (1.93 million cases and 935,000 deaths)
- Stomach cancer (1.09 million cases and 769,000 deaths)
- Liver cancer (906,000 cases and 830,000 deaths)
- Prostate cancer (1.41 million cases and 375,000 deaths)
- Skin cancer (nonmelanoma) (1.20 million cases and 57,000 deaths)

Cancer has a complex set of causes and consequences. Cancer occurs as a result of alteration in cellular functions. It is caused by gene changes that control how the cells function, especially how they grow and divide. In many cases, the cell's DNA is damaged by harmful environmental substances, such as toxic chemicals (benzene, asbestos, vinyl chloride, radon, and arsenic), the chemicals in tobacco smoke, and exposure to ultraviolet rays from the sun. Also, the genetic changes that cause normal cells to change to cancer cells can be triggered by errors that occur when the cell divides.

There is no single cause of cancer. Cancer development depends on things such as family history (genetics), health, nutrition, personal habits, and the environment. Genetic factors, by themselves, account for only a small fraction of cancers. Genetic factors do have an important influence on a person's chance of developing cancer when combined with outside factors. These factors are either voluntary (such as cigarette smoking, diet, and sexual behavior) or involuntary (such as breathing polluted air or drinking contaminated water).

- Cigarette smoking is the leading cause of cancer. Cigarette smoke contains more than 3,800 individual chemicals, and more than 40 are carcinogenic (cancer-causing).
- Portions of the diet, especially fatty foods and alcoholic beverages, also are linked to cancer.
- Skin exposure to ultraviolet radiation in sunlight is the primary cause of melanoma, a skin cancer.
- Sexual behavior that helps spread sexually transmitted diseases is intricately linked to cervical cancer in women.
- Environmental pollution by chemicals in drinking water, air, food, and in the workplace may contribute to cancer. The harmful health effects of chemicals depend on the dose, the strength of the chemical compound, the length of exposure, and the general health of the individual. Outside of the workplace, very few cancer cases are believed to be caused by exposure to environmental chemicals.

Most cancers may be prevented through the identification and control of external factors. Approximately 30% of cancers are linked to cigarette smoking. The remaining 70% are likely the result of interaction among various factors.

Diabetes

Diabetes is a chronic metabolic disease characterized by elevated levels of blood glucose (blood sugar), which leads over time to serious damage to the heart, blood vessels, eyes, kidneys, and nerves. It occurs when the pancreas is no longer able to make insulin or when the body cannot utilize the insulin it produces (insulin resistance). Insulin is a hormone made by the pancreas that acts like a key to facilitate glucose from the food we eat passing from the bloodstream into the cells to produce energy. Within minutes of its consumption, carbohydrate is first broken down into glucose in the blood; insulin is then required to transport the glucose into the cells. Not being able to produce or use insulin effectively leads to elevated glucose levels in the blood (hyperglycemia), resulting in damage to the body and failure of various organs and tissues, including heart disease, vision loss, and kidney disease.

There are three main types of diabetes: type 1, type 2, and gestational diabetes (diabetes while pregnant).

Type 1 diabetes is thought to be caused by an autoimmune reaction (the body attacks itself by mistake). This reaction stops the body from making insulin. Approximately 5% to 10% of the people with diabetes have type 1. Symptoms of type 1 diabetes often develop quickly. This disease is usually diagnosed in children, teens, and young adults, with daily insulin injections being necessary for them to survive.

With type 2 diabetes, the body does not use insulin well and cannot keep blood sugar at normal levels. About 90% to 95% of people with diabetes have type 2. It develops over many years and is usually diagnosed in adults (but is increasingly being diagnosed in children, teens, and young adults). Symptoms of type 2 diabetes often develop slowly and may not be noticed as quickly as in type 1. As with type 1, there is no cure for type 2 diabetes. Type 2 diabetes can be prevented or delayed with healthy lifestyle changes, such as:

- Losing weight
- Eating healthy food
- Being active

Gestational diabetes develops in pregnant women who have never had diabetes. Like other types of diabetes, gestational diabetes affects how the cells use sugar (glucose). This disease causes high blood sugar that can affect the pregnancy and the baby's health. Gestational diabetes is usually temporary and can be controlled while pregnant. Upon delivery, the woman's glucose will return to normal levels. However, gestational diabetes increases the woman's risk for type 2 diabetes later in life. The baby is also more likely to have obesity as a child or teen and to develop type 2 diabetes later in life.

Prediabetes is defined as higher than normal blood sugar levels. Unmanaged prediabetes leads to type 2 diabetes in about 50% of affected people over the next 5 to 10 years. Many people have no symptoms of prediabetes and it may exist for years. Losing weight, exercising regularly, and eating a healthy diet can reverse prediabetes and prevent type 2 diabetes from developing.

According to the International Diabetes Federation's (IDF) latest global data and projections on diabetes in 2021:

- Approximately 537 million adults (20–79 years) have diabetes.
- The total number of people living with diabetes is projected to rise to 643 million by 2030 and to 783 million by 2045.
- Three in four adults with diabetes live in LMICs.
- Almost one in two (240 million) adults living with diabetes are undiagnosed.
- Diabetes caused 6.7 million deaths.
- Diabetes caused at least 966 billion USD in health expenditures—9% of total health spending on adults.
- More than 1.2 million children and adolescents (0–19 years) are living with type 1 diabetes.
- One in six live births (21 million) are affected by diabetes during pregnancy.
- An estimated 541 million adults are at increased risk of developing type 2 diabetes.

Obesity

Obesity is one of the greatest public health challenges of the 21st century in both developed and developing countries. In 1997, WHO recognized obesity as a global health problem. In 2016, more than 1.9 billion adults were overweight worldwide. Among them, more than 650 million were obese. Obesity is a global burden that significantly increases the risk of NCDs. It is associated with a higher risk of morbidity, disability, and death. Its level of impact, as a risk factor for mortality, is similar to that of smoking. Major risk factors for mortality are increased cardiovascular incidents, such as coronary heart disease, hypertension, stroke, type 2 diabetes, and some types of cancer (e.g., breast cancer in postmenopausal women, endometrial cancer, and colon and kidney cancer).

Overweight and obesity are defined as abnormal or excessive fat accumulation that presents a health risk. A body mass index (BMI) over 25 is considered overweight, and a BMI over 30 is obese. This issue has grown to epidemic proportions, with over 4 million people dying each year due to being overweight or obese in 2017, according to the global burden of disease report.

Rates of overweight and obesity continue to grow in adults and children. From 1975 to 2016, the prevalence of overweight or obese children and adolescents aged 5–19 years increased more than fourfold, from 4% to 18% globally.

Obesity is one side of the double burden of malnutrition. In fact, today, more people are obese than underweight in every region except sub-Saharan Africa and Asia. Once considered a problem only in high-income countries, overweight and obesity are now dramatically rising in LMICs, particularly in urban settings. The vast majority of overweight or obese children live in developing countries, where the rate of increase has been more than 30% higher than that in developed countries.

Financially, being overweight and obese are relevant public health problems. It was estimated that the cost of health care for people who are overweight and obese is significantly higher than for those with normal weight. Moreover, in 2014, the global economic burden of obesity accounted for 2.8% of the global gross domestic product (GDP); it is predicted to reach 3.3% of the global GDP by 2060.

Obesity is a complex disease, with many factors contributing to excess weight gain. Usually, obesity results from inherited, physiologic, and environmental factors; medications; and unhealthy diet, physical activity, exercise choices, eating patterns, and sleep routines. The response to this epidemic has been a global action plan, with WHO, United Nations (UN), World Bank, World Obesity Federation, Organization for Economic Cooperation and Development, and various other government and nongovernmental organizations (NGOs) supporting initiatives and strategies that focus on the prevention and management of obesity over the life course, including developing targets.

Mental Health and Mental Disorders

Mental health is a state of mental well-being that enables people to cope with the stresses of life, realize their abilities, learn well and work well, and contribute to their community. It is an integral component of health and well-being that underpins our individual and collective abilities to make decisions, build relationships, and shape the world we live in. Mental health is a basic human right. And it is crucial to personal, community, and socioeconomic development.

Mental health is more than the absence of mental disorders. It exists on a complex continuum, which is experienced differently from one person to the next, with varying degrees of difficulty and distress and potentially very different social and clinical outcomes.

Mental health conditions include mental disorders and psychosocial disabilities as well as other mental states associated with significant distress, impairment in functioning, or risk of self-harm. People with mental health conditions are more likely to experience lower levels of mental well-being, but this is not always or necessarily the case.

A mental disorder is characterized by a clinically significant disturbance in an individual's cognition, emotional regulation, or behavior. It is usually associated with distress or impairment in important areas of functioning. There are many different types of mental disorders. Mental disorders may also be referred to as mental health conditions. The latter is a broader term covering mental disorders, psychosocial disabilities, and (other) mental states associated with significant distress, impairment in functioning, or risk of self-harm.

In 2019, one in every eight people, or 970 million people worldwide, lived with a mental disorder, with anxiety and depressive disorders being the most common.[1] In 2020, the number of people living with anxiety and depressive disorders rose significantly because of the COVID-19 pandemic. Initial estimates show a 26% and 28% increase, respectively, for anxiety and major depressive disorders in just one year.[2] While effective prevention and treatment options exist, most people with mental disorders do not have access to effective care. Many people also experience stigma, discrimination, and violations of human rights (see **Figure 3-5**).

NCDs have been a persistent issue in developed countries for a long time. However, they are now becoming a major concern in developing nations due to their transition from low-income to middle-income status, the impact of globalization on consumption patterns, and the aging of populations. NCDs are considered one of the significant challenges for sustainable development in the 21st century. Thus, global efforts to address this health issue have gained more attention worldwide, including in the United States.

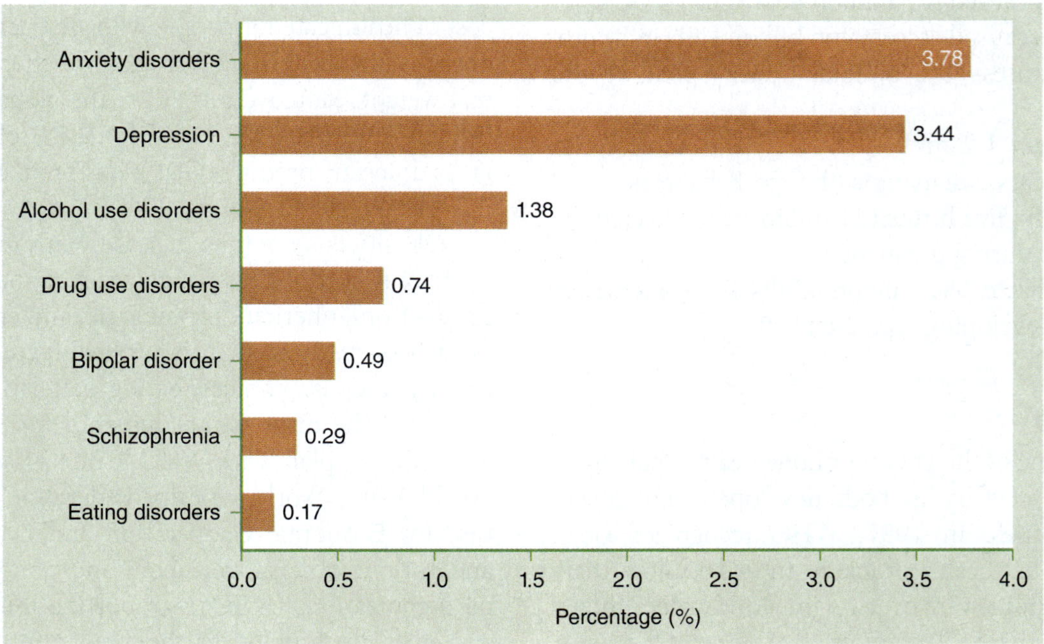

Figure 3-5 Prevalence by mental and substance use disorder, world, 2019

Reproduced from Dattani S, Rodés-Guirao L, Ritchie H, Roser M. Mental health. OurWorldInData.org. 2023. https://ourworldindata.org/mental-health.

Infectious Disease

Infectious diseases are illnesses that are spread from person to person, either directly or indirectly. They may spread in a variety of ways. Some require an intermediary host, such as diseases that are vector-borne (yellow fever virus, West Nile virus, Lyme disease, and Zika virus) and diseases that require zoological hosts for part of their life cycles and development (malaria, schistosomiasis). Others are spread through direct contact (impetigo, gonorrhea, syphilis, Ebola), contact with infected surfaces or fomites (*Staphylococcus aureus* infection, rhinovirus), ingestion of contaminated water (cholera, giardiasis), infection via the blood (hepatitis B and C, HIV), ingestion of fecal material (hepatitis A, *Escherichia coli*), intake via the respiratory system (tuberculosis, severe acute respiratory syndrome [SARS]), or direct contact with infected animals (tularemia). Many diseases can be spread in more than one way.

Infectious diseases have experienced a major comeback in the last four decades. In the 1970s, many public health and medical professionals believed that the age of infectious disease was mostly over because of successful vaccination development, a reduction of potential disease vectors through pesticide use, vast increases in basic public health sanitation, and identification and knowledge about infectious disease life cycles and modes of transmission. Most health professionals living in industrialized nations thought little of infectious diseases and turned their attention to chronic disease and its management. Within this environment of complacency appeared a newly recognized pathogen in the 1980s, the human immunodeficiency virus (HIV). HIV turned out to be the first of many new emerging and re-emerging infectious diseases that caught health professionals unprepared. Since the early 1980s, public health and healthcare systems have faced a number of new infectious diseases and new challenges with some diseases thought conquered.

The report of a new sexually transmitted disease that led to almost certain death was a concept that shocked everyone—from professionals in the medical community to the average person on the street. How could this occur? The emergence of HIV was quickly followed by other infectious diseases, including Ebola virus, SARS, avian flu, and Zika virus. In addition, some infectious diseases began to spread to new areas of the world, such as West Nile virus entering North America from Africa, Ebola spreading out from West Africa, and SARS spreading from Asia to Canada. Further contributing to this situation, the role of commercial airline traffic in spreading disease throughout the world changed from being a theoretical concern to a public health reality. And more importantly, we came to realize that the infusion of healthcare workers into endemic areas of some diseases created new fears in their home countries. As Ebola outbreaks in Africa appeared on our television screens, we were stunned to learn that this disease jumped from other primates to humans. Now we nervously watch for new cases of avian flu for the same reason. HIV in Africa reminds us of those historical plague epidemics that changed the basic population structure of societies as vast numbers of people died within short time periods. Those old infectious diseases that we thought were under control suddenly started to reappear or grow in prevalence. Malaria, for instance, is on the rise. Some infectious agents have now developed resistance to treatment. A virulent new form of tuberculosis has appeared that is also resistant to most treatments. Nature seems to thwart us at each turn. Those in the business of providing healthcare services and those who conduct disease surveillance must very seriously assess the burden of infectious diseases on the populations they serve and be prepared to address them through prevention, early detection, and treatment. Countries with healthcare resources that reach out as responders in emergency outbreaks around the world must prepare their own people with the knowledge and equipment necessary to prevent transmission to themselves and to those at home when they return.

As we progress through the early 21st century, developed countries are becoming increasingly aware of the health problems and needs of developing countries. This is not just because the developed countries are concerned that diseases endemic to developing countries may pose a hazard for their own citizens, but also out of a sense of justice and social responsibility. Because of real-time communication through technology such as the Internet and dedicated 24-hour news programming, an increase in international travel to developing countries, and demographic changes caused by immigration, people from all over the world are more aware of the conditions under which many people live. As our global awareness has increased, so has our sense of interconnectedness to those beyond our borders.

Global awareness has motivated governments, private organizations, and international organizations to come to the aid of people and nations with large burdens of illness. Unfortunately, special interests, politics, international corruption, and incompetence have thwarted many of these well-meaning efforts. Conditions in developing countries often contribute to the disease burden caused by infectious diseases. Many developing countries lack not only adequate healthcare services but also many of the public health advancements and infrastructure that developed countries experienced and enjoyed in the early part of the 20th century. Conditions in many developing countries include poverty, undernutrition, poor sanitation, lack of potable water, little or no access to healthcare services, and low levels of education. Recent studies have shown that undernutrition is a leading contributor to childhood deaths from infectious disease. Of the estimated 10 million children who die each year, the majority die from preventable causes: pneumonia and diarrhea, followed by malaria, AIDS, and measles.[5,6]

It is essential for healthcare delivery systems to provide effective interventions for infectious diseases, including both prevention and treatment. These systems must also work to collect and provide timely and accurate health statistics for both the planning and monitoring of the use and provision of health services by the populations they serve. It is further incumbent upon healthcare services to work with their communities to reach out with interventions to those in the population who cannot or will not access services. It is equally important for countries to develop plans for improvement of infrastructure, community education, and economic development, which have been shown to significantly improve the health status of populations.

Vector-Borne Diseases

Of great concern to epidemiologists worldwide is the resurgence of vector-borne diseases. This resurgence is due to a number of factors, including resistance to pesticides, poor environmental and ecosystem management, resistance to drugs used for treatment, the shifting of health policy from prevention to emergency response, genetic changes in pathogens, climate change, deforestation, and changes in agricultural practices.[7] The newest of these challenges is the Zika virus, which was endemic in Africa and Asia in humans in the early 1950s but first caused an outbreak in the South Pacific in 2007 among populations with no resistance. This virus suddenly came to public awareness through its teratogenic properties in South America. The idea of globalization and interconnectedness took on a whole new meaning as people from around the world gathered in Brazil for the Olympics. Many athletes risked their safety to attend. We would never have imagined in the 1970s that the Olympics in 2016 would be impacted by an infectious disease. This trend is changing the world and requires a different type of thinking to manage infectious diseases. Health systems must be prepared for these diseases, the old and the new.

Vector-borne diseases are those that require a blood-sucking agent (arthropod) to transmit the pathogen among vertebrate hosts. These diseases can be grouped according to three types of pathogens: parasitic, bacterial, and viral. Until World War II, vector-borne diseases were the number one cause of morbidity around the world. Since the early 1990s, vector-borne diseases have contributed significantly to the burden of disease in most areas of the developing world, and they continue to spread to the developed world. **Table 3-4** summarizes the three categories of vector-borne diseases and their geographic distribution in the world today.

Malaria

The vector-borne disease of greatest concern worldwide is malaria. Malaria is caused by a protozoan parasite that invades the red blood cells of humans. It is spread by mosquitoes in the genus *Anopheles*; after biting one infected person, they go on to bite someone else, thus transmitting the disease. It is important to note that part of the life cycle of the parasite occurs in the mosquito and is required for disease transmission. Common symptoms include malaise, febrile episodes with cerebral damage, hypoglycemia, respiratory distress, anemia, chronic debilitation, malnutrition, and neurologic syndromes. Malaria in endemic areas presents itself in two basic forms. For those under the age of 5 years and travelers without previous exposure, the parasitemia results in acute symptoms and can eventually lead to death. In Africa, the majority of deaths from malaria are among children.[6] People who live in endemic areas and who have survived early childhood episodes of malaria often develop a level of immunity. In this case, malaria may present with mild symptoms, including general malaise, general debilitation, and periods of low fever. Frequently, adults with malaria may be completely asymptomatic.

Untreated mild or asymptomatic cases preserve a reservoir of parasites for transmission to others via mosquito vectors because the symptoms may be so mild that adults do not seek treatment. This asymptomatic pool of people poses the biggest obstacle to eradicating malaria. In order to eradicate malaria, it is necessary to find and treat these individuals and use new drugs and treatment regimens that eliminate the parasites from the blood of humans. The call to public health is surveillance, finding asymptomatic cases, and treating those cases quickly and effectively. This also calls for the development and use of highly sensitive diagnostic tools. Treating a population as a whole prophylactically has been controversial.

Table 3-4 Geographic Distribution of Major Vector-Borne Diseases by Type of Pathogen

Country	Parasitic Disease	Bacterial Disease	Arboviral Disease
North America	Malaria	Tularemia, tick-borne relapsing fever, Lyme disease	Encephalitis types: Eastern equine, La Crosse, Venezuelan equine, St. Louis, West Nile virus, dengue, Zika virus (emerging)
South American and Central America	Malaria	Plague	Venezuelan Eastern equine encephalitis, St. Louis encephalitis, dengue fever, yellow fever, Zika virus
Europe	—	Lyme disease, tularemia	Sindbis, tick-borne encephalitis, Dengue fever, Crimean-Congo hemorrhagic fever
Africa	Malaria, leishmaniasis, African trypanosomiasis	Louse-borne typhus, plague	Rift Valley fever, Kyasanur Forest disease, dengue fever, yellow fever, Crimean-Congo hemorrhagic fever, chikungunya
Asia	Malaria, lraeishmaniasis	Plague	Chikungunya, dengue, Japanese encephalitis, California encephalitis, Sindbis, Crimean-Congo hemorrhagic fever, tick-borne encephalitis
Australia	—	—	Dengue, Japanese encephalitis, Murray Valley encephalitis, Ross River hemorrhagic fever

Data from Centers for Disease Control and Prevention. List of VHF diseases. June 6, 2016. Accessed August 8, 2016. http://www.cdc.gov/vhf/diseases.html; Centers for Disease Control and Prevention. Division of Vector-Borne Diseases. April 2, 2016. Accessed July 20, 2016. https://www.cdc.gov/ncezid/divisions-offices/about-dvbd.html; Centers for Disease Control and Prevention. Technical fact sheet: Eastern equine encephalitis. April 5, 2016. Accessed August 8, 2016. http://www.cdc.gov/EasternEquineEncephalitis/; Centers for Disease Control and Prevention. La Crosse encephalitis. April 11, 2016. Accessed August 8, 2016. http://www.cdc.gov/lac/; Centers for Disease Control and Prevention. Arboviral diseases, neuroinvasive and non-neuroinvasive 2015 case definition. Accessed August 8, 2016. https://ndc.services.cdc.gov/case-definitions/arboviral-diseases-neuroinvasive-and-non-neuroinvasive-2015/; Heymann DL. *Control of Communicable Disease Manual.* American Public Health Association; 2015:33–43.

Treatment of malaria has become complicated over time, as some of the species of malaria (*P. malariae*, *P. falciparum*, *P. vivax*, and *P. ovale*) have developed resistance to more commonly used treatment drugs. As of now, there are no vaccines for malaria.[6] Long-term chemoprophylaxis with malaria-preventing drugs is not a viable option, as it can result in further resistance and poses other risks and side effects to the individual. The current recommendation is to provide targeted groups (pregnant women and small children) in endemic areas with intermittent therapeutic doses of malaria treatment.[1] Other options include programs to eliminate mosquito breeding sites and to educate people in the use of bed nets, which can weaken the chain of infection. However, only the successful treatment of asymptomatic people will move us further toward eradication of malaria globally.

Of all the vector-borne diseases, malaria is believed to cause the greatest morbidity burden around the world. A worldwide campaign that started in 1955 and operated through the mid-1960s resulted in a substantial reduction in malaria in areas where it was endemic.[6] As efforts abated, a resurgence of malaria occurred. This was primarily caused by the ban of DDT and the discontinuation of programs to reduce mosquito breeding areas, resulting in a decrease in vector control. The initial successful efforts show how public health measures, when appropriate, can have a significant impact on vector-borne diseases and can result in less reliance on treatment. Perhaps most importantly, as many sub-Saharan countries earned independence in the 1950s and 1960s, the ensuing political instability, escalation of foreign debt, and decrease in international aid resulted in the collapse of the public health and healthcare systems in many countries. The result of these multifaceted factors is that malaria has returned with a vengeance. Not until 1998 were efforts once again renewed to reduce malaria levels by introducing the Roll Back Malaria program. The Roll Back Malaria program is a partnership with WHO, UNICEF,

UNDP, and the World Bank that had a goal of reducing the number of cases of malaria by one-half by the year 2010. This program has had limited success in great part because of lack of adequate funding.[8] Recently renewed efforts to bring the disease under control have been funded by new organizations, such as the Bill and Melinda Gates Foundation[9] and the Global Fund to Fight AIDS, Tuberculosis, and Malaria.

The population at risk for malaria increased significantly during the 20th century. The at-risk population grew from 0.9 billion to 3.0 billion people from 1900 to 2002, with 48% of the world's population currently at risk.[10] Of all cases, 90% occur in sub-Saharan Africa, although malaria exists in more than 100 countries. It resulted in over 600,000 deaths in 2012, 77% of which were children under the age of 5 years. In 2018, it was estimated that 228 million people had malaria and 405,000 died, most of whom were under the age of 5.[11] Martens and Hall report that migration of populations caused by urban relocation and the flight of refugees increase the distribution of malaria regionally into areas that were previously malaria free. This type of population migration results from crises, such as environmental changes, economic necessity, war and conflict, and natural disasters, all of which result in populations moving to neighboring areas to escape these conditions.[12] Often this results in people moving into city shantytowns without any services, such as potable water, electricity, or sanitation. These conditions are more likely to exist in areas where poverty is common and where malaria is endemic.[11] Complicating matters even further the surveillance, treatment, public health interventions, and disease reservoirs vary from one region to another, making efforts geared toward eradication all the more difficult.

Because of the debilitating nature of malaria, the disease has a major impact on the economies of the regions and countries where it is endemic, reducing productivity, lowering rates of economic growth, impeding development, and discouraging savings and investment.[13] Control of malaria mostly has a clear association with economic development, although until now malarial control has mostly occurred outside of Africa. After an area becomes malaria free, the growth in the economy over the next five years is significantly higher than in neighboring countries for which malaria remains a significant problem. A study of the association between malaria and economic growth looked at the years between 1965 and 1990 and found that in areas with high incidence and prevalence of malaria, the economy grew 1.3% less per person per year, but a reduction in malaria by 10.0% was associated with a 0.3% increase in GDP growth.[14]

Zika Virus

Over the past two decades, we have experienced a number of emerging or re-emerging infectious diseases posing new threats in new places—for example, West Nile virus becoming endemic in North America. While we have eradicated smallpox and hope to soon eradicate polio, many new diseases are vector-borne, making their eradication highly unlikely, if not impossible. An excellent example of such an emerging virus is the Zika virus, which came to prominent attention in 2015.[15]

Zika virus, which was of little significance throughout equatorial Africa and Asia between 1960 and 1980, emerged in the South Pacific as an epidemic on Yap Island in 2007 in a mild form. In 2013 to 2014, it emerged again in a number of South Pacific Island nations, and for the first time its association with birth defects was noted. In March 2015, Brazil detected its first case, and by January 2016, Zika was in 18 additional countries in South America and in the Caribbean. In July 2016, the United States announced its first case and found an endemic area in north Miami. There were also a few cases in Texas.[16] Since this time period, no additional cases of Zika have been found in the United States or in the world.[17]

This disease, which is spread primarily by the *Aedes aegypti* and *Aedes albopictus* mosquitoes, has no treatment or vaccination. Furthermore, the virus can be spread from pregnant mothers to their fetuses, through sexual contact with partners, and theoretically through blood products, although there are no recorded cases of this type of transmission to date. The vector mosquitoes are commonly found throughout the world in certain climate zones, including the southern United States and Europe. These zones are expanding each year with climate change and global warming. The same mosquitoes transmit dengue and chikungunya disease. California has reported the presence of mosquitos known to transmit Zika,[18] which arrived in the United States on goods imported from Asia and are known as the Asian tiger mosquito (*Aedes albopictus*).

Our efforts today are focused on reducing mosquito populations in infected areas. Unfortunately, widespread spraying of insecticides results in its own problems due to toxic exposure of wildlife. In many areas of the world, populations are left with few options except to reduce standing water, which serves as breeding sites. The vector mosquitoes are both daytime and nighttime biters, so the use of bed nets is limited in its impact. Only three insecticides for personal use are effective: DEET, IR 3535, and icaridin.[19]

The emergence of Zika on the world stage is an excellent example of "one health." This new discipline looks at the entire environment, physical and social, and the interaction and interconnectedness of all things in the environment that contribute to human health. In the case of Zika, climate changes and increasing temperatures have increased the zones where the two types of vector mosquitoes can live and breed. Global travel has moved the virus from Africa and Asia to Central and South America, the Caribbean, and North America. Pesticide use is limited and may contribute to further deterioration of other species' habitats and harm humans. The social and environmental systems in many countries are not prepared to develop and enforce policies that might contain the virus's spread. Healthcare systems are not prepared to test for and treat the disease, nor are they set up to deal with the terrible consequences of the microcephaly associated with the transmission of the virus from mother to fetus. The concept of one health encourages us to understand the complete interconnectedness of all human, social, and physical systems on the planet and its impact on human health and well-being.[20]

Waterborne Diseases

Waterborne diseases generally invade the gastrointestinal system, although some parasitic forms found in water can enter the body through the skin, such as schistosomiasis (blood fluke/trematode), and cause damage to other areas of the human body. Of particular importance are those infections that are caused by viruses (rotaviruses), bacteria (*Vibrio cholerae, E. coli*), and parasites (*Entamoeba histolytica*), to name a few. In addition, water is critical in the reproduction and development of a number of insect vectors that contribute to disease burden. Finally, water is a place where a number of toxins, chemicals, and metals concentrate, such as arsenic, mercury, and chromium.[21]

These contaminants pose health hazards as they enter the food chain, as well as through direct exposure to skin during water activities close to their sources. In the developing world, many waterborne infections result in diarrhea that can often be life-threatening because of loss of fluids and salts. Chronic diarrheal infections can lead to poor absorption of nutrients, malnutrition, malaise, stunted growth, and chronic disability. The impact of waterborne diseases on children in developing countries can be devastating, with these diseases being a leading cause of death among children worldwide. In all regions of the world, flooding and contamination of water systems can cause disease, especially with climate change and an increase in the number, duration, and severity of storms and flooding events.[22]

Diarrheal Disease

Each day, over 2,000 children die from diarrheal illness worldwide. Approximately 11% of child deaths are due to diarrheal illness globally, and one in every nine children under the age of 5 dies from this disease. For children with HIV/AIDS, the mortality rate is 11 times greater. Diarrheal illness in children leads to poor growth and to disabilities associated with cognitive development. In addition, diarrheal illness is a major contributor to malnutrition. Conversely, malnutrition increases the susceptibility of children to the pathogens that cause diarrhea. Although there are many causes of diarrheal illness, the most prevalent cause is rotaviruses.[23]

The most common mode of transmission for all diarrheal illnesses is through contaminated water (88%), especially water contaminated with feces. The most common cause in children is rotaviruses, which are often present in contaminated water sources. Around 5% of all deaths in children under the age of 5 years are caused by these viruses. Of diarrheal episodes seen in outpatient clinics in developing countries, up to 35% of them are caused by rotaviruses.[24] In addition, rotavirus is estimated to cause 440,000 deaths per year, 2 million hospitalizations per year, and over 110 million visits to clinics.[25-28] A specific vaccine for rotavirus is available and has been determined to be highly effective. Vaccination programs for rotavirus infection, however, face numerous challenges in developing countries, with many being underfunded, poorly organized, and with limited access to needed supplies.

The chain of infection for nearly all diarrheal illness is through fecal contamination of water or food (most commonly water), and the low level of sanitation in most developing countries remains a major obstacle to relieving this burden. Today, nearly 1.1 billion people do not have access to a clean and sustainable water source,[29] and 84% of those people live in rural areas. In these areas, the lack of potable water for cleaning and preparing food, handwashing, and bathing, not to mention drinking, results in a continuous cycle of diarrheal diseases. This problem is compounded by the fact that 2.6 billion people in the world have no access to a sanitary toilet facility and must defecate in uncontrolled areas. This contributes to the problem in many ways, as uncovered excrement can contaminate food and water supplies, and an inability to wash hands properly can facilitate the spread of pathogens from person to person. In developed countries, the 20th century saw the introduction of clean water sources for the bulk of their populations, as well as municipal wastewater disposal. This single achievement is cited as one of the major reasons developed countries saw a substantial drop in infectious diseases in the early part of the 20th century.[30]

There have been a number of efforts to reduce this disease, starting with an active vaccination program for rotaviruses. In addition, there have been efforts to promote exclusive breastfeeding of infants for the first 6 months of life.[31] UNICEF estimates that 13% of all under-5 deaths in developing countries could be prevented by exclusive breastfeeding, making it the most powerful means of preventing child mortality. In terms of the importance of healthcare systems, mortality from diarrheal diseases can also be prevented through the use of oral rehydration therapy (ORT). The adoption of ORT has reduced the incidence of associated morbidities and moralities; however, over the past 30 years, its use still remains low, at around 33% in developing nations.[31] Finally, the improvement of water supplies for drinking and the improvement of hygiene and sanitation are vital to bringing an end to this kind of illness.[32] In comparing and evaluating countries' health systems, the level of sanitation is vital to understanding of the health status of the population.

Cholera

Cholera is caused by a bacterium, *Vibrio cholerae*, and is one of three diseases that are required to be reported to WHO.[1] In 1992, WHO organized the Global Task Force on Cholera Control to reduce the number of outbreaks and to address the social and economic conditions that lead to periodic epidemics.[33] Cholera is endemic to parts of India and Bangladesh, but periodic outbreaks occur in South America and Africa as well. This disease can spread quickly, especially during natural or human-made disasters that disrupt water and sewage treatment systems. Like other etiologic agents that cause diarrheal illness, cholera is spread through contaminated water, exposure to feces, and person-to-person contact, especially between patients and caregivers. Cholera takes advantage of crises and overcrowding.

Cholera is an extremely virulent disease and can cause death in both children and adults within hours of onset of diarrhea, which leads to severe dehydration. Of those with cholera, 75% are asymptomatic but continue to shed the bacteria for 7 to 14 days, making transmission to others more likely. During periods of environmental stress due to disasters, healthcare workers and first responders should be aware of water and sewage treatment systems that have been compromised, and should be vigilant for signs of the disease.

Following the earthquake in Haiti in 2010, a serious outbreak of cholera occurred. Politically, this has become a point of contention between the government of Haiti and the United Nations. It is believed that UN healthcare workers from Nepal, who came to Haiti to respond to this emergency, were responsible for bringing cholera with them and contaminating the water supply in Haiti.[34]

Respiratory Infections

Respiratory infections are generally categorized as upper or lower respiratory infections. Infections of the upper respiratory tract include the common cold, viral and group A streptococcal pharyngitis, and middle ear infections. Upper respiratory infections are found worldwide and in all populations regardless of socioeconomic status or general living conditions. Generally, when indicated, treatment of upper respiratory infections is successful; as a result, they do not contribute to mortality. Many of these types of infections require only supportive care.

Lower respiratory infections, however, can often be very serious and lead to death, especially among children.[35] Lower respiratory infections are caused by viruses and bacteria, often simultaneously. The most common viral causes of lower respiratory infection are influenza, parainfluenza, syncytial virus, and adenovirus. Bacterial causes include *Streptococcus pneumoniae, Haemophilus influenzae*, and *Staphylococcus aureus*. It is estimated that over 2 million children die from pneumonia and other lower respiratory infections each year, making this cause the number one killer of children less than 5 years old. Worldwide, the mortality of children under the age of 5 years from pneumonia is 12%, not including neonatal deaths with a pneumonia-related etiology. Most of these deaths occur in poorer countries; however, children who live in poverty in industrialized countries are at greater risk of dying from pneumonia than those not living in poverty.[36] Children from low-income groups are exposed to a number of risk factors, including indoor air pollution, cigarette smoke, poor housing, poor nutrition, and limited access to health care for proper diagnosis and treatment.

Respiratory infections are spread from person to person through aerosols (coughing and breathing) when close, through person-to-person contact such as with the face and hands, and through inanimate objects that have been touched or used for eating and drinking and then used by others. The campaign for handwashing and coughing in your arm is an effort in the United States to reduce transmission of these types of respiratory illnesses. In addition, the widespread use of hand wipes and disinfectants is the result of trying to reduce respiratory illnesses in developed countries. These strategies became core methods to reduce the spread of COVID-19 (also a respiratory illness) in 2020 and beyond. Eventually, the use of masks was added to the list.

Tuberculosis

Tuberculosis is caused by *Mycobacterium tuberculosis* and is spread through aerosol exposure from an infected person. It is considered a problem in every low-income country in the world. It is estimated that nearly one-third of the world's population is infected with tuberculosis.[1] The immune systems of healthy people successfully keep this organism in check, even while the bacteria remain alive in their systems. However, in people with a compromised immune system, often associated with circumstances such as poverty, poor nutrition, and stress, the infection may become active and create a clinical case. Under such circumstances, the immune system can no longer protect the body from the organism. Other conditions in developing countries that contribute to TB transmission are close living conditions due to overcrowding and lack of healthcare services that could successfully identify and treat new cases of tuberculosis. Even in developed countries, the public health systems must be vigilant for new cases of tuberculosis, especially among those with impaired immune systems, including people living with HIV, and those infected with drug-resistant strains of the bacteria.

The treatment recommended for tuberculosis is multiple-drug therapy. Success in limiting the spread of tuberculosis is dependent on rapid detection and treatment of active cases in this manner. Some industrialized countries have historically treated asymptomatic infected individuals with daily doses of the drug isoniazid for up to 1 year, but this approach has led to drug resistance. In developing countries, the strategy for treatment has been a "directly observed short-course therapy," which has proved to be more effective in circumstances where constraining factors would otherwise result in noncompliance with a daily regimen.[37] Also, in many low-income countries, infants are given a BCG (bacilli Calmette-Guérin) vaccination. This strategy has been successful in reducing tuberculous meningitis but has had limited success in treating pulmonary tuberculosis. Currently, the biggest concern in controlling tuberculosis is antimicrobial drug resistance.

Multidrug-resistant tuberculosis (MDR TB) became increasingly more prevalent in all areas of the world, developing and developed, in the mid-1980s. Treatment of TB with antibiotics started in 1947 and had a dramatic effect in reducing TB in industrialized countries. Until the advent of antibiotic treatment, the mortality rate for people with TB was 50%. In 1985, MDR TB appeared. This new development is believed to be the result of patients not taking their medication properly (i.e., not completing doses over time). In the 1990s, new strains appeared that are resistant to virtually all antituberculosis drugs, and the mortality rate returned to 50% among those infected with these new strains, which are referred to as extensively drug-resistant tuberculosis (XDR TB). These fast-paced events have taken us nearly full circle, back to pre-1947. Tuberculosis is once again a major fixture of concern among public health and medical personnel.[38]

New concerns for tuberculosis have emerged as people living with HIV have become increasingly at risk for contracting tuberculosis because of the compromised nature of their immune systems. In sub-Saharan Africa, it is estimated that 60% of patients with TB are also living with HIV/AIDS.[39] Among infected people in general, only 10% develop active cases of tuberculosis, but among those living with HIV, 50% develop active cases.[40] In addition, increases in homelessness, incarceration, and even urban hospitalization have contributed to the transmission and increased prevalence of TB. Internationally, the movements of people through immigration and as refugees of war make the control of this disease more complex, as well as more urgent.

Influenza

Three general types of viruses cause seasonal influenza: viruses A, B, and C. In addition, there are subtypes of virus A. Virus C causes a mild form of influenza. Seasonal and sporadic outbreaks of influenza are generally caused by viruses A and B. Influenza has a nasty history, causing pandemics in 1918 (Spanish flu H1N1), 1957 (Asian flu, H2N2), and 1968 (Hong Kong flu, H3N2). Because there are multiple strains of influenza and these strains experience genetic shifts from time to time, new strains can appear with new characteristics and infect populations that may have been exposed previously but now are at risk. Since 1977, eight new strains have appeared and caused outbreaks in various locations. Of particular interest is the strain H5N1, which is found in birds and pigs and makes the jump to humans during close contact.

A limited number of antiviral drugs are available to combat influenza. In addition, replication of the viruses often results in genetic shifts through coding mutations, making it difficult for public health professionals to determine which virus subtype will be responsible for illness in any given season or global location. Each year, a vaccine is made with the best guess for what the flu season will bring; sometimes it is on the mark, and other times it results in an ineffective vaccine for that season's influenza. The most common reservoir for influenza viruses is aquatic birds, but bats have also been implicated.

People at greatest risk are generally children, older adults, and people with compromised immune systems. Immunity for some individuals may exist based on prior exposure to a specific strain earlier in life. Since influenza is spread through airborne droplets, droplets on surfaces, and direct person-to-person contact, good hygiene is basic to preventing transmission.

Sexually Transmitted Diseases

Until the advent of HIV in the early 1980s, little time or interest was spent on sexually transmitted infections (STIs), especially from a global perspective. Given the nature of HIV with its high mortality rate and extensive comorbidities, HIV infection and STIs have taken on lives of their own in the collective minds of governments. Rates of more common STIs, such as syphilis and gonorrhea, are often predictors of previously undetected HIV infections. Because of this relationship, surveillance of STIs is an important part of public health, as is disease prevention through education, provision of barrier prophylaxes, family planning, and treatment. Most recently, the emergence of the Zika virus raises further concerns because it is a disease that causes flu-like symptoms, is generally spread by mosquitoes, and is now found to pass between sex partners and ultimately between mother and fetus, with potentially catastrophic results.[41,42]

STI control has many obstacles. STIs are often asymptomatic. There are few treatments that are easy to administer in a single dose, and worldwide there is a dearth of easy and inexpensive laboratory tests available for detection. In addition, social and cultural practices often aid in the transmission process. This includes practices of polygamy, attitudes toward sexual conquests among young men, the wide use of sex workers around the world, beliefs regarding the use of condoms, taboos surrounding the teaching of sex education and family planning, and limited access to health care for women.

The primary etiologic agents of STIs are bacteria and viruses. Tracking of STIs is complicated by the fact that some—including syphilis, gonorrhea, HIV/AIDS, and hepatitis B—can also be transmitted by blood products, whereas other STIs, like chlamydia, can be transmitted through physical contact between mother and newborn child (see **Table 3-5**).

Table 3-5 Principal Sexually Transmitted Diseases of Interest to Global Public Health

Etiologic Agent	Disease	Transmission to Newborns	Transmission Through Blood Products
Treponema pallidum (spirochete)	Syphilis	yes	yes
Neisseria gonorrhoeae (bacteria)	Gonorrhea, pelvic inflammatory disease	yes	yes
Chlamydia trachomatis (bacteria)	Cervicitis, urethritis, lymphogranuloma venereum, pelvic inflammatory disease	yes	no
Human immunodeficiency virus	AIDS	yes	yes
Herpes simplex virus	Genital herpes	yes	no
Human papillomavirus	Genital warts, cervical dysplasia, cervical carcinoma	unknown	no
Hepatitis B virus	Acute and chronic hepatitis, cirrhosis, hepatocellular carcinoma	yes	yes
Zika virus	Flu-like symptoms	yes	unknown

Data from Merson MH, Black RE, Mills AJ. *International Health: Diseases, Programs, Systems, and Policies.* 2nd ed. Jones and Bartlett Publishers, 2006; Centers for Disease Control and Prevention. Zika virus: what you need to know. May 20, 2019. Accessed June 8, 2023. http://www.cdc.gov/zika/about/needtoknow.html; Heymann DL. *Control of Communicable Disease Manual.* American Public Health Association; 2015:99–101, 237–241, 257–264, 275–282, 287–294, 298–301, 595–600.

The link is now well established between human papillomaviruses and various cancers, including cervical, vulvar, vaginal, penile, anal, and oropharyngeal. The availability of a vaccine for these viruses has brought this issue to the forefront of public health policy. The vaccine holds out hope for reducing the incidence of some types of cancer, but at the same time, it comes with problems of cost, distribution in poor countries, and ethical issues surrounding the use of this vaccine in girls and boys as young as 11 years old. Professionals believe that in order for the vaccination to be successful, it must be administered early before the chance of being sexually active is real. Given that the total mortality for cervical cancer worldwide was estimated to exceed 300,000 in 2013,[43] the decision of whether to vaccinate against HPV highlights the difficult dilemma faced by healthcare providers when deciding how to allocate funds. In contrast, the measles vaccination, which cost under USD 1 for a full series, is still underused in many countries around the world. Measles has been responsible for over 700,000 deaths annually, all of which could have been prevented by properly administered vaccinations. In the United States and other developed countries, the wisdom of paying for this vaccine is evidence-based, and most healthcare insurance now pays for this inoculation.[41]

HIV/AIDS

When HIV emerged in the early 1980s, the developed world was not prepared for a new infectious disease. Many healthcare professionals were surprised and were caught unprepared. However, the onset of this epidemic inspired efforts worldwide not only to confront HIV but also to put renewed emphasis on all infectious diseases and their identification, control, and treatment. In addition, the emergence of HIV and its rapid spread around the world, as well as its diffusion to different types of populations through sexual contact, have served to identify the potential for rapid changes in disease patterns. Factors contributing to these changes include globalization, cultural and social contexts, resource availability, and the increasing ease of international transportation. The emergence of HIV/AIDS provided a new infectious disease challenge for all of public health and healthcare delivery.[44]

In 2015, 1.1 million people died of AIDS, while 37.6 million continued to live with HIV/AIDS, including 25.6 million people in sub-Saharan Africa. During that time, there were 2.1 million new cases. Although since 2000 there has been a 35% reduction in new cases, the challenges remain. Only 54% of those infected know their status.[44] One of the most powerful ways to control new infections is to find and confirm new infections and engage in counseling on transmission and treatment. This approach goes back to the old public health practice of case finding. A rapid diagnostic test is available, and results can be obtained within 1 day. However, many areas of the developing world do not have these tests available, and determination of infection is either not done or is time consuming and expensive. Many HIV/AIDS programs are unable to gain cooperation for testing due to social and cultural factors.

The advent of treatment is making an impact for those who can obtain the antiretrovirals (ARVs). At the end of 2015, it was reported that 17.0 million people living with HIV/AIDS were under treatment with ARV. NGOs such as the Bill and Melinda Gates Foundation seek to find vaccines and to develop long-acting prevention measures, as well as to expand and simplify HIV treatments. Their focus has been in the worst-hit areas of sub-Saharan Africa. They have provided more than 3 billion USD to the cause and have partnered with the Global Fund to Fight AIDS, Tuberculosis, and Malaria.[45] The Global Fund is directly responsible for ensuring that 9.2 million people, of the total 17.0 million who take ARVs, receive ARVs through their partnerships with local experts in areas with the most need around the globe. It brings donors together to make a major impact on HIV/AIDS, as well as tuberculosis and malaria.[44] The importance of health care and public health systems meeting the challenge of HIV/AIDS is vital for success in limiting this terrible disease. In developed countries, successful treatment with ARVs has turned HIV into a chronic disease when patients are treated appropriately over a lifetime.[46]

Despite this progress, HIV/AIDS should not be underestimated. This disease, left unchecked, can have long-term social consequences. In some areas of Africa, nearly an entire generation has succumbed to AIDS, leaving societies without workers, parents, or incomes, creating a myriad of other problems. The good news, as stated previously, is that the number of new cases decreased by 35% between 2000 and 2015, indicating that the constant and tireless work of scientists, healthcare providers, and public health professionals can, and does, make an impact.[41]

Zoonotic Infections

Zoonosis is "an infection or infectious agent transmitted under natural conditions from vertebrate animals to humans."[41] The interaction between people and animals can lead to diseases. Some of these diseases are quite common, such as salmonella (*Salmonella enterica*) from uncooked or undercooked turkey or chicken, or direct handling of infected animals. Other, less prevalent diseases include hantavirus disease, a hemorrhagic disease contracted through contact with rodent urine and feces; *Campylobacter* enteritis (*C. jejuni*), which is contracted through ingestion of undercooked meat or directly handling puppies, kittens, or farm animals; tularemia (*Francisella tularensis*), a bacterial zoonotic infection contracted through handling infected animals, especially during hunting and dressing small game such as rabbits and hares; and trichinellosis (*Trichinella spiralis*), an intestinal nematode caused by ingestion of uncooked infected pork.[41]

Avian Influenza

Seven types of influenza (type A) viruses can be transmitted directly to humans from animals and cause illness, but the one of most concern is H5N1, which causes avian flu. Avian flu surfaced in Southeast Asia in 1997 with the first case of bird-to-person transmission of H5N1. It is now considered to be endemic in poultry in Southeast Asia, posing a serious hazard for people routinely handling poultry in processing, markets, and farming. There have been only a few cases that have demonstrated direct transmission from one human to another, and those occurred only between a severely ill patient and close caregivers. Outbreaks of avian flu among poultry and migratory birds are carefully monitored, as are any human cases. The case fatality rate of this disease in humans is high (30%–50%). In addition to birds, H5N1 can be transmitted from sick pigs to humans who are in direct contact with them, although this is rare, especially in developed countries where agricultural practices reduce the risk of disease. In 1976 at Fort Dix, New Jersey, four soldiers became infected with swine flu, which was transmitted from person to person. These cases created a panic and subsequently led to a vaccination program for swine influenza in the United States. This was a rare incident, however.[41]

With these types of diseases, it is incumbent upon the public health surveillance systems and laboratories to quickly identify cases and confirm them through lab tests. The Laboratory Response Network (LRN) maintains a global system of laboratories that work together to help rapidly identify pathogens. The LRN was created in 1999 between the Federal Bureau of Investigation and the Association of Public Health Laboratories. It joins state and local public health laboratories, federal and military laboratories, and international laboratories in Canada, the United Kingdom, Australia, Mexico, and South Korea. The federal laboratories in the United States include those at the Centers for Disease Control and Prevention, U.S. Food and Drug Administration, and U.S. Department of Agriculture, which can do animal testing.[47]

Ebola Virus

Ebola virus was first identified in 1976 in the Congo; there were 318 cases in this outbreak, of whom 280 died. As the virus was researched, it was found that the reservoir in nature is several species of bats. It was also found that the virus infects a variety of primate species, resulting in die-offs of primate populations in local areas. The spread to humans is the result of contact between humans and infected primates, alive or dead. Monkey meat, for example, is commonly prepared and eaten in sub-Saharan Africa. If it is not cooked thoroughly, Ebola can be transmitted. The virus can also be contracted simply by handling a primate.

Including the first outbreak, there were 17 outbreaks of Ebola between 1976 and 2014. The last outbreak was in the West African nations of Guinea, Liberia, Sierra Leone, Nigeria, and Senegal, resulting in 3,707 cases and 1,848 deaths. Due to the huge international response, which included nurses, doctors, public health professionals, lab workers, and the military, two cases were imported to the United States. Ultimately, one person died and two additional healthcare workers were infected in U.S. hospitals.[48]

Once humans are infected with the Ebola virus, person-to-person transmission is quick and aggressive. Any contact with infected blood, urine, vomit, feces, secretions, organs, or semen can cause infection. Given that the symptoms of patients include diarrhea, vomiting, and bleeding from body orifices, caregivers are at immediate and high risk. Proper care for healthcare workers is to use full-barrier protection, including respirators, face shields, and nonporous garments and gloves while caring for patients. There is no antiviral known to cure Ebola at this time.[41]

Because of the ease of transmission and the high mortality rate, Ebola outbreaks, especially the one in 2014, raise major concerns for containing outbreaks, managing patients and healthcare workers, and providing supportive health services. These issues are paramount in the minds of national leaders around the world and especially among international healthcare agencies and workers. In order to address these types of outbreaks, emergency preparedness is essential—not only for those health and public health systems and healthcare workers in country, but for all governments and healthcare workers. The ability to bring diseases, such as Ebola (easily transmitted to other humans and with high mortality rates), to other countries was demonstrated in 2014. As a result, the United States and many developed nations have structured new policies and made preparations to engage in containing these outbreaks both at home and abroad. Unfortunately, the countries in sub-Saharan Africa are some of the poorest in the world, and they have the worst infrastructure, especially for healthcare services, to deal with a disease as devastating as Ebola. In addition, many local, cultural, religious, and social customs increase the likelihood of transmission. Ebola has served to demonstrate the need for all nations to come together and work on solutions to diseases that diminish human life.[37]

The Future of Infectious Disease

Infectious disease clearly demonstrates the need for good public health and healthcare systems globally. Prevention, early diagnosis, and treatment are the cornerstones of disease control. The 10 essential services of public health mentioned in the introduction of this chapter begin to come into focus as critical to limiting the impact of infectious disease.

The challenges we are facing today are great, and all impact the emergence, re-emergence, and transmission of communicable disease. These challenges include climate change, violence/war, population migration, rapid global transportation and communication, declining infrastructure, poverty, antibiotic resistance, and viral and bacterial mutations.

Climate Change

Climate change has an impact on all countries. In recent years, the United States has suffered an inordinate number of serious storms that have brought flooding and destruction, as well as extreme drought that threatens water supplies and results in serious fires.[49] These types of events are also seen worldwide. Droughts cause many people to migrate to other areas. Floods increase breeding areas for disease vectors and increase the risk of waterborne diseases; rising sea levels cause disruption to coastal communities; and the pollution associated with climate change and the warming of the earth are clearly linked to many diseases. These diseases include asthma (increased allergens), cardiovascular disease, insufficient food resources, and increases of stress. The importance of climate change cannot be underestimated.[50]

Population Migration

Migration of populations is a critical issue in infectious disease. Bringing populations together introduces new disease agents, and many new migrants live in close quarters, have poor sanitation and water sources, and have limited access to health care. Populations move for many reasons, with war and anarchy (no government) being the principal drivers today. In 2016, the number of forcibly displaced people on a global basis was estimated at 65.3 million. More than 21 million people had refugee status, and 10 million people were considered stateless (denied a nationality). Each day, 34,000 more people are displaced.[51]

Countries with the highest number of refugees have a high burden put on their own resources. The countries with the most refugees are Turkiye (2.5 million refugees), Pakistan (1.6 million), Lebanon (1.1 million), Iran (980,000), Ethiopia (736,000), and Jordan (665,000). In addition, drought moves farming families into urban areas, as does perceived economic opportunity through the mechanism of "urbanization." Concentrations of displaced people in urban areas have the same environmental characteristics as those found in refugee situations: crowding, poor sanitation, inadequate drinking water, lack of health care, poor nutrition, and exposure to vectors.

Poverty

Poverty takes a toll: Poorer people in all countries experience lower health status than their wealthier counterparts, and wealthier nations consistently experience better health status among their citizens compared with poorer countries. Although the millennium goal of cutting the poverty rate in half from 1990 to 2015 was actually met in 2010, 12.7% of the world's population (896.0 million) live with incomes at or below USD 1.90 per day, and 2.1 billion people live with incomes at or below USD 3.10 per day. Poverty contributes to the infectious disease burden because of substandard housing, poorer educational systems and opportunities, less access to quality healthcare services, crumbling infrastructure (roads, water systems, wastewater systems), increased pollution, and often more violence. Lifting people out of poverty improves health status, and improving economic opportunities for all is an important part of improving health at all levels and reducing both communicable diseases and NCDs.[52]

Drug-Resistant Infectious Bacteria

Drug-resistant etiologic agents are on the rise and are contributing to an increase in morbidity and mortality. As discussed previously, the re-emergence of tuberculosis as a disease to be reckoned with is due to the development of resistance to common treatments by the TB bacterium itself. For 70 years, healthcare professionals have successfully relied on a wide choice of antibiotics to cure a number of infectious diseases. Unfortunately, over time, a number of these "miracle drugs" have become less effective as the bacteria have found ways to resist the effects of the antibiotics.[53]

The Centers for Disease Control and Prevention has identified 18 bacteria that are resistant to antibiotics. **Table 3-6** outlines these 18 organisms and puts them into the three categories outlined by the CDC: urgent threat, serious threat, and concerning threat.

Lack of Infrastructure

Many countries lack the infrastructure needed to reduce the number of infectious diseases in their region. Most important of these is providing drinkable water to populations, as well as improving

Table 3-6 Drug-Resistant Bacteria, Threat Level, and Disease/Symptoms

Organism	Disease/Symptoms
Urgent Threats	
Clostridium difficile	Diarrhea associated with hospital stays
Carbapenem-resistant Enterobacteriaceae	Bloodstream infection associated with hospital stays; 50% mortality rate
Carbapenem-resistant *Acinetobacter*	Bloodstream infections associated with hospitalizations
Neisseria gonorrhoeae	Common STI, gonorrhea
Serious Threats	
Drug-resistant (DR) *Campylobacter*	Fever, diarrhea
Fluconazole-resistant *Candida*	Fungus, on skin or in bloodstream
Extended-spectrum β-lactamase–producing Enterobacteriaceae	Extended-spectrum β-lactamase: enzyme that allows bacteria to develop resistance to various penicillins and cephalosporins
Vancomycin-resistant *Enterococcus*	Surgical sites, bloodstream infections
MDR *Pseudomonas aeruginosa*	Associated with hospitals; can attack numerous sites
MDR *Salmonella enterica* serotype Typhi	Typhoid fever
DR nontyphoidal *Salmonella*	Diarrhea, fever, associated with foodborne illness
DR *Shigella*	Diarrheal illness with fever and cramps
Methicillin-resistant *Staphylococcus aureus*	Skin and wound infections
DR *Streptococcus pneumoniae*	Leading cause of pneumonia and meningitis
DR tuberculosis	Tuberculosis
Concerned Threats	
Erythromycin-resistant group A *Streptococcus*	Associated with pharyngitis, toxic shock syndrome, necrotizing fasciitis (flesh-eating bacteria), scarlet fever, rheumatic fever, and impetigo
Clindamycin-resistant group B *Streptococcus*	Bloodstream infections, pneumonia, meningitis, and skin infections
Watch List Threats	
Azole-resistant *Aspergillus fumigatus*	Lung and blood infections
Drug-resistant *Mycoplasma genitalium*	Urethritis in men and cervicitis in women
Drug-resistant *Bordetella pertussis*	Whooping cough, bacterial respiratory infection

Modified from Centers for Disease Control and Prevention. 2019 antimicrobial resistance: threats. November 23, 2021. Accessed June 8, 2023. https://www.cdc.gov/antimicrobial-resistance/media/pdfs/2019-ar-threats-report-508.pdf.

sanitation (wastewater treatment). Globally, in 2016, 780 million people lived without improved water resources and 2.5 billion people lived without improved sanitation. Seven out of 10 of these people lived in rural areas. It is estimated that for every USD 1 invested in improving these most basic life-assuring systems, the economic benefit is between USD 5 and USD 46. In the early part of the 20th century in the United States, infectious diseases were rampant, but with the building of water-treatment facilities and wastewater management systems, infectious disease rapidly declined. It is expected that the improvement of water resources and sanitation in many areas of the developing world will produce many of the same benefits, reducing water-borne, soil-transmitted, and hygiene-related diseases.[54]

Globalization

In a world of rapid transportation and communication, the spread of infectious disease has become a concern for all public health and healthcare workers worldwide. As demonstrated by the Ebola outbreak in 2014 in West Africa, the introduction of West Nile virus to the United States, and the spreading of the Zika virus to Florida in a matter of months, developed countries cannot rest on their past achievements. In fact, in the case of COVID-19, developed countries, where people move about easily and are more mobile (eating out, movies, shopping, sporting events, visiting relatives for major events) may be at a greater risk of transmission. Culture/practices, mobility, poverty, education, and politics are essential to understanding the way disease is transmitted in a particular location and under specific conditions. People in developed countries can no longer turn a blind eye to poverty, violence, political strife, and diseases that plague people around the world. Globalization leads us to know and understand the injustices suffered by others, just as rapid communication brings a glimpse of the developed world to all others on the planet. This interconnectedness of us all may lead to improvements in health status for everyone. Today, the phrase "no man is an island" is exceedingly poignant. There are emerging diseases that are truly new diseases (HIV, SARS, Lyme disease, *E. coli*, hantavirus, dengue fever, West Nile disease, and Zika), and some diseases have re-emerged (malaria, tuberculosis, cholera, pertussis, influenza, pneumococcal infections, and gonorrhea) after having been in a decline. Many factors can trigger a re-emergence, such as an environmental disaster, breakdown in public health systems, or population migration.

Data from Johns Hopkins Medicine. 2023. Accessed June 8, 2023. https://www.hopkinsmedicine.org/health/conditions-and-diseases/emerging-infectious-diseases#:~:text=Emerging%20diseases%20include%20HIV%20infections,been%20on%20a%20significant%20decline.

Public Health and Healthcare Services

The challenges of infectious disease and disease transmission seem overwhelming. Successful intervention in these diseases depends on the good practice of public health and healthcare services. It requires all public and healthcare professionals to be vigilant and well prepared for their jobs. It is incumbent upon countries to ensure their health systems include adequate training, access to appropriate equipment and medication, and good policies related to disease transmission (e.g., providing healthcare workers with barrier protection and knowledge of its proper use, or having adequate vaccine).

Of particular importance in meeting the challenges of infectious disease is the constant surveillance for disease. This requires that public health professionals collect and maintain health records and information and means of quick communication of information throughout the country and the world. It requires that healthcare professionals are well educated, are prepared for rapid and accurate diagnosis, have the means for proper treatment, and work with good policies to prevent further transmission.

Community health workers need the skills to investigate outbreaks, understand the dynamics of the diseases they confront, and educate the public about how to protect themselves from transmission. It is vital that public and healthcare professionals are able to link people to the proper healthcare services and treatments as quickly as possible.

Countries must be able to assess their infectious disease burdens, develop policies that address public education, provide proper training for professionals, and have a plan for emergency preparedness and acute intervention. Governments need to prepare communities to help with the intervention of infectious diseases and need to support community efforts. Laws and regulations should be enforced to limit the spread of disease and protect the population. For example, they may require vaccination of school-aged children, quarantine infected people if appropriate, and require the use of safety products, such as seat belts or helmets.

Finally, all nations must engage in new research to find new treatments, cures, and innovative solutions to limit these diseases. They must also engage in constant evaluation of the services people receive and the systems that support those services. An example of this is shown in **Box 3-2**. As evidenced in this section, public and healthcare professionals, politicians, and citizens cannot afford to "drop the ball" when infectious disease is concerned.

Box 3-2 Neglected Tropical Diseases: Lymphatic Filariasis Elimination Program

The microscopic threadlike worm (*Wuchereria bancrofti*) invaginates the lymphatic nodes and vessels, where it then reproduces, creating millions of microfilariae. Microfilariae are transmitted from person to person via mosquito bites. The worms become adults in approximately 6 months, and the adult worms live for approximately 6 years. When the adult worms die, the person's bodily response causes inflammation of the vessels, resulting in lymphedema (swelling) of limbs, legs, breasts, or genitalia. According to the Centers for Disease Control and Prevention (CDC), lymphatic filariasis (LF) is "one of the world's neglected tropical diseases (NTDs), affecting more than 1 billion people" (2011). Although most infected people are asymptomatic, 30% of infected people develop debilitating manifestations, which affect their ability to be productive.

Current statistics indicate that LF affects over 120 million people in 73 countries worldwide. However, this is a neglected tropical disease that can be eliminated. In 2000, WHO launched the Global Lymphatic Filariasis Elimination Program with a target elimination deadline of 2020. In the Americas, 11.3 million people are at risk for acquiring the disease. Mass public health efforts reduced the transmission in Costa Rica, Suriname, and the Republic of Trinidad and Tobago. However, there is still active transmission in four countries in the Americas: Brazil, the Dominican Republic, Haiti, and Guyana.

The public health strategy to interrupt transmission requires the health agency to map the endemic areas, administer drugs to break the transmission cycle, and reduce microfilaraemia.

Mapping

Statistics generated by the Ministry of Health indicate the LF antigen is prevalent in seven of the 10 geographic regions in Guyana.

Administering the Drugs

In 2003, the Ministry of Health collaborated with the Pan American Health Organization (PAHO)/WHO to implement phase one of the Transmission Interruption Plan. This phase included social mobilization, distribution, promotion, and use of diethylcarbamazine (DEC)-fortified salt, and monitoring and evaluation of the progress at sentinel sites. The scientific efficacy of DEC-fortified salt in reducing microfilaraemia is well established and has been documented in pilot studies in Brazil, Haiti, India, and the United Republic of Tanzania. In fact, the DEC-fortified salt causes few or no adverse reactions compared with the DEC tablet (2007). As such, officials in Guyana launched a national program that introduced DEC-fortified salt into the competitive market. This was accompanied by social marketing activities to increase consumer demand. These efforts included television ads, health education seminars, appearances at health expositions, and door-to-door counseling.

Challenges with Implementing the Program

Guyana is classified as the second poorest country in South America and the Caribbean, with a per capita GDP of USD 800 in 1999 (2001). All of the healthcare initiatives are coordinated by the minister of public health and their ministry. Some of the challenges with this program were:

1. The lead agency for health promotion is the Division of Health Sciences Education, which is involved in training health staff and NGOs. However, the Ministry of Health (MoH) lacked sufficient health staff to coordinate mass countrywide drug/salt marketing education activities. As such, a partnership with PAHO/WHO resulted in a project launch funded by PAHO/WHO for training and development of a team specifically geared toward countrywide health education, DEC-fortified salt promotion, and active marketing and sales of the salt.
2. DEC-fortified salt needed to be imported and sold not as a drug but as a food product. As such, the MoH partnered with the salt producers and importers to ease the importation regulations.
3. Salt sales decreased with disruptions to the salt supply and reduced consumer confidence after the salt became discolored (turned blue over time). The MoH increased quality control and collaborated with PAHO/WHO on a second social mobilization campaign to restock the retail suppliers and quell the concerns of the population.
4. DEC-fortified salt competed with cheaper alternatives, which were not fortified with DEC or iodine. The MoH and government partnered with importers and salt producers to increase the supply and consumer demand for the salt, as this targeted both the iodization and LF programs.

The production of DEC-fortified salt for mass treatment stopped in 2007 after the importation of approximately 900 tons of salt from the time the program launched in July 2003. In 2008, the MoH embarked on phase two, which included evaluation of phase one, identification of *hotspots* using surveillance information, mass drug administration with tablets (DEC-fortified salt and albendazole), and monitoring and evaluation of sentinel sites. Once again, the MoH partnered with PAHO/WHO and the Inter-American Development Bank (IDB) for support. The MoH has even indicated that this LF elimination program is integrated with the Georgetown Sanitation

Improvement Program, which was supported by both the IDB and Guyana Water Incorporated. The healthcare system in Guyana is able to achieve successful results because of its public/private partnerships. These partnerships not only offset the financial and human resource constraints of the country's healthcare system, but also strengthen the health system's ability to reduce the burden of diseases, especially neglected tropical diseases that can be eliminated.

Contributing author: Gabrielle Walcott-Bedeau MD, MMSci, PGCME

References

Centers for Disease Control and Prevention, Center for Global Health, Division of Parasitic Diseases and Malaria. Lymphatic filariasis: elimination in the Americas. https://www.cdc.gov/neglected-tropical-diseases/?CDC_AAref_Val=https://www.cdc.gov/globalhealth/ntd/resources/lf_americas_at_a_glance.pdf. Published September 2011. Accessed October 20, 2016.

Commonwealth Health Online. Health systems in Guyana. http://www.commonwealthhealth.org/americas/guyana/health_systems_in_guyana/. Published 2016. Accessed October 20, 2016.

Lammie P, Milner T, Houston R. Unfulfilled potential: using diethylcarbamazine-fortified salt to eliminate lymphatic filariasis. *Bulletin of the World Health Organization*. https://iris.who.int/handle/10665/269971. Published July 2007. Accessed October 20, 2016.

Pan American Health Organization. Health systems and services profile of Guyana. http://www.paho.org/hq/dmdocuments/2010/Health_System_Profile-Guyana_2001.pdf. Published December 14, 2001. Accessed October 20, 2016.

Persaud S. Tenth Regional Lymphatic Filariasis Elimination Program. www.pancap.org/NTD_%20Guyana.pptx

World Health Organization. Country cooperation strategy at a glance: Guyana. http://www.who.int/countryfocus/cooperation_strategy/ccsbrief_guy_en.pdf. Published May 2013. Accessed October 20, 2016.

References

1. World Health Organization. Global status report on noncommunicable diseases 2010. Published 2011. Accessed April 3, 2023. https://apps.who.int/iris/bitstream/handle/10665/44579/9789240686458_eng.pdf?.
2. Wagner KH, Brath H. A global view on the development of non-communicable diseases. *Prev Med*. 2012;54(1):S38-S41.
3. Checkley W, Ghannem H, Irazola V, et al. Management of NCD in low- and middle-income countries. *Glob Heart*. 2014;9(4):431-443. doi: 10.1016/j.gheart.2014.11.003 PMID: 25592798; PMCID: PMC4299752.
4. Benziger CP, Roth GA, Moran AE. The Global Burden of Disease Study and the preventable burden of NCD. *Glob Heart*. 2016;11(4):393-397. doi: 10.1016/j.gheart.2016.10.024. PMID: 27938824.
5. World Health Organization. Noncommunicable disease fact sheets. Published September 16, 2022. Accessed April 15, 2023. https://www.who.int/news-room/fact-sheets/detail/noncommunicable-diseases
6. Roser M, Ritchie H, Spooner F. Burden of disease. OurWorldInData.org. Published 2021. Accessed April 15, 2023. https://ourworldindata.org/burden-of-disease [Online Resource]
7. Sears ME, Genuis SJ. Environmental determinants of chronic disease and medical approaches: recognition, avoidance, supportive therapy, and detoxification. *J Environ Public Health*. 2012;2012:356798. doi: 10.1155/2012/356798. PMID: 22315626; PMCID: PMC3270432.
8. World Health Organization. The top 10 causes of death. Published December 9, 2020. Accessed April 18, 2023. https://www.who.int/news-room/fact-sheets/detail/the-top-10-causes-of-death.
9. Egger G, Stevens J, Binns A, Morgan B. Psychosocial determinants of chronic disease: implications for lifestyle medicine. *Am J Lifestyle Med*. 2019;13(6):526-532. doi: 10.1177/1559827619845335 PMID: 31662714; PMCID: PMC6796226.
10. Bahall M, Bailey H. The impact of chronic disease and accompanying bio-psycho-social factors on health-related quality of life. *J Family Med Prim Care*. 2022;11(8):4694-4704. doi: 10.4103/jfmpc.jfmpc_2399_21. PMID: 36352993; PMCID: PMC9638608.
11. Centers for Disease Control and Prevention. Malaria. Accessed May 29, 2023. https://www.niaid.nih.gov/search?search=Malaria April 24m 2020.
12. Prüss-Ustün A, Vickers C, Haefliger P, Bertollini R. Knowns and unknowns on burden of disease due to chemicals: a systematic review. *Environ Health*. 2011;10:9 https://doi.org/10.1186/1476-069X-10-9.
13. World Health Organization. The public health impact of chemicals: knowns and unknowns—data addendum for 2019. Published July 6, 2023. Accessed April 16, 2023. https://www.who.int/publications/i/item/WHO-HEP-ECH-EHD-21.01.
14. World Health Organization. The top 10 causes of death. Published December 9, 2020. Accessed April 17, 2023. https://www.who.int/news-room/fact-sheets/detail/the-top-10-causes-of-death.
15. World Health Organization. Cardiovascular diseases (CVDs). Published June 21, 2021. Accessed April 26, 2023. https://www.who.int/news-room/fact-sheets/detail/cardiovascular-diseases-(cvds).
16. NCD Alliance. Cardiovascular diseases. Accessed April 18, 2023. https://ncdalliance.org/why-ncds/ncds/cardiovascular-diseases ND.
17. International Diabetes Federation. *IDF Diabetes Atlas*. 10th ed. International Diabetes Federation; 2021. http://www.diabetesatlas.org.

18. Centers for Disease Control and Prevention. Zika virus, 2023. Retrieved May 29, 2023. https:/CDC.gov/zika.
19. World Health Organization. Obesity and overweight. Published June 9, 2021 Accessed April 20, 2023. https://www.who.int/news-room/fact-sheets/detail/obesity-and-overweight.
20. UC Riverside: Center for Invasive Species Research. Accessed May 29, 2023. https://cisr.ucr.edu/invasive-species/asian-tiger-mosquito.
21. World Health Organization. Obesity. Accessed April 20, 2023. https://www.who.int/health-topics/obesity#tab=tab_1.
22. Sahoo K, Sahoo B, Choudhury AK, Sofi NY, Kumar R, Bhadoria AS. Childhood obesity: causes and consequences. *J Family Med Prim Care*. 2015;4(2):187-92. doi: 10.4103/2249-4863.154628 PMID: 25949965; PMCID: PMC4408699.
23. Merson MH, Black RE, Mills AJ. International public health: diseases, programs, systems, and policies. 2nd ed. Sudbury, MA: Jones and Bartlett Publishers; 2006.
24. Basch PF. *Textbook of International Health*. New York: Oxford University Press; 1999.
25. Lopez AD, Murray CC. The global burden of disease, 1990–2020. *Nat Med*. 1998; 4(11):1241-1243.
26. Murry CJL. Quantifying the burden of disease: the technical basis for disability-adjusted life years. *Bull World Health Organ*. 1994;72(3):429-445.
27. Skolnick RS. *Essentials of Global Health*. Sudbury, MA: Jones and Bartlett Publishers; 2008.
28. Moorthy VS, Good MF, Hill AV. Malaria vaccine development. *Lancet*. 2004;363(9403):150-156.
29. McKenzie JF, Pinger RR, Kotecki JE. *An Introduction to Community Health*. Sudbury, MA: Jones and Bartlett Publishers; 2005.
30. Sachs JD. A new global effort to control malaria. *Science*. 2002;298(5591):122-124.
31. Aghsaeifard Z, Heidari G, Alizadeh R. Understanding the use of oral rehydration therapy: a narrative review from clinical practice to main recommendations. *Health Sci Rep*. 2022;5(5):e827. doi: 10.1002/hsr2.827. PMID: 36110343; PMCID: PMC9464461.
32. Yamey G. Roll back malaria: a failing global health campaign. *BMJ*. 2004;328:1086. Accessed June 12, 2023. https://www.bmj.com/content/328/7448/1086.
33. Hay SI, Guerra CA, Tatem AJ, Noor AM, Snow RW. The global distribution and population at risk of malaria: past, present, and future. *Lancet Infect Dis*. 2004;4(6):327-336.
34. Martens P, Hall L. Malaria and the move: human population movement and malaria transmission. *Emerg Infect Dis*. 2000; 6(2):103-109.
35. Sachs J, Malaney P. The economic and social burden of malaria. *Nature*. 2002;415(6872):680-685.
36. Centers for Disease Control and Prevention. Impact of malaria. Published March 26, 2014. Accessed July 22, 2016. http://www.cdc.gov/malaria/malaria_worldwide/impact.html.
37. World Health Organization. Zika virus and complications. Published 2022. Accessed June 12, 2023. https://www.who.int/topics/zika/en.
38. World Health Organization. Zika situation report. Published 2023. Accessed June 12, 2023. https://www.who.int/news-room/feature-stories/detail/the-history-of-zika-virus.
39. Centers for Disease Control and Prevention. What you can do to protect yourself. Updated August 31, 2022. Accessed June 12, 2023. https://www.cdc.gov/zika/prevention/.
40. One Health Activities. Published May 2023. Accessed June 12, 2023. www.cdc.gov/onehealth/.
41. Centers for Disease Control and Prevention. Published 2016. Accessed June 12, 2023. https://wwwn.cdc.gov/tsp/PHS/PHS.aspx?phsid=18&toxid=3.
42. World Health Organization. Climate change and health. Published 2023. Accessed June 12, 2023. https://www.who.int/health-topics/climate-change#tab=tab_1.
43. Centers for Disease Control and Prevention. Global water, sanitation and hygiene (WASH). Published March 2020. Accessed June 12, 2023. http://cdc.gov/healthywater/global/diarrhea-burden.html.
44. Fontaine O, Garner P, Bhan MK. Oral rehydration therapy: the simple solution for saving lives. *BMJ*. 2007;334(suppl 1):s14.
45. Parashar UD, Hummelman EG, Bresee JS, et al. Global illness and deaths caused by rotavirus disease in children. *Emerg Infect Dis*. 2003;9(3):565-572.
46. Bern C, Martines J, de Zoysa I, Glass RI. The magnitude of the global problem of diarrhoeal disease: a ten-year update. *Bull World Health Organ*. 1992;70(6):705-714.
47. Kosek M, Bern C, Guerrant RL. The global burden of diarrhoeal disease, as estimated from studies published between 1992 and 2000. *Bull World Health Organ*. 2003;81(3):197-204.
48. Deeks SG, Lewin SR, Halir DV. The end of AIDS: HIV as a chronic infection. *Lancet*. 2013;382(9903):1525-1533. Retrieved June 3, 2023. doi: 10.1016/S0140-6736(13)61809-7. https://www.ncbi.nlm.nih.gov/pmc/articles/PMC4058441/.
49. World Health Organization, UNICEF. *Meeting the MDG Drinking Water and Sanitation Target: The Urban and Rural Challenge of the Decade*. Geneva, Switzerland: WHO Press; 2006. Accessed March 25, 2008. http://www.childinfo.org/areas/water/pdfs/jmp06final.pdf.
50. Epidemiology Program Office, Office of the Director, Centers for Disease Control and Prevention. Achievements in public health, 1900–1999: changes in the public health system. *JAMA*. 2000;283:735-738.
51. Bryce J, Pinto-Boschi C, Shibuya K, Black RE. WHO estimates of the causes of death in children. *Lancet*. 2005;365: 1147-1152.
52. UNICEF. *Progress for Children: a World Fit for Children Statistical Review*. 6th ed. New York, NY: UNICEF Division of Communication; 2020. Accessed June 12, 2023. http://childinfo.org/areas/childmortality/Progress_for_Children.pdf.
53. World Health Organization. Manary M, et al. Systems review of the cause of children with diarrhea in community-based management of severe acute malnutrition. Published September 2020. Accessed June 12, 2023. https://www.who.int/news-room/fact-sheets/detail/diarrhoeal-disease.
54. World Health Organization. Cholera. Published June 2018. Accessed June 12, 2023. https://www.who.int/news-room/fact-sheets/detail/cholera.

CHAPTER 4

Global Health Systems Politics, Economics, and Policy

Walter J. Jones and Jiebing Wen

The Worldwide Challenge of Health Policymaking in the 21st Century

Health care is one part of society that has always been subject to varying degrees of public scrutiny and regulation, and thus there is health policymaking, in one guise or another. Since medicine originated thousands of years ago within such important social institutions as religion, societies have recognized that healthcare organizations and practices have a social dimension that needs to be monitored.[1] Governments and other social/community organizations have intervened in health care because national societies have viewed it as at least partly a social service, not an economic good. Government intervention often takes place because of market imperfections or failure, or due to national/social political imperatives that override the prerogatives of the healthcare market.[2-4]

As will be discussed later, the biggest policymaking challenges faced by nations around the world are broadly similar, and they represent efforts to manage a medical/scientific revolution that has positively and profoundly transformed the life prospects of humanity. Using almost any metric of performance, there is no area of human endeavor that has been more successful in the last 150 years than health care. In that very success lies the worldwide problems we now face. As physician and social theorist William Schwartz notes:

> Even the prospect of dependable and sustained progress against disease—let alone the achievement of a medical utopia—emerged only after World War II .... [At the end of] the hundred-year span ... beginning with ... the 1950s and ending in the year 2050 ... it seems conceivable that most of today's debilitating and fatal diseases will be preventable or curable. ... That is the utopian vision for medicine that now, for the first time, appears to have a scientific foundation. The critical question is at what price—economically, politically, and ethically—that vision will be realized.[5]

Due to the cost and complexity of modern health care, all nations now have problems controlling costs, providing effective access to care, ensuring a reasonable level of quality of care, controlling the introduction and use of technology, and validly measuring individual and community health outcomes. Inevitably, at the same time, nations are attempting to address these common health system aspects while possessing widely varying national cultures, governmental structures, economies, political systems, and population/subpopulation health statuses and lifestyles.[6] Not surprisingly, then, what U.S. policymakers are considering with respect to health system reform often differs considerably from that contemplated by their counterparts in nations such as the United Kingdom, Brazil, Russia, and China.[7-9]

It will be argued here that, despite these differences, the general range of policymaking issues and options faced by nations can be productively analyzed and compared by using well-defined models of what can be called *micro* and *macro* health policymaking. To consider health policymaking issues and activities around the world, we must first understand how to think about health policymaking.

How to Think About Health Policymaking—Micro and Macro Models

It must be remembered that in the most fundamental way, health policymaking (like any other area of policymaking) is a *political* process. There may be varying technical and clinical issues at stake in any given action, and the particular actors in the policy process may differ markedly. Most policymaking (whether it is taking place within a democratic or nondemocratic framework) usually involves both governmental and nongovernmental individuals and organizations. Nevertheless, all policy activities are critically determined by the interactions of individuals and interest groups within the society over the distribution of its resources. It is, at bottom, politics—in the words of Harold Lasswell, "who gets what, when, how."[10]

As suggested previously, health policymaking can be analyzed successfully using both micro and macro frameworks. In some ways, these policy frameworks are analogous to microeconomics (the study of economic interactions at the level of individual producers and consumers) and macroeconomics (the analysis of economic activity at the sector, regional, national, and international levels). For the purposes of policy analysis, they are interrelated and should both be used if the dynamics, substance, and outcomes of health policymaking are to be fully understood.

Micro Policymaking—The Policy Marketplace Model

The marketplace model of policymaking is outlined most completely in the work on health legislative policymaking done by Paul J. Feldstein.[11] As the term indicates, it is adapted from economic theory, with suppliers and demanders, as in the economic marketplace. The policy marketplace model has the following characteristics:

- Like its economic counterpart, the policy marketplace model assumes that individuals and groups are constantly interacting to satisfy their needs. All policy actors are both suppliers and demanders, since they must exchange some commodity in the marketplace to purchase the other goods that they want. For example, politicians supply favorable policies. In democratic states, these usually include financial subsidies, regulations, and additional health-related services for constituency groups, such as senior citizens, hospitals, and medical schools. In exchange, the politicians receive political support, which could include financial contributions, votes, and other desirable commodities.[11] In dictatorships such as Zimbabwe, the exchanged goods could also include such items as access to basic health services in exchange for support from armed groups (including the nation's military and police forces) used to suppress the mass public.[12]
- As in the economic marketplace, the policy marketplace around the world features disparities in power.[13] Individuals and groups that can supply more can demand more in exchange. In the United States, physicians, senior citizens, hospitals, pharmaceutical and insurance companies, and academic health centers are among the "haves," since they are politically organized, particularly through interest groups and professional associations, such as the American Hospital Association, the American Medical Association, and AARP. Members of these groups receive relatively generous government services and legal protections. In contrast, politically unorganized groups in nations as diverse as the United States and India are often less educated, less politically powerful, and poorly situated geographically, and as a consequence, they receive substandard or no medical services.[14,15]
- In the policy marketplace, the currency used in exchanges can be money, but it usually also involves other factors such as superior leadership, more effective organization, access to and greater articulation through communications media, and greater group-member intensity (the willingness of group members to exert great efforts to advance the interests of the group).[16,17] The latter is evident in U.S. health policymaking with disease-specific and victim groups, such as family members of the

mentally ill and as people with HIV/AIDS,[18-20] and it is evident in the post–World War II development of the Japanese health insurance system.[21] Money matters, but power in the policy marketplace involves much more than money.

- To gain control over their relevant areas of the marketplace, nongovernmental groups will attempt to forge enduring alliances with governmental agencies. For example, disease-specific groups in the United States lobby for more federal government funding for research via the National Institutes of Health in their area of disease. In the distinctive policy marketplaces of the United States, Canada, the United Kingdom, and France, pharmaceutical companies attempt to influence regulation by interacting differently with the relevant national health policymakers.[22] More politically powerful groups will be more successful at this than the "have-nots." Often, these groups will engage in their activities via enduring *iron triangles* or more transient *issue networks* of power and influence.[23] As a result of these organized group activities, it cannot be assumed that government in any given policy system will protect "the little guy"—those without group affiliations. Indeed, more often than not, governmental regulations reinforce power disparities in health policymaking.[11]

Macro Policymaking—The Policy Systems Model

In contrast to the marketplace of micro policymaking, the *macro* level of policymaking can be best conceived of as the continual evolution of a complex system. Systems theory was developed in the disciplines of engineering and ecology. It was first applied to political systems by Easton[24] and has been modified to describe health policymaking by Longest.[14] As applied to policy systems, systems theory has the following characteristics:

- *Complexity*—Numerous influences interact to produce a system that is continually in flux while generally attaining some level of equilibrium or stability. Individuals, social groups, and organizations are all actors in the policy process.
- *Interrelatedness*—Most significant activities are connected to one another by feedback loops and both direct and indirect impacts. All policy actions create reactions within the system, some perhaps modifying the system itself.
- *Cyclical process*—With complexity and interrelatedness, the policy process does not have a definite beginning or end; it continues on as long as organized society continues to exist. There are no permanent policy successes or failures.

As noted, the system's model is cyclical, so strictly speaking, there is no start or finish—just a continual cycle in which any beginning is arbitrary. In Longest's model, the policy process has the following stages:

1. *Recognition of inputs*. There are numerous elements of feedback from previous policy decisions (health outcomes, budgets, programs, elections, and so forth). These include support for and opposition to current policies as well as demands for modifications of these policies. These inputs are recognized by policy actors (including elected officials, interest group leaders, and regulators) and lead to their reactive efforts to engage in further policy activities.
2. *Policy formulation*. Significant policy actors attempt to develop new policies to address these new inputs. In advanced nations, these efforts usually center on formal policymaking structures, such as executive, legislative, judicial, and regulatory institutions. Executive orders are issued, legislation passes through Congress or a similar assembly, and lawyers bring cases for consideration before judicial bodies or regulatory agencies take up issues brought before them. As with the other stages of policymaking, the actions of policy formulation cannot be separated from politics and political considerations. As suggested in a study of health policymaking in advanced, industrial democracies, there is no such thing as apolitical policy formulation.[25]
3. *Policy outputs*. Efforts at formulation can result in a variety of policy outputs. The most obvious and conventional include statutory laws and regulatory directives (passed by legislatures but subsequently implemented by regulatory agencies). These actions can also contain subsidy and taxation provisions, thus redistributing wealth from one area of society to another. One output can in fact be a *nondecision*—a phenomenon first described by Crenson[26] and defined as a decision to do nothing, which itself creates political and policy impacts, such as when the U.S. Congress blocked Bill Clinton's Health Security Act in 1994 without ever holding any formal hearings or votes.[27,28]

   Many policy outputs also intentionally provide some element of political symbolism. As described by Edelman, a political scientist at the University of Wisconsin, symbolic politics is virtually inseparable from policymaking because it provides both policymakers and the mass public with threatening and/or reassuring images that emotionally condense often-complex arguments into easily accessible reactions.[29] Often, these symbols include evocative legislative titles, such as the Medicare Modernization Act of 2003, which added not only a prescription drug benefit for seniors in the United States but also multibillion-dollar subsidies for the U.S. health insurance and pharmaceutical industries. Who could oppose "modernization"? Similarly, the Patient Protection and Affordable Care Act of 2010 (ACA), which was enacted by the Obama administration in the teeth of determined Republican party opposition, has a title that implies the victory of the average American over the costly medical/industrial complex. However, the legislation actually includes considerable financial concessions to the health insurance and pharmaceutical industries, providing them with additional subsidized customers for their products.[30] As Edelman notes, symbols can often be used in policymaking to distract the public from policy details that powerful and focused interest groups have worked out for their own benefit (if not the general public's).[29]

4. *Implementation*. Any policy output that is not a nondecision has to be implemented to have a social impact, and that implementation can be highly variable.[31,32] Government agencies must often work through nongovernmental elements of society to implement policies, and the values, political skills, and preferences of leaders in these organizations often determine whether or not (and, if so, how) a new governmental policy is realized through implementation.[14] Due to the vagaries of implementation, the actual impacts of policies are often unanticipated.[33,34]
5. *Outcomes*. Policies create individual, group, and social impacts. In health policy, the most obvious outcome may involve changes in individual, group, and social health resource consumption and health status. Usually, however, health policies have nonhealth outcomes that may be equally important politically. There are always winners and losers. Some individuals and groups get more resources, while others pay. Some have their needs attended to, while others' needs are neglected. Policy outcomes may also have profound long-range impacts that were unanticipated, such as the creation of new ethical issues (for example, in the case of new technological development resulting from the Human Genome Project), and the need for explicit resource rationing (for example, when government research funding leads to useful but costly new medical technologies and procedures).[35]
6. *Feedback and subsequent modification*. As previously mentioned, the outputs and outcomes of policy cycles include reactions in society and related efforts to further develop policy. In policy cycles, outputs and outcomes create the reactions in society mentioned earlier and related further efforts at policy development. The policy agenda is refreshed, and the cycle continues onward. Often, the success of a previous cycle (say, the enactment of Medicare and Medicaid to address the lack of healthcare access for seniors and some low-income categories) leads to the challenges faced in a subsequent cycle (for example, how to cope with the unsustainable healthcare demands and cost inflation triggered by events such as the introduction of large government health insurance programs such as Medicare and Medicaid).[36,37] Health policymaking does result in great benefits for individuals and society, but it also seems a compounding hassle when viewed in terms of day-to-day activities.

Looking at U.S. Policy Responses to the COVID-19 Pandemic Through the Lens of Micro and Macro Models

As of April 2023, the United States had surpassed 104 million infections from SARS-CoV-2, the virus that causes COVID-19, and more than 1 million deaths from this disease.[38] Since 2020, COVID-19 has become the third leading cause of death.[39] The adverse effects of COVID-19 are not limited to deaths. An estimated 1 in 13 U.S. adults have "long COVID" symptoms, defined as symptoms involving multiple organs and affecting many systems that last at least 3 months after first infection.[40] "Long COVID" is associated with increased healthcare costs and losing productivity.[41] The most recent estimates show that total costs of COVID-19 for the United States from 2020 to 2021 were approximately $16 trillion USD when combining health and life loss, mental health, and economic damages, with mental health issues being the primary concern given the rapid economic recovery since 2021.[42,43]

Most public policy responses to the COVID-19 pandemic since March 2020 occurred through national and state emergency declarations, which gave government flexibilities to waive or reduce red tape in a wide range of policy areas, such as stay-at-home (SaH) orders and mask mandates, as well as Medicare, Medicaid, and private health insurance coverage policies.[44] The Coronavirus Aid, Relief, and Economic Security (CARES) Act passed by the U.S. Congress in March 2020 was the most important legislation to support economic relief and recovery in response to the COVID-19 pandemic.[45] Besides loans and grants to business and funding for state and local governments, the CARES Act provided approximately $12.4 billion in initial funding to pharmaceutical companies, such as Pfizer-BioNTech and Moderna, for the COVID-19 vaccines, diagnostics, antiviral therapeutic development, and delivery through Operation Warp Speed (OWS). OWS was a public–private partnership between the Department of Health and Human Services (HHS), other government agencies, and pharmaceutical companies. For example, Pfizer-BioNTech received approximately $1.95 billion from OWS for 100 million doses of vaccines and Moderna received approximately $3.2 billion from OWS for vaccine development and manufacturing, as well as for 200 million doses of vaccines.[46] The emergency approval of the first COVID-19 vaccine based on messenger-RNA (mRNA) technology by Pfizer-BioNTech on December 11, 2020, significantly accelerated the pace of "back to normal" by building herd immunity through immunization to save lives and ensure health system functioning within its capacity. The success of the mRNA vaccines in protecting against severe disease and fending off infection in at least a limited period is widely considered to be the most important factor enabling the society to get "back to normal." After 3 years, public precautions toward COVID-19 have broadly faded, with low updated COVID-19 vaccine uptake. As of November 2023, only about 15% of U.S. adults age 18 or older and 5% of children had gotten the updated COVID-19 vaccines.[47] However, vaccination and masking remain the cost-effective way to curb the spread of COVID-19.[47,48]

From the health policy perspective, it is important for us to look back and answer a crucial question: Where are we heading out of the COVID-19 pandemic? There are different ways to answer the question. Here we answer it through the lens of micro and macro models.

From the micro perspective, the major actors are federal and state policymakers, physicians, hospitals, pharmaceutical and insurance companies, academic health centers, and vulnerable populations. For example, in response to the demand for maintaining healthcare flexibilities and waivers during the COVID-19 pandemic from healthcare providers, insurance companies, and people, the Biden administration extended the National Emergency Declaration to April 10, 2023, and the public health emergency (PHE) until May 11, 2023. Another two separate emergency declarations (pursuant to Section 564 and under Public Readiness and Emergency Preparedness, respectively) by the HHS allowed emergency use authorization (EUA) for COVID-19–related medical measurements and liability immunity for related activities, thereby shielding COVID-19 vaccine manufacturers and distributors from legal liability as the result of vaccine side effects. Without those emergency declarations, public and private insurers would have needed to cover the large proportion of costs for COVID–19–related tests, treatments, and services, and millions of privately insured citizens would have faced out-of-pocket costs for many COVID–19–related medical services. States also received a 6.2 percentage point increase in their federal matching rate for Medicaid under certain conditions.[44] Pharmaceutical companies are expected to continue research on universal COVID-19 vaccines and treatments, which may promote better preparedness for future pandemics, especially the application of mRNA technology in various therapeutics.[49] In addition, Democratic-affiliated states had more promptly adopted SaH orders, mask and vaccine mandates, and higher COVID-19 vaccination rates and lower COVID-19 infection and death rates compared with Republican-affiliated states.[50,51] The public health measures in response to the COVID-19 pandemic triggered vigorous political debates about state autonomy and individual freedom.[52] Some studies have found that the initial responses saved millions of lives and prevented the healthcare system from collapsing.[53,54] However, the damages brought by the COVID-19 restrictions, especially the toll on mental health and small businesses, were also significant. The public appetite for broad drastic measures is virtually nonexistent now, so "living with COVID-19" is the most preferred policy direction.[55,56]

From the macro perspective, the input by the federal government in the development of COVID-19 vaccines was perhaps the most successful government-sponsored public health program.[57] The federal government was able to efficiently use taxpayer dollars to support fast-track development of the COVID-19 vaccines while minimizing the risk of a lack of demand for the vaccines through purchasing commitments. Because of the OWS, which later transformed into the White House COVID-19 Response Team in February 2021, the COVID-19 vaccine makers were able to secure sustained resources in the development of the COVID-19 vaccines. Government purchase contracts also allowed the COVID-19 vaccine makers to achieve economies of scale. The COVID-19 pandemic once again proved that in light of a public health emergency, government intervention is necessary to ensure quick and effective responses. The emergent policy responses effectively cut back red tape but also ensured sufficient regulations for the safety of COVID-19 vaccines through the FDA's rigorous and scientific emergency use authorization (EUA). The U.S. government is estimated to have spent $19.3 billion on COVID-19 vaccine development, which is a fraction of the $5 trillion in the total economic stimulus package. Public health spending proved to be the most cost-effective way to address the economic challenges in this public health crisis.[46,57]

However, as previously mentioned, the outputs and outcomes of policy cycles include reactions in society and related efforts to further modify policy. During the COVID-19 pandemic, the CDC was criticized as too data dependent, lacking an effective public communication strategy, and not acting quickly against new variants, as well as focusing too much on containing the virus, instead of factoring in other collateral damages, such as the toll on mental health, during its initial 2020 response. In response to the criticisms, the CDC reorganized to improve its responses in public emergencies, including increasing the use of available data and making communication more public friendly. In addition, the Biden administration continued the investment in COVID-19 vaccines and treatments.[58] With the U.S. Congress providing $1.15 billion to support research on "long COVID," such as the Long Covid Initiative by Brown School of Public Health, there is hope for better understanding and treatment of this long-term condition. Moreover, the FDA is working on a simplified annual booster plan to reduce future uncertainty associated with "living with COVID-19."[59] It is clear that the U.S. government's involvement in the development of vaccines and treatments will continue to be crucial in fighting the COVID-19 pandemic. Nevertheless, there have not been any permanent policies that commit resources for monitoring and managing the ongoing pandemic even though SARS-CoV-2 continues circulating and public precautions are waning.[47] It is important that public and private partnerships work toward a more proactive approach to prevent and prepare for the long-term impacts of COVID-19.

Possible Responses to the Convergence of Policy Problems

Since the rise of modern medicine in the 19th and 20th centuries, national variations in health organization, practice, and policies have been gradually affected by a growing convergence due to technologic change and social globalization.[60,61] Recent international surveys of health system changes emphasize that nations are all coping with the same major problems, including cost containment, access barriers to large population subgroups, the impact of rapidly developing new technologies, ensuring a reasonably high-quality standard for care, and measuring health outcomes.[6]

1. *Cost containment.* All nations face the problem that the cost of providing modern health care with currently accepted standards and technologies is outrunning patients' abilities to generate the wealth to pay for it. Nations that do not have true national healthcare systems, such as the United States, may be racing toward the cliff of runaway healthcare costs faster than most European nations, which have historically possessed national structures for healthcare organization and delivery.[62] But all nations are being forced to confront the issue of allocating scarce healthcare resources. According to the Organization for Economic Cooperation and Development (OECD), healthcare expenditures "will outpace GDP growth over the next 15 years in almost every OECD country.... Health spending per capita will grow at an average annual rate of 2.7% across the OECD and will reach 10.2% of GDP by 2030, up from 8.9% in 2018."[6]

   The need for cost containment entails consideration of the cost-effectiveness of health technologies and procedures.[63] Frequently, the most cost-effective technology is not the most recently developed, particularly in areas where it appears that healthcare research and development are approaching, or have reached, the "flat of the curve."[64] Cost containment requirements also include the imperative to sometimes say *no*, even when the added consumption of health resources might benefit individual and/or population health in some way.[65] The removal of "waste" in health services delivery is certainly desirable, but the ultimate challenge in cost containment is controlling and limiting the application of potentially useful health services.

2. *Access to care.* Whether they are economically advanced and wealthy or relatively poor and less developed, all nations have at least some subpopulations that are relatively disadvantaged in their access to necessary health services. However, it is often difficult to address these needs since they usually require the expenditure of additional resources (clearly limited, as noted earlier). In addition, the redistribution of national resources to "have-not" groups is often administratively and technically difficult (it is hard to reach vast rural populations in nations such as China, for example), and politically divisive (politically active and articulate "have" groups in all nations usually want to keep their share of national wealth rather than having a significant part of it taken away and given to others).[66]

   Often, poorer citizens in nations such as Bolivia, Vietnam, and Moldova have to rely on under-the-table payments (often constituting bribery) to get even the most essential healthcare services from underpaid and overworked providers.[67] In extreme situations of political instability and repression, healthcare institutions can break down entirely. This was the case in the Tigray region of Ethiopia during a civil war that began in 2020, where healthcare facilities were targeted for destruction by Ethiopian military forces.

   An equally horrifying medical disaster has taken place in Syria as the result of a civil war that began in 2011. In late 2024, Syrian rebels seized the capital of Damascus and overtook the Assad family's brutal rule of the country. The Syrian people are reeling from the decade-long conflict and crisis, which includes the decimated healthcare system. Many hospitals and primary care facilities are nonfunctional.[68]

   At the same time, wider access to basic health services would save hundreds of millions of people worldwide from death and disability and would serve as a powerful tool in antipoverty efforts.[69-71] The case for greater access to health care is, therefore, both sensible from the standpoint of national interests and urgent as a global moral imperative.[72,73] When the wealthiest nations in the world help the poorest and sickest people in the world, they wind up doing well for themselves by doing good for others. (Indeed, if this was not the case, the outlook for the poorest and the sickest would be even worse than it is now.)

3. *Impact of new technologies.* Health technologies have continuously and rapidly evolved in the last century, usually becoming more complex and costly. These technologies, in areas as varied as assistive technologies, pharmaceuticals, and surgical techniques, often provide major health benefits to their recipients.[74] Most dramatically, the rapid development and deployment of vaccines using new mRNA technology in 2020 saved millions of lives worldwide during the COVID-19 pandemic. But all nations, as part of the challenge of facing cost containment difficulties, have to balance the allocation of limited resources to these new technologies against older but cheaper services (often in the realm of primary care) that may help larger numbers of people, but less dramatically or visibly. This leads to both economic and ethical conflict, since such decision making inevitably does involve "playing God," sometimes with life-and-death consequences.[75] National governments must respond to continuous and virtually unlimited demands from individuals and groups with limited resources. The allocation of these scarce resources involves explicit or implicit rationing that inevitably benefits some individuals and groups at the expense of others.

4. *Quality of care considerations.* As healthcare technologies become more complex, the issue of quality assurance looms larger. Health professionals often cannot monitor technologies through simple observation—detailed technologies are required to provide constant readings.[76] In addition, there have been breakthroughs in data collection and analysis during the last two decades, particularly with respect to the development of computerized data entry and aggregation (often via Internet-based means). For the first time in history, it is possible to aggregate large numbers of patient encounters and detect variations in care quality, along with their consequences, such as medical errors. Major studies that have been done in the United States, the United Kingdom, Canada, and Australia constitute the first steps in defining and understanding the level of medical errors.[76-79] However, as noted in a PriceWaterhouseCoopers (PWC) report[123], "no one really knows how many errors or adverse

events occur because of gaps in reporting processes and differences in definition."[6]

The revolution in health information technology means that nations can consciously guide healthcare quality assurance and improvement, with enormous benefits accruing to both patients and providers. Of course, to benefit from these technologies, nations must also develop the necessary data collection systems, along with the trained professionals to administer and utilize them. As with other aspects of health technologies, this can pose major challenges for less economically developed nations, such as India.[80]

5. *Measuring health outcomes.* In the long run, the greatest potential benefit from new health information technologies is that they increase the likelihood that health status and outcomes can be measured and related back to health services utilized, as well as individual and community lifestyles and practices. The *health outcomes movement* has the potential to make health service delivery much more cost-effective, as well as to reduce medical errors and to clarify which aspects of health care and behavior are more or less important.[81]

It must be noted that an important part of this is showing to what extent health services and new technologies cannot substitute for improved individual and community health lifestyles. For example, whatever funding the nation of China puts into its health system for treatment of lung cancers, it is clear that the funding cannot substitute for a concerted effort to reduce the rapid increase in national tobacco consumption, which will result in the deaths of tens of millions over the next few decades.[82] A 2015 report by the National Research Council at the National Academies of Science suggested that 50% of premature deaths in the United States can be accounted for by one or more quantified lifestyle and environmental risks.[83] Unfortunately, it is also true that nations differ in their abilities to afford and apply the systems needed for effective health outcomes research, as well as the subsequent system reforms driven by research results, with poorer nations being especially hampered.

Internationally, there is a general consensus about the existence of the previously mentioned healthcare system problems. Within each country, there has also been some debate (if only at the upper policymaking level) over how the nation should respond to these challenges. China, a rapidly developing but still relatively low-income nation that has never really had a structured national health system, faces enormous challenges in organizational development and funding.[66] Developed nations with existing national health systems, such as Australia and Japan, are talking about to what extent (and if so, how) private-sector components should be introduced and integrated to improve provider responsiveness to consumer demands.[84,85]

The United States is unique internationally in that it is a very wealthy nation with a lavishly funded healthcare sector but lacks an effective structure to direct spending and system restructuring. So, while the U.S. system can produce some of the best high-technology health care in the world and leads in research and development spending, it wastes money on an epic scale and suffers from glaring disparities in health insurance coverage and access to care.[65] As the United States has the highest proportion of GDP devoted to health care, and with cost inflation generally recognized as ultimately unsustainable, health reform has been and will continue to be a major item on the nation's policy agenda. Reform proposals have been put forth by political liberals (such as the introduction of a *single payer system* like that in Canada as well as enhanced employer coverage within existing insurance structures) and conservatives (such as the increased use of individual healthcare purchasing through Health Savings Accounts).[86,87]

In the international study done by PWC,[6] three clear findings emerged:

- The globalization of health brings enormous opportunities, but is overshadowed by common threats. Bloated costs, uneven quality, and inequitable or mismanaged access threaten the sustainability of health organizations, systems, and populations. The most important attribute of reformed national healthcare systems in the coming years will be sustainability. "To be sustainable, health executives will need information, metrics, and transparency to support decision making .... Transparency enables a comparative focus on access as well as the cost and quality of care."
- Increasingly, with ever-growing global communication among national health policymakers, it appears that *convergence* will characterize policy reform efforts. In the words of the PWC study authors, there will be significant "global convergence, as best practices are shared, and industry-wide convergence, as the barriers among pharmaceuticals, providers, clinicians, biotech, and payers melt away." If sustainability is the key objective for health policymakers around the world, what aspects of reform do they need to focus on to get there? Like most others who have

considered the issue, the PWC analysts believe that there are some critical factors. The PWC list includes:

1. *A quest for common ground*. Essentially, this is an effort to develop national political consensus on the public/private sector division of healthcare responsibilities, along with social agreement about some basic level of guaranteed access to basic health services for all citizens.
2. *A digital backbone*. This refers to the use of nationwide integrated clinical and administrative information systems to increase the efficiency of the healthcare system, as well as to provide data that can be utilized for program evaluation and outcomes research efforts.
3. *Incentive realignment*. This feature centers on the nation's citizens who are healthcare recipients and contends that a sustainable national system must "ensure and manage access to care while supporting accountability and responsibility for healthcare decisions."[6]
4. *Quality and safety standardization*. This feature focuses on provider accountability and responsibility, suggesting that there needs to be transparent quality and safety standards so that consumer trust can be established and maintained in the nation's healthcare services.
5. *Strategic resource deployment*. This is more vaguely defined in the PWC study, since it suggests the need for resource allocation that "appropriately satisfies competing demands on systems" to balance cost containment and access requirements without being able to provide any real definition of what might constitute *appropriate satisfaction*.[6] This indicates the contingent nature of this feature, since it will most clearly be determined by the political balance of power within each society.
6. *Climate of innovation*. This feature suggests that nations need to embrace innovation in both technology and processes in order to improve the functioning of the healthcare system.
7. *Adaptable delivery roles and structures*. The PWC report calls for patient-centered care that is maximized in varying circumstances by the adoption of variable care practices and clinical roles.

Surveying the current state of national health systems around the world, what can be concluded with respect to the progress being made in policymaking in these areas?

Two of the previously mentioned sustainability features are primarily technological in nature and can be assessed fairly easily. Some nations have moved materially toward a true *digital backbone* (#2), but only a few. The Netherlands has pioneered in using health information systems to improve healthcare quality within a constrained national budget.[88] Both Canada and the United Kingdom have also worked toward developing national integrated electronic medical records.[89] However, these nations already have truly integrated national health systems; the Netherlands has a national employer-based system, the United Kingdom has a National Health Service, and Canada has a single payer system administered by its provinces.[86] There may be significant problems with national health systems, but it is easier to implement uniform technical and structural reforms within them. In all of these nations, the policy marketplace has been dominated by forces (particularly the government and organized labor, along with general public opinion) in favor of national health care. As will be discussed later, if that decision is made (or not made), choices concerning structure, including of information systems, are significantly affected.

In contrast, the United States is very wealthy and spends an enormous amount on health care, but lacks such a national governing structure. In the policy marketplace, there is bitter political controversy over the structure and functioning of the ACA, and industry groups tend to further system fragmentation through their own interests in controlling market share. Consequently, U.S. health care has failed to produce a viable health information system through market mechanisms.[90] Smaller providers in the United States, particularly home health agencies and skilled nursing facilities, have clearly lagged behind larger private- and public-sector health systems in adopting health information technologies.[91]

In recent years, the need for national health information integration has become so evident that it united conservatives like Newt Gingrich and liberals like Hillary Clinton in support of national policy initiatives.[92] A conservative Republican president, George W. Bush, followed through on this call by supporting the establishment of a National Health Information Infrastructure (NHII), which is supposed to be a "comprehensive knowledge-based network of interoperable systems of clinical, public health, and personal health information."[93] In the case of the United States, the policy marketplace has shifted to support national health information system restructuring due to growing concerns by payers (that a lack of a national information infrastructure is not cost-effective) and patients/consumers (primarily due to desires for increased quality improvement and safety and for easier personal access to care information).

Since they usually lack the funds and technical expertise, most poor and less developed nations are far from attaining the digital backbone sustainability goal put forth by PWC. For example, in Mexico, the Ministry of Health is responsible for overall health system functioning, but provider funding is very fragmented (much of it coming from patient self-payment), and there is essentially no functioning national information system. The nation's healthcare problems are so great, and government funding so limited, that it will be many years before the system will be sufficiently coherent to permit a digital backbone.[94] For these nations, sustained economic growth will be necessary to generate the required capital for health system upgrades.

Some of the same conclusions are reached in a global examination of quality and safety standardization (#4). In Europe and Canada, physicians have taken a leadership role in forwarding these causes. In the U.S. policy marketplace, the prominence of patient advocacy groups has provided a different avenue to advance demands for quality and safety assurance.[6] The Health and Medicine Division (formerly the Institute of Medicine) of the National Academies of Science has provided a reasonably clear blueprint as to how the United States can cross the quality chasm.[95] Generally, in economically advanced nations, there are important and increasingly influential groups that are effectively demanding higher quality standards, although there are still debates about the extent to which these standards should be dictated by the government, as opposed to the private sector.[96]

As with the digital backbone, less economically advanced nations generally do not yet have the funds or organizational structure to provide system-wide quality and safety standards, whatever the political preferences might be. A study of practice quality in Indonesia, Tanzania, India, Paraguay, and Mexico suggests substantial variation within each country and different factors leading to each country's pattern of variation. As the study's authors conclude, "questions relating to practice quality [in low-income countries] remain unanswered in the literature, because the quality of health care in low-income countries is difficult to measure."[97] Until data collection and database development related to the quality of care are improved in these nations, they will not have the necessary inputs to even begin developing and monitoring system-wide quality standards.

The same thing can be said for safety standards. Many poorer nations do not have well-established and effective regulatory structures for overseeing medical safety. China has been particularly visible with respect to safety problems. It is the largest supplier of pharmaceutical ingredients in the world, and there have been major problems reported with some medical products.[98] China's chief food safety watchdog has said that almost 20% of products made for consumption in China were found to be substandard.[99] It appears that neither government nor voluntary private-sector safety guidelines and agreements are effective in China, where there is high turnover in manufacturers and their executives.[100] These ongoing problems resulted in the United States and China signing a Memorandum of Agreement on December 11, 2007, to establish a bilateral mechanism to ensure the safety of drugs, excipients, and medical devices exported from China to the United States.[101] This has resulted in a permanent FDA presence in China as a condition for continued exports to the United States. China is making major efforts to improve "pharmacovigilance," but the nation faces numerous cost and organizational challenges, particularly in integrating traditional Chinese medicines (TCM) into a unified drug surveillance system.

Beyond the two previously described factors, a digital background and system-wide quality and safety standards, it should be noted that the others listed in the PWC report ("a quest for common ground," "incentive realignment," "strategic resource deployment," "climate of innovation," and "adaptable delivery roles and structures") are fundamentally political in nature. Their definition within each nation depends on ideologic decisions that in turn will come from widely varying political systems and structures. These varying decisions made by each will reflect tradeoffs between multiple valued objectives. So, to understand the nature of what nations will be doing in health care in the coming decades, we must understand the nature of tradeoffs, and how these tradeoffs relate to national systems of ideology and ethics in health and nonhealth areas.

The Nature of National Health Tradeoffs, Ideology, and Ethics

In policymaking, tradeoffs come from the inescapable fact that all policy decisions involve the use of finite resources, and to use them in one area means that they may not be available to be deployed in alternative areas. As economist Arthur Okun suggested,

"Tradeoffs are the central study of the economist. 'You can't have your cake and eat it too' is a good candidate for the fundamental theorem of economic analysis."[3] But resources in policy analysis can also be intangible and involve such value-laden tradeoffs as individual choice versus government dictation, or political equity versus economic efficiency. That means that tradeoffs must involve ideology and ethics as well as economics.

The importance of tradeoffs in health policymaking—and differing decisions on tradeoffs—have been widely recognized, both within and among nations. Dervaux, Leleu, and Valdmanis conducted an expanded data envelopment analysis of World Health Organization (WHO) and individual national rankings of five health objectives: life expectancy, health distribution, health system responsiveness, responsiveness distribution, and financial contribution fairness. The authors agreed with the WHO Commission for Macroeconomics and Health that any global perspective on health policy priorities needs to be complemented by individual national health policy priority analyses and choices.[102]

When it comes to tradeoffs between economic efficiency and political equity, some researchers have attempted to provide tools that contain explicit criteria. Focusing on developing nations, James et al. suggest that more explicit analysis can aid efforts to attain social justice.[103] In their work, the researchers list and explain a number of efficiency and equity criteria to guide priorities, including cost-effectiveness, horizontal equity, and vertical equity.[103] Ross states that social justice is a "central obligation of civil society where the measure of the ethical integrity of a society is how it treats its most vulnerable members."[104]

Particularly in wealthy nations with expensive healthcare systems, policymakers and clinicians are starting to develop guidelines for tradeoffs in healthcare decision making. New York State health officials have now developed protocols for the allocation of ventilators in the event of an H5N1 influenza pandemic. The lead author of their study, Dr. Tia Powell, calls for the public to confront such triage issues, so that these decisions reflect community views as well as ethical and clinical standards. "It's not really a technical solution. … It's values. And the people are the experts on that."[105] Another example of this is in cancer treatment. According to *The New York Times*, medical groups, such as the American Society of Clinical Oncology, are now recommending that physicians weigh the costs as well as the effectiveness of treatments when making cancer care decisions. This group is developing a scorecard to evaluate drugs on cost and value as well as efficacy and side effects.[106]

There are clear political obstacles to explicit tradeoff analysis in health policymaking. The public in most nations does not have a clear understanding of the inescapability of tradeoffs, especially if they suspect that they entail rationing of popular services.[107] As some have observed, all Americans ask for is cheap, fast, and high-quality health care, but they do not understand that they can never get health care with more than two out of those three characteristics in a real-world healthcare system with limited resources and potentially unlimited demands. Research on public response to possible cost-quality tradeoffs in clinical decisions indicates that reactions are unpredictable and not necessarily clinically or economically logical.[102] Conversely, findings suggest that a significant portion of the public (at least in the United States) would be willing to accept cost–quality tradeoffs, if they are provided with clear information on the cost-effectiveness of specific treatments. Most recently, these issues have been faced in the difficult and contentious area of COVID-19 resource allocation decision making.

At the global level, it is just as difficult to analyze tradeoffs. In research conducted for the WHO Advisory Committee on Health Research, Schunemann et al. reviewed the available literature on "determining which outcomes are important for the development of guidelines" and found "limited relevant research evidence."[107] The authors offered the general recommendation that methods to examine tradeoffs and their impact on outcomes should employ "systematic and transparent methods involving key stakeholders, including consumers and people from different cultures, to help ensure that all important outcomes are considered."[108] Of course, this recommendation only addresses procedural issues and does not touch on the substance of which choices should be made. Moreover, the division and debate over the substance of health reform is the primary challenge facing national publics and their policymakers.

As noted earlier, there is a convergence of opinion (at least, at the policy elite level) that current national health systems are unsustainable because of growing cost, access, and quality problems. In the ongoing global discussion about tradeoffs and possible health system reforms, it is equally clear that there is no current consensus—only a diversity of ethical perspectives and ideological positions.

One thing is clear: National deliberations over health reform policymaking cannot take place without recognizing that there are ethical and ideologic disagreements at the heart of the debates. Unfortunately, all too often, policymakers do engage in de facto social experiments without ethical review and debate, both among themselves and with their nation's citizens.[109] In an analysis of the role of justice and solidarity in priority setting in health care,[110] two ethicists point out that one major reason for this is that some nations do not have the ideologies or institutions of inclusive social participation and modern economics that provide the foundation for a balanced debate over tradeoffs in health system reform. One analyst contends that "in a political process, where reforms are implemented by democratically controlled agencies, the analogy to informed consent is democratic oversight of the reform process. Unfortunately, this analogy is problematic wherever democratic control of institutions is weak ... and wherever powerful external agencies offer large incentives and are not themselves held accountable for the reforms they impose."[111]

Scholars have developed a variety of perspectives related to this. The economist Hernando de Soto has contended that many poor nations, particularly in the "post-communist" world, have not developed the social habits of the rule of law that permit widely accepted policies for resource use. Absent these, decisions on resource allocation in all areas of society—including health care—are made largely on the basis of "might makes right." The less powerful are largely disenfranchised and simply attempt to evade the rule of the powerful (usually through governments) by the use of black markets.[112] According to the social philosopher John Rawls, "One may think of a public conception of justice as constituting the fundamental charter of a well-ordered human association."[113] In societies with volatile political and social systems in transition (including nations experiencing rapid economic and social growth, such as China and India), the principles of justice and popular participation are often not well established or widely shared, which means that health policymaking may be essentially the imposition of the will of political elites. In the long run, such policymaking may contribute to, rather than reduce, social and political instability.

Justice has both individual and social components. Ethical health policymaking implies an acceptance of *individual autonomy*—the belief that individuals have the right to their own beliefs and values and to related decisions and choices with respect to the use of health services. Some of the most politically charged policy debates occur when the principle of autonomy clashes with social/communal welfare principles of treatment, as in the case of Terri Schiavo in the United States.[114] *Whose Life Is It Anyway?* is a noted play and movie that considers the dilemma of which set of priorities should prevail over life-and-death decisions—that of the individual whose life is in question or that of a society, which has to put forth and defend laws regulating medical treatment. The debate over COVID-19 vaccine mandates for school-age children and various categories of employees beginning in 2021 featured strong (at times violent) disagreement between those prioritizing personal choice and those maintaining that public/community health needs require individual compliance with vaccine mandates.

In health policymaking, the social component is reflected primarily in the debate over *distributive justice*, or the fairness in the distribution of health benefits and burdens in society.[14] In most nations, the question of fairness is debated endlessly by the various participants in the policy marketplace. The economist Thomas Rice, criticizing the United States in 1998 for its unique status as the only economically advanced nation without some system of national health insurance, articulated the egalitarian view of justice, in which equal access to health services (at least to an essential minimum package of services) for all citizens, regardless of income or class, is of central importance. In doing so, he made the ethical case for U.S. adoption of national health insurance.[115]

In most Western nations (particularly in the United States), there is also a libertarian perspective of fairness that would argue Rice's preferences are decidedly unfair. Libertarians (who adhere to a mix of beliefs found both on the political left and on the political right) tend to believe that individual freedom is the most important social value. *Fairness* means that individuals have the freedom to choose to do what they wish with their own resources, and that the best set of policies rests on the belief in a minimal state, enforcing basic laws and regulatory "rules of the game" but not attempting to dictate economic outcomes or to engage in large-scale redistribution of wealth.[116,117] In contrast to Rice, libertarian health economists prescribe individual choice and responsibility as the best ways to *reform* U.S. health care.

Health policymaking is certainly a matter of data collection and analysis, of research and forecasting, of power struggles within national policy marketplaces. Like other aspects of public policy, it is also an "inescapably moral enterprise."[118] Because of that, health policymaking and analysis will be sterile and ultimately ineffective if the policymakers and analysts do not realize—whether they want to or not—that "policy and ethics both ask the same question: 'what is the good, and how do we achieve (create, protect, cultivate) it?'"[119]

Conclusion: Health Policymaking Around the World—Uncertain Times and Futures

It is not at all clear how the nations of the world, with greatly differing political, economic, healthcare, and social systems, are going to meet the health system challenges in the next 20 years. Most wealthy countries, with aging populations, are beginning to hit the financial wall, with unpredictable consequences. In the United States, any reasonably balanced investigation of the numbers—rising demand for more (and more technologically intensive) health care, an aging population, declining employer-based insurance, increasing number of uninsured individuals, and, above all, a healthcare cost inflation rate that outruns economic growth by a significant margin—will reveal that sometime between 2025 and 2035, when essentially all of the "baby boomers" will have retired and expect to get all of the health care they want and "deserve" from Medicare, financing the U.S. healthcare system as it is currently structured will not add up. Something will have to give.

In the absence of the establishment of a true national healthcare system, the supply/demand imbalance is already creating de facto rationing, with insured individuals waiting longer and longer and paying more and more to get ever more tightly limited care. If the U.S. healthcare system hits the financial wall, many individuals who cannot afford to even make copayments on ACA insurance purchased through state exchanges will fall completely through the cracks, since the ad hoc public and charity healthcare system will come apart at the seams. This is a profoundly depressing vision for anyone who believes that access to some effective level of basic health care should be a right that all citizens possess.

U.S. reformers who want to avoid these dire straits generally advocate increased cost controls on health system expenditures and/or increased taxes on upper-income citizens. Some advocate eliminating private health insurance and moving to a single payer system ("Medicaid for all").[119] They will experience major political difficulties in getting any post–ACA proposal enacted. Most efforts to enact national health reform, including the ACA, are sold to the public as giving everyone the right to relatively easy access to comprehensive health services, with only modest costs. As was seen in 1993 to 1994, the largely insured public reacted badly when they found out that they would actually have to adjust their own healthcare arrangements and pay out themselves to provide insurance for those fellow citizens who were going without.

There has also been a significant backlash against the ACA, with claims of decreased access, with health providers withdrawing from markets, and with employers eliminating jobs or reducing work hours to reduce their obligations to fund expanded health insurance.[120] Access was further reduced when the U.S. Supreme Court, in its *National Federation of Independent Business v. Sebelius* decision in 2012 made a key element of the ACA, state Medicaid expansion, optional rather than mandatory.[121] Many states with Republican-dominated governments immediately announced that they would not expand their state Medicaid systems. Most Republicans in Congress still advocate "repeal and replace" for the ACA while being extremely vague on exactly what the replacement might be. However, as time has gone by, more and more states (41 plus the District of Columbia, as of January 2025) have expanded Medicaid as part of the ACA, including many states led by Republican governors.[122] Yet, even the ACA does not squarely confront the dilemma of a continuing large gap between healthcare demand and affordable supply and ongoing cost inflation exceeding the economic growth required to pay for care.

The problems of cost containment and access in the United States have continued to mount. There is no question of maintaining the current "system"—it is visibly coming apart before our eyes. Either we shape the future healthcare system now, or we will inherit the disorder of our old healthcare system as it slowly unravels.

Any examination of the experiences of those nations that do have comprehensive national health systems, such as the National Health Service in the United Kingdom, shows that national health insurance means national health rationing, like it or not, with real consequences for patient health and well-being.[65] In any event, European nations, with rapidly aging populations and relatively expansive social expectations for public health and welfare spending, will have their own political conflicts. However, with structured healthcare systems, they appear to have the potential to develop some political consensus over providing health care within tighter financial limits.

The situation in many developing nations will be incomparably more difficult. It is hard to see how most African nations, with their unstable political systems and desperately poor populations, could afford to even approach "advanced nation" healthcare provision any time in the foreseeable future. Some Asian countries, such as South Korea, Singapore, and Taiwan, have already reached very high economic development levels and so can afford the most modern health care. But China and India, even with their strong economic growth rates in the last decade, will continue to face the prospect of rapidly growing (and potentially politically explosive) social inequities, with growing numbers of relatively well-off urban residents, and hundreds of millions of low-income individuals in their rural hinterlands and urban slums.

The world is entering what will undoubtedly be a turbulent period, with national healthcare systems everywhere requiring major overhauls of one form or another. There is no past template that nations can employ to respond to this challenge. However, it is very important to remember that any response to escalating healthcare costs must recognize that health care has never been, and can never be, treated as a purely market good. There is clearly a role for competition and economic incentives in providing and selecting health care. At the same time, any long-range response that brings healthcare supply and demand into a sustainable balance—by regulatory fiat or by market competition—will have to recognize that, as citizens, community members, and human beings, we must all care enough about each other to ensure that none of us lacks the essential healthcare services that we can afford to provide.

To end on a note of optimism, it is important that we do not lose sight of the ongoing achievements of modern health care that have transformed the lives of citizens in wealthy nations and are now doing the same for a majority of the poor in the rest of the world. A renewed sense of economic limits in health care need not be in opposition to this worldwide trend. In fact, recognizing the limits is almost certainly a requirement for continuing to make progress. Here it is appropriate to conclude with another quotation from the scholar and visionary cited at the beginning of this chapter, Dr. William Schwartz:

> Where does all this leave us as we try to sort out the challenges that face us at the beginning of a new century? We are enticed by visions of triumph over disease but disturbed by the near-term prospect of denying useful care to some patients .... The next 25 years will be especially challenging and possibly divisive ones, but it is important that we not lose sight of the utopian visions that are emerging. The possibility of mastery over a broad range of illnesses is no longer the sole property of philosophers and science fiction authors. Our challenge will be to tackle the ethical and social issues that accompany medical progress with the same rigor that we apply to the scientific challenges themselves. Above all, we must ensure that in the sacrifices required to realize our visions, especially in the critical area of healthcare rationing, we do not compromise fairness and equity, without which the conquest of disease would be a hollow victory.[5]

References

1. Porter R. *The Cambridge History of Medicine*. Cambridge, UK: Cambridge University Press; 2006.
2. Rawls J. *A Theory of Justice*. Cambridge, MA: Harvard University Press; 1971.
3. Okun A. *Equality and Inefficiency: The Big Tradeoff*. Washington, DC: Brookings Institution; 1975.
4. Rice T. *The Economics of Health Reconsidered*. Chicago, IL: Health Administration Press; 1998.
5. Schwartz WB. *Life without Disease: The Pursuit of Medical Utopia*. Berkeley, CA: University of California Press; 1998.
6. Organization for Economic Cooperation and Development. Health spending set to outpace GDP growth to 2030. Accessed August 1, 2023. https://www.oecd.org/health/.
7. World Economic Forum. *Future of Healthy: How to Realize Returns on Health*. Geneva, Switzerland: January 2016.
8. Anderson OW. *The Health Services Continuum in Democratic States*. Ann Arbor, MI: Health Administration Press; 1989.
9. Capital Health, Global Strategy Initiative. *Crisis Response: Global Health Care Strategy in the 21st Century. Report on Symposia*. Washington, DC/Paris, France; 2004.
10. Lasswell H. *Politics: Who Gets What, When, How*. New York, NY: World Publishing; 1951.
11. Feldstein PJ. *The Politics of Health Legislation: An Economic Perspective*. Chicago, IL: Health Administration Press; 2006.
12. Gande C. Zimbabwean government triples army officer pay ahead of elections. *VOA News Com*. 2008. Accessed February 24, 2008. http://www.voazimbabwe.com/a/a-13-56-74-2008-02-21-voa45-68976302/1470185.html.
13. Blank RH, Burau V. *Comparative Health Policy*. New York, NY: Palgrave Macmillan; 2004.

14. Longest BB. *Health Policymaking in the United States*. 6th ed. Chicago, IL: Health Administration Press; 2015.
15. Das J, Hammer J. Location, location, location: residence, wealth, and the quality of medical care in Delhi, India. *Health Aff*. 2007;26(3):w338-w351. doi: 10.1377/hlthaff.26.3.w338.
16. Olson M. *The Logic of Collective Action*. Cambridge, MA: Harvard University Press; 1965.
17. James C, Carrin G, Savedoff W, Hanvoravongchai P. Clarifying efficiency–equity tradeoffs through explicit criteria, with a focus on developing countries. *Health Care Analysis*. 2005;13(1):33–51.
18. Denenberg R. The community: mobilizing and accessing resources and services. In: Cohen FL, Durham JD, eds. *Women, Children, and HIV/AIDS*. New York, NY: Springer; 1993.
19. Foreman C. Grassroots victim organizations: mobilizing for personal and public health. In: Cigler AJ, Loomis BA, eds. *Interest Group Politics*. 4th ed. Washington, DC: Congressional Quarterly Press; 1995.
20. Koyanagi C, Bevalacqua JJ. Managed care in public mental health systems. In: Hackey RB, Rochefort DA, eds. *The New Politics of State Health Policy*. Lawrence, KS: University Press of Kansas; 2000:186-206.
21. Steslicke WE. Development of health insurance policy in Japan. *J Health Polit Policy Law*. 1982;7(1):197–226.
22. Wiktorowicz ME. Emergent patterns in the regulation of pharmaceuticals: institutions and interests in the United States, Canada, Britain and France. *J Health Polit Policy Law*. 2003;28(4):615–658.
23. Weissert CS, Weissert, WG. *Governing Health*. 2nd ed. Baltimore, MD: Johns Hopkins University Press; 2002.
24. Easton D. *A Systems Analysis of Political Life*. Chicago, IL: University of Chicago Press; 1979.
25. Wilsford D. States facing interests: struggles over health policy in advanced, industrial democracies. *J Health Polit Policy Law*. 1995;20(3):571–613.
26. Crenson MA. *The Unpolitics of Air Pollution*. Baltimore, MD: Johns Hopkins University Press; 1971.
27. Yankelovich D. The debate that wasn't: the public and the Clinton plan. *Health Aff*. 1995;14(1):7–23.
28. Skocpol T. The rise and the resounding demise of the Clinton plan. *Health Aff*. 1995;14(1):66–85.
29. Edelman M. *The Symbolic Uses of Politics*. Urbana, IL: University of Illinois Press; 1964.
30. Starr P. *Remedy and Reaction*. New Haven, CT: Yale University Press; 2013.
31. Brown LD. Getting there: the political context for implementing health care reform. In: Brecher C, ed. *Implementation Issues and National Health Care Reform*. Washington, DC: Josiah Macy, Jr. Foundation; 1992:13–46.
32. Thompson FJ. The evolving challenge of health policy implementation. In: Litman TJ, Robins LS, eds. *Health Politics and Policy*. 3rd ed. New York, NY: Delmar Publishers; 1997:155–175.
33. Pressman JL, Wildavsky A. *Implementation*. Berkeley, CA: University of California Press; 1973.
34. Sparer MS, Brown LD. States and the health care crisis: limits and lessons of laboratory federalism. In: Rich RF, White WD, eds. *Health Policy, Federalism and the American States*. Washington, DC: Urban Institute Press; 1996: 181–202.
35. Wenk E. *Margins for Survival: Overcoming Political Limits in Steering Technology*. New York, NY: Pergamon Press; 1979.
36. Moon M. *Medicare Now and in the Future*. 2nd ed. Washington, DC: Urban Institute Press; 1996.
37. Oberlander J. *The Political Life of Medicare*. Chicago, IL: University of Chicago Press; 2003.
38. Centers for Disease Control and Prevention (CDC). 2023. https://archive.cdc.gov/#/details?q=covid%20data&start=0&rows=10&url=https://www.cdc.gov/coronavirus/2019-ncov/covid-data/faq-surveillance.html.
39. Ahmad FB, Anderson RN. The leading causes of death in the US for 2020. *JAMA*. 2021;325(18):1829–1830. doi: 10.1001/jama.2021.5469.
40. National Center for Health Statistics. U.S. Census Bureau, Household Pulse Survey, 2022–2023. Long COVID. Generated interactively. https://www.cdc.gov/nchs/covid19/pulse/long-covid.htm.
41. Bach K. New data shows long Covid is keeping as many as 4 million people out of work. Brookings. 2022. https://www.brookings.edu/research/new-data-shows-long-covid-is-keeping-as-many-as-4-million-people-out-of-work/.
42. Cutler DM, Summers LH. The COVID-19 pandemic and the $16 trillion virus. *JAMA*. 2020;324(15):1495–1496. doi: 10.1001/jama.2020.19759.
43. Bruns R, Teran N. *Weighing the Cost of the Pandemic. Knowing What We Know Now, How Much Damage Did COVID-19 Cause in the United States*? Institute for Progress; 2022. https://progress.institute/weighing-the-cost-of-the-pandemic/.
44. Cubanski J, Kates J, Tolbert J, Guth M. *What Happens When COVID-19 Emergency Declarations End? Implications for Coverage, Costs, and Access*. Kaiser Family Foundation; 2023. https://www.kff.org/coronavirus-covid-19/issue-brief/what-happens-when-covid-19-emergency-declarations-end-implications-for-coverage-costs-and-access/.
45. Senate Bill 3548. 116th U.S. Congress. 2020. https://www.congress.gov/bill/116th-congress/senate-bill/3548/text.
46. Barone E. The Trump administration's "Operation Warp Speed" has spent $12.4 billion on vaccines. How much is that, really? *Time*. 2020. https://time.com/5921360/operation-warp-speed-vaccine-spending/.
47. Lee BY. Only ~14% of U.S. adults have gotten latest Covid-19 vaccine update 2023. *Forbes*. 2023. https://www.forbes.com/sites/brucelee/2023/11/18/only-14-of-us-adults-have-gotten-latest-updated-covid-19-vaccine/?sh=7482bb8e2f6c.
48. Brüssow H, Zuber S. Can a combination of vaccination and face mask wearing contain the COVID-19 pandemic? *Microb Biotechnol*. 2022;15(3):721–737. doi: 10.1111/1751-7915.13997. Epub 2021 Dec 28. PMID: 34962710; PMCID: PMC8913850.
49. Cohen J. Why efforts to make better, more universal coronavirus vaccines are struggling. *Science*. 2022. https://www.science.org/content/article/why-efforts-make-better-more-universal-coronavirus-vaccines-are-struggling.
50. Adolph C, Amano K, Bang-Jensen B, et al. Governor partisanship explains the adoption of statewide mask mandates in response to COVID-19. *State Polit Policy Quart*. 2022;22(1), 24–49. doi: 10.1017/spq.2021.22.
51. Güss CD, Boyd L, Perniciaro K, Free DC, Free JR, Tuason MT. The politics of COVID-19: differences between US red and blue states in COVID-19 regulations and deaths. *Health Policy OPEN*. 2023;5:100107. https://doi.org/10.1016/j.hpopen.2023.100107.

52. Scott D. California mandated masks. Florida opened its restaurants. Did any of it matter? *Vox*. 2021. https://www.vox.com/coronavirus-covid19/22456544/covid-19-mask-mandates-lockdown-debate-evidence.
53. Zhang X, Warner ME. COVID-19 policy differences across US states: shutdowns, reopening, and mask mandates. *Int J Environ Res Public Health*. 2020;17(24):9520. doi: 10.3390/ijerph17249520 PMID: 33353158; PMCID: PMC7766317.
54. Yakusheva O, van den Broek-Altenburg E, Brekke G, Atherly A. Lives saved and lost in the first six months of the US COVID-19 pandemic: a retrospective cost-benefit analysis. *PLoS One*. 2022;17(1):e0261759. https://doi.org/10.1371/journal.pone.0261759.
55. Smith-Schoenwalder C. How COVID-19 will shape the 2022 midterm elections. *U.S. News*. 2022. https://www.usnews.com/news/elections/articles/the-coronavirus-and-the-2022-elections.
56. Portnoy J. Local Covid tracking sites adapt to new era of coronavirus pandemic. *The Washington Post*. 2023. https://www.washingtonpost.com/dc-md-va/2023/05/02/covid-dashboard-health-emergency/.
57. Frank RG, Dach L, Lurie N. It was the government that produced COVID-19 vaccine success. *Health Affairs*. 2021. doi: 10.1377/hblog20210512.191448.
58. NPR. 2022. https://www.npr.org/2022/08/17/1117904729/cdc-reorganization-walensky-covid.
59. National Institutes of Health. NIH launches new initiative to study "long COVID." https://www.nih.gov/about-nih/who-we-are/nih-director/statements/nih-launches-new-initiative-study-long-covid.
60. Torrens PR. Historical evolution and overview of health services in the United States. In: Williams SJ, Torrens PR, eds. *Introduction to Health Services*. 5th ed. New York, NY: Delmar Publishers; 1999:chap 1.
61. Friedman TL. *The World Is Flat*. New York, NY: Farrar Straus & Giroux; 2005.
62. Davis K, Anderson GF, Rowland D, Steinberg EP. *Health Care Cost Containment*. Baltimore, MD: Johns Hopkins University Press; 1990.
63. Gold MR, Siegel JE, Russell LB, Weinstein MC. *Cost-Effectiveness in Health and Medicine*. New York, NY: Oxford University Press; 1996.
64. Lee RH. *Economics for Healthcare Managers*. Chicago, IL: Health Administration Press; 2015.
65. Aaron H, Schwartz WC. *Can We Say No? The Challenge of Rationing Health Care*. Washington, DC: Brookings Institution; 2005.
66. Hu K. Challenges facing the Chinese health care system. *Asia Pacific Journal of Public Health*. 2020;33(1). doi.org/10.1177/1010539520968464.
67. Lewis M. Informal payments and the financing of health care in developing and transition countries. *Health Aff*. 2007;26(4):984–997.
68. International Rescue Committee. Emergency Watchlist 2025. Crisis in Syria: What to Know and How to Help. Accessed January 27, 2025. https://www.rescue.org/article/crisis-syria-what-know-and-how-help.
69. World Bank. *Global Monitoring Report 2005, Millennium Development Goals: From Consensus to Momentum*. Washington, DC: World Bank; 2005.
70. Sachs JD. *The End of Poverty*. New York, NY: Penguin Press; 2006.
71. Martin G, Grant G, D'Agostino M. Global health funding and economic development. *Global Health*. 2012;8(8). doi: 10.1186/1744-8603-8-8.
72. Brower J, Chalk C. *The Global Threat of New and Reemerging Infectious Diseases*. Santa Monica, CA: RAND Corp.; 2003.
73. Roychoudhuri O. The end of poverty: an interview with Jeffrey Sachs. *Mother Jones*. May 6, 2005. Accessed January 28, 2008. http://www.motherjones.com/news/qa/2005/05/jeffrey_sachs.html.
74. Newman PJ, Weinstein MC. The diffusion of new technology: costs and benefits to health care. In: Gelijns AC, Halm EA, eds. *The Changing Economics of Medical Technology*. Washington, DC: National Academy Press; 1991:21–34.
75. Ubel PA. *Pricing Life: Why It's Time for Health Care Rationing*. Cambridge, MA: MIT Press; 2001.
76. Wilson RM, Runciman WB, Gibberd RW, et al. The quality in Australian health care study. *Med J Aust*. 1995;163: 458–471.
77. Kohn L, Corrigan JM, Donaldson MS, eds. *To Err Is Human: Building a Safer Health System*. Washington, DC: National Academy Press; 2000.
78. Vincent C, Neale G, Woloshynowych M. Adverse events in British hospitals: preliminary retrospective record review. *BMJ*. 2001;322(7285):517–519.
79. Baker GR, Norton PG, Flintoft V, et al. The Canadian adverse events study: the incidence of adverse events among hospital patients in Canada. *CMAJ*. 2004;170(11):1678–1686.
80. Anonymous. India's fake doctors: quackdown. *Economist*. 2008:386(8568):58–59.
81. Epstein AM. The outcomes movement: will it get us where we want to go? *N Engl J Med*. 1990;323:266–270.
82. China's cigarette threat. *BBC News*. November 19, 2007. Accessed January 8, 2008. http://news.bbc.co.uk/1/hi/health/216998.
83. *Measuring the Risks and Causes of Premature Death: Summary of a Workshop*. Institute of Medicine, National Academy of Sciences; 2015. Accessed October 25, 2016. https://www.nap.edu/catalog/21656/measuring-the-risks-and-causes-of-premature-death-summary-of.
84. Hall J. Incremental change in the Australian health care system. *Health Aff*. 1999;18(3):95–110.
85. Ikegami N, Campbell JC. Health care reform in Japan: the virtues of muddling through. *Health Aff*. 1999;18(3):56–75.
86. White J. *Competing Solutions: American Health Care Proposals and International Experience*. Washington, DC: Brookings Institution; 1995.
87. Cogan JF, Hubbard RG, Kessler DP. *Healthy, Wealthy, and Wise*. Washington, DC: American Enterprise Institute Press; 2005.
88. Grol R. *Quality Development in Health Care in the Netherlands*. Commonwealth Fund report, Commission on a High Performance Health System, Pub. 910. Accessed October 25, 2016. http://www.commonwealthfund.org/~/media/files/publications/fund-report/2006/mar/quality-development-in-health-care-in-the-netherlands/grol_qualitynetherlands_910-pdf.pdf.
89. Anderson GF, Frogner KK, Johns RA, Reinhardt UE. Health spending and use of information technology in OECD countries. *Health Aff*. 2006;25(3):819–831.
90. Kleinke JD. Dot-gov: market failure and the creation of a national health information technology system. *Health Aff*. 2005;24(5):1246–1262.

91. Kaushal R, Bastes DW, Poon EG. Functional gaps in attaining a national health information network. *Health Aff.* 2005;24(5):1281–1289.
92. Donald B. Newt Gingrich pushing "wired" hospitals. Associated Press. June 22, 2004.
93. U.S. Department of Health and Human Services. FAQs about NHII. Accessed January 29, 2008. http://aspe.hhs.gov/sp/NHII/FAQ.html.
94. Barraza-Llorens M, Bertozzi S, Gonzalez-Pier E, Gutierrez JP. Addressing inequity in health and health care in Mexico. *Health Aff.* 2002;21(3):47–56.
95. Institute of Medicine. *Crossing the Quality Chasm.* Washington, DC: National Academy Press; 2001.
96. Schoenbaum SC, Audet AJ, Davis K. Obtaining greater value from health care: the roles of the U.S. government. *Health Aff.* 2003;22(6):183–190.
97. Das J, Gertler PJ. Variations in practice quality in five low-income countries: a conceptual overview. *Health Aff.* 2007;26(3):w296-w309. doi: 10.1377/hlthaff.26.3.w296.
98. Harris G, Bogdanich W. Drug tied to China had contaminant, F.D.A. says. *New York Times*. March 6, 2008. Accessed March 10, 2008. http://nyti.ms/2dO4GIn.
99. China executes former FDA chief amid product safety crisis. *CBC News*. July 10, 2007. Accessed January 10, 2008. http://www.cbc.ca/world/story/2007/07/10/china-tainted-products.html.
100. More disturbing news about contaminated imports. *Consumer Reports*. Accessed October 26, 2016. http://www.consumerreports.org/cro/news/2007/06/more-disturbing-news-about-contaminated imports/index.htm
101. FDA–SFDA China, agreement on the safety of drugs and medical devices. U.S. Food and Drug Administration. Published December 11, 2007. Accessed October 26, 2016. http://www.fda.gov/InternationalPrograms/Agreements/MemorandaofUnderstanding/ucm107512.htm.
102. Dervaux B, Leleu H, Valdmanis V. Estimating tradeoffs among health care system's objectives. *Health Serv & Outcomes Res Method.* 2004;5:39–58.
103. James M, Hoff T, Davis J, Graham R. Leveraging the power of the media to combat HIV/AIDS. *Health Aff.* 2004;24(3): 854–857.
104. Ross, D. Social Justice. Encyclopedia of Sustainable Management, 2020. DOI: https://doi.org/10.1007/978-3-030-02006-4_186-1.
105. Dean C. Guidelines for epidemics: who gets a ventilator? *New York Times*. March 25, 2008. Accessed March 25, 2008. http://nyti.ms/1OPpFRR.
106. Pollack, A. Cost of treatment may influence doctors. *New York Times*. Accessed October 25, 2016. http://www.nytimes.com/2014/04/18/business/treatment-cost-could-influence-doctors-advice.html.
107. Baily MA. "Rationing" and American health policy. *J Health Polit Policy Law*. 1984;9(3):489–501.
108. Schunemann HJ, Oxman AD, Fretheim A. Improving the use of research evidence in guideline development: determining which outcomes are important. *Health Policy Res and Sys*. 2006;4(18). doi: 10.1186/1478-4505-4-18.
109. Daniels N. Toward ethical review of health system transformations. *Am J Public Health*. 2006;96(3):447–451.
110. Hoedemaekers R, Dekkers W. Justice and solidarity in priority setting in health care. *Health Care Analysis*. 2003;11(4):325–343.
111. Daniels N. Toward ethical review of health system transformations. *Am J Public Health*. 2006;96(3):447–451.
112. de Soto H. *The Mystery of Capital*. New York, NY: Basic Books; 2003.
113. Rawls J. *A Theory of Justice*. New York: NY: Oxford Paperbacks; 1971.
114. Goodnough A, Hulse C. Feeding-tube case roils Washington and Florida. *New York Times*. March 18, 2005. Accessed August 5, 2016. http://hdl.handle.net/10822/982594.
115. Rice TH. *The Economics of Health Reconsidered*. 3rd ed. Chicago, IL: Health Administration Press; 2009.
116. Friedman M, Friedman R. *Free to Choose: A Personal Statement*. New York, NY: Manner Books; 1990.
117. Nozick R. *Anarchy, State, and Utopia*. New York, NY: Basic Books; 1974.
118. Kenny N, Giacomini M. Wanted: a new ethics field for health policy analysis. *Health Care Anal*. 2005;13:247.
119. Gaffney AW, Verhoef PA, Hall JB. Should pulmonary/ICU physicians support single payer health care reform? Yes. *Chest*. 2016;150(1):14–15.
120. Antos J, White J. Can we afford four more years of Obamacare? *Inside Sources*. American Enterprise Institute. Accessed August 5, 2016. http://www.aei.org/publication/can-we-afford-four-more-years-of-obamacare/2016.
121. Kaiser Family Foundation. A guide to the Supreme Court's decision on the ACA's Medicaid expansion. *Focus on Health Reform*. August 2012. Accessed August 8, 2016. https://kaiserfamilyfoundation.files.wordpress.com/2013/01/8347.pdf.
122. Kaiser Family Foundation. Status of state Medicaid expansion decisions: interactive map. Published November 9, 2022. Accessed January 9, 2023. https://www.kff.org/medicaid/issue-brief/status-of-state-medicaid-expansion-decisions-interactive-map/.
123. PricewaterhouseCoopers' Health Research Institute, HealthCast 2020: *Creating a Sustainable Future*. Available at https://www.pwc.com/il/he/publications/assets/2healthcast_2020.pdf.

CHAPTER 5

Role of International Organizations in Health Systems

Allen Johnson, Veronica Leary, and Raheleh Mohammadi

Introduction

Although national health systems have an important role in providing health services, they are not the only entities that are tasked with improving and ensuring the health of individuals and populations. There is a spectrum of organizations that directly and indirectly contribute to global health, including foundations, development banks, nongovernmental organizations, bilateral agencies, and intergovernmental organizations. Myriad organizations and agencies that are independent from governments or larger health systems work to provide conditions conducive to good health. Additionally, partnerships among nation-states have been ever present in global health through collaborative efforts to prevent conflict, famine, and disease. The focus of this chapter is on organizations beyond national health systems that broadly fall into one of the two categories: intergovernmental organizations and nongovernmental organizations.

Intergovernmental Organizations

Intergovernmental organizations (IGOs, also referred to as international governmental organizations) are organizations composed primarily of sovereign states, referred to as member states. IGOs are established by treaty among member states, and the treaty acts as a charter for creating the group. Although formally established by treaty, IGOs are distinct agencies and differ from organizations of sovereign states unified by treaties like the North American Free Trade Agreement (NAFTA). IGOs are also distinguished from informal groupings or coalitions of states, such as the Group of Seven (G7). IGOs vary in function, membership, membership criteria, goals, and scope, which are often outlined in the treaty or charter that established the organization. IGOs are developed to address mutual interests with unified aims to resolve conflict and improve international relations, promote international cooperation on matters such as environmental protection, promote human rights and social development (education, health), render humanitarian aid, and foster economic development. Some are more general in scope, whereas others may have specific missions. The largest IGO is the United Nations (UN).

The United Nations System

After World War I, the League of Nations was created in 1920 as the first IGO with the purpose of achieving world peace.[1] At its height, the League was composed of 58 member states.[2] However, the start of World War II made it apparent that the League of Nations had failed at its primary goal. In 1941,

Franklin Roosevelt and Winston Churchill signed a "Declaration by United Nations" as a pact to fully cooperate in the war against the Axis powers. In addition, the declaration outlined the necessity to defend life, liberty, religious freedom, and human rights.[3] Later, 47 additional states, including the Soviet Union and China, signed the pact.[4,5] In 1945, a delegation of representatives from 50 governments met in San Francisco for the United Nations Conference on International Organization. It was the culmination of a process that started in 1944 to create a new IGO that would formally replace the now defunct League of Nations. On October 24, 1945, the United Nations Charter was ratified, and the UN was officially established.[6] Over the past 79 years, the United Nations, its agencies, and affiliated specialized agencies have been awarded the Nobel Peace Prize 12 times.[7]

The UN is composed of 193 member states and is divided into six main branches: the General Assembly, Security Council, Economic and Social Council, International Court of Justice, Secretariat, and Trusteeship Council. Each branch has its own unique role and function within the UN to help achieve the mission of world peace, friendly relations among nations, and international cooperation on economic, social, environmental, and humanitarian issues.[8,9] In addition to the six main branches, the UN system includes 11 funds and programs, 15 specialized agencies, and many other affiliated groups.[10] To ensure effective communication among its members, Arabic, Chinese, English, French, Russian, and Spanish are official languages of the UN, with documents presented in all six languages.[11] The UN headquarters is located in New York City. Although it is situated in the United States, the land occupied by the UN headquarters is under the sole administration of the UN and not the U.S. government. The UN has three additional headquarters, located in Geneva, Switzerland; Vienna, Austria; and Nairobi, Kenya. Each site is considered an international territory and is exempt from the jurisdiction of local law.[12]

The General Assembly is the main representative arm of the UN. The General Assembly oversees the UN budget, receives reports from various UN system organizations, and makes policies and recommendations for resolutions. The General Assembly also has the power to appoint or dismiss nation-states from various roles within the UN, including Security Council roles and UN membership. Member states are equally represented in the General Assembly, with all 193 given one vote per state. An appointed president of the General Assembly, the secretary-general, presides over its annual meetings. Resolutions pass with a simple majority vote among those present and voting. However, if the membership deems an issue to be critical, the issue must pass with a two-thirds majority. Such issues are usually matters of budget, appointments, dismissals, peace, and security.[8] The General Assembly may also be called to meet outside of its regularly scheduled meetings for emergency special sessions. Such sessions may be convened either at the request of the Security Council or at the request of a majority of the member states. If the Security Council is at an impasse on resolution, it may hold an emergency special session to deal with a breach of peace. In such an event, the General Assembly has the power, with a two-thirds majority vote, to recommend use of armed forces.[13] Special sessions may also be called to confront a range of humanitarian issues, such as the one called in 2001 to discuss the HIV/AIDS pandemic.[14]

According to the UN Charter, the role of the Security Council is to maintain international peace and security. Additionally, the Council has the power to add new members to the UN as well as to alter the UN Charter. All UN member states must comply with resolutions of the Security Council charged with establishing peacekeeping operations, sanctions, and authorizing military actions. The 15-member council is composed of 10 appointed, nonpermanent member states and five permanent members.[8] The five permanent members of the security council are the United States, the United Kingdom, France, Russia (replacing the Soviet Union in 1991), and China.[15] All Security Council decisions must pass with a nine-member assenting vote. However, a negative vote by one of the five permanent members on any resolution is an effective veto.[16]

The Economic and Social Council has the primary role of UN economic, social, and environmental policy review and implementation. Composed of 54 member states, 14 specialized agencies of the UN system, and over 3,200 partner nongovernmental organizations, the Council coordinates the effort of agreed-upon development goals. Members of the Economic and Social Council are elected by the General Assembly for 3-year terms.[8,17]

The International Court of Justice is the judicial branch of the UN. Its primary responsibilities are to settle disputes among member states in accordance with international law and to give legal counsel on questions referred by other UN departments and specialized agencies.[8] The Court is composed of 15 judges elected to 9-year terms by the General Assembly and Security Council.[18] All 193 members of the UN must comply with the court's decisions, and its orders are enforced by the Security Council.[19] Situated in The Hague (the seat of the Dutch government), within the Netherlands, the Court is the only primary organization of the UN not headquartered in New York City.[8]

The UN Secretariat is composed of the secretary-general as well as 44,000 civil servants. Its primary purpose is to carry out the mandates of the other five main branches, including day-to-day operations, peacekeeping operations, research, and communication with nonstate participants. The secretary-general is the head of the Secretariat and is appointed to a renewable 5-year term by the General Assembly after a recommendation from the Security Council.[8,20]

Working together with the UN main body, its funds, programs, and specialized agencies are integral to the achievement of the UN mission.

UN Funds and Programs

Throughout its history, the UN General Assembly has established several programs and funds to address various humanitarian and development concerns. Each of the funds and programs is headed by an Executive Director and is governed by an Executive Board. These bodies report to the General Assembly through the Executive Board. Following are a few notable UN funds and programs.

United Nations Children's Emergency Fund In 1946, the General Assembly created the United Nations Children's Emergency Fund (UNICEF) to provide food and health care for children of countries that were ravaged by World War II. Since then, the goal of the organization has expanded to the development of sustainable community-based systems that provide for the well-being of all children. UNICEF currently operates in 190 countries and relies on member state contributions as well as private donations. For its efforts and achievements, UNICEF was awarded the Nobel Peace Prize in 1965.[21]

United Nations Development Programme Founded in 1965, the United Nations Development Programme (UNDP) serves as the global development network of the UN. Funded entirely by member states, the UNDP works to help 170 countries reach their development goals. The scope of the UNDP is broad and includes the reduction of poverty, inequality, and HIV/AIDS, as well as the creation of sustainable environmental, energy, and crisis prevention projects. To measure its progress, the UNDP releases an annual Human Development Report.[22] Central to the UNDP's role as the UN's primary development agency are its aims to help countries achieve the Sustainable Development Goals (SDGs)—17 goals set forth by the UN and its member states.[23]

United Nations High Commissioner for Refugees Founded in 1950, the United Nations High Commissioner for Refugees (UNHCR) is a UN agency focusing on the protection and well-being of refugees. It strives to make sure that all people have the ability to seek safe asylum in another country when necessary. It also works to protect the ability of refugees to voluntarily integrate into the society of the host country, relocate to another country, or return home. The UNHCR has also been instrumental in advising host countries to suspend negative asylum decisions during refugee crises, and it supplies information regarding the effects of diaspora. For its efforts, the UNHCR was awarded the Nobel Peace Prize in 1954, and again in 1981.[24,25]

World Food Programme Considered the largest humanitarian organization focused on hunger in the world, the goal of the World Food Programme (WFP) is to ensure every person has sustained access to food necessary for a healthy life. Founded in 1961, the WFP works in 120 countries and territories and provides food assistance to an estimated 158 million people each year. In addition to food aid, the WFP works on community-level projects that help reduce the risk of food shortage and malnutrition. A recent additional project of the World Food Programme is providing security of food and water deliveries in deprived territories or countries. It is funded by a combination of member-state support and private donations.[26,27]

UN Specialized Agencies

Specialized agencies are autonomous organizations working with the UN and each other through the coordination of the United Nations Economic and Social Council. Specialized agencies may or may not have been originally created by the UN, but they are incorporated into the UN system. Although they are part of the UN system, specialized agencies typically have their own member states separate from UN member states. As such, funding for these agencies is through their own member states and direct donations. A few notable specialized agencies are described next.

International Monetary Fund The International Monetary Fund (IMF) is composed of 189 member states working to foster global monetary cooperation, secure financial stability, facilitate international trade, promote high employment and sustainable economic growth, and reduce poverty around the world. The IMF promotes international cooperation, trade, exchange-rate stability, and sustainable economic growth. The IMF collects money from member states to create a monetary reserve. Countries may borrow from the IMF reserve to stabilize their economy or invest in development projects. Additionally, the IMF may assist in the management of international payment difficulties and financial crises. The IMF also monitors housing trends as per its Global Housing Watch.[10,28-30]

World Bank The World Bank's primary goals are to reduce poverty by providing grants, low-interest loans, and interest-free credit to developing countries and to promote foreign investment and international trade. Founded in 1944, two of the main branches, the International Bank for Reconstruction and Development and the International Development Association, now have 189 member countries and staff in 170 countries. To become a member of the World Bank, a country must first join the IMF. Although not a UN agency, the World Bank coordinates with the UN on a number of economic development projects.[10,31]

World Health Organization Founded in 1948, the World Health Organization (WHO) is a specialized agency of the UN focused on global public health.[32] Its overall mission is "the attainment of all people to the highest level of health."[33] Through research, health policymaking, education initiatives, and disease monitoring and intervention, the WHO seeks to stop the spread of communicable diseases and lessen the burden of chronic disease. Currently involved in the fight against HIV/AIDS, malaria, and tuberculosis, the WHO is also a major partner in the Global Polio Eradication Initiative. Its *World Health Report* publication highlights health concerns relating to each of its member states. The WHO currently has 194 member countries and works in more than 150 locations to provide resources (and information) to combat various communicable and noncommunicable diseases.[34] The WHO collaborates with five hosted (and formal) partnerships, 100 collaborative arrangements, and 800 collaborative centers through a network that covers 80 countries.[35] It gets its funding through two primary sources: assessed contributions (a percentage of a member country's annual GDP and amounting to 20% of the WHO's total revenue) and voluntary contributions (from member states, various IGOs, philanthropic organizations, and the private sector, and amounting to 80% of its total revenue).[36] Much like the IMF and UNDP, the WHO is concerned with helping countries to attain the 17 SDGs through initiatives such as the Triple Billion targets—a project that uses 46 outcome indicators (including 39 SDG indices) that cover a range of health topics in order to ascertain the health life expectancy index as a summary measure of population health and as a baseline for member states' progress.[37] A further aim of the WHO is to expand universal health coverage to 1 billion people as per its Triple Billion targets.[32,38]

A Look at Other Intergovernmental Organizations

Although the UN is the largest IGO with great influence and participation around the world, it is by no means the only one. The following section summarizes a few of the world's largest and most influential non-UN IGOs.

European Union

Founded in 1992, the European Union (EU) is an intergovernmental organization that possesses some of the powers of a sovereign nation and some of the roles of an international organization—including as a funding source. In particular, the EU is a regional IGO that formulates foreign and security-related policies via its 24 member states. The EU's structure entails four components: the European Council (which consists of the leaders of its member states); the Council of the European Union (which consists of ministers from various member states); the European Commission (which consists of 27 commissioners from each of its member states); and the European Parliament (which consists of officials who are elected every 5 years). The European Council is the primary organization—having been established in 2009—that sets the EU's political priorities. The Council of the EU passes legislation, coordinates economic policies for EU member states, develops the EU's foreign and defense policies, and signs agreements with EU members and non-EU countries/territories. The European Commission proposes new laws to the parliament and the council, allocates funding, enforces EU laws, and represents the EU internationally. The European Parliament passes laws in conjunction with the Council, adopts the EU budget, and scrutinizes the EU's actions to ensure those actions are democratic in nature.[39]

African Union

The African Union, composed of 55 member states, was founded in 2002 as a successor to the Organization of African Unity (which was founded in 1963).[40] Its aims are to foster international cooperation, peace, and economic and social development among African peoples. The African Union functions with its own Secretariat; Assembly; Economic, Social, and Cultural Council; Peace and Security Council; and peacekeeping force. Its highest decision-making body, the Assembly of the African Union, is composed of the heads of state of all 55 of its member states.[41]

International Criminal Court

Founded in 2002 as part of the Rome Statute and located in The Hague, the International Criminal Court (ICC) is an international tribunal whose purpose is prosecuting individuals for international war crimes, crimes against humanity, and genocide. The ICC initiates prosecution following investigations and requests by individual states or by the UN Security Council. The ICC may also take up an investigation when a country's national courts are unwilling to prosecute an individual. Currently, 123 countries are members of the ICC.[42]

Organisation for Economic Co-operation and Development

Originating in 1948 as the Organisation for European Economic Co-operation to help administer the Marshal Plan, this IGO was re-formed in 1961 as the Organisation for Economic Co-operation and Development (OECD). The mission of the OECD is to implement policies that improve the economic and social wellbeing of people around the world. The 37 democracies that constitute the OECD generally have high-income economies and a high Human Development Index score. Through government collaboration and analysis of successful strategies and underlying global issues, the OECD provides a forum for implementing quality-of-life improvements for every country.[43] The OECD publishes an annual report detailing the economic, environmental, and social statistics, including health measures, of its member states.

World Trade Organization

The World Trade Organization (WTO) was founded in 1995 and currently is composed of 164 member states and 24 observer states. It has the explicit purpose of regulating international trade. The WTO oversees the implementation of trade deals and serves as a forum for its member states to settle trade disputes. It provides assurance among consumers and producers that international markets will remain open to them. The philosophy of the WTO is that by removing trade barriers, it also removes barriers among peoples and nations. Although not formally a UN specialized agency, the WTO has cooperative agreements with the UN.[44]

Nongovernmental Organizations

The term *nongovernmental organization* (NGO) remains vaguely defined. In general, NGOs are broadly defined as "legal entities created by private individuals, private organizations, publicly traded organizations, or in some combination where governmental influence, supervision, and management are removed, or at least greatly minimized, from the NGO's strategic and operational mission."[45] The term came into currency in 1945 because of the need for the UN to differentiate in its charter the participation rights for intergovernmental specialized agencies versus international private organizations. At the UN, virtually all types of private bodies can be recognized as NGOs. They only have to be not-for-profit, noncriminal, independent from government control, and not seeking to challenge governments either as a political party or by a narrow focus on human rights.[46] The definition generally used by the U.S. Peace Corps to define an NGO is "a specific type of organization that is not part of government and that possesses the following four characteristics:

1. Works with people to help them improve their social and economic situations and prospects
2. Was formed voluntarily
3. Is independent, controlled by those who have formed it or by management boards representing the organization's stakeholders
4. Is not for profit; although NGOs engage in revenue-generating activities, the proceeds are used in pursuit of the organization's aims."[47]

NGOs participate in a wide and varied spectrum of advocacy and operations around the globe. From locally based groups meeting in private homes to global giants with budgets in the hundreds of millions of U.S. dollars, NGOs make significant contributions to global health based on their unique missions. NGOs engage in a wide array of activities involving political advocacy, the environment, health care, women and children's rights, economic development, and many other issues. By definition, NGOs are independent from government influence; therefore, they are often in a unique position to address issues that governments do not. Operating in a milieu lacking constraints from bureaucratic or political considerations, NGOs are often able to provide leadership and resources for producing and advocating for public policy when government agencies are unable or unwilling to do so. NGOs are often activists or advocates that operate with funding secured through IGOs. They frequently promote grassroots initiatives and pressure IGOs and governments to invest in specific issues.[48] The efficiency of NGOs is, in part, attributed to their grassroots approach. According to the UN, the strength of NGOs lies in their "proximity to their members or clients, the flexibility and the high degree of people's involvement and participation in their activities, which leads to strong commitments, appropriateness of solutions and high acceptance of decisions implemented."[49]

NGOs are not formally part of the UN system; rather, some NGOs work closely with the UN in consultative capacities. Having participated in the work of the UN from its inception, NGOs first took a role in formal UN deliberations through the Economic and Social Council in 1946. Initially, 41 NGOs were granted consultative status by the Council; by 1992, more than 700 NGOs had attained that level of credibility. The number has been steadily increasing ever since, and today 5,451 NGOs collaborate with the UN.[50]

NGOs have grown substantially since the 1990s—with the first proliferation of international NGOs occurring during the AIDS crisis—to 47,000 NGOs in 2001. The World Bank estimates that NGOs now contribute to 15% of total overseas development aid—with that trend likely to increase in the next decade.[51] There are over 1.5 million NGOs operating in the United States alone.[52] The amount of resources controlled and distributed by these organizations varies greatly and can be quite extensive. For instance, one of the largest in terms of budget and scope, World Vision, had annual expenses in 2022 of over 1.3 billion USD,[53,54] as much as 20 times the gross domestic product (GDP) of some of the smaller countries around the world.[55] Based on firm financial growth, the largest NGOs continue to expand in both their funding and their mission.

Classifying NGOs

Nationally and internationally, the broad range of NGOs has become so expansive that the establishment of a single classification system is exceedingly difficult. The World Bank classifies NGOs into two categories: operational and advocacy.[56] According to the WHO, the primary purpose of an operational NGO is the design and implementation of development-related projects, whereas advocacy NGOs have a primary purpose of defending or promoting a specific cause. NGOs can be further classified as either relief-oriented or development-oriented based on the development status of the countries in which they work, the nature of their work, and whether they are faith-based or secular or any combination thereof. Due to the extensive variations among NGOs, a list of acronyms has been developed to aid in the classification of such organizations. Some examples of these include the following:

FONGO—Funder-organized NGO

RINGO—Religious international NGO

PVO—Private voluntary organization

CBO—Community-based organization

CSO—Civil society organization

BONGO—Business-organized NGO

TANGO—Technical assistance NGO

A Look at Some of the Largest International NGOs

The following section summarizes the NGO "global giants," which have hundreds, even thousands, of employees and budgets in the hundreds of millions of dollars. This list, although certainly not exhaustive, represents some of the largest and most established NGOs working in the world today.

Amnesty International

Amnesty International (commonly known as Amnesty) was founded in 1961 in London. It was originally established to facilitate the release of political prisoners. Amnesty has since grown into an organization aimed at upholding the whole spectrum of human rights, including abolishing the death penalty, protecting sexual and reproductive rights, combatting discrimination, and defending refugee and migrant rights. It draws attention to human rights abuses, and it campaigns for compliance with international laws and standards. Amnesty International is almost entirely composed of voluntary members, with only a small number of professional staff, and is structured as groups or sections. Sections entail the coordination of basic activities; larger sections focus on activities that require larger numbers of people and, at times, the inclusion of professional staff. As of 2019, there were 63 sections globally.[57] Amnesty currently has over 7 million members and supporters worldwide.[58] The organization was awarded the Nobel Peace Prize in 1977.

BRAC

BRAC (formally Bangladesh Rural Advancement Committee) is an international development organization based in Bangladesh. Established in 1972 as a small-scale relief and rehabilitation project to help returning war refugees, today BRAC is the largest NGO in the world in terms of number of employees. BRAC employs over 100,000 people, roughly 70% of whom are women. The organization's activities involve economic development, education, public health, and gender equality. BRAC's Economic Development Program includes the use of microcredit. It provides collateral-free loans to mostly poor, landless, rural women, enabling them to generate income and improve their standards of living. Reaching nearly 4 million borrowers, BRAC has provided loans to those who, due to extreme poverty, have been otherwise unable to secure other financial sources. BRAC's microcredit program has funded over 5.09 billion USD in loans, with 95% of its borrowers being women. BRAC has served 7.4 million clients and 5.6 million borrowers.[59] According to BRAC, the repayment rate is over 98%.[60,61]

CARE International

Founded in 1945 to provide relief to World War II survivors, CARE is committed to promoting social change and ending global poverty. CARE currently works in over 100 countries around the world. A leading humanitarian organization fighting global poverty, CARE's philosophy is that women are essential with regard to helping families and communities escape poverty. Women are at the heart of CARE's community-based efforts to improve basic education, prevent the spread of HIV, increase access to clean water and sanitation, expand economic opportunity, and protect natural resources. CARE promotes the UN's SDGs through both direct and indirect pathways in order to reach women and families. As of 2022, 61% of total participants had been reached via 1,631 projects/initiatives.[62] CARE also provides emergency aid to survivors of war and natural disasters.[63]

Human Rights Watch

The largest human rights organization based in the United States, Human Rights Watch conducts fact-finding investigations into human rights abuses around the world. Founded in 1978 as Helsinki Watch to monitor human rights in the former Soviet Union, Human Rights Watch publishes numerous books and reports every year, generating extensive coverage of human rights issues in both local and international media. Human Rights Watch also meets with government officials to urge changes in policy and practice. Under extreme circumstances, it presses for the withdrawal of military and economic support from governments that egregiously violate the rights of their people.[64] Human Rights Watch consists of 550 individuals—representing over 70 nationalities—who advocate for vulnerable populations.[65]

International Committee of the Red Cross/Crescent

The International Committee of the Red Cross (ICRC) is based in Geneva and is a three-time Nobel Prize Laureate. The ICRC is mandated to protect victims of international and internal armed conflicts. Such victims include prisoners, refugees, civilians, and other noncombatants. Under the ICC statute, the states retain primary responsibility for the prosecution of international crimes. However, Geneva Conventions & Additional Protocol I of 1977 requires that states prosecute individuals accused of war crimes or that they extradite such individuals for prosecution. Given that the ICC prosecutes individuals—not nations—the ICRC was given immunity from providing evidence to the ICC per Rule 73 of the Statute. This exception allows the ICRC to intercede in domestic and international conflicts without states being fearful of the ICRC witnessing any human rights violations.[66]

The ICRC is part of the International Red Cross and Red Crescent Movement, which—along with the ICRC—includes the International Federation of Red Cross and Red Crescent Societies (encompassing 190 national societies). The ICRC is the oldest and most honored organization within the Movement and one of the most widely recognized humanitarian organizations in the world. Today, the ICRC is based in around 80 countries and has a total of more than 12,000 staff.[67] Financing for the ICRC consists of voluntary contributions from the states involved in the Red Cross and Crescent Societies, the Geneva Convention, and various IGOs (e.g., the EU), and totaled CHF 2.8 billion as of 2023.[68]

Médecins Sans Frontières (Doctors Without Borders)

Médecins Sans Frontières (MSF) is an independent humanitarian medical aid agency that is committed to providing medical aid wherever it is needed.

Founded in 1971, MSF has 20 country offices and provides emergency medical aid in more than 70 countries. Its teams are composed of doctors, nurses, and other professionals, medical and nonmedical, working alongside locally hired staff. MFS has approximately 45,000 medical and ancillary workers.[69] Working in teams in 63 countries around the world, MSF workers have provided around 12.5 million medical consultations, have admitted over 1 million patients to hospitals and clinics throughout the world, and have helped deliver more than 194,000 babies.[70,71] MSF won the Nobel Peace Prize in 1999.

Oxfam International

The name *Oxfam* comes from the British group Oxford Committee for Famine Relief, founded in 1942 during World War II. Oxfam International is a confederation of 21 independent NGOs working with thousands of partner organizations in more than 90 countries with the common goal of ending global poverty and related injustice Oxfam has reached an estimated 15.6 million people through 994 initiatives.[72] It works with communities, allies, and partner organizations undertaking long-term development, emergency work, research, and advocacy. Oxfam focuses on a broad range of issues, including trade, conflict, debt and aid, and education.[73]

Partners in Health

Partners in Health (PIH) was founded in 1987 in Boston, Massachusetts, to deliver health care to the poorest areas of Haiti. Today, PIH has programs in nine countries on four continents. With a mission to provide a preferential option for the poor in health care, PIH works globally to bring the benefits of modern science to those most in need through service delivery, training, research, and advocacy.[74] Through its network of paid professionals and unpaid volunteers, PIH had carried out 3 million outpatient clinic visits and 2.2 million home visits, as well as 2.2 million women's wellness checkups, as of 2023.[75] Paul Farmer, one of the founders of PIH and a major contributor to public health efforts around the world, passed away in 2022. "O for the P" is a saying used widely in the organization that was coined by Farmer: It stands for "Preferential Option for the Poor" and is a guiding principle for PIH. It is a kind of "If you know, you know" statement that pays homage to a highly dedicated public health professional.

Save the Children International

Save the Children International promotes children's rights, provides relief, and helps support children in developing countries. Headquartered in the United Kingdom, it aims to improve the lives of children through better education, health care, and economic opportunities, as well as to provide emergency aid in natural disasters, war, and other conflicts. A total of 29 national organizations are members of Save the Children International; this global network of organizations supports local partners in over 120 countries around the world.[76] As of 2021, Save the Children International supported 3.2 million women and 10.1 million children through its nutrition initiatives; it also supplied an access to education to 12 million children, including 6.2 million girls.[77]

World Vision International

World Vision International is a Christian humanitarian organization that is dedicated to working with children, families, and communities worldwide and enabling them to reach their full potential by tackling the causes of poverty and injustice. World Vision first began caring for orphans and other children in need in South Korea in 1950, and then expanded throughout Asia. Today, World Vision International works in nearly 100 countries around the world and has expanded its mission to include community development and advocacy for the poor. Its child sponsorship program has been successful in attracting donors who send funds each month to provide support for sponsored children and projects.[78] The World Vision Program constitutes the World Food Programme's largest food distributor partnership, having supplied malnourished children with proper nutrition and leading to an 89% recovery rate through its services.[79]

The Relationship Between NGOs and IGOs

Near the end of the Cold War, civil society became an increasingly important alternative to state actions, wherein societal participation extended beyond the auspices of state governments or intergovernmental partnerships. NGOs became increasingly important to solving international issues with the concomitant rise of civil society, globalization, and the AIDS pandemic. As such, NGOs have attained greater levels of legitimacy at the local (grassroots), national, and global levels.[51] In recent years, NGOs and IGOs have become integral components of global governance and various interorganizational collaborations. As noted previously, IGO-NGO collaborations may entail formal or informal partnerships given the needs of both organizations, the scope of projects, and impediments created by other NGO-IGO or governmental partnerships. Collaborations between NGOs and IGOs entail complex dynamics and are best understood by the six phases of policymaking: agenda setting, policy analysis, policy formulation, policy decision making, implementation, and policy evaluation/revision.[80] In particular, NGO-IGO partnerships entail the exchanges of material and/or immaterial resources such that their collaborations optimize those resources and—in some instances—expedite initiatives. For example, NGOs may exert "soft influences" on governmental agencies or IGOs by raising awareness, garnering public support, or reframing concerns.[48] IGOs can provide political and/or financial support, as well as other material and immaterial resources—such as paid staff, unpaid volunteers, or expertise within a field or initiative format. An IGO may, therefore, elect to collaborate with an NGO to gain perspective on a particular issue and its potential solution(s); or it may seek collaboration with an NGO for assistance with the implementation stage of an initiative. NGOs may also be useful to IGOs in the evaluation or compliance stages of policymaking, wherein NGOs can determine if initiatives are being upheld or policies are being properly evaluated. Similarly, NGOs may wish to partner with IGOs for funding; they may pair with IGOs for political influence or expertise; or they may seek out IGOs to attain additional data, or to monitor various governmental policies and/or evolving statutes.[48] Consequently, NGOs and IGOs entail flexible and effective formats for initiatives that go beyond typical government constraints.

References

1. Tomuschat C. *The United Nations at Age Fifty: A Legal Perspective.* Vol. 23. Martinus Nijhoff Publishers; 1995.
2. United Nations. Chronology of the League of Nations. Accessed October 30, 2019. http://www.unog.ch/80256EDD006B8954/(httpAssets)/3DA94AAFEB9E8E76C1256F340047BB52/$file/sdn_chronology.pdf.
3. Aandahl F. *Foreign Relations of the United States: The Conferences at Washington, 1941–1942, and Casablanca, 1943.* Vol. 8414. U.S. Government Printing Office; 1968.
4. Roll DL. *The Hopkins Touch: Harry Hopkins and the Forging of the Alliance to Defeat Hitler.* New York, NY: Oxford University Press. 2013;117:14.
5. Osmańczyk EJ. *Encyclopedia of the United Nations and International Agreements, a Cura di Anthony Mango.* Vol. 4. Taylor & Francis; 2004.
6. United Nations. 1945: The San Francisco Conference. Accessed June 26, 2023. http://www.un.org/en/sections/history-united-nations-charter/1945-san-francisco-conference/index.html.
7. The Nobel Prize. Nobel Foundation. 2023. Accessed April 8, 2023. https://www.nobelprize.org/prizes/lists/nobel-prize-awarded-organizations/.
8. United Nations. Main organs. Accessed October 6, 2023. https://www.un.org/en/about-us/main-bodies.
9. United Nations. United Nations Charter. Accessed January 27, 2025. https://www.un.org/en/about-us/un-charter.
10. United Nations. Funds, programmes, specialized agencies and others. Accessed June 26, 2023. https://www.un.org/en/about-us/un-system.
11. United Nations. Official languages. Accessed February 14, 2023. https://www.un.org/en/our-work/official-languages#:~:text=There%20are%20six%20official%20languages,%2C%20French%2C%20Russian%20and%20Spanish/.
12. Fomerand J. *The A to Z of the United Nations.* Vol. 28. Scarecrow Press; 2009.
13. United Nations. Emergency special sessions. Accessed January 2, 2022. https://www.un.org/en/ga/sessions/emergency.shtml.
14. UN Department of Public Information; Joint United Nations Programme on HIV/AIDS. United Nations General Assembly Special Session on HIV/AIDS. New York, NY: United Nations; 2001.
15. United Nations. United Nations Security Council. Accessed March 9, 2022. http://www.un.org/en/sc/members/.
16. Fasulo L. *An Insider's Guide to the UN.* New Haven, CT: Yale University; 2004.
17. United Nations. United Nations Economic and Social Council. Accessed March 18, 2022. https://www.un.org/ecosoc/en/content/about-us.
18. Harris DJ. *Cases and Materials on International Law.* 7th ed. London, UK: Sweet & Maxwell; 2010.
19. United Nations. Chapter XIV of the UN Charter (Articles 92–96). Accessed April 13, 2021. https://www.un.org/en/about-us/un-charter/chapter-14.
20. United Nations. Secretariat. Accessed February 3, 2021. http://www.un.org/en/sections/about-un/secretariat/index.html.
21. United Nations Children's Emergency Relief Fund. About. Accessed February 4, 2022. https://www.unicef.org/about-unicef.
22. United Nations Development Programme. A world of development experience. Accessed April 17, 2020. http://www.undp.org/content/undp/en/home/operations/about_us.html.
23. United Nations Development Programme. Sustainable goals. 2023. Accessed July 1, 2020. https://www.undp.org/safer.
24. United Nations High Commissioner for Refugees. About us. Accessed August 25, 2019. https://www.unhcr.org/about-unhcr.
25. United Nations High Commissioner for Refugees. Parents scale-up relief efforts as cross-border movements from Sudan increase. Accessed September 3, 2023. https://www.unhcr

.org/news/unhcr-partners-scale-relief-efforts-cross-border-movements-sudan-increase.

26. World Food Programme. Who we are. Accessed October 17, 2020. https://www.wfp.org/who-we-are.
27. United Nations Environment Program. WFP and UNEP bolster global food and water delivery. Accessed November 17, 2023. https://www.unep.org/news-and-stories/press-release/wfp-and-unep-bolster-global-food-and-water-security.
28. International Monetary Fund. About the IMF. Accessed December 7, 2018. https://www.imf.org/en/About.
29. Lipscy PY. Explaining institutional change: policy areas, outside options, and the Bretton Woods institutions. *Am J Polit Sci.* 2015;59(2):341–356.
30. International Monetary Fund. Research. 2022. Accessed January 20, 2022. https://www.imf.org/en/Research.
31. World Bank. Who we are. 2023. Accessed January 30, 2011. https://www.worldbank.org/en/home.
32. World Health Organization. History. Accessed February 21, 2023. https://www.who.int/about/history.
33. World Health Organization. Constitution of the World Health Organization. Accessed https://apps.who.int/gb/bd/PDF/bd47/EN/constitution-en.pdf.
34. World Health Organization. Our work. 2023. Accessed December 9, 2023. https://www.who.int/our-work.
35. World Health Organization. About WHO: collaboration. 2023. Accessed January 29, 2022. https://www.who.int/about/collaboration.
36. World Health Organization. About WHO: funding. 2023. Accessed February 8, 2021. https://www.who.int/about/funding.
37. World Health Organization. Data: the Triple Billion targets. 2023. Accessed March 5, 2019. https://www.who.int/data/stories/the-triple-billion-targets-a-visual-summary-of-methods-to-deliver-impact.
38. World Health Organization. Frequently asked questions. 2023. Accessed March 14, 2022. https://www.who.int/about/frequently-asked-questions.
39. University of Cincinnati. Intergovernmental agencies: the European Union. 2021. Accessed April 21, 2021. https://guides.libraries.uc.edu/c.php?g=222419&p=1472111.
40. African Union Commission. About the African Union. 2023. Accessed May 8, 2021. https://au.int/en/overview.
41. East African Center for Law and Justice. The AU: mission, goals, organs and objectives. Accessed June 7, 2020. https://eaclj.com/general/24-general-east-africa/103-the-au-mission-goals-organs-and-objectives.html.
42. International Criminal Court. About the Court. Accessed June 10, 2024. https://www.icc-cpi.int/about/the-court#:~:text=%E2%80%8BThe%20International%20Criminal%20Court,and%20the%20crime%20of%20aggression.
43. Organisation for Economic Co-operation and Development. About. Accessed July 5, 2023. https://www.oecd.org/about/#:~:text=The%20Organisation%20for%20Economic%20Co,and%20well%2Dbeing%20for%20all.
44. World Trade Organization. The WTO… in brief. Accessed July 9, 2022. https://www.wto.org/english/thewto_e/whatis_e/inbrief_e/inbr_e.htm.
45. Duke University. NGO database. Accessed August 15, 2022. https://library.duke.edu/research/subject/guides/ngo_guide/ngo_database.
46. Willetts P. What is a non-governmental organization? *Conventions, Treaties and Other Responses to Global Issues.* 2002; 2(11):229–248.
47. *An NGO Training Guide for Peace Corps Volunteers*. Peace Corps; 2003.
48. Steffek J. Explaining cooperation between IGOs and NGOs: push factors, pull factors, and the policy cycle. *Rev Intl Stud.* 2013;39(4):993–1013.
49. United Nations Department of Economic and Social Affairs. Accessed August 9, 2021. https://esango.un.org/civilsociety/login.do.
50. United Nations Department of Economic and Social Council. List of nongovernmental organizations in consultative status with the Economic and Social Council as of September 1, 2013.
51. Leverty S. *NGOs, the UN and APA*. Washington, DC: American Psychological Association; 2008. https://wwwapaorg/international/unitednations/publications#:~:text=APA%20is%20also%20a%20member%20of%20the%20Conference,to%20the%20principles%20and%20programs%20of%20the%20UN.
52. Bureau of Democracy, Human Rights and Labor. Fact sheet: non-governmental organizations (NGOs) in the United States. U.S. Department of State. Accessed November 18, 2022. https://www.state.gov/bureaus-offices/under-secretary-for-civilian-security-democracy-and-human-rights/bureau-of-democracy-human-rights-and-labor/.
53. World Vision. Letter from the CFO: financial results for 2015. Accessed September 4, 2023. https://www.worldvision.org/wp-content/uploads/2015-letter-from-cfo.pdf.
54. Statista. World Vision's operating expenses from 2012 to 2022, by source. 2022. https://www.statista.com/statistics/262578/world-visions-operating-expenses/#:~:text=In%202022%2C%20the%20total%20operating,have%20increased%20steadily%20since%202017.
55. International Monetary Fund. *World Economic Outlook Database: Data for 2015*. New York, NY: IMF; May 2016.
56. World Bank. Guidelines for non-government organizations. Accessed July 22, 2023. https://www.worldbank.org/content/dam/documents/sanctions/other-documents/osd/User%20Friendly%20Version%20of%20the%20Anti-Corruption%20Guidelines.pdf.
57. Amnesty International. Structure and people. Accessed August 10, 2023. https://www.amnesty.org/en/about-us/how-were-run/structure-and-people/.
58. Amnesty International. Who we are. Accessed March 10, 2023. https://www.amnesty.org/en/who-we-are/.
59. BRAC. Advancing financial inclusion: BRAC microfinance in 2019. Accessed April 15, 2023. http://blog.brac.net/advancing-financial-inclusion-brac-microfinance-in-2019/.
60. BRAC. BRAC at a glance. Accessed January 2, 2023. https://www.brac.net/sites/default/files/BRAC-at-a-glance-december-2012.pdf.
61. BRAC. What we do. Accessed January 2, 2023 https://www.bracuk.net/.
62. CARE International. Impact data. 2023. Accessed January 2, 2023. https://www.care-international.org/impact-data.
63. CARE. Where we work. Accessed January 2, 2023. https://www.care.org/our-work/where-we-work/.
64. Human Rights Watch. About us. Accessed January 2, 2023. https://www.hrw.org/about/about-us.
65. Human Rights Watch. About us. 2023. Accessed January 2, 2023. https://www.hrw.org/about/about-us.
66. International Committee of the Red Cross. International Criminal Court. 2010. Accessed January 2, 2023. https://www.icrc.org/en/document/international-criminal-court.

67. International Federation of Red Cross and Red Crescent Societies. Annual report 2014. Accessed January 2, 2023. https://reliefweb.int/report/world/ifrc-annual-report-2014.
68. Committee of the Red Cross. Finances. 2023. Accessed January 2, 2023. https://www.icrc.org/en/who-we-are/finances.
69. Doctors Without Borders. Our history. Accessed January 2, 2023. https://www.doctorswithoutborders.org/who-we-are/our-history.
70. Doctors Without Borders. Who we are. Accessed January 2, 2023. https://www.doctorswithoutborders.org/who-we-are.
71. Doctors Without Borders. Finances, reporting and accountability. 2023. Accessed January 2, 2023. https://www.doctorswithoutborders.org/who-we-are/finances-reporting-accountability.
72. Oxfam. About us: the future is equal. 2023. Accessed January 2, 2023. https://www.oxfamamerica.org/about-us/?en_txn7=sitelink&&en_txn10=BRAND.OXF-GS-ALL-SLK-SLK-18P-ALL-EOYSLK1-PURCHASE&hsa_acc=8955072673&hsa_cam=1400171002&hsa_grp=61974898493&hsa_ad=643251440636&hsa_src=g&hsa_tgt=kwd-24291640&hsa_kw=oxfam&hsa_mt=e&hsa_net.
73. Oxfam. FAQ. Accessed January 2, 2023. https://www.oxfamamerica.org/about-us/contact-us/faqs/.
74. Partners in Health. Countries. Accessed January 2, 2023. https://www.pih.org/injusticehasacure?utm_content=brand1responsive&ms=pdgg&gad=1&gclid=CjwKCAjwge2iBhBBEiwAfXDBR3tCJWpT5L-IY8VRzzLLAscHdukFcHlqHaB3YTlW2Fh33LJFWGEXzRoCtDQQAvD_BwE.
75. Partners in Health. Your impact. 2023. Accessed January 2, 2023. https://www.pih.org/injusticehasacure?utm_content=brand1responsive&ms=pdgg&gad=1&gclid=Cj0KCQjw9deiBhC1ARIsAHLjR2DFKVn7JbddhjU2NBs5UxbyAL8GYWIYupd70v6lufg4l2-ctFGUzPAaAhi1EALw_wcB.
76. Save the Children International. About us. Accessed January 2, 2023. https://www.savethechildren.net/about-us.
77. Save the Children. What we do. 2023. Accessed January 2, 2023. https://www.savethechildren.org/us/what-we-do.
78. World Vision. Our impact. Accessed January 2, 2023. https://www.wvi.org/our-impact.
79. World Vision. Global hunger has reached unprecedented levels. 2023. Accessed January 2, 2023. https://www.worldvision.org.
80. Benoit F. Public policy models and their usefulness in public health: The stages model. 2014. https://ccnpps-ncchpp.ca/public-policy-models-and-their-usefulness-in-public-health-the-stages-model/.

PART II

Health Systems by Country

The Americas Region

European Region

Middle East and African Region

Asia and Pacific Region

CHAPTER 6

United States

Leiyu Shi

Country Description

Table 6-1 United States

Nationality	Noun: American(s) Adjective: American
Ethnic groups*	White 61.6%, Black or African American 12.4%, Asian 6%, Amerindian and Alaska Native 1.1%, Native Hawaiian and other Pacific Islander 0.2%, other 8.4%, two or more races 10.2% (2020 est.)
Religions	Protestant 46.5%, Roman Catholic 20.8%, Mormon 1.6%, other Christian 1.7%, Jewish 1.9%, Buddhist 0.7%, Muslim 0.9%, Hindu 0.7%, other or unspecified 1.8%, unaffiliated 22.8%, don't know/refused 0.6% (2014 est.)
Language	English only 78.2%, Spanish 13.4%, Chinese 1.1%, other 7.3% (2017 est.)
Literacy	Definition: age 15 and over and can read and write Total population: 99% Male: 99% Female: 99% (2003 est.)
Government type	Constitution-based federal republic; strong democratic tradition
Date of independence	July 4, 1776 (from Great Britain)
Real gross domestic product (GDP) per capita	74,600 USD (2023 est. based on 2021 dollar)
Real GDP with growth rate	27.721 trillion USD with a 2.89% growth rate (2023 est. based on 2021 dollar)
Unemployment rate	5.46% (2021 est.)
Natural hazards	Tsunamis, volcanoes, and earthquake activities around the Pacific Basin; hurricanes along the Atlantic and Gulf of Mexico coasts; tornadoes in the Midwest and Southeast; mud slides in California; forest fires in the West; flooding; permafrost in northern Alaska, a major impediment to development

(continues)

Table 6-1 United States *(continued)*

Environment: current issues	Air pollution resulting in acid rain in both the United States and Canada; carbon dioxide from the burning of fossil fuels; water pollution from runoff of pesticides and fertilizers; careful management of limited natural freshwater resources in much of the West; deforestation; mining; desertification; species conservation; invasive species
Population	339,665,118 (2023 est.)
Age structure	0–14 years: 18.1% (male 31,618,532/female 30,254,223) 15–64 years: 63.4% (male 108,553,822/female 108,182,491) 65 years and over: 18.5% (male 28,426,426/female 34,927,914) (2024 est.)
Median age	Total: 38.9 years Male: 37.8 years Female: 40 years (2022 est.)
Population growth rate	0.67% (2024 est.)
Birth rate	12.2 births/1,000 population (2024 est.)
Death rate	8.5 deaths/1,000 population (2024 est.)
Disease burden	Communicable disease deaths: 31/100,000 population Noncommunicable disease deaths: 413/100,000 population Injury deaths: 44/100,000 population (2016 est.)
Net migration rate	3 migrant(s)/1,000 population (2024 est.)
Sex ratio	At birth: 1.05 male/female 0–14 years: 1.04 male/female 15–64 years: 1 male/female 65 years and over: 0.81 male/female Total population: 0.97 male/female (2024 est.)
Infant mortality rate	Total: 5.12 deaths/1,000 live births Male: 5.49 deaths/1,000 live births Female: 4.73 deaths/1,000 live births (2024 est.)
Life expectancy at birth	Total population: 80.9 years Male: 78.7 years Female: 83.1 years (2024 est.)
Total fertility rate	1.84 children born/woman (2024 est.)
HIV/AIDS adult prevalence rate	1 per 1,000 people (2024 est.)
Number of people living with HIV/AIDS	1,200,000 (2024 est.)
HIV/AIDS deaths	19,310 (2022 est.)

*Hispanic people may be of any race, so they are also included in applicable race categories.

Data from Central Intelligence Agency. United States. In: *The World Fact Book, 2023.* Accessed January 22, 2025. https://www.cia.gov/the-world-factbook/countries/united-states/.

Introduction

The United States has a unique system of healthcare delivery (refer to **Table 6-1** for summary information on the United States, including top health statistics). Unlike other developed countries where health care is perceived as a right and almost all citizens are entitled to receive at least basic healthcare services, the United States still has a significant number of people who are without health insurance despite healthcare reform efforts (i.e., the Affordable Care Act, nicknamed ObamaCare). The United States also witnesses significant disparities in health status across racial/ethnic and socioeconomic groups and between those who are insured versus uninsured. The U.S. healthcare delivery "system" is not a system in the true sense, even though it is called a system when reference is made to its various features, components, and services. The system is fragmented because there are numerous private insurance plans and tax-supported public programs. The system has periodically undergone incremental changes, mainly in response to concerns about cost, access, and quality. Despite these changes, providing at least a basic package of health care at an affordable price to every American remains an unrealized goal. People outside of the United States sometimes wonder why Americans do not have a national healthcare system. The answers lie in the way American culture was shaped by a history that resulted in self-reliance, an aversion to excessive taxes, and a preference for limited government. Also, within the country today, sentiments about health care are paradoxical. Influenced by the American media, Americans have come to believe that the healthcare system may need major reform, but at an individual level, they are mostly satisfied with their own care thanks to largely subsidized, employment-based health insurance.

The main objective of this chapter is to give a general overview of the United States as a nation and to furnish a broad understanding of the healthcare delivery system. For a more in-depth understanding and systematic analysis of U.S. health care, readers may wish to consult additional textbooks, including those by the author.[1,2]

History

The first Americans are believed to be people who crossed from Asia to North America over a narrow land strip that connects Siberia to Alaska and that is now submerged below the Bering Strait.[3] This migration likely occurred millennia before the White people arrived from Europe. Gradually, many of these Native Americans/Indigenous Americans and Alaskan Natives, as we call them today, migrated southward. By the time the Europeans arrived, the indigenous population had spread throughout the North American continent.

In the 15th century, European sailors began exploring new routes to India by sailing west from Spain and Italy. The modern history of the Americas began with the voyage of Christopher Columbus, who crossed the Atlantic and reached the Bahamas in 1492.[3] In subsequent expeditions, he discovered other islands in the Caribbean Sea. Although Columbus was credited with discovering the New World, he never reached the continent of North America[4]; however, after the New World had been explored, other adventurers, such as Juan Ponce de León and John Cabot, reached North America's eastern shores. The voyage of John Cabot, an Italian, was commissioned by the British king. Cabot's voyage to North America later provided the basis for England's claim over the continent. Later, King Francis I of France sent Giovanni da Verrazano, an Italian adventurer, and subsequently Jacques Cartier, a French explorer, to lay claims on parts of North America on behalf of France. The Dutch hired Henry Hudson, an English navigator, who also reached North America. However, America was named after another Italian explorer, Amerigo (Americus in Latin) Vespucci, who likely explored the American coast farther than any navigator of his time in at least two voyages; the accounts of his voyages were published in Europe.[5]

The first European colony in what would become the United States was established by neither England nor France but by the Spanish forces of Pedro Menéndez in what is now Florida. Menéndez destroyed a group of French settlers in northern Florida in 1565. The British, under the leadership of Walter Raleigh, established the first British colony in 1585, on Roanoke Island off the coast of North Carolina. Although this colony did not last long, the British finally succeeded in establishing a more long-lived a more long-lived colony in Jamestown, Virginia, in 1607. This was the first permanent English settlement in what later became the United States. Virginia soon became prosperous by growing tobacco on plantations. These plantations required a labor force in excess of the available supply. In 1619, a Dutch ship brought the first group of African people (who were later enslaved) to Virginia. By the 18th century, the atrocity of slavery became an integral part of the economic and social composition of Virginia.[6] Around 1795, the rapid increase in cotton cultivation brought these people who were enslaved to other parts of the South.[7]

The early 1600s saw the beginning of a great tide of emigration from Europe to North America. Between 1620 and 1635, economic difficulties swept England. Many people could not find work. Even skilled artisans could earn little more than a bare living. Poor crop yields added to the distress. Other European emigrants left their homelands to escape political oppression, to seek freedom, to practice their religions, or to find opportunities denied them at home. Britain continued to establish colonies in Plymouth (now Massachusetts), Maryland, Rhode Island, Connecticut, the Carolinas, New Jersey, and Pennsylvania. The New England colonies flourished from profits gained through commerce in fishing. The French established their settlements in what is now Quebec, Canada, and in Alabama and Louisiana. The Dutch established some scattered footholds, but theirs was never a strong colony in terms of political power or stability.[6] The Spaniards also established settlements mainly in the southern parts of North America. Around 1732, Britain founded a colony in Georgia to avert any threats of Spain's expansion into South Carolina.[6] In 1664, under the threat of an armed conflict, the Dutch surrendered New Amsterdam to the British, and the colony was renamed New York.[3] The French lost control of their colonies after they were defeated by the British. The British then had 13 colonies, all located east of the Mississippi River, that were secure for the first time in almost a century from attack by another power.[6]

A chain of events led to the War for American Independence. The Anglo-French wars were fought in both America and Europe and had dragged on from 1689 to 1763. The British wanted the colonies to bear part of the burden of new taxes. The American Revenue Act (Sugar Act) of 1764 and the Stamp Act of 1765 were passed by the British Parliament as means of raising revenues from Americans. The Currency Act of 1764 prohibited the American colonies from issuing paper currency. The Townshend Revenue Act of 1767 imposed taxes on tea, lead, paper, glass, and paint imported into the colonies.[6] The Americans bitterly resented these taxes. Boycotts, protests, and skirmishes between the citizens and British troops posted in Boston brought on the Boston Massacre of 1770, in which three Bostonians were killed and two were mortally wounded. The incident inflamed public opinion.[6] The Tea Act of 1773 gave the British East India Company monopoly status to sell tea to the colonies. This action resulted in the event referred to as the Boston Tea Party, in which American radicals boarded the ships carrying prime tea and dumped about 350 chests of tea into Boston harbor as a gesture of protest. Retaliation from Britain brought on the Coercive Acts of 1774. Although these acts were designed to coerce the Massachusetts colony into submissiveness, they had the opposite effect.[6] The American Revolution was born as a result of the tyranny under Great Britain, an experience that most Americans felt was oppressive and unjustified. Later, the framers of the U.S. Constitution were careful to place limits on the government's power over individual freedoms.

Not surprisingly, the Revolutionary War began in the Boston area, with fighting between armed citizens and British forces first taking place in 1775. On June 10, 1776, the Continental Congress appointed a committee under the leadership of Thomas Jefferson to draft the Declaration of Independence. On July 4 of that year, Congress approved the Declaration of Independence, according to which the 13 colonies in North America were "free and independent states" and became the United States of America. The Revolutionary War came to an end on October 19, 1781, when the American army, under the command of George Washington and with the help of the French, defeated the British forces at Yorktown, Virginia. In 1783, the Treaty of Paris endorsed the independence of the colonies from Great Britain. In 1789, George Washington became the first president of the United States.

When the population of a state reached 60,000 free inhabitants, it was eligible to join the union (the United States). During Washington's tenure as president, Vermont, Kentucky, and Tennessee were added to the union. In later years, the country acquired land from France, Spain, Great Britain, Mexico, and Russia and annexed the Republic of Texas and the Republic of Hawaii. In 1959, Alaska and Hawaii became the 49th and 50th states, respectively, to join the union. The United States also has a few territories, all islands or groups of islands, that are under the jurisdiction of the federal government. The main territories are Puerto Rico, U.S. Virgin Islands, American Samoa, Guam, and Northern Mariana Islands. The nation's capital is Washington, DC (District of Columbia), which is a federal district.

Size and Geography

The total area of the United States is 3.79 million square miles (9.83 million square kilometers). Of this area, 93.0% is land (**Figure 6-1**).[8] The estimated population in 2023 was 339.7 million. The United States occupies roughly 6.5% of the world's surface (about the same as China, and a little over half as much as Russia) and has about 4.4% of the world's population.

Forty-eight states and the District of Columbia are situated between Canada and Mexico and between the Atlantic and Pacific oceans. Alaska and Hawaii are physically separate from the rest of the country (see the U.S. map). Alaska occupies the northwestern corner of the North American continent, with Canada to its east and Russia to the west across the Bering Strait. Hawaii consists of eight major islands and over 100 small ones. The main Hawaiian Islands are located approximately 2,400 miles (3,900 kilometers) southwest of the U.S. mainland in the mid-Pacific Ocean.

The 50 states are significantly different in sizes. Alaska is the largest state and is about 425 times larger

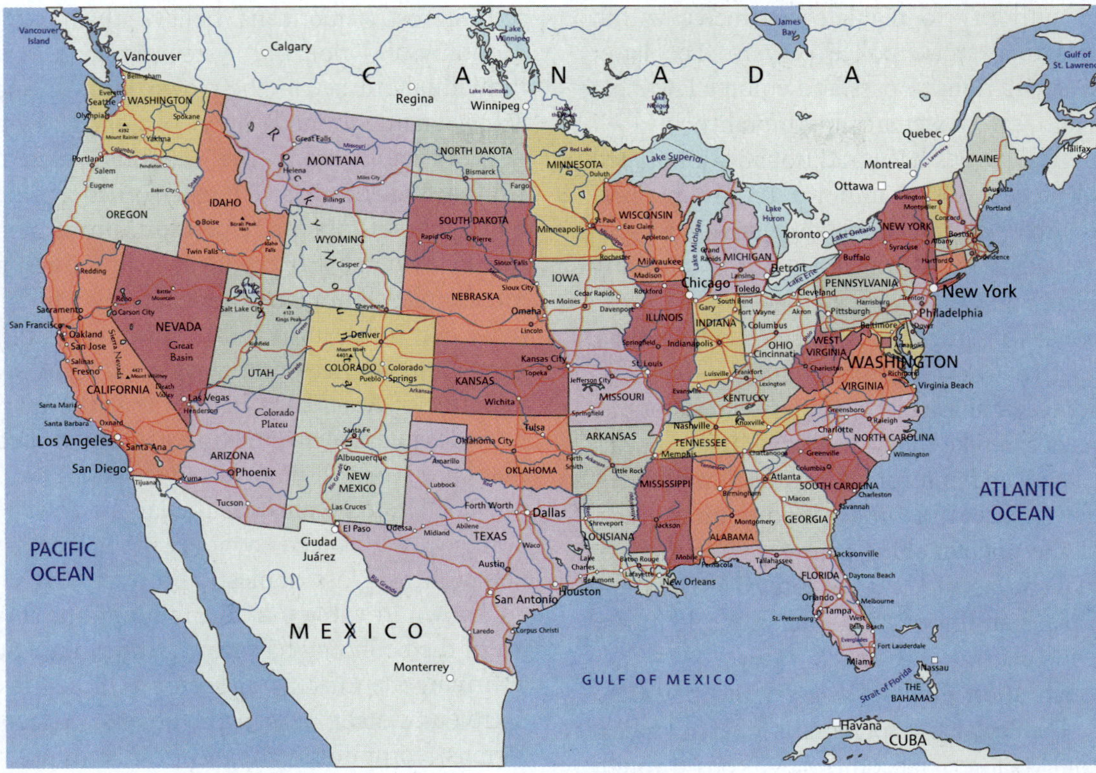

Figure 6-1 Map of the United States

than the smallest, Rhode Island. The three largest states, Alaska, Texas, and California, make up about 30% of the entire country. The most populous states are California (39.1 million), Texas (27.5 million), and Florida (20.3 million). Wyoming (586,107), Vermont (626,042), and North Dakota (756,927) have the least number of people.[9]

Government and Political System

The United States is a representative republic in which those who govern are popularly elected by those who are governed. All U.S. citizens who have attained the age of 18 have the right to vote. As the supreme law of the land, the Constitution of the United States (adopted on September 17, 1787) incorporates several key principles of government: (1) government by the people, which means that it is the people who form the government; (2) limited government, which means that government can only do what the people allow it to do through exercise of a duly developed system of laws[10]; (3) federalism, according to which the central government shares sovereign powers with the state governments[10]; (4) separation of powers, which divides political power among the three branches of government: the legislative, the executive, and the judicial; (5) checks and balances that emanate from separation of powers and enable inspection and restraint of one part of the political system by another[7]; (6) respect for individual worth, a principle that was first embraced in the Declaration of Independence and that has been used as a measure of the value of social institutions to individuals[7]; (7) equal opportunity, which stresses individual worth by making available to each individual the opportunity to develop their abilities and interests[7]; and (8) a Bill of Rights that protects individual liberties against violations by the government. These rights were added to the Constitution in the form of 10 amendments that were ratified by all states in 1791. The First Amendment protects the right to freedom of religion and freedom of expression from government interference.

The federal government has three branches: legislative (the Senate and House of Representatives), executive (the president and cabinet departments), and judicial (federal courts and the U.S. Supreme Court). Each of the states also has its own constitution and its own legislative, executive, and judicial branches. In general, the states can do anything that is not prohibited by the U.S. Constitution or that is contrary to federal policy. The major reserved powers of the state include the authority to regulate commerce within the state and to exercise police powers. The latter refers to the state's right to pass and enforce laws that promote health, safety, welfare, and morality.[10]

Two political parties have traditionally dominated the political process. Other minor party groups have appeared on the political scene, but none has succeeded in replacing the two major parties,[7] currently the Republican and Democratic parties.

In response to issues that politicians believe their constituents face, the government makes decisions and takes actions that are broadly referred to as public policy. Policies can take the form of new laws; repeals of existing laws; and interpretations and implementations of laws, executive orders, and court rulings. Throughout the policymaking process, the system of constitutional checks and balances prevails. The president often plays an important leadership role in key policy issues.

The Constitution grants Congress the power to make laws. The legislative process is often cumbersome as a bill (before it becomes law) goes through both houses of Congress and various committees and subcommittees. Numerous organizations, called interest groups, which represent common objectives of their members, try to influence policymakers to protect their members' interests. In the end, if the president signs the approved bill, it becomes law. The president also has the power to veto (overturn) a bill passed by Congress. Unless a presidential veto is overruled by a two-thirds majority of Congress, it fails to become law. Even after a law has been passed, policymaking continues in the form of interpretation and implementation by the federal agency responsible for implementing the law. For example, the Department of Health and Human Services oversees more than 300 programs related to health and welfare services. It is responsible for 12 different agencies that deal with such diverse areas as issues related to public health, approval of new drugs, healthcare research, services for the elderly, and substance abuse.

Macroeconomics

America is called a "land of plenty." The nation is richly blessed with natural resources. In large part, the nation's spectacular economic growth has been credited to the enterprising way in which Americans have used the nation's resources.[7] The seeds of American capitalism are found in the Constitution. At the foundation of American capitalism is the belief that individuals know best what is in their self-interest. Americans believe that their market economy and political system provide avenues for individuals to act in their own interest and realize achievement limited only by one's own potential and motivation. The economic system in the United States is based largely on the principles of a free market, open competition, profit motive, and private ownership of the means of production. These forces unleash human potential to maximize productivity and innovation and to produce and distribute goods and services that people value. A significant majority of Americans believe that the marketplace provides people with the opportunity to succeed and that hard work is the ticket to success.[11]

The United States has the largest and most technologically advanced economy in the world. Components of the gross domestic product (GDP) in 2022 are shown in **Table 6-2**. Even though the service sector of the economy has grown, the United States has a thriving manufacturing sector in industries such as petroleum, steel, aerospace, defense, telecommunications, computers, chemicals, electronics, mining, pharmaceuticals, and consumer goods.

U.S. residents enjoy one of the highest standards of living in the world. The labor force is among the most productive, and unemployment is relatively low (4–9%). Roughly one-third of the civilian labor force has college degrees. Both full- and part-time workers work 38.3 hours per week, on average. In 2010, the median weekly earning for full-time workers was $747. Among employed civilians, approximately

Table 6-2 Components of the U.S. GDP, 2023

	Trillions of Dollars	Percentage
Total GDP	27.72	100.0
Consumption	18.6	68
Goods	6.2	23
Services	12.4	44.8
Private investment	4.8	18
Government spending	4.7	17
Federal	1.8	6
State and local	3	11
Exports minus imports	−0.8	−3

Data from U.S. Bureau of Economic Analysis. National data. 2023. Accessed March 24, 2023. https://www.bea.gov/sites/default/files/2023-02/gdp4q22_2nd.pdf.

13% worked for various levels of government; the remaining 87% were employed in the private sector.[8] In 2023, the size of the average family in the U.S. was 3.15, and the median annual family income was $80,610.

Demographics

America is largely a nation of immigrants and minority groups, although Native American and Black people are not immigrants (Native Americans were here when the Europeans arrived and African people who were enslaved came against their will as captives). In 2021, 13.7% of the total population was foreign born.[12] Between 2019 and 2021, 337,000 foreign-born individuals entered the country. This number is a sharp decrease in foreign-born individuals entering the country compared with the 407,000 individuals who entered the country between 2019 and 2021 and the 1.3 million individuals who entered between 2014 and 2016.[13] The slowing growth of immigrants reflects the decreased growth in the overall U.S. population. Hispanic and Latino people represent the largest number of foreign-born residents (**Table 6-3**).

The fertility rate per 1,000 U.S. women residents declined from 70.9 in 1990 to 54.5 (estimated) in 2023. Over the 23-year span of time the fertility rate slowly decreased. According to data from Migration Policy Institute, the number of new U.S. legal permanent residents was 1,173,000 in 2023.[14]

Table 6-4 provides the racial/ethnic mix, age categories, and gender mix of the U.S. resident population. In 2020, life expectancy at birth was 77.28 years [80.2 years for females (2019); 74.5 years for males; 76.4 years for White people; 71.5 years for Black people]. A man aged 65 years could expect to live to an age of 85 years, and a woman aged 65 years could expect to live to an age of 84.8 years.[15,16]

In 2020, 82.66% of the population lived in urban areas. Poverty rates vary by rural versus urban residence. In 2019, the rural population had a higher poverty rate among all racial groups compared with those who lived in an urban area. Black people experienced the highest unemployment rate of 30.7% in

Table 6-3 Foreign-Born Population, 2023

Region	Population (thousands)	Percentage
Total resident population	44,799	100.0
Latin America (Caribbean, Central America, South America)	23,628	52.7
Asia	13,426	30.0
Europe	4,148	9.3
Other (Africa, Oceania, Northern America, and born at sea)	3,598	8.0

Data from U.S. Census Bureau. Current population survey: annual social and economic supplement, 2021. Accessed March 24, 2023. https://www.census.gov/data/tables/2021/demo/foreign-born/cps-2021.html.

Table 6-4 Racial/Ethnic Mix, Age Categories, and Gender Mix of the U.S. Resident Population, 2023

Race/Ethnicity	Population	Percentage
Total resident population	334,914,895	100.0
White	252,065,704	75.2
Black/African American	45,757,433	13.6
Asian	21,386,914	6.1
American Indian/ Alaskan Native	4,486,417	1.3
Native Hawaiian/ Pacific Islander	899,815	0.2
Two or more races	10,318,612	3.0
Hispanic or Latino origin	65,219,145	18.9
Age categories		
Less than 5	18,511,160	5.5
5–14	40,987,321	12.2
15–29	65,905,012	19.7
30–49	87,731,859	26.0
50–64	62,531,182	18.6
65–74	34,685,284	10.3
75–84	18,368,097	5.4
85 and over	6,194,980	1.8
Gender mix		
Male	165,749,400	49.5
Female	169,165,495	50.5

Data from U.S. Census Bureau. National population by characteristics. 2023. https://www.census.gov/data/tables/time-series/demo/popest/2020s-national-detail.html.

rural areas and 20.4% in urban areas. The lowest poverty rates are found among White non-Hispanic people: 12.7% in rural areas and 8.2% in urban areas.[17]

The religious makeup of the U.S. population in 2023 was 33% Protestant, 22% Roman Catholic, 1% Mormon, 13% other Christian, 2% Jewish, 1% Buddhist, 1% Muslim, 5% atheist, 5% agnostic, and 17% "nothing in particular."[18]

Brief History of the Healthcare System

Pre–World War II

From colonial times to the beginning of the 1900s, medical education and practice were far more advanced in Great Britain, France, and Germany than they were in the United States. The practice of medicine in the United States had a strong domestic (rather than professional) character because medical procedures were primitive. Medical education was not grounded in science. Consequently, medical practice was more a trade than a profession. The nation had only a handful of hospitals that existed in very large cities, such as New York, Boston, and Philadelphia. There was no health insurance—private or public.

Post–World War II

The postindustrial era was marked by the growth and development of a medical profession that benefited from urbanization, new scientific discoveries, and reforms in medical education. American physicians became professionally organized. To this day they remain a powerful force in resisting proposals for a national healthcare program.

The system for delivering health care in America took its current shape during this period. Private practice of medicine became firmly entrenched as *physician* became a cohesive profession and physicians opted for specialization and gained power and prestige. The hospital emerged as a repository for high-tech facilities and equipment.

History of Health Insurance

The first broad-coverage health insurance in the United States emerged in the form of workers' compensation. It was originally designed to make cash payments to workers for wages lost because of job-related injuries and diseases. Later, compensation for medical expenses and death benefits to survivors were added.

Health insurance began in the form of disability coverage that provided income during temporary disability caused by bodily injury or sickness. During the early 1900s, medical treatments and hospital care became socially acceptable; however, they were also becoming increasingly more expensive, and people could not predict their future needs for medical care or the costs. These developments pointed to the need for some kind of insurance to spread an individual's financial risk over a large number of people. Between 1916 and 1918,[16] state legislatures, including those in New York and California, attempted to enact legislation compelling employers to provide health insurance, but their efforts were unsuccessful.

Health insurance became a permanent feature of employment benefits during World War II. During this period, wages were frozen, and employees accepted employer-paid health insurance to compensate for the incremental losses from their salaries. Thus, health insurance became an important component of collective bargaining between unions and employers. Subsequently, employment-based health insurance expanded rapidly, and private health insurance became the primary vehicle for the delivery of healthcare services in the United States. It is estimated that private health insurance grew from a $1.0 billion industry in 1950 to an $8.7 billion industry by 1965.

Before 1965, private health insurance was the only widely available source of payment for health care, and it was available primarily to middle-class working people and their families. The elderly, the unemployed, and the poor had to rely on their own resources, on limited public programs, or on charity from hospitals and individual physicians. In 1965, Congress passed the amendments to the Social Security Act that created the Medicare and Medicaid programs. The government thus assumed direct responsibility for insuring two vulnerable population groups—the elderly and the poor.

Although adopted together, Medicare and Medicaid reflected vastly different traditions. Medicare was upheld by broad grassroots support and, being attached to Social Security, had no class distinction. Medicaid, in contrast, carried the stigma of public welfare. Medicare had uniform national standards for eligibility and benefits; Medicaid varied from state to state in terms of eligibility and benefits. Medicare covered anyone at or over the age of 65 years. Medicaid became a means-tested program, which confined eligibility to people below a predetermined income level. Consequently, many of the poor did not qualify because their incomes exceeded the means-test limits.

The creation of Medicare and Medicaid had a drastic impact on both federal and state budgets, but the federal government bore the greatest brunt. Federal healthcare expenditures increased at an average annual rate of 30.0%, whereas total federal expenditures increased at a rate of only 11.3%. To curb inflation, President Richard Nixon implemented the Economic Stabilization Program in 1971. Under this program, wages and prices were frozen, including those in the healthcare industry. The Health Maintenance Organization (HMO) Act of 1973 was passed during the Nixon administration after price controls had failed to be effective. The main rationale behind the new law was to create competition in the healthcare marketplace. The law required employers with more than 25 workers to offer an HMO plan as an alternative to the standard health insurance plans, which were already in wide use.

During the 1990s, managed care was largely credited with containing double-digit inflation in healthcare costs. The beginning of the 21st century, however, has once again been marked with an increase in healthcare spending.

The Current Healthcare System

Facilities

Health care is the largest industry in the United States. From a technological standpoint, the nation has a highly developed infrastructure for the delivery of medical services. It has modern healthcare facilities, high-caliber medical schools, university-based curricula to prepare healthcare managers and public health professionals, research organizations, a large pharmaceutical industry, manufacturers of medical devices, and providers of long-term care and rehabilitation services. The private sector owns most of the infrastructure. The government, however, plays a critical supportive role. The public health infrastructure, for example, is in the public domain. The government is also a major financier of health services research and medical education. It operates the military and veterans health systems. It supports the delivery of care for certain vulnerable populations and funds the Indian Health Service (IHS) for American Indians and Alaska Natives. By having state-of-the-art technology, the United States offers medical services by highly trained physicians in its world-renowned facilities that are the envy of the world. However, this focus on high technology and specialization has certain negative effects. Specifically, it raises the cost of medical care, which produces imbalances in access due to differences in health insurance. It also influences medical education, practice of medicine, and technology-driven competition among hospitals.

Workforce

In 2021, there were 949,658 professionally active doctors of medicine (MDs) in the United States, which amounted to 29.1 physicians per 10,000 civilian population.[19] Roughly 49.1% of the physicians worked in private office-based practice[20]; the rest worked in hospitals or other professional settings related to teaching, research, or administration.[21] Approximately 25% of all practicing physicians were graduates of foreign medical schools; however, they must take rigorous examinations and undergo further training before they can practice in the United States.[22] Compared with most European nations, the United States has a greater aggregate supply of physicians, but their distribution shows certain imbalances. A lopsided focus on technology has over time caused the supply of medical specialists to outpace the supply of primary care physicians. For example, in 2022 the specialties with the largest number of active physicians were the primary care specialties of internal medicine, family medicine, and pediatrics.[23] Besides a specialty-oriented medical education, disparities in income offer another reason why the majority of medical students in the United States opt for specialty training. For example, according to data from the American Medical Association, general surgeons can make 40.0% to 80.0% more than physicians in family practices. A high proportion of specialists in medicine drive up the use of technology and the cost of health care.

Besides imbalances in primary and specialty care, locations outside of the metropolitan areas experience shortages of physicians. Approximately 20% of the U.S. population lives in nonmetropolitan areas, but only 11% of the physicians practice in these areas.[24] These data support why three out of five rural regions are designated as health professional shortage areas.[21] People needing medical care in these areas may experience increased travel time to see a physician, which can deter timely and appropriate health care. Scarcity of physicians may result in higher caseloads, so patients face increased time to get appointments and wait longer in physicians' offices before they receive care.[24]

Nurses constitute the largest group of healthcare professionals. Like physicians and other healthcare professionals, nurses must be licensed to practice in their respective states of employment. Depending on their level of education and competency assessment, nurses can be licensed as registered nurses (RNs) or as licensed practical/vocational nurses (LPNs/LVNs); 84.1% of all nurses are RNs. RNs must complete a 4-year bachelor's degree, a 4-year diploma, or a 2-year or 3-year associate's degree.[25] Nurses can also specialize beyond their RN training to become advanced practice nurses.

Dentists, optometrists, psychologists, podiatrists, pharmacists, and chiropractors must complete doctoral-level education to qualify for licenses in their respective fields. Audiologists and speech/language pathologists must have master's-level preparation. Healthcare professionals who generally are required to complete a 4-year bachelor's degree include physical therapists, occupational therapists, clinical laboratory technologists, and dietitians. Educational requirements for numerous other types of allied health professionals vary from one state to another and require between 1 and 4 years of training.

Inpatient Institutions

Depending on patient needs, institutional care that requires overnight stays is delivered in general acute care hospitals, specialty hospitals (including rehabilitation hospitals and psychiatric facilities), and long-term care facilities. The construction and operation of these institutions is governed by federal laws; state regulations; city ordinances; standards of the Joint Commission on Accreditation of Healthcare Organizations; and national codes for building, fire protection, and sanitation. The Joint Commission on Accreditation of Healthcare Organizations is a private, nonprofit organization that sets standards and accredits various types of healthcare facilities for ongoing verification of compliance with the standards.

The military medical care system and the Veterans Administration (VA; described later) operate federal hospitals that are largely inaccessible to the general public. Most of the remaining hospitals in 2022 were community hospitals, which are accessible to the general public; there were almost 5,139 in operation with over 789,354 beds.[26] In 2022, the United States had 2.4 community hospital beds per 1,000 population residents,[21] far fewer than what most developed countries have. Hospitals in the United States come under three main types of ownership: private nonprofit, private for profit, and government owned. Private nonprofit organizations, such as community associations and churches, operate nonprofit hospitals. By law, these hospitals must reinvest the profits in the hospitals' operations and must not distribute them to any individuals. For-profit hospitals are proprietary or investor owned. They are operated for the financial benefit of the stockholders; however, hospitals operate in a competitive environment, and they must often compete on the basis of high-quality, cost-efficient services. In 2022, 57.6% of the nation's community hospitals were operated as nonprofit, 23.9% were operated as for profit, and 18.5% were operated by state or local governments.[21,26] Approximately 400 teaching hospitals (including 64 VA medical centers) belong to the Council of Teaching Hospitals and Health Systems. These hospitals generally have substantial teaching and research programs, are affiliated with medical schools of large universities, and train the majority of physician residents in the United States.

Specialty hospitals in the United States are establishments that primarily treat specific types of medical conditions (such as cardiac or orthopedic), provide specialized rehabilitation care, or specialize in treating certain types of patients (such as women or children). The exact number of such hospitals is unknown, but their numbers are increasing. In addition, in 2020, there were nearly 1,905 mental health institutions (over 132,000 beds) that provide 24-hour hospital and residential treatment.[27] In 2018, approximately 15,600 nursing homes with over 1.7 million beds delivered 24-hour long-term care to mostly elderly patients.[21,28] Nursing homes mainly provide skilled nursing care, which is medically oriented care, approved by physicians and provided by and under the direction of licensed nurses, for complex chronic conditions and often includes rehabilitation therapies. In addition to these nursing homes, there are a large number of assisted living and personal care facilities that mainly provide assistance with activities of daily living.

Outpatient Settings

Outpatient (ambulatory care) services are delivered in a variety of settings, depending on factors such as the type of care needed, location, and whether the person has health insurance. Development of new technology and innovations in payment methods to providers have led to a decline in the utilization of inpatient hospitals and an expansion of outpatient services in both volume and scope. Many procedures that previously required a hospital stay are now performed on an outpatient basis. In the United States, the average of 2.4 community hospital beds per 1,000 population residents and the average length of stay of 6.2 days are among the lowest in the world.[29] The number of community hospital beds per capita decreased from 2.6 per 1,000 residences in 2009 to 2.4 per 1,000 in 2019. Average length of stay was also decreasing. Consequently, many hospitals seek to provide both inpatient and outpatient services to remain profitable. In 2020, 11% to 14% of all ambulatory visits occurred in hospitals' outpatient units (an increase from 6.2% in 1992).[30] Of course, most outpatient visits take place in physicians' offices (44.2% in 2020).[21] Hospital emergency rooms, however, are commonly used by the insured and the uninsured alike for both urgent and nonurgent conditions.[31] Heavy use for nonemergencies results in overcrowding and waste of resources. For nonurgent care, emergency rooms are often used by those who do not have routine access to primary care.[32] In 2021, 5.3% of children under the age of 18 and 12.2% of nonelderly adults did not have a usual source of care.[21] After the creation of the State Children's Health Insurance Program (SCHIP; discussed later), the proportion of children who lacked a usual source of care declined from 7.7% in 1993–1994 to 3.8% in 2013–2014, but then increased to 5.3% in 2021.[33,34]

Home health has been among the fastest-growing sectors in U.S. health care. Over 70% of home health patients are elderly. Home health commonly includes part-time or intermittent nursing care, rehabilitation services, nutritional consultations, and assistance with activities of daily living. Since the early 1980s, specialized high-technology home therapies have proliferated. They include intravenous antibiotics, oncology therapy, hemodialysis, nutrition, ventilator care, and telehealth technologies for remote in-home patient monitoring. Overall, home health has proven to be cost-effective because it decreases the use of hospitals, emergency departments, and nursing homes.

Other main outpatient settings in the United States include walk-in clinics that provide the convenience of evening and weekend hours with no prior appointments; urgent care centers that operate 24 hours a day, 7 days a week; free-standing surgicenters that perform outpatient surgeries; laboratories; imaging centers; dialysis centers; pharmacies; and rehabilitation centers. Retail medical clinics have started to open in major stores where people commonly shop for everyday items.

The federal government provides funding for more than 13,400 health centers and 100 Health Center Programs.[35] These centers are located in defined, medically underserved areas, where they provide primary care, mental health care, and dental care to mostly low-income and uninsured populations.

Public Health

Public health services in the United States are typically provided by local health departments, and the range of services offered varies greatly by locality. The programs are generally limited in scope. They include well-baby care, sexually transmitted infection (STI) clinics, family planning services, screening and treatment for tuberculosis, and outpatient mental health care.

The Subsystems of U.S. Healthcare Delivery

The United States does not have a well-integrated and coordinated healthcare delivery system enjoyed by everyone. Instead, there are multiple subsystems that developed either through market forces or as a result of policy initiatives to address the needs of certain population segments. The major subsystems are described next.

The Managed Care System

Managed care is a system of healthcare delivery that (1) seeks to achieve efficiencies by integrating the basic functions of healthcare delivery, (2) employs mechanisms to control (manage) utilization of medical services, and (3) determines the price at which the services are purchased and consequently how much the providers get paid. It is the most dominant healthcare delivery system in the United States today and is available to most Americans.

The primary financiers of the managed care system are employers and the government; however, it is not a private–public partnership. Employers purchase insurance for their own employees, but they do so voluntarily. As a result, many small employers do not provide health insurance to their employees. Meanwhile, because employer-based health insurance requires cost sharing, many workers choose not to participate even when the employer pays the bulk of the premium costs. Because of variations in the government programs, beneficiaries are required to obtain healthcare services through either a managed care organization (MCO) or alternative plans. There are two main types of MCOs: HMOs and preferred provider organizations (PPOs). An MCO functions like an insurance company and promises to provide healthcare services contracted under the health plan to the enrollees of the plan.

The terms *enrollee* and *member* refer to the individual covered under the plan. The contractual arrangement between the MCO and the enrollee—including the array of covered health services that the enrollee is entitled to—is referred to as the health plan (or *the plan*, for short). The health plan generally uses selected providers from whom the enrollees can choose to receive routine services. HMOs typically require in-network access—that is, the enrollees must receive services from the providers selected by the HMO. PPOs, in contrast, allow out-of-network access—that is, the enrollees can choose to receive services either from providers who participate in the PPO's selected network or from providers who are not part of the network. The enrollee incurs higher out-of-pocket costs when out-of-network providers are used. Nevertheless, because of the option to choose one's providers, PPO plans have been more popular than HMO plans. Particularly in HMOs, primary care providers or generalists manage routine services and determine the appropriateness of referrals to higher-level or specialty services. In these plans, generalists are often referred to as gatekeepers. Some HMOs may deliver services partially through the plan's own hired physicians, but most services are delivered through contracts with providers, such as physicians, hospitals, and diagnostic clinics.

Although the employer finances the care by purchasing a plan from an MCO, the MCO is the one responsible for negotiating with providers. HMOs typically use capitation arrangements to pay providers. Under capitation, a negotiated fixed amount per enrollee is paid each month to the provider. This fixed amount is commonly referred to as the per-member-per-month rate. Risk is shared between the HMO and the provider who receives the per-member-per-month rate, because, in exchange for this payment, the provider is obligated to deliver whatever contracted services the enrollees might need. PPOs commonly pay the providers a discounted fee that has been negotiated between the PPO and the provider. Providers are willing to discount their services in exchange for being included in the PPO's network and being guaranteed a patient population. As insurers, health plans must make actuarial projections of the expected cost of healthcare utilization. They bear the risk that the cost of services delivered could exceed the premiums collected. By underwriting this risk, a plan assumes the role of insurer.

The Military and Veterans Systems

The military medical care system is available free of charge to active-duty military personnel.[36] Despite its inherent deficiencies,[37] compared with other healthcare delivery modes in the United States, the military system is a relatively well-organized and integrated system, which is operated by the U.S. Department of Defense. Comprehensive services cover prevention as well as treatments provided by salaried healthcare personnel. Routine ambulatory care is often available at a dispensary, sick bay, first-aid station, or medical station located close to the military personnel's workplace. Routine hospital services are provided in dispensaries located in military bases, in sick bays aboard ships, and in small base hospitals. Complicated hospital services are provided in regional military hospitals. Dependents of service members, retirees and their dependents, and survivors of deceased members can receive medical care through an insurance program called TriCare. This program permits the beneficiaries to receive care from military as well as private medical care facilities. Although patients have little choice regarding how services are provided and there remain significant racial disparities in care,[38] in general the military medical care system provides relatively good-quality health care.

War veterans are entitled to receive a wide array of medical and long-term care services through facilities operated by the VA. The VA system provides a broad spectrum of medical, surgical, and rehabilitative care. It is one of the largest, oldest formally organized healthcare systems in the world. The VA, predecessor to the current Department of Veterans Affairs, was established in 1930. In addition to medical care, its mission includes education, training, research, and contingency support and emergency management for the Department of Defense medical care system. The VA system operates 171 medical centers, with at least one located in each state, Puerto Rico, and the District of Columbia. VA facilities also include 1,298 sites of care (including 171 VA Medical Centers and 1,113 outpatient sites). In 2022, over 9 million people received care in VA facilities. The VA delivery system is organized under 18 geographically distributed Veterans Integrated Service Networks. Healthcare spending for 2022 was approximately $68 billion.[39]

The System for Vulnerable Populations

Vulnerable populations include people who are at increased/higher risk for poor health conditions or people who live/work in settings that put them at increased/higher risk of becoming infected or exposed to hazards. In 1965, the U.S. Congress passed two major amendments to the Social Security Act that created the Medicare and Medicaid programs, and the government assumed direct responsibility to pay for some of the health care on behalf of two vulnerable population groups—the elderly and the poor.[21] Medicaid and Medicare are prime representations of the public sector in the amalgam of private and public approaches for providing access to health care in the United States. Originally created for the elderly, the Medicare program now covers 64 million Americans, including low-income disabled individuals below the age of 65 and people who have end-stage renal disease. The Medicaid program finances healthcare services for the indigent who qualify based on assets and income below the threshold levels established by each state. The program serves nearly 83 million poor Americans.[40]

In 1997, the SCHIP was enacted to provide health insurance to children living in low-income families that did not qualify for Medicaid. Of the 74.2 million children in the United States, about 56% are enrolled in either Medicaid (34.7 million) or SCHIP (7.0 million).[41] In the three main public programs, the government finances the insurance, but healthcare services are received mainly through private providers. Medicaid and SCHIP enrollees incur few out-of-pocket costs, but Medicare enrollees pay for approximately half of their healthcare costs. This is mainly due to high deductibles, copayments, and certain noncovered services—such as dental, vision, and hearing aids—and gaps in prescription drug coverage (coverage was added to the program in 2005). Those who are poor or experience poverty can qualify for both Medicaid and Medicare, in which case Medicaid pays for the gaps in Medicare coverage. Most other enrollees purchase private health insurance (Medigap) to pay for noncovered Medicare expenses.

Other vulnerable populations—especially the uninsured who may live in economically disadvantaged communities, immigrants, and those living in geographically disadvantaged communities—receive care from safety net providers, including community health centers, physicians' offices, hospital outpatient departments, and emergency rooms, of which community health centers are expressly designed for the underserved. Consistent with their unique role and mission, safety net providers offer comprehensive medical and enabling services (e.g., interpretation, transportation, outreach, and nutrition and social support services) that address the needs of vulnerable populations.

For over 50 years, federally funded health centers have provided primary and preventive health services to rural and urban underserved populations.[35] The Bureau of Primary Health Care, within the Department of Health and Human Services' Health Resources and Services Administration, provides federal support for community-based health centers, including programs for migrant and seasonal farm workers and their families, people experiencing homelessness, persons experiencing unstable housing, and school-age children. In addition to essential primary care and preventive services, health centers provide enabling services, such as case management, transportation, health education, language translation, and childcare. These services facilitate regular access to care for predominantly minority (or emerging majority), low-income, uninsured, and Medicaid patients. By 2023, the nationwide network of nearly 1,400 reporting health centers delivered essential primary and preventive care at nearly 15,000 sites serving 30 million users, which includes one in three people living in poverty and one in five rural residents.[35,42] Health centers have contributed to significantly improved health outcomes for the uninsured and Medicaid populations and have reduced disparities in health care and health status across socioeconomic and racial/ethnic groups.[43,44]

America's safety net, however, is by no means secure, and the availability of safety net providers varies from community to community. Vulnerable populations residing in communities without safety net providers have to forgo care or seek care from hospital emergency rooms. Safety net providers face enormous pressures due to high demand, particularly in communities that have an increasing number of uninsured and poor. The inability to shift costs for uncompensated care onto private insurance has become a significant problem because revenues from Medicaid, the primary source of third-party financing for core safety net providers, are inadequate because of funding constraints.

The Indian Health System

American Indians and Alaska Natives are the only ethnic groups for which the federal government has taken direct responsibility for health care. Also, as citizens of the United States, these groups are eligible to participate in all public, private, and state health programs available to the general population. The Indian Health Service (IHS), an agency of the federal government, is the principal healthcare provider and health advocate for these groups. The agency provides health services to approximately 2.56 million people who belong to more than 574 federally recognized tribes in 37 states.[45] The policy of self-determination underlies healthcare services for these citizens. Accordingly, the tribes have three options for receiving health care: (1) directly from the IHS; (2) through contracting with the IHS to have the administrative control, operation, and funding for health programs transferred to American Indian and Alaska Native tribal governments; or (3) through contracting with the IHS and assuming even greater control and autonomy for the provision of tribes' healthcare services. The IHS operates 46 hospitals and over 600 health centers, clinics, and health stations.[46]

Integrated Delivery Systems

An integrated delivery system (IDS) may be defined as a network of organizations that provides, or arranges to provide, a coordinated continuum of services to a defined population and is willing to be held clinically and fiscally accountable for the outcomes and health status of that population. For over a decade now, organizational integration to form IDSs has been the hallmark of the U.S. healthcare industry. Integration of the U.S. healthcare delivery system has occurred in response to cost pressures, development of new alternatives for the delivery of health care, the growing power of MCOs, and the need to provide services more efficiently to populations spread over large geographic areas. An IDS represents various forms of ownership and other strategic linkages among major participants, such as hospitals, physicians, and insurers. The objective is to achieve greater integration of healthcare services along the continuum of care.

Evaluation of the Healthcare System

The healthcare system of a nation is influenced by external factors, including the political climate, economic development, technological progress, social and cultural values, the physical environment, and population characteristics, such as demographic and health trends. The combined interaction of these forces influences the course of healthcare delivery in the United States. In the following sections, we summarize the following basic characteristics that differentiate the U.S. healthcare delivery system from that of other countries.

- No central governing agency and little integration and coordination
- A technology-driven delivery system focusing on acute care
- High cost, unequal access, and average outcome
- Delivery of health care under imperfect market conditions
- Government as a subsidiary to the private sector
- Market justice versus social justice, which is pervasive throughout health care
- Multiple players and balance of power
- Quest for integration and accountability

No Central Governing Agency and Little Integration and Coordination

The U.S. healthcare system provides a conspicuous contrast to the healthcare systems of other developed countries. The centrally controlled universal healthcare systems of most developed countries authorize financing and delivery of health care for all residents. The U.S. system is not centrally controlled and has a very complex structure of financing, insurance, delivery, and payment mechanisms. Private financing, which is predominantly through employers, accounts for approximately 54% of total healthcare expenditures; the government finances the remaining 46%.

The less complex structure of a centrally controlled healthcare system improves efficiency by managing total expenditures through global budgets and by governing the availability and utilization of services through central planning. Because the United States has such a large private system of financing, insurance, and delivery, the majority of insurers and providers are private businesses, independent of the government. Nevertheless, the federal and state governments play an important role in healthcare delivery. They finance healthcare services for publicly insured patients, such as those covered under Medicare and Medicaid. They also determine public-sector expenditures and establish reimbursement rates for services delivered to Medicare and Medicaid patients. The government uses various payment mechanisms for providers. Currently, almost all inpatient and home healthcare services delivered to Medicare and Medicaid patients are reimbursed according to a variety of prospective payment methods. Physician reimbursement rates are derived using complex formulas that take into account factors such as time, skill, and intensity of physician work; beginning in 1983, a gradual departure occurred from the previous cost-based reimbursement methods. The government also formulates standards of participation through health policy and regulation and requires providers to comply with the standards and receive federal certification in order to deliver care to Medicare and Medicaid patients. Certification standards are also regarded as minimum standards of quality in most sectors of the healthcare industry.

The insurance and delivery functions are separated in the main government programs (Medicare, Medicaid, and SCHIP) because the government provides insurance but services are delivered through the private sector. Even in the military and VA systems, some services are contracted through the private sector.

A Technology-Driven Delivery System Focusing on Acute Care

The United States is a hotbed of research and innovation in new medical technology. Because of its cost implications, almost all nations try to limit the diffusion and utilization of technology through central planning and control. Lack of such controls in the United States promotes innovation, rapid diffusion, and utilization of new technology. Advances in science and technology often create demand for new services despite shrinking resources to finance sophisticated care. Other factors also contribute to increased demand in expensive technological care: Patients assume that the latest innovations offer the highest quality, physicians want to try the latest gadgets, and competition among hospitals is often driven by the acquisition of technology. After organizations acquire new equipment and facilities, they are often under pressure to recoup the capital investments. Legal risks for providers and health plans alike may also play a role in discouraging denial of new technology.

Although technology has ushered in a new generation of successful interventions, the negative outcomes resulting from its overuse are many. For example, the expense of highly technical interventions increases insurance payments to providers. Insurance premiums rise, and it becomes more difficult for employers to expand coverage. Broad exposure to technology early in medical training not only affects clinical preferences but also future professional behavior and practice patterns. Because medical specialization revolves around technology, an oversupply of specialists in the United States has compounded the rate of technology diffusion. In this technology-driven environment, the healthcare system suffers from inadequate resources and mechanisms to address the growing needs of people with chronic conditions and comorbidities. Given the rising number of elderly in the U.S. population, the system that is primarily driven by the acute care model will be overburdened unless appropriate steps are taken to shift resources from acute to chronic care.

High Cost, Unequal Access, and Mixed Outcomes

Although data on healthcare spending in various countries are not always comparable because of differences in accounting for the expenditures, experts generally agree that compared with any other developed country in the world, the United States spends the most. For example, in 2014, U.S. healthcare spending was $9,523 per capita, or 17.5% of the GDP.[47] In 2023, U.S. healthcare spending reached in 2023, U.S. healthcare spending reached 4.8 trillion, about $14,570 per person.[48] The average annual healthcare cost inflation in 2023 was 7.5%. This was higher than the 4.6% increase from 2021 to 2022.[49] The high cost of health care has ramifications for the expansion of health insurance to the uninsured, the long-term solvency of publicly financed programs, and other issues of equity and health disparities that remain unaddressed.

Access means the ability of an individual to obtain healthcare services when needed. In the United States, access is restricted to (1) those who have health insurance through their employers, (2) those covered under a government healthcare program, (3) those who can afford to buy insurance out of their private funds, and (4) those who are able to pay for services privately. Health insurance is the primary means for ensuring access, although some uninsured Americans receive care through the safety net. In early 2015, 29 million Americans of all ages (9.2% of the population) were uninsured—that is, they were not covered under a private or public health insurance program.[50] Despite the ACA, 27.5 million nonelderly individuals were uninsured in 2021.

For consistent, basic, and routine primary care, the uninsured are unable to see a physician unless they can pay the physician's fees. Those who cannot afford to pay generally wait until health problems develop, at which point they may be able to receive services free of charge in a hospital emergency department. The Emergency Medical Treatment and Labor Act of 1986 requires screening and evaluation of every patient, necessary stabilizing treatment, and admitting, when necessary, regardless of ability to pay. Uninsured Americans, therefore, are able to obtain medical care for acute illness. Hence, one can say that the United States does have a form of universal catastrophic health insurance, even for the uninsured.[51]

It is widely acknowledged that absence of insurance inhibits patients' ability to receive well-directed, coordinated, and continuous health care through access to primary care services and, when needed, referral to specialty services. Experts generally believe that inadequate access to basic and routine primary care services is the main reason that the United States, in spite of being the most economically advanced country, lags behind other developed nations in measures of population health such as infant mortality and overall life expectancy. This belief, however, remains largely unsubstantiated, mainly in view of the fact that the health status of a population is based on many factors, including individual lifestyles and behaviors.

Delivery of Health Care Under Imperfect Market Conditions

Under national healthcare programs, patients have varying degrees of choice in selecting their providers; however, true economic market forces are virtually nonexistent. In the United States, even though the delivery of services is largely in private hands, health care is only partially governed by free market forces. The delivery and consumption of health care in the United States do not quite meet the basic tests of a free market. Hence, the system is best described as a quasi-market or an imperfect market.

Some key features characterize all free markets. In a free market, multiple patients (buyers) and providers (sellers) act independently. In addition, patients should be able to choose their provider based on price and quality of services. If it were this simple, patient choice would determine prices by the unencumbered interaction of supply and demand. Theoretically at least, prices are negotiated between payers and providers; however, in many instances, the payer is not the patient, but rather a managed care organization, Medicare, or Medicaid. Because prices are set by agencies external to the market, they are not freely governed by the forces of supply and demand.

For the healthcare market to be free, unrestrained competition must occur among providers on the basis of price and quality. Generally speaking, free competition exists among healthcare providers in the United States. The consolidation of buying power into the hands of private health plans, however, has forced providers to form alliances and integrated delivery systems on the supply side. In certain geographic sectors of the country, a single giant medical system has taken over as the sole provider of major healthcare services, restricting competition. As the healthcare system continues to move in this direction, it appears that only in large metropolitan areas will there be more than one large, integrated system competing to get the business of the health plans.

A free market requires that patients have information about service options. Free markets operate best when consumers are educated about the products they are using. Patients, however, are not always well informed about the decisions that need to be made regarding their care. Choices involving sophisticated technology, diagnostic methods, interventions, and pharmaceuticals can be difficult and often require physician input. Acting as advocates, primary care providers can reduce this information gap for patients. Recently, healthcare consumers have taken more initiative to educate themselves using Internet resources for gathering medical information. Also, pharmaceutical product advertising is having an impact on consumer expectations and is increasing awareness of available medications.

In a free market, patients have information on price and quality for each provider. Current pricing methods for healthcare services further confound free market mechanisms. Hidden costs make it difficult for patients to gauge the full expense of services ahead of time. Item-based pricing, for example, refers to the costs of adjunct services that often accompany major procedures such as surgery. Patients are usually informed of the surgery's cost ahead of time but cannot anticipate the cost of anesthesiologists, pathologists, and hospital supplies and facilities, thus making it extremely difficult to ascertain the total price before services have actually been received. Package pricing and capitated fees can help overcome these drawbacks by providing a bundled fee for a package of related services. Package pricing covers services bundled together for one episode, which is less encompassing than capitation. Capitation covers all services an enrollee may need during an entire year.

In recent years, care quality has received much attention. Performance rating of health plans has met with some success; however, apart from sporadic news stories, the public generally has scant information on the quality of healthcare providers.

In a free market, patients must directly bear the cost of services received. The purpose of insurance is to protect against the risk of unforeseen catastrophic events. Because the fundamental purpose of insurance is to meet major expenses when unlikely events occur, having insurance for basic and routine health care undermines the principle of insurance. Health insurance coverage for minor services, such as colds, coughs, and earaches, amounts to prepayment for such services. There is a moral hazard that after enrollees purchase health insurance, they will use healthcare services to a greater extent than if they had to pay for such services themselves. If the patient has to bear the full cost, the patient may even forgo certain referrals.

Moral hazard can be contained by a new type of health insurance arrangement that seems to be gaining some initial momentum. Under certain qualifying conditions, individuals can have a Health Savings Account (HSA), which is a tax-sheltered trust account that the individual owns for the purpose of paying qualified medical expenses. The HSA account works in conjunction with a high-deductible health plan. In order to have an HSA, the individual must enroll in a high-deductible health plan. Healthcare expenses are paid out of the HSA. Insurance kicks in once the annual deductible is met.

In a free market for health care, patients as consumers make decisions about the purchase of healthcare services. In addition to the factors discussed earlier, at least two more factors limit the ability of patients to make decisions. First, decisions about the utilization of health care are often determined by need rather than price-based demand. Need has generally been defined as the amount of medical care that medical experts believe a person should have to remain or become healthy.[52] Second, the delivery of health care can result in creation of demand. This follows from self-assessed need, which, when coupled with moral hazard, leads to greater utilization. This creates an artificial demand because prices are not taken into consideration. Practitioners who have a financial interest in additional treatments also create artificial demand,[53] commonly referred to as provider-induced demand.

Government as Subsidiary to the Private Sector

In most other developed countries, the government plays a central role in the provision of health care. In the United States, the private sector plays the dominant role. This can be explained to some degree by the American tradition of reliance on individual responsibility and a commitment to limiting the power of the national government. As a result, government spending for health care has been largely confined to filling in the gaps left open by the private sector. These gaps include environmental protection, support for research and training, and care of vulnerable populations.

Market Justice Versus Social Justice: Pervasive Throughout Health Care

Market justice and social justice are two contrasting theories that govern the production and distribution of healthcare services in the United States. The principle of market justice ascribes the fair distribution of health care to the market forces in a free economy. Medical care and its benefits are distributed on the basis of people's willingness and ability to pay.[54] In contrast, social justice emphasizes the well-being of the community over that of the individual; thus, the inability to obtain medical services because of a lack of financial resources would be considered unjust. A just distribution of benefits must be based on need, not simply on one's ability to purchase services in the marketplace. In a partial public and private healthcare system, the two theories often operate side by side; however, market justice principles tend to prevail. Unfortunately, market justice results in the unequal allocation of healthcare services, neglecting critical human concerns that are not confined to the individual but that have broader negative impacts on society.

Multiple Players and Balance of Power

The U.S. healthcare system involves multiple players. The key players in the system have long been physicians, administrators of health service institutions, insurance companies, large employers, and the government. Big business, labor, MCOs, insurance companies, physicians, and hospitals are powerful and politically active special interest groups, which are represented before lawmakers by high-priced lobbyists. Each player has a different economic interest to protect. The problem is that the self-interests of the various players are often at odds. For example, providers seek to maximize government reimbursement for services delivered to Medicare and Medicaid patients, but the government wants to contain cost increases. The fragmented self-interests of the specific players produce countervailing forces within the system. In an environment that is rife with motivations to protect conflicting self-interests, achieving comprehensive system-wide reforms is next to impossible, and cost containment remains a major challenge. Consequently, the approach to healthcare reform in the United States is characterized as incremental or piecemeal.

Quest for Integration and Accountability

The use of primary care as the organizing hub for continuous and coordinated health services has historically been recognized in the United States. It was envisioned that through primary care, other healthcare services would be integrated in a seamless fashion. Although this model gained popularity with the expansion of managed care, its development stalled before it could reach its full potential. The large-scale transition of healthcare delivery to the managed care system in the 1990s was met with widespread criticism, which turned into backlash from consumers, physicians, and legislators. As a result, various compromises were reached. The HMO model that was based on primary care and gatekeeping became less popular than was initially foreseen by its proponents. A compromised PPO model has become dominant in U.S. healthcare delivery; however, current political debates seem to support the need for a model of healthcare delivery that is based on primary care. The PPO model also emphasizes the importance of the patient–provider relationship and how it can best function to improve the health of each individual; however, such a system would fall short of meeting any population-wide objectives without universal access to basic health care.

In 2007, the state of Massachusetts implemented a program that promised to achieve nearly universal health coverage in the state. Under legal penalties, the program called for all residents to obtain health insurance and for all employers to offer a basic insurance plan that workers could buy with pretax dollars. Government subsidies were made available to low-income individuals to buy insurance; those experiencing poverty had their premiums paid by the state. A central clearinghouse brokered the purchase of insurance and established rules and procedures. After 6 years of implementation, the reform initiative demonstrated the potential for expanding coverage and improving access to care by embracing a model of shared responsibility. With the lowest rate of uninsured in the country, the Massachusetts experience became a model for federal health reform[55]; the Patient Protection and Affordable Care Act (ACA) was passed by Congress and then signed into law by President Obama on March 23, 2010.[56]

The ACA was enacted to increase the affordability of health insurance, to lower the uninsured rate by expanding public and private insurance coverage, and to reduce the costs of health care. It introduced mechanisms like mandates, subsidies, and insurance exchanges.[57] Since the ACA was enacted, the U.S. healthcare system has taken important steps toward providing all Americans with quality, affordable health care. About 40 million uninsured people have gained health insurance coverage since the ACA was enacted in 2010. These benefits include health insurance through the marketplace and Medicaid enrollment.[58]

In 2021, New York passed a bill to prevent healthcare providers from garnishing wages from patients for unpaid bills or placing home liens.[59] Nearly 70% of New Yorkers believe that they would be unable to afford care for major illnesses, which explains why 38% of them sacrifice health care due to cost. This bill aims to increase access to health care by removing the fear of losing a wage or home. The practices of home liens and garnishing wages disproportionately impact those living in less densely populated and low-economic-status counties. The bill seeks to bolster health equity and overall access to care.

Often, behavioral health is not included in the primary care setting. One model integrated primary care services in a specialty mental health clinic to promote positive behavioral health.[60] The results indicated that there was a significant increase in stays at the hospital compared with the status quo. This might suggest that the integration could lead to newly identified unmet medical needs.

Health information technology (HIT) is generally defined as use of an electronic system to store and share health data. Implementing a common database for information can reduce administrative costs and lead to faster and more accurate treatment. Although 91% of ambulatory care providers use an electronic health record, only one-third of clinics use HIT. In Hawaii, during the 2023 state legislative session, a bill was introduced (but failed) that established a working group to develop a health data exchange framework with the health department.[61] The bill sought to enable and require real-time access to health information among healthcare providers and payers through mandated standards-based health data sharing. This secure and efficient exchange of patient health information could improve health outcomes, enhance communication among health providers, and foster a more client-centered approach to medicine.

Telehealth increased exponentially during the COVID-19 pandemic as a means to reduce the spread of COVID-19. The use of telehealth is not a panacea in primary health care, but it could significantly impact increased access to care for medically underserved populations.[62] For rural communities where the doctor-to-population ratio is disproportionately lower compared with the rest of the country, telehealth helps reduce the physical boundaries linked to in-person appointments. Integral to the relationship between patients and providers is the concept of accountability. For providers, accountability means delivery of care that is efficient, ethical, and of high quality. From the patient's standpoint, it means taking individual responsibility to safeguard one's own health and to use available resources sensibly.

COVID-19 Pandemic

Beginning in December 2019, patients in Wuhan, Hubei, began experiencing unusual symptoms and did not respond positively to standard treatment practice. On January 7, 2020, China identified the cases as a new virus—SARS-CoV-2, whose symptoms included fever and shortness of breath. The initial cases all seemed to connect to a Huanan Seafood Market.

The CDC began screening for the coronavirus in three airports.[63,64] Despite the screening, the first documented case of COVID-19 in the United States was confirmed on January 20, 2020. The FDA approved the first diagnostic test on February 4; however, the results were deemed untrustworthy on February 8. The CDC created a hospitalization surveillance network to track the number of cases on March 1. COVID-19 was then determined to be a pandemic by the World Health Organization (WHO) after more than 118,000 cases and 4,291 deaths on March 11. A travel ban was issued for 26 European countries on March 13, and states began to issue shutdowns to reduce the spread of COVID-19.

COVID-19 highlighted the different roles among the states and the federal government in mitigating the pandemic. The CDC provided large-scale information surrounding the pandemic; the FDA managed approval for the testing kits and vaccines for COVID-19; and the federal government impacted the travel restrictions, healthcare coverage, and direct payment plans. By comparison, the state government had the power to determine the policies to implement based on the information provided by the CDC, resulting in 50 different approaches to mitigate the impact of COVID-19.

Moderna began the first human trials of the COVID-19 vaccine on March 17, 2021. Medicare and Medicaid began to temporarily expand telehealth benefits. COVID-19 revealed the positives of integrating virtual services into the medical field. On March 27, 2021, the CARES Act became law, providing direct payments and expanding unemployment insurance. With 26.5 million Americans filing for unemployment by mid-March 2021 and the pre-existing inequities in health care, a report revealed one in seven Americans in April 2021 shared that they did not seek care for a fever or dry cough due to cost concerns. Avoiding treatment for similar symptoms to COVID-19 could have increased the spread of COVID-19.

The vaccines began to roll out in December 2021 and reached 20 million people by December 31. At the end of 2024, the United States surpassed 95 million infections and more than 1.1 million deaths.

As of January 2025, the number of cases, deaths, and hospitalization have decreased, and most communities have a low level of COVID-19. The CDC has updated the Child and Adolescent Immunization Schedule to include the COVID-19 vaccine.

Conclusion

The United States does not have a well-integrated healthcare delivery system for all citizens. Instead, there are multiple subsystems developed either through market forces or through public initiatives to address the needs of certain population segments. The subsystems include managed care, the military and VA systems, the system for vulnerable populations, and the emerging integrated delivery system. The basic features that characterize the unique healthcare delivery system in the United States include the absence of a central agency to govern the system, little integration and coordination, a technology-driven delivery system focusing on acute care, a costly system that produces unequal access and average outcomes, delivery of health care under imperfect market conditions, government as subsidiary to the private sector, the conflict between market justice and social justice, multiple players and balance of power, and quests for integration and accountability.

References

1. Shi L, Singh DA. *Delivering Health Care in America: A Systems Approach*. 6th ed. Burlington, MA: Jones & Bartlett Learning; 2015:649.
2. Shi L, Singh DA. *Essentials of the U.S. Health Care System*. 3rd ed. Burlington, MA: Jones & Bartlett Learning; 2013.

3. Bedford HF, Colbourn T. *The Americans: A Brief History to 1877*, part 1. New York, NY: Harcourt Brace Jovanovich; 1972.
4. Konstam A. *Historical Atlas of Exploration: 1492–1600*. New York, NY: Checkmark Books; 2000.
5. Bryant WC, Gay SH, Brooks N. *Scribner's Popular History of the United States*. New York, NY: Charles Scribner's Sons; 1897.
6. Bradley HW. *The United States 1492–1877*. New York, NY: Charles Scribner's Sons; 1972.
7. Karlen HM. *The Pattern of American Government*. 2nd ed. Beverly Hills, CA: Glencoe Press; 1975.
8. U.S. Census Bureau. *Statistical Abstract of the United States, 2012*. Washington, DC: U.S. General Printing Office; 2012.
9. U.S. Census Bureau. QuickFacts. Statistics for all states and counties. January 2016. Accessed April 14, 2016. https://www.census.gov/quickfacts/table/PST045215/00.
10. Sidlow E, Henschen B. *America at Odds: An Introduction to American Government*. 2nd ed. Belmont, CA: Wadsworth/Thomson Learning; 2000.
11. Gosling JJ. *Economics, Politics, and American Public Policy*. Armonk, NY: ME Sharpe; 2008.
12. Ward N. Frequently requested statistics on immigrants and immigration in the United States. Migration Policy Institute. March 14, 2023. Accessed March 24, 2023. https://www.migrationpolicy.org/article/frequently-requested-statistics-immigrants-and-immigration-united-states#:~:text=In%202021%2C%20immigrants%20comprised%2013.6,share%20they%20comprised%20in%202019.
13. Migration Policy Institute. Annual number of U.S. legal permanent residents, fiscal years 1820–2014. Accessed October 24, 2016. http://www.migrationpolicy.org/programs/data-hub/us-immigration-trends#history.
14. U.S. Department of Homeland Security. U.S. lawful permanent residents: 2014. Accessed October 24, 2016. https://www.dhs.gov/sites/default/files/publications/Lawful_Permanent_Residents_2014.pdf.
15. Kochanek KD, Murphy SL, Xu JQ, Tejada-Vera B. Deaths: final data for 2014. In: *National Vital Statistics Reports*; 2016;65(4). Hyattsville, MD: National Center for Health Statistics.
16. DeNavas-Walt C, Proctor BD, Smith J. *Income, Poverty, and Health Insurance Coverage in the United States: 2014*. Washington, DC: U.S. Government Printing Office; 2015.
17. U.S. Department of Agriculture. *Rural America at a Glance*. 2015 ed. Accessed April 15, 2016. http://www.ers.usda.gov/media/1952235/eib145.pdf.
18. PRRI Staff. 2023 PRRI Census of American Religion: County-Level Data on Religious Identity and Diversity. August 29, 2024. Accessed January 27, 2025. https://prri.org/research/census-2023-american-religion/.
19. Number of people per active physician by specialty, 2021. Association of American Medical Colleges. Published December 2021. Accessed March 24, 2023. https://www.aamc.org/data-reports/workforce/data/number-people-active-physician-specialty-2021.
20. AMA analysis shows most physicians work outside of private practice. American Medical Association. Published May 2021. Accessed March 24, 2023. https://www.ama-assn.org/press-center/press-releases/ama-analysis-shows-most-physicians-work-outside-private-practice.
21. National Center for Health Statistics. *Health, United States, 2015*. Hyattsville, MD: U.S. Department of Health and Human Services; 2016.
22. How IMGs have changed the face of American medicine. American Medical Association. Published October 2021. Accessed March 24, 2023. https://www.ama-assn.org/education/international-medical-education/how-imgs-have-changed-face-american-medicine.
23. Association of American Medical Colleges. U.S. Physician Workforce Data Dashboard: 2023 Key Findings and Definitions. Accessed January 29, 2025. https://www.aamc.org/data-reports/data/2023-key-findings-and-definitions.
24. Peter J. Attracting the next generation of physicians to rural medicine. Association of American Medical Colleges. Published February 2020. Accessed March 24, 2023. https://www.aamc.org/news-insights/attracting-next-generation-physicians-rural-medicine.
25. Smiley RA, Ruttinger C, Oliveira CM, et al. The 2020 National Nursing Workforce Survey. *J Nurs Reg*. 2021; 12(suppl 1):S1–S48.
26. Fast facts on U.S. hospitals. American Hospital Association. Published January 2022. Accessed March 24, 2023. https://www.aha.org/statistics/fast-facts-us-hospitals.
27. National Mental Health Services Survey. Substance Abuse and Mental Health Services Administration. Published September 2021. Accessed March 24, 2023. https://www.samhsa.gov/data/sites/default/files/reports/rpt35336/2020_NMHSS_final.pdf.
28. Nursing home care. Centers for Disease Control and Prevention. Published December 2022. Accessed March 24, 2023. https://www.cdc.gov/nchs/fastats/nursing-home-care.htm.
29. Public-use data files. Centers for Disease Control and Prevention. Published February 2022. Accessed March 24, 2023. https://www.cdc.gov/nchs/data_access/ftp_data.htm.
30. Number of outpatient visits in the United States in 2020, by ambulatory health care service. *Statista*. Published August 2022. Accessed March 24, 2023. https://www.statista.com/statistics/1323185/number-of-outpatient-visits-by-type-of-ambulatory-health-care-service-in-the-us/#:~:text=In%202020%2C%20around%201.5%20billion,outpatient%20service%20was%20dentist%20offices.
31. Tolbert J. Key facts about the uninsured population. Kaiser Family Foundation. Published December 2022. Accessed March 24, 2023. https://www.kff.org/uninsured/issue-brief/key-facts-about-the-uninsured-population/#:~:text=The%20uninsured%20rate%20among%20children,for%20adults%20(Figure%205).
32. Hsuan C. Emergency departments in the United States treating high proportions of patients with ambulatory care sensitive conditions: a retrospective cross-sectional analysis. *BMC Health Serv Res*. 2022;22:854.
33. Keisler-Starkey K, Bunch LN. Health insurance coverage in the United States: 2021. September 13, 2022. Report Number P60-278. Accessed January 27, 2025. https://www.census.gov/library/publications/2022/demo/p60-278.html.
34. Mykyta L, Keisler-Starkey K, Bunch L. More Children Were Covered by Medicaid and CHIP in 2021. September 13, 2022. Accessed January 27, 2025. https://www.census.gov/library/stories/2022/09/uninsured-rate-of-children-declines.html.
35. Health center program: impact and growth. Bureau of Primary Health Care, Health Resources and Services Administration. Published August 2022. Accessed March 24, 2023. https://bphc.hrsa.gov/about-health-centers/health-center-program-impact-growth.

36. Veterans Health Administration. Published August 2022. Accessed March 24, 2023. https://www.va.gov/health/aboutvha.asp.
37. Bonenberger A. VA Still Challenged to Provide Veterans Timely Health Care, Watchdog Says. Military.com. Published June 2, 2023. Accessed January 29, 2025. https://www.military.com/daily-news/2023/06/02/va-still-challenged-provide-veterans-timely-health-care-watchdog-says.html.
38. Saha S, Freeman M, Toure J, Tippens KM, Weeks C, Ibrahim S. Racial and ethnic disparities in the VA health care system: a systematic review. *J Gen Intern Med*. 2008 May;23(5):654–671. Accessed January 29, 2025. https://www.ncbi.nlm.nih.gov/pmc/articles/PMC2324157/.
39. Department of Veterans Affairs. *Fact Sheet: Facts About the Department of Veterans Affairs*. Washington, DC: VA Office of Public Affairs; 2016.
40. CMS releases latest enrollment figures for Medicare, Medicaid, and Children's Health Insurance Program (CHIP). Centers for Medicare and Medicaid Services. Published December 2021. Accessed March 24, 2023. https://www.cms.gov/newsroom/news-alert/cms-releases-latest-enrollment-figures-medicare-medicaid-and-childrens-health-insurance-program-chip.
41. Conmy AB. Children's health coverage trends. Assistant Secretary for Planning and Evaluation, U.S. Department of Health and Human Services. Published March 2023. Accessed March 24, 2023. https://aspe.hhs.gov/sites/default/files/documents/77d7cc41648a371e0b5128f0dec2470e/aspe-childrens-health-coverage.pdf.
42. Bureau of Primary Health Care. *BPHC-UDS Annual Report*. Washington, DC: BPHC; 2014.
43. Politzer RM, Schempf AH, Shi L, Starfield B. The future role of health centers in improving national health. *J Pub Health Pol*. 2003;24(3):296–306.
44. Shi L, Politzer R, Regan J, Lewis-Idema D, Falik M. The impact of managed care on vulnerable populations served by community health centers. *J Ambu Care Manag*. 2001; 24(1):51–66.
45. Indian Health Service. IHS fact sheets. August 2020. Accessed March 24, 2023. https://www.ihs.gov/newsroom/factsheets/ihsprofile/.
46. Indian Health Service. IHS fact sheets. January 2016. Accessed April 15, 2016. https://www.ihs.gov/newsroom/factsheets/.
47. Centers for Medicare and Medicaid Services. National health expenditure fact sheet. Accessed October 24, 2016. https://www.cms.gov/research-statistics-data-and-systems/statistics-trends-and-reports/nationalhealthexpenddata/nhe-fact-sheet.html.
48. Centers for Medicare and Medicaid Services. NHE Fact Sheet. Page last modified December 18, 2024. Accessed January 29, 2025. https://www.cms.gov/data-research/statistics-trends-and-reports/national-health-expenditure-data/nhe-fact-sheet.
49. McGough M, Wager E, Winger A, Panchal N, Cotter L. How has U.S. spending on healthcare changed over time? Peterson-KFF Health System Tracker. December 20, 2024. Accessed January 27, 2025. https://www.healthsystemtracker.org/chart-collection/u-s-spending-healthcare-changed-time/.
50. Cohen RA, Martinez ME. Division of Health Interview Statistics, National Center for Health Statistics. Health insurance coverage: estimates from the National Health Interview Survey. January–March 2015. Accessed April 15, 2016. http://www.cdc.gov/nchs/data/nhis/earlyrelease/insur201508.pdf.
51. Altman SH, Reinhardt UE. Introduction: where does health care reform go from here? An uncharted odyssey. In: Altman SH, Reinhardt UE, eds. *Strategic Choices for a Choices for a Changing Health Care System*. Chicago, IL: Health Administration Press; 1996:xxi–xxxii.
52. Feldstein PJ. *Health Care Economics*. 4th ed. New York, NY: Delmar Publishing; 1993.
53. Hemenway D, Fallon D. Testing for physician-induced demand with hypothetical cases. *Med Care*. 1985;23(4): 344–349.
54. Santerre RE, Neun SP. *Health Economics: Theories, Insights, and Industry Studies*. Chicago, IL: Irwin; 1996.
55. Kaiser Family Foundation. Massachusetts health care reform: six years later. May 2012. Accessed April 15, 2016. https://kaiserfamilyfoundation.files.wordpress.com/2013/01/8311.pdf.
56. Patient Protection and Affordable Care Act, 42 U.S.C. § 18001. 2010.
57. Kaiser Family Foundation. Summary of the Affordable Care Act. April 2013. Accessed April 15, 2016. http://files.kff.org/attachment/fact-sheet-summary-of-the-affordable-care-act.
58. Vankar P. Affordable Care Act – Statistics & Facts. Published February 28, 2024. Accessed January 23, 2025. https://www.statista.com/topics/3272/obamacare/#topicOverview.
59. Innovation in delivery: how can the U.S. health care system connect people with appropriate care? RAND Corp. April 2021. Accessed March 24, 2023. https://www.rand.org/health-care/focus-areas/delivery-improvements.html#:~:text=Innovations%20in%20health%20care%20delivery%20aim%20to,patients%27%20needs%20at%20the%20center%20of%20care.
60. Dinowitz J. Protects patients from certain penalties due to money judgments arising from actions brought by hospitals or health care professionals. Published November 2022. Accessed March 23, 2023. https://www.nysenate.gov/legislation/bills/2021/A7363.
61. Nakashima M. Relating to health data sharing. Published February 2023. Accessed March 23, 2023. https://www.capitol.hawaii.gov/session/measure_indiv.aspx?billtype=HB&billnumber=517&year=2023.
62. Telehealth and telemedicine. Centers for Disease Control and Prevention. Published July 2020. Accessed March 24, 2023. https://www.cdc.gov/phlp/php/publications/research-anthology-telehealth-and-telemedicine.html.
63. COVID-19 timeline. Centers for Disease Control and Prevention. March 2023. Accessed March 24, 2023. https://www.cdc.gov/museum/timeline/covid19.html.
64. Spring into action. Centers for Disease Control and Prevention. March 2023. Accessed March 24, 2023. https://www.cdc.gov/coronavirus/2019-ncov/covid-data/covidview/index.html.

CHAPTER 7

Canada

R. Paul Duncan, Michael E. Morris, Gaia L. Zori, and Linda A. McCarey

Country Description

Table 7-1 Canada

Nationality[1]	Noun: Canadian(s) Adjective: Canadian
Ethnic groups[1]	Canadian 32.3%, English 18.3%, French 13.6%, Scottish 13.9%, Irish 13.4%, German 9.6%, Italian 4.6%, Chinese 5.1%, North American Indian 4.4%, other 47.7%* (2016 est.)
Race[2]	White 67.4%, South Asian 6.9%, Indigenous Peoples 4.9%, Chinese 4.5%, Black 3.8%, Filipino 2.5%, Arab 1.9%, Latin American 1.6%, West Asian <1%, Southeast Asian <1%, Korean <1%, Japanese <1%, Other <1%, Multiple population groups 3.2% (2020 est.)
Religions[3]	Christian 63.2% (includes Catholic 32.0%, Anglican 3.8%, Christian Orthodox 1.4%, Baptist 1.4%, Lutheran 1.2%, Presbyterian 1.4%, United Church 3.8%, Pentecostal 0.8%, other Christian 7.1%, Christian with no other specification 10.3%), Buddhist 1.4%, Hindu 1.7%, Jewish 1.0%, Muslim 3.7%, Sikh 1.4%, Other 1.3%, No religion and secular perspectives 26.3% (2021 est.)
Language	English (official) 58.7%, French (official) 22.0%, Punjabi 1.4%, Italian 1.3%, Spanish 1.3%, German 1.3%, Cantonese 1.2%, Tagalog 1.2%, Arabic 1.1%, other 10.5% (2011 est.)
Literacy	Definition: Age 15 and over and can read and write Total population: 99% Male: 99% Female: 99% (2022 est.)
Government type[1]	Federal parliamentary democracy (Parliament of Canada) under a constitutional monarchy; a Commonwealth realm; federal and provincial authorities and responsibilities regulated in constitution
Date of independence[1]	July 1, 1867 (union of British North American colonies); December 11, 1931 (recognized by the United Kingdom per Statute of Westminster)
Gross domestic product (GDP) per capita[1]	USD 53,371 (2023 est.)
Unemployment rate[1]	6.8% (2024 est.)

Table 7-1 Canada

Natural hazards[1]	Continuous permafrost in the north is a serious obstacle to development; cyclonic storms form east of the Rocky Mountains as a result of the mixing of air masses from the Arctic, Pacific, and North American interior, and they produce most of the country's rain and snow east of the mountains; volcanism is possible, but the vast majority of volcanoes in western Canada's Coast Mountains remain dormant
Environment: current issues[1]	Metal smelting, coal-burning utilities, and vehicle emissions impacting agricultural and forest productivity; air pollution and resulting acid rain severely affecting lakes and damaging forests; ocean waters becoming contaminated due to agricultural, industrial, mining, and forestry activities; shrinking polar ice cap
Population[1]	38,232,593 (2022 est.)
Age structure[1]	0–14 years: 15.99% (male 3,094,008/female 2,931,953) 15–24 years: 11.14% (male 2,167,013/female 2,032,064) 25–54 years: 39.81% (male 7,527,554/female 7,478,737) 55–64 years: 14.08% (male 2,624,474/female 2,682,858) 65 years and over: 18.98% (male 3,274,298/female 3,881,126) (2020 est.)
Median age[1]	Total: 41.8 years Male: 40.6 years Female: 42.9 years (2020 est.)
Population growth rate[1]	0.75% (2022 est.)
Birth rate[1]	10.17 births/1,000 population (2022 est.)
Death rate[1]	812 deaths/100,000 population (2022 est.)
Disease burden[4]	Age-adjusted communicable disease deaths: 18.6/100,000 population Age-adjusted noncommunicable disease deaths: 301.5/100,000 population Age-adjusted deaths due to external causes: 26.8/100,000 population (2024 est.)
Net migration rate[1]	5.46 migrant(s)/1,000 population (2022 est.)
Gender ratio[1]	At birth: 1.05 male/female 0–14 years: 1.06 male/female 15–24 years: 1.06 male/female 25–54 years: 1.01 male/female 55–64 years: 0.98 male/female 65 years and over: 0.75 male/female Total population: 0.98 male/female (2022 est.)
Infant mortality rate[1]	Total: 4.38 deaths/1,000 live births Male: 4.66 deaths/1,000 live births Female: 4.08 deaths/1,000 live births (2022 est.)
Life expectancy at birth[1]	Total population: 83.8 years Male: 81.52 years Female: 86.21 years (2022 est.)
Total fertility rate[1]	1.57 children born/woman (2022 est.)
HIV incidence rate[5]	4.0/100,000 population (2020 est.)
Number of people living with HIV[5]	62,790 (2020 est.)
HIV/AIDS deaths	129 (2024 est.)

*Percentages add up to more than 100% because respondents were able to identify more than one ethnic origin.

Data from Central Intelligence Agency. The World Fact Book, 2021: Canada. https://www.cia.gov/the-world-factbook/about/archives/2021/countries/canada/; Statistics Canada. Table 98-10-0324-01. Visible minority and population group by generation status: Canada, provinces and territories, census metropolitan areas and census agglomerations with parts. https://www150.statcan.gc.ca/t1/tbl1/en/tv.action?pid=9810032401; Statistics Canada. Religiosity in Canada and its evolution from 1985 to 2019. https://www150.statcan.gc.ca/n1/pub/75-006-x/2021001/article/00010-eng.htm; Pan American Health Organization. Country profile: Canada. https://hia.paho.org/en/countries-22/canada-country-profile; Government of Canada. Estimates of HIV Incidence, prevalence and Canada's progress on meeting the 90-90-90 HIV targets, 2020. https://www.canada.ca/en/public-health/services/publications/diseases-conditions/estimates-hiv-incidence-prevalence-canada-meeting-90-90-90-targets-2020.html#a2.

History

Archeological records indicate that Canada has some of the first lands in North America to be inhabited by humans. People settled the area roughly 10,000 years ago. At the time of Columbus's voyage, there had been a highly developed and flourishing society in Canada for over 1,000 years.[6]

It is now widely held by historians that the Norse, led by Leifur Eiriksson, were the first Europeans to set foot on Canadian soil, around the year 1000 CE. Eiriksson's and the subsequent Norse ventures to North America were short lived and yielded little lasting sway over the development of Canadian society.[7,8]

In contrast, a new era of European arrivals was initiated in 1497 with the voyage of Englishman John Cabot, the first post-Columbian explorer to land upon the shores of Canada.[7,9] The Treaty of Paris, 1763, represents a critical turning point in Canadian history. With the English victory in the Seven Years' War, the dual colonial structure of Canada was at an end. In its place arose an English hegemony over the Canadian colonies that would be sustained for the next century.[7,9]

With its inauguration on July 1, 1867, the British North America Act established the Dominion of Canada. The foundations of a nation were thus laid with the unification of the Canadian colonies as a single entity.[9] Under the terms of confederation, the provinces were granted authority over broad areas of governance, and thus, they represented a powerful force within the new nation. From the outset, the issue of balancing the delegation of authority between the national government and the provinces was contentious.

During the last half of the 19th century and the early years of the 20th century, Canada began to expand westward, extending the nation fully across the North American continent. As the newly formed provinces were added to the Dominion, a stronger and more prosperous nation-state grew. This expansion also served to reinforce the Canadian ethic of communal action, as the challenges of inhabiting the vast rural territory made local and regional coordination essential for successful settlement.[9,10]

Canadians suffered greatly during the Depression in the 1930s. The enormity of the economic disaster overwhelmed the resources of individuals and local governments. Because of the scale of the crisis, Canadians began to focus more on communal action and on an expanded role for the state in the lives of their citizens. As a result, many of Canada's social welfare programs at the provincial and national levels can trace their origins to this time period.[11] This era also provided the catalyst for the evolution of the modern Canadian healthcare system.[12]

World War II had three primary effects on Canadian society. First, it served to further galvanize the national identity of Canada, both among its own citizenry and in the international community.[9] A second influence of the war was the substantial increase in population that came in the wake of the Allied victory. This rise was fueled by a spike in birth rates and by a wave of immigration from around the world.[13] The third significant result of World War II, specifically of the fighting efforts, was the shift in taxation powers among the various levels of the Canadian government.

With the patriation of the British North America Act in 1982, Canada formally became a fully independent nation. It is recognized as a world leader in peacekeeping and as an influential actor in the international economy.

Size and Geography

Table 7-1 displays the key characteristics of Canada. Canada is geographically the second largest nation in the world and the largest on the North American continent, covering 9.9 million square kilometers (3.8 million square miles; see **Figure 7-1**).

Spanning the width of the continent, Canada has a varied environment ranging from its coastal regions, to the arid plains of the interior, to the polar cap of the north. Although some population centers are spread across the nation's land mass, roughly two-thirds of the population reside along the southern border. The population density of Canada is 4.2 people per square kilometer, but this figure is misleading because more than 80% of the population resides in relatively dense urban areas.[14] In metropolitan areas, the population concentration is 2,250 people per square kilometer, roughly comparable to that of England. The rural areas in the west and north are very sparsely populated.[14]

Government and Political System

It is often said that the essence of the Canadian perspective on government and society is captured in one brief phrase from the Constitution Act of 1867, "Peace, Order and Good Government." These few words convey the Canadian dedication to the practical application in government of communally held values and collective action. Equality represents the foundation on which the civil union in Canada is

Figure 7-1 Map of Canada

constructed, and this core value is infused throughout government policy actions and debates at the federal, provincial/territorial, and local levels, particularly regarding health policy.[15]

As established under the British North America Act, 1867, and subsequently patriated on April 17, 1982, the governmental structure of Canada is a constitutional monarchy. Under this system, Queen Elizabeth II and, since September 8, 2023, King Charles III of Great Britain and the United Kingdom have ruled as monarch of Canada but have no governing role. The functional government of Canada is an English-style parliamentary democracy with a federal structure. The federal system of rule that exists in Canada delegates governing authority to the national and provincial governments; thus, the provincial governments are sovereign entities in their own right and not merely extensions of the national government.[15]

The national government, based in the city of Ottawa, is led by the prime minister, the elected leader of the political party that garnered the largest number of parliamentary seats in the previous parliamentary elections. Parliament is a bicameral body consisting of the 105 members of the Senate, who are appointed by the Monarch's representative, the governor general, and the House of Commons, whose 338 members are elected by popular vote of the citizenry.[16] Among the varied levels of government in Canada, taxation authority is broadest for the national government, which holds constitutional authority to levy personal/corporate income taxes and value-added taxes on goods and services, and has the exclusive power to impose excise taxes and duties on imported goods.[17]

The 10 provincial and three territorial governments are headed by their respective premiers, who are elected by the predominant party in the provincial assemblies. In all 13 jurisdictions, the legislatures are unicameral assemblies. The breadth of provincial and territorial taxation authority is roughly equivalent to that of the national government. The exception is excise taxes and duties, which are solely the purview of Ottawa.[17]

Political parties emerged in Canada during the 1830s and were, in essence, a colonial reflection of the British two-party system, composed of the Liberal party and the Conservative party. By 1921, the Progressive party had established a tradition of a multiparty system within Canada.[18] Over the following decades, three to five substantial political parties have existed in Canada, and minor and regional parties have played pivotal roles in many elements of Canadian governance, particularly in relationship to the development of national health insurance.[19,20]

Macroeconomics

Canada, a member of the Group of Seven, is recognized as one of the leading market-based economies in the world. Government estimates place the total gross domestic product (GDP) for 2021 at $1.99 trillion, with a per capita GDP of $51,988 USD based on 2021 population estimates.[21] Other indicators of the health of the economy include the rate of inflation and the unemployment rate. In November 2022, the core consumer price index rose by 6.8% year over year,[22] and the unemployment rate as of December 2022 was 5.0%.[23] As with the global economy, the COVID-19 pandemic has had a notable impact on the Canadian economy. During the pandemic, many economic activities were partially or fully restricted as part of public health measures aimed at slowing the spread of infection.[24] As a result, production and employment were substantially reduced, leading to a significant decrease in income and a rise in unemployment. While the GDP had largely recovered to prepandemic levels by the end of 2021, per capita GDP had not. Canada's GDP per capita growth decreased by an average of 1.3% per year during the pandemic from 2020 to 2021, down from 1.0% during the period from 2010 to 2019.[24]

Since the turn of the 20th century, the Canadian economy has evolved from its predominately natural resource–driven origins to encompass a richly diverse array of market sectors. The service sector is the largest element of the Canadian economy, representing roughly 70% of GDP in the year 2021, up from 49% in the years immediately after World War II. Manufacturing accounted for less than 30% of GDP in 2021.[25]

Key industries include trade, health care and social services, finance and insurance, machinery and auto manufacturing, production of natural gas and oil, mining, and agriculture. As is true with the population of Canada, all sectors of the economy—with the exclusion of the gas, oil, and mining sectors—are heavily concentrated along the southern border. Agricultural production is primarily found in the central and western provinces. The financial and insurance industries are disproportionately headquartered in the provinces of Ontario and Quebec.

Canada has a highly developed infrastructure, with a national system of roads and highways covering 1.4 million kilometers. An extensive rail system provides 72,093 kilometers of track covering all areas of Canada. Air travel is available throughout the country from a system of 13 international airports located in the major metropolitan cities and more than 300 smaller terminals spread across the nation.[26]

Public schools, administered by the local and provincial governments, are provided at no direct cost to students throughout the nation for elementary and secondary education.[27] From 2012 to 2013 and 2021 to 2022, public school funding increased from $61.5 billion to $82.5 billion Canadian dollars.[28] Attendance is mandatory for children under certain ages, although the age varies by jurisdiction. Private schools are also allowed under the educational system.[27] Canada possesses a world-class postsecondary educational system. Universities in Canada not only educate Canadians but also attract students from Asia, Europe, the United States, and around the world. In 2017, international students accounted for 15% of students enrolled in tertiary education, an increase from 5% in 2000.[29]

Demographics

As of July 1, 2022, Canada's population exceeded 38 million people.[30] The average age of Canadians in 2022 was 41.7 years, an increase of nearly 4 years since 2002.[31] In 2022, 18.8% of Canadians were at least 65 years of age, and the gap is widening between the number of people in this age group and that of people aged 0 to 14 years (15.6%).[31] It is the increase in the over-65 population causing the population shift; there were 3,506,480 people over 65 years old in 1995 compared with 7,329,910 in 2022.[31] Nearly half of the Indigenous population in 2011 was younger than 24 years of age. Indigenous peoples—Inuit, Métis, or First Nation heritage—represented 4.3% of the population in 2011.[32]

Data from the 2021 census indicate that 30.3 million Canadian citizens aged 15 and older have a certificate, diploma, or degree. Those with a high school diploma make up 26.7%, and the same percentage (26.7%) have a bachelor's degree or higher.[33,34]

The median after-tax income of individuals was $34,500 Canadian dollars in 2020. For families of two or more, the median was $92,400 in after-tax earnings.[35] As measured by the Gini coefficient, income distributions across families indicate that from the late 1970s to 2015 there was a slight widening of the income gap among Canadians. The coefficient for income inequality increased from 0.29 to 0.32 during this period.[35,36]

Data from the General Social Survey show that during 2017 to 2019, the majority (63.2%) of

Canadians were followers of various denominations of the Christian faith. During that time, Catholics represented the most prevalent group (32.0%). Other Christian faiths accounted for an additional 10.3%. Canadians reporting no religion represented 26.3% of the population. Muslims were the most prominent non-Christian religion, representing 3.7% of Canadians. Adherents of the Jewish, Buddhist, Sikh, and Hindu faiths each accounted for approximately 1.0% of the population. The remaining population represented a variety of religious beliefs.[37]

Patterns of morbidity and mortality in Canada have changed greatly since the turn of the 20th century. Cancer is the leading cause of mortality in the nation, accounting for 26.6% of deaths in 2022, followed by heart disease, accounting for 17.7% of deaths.[38] Recent data reveals that 1 in 12 Canadian adults over the age of 20 live with a diagnosed heart disease. Men are two times more likely than women to experience a heart attack.[39]

Diabetes, another known risk factor for cardiovascular disease, has been steadily rising in the Canadian population. Among the overall population, the prevalence of diabetes was 9.4% in 2020 to 2021, with men (10.1%) slightly more likely than women (8.7%) to be diagnosed with the condition.[40] Diabetes prevalence increases with age, from about 2.0% in Canadians in their 30s, to about 27% in those aged 75 to 79 years.[41]

Obesity has been repeatedly linked in the medical literature to cardiovascular disease, diabetes, and hypertension. In 2022, about 30% of Canadians were classified as obese.[42] The trend toward greater levels of obesity is demonstrated among most age groups. The rate of increase among 35 to 49 and 50 to 64 year olds rose the highest.[43] The observation that physical activity helps to moderate obesity is demonstrated by the fact that 27.0% of sedentary Canadian men were found to be obese, compared with 19.0% of active men.[41] A hopeful sign for the future is that the levels of physical activity among the population in Canada appear to be rising. In 2019, 49.2% of adults aged 18 to 79 reported meeting the recommended target of at least 150 minutes of moderate or vigorous intensity physical activity each week, compared with 41.4% in 2009.[44]

Cancer continues to be the leading cause of mortality in the country. Estimates for 2021 indicate that 229,200 cases of cancer were diagnosed in Canada, and 84,600 people died from the disease.[45] Breast cancer and prostate cancer were, respectively, the most common forms of cancer for women and men. Lung cancer remains the most common cancer-related cause of death in both genders, responsible for an estimated 25% of all cancer deaths in 2021.[45]

The prevalence of illness and chronic conditions is considerably higher in certain subpopulations, such as the First Nations. In 2012, 49% of First Nations people aged 15 years and older living off reservations reported excellent or very good health, compared with 62% (age standardized) of the total population of Canada.[46] In 2017, 47.7% of Canadian individuals with Indigenous identity reported excellent or very good self-perceived general health.[47] Comparable disparities have been observed in Canada's Black population.[48]

Brief History of the Healthcare System

Sociocultural factors play a fundamental role in the evolution of a nation's health system.[49] To understand the structures and performance of the current Canadian healthcare system better, some context is valuable. As will become clear, the steps leading to Canada's contemporary healthcare financing and delivery system do not dramatically differ from those observed in most of the Western democracies.

Pre–World War II

From the earliest era of European influence and continuing until the beginning of the 20th century, health care in Canada was focused on the relationship between a physician and a patient. Independent physicians and surgeons, practicing in the private sector, provided services to patients predominantly in the physician's office or the patient's home. The fiscal dimension of this type of care would be characterized as a private mercantile exchange. Hospitals, until the late 19th century, were viewed as places to be avoided, as the level of care was sadly lacking. Socially, hospitals were stigmatized through their association with the poor.[19]

Throughout the 19th century, government's role in health care was limited. Some support was given to the establishment of facilities to care for the poor, but for the most part, this service was provided by religious orders. It should be noted that Canada's first hospital opened in Quebec in 1639, and that hospitals proliferated more rapidly in Canada than in other areas of North America.[19]

Other areas of governmental involvement in health care before the 20th century were primarily sanitation, quarantine during times of epidemics, and medical licensure. Infectious disease was the primary pathologic process of concern during this period. As late as 1849, a single cholera outbreak was responsible for the deaths of 2% of the population of Quebec.

Throughout the 19th century and after the turn of the 20th century, the status of the physician began to ascend within Canadian society. Advances in medical knowledge allowed the provision of more effective care.

As Canada emerged from World War I, infectious disease remained the predominant challenge. Public hygiene, the Spanish influenza, and other population health issues catalyzed the development of the public health infrastructure under the direction of the provincial governments. In 1919, the federal government began to provide a coordinating hand to the provincial public health efforts and created the national hygiene grants program to fund these efforts. The first school of public health was opened in Canada in 1920 to provide the trained workforce needed to pursue the aims of infectious disease control.[19]

The concept of communal resource pooling again rose in Saskatchewan in 1920 when Union Hospital Districts were formed among adjacent rural towns to fund the construction and operation of hospitals. These collective actions, though limited to the rural areas of Canada, are viewed by some as the seeds of what would become the nation's modern healthcare system.[50]

With the provincial election of 1944, the process of reorganizing health care reemerged. The Cooperative Commonwealth Federation (CCF) party came to power in Saskatchewan under the banner of progressive reformation of government and its role in society. A socialist leaning party, the CCF vigorously promoted the agenda of "socialized health services."[50]

Post–World War II

At the close of World War II, the national environment seemed ripe for the establishment of a national health insurance program. A bill was drafted in Ottawa for such a program, but because of a conflict over the allocation of taxation powers between the federal and provincial governments, the bill failed to pass.[12] From this debate, it became clear that the provinces were divided in their opinions based on their level of prosperity. The wealthier provinces, especially Ontario, wanted to trim the federal government's power to levy taxes, which had been expanded during the war. The poorer provinces, such as Saskatchewan, were in favor of keeping tax policies in place as they were, in exchange for federal cash transfers to support social programs at the provincial level.[12]

In the wake of this stalemate at the federal level, the provincial governments once more provided the impetus for change. In 1946, Saskatchewan's government, led by the CCF, implemented the Hospital Services Plan. This program provided payment for all hospital-based services rendered in the province. Initially, reimbursement was based on a per diem system, but this was soon recognized as contributing to an unwarranted increase in utilization. Subsequently, a prospective global budget was developed in which the hospital was paid a flat monthly rate for the care of all patients treated at the facility. The rate was based on an estimated 90% occupancy rate for the hospital.[50] This method became a hallmark of hospital service financing throughout Canada.

Other provinces soon adopted Saskatchewan's Hospital Services Plan as the template for hospital payment plans developed under the new federal legislation. By 1961, all 10 provinces were participating in the federal match program, providing near-universal coverage for hospital services. The National Hospital and Diagnostic Services Act served to establish the constitutionality of a federal role in health care, which, under the British North America Act, was ostensibly a provincial matter.[50,51] The resulting program of insurance for medical care (both diagnostic and therapeutic) was popular and perceived as a success by the federal government, the provincial governments, and the vast majority of Canadians.

The federal government capitalized on the innovations of the provinces, and in 1966, the Medical Care Act was passed by the national parliament. This act established universal coverage for physician services under provincially administered programs. Financing of the plan was a mixed model similar to that under the National Hospital and Diagnostic Services Act, with the federal government matching provincial expenditures at roughly a 50% rate for physician services.[52] This part of the system was quickly labeled Medicare (sometimes causing terminology confusion when Canada–United States comparisons are pursued).

As was the case for the National Hospital and Diagnostic Services Act, provinces had considerable latitude in developing their health plans under the Medical Care Act. Many of the provinces adopted a more rigid stance than Saskatchewan on dealing with physician balance billing. While the practice continued to exist in principle, physicians who wanted to pursue balance billing were required to opt out of the government-sponsored plan. The physician could either accept the government fee schedule rate as payment in full for all services rendered to patients, or they could practice outside of the insurance program entirely, receiving no payments from the government. Given the consistent stream of revenue the government program offered, few physicians were willing to opt out.[50] The Medical Care Act had the effect of creating near-universal coverage for office and clinic-based physician care and all closely related diagnostic services.

After enactment of the two federal programs, the National Hospital and Diagnostic Services Act and the Medical Care Act, utilization and costs were observed to rise across the country. In response, the Federal–Provincial Fiscal Arrangements and the Established Programs Financing Act were passed in 1977 to provide a stronger incentive for the provinces to control escalating costs of health care by exposing them to more of the risk for such cost increases in their programs. Through a system of block grant transfers, the federal government's contributions were reduced in 1977 to a figure that equaled roughly 25% of provincial hospital and physician expenditures.[51] Block grants effectively severed any direct connection between the costs of health care provided and the amount of the federal government's contributions to support the care.[50,53]

The Canada Health Act of 1984 served to integrate the three previously enacted pieces of federal legislation into one national framework for health insurance. This unified system of insurance/financing has come to be known as Medicare, adopting the common name previously used to denote insurance provided under the 1966 Medical Care Act. Provisions of the act stipulated that the provinces would continue to devise and administer the health insurance system under guidelines set out by Ottawa and known as the five principles (**Table 7-2**),[51] which outline the framework within which provinces develop their own unique health insurance systems.

During the 1990s, stress within the economy triggered a key policy issue. In response to escalating levels of national debt, Ottawa imposed significant reductions in federal expenditures. At the federal level, these cuts were successful in reining in both the growth in spending and the debt. From 1998 to 2009, there was a 1.9% increase in revenue and a 2.9% reduction in debt charges; however, this trend did not continue in the wake of the 2008 global recession.[54]

Since 1996, the Canada Health and Social Transfer and its successor, the Canadian Health Transfer block grant system, have been the primary method used to provide federal financial support for health programs, including Medicare. In its first year, this system reduced federal cash transfers to the provinces by \$2.5 billion to \$7.0 billion Canadian dollars, depending on the estimate. Block grants ostensibly allow for great flexibility at the provincial and territorial level. Given the climate of budgetary restraint that has been consistent in Ottawa over

Table 7-2 Five Principles of the Canada Health Act

Public administration	The plan must be administered and operated on a nonprofit basis by a public authority.
Comprehensiveness	Province/territorial health insurance plans must cover all medically necessary health services provided by hospitals and physicians. They must also cover hospital-based dental surgeries.
Universality	All insured residents must be entitled to all of the insured health services provided by the provincial/territorial healthcare plan on equal terms.
Portability	Residents moving from one province/territory to another are entitled to continued coverage under their original health insurance plan until any waiting periods required by the new jurisdiction are met. The waiting periods may not exceed three months.
Accessibility	Insured people must have uniform and reasonable access to hospital, physician, and dental surgery services available in that location.

Data from Health Canada. Canada Health Act annual report 2006–2007. http://www-.hc-sc.gc.ca/hcs-sss/alt_formats/hpb-dgps/pdf/pubs/chaar-ralcs-0607/chaar-ralcs-0607_e.pdf.

the past decade, many at the provincial level see the Canada Health and Social Transfer system as simply a method to reduce federal support for provincially administered programs like Medicare. This has served to create tension within the federal structure of Canada, as the provinces felt excluded from the initial decision process for the creation of the Canada Health and Social Transfer system and continue to feel that the financing arrangements place a disproportionately heavy burden on them to operate the Medicare program with insufficient resources.[53,55,56]

The Current Healthcare System

The contemporary healthcare system in Canada is characterized by mixed sources of funding, delivery, and administration of services. The sources vary, depending on the nature of the services being rendered and the person being treated. Hospital and physician services for approximately 97% of Canadians are covered under Medicare, the jointly funded federal/provincial health insurance system whose emergence was described in the previous section and that will be the focus of the remainder of this chapter.[57]

Health services for people of First Nations and Inuit descent are solely the purview of the federal government and are handled outside of the Medicare framework. Similarly, healthcare services for veterans, members of the armed forces, and members of the Royal Canadian Mounted Police fall solely under the auspices of the federal government.[57] Together, these segments of the population total roughly 1 million people.[58]

For both the joint programs and the federal-only programs, a number of services are not covered, including portions of dental care, residential care, and pharmaceutical costs. They are funded outside of the national health insurance plans, either directly by the individual or through private-sector insurance.[57]

In recent years, the Canadian health system has begun to face the repercussions of the policy decisions made in the 1980s and 1990s. With decreased financial support for the Medicare program, particularly from the federal level, investment in the maintenance and expansion of the healthcare infrastructure declined, creating a number of problems. At the core of these issues is a concern over physical access to healthcare services. Waiting times for services, particularly technologically complex or procedure-oriented services, have repeatedly been highlighted by critics as a problem point for the healthcare system. Concern over a lack of infrastructure, such as computed tomography (CT) and magnetic resonance imaging (MRI) scanning machinery, as well as a shortage of physicians and other healthcare professionals, has garnered considerable attention both in the public eye and among policy circles.

The delivery of health care in Canada involves both public and private transactions. Physicians and residential care facilities are mostly nongovernmental entities. The hospital sector is substantially composed of facilities operated by local and provincial governments. In addition, not-for-profit private-sector hospitals, particularly religiously affiliated institutions, constitute a smaller yet highly significant source of hospital-based care.[57]

The governmental component must be seen in context. As noted, a long history of geographic dispersion and independent local action created a federal structure characterized by strong provincial governments and created an interest in local (municipal) autonomy where appropriate. This tradition, coupled with well-documented innovation by provincial governments in the healthcare arena, contributed to the development of the observed structure and to the considerable latitude of action.[59] The provinces have adopted a wide variety of approaches for their health insurance plans; thus, it is frequently argued that Canada has (at least) 13 healthcare systems, not one.[60]

Facilities

Canada operates an extensive physical infrastructure for health care. Primary care services are provided in a variety of settings. Private physician offices constitute by far the most common venue for the delivery of primary care.[61] Primary health services are also delivered in ambulatory care clinics and in community health centers.[57]

In another example of this recurring theme, community health centers emerged as a result of provincial innovation—in this case, Quebec's. The concept spread to Ontario and then across the nation.[61] Although community health centers provide a significant amount of care, they continue to represent a much smaller provider source compared with private physician practices. As of 2019, there were just over 200 community health centers, with close to 50% located in Ontario.[62]

There were 702 hospitals offering an estimated 96,849 beds in Canada during the year 2020.

Of these hospitals, 695 were publicly owned, including by federal, municipal, provincial, and regional/district entities.[63] The number of acute care hospital beds in Canada has declined significantly since reaching a peak of 179,256 beds in 1989. Between 1986 and 1995, the number of hospitals decreased from 1,224 to 978; public hospitals decreased from 1,053 to 901, and private hospitals declined by almost two-thirds (from 59 to 22). A significant portion of these closures occurred among smaller hospitals, particularly those located in rural areas. Saskatchewan, for instance, witnessed the closure of 52 of its rural hospitals during the early 1990s.[64,65]

In summary, these closures reduced the number of acute care beds from 178,137 in 1986 to 156,547 by 1995.[66] Some of this decline in the number of hospitals and beds reflects the transition of a number of hospitals to residential care facilities as well as the reclassification within other facilities of a portion of their acute care beds for long-term care use.[67] In the mid-1990s, 14,000 beds were reclassified for residential care use in the provinces of Alberta and Quebec alone.[67] In 2013, Canada had 270 acute care hospital beds per 100,000 population, down from 400 per 100,000 in 1990. This mirrors the trend among other nations in the Organization for Economic Cooperation and Development (OECD), where the average rate of acute care beds dropped from 510 per 100,000 people to 480 beds per 100,000 residents.[68]

In 2009–2010, there were 4,633 residential care facilities operating in Canada with 265,220 approved beds. Of these, 2,136 (46.1%) were designated for the care of the elderly population; 2,202 (47.5%) were mental health institutions; and the remaining 295 facilities were dedicated to an array of different specialties, including care of the physically disabled and delinquent youths. The distribution of facilities yields 212,948 beds staffed and in operation for the care of the elderly population, 39,644 for mental health patients, and 9,353 for the other types of institutions.[69] Of note, Canada's nursing and residential care facilities were adversely impacted by the COVID-19 pandemic. In 2020, the number of residents fell 4.3% year over year, largely driven by decreased admissions leading to fewer residents in nursing care facilities and community care facilities for the elderly.[70]

Long-term care facilities in Canada are distributed somewhat differently than hospitals in terms of ownership, with the private for-profit sector representing a far more substantial component of the mix. Recent studies indicate that there are notable differences between the for-profit facilities and those operated under other modes of ownership. For-profit elderly care facilities have lower staff-to-patient ratios than other institutions. In 2009–2010, the number of accumulated paid hours per resident-day, a measure of the level of staffing of long-term care facilities, was found to be 5.2 for all facilities, and 4.9 in facilities for the elderly.[71]

Public health in Canada is, for the most part, a distinct entity from the delivery of medical care. The focus of public health activities in Canada is not on supporting the delivery of healthcare services as it is in many nations, but rather on population health issues, such as community health assessment, disease surveillance, health promotion, disease and injury prevention, and health protection.

Under the Canadian system, public health departments are within the purview of provincial and local governments. The roles between the two levels of government vary from province to province, with Ontario being the most reliant on local government funding and administration. In recent years, reports by the Krever Commission and the Auditor General of Canada have raised concerns over the existing funding and infrastructure for the support of public health functions.[60] The federal government's public health role has traditionally been limited.

Workforce

Human resources are a critical element of any healthcare system. Canada has focused considerable attention on this area, particularly since the 1990s, when it was perceived that the numbers of physicians and nurses were declining. The First Ministers Accord of 2003 designated healthcare human resources planning a high priority in the Canadian health policy sphere. Beyond its inherent importance in the delivery of care for patients, health care is among the nation's largest sources of employment, with over 1 million direct employees, representing 6.0% of the workforce. In 2010, 24.8% of healthcare costs were directly attributable to human resource costs.[72] Although health expenditures in Canada increased during the 2020 and 2021 COVID-19 pandemic, this pattern of cost distribution largely returned in 2022, when physicians and other professionals accounted for 23.9% of total health spending.[73]

As of 2020, there were 92,173 physicians practicing in Canada, a ratio of roughly 242 physicians per 100,000 population.[74] This is comparable to the ratios in the United States—260 per 100,000 people—and the United Kingdom—280 per 100,000 people—but is below the OECD average of 330 physicians per 100,000 people.[68] Canada has seen more than a 0.9% increase in the number of physicians each year since 2019.[74]

Approximately half (50.4%) of practicing Canadian physicians in 2021 were in the primary care field of family medicine. Medical specialists other than surgeons accounted for 37.7% of physicians, while surgeons accounted for 11.8%. The remaining fraction of physicians are classified as medical scientists.[75] The percentage of primary care physicians in the workforce is notably higher than the 36.0% observed in the United States but lower than the 56.0% found in Australia.[76]

Of physicians, 72.1% were educated in one of the 17 accredited Canadian medical schools, and 25.6% were trained in other countries—most notably the United Kingdom, South Africa, and India; the remaining had unknown places of MD graduation.[75,77] Physicians are required to hold the medical doctor (MD) degree.

Due to an increasing number of younger physicians entering the workforce, the average age of physicians remained relatively stable from 2010 to 2014 (50.0 and 50.1 years, respectively). In 2014, the proportion of physicians under age 40 (24.5%) was approximately equal to the proportion of physicians aged 60 and over (25.2%).[74] By 2021, this proportion had shifted slightly, with physicians under age 40 representing 29.1% of all physicians in Canada compared with 24.6% for those aged 60 and over.[75]

The change in the demographics of the physicians presents a challenge for the future, as research indicates that both female physicians and older physicians, on average, work fewer hours per week and see fewer patients than their younger male counterparts.[77]

In 2021, there were 312,382 registered nurses (RNs) in Canada, or 816.8 RNs for every 100,000 people. In addition, there were 347 licensed practical nurses (LPNs) per 100,000 people in the population. The overall ratio of roughly 1,235 practicing nurses per 100,000 population puts Canada above the 977 per 100,000-person average of G8 countries (excluding Russia) in 2010.[72,78]

Between 1997 and 2011, the number of practicing nurses rose by 16.3%. The trend of growth has continued, and the 312,382 registered nurses practicing in 2021 represents a 2.5% increase over 2020.[79] The average age of nurses also rose slightly during this period: from 43 to 45 years old for registered nurses, and from 41 to 42 years old for licensed practical nurses. In 2021, registered nurses and licensed practical nurses who were over the age of 55 represented 20.6% and 15.4% of the workforce, respectively.[80] As was seen with their physician counterparts, the nursing workforce is growing older at the same time as the general population ages and demands greater access to healthcare services (see **Table 7-3**).

Table 7-3 Number of Health Professionals per 100,000 Canadians, 2021

Health Profession	Number per 100,000 Population
Optometrists	18
Chiropractors	25
Respiratory therapists	32
Dietitians	33
Psychologists	52
Physiotherapists	70
Dentists	61
Occupational therapists	53
Pharmacists	119
Social workers	177
Physicians	245
Registered nurses (including nurse practitioners)	816
Licensed practical nurses	347
Nurse practitioners	19

Data from Canadian Institute for Health Information. *Health Workforce in Canada, 2017 to 2021: Overview—Data Tables.* CIHI; 2022.

Technology and Equipment

Canada's healthcare system possesses a considerable infrastructure of advanced medical imaging and diagnostic equipment. The CT scan machine was introduced in Canada in 1973. In 2019–2020, there were 549 machines located throughout the country.[81] This represents 14.5 CT scan machines per million people in the population. In 2014, the United Kingdom reported 7.9 per million, and the United States had 44.9 per million in 2019.[81] Among the 37 OECD countries with available data in 2020, Canada ranked 30th in CT units per million population.[81] The OECD average for 2013 was 24.4 CT scan machines per million.[68]

Since 2000, there has been a considerable growth in freestanding private-sector imaging facilities offering CT and MRI scans. In 2003, there were 9 CT machines in freestanding clinics. That number rose to 25 by 2012, which represented 5% of CT machines in the country, and remained at 22 by 2020. Similarly, there were 26 MRI machines located in freestanding clinics in 2003; by 2012, there were 66, which represented 21% of the nation's scanners, and the number remained at 65 MRI units at 60 free-standing institutes through 2020.[81] Interestingly, the funding for these free-standing facilities is different from that for hospital-based machines. For hospitals, the primary source of revenue is the government's health insurance plan; for the freestanding facilities, the primary sources of revenue are private insurance and out-of-pocket payments.

Imaging capacity (whether public or private, hospital-based or freestanding) is largely an urban phenomenon. In Toronto, Montreal, Vancouver, and other large urban settings, the availability of such technology is comparable to, and in some cases slightly less than, that in other industrialized nations. Access to advanced imaging technology in the more sparsely populated areas, such as the Northwest Territories, Newfoundland, and Labrador, is considerably more limited (see **Table 7-4**).[81]

Table 7-4 Medical Imaging Technology per Million Canadians, 2019–2020

Imaging Technology	Number per Million Population
CT scanners	14.5
MRI scanners	10.0
PET/MRI scanners	0.1
PET/CT scanners	1.5
SPECT scanners	8.1
SPECT/CT scanners	7.2

Data from *The Canadian Medical Imaging Inventory 2019–2020*. CADTH; 2021 (CADTH health technology review)

Evaluation of the Healthcare System

Cost

Overall spending on the healthcare system in 2022 reached $331 billion Canadian dollars, approximately $8,563 per Canadian. This represents a 0.8% increase over the prior year, following high growth of 13.2% in 2020 and 7.6% in 2021. Prior to the COVID-19 pandemic, growth in health spending averaged 4% per year from 2015 to 2019. It was estimated that in 2019, total expenditures totaled $269 billion Canadian dollars or approximately $7,166 per Canadian.[73] Expenditures were projected to vary by province within a range of 7% to 15% from the mean. New Brunswick was projected to have the lowest per capita total health expenditure in 2022 at $7,935, and Newfoundland and Labrador to have the highest at $9,750 per person. Expenditures in the territories were projected to be considerably higher in 2022, with Nunavut being the highest at $23,955 per capita.[82] This is primarily due to the small populations and vast geography of the territories. The relationship pattern for provincial and territorial spending has been consistent over the recent past.[54]

Trends in overall healthcare expenditures have varied significantly since 1975. From 1975 until 1991, healthcare costs in Canada rose at a rate of 2.7% per year. As the effect of budget cuts during the 1990s took hold, spending on health decreased dramatically. From 1991 to 1996, healthcare expenditures declined at 0.5% per year, a value less than the overall rate of inflation in the economy, thus representing real dollar cuts in resources. As budgetary restraints were loosened in the late 1990s and early 2000s, the rate of spending began to increase once more. Between 1996 and 2010, the rate of increase in spending rose to 3.3% per year. From 2010 to 2013, spending decreased by an average of 0.6% per year.[54] By the second half of the decade, health spending per capita increased by an average of 1.2% per year. Total health expenditures in Canada reached $331 billion Canadian dollars in 2022, or $8,563 per capita. This follows a surge in spending due to the COVID-19 pandemic, particularly in 2020. Continued spending growth was expected in 2022 as health care that was deferred during the pandemic returned, and demographic factors such as population aging and population growth further contribute to increased spending.[73]

As a percentage of economic output, healthcare expenditures in 2019 represented 11.7% of the nation's GDP. Healthcare expenditures increased to 13.8% of the nation's GDP in 2020.[73] By province, Nova Scotia and Manitoba had the highest spending in relation to the budget, estimated to be 46.0%. Quebec had the lowest spending: 30.0% of the budget. Among the territories, the range varied from Yukon, which spent 18.0% of the budget in 2013, to Nunavut, which is estimated to have spent 29.0%.[54]

Growth in healthcare expenditures as a percentage of GDP displays a trend quite similar to overall spending. In 1975, spending on health care represented 7.0% of GDP. During recession periods, such as that experienced in Canada during the early 1980s, the rate of healthcare spending as a percentage of GDP rose sharply from 6.8% in 1979 to 8.3% in 1983. This reflected the steady rise in healthcare costs as national production slipped. A similar effect was witnessed with the recession in the early 1990s, and for the first time, healthcare expenditures as a percentage of GDP reached 10% in 1992. The effects of government spending cuts lowered health expenditures during the mid-1990s, and as the economy began to expand during the post-recession period, the percentage of GDP consumed by health care dropped to 8.7% in 1997. Between 1998 and 2010, healthcare spending expanded slightly faster than the overall economy, reaching 11.6% of GDP in 2010. Subsequent to the 2009 recession, and prior to COVID-19, health spending growth had been slower than growth in the overall economy, declining to 10.9% of GDP in 2013.[54]

Financing of the Canadian healthcare system is achieved through the convergence of multiple streams of funding. The three primary sources of financing are the Medicare system, out-of-pocket payments by individuals, and private insurance. Since 1997, the division of spending on health care has been relatively set, with the public sector contributing roughly 70.0% of funding and the private sector generating 30.0% from out-of-pocket payments, private insurance payment for services not covered under Medicare, and nonconsumption revenue.[83] In 2019, the overall per capita spending of $7,166 Canadian dollars consisted of $5,010.50 from public sources and $2,155.30 from private sector funds.[73] Among private-sector funding, there has been a significant shift in recent years in the mix of out-of-pocket payments and private health insurance coverage. In 1988, 29.2% of private-sector spending was contributed by private insurance; by 2013, that percentage had risen to 41.3%.[54]

Medicare spending represents the majority of healthcare spending in Canada. Funding for Medicare is derived from tax revenues collected at both the federal and provincial levels. Federal support is delivered through Canada Health Transfer per-capita block grants to the provinces.[54,83,84] Prior to 2014, block grants were composed of two components: actual cash transfers and tax point transfers. Beginning in 2014/2015, Health Transfers converted to cash only, to provide comparable treatment for all residents regardless of where they live.[85] The actual percentage of expenditures under Medicare that the federal government pays compared with what the provinces pay has varied considerably over time. In 1980, the federal government contributed 30.6% of public funds allocated to health care; this figure dropped to 21.5% by 1996.[86]

Payment systems for healthcare services vary by provider type and the nature of the service being rendered. Hospitals, regardless of ownership status, are paid through the provincial government based on a global budget for the year. Physician services, in most cases, are handled on a fee-for-service basis. The fee schedule is negotiated annually between the provincial government and the province's medical association.[54,86] Physicians may also be paid under a blended system of fee-for-service and incentive-based payments. This is particularly common with those working in large group practices and community health centers. Some physicians are salaried employees.[54]

Pharmaceuticals are paid for under a mixed method that varies considerably by province. Quebec has a comprehensive prescription drug plan that is financed through tax revenues and that covers the cost of most outpatient drugs. In the majority of Canadian provinces, some portion of outpatient drug costs are supplemented by the government at least for specific segments of the population, such as people with lower incomes and the elderly. For the remainder of the population, the bulk of outpatient prescription drug costs are paid for through private insurance or out-of-pocket payments. This issue is complicated by the fact that provincial laws prohibit the marketing of insurance products for services covered under public health insurance.[73]

Quality

The quality of a healthcare system can be measured in numerous dimensions. Three measures are population health, system efficiency, and patient perception/satisfaction. Several clinical measures are routinely used for the comparative assessment of healthcare systems. These include infant mortality rates, life expectancy, and immunization rates. Efficiency measures refer to wait times for procedures or services.

The overall infant mortality rate in Canada in 2022 was 4.3 infant deaths per 1,000 live births. This rate represents a slight decrease from 1980, when the infant mortality rate was 10.9 per 1,000 live births. The rates differed by gender, with deaths among male infants occurring at a rate of 4.5 per 1,000 live births and among female infants at a rate of 4.0 deaths per 1,000 live births.[87] This is close to the OECD national average of 4.1 infant deaths per 1,000 live births in 2018. Infant mortality rates are higher in the United States, at 5.6 deaths per 1,000 live births, and lower in the United Kingdom, at 3.7 infant deaths per 1,000 live births in 2019.[63] The overall rates in Canada do not present the full picture, as the infant mortality rate is significantly higher in some subpopulations. Residents of rural Nunavut Territory had an infant mortality rate in 2022 of 5.6, which is greater than the national average that year. Similarly, members of the First Nations have been found to have higher infant mortality rates than the nation as a whole. Disparities also exist in infant mortality rates between people in the top quartile of income and those in the bottom quartile.[88]

Life expectancy at birth has been rising among Canadians. In 2020, the overall life expectancy at birth was 81.7 years. In 2020, men had an expected longevity of 79.5 years and women lived, on average, 84.0 years.[63] Each of these longevity markers is significantly above the OECD averages and surpasses those of both the United Kingdom and the United States.[89] Disparities in life expectancy do, however, continue to exist within certain subpopulations. Men of Indigenous heritage live, on average, 7.0 years less than the national average. Likewise, Indigenous women live an average of 5.0 years less than the Canadian average.[88] The data are unclear regarding variations in life expectancy among other minority groups, although some differences in mortality have been observed between White and Black adult Canadians, depending in part on cause of death.[90,91]

Immunization rates in Canada are high across the population. In 2019, 90% of children received an immunization for measles, mumps, and rubella by their second birthday. Similarly, 90% of children received an immunization for polio by age 2. Rates of other internationally recommended childhood vaccinations are also high. Approximately 80% of adolescents aged 12 to 14 years were immunized for HPV, and by age 17, almost 90% of children were immunized for hepatitis B.[92]

Waiting time for appointments is an issue that has garnered considerable attention in the Canadian healthcare system. A 2020 survey indicated that Canadians waited longer to see a physician than did their counterparts in 10 other countries, including the United States, the United Kingdom, Germany, and Australia. When attempting to see a specialist, 38% of Canadians waited less than 1 month, and another 62% waited for 4 months or more—the lowest and highest proportions, respectively, of the 11 countries surveyed.[93] Similarly, wait times for diagnostic testing varied among the provinces. Median wait times for MRIs ranged from 32 to 55 days.[94] Wait times are a significant issue with Canadians, although only about one-fifth of the population considers the current circumstances "unacceptable."

Overall, Canadians are quite satisfied with their healthcare system. In 2005, 84.4% of Canadians rated their satisfaction with health services as "very satisfied" or "somewhat satisfied." These results have been stable since 2000.[95] Furthermore, in a 2020 survey, 65% of Canadians rated the overall performance of their healthcare system as "good" or "very good."[93] For the most part, Canadians are satisfied with their system and, in some studies, are noted to be proud of its fundamental attributes, especially the degree of equity it achieves. It is a subtle but important point that can easily be lost in cross-national comparisons; Canadians are particularly proud of the perceived fairness of their system. Changes not experienced in an equitable manner would not be viewed as improvements.

Access

Universal coverage is one of the five core principles of the Canadian healthcare system. All residents of Canada not specifically designated as being covered under another federal health insurance program are entitled to coverage for hospital and physician services under the national health insurance plan, Medicare. The cornerstone of the Canadian philosophy of health care is equality among people.[55] Since the introduction of Medicare, it has been an expressed intent that a two-tiered system of health care not only be avoided but actively prevented from developing in Canada. It is felt that need, not financial position, should be the basis on which the allocation of healthcare resources is decided. Although disparities in health care do exist in Canada, they are based on processes that are not rooted in strictly defined financial access to physician and hospital services.[54]

Health insurance coverage substantially reduces financial barriers to obtaining care but does not eliminate all of them. Other expenses (e.g., transportation to site of care and the costs of uncovered services) are also impediments. The influence of such costs is disproportionately felt by people with lower incomes, creating differential impacts on access to care.

Beyond financial issues, access to care can be constrained by geographic, social, cultural, psychological, and other attributes of both the potential recipient of care and the potential provider of services. In Canada, the wide expanses of rural areas and the resulting travel times are a significant barrier to access. Similarly, harsh winter weather and language issues (including French/English differences, and communication by recent immigrants or others for whom either French or English would be a second language) have been cited as impeding access to care. For the most part, the Canadian population views access to care in much the same way that it views other elements of the system, strongly emphasizing questions of equity and fairness.

Virtually all Canadians are covered by one of the varieties of health insurance programs sponsored by some level of government; however, a relatively small number of people (200,000–500,000) remain uninsured.[96] The people who fall into this category are primarily recent immigrants and refugees to Canada, expatriates, and others for whom participation in health insurance coverage is pending final resolution of their immigration or residence status.[97]

Current and Emerging Issues and Challenges

Canada will face several healthcare challenges as the 21st century proceeds. Among the more prominent issues facing the Canadian system are the financial sustainability of the system as currently structured, questions about access to care (generally focused on system capacity), concerns about outpatient pharmaceuticals, debates about the appropriate role of the private sector, and continuing conversations about the importance of equity in assessing system performance.

In recent years, there has been considerable discussion regarding the sustainability of the Canadian healthcare system.[98,99] If considering solely the financial capacity of the nation as a whole to shoulder the rising costs of health care, international comparisons of health expenditures as a percentage of GDP indicate that Canada is operating well within a supportable and sustainable range.[68,98–100] Although annual federal budget surpluses prior to COVID-19 indicated that the nation was in a solid position to sustain the healthcare system,[22] the economic challenges of the pandemic have placed a near-term revenue strain on governments at both the federal and provincial levels.[101–103] While budget deficits have declined since their peaks in 2021, the financial strains of COVID-19 have helped to fuel a resurgence in calls at the provincial level for the federal government to bear an increased share of the costs of health care.[104,105] Federal overtures for increases in the transfers to the provinces for health care have been met with skepticism by provincial leaders, who want longer-term commitments from Ottawa, not temporary or one-time increases in the transfers.[104]

The 2002 Commission on the Future of Health Care in Canada, commonly referred to as the Romanow Commission, considered the topic of sustainability and determined that the real issue was not the actual financial burden but rather the willingness of the Canadian people and their governments to accept and bear the expense of universal health care. With respect to this, the commission found that Canadians were resolved to the preservation of their healthcare system in the face of increased costs of health care as long as the system was responsive to the needs and expectations of the people.[98] From this perspective, the financial sustainability of the system is intimately tied to its performance in terms of meeting the requirements of the Canadian people. The terminology is noteworthy—needs, requirements, and expectations are not the same as demand in the sense that the latter term is employed in orthodox economic terminology. Thus, it seems clear that the central element of Canadian health policy conversations in the coming years will be bending the cost curve while maintaining access to timely, high-quality health care.[98,106]

Achieving these diverse aims will be particularly challenging given the ever-changing political landscape of a democratic nation and the shift that has occurred over the last decade in the health policy dynamic between Ottawa and the provinces. Since 2011, the central government has attempted to divest itself of much of the guidance and administrative responsibilities for the healthcare system.

This shift has led to an even greater level of reliance on the provincial and territorial governments. This expands the traditional role of the provinces as the incubators of innovation, making them now drivers in bending the cost curve while addressing issues of access and quality.

Provincial-level reforms to control costs, improve access, and enhance the quality of care have focused on several areas, most notably the regionalization of healthcare system decision making,[107] primary care system reform,[108–110] and, to a lesser degree, hospital payment reform.[111] While the varied initiatives undertaken by the various provinces to improve these systems-level objectives have produced some encouraging results, no clear directions forward have as of yet emerged.

It is important to recognize that problems with access to care in the Canadian context do not refer to the same financial access (insurance coverage) issues that exist in the United States and in many other nations. Rather, the focal concerns in Canada are primarily questions of availability (including distance, travel times, and wait times, coupled with social, psychological, demographic, and similar elements of use and access, all noted by Andersen[112] and many other analysts of healthcare utilization).[113] In recent years, this part of the access conversation has focused heavily on waiting times and on a general perception that waiting times can and should be reduced by increasing service capacity.

It is reasonably well documented that waiting times for a significant number of services and procedures are longer in Canada than in comparable nations.[114] This international comparison, however, is less significant than the emerging perception among a substantial number of Canadians that some wait times, especially for appointments with primary care doctors, specialty referrals, some imaging procedures, and a relatively specific list of surgical interventions, are simply too long.[115]

In general, wait times for services can be attributed to both supply and demand factors, and given the evolving circumstances of the Canadian healthcare sector, it would seem likely that wait times will lengthen without some alteration in the status quo. Changes in the supply of and demand for health care caused by the shifting demographics of both the general population and the healthcare professions represent one of the most significant factors related to access to care that Canadians will have to face in the coming years. As the population continues to age, greater demands will be placed on the healthcare system. The human resources necessary to meet the evolving needs of the population must be identified, trained, and placed. This will be a challenge as the physician workforce transitions into a cohort that is older and more evenly distributed in terms of gender. Both older physicians and female physicians, on average, work fewer hours than their younger male colleagues.[72] This presents a situation in which either the number of physicians per population must be increased or steps must be taken to increase the productivity of the existing physician supply or to provide for a comparable set of services from other professionals. One such step that is currently taking form in Canada is the integration of nurse practitioners into the healthcare setting. While in 2000 only seven jurisdictions in Canada permitted the licensure of nurse practitioners,[72] now all 13 provinces and territories have licensing statutes in place.

The overall supply of physicians is not the only concern related to healthcare availability. Access to primary care physicians also continues to be an issue in many areas of Canada. Although physicians practicing in the primary care fields of family medicine and general practice represent more than 51% of Canadian physicians, it has been observed that getting appointments with them can be difficult.[72] Efforts to increase the availability and accessibility of primary care practitioners to meet the demands of the Canadian people (especially those residing in rural, sparsely populated areas) will certainly be a significant policy focus of the next decade.[98]

As a result of budget cuts in the 1980s and 1990s, the infrastructure for providing many technologically advanced services has not expanded at a rate that aligns with the growth in demand for these services.[116] This gap in the available supply of physical infrastructure has compounded issues arising from the decline in the real number of physicians practicing in Canada. Similarly, the construction of new hospital capacity, additional long-term care beds, assisted-living facilities, and other capital-intensive projects lagged over the same period. While efforts to increase and enhance primary prevention and other public (population) health initiatives may serve to mitigate this downward trend in the availability of some medical services, the gap between capacity and demand will remain a significant policy issue.

In the five decades since Canada's Medicare program was introduced in the 1960s, there have been considerable changes in the manner in which medical services are provided. Fifty years ago, hospital costs were overwhelmingly the "big-ticket" component of total costs. Physician services were a somewhat distant second. Long-term care was a far distant third, and pharmaceuticals were just barely part of the picture. In 2014, outpatient pharmaceuticals constituted the second leading cost among national health expenditures,[54] accounting for $33.9 billion Canadian dollars, 15.7% of total healthcare spending. This figure does not include expenditures on many of the most expensive drugs (such as cancer treatment drugs) that are delivered only in inpatient settings as a part of hospital care. Under the federal legislation that enacted Medicare, outpatient drugs are not a required item of the provincial plans. Many provinces do offer coverage for certain segments of the population, but the scope varies greatly by province, ranging from a low in 2008 of 9.0% of the population receiving either direct coverage or premium supplements in Manitoba to 43.0% in Quebec. Over 75.0% of Canadians have some form of prescription drug coverage, primarily private-sector insurance.[117] Estimates from 2023 suggest that 43% of outpatient pharmaceutical spending was paid for through public-sector sources, with the remaining 58.0% coming from private insurance (37%) and out-of-pocket funds (20%).

In a nation where there is virtually universal insurance coverage for major medical expenses from hospitalization and physician services, having nearly a quarter of the population be without coverage for the second leading source of medical expenses represents a significant issue. This issue is compounded by the wide variation in the degree of coverage provided under both public- and private-sector drug plans. These geographic variations in coverage have led to significant concerns over the equity of the system. Compounding the concerns over equity is the view, in many circles, that by having such a fragmented system of insurance for pharmaceuticals, the system is forfeiting the opportunity to leverage scale to negotiate better pricing with manufacturers. Addressing cost and equity issues in outpatient pharmaceuticals is likely to be a pressing issue in the coming years whether it continues to be addressed at the provincial level or through a national effort. In a different vein, outpatient drugs present another challenge for the Canadian healthcare system: cross-border sales to citizens of the United States. Because of the regulation of prices for patented medicines in Canada, the consumer costs are lower for some brand-name medications than in the United States. As a result, at least since the 1990s, there has been a growing business in the sale of prescription drugs to Americans both in traditional over-the-counter sales and through Internet pharmacies. Some estimates place the total upward of $1.2 billion Canadian dollars in annual sales, accounting for about 10% of Canadian retail pharmaceutical sales.[118]

There has been a growing concern in recent years over the potential of this cross-border industry to jeopardize drug availability in Canada or to prompt U.S. drug manufacturers to either withhold sale of medications to Canada or greatly increase their wholesale prices. Some anecdotal evidence supports the contention that localized drug shortages in Canada are attributable to the international resale of pharmaceuticals.[118] The 2003 granting of prescription drug coverage for U.S. Medicare participants in the United States was expected to decrease the total demand for medications from Canada. Even so, in the years to come, this friction point in Canadian–U.S. relations will need to be addressed.

There has also been some movement in Canada toward developing private health insurance products to support the financing of services that are also covered under Medicare. In a widely reported 2005 decision, the Canadian Supreme Court struck down Quebec's statute prohibiting the sale of insurance products that would provide payment for any services covered under the provincial Medicare plan.[119] Technically, this decision is germane only to Quebec, but other similar cases are under consideration in courts across Canada. In response to this judicial direction, some political forces are being marshaled to accomplish whatever constitutional change is necessary to effectively overturn the court's ruling.

At the core of the Supreme Court's ruling is that the government has a responsibility to provide the services covered under Medicare in a timely fashion to prevent undue pain and risk of death. If the government fails to meet these obligations, the statutory prohibition of people going outside of the public system to obtain care is unconstitutional under the laws of Quebec.[120] Although the long-term consequences of the movement toward privatization and the Supreme Court's decision are not clear at present, this certainly will be a central element in the future health policy debate in Canada.

Beyond these questions of supply, the changing composition of medical care, and some unique relationship issues that arise because of its proximity to the United States, Canada faces an ongoing, perhaps perpetual, review and reconsideration of a fundamental philosophical question. Since the inception of publicly financed health insurance in Canada, the nation's health care and health policy conversations have entailed a delicate balancing act with three core values: (1) a respect for and commitment to communal action; (2) a faith in the abilities and power of free market economics, competition, and the private sector; and (3) a belief that the distribution of services, perhaps especially health services, should be achieved in a manner that is equitable, fair, and just. Balancing these three core values led to the development of a system that uses community orientation for financing and making major capital decisions; leaves the individual medical care transactions in the private realm of the patient, the family, and the provider; and expects everyone to play the same game, on the same field, and by the same rules. This conversation can perhaps be best understood by returning to the question of waiting times.

In 1978, Canadians were the most satisfied nation in the world with regard to their healthcare system. By 2001, a significant majority of Canadians felt that the country needed to make "fundamental changes."[121] Much of this continuing conversation has focused on waiting lists and a public perception that waiting lists for care in Canada are creating a migration of patients to the United States to receive healthcare services. Some estimates have placed the expenditures outside Canadian borders in the range of $1 billion Canadian dollars per year.

It is clear that, to some degree, this phenomenon is real. In fact, a few Canadian provinces have standing agreements with providers in the United States to handle overflow demand for certain services at their facilities. Indeed, some such agreements are reciprocal. Canadian hospitals located near the international border are part of emergency surge plans and offer other capacity management support to their U.S. colleagues. There is no question that some level of cross-national service delivery occurs. Some of these arrangements are contractually sanctioned. Some reflect the capacity of wealthy individuals to obtain whatever care they seek in whatever setting they prefer and at whatever time meets their priorities, presuming that they have the resources necessary to implement those decisions. Despite the publicity, the evidence, when taken together, suggests that this is a relatively infrequent phenomenon. A 2002 study indicated that the majority of healthcare expenditures by or on behalf of Canadians in the United States were the result of incidental occurrences while traveling on vacation or business and were not due to some form of medical tourism.[122]

Concern about waiting times has given rise to renewed consideration of whether Canadians would, in general, prefer that the system continues under its current form, guided by the five principles of the Canada Health Act, or that it be modified to embrace a greater degree of privatization in the organization and financing of health services. Although there are, and have always been, some advocates who argue for a greater private role in Canadian health care, the momentum behind the current discussion can be traced back to the perception of increased difficulties in obtaining services that began during the 1990s.[123]

At the crux of this privatization agenda is the view that the current system is failing to meet the needs of the population in terms of timely health services and that the rigors of market opportunities and constraints might be valuable in providing more services. Given the historical commitment of the nation to free market principles, it certainly should be no surprise that this proposition would be considered. It is seen by many as an obvious way to bolster the infrastructure for the delivery of high-technology services, which are perceived as being in short supply.[120] Such proposals, however, are quickly extended to a discussion of whether any newly developed "private" capacity would be universally accessible or available only to some subset of the population who would be willing and able to use the new services by virtue of their private economic circumstances. Opponents of increased privatization assert that private capacity would violate the "just, fair, and equitable principle" that is a hallmark of the Canada Health Act.[55] Proponents of market initiatives contend that new, private capacity, even if it is available only to some, would "free up" public capacity and hence make access better for all. This stance has not gained much traction to date.

COVID-19 Pandemic

The first known diagnosis in Canada of SARS-CoV-2, the virus that leads to COVID-19, was in Toronto on January 25, 2020.[124] As of January 23, 2023, the total number of COVID-19 cases in Canada had reached almost 4.54 million, with the bulk of cases occurring in Ontario and Quebec.[125] Canada experienced seven distinct surges of COVID-19 between April 2020 and May 2022. By August 2022, there were 44,000 confirmed deaths, most of which occurred during these outbreak periods.[4] Furthermore, an estimated 26,248 excess deaths were reported in the period of March 2020 through October 2021, which correlates to 5.8% more deaths than would otherwise be expected.[126] In the early stages of the pandemic, excess deaths occurred primarily among adults over age 65 with COVID-19, but there was a later increase among younger Canadians, as well.[126] Compared with most other Group of 10 (G10) countries, Canada largely performed better on several measures of the direct impacts of the pandemic, including lower numbers of individuals infected, lower numbers of individuals who died from COVID-19, and lower excess deaths.[124] As an illustration, Canada's rate of COVID-19–related deaths was 919 per million, the second lowest among comparable countries, and significantly lower than the cumulative rate of COVID-19–related deaths of 2,730 per million in the United States.[124] It is important to note that the health impacts of COVID-19 were not universal, and social inequality contributed to substantial differences in COVID-19 cases, hospitalizations, and death.[127] Overall, the COVID-19 mortality rate in Canada was significantly higher among Indigenous populations and for some (but not all) minority group populations, compared with the overall national rate.[128]

Public health in Canada has federal, provincial, and regional oversight, and Canadian provinces primarily determined which strategies to employ for containment and mitigation of COVID-19.[129] Canadian provinces and territories implemented various public health control measures including, but not limited to, school closures, closing nonessential businesses such as bars and restaurants, mandating the use of masks in public spaces, and limiting contact among people.[130] Social distancing was a key measure adopted in Canada, and by late March 2020, all provinces had mandated closing of schools, universities, public playgrounds, and nonessential businesses, with federal and provincial government encouraging all nonessential individuals to stay home.[129] Social interactions with individuals not living in the same household were actively discouraged, and gatherings outside of households were limited to a size of five to 10 people, with variation by province.[129] Canada also issued a series of travel warnings and restrictions in 2020, ranging from urging citizens to avoid nonessential travel to China to ending the allowance of entry of foreign nationals from any country other than United States. In March 2020, Canada closed the land border with the United States for the first time since Canada was founded.[129] The Quarantine Act, established in 2005 in response to the severe acute respiratory syndrome (SARS) crisis of 2003,[131] was also implemented, requiring everyone who entered the country to self-quarantine for 14 days.[129]

Additional crucial public health measures during the COVID-19 pandemic included testing for COVID-19, masking, and vaccination efforts. The capacity for COVID-19 polymerase chain reaction (PCR) testing in the early stages of the pandemic was limited in many regions of Canada but gradually increased and was widely available throughout the country by June 2020.[129] Public health agencies in Canada expanded the workforce for contact tracing efforts, and mask mandates were instituted in Quebec, Nova Scotia, and parts of Ontario and Alberta in July 2020.[129] Health Canada approved the first vaccine (Pfizer-BioNTech) on December 9, 2020.[132] Through 2022, people in Canada had received a variety of vaccine series, with the most common series containing only the Pfizer-BioNTech vaccine.[133] Vaccination mandates were instituted in 2021 in multiple sectors in Canada, including vaccine mandates for employees from both public and private enterprises, mandated proof of vaccination for entry to nonessential services from provincial governments, and mandated vaccination for air and train travel from the federal government.[134] Overall, Canada was among the slowest countries to begin vaccination, but vaccination rates quickly increased in the second half of 2021 and, as of February 2022, Canada had the highest proportion of fully vaccinated people at 79.9%.[124,132] Comparatively, and despite having the most rapid initial uptake, the United States had the lowest proportion of fully vaccinated people at 63.9%.[124]

A potential area of future public health concern for Canada is the relatively low rate of individuals who have received third and fourth doses of the vaccine, with only 51% of the Canadian population receiving a third dose.[134] As of January 1, 2023, 25% of the Canadian population had completed the primary series or received a booster dose of a COVID-19 vaccine within the previous 6 months.[133]

Canada enacted some of the most restrictive public health measures across a broad range of domains, such as those previously described related to school closures and restrictions on public gatherings, in efforts to mitigate the spread of COVID-19. In the early stages of the pandemic, Canadians were generally compliant with the COVID-19 precautions instituted, with some variation. Characteristics found to be associated with lower levels of compliance included being male, being younger than 35 years old, and living in one of the territorial capitals or in a rural area.[124,130] Studies have found that women and older adults in Canada have more trust in public health measures and are more confident in their ability to comply with precautions enacted.[130] Although public adherence to the public health measures enacted was high during the first wave of the COVID-19 pandemic, orders to remain at home during the second and third waves were comparatively more contentious, and there was a smaller reduction in mobility and personal contact following government mandates in subsequent surges.[132] Protests developed in Ottawa, Canada's capital city, in February 2022 in opposition to public health measures affecting cross-border trucking and expanded to include demands for removal of all COVID-19 mandates and restrictions.[134] The protests continued for 4 weeks, and the prime minister instituted the Emergency Measures Act for the first time in Canadian history. Prior to the protests, the majority of provinces already had plans to ease most restrictive measures, such as proof of vaccination requirements and masking mandates, and the provinces followed through and removed most public health measures.[134] The federal government additionally removed COVID-19 testing requirements for entry to Canada in April 2022.[134] Nonetheless, despite the challenges discussed, there has generally been a favorable response to COVID-19 public health initiatives in Canada and relatively high levels of compliance among the population.

The pandemic has had significant direct and indirect health impacts in Canada and will affect the future health of Canadians for years to come. Canada has implemented plans to strengthen surveillance and public health guidance, including the creation of the Centre for Research on Pandemic Preparedness and Health Emergencies in January 2022, with an ongoing investment of $18.5 million Canadian dollars per year. In collaboration with other federal departments and agencies, as well as domestic and international stakeholders, this center aims to be a leader in "preventing, preparing for, responding to, and recovering from existing and future pandemics and public health emergencies."[4]

Conclusion

During the 1980s and 1990s, Canada made political and fiscal decisions that curtailed the development of the nation's physical healthcare infrastructure and perhaps its supply of healthcare personnel. The consequences of these decisions are particularly evident in the areas of diagnostic technology and complex procedures. Waiting times for these services continue to range beyond those of comparable nations. Privatization initiatives have taken place for these services, including an increase in the number of private imaging service delivery sites (freestanding CT and MRI clinics). For proponents of some privatization, there is hope that the approach taken to imaging might be extended to include such services as complex procedural interventions and appointments with specialists. For those opposed to any privatization not universally accessible, the same outcome is viewed with concern.[135]

Canadians still overwhelmingly support their healthcare system, and this support is indicated by favorable satisfaction rates. Their satisfaction with the system includes giving it very high marks for fairness and its achievement of community obligations, but concerns over individual access to certain areas of care are pervasive. The late Paul Farmer famously postulated a distinction between healthcare issues in a context of affluence from those in a context of lower wealth and incomes.[136] In general, Canada is a relatively wealthy nation and Canadians are overall an affluent, well-educated population. Their needs and expectations in terms of health care reflect that status and are compounded by geographic, economic, and cultural proximity to the United States. To preserve the essential features of their healthcare system will require that the nation confront and meaningfully address the needs and expectations experienced at both the individual and community levels.[98] In the near term, it appears that efforts to overcome the challenges and reach the health system's multifaceted objectives will be driven by and played out in the provinces and territories.

References

1. Central Intelligence Agency. Canada. In: *The World Factbook. 2021*. Accessed January 20, 2023. https://www.cia.gov/the-world-factbook/about/archives/2021/countries/canada.
2. Statistics Canada. Table 98-10-0324-01. Visible minority and population group by generation status: Canada, provinces and territories, census metropolitan areas and census agglomerations with parts. Accessed February 5, 2024. https://www150.statcan.gc.ca/t1/tbl1/en/tv.action?pid=9810032401.
3. Statistics Canada. Religiosity in Canada and its evolution from 1985 to 2019. Accessed February 15, 2023. https://www150.statcan.gc.ca/n1/pub/75-006-x/2021001/article/00010-eng.htm.
4. Pan American Health Organization. Health in the Americas. Canada—country profile. 2022. Accessed January 24, 2023. https://hia.paho.org/en/countries-22/canada-country-profile#mortality.
5. Government of Canada. Estimates of HIV incidence, prevalence and Canada's progress on meeting the 90-90-90 HIV targets. 2020. Accessed February 15, 2023. https://www.canada.ca/en/public-health/services/publications/diseases-conditions/estimates-hiv-incidence-prevalence-canada-meeting-90-90-90-targets-2020.html#a2.
6. Dickason O. *Canada's First Nations: A History of Founding Peoples from Earliest Times*. 3rd ed. Toronto, ON: Oxford University Press; 2002.
7. Bumsted J. *The Peoples of Canada: A Pre-Confederation History*. 2nd ed. Toronto, ON: Oxford University Press; 2003.
8. Brune N. A history of Canada online. Accessed February 15, 2008. http://canadachannel.ca/2/2Avikings.php.
9. Morton D. *A Short History of Canada*. 6th ed. Toronto, ON: McClelland & Stewart; 2006.
10. Bumsted J. *The Peoples of Canada: A Post-Confederation History*. 3rd ed. Toronto, ON: Oxford University Press; 2007.
11. Horn M. *The Great Depression of the 1930s in Canada*. Canadian Historical Association; 1984. Accessed October

2016. http://www.collectionscanada.gc.ca/cha-shc/008004-%0A119.01-e.php?&b_id=H-39ψnbr=1&brws=y&&page_id=H-39-EN-4671406&&&&&PHPSESSID=bgbuuv4ucgkg1rs6rt0dpq1267.

12. Ostry A. The roots of North America's first comprehensive public health insurance system. *Hygiea Internationalis*. 2001;2(1):25-44. Accessed October 16, 2016. http://www.ep.liu.se/ej/hygiea/ra/007/paper.pdf.
13. Statistics Canada. 2021 Census of population—Canada. Accessed January 2023. https://www12.statcan.gc.ca/census-recensement/2021/dp-pd/prof/details/page.cfm?Lang=E&DGUIDList=2021A000011124&GENDERList=1,2,3&STATISTICList=1&HEADERList=0&SearchText=Canada.
14. Statistics Canada. Population, urban and rural, by province and territory. Accessed May 11, 2016. http://www.statcan.gc.ca/tables-tableaux/sum-som/l01/cst01/demo62a-eng.htm/.
15. Government of Canada. *Canadians and Their Government: A Resource Guide*. Published 2008. Accessed October 25, 2016. http://publications.gc.ca/collections/collection_2009/pc-ch/CH4-70-2008E.pdf.
16. Elections Canada. *The Electoral System of Canada*. 4th ed. 2015. Accessed October 16, 2016. http://www.elections.ca/content.aspx?section=res&dir=ces&document=index&lang=e.
17. Government of Canada. *The Structure of the Canadian Government*. 2007. Accessed February 25, 2008. http://canada.gc.ca/howgoc/glance_e.html.
18. Underhill FH. *Canadian Political Parties*. Canadian Historical Association; 1974. Accessed October 2016. http://www.collectionscanada.gc.ca/cha-shc/008004-119.01-e.php?&b_id=H-8ψnbr=1&brws=y&&PHPSESSID=bgbuuv4ucgkg1rs6rt0dpq1267.
19. Bernier J. *Disease, Medicine, and Society in Canada: A Historical Overview*. Canadian Historical Association; 2003:63. Accessed October 25, 2016. http://www.collectionscanada.gc.ca/cha-shc/008004-119.01-e.php?&b_id=H-63ψnbr=1&brws=y&&PHPSESSID=bgbuuv4ucgkg1rs6rt0dpq1267.
20. Maioni A. Parting at the crossroads: the development of health insurance in Canada and the United States, 1940–1965. *Comp Polit*. 1997;29(4):411-431. doi:10.2307/422012.
21. World Bank. Data by country, Canada. Accessed January 20, 2023. https://data.worldbank.org/country/canada.
22. Statistics Canada. Consumer price index, November 2022. Accessed January 20, 2023. https://www150.statcan.gc.ca/n1/daily-quotidien/221221/dq221221a-eng.htm?indid=3665-1&indgeo=0.
23. Statistics Canada. Labour force characteristics by province, monthly, seasonally adjusted. Accessed January 20, 2023. https://www150.statcan.gc.ca/t1/tbl1/en/tv.action?pid=1410028703.
24. Wang W. The COVID-19 pandemic and gross domestic product per capita growth in Canada. In: *Economic and Social Reports*. Statistics Canada; 2022. Accessed February 21, 2023. https://www150.statcan.gc.ca/n1/pub/36-28-0001/2022005/article/00002-eng.htm.
25. Statistics Canada. Gross domestic product (GDP) at basic prices, by industry, monthly, growth rates. 2022. Accessed January 23, 2023. https://www150.statcan.gc.ca/t1/tbl1/en/tv.action?pid=3610043402.
26. Transport Canada, Government of Canada. Advisory Circular (AC) No. 302-032. 2019. Accessed January 23, 2023. https://tc.canada.ca/en/aviation/reference-centre/advisory-circulars/advisory-circular-ac-no-302-032#toc55.
27. Council of Ministers of Education, Canada. *The Development of Education*. 2008. Accessed January 18, 2023. http://www.cmec.ca/Publications/Lists/Publications/Attachments/122/ICE2008-reports-canada.en.pdf.
28. Zwaagstra M, Shang M, Kardos A. Six Out of 10 Provinces Increased Per-Student Spending on Public Schools, Even After Adjusting for Inflation. Fraser Institute. August 22, 2024. Accessed January 23, 2025. https://www.fraserinstitute.org/studies/education-spending-in-public-schools-ic-canada-2024#:~:text=Education%20Spending%20in%20Public%20Schools%20in%20Canada%2C,in%202012/13%20to%20$82.5%20billion%20in%202021/22.&text=*%20Per%2Dstudent%20spending%20adjusted%20for%20inflation%20(price,by%205.1%%20nationally%20from%202012/13%20to%202021/22.
29. Statistics Canada. Tourism and the Centre for Education Statistics Education indicators in Canada: an international perspective, 2020. Accessed February 21, 2023. https://www150.statcan.gc.ca/n1/pub/81-604-x/81-604-x2020001-eng.pdf.
30. Statistics Canada. Quarterly demographic estimates, April to June 2022. Accessed January 23, 2023. https://www150.statcan.gc.ca/n1/pub/91-002-x/91-002-x2022002-eng.htm.
31. Statistics Canada. Annual demographic estimates: Canada, provinces and territories, 2022. Accessed January 19, 2023. https://www150.statcan.gc.ca/n1/pub/91-002-x/91-002-x2022002-eng.htm.
32. Statistics Canada. Aboriginal peoples in Canada: First Nations people, Métis and Inuit. 2011. Accessed January 23, 2023. https://www12.statcan.gc.ca/nhs-enm/2011/as-sa/99-011-x/99-011-x2011001-eng.cfm#a6.
33. Statistics Canada. 2021 Census of Population. Statistics Canada Catalogue no. 98-316-X2021001. Ottawa. Released November 15, 2023. Modified August 2, 2024. Accessed February 4, 2025. https://www12.statcan.gc.ca/census-recensement/2021/dp-pd/prof/details/page.cfm?LANG=E&GENDERlist=1,2,3&STATISTIClist=1,4&DGUIDlist=2021A000011124&HEADERlist=37&SearchText=Canada.
34. Statistics Canada. Table 98-10-0387-01. Highest level of education by geography: census divisions. Modified February 5, 2025. Accessed February 5, 2025. https://www150.statcan.gc.ca/t1/tbl1/en/tv.action?pid=9810038701.
35. Statistics Canada. Distribution of total income by census family type and age of older partner, parent or individual. Accessed January 2023. https://www150.statcan.gc.ca/t1/tbl1/en/tv.action?pid=1110001201.
36. World Bank. World development indicators data bank. Accessed January 23, 2023. https://databank.worldbank.org/reports.aspx?frmsrc=search&CNO=2&country=&series=SI.POV.GINI&period=.
37. Statistics Canada. Religiosity in Canada and its evolution from 1985 to 2019. Published 2021. Accessed January 23, 2023. https://www150.statcan.gc.ca/n1/pub/75-006-x/2021001/article/00010-eng.htm.
38. Government of Canada. Fourth annual report on medical assistance in dying in Canada 2022. Modified October 26, 2023. Accessed January 24, 2025. https://www.canada.ca/en/health-canada/services/publications/health-system-services/annual-report-medical-assistance-dying-2022.html.
39. Government of Canada. Heart disease in Canada. Modified July 28, 2022. Accessed January 24, 2025. https://www.canada.ca/en/public-health/services/publications/diseases-conditions/heart-disease-canada.html.
40. Government of Canada. Snapshot of diabetes in Canada, 2023. Public Health Agency of Canada. Modified January 30, 2024. Accessed January 24, 2025. https://www.canada.ca

/en/public-health/services/publications/diseases-conditions/snapshot-diabetes-canada-2023.html.

41. Pan American Health Organization. Health in the Americas, 2017. Accessed January 19, 2023. https://iris.paho.org/bitstream/handle/10665.2/34321/9789275119662_eng.pdf?sequence=6&isAllowed=y.
42. Statistics Canada. An overview of weight and height measurements on World Obesity Day. Modified March 4, 2024. Accessed January 24, 2025. https://www.statcan.gc.ca/o1/en/plus/5742-overview-weight-and-height-measurements-world-obesity-day.
43. Statistics Canada. Health fact sheets: overweight and obese adults, 2018. Data modified June 25, 2019. Accessed January 24, 2025. https://www150.statcan.gc.ca/n1/pub/82-625-x/2019001/article/00005-eng.htm.
44. Statistics Canada. Household population meeting/not meeting the 2020 Canadian physical activity guidelines. Accessed January 2023. https://www150.statcan.gc.ca/t1/tbl1/en/tv.action?pid=1310082101.
45. Government of Canada. Canadian cancer statistics 2021. Accessed January 19, 2023. https://cdn.cancer.ca/-/media/files/research/cancer-statistics/2021-statistics/2021-pdf-en-final.pdf.
46. Statistics Canada. Aboriginal Peoples Survey, 2012. Social determinants of health for the off-reserve First Nations population, 15 years of age and older, 2012. Accessed January 23, 2023. https://www150.statcan.gc.ca/n1/pub/89-653-x/89-653-x2016010-eng.htm.
47. Statistics Canada. Self-perceived general health by Aboriginal identity, age group and sex. Table 41-10-0020-01. 2020. Accessed January 2023. https://www150.statcan.gc.ca/t1/tbl1/en/tv.action?pid=4110002001.
48. Government of Canada. Social determinants and inequities in health for Black Canadians: a snapshot. 2020. Accessed January 30, 2024. https://www.canada.ca/en/public-health/services/health-promotion/population-health/what-determines-health/social-determinants-inequities-black-canadians-snapshot.html/.
49. Starr P. *The Social Transformation of American Medicine*. Basic Books; 1982.
50. Roemer M. *National Health Systems of the World, Volume I: The Countries*. New York, NY: Oxford University Press; 1991.
51. Vayda E. The Canadian health care system: an overview. *J Public Health Policy*. 1986;7(2):205-210. doi:10.2307/3342258.
52. Iglehart JK. Revisiting the Canadian health care system. *N Engl J Med*. 2000;342(26):2007-2012. doi:10.1056/NEJM200006293422624.
53. Rocher F, Smith M. *Federalism and Health Care: The Impact of Political-Institutional Dynamics on the Canadian Health Care System*. Commission on the Future of Health Care in Canada. Discussion Paper No. 18. Published 2002. Accessed February 22, 2008. https://qspace.library.queensu.ca/bitstream/1974/6884/23/discussion_paper_18_e.pdf.
54. Canadian Institute for Health Information. National health expenditure trends 1975–2015. Published 2015. Accessed October 16, 2016. https://secure.cihi.ca/free_products/nhex_trends_narrative_report_2015_en.pdf.
55. Premont M. *The Canada Health Act and the Future of Health Care Systems in Canada*. Commission on the Future of Health Care in Canada. Discussion Paper No. 4. Published 2022. Accessed February 25, 2008. http://www.hcsc.gc.ca/english/pdf/romanow/pdfs/4_Premont_1E.pdf.
56. Marmor T, Maioni A. *One Issue, Two Voices Health Care in Crisis: The Drive for Health Reform in Canada and the United States*. Woodrow Wilson International Center for Scholars; 2008:9. Accessed April 20, 2008. https://papers.ssrn.com/sol3/papers.cfm?abstract_id=1259253.
57. Health Canada. Canada's health care system. Published 2012. Accessed January 23, 2023. https://www.canada.ca/en/health-canada/services/health-care-system/reports-publications/health-care-system/canada.html.
58. Health Canada. First Nations and Inuit health. Accessed January 23, 2023. https://www.sac-isc.gc.ca/eng/1569861171996/1569861324236.
59. Kohn R, Radius S. Two roads to health care: U.S. and Canadian policies, 1945–1975. *Med Care*. 1974;12(3):189-201. doi:10.1097/00005650-197403000-00001.
60. Canadian Institutes of Health Research. The future of public health in Canada: developing a public health system for the 21st century. Published 2003. Accessed March 7, 2008. http://rnao.ca/sites/rnao-ca/files/Future_of_Public_Health_in_Canada_2003.pdf.
61. Hutchison B, Abelson J, Lavis J. Primary care in Canada: so much innovation, so little change. *Health Aff*. 2001;20(3):116-131. doi:10.1377/HLTHAFF.20.3.116.
62. Canadian Association of Community Health Centers. From coverage to access and impact: the evolving role of community health centres in Canada's publicly funded health care system. Accessed January 23, 2023. https://www.nwrpca.org/news/469965/The-Evolving-Role-of-Community-Health-Centres-in-Canadas-Publicly-Funded-Health-Care-System.htm.
63. Organisation for Economic Co-operation and Development. Health Status Data. Accessed January 23, 2023. https://stats.oecd.org/index.aspx?DataSetCode=HEALTH_STAT.
64. Barer M, Morgan S, Evans R. Strangulation or rationalization? Costs and access in Canadian hospitals. *Healthcare Quarterly*. 2003;7(1). doi:10.12927/HCQ.2003.17241.
65. Liu L, Hader J, Brossart B, et al. Impact of rural hospital closures in Saskatchewan, Canada. *Soc Sci Med*. 2001;52(12):1793-1804. doi:10.1016/S0277-9536(00)00298-7.
66. Tully P, Saint-Pierre E. Downsizing Canada's hospitals, 1986/87 to 1994/95. *Health Rep*. 1987;8(4):33-39.
67. Canadian Institute for Health Information. Hospital trends in Canada: results of a project to create a historical series of statistical and financial data for Canadian hospitals over twenty-seven years. Published 2005. Accessed April 9, 2008. https://secure.cihi.ca/free_products/Hospital_Trends_in_Canada_e.pdf.
68. Organisation for Economic Co-operation and Development. *Health at a Glance 2015: OECD Indicators*. Paris: OECD Publishing; 2015. doi:10.1787/health_glance-2015-en.
69. Statistics Canada. Residential care facilities, 2009/10. Residential care facilities by ownership, facility characteristics and geography—Canada. Accessed January 23, 2023. https://www150.statcan.gc.ca/n1/pub/83-237-x/2012001/t001-eng.htm.
70. Statistics Canada. Nursing and residential care facilities in 2020. *The Daily*. 2002. Accessed January 23, 2023. https://www150.statcan.gc.ca/n1/daily-quotidien/221102/dq221102c-eng.htm.
71. Statistics Canada. Accumulated paid hours during year per resident-day in operating residential care facilities by facility characteristics and geography—Canada. Accessed May 12, 2016. http://www.statcan.gc.ca/pub/83-237-x/2012001/%0Atablesectlist-listetableauxsect-eng.htm%0A.
72. Canadian Institute for Health Information. *Canada's Health Care Providers, 1997 to 2011: A Reference Guide*.

2013. Accessed May 8, 2016. https://secure.cihi.ca/estore/productFamily.htm?pf=PFC2161&lang=en&media=0.

73. Canadian Institute for Health Information. National health expenditure trends, 2022. Published 2022. Accessed January 23, 2023. https://www.cihi.ca/en/national-health-expenditure-trends-2022-snapshot.
74. Canadian Institute for Health Information. A profile of physicians in Canada, 2020 [infographic]. Accessed January 23, 2023. https://www.cihi.ca/en/a-profile-of-physicians-in-canada-2020.
75. Canadian Institute for Health Information. *Supply, Distribution and Migration of Physicians in Canada*. Ottawa, ON: CIHI; 2022. doi:10.12/sorting/datetime-moment.js.
76. Bindman AB, Forrest CB, Britt H, et al. Diagnostic score of and exposure to primary care physicians in Australia, New Zealand, and the United States: cross sectional analysis of results from three national surveys. *BMJ*. 2007;334(7606):1261. doi:10.1136/BMJ.39203.658970.55.
77. Chan B. From perceived surplus to perceived shortage: what happened to Canada's physician workforce in the 1990s. Published 2002. Accessed February 15, 2008. https://secure.cihi.ca/free_products/chanjun02.pdf.
78. Canadian Institute for Health Information. Health workforce in Canada, 2017 to 2021—data tables. Published 2022. Accessed January 23, 2023. https://www.cihi.ca.
79. Canadian Nurses Association. Nursing statistics: highlights from the 2021 pan-Canadian statistics on regulated nurses from the Canadian Institute for Health Information (CIHI). Accessed January 23, 2023. https://www.cna-aiic.ca/en/nursing/regulated-nursing-in-canada/nursing-statistics.
80. Canadian Institute for Health Information. Nursing in Canada, 2021: data tables. 2022. Accessed January 23, 2023. https://www.cna-aiic.ca/en/nursing/regulated-nursing-in-canada/nursing-statistics.
81. Canada's Drug and Health Technology Agency. The Canadian medical imaging inventory 2019–2020. Accessed January 23, 2023. https://www.cadth.ca/canadian-medical-imaging-inventory-2019-2020/.
82. Canadian Institute for Health Information. Health expenditure data in brief. Published November 2021. Accessed January 23, 2023. https://www.cihi.ca/sites/default/files/document/health-expenditure-data-in-brief-en.pdf.
83. Canadian Institute for Health Information. Exploring the 70–30 split: how Canada's health care system is financed. Published 2005. Accessed March 28, 2008. https://secure.cihi.ca/estore/productSeries.htm?pc=PCC292.
84. Department of Finance, Canada. History of health and social transfers. Published 2008. Accessed March 28, 2008. https://www.fin.gc.ca/fedprov/his-eng.asp.
85. Department of Finance, Canada. Canada Health Transfers. Accessed October 27, 2016. https://www.fin.gc.ca/fedprov/cht-eng.asp.
86. Naylor C. Health care in Canada: incrementalism under fiscal duress. *Health Aff*. 1999;18(3):9-26. doi:10.1377/HLTHAFF.18.3.9.
87. O'Neill A. Canada: Infant mortality rate from 2012 to 2022. Statista. November 4, 2024. Accessed January 24, 2025. https://www.statista.com/statistics/806726/infant-mortality-in-canada/.
88. Public Health Agency, Canada. Reducing health disparities-roles of the health sector: discussion paper. Published 2005. Accessed April 3, 2008. http://www.phac-aspc.gc.ca/ph-sp/disparities/pdf06/disparities_discussion_paper_e.pdf.
89. Statistics Canada. Life expectancy at birth, by sex, by province, 2012. Accessed January 23, 2023. https://www150.statcan.gc.ca/t1/tbl1/en/tv.action?pid=1310071001.
90. Statistics Canada. Health reports: mortality inequalities of Black adults in Canada. February 15, 2023. Accessed February 5, 2024. doi: https://www.doi.org/10.25318/82-003-x202300200001-eng.
91. Public Health Agency, Canada. Key health inequalities in Canada: a national portrait. Published August 2018. Accessed February 5, 2024. https://www.canada.ca/content/dam/phac-aspc/documents/services/publications/science-research/key-health-inequalities-canada-national-portrait-executive-summary/key_health_inequalities_full_report-eng.pdf.
92. Government of Canada. Vaccination coverage in Canadian children: results from the 2019 childhood National Immunization Coverage Survey (cNICS). Accessed January 20, 2023. https://www.canada.ca/en/public-health/services/publications/vaccines-immunization/2019-childhood-national-immunization-coverage-survey-results.html#a6.4.
93. The Commonwealth Fund. How Canada compares: results from the Commonwealth Fund's 2020 international health policy survey of the general population in 11 countries. Published 2021. Accessed January 20, 2023. https://www.cihi.ca/sites/default/files/document/how-canada-compares-cmwf-survey-2020-chartbook-en.pdf.
94. Canada Institute for Health Information. *Health Care in Canada, 2012: A Focus on Wait Times*. Accessed May 11, 2016. https://secure.cihi.ca/free_products/HCIC2012-FullReport-ENweb.pdf.
95. Health Canada. *Healthy Canadians 2010: A Federal Report on Comparable Health Indicators*; 2011.
96. Barnes S. Health care access for the uninsured in Ontario Symposium Report. 2016. Accessed January 30, 2024. https://www.wellesleyinstitute.com/wp-content/uploads/2017/01/Health-Care-Access-for-the-Uninsured-Symposium-Report.pdf.
97. Caulford P, Vali Y. Providing health care to medically uninsured immigrants and refugees. *CMAJ*. 2006;174(9):1253. doi:10.1503/CMAJ.051206.
98. Romanow R. *Commission on the Future of Health Care in Canada: Final Report*. Published 2002. Accessed February 1, 2008. http://www.cbc.ca/healthcare/final_report.pdf.
99. Dhalla I. Canada's health care system and the sustainability paradox. *CMAJ*. 2007;177(1):51. doi:10.1503/CMAJ.061064.
100. Evans R. Economic myths and political realities: the inequality agenda and the sustainability of Medicare. In: Campbell B, Marchildon G, eds. *Medicare: Facts, Myths, Problems, Promise*. Toronto, ON: James Lorimer; 2007:113-155.
101. Statistics Canada. Consolidated Canadian government finance statistics, 2020. *The Daily*. Accessed February 13, 2023. https://www150.statcan.gc.ca/n1/daily-quotidien/211122/dq211122a-eng.htm.
102. Reuters. Canada records C$314.0 billion budget deficit in fiscal 2020/21. Accessed February 13, 2023. https://www.reuters.com/world/americas/canada-records-c3140-billion-budget-deficit-fiscal-202021-2021-05-28/.
103. Powers L. Ontario budget 2021: Deep deficits as province plots COVID-19 recovery. CBC News. Published 2021. Accessed February 13, 2023. https://www.cbc.ca/news/canada/toronto/ontario-budget-2021-covid-19-doug-ford-1.5962279.

104. Canadian Health Coalition. Provinces reject federal government's offer of more health care funding. Accessed February 13, 2023. https://www.healthcoalition.ca/provinces-reject-federal-governments-offer-of-more-health-care-funding/.
105. CBC News. Premiers emerge from Winnipeg meeting united in call for more federal health-care funding. Published 2022. Accessed February 13, 2023. https://www.cbc.ca/news/canada/manitoba/premier-meeting-winnipeg-health-care-1.6680796.
106. Stolberg HO. The Canadian health care system: past, present, and future. *J Am Coll Radiol*. 2004;1(9):659-670. doi:10.1016/J.JACR.2004.03.021.
107. Barker P, Church J. Revisiting health regionalization in Canada: more bark than bite? *Int J Health Serv*. 2017;47(2):333-351. doi: 10.1177/0020731416681229.
108. Marchildon GP, Sherar M. Doctors and Canadian medical care: improving accountability and performance. *Healthcare Papers*. 2018;14(4):14-26.
109. Church J, Skrypnek R, Smith N. Improving physician accountability through primary care reform in Alberta. *Healthcare Papers*. 2018;14(4):48-55.
110. Rosenberg L. Healthcare delivery and physician accountability in Quebec: a system ready for change. *Healthcare Papers*. 2018;14(4):32-40.
111. Laberge M, Brundisini FK, Champagne M, Daniel I. Hospital funding reforms in Canada: a narrative review of Ontario and Quebec strategies. *Health Res Policy Syst*. 2022;20(1). doi:10.1186/s12961-022-00879-2.
112. Andersen R. Revisiting the behavioral model and access to medical care: does it matter? *J Health Soc Behav*. 1995;36(1):1-10.
113. Baxter N. Equal for whom? Addressing disparities in the Canadian medical system must become a national priority. *CMAJ*. 2007;177(12):1522-1523. doi:10.1503/CMAJ.071578.
114. Health Council of Canada. Fixing the foundation: an update on primary care and home care renewal in Canada. Published 2008. Accessed April 14, 2008. http://publications.gc.ca/collections/collection_2008/hc-sc/H174-14-2008E.pdf.
115. Soroka S. *A report of the Health Council of Canada: Canadian Perceptions of the Health Care System*. Health Council of Canada. Council of Canada; 2007. Accessed April 9, 2008. http://www.queensu.ca/cora/_files/PublicPerceptions.pdf.
116. Canadian Institute for Health Information. MIT selected medical imaging equipment in Canada, MIT 2012 data release—static figures and tables. Published 2012. Accessed May, 2016. https://www.cihi.ca/en/types-of-care/specialized-services/medical-imaging/mit-selected-medical-imaging-equipment-in-canada.
117. Demers V, Melo M, Jackevicius C, et al. Comparison of provincial prescription drug plans and the impact on patients' annual drug expenditures. *CMAJ*. 2008;178(4):405-409. doi: 10.1503/CMAJ.070587.
118. Voelker R. Northern Rx-posure: US, Canada clash on cross-border medication sales. *JAMA*. 2003;290(22):2921-2925. doi: 10.1001/JAMA.290.22.2921.
119. Ouellet R. The Chaoulli decision: a debate in which physicians must be heard. *CMAJ*. 2005;173(8):896. doi: 10.1503/CMAJ.051132.
120. Steinbrook R. Private health care in Canada. *N Engl J Med*. 2006;354(16):1661-1664. doi: 10.1056/NEJMP068064.
121. Tuohy CH. The costs of constraint and prospects for health care reform in Canada. *Health Aff*. 2002;21(3):32-46. doi: 10.1377/HLTHAFF.21.3.32.
122. Katz SJ, Cardiff K, Pascali M, et al. Phantoms in the snow: Canadians' use of health care services in the United States. *Health Aff*. 2002;21(3):19-31. doi: 10.1377/HLTHAFF.21.3.19.
123. Kenny N, Chafe R. Pushing right against the evidence: turbulent times for Canadian health care. *Hastings Cent Rep*. 2007;37(5):24-26. doi: 10.1353/HCR.2007.0073.
124. Razak F, Shin S, Naylor CD, Slutsky AS. Canada's response to the initial 2 years of the COVID-19 pandemic: a comparison with peer countries. *CMAJ*. 2022;194(25):E870-E877. doi: 10.1503/CMAJ.220316/tab-related-content.
125. Government of Canada. COVID-19 epidemiology update: key updates. Published January 23, 2022. Accessed January 24, 2023. https://health-infobase.canada.ca/covid-19/.
126. Statistics Canada. COVID-19 in Canada: a two-year update on social and economic impacts. Published 2020. Accessed January 24, 2023. https://www150.statcan.gc.ca/n1/pub/11-631-x/11-631-x2022001-eng.htm.
127. Government of Canada. Social inequalities in COVID-19 deaths in Canada. Accessed January 23, 2023. https://health-infobase.canada.ca/covid-19/inequalities-deaths/technical-report.html.
128. Gupta S, Aitken N. COVID-19 mortality among racialized populations in Canada and its association with income. StatCan COVID-19: data to insights for a better Canada. Published 2022. Accessed January 23, 2023. https://www150.statcan.gc.ca/n1/pub/45-28-0001/2022001/article/00010-eng.htm.
129. Detsky AS, Bogoch II. COVID-19 in Canada: experience and response. *JAMA*. 2020;324(8):743-744. doi: 10.1001/JAMA.2020.14033.
130. Cabot J, Bushnik T. Compliance with precautions to reduce the spread of COVID-19 in Canada. *Health Rep*. 2022;33(9). doi: 10.25318/82-003-X202200900001-ENG.
131. *The Canadian Encyclopedia*. Quarantine Act. Accessed February 16, 2023. https://www.thecanadianencyclopedia.ca/en/article/quarantine-act.
132. Detsky AS, Bogoch II. COVID-19 in Canada: experience and response to waves 2 and 3. *JAMA*. 2021;326(12):1145-1146. doi: 10.1001/JAMA.2021.14797.
133. Government of Canada. COVID-19 vaccination coverage in Canada. Published 2023. Accessed January 24, 2023. https://health-infobase.canada.ca/covid-19/vaccination-coverage/#a1.
134. Detsky AS, Bogoch II. COVID-19 in Canada: the fourth through seventh waves. *JAMA Health Forum*. 2022;3(11):e224160-e224160. doi: 10.1001/jamahealthforum.2022.4160.
135. Health Canada. Canada Health Act annual report 2006–2007. Published 2007. Accessed October 16, 2016. http://www.hc-sc.gc.ca/hcs-sss/alt_formats/hpb-dgps/pdf/pubs/chaar-ralcs-0607/chaar-ralcs-0607_e.pdf.
136. Kidder T. *Mountains Beyond Mountains: The Quest of Dr. Paul Farmer, a Man Who Could Cure the World*. New York, NY: Random House; 2003.

CHAPTER 8

Mexico

Carrie Shaver, Ronn Pineo, Kelcie Creel, and Chelsea Pritchard

Country Description

Mexico	
Nationality	Noun: Mexican(s) Adjective: Mexican
Ethnic groups	Mestizo (Amerindian-Spanish) 62%, predominantly Amerindian 21%, Amerindian 7%, other 10% (mostly European) (2012 est.) *Note: Mexico does not collect census data on ethnicity*
Religions	Roman Catholic 78%, Protestant/Evangelical Christian 11.2%, Other 0.002%, Unaffiliated, including atheism 10.6% (2020 est.)
Language	Spanish only 93.8%, Spanish and Indigenous languages 5.4%, Indigenous only 0.6%, unspecified 0.2%; Note: Indigenous languages include various Mayan, Nahuatl, and other regional languages (2020 est.)
Literacy	Definition: age 15 and over and can read and write Total population: 95.2% Male: 96.1% Female: 94.5% (2020)
Government type	Federal presidential republic
Date of independence	September 16, 1810, from Spain (celebrated) and September 21, 1821, (achievement)
Gross domestic product (GDP) per capita	10,045.68 USD (2021 est.)
Unemployment rate	4.38% (2021 est.) *Note: underemployment may be as high as 25% due to reliance on the informal work sector*
Natural hazards	Tsunamis along the Pacific coast; volcanoes and destructive earthquakes in the center and south; and hurricanes on the Pacific, Gulf of Mexico, and Caribbean coasts

Mexico

Environment: current issues	Scarcity of hazardous waste disposal facilities; rural to urban migration leading to crowding in cities; natural freshwater resources scarce and often polluted; raw sewage and industrial effluents polluting rivers in urban areas; deforestation; widespread erosion; desertification; deteriorating agricultural lands; serious air and water pollution in the national capital, most urban centers, and especially along U.S.–Mexico border; land subsidence in Valley of Mexico caused by groundwater depletion *Note: Mexico considers the lack of clean water and deforestation national security issues*
Population	130,262,220 (2021 est.)
Age structure	0–14 years: 26.01% (male 17,111,199/female 16,349,767) 15–24 years: 16.97% (male 11,069,260/female 10,762,784) 25–54 years: 41.06% (male 25,604,223/female 27,223,720) 55–64 years: 8.29% (male 4,879,048/female 5,784,176) 65 years and over: 7.67% (male 4,373,807/female 5,491,581) (2020 est.)
Median age	Total: 29.3 years Male: 28.2 years Female: 30.4 years (2020 est.)
Population growth rate	0.51% (2022 est.)
Birth rate	13.55 births/1,000 population (2022 est.)
Death rate	7.71 deaths/1,000 population (2022 est.)
Net migration rate	−0.76 migrant(s)/1,000 population (2022 est.)
Gender ratio	At birth: 1.05 male/female 0–14 years: 1.05 male/female 15–24 years: 1.09 male/female 25–54 years: 0.91 male/female 55–64 years: 0.84 male/female 65 years and over: 0.75 male/female Total population: 0.96 male/female (2022 est.)
Infant mortality rate	Total: 11 deaths/1,000 live births Male: 12.1 deaths/1,000 live births Female: 10.9 deaths/1,000 live births (2022 est.)
Life expectancy at birth	Total: 11.86 deaths/1,000 live births Male: 13.11 deaths/1,000 live births Female: 10.55 deaths/1,000 live births (2022 est.)
Total fertility rate	1.68 children born/woman (2022 est.)
HIV/AIDS adult prevalence rate	0.4% (2021 est.)
Number of people living with HIV/AIDS (adults and children)	360,000 (2021 est.)
HIV/AIDS deaths (adults and children)	4,600 (2021 est.)

USD = U.S. dollars.

Data from Central Intelligence Agency. The World Fact Book: Mexico. https://www.cia.gov/the-world-factbook/countries/Mexico/ and https://www.unaids.org/en/regionscountries/countries/Mexico.

From the stunning beaches of Cancun to the ancient ruins of Chichen Itza, Mexico is full of natural and cultural wonders. With over 200,000 different species, Mexico is home to 10–12% of the entire world's biodiversity.[1] The country also has some of the most diverse and historic architecture in the world, ranging from pre-Columbian Mesoamerican pyramidal structures to the Spanish-influenced Palacio de Bellas Artes in Mexico City. Mexico is a country of vibrant colors and sounds, from the vivid hillside buildings of Guanajuato to the lively music of Mariachi bands. The country's populace is renowned for their warmth and hospitality and their food for its bold flavors and fresh ingredients.

Mexico is also a country with a rich and complicated history. Over the centuries, the nation has faced numerous challenges, including many wars, political upheavals, and recurrent periods of economic instability, which influenced its economic advance and social reform efforts. Understanding the historical context and current realities of Mexico is crucial to appreciating the country's unique culture and navigating the ongoing social, political, and economic issues, especially as it relates to public health and the provision of health care.

Geography

Mexico is located in southern North America, sharing borders with the United States to the north and with Belize and Guatemala to the southeast. It is the third largest country in Latin America, after Brazil and Argentina. The country has a diverse geography that ranges from high mountains, arid deserts, dense tropical rainforests, to coastal plains. The most prominent mountain range is the Sierra Madre, which runs parallel to the Gulf of Mexico and the Pacific Ocean. The highest peak in Mexico is Pico de Orizaba, standing at an impressive 5,636 meters above sea level. The country also has numerous active volcanoes, including Popocatepetl and Colima.[2] Mexico's long coastline stretches over 9,330 km, including the Gulf of Mexico, the Pacific Ocean and the Gulf of California, and the Caribbean Sea.[3] The Gulf of Mexico has rich oil reserves, which play a crucial role in the Mexican economy and provide a large share of government revenues.[4]

Mexico also has a unique geography in terms of its climate. The country is divided into several distinct regions, each with its own weather patterns. The northern regions experience a desert climate with hot summers and mild winters, while the central regions have a temperate climate with rainy summers and dry winters. The southern regions have a tropical climate, with high temperatures and heavy rainfall throughout the year. As such, Mexico is able to cultivate a wide variety of crops, from corn and wheat in the north to coffee and bananas in the south (see **Figure 8-1**).[3]

The size and considerable variety of the landscape and climate create one of the key challenges for crafting healthcare policy for Mexico. Author Lesley Byrd Simpson sought in the title of his classic 1960 study of Mexican history to accurately reflect the great physical and cultural complexity of the nation. The title Byrd Simpson settled on, "Many Mexicos," remains quite apt.[5]

Mexico/U.S. Border Region

An advantage of living in a community near the U.S. border in Mexico is economic opportunity. Manufacturing jobs that supply goods to the United States and elsewhere in the world are critical in the supply chain of a myriad of sectors and are perpetually in demand.[6] The northern Mexican states that border the United States have comparatively lower poverty rates compared with other Mexican states. The poorest Mexican states are in the far south, Chiapas and Guerrero, which in 2022 had poverty rates of 67% and 60%, respectively, whereas poverty rates in the northern border states range from 18% to 20%.[7]

Yet, for all these economic advantages, the northern borderlands now show poor health conditions in several ways. Noncommunicable diseases (NCD), including cardiovascular disease and diabetes, are leading causes of deaths there, as in the rest of the country.[8] Certainly, to some extent this problem is related to diet. Rates of diabetes are higher than the national average in the states of Coahuila and Tamaulipas.[9] The states of Baja California and Sonora have had excess mortality due to ischemic heart disease, diabetes, and cirrhosis of the liver during the last decade compared with other Mexican states.[10,11] Mexico as a nation is confronting an obesity epidemic, with all of the attendant health concerns.[12] Mexico has in some respects the worst of two worlds, with developed world health concerns that are especially pronounced in the richer northern districts, and developing world health problems plaguing poor rural districts, especially in Chiapas and Oaxaca to the south.

Government and Political System

Mexico is a federal presidential representative democratic republic where the president is both the head of state and the head of government. The political system is based on the constitution of 1917, which established a three-branch government: executive, legislative, and judiciary. The president is elected for a 6-year term and cannot be re-elected. The Mexican Congress is composed of the Senate and the Chamber of Deputies, which are responsible for creating and enacting laws, and exercising fiduciary responsibilities. The judiciary is independent of the other branches of government and is responsible for interpreting the constitution and laws.[13]

Figure 8-1 Map of the country of Mexico

Courtesy of the Central Intelligence Agency.

The country has a multi-party system, with the Institutional Revolutionary Party (PRI) holding power for most of the 20th century. However, since the 1990s, Mexico has undergone a democratic transition, with several parties gaining representation and holding the presidency.[14] The right-of-center National Action Party (PAN) held power from 2000 to 2012, followed by the return of the centrist PRI until 2018, when Andrés Manuel López Obrador of the left-wing National Regeneration Movement (MORENA) won the presidency.[15] López Obrador's campaign focused on reducing corruption, increasing social welfare programs, and promoting economic growth.[16] MORENA has held powerful majorities in the Congress, allowing President López Obrador to enact his agenda.

One of the biggest challenges facing Mexico's political system is corruption, which has been a pervasive problem throughout the country's history.[17] The Mexican government has taken steps to combat corruption, including the creation of specialized anti-corruption agencies, but progress has been slow. The issue remains a significant concern, and stood at the center of President López Obrador's policies for healthcare reform.[18]

Another challenge for Mexico's government is organized crime. Drug cartels have significant power in some areas of Mexico, and violence related to these crime organizations remains a significant problem. Mexico's high homicide rates are a direct result of the activities of these illegal drug organizations. Each successive *sexenio* (the 6-year presidential term) has sought to implement strategies to address this issue, including increased security measures and efforts to reduce drug trafficking, but progress has been poor.[18] Directly confronting the cartels has served only to escalate violence, killing many innocents in the process. Some have likened strategy of using the military to battle the cartels to trying to hammer mercury. Reformers have long called for exploring decriminalization of illegal drugs, hoping that the cartels might be more dedicated to just making money than only making money illegally. Some reformers look to the gradual legalization of recreational marijuana in the United States as a model for change.

Mexico's political system faces criticism for its lack of inclusivity and representation. Indigenous peoples, women, and other groups have historically faced discrimination and have limited representation in government.[19,20] However, the country has made some strides in recent years, including the election of the first Indigenous woman to the Senate in 2018 and the appointment of women to key government positions. Efforts to promote diversity and inclusion are ongoing and remain a priority for many activists and politicians in Mexico.

Macroeconomics

Mexico is one of the largest and most important economies in Latin America. With a population of over 130 million people, it is the second-largest economy in the region, after Brazil. It is among the 15th largest economies in the world. It is primarily driven by manufacturing and services sectors, with significant contributions from agriculture, mining, and energy (see **Table 8-1**).[21]

Mexico has a mixed economy, with both the private and public sectors playing important roles. The government is involved in key sectors such as energy, telecommunications, and transportation. However, in the years from 1982 to 2018, Mexico joined the Latin American movement toward the adoption of neoliberal or free market economic policies. Each successive *sexenio* deepened this impulse, from President Miguel de la Madrid (1982–1988) through President Enrique Peña Nieto (2012–2018). Neoliberalism in Mexico brought a sharp change from prior state-led development economic policies (1934–1982), launching a continually advancing trend toward privatization, with the government sale of state-owned enterprises to private companies.[22] Mexico is a member of several international organizations, including the World Trade Organization (WTO) and the Organization for Economic Cooperation and Development (OECD). The country has

Table 8-1 Mexican Economy

Mexican Economy		
Total Gross Domestic Product (GDP)	385.540 billion USD (2020) 487.227 billion USD (2021)	8,655 USD per capita (2020) 10,046 USD per capita (2021)
GDP Growth, annual	−9.94% (2020) 10.4% (2021)	In 2021, increased by 19.94 percentage points to 10.4%, recovering from the initial economic impact of the COVID-19 pandemic.
Imports of Goods and Services, percentage of GDP	13.61% (2020) 14.95% (2021)	Mexico imports for 2021 totaled 541.76 billion USD, a 32.75% increase from 2020. Imports for 2020 totaled 408.11 billion USD, a 17.7% decline from 2019. Major imports include machinery, electrical equipment, steel, chemicals, and agricultural products.
Exports, percentage of GDP	16.61% (2020) 18.03% (2021)	Mexico exports for 2021 totaled 522.53 billion USD, a 21.38% increase from 2020. Exports for 2020 totaled 430.50 billion USD, a 12.61% decline from 2019. Major exports include motor vehicles, parts, and accessories, minerals, crude petroleum, and agricultural products.
Personal Remittances, Received	651.020 million USD (2020) 911.592 million USD (2021)	Remittances have grown from 1.9% of 2012 GDP to 4.2% GDP in 2022.
Travel and Tourism, percentage of GDP	5.3% (2020) 6.1% (2021)	4.755 billion USD and 271 million employed (1:12 jobs) in 2020. 5.812 billion USD and 289 million employed (1:11 jobs).

USD = U.S. dollars.

Data from the following sources. Accessed April 21, 2023.
World Bank Databank. World development indicators. https://databank.worldbank.org/source/world-development-indicators/.
Statista. Mexico's economy & society. https://www.statista.com/study/48363/Mexico/.
Macrotrends. Mexico imports 1960-2023. https://www.macrotrends.net/countries/MEX/Mexico/imports#:~:text=Mexico%20imports%20for%202021%20was,a%2017.7%25%20decline%20from%202019.
Macrotrends. Mexico exports 1960-2023. https://www.macrotrends.net/countries/MEX/Mexico/exports#:~:text=Data%20are%20in%20current%20U.S.,a%2021.38%25%20increase%20from%202020.
World Travel and Tourism Council. Mexico: annual research key highlights. https://wttc.org/research/economic-impact.

also signed numerous trade agreements, including the 1994 North American Free Trade Agreement (NAFTA). NAFTA, renamed in Mexico T-MEC [*Tratado entre Mexico, Estados Unidos y Canadá*, or Treaty between Mexico, the United States, and Canada], has greatly influenced its economic development through increased integration with the United States and Canada. Roughly 80% of its exports go to the United States, and in 2021, Mexico was the second largest export market in the United States.[23] Over time, strong criticism of neoliberal policies has emerged as real wages and job security have declined; collective bargaining rights and union strength have been weakened; and migration of Mexican workers to the United States for better wages and working conditions has again increased.[24]

Inflation has at times been a large concern for Mexico's economy. The country has struggled with high inflation rates in the past, with rates reaching as high as 100% in the 1980s. However, in recent years, the government has been successful in bringing inflation under control. Inflation was at 3.4% in 2020, within the government's target range of 3–4%. Like most nations in the endemic COVID-19 environment, inflation rose in 2022 to 8.7% (in August).[24-26]

The Mexican peso is the country's currency and is freely traded on international currency markets. The country has a floating exchange rate, which means that the peso's value is determined by market forces. This can lead to volatility in the currency's value, which can affect the country's exports and imports. The government can intervene in the currency markets to stabilize the peso's value, if necessary.

While globalization opened world markets to Mexico, barriers to sustainable economic growth persist. Mexico's economy has experienced significant growth in recent years, but compared with similar countries, it has underperformed. Between 1980 and 2021, its economic growth averaged 2.1% per year.[21] Income inequality and poverty must be reduced, infrastructure and access to finance improved, and governmental transparency and checks and balances strengthened in order to limit corruption.

While Mexico is one of the largest and most economically advanced nations in Latin America, it has some of the lowest socioeconomic metrics in the hemisphere, especially in the regions where Indigenous people make their homes. Much of the country's wealth is concentrated in the hands of a small, wealthy elite, leaving many Mexicans struggling to make ends meet. In Mexico, 1% of the population controls 40% of the wealth.[27] Multidimensional measurements of poverty are collected by a decentralized public body established by the National Council for the Evaluation of Social Development Policy. Data collected include the following indicators: percentage of population in poverty, rates of well-being and access to fundamental services such as education, health services, social security, and infrastructure (see **Table 8-2**). When

Table 8-2 Mexican Poverty and Inequality Indicators, 2016–2020

Indicators	Percentage			Population (millions)		
	2016	2018	2020	2016	2018	2020
Poverty						
Population in poverty	43.2	41.9	43.9	52.2	51.9	55.7
Due to poor well-being	25.3	26.4	23.7	30.5	32.7	30.0
Due to income	7.6	8.0	8.9	9.1	9.9	11.2
Social well-being						
Lack of access to educational services	18.5	19.0	19.2	22.3	23.5	22.4
Lack of access to health services	29.2	21.5	18.2	3.5	25.3	21.8
Lack of access to social security	54.1	53.5	52.0	65.4	66.2	66.0
Lack of access to quality housing	12.0	11.0	9.3	14.5	13.6	11.8
Lack of access to urban services and utilities	19.2	19.6	17.9	23.1	24.3	22.7
Lack of access to food and nutrients	21.9	22.2	22.5	26.5	27.5	28.6

Data from Consejo Nacional de Evaluacion de la Politica de Desarrollo Social (CONEVAL). Poverty measurement. https://www.coneval.org.mx/Medicion/MP/Paginas/Pobreza_2020.aspx.

compared against other nations in Latin America and the Caribbean, Mexico performs poorly with respect to economic inequality and the percentage of the population that lives in poverty.

Mexico's labor force is large and diverse, with significant numbers of workers in both the formal and informal sectors. The country has a minimum wage, which is set by the government and varies, depending on the region. However, the minimum wage is relatively low compared with other countries in the region, which has led to concerns about worker exploitation and poverty. About half of economically active Mexicans work day-to-day in informally arranged jobs, as street peddlers, or as day workers, as housemaids, or in other similar activities.[28]

One area where economic inequality has had a particularly profound impact is health care. Despite repeated initiatives to improve access and quality, Mexico's healthcare system remains inadequate, especially for the many living in poverty. The country's healthcare infrastructure was built over time into a system that is highly fragmented. What Mexico offers is an array of programs, each specifically designated for one set of people or another. There are dedicated facilities for private-sector, salaried employees; another set of facilities for government employees; another for oil workers; yet more for the branches of the military; the efficient, well-run, and professionally staffed private facilities for those who can pay whatever it costs, straight out of pocket; and finally, the overburdened and underfunded facilities for the other half of the population, the ordinary people of limited means. Attempting to access this often-bewildering healthcare system and wade through the thickets of bureaucratic red tape can be a frustrating and too often fruitless undertaking for many Mexicans desperately seeking care for themselves or their loved ones. As a result, Mexico's population health outcomes belie its status as a relatively wealthy nation.

Mortality and Morbidity

In Mexico, mortality and morbidity from chronic conditions dominate the epidemiologic profile. NCDs are the leading cause of death (see **Table 8-3**). In the 2010s, the federal government developed prevention plans, regulations, and policies (PRP) to address social and environmental factors, many of which emphasized nutrition. However, the healthcare system's underfunding has made it difficult to provide chronic disease prevention and treatment, especially for an aging population. There is a shortage of specialty physicians to treat the most common NCDs, such as heart disease, diabetes, and obesity.[29] Advocates have since called for robust PRP implementation and effectiveness evaluation and additional PRP to integrate clinical, social, and environmental approaches to physical activity.[8] Significant political commitment and resources beyond current levels are needed to comprehensively address core social determinants of health (SDH).

Table 8-3 Major Causes of Death, 2022

2022 Rank Order	Disease or Condition
1	Ischemic heart disease
2	Diabetes
3	Malignant tumors
4	Liver disease
5	COVID-19
6	Accidents
7	Cerebrovascular diseases
8	Assaults
9	Influenza and pneumonia
10	Obstructive chronic lung diseases

Data from Institute for Health Metrics and Evaluation 2022. https://www.healthdata.org/Mexico.

According to recent data, cancer is a significant contributor to mortality in Mexico. The most prevalent cancers are breast, cervical, and colorectal cancer in women and prostate, lung, and colorectal cancer in men.[30] The country has recently developed registries to assess cancer prevalence and mortality estimates. For those at risk, diagnosis is difficult to access. In 2021, Mexico had 9.6 mammography machines per 100,000 residents, most of which were located in hospitals. By comparison, the United States had 70 machines per 100,000 residents. Mexico's mammography screening guidelines for apparently healthy women between 40 and 69 years of age call for a biannual scan. Additional breast imaging units and radiologists would improve detection and shorten the length of time until diagnosis.[31–32]

Accessing cancer treatment is equally difficult. Compared with other OECD countries, there are fewer oncologists and radiotherapy equipment per 100,000 residents (2.2 radiotherapy machines, 7 computed tomography machines, and 2.6 magnetic resonance imaging machines).[33-35] Integrated patient care is further challenged by the gaps in coverage for workers who frequently go between the informal and formal sectors, which dictate what coverage and which facilities are accessible.[29] Concentrations of resources in large hospitals in urban centers throughout the country create further barriers to access for more rural residents who may not have the ability to travel to the city for care for their chronic condition.[27,29] Women who reside in municipalities with a large concentration of Indigenous people contend with systemic barriers to breast cancer screening, which suggests that racial discrimination plays a role in breast cancer outcomes.[36]

Communicable diseases have also been a significant public health concern in Mexico, with the country facing several outbreaks in recent years. Other than the COVID-19 global pandemic, the most notable outbreak was the H1N1 influenza epidemic in 2009, which affected over 70,000 people and resulted in more than 1,000 deaths.[37] Other communicable diseases that have posed a threat to public health in Mexico include tuberculosis, Zika virus, Chikungunya, and dengue fever.[38] The Mexican government has implemented various measures to contain the spread of these diseases.

Mexico's public health response to communicable diseases has been a combination of prevention, surveillance, and control measures. The country's health authorities have developed and implemented various prevention strategies, including vaccination campaigns, health education programs, and initiatives to improve hygiene practices. Surveillance systems have also been put in place to monitor the spread of diseases and detect outbreaks early. Control measures include the implementation of quarantine and isolation measures, contact tracing, and treatment protocols.

Mexico's vaccination program has been a critical part of the country's public health response to communicable diseases. The program aims to provide free vaccines to all Mexican citizens, and it has been successful in reducing the incidence of vaccine-preventable diseases such as measles, mumps, and rubella. The country has also made significant progress in controlling tuberculosis, with a 30% decrease in cases reported between 2010 and 2020. The prevalence of completely unvaccinated children in Mexico is low, with 0.3% of children in 2012 and 0.8% of children in 2021 receiving no vaccines.[39] However, additional work is needed to strengthen information systems, health promotion, training, and timely vaccination availability.[40]

Brief History of the Healthcare System

The pluralist Mexican healthcare system incorporates traditional Indigenous and African medicine elements with modern systems.[41] Indigenous cultures in Mexico that predate Spanish conquest by thousands of years include nearly 70 distinct ethnolinguistic groups in what is considered modern-day Mexico.[42] The African influence in Mexican health care originates from the use of imported slave labor during the colonization of Mesoamerica in the early 16th century. The unique interaction of these approaches to health can be observed in the modern era, although the dominant system is the European hospital model embraced by the Spanish colonialists in the 18th century.[41]

The modern Mexican health system dates to 1943 when three important institutions were created: the Ministry of Health (MoH), the *Instituto Mexicano del Seguro Social* (Mexican Institute for Social Security or IMSS), and Mexico's Children's Hospital. The MoH now consists of 12 National Institutes of Health, charged with tertiary care, training of specialists, and performing scientific research. IMSS continues to serve middle-class salaried employees today. In 1959, all government workers achieved their most significant social victory with the creation of the *Instituto de Seguridad y Servicios Sociales de los Trabajadores del Estado* (Institute for Social Security and Services for State Workers or ISSSTE). These two institutions, the IMSS and the ISSSTE, dominate the healthcare situation for salaried workers in Mexico today, insuring and providing care for approximately two-thirds of the population.[29]

Effective efforts to increase access to care for unsalaried, informal-sector workers began in the early 2000s with the introduction of *Seguro Popular* (2003–2020). At its peak, *Seguro Popular* covered 42% of the portion of the population that was not eligible for other public coverage.[27] The Institute for Social Health and Wellbeing (INSABI, 2020–2022) replaced *Seguro Popular* in 2020 as part of the newly elected President López Obrador's promise to champion national healthcare reform.[29] However, INSABI was short-lived, lasting from 2020 to 2022. President López Obrador disbanded INSABI, citing concerns about corruption. IMSS-Bienestar, a program established in 1973, was then extended from its original mission of serving only the rural poor without health coverage to all in need as long as their state chose to participate. In 2022, 19 of the 32 federal units were actively participating in the IMSS-Bienestar programs and were serving 11.6 million people.[43]

The private healthcare sector exists for those able to afford it and is also used by international travelers seeking more affordable services. Among the domestic population, only a very small portion are able to obtain private healthcare services.

While access to health care is guaranteed in the Mexican Constitution, a significant proportion of the country has no access to health care, about 27% in 2022, with the rural, Indigenous poor being the most impacted in southern states such as Oaxaca and Chiapas.[27] The prevailing healthcare delivery model, which is mostly hospital based and specialty oriented, dramatically increases healthcare costs. In addition, many households face significant financial burdens in seeking care, with out-of-pocket spending accounting for a large portion of the national expenditure on health care compared with other OECD countries.[29]

Current Healthcare System Organization, Costs, and Facilities

The Mexican healthcare system is a medley of different subsystems. The public sector is composed of five systems, four of which insure formal-sector employees and their families: the Mexican Institute of Social Security (IMSS), the Institute for Social Security and Services for State Workers (ISSSTE), Social Security Institute for the Mexican Armed Forces (ISSFAM), and *Petróleos Mexicanos* (PEMEX). The Mexican Institute of Social Security Wellness Program (IMSS-Bienestar) is the sole insurer and provider for the half of the total population that is employed in the informal sector. The private sector is mostly unregulated, expensive, and funded by private health insurance that only the wealthiest can afford—only 2.3% of the population.[27] **Table 8-4** shows the components of the healthcare system.

IMSS and ISSSTE administer care through their own networks of hospitals and clinics and combined are the largest provider of services in the nation. The private sector provides another option for care for both citizens who are able to self-pay and international medical tourists. Many major pharmacy chains throughout Mexico have begun to offer physician consultation services.[44] These physicians, paid out-of-pocket by the customers, usually prescribe medications that then can be purchased on-site.[45] Traditional healers, known as *curanderos*, offer cost-effective home care that is deeply rooted in tradition. They are highly respected within their communities and are considered a trusted source of care.[46]

Health care in Mexico is chronically underfinanced and under-resourced.[29] Among the OECD nations, Mexico's government has consistently spent very little on health care in the last decade, with a maximum of about 6% of GDP spent on health care in 2016. In 2020, Mexico ranked third in least spending per capita among the OECD countries at $620 USD per capita, ahead of China and India (2023). U.S. government spending was $10,052 USD per capita, by comparison.[47] Conversely, Mexico spends a great share of its GDP on pharmaceuticals, ranking 8th at 21.5%, along with Eastern European nations such as Lithuania, Latvia, Hungary, Greece, and Bulgaria.[48] Nationally, Mexico had 1.2 physicians, 2.9 nurses, and 10 hospital beds per 100,000 residents in 2020–2021.[49–51] This was significantly below OECD averages and recommendations—3.2 doctors and 8.8 nurses per 100,000 residents.[27]

Table 8-4 Mexican Healthcare System

Public Subsystem Components						Private Sector
	Mexican Institute of Social Security (IMSS)	Institute for Social Security and Services for State Workers (ISSSTE)	Mexican Institute of Social Security Wellness Program (IMSS-Bienestar)	Social Security Institute for the Mexican Armed Forces (ISSFAM)	Petróleos Mexicanos (PEMEX)	For-profit, private hospitals, clinics, and physician practices, including medical tourism
Funding source	Federal allocations, employer contributions, and payroll taxes*					Out-of-pocket fees paid by patients and private health insurance

Public Subsystem Components						Private Sector
Services	Hospital care, ambulatory clinics, physician visits, outpatient and preventive care					Depends on coverage but can include long-term care, plastic surgery, physician consultation services in pharmacies, and traditional medicine
Participation eligibility	Formal-sector employees in private enterprises	Federal and state government employees, retirees, spouses, and underage children	Informal-sector workers ineligible for coverage through an employer or other social security coverage	Members of the Army and Navy, their families	Employees of the oil company PEMEX, their families	Those with private health insurance or those willing to pay out-of-pocket

*IMMS-Bienestar is funded jointly by participating states and the federal government.

Data from Sánchez-Talanquer M, González-Pier E, Sepúlveda J, et al. México's response to COVID-19: a case study. UCSF Institute for Global Health Sciences. April 12, 2021. https://globalhealthsciences.ucsf.edu/wp-content/uploads/2024/02/mexico-covid-19-case-study-english.pdf; Villarreal V. How do Mexicans get healthcare? Wilson Center. October, 2, 2022. Accessed April 16, 2023. https://www.wilsoncenter.org/article/infographic-how-do-mexicans-get-healthcare.

Long wait times to see a doctor for an appointment or to receive medical treatment for public-sector patients have been a prevailing issue in healthcare quality in Mexico in the last decade. A lack of personnel and a lack of space are two reasons for many cancellations and long waits. It is estimated that of all the available examination rooms or surgery suits that could be available, only half of them exist in the public sector.[52] Medical professionals are often lured away from the public sector to the private sector by better pay, equipment, and the promise of a safe work environment, leaving public facilities and the workforce further disadvantaged and public-sector patients with worse health outcomes. In the president's National Development Plan for 2019–2024, a lack of quality and uniformity in the nation's healthcare systems was acknowledged and an approach to reduce barriers to accessing quality health care was outlined. The first step was making permanent the fight against corruption in the entire healthcare sector.[53] Corruption within the government and its agencies was a common theme of the López Obrador administration and a main reason why mass layoffs of medical professionals occurred in 2019 ahead of the COVID-19 pandemic. Although this accomplished the campaign goal of reducing government spending, it created a dire situation when the COVID-19 pandemic came to Mexico in early 2020.[29]

Mexico has a dearth of well-equipped healthcare facilities. Existing facilities are concentrated in wealthier states and cities such as Mexico City, which has three to four times more physicians compared with the rest of the nation.[29] Healthcare spending in Mexico was curbed significantly in 2019 by mass layoffs of contracted healthcare workers and by closing epidemiologic surveillance centers.[29] Mexican health officials have recognized this shortage in healthcare providers and recommended hiring foreign doctors from Cuba. As of 2022, 500 Cuban doctors had arrived.[27] However, political tensions between Cuba and the United States could have negative economic implications for Mexico and could delay or prevent this type of initiative.

Even though Mexico spends a large percentage of its total healthcare expenditures on prescription medications, shortages and delays in filling prescriptions persist. In 2021, complaints from IMSS patients about their pharmacy's inability to fill their prescriptions in a timely manner rose by over 1,000% from 2020.[27] This is linked to the major changes to the healthcare sector's purchasing schema when *Seguro Popular* ended and INSABI began. The new program transferred purchasing medications from IMSS first to the Ministry of Finance and Public Credit, which lacked the coordination and experience to handle purchasing medications for the entirety of Mexico. By July 2020, prescription medications were being bought from only four companies, down from 60, which monopolized the market and drove up costs. Out-of-pocket costs for medical services skyrocketed by over 40% between 2018 and 2020, resulting in underutilization increases of as much as 14% in the poorest states in the south. In 2020, over 70% of Mexicans sought health care in full or partially in the private sector as the COVID-19 pandemic all but crippled the public subsystems.[27]

COVID-19 Pandemic

Mexico's healthcare system was undergoing major changes during the first year of the COVID-19 pandemic, as mentioned earlier.[54,55] It was likely that these changes hampered the systems' response capacity and contributed to the high burden of disease and death: Mexico experienced an excess mortality rate from COVID-19 of 43% in 2020, with the central and northern states being the most impacted.[29]

On the day the first confirmed case of COVID-19 was reported in Mexico in late February 2020, President López Obrador made a public statement emphasizing that his priority was not to overstate the possible severity of the disease. Some states took the lead in COVID-19 mitigation efforts.[54] For example, several states, including Guanajuato, Jalisco, Michoacán, Nuevo León, Tamaulipas, Tlaxcala, Veracruz, and Yucatán, established social distancing protocols ahead of any national recommendations.[56]

Despite the initial challenges, Mexico's response to the COVID-19 pandemic was robust, with the government implementing measures such as lockdowns, mask mandates, and testing and tracing programs to control the spread of the virus in the early spring of 2020. As the pandemic continued into the summer of 2020, and given the context of the United States' international border closure, both federal and state leaders in Mexico prioritized lifting lockdowns and easing social distancing measures.[56]

Mexico's diminished capacity to effectively manage the pandemic stemmed from severe socioeconomic inequality and a fragmented healthcare system. Indeed, patient outcomes from COVID-19 varied between healthcare subsystems. Among hospitalized patients in IMSS care settings, the case fatality rate was 50% or higher in 2020. This rate was much higher than in both ISSSTE and private hospitals, 38% and 20%, respectively.[29]

In 2021, the primary focus of the vaccination campaign in Mexico was on economic recovery, which also greatly influenced decisions regarding vaccine distribution. Mexico primarily relied on the AstraZeneca vaccine, which uses a viral vector format similar to the Johnson & Johnson vaccine used in the United States.[56] Pfizer and Sinovac were additional brands of vaccine distributed in Mexico.[57]

President López Obrador proposed a national distribution plan that prioritized vaccinating working-age individuals in municipalities situated along the U.S.–Mexico border, with the primary objective of expediting the reopening of the border. However, this strategy had the consequence of neglecting key groups residing in the border region, particularly rural inhabitants and older individuals. Consistent with previous health promotion initiatives, the vaccination rate in the southern state of Chiapas, which is predominantly inhabited by Indigenous communities, was notably slower.[56]

Of all healthcare workers who succumbed to COVID-19, physicians had the highest mortality rates, accounting for 46% of confirmed deaths.[56] Nurses suffered the largest burden of infections, totaling 40% of cases among healthcare professionals. Personal protective equipment, if available, was reused or worn far beyond its effectiveness and may have significantly contributed to the morbidity and mortality from COVID-19 in the healthcare workforce.[29] Per the Pan American Health Organization (PAHO), Mexican healthcare worker mortality from COVID-19 in 2020 was 45% of total deaths in the 17 Latin American nations that were surveyed.[56]

Conclusion

Health outcomes in Mexico should reflect the nation's size, the strength of its economy, and the vast resources available to government authorities. Despite its advantages compared with other Latin American countries, health outcomes in Mexico have not improved at similar rates. There are concerns that the reconfiguration of healthcare subsystems may leave substantial gaps in coverage for the most vulnerable. Mexico's healthcare system remains fragmented, and this fragmentation serves as a barrier to providing high-quality, equitable healthcare services. As other chapters in this volume demonstrate, there are clear advantages to having a single unified health system, as found in Costa Rica and in Cuba. But the construction of those unitary systems depended on finding the political will to do so, or perhaps even more, the serendipity of unique historic settings and rare political openings that allowed for this.

Worst off are the regions of Mexico that are home to the nation's Indigenous populations. Health disparities and inequities continue to impact these communities. They face a range of challenges, including poverty, lack of access to healthcare services, and language barriers. Mexico's healthcare system must address these disparities if it is to meet the needs of its diverse populations. While Mexico's healthcare system has made progress in recent years, there is still much work to be done. The country's relative wealth should enable it to achieve better health outcomes.

References

1. Mexico. BIOFIN. Updated 2021. Accessed April 29, 2023. https://www.biofin.org/mexico#:~:text=Mexico%20is%20a%20mega%20diverse,be%20found%20in%20its%20territory.
2. Pico de Orizaba, Mexico. NASA Earth Observatory. Updated February 10, 2011. Accessed April 29, 2023. https://earthobservatory.nasa.gov/images/49462/pico-de-orizaba-mexico#:~:text=The%20snow%2D%20and%20ice%2Dclad,tallest%20volcano%20in%20North%20America.
3. Central Intelligence Agency. Explore all countries—Mexico. In: *The World Factbook*. Updated April 26, 2023. Accessed April 29, 2023. https://www.cia.gov/the-world-factbook/countries/mexico/.
4. Mexico: country commercial guide. U.S. Department of Commerce International Trade Administration. Updated September 9, 2022. Accessed April 29, 2023. https://www.trade.gov/country-commercial-guides/mexico-oil-and-gas.
5. Byrd Simpson L. *Many Mexicos*. University of California Press; 1960.
6. Beaubien J. Border-town factories give manufacturers edge. *NPR*. November, 2011. https://www.npr.org/2011/11/20/142536024/border-town-factories-give-manufacturers-an-edge.
7. Sanchez J. Share of population living in poverty in Mexico in 2022, by state. Statista. July 5, 2024. Accessed January 25, 2025. https://www.statista.com/statistics/1036147/poverty-rate-mexico-state/.
8. Aceves B, Ingram M, Nieto C, et al. Non-communicable disease prevention in Mexico: policies, programs and regulations. *Health Promot Int*. 2020;35(2):409-421. doi: 10.1093/heapro/daz029.
9. Manzanares-Rivera JL. Expenditure patterns and social determinants of type II diabetes epidemic in the Coahuila–Texas border. *Papeles de Población*. 2016;22(89). http://www.scielo.org.mx/scielo.php?pid=S1405-74252016000300255&script=sci_arttext&tlng=en.
10. Aburto JM, Riffe T, Canudas-Romo V. Trends in avoidable mortality over the life course in Mexico, 1990–2015: a cross-sectional demographic analysis. *BMJ*. 2018;8(7):1-11.
11. Diamond M, Testa L, Novak C, et al. *A Population in Peril: A Health Crisis Among Asylum Seekers on the Northern Border of Mexico 2020*. Harvard Global Health Institute; 2020.
12. Barquera S, Rivera JA. Obesity in Mexico: rapid epidemiological transition and food industry interference in health policies. *Lancet Diabetes Endocrinol*. 2020;8(9):746-747. doi: 10.1016/S2213-8587(20)30269-2.
13. Bartley P, Monterrosas E, Ruiz PP. Resisting a hostile and insecure environment for defending rights in Mexico. In: *Protecting Human Rights Defenders at Risk*. Routledge; 2020:104-129.
14. Barrow LK. Party on? Politicians and party switching in Mexico. *Politics*. 2007;27(3):165-173.
15. Greene KF, Sánchez-Talanquer M. Latin America's shifting politics: Mexico's party system under stress. *J Democracy*. 2018;29(4):31-42. doi: 10.1353/jod.2018.0060.
16. Berg NM, Welsh P, Ford K, Romero HM. AMLO 2021: is the Mexican administration's fight against corruption all rhetoric? Ropes & Gray. June 2021. https://www.ropesgray.com/en/newsroom/alerts/2021/june/amlo-2021-is-the-mexican-administrations-fight-against-corruption-all-rhetoric.
17. Morris SD. Corruption and the Mexican political system: continuity and change. *Third World Quarterly*. 1999; 20(3):623-643.
18. Palifka BJ. Corruption, organized crime and the public sector in Mexico. In: *Handbook on Corruption, Ethics and Integrity in Public Administration*. Edward Elgar Publishing; 2020: 274-288.
19. Craske N. Mexican women's inclusion into political life: a Latin American perspective. In: *Women's Participation in Mexican Political Life*. Routledge; 2019:41-62.
20. Yörük E, Öker I, Şarlak L. Indigenous unrest and the contentious politics of social assistance in Mexico. *World Development*. 2019;104618.
21. World Bank. Mexico overview. Accessed April 30, 2023. https://www.worldbank.org/en/country/Mexico/overview#:~:text=Its%20economic%20growth%20averaged%20just,to%20the%20COVID%2D19%20pandemic.
22. MacLeod D. *Downsizing the State: Privatization and the Limits of Neoliberal Reform in Mexico*. Penn State Press; 2004.
23. Silva V. A new dawn or a false hope for Mexico's left? Overcoming neoliberal legacies in an uncertain world. *Latin Am Perspect*. 2023; 0094582X231164127.
24. U.S. Department of State. 2022 investment climate statements: Mexico. 2022. https://www.state.gov/reports/2022-investment-climate-statements/Mexico/.
25. Agarwal R, Kimball M. Will inflation remain high? International Monetary Fund. 2002. https://www.imf.org/en/Publications/fandd/issues/2022/03/Future-of-inflation-partI-Agarwal-kimball.
26. Instituto Nacional de Estadística y Geografía (INEGI) [National Institute of Statistics and Geography]. *Índice Nacional de Precios al Consumidor* [National Consumer Price Index]. https://www.inegi.org.mx/temas/inpc/.
27. Villarreal V. How do Mexicans get healthcare? Wilson Center. 2022. Accessed April 16, 2023. https://www.wilsoncenter.org/article/infographic-how-do-mexicans-get-healthcare.

28. Tilly C, Rojas-García G. Shifting tides of informal worker resistance in Mexico: a domestic work-construction contrast. *Bull Latin Amer Res*. 2021;40(3):352-368.
29. Sánchez-Talanquer M, González-Pier E, Sepúlveda J, et al. Mexico's response to COVID-19: a case study. UCSF Institute for Global Health Sciences. April 2021. https://globalhealthsciences.ucsf.edu/sites/globalhealthsciences.ucsf.edu/files/mexico-covid-19- case-study-english.pdf.
30. Beltran-Ontiveros SA, Contreras-Gutierrez J, Lizarraga-Verdugo E, et al. National Burden and Trends for 29 Groups of Cancer in Mexico from 1990 to 2019: A Secondary Analysis of the Global Burden of Disease Study 2019. *Cancers*, 2023;16(1):149. Accessed January 25, 2025. https://pmc.ncbi.nlm.nih.gov/articles/PMC10778521/.
31. Organization for Economic Cooperation and Development. Mammography machines (indicator). 2023. Accessed April 23, 2023. doi: 10.1787/685c9c5e-en.
32. Ramírez-Galván YA, Cardona-Huerta S, Elizondo-Riojas G, et al. Value of a breast imaging unit in the detection of breast cancer in Mexico. *eCancer.* 2021;15,1272.
33. Organization for Economic Cooperation and Development. Radiotherapy equipment (indicator). 2023. Accessed April 23, 2023. doi: 10.1787/47a5492f-en.
34. Organization for Economic Cooperation and Development. Computed tomography (CT) scanners (indicator). 2023. Accessed April 23, 2023. doi: 10.1787/bedece12-en.
35. Organization for Economic Cooperation and Development. Magnetic resonance imaging (MRI) units (indicator). 2023. Accessed April 23, 2023. doi: 10.1787/1a72e7d1-en.
36. Armenta-Paulino N, Wehrmeister FC, Arroyave L, et al. Ethnic inequalities in health intervention coverage among Mexican women at the individual and municipality levels. *eClinicalMedicine*. 2021;43:101228. doi: 10.1016/j.eclinm.2021.101228.
37. Agüero JM, Beleche T. Health shocks and their long-lasting impact on health behaviors: evidence from the 2009 H1N1 pandemic in Mexico. *J Health Econ*. 2017;54:40-55.
38. Oppong JR. Globalization of communicable diseases. *Intl Encyclo Human Geog*. 2020;223-228. doi: 10.1016/B978-0-08-102295-5.10438-X.
39. Gutierrez JP, Johri M. Socioeconomic and geographic inequities in vaccination among children 12 to 59 months in Mexico, 2012 to 2021. *Rev Panam Salud Publica*. 2023;47:e35. doi: 10.26633/RPSP.2023.35.
40. Díaz-Ortega JL, Ferreira-Guerrero E, Trejo-Valdivia B, et al. Cobertura de vacunación en niños y adolescentes en Mexico: esquema completo, incompleto y no vacunación [Vaccination coverage in children and adolescents in Mexico: vaccinated, under vaccinated and non vaccinated]. *Salud Publica Mex*. 2013;55(suppl 2):S289-S299.
41. Cueto M, Palmer S. Indigenous medicine, official health, medical pluralism. In: *Medicine and Public Health in Latin America: A History: New Approaches to the Americas*. Cambridge, UK: Cambridge University Press; 2014:10-57 doi: 10.1017/CBO9781139152174.002.
42. Mexico. International Work Group for Indigenous Affairs. April 2022. Accessed April 17, 2023. https://www.iwgia.org/en/mexico.html.
43. Maia L. Mexico: how does the health system work and what are the challenges of Mexican public health. Green Rock. Accessed January 25, 2025. https://www.greenrock.vc/en/blog/mexico-how-does-the-health-system-work-challenges-of-mexican-public-health.
44. López-Manning M, García-Díaz R. Doctors adjacent to private pharmacies: the new ambulatory care provider for Mexican health care seekers. *Value Health Region Iss*. 2017(14):81-88.
45. May B. How to see a doctor at the pharmacy. *Mexico Living*. April 2019; 5. https://Mexicoliving.org/how-to-see-a-doctor-at-the-pharmacy/.
46. Torres C. The teaching of Curanderismo traditional medicine through a free online course. *UNM Newsroom*. May 2019. http://news.unm.edu/news/the-teaching-of-curanderismo-traditional-medicine-through-a-free-online-course.
47. Organization for Economic Cooperation and Development. Health spending (indicator). 2023. Accessed April 23, 2023. doi: 10.1787/8643de7e-en.
48. Organization for Economic Cooperation and Development. Pharmaceutical spending (indicator). 2023. Accessed April 23, 2023. doi: 10.1787/998febf6-en.
49. Organization for Economic Cooperation and Development. Hospital beds (indicator). 2023. Accessed April 23, 2023. doi: 10.1787/0191328e-en.
50. Organization for Economic Cooperation and Development. Doctors (indicator). 2023. Accessed April 23, 2023. doi: 10.1787/4355e1ec-en.
51. Organization for Economic Cooperation and Development. Nurses (indicator). 2023. Accessed April 23, 2023. doi: 10.1787/283e64de-en.
52. Doubova SV, García-Saiso S, Pérez-Cuevas R, et al. Quality governance in a pluralistic health system: Mexican experience and challenges. *Lancet Glob Health*. 2018;6(11):e1149-e1152.
53. Federal, Mexico Poder Ejecutivo. *Plan Nacional de Desarrollo: 2019–2024*. 2019;240-241. https://lopezobrador.org.mx/wp-content/uploads/2019/05/PLAN-NACIONAL-DE-DESARROLLO-2019-2024.pdf.
54. Knaul FM, Touchton M, Arreola-Ornelas, et al. Punt politics as failure of health system stewardship: evidence from the COVID-19 pandemic response in Brazil and Mexico. *Lancet Regional Health—Americas*. 2021;4:100086.
55. Verguet S, Hailu A, Teshome Ergata G, et al. Toward universal health coverage in the post-COVID-19 era. *Nat Med*. 2021;27(3):380-387.
56. Pineo R, Shaver C, Creel K, Pritchard C. COVID-19 in Latin America and the Caribbean with a special focus on Perú, Mexico, and Cuba. *J Dev Soc*. 2023;39(1):7-39.
57. Kane Jiménez S, Gandy A. Infographic: Mexico's vaccine supply and distribution efforts. Wilson Center. 2021. https://www.wilsoncenter.org/article/infographic-Mexicos-vaccine-supply-and-distribution-efforts.

CHAPTER 9

Brazil

Marcia Cristina Zago Novaretti, Thomas Maryon, and Antonio Pires Barbosa

Country Description

Table 9-1 Brazil

Nationality	Noun: Brazilian(s) Adjective: Brazilian
Ethnic groups	Mulatto (mixed White and Black) 45.3%, White 43.5%, Black 10.2%; Asian 0.6%; Indigenous 0.4% (2022 est.)
Religions	Roman Catholic 56%, other Catholic 0.4%, Protestant 34% (includes Adventist, Pentecostals, Reformers, other Protestant), other Christian 0.5%, Spiritist 1.5%, none 8% (2022 est.)
Language	Portuguese (official and most widely spoken); English and Spanish (most focused on by second-language learners; less common: German, Italian, Japanese, many minor Amerindian languages
Literacy	Definition: Percentage of population age 15 and over who can read and write. Total population: 93.2% (2018 est.) Male: 93% Female: 93.4%
Government type	Federal presidential republic
Date of independence	September 7, 1822 (from Portugal)
Gross domestic product (GDP) per capita	14,600 USD (2021 est.)
Unemployment rate	14.4% (2021 est.)
Natural hazards	Recurring droughts in northeast; floods and occasional frost in south
Environment: current issues	Amazon Basin deforestation destroys habitat and endangers a multitude of local indigenous plants and animals; lucrative illegal wildlife trade; air and water pollution in Rio de Janeiro, São Paulo, and several other large cities; land degradation and water pollution from improper mining activities; wetland degradation; severe oil spills
Population	214,326,223 (December 2021)

(continues)

Table 9-1 Brazil *(continued)*

Age structure	0–14 years: 21% (male 49.1%/female 50.9%) 0–14 years: 21.11% (male 22,790,634/female 21,907,018) 15–24 years: 16.06% (male 17,254,363/female 16,750,581) 25–54 years: 43.83% (male 46,070,240/female 46,729,640) 55–64 years: 9.78% (male 9,802,995/female 10,911,140) 65 years and over: 9.21% (male 8,323,344/female 11,176,018) (2020 est.)
Median age	Total: 33.2 years Male: 32.3 years Female: 34.1 years (2020 est.)
Population growth rate	0.7% (2022 est.)
Birth rate	13.96 births/1,000 population (2022 est.) country comparison to the world: 127
Death rate	6.81 deaths/1,000 population (2022 est.) country comparison to the world: 125
Disease burden	**Communicable disease deaths:** 13.71% of the total population **Noncommunicable disease deaths:** 74.74% of the total population **Injury deaths:** 11.55% of the total population (2019 est.) Communicable disease deaths increased significantly during and after the COVID-19 pandemic.
Net migration rate	−0.19 migrant(s)/1,000 population (2023 est.)
Gender ratio	At birth: 1.05 male/female 0–14 years: 1.04 male/female 15–24 years: 1.03 male/female 25–54 years: 0.98 male/female 55–64 years: 0.9 male/female 65 years and over: 0.58 male/female Total population: 0.97 male/female (2022 est.)
Infant mortality rate	Total: 13.31 deaths/1,000 live births Male: 14.75 deaths/1,000 live births Female: 11.8 deaths/1,000 live births (2022 est.)
Life expectancy at birth	Total population: 75.92 years Male: 72.5 years Female: 79.5 years (2022 est.)
Total fertility rate	1.8 children born/woman (2022 est.)
HIV/AIDS adult prevalence rate	0.6% (2021 est.)
Number of people living with HIV/AIDS	990,000 (2022 est.)
HIV/AIDS deaths	13,000 (2022 est.)

USD = U.S. dollars.

Data from IBGE 2022 Brazilian Institute of Geography and Statistics. https://www.ibge.gov.br/en/home-eng.html. Accessed February 24, 2023.
Central Intelligence Agency. The World Fact Book, 2020: Brazil. https://www.cia.gov/the-world-factbook/countries/brazil. Accessed February 24, 2023.
Pan American Health Organization. Brazil - country profile. October 13, 2024. https://hia.paho.org/en/country-profiles/brazil. Accessed January 27, 2025.
United Nations: UNAIDS. https://www.unaids.org/en/regionscountries/countries/brazil. Accessed January 27, 2025.

History

Brazil was discovered in 1500 by Portuguese explorer Pedro Cabral by accident as part of a journey to find India by traveling west on the Atlantic Ocean; this venture was undertaken to secure trade and to advance the Catholic faith.[1] For more than three centuries, Brazil remained a colony of Portugal. In 1882, Brazil gained its independence and maintained a monarchical form of government until slavery was abolished in 1888. In 1889, the formation of a republic was proclaimed by the military.[2] Political control of Brazil was dominated by its coffee growers and exporters until populist leader Getulio Vargas ascended to power in 1930.[3] Populist and military government existed for greater than a half century until 1985, when the military regime peacefully ceded power to civilian rulers.[4] Brazil continues to this day to be governed in the federal republic model.

Size and Geography

Brazil is by far the largest and most populated country in South America, bordering the Atlantic Ocean for 7,491 kilometers and sharing land borders with Argentina, Bolivia, Colombia, French Guiana, Guyana, Paraguay, Peru, Suriname, Uruguay, and Venezuela. It occupies the fifth largest area mass in the world; at over 8.5 million square kilometers, it is the largest country in the southern hemisphere.[3] There are now over 214 million people living in Brazil, and nearly 88% of the population lives in urban areas (see **Table 9-1**). With nearly 20 million people, São Paulo is the largest urban area in Brazil, followed by Rio de Janeiro with approximately 12 million inhabitants. Brasilia, the nation's capital, has approximately 3.8 million residents. Urbanization has been occurring at the rate of approximately 1.15% per year.[3] The climate is mostly tropical, including the Amazon rain forest, and is more temperate in the southern part of the country.

Brazil continues to be the net recipient of immigrants, with the Southeast region being the prime relocation area (Brazil officially has five major regions; see **Figure 9-1**). In the mid-19th century, the importation

Figure 9-1 Map of Brazil

of African slaves was made illegal. At that point, Brazil sought Europeans to work in agriculture—particularly in the coffee-growing business—including Italians, Portuguese, Spanish, and Germans. Later, Japanese immigrants flocked to Brazil. More recently, immigrants have come from Argentina, Chile, and the Andean countries (many as unskilled illegal migrants) or are returning Brazilian nationals.[3]

While Brazil has a growing middle class (estimated to be more than half of the population), poverty levels and income disparities remain high. This is particularly true in the Northeast, North, and Central-West regions, and disproportionately so for women, Black, mixed-race, and Indigenous populations. These disparities lead to a sense of social exclusion and contribute to Brazil's high crime rate, with violent crime found in densely populated urban areas and favelas (slums).[3]

Government and Political System

The conventional long-form name of the country of Brazil is *República Federativa do Brasil*; in English, this is translated as *Federative Republic of Brazil*. As the long-form name implies, Brazil is a federal republic, which means that the powers vested in the central government through the Brazilian constitution are restricted, and the component parts (states and municipalities) retain a degree of self-government. The constitution of Brazil is considered the supreme law of the country, and health care is guaranteed as a constitutional right. The ultimate sovereign power remains with the voters, who retain the ability to choose their governmental representatives in the voting process.[3]

There are 26 states and a federal district (Brasilia) represented in the federal Brazilian government, and each state has its own governor and legislature. The 1988 constitution (as amended over time) extends broad powers to the federal government, which is made up of executive, legislative, and judicial branches. The president is the head of the executive branch, holds office for 4 years—with the right to reelection for an additional 4-year term—and appoints the cabinet. The president may unilaterally intervene in state affairs, and serves as both head of state and head of the government.[5]

Brazil's bicameral legislature consists of an upper Federal Senate and a lower Chamber of Deputies. The 81 senators are elected for 8 years, and the 513 deputies are elected for 4 years. Each state is eligible for a minimum of eight seats in the chamber. The largest state delegation is from São Paulo's, and is capped at 70 seats.[6] The main political parties include the Brazilian Democratic Movement, Democrat, Democratic Labor, Brazilian Social Democracy, Workers, and Progressive parties.[7]

The third branch of government is the judiciary. The highest court in Brazil is the Supreme Federal Court, with 11 justices. There are various subordinate courts, including the Federal Appeals Court, the Superior Court of Justice, the Superior Electoral Court, regional federal courts, and the state court system.[6]

Macroeconomics

Major Industries

Brazil has several well-developed economic sectors, including agricultural, manufacturing, mining, and service industries, and has also undertaken the development of its vast interior. Brazil has abundant natural resources, a large labor pool, and a growing middle class. Its economy is very large compared with all of the other South American countries, and it is becoming an even greater presence in the world markets.

Since 2003, Brazil has steadily enhanced its macroeconomic stability, reducing its debt burden by shifting it toward real denominated and domestically held instruments and by building up foreign reserves. In 2008, Brazil became a net external creditor, and two ratings agencies awarded investment-grade status to its debt. After strong growth in 2007 and 2008, the global financial crisis rocked Brazil. Brazil experienced two quarters of recession as global demand for Brazil's commodity-based exports constricted and external credit withered. However, Brazil was one of the first emerging markets to begin recovering. In 2010, consumer and investor confidence revived, and GDP growth reached 7.5%, the highest growth rate in the past 25 years. Rising inflation then led Brazilian authorities to take measures to slow down the economy. These steps and the world's economic slowdown affected Brazil's growth potential from 2011 to 2013. Brazil´s economy was recovering when it was hit by the COVID-19 pandemic.

Brazil's traditionally high level of income disparity has declined for each of the last 14 years. Brazil is an attractive location for foreign investors because of its historically high interest rates. The unemployment rate had been at historic lows, but began rising again, to over 8.7%, in 2012.[3] The government has been compelled to intervene in foreign exchange markets and raise taxes on some foreign capital inflows, as large capital inflows over the past several years have contributed to the appreciation of the currency, harming Brazilian manufacturing to an appreciable extent. Dilma Rousseff, Brazil's president from 2011 to 2016, retained the previous administration's commitment to a floating exchange rate, fiscal restraint, and inflation targeting by the central bank.[3]

The 5 main export destinations for Brazilian products in 2022 were China (26.8%), the United States (11.4%), Argentina (4.5%), the Netherlands (3.6%), Spain (3.0%). The 5 main countries from which Brazil imported products in 2022 were China (23.8%), the United States (18.6%), Argentina (4.7%), Germany (4.6%), and India (3.3%).[8] Brazil is the largest exporter of soybeans and soybean oil to China, and it exports iron ore in large quantities for Chinese steel production. The main products that Brazil imports from China are electric equipment, machines, and mineral fuels. The main products exported to the United States are mineral fuel, oil, iron, steel, machinery, and beverages. The top import categories are machinery, mineral fuel, aircraft, electrical machinery, and optic and medical instruments.[9]

Infrastructure and Transportation

There are more than 1.58 million kilometers of roadways in Brazil.[3] The Brazilian-paved highway system is one of the largest in the world, but it is seen as inadequate for the growing needs of the country. Great efforts were made to improve the roadways for the 2014 FIFA World Cup and for the 2016 Olympic Games and to better connect the industrial parts of the nation with the less-developed areas. An estimated 1.2 billion people travel the highways in Brazil each year.[10] Railways were nationalized in Brazil in the past, but rail services are now under the control of various public and private operators. There are approximately 50 major commercial airports in the country, with more than 115 million air passengers yearly.[10]

Approximately 90% of Brazil's power is secured from hydroelectric plants, and fossil fuel and nuclear plants have met the remainder of the power needs. By law, only state-owned power companies can produce power in Brazil, and this has proven a fairly reliable system to date.[10] Brazil is blessed with approximately 50,000 kilometers of navigable waterways. There are 15 or so major seaports and harbors along the coast and the Amazon and Paraguay Rivers.[10]

Demographics

Age Distribution of the Population

Brazil is the sixth most populated country in the world, with just over 214 million people in 2022, representing approximately 2.8% of the world's overall population. It was not until the year 2013 that Brazil first exceeded a population of 200 million, and its population continues to grow faster than previously estimated largely due to the expanding middle class, which enjoys a longer lifespan than previous generations.[11] As of 2020, there was favorable age distribution in Brazil, with nearly 37% of the population under 25 years of age and with just over 9% of the population 65 years and over.[3]

Like many industrialized countries, Brazil has experienced a decline in fertility rate since the 1970s, when women had 4 children, on average. The birth rate in 2020 was estimated to be 1.658 children per woman, largely attributed to more women entering the workforce and electing to wait longer before having offspring. It is estimated that the birth rate will decline to 1.5 by 2034 and will remain approximately at that level through 2060.[11] It is projected that the current favorable age structure will begin to shift around 2025, with the labor force shrinking somewhat and the elderly cohort starting to represent an increasing share of the total population. Poverty among the elderly has been nearly eliminated due to funded public pensions, and Bolsa Familia and other social programs have lifted tens of millions out of poverty.[3]

Education Levels of Population

The literacy rate in Brazil (age 15 and over who can read and write) in 2018 was 93.2%.[3] The federal government of Brazil regulates education through the Ministry of Education, which sets forth guiding principles for education programs throughout the country. Federal funding is used to develop state and local education programs. The national budget for education in 2020 was 6% of GDP, and the federal government intends to increase this number over time to 7.0%.[6] The compulsory level of education in Brazil is 9 years, compared with 12 years in the United States, Great Britain, and Peru; 13 years in Germany and Argentina; and 8 years in Turkiye and Bolivia.[12] Approximately 11.0% of the working-age population has a university degree, and college graduates earn, on average, 2.5 times as much as those without degrees and 5.0 times as much as the majority of the population, who never complete secondary school. There are approximately

2,400 universities or colleges of further education in Brazil, the majority of which are private institutions.[13]

Religion

In census data, approximately 90% of the Brazilian population revealed that they subscribe to some religious ideal, making Brazil more religiously inclined than any other South American country.[10] Brazil is, and has historically been, made up largely of members of the Catholic faith (nearly 65% of the population identifies itself as Catholic), and another 22% of the population identifies itself as Protestant Christian.[3] Today, there are more Catholics in Brazil than in any other county of the world. Only about 1% of the population identifies itself today as not believing in God or a supreme being.[10]

The Catholic faith was brought to Brazil when Portuguese and other European settlers arrived with the aim of "civilizing" the local native people. Churches, schools, and hospitals were built, all buttressing the doctrines of the Catholic faith. In the 19th century, Catholicism was made the official religion of Brazil, which meant that Catholic priests were paid a salary by the government, and the Catholic hierarchy was included in the political affairs of the country. As such, Catholicism became an integral part of the administration of Brazil and of its people, and many of the Brazilian festivals are based on the Catholic religion.[10]

Protestant denominations in Brazil include Methodist, Episcopal, Pentecostal, Lutheran, Baptist, and nondenominational Protestant. Non-Christian religions include Judaism, Islam, Buddhism, Shintoism, Rastafarianism, Candomblé, Umbanda, and Spiritism.[10]

Distribution of Major Morbidity in the Country

The top 10 causes of death in Brazil as of 2021 are provided here, per 100,000 population, along with: COVID-19, 219.5; ischemic heart disease, 85.7; stroke, 64.2; lower respiratory infections, 38.3; interpersonal violence, 32.3; diabetes mellitus, 31.2; chronic obstructive pulmonary disorder, 24.7; kidney disease, 24.1; Alzheimer's and other dementia diseases, 18.9; road injury, 15.7.[14]

Brief History of the Healthcare System

The story of the Brazilian healthcare system is connected deeply to the political, economic, demographic, and social changes that have occurred through the centuries. Brazil was a colony of Portugal from 1500 until 1822, when it gained political independence. During these centuries, gold, gemstones, and many other natural resources were transferred to Portugal, and Portugal left Brazilian natives and most of its immigrants in extreme poverty. Slavery persisted in Brazil for more than two centuries. During this period, raw materials were also used for payment to the English, who intermediated slave trade worldwide. In 1888, slavery was abolished. Brazil turned into a federal republic in a relatively peaceful process in 1889, and this remains the political form of government to the present time.

Health Care in the Colonial Period (1500–1808)

In the colonial period, Brazil was under the political, economic, and cultural control of Portugal. The first news that arrived in Europe about Brazil was a description of a new land characterized by naïve Indigenous peoples and exuberant tropical flora and fauna, resembling an idyllic paradise. Based on these reports, countless expeditions sailed to the New Continent with the purpose of finding gold and securing rapid wealth. These adventurous men were soldiers, beggars, fugitives, and people with financial problems in their homeland. They brought with them numerous diseases, such as tuberculosis, syphilis, malaria, gonorrhea, and measles. Pestilent diseases and local wars contributed enormously to the extermination of many Native tribes. Smallpox was brought to Brazil by slaves and became the main cause of death in the colony.[15]

The combination of Indigenous conflict, disease, and inadequate sanitation led Portugal to deploy, as early as the 16th century, people appointed to positions of chief physician and chief surgeon. However, few doctors chose to venture across the ocean to work in Brazil. In 1746, there were only six medical doctors who had graduated in Europe and who were available in all of Brazil. Healers and traditional healers, although prohibited by law to act as medical doctors, were frequently consulted and were respected by the population.[15]

The organization of health care during this period was in its most primal form. During the colonial period, there were no hospitals in Brazil that were similar to those that existed in Europe. There were only the so-called *santa casas*, large infirmaries maintained by the Jesuits. The first *santa casa* was installed in Olinda (Northeast region) in 1539. After that, they were installed in Santos (1543), Bahia (1549),

São Paulo (1560), Rio de Janeiro (1582), and Belem (1619). Today, there are *santa casas* in almost all cities in Brazil, many of them in small cities. It is relevant that the *santa casa* system in many ways led to future government-sponsored healthcare assistance in Brazil.[16]

Health Care During the Imperial Phase (1808–1888)

Napoleon invaded Portugal in 1808, prompting Dom João VI, King of Portugal, and his entourage to transfer royal activities to Brazil. The king established the first schools of medicine in Brazil, initially in the state of Bahia and then in Rio de Janeiro. The opening of ports to other countries allowed an increase of commerce and economic prosperity in the country. Cultural and social life flourished, and Rio de Janeiro was brought into a golden age. International artists, scientists, engineers, architects, and lawyers visited Rio de Janeiro, and some of them moved to Brazil.

Health-related programs and structures were developed to provide better health care to the Portuguese court, including vaccination against smallpox and sanitary control of ports and epidemics. In spite of this, from 1820 to1840, yellow fever, smallpox, measles, and typhoid fever epidemics devastated Rio de Janeiro, leaving more than 4,000 dead in a single year (1849). The imperial government established the first Public Health Care Commission, with the purpose of developing sanitation policies and epidemic control procedures. Soon thereafter, a Central Public Hygiene Joint Commission started controlling medical activities, vaccinations, food handling, pharmacies, and public health planning.

The general public's access to health care improved during the imperial phase. However, these new programs and strategies did not effectively control the epidemics of that time. Tuberculosis was not the focus of sanitary vigilance during the imperial phase because it was more commonly found among the enslaved residents. Yellow fever caused more deaths among Europeans, and it was easier to control yellow fever, so yellow fever was emphasized in terms of medical attention. Hospitals were created specifically to isolate patients with tuberculosis in an attempt to control the dissemination of this disease.[16]

Health Care in the Old Republic Period (1889–1930)

The Old Republic period can be characterized as the time of a "liberal oligarchic state." The federal government emphasized immigration to bolster the economy's agricultural workforce after the abolition of slavery. Consequently, efforts were necessary to control pestilential diseases and other widespread diseases (tuberculosis, syphilis, and rural endemic diseases) that were common in the imperial phase. This was especially true for protection of the coffee farms and for the incipient industries that were developing.

Rio de Janeiro and São Paulo developed effective measures against yellow fever, smallpox, and typhoid fever, but there was a lack of focus on the fight against tuberculosis.[15] At the end of 19th century and the beginning of the 20th century, Dr. Clemente Ferreira from São Paulo initiated a philanthropic action, Leagues Against Tuberculosis, that spread all over Brazil. These leagues provided epidemiologic data and economic analysis and promoted effective interactions with the government. Public institutes for healthcare research and assistance were launched in São Paulo (Butantan Institute, Emilio Ribas Institute, Biological Institute) and in Rio de Janeiro (Oswaldo Cruz Institute).

A federal law in 1904 established a healthcare crusade to eradicate yellow fever through mandatory vaccination, which then precipitated the Vaccination Revolt. Large parts of the population resisted the exposure of women's arms to strangers for vaccination, as well as the mandatory forced entry into homes by police and health workers to conduct vaccination. There were physical confrontations, looting, and civil disobedience, culminating in the deaths of several civilians. The government was considered responsible for the mayhem, and subsequently it repealed the mandatory vaccine program, instead settling on a more acceptable optional vaccination approach.

In 1920, a new concept of sanitary vigilance was implemented that introduced sanitary education and specific departments for vigilance toward and control of other diseases, such as leprosy and venereal diseases. Hospital assistance, pediatric care, and endemic rural diseases—such as Chagas disease, schistosomiasis, malaria, filariasis, trachoma infection, and leishmaniasis—received attention through specific programs. The Special Strategic Health Care Service was created during World War II with the mission to provide health care in a strategic manner, and after the war it continued to provide services to underrepresented areas.[16]

Health Care During the Vargas Dictatorship (1930–1945)

The time that Getulio Vargas was in control in Brazil is known as the "authoritarianism period." Vargas governed through federal decrees until 1934, when a new

Federal Constitution was published. Reforms institutionalized public health through the Ministry of Education and Public Health and institutionalized social security and occupational health through the Ministry of Labor, Industry, and Commerce. Intensification of public health campaigns against yellow fever, tuberculosis, rural endemic diseases, and nutritional deficiencies reached most of the Brazilian states. Pension institutes extended insurance security to the majority of urban workers.[15,17]

Health Care in the Post-Vargas Era to 1988

After the Vargas deposition, there was a period of democratic instability until 1964 that was characterized by rapid urbanization, immigration, and the first arrival of the automobile industry in Brazil. Although the creation of the Ministry of Health (1953) allowed for better organization of health assistance, the public health system was fragmented and made up of several unconnected programs. During this period, there was an expansion of hospital care and an emergence of the private healthcare sector.

During the time of the military dictatorship (1964–1985), public health budget reductions resulted in the recrudescence of dengue, meningitis, and malaria. Public health care was chaotic, and Brazilian quality of life stagnated. Nevertheless, during the 1970s, Brazil experienced impressive economic growth, with disproportional improvement of quality of life for the most privileged in society. Significant advances for the general population occurred only beginning in 1983, when an interministerial project, Integrated Actions in Health, simultaneously focused on prevention, therapeutics, and education in health care. The National Social Security Healthcare Institute funded states and municipalities to expand healthcare coverage. The period of military government was hallmarked by a number of political interventions that provided privileges to the private medical sector.[17]

Health Care in the Era of Democracy (1988–Present)

At the end of the 1980s and the beginning of the 1990s, an economic crisis engulfed Brazil and contributed to a great loss of income and hyperinflation. Fernando Collor de Mello, the president elected in 1990, facilitated policies that expanded importation of goods and generated significant unemployment—with the loss of almost 920,000 jobs in a single fiscal year. He was impeached in 1992 following allegations of corruption.

The Brazilian Federal Constitution (BFC), published in 1988, drove the country toward a completely new health system, in addition to triggering major political and social changes. The definition of health as a "citizen's right and duty of the state," first in the Eighth National Health Conference in 1986 and then reinforced in BFC (art. 196), established a new dynamic for the social welfare model in the country.[18,19] It made possible the creation of the Universal Health System (SUS), composed of the core traits of equity, comprehensiveness, universality, and decentralization of health care.[18] SUS brought important developments in the organization of health care, cooperation between the public and private sectors, and social participation in control of policies and services.[19,20] Consequently, health care in Brazil was segmented into two large nuclei of assistance: SUS, directed to the whole population and emphasizing primary care, and the private healthcare (or supplemental) system, for that portion of the population insured with private health plans. Since then, the evolution of the Brazilian health system has shown substantial differences, mainly due to an inability of the government to meet and to guarantee Federal Constitution healthcare principles. **Table 9-2** shows the key differences between SUS and private health care in Brazil.

Brazil began the process of acquiring and distributing free antiretroviral drugs (medications that hinder the multiplication of HIV) in 1988, and it is recognized as one of the few countries that provide free treatment for all HIV-infected individuals. In 1994, Brazil set a course for economic stability after the institution of the Plano Real, a currency and monetary reform model. Incomes began to recover, although in a sporadic fashion. The Family Health Program was also set up in 1994 but has not been fully implemented in all Brazilian cities, even though it is considered a key component of the SUS.[19]

The SUS has gone through several phases since its inception. In the initial years (1990–2002), management focused on role differentiation among the federal, state, and municipal levels. The federal Ministry of Health served in a regulatory and policymaking function, delegating to the states and municipalities the responsibilities for activities related to high- and intermediate-complexity healthcare levels.[20] During this period, the basis of regulation consisted of establishing operational mechanisms for financial transfers for three levels of care (primary care, medium-complexity care, and high-complexity care) on a productivity basis, similar to the "fee-for-service" model. Simultaneously, the private sector's cost-control actions focused on the more expensive

Table 9-2 Major Differences Between Public (SUS) and Private Health Care in Brazil After 1988

	Public Health Care (SUS)	Private Health Care
Population coverage	All individuals on Brazilian soil (citizens or not)	Exclusively for healthcare plan subscribers
Focus	Primary care, including hospital care	Both outpatient and hospital care
Funding	Federal fiscal resources	Individual and employer payments
Management	Federal, state, and municipal	Targeted by functions (providers and payers)
Sanitary and health vigilance activities	Yes	No
Pharmaceutical assistance	Yes, for primary care	Varies by type of health plan
Scope	Entire liability of high-cost therapeutics, procedures, and transplants	Generally all required services based on medical necessity and covered benefits are included. Often includes preventive and wellness services. Approved covered services, treatments, and procedures are systematically reviewed.
Investments in infrastructure	Low	High
Investments in technology	Low	High
Compensation for health professionals	Low—causing reduced efficiency and high personnel rotation	Adequate for market

clinical procedures and the requirement for prospective authorizations for high-complexity cases.

In 1999, the National Health Surveillance Agency was formed with the responsibility of providing surveillance and control of healthcare services and products in Brazil.[21] A few months later, the Supplementary Health Care Agency was established to regulate and oversee private healthcare plans.[22] The generic drug program in Brazil, based on the American and Canadian models, was launched in 1999 and allowed access to medications for large portions of the population. The generic drug program gained rapid popularity and support from employers and the general population.[23]

A constitutional amendment was passed in 2000 that defined the duties of federal, state, and municipal governments as related to SUS financing, and it determined the minimum percentage allocation of public budgets for health care. In the second phase (2002–2006), there was an expansion of SUS services among the Brazilian states. A National Mobile Emergency Care system (similar to 911 in the United States) was set up in Brazil in 2003, effectively reducing deaths and severe injuries.

In 2006, the Pact for Health Act established within the SUS prioritized health prevention and promotion standards. This program was originally conceived in 1998, and it progressively became a more effective health policy, reaching over 55% of Brazilians in 2012. The Pact for Health also expanded the Family Health Program and its multiprofessional family health support teams to all Brazilian states. In 2006, the Health Promotion Program, the National Primary Care Policy, and the National Oral Health Policy provided substantial advances in health care, especially for underprivileged populations. At the same time, new legal requirements were put in place to protect consumer rights and to promote changes in the private sector, with the purpose of ensuring mechanisms for access to private hospitals and for the maintenance of financial reserves for the third-party payer market.

From 2008 to the present, the Brazilian public health system has been incorporating the concept of service networks. There are five Healthcare Service Networks: (1) an Urgent and Emergency Network, designed for acute events of trauma, cardiovascular diseases, stroke, and acute complications of chronic and other disorders; (2) the Maternal–Infant Stork Network (Rede Cegonha in Portuguese) with the main goal of enhancing actions related to mother–child health, promoting obstetric and child health care;

(3) a Chronic Diseases Network, focused on chronic hypertension, diabetes mellitus, and oncology; (4) a Psycho-Social Network, focused on mental health care and alcohol and drug addiction; and (5) a Special Needs People Network, focused on rehabilitation and social reintegration of individuals experiencing postacute events.[20] In the private sector, the implementation of quality programs (ISO, National Organization Certification) and international accreditation (Joint Commission) in hospitals and clinics has become more common, and it has validated these facilities' commitment to excellence in patient care and safety. Recently, there has been a merging of clinics, hospitals, and healthcare insurance providers under large employee pension plans.

After the approval of a 2012 constitutional change for the health sector that allowed the participation of foreign investments, a process of consolidation has begun. Initially, private health plan operators began investing resources. More recently, with the development of large medical and hospital networks focused on secondary and tertiary healthcare delivery, large, international investment funds have arrived, whose primary focus historically has not been healthcare-related investment. These funds are now investing in the Brazilian healthcare system. A survey carried out by the National School of Public Health of the Osvaldo Cruz Foundation identified, based on data from the Central Bank of Brazil, the presence of 13 large international investment funds in Brazilian healthcare delivery. Only three of the funds are primarily healthcare-focused in their country of origin. The entry of foreign investments into the health system in Brazil has introduced an additional player into the existing group of stakeholders in the management of the supplementary (private) health system in Brazil.

The present system is now well established and is a source of national pride given the steady improvement in access to healthcare services and the overall improvement in healthcare status and quality indicators. These gains, however, are not exclusively a consequence of the Brazilian healthcare model. Over the last few years, Brazil has also stabilized economically and has evolved toward the preservation of democratic values and the search for equity and justice for all of its citizens, today and into the future.

The Current Healthcare System

A poll in 2022 showed that health care is the top priority for Brazilians.[24,25]

The majority of the population, almost 74%, depends exclusively on the Brazilian public healthcare (SUS) system. SUS is a hierarchical, universal, and integrated system. Although the Brazilian public healthcare plan requires universality of coverage, this is still not a reality. Brazilian health care is available to every person who needs health care in the country, whether or not the individual happens to be a Brazilian citizen. This model has attracted an influx of immigrants from other Latin American countries, especially when people from afar receive a diagnosis of a severe and/or complex disease (cancer, cardiac surgery, or brain surgery, for example). There are no reimbursement compacts for health care among the Latin American countries. Consequently, even though Brazil has spent more on health care in the last decade, it does not necessarily reflect that it has yet to achieve the highest level of healthcare services and outcomes.

The Brazilian public healthcare system provides a wide range of services, from primary care to highly complex surgical procedures. However, these broad-scoped services are not yet fully available in all Brazilian states. In some states, where the public healthcare services are well organized, internal immigration from other Brazilian states is a daily reality. Located in the state of São Paulo (in the Southeast region of the country), Clinicas Hospital Complex, with 2,400 inpatient beds in 2022, is the largest university hospital in Brazil. Doctors at that hospital performed over 50,000 surgeries and approximately 232,000 urgent and emergent consultations in 2022. Almost 3% of all admissions involve patients from other Brazilian states.[26] It is very difficult to develop a comprehensive strategic plan for public healthcare services due to these kinds of intensive internal and external immigration realities and funding challenges.

Facilities

The Brazilian healthcare system has been marked by inequity. In July 2022, there were 7,191 hospitals in Brazil, mainly in the Sao Paulo and Minas Gerais states, in the Southeast region. Total beds available in both public and private settings numbered 427,047, or 1.99 beds per 1,000 inhabitants. According to the national standards, the minimum number of beds available should be 2.5 to 3.0 per 1,000 inhabitants. In 2022, there was a gap of 107,953 to 214,953 beds throughout the country. There has been a slow decline in the number of total hospital beds in Brazil since 2004.[27] Of total existing beds in October 2022, 263,793 were exclusively for non-SUS individuals, resulting in 2.5 beds per 1,000 inhabitants. However, bed distribution varies from state to state in number and in complexity of health care available. Despite the efforts made by the federal government in the last 10 years, there is still a shortage of beds, particularly for intensive care, neonatal intensive care, oncology, and emergency care for the public healthcare sector. In intensive care (adults, pediatric, neonatal, and burns), there were 41,559 total beds available, or 2.02 beds per 10,000 inhabitants in October 2016. However, while there were 1.32 intensive care beds per 10,000 inhabitants for public care, there were 4.11 intensive care beds per 10,000 inhabitants for private care. In the state of Maranhão (Northeastern region), there was only 1.00 intensive care bed per 10,000 inhabitants in two hospitals, far less than in the state of Rio de Janeiro (Southeastern region), which had 3.54 intensive care beds per 10,000 inhabitants in 47 hospitals.[28]

There were 385,679 healthcare facilities registered in Brazil in 2023, 28.8% of them public. Of this total, 153,082 provided medical consultation for spontaneous demand, and of these, 37.4% were public institutions. The Brazilian healthcare system consisted of approximately 5,363 general hospitals, 999 specialized hospitals, 1,524 day-hospitals, 1,214 general emergency care units, and 127 specialized emergency care units. About 61.3% of healthcare facilities were designed for patients referred from primary or emergency care. A total of 178,900 medical offices were distributed throughout Brazil, mainly in the Southeast region (53.4%).[29]

In February 2023, there were 48,711 public primary care units registered, 32.6% in the Southeast region; 113 fluvial mobile healthcare units provided primary care in remote areas, mainly in the Amazon region; and 415 healthcare clinical locations were provided to Brazilian Natives. There are 6,081 mobile emergency units interspersed throughout the country. In Brazil, there were 5,152 blood testing sites, with 38.7% of them being found in the Southeast region in February 2023. According to the Brazilian Institute of Geographics and Statistics, almost 42.1% of all Brazilians lived in the Southeast region during that time. A total of 163 public centers for obesity care (February 2023) have been developed as a result of the substantial percentage of overweight (55.4%; male 57.1%, female 53.9%) and obese (19.8%; male 18.7%, female 20.7%) people living in Brazil.[29]

Pharmaceutical assistance in Brazil is provided through a generic drug program, free medication distribution at public primary care units, and an agreement with pharmacies throughout the country to promote the free distribution of subsidized medicines. The Brazilian Generic Drugs Program, based on similar programs found in the United States and Canada, was initiated 25 years ago with the goal to increase access to medications and keep costs low. Today, there are more than 21,000 generic drugs in the formulary for treatment of almost 80% of the most common diseases in the country. The number of pharmacies was the highest in the world, with 118,000 in 2022, resulting in a proportion of one pharmacy per 1.813 inhabitants—substantially higher than the ratio recommended by the World Health Organization of one pharmacy per 10,000 inhabitants.[30] This huge number of pharmacies brings about inspection difficulties, especially in towns located far from large urban centers.

Workforce

More healthcare personnel are needed in Brazil, and in a better dispersion pattern throughout the nation. According to the Brazilian Demographic Study 2022, Brazil has 2.31 practicing physicians per 1,000 population, which is far below the ratio in Argentina (3.1 per 1,000).[31] The physician distribution in Brazil has been unequal and markedly concentrated in larger cities. In the North region, there were only 1.01 physicians per 1,000 population, while in the Southeast, there were 2.67 per 1,000 inhabitants in 2013. In Maranhão state (northeastern region), the density of physicians was only 0.70 per 1,000. The number of physicians overall has increased over the past 30 years, especially due to the opening of private medical schools.[31]

The Brazilian physician profile has been changing dramatically. Since 2009, the number of female doctors graduated has surpassed the number of male doctors, and by 2022, female doctors represented 54.50% of practicing physicians under 29 years of age.[32] In 2023, the average age of all physicians in active practice in the country was 44.7 years, including nonspecialists, generalists, and specialists. In 2023, there were 495,716 practicing physicians (51.5% men and 48.5% women).[33] Approximately 215,640 physicians (55.50%) worked in government settings at federal, state, and municipal levels. The number of generalist physicians was approximately 186,688 (37.7%), but they were not heterogeneously distributed. Although 56.40% of physicians worked in the Southeast region, there were 1.09 generalists per 1,000 inhabitants in this region in 2013. Specialists represented 53.60%, and of these, 29% had two or more Brazilian board certifications. The North and Northeast regions had fewer specialists than generalists with ratios of 0.81 and 0.92, respectively.[33]

Brazil had the largest number of dentists per capita in the world in 2023, with approximately 383,996 in active practice. However, the distribution of dentists has been marked by inequity. Approximately 59% of all

Brazilian dentists work in the Southeast region. Two-thirds of them are active in private clinics, and there is ongoing difficulty with getting dentists to work regularly in small cities. Consequently, the majority of Brazilians have not had access to ongoing dental care because they depend exclusively on public health care.[33]

The Brazilian Federal Board of Nursing estimates that there were 2,786,240 health professionals (excluding physicians and dentists) in Brazil in 2023. The number of registered nurses reported was 3.2 per 1,000 inhabitants, which is below the ratio recommended by WHO of 2.00 per 1,000 inhabitants.[34] Approximately 53.8% of nurses were actively working in the Southeast region. During that time, there were also 6.57 practical nurses per 1,000 inhabitants. The majority of these nursing professionals were 26 to 45 years old (75.6%) and female (82.1%).[35]

Technology and Equipment

Substantial efforts have been made to increase the availability of diagnostic capabilities in Brazil. Even though the federal regulation, Portaria 1101, recommended one magnetic resonance imaging (MRI) unit per 500,000 inhabitants, the proportion of MRI units in use in Brazil in February 2023 was approximately 1.0 per million population. In comparison, at that time, the Organization for Economic Co-operation and Development (OECD) average was 9.80 MRI units per million. For nonpublic health care, there were 1.49 MRI units per million population in Brazil, while in public setting care there were only 0.69 MRI units per million. Unfortunately, the distribution of MRI units has been unequal among Brazilian states and between the public and private sectors. The Southeast region accounted for 53.4% of total MRI units available in Brazil and 41.3% were exclusively for the private sector in 2023.

According to the National Standards, the number of computed tomography (CT) scanners was adequate at 2.92 per million population as of February 2023; however, there were 2.21 times more of these CT units available to the non-SUS population.

Evolution of the Healthcare System in Brazil

Cost Approach

Unlike the health systems from other OECD member countries, the Health System in Brazil (called Sistema Unico de Saude, SUS) was defined in constitutional principles and specific legislation.[18] Also established was the contribution of fiscal resources from the central government, the federal states, and the municipalities. The Brazilian Federal Constitution (BFC) also allowed for the involvement of private resources in the provision of services to Brazilian citizens.[18,21]

The system to finance and fund health assistance was organized in two categories: a public system, theoretically responsible for providing universal coverage to the population of 214 million people; and a private (supplementary) system, providing care to 64.2 million users who are covered by health insurance.[36] The private system is financed by individuals/families (approximately 48% of the total) or companies (approximately 52% of the total), and is provided as an employment benefit to employees.[28]

The coverage provided to users of the public system focuses on three areas of direct care and areas of technical support[20]:

- Primary care—in extensive modalities to the whole population.
- Care of medium and high complexity—in outpatient and inpatient forms.
- Pharmaceutical assistance, with free-of-charge medications, by component:
    - *Basic component*—primary care medication, including for maternal and infant care and for some chronic illnesses.
    - *Strategic component*—medication for endemic illnesses that have an economic impact. Among these, the most important items include biopharmaceuticals, blood products, and medication for the treatment of HIV/AIDS, tuberculosis, and leprosy.
    - *Speciality component*—high-cost medication for the care of special pathologies; regulated by protocols and clinical-therapeutic guidelines.

Furthermore, the public system sets aside resources from its budget for sanitary and epidemiological surveillance, investments in replacement of medical technology facilities, and training of human resources and management in its three levels.

The coverage provided by the private system is organized by means of assistance networks, which integrate clinics and private practices, outpatient diagnostic centers, hospitals, and day (day care) hospitals. The suppliers of care, in general, adhere to the following models: (1) units owned by health insurance companies; (2) units owned by philanthropic or not-for-profit organizations; (3) private units; and (4) clinics, practices, and units of autonomous physicians or other healthcare professionals. Access to these units is regulated according to the degree of complexity of care and restricted to those persons covered by health insurance. Generally, these units are able to perform consultations, diagnostic tests, hospital admissions, and procedures, and—depending on the contract format—care is arranged between service providers and health plan companies.[37]

The public healthcare system can arrange for services and procedures of high complexity from nonprofit organizations. These services and procedures are regulated by a system of information and central authorization. For example, they include the execution of procedural diagnoses by MRI and CT scanners, cancer treatment, organ and bone marrow transplantation, invasive vascular procedures, physical rehabilitation, and the dispensing of high-cost medications.[38,39]

Total Expenditures for Health Care in Brazil

As in other parts of the world, expenditures for health care in Brazil have increased at a rate higher than the economic growth rate. According to data from the National Congress and the National Agency for Supplementary Health, the budget for SUS grew by 95.0% in real terms between 2001 and 2011, with greater impacts being felt on the resources of federal states and municipalities.[40] For instance, between 2006 and 2011, the budget (adjusted for inflation) of the public system increased by 41.7%, which corresponds to a variation of $51.6 billion USD to $95.4 billion USD. Over the same period, the covered population increased from 174.0 million to 193.5 million citizens.[41] Among the most important causes of this growth are the increased frequency of chronic degenerative diseases, aging of the population, external causes (especially trauma), and expansions of the covered population.

Total expenditures for health care in Brazil varied between 8.5% and 9.05% of the GDP from 2020 to 2022, with budget growth typically above inflation. In 2022, 9.0% of the GDP was devoted to health care. Of this, 59.1% was spent by the private sector. Similarly, spending within the private funding system has evolved with the incorporation of a large contingency of citizens as a result of decreased unemployment rates found in the country. Data from the National Agency for Supplementary Health indicate that in February 2023, the population with health care financed by families and companies (by the private system) leaped from 31 million users to the current 64.2 million users.[42,43]

Currently, the annual per capita expense for the public system is approximately $853.39 USD, with SUS having provided more than 114.3 million hospitalizations, 4.1 million surgeries, 84,000 transplants, 531.0 million consultations, and 4.8 million ambulatory procedures. The per capita expense for the private system is estimated at $1,423 USD, including 8.6 million hospitalizations and 285.0 million consultations and ambulatory procedures.[44]

Structure of the Public Services

Managers and healthcare professionals in Brazil largely agree that the implementation of SUS considerably increased patients' access to primary care and to emergency services. As a result, for instance, there has been a greatly improved rate of prenatal care and immunization.[45] Many changes have taken place to make SUS more effective in providing healthcare assistance. Considerable efforts are being made to improve the quality of primary care as well as to reduce the rate of hospitalizations. The introduction in 2011 of a federal program to measure the performance of primary care units is one adopted approach that has already shown promising results.[46]

The Brazilian federal government also decided to become less dependent on the importation of strategic medicines. A federal plan was initiated that established public companies devoted to producing blood derivatives. For example, to support federal healthcare programs that provide free medication to all patients with AIDS and hepatitis C, as well as other high-cost medicines and vaccines, publicly held pharmaceutical laboratories (including Farmanguinhos, Fundação para o Remédio Popular, São Paulo's Instituto Butantan) were modernized and received substantial grants.

In 2006, SUS initiated a series of changes to improve operations at local and state levels, with the institution of decision-making boards and an emphasis on primary care. These changes brought about an intense program of medical and health education and the implementation of family health teams (which include one general physician, one nurse, practical nurses, and community agents) responsible for the care of communities of up to 1,000 families and the management of the use of health resources in each segment. As of 2020, there were 43,000 teams in the Family Health Program reaching 64% of the national population.

Another important initiative took place in 2011 with the creation of Healthcare Service Networks, which were based on conditions that required integrated services of several units and specialized equipment. The networks were coordinated by a unique information, communication, and control system. Five extensive networks were implemented, including networks for urgent and emergency care, networks for perinatal care, networks for chronic conditions, and networks for psychosocial care. These networks provide care and rehabilitation programs for conditions such as cardiovascular and cerebrovascular emergencies and trauma, the cycle of pregnancy from birth to 1 year of life, hypertension, diabetes, cancer, and mental disturbances including addiction.[47]

Quality

Between 1990 and 2017, there were a few indicators of improvement in the health of the population, such as a decrease in maternal mortality from 143.2 to 60 per 1,000 inhabitants (since 2018 the rate of maternal mortality has steadily been increasing every year) and a decrease in infant mortality from 45.3 to 13.3 per 1,000 live births.[14,48,49] This improvement seems to be related to improvements in sanitation and drinking water—both determinants of health but not directly within the scope of action coordinated by SUS—as well as the development of health programs related to maternal and infant health, perinatal care, breastfeeding, oral rehydration, and vaccine campaigns.[28] In addition, in the South and Southeast, regions in which the greatest share of population and the greatest volume of industrial production are concentrated, infant mortality rates range between 7.8 and 13.0 deaths per 1,000 live births. When one considers the first 5 years of life, the child mortality rate was 13.17 per 1,000 children in general; in nonindustrialized areas, it was 16.0 per 1,000, during this time frame.

Infant Mortality

The main causes of childhood mortality in Brazil are associated with perinatal conditions and respiratory diseases. For people between 15 and 40 years of age, mortality is due mainly to external causes (traffic accidents, chiefly). For people older than 40, mortality is due to cancer and cardiovascular and cerebrovascular diseases. With the implementation of the Networks of Care, the levels of morbidity and mortality have dropped appreciably. For example, the implementation of the Maternal Infant Network in the North and Northeast regions produced a 56% decrease of maternal mortality in these regions between 2020 and 2013.[49]

Other Health Indicators

Immunization program coverage rates for children are high, and they are improving for the elderly. The vaccination rate varies between 83% and 97% for the population at risk. Recently, the immunization against hepatitis B, HPV in preadolescent girls, and influenza gained more attention.[50] It is hoped that in the end, there will be a decrease in demand for hepatic transplants, fewer cervix cancer cases, and a reduction of influenza complications for populations at risk.

Another point that deserves attention relates to the increase of Family Health Program coverage (PSF) for the users of SUS. Between 1998 and 2019, the proportion of older adults registered increased from 4.4% to 64.2%.[51] The degree of coverage varied by region and municipality. One of the positive observations from the program is that the higher the coverage within PSF in a group of municipalities, the greater the decrease in postneonatal infant mortality is; this is associated with a decrease in the number of deaths due to diarrhea and respiratory infections.[52] Other studies suggest a reduction of 15% of avoidable hospitalizations in the years following 1999.[53]

Access

Equity/Universality

The coverage of the public healthcare system in Brazil, as mentioned earlier, is universal and also includes the population otherwise covered by health insurance plans. The main differences between the two models relate to available structures in terms of hospitality, readiness, and assertiveness. Due to a lack of coordination between supply and demand within the system, the concept of "systemic regulation" emerged. That is, access to available resources is largely free, and access to resources that are more complex requires special authorization. Often, because of a lack of generally agreed-upon protocols and therapeutic guidelines, one can observe the installation of mechanisms for managing resources that do not meet the real needs of users in terms of availability, time, and quality. One of the consequences has been an observed increase in lawsuits by disgruntled users pursuing fulfillment of their perceived constitutional rights.[54]

Despite these issues, there have been substantial improvements in standards of care, with new models of procurement of public services by nongovernmental organizations. In addition, a system of regulatory mechanisms has been developed that are based on scientific evidence and/or protocols for economic evaluation of healthcare activities.

The supply of healthcare services has been impacted by changes in demographic characteristics, educational and cultural levels, economic production, and industrial and urban concentrations in different regions of the country. One of the consequences is the concentration of resources of greater complexity in large cities and states in the South and Southeast regions. The distribution of users of health insurance plans is similar, with large participation in the South and Southeast regions, where some cities have over 45% of their populations with health insurance coverage. Wide differences in health insurance coverage exist in other states and regions. In one capital of the North region, for example, approximately 20% of the population maintains a health plan or private health insurance.[18]

Current and Emerging Issues and Challenges

Like other developing countries, Brazil is witnessing important demographic and epidemiologic transitions that are at the root of national healthcare system problems. Brazil faces rapid aging of the population and consequent increases in the prevalence of chronic degenerative diseases. Coupled with this, there is growth in morbidity and mortality in younger populations due to external causes. Projections from IBGE, the National Geographic and Statistic Institute, estimate a stabilization of population around 217 million between 2030 and 2035.[55] These issues will require deep changes in the profile of health facilities, especially in the public sector.

The following issues in Brazilian health care are in need of resolution:

- Addressing the financial and allocation alternatives for provision of resources that complement the current cost models, even if this means an increase in overall spending.
- Restructuring healthcare facilities to treat chronic diseases and their complications more effectively.
- Incorporating new medical technologies.[56]
- Implementing a rigorous approach to ensure high standards of quality and safety for users and patients in outpatient and inpatient settings, especially in mid- and high-complexity care.
- Reviewing medical education programs, with an eye toward the use of evidence-based care protocols and assessments of economical approaches.[56]
- Promoting outpatient and home care.
- Implementing a national electronic health registry that allows the system to identify and evaluate major situations of overspending and off-protocol therapeutic treatments and procedures.[56]
- Reviewing the role of health boards, which are currently responsible for local health control and have political influence in determining spending on municipal and state levels.
- Reviewing and restraining the judiciary, with the goal to reduce interference in the determination of not-scientifically-proven therapeutic procedures, such as in dubious and experimental treatments of cancer.
- Preventing and controlling emerging epidemics, such as those caused by dengue, Zika, and chikungunya, and more recently, the installation of control and surveillance systems for the spread of SARS-CoV-2.

Solutions to these issues will require the cooperation of multiple stakeholders and interest groups in both the public and private sectors. Indeed, one must understand that the Federal Constitution was enacted in a peculiar historical moment at the end of the military period during the transition to full democracy.[18] At that time, many of the approved platforms of the constitutional body included the incorporation of citizen rights and obligations, for which the government had not identified financial resources. As a consequence of this movement, the system now exhibits a series of malfunctions and process failures to which health managers and planners devote much time and effort. For example, investments in new beds and adding new critical care units have been virtually stymied in the public system since the 2000s.

The private system, in turn, has seen important conflicts arise among payers, hospitals, and physicians related to standards of compensation. The private sector, together with some nonprofit organizations, has been largely responsible for the implementation of newer medical technologies and in "making their case" through clinical/economic evaluation studies. Competition continues between funds and payers in this area, as the natural result of entities wishing to attract and increase their number of users in the system.

The emerging epidemic caused by the Zika virus spread rapidly in Brazil. It is thought that the Zika virus infection was brought onto Brazilian soil in 2013 during the Confederation Soccer Championship. This virus was rapidly transmitted to different Brazilian states because its vector, the *Aedes aegypti* mosquito, is highly prevalent in Brazil. As of April 2016, Zika virus infection was reported throughout all of Brazil. Approximately 80% of adult-infected individuals are asymptomatic. The most common symptoms are fever, joint pain, rash, and conjunctivitis. In those who develop symptoms, the disease is usually mild and lasts from several days to a week.[57] There are reports of Guillain-Barré syndrome in adults also affected by Zika virus infection. In fetuses, Zika virus can be devastating. The Brazilian Secretary of Health has confirmed over 2,063 newborns with microcephaly due to Zika virus, and more than 3,505 cases were under investigation from November 2015 to October 2016.[58] In 2023 the reported number of microcephaly cases among newborns in Brazil was 318.[59] This number of cases is nowhere near the amount during the Zika epidemic in 2015–2016. It has been suggested that Zika virus infection can also cause arthrogryposis, brain calcifications, and excessive and redundant scalp skin in newborns, so some researchers use the term "congenital Zika syndrome."[60] Pregnant women are advised to use appropriate insect repellents and long clothing.

In more recent times, during the Global Health Emergency decreed by the World Health Organization due to the spread of SARS-CoV-2, the country sought to adjust its health structures to meet the needs of the population. Despite the measures taken, what was observed was a heterogeneity of actions and policies among the various states, many of them resulting from political practices and decisions by health authorities that contradicted the best scientific evidence. Basically, actions were carried out that substantially increased the capacity in some states with the expansion of beds for critically ill patients, creation of field hospital units, reorganization of models for the allocation of health professionals, and the logistics of materials, equipment, and medicines.

In addition, the roles of the National Health Surveillance Agency (ANVISA) and the National Commission for the Incorporation of Health Technologies (Conitec) were reinforced in mediating and defining which practices and measures could be taken to face the pandemic in Brazil. As a result of the actions of these organizations, the country gradually managed to overcome the previous denialist and anti-scientific discourse and incorporate evidence-based practices, for example, the implementation of a vigorous and effective immunization program for its population. It should be noted that such measures did not definitively eliminate the political conflict that permeated the Brazilian Society, with a certain degree of disinvestment occurring in the sector and the increased relevance of the roles of the SUS in the configuration and delivery of primary health care.

The following represent the myriad healthcare actors, interests, associated problems, and possible resolution alternatives that can be identified for Brazil's foreseeable future:

- *Customers/patients* are individuals who expect immediate access and positive clinical results in the system. There is widespread overuse of the healthcare system, especially when individuals are not satisfied with the treatment that has been rendered and go elsewhere for additional and/or different treatment. Amelioration may occur with the implementation of the Brazilian National Electronic Health Records, which will allow for monitoring of public health actions in real time.
- *Public system providers* (including public hospitals and public ambulatory care units) are caregivers that often are perceived as not as accountable as providers in the private system. Payments to public-sector providers are often substantially less than payments in the private sector, so public-sector productivity is often not as high, and complacency is often seen as more acceptable than what is typically found in the private sector. Improvements are contingent on the establishment of new contractual relationships that reward productivity and eliminate ineffective practices. Improvements may also depend on important changes in legislation dealing with organized labor in the public sector, in terms of curtailing certain worker rights.
- *Private system providers* (including private hospitals and clinics) generally seek to optimize mark-up and profitability margins for healthcare services rendered, and they face strong pressure on prices based on negotiations with third-party payers. In Brazil, physicians are considered part of the private system, in terms of offering private services to clinic outpatients and hospital inpatients.
- *Third-party payers* are important in the private sector and predominantly represent insurance companies and health plans. Third-party payers depend on the performance of the economy as a whole and, therefore, are vulnerable to periods of economic downturn and low production. Third-party payers need to develop funding mechanisms to help them weather economic slumps and to allow smaller carriers to avoid closure or merging.
- The *federal government* provides a major regulatory element of the system and is responsible for the administration of budgetary resources for the public system. The federal government faces ongoing problems with the changing epidemiologic profile and the transitioning geodemographic and structural aspects of the system. A major point of discussion is the need for more resources from the social security budget and the pressure to expand the scope of assistance. For example, an argument has surfaced in recent times that even diapers should be covered by the public system. The federal government generally

has guided its healthcare activities toward overall equity of access and universal coverage.

- The *judiciary and legal systems* interpret the Federal Constitution healthcare mandates and strive to balance the need for protections of individual rights. At times, the courts have been a factor driving imbalance in overall health planning as they consider coverage claims in both the private and public healthcare systems, often without sufficiently evaluating technical issues of healthcare assistance on a scientific basis. To remedy this, the courts should defer to an administrative mechanism that verifies a priori the effectiveness of clinical modalities based on best evidence and outcomes research grounded in scientific methodology.
- The *medical technology and pharmaceutical industries* are greatly affected by the infusion of foreign capital. There is a tendency to launch only products that have higher mark-ups. This sector underwent a major overhaul recently with the introduction of the production of essential and strategic items (e.g., generics) within Brazil in an effort to reduce the dependence on imported medicines.
- *Investors and controllers of foreign money* that arrived in the country have been working to consolidate the supplementary health system through the concentration of health plan operators and the formation of large service networks in hospitals, clinics, and diagnostic support services.

The political situation in Brazil took an extraordinary turn in May 2016, when Brazil's Senate voted to convene a presidential impeachment trial of Dilma Rousseff, who then was suspended from her executive duties and replaced by Michel Temer, who stepped up from vice president to acting president. The Senate voted overwhelmingly in favor of conviction of Rousseff, so Temer served out the remainder of Rousseff's term until January 1, 2019.[3] In the meantime, there has been great uncertainty as to what may occur next in the political arena in Brazil, including the possibility of further corruption investigations and prosecutions of other political office holders.[61] An ongoing federal investigation called the Car Wash Operation (Operação Lava Jato) has implicated officials at all levels in Brazilian government, and many prosecutions have resulted.[62] In the last 2 years, however, the Car Wash Operation suffered many setbacks. Brazil's former president, Luis Ignacio Lula da Silva, was initially convicted and served in a federal prison due to charges of corruption. When this process was reviewed by the Brazilian Supreme Court, Lula was set free. He again became a candidate for the Brazilian presidency and won the election. Since January 2023, Lula has been the president of Brazil.

COVID-19 Pandemic

Brazil has a well-known, successful vaccination program, providing a comprehensive vaccination for free for all Brazilians. Developing a strategy to deliver COVID vaccines to Brazilian people was not that difficult. As a result, 90.2% of the Brazilian population has taken at least one COVID-19 vaccine dose and 83.8% are completely vaccinated. This is a landmark when you consider the number of individuals vaccinated, Brazilian geography (some areas are only reached by small planes or boats).[63]

Conclusion

There are many aspects of the Brazilian healthcare experience that are worthy of being benchmarks in other countries, particularly as related to overall coverage of the population and conceptual innovation. There are many opportunities to extend and improve the quality of care, in both the public and private systems. In essence, the Brazilian healthcare system has been a unique construction of Brazilian society, and one can expect that the following aspects will be maintained into the future: the pursuit of equity, universal access, community-level participation in its control, and broad collaboration from all players in the planning and design of the model.

References

1. Smith A. *A History of Brazil*. New York, NY: Routledge; 2013.
2. Fausto B. *A Concise History of Brazil*. Cambridge, UK: Cambridge University Press; 1999.
3. Central Intelligence Agency. Brazil. In: *The World Factbook*. Updated March 1, 2020. Accessed February 10, 2023. https://www.cia.gov/library/publications/the-world-factbook/geos/br.html.
4. Levine R. *The History of Brazil*. Westport, CT: Greenwood; 1999.
5. Michigan State University. globalEDGE: Brazil. Published 2016. Accessed October 27, 2016. http://globaledge.msu.edu/countries/brazil/government.
6. Farlex. Brazil. In: *The Free Dictionary*. Published 2016. Accessed October 27, 2016. http://encyclopedia2.thefreedictionary.com/Brazil.

7. Mello J. Political parties in Brazil. In: *The Brazil Business*. Updated October 11, 2013. Accessed October 27, 2016. http://thebrazilbusiness.com/article/political-parties-in-brazil.
8. Trading Economics. Brazil exports by country. Accessed February 2, 2025. https://tradingeconomics.com/brazil/exports-by-country.
9. Farah A. Largest trading partners for Brazil. In: *The Brazil Business*. Updated October 24, 2013. Accessed October 27, 2016. http://thebrazilbusiness.com/article/largest-trading-partners-of-brazil.
10. Brazil.org. Updated March 23, 2016. Accessed October 27, 2016. http://www.brazil.org.za.
11. Brazil. In: *World Population Review*. Updated March 2016. Accessed October 27, 2016. http://worldpopulationreview.com/countries/brazil-population/.
12. Nation Master. Compulsory education duration: countries compared. Published 2012. Accessed October 27, 2016. http://www.nationmaster.com/country-info/stats/Education/Compulsary-education-duration.
13. *The Economist*. Higher education in Brazil: the mortar-board boom. Published September 15, 2012. Accessed October 27, 2016. http://www.economist.com/node/21562955/print.
14. World Health Organization Data. Brazil. Accessed January 27, 2025. https://data.who.int/countries/076.
15. Bertolli Filho C. *História da Saúde Pública no Brasil*. 11th ed. Atica, Brazil; 2008.
16. Rosemberg AMF. Breve historia da saúde pública no Brasil. In: Rouquayrol MZ, Gurgel M. *Epidemiologia & Saúde*. 7th ed. Rio de Janeiro, Brazil: Medbook; 2013.
17. Paim J, Travassos C, Almeida C, Bahia L, Macinko J. The Brazilian health system: history, advances, and challenges. *Lancet*. 2011;377(9779):1778-1779.
18. Mendes A, Marques RM. Saúde e Sociedade. Democracia, saúde pública e universalidade: o difícil caminhar. *Saúde e Sociedade*. 2007;16(3):35-51.
19. Agência Nacional de Vigilância Sanitária. Registros de medicamentos. Published September 2016. Accessed November 1, 2016. http://www.anvisa.gov.br/medicamentos/registro/index.htm.
20. Brasil—Ministério da Saude. Norma operacional da assistência à Saude—NOAS—SUS. Published February 27, 2002. Accessed April 4, 2016. http://bvsms.saude.gov.br/bvs/saudelegis/gm/2002/prt0373_27_02_2002.html.
21. Brasil. Lei 9961 de 28 janeiro de 2000. Cria a Agencia Nacional de Saude Suplementar e dá outras providencias. Updated 2004. Accessed March 25, 2016. http://www.planalto.gov.br/ccivil_03/leis/L9961.htm.
22. Brasil. Emenda Constitucional n.º 29 de 13 setembro de 2000. Altera os arts. 34, 35, 156 e 198 da Constituição Federal de 1988 e dá outras providências. Published September 14, 2000. Accessed March 25, 2016. http://www.planalto.gov.br/ccivil_03/constituicao/Emendas/Emc/emc29.htm.
23. Brasil. Lei 9.787, de 10 de fevereiro de 1999. Altera a Lei n.º 6.360, de 26 de setembro de 1976, que dispõe sobre a vigilância sanitária, estabelece o medicamento genérico, dispõe sobre a utilização de nomes genéricos em produtos farmacêuticos e dá outras providências. Diário oficial da união; 11 fev 1999.
24. Barbosa EC. 25 Anos do Sistema Único de Saúde: Conquistas e Desafios. *Revista de Gestão em Sistemas de Saúde*. 2013;2(2):85-102.
25. Health is the greatest concern of Brazilians Surce: Senate Agency. Accessed February 24, 2023. https://www12.senado.leg.br/noticias/materias/2022/12/12/datasenado-saude-e-a-maior-preocupacao-do-brasileiro.
26. Bassette F. Número de pacientes de outros Estados cresce 89% no HC. Published May 31, 2006. Accessed April 12, 2016. http://www1.folha.uol.com.br/fsp/cotidian/ff3105200611.html.
27. World Bank. Brazil data. Updated 2016. Accessed March 25, 2016. http://data.worldbank.org/country/brazil.
28. Portaria n.º 1101/GM. (2002, 12 de junho). Parâmetros de cobertura de assistência do Sistema Único de Saúde. Published 2012. Accessed April 4, 2016. http://www1.saude.ba.gov.br/regulasaude/2009/PN%20PORTARIAS%202009/nvos%20pdfs%202009/PT%20GM%201101%2012.06.2002.pdf.
29. Vigitel 2014 Vigilância de fatores de risco e proteção para doenças crônicas por inquérito telefônico. Published 2014. Accessed November 1, 2016. http://www.abeso.org.br/uploads/downloads/80/553a243c4b9f3.pdf.
30. Folha De S. Paulo, Datafolha/Instituto de Ciência, Tecnologia e Qualidade: Censo Demográfico Farmacêutico. Published January 20, 2014. Accessed March 25, 2016. http://folha.com/no1399934.
31. World Health Organization. Global Health Observatory data repository. Published 2013. Accessed March 25, 2016. http://apps.who.int/gho/data/node.main.A1444.
32. CREMESP. Demografia médica no Brasil. Published February 2013. Accessed March 25, 2016. http://www.cremesp.org.br/pdfs/DemografiaMedicaBrasilVol2.pdf.
33. Demografia Médica no Brasil 2: Cenários e Indicadores de Distribuição (PDF). Conselho Federal de Medicina (CFM) Tabela 7—Distribuição de médicos registrados (CFM) por 1.000 habitantes, segundo Unidades da Federação. Brasil; 2013: 256.
34. World Health Organization. Working together for health. *World Health Report 2006*. Geneva, Switzerland: WHO; 2006:237.
35. A Enfermagem. Perfil da enfermagem. Published 2012. Accessed November 1, 2016. http://aenfermagem.com.br/materia/perfil-da-enfermagem/.
36. Agencia Nacional de Saude Suplementar. Cadernos de informação em Saude. Published December 2013. Accessed March 25, 2016. http://www.ans.gov.br/index.php/a-ans/sala-de-noticias-ans/numeros-do-setor/1485-ans-publica-caderno-de-informacao-da-saude-suplementar-.
37. Agencia Nacional de Saude Suplementar. Guia ANS de Planos de Saude. Published 2013. Accessed March 25, 2016. http://www.ans.gov.br/index.php/planos-de-saude-e-operadoras/contratacao-e-troca-de-plano.
38. Agencia Nacional de Saúde Suplementar. Nova listagem de coberturas obrigatórias entra em vigor. Published 2011. Accessed November 1, 2016. http://www.ans.gov.br/sala-de-imprensa/releases/consumidor/1268-nova-listagem-de-coberturas-obrigatorias-entre-em-vigor highlight=WyJyZXNvbHVcdTAwZTdcdTAwZjVlcyIsInNvYnJlIiwicm9sIiwiZGUiLCJwcm9jZWRpbWVudG9zIiwiJ3Byb2NlZGltZW50b3MiLCJzb2JyZSByb2wiLCJzb2JyZSByb2wgZGUiLCJyb2wgZGUiLCJyb2wgZGUgcHJvY2VkaW1lbnRvcyIsImRlIHByb2NlZGltZW50b3MiXQ.
39. Associação Nacional de Hospitais Privados. Observatório, 2015. Published 2016. Accessed November 1, 2016. http://anahp.com.br/produtos-anahp/observatorio/observatorio-anahp-ingles-2015.
40. Brasil. Câmara dos Deputados. Consultoria de Orçamento e Fiscalização Financeira. Nucleo de Saude, 2011. Updated 2016.

Accessed March 25, 2016. http://www2.camara.leg.br/a-camara/estruturaadm.

41. Brasil—Ministério da Saude—Indicadores e Dados Básicos—IDB—2012—E—Indicadores de Recursos. Published 2012. Accessed March 25, 2016. http://tabnet.datasus.gov.br/cgi/tabcgi.exe?idb2012/e0601.def.
42. Brasil. MS. Indicadores e Dados Básicos - IDB - 2009 - E - 4 - Indicadores de recursos—Gasto com consumo percentual em saude sobre PIB ajustado, por setor. Published 2012. Accessed March 25, 2016. http://tabnet.datasus.gov.br/cgi/idb2012/e04.htm.
43. Agencia Nacional de Saude Suplementar—ANS—Caderno de informaçaõ da saude suplementar—2011. Published December 2013. Accessed March 25, 2016.http://www.ans.gov.br/images/stories/Materiais_para_pesquisa/Perfil_setor/Caderno_informacao_saude_suplementar/2013_mes12_caderno_informacao.pdf.
44. Brasil. MS. Informações de Saude: Indicadores de produção assistencial 2015. Published 2015. Accessed November 1, 2016. http://www2.datasus.gov.br/DATASUS/index.php?area=0202&id=19451&VObj=http://tabnet.datasus.gov.br/cgi/deftohtm.exe?sih/cnv/qr.
45. Bahia L. A privatização no sistema de saúde brasileiro nos anos 2000: tendências e justificação In: Santos NR, Amarante PD, *orgs, Gestão Pública e Relação Público Privado na Saúde*. Rio de Janeiro, Brazil: Cebes; 2011.
46. Marins M, Daher DV. O programa nacional de melhoria do acesso e qualidade da atenção básica (PMAQ-AB). Relato de experiência. *Revista Enfermagem Profissional*. 2014;1(2), 331-337.
47. Brasil. Indicadores de transição do Pacto pela Saude e Contrato Organizativo da Ação Pública de Saude (COAP); 2012. Published February 27, 2015. Accessed March 25, 2016. http://tabnet.datasus.gov.br/cgi/pacto/2012/pactmap.htm.
48. Brasil - Ministério da Saude - Indicadores e Dados Básicos - IDB - 2012-3 Indicadores epidemiológicos - Taxas de mortalidade infantil. Published 2016. Accessed March 25, 2016. http://tabnet.datasus.gov.br/cgi/idb2012/matriz.htm#mort.
49. Brasil. Portal da Saude. Rede Cegonha: Indicadores de impacto sobre a assistencia integrada. Published 2012. Accessed March 25, 2016. http://dab.saude.gov.br/portaldab/ape_redecegonha.php.
50. Brasil. Portal da Saude. Programa Nacional de Imunização. Published 2015. Accessed April 7, 2016. http://pni.datasus.gov.br/sipni/documentos/Protocolo_MRC_vers%E3o_27-01-2015.pdf.
51. Kessler M, Thumé E, Marmot M, et al. Family health strategy, primary health care, and social inequalities in mortality among older adults in Bagé, Southern Brazil. *Am J Public Health*. 2021:111(5):927-936. Accessed January 27, 2025. https://pmc.ncbi.nlm.nih.gov/articles/PMC8034023/.
52. Rasella D, Aquino R, Barreto ML. Impact of the Family Health Program on the quality of vital information and reduction of child unattended deaths in Brazil: an ecological longitudinal study. *BMC Public Health*. 2010;10:380. doi: 10.1186/1471-2458-10-380.
53. Guanais F, Macinko J. Primary care and avoidable hospitalizations: evidence from Brazil. *J Ambul Care Manage*. 2009;32:114-121.
54. Diniz D, Machado TRC, Penalva J. A judicialização de saude no Distrito Federal, Brasil. *Ciência e Saude Coletiva*. 2014;19(2):591-598. doi: 10.1590/1413-81232014192.23072012.
55. Instituto Brasileiro de Geografia e Estatística: Projeção da população do Brasil por sexo e idade: 2000–2060. Published 2015. Accessed April 4, 2016. http://www.ibge.gov.br/home/estatistica/populacao/projecao_da_populacao/2013/.
56. Vecina Neto G, Malik AM. *Gestão em Saude*. Rio de Janeiro: Guanabara Koogan; 2011.
57. de Carvalho NS, de Carvalho BF, Fugaça CA, Dóris B, Biscaia ES. Zika virus infection during pregnancy and microcephaly occurrence: a review of literature and Brazilian data. *Brazil J Infect Dis*. 2016;20(3):282-289.
58. Saúde. Published 2016. Accessed November 1, 2016. http://combateaedes.saude.gov.br/images/pdf/informe_microcefalia_epidemiologico48.pdf.
59. Mendoza J. Number of microcephaly cases among newborns in Brazil from 2010 to 2023. Statista. November 29, 2024. Accessed January 27, 2025. https://www.statista.com/statistics/507576/microcephaly-cases-among-newborns-in-brazil/#:~:text=Congentinal%20Zika%20virus%20syndrom%20in%20Brazil%20The,affected%20state%20in%20the%20country%20was%20Pernambuco.
60. Rasmussen SA, Jamieson DJ, Honein MA, Petersen LR. Zika virus and birth defects: reviewing the evidence for causality. *N Engl J Med*. 2016;374:1981-1987. doi: 10.1056/NEJMsr1604338.
61. Anderson JL. A way forward for Brazil. *The New Yorker*. Published June 1, 2016. Accessed October 27, 2016. http://www.newyorker.com/news/daily-comment/a-way-forward-for-brazil.
62. Alves L. Brazil's former Speaker arrested on corruption charges. *The Rio Times*. Published October 20, 2016. Accessed November 1, 2016. http://riotimesonline.com/brazil-news/rio-politics/brazils-former-speaker-arrested-on-corruption-charges/.
63. Mathieu E, Ritchie H, Rodés-Guirao L, et al. Coronavirus (COVID-19) vaccinations. Our World in Data. Published 2020. Revised 2024. Accessed February 7, 2025. https://ourworldindata.org/covid-vaccinations.

CHAPTER 10

Cuba

Ronn Pineo, Carrie Shaver, Kelcie Creel, and Chelsea Pritchard

Country Description

Table 10-1 Cuba

Nationality	Noun: Cuban(s) Adjective: Cuban
Ethnic groups	White 64.1%, Multiracial 26.6%, Afro-Cuban 9.3% (2012 est.) *Note: Data represent racial self-identification from Cuba's latest national census.*
Religions	Christian 58.9%, folk religion 17.6%, Buddhist <1%, Hindu <1%, Jewish <1%, Muslim <1%, other <1%, none 23.2% (2020 est.) *Note: Folk religions include religions of African origin, spiritualism, and others intermingled with Catholicism or Protestantism. Data are estimated because no authoritative source on religious affiliation exists for Cuba.*
Language	Spanish (official)
Literacy	99.67% *Note: Adult literacy rate includes people 15 years of age and older who can read and write a short statement about their everyday life.*
Government type	Communist state
Date of independence	U.S. recognition of Cuban independence, May 19, 1902. Following the defeat of Spain in 1898, the United States remained in Cuba as an occupying power until the Republic of Cuba was formally installed on May 19, 1902. Date of independence from Spain, October 10, 1898. Carlos Manuel de Céspedes issued the first call for independence, the *grito de Yara* (for the town in eastern Cuba where the call was first given).
Gross domestic product	Total GDP: 107.35 billion USD (2020) GDP per capita: 9,499.59 USD (2020)
Unemployment rate	2.76% (2021 est.) 2.62% (2020 est.) 1.74% (2019 est.) *Note: Data are official rates; unofficial estimates are nearly double. The Cuban workforce relies heavily on informal labor.*

Table 10-1 Cuba

Natural hazards	Coasts are subject to hurricanes from August to November (in general, the country averages about one hurricane every other year); droughts are common.
Environment: current issues	Soil degradation and desertification (brought on by extensive farming techniques and natural disasters) are the main environmental problems; biodiversity loss; deforestation; air and water pollution.
Population	10,985,974 (2023 est.)
Age structure	0–14 years: 16.39% (male 926,457/female 874,347) 15–64 years: 66.81% (male 3,692,573/female 3,647,316) 65 years and over: 16.8% (male 835,005/female 1,010,276) (2022 est.)
Median age	Total: 42.1 years Male: 40.2 years Female: 43.8 years (2020 est.)
Population growth rate	−0.19% (2023 est.)
Birth rate	9.99 births/1,000 population (2023 est.)
Death rate	9.37 deaths/1,000 population (2023 est.)
Disease burden	Communicable disease deaths: 75.79/100,000 population Noncommunicable disease deaths: 530.2/100,000 population Injury deaths: 24.87/100,000 population (2019 est.)
Net migration rate	−2.53 migrant(s)/1,000 population (2023 est.)
Gender ratio	Total population: 0.93 male/female At birth: 1.06 male/female 0–14 years: 1.07 male/female 15–64 years: 1 male/female 65 years and over: 0.71 male/female (2023 est.)
Infant mortality rate	Total: 4.07 deaths/1,000 live births Male: 4.58 deaths/1,000 live births Female: 3.52 deaths/1,000 live births (2023 est.)
Life expectancy at birth	Total population: 79.87 years Male: 77.53 years Female: 82.35 years (2023 est.)
Total fertility rate	1.71 children born/woman (2023 est.)
HIV/AIDS adult prevalence rate	0.5% (2021 est.)
Number of people living with HIV/AIDS	36,000 (2021 est.)
HIV/AIDS deaths	471 total deaths since 2020 3.76 per 100,000 (2020 est.)

USD = U.S. dollars.

Data aggregated from the following sources. Accessed April 10, 2023. Central Intelligence Agency. *The World Fact Book, 2023*: Cuba. https://www.cia.gov/the-world- factbook/countries/cuba/; Statista. *Health in Cuba: Statistics & Facts*. https://www.statista.com/topics/8690/health-in-cuba/; UNAIDS. *Country Factsheets: Cuba, 2021*. https://www.unaids.org/en/regionscountries/countries/cuba; World Bank Open Data. *GDP—Cuba*. https://data.worldbank.org/indicator/NY.GDP.MKTP.CD?locations=CU; World Health Organization. *The Global Health Observatory: Global Health Estimates—Leading Causes of Death*. https://www.who.int/data/gho/data/themes/mortality-and-global-health-estimates/ghe-leading-causes-of-death.

Cuba is a small, underdeveloped, and low-resource island nation (see **Table 10-1** for a detailed description of the country). If it can deliver excellent public health care, so, too, can any nation. Cuba's per capita gross domestic product (GDP) is about one-tenth that of the United States and about half of that of Mexico or Brazil. While Cuba spends about one-twentieth per capita on health care compared with the United States, and roughly one-tenth of what Mexico and Brazil spend per capita, Cubans nevertheless enjoy longer life expectancy than people in the United States (79 years in Cuba compared with 78 years in the United States), in Mexico (77 years), in Brazil (75 years), in Latin America as a whole (75 years), and in the developing world as a whole (66 years).

Cuba also has a superior childhood mortality rate (the number of deaths to age 5 per 1,000 live births per year) of 6, compared with 8 in the United States. What is all the more remarkable is that Cuba has realized its healthcare achievements in the face of significant challenges, from punishing covert operations in prior years carried out by the U.S. Central Intelligence Agency (CIA), the end of Soviet aid in the late 1980s, and the continuing U.S. economic embargo.[1–5]

Current Relations with the United States: Failed Rapprochement

President Barack Obama (2009–2017) opened a new chapter in U.S. policy toward Cuba, beginning in January 2015, by relaxing key trade and travel restrictions. Building upon these changes, the nations exchanged ambassadors in the summer of 2015. The administration of Donald J. Trump (2017–2021), however, reversed much of the Obama administration's policies toward Cuba, retightening trade and travel restrictions. On November 9, 2017, President Trump put in place tougher restrictions on travel to Cuba, as well as making it again more difficult for U.S. companies to do business with Cuban enterprises associated with the Cuban military, something that is common in the Cuban economy. Then, following a series of medical issues that mysteriously developed among American diplomats in Cuba, President Trump withdrew nearly all U.S. officials from the Havana embassy.[6–8]

Under the administration of President Joseph Biden, beginning in 2021, the embassy in Havana was staffed once again, but otherwise, the Trump era restrictions were not substantially reversed. Americans still cannot visit Cuba as tourists. The U.S. trade embargo remained in place and cannot be ended without an act of the U.S. Congress. While the suffering of some past American diplomatic personnel stationed in Havana cannot be denied, a conclusive explanation of the origin of their problems has remained elusive. Recent research has come to reject the notion of a sonar attack by a foreign adversary, a view that has sometimes been offered to explain the conditions experienced.

History of Cuba

Cuba's history is marked by colonization, slavery, revolution, and the emergence of a one-party government led by Fidel Castro and the Communist Party. Under Spanish colonialism, the port of Havana served as a hub for transatlantic trade. Enslaved Africans were brought to the island, especially as the forests were cleared and sugar was planted in the 18th century. Cuba escaped from Spanish colonialism in 1898 but continued as a de facto U.S. colony until the 1959 Revolution. Within a couple of years, Cuba transitioned to dependency on the Soviet Union as a significant recipient of aid; and after that, on socialist Venezuela as an aid recipient. Cuba now, for the first time since the Spanish conquest, is on its own.[6,9]

Before the Revolution: Economic and Social Conditions

The United States dominated the Cuban economy in the years before the Revolution, controlling 80% of Cuba's trade. U.S. firms ran the public utilities, the railroad, and all of the oil refineries. Two-thirds of food production came from U.S.-owned agrobusiness enterprises. U.S. developers owned half of the arable land on the island.

Cuba was a nation of great inequality, which had grave implications for public health. Eight percent of landholders owned three-quarters of the land. At least a quarter of the working-age population was unemployed much of the time. Meanwhile, one-fifth of the population received 58% of the income, while the bottom fifth took in just 2%, one of the lowest rates for the bottom 20% in the world, then or now.[10,11] Rural districts in the eastern, Afro-Cuban section of the island endured especially impoverished conditions. In the years just before the Revolution, Cuban annual per capita income reached $374 USD in the cities but was only US $91 in the countryside; 87% of urban homes had electricity, but only 9% or rural ones did. Only 4% of the rural population could afford to eat meat regularly. More than one in 10 rural dwellers suffered from tuberculosis.[10–12]

Revolution

In the mid-20th century, Cuba underwent a revolution that brought Fidel Castro and the Communist Party to power. In 1959, Castro completed the successful revolution against the U.S.-backed government of Fulgencio Batista. Castro soon declared Cuba to be a socialist state. Following the triumph of the Revolution, tension developed with the United States, falling into a downward spiral of action and over-reaction. In 1961, the United States established an economic embargo against Cuba, seeking to stop all nations from trading with the nation. This U.S. policy has brought serious health repercussions for Cuba, halting the importation of food, medicine, and medical equipment. According to Amnesty International, "the export of medicines and medical equipment [from the United States to Cuba] continues to be severely limited and has a detrimental impact on . . . health."[1,12–17] As a partial solution, Cuba was fast developing the capacity to produce most of its own medicines by the 1980s.[6,15]

The "Special Period"

Throughout the 1960s and into the 1980s, Cuba aligned with the Soviet Union and received in return significant economic aid. This led to tensions between Cuba and the United States, including the Cuban Missile Crisis in 1962. However, after the collapse of the Soviet Union in 1991, Cuba faced significant economic challenges, labeled the "Special Period" by the Communist Party government. Cuba's annual $5 billion USD in aid allocation from the Soviet Union began to plummet dramatically, then was halted altogether. This cut in support brought devastation to Cuba, with its GDP dropping by an astonishing one-third from 1989 to 1993. Cuba's total foreign trade fell by 80%. Gasoline, previously provided at below cost by the Soviets, dried up. In 1987, Cuba had imported 7.8 million tons of Soviet oil; in 1995, it took in just 3 million tons. As gasoline grew scarce, many Cubans turned to bicycles for transportation. On farms, oxen replaced tractors. Recovery was slow. By 2000, the Cuban economy was still 18% below its 1989 level.[12,18–20]

Food imports fell by at least half between 1989 and 1993, leading to a one-third drop in average caloric intake per person. The average weight of adult men in Cuba dropped by over 20 lb. As cuts came to Cuba's social support programs, the government gathered communities together to share information and to seek consultation. Starting in 1994, Castro relaxed the prohibition on farmers' markets, making vegetables much more widely available. Cuba began steadily shifting from vast, Soviet-style collective farms to community and individual plots. The government set in place food rationing programs, with at least half of island agricultural production targeted for food rations. With the vast drop in food imports, urban people planted vegetable gardens in their backyards or in nearby vacant lots. As Cubans shifted their diets from imported foods high in fat, sugar, and salt to home-grown fresh vegetables, rates of heart diseases and hypertension fell markedly. By 1998, Havana residents had sown over 26,000 community gardens, usually collective efforts, with everyone in the neighborhood expected to participate.

By the end of the 1990s, Cuba had recovered in food production, reaching levels nearly twice those at the start of the decade. Nevertheless, Cuba continues to import food to meet most of its needs. The response by Castro to the food crisis during the special period demonstrated at least one benefit of an authoritarian system: The government could act immediately and in a cohesive manner without having to line up political support or make compromises with quarreling political interests.[2,12,16,19–23]

The U.S. Congress tightened the economic embargo on Cuba in 1992 under the Torricelli bill, banning vessels from coming to the United States if they had called in Cuba within the past 6 months. In 1996, the U.S. Congress, with the Helms-Burton Act, added fines and even jail time for those individuals or companies that traded with Cuba. As a consequence, the special period brought a serious deterioration in potable water and sewer services in Cuba. The percentage of chlorinated potable water dropped from 98% in 1988 to just 26% in 1994. Deaths from diarrheal diseases more than doubled, and Cuba likewise saw many more low-birth-weight babies in these years.[1,2] The embargo remains a central impediment to the health of the Cuban economy; lifting the U.S. embargo would likely boost Cuba's GDP by 5% or 6% annually, and would substantially improve access to food and hard-to-get medicines and medical supplies.

Size and Geography

Cuba is a small nation, 42,427 square miles (about the size of Virginia, or smaller than the Netherlands), running some 785 miles east to west. The population of Cuba is 11 million (about the size of Ohio, or smaller than Chad), with the capital city of Havana numbering 2 million people. Although the socialist government has made considerable efforts to improve rural conditions, many modern services can be harder to find outside of Havana. The eastern portion of the island is historically the region with the largest Afro-Cuban population (see **Figure 10-1**). With Cuba's disproportionate economic focus on Havana, the eastern

Figure 10-1 Map of Cuba

Courtesy of the Central Intelligence Agency.

district has long been ignored. This region of the country has long shown the worst rankings in standard health metrics.

Government and Political System

Cuba is a single-party state, governed by President Miguel Díaz-Canel and the leadership of the *Partido Comunista de Cuba* (Communist Party of Cuba or PCC). Cuba's political system is summarized in **Table 10-2**. Political oppression remains a serious concern in Cuba, although this situation was hardly unique to the Castros and the present Communist Party leadership. The pre-Revolution Batista regime's brutal repression of all political opponents, real and imagined, contributed much to its own downfall. Fidel Castro (in power from 1959 to 2008) could be fiercely intolerant of dissent: By 1965, he had jailed some 20,000 political prisoners, opponents of the Revolution. From 1959 to 2000, at least 1 million people left Cuba, a total of 10% to 15% of the population, although many of these people were economic refugees, not individuals fleeing political persecution. Problems have continued. Vast demonstrations in July 2021, protesting economic and political conditions, led to many arrests. Even in April 2023, more than 900 political opponents remained in jail. In 2022 and 2023, Cuba began to experience the largest emigration in its history, with at least 200,000 people leaving the island, driven away by economic shortages and the lack of political freedoms. Cuban speech remains restricted, with only state-run mass media permitted.[24,25]

Table 10-2 Cuba Political System

Government type	Single party state
Government structure	Executive branch Unicameral legislative branch Judicial branch
Political party and leader	Cuban Communist Party (PCC) Miguel Díaz-Canel (President) Manuel Marrero Cruz (Prime Minister)
Constitution	Latest version ratified in 2019
Legal system	Civil law system is based on Spanish civil code

Data from Central Intelligence Agency. Cuba. In: *The World Factbook*. Published 2023. Accessed February 20, 2023. https://www.cia.gov/the-world-factbook/countries/cuba/#government.

Macroeconomics, Business, and Economic Environment

Cuba's economy is largely state controlled and heavily influenced by government policies. The country has a history of economic difficulties, which are often attributed to the U.S. trade embargo that has been in place since 1961. However, the Cuban government has also been criticized for its rigid economic policies and the lack of incentives for entrepreneurship and private enterprise.

Despite the challenges, the country has a well-educated population, with a literacy rate of over 99%. In recent years, the government has made efforts to attract foreign investment and develop its tourism industry. Cuba has a wealth of cultural and historical attractions, and the government has been working to improve infrastructure and expand hotel accommodations for tourists.

Since 1959, while most Cuban economic indicators have declined, most social and health indicators have improved markedly, especially in rural zones that had the most catching up to do. At the time of the Revolution, Cuba was already well ahead of most Latin American nations in general economic conditions, boasting the third highest GDP per capita in the region, after Venezuela and Uruguay. By 2005, however, Cuba had slumped to twelfth in Latin American per capita GDP. In 2021 and 2022, the Cuban GDP grew at a slow rate of 1% to 2% annually, and the forecast for the next several years is not encouraging.[16,18,26]

Steps Toward Economic Opening in Cuba: Adoption of "Market Socialism"

During the special period of the 1990s, Fidel Castro took the first tentative steps toward opening the economy to some elements of a free market. But by 1996, as Cuba began to recover, Fidel slowed the opening process before reversing this impulse entirely in 2003. A new donor, Venezuela, under leftist ally Hugo Chávez (1999–2013), began to offer generous aid to Cuba, especially low-cost oil that Cuba could use or resell on the international market.[18,27]

In the midst of all this came a change of political leaders. Fidel fell ill in 2006 with diverticulitis and his brother Raúl Castro took over as acting president. In 2008, Raúl Castro became president, elected by the Cuban national assembly. He retired from this post in 2018 after the second of two 5-year terms, at age 87.

Responding to Cuba's long-term problem of low productivity, Raúl started a series of basic economic transformations, steps that grew out of his experiences in managing the Cuban military's many economic enterprises. The changes were long overdue. As Fidel admitted in 2010, "the Cuban model doesn't even work for us anymore."[28] Ordinary Cubans can now take advantage of vastly more opportunities to work for themselves or start their own small businesses. Before Raúl Castro's reforms, approximately 15% of the labor force worked outside of the state-run sector, but today, about 40% do. As Cuban scholar William LeoGrande has termed it, Cuba has a "market socialist economy," a change designed to help distribute goods more efficiently.[29] However, since 2019, when President Díaz Canel assumed power, Cuba has slow walked any further opening of the economy.[18,25,27,29,30] A summary of the Cuban economy in 2020 is displayed in **Table 10-3**.

Brief History of the Healthcare System

Beginning in 1984, Cuba started the implementation of its "one doctor plus one nurse team" approach (called Basic Health Teams), with each team unit caring for 80 to 150 families. The healthcare teams

Table 10-3 Components of the Cuban Economy

Cuban Economy, 2020		
Total GDP	**107.35 Billion USD**	**9499.6 USD per capita**
GDP growth, annual	−10.9%	In 2021, increased by 12.2 percentage points to 1.3%, recovering from the initial economic impact of the COVID-19 pandemic.
General government spending	41.7 billion USD	

(continues)

Table 10-3 Components of the Cuban Economy *(continued)*

Cuban Economy, 2020		
Total GDP	**107.35 Billion USD**	**9499.6 USD per capita**
Households and nonprofit institutions serving households consumption	286.78 billion USD	Market value of all goods and services purchased by households, including the expenditures of nonprofit or nongovernmental institutions serving households.
Imports	8.07 billion USD, a 26.47% decline from 2019	Main imports are machinery, food, and fuel products. 2019: 10.97 billion USD, a 12.7% decline from 2018. 2018: 12.57 billion USD, an 11.17% increase from 2017.
Exports	8.77 billion USD, a 30.58% decline from 2019	Major exports include medical internationalism programs, nickel, cane sugar, cigars, fuel, beverages, metallic ores, fish, cement, oil, and thyroid extract. 2019: 12.63 billion USD, a 13.06% decline from 2018. 2018: 14.53 billion USD, a 3.1% increase from 2017.
Travel and tourism	6.50 billion USD	Leisure travel, medical tourism, and informal/illegal sale or illicit goods tourism.

Data from the following sources. Accessed April 10, 2023. Statista. *Cuba's Economy & Society*. https://www.statista.com/study/48428/cuba/; Macrotrends. *Cuba Imports 1970–2023*. https://www.macrotrends.net/countries/CUB/cuba/imports; Macrotrends. *Cuba Exports 1970–20*. https://www.macrotrends.net/countries/CUB/cuba/exports.

live in the communities that they serve, or at least as much as is feasible given continuing housing shortages, with the goal of coming to better understand local health issues. Usually, the doctor's offices are on the first floor of their clinic, where the staff treat patients most mornings. Upstairs are the healthcare team's living quarters, with the dwellings provided free of charge. In this way, the healthcare professional teams are much more likely to notice medical conditions of the people they serve before most afflictions can grow to become too serious. The teams use their house calls as opportunities to remind residents to take their medications (supplied free or at very low price-controlled costs) and to exercise more, and usually quiz their patients closely about their daily diets. During the special period, Castro charged teams with a nationwide effort to assure food security, directing the teams to check on basic food supplies in each household. Today, most healthcare teams endeavor to see every individual in their community at least twice a month, whether household members are sick or in good health.

In recent years, Cuba has sometimes added public health experts to the doctor/nurse teams. The public healthcare specialist's core tasks focus on mosquito abatement, monitoring of potable water supplies, and inspecting sewer line hook-ups. Cuba has made a massive commitment of labor power to health, with more than one of 10 workers in the nation employed in some way in the health service sector.

Cuban Medical Internationalism

Cuba is committed to medical internationalism, sending medical missions all over the world and seeking to help fellow developing nations. Cuba makes an oversized contribution in this regard: Its international medical assistance is greater than that offered by all of the developed nations of the world combined. Cuba has posted over 130,000 medical personnel in 107 nations. By 2011, one in every 241 Cubans was serving abroad in a foreign aid program, in medical or other social outreach initiatives. Estimates place the number of lives saved by Cuban medical internationalism at over 2 million people.[1,31–35] Cuba has medical brigades in over 30 nations in Africa and many in the Pacific islands. It also sends many other professionals abroad, especially teachers to assist in literacy campaigns in Spanish-speaking nations.

Meanwhile, some in Cuba have questioned the wisdom of sending so many doctors abroad. Complaints from Cuban patients have emerged, with some arguing that waiting times at clinics have increased with the placement of so many Cuban doctors overseas. With many doctors abroad, the workload per doctor in Cuba rose from around 600 patients to as many as 1,500 patients. By 2008, a quarter of Cuban physicians were working abroad, with nearly 37,000 health professionals stationed in some 72 nations. By 2012, some 41,000 medical workers were abroad, working in 68 countries. Some reports concluded that a third or as many as half of all Cuban doctors had been exported, sent to earn money for the Revolution, if not earning enough for themselves or their families. Serious money is involved: More than a quarter of Cuba's export earnings come from income gained through its medical internationalism programs. Today, the largest share of Cuba's export earnings comes from its medical missions abroad.

The Biotechnology Sector in Cuba

Shortly after the Revolution, Fidel Castro demanded that the foreign-owned drug companies in Cuba lower drug prices. When the companies refused, Castro seized the enterprises and all of their assets. From this beginning, and with gathering speed in the 1980s, biotechnology became an important sector of economic achievement and scientific advance for Cuba.[36,37]

In May 2002, then U.S. Undersecretary of State for Arms Control, John Bolton, announced that "the United States believes that Cuba has at least a limited offensive biological warfare and research and development effort." "Cuba has provided dual-use biotechnology to other rogue states," the undersecretary suggested.[38] But Bolton's views were not grounded in fact; the Cuban biotechnology industry is entirely focused on humanitarian and medical purposes. The evidence is overwhelming. Today, there are a number of drug manufacturing facilities in Cuba making pharmaceutical generics and vaccines. Cuban facilities, including the flagship Carlos J. Finlay Institute and BioCubaFarma, which together produce a vast amount of medicines and medical equipment in Cuba.[39] Cuba has made particularly significant progress in pioneering a hepatitis B vaccine. Of the 13 vaccines that Cuban children routinely receive, eight are produced in the country. The biotech sector in Cuba responds to the needs identified at the local level, which are carefully documented in the data collection and reports that are a main focus of health care. The Cuban biotechnology sector focuses on the quantifiable areas of greatest human need; it does not have to be concerned with producing profits, nor, given the Cuban legal landscape, does it have to worry about being sued. The Cuban biotechnology sector does not claim patent rights to its discoveries, making the medicines readily available to people in need around the globe.[1,22,37,38,40]

Cuba exports pharmaceuticals to 40 nations, sending some 38 different products, all at lower prices than global pharmaceutical firms offer. Cuba also manufactures mosquito sprays, especially those used in Africa to combat malaria. Cuba's policies of making pharmaceuticals available to ordinary people in developing nations stands in contrast to the approach taken by the for-profit, multinational pharmaceutical companies, which routinely seek to secure monopoly rights over drugs they have developed, or to which they purchased the rights. There is a desperate global need for medications and vaccinations for use by people in the tropics, generally the lowest-resource regions in the world. Some researchers refer to this as the 10/90 gap, where 90% or more of research and development of medicines are directed toward 10% or less of the world's population. Consequently, Cuba's biotechnology sector is seeking to address this global healthcare gap, in solidarity with global communities.[33,41]

The Current Healthcare System

Cuban Health Care: Prevention and Community Involvement

Cuba has developed its own unique system (**Table 10-4**), one that seeks to be highly responsive to the special conditions and challenges each local population faces. Health care, education, housing, transportation, and basic necessities are all either free or available at a nominal charge. The Cuban medical system focuses on consultation with patients and local communities; disease prevention; and directing scarce resources toward the groups most in need, especially expectant mothers, infants, children, and the infirm elderly. Cuba practices social medicine, dealing more with the conditions that lead to poor health (nutrition, potable water, sanitation, vaccination, mosquito control) and giving less focus to expensive curative treatments. Commitment to this approach was underscored in the 1976 constitution in article 50, which assured universal health care. Deepening this pledge, Cuba often works cooperatively with the WHO and the Pan American Health Organization (PAHO), responding actively to special initiatives from these and other international health agencies or special health initiatives, which provide much-needed financing as well as external ratification for Cuba's healthcare model.[31] Cuba also uses a great deal of natural/traditional/complementary alternative medicine and homeopathic medicine. While the efficacy of these approaches remains a

Table 10-4 Components of the Healthcare System

	Public Sector	Medical Tourism Sector
Funding	The National Health System (SNS) is a government-sponsored healthcare system funded by allocations from the national budget. Díaz-Canal pledged 27.5% of the national GDP to health care and social welfare.	Private companies abroad sponsor patients to travel to Cuba; patients pay the agency, which pays the facility either in full or through financing
Provider organizations	Family doctor-and-nurse teams at the community level supported by community polyclinics. Polyclinics and doctor–nurse teams supervised by a Basic Work Group. Basic Work Groups include the polyclinic supervisor, medical specialists, and often a social worker. Hospitals and medical institutes at the municipal and national level.	Public-sector facilities broker relationships with Canadian or American NGOs to take on medical tourists
Services	Community level: Emphasis on preventive care and population health within communities Polyclinics: Provide specialty care, laboratory tests, dentistry, and rehabilitation care Hospitals and medical institutes: Specialty tertiary care, research	Popular medical tourism procedures include cosmetic surgery, spinal surgery, weight-loss surgery, cancer treatments, and physiotherapy
Participation eligibility	All Cubans have a right to access health care through the SNS as guaranteed by the Cuban constitution	Patients' access to medical tourism in Cuba depends on their nation of origin. Canadians have full privileges to travel to Cuba but U.S. citizens' access hinges on special permissions to travel to the island. U.S. patients tend to access medical tourism from other Latin American countries before Cuba.

Data from the following sources. Accessed April 10, 2023. Keck CW, Reed GA. The curious case of Cuba. *Am J Public Health.* 2012;102(8):e13–e22. https://journalofethics.ama-assn.org/article/health-equity-cuban-style/2021-03; https://www.commonwealthfund.org/blog/2016/fidel-castros-health-care-legacy; https://www.nytimes.com/2015/02/18/world/americas/americans-may-see-appeal-of-medical-tourism-in-cuba.html; https://ajph.phapublications.org/doi/full/10.2105/AJPH.2012.300822.

matter of controversy, these methods do have the benefit of finding popular acceptance in parts of Cuba, and these approaches can be much more affordable, especially as the nation struggles under the continuing U.S. economic blockade, which can make orthodox medicines and equipment very difficult to obtain.

Public Health Care in Cuba: Potable Water, Sanitation, and Preventive Medicine

Cuba has made great strides in the provisioning of potable water and in providing sanitation services, extending water and sewer lines beyond urban areas into hard-to-reach rural areas. In 1970, 56% of the Cuban population had access to potable water. By 1999, 92% did. According to the PAHO, by 2010, 94% of Cubans had access to potable water, compared with 79% in the developing world as a whole. In 2022, 97.6% of Cubans had access to drinking water.[42] PAHO reported that in 2010, 91% of Cubans had sewer hook-ups for their homes, up from only 44% of homes in 1970.[2,3,11]

Vaccination coverage has shown strong positive growth. After early smaller efforts beginning in 1962, Cuba launched a mass vaccination program in the early 1970s, training lay people to inject the vaccines. There was no apparent ill effect from this approach, as one does not have to be a doctor to safely provide an injection and some vaccines can be given orally. During the early years, the Revolution placed the greatest emphasis on its polio vaccination program and its malaria-vector eradication campaigns, achieving considerable success.

By the late 1980s and into the early 1990s, Cuba's public health and vaccination efforts had brought great victories. Beyond the elimination of polio, which previously had afflicted 1,162 in the decade from 1957 to 1967, came other diseases eliminated or controlled: tetanus (eliminated in 1972), diphtheria (eradication in 1979), measles (eliminated in 1993, even as thousands still contract the disease each year in Latin America), whooping cough (over 1,000 cases in Cuba in 1970 but near-total eradication in 1996), rubella (the last case in 1995), and the near eradication of typhoid fever. Before the Revolution, more than one in 10 suffered from tuberculosis (TB), but today, TB has been all but eliminated in Cuba. (Because the bacille Calmette-Guerin [BCG] tuberculosis vaccination is only partially effective, Cuba still experiences 35 to 40 deaths from the disease each year.) Cuba's vaccine coverage is stronger than that in most other regions in the world. For instance, the United States has an overall childhood vaccination rate of 70%; in Cuba, this rate is 99%.[11–13,18,22,31,43,44]

Another disease that has been a significant concern for the country is dengue fever, which is a vector-borne illness, spread by the *Aedes aegypti* mosquito. It causes flu-like symptoms and can sometimes develop into a severe form known as dengue hemorrhagic fever (DHF). In response to the dengue outbreak that occurred in the country in the 1980s, Cuba implemented a comprehensive program for control and prevention. Warming of the global climate in recent years has opened up more breeding areas, bringing with it many more cases of dengue. The number of cases has surged, with 400 million cases of dengue worldwide each year, resulting in at least 21,000 deaths. There are several types of dengue, and those who have suffered previously from one strain of dengue are especially at risk of death if they contract one of the other forms. In 2019, the worst recent spike in dengue cases occurred in Latin America and the Caribbean, with more than 3 million cases and over 1,800 DHF deaths. In Cuba, there were 3,259 reported cases but no deaths from dengue that year.[12,45–47] The Cuban dengue fever control program has been recognized for its effectiveness and innovative strategies, making it a model for other countries to follow.

Cuba remains very aggressive about mosquito abatement, with public health inspectors aided by the army, neighborhood organizations, and even school children helping to identify potential breeding sites. Cuba uses a highly intrusive approach, if a highly effective one, with public sanitation workers and their auxiliaries heading right into people's backyards, tipping over all the containers holding standing water, and spraying an oil-based pesticide. Those people who try to chase off the health inspectors and the auxiliary brigades can receive heavy fines. Overall, this method has worked, but Cuba's gains against dengue remain at risk, with reinfection a constant threat. Cuba remains an island surrounded by a sea of dengue.

The principal dengue mosquito vector, the *Aedes aegypti,* spreads other diseases, too—Zika, chikungunya, and yellow fever. Cuba has had just 62 reported cases of chikungunya, all but two imported. Zika first arrived in Cuba in early 2016, but renewed mass spraying campaigns began even before the first case of Zika was reported. By the end of the year, Cuba had 187 confirmed cases. (The two pregnant women who were diagnosed with Zika elected to have abortions.) By way of comparison, mid-2016 Honduras had 30,087 confirmed cases of Zika. All told, from malaria, dengue, yellow fever, and chikungunya to Zika, Cuba has been the least afflicted nation in the region from all mosquito-borne diseases.[12,43,46,48–53]

Before the Revolution, the leading causes of death in Cuba were generally infectious diseases such as malaria and TB. Now roughly three-quarters of all deaths are the same ones found in the developed world—that is, chronic diseases, including heart disease, strokes, and cancer. By way of comparison, in the United States, infectious diseases accounted for 30% of all deaths in 1900, but only 3% in 2000. Cuba is like the United States now in this regard, whereas the other low-resource nations of the world are more like the United States in 1900 (see **Table 10-5**).

Table 10-5 Major Causes of Death, 2021

Rank Order	Disease or Condition (2021)
1	COVID-19
2	Ischemic heart disease
3	Stroke
4	Chronic obstructive pulmonary disease (COPD)
5	Alzheimer's disease and other dementias
6	Hypertensive heart disease
7	Lower respiratory infections
8	Trachea, bronchus, lung cancers
9	Prostate cancer
10	Colon and rectum cancers

Data from World Health Organization Data Platform. *WHO Mortality Database.* Accessed January 27, 2025. https://data.who.int/countries/192.

Evaluation of the Healthcare System

Infant Mortality Rates

Significant improvement in the infant mortality rate stands as perhaps the great achievement of the Revolution. The Cuban infant mortality rate (the number of deaths, age 0 to 1, per 1,000 live births, per year) was 33.4 in 1958, rising after the Revolution to 46.7 in 1969 as nearly half of Cuba's 6,912 doctors left the island. But beginning in the 1970s, Cuba embarked on a determined effort to reduce its infant mortality rate. The focus was continuing care for expectant mothers with dedicated facilities for higher-risk pregnancies. By mid-decade, Cuba had brought its infant mortality rate down to 28, the lowest level anywhere in Latin America at the time. By 1984, the Cuban infant mortality rate had fallen to 15, a level lower than that in most of the developing world in that decade.

By 2008, Cuba's infant mortality rate stood at 5.3 per 1,000 live births per year, compared with 22 in all of Latin America. By 2013, Cuba's rate had dropped to 4.70, lower than the rate found in the United States, 6.17. In 2021, the Cuban infant mortality rate was 4.0; in the United States, it was 5.6.[54,55] A significant factor is the emphasis on preventive and primary healthcare services in Cuba, which ensures that pregnant women receive comprehensive prenatal care and education. The country's commitment to universal health care, with a focus on community-based and accessible services, plays a crucial role in providing early detection and intervention for potential health issues during pregnancy and infancy. Additionally, Cuba's strong emphasis on social determinants of health, such as education and social support, contributes to overall better maternal and child health outcomes.

Cuba has lowered its childhood mortality rates (or under-5 mortality per 1,000 live births, per year) in the years following the Revolution. In 1970, Cuba's childhood mortality rate was nearly 40 per 1,000 live births per year. But by 2004, the childhood mortality rate in Cuba was 11 for boys and 8 for girls, compared with Bolivia, with roughly the same per capita income, at 84 for boys and 76 for girls. By 2013, Cuba's childhood mortality rate stood at 5.7, not as good as Japan at 3, but better than the United States at 6.6 and better than Latin America as a whole, at 17. This situation has persisted year after year: Cuba's childhood mortality rate continues to be lower than that of the United States, and much better than that for the region as a whole.[2,3,11,12,44,53,56–58]

For newborns and infants, Cuba focused its efforts on providing rehydration for children suffering from diarrhea, the leading cause of infant death around the developing world. After the country opened its rural rehydration clinics, deaths from infant diarrhea swiftly fell from 25.8 per 100,000 child per year in 1965 to 3.1 in 1980. In Cuba today, all infants up to 1 year old must have their mother take them to see a doctor 15 times per year; those children between 1 and 4 years have 12 required visits; and then those up to age 14 usually have 11 required visits with a pediatrician per year. By age 14, most Cuban children will have seen a doctor 38 times; by way of comparison, the average child in the United States will have had 22 visits with a doctor by age 20.[12]

It could well be that Cuba's calculation of the infant mortality rate—counting as stillborn those infants born alive but who die shortly after birth—reduces its overall death reporting. Cuba has the highest stillborn rate, or infant deaths counted as stillborn, of any nation in Latin America, with a rate about three times higher than the average.[59] Nevertheless, Cuba's infant mortality rate is still extraordinarily good.[60]

HIV/AIDS

Cuba has been widely recognized for its comprehensive and successful response to the HIV/AIDS epidemic, which began in the early 1980s. The country's public health response has been characterized by a commitment to universal access to prevention, care, and treatment services, as well as a focus on community-based approaches and the empowerment of people living with HIV/AIDS. These efforts have resulted in low HIV prevalence rates, high treatment coverage, and strong political support for HIV/AIDS prevention and care.

The initial public health response was typified by stigma and authoritarianism. Blood collected for transfusions was discarded due to the potential risk of HIV infections. From 1986 to 1994, Cuba's HIV/AIDS patients were forced into quarantine. At the height of their operation, about 10,000 people were held in the 14 sanatoriums. In order to leave the grounds, patients had to be accompanied by a staff member at all times. Many gay Cubans fled the island, rejecting the idea of being sent to a quarantine and horrified by the aggressively anti-gay attitude of Fidel Castro, which led to the hostile actions taken against LBGTQ individuals by the Cuban government.

In the years since then, Cuba has implemented a comprehensive approach to HIV prevention and care, including widespread testing and counseling, condom distribution, harm reduction programs for people who inject drugs, and the provision of antiretroviral therapy (ART) to all those who need it. As a result, Cuba has achieved an HIV prevalence rate of 0.1%, one of the lowest in the world.

Another important aspect of Cuba's HIV/AIDS response has been its focus on community-based approaches. The country has established a network of HIV/AIDS support groups, which provide education, counseling, and other services to people living with HIV/AIDS and their families. These groups are also involved in the development of policies and programs related to HIV/AIDS, ensuring that the perspectives and needs of people living with HIV/AIDS are taken into account.

Cuba's HIV/AIDS response has also been characterized by a strong commitment to research and innovation. The country has been a leader in the development of new HIV prevention technologies, including the use of pre-exposure prophylaxis (PrEP) and the development of a therapeutic vaccine for HIV. Cuba has also been actively involved in international collaborations to share its expertise and contribute to the global effort to end the HIV/AIDS epidemic.

Cuba has the lowest incidence rate of HIV/AIDS in the Caribbean, and indeed one of the lowest rates in the world. The country's commitment to universal access to prevention, care, and treatment services, community-based approaches, research and innovation, and the empowerment of people living with HIV/AIDS has enabled it to achieve low HIV prevalence rates and high treatment coverage. While challenges remain, Cuba's success in addressing the HIV/AIDS epidemic offers important lessons for the global effort to end the epidemic.[12,61,62]

COVID-19 Pandemic

The one nation in Latin America and the Caribbean that might have been expected to have had the least negative experience with the COVID-19 pandemic would be Cuba, long the leader in public health measurements. But after initially very low numbers of cases and deaths, Cuba lamentably moved back to join the rest of the world in COVID-19 miseries.

Cuba certainly benefited, at least at the start of the pandemic, from the isolation afforded by its island geography. When the pandemic first emerged, Cuba quarantined anyone arriving who showed the symptoms of viral infections. Within days, Cuba had halted all incoming flights.[63] But measures like this could only work in the short term. Although Cuba managed comparatively well during the first part of the pandemic, this success did not continue with each follow-on wave and iteration of coronavirus.

Cuba's overall situation during the pandemic was shaped by the strength of its public healthcare system. As the virus appeared, Cuban medical professionals, organized into doctor/nurse/public health worker teams from the over 11,000 *consultorios*, went door to door in their designated catchment zones.[64] With the additional assistance of 28,000 medical students, Cuban healthcare professionals scouted for any possible COVID-19 case, tested, and then isolated those identified with the virus.[63,65] Testing in Cuba kept up with the challenge of the pandemic, with 27 laboratories operating on the island.[64,66,67] At first, those with a confirmed case of COVID-19, as well as those exposed to the virus, were sent to one of the 200 quarantine facilities set up to deal with the crisis.[68] This imposition was eventually relaxed, with a home quarantining system taking its place. By monitoring and isolating the situation in each household, the Cuban healthcare system allowed the country to effectively beat back the first wave of the pandemic.[69,70]

The strength of the biotechnical industries in Cuba offered some victories against the coronavirus. Alone in Latin America and the Caribbean, Cuba created its own COVID-19 vaccines. Cuba's biotechnology industry, BioCubaFarma, developed several coronavirus vaccines.[70,71] Based on older vaccine technologies, both Cuban vaccines require only normal refrigeration, not the super-low temperatures necessary for mRNA vaccines like those developed by Pfizer and Moderna.[72] The Cuban vaccines come in a series of three doses, a requirement that complicates matters: It necessitates tracking of those who got just one shot or two, following up, and making sure everyone gets all three. It eases things somewhat that mixing Abdala and Soberana 02 shots is acceptable, but it is clear that some Cubans who were vaccinated did not complete the three-shot regimen. Established social connection organizations, the Committees for the Defense of the Revolution and the Women's Federation, greatly facilitated the efficiency of the COVID-19 vaccination rollouts.[70] These groups provided information and mobilized neighbors to get the vaccine.

A key issue for Cuba was the continuing U.S. economic embargo, making medicines and medical supplies often impossible to obtain. As the Delta and Omicron variants swept the world, with 43,000 confirmed cases in Cuba just 2 weeks in early January 2022, ventilators, oxygen, and other life-saving equipment were in short supply.[73]

A special challenge for Cuba during the pandemic was the age distribution of its population. Cuba has one of the most elderly populations in the world. One in five Cubans (20%) is age 60 or older.[74] By comparison, the United States, only 17% of the population is age 60 or over. Given this fact, Cuba was predisposed to suffer more from the pandemic.

Initially, Cuba showed low excess mortality—that is, the number of deaths beyond what would otherwise have ordinarily been expected. As of July 15, 2021, Cuba had recorded 2,553 excess deaths, or 22.6 per 100,000, above the ordinary level.[64] In the context of the global pandemic, this was a comparatively good overall situation. However, with the emergence of the Delta variant in the autumn of 2021, and then Omicron in late 2021, conditions in Cuba shifted, turning increasingly more deadly.[69] Cuba's excess mortality rate rose by early 2022 to at least five times the previously estimated level. But even as excess mortality spiked, Cuba's officially reported COVID-19 deaths did not. The two metrics began to vary significantly. Many healthcare researchers have concluded that Cuba was not accurately reporting coronavirus deaths.

Conclusion

At the Summit of the Americas meeting held in Trinidad and Tobago in April 2009, shortly after Barack Obama took office, the U.S. president commented on Cuba's international medical support programs: "It's a reminder for us in the United States, that if our only interaction with many … [Latin American] countries is drug interdiction, if our only interaction is military, then we may not be developing the connections that can, over time, increase our influence and have a beneficial effect."[74]

Cuba provides an example of what can be achieved in public health care in a low-resource environment. The Cuban healthcare system, focused on progress in sanitation, preventive medicine, steady contact with health professionals, community consultation, and natural/traditional/complementary alternative medicine access may serve as an international health system model. This system provides a model worthy of emulation, especially for the developing world. But there are also lessons for the wealthier nations.

It is worth remembering that nearly all infectious diseases have an incubation period of 36 hours or more—that is, a day and a half before a person is too ill to get on a plane and travel. Given this, attacking diseases in remote areas of the world is in the interest of every living person on the planet. Microbes can travel far and fast; dealing with disease challenges the world over protects the health of everyone. Good health care need not be available only to affluent city dwellers; it can and must be available to all. We all must do this together because it is in everyone's personal self-interest, because it is the smart thing to do, and, most importantly, because it is the right thing to do. As the world's public health authorities rightly asserted in the declaration of Alma Ata in 1978, we must do so because health care is a basic human right for all.

References

1. Gorry C, Keck CW. The Cuban health system: in search of quality, efficiency, and sustainability. In: *A Contemporary Cuba Reader: The Revolution under Raúl Castro*. Rowman & Littlefield; 2015.
2. Sixto FE. *An Evaluation of Four Decades of Cuban Healthcare*. Association for the Study of the Cuban Economy. Published November 30, 2002. Accessed April 20, 2023. https://www.ascecuba.org/asce_proceedings/an-evaluation-of-four-decades-of-cuban-healthcare/.
3. Pan American Health Organization. *Health Situation in the Americas, 2012: Basic Indicators*. Washington, DC: PAHO; 2012.
4. Garrett L. Castrocare in crisis. *Foreign Affairs*. Published July 1, 2010. https://www.foreignaffairs.com/articles/americas/2010-07-01/castrocare-crisis.
5. Hill F. Prevention is better than cure in Cuban healthcare system. *BBC News*. Published December 13, 2015. http://www.bbc.com/news/health-35073966.
6. Mattingly A. The changing face of Cuba. *World Policy J*. 2015;32(4):37-49. doi: 10.1177/0740277515623745.
7. Lamrani S. The Bolivarian alliance for the peoples of our America: the challenges of social integration. *Intl J Cuban Stud*. 2012;4(3-4):347-365.
8. Latin American Weekly Report. Cuba seeks foreign assistance over sonic attack allegations. *Latin News*. Published 2017. https://www.latinnews.com/component/k2/itemlist/category/33.html?archive=true&archive_id=33&period=2017.
9. Feinberg RE. What will be Raúl Castro's legacy? Brookings Institute. 2017. Accessed December 14, 2017. https://www.brookings.edu/blog/order-from-chaos/2017/12/04/what-will-be-raul-castros-legacy/.
10. Staten CL. *The History of Cuba*. New York, NY: Palgrave MacMillan; 2005.
11. Cuba. *Desarrollo social: caracterización general [Social development: General characterization]*. Accessed September 2017. http://www.cubagob.cu/des/car_gral.htm.

12. Whiteford LM, Branch LG. *Primary Health Care in Cuba: The Other Revolution*. Roman & Littlefield; 2008.
13. LeoGrande WM. Normalizing US–Cuba relations: escaping the shackles of the past. *Intl Aff.* 2015b;91(3):473-488.
14. Scheye E. The impact of the world economic crisis on Cuba's health care system and biotechnology sector. *Cuba Trans.* 2009;19:383-388.
15. Drain PK, Barry M. Fifty years of US embargo: Cuba's health outcomes and lessons. *Science.* 2010;328:572-573.
16. Bustamante MJ. Cuba in the crosshairs. *NACLA Rep Americas.* 2017;49(2):212-220.
17. Latin American Economy & Business. *Cuba: A Highly Uncertain Outlook for 2017*. 2017;8-10.
18. Mesa-Lago C. Economic and social balance of 50 years of Cuban revolution. *Cuba Trans.* 2009;19:368-382.
19. Huish R. Going where no doctor has gone before: the role of Cuba's Latin American School of Medicine in meeting the needs of some of the world's most vulnerable populations. *J R Inst Public Health.* 2008;112:552-557.j.puhe.2008.03.00120211016-13528-yl91bn-libre.pdf (d1wqtxts1xzle7.cloudfront.net).
20. De Vos P, Van der Stuyft P. Socio political determinants of international health policy. *Int J Health Serv.* 2015;45(2): 363-377.
21. Kirk JM. Cuban medical internationalism and its role in Cuban foreign policy. *Diplomacy & Statecraft.* 2009;20: 275-290.
22. Huish R. Where no doctor has gone before: Cuba's place in the global health landscape. In: *Waterloo.* Wilfrid Laurier University Press; 2013.
23. Wright J. The little-studied success story of post-crisis food security in Cuba: does lack of international interest signify lack of political will. *Int J Cuban Stud.* 2012;(2):130-153.
24. Staten CL. *The History of Cuba*. New York, NY: Palgrave MacMillan; 2005.
25. Kapcia A. Celebrating 50 years—but of what exactly and why is Latin America celebrating it? *Bull Lat Am Res.* 2012;31: 58-76.
26. Pérez Jr LA. *Cuba: Between Reform and Revolution*. New York, NY: Oxford University Press;1988.
27. Henken TA, Ritter ARM. Overcoming Cuba's internal embargo. *Curr History.* 2015;73-76.
28. Sweig JE, Bustamante MJ. Cuba after communism. *Foreign Affs.* 2012;92(4):101–114.
29. LeoGrande WM. Cuba's perilous political transition to the post-Castro era. *J Lat Am Stud.* 2015a;47:377-405.
30. Burbach R, Fox M, Fuentes F. *Latin America's Turbulent Transitions: The Future of Twenty-First-Century Socialism.* Halifax, NS: Fernwood Publishing; 2013.
31. Thomas JG. Historical reflections on the post-soviet Cuban health-care system, 1992–2009. *Cuban Stud.* 2016;44: 189-213.
32. Kirk JM. Cuban medical internationalism under Raúl Castro. *Bull Lat Am Res.* 31(suppl)2012;77-90.
33. Kirk JM. Cuban medical internationalism and its role in Cuban foreign policy. *Diplomacy & Statecraft.* 2009;20: 275-290.
34. Feinsilver JM. Fifty years of Cuba's medical diplomacy: from idealism to pragmatism. *Cuban Studies.* 2010;41: 85-104.
35. Erisman HM. Brain drain politics: the Cuban medical professional parole programme. *Int J Cuban Stud.* 2012;4(3-4): 269-290.
36. Cueto M, Palmer S. *Medicine and Public Health in Latin America: A History.* Cambridge, UK: Cambridge University Press; 2015.
37. Scheye E. The impact of the world economic crisis on Cuba's health care system and biotechnology sector. *Cuba in Transition.* 2009;19:383-388.
38. Pérez-Stable M. The United States and Cuba since 2000. In: Domínguez JI, Fernández de Castro R, eds. *Contemporary US–Latin American Relations: Cooperation or Conflict in the 21st Century?* New York, NY: Routledge; 2010.
39. Biopharma Dealmakers. BioCubaFarma: bringing Cuban biopharma to the world. Springer Nature. Accessed January 27, 2025. https://www.nature.com/articles/d43747-020-00522-5#:~:text=The%20CIGB%E2%80%94one%20of%2034%20companies%20and%20institutes,diagnostic%20systems%2C%20functional%20foods%2C%20and%20aquaculture%20products.
40. Huish R. Where no doctor has gone before: Cuba's place in the global health landscape. In: *Waterloo.* Wilfrid Laurier University Press; 2013.
41. Labonte R. Globalization, health, and the free trade regime: Assessing the links. In: Harris, RL, Seid MJ, eds. *Globalization and Health*. Leiden, Netherlands: Brill; 2004.
42. Statista. Share of population with access to drinking water in Cuba from 2013 to 2022. Accessed January 27, 2025. https://www.statista.com/statistics/1086349/cuba-drinking-water-access/.
43. Cuba, Ministerio de Salud Pública [Ministry of Public Health]. *Dirección de Registros Médicos y Estadístico de Salud [Office of Medical Registries and Health Statistics]. 2014 anuario estadístico de salud [2014 annual health statistics].* Havana, Cuba; 2015.
44. Erwin PC, Bialek R. A matter of perspective: seeing Cuban and United States health systems through a cultural lens. *Am J Public Health.* 2015;105(8):1509-1511.
45. Saker L, Lee K, Cannito B. Infectious disease in the age of globalization. In: Kawachi I, Wamala S, eds. *Globalization and Health.* Oxford, UK: Oxford University Press; 2007.
46. Macías Miranda CD, et al. Características clínicas y epidemiológicas de la epidemia de dengue en el municipio de Santiago de Cuba [Clinical characteristics and epidemiology of the dengue epidemic in the municipality of Santiago, Cuba]. *Medisan.* 2013;17(8):3043-3049.
47. Pan American Health Organization. *Reported Cases of Dengue Fever in the Americas.* Washington, DC. Accessed March 22, 2023. https://www3.paho.org/data/index.php/en/mnu-topics/indicadores-dengue-en/dengue-nacional-en/252-dengue-pais-ano-en.html.
48. Pan American Health Organization. *Zika: Epidemiological Report Cuba.* Washington, DC; March 2017.
49. Kahn C. Cuba fights off Zika. *NPR.* September, 2016; Accessed December 15, 2017. https://www.npr.org/2016/09/17/494360229/zika-reaches-cuba.
50. Reardon S. Mosquito guns and heavy fines: how Cuba kept Zika at bay for so long. *Nature.* August 2016. Accessed December 1, 2017. https://www.nature.com/news/mosquito-guns-and-heavy-fines-how-cuba-kept-zika-at-bay-for-so-long-1.20429.
51. Waters R. Cuba is waging an organized, intrusive war on Zika. *STAT.* November, 2016. Accessed December 7, 2017. https://www.statnews.com/2016/11/08/zika-in-cuba/.
52. Weissenstein M. Cuba reports remarkable success in containing Zika virus. *AP.* 2016. Accessed December 10,

2017. http://www.businessinsider.com/ap-cuba-reports-remarkable-success-in-containing-zika-virus-2016-9.

53. Spiegel JM, Yassi A. Lessons from the margins of globalization: appreciating the Cuban health paradox. *J Public Health Policy.* 2004;25(1):85-110.
54. World Bank. *Cuba Data.* Accessed March 2023. https://data.worldbank.org/country/cuba?view=chart.
55. Stateline. Babies kept dying in Baltimore: people worked together to understand why. *Maryland Matters.* November 2021. Accessed March 27, 2023. https://www.marylandmatters.org/2022/11/01/babies-kept-dying-in-baltimore-people-worked-together-to-understand-why/#:~:text=By%202019%2C%20the%20city%20had,higher%20than%20for%20white%20infants.
56. Stusser RJ. Demystifying the Cuban health system: an insider's view. *Cuba in Transition.* 2011;21:222-234.
57. Maceira D. *Comparative Health Systems in Latin America: Organization, Results and Equity.* Buenos Aires, Argentina: Centro de Estudios de Estado y Sociedad [Center for Studies of the State and Society].
58. Wang H, et al. Global, regional, and national levels of neonatal, infant, and under-5 mortality during 1990–2013: a systemic analysis of the Global Burden of Disease study 2013. *Lancet.* 2014;384:957-979.
59. Gonzalez RM. Infant mortality in Cuba: myth and reality. *Cuban Stud.* 2015;43:19-39.
60. Stusser RJ. Demystifying the Cuban health system: an insider's view. *Cuba in Transition.* 2011;21:222-234.
61. de Mayo J. Cuba's HIV sanatoriums: prisons or public health tool? In: *NACLA: Report on the Americas.* November 2017.
62. Sweig JE. *Cuba: What Everyone Needs to Know.* Oxford, UK: Oxford University Press; 2012.
63. Reed G. Stemming COVID-19 in Cuba: strengths, strategies, challenges. Francisco Durán, MD, National Director of Epidemiology, Ministry of Public Health, Cuba. *MEDICC Rev.* 2020;22(2):47-49. Accessed July 12, 2022. https://www.scielosp.org/article/medicc/2020.v22n2/47-49/en/.
64. Powell MA, Erwin PC, Mas Bermejo P. Comparing the COVID-19 responses in Cuba and the United States. *Am J Public Health.* 2021;111(12):2186-2193. Accessed July 13, 20220. https://pubmed.ncbi.nlm.nih.gov/34878871/#:~:text=Through%20July%2015%2C%202021%2C%20the,higher%20in%20the%20United%20States.
65. Yaffe H. Leading by example: Cuba in the Covid-19 pandemic. *Counterpunch.* 2020. Accessed July 13, 2022. https://www.counterpunch.org/2020/06/04/leading-by-example-cuba-in-the-covid-19-pandemic/.
66. Gamboa Díaz Y, Valdés ML, García Vargas A, Domínguez Arencibia B. Impacto económico de la COVID-19 en sistema de salud Cubano y capacidad de repuesta [Economic impact of COVID-19 on the Cuban health system and response capacity]. *Cuba.* Revista de información para directivos de la salud [*Journal of health directive information*]. 2022;37:e_1131. Accessed July 11, 2022. http://www.revinfodir.sld.cu/index.php/infodir/article/view/1131#:~:text=Introducci%C3%B3n%3A%20La%20pandemia%20de%20COVID,demanda%20un%20fortalecimiento%20de%20las.
67. Looney RE. COVID-19 in the Caribbean: a reticent recovery? In: *Europa World Online.* Routledge; 2021.
68. Ashton J. Shoe leather epidemiology in the age of COVID: lessons from Cuba. *J R Soc Med.* 2020;113(7):282-283.
69. Silva-Ayçaguer LC, Ponzo-Gómez J. A year in the COVID-19 epidemic: Cuba and Uruguay in the Latin American context. *MEDICC Rev.* 2022;23:65-73.
70. Kunzmann M. Cuba and Covid: an update. Cuba Studies. International Institute for the Study of Cuba. 2021. Accessed July 11, 2022. https://cubastudies.org/cuba-and-covid-an-update/.
71. Taylor L. Why Cuba developed its own Covid vaccine–and what happened next. *BMJ.* 2021;374N1912. Accessed July 13, 2022. https://www.bmj.com/content/374/bmj.n1912.
72. Head M. Cuba's COVID vaccines: the limited data available suggests they're highly effective. *The Conversation.* 2021. Accessed July 13, 2022. https://theconversation.com/cubas-covid-vaccines-the-limited-data-available-suggests-theyre-highly-effective-172725.
73. Puig Meneses Y. Cumplir con los protocolos: clava para avanzar en el control de la COVID-19 [Complying with protocols: key to advancing the control of COVID-19]. *Granma.* 2022. Accessed July 12, 2022. https://www.juventudrebelde.cu/cuba/2022-01-22/cumplir-con-los-protocolos-clave-para-avanzar-en-el-control-de-la-covid-19.
74. Morales C, Fitzgerald J. Experiences and lessons from Cuba on the road to universal health in the Americas. *Pan Am J Public Health.* 2018;42.

CHAPTER 11

United Kingdom

Victor Weeden, Tony Garthwaite, Sophie Randall, and Sion Tetlow

Country Description

Table 11-1 United Kingdom (other than where stated)

Nationality	Noun: Briton(s), British (collective plural) Adjective: British
Ethnic groups (England and Wales)	White 91.7%, Asian/Asian British/Asian Welsh 9.3%, Black/Black British/Black Welsh/Caribbean/African 2.5%, other 1.8% (2022 est.)
Religions	Christian (includes Anglican, Roman Catholic, Presbyterian, Methodist) 46.2%, Muslim 6.5%, Hindu 1.7%, Sikh 0.9%, other 0.6%, Jewish 0.5%, unspecified 6%, none 37.2% (2022 est.)
Language	English Recognized regional languages: Scots (about 30% of the population of Scotland), Welsh (about 30% of the population of Wales), Irish (about 12% of the population of Northern Ireland), Gaelic (about 1% of the population of Scotland), Cornish (about 1% of the population of Cornwall as main language) (2022 est.)
Government type	Parliamentary constitutional monarchy, a Commonwealth realm
Date of independence	April 12, 1927 (Royal and Parliamentary Titles Act established the name United Kingdom of Great Britain and Northern Ireland)*
Gross domestic product (GDP) per capita	45,000 USD (2021 est.)
Unemployment rate	4.53% (2021 est.)
Natural hazards	Winter windstorms, floods
Environment: current issues	Air pollution improved but remains a concern, particularly in the London region; soil pollution from pesticides and heavy metals; declines in marine and coastal habitats brought on by pressures from housing, tourism, and industry

(continues)

Table 11-1 United Kingdom (other than where stated) *(continued)*

Population	67,791,400 (2022 est.) England 84.3% Scotland 8.1% Wales 4.7% Northern Ireland 2.8%
Age structure	0–14 years: 17.63% (male 5,943.435/female 5,651,780) 15–24 years: 11.49% (male 3,860,435/female 3,692,398) 25–54 years: 39.67% (male 13,339,965/female 12,747,598) 55–64 years: 12.73% (male 4,139,378/female 4,234,701) 65 years and over: 18.48% (male 5,470,116/female 6,681,311) (2020 est.)
Median age	Total: 40.6 years Male: 39.6 years Female: 41.7 years (2020 est.)
Population growth rate	0.53% (2022 est.)
Birth rate	10.79 births/1,000 population (2022 est.)
Death rate	9.07 deaths/1,000 population (2022 est.)
Net migration rate	3.59 migrant(s)/1,000 population (2022 est.)
Gender ratio	At birth: 1.05 male/female 0–14 years: 1.05 male/female 15–24 years: 1.01 male/female 25-54 years: 1.03 male/female 55–64 years: 0.99 male/female 65 years and over: 0.73 male/female Total population: 0.99 male/female (2022 est.)
Infant mortality rate	Total: 3.82 deaths/1,000 live births Male: 4.27 deaths/1,000 live births Female: 3.35 deaths/1,000 live births (2022 est.)
Life expectancy at birth	Total population: 81.94 years Male: 79.95 years Female: 84.04 years (2022 est.)
Total fertility rate	1.63 children born/woman (2022 est.)
Current health expenditure	12% of GDP (2020 est.)
Physician density	3 physicians/1,000 population (2020)
Hospital bed density	2.5 beds/1,000 population (2021)

USD = U.S. dollars

*Earlier dates related to independence are 927 C.E. when minor English kingdoms united; March 3, 1284, when the Statute of Rhuddlan was enacted, uniting England and Wales; 1536 when the Acts of Union formally incorporated England and Wales; May 1, 1707, when Acts of Union formally united England and Scotland as Great Britain; January 1, 1801, when Acts of Union formally united Great Britain and Ireland as the United Kingdom of Great Britain and Irelanvd; December 6, 1921, when Anglo-Irish Treaty formalized partition of Ireland—six counties remain part of the United Kingdom and Northern Ireland.

Data from Central Intelligence Agency. The World Fact Book, 2008: United Kingdom. Accessed February 23, 2023. https://www.cia.gov/library/publications/the-world-factbook/geos/uk.html, and Office for National Statistics2 https://www.ons.gov.uk/3.

History

The United Kingdom is a sovereign nation composed of the four constituent countries of England, Scotland, Wales, and Northern Ireland. **Table 11-1** shows pertinent details about the United Kingdom. It is also commonly referred to as Great Britain and Northern Ireland. In the past, England was the dominant country, controlling all aspects of U.K. governance. However, Scotland, Wales, and Northern Ireland now have significant autonomy and their own governmental structures. As a result of the devolution of powers, each country is responsible for providing health care for its citizens. Devolution enables the four countries to apply different policies and structures to their health systems, influenced by their individual socioeconomic and demographic profiles, and political priorities. Significantly, however, they have limited tax-raising powers or control over welfare payments, so their overall revenue is still largely controlled by the U.K. government, which allocates block grant funding. It is not possible in this chapter to provide an analysis of these differences or their outcomes on population health. However, to illustrate the relevance of devolution, during the COVID-19 pandemic, each nation followed different approaches to issues like social distancing measures, face coverings, and self-isolation rules. Devolution is also being applied to regions of England, most notably Greater Manchester and West Midlands, and this is also leading to more discretion to organize health services differently. Because England is the largest of the four countries, the majority of information and statistics contained in this chapter will, however, focus on its National Health Service (NHS).

The U.S. Central Intelligence Agency's *The World Factbook* has been collecting geographic, political, and demographic information on all countries of the world for over 2 decades. The demographic, economic, and political information regarding the United Kingdom is based largely on extracts from the 2023 edition of the *The World Factbook*.[1] and the U.K.'s Office for National Statistics (ONS),[2] unless otherwise stated.

At the height of its economic and political power in the 19th century, it was said that the sun never set on the British Empire. In the beginning of the 20th century, however, two world wars seriously diminished the Empire's political and economic hold on its territories. During the second half of the 20th century and continuing into the 21st, the United Kingdom rebuilt itself into a modern and prosperous European nation.

As one of the five permanent members of the United Nations Security Council, a founding member of the North Atlantic Treaty Organization (NATO), and a member of the Commonwealth of Nations, the United Kingdom pursues a global approach to foreign policy.

The United Kingdom was an active member of the European Union (EU) after its accession in 1973, although it chose to remain outside of the Economic and Monetary Union and maintain its own currency. In 2016, the U.K. government, under pressure from elements of the Conservative Party and acknowledging some public frustration with the remoteness of the Brussels-based bureaucracy and free movement of labor from EU countries into the United Kingdom, held a referendum on whether the United Kingdom should leave the European Union. The result was a 52% to 48% vote in favor of Brexit (British + exit). Following much political and constitutional debate, the United Kingdom discontinued its EU membership on January 31, 2020. The vote was generally split between the young, who wished to stay, and older people, who wished to exit. Further demographics indicated that Scotland, the areas around London, and Northern Ireland were in favor of staying. In the case of the latter, a protocol was established to reflect the country's unique position as the United Kingdom's only land border with the EU and the need to ensure peace and security on the island of Ireland. This protocol remains a source of consternation for many in terms of its relative significance for economic prosperity, peace, and the maintenance of Northern Ireland within the United Kingdom.

Constitutional reform is also a significant issue in the United Kingdom. The Scottish Parliament, National Assembly for Wales, and Northern Ireland Assembly were established in 1999, affording these countries a greater role in self-rule. In 2014, the United Kingdom remained intact following a referendum for Scottish independence, but calls for independence remain high, not least because of the continued control of the Scottish government by the Scottish Nationalist Party.

The United Kingdom has played a huge role in shaping the democratic political structure of many Western societies. As a country steeped in tradition and institutionalism, the United Kingdom does not have a common set of governing documents similar to the United States' Declaration of Independence, Constitution, or Bill of Rights. It is one of the few countries of the world without a written constitution. Rather, the English system of government traces many of its roots back to the Magna Carta of 1215, which outlined and protected certain individual rights. These rights were later validated and augmented through various Acts of Parliament over the subsequent 900 years. The result is a highly evolved democratic country with respect to certain individual freedoms, while maintaining certain expectations from the government for what Americans might call socialized practices. Among one of these expectations is free and universal health care for all citizens.

Size and Geography

The United Kingdom is 241,590 square kilometers in size. This is equivalent to the U.S. state of Oregon. The bulk of the land is in agricultural use, with 25.12%

in crops and 45.7% in pasture. Natural resources include coal, petroleum, natural gas, tin, limestone, iron ore, and salt.

As an island nation, the United Kingdom is located at the northwest corner of Europe. With weather primarily influenced by the warm waters of the Gulf Stream, the climate is temperate despite the United Kingdom's relatively northern latitude. Approximately 50% of days are overcast.

Population Centers

Approximately 67 million people inhabit the United Kingdom, with just over 9.65 million people residing in London (2023 estimate). Other larger urban centers in England include Manchester (2.79 million), Birmingham (2.67 million), West Yorkshire (1.93 million), Glasgow (1.70 million), and Southampton/Portsmouth (952,000). The population of Scotland is approximately 5.5 million, Wales 3.1 million, and Northern Ireland 1.9 million. (See **Figure 11-1** for a map of the United Kingdom.)

Government and Political System

The United Kingdom's government is a constitutional monarchy. The chief of state is the monarch, currently King Charles III. He holds his position by birthright, but has no real governing role. The head of government is the prime minister (PM), the leader of the political party with the largest share of parliamentary seats. Since 2019, the United Kingdom has had no fewer than four PMs, largely as a result of political differences in the Conservative Party relating to Brexit, response to the pandemic, and management of the economy. In 2024, Keir Starmer became leader of the Labour Party and PM. The PM appoints cabinet members to run various government departments. Members of the cabinet are department heads and must be members of Parliament. The legislative branch is a bicameral parliament that consists of the House of Lords and House of Commons. The House of Lords currently has 781 seats, the vast majority held by life peers, with members appointed by the monarch on advice of the PM. The House of Commons has 650 members popularly elected from single-seat constituencies; they serve 5-year terms.

The judicial branch of government is the Supreme Court, established by the Constitutional Reform Act of 2005. The court consists of 12 justices selected by a judicial commission and appointed by the monarch upon the PM's recommendation.

At the last national election in 2024, the Labour Party won the general election with 63% of the vote. The Conservative Party won a total of 121 seats, and the Liberal Democrats won 72 seats. The results gave the Labour Party control of the government.[3]

In September 1997, a majority of voters in Scotland and Wales voted to establish a Scottish Parliament and a National Assembly for Wales. A semiautonomous government in Northern Ireland was established under what is commonly referred to as the Good Friday Agreement and was affirmed by voters in 1998. One area of responsibility that devolved under legislation passed by the U.K. Parliament was control over the delivery of healthcare services within each of the countries.[4] Each country has its own structure for planning, monitoring, and delivering healthcare services within its boundaries.

Macroeconomics

The United Kingdom has enjoyed one of the most prosperous periods of sustained growth in all of Europe. Despite its relatively small geographic size and relative scarcity of natural resources, the United Kingdom has the second largest economy in Europe, after Germany.[5] As in many developed countries, services are the primary drivers of the economy, particularly banking, insurance, and business services. Most economic output is accounted for by manufacturing, construction, and agriculture, forestry, and fishing.[6]

In 2020, the U.K. economy shrank by a record 9.4% due to the economic fallout of the COVID-19 pandemic.[7] In some ways, the U.K. economy has successfully recovered from the sudden shock of the pandemic. Looking at the broader picture, however, GDP was flat in the 3 months to December 2022 compared with an annual GDP growth rate of 7.5% in 2021.[7] The unemployment rate quickly recovered to its prepandemic levels of less than 4%. The inflation rate, by contrast, increased rapidly toward the end of 2021 and reached a 30-year high of 6.2% in February 2022.[7] It has been double figures since then, highlighting that despite the initial economic recovery, the United Kingdom looks set to enter its worst cost-of-living crisis since the 1970s, driven by rising prices, tax increases, and geopolitical instability.[7]

In 2024, 83%[8] of U.K. employees worked in service industries. This has increased from 76.9% in 1998. By contrast, in 2024, 8.1% of U.K. employees worked in production industries. This has decreased from 17.1% in 1998.[8] Major industries include aircraft/aerospace, railroad equipment, machine tools, electronics, chemicals, automobiles, and natural gas.

Figure 11-1 Map of the United Kingdom

The United Kingdom is serviced by major airports located in London, Birmingham, and Manchester, and numerous regional airports. There are seven major seaports, with container facilities located at Felixstowe, London, Southampton, Tees, and Liverpool.[9]

The United Kingdom boasts an advanced communications infrastructure, with phone services provided by a mix of buried cable, microwave, and fiber-optic systems. The British Broadcasting Corporation (BBC) is the largest broadcasting system in the world, operating international, national, and local broadcasting operations. The BBC operates radio, television, and streaming services.[10-12]

Demographics

Age Distribution of the Population

The estimated population of the United Kingdom in 2022 was 67,791,400.[1] The median age is 40.6 years (male 39.6, female 41.7). The annual growth rate of the population is 0.53%, reflecting a birth rate of 10.79 per 1,000, a death rate of 9.07 per 100,000, and an immigration rate of 3.59 per 1,000. The dependency ratio is 57.70%.

Population Race and Ethnicity

The total population of England and Wales was 67 million in 2021, and 81.7% of the population was White.[13] People from Asian ethnic groups made up the second largest percentage of the population (9.3%), followed by Black (4.0%), mixed (2.9%), and other (2.1%) ethnic groups. Of the 19 ethnic groups, White British people made up the largest percentage of the population (74.4%), followed by people in the White "other" (6.2%) and Indian (3.1%) ethnic groups. From 2011 to 2021, the percentage of people in the White British ethnic group decreased from 80.5% to 74.4%. The percentage of people in the White "other" ethnic group increased from 4.4% to 6.2%—the largest percentage point increase of all ethnic groups. The number of people who identified as "any other ethnic background" rose from 333,100 to 923,800.

Regional Ethnic Diversity

According to the 2021 Census, London was the most ethnically diverse region in England and Wales.[13] Of all regions, London had the smallest percentage of people who identified as White British, and the North East and Wales had the largest percentage. More White people lived in the South East than anywhere else, and more people from the Black, Asian, mixed, and "other" ethnic groups lived in London than anywhere else. Newham in London was the most ethnically diverse of all local authorities in England and Wales.

Population Socioeconomic Status

The 2021 census did not update these figures, but according to the 2011 census, people from the White ethnic group made up a smaller share of those classified as "never worked and long-term unemployed" (at 71.1%) compared to their share of the general population (86.0%).[14] People from the Asian and Black groups made up larger shares of the "never worked and long-term unemployed" group (at 17.5% and 6.2%, respectively) compared to their shares of the general population (7.5% and 3.3%, respectively). Approximately 15.5% of people from the Indian ethnic group were in higher managerial and professional occupations (the highest socioeconomic group), the highest percentage of all ethnic groups. In every ethnic group, a higher percentage of men than women were in higher managerial and professional occupations. In nearly every ethnic group, a higher percentage of women than men were classified as "never worked or long-term unemployed."

Education Levels of the Population

The United Kingdom has a literacy rate of 99%.[13] This outcome is a result of a state-funded education policy that mandates primary school attendance through age 16 years. The primary school population has been rising since 2009, but peaked in 2019 and has been dropping due to reductions in birth numbers since 2013—although the larger drop in 2021 might have been connected to the pandemic. As a result, attendance in secondary education (11–18) is expected to increase as well, with a peak in 2024.[11] Approximately 53.4% of students elect to enter higher education (university).[12]

Major Religious Groups

U.K. residents who profess a religious affiliation, are predominantly Christian (46.2%). There are also significant populations of Muslim (6.5%) and Hindu (1.7%) people, in addition to residents who do not follow a religion (37.2%).[13] The growth of these non-Christian religions is due to increasing numbers of descendants of immigrants from countries formerly part of the British Empire and due to the expansion of the European Union.

Brief History of the Healthcare System

The United Kingdom has a National Health Service (NHS), which was established by an Act of Parliament in 1946.[14] This action followed years of study and consideration by the government. The greatest changes in health care were the nationalization of the hospital system, payment for care by the government, and universal coverage for all residents of the United Kingdom. By 1948, all of the pieces were in place for implementation, and on July 5, 1948, the NHS was born.

Before the establishment of the NHS, hospital services were provided by a combination of private *voluntary hospitals*, tax-supported public hospitals, and *cottage hospitals* in smaller communities and rural areas.[15] Specialty care was provided by hospital-based outpatient departments; primary care was delivered by community-based general practitioners (GPs).

Hospitals were established to provide medical care for sick, poor people. The wealthier classes were generally attended at home by their physicians. To provide this care, altruistic individuals would organize into charitable groups to raise the necessary funding for a hospital, or individuals would endow an established facility or the development of a hospital. Providing care free of charge initially, financial constraints generally led these hospitals to ask patients to voluntarily pay what they could toward the provision of care.

In the hospitals, appointed physicians and surgeons managed patient care. These staff provided general care for all conditions for which patients were admitted. Staff appointments were few in number and were particularly prized. It was the goal of many resident medical officers to achieve an appointment to the attending staff. These staff positions did not pay well, if at all, and attending physicians supported themselves with fees from private patients and from medical students and resident medical officers who paid the attending physician or surgeon for training. In smaller cities, the hospital could be staffed with resident medical officers (trainees) overseen by local GPs and with regular visitations by out-of-town specialists. The voluntary hospitals saw themselves as providers of care for the acutely ill who would benefit from a short stay and treatment or surgery. Thus, in many cases, patients with chronic illness and infectious diseases were turned away.

Public hospitals generally developed separately from the voluntary hospitals and infirmaries associated with workhouses.[15] Initially, the workhouses were intended for the able-bodied who were temporarily without work, but they increasingly became final destinations for the chronically ill, the elderly, and the mentally ill. In many instances, the number of infirmary beds quickly outnumbered the beds available for the indigent. These infirmaries were also facilities to which the voluntary hospitals would refer or transfer infected and chronically ill patients. In the early 20th century, local county governments took over the operation of the workhouses and infirmaries with some financial support from the central government; the rest of the funding came from local taxes. Under the new arrangements, the counties could separate the hospital section of these institutions and assign them to public health committees for operation. Many local general hospitals in operation today began their existence as workhouse infirmaries, and some of these hospitals still use their original infirmary buildings.

Cottage hospitals were small, rural facilities, generally established and attended by a local GP. A number of these hospitals are still in operation and are now more likely to be referred to as community hospitals. Advantages to the cottage-style hospital are care closer to home and medical staff familiar with the health histories of the patients. Visiting consultants from the local general hospital or teaching hospital held specialty outpatient clinics.

Before the NHS, general practice was provided by apothecaries and physicians who were trained in the teaching hospitals and had returned to their communities to establish a practice or who failed to receive an appointment to a hospital staff position. Apothecaries traced their lineage to herb merchants who compounded and sold medicine preparations.[16] In the Rose decision of 1704, the House of Lords decided that apothecaries could both prescribe and dispense medicine for the treatment of illness, establishing apothecaries as the forefathers of the modern GP. In 1815, the apothecary society was given statutory authority to administer examinations and license doctors in England and Wales. In addition to seeing patients in surgery, GPs visited patients in their home and attended deliveries at the request of midwives.

Before the establishment of the NHS, health care was paid for mostly out of pocket by those who could afford it. Voluntary and public hospitals provided inpatient care and some outpatient care to the poor for free or for whatever the patient could afford to pay toward their care. Beginning in the 19th century, trade unions, fraternal societies, and other groups established provident dispensaries, providing free medical care to their members and sometimes their families.[14] In most cases, primary care and prescriptions were paid for by the society; inpatient care was generally not covered because services were available for free at the local charitable or public hospital. Some societies also provided coverage for worker families for an additional fee. In the mid to late 19th century, worker participation in these programs became compulsory. These provident societies collected a regular contribution from their members (essentially the forerunner of the prepaid health plan).

Government payment for health services was established in the United Kingdom when David Lloyd George introduced the Liberal Welfare Reforms between 1906 and 1914. One of these provisions was the 1911 National Health Insurance Act.[14] This act provided payment for workers' medical care, funded by employee, employer, and government contributions. Eligibility for care was subject to income limits. As with the provident society, payment through the National Insurance Act covered payment for GP services and drugs; hospital services were still provided by public and private hospitals for free. Dental and other services were not covered. It was after the 1911 act that GPs generally chose to be paid under capitation arrangements with local insurance committees.

The Current Healthcare System

The National Health Service

The NHS operates across all four U.K. nations. NHS England is an arm's-length body, funded by the government to deliver a public service but operating independently from the government, that sets the priorities and direction of the NHS. NHS England is the commissioning body for primary care, pharmacy, dental, and other specialized services. In contrast, the national health services of, for example, Wales and Scotland are more directly involved in the provision of both primary and secondary care.

The NHS was established by Act of Parliament in 1947 and was realized in 1948. The NHS was the result of the tireless efforts of the minister of health at that time, Aneurin Bevan, and was based on three core principles:

- That it met the needs of everyone
- That it be free at the point of delivery
- That it be based on clinical need, not the ability to pay

These three principles remain the core of the NHS as it delivers healthcare services to the citizens of the United Kingdom. In 2011, the then Department of Health published the NHS Constitution, which has been updated since.[17] Within this document are seven key principles that guide the NHS in everything it does. These principles are listed in **Box 11-1**. The Constitution also outlines rights and responsibilities of the NHS to the public and its staff as well as responsibilities of the public and staff to the NHS.

Box 11-1 NHS Key Principles

1. The NHS provides a comprehensive service available to all.
2. Access to NHS services is based on clinical need, not an individual's ability to pay.
3. The NHS aspires to the highest standards of excellence and professionalism.
4. The patient will be at the heart of everything it does.
5. The NHS works across organizational boundaries and in partnership with other organizations in the interest of patients, local communities, and the wider population.
6. The NHS is committed to providing the best value for taxpayers' money.
7. The NHS is accountable to the public, communities, and patients that it serves.

Reproduced from NHS. The NHS constitution for England. 2021. https://www.gov.uk/government/publications/the-nhs-constitution-for-england/the-nhs-constitution-for-england.

The NHS has circa 1.4 million staff members across the United Kingdom.[18] In 2021–2022, there were an estimated 590 million patient interactions across all of its services[19] (GPs, community services, mental health services, hospitals, NHS 111, and ambulance services), with 142 million patient interactions in hospitals.[18] According to the NHS, a typical day includes over 835,000 people visiting their GP practice or practice nurse, 94,000 hospital emergency admissions, 50,000 people visiting A&E departments, 49,000 outpatient consultations, and 36,000 patients for planned treatments in hospital.[20]

The NHS in England is headed by a chief executive who leads a management team consisting of a deputy chief executive and chief financial officer, a chief operating officer, a chief delivery officer, a chief nursing officer, a chief strategy officer, and a chief executive of health education England and chief workforce officer of NHS England; a national medical director; and national directors for commissioning operations, commissioning strategy, transformation, and corporate operations.[21] In addition, there are regional directors for London, the South East, the East of England, the Midlands, the South West, the North East, Yorkshire, and the North West.

The Health and Care Act received royal assent in April 2022. The main purpose of this act is to establish a legislative framework that supports collaboration and a partnership working to integrate services for people. Among a wide range of other measures, the act includes changes to public health, social care, and the oversight of quality and safety.[22]

At the heart of the changes brought about by the act is the formalization of integrated care systems (ICSs). ICSs are partnerships that bring providers and commissioners of NHS services across a geographic area together with local authorities and other local partners to collectively plan health and care services to meet the needs of their local population. This solidifies the move away from the old legislative focus on competition to a new framework that supports collaboration.

Each ICS is now made up of two parts: an integrated care board (ICB) and an integrated care partnership (ICP). ICBs are tasked with the commissioning and oversight of most NHS services and are accountable to NHS England for NHS spending and performance. ICPs bring together a wider range of partners, not just the NHS, to develop a plan to address the broader health, public health, and social care needs of the population. ICSs have the potential to reach beyond the NHS to work alongside local authorities and other partners to address the wider determinants of health.

A key premise of ICS policy is that much of the activity to integrate care and improve population health will be driven by organizations collaborating over smaller geographies within ICSs, often referred to as "places," and through teams delivering services and working together on even smaller footprints, usually referred to as "neighborhoods." Unlike previous reforms, which have overspecified at a local level, the Health and Care Act gives local leaders flexibility in how they set up these more local arrangements.

The act also does a number of things beyond progressing integration, including formalizing the merger of NHS England and NHS Improvement; the resulting body, NHS England, is now responsible for providing "unified, national leadership for the NHS." The act also introduces targeted changes to public health (for example, limiting the advertisement of junk food), to social care by creating a framework for assuring commissioners and sharing data, and to the quality and safety of care by formalizing the role of the Health Services Safety Investigations Body—an independent body to investigate patient safety issues in England.

The Department of Health and Social Care

Each country in the United Kingdom (England, Wales, Scotland, and Northern Ireland) has a cabinet-level secretary or minister of health who makes political decisions on health care in general and on the NHS in particular. The individual countries' health ministers are accountable to their respective legislative bodies. Some policies are generated from the central government in London and then implemented via the U.K. Department of Health and Social Care (DHSC), the Scottish Executive Health Department, the Department of Health and Social Services in Wales, and the Department of Health, Social Services, and Public Safety of Northern Ireland. Although all are based on the English system, there are significant differences in the structure and delivery of services in each of the four countries.

Government control of health care in England resides in the DHSC,[23] which also influences matters affecting health care, as reserved under the devolution agreements. The U.K. Parliament funds the DHSC and provides block grants to fund health services in the other countries. Each country's legislature is then responsible for allocating funds for their respective health services. England's responsibilities include:

- Creating national policies
- Providing long-term vision
- Providing funding for delivery and continuity of services
- Championing innovation and improvement
- Promoting honesty, openness, and transparency

Box 11-2 lists the DHSC's priorities from 2021 to 2022. The DHSC is a ministerial department that is headed by the secretary of state for health (also known as the health secretary). The secretary is appointed by the prime minister and is a sitting member of Parliament. The secretary is also assisted by a cabinet of ministers and under-secretaries. See **Box 11-3** for a list of these offices and their responsibilities. Ministers and under-secretaries are political appointees drawn from members of the House of Commons or the House of Lords.

The senior civil servant of the DHSC is the permanent secretary responsible for the day-to-day operation of the department. The permanent secretary is also the chief accounting officer for the department and is responsible to Parliament for how the department spends it appropriations. The permanent secretary is a member of the department board that brings together ministerial and civil service leadership

Box 11-2 Department of Health and Social Care Priorities, 2021–2022

- Protect the public's health through the health and social care system's response to COVID-19
- Improve healthcare outcomes by providing high-quality and sustainable care at the right time in the right place and by improving infrastructure and transforming technology
- Improve healthcare outcomes through a well-supported workforce
- Improve, protect, and level up the nation's health, including through reducing health disparities
- Improve social care outcomes through an affordable, high-quality, and sustainable adult social care system

Reproduced from Department of Health and Social Care. About us: our priorities 2021-2022. https://www.gov.uk/government/organisations/department-of-health-and-social-care/about.

with nonexecutives from outside of the government who can provide independent support and challenge. The departmental board provides the collective strategic and operational leadership of DHSC, meets on a quarterly basis, and has responsibility for:

- Supporting ministers and the department on strategic issues linked to the development and implementation of the government's objectives for the health and social care system
- Horizon scanning for emerging issues
- Ensuring that there is strategic alignment across the health and care system
- Overseeing the sound financial management of the department
- Overseeing the management of risks within the department and its arm's-length bodies (ALBs)
- Overseeing the department's portfolio of major programs and projects

Box 11-3 Ministers and Parliamentary Under-Secretaries

Parliamentary Under-Secretary of State (Minister for Primary Care and Public Health)

- Primary care:
  - General practice
  - Pharmacy
  - Eye care
  - Primary care backlogs
  - Primary care workforce
  - 50 million GP appointments
  - Dentistry
  - Prescription charges
- Blood, transplant, and organs
- Office for Health Improvement and Disparities (OHID):
  - Tobacco
  - Obesity
  - Alcohol, drugs, and addiction
  - NHS health checks
  - Children's health, Start for Life
  - Sexual health
- Long COVID
- Antimicrobial resistance (AMR) and global health security
- Sponsorship of:
  - NHS Blood and Transplant (NHSBT)
  - Food Standards Agency (FSA)

Parliamentary Under-Secretary of State (Minister for Mental Health and Women's Health Strategy)

- Women's health
- Maternity services
- Gender identity services
- Cosmetic regulation
- DHSC litigation
- Mental health:
  - Children and young people and early intervention
  - Mental Health Act
  - Suicide prevention and crisis prevention
- Bereavement
- Disabilities, including autism
- Offender health
- Patient safety:
  - Clinical negligence
  - Historic inquiries
  - Quality regulation
  - Death certification
  - Indemnity
  - Patient Safety Commissioner
- Vaccine Damage Payment Scheme (see www.gov.uk)
  - One-off tax-free payment of 120,000 GPB
  - Eligibility determined based on whether severe individual disability was caused by vaccination against one of 19 listed diseases (includes COVID-19)
- Patient experience:
  - Ombudsman, complaints
  - Whistleblowing, health ethics
- U.K. Health Security Agency (UKHSA):
  - COVID-19—status certification, variant tracing, shielding
  - Environmental health (air quality, chemicals, radiation)
  - Health security at the border
  - Infectious diseases (including monkeypox)
  - Seasonal flu
- Vaccines:
  - COVID-19 vaccine deployment and uptake
  - Routine immunizations and vaccinations

- Emergency preparedness including Ukraine
- Sponsorship of:
  - Healthcare Safety Investigation Branch (HSIB)
  - Care Quality Commission (CQC)
  - NHS Resolution
  - Human Fertilisation and Embryology Authority (HFEA)
  - Human Tissue Authority (HTA)
  - UKHSA

Minister of State (Minister for Social Care)

- Primary care:
  - General practice
  - Pharmacy
  - Eye care
  - Primary care backlogs
  - Primary care workforce
  - 50 million GP appointments
  - Dentistry
  - Prescription charges
- Blood, transplant, and organs
- Office for Health Improvement and Disparities (OHID):
  - Tobacco
  - Obesity
  - Alcohol, drugs, and addiction
  - NHS health checks
  - Children's health, Start for Life
  - Sexual health
- Long COVID
- Antimicrobial resistance (AMR) and global health security
- Sponsorship of:
  - NHS Blood and Transplant (NHSBT)
  - Food Standards Agency (FSA)

Minister of State (Minister for Health)

- NHS operational performance
- Implementation of the Health and Care Act
- Finance, efficiency, and commercial
- NHS capital, land, and estates
- NHS workforce
- Transformation, including reconfigurations
- Diagnostics
- Devolved administrations, Crown dependencies, and overseas territories
- Secondary legislation
- Maternity care
- Women's health
- EU future relationship, Northern Ireland Protocol, and international trade
- Sponsorship of NHS England (NHSE) and Health Education England (HEE)

Data from Department of Health and Social Care. https://www.gov.uk/government/organisations/department-of-health-and-social-care.

Two board subcommittees further advise the board on individual issues. The permanent secretary heads a management team of senior civil servants with specific duties. **Box 11-4** lists the DHSC management team.

Box 11-4 Department of Health Management Team

Permanent Secretary
Second Permanent Secretary
Director General, Health Improvement, and Disparities
Director General, Adult Social Care
Chief Medical Officer
Chief Scientific Adviser
Director General, Global Health
Director General, Finance
Director, Human Resources
Director General, NHS Policy, and Performance
Director, Ministers, Accountability, and Strategy
Director, Information Risk Management, and Assurance
Plus 3 nonexecutive directors

Reproduced from U.K. Government. Department of Health and Social Care: about us. Accessed February/March 2023. https://www.gov.uk/government/organisations/department-of-health-and-social-care/about.

The DHSC is supported by and collaborates with several government agencies and partner organizations in the development and delivery of health and social care in the United Kingdom. A list of the key bodies is shown in **Box 11-5**.

Primary Care

The first point of contact with the NHS is typically the general practice (GP) surgery. GPs act as gatekeepers for secondary care. General practices are the small- to medium-sized businesses whose services are contracted by NHS commissioners to provide generalist medical services in a geographic or population area. In September 2022, there were approximately 27,500 GPs (full-time equivalents) in England.[24] Residents of England who are eligible for health care are required to register with a general practice. While patients nominally have their choice of GP, choice may be limited because GPs reach their patient limits and stop accepting new patients. To overcome this and create more collaborative partnerships, GP practices work together with community, mental health, social care, pharmacy, hospital, and voluntary services in their local areas in groups of practices known as primary care networks (PCNs).

Box 11-5 Key DHSC Agencies and Partner Organizations

NHS England
Care Quality Commission
National Institute for Health and Care Excellence
U.K. Health Security Agency
NHS Digital (since July 2016, legal name remains Health and Social Care Information Centre)
Health Education England
Health Research Authority
NHS Blood and Transplant
Medicines and Healthcare Products Regulatory Agency (MHRA)
NHS Business Services Authority
NHS Resolution (NHS Litigation Authority)
Human Fertilization and Embryology Authority
Human Tissue Authority (HTA)
NHS Counter Fraud Authority

Data from U.K. Government. Department of Health and Social Care: about us. Accessed February/March, 2023. https://www.gov.uk/government/organisations/department-of-health-and-social-care/about.

These build on existing primary care services and enable greater provision of proactive, personalized, coordinated, and more integrated health and social care for people close to home.

Every individual or partnership of GPs must hold an NHS GP contract to run an NHS-commissioned general practice. These set out mandatory requirements and services for all general practices, as well as making provisions for several types of other services that practices may also provide, if they so choose.

General practices are contracted to perform five broad types of service for the NHS, although some are optional. Essential services are mandatory for a practice to deliver to registered patients and temporary residents in its practice area. They include the identification and management of illnesses, providing health advice, and referral to other services. GPs are required to provide their essential services during core hours. Out-of-hours services are those provided outside core working hours. A practice is assumed to provide these by default but can opt out. Where a practice opts out, as most practices do, commissioners have the responsibility for contracting a replacement service to cover the general practice area population.

The core parts of a general practice contract are to[25]:

- Agree to the geographic or population area the practice will cover
- Require the practice to maintain a list of patients for the area and set out who this list covers and under what circumstances a patient might be removed from it
- Establish the essential medical services that a general practice must provide to its patients
- Set standards for the premises and workforce and requirements for inspection and oversight
- Set out expectations for public and patient involvement
- Outline key policies, including indemnity, complaints, liability, insurance, clinical governance, and termination of the contract

In addition to these core arrangements, a general practice contract contains several optional agreements for services that a practice might enter into, usually in return for additional payment.

The PCN model follows similar approaches in Wales, Scotland, and Northern Ireland. Each of the 1,250 PCNs across England is based on GP registered patient lists, typically serving natural communities of between 30,000 and 50,000 people (with some flexibility). They are regarded as small enough to provide the personal care valued by both people and GPs, but large enough to have impact and economies of scale through better collaboration between GP practices and others in the local health and social care system. PCNs are led by clinical directors who may be a GP, general practice nurse, clinical pharmacist, or other clinical professional working in general practice.

Over 99% of general practices are part of a PCN. They must sign the Network Directed Enhanced Service (DES) contract, which details their core requirements and entitlements. The provisions of the DES become part of the practice's primary medical services contract.

PCNs will eventually be required to meet a set of seven national service specifications: structured medication reviews, enhanced health in care homes, support for early cancer diagnosis, anticipatory care (with community services), personalized care, cardiovascular disease case-finding, and locally agreed action to tackle inequalities. To do this, PCNs are expected to provide a wider range of primary care services to patients, involving a wider set of staff roles than might be feasible in individual practices—for example, first-contact physiotherapy, extended access, and social prescribing.

Networks are also the footprint around which integrated community-based teams will be expected to develop, and community and mental health services will be expected to configure their services around PCN boundaries. These teams will provide services to people with more complex needs, undertaking proactive and anticipatory care.

Performance-related payments are made under the Quality and Outcomes Framework (QOF).[26] The QOF accounts for around 10% of a practice's income. It is a voluntary program that practices can opt into to receive payments based on good performance against a number of indicators. In 2018–2019, more than 95% of practices took part. The framework covers a range of clinical areas—for example, management of hypertension or asthma; prescribing safety; and ill health prevention activity. Each area has a range of indicators that equate to a number of QOF points. **Box 11-6** lists the outcomes and indicators in the NHS QOF for 2020–2021. At the end of the financial year, the practice receives an amount of money, based on its QOF points.

Secondary Care

Secondary care (sometimes referred to as "hospital and community care") may be either elective (for procedures such as a cataract operation) or urgent

Box 11-6 List of Outcomes and Indicators in the NHS Outcomes Framework for 2020–2021

Domain 1: Preventing people from dying prematurely

Overarching indicators

1a. Potential years of life lost from causes considered amenable to health care
- Adults
- Children and young people

1b. Life expectancy at 75
- Males
- Females

1c. Neonatal mortality and stillbirths

Improvement areas

- Under-75 mortality rate from cardiovascular disease
- Under-75 mortality rate from respiratory disease
- Under-75 mortality rate from liver disease
- Under-75 mortality rate from cancer
- One-year survival from all cancers
- Five-year survival from all cancers
- One-year survival from breast, lung, and colorectal cancer
- One- and five-year survival after being diagnosed at stage 1 or 2
- Excess under-75 mortality rate in adults with serious mental illness
- Excess under-75 mortality rate in adults with common mental illness
- Suicide and mortality from injury of undetermined intent among people with recent contact from NHS services
- Infant mortality
- Five-year survival from all cancers in children
- Excess under-60 mortality rate in adults with learning disability

Domain 2: Enhancing quality of life for people with long-term conditions

Overarching indicators

2. Health-related quality of life for people with long-term conditions

Improvement areas

- Proportion of people feeling supported to manage their condition
- Employment of people with long-term conditions
- Unplanned hospitalization for chronic ambulatory care sensitive conditions (ages)
- Unplanned hospitalization for asthma, diabetes, and epilepsy in under-19s
- Health-related quality of life for carers
- Employment of people with mental illness
- Health-related quality of life for people with mental illness
- Estimated diagnosis rate for people with dementia
- A measure of the effectiveness of postdiagnosis care in sustaining independence and improving quality of life
- Health-related quality of life for people with three or more long-term conditions

Domain 3: Helping people to recover from ill health or injury

Overarching indicators

3a. Emergency admissions for acute conditions that do not usually require hospital admission

3b. Emergency readmissions within 30 days of discharge from hospital

Improvement areas

- Total health gain as assessed by patients for elective procedures—physical health-related procedures
- Total health gain as assessed by patients for elective procedures—psychological therapies
- Recovery in quality of life for patients with mental illness
- Emergency admissions for children with lower respiratory tract infections
- Survival from major trauma
- Proportion of stroke patients reporting improvements in activity/lifestyle on the Modified Rankin Scale at 6 months

(continues)

Box 11-6 List of Outcomes and Indicators in the NHS Outcomes Framework for 2020–2021 *(continued)*

- Hip fracture: proportion of patients recovering to their previous levels of mobility at 30 days
- Hip fracture: proportion of patients recovering to their previous levels of mobility at 120 days
- Proportion of older people (65 and over) who were still at home 91 days after discharge from hospital into reablement/rehabilitation services
- Proportion offered rehabilitation following discharge from acute or community hospital
- Decaying teeth

Domain 4: Ensuring that patients have positive care experiences

Overarching indicators

4a. Patient experience of primary care
- GP services
- GP out-of-hours services
- NHS dental services

4b. Patient experience of hospital care

4c. Friends and family test

4d. Patient experience characterized as poor or worse
- Primary care
- Hospital care

Improvement areas

- Improving people's experience of outpatient care
- Improving hospitals' responsiveness to personal needs
- Improving people's experience of accident and emergency services
- Improving access to primary care services
- Access to NHS dental services
- Improving women's and their families' experience of maternity services
- Bereaved carers' views on the quality of care in the last 3 months of life
- Patient experience of community mental health services
- Children and young people's experience of inpatient services
- Improving people's experience of integrated care

Domain 5: Treating and caring for people in a safe environment and protecting them from avoidable harm

Overarching indicators

5a. Deaths attributable to problems in health care

5b. Severe harm attributable to problems in health care

Improvement areas

- Deaths from VTE-related events within 90 days post discharge from hospital
- Incidence of healthcare-associated infection—MRSA bacteremia
- Incidence of healthcare-associated infection—*C. difficile*
- Proportion of patients with category 2, 3, or 4 pressure ulcers
- Hip fractures from falls during hospital care
- Admission of full-term babies to neonatal care
- Patient safety incidents reported

Data from NHS Outcomes Framework 2020/21 Indicator and Domain Summary Tables. https://digital.nhs.uk/data-and-information/publications/statistical/nhs-outcomes-framework.

in the case of emergencies. Tertiary care is highly specialized treatment, such as neurosurgery, transplants, plastic surgery, and secure forensic mental health services.

As of April 2020, there were 217 NHS providers of secondary and tertiary care, split across 147 foundation trusts and 70 NHS trusts. They included:

- 80 acute providers
- 10 ambulance services
- 15 community providers
- 44 integrated providers
- 22 mental health providers
- 30 combined mental health and learning disability community providers
- 16 specialist providers[27]

Almost all specialty physicians and surgeons are employed by NHS hospitals. Physicians and surgeons are paid salaries by the hospital. Hospitals have been under public ownership since the establishment of the NHS in 1948. Hospitals are organized either as an NHS trust, accountable to the DHSC, or as a foundation trust; each type is regulated by NHS England. Foundation trusts[28] are not-for-profit, public benefit corporations created to devolve decision making from central government to local organizations and communities. They are not directed by government, so they have greater freedom to decide, with their governors and members, their own strategy and the way their services will be run. NHS foundation trusts are accountable to their local communities through their members and governors, their commissioners through contracts, Parliament, the Care Quality Commission (CQC), and NHS England. Foundation trust status is awarded to hospitals that have shown they demonstrate the highest clinical standards, quality leadership, and a great record of patient responsiveness and safety.

NHS foundation trusts have a unique governance structure, which is substantively different from that of other providers and means the public are effectively their shareholders. They also sit on the government's balance sheet. NHS foundation trusts can set up subsidiaries and joint ventures for the purposes of, or in connection with, their functions. In other words, they can carry out their principal function of delivering health care for the purposes of the NHS through another body.

Other Health Care

NHS services are also delivered by a number of other organizations, such as ambulance trusts, which provide emergency and nonemergency transport. Primary care dentists are self-employed and can provide a mixture of private and NHS-funded care. Delivery of services provided via the NHS is agreed under contract between the NHS and the dentist.

The emphasis of U.K. health care is on collaborative working, exemplified in England by integrated care systems (ICS).[29] The purpose of ICSs is to bring partner organizations together to:

- Improve outcomes in population health and health care
- Tackle inequalities in outcomes, experience, and access
- Enhance productivity and value for money
- Help the NHS support broader social and economic development

Collaborating as ICSs should help health and care organizations tackle complex challenges, including:

- Improving the health of children and young people
- Supporting people to stay well and independent
- Acting sooner to help those with preventable conditions
- Supporting those with long-term conditions or mental health issues
- Caring for those with multiple needs as populations age
- Getting the best from collective resources so people get care as quickly as possible

Nursing home services are provided predominantly by the private sector and are regulated by the government.

Social Care

Social care in the United Kingdom is a means-tested service commissioned through local authorities (councils) and provided predominantly by the private sector. More than 1.5 million people worked in adult social care in England in 2021–2022,[30] more than the number who worked in the NHS. About 16% of the workforce is non-British, and this sector has been particularly affected by Brexit and the removal of free movement of labor from EU countries. Vacancy rates in May 2022 were at 10.3%. Care can be paid for privately, by the state, or a mixture of both, subject to asset limitations. People below a certain asset threshold are eligible for government-supported care.[31] In 2019–2020, 838,530[31] people received publicly funded long-term social care, primarily in care/nursing homes or in their own homes. In addition, there were 231,295 episodes of short-term care provided. Overall, around 43% of people who request support receive some form of service, a further 28% receive advice or signposting, and 29% receive nothing. Most social care staff are employed by small- and medium-sized private providers (of which there are around 18,200 in total). There are also approximately 135,000 roles directly employed by individual users of care services.

Policies for adult social care are increasingly focused on preventive strategies and care at home or in the community, although institutional care still exists in the form of residential care homes. Traditionally, social care has been undervalued in terms of its impact on population well-being,[32] but its importance and value to the provision of health care was brought into sharp relief during the COVID-19 pandemic. Various governments have promised and failed to solve what they describe as the social care problem, with the most recent attempt being to cap the amount people have to pay for care over their lifetime. Health and social care are now being much more widely viewed as part of a whole system with integrated care systems, where professionals and agencies work in harmony. This approach is seen as the way of chieving greater coordination and seamlessness within service delivery.

Facilities

Estimating the number of hospitals providing services in England is challenging. All NHS hospitals are managed by acute, mental health, specialist, or community trusts; as of 2021, there were 219 trusts, including 10 ambulance trusts.[33] However, the number of NHS trusts does not correlate to the number of hospitals, as many trusts run more than one hospital. The following are key statistics relating to the number of NHS beds and their usage.[34] There were an estimated 141,000 hospital beds in England as of 2019–2020. This number has been more than halved over the past 30 years, from around 299,000 in 1987–1988. Due to several advances in medical care, increasing numbers of patients spend less time in the hospital now than they would have previously. The average length of stay in an NHS hospital fell from around 8.4 days in 1998–1989 to 4.5 days in 2019–2020. The average length of stay fell even further during the COVID-19 pandemic (to 4.3 days in 2020–2021, although data are not yet available to show whether these reductions will be sustained. In emergency care, there were 1.7 million more attendances and 1.1 million more admissions at A&E departments in 2019–2020 than there were in 2011–2012, with the total being around 15.8 million attendances and 4.7 million admissions. The number of referrals to outpatient services increased from 4.1 million in 2008–2009 to 5.9 million in 2019–2020—an overall increase of 42% with an average increase of 3.2% a year.[33] Factors such as population growth and the aging of the population account for some of the increase; however, the same changes in technology and medical care likely combine with the previous factors to explain the increases.

Technology and Equipment

NHS trusts are also responsible for providing access to diagnostic technology. In 2021, there were an estimated 8.6 MRI scanners per 1 million people; there were an estimated 10 CT scanners per 1 million people in 2021.[35]

Private Versus Public Components

In addition to having healthcare coverage under the NHS, people residing in the United Kingdom can take out private medical insurance (PMI).[36] PMI is also called voluntary insurance because the purchaser participates voluntarily. There is considerable overlap in the services covered, duplicating many services available to the purchaser through the NHS, to which the purchaser retains access. Benefits of PMI include faster access to treatment, a wider choice of specialists, more comfortable care treatment environments, and more convenient timing of treatment.

PMI is available as a prerequisite of employment or through the individual market. PMI is offered at different levels of coverage, the widest range of services being covered by more expensive comprehensive policies. Budget policies are cheaper but may cover fewer services or have conditions on usage. The take-up of private health care has increased in recent years, which has sparked criticism of the United Kingdom moving toward a two-tier public/private system.[37]

Workforce

The NHS employs more than 1.4 million,[18] making it the largest single employer in the United Kingdom and one of the top 20 employers in the world. There are approximately 716,258 professionally qualified clinical staff (e.g., doctors, nurses, ambulance staff), 434,196 workers supporting those clinical staff, and 226,220 NHS infrastructure support staff. There were an estimated 124,000 vacancies in the NHS at the end of 2022 and a vacancy rate of 8.9%.

Medical Education

There are 44 universities offering medical degrees in the United Kingdom.[38] Entry into medical education can take two paths. The first, traditional method is entry directly from secondary education, culminating 5 to 6 years later in the undergraduate medical degree of bachelor of medicine or bachelor of surgery (or chirurgy). Alternatively, after receiving a first bachelor's degree, medical education may be completed in 4 years. Some universities require the first bachelor's degree to be in a science, while others have no specific requirements. Upon graduation, students are awarded a primary medical qualification.

After graduation from undergraduate training, new graduates complete a 2-year foundation training program. This is equivalent to a rotating internship, with trainees rotating through different specialties every 3 or 4 months. Successful completion of the first foundation year leads to registration with the General Medical Council (GMC). The GMC is one of two medical licensing agencies in the United Kingdom. After the second year, the trainee can apply to specialty training programs either as a GP or as a physician or surgeon. Training can take up to 8 years for some specialties. Health Education England has developed several objectives to increase the number of health professionals and transform the workforce.[39]

Evaluation of the Healthcare System

Cost

Almost 99% of NHS funding comes from general tax collections (80%) and National Insurance (19%) contributions.[40] The balance is collected each year in user fees, mainly from prescription and dental copayments. The budget for the NHS overall was £192 billion or about $250 billion USD in 2023–2024.[41] At present, the NHS is experiencing the longest and most severe slowdown in funding in its history. This has raised questions about the sustainability of its funding model.[42] The United Kingdom ranks only 15th among OECD nations in spending on health care.[43]

In September 2021, the "Build Back Better" plan was announced,[44] providing the NHS with a significant funding increase and stability for parts of its budget over the next 3 years. The new funding totaled £30.3 billion across health and social care in England. Of this, £5.4 billion was reserved for social care reform. The new funding was intended to come in the form of the Health and Social Care Levy, but it is unclear how this will be resourced, as the levy and initial decision to raise funds via a 1.25 percentage point increase on National Insurance contributions was subsequently reversed.[45]

In 2021, the United Kingdom spent about 11.9 % of its GDP on health care,[48] a total of £3,227 per person.[47] Spending is growing at a rate of around 2%.[46] The workforce accounted for about 46% of healthcare spending.[48] Most private expenditures are for over-the-counter medications, other medical products, and PMI.

Quality

The Care Quality Commission (CQC) is responsible for regulating health and social care for adults in England.[49] This includes care provided by the NHS, local authorities, and the private and voluntary sectors. All providers must be registered with the CQC, which applies national quality standards and investigates consumer complaints.

The National Institute for Health and Care Excellence (NICE)[50] is responsible for development of treatment guidelines for common conditions across primary and secondary care. NICE is also responsible for determining which pharmaceuticals are approved for use in the NHS in England and Wales. The NHS publishes information on quality at the organization, department, and physician levels.

In 2021, average life expectancy at birth for U.K. residents was estimated at 81.94 years.[1] Infant mortality was 3.82 per 1,000 live births,[1] and maternal mortality was 7 per 100,000 live births,[1] compared with EU rates of 3 per 1,000[51] and 8 per 100,000,[52] respectively. The diphtheria/tetanus/polio/pertussis/Hib vaccination rate in the United Kingdom is 93.8% by the second birthday. The measles/mumps/rubella vaccination rate is 90.3%, and the rate for the pneumococcal conjugate vaccine is 93.2%.[53] All of the population has access to improved water and sanitation.

In 2018, ischemic heart disease was the leading cause of death in the United Kingdom, followed by dementia, malignant neoplasm of the bronchus, trachea, and lung; chronic lower respiratory diseases; cerebrovascular diseases; influenza; and pneumonia.[54]

Patient Satisfaction

Surveys published in 2022 and 2023 by two of the United Kingdom's most respected research bodies offer important insights into public perception of the NHS.[55,56] They report that the founding principles of the NHS are afforded high levels of support from the general public. Approximately 90% of people believe that the NHS should be free at the point of delivery, 89% believe that it should provide a comprehensive service available to everyone, and 84% believe that the NHS should be primarily funded through taxation. However, recent NHS pressures have affected public opinion, such that only 34% of people currently believe that the NHS is providing a good service nationally. Of those who are satisfied with the NHS overall, the top reason was because the NHS is free at the point of use, followed by the quality of NHS care and the range of services provided. In addition, 77% of people surveyed say that the NHS makes them proud to be British and 85% think that NHS staff are overstretched but doing their best.

Satisfaction with the NHS in 2021 fell to 36%, the lowest level of satisfaction since 1997 and a 17 percentage point decrease from 2020. More people (41%) were dissatisfied with the NHS than satisfied. The main reason for this was waiting times for GP and hospital appointments, staff shortages, and a view that the government does not spend enough money on the NHS, with 71% thinking that health and care services are underfunded. Additionally, only 8% of people believe that the government has the right policies for the NHS.

Access

One of the major issues with the NHS has been waiting times for urgent and elective care; this has recently become even more significant following the effects of the COVID-19 pandemic.[57] The goal for nonurgent surgery is to be seen within 18 weeks, but this has had been met since 2016; as of 2021, 3,000 people had been waiting for more than 2 years.[58] Trauma and orthopedics have the longest waitlist of more than 600,000 people. Across all specialties, the number of people referred is greater than the number receiving treatment, meaning that waitlists are likely to grow. Wait time in A&E departments are similarly lengthening; the target of 95% of people being seen in 4 hours or fewer has not been met since 2015.[59]

There are acute access problems in dentistry. In 2022, 91% of NHS practices were not accepting new adult patients; 23% (1,124) said they had an open waiting list, with the wait time of 16% of those being a year or longer (or were unable to say how long it would be). Seventy-nine percent of NHS practices were not accepting new child patients.[59]

Innovation

The government aims to speed up the pipeline for developing innovations in the NHS,[60] so that proven and affordable innovations get to patients faster. It promises to create a simpler, clearer system for medtech and digital technologies that will apply across England. This will include a new advisory service for innovators, linked to the Academic Health Science Networks (AHSNs). The NHS aims to increase the number of people registering to participate in health research to 1 million by 2023–2024. The government's ambition is to treble industry contract and R&D collaborative research in the NHS over 10 years, to nearly £1 billion. As part of the NHS's contribution to the U.K. government's broader aims to reach 5 million genomic tests and analyses over the same time frame, the new NHS Genomic Medicine Service will sequence 500,000 whole genomes by 2023–2024.

The NHS Innovation Lab[61] was established in 2020 to rapidly trial innovative ideas in real-world health and social care settings. It is particularly interested in technologies that have the potential for widespread impact within a 2- to 5-year time frame.

Wherever possible, solutions are co-designed with patients, clinicians, and other stakeholders to test whether a particular technology will be fit for purpose in addressing a challenge. The benefits it could bring are evaluated and potential barriers to adoption identified. This helps inform national program priorities and product roadmaps. The Innovation Lab's own project roadmap is driven by user needs and real-world problems and is shaped by engagement with staff from across the health and social care sectors.

Summary

Numerous statistics point to the NHS failing to meet the reasonable expectations for a modern health system in an economically advanced country. A Parliamentary briefing[62] reported that the number of people on a waiting list for hospital treatment in England rose to a record of 7.2 million in January 2023. The waiting list rose consistently between 2012 and 2019 and has risen more quickly since early 2021. The 18-week treatment target has not been met since 2016. The number of people visiting A&E departments in February 2023 was similar to prepandemic levels. The percentage of patients waiting over 4 hours in hospital A&E rose consistently between 2015 and 2020. A new record high was reached in December 2022, but performance has subsequently improved slightly. The 62-day waiting time standard for cancer (measured from urgent GP referral to treatment) has not been met in recent years. Performance declined between 2013 and 2018. Since the pandemic, it has fallen further, with 54.4% of patients waiting less than 62 days for treatment in January 2023 (target: 85%). NHS staff numbers have increased, with 21% more doctors and 16% more nurses than 5 years ago. However, the NHS vacancy rate rose from 8.3% to 8.9% over the past year. Ambulance response times have increased, with the average response to a Category 2 call at over 1.5 hours in December 2022, compared with a target of 18 minutes. Performance has subsequently improved but remains outside of the target.

Permanent U.K.-wide staff shortages are estimated to exceed 100,000 in the NHS and 112,000 in social care. The latter shortage has resulted in care providers not being able to alleviate pressure on the NHS by enabling people to return home from hospital. Industrial actions (i.e., strikes) have been taken by many health-sector groups, including ambulance workers, nurses, and junior doctors.

The reasons for this worrying assessment of the current state of the NHS are complex, with many embedded in history and others being associated with the COVID-19 pandemic. The lack of integration of health and social care is contributing to too many people remaining in hospitals awaiting social care packages that would allow their timely discharge. Decisions in the past to reduce hospital beds in favor of community-based care were laudable but not accompanied by sufficient resources to ensure their success. Different governance and political management structures reinforce the differences between a national service free at the point of delivery (health) and a local means-tested service (social care). There has been a traditional undervaluing of social care as an important ingredient of a whole-system approach. Despite government efforts over the decades to create a climate where meaningful integration can occur, the consequences of this fragmented approach remains a cause for concern.[32]

Fragmentation also occurs within the NHS, which creates a lack of cohesion among the various professional and managerial disciplines, leading to public frustration about service delivery. Some may argue that the challenge of creating a seamless approach within such a large and complex organization is simply too great, with continuing piecemeal governmental initiatives to reorganize the NHS preventing new systems and structures from becoming sufficiently embedded. Both the NHS and social care are vulnerable to government fiscal and monetary policies, and austerity measures since 2010 have had a significant impact on the NHS's ability to provide a consistently high quality of service.

Despite all of this, the founding principles of the NHS have high levels of support from the general public.[56] This support is being threatened by the current level of performance, however, as evidenced by the relatively low and decreasing level of public satisfaction reported earlier. Only 8% of people believe that the government has the right policies for the NHS, and this lack of confidence in political leadership is impacting the public and staff confidence and morale.

COVID-19 Pandemic

The NHS is facing many of the same challenges as other health systems in industrialized countries. A growing and aging population is increasing demand on the service and the impact of the COVID-19 pandemic is likely to be felt for many years to come. Wider geopolitical issues, such as the war in Ukraine and its associated fuel and cost of living crises, have added pressure to already struggling physical and mental health services. However, a mix of employment-related issues, such as low morale, dissatisfaction with pay rates, and the loss of free movement of labor from the EU since Brexit, are domestic issues that have produced unprecedented challenges in recruiting and retaining a skilled and sustainable workforce. The workforce crisis is certainly an immediate priority for the NHS to address. Stabilizing the workforce by settling pay disputes and investing in stronger recruitment and retention strategies will be crucial.

The King's Fund[63] produced valuable ongoing position statements[64] on the big issues in health and social care. It agrees that urgent action is required to tackle a vicious cycle of shortages and increased pressures on staff, which has been exacerbated by the COVID-19 pandemic. It has also concluded that:

- Urgent action is needed to tackle deep and widening health inequalities in England.
- The social care system remains under intense pressure with an unstable provider market, a workforce crisis, and high levels of unmet need: Unless these problems are addressed, it will continue to fail the people who rely on it.
- Waits for care are likely to get worse before they get better, with the government estimating that waiting lists would continue to grow through 2024. It will be several years before waiting lists and waiting times return to prepandemic levels, and even longer until performance standards are met again. Politicians and NHS leaders must be honest with the public about this.
- Growing demand and a shortage of GPs have left general practices cracking at the seams; additional investment and continued support to develop the primary care workforce is needed to improve access to high-quality care.
- Recent increases in the NHS budget were welcome and necessary, but the systemic challenges the NHS faces, particularly around workforce pressures, have grown and the outlook for COVID-19 recovery is uncertain.
- The COVID-19 pandemic reinforced the need for a much greater focus on and investment in prevention and public health.
- Mental health services are receiving much-needed attention and funding after years of underinvestment and neglect, but there are still problems with access and the quality of care experienced by people using services.
- Health and care services need to be better coordinated and work together more effectively to meet people's needs and improve their experience of care.
- Digital technologies bring many opportunities to improve people's health and experiences of services, but realizing their potential will require investment and thoughtful implementation.
- Collaborative, inclusive, and compassionate leadership is essential to deliver the highest-quality care for patients and tackle deep-seated cultural issues in the NHS, including unacceptable levels of work-related stress, bullying, and discrimination.

The King's Fund analysis accurately represents the current and emerging issues and challenges for health and social care in the United Kingdom. It concludes that the NHS's long-term plan for England offers an opportunity to finally deliver on the longstanding ambition to provide more care closer to home, but only if commitments to increase funding and give more priority to community health services are honored and severe workforce shortages are tackled.

References

1. *The World Factbook. United Kingdom*. Washington, DC: Central Intelligence Agency. Accessed February 23, 2023, https://cia.gov/library/publications/the-world-factbook/geos/print_uk.html.
2. U.K. Office for National Statistics. Accessed February/March 2023. https://www.ons.gov.uk/.
3. BBC News. UK general election 2024 results. Accessed January 30, 2025. https://www.bbc.com/news/election/2024/uk/results.
4. Cylus J, Richardson E, Findley L, et al. United Kingdom: health system review. *Health Syst Trans*. 2015;17(5):1-125.
5. *The World Atlas*. The biggest economies in Europe. Accessed February/March 2023. https://www.worldatlas.com/articles/the-biggest-economies-in-europe.html.
6. U.K. Office for National Statistics. Economic output. Accessed February/March 2023. https://www.ons.gov.uk/economy/economicoutputandproductivity/output.
7. *Statista*. The UK economy: statistics and facts. Accessed February/March 2023. https://www.statista.com/topics/6500/the-british-economy/#topicOverview.
8. Brien P. Service industries: Economic indicators. UK Parliament. House of Commons Library. Published February 5, 2025. Accessed February 8, 2025. https://commonslibrary.parliament.uk/research-briefings/sn02786/#:~:text=The%20service%20industries%20include%20the%20retail%20sector%2C,and%2083%%20of%20employment%20in%20April%E2%80%93June%202024.
9. Marine Insight. 7 major ports in United Kingdom. Accessed February/March 2023. https://www.marineinsight.com/know-more/7-major-ports-in-the-united-kingdom/.
10. UNA-UK. International Literacy Day factsheet. Accessed February/March 2023. https://una.org.uk/international-literacy-day-factsheet#:~:text=In%20the%20UK%20the%20literacy%20rate%20is%2099%25%2C,miss%20out%20on%20a%20whole%20host%20of%20opportunities.
11. U.K. Government. National pupil projections 2022. Accessed February/March 2023. https://explore-education-statistics.service.gov.uk/find-statistics/national-pupil-projections#releaseHeadlines-tables.
12. U.K. Government. Participation measures in higher education 2019/20. Accessed February/March 2023. https://explore-education-statistics.service.gov.uk/find-statistics/participation-measures-in-higher-education/2019-20.
13. Office for National Statistics. Census 2021. Accessed February/March 2023. N.B. Data relates to England and Wales only. https://www.ons.gov.uk/peoplepopulationandcommunity/culturalidentity/religion/bulletins/religionenglandandwales/census2021.
14. Roemer MI. National health systems throughout the world. *Annu Rev of Public Health*. 1993;14(1):335-353.
15. Rivett G. The development of the London hospital system, 1823–2015. Accessed May 22, 2015. www.nhshistory.net.
16. Worshipful Society of Apothecaries of London. History. origins. Accessed May 22, 2016. http://www.apothecaries.org/charity/the-archives.
17. U.K. Government. The NHS Constitution for England. Accessed February/March 2023. https://www.gov.uk/government/publications/the-nhs-constitution-for-england/the-nhs-constitution-for-england.
18. Rolewicz L, Palmer B, Lobont C. The NHS workforce in numbers. Nuffield Trust. Published July 2, 2024. Accessed January 30, 2025. https://www.nuffieldtrust.org.uk/resource/the-nhs-workforce-in-numbers.
19. NHS Confederation. Key statistics on the NHS. August 18, 2023. Accessed January 30, 2025. https://www.nhsconfed.org/articles/key-statistics-nhs.
20. NHS. Working in the NHS. Accessed February/March 2023. https://www.jobs.nhs.uk/about_nhs.html.
21. NHS. NHS executive group. Accessed February/March 2023. https://www.england.nhs.uk/about/nhs-executive-group/.
22. King's Fund. The Health and Care Act: 6 key questions. Accessed February/March 2023. https://www.kingsfund.org.uk/publications/health-and-care-act-key-questions#:~:text=The%20main%20purpose%20of%20the,oversight%20of%20quality%20and%20safety.
23. U.K. Government. Department of Health and Social Care: about us. Accessed February/March 2023. https://www.gov.uk/government/organisations/department-of-health-and-social-care/about.
24. Nuffield Trust. NHS staffing tracker, general practice. Accessed February/March 2023. https://www.nuffieldtrust.org.uk/nhs-staffing-tracker/general-practice#general-practice.
25. King's Fund. GP funding and contracts explained. Accessed February/March 2023. https://www.kingsfund.org.uk/publications/gp-funding-and-contracts-explained.
26. NHS Digital. NHS Outcomes Framework. Accessed February/March 2023. https://digital.nhs.uk/data-and-information/publications/statistical/nhs-outcomes-framework.
27. NHS Providers. The NHS provider sector. Accessed February/March 2023. https://nhsproviders.org/topics/delivery-and-performance/the-nhs-provider-sector.
28. NHS Improvement. Oversight of NHS-controlled providers. Accessed February/March 2023. https://www.england.nhs.uk/wp-content/uploads/2020/08/NHS-controlled_providers_policy_position_12feb.pdf.
29. NHS England. What are integrated care systems? Accessed February/March 2023. https://www.england.nhs.uk/integratedcare/what-is-integrated-care/.
30. UK Parliament. House of Commons Library. Adult social care workforce in England. Accessed February/March 2023. https://commonslibrary.parliament.uk/research-briefings/cbp-9615/#:~:text=Around%201.5%20million%20people%20worked,more%20than%20in%20the%20NHS.
31. King's Fund. Key facts and figures about adult social care. Accessed February/March 2023. https://www.kingsfund.org.uk/audio-video/key-facts-figures-adult-social-care.
32. Garthwaite T. Social care. In: Prowle MJ, ed. *Reforming UK Public Policy Through Elected Regional Government*. London, UK/New York, NY: Routledge; 2023.
33. King's Fund. Key facts and figures about the NHS. Accessed February/March 2023. https://www.kingsfund.org.uk/audio-video/key-facts-figures-nhs.
34. King's Fund. NHS hospital bed numbers: past, present, future. Accessed February/March 2023. https://www.kingsfund.org.uk/publications/nhs-hospital-bed-numbers#footnote1_e1j2mog.
35. Organization for Economic Cooperation and Development. Computed tomography (CT) scanners (indicator). doi: 10.1787/bedece12-en. Accessed February/March 2023. https://data.oecd.org/healtheqt/computed-tomography-ct-scanners.htm#indicator-chart.

36. Foubister T, Thomson S, Mossialos E, McGuire A. *Private Medical Insurance in the United Kingdom*. Copenhagen, Denmark: WHO Regional Office for Europe; 2006.
37. *The Guardian*. England is sleep walking towards a two tier health system. Accessed February/March, 2023. https://www.theguardian.com/commentisfree/2021/jul/27/uk-two-tier-health-system-private-healthcare-nhs-waiting-lists#:~:text=There%20are%20about%2090%20private,across%20the%20UK%20in%202019.
38. British Medical Association. UK medical schools. Accessed February/March 2023. https://www.bma.org.uk/advice-and-support/studying-medicine/becoming-a-doctor/uk-medical-schools.
39. Health Education England. Strategic goals and 2021/2022 objectives. Accessed February/March 2023. https://www.hee.nhs.uk/about/work-us/recovery-delivery-hee-business-plan-202122/hee-strategic-goals-202122-objectives.
40. King's Fund. How the NHS is funded. Accessed February/March 2023. https://www.kingsfund.org.uk/projects/nhs-in-a-nutshell/how-nhs-funded.
41. Issa Z, Watt T, Fozzard K. Health care funding: The latest funding figures for England. The Health Foundation. Accessed January 30, 2025. https://www.health.org.uk/reports-and-analysis/analysis/health-care-funding.
42. King's Fund. How health care is funded. Accessed February/March 2023. https://www.kingsfund.org.uk/publications/how-health-care-is-funded.
43. Organization for Economic Cooperation and Development. Health spending. https://data.oecd.org/healthres/health-spending.htm.
44. King's Fund. The comprehensive spending review: what more for health and social care spending. Accessed February/March 2023. https://www.kingsfund.org.uk/publications/comprehensive-spending-review-health-and-care-spending.
45. *UK Government News*. National Insurance increase reversed. Accessed February/March, 2023. https://www.gov.uk/government/news/national-insurance-increase-reversed.
46. *Statista*. Total healthcare expenditure as a share of GDP in the United Kingdom from 1980 to 2021. Accessed February/March 2023. https://www.statista.com/statistics/317708/healthcare-expenditure-as-a-share-of-gdp-in-the-united-kingdom/#:~:text=Healthcare%20spending%20in%20the%20United%20Kingdom%20%28UK%29%20as,UK%20amounted%20to%2011.9%20percent%20of%20the%20GDP.
47. Office for National Statistics. Healthcare expenditure, UK Health Accounts: 2018. Accessed February/March 2023. https://www.ons.gov.uk/peoplepopulationandcommunity/healthandsocialcare/healthcaresystem/bulletins/ukhealthaccounts/2018.
48. King's Fund. Key facts and figures about the NHS. Accessed February/March, 2023. https://www.kingsfund.org.uk/audio-video/key-facts-figures-nhs.
49. Care Quality Commission. About us. Accessed February/March 2023. https://www.cqc.org.uk/about-us.
50. National Institute for Health and Care Excellence. About Us. Accessed February/March 2023. https://www.nice.org.uk/about.
51. World Bank. Mortality rate infant (per 1,000 live births)—European Union. Accessed February/March 2023. https://data.worldbank.org/indicator/SP.DYN.IMRT.IN?locations=EU.
52. *Our World in Data*. Mortality risks per pregnancy. Accessed February/March 2023. https://ourworldindata.org/maternal-mortality#:~:text=The%20average%20rate%20in%20the%20European%20Union%20is,times%20more%20likely%20to%20die%20with%20each%20pregnancy.
53. Nuffield Trust. Vaccination coverage for children and mothers. Accessed February/March 2023. https://www.nuffieldtrust.org.uk/resource/vaccination-coverage-for-children-and-mothers-1.
54. Office for National Statistics. Leading causes of death UK. Accessed February/March 2023. https://www.nuffieldtrust.org.uk/resource/vaccination-coverage-for-children-and-mothers-1.
55. King's Fund. Public satisfaction with the NHS and social care in 2021: Results from the British Social Attitudes survey. Accessed February/March 2023. https://www.kingsfund.org.uk/publications/public-satisfaction-nhs-social-care-2021.
56. Health Foundation. Public perceptions of the NHS: a winter of discontent. Accessed February/March 2023. https://www.health.org.uk/publications/long-reads/public-perceptions-of-the-nhs-a-winter-of-discontent?utm_campaign=13796154_Ipsos%20polling%20wave%203%20%20February%202023%20%20WARM&utm_medium=email&utm_source=The%20Health%20Foundation&dm_i=4Y2,87P6I,8HIT3B,XP0S5,1.
57. King's Fund. Patient waiting times. Accessed February/March 2023. https://www.kingsfund.org.uk/projects/nhs-in-a-nutshell/patient-waiting-times.
58. King's Fund. Waiting times for elective (non-urgent) treatment: referral to treatment. Accessed February/March 2023. https://www.kingsfund.org.uk/projects/nhs-in-a-nutshell/waiting-times-non-urgent-treatment.
59. King's Fund. What's going on with A&E waiting times. Accessed February/March 2023. https://www.kingsfund.org.uk/projects/urgent-emergency-care/urgent-and-emergency-care-mythbusters.
60. NHS. Research and innovation to drive future outcomes improvement. Accessed February/March 2023. https://www.longtermplan.nhs.uk/online-version/chapter-3-further-progress-on-care-quality-and-outcomes/better-care-for-major-health-conditions/research-and-innovation-to-drive-future-outcomes-improvement/.
61. NHS England. Innovation Lab: our projects. Accessed February/March 2023. https://transform.england.nhs.uk/innovation-lab/#:~:text=Our%20roadmap%20is%20aligned%20to%20our%20five%20priorities%2C,5%20improve%20safety%20across%20health%20and%20care%20systems.
62. House of Commons Library. NHS Key Statistics England, March 2023. Accessed February/March, 2023. https://researchbriefings.files.parliament.uk/documents/CBP-7281/CBP-7281.pdf.
63. The King's Fund is a well-respected independent charitable organisation working to improve health and care in England. Accessed February/March 2023. https://www.kingsfund.org.uk/about-us.
64. King's Fund. The King's Fund position: what do we think about key health and care issues? Accessed February/March 2023. https://www.kingsfund.org.uk/projects/positions.

CHAPTER 12

France

Stephanie Baiyasi, Sophie Kobouloff, and Zigmond Kozicki

Country Description

Table 12-1 France

Official name	French Republic (*République Française*)
Nationality	Noun: Frenchman (men) Frenchwoman (women) Adjective: French
Ethnic groups	Celtic and Latin with Teutonic, Slavic, North African (Algerian, Moroccan, Tunisian), Indochinese, Basque minorities Overseas departments: Black, White, Mulatto, East Indian, Chinese, Amerindian
Religions	Roman Catholic 47%, Muslim 4%, Protestant 2%, Buddhist 2%, Orthodox 1%, Jewish 1%, other 1%, none 33%, unspecified 9% (2022 est.)*
Language	French (official) 100%, declining regional dialects and languages (Provencal, Breton, Alsatian, Corsican, Catalan, Basque, Flemish, Occitan, Picard) Overseas departments: French, Creole patois, Mahorian (a Swahili dialect)
Government type	Semi-presidential republic
Date of independence	No official date of independence**
Real gross domestic product (GDP) per capita	44,460 USD (2023)
Unemployment rate	7.4% (2024) 7.1% (2023) 7.1% (2022)
Natural hazards	Metropolitan France: flooding; avalanches; midwinter windstorms; drought; forest fires in south near the Mediterranean Overseas departments: hurricanes (cyclones); flooding; volcanic activity (Guadeloupe, Martinique, Reunion)
Environment: current issues	Some forest damage from acid rain; air pollution from industrial and vehicle emissions; water pollution from urban wastes, agricultural runoff

Table 12-1 France

Population	68,305,148 (2022 est.)***
Age structure	0–14 years: 18.36% (male 6,368,767/female 6,085,318) 15–24 years: 11.88% (male 4,122,981/female 3,938,938) 25–54 years: 36.83% (male 12,619,649/female 12,366,120) 55–64 years: 12.47% (male 4,085,564/female 4,376,272) 65 years and over: 20.46% (male 6,029,303/female 7,855,244) (2020 est.)
Median age	Total: 41.7 years Male: 40 years Female: 43.4 years (2020 est.)
Population growth rate	0.32% (2022 est.)
Birth rate	11.66 births/1,000 population (2022 est.)
Death rate	9.54 deaths/100,000 population (2022 est.)
Current health expenditure	12.3% of GDP (2021)
Net migration rate	1.06 migrant(s)/1,000 population (2022 est.)
Gender ratio	At birth: 1.05 male/female 0–14 years: 1.05 male/female 15–24 years: 1.05 male/female 25–54 years: 1.02 male/female 55–64 years: 0.94 male/female 65 years and over: 0.64 male/female Total population: 0.96 male/female (2022 est.)
Infant mortality rate	Total: 3.15 deaths/1,000 live births Male: 3.53 deaths/1,000 live births Female: 2.74 deaths/1,000 live births (2022 est.)
Life expectancy at birth	Total population: 82.59 years Male: 79.53 years Female: 85.79 years (2022 est.)
Total fertility rate	2.03 children born/woman (2022 est.)
HIV/AIDS adult prevalence rate	0.3% (2023 est.)
Major infectious diseases	Widespread ongoing transmission of a respiratory illness caused by the novel coronavirus (COVID-19) is occurring throughout France; as of August 18, 2022, France had reported a total of 33,275,006 cases of COVID-19 or 51,161.33 cumulative cases of COVID-19 per 100,000 population with a total of 149,848 cumulative deaths or a rate 230.39 cumulative deaths per 100,000 population; as of August 16, 2022, 80.89% of the population had received at least one dose of the COVID-19 vaccine

USD = U.S. dollars

*France maintains a tradition of secularism and has not officially collected data on religious affiliation since the 1872 national census, which complicates assessments of France's religious composition; an 1872 law prohibiting state authorities from collecting data on individuals' ethnicity or religious beliefs was reaffirmed by a 1978 law emphasizing the prohibition of the collection or exploitation of personal data revealing an individual's race, ethnicity, or political, philosophical, or religious opinions; a 1905 law codified France's separation of church and state.

**In 486 CE, Frankish tribes unified under Merovingian kingship; on August 10, 843 CE, Western Francia was established from the division of the Carolingian Empire; on July 14, 1789, the French monarchy was overthrown; on September 22, 1792, the First French Republic was founded; on October 4, 1958, the Fifth French Republic was established.

***This population figure is for metropolitan France and five overseas regions; the metropolitan France population is 62,814,233 (July 2015 est.).

Data from Central Intelligence Agency. The World Factbook, 2022: France. Accessed December 5, 2022. https://www.cia.gov/the-world-factbook/countries/france/; Institut national de la statistique et des etudes economiques (INSEE). In Q3 2024, the unemployment rate was virtually stable at 7.4%. Published November 13, 2024. Accessed January 31, 2025. https://www.insee.fr/en/statistiques/8283457; and World Bank Group. GDP per capital (current US$) – France. Accessed January 31, 2025. https://data.worldbank.org/indicator/NY.GDP.PCAP.CD?locations=FR.

History

France's history started long ago with the first tribes. At the beginning of the third millennium BCE, there were around 2 million people[1] living off agriculture, hunting, and fishing.

From 58 to 51 BCE to the 5th century, Rome dominated the country, and a brilliant Gallo-Roman culture thrived until the Barbarians ended Rome's domination and spread chaos. In the 500s CE, Clovis and the Germanic tribes, called the Franks, pushed the invaders out, and the land of Francie (the archaic name of France) became a mosaic of kingdoms ruled by several kings and one emperor, Charlemagne (768–814), who expanded his kingdom from the Ebro River (Spain) to the Elbe River (Czech Republic). When this vast empire broke into pieces, the western part of it became France in 843.[2]

During the Renaissance (from 1483), France was ruled by a succession of conquering kings who increased their power. The end of the century brought a deterioration of the economy, expansion of the colonial conquests in Africa and Asia, and political instability. The 20th century started with a rise of leftist parties. Under their influence, the separation of church and state was officially declared in 1905. The poor state of the economy led to social unrest and resentment toward Germany. World War I (1914–1918) gave France back its two lost regions.

In 1939, World War II began and France was occupied by Germany. The French Resistance and the Allies defeated occupying Germany in 1944 and created the Fourth Republic, which lasted until 1958. Post–World War II economic development was also favorable for the creation of social legislation. In 1958 the current Fifth Republic was born. The Fifth Republic saw the entrance of France into the European Economic Community under President Charles de Gaulle and industrial and commercial development occurred. From 1981 to 1986, the Socialists were voted into power and François Mitterrand became the first socialist president of the Fifth Republic.[3] The socialist government gave more power to the regions. In 1995, President Jacques Chirac's liberal government reduced public spending and began the reform of social security.[4] This brought Socialists back to power at the ministerial level, and they passed social reforms, including the 35-hour workweek and universal healthcare coverage (1999).

In 2007, conservative Nicolas Sarkozy was elected president and in line with the European Union (EU), Sarkozy pushed back retirement age to 62. His reforms made him very unpopular, and he lost the next presidential elections to Socialist Francois Hollande (2012–2017). During Hollande's time in office, the economic situation in France plummeted and unemployment rose to unseen numbers.[5,6] Despite a few reforms, Hollande succeeded in alienating most of the French people.[7]

In May 2017, centrist Emmanuel Macron, defeated Marine Le Pen (a far-right member of the National Rally political party) and was elected president of France. Macron quickly became a presence on the world stage. Domestically, he had intensifying criticism.

The coronavirus SARS-CoV-2 (COVID-19) pandemic in 2020 caused an economic contraction. Despite more than 25 million of the French population contracting COVID-19, the country had a robust job retention scheme and a high rate of vaccination, and this spared the French population the high unemployment and death rates seen in other countries.[7]

Emmanuel Macron was re-elected in 2022 with 58% of the vote, becoming the first French president in two decades to win a second term.[8] The challenges he faced included the war in Ukraine, inflation, gas/electricity price increase, pension reform, climate transition, and other social movements.[9] France remains one of the most modern countries in the world and a leader among European nations.[7,10]

Size and Geography

Table 12-1 provides key statistics for France. France is commonly referred to as a hexagon. Metropolitan France is in western Europe, north of Spain and Andorra, with the Bay of Biscay to the west and the Mediterranean Sea to the southeast. Belgium, Luxembourg, Germany, Switzerland, Italy, and Monaco lie on its eastern boundary, and the English Channel lies to the north. Covering an area of around 551,500 square kilometers, France is slightly smaller than Texas.[10] (See **Figure 12-1**.)

France is also composed of various territories around the globe. These include French Guiana in northern South America; Guadeloupe and Martinique, which are Caribbean islands; the Reunion, an island in the Indian Ocean; Saint Pierre and Miquelon in the Atlantic Ocean; Mayotte, one of the Comoros Islands; Wallis and Futuna, New-Caledonia, and French Polynesia; and many other territories around the globe. These remains of the former French colonies double the area of France (over 559,000 square kilometers) and provide the country with a political presence

Figure 12-1 Map of France

in the world as well as total control over the globe's largest exclusive economic maritime zone of more than 11 million square kilometers.[11] With a current population of 65.6 million people (2022 est.)[12] in metropolitan France (67.8 million including the overseas territories),[13] it is the second largest country by population in the EU, right after Germany.[14] Almost 9% of the approximately 750 million Europeans live in France.[15,16]

Government and Political System

The government of the French Republic is a semi-presidential system, which means that both the president and the prime minister actively participate in the daily operations of the state. This form of government was determined by the French Constitution of the Fifth Republic. The Constitution provides for a separation of powers; the national government of France is divided into executive, legislative, and judicial branches.

The legislative power is in the hands of the Parliament, which is composed of the National Assembly and the Senate. It passes statutes and votes on the budget, and it controls the action of the executive. The constitutionality of the statutes is checked by the Constitutional Council, whose members are appointed by the president of the Republic, the president of the National Assembly, and the president of the Senate. The National Assembly can revoke the entire government, including the prime minister, through a "censure motion."

The independent judiciary branch is based on a civil law system that evolved from the Napoleonic codes and is divided into the judicial branch, which deals with civil law and criminal law, and the administrative branch, which deals with appeals against executive decisions. The French government includes organizations that check abuses of power and independent agencies. France is a unitary state, but the administrative subdivisions (the regions, departments, and communes) have various legal functions, and the national government is prohibited from intruding into their normal operations. Each entity is headed by elected assemblies.

As a founding member of the European Coal and Steel Community, which later became the European Union (EU), France has had to transfer part of its sovereignty to European institutions, something that has been included in the country's Constitution. The French government must adopt and follow all European treaties, directives, and regulations.[17]

Macroeconomics

France ranks among the leading European countries and is one of the most modern countries in the world. France has the fifth strongest economy in the world with an estimated GDP of $3.011 trillion USD.[18] The COVID-19 pandemic contributed to a 7.8% drop in GDP in 2020. The 2014 Russian–Ukrainian war and the recovery from the COVID-19 pandemic have impacted supply chains and put pressure on prices. In the third quarter of 2022, the French unemployment rate was virtually stable at 7.3%.[4,19]

France is the sixth largest exporter of goods and services in the world.[20] Currently, services are the main contributor to the country's economy, with over 70% of its GDP stemming from this sector. In manufacturing, France is one of the global leaders in the automotive, aerospace, and railway sectors as well as in cosmetics and luxury goods. France has a highly educated labor force and the highest number of science graduates per thousand workers in Europe.[21]

The structure of the French economy has evolved during the past decades and remains diversified and resilient. Such institutional strengths as strong protection of property rights and a fairly efficient regulatory framework facilitate entrepreneurial activity.[22] The GDP or purchasing power parity (PPP) of was $3.031 trillion USD in 2023.[23] The GDP per capita was $44,460 USD in 2023, with a national unemployment rate of 7.1%.[24] The top individual and corporate tax rates are, respectively, 45% and 25%. The tax burden equals 45.4% of GDP. Three-year government spending and budget balance averages are, respectively, 58.6% and −6.1% of GDP. Public debt equals 110.6% of GDP.[23]

Demographics

As of January 1, 2022, the total population of metropolitan France and French overseas departments was estimated at 67.813 million.[25] The number of people living in France has increased steadily since 1982.[26] In 2021, 738,000 children were born and 657,000 people died, putting the natural increase at 81,000. Net migration is estimated at 140,000.[27] France's demographic increase is today one of the most dynamic of the EU. The current fertility rate for France in 2023 is just below two children per woman (1.848).[28] France is, along with Ireland, the EU country with the highest fertility rate.

Ethnic Groups in France

According to French law, it is illegal for the government to collect data on the ancestry and ethnicity of its citizens. The French population is believed to be made up of White, North African, Black, and Asian origin. The French population is vast and diverse.[29]

Religion

Since 1905, church and state have been officially separated in France, and secularity is a notion strongly defended. Religion is a private matter, and on principle, the French state does not conduct any religious polls or census. Therefore, information about religions in France can only be based on estimates and extrapolations of nongovernment polls.

Although France is a traditionally Catholic country whose history has been molded in part by the church, the influence of the church has enormously diminished. The total number of Catholic baptisms dropped from over 334,000 in 2008 to under 205,000 in 2019,[30] and a large part of the population claims to be agnostic or atheist. A 2020 survey of the feeling of belonging to a religion among people in France showed that nearly half (47%) felt a link to Catholicism, 4% to Islam, 2% each to Protestantism, 2% to Buddhism, and 1% each to Judaism, Orthodox Christianity, or another religion. Thirty-three percent indicated a feeling of belonging to no religion and 9% declined to answer.[31]

Health Status of the Population

The infant mortality rate for France in 2020 was 2.890 deaths per 1,000 live births,[32] which is lower than the EU rate in 2020 of 3.224 deaths per 1,000 live births.[33] The French also enjoy very high ratios of healthy-life years (HLYs), which can be thought of as the disability-free life expectancy; a French woman born in 2022 can expect 65.3 years of healthy life, and a French man can expect 63.9 HLYs.[34] However, nearly two in five French adults reported having a chronic condition in 2019, even though about two-thirds of these adults reported being in good health.[35] Rates of cancer in France are higher than for the EU on average. Drivers of French mortality are behavioral and environmental risk factors such as tobacco use, dietary risks, alcohol consumption, low physical activity, and air pollution.[35] Healthcare availability seems to be unequal throughout the territory, and prevention campaigns do not seem effective enough. Children born prior to 2018 had among the worst measles/mumps/rubella (MMR) vaccination statistics.[36] Since January 1, 2018, however, MMR vaccination has been mandatory for infants born in France and most of the children born in 2019 were immunized.[37]

Brief History of the Healthcare System

From the 19th Century to 1945: Public Health at the Heart of the System

Medical progress and discoveries led to the adoption of laws and rules to address sanitary problems and improve people's health. These included laws on sanitary practices to contain epidemics (1822), laws on treatments and procedures for mental diseases (1838), spring water management and water sanitation (1856), mandatory vaccinations, disinfection procedures, mandatory reports of transmissible diseases, and regulation of new constructions (1902).[38] By the beginning of the 20th century, the 1902 law put the responsibility for its application in the hands of French mayors, who officially became the protectors and defenders of public health. In 1920, the creation of the Ministry of Health in charge of hygiene, assistance, and social planning put health care back under the authority of the central state. In 1941, the hospital law put most of the hospital management under direct control of the Ministry of Health, as opposed to the exclusively communal management of the hospitals established in 1796.

Financing Through Mutual Benefit Companies as Opposed to Public Assistance

From the beginning, health care in France was self-paid by the people who used it. You called the doctor, and you paid for the service. Then, at the beginning of the 19th century, the notion of social protection began to develop as a form of provision for the future. Everyone had to pay their own health expenses and had to plan for them. That was the funding concept for the mutual benefit movement. In 1898, mutual benefit companies were removed from state control, and a mutuality code was published to define their roles and missions. By 1900, the number of mutual benefit associations had reached 13,000, with 2.5 million members. In 1940, these associations had nearly 10 million members,[39] and they are still an important force in French political life.

Transition to the Notion of Insurance

Until 1898, the victim of a work-related accident had to prove that the employer was at fault in order to get coverage for their medical expenses. In 1898, new legislation stated that in a case of a work accident, the employer would have to support all of the related expenses for the employee. To protect themselves against this risk, employers called upon insurance companies to cover their employees.

The 1898 law covered only industry workers. In 1930, an Act on Social Insurance created compulsory protection for employees in industry and business whose earnings fell below a certain level. It provided insurance in five areas: illness, maternity, disability, old age, and death. By the outbreak of World War II (in 1939), two-thirds of the French population was covered for illness.[40] However, this social protection applied only to employed people, leaving a large part of the French population without coverage.

The institutionalization of the insurance system further developed the role of the hospital through a 1943 decree to treat the sick, the elderly, the disabled, the incurable, and pregnant women, as well as those whose treatment was in charge of the public collectivities and of insurance companies. All of these laws and decrees set the basis for the future evolution of the healthcare system that would take shape after World War II.

La Sécurité Sociale

The present system of social security, including statutory health insurance, was established in 1945, at the end of World War II, to give everyone the guarantee of subsistence and support of their family under decent conditions. Its creation also called for the development of a vast nationwide mandatory mutual aid organization that would be extremely general and open in terms of the people it covered and the risks it guarded against. To implement this plan, the 1945 ruling replaced the many insurance organizations with a single network of coordinated insurance departments. The goal was to extend coverage to all individuals, regardless of their employment status.

The conditions covered by social security in 1945 were sickness, maternity, disability, old age, and death. A 1946 addition included a child benefit and protection for work-related accidents. Today, social security covers five areas of risk: sickness/maternity/disability/death, family, old age, widowhood, and work accidents or profession-related sickness.

When Social Security was funded, it was based on the work insurance system created in 1898 and on the 1930 Social Insurance Act. Thus, it concerned only industry workers and their families. Later, statutory health insurance coverage was extended to state employees (in 1947), artisans and other workers (in 1948), farmers (in 1961), and self-employed nonagricultural workers (in 1966). This process of expanding coverage was recognized in the statutes of 1974, which established a system of personal insurance for those who did not fall into any of the categories already covered. To obtain this insurance, individuals had to pay a contribution, or request that the department contribute on their behalf.

Universal Health Coverage

The year 1999 was a milestone in French health care: An act established universal statutory health coverage, *Couverture Maladie Universelle* (CMU), for any person with permanent residence in France. For people whose income was below a certain level, this access to medical coverage was free, emphasizing the French philosophy of national solidarity.

Together with the CMU, the legislature created Complementary Universal Health Coverage (CMU-C), with the goal of helping people receive voluntary health insurance to cover all expenses not included in the basic social security scheme. Despite those measures, the system still excluded people whose income was just slightly over the minimum income level defined to become a CMU and CMU-C recipient. Therefore, in 2004, the Complementary Health Aid (ACS) program was created. People with resources between the CMU level and the CMU level plus 15.0% could benefit from a government-fixed reduction for voluntary health insurance premiums. By the end of 2007, 7.4% of the population benefited from the CMU and the CMU-C.[41] Finally, for destitute people who were ineligible for the CMU for lack of proof of stable or regular residency in France, the State Medical Aid (Medicaid or AME) was established, putting all of their medical care expenses under the responsibility of the state.

Enrollment in France's statutory health insurance (SHI) system is mandatory.[42] The system covers most costs for hospital, physician, and long-term care, as well as prescription drugs; patients are responsible for coinsurance, copayments, and balance bills for physician charges that exceed covered fees. The insurance system is funded primarily by payroll taxes (paid by employers and employees), a national income tax, and tax levies on certain industries and products. Ninety-five percent of citizens have supplemental insurance to help with these out-of-pocket costs, as well as dental, hearing, and vision care.[42]

Financing and Regulating Health Care

In 1945, the founders of the system hoped that better access to health care would help keep the population in good health, thus reducing the need for care and health expenditures. In the 1960s, healthcare consumption expanded tremendously, while revenues did not. With the economic difficulties of the 1970s, financial constraints became a main driver of healthcare policies. "The social security (CSG) contribution rates for health insurance have steadily increased to cover spending on health care."[43]

Since 2009, CSG and the central government have had a larger role in managing healthcare provision at the local level.[44] In 2019, the public and private compulsory health insurance plans funded 83.7% of the health spending in France, with the revenue for these plans coming from social security contributions (from employers and employees), income taxes, and taxes on tobacco and alcohol. Healthcare spending in 2019 was higher in France (11.1% of GDP) than in the rest of the EU (9.9%).[44]

The French Health and Social Protection System

The early public assistance and welfare systems were progressively replaced with a social insurance system, introduced at the end of the 19th century and continued throughout the first half of the 20th century. However, social protection in its current form was only introduced shortly after World War II. From 1946, the right to social protection was recognized in the preamble of the French Constitution. The French social protection system principles, in place since the end of World War II, still apply today:

- *Universality*: All nationals and residents are covered by the system, and it is compulsory to sign up with the social protection organizations.
- *All-encompassing*: The French system covers every possible eventuality in life (health, parenthood, old age, disability, industrial accidents and professional illnesses, family benefits and dependency, as well as unemployment).
- *Solidarity*: The French social protection system stems from the professional insurance schemes introduced before World War II. Today it combines this insurance-based approach—particularly with contributions deducted from employment income—with measures reliant on solidarity and collective financing.[45]

Description of the Current Healthcare System

When studying the French healthcare system, one must keep in mind that social security is the main framework and that all the actors, decisions, implementations, and policies relate to social security. In describing the current health system, one must begin by looking at the care supply, which includes hospitals and health professionals. See **Figure 12-2**.[42]

Facilities

In France, hospitals are core to the healthcare system.[40] Hospitals are planned using a medical map (quantitative) and the regional strategic health plan (qualitative).[46] The medical map divides each section into healthcare regions and psychiatric regions. The Ministry of Health is required to authorize expensive equipment and specialized care. French medical institutions can be roughly divided into three categories: public hospitals, private not-for-profit hospitals, and private for-profit hospitals and clinics.[47]

The American Hospital of Paris, founded in 1906, is a private, not-for-profit, community hospital that is certified under the French healthcare system.[48] Located in Neuilly-sur-Seine, in the western suburbs of Paris, it has 187 surgical, medical, and obstetric beds.[48] The clinic initially focused on the treatment of Americans living in Paris, but in 1918, it opened its doors to all patients. The current hospital annually helps about 200,000 patients from all over the world to overcome acute/chronic diseases and cancer of varying severity. "This hospital has dual accreditation: the Joint American Commission for Hospital Accreditation and the Supreme French Commission for Health Combining the main achievements of French and American medicine; the hospital has become one of the leading medical institutions in the world."[49]

In 2020, there were 2,989 hospitals in operation in France,[50] compared to 3,192 in 2013.[51] Public hospitals tend to be larger in size than private hospitals and account for about one-third of all hospitals.[52,53] These public hospitals provide for research and training of medical students and personnel and are generally well equipped. There are four levels of public hospitals. General hospitals account for roughly 54% of public hospitals and are the most common type of public hospital. They provide a range of acute care services, rehabilitation, and long-term care, and may also provide psychiatric care. Local hospitals account for roughly 34% of public hospitals and are community-level structures offering acute care, follow-up care and rehabilitation, and long-term care. Most doctors who work in local hospitals are self-employed private practitioners. Specialized hospitals account for 9% of public hospitals and include psychiatric hospitals. Regional hospitals account for roughly 3% of public hospitals and provide a higher level of specialization and technical capacity; many of these are linked to a university and operate as teaching and research hospitals.

Nonprofit private hospitals number 670 (22.4% of all hospitals),[54] down from 1,400 in 2008. Private for-profit hospitals used to be most numerous, at 1,750, and specialized most often in medical, surgical, or obstetric procedures; their number is now down to 972 (32.5%).[55] Although all hospitals receive a per diem payment, the services covered by that rate vary based on hospital type. Public hospitals receive a single per diem rate that covers all services provided, while private for-profit hospitals bill medical fees and other items, such as prostheses, separately. Patients also contribute 20% of the cost of hospital stays per day.

The number of hospital beds has decreased in recent years. In 2020, there were 5.7 beds per 1,000 patients, down from 6.3 beds per 1,000 patients in 2013. "This number is still above the OECD average (4.3).[56] Every year, the regional courts of auditors identify most hospitals for their low occupancy rates. Hospital costs represent 38.9% of France's total health expenditures; the European average is 37.4%."[57] Over the past 10 years, France has closed nearly 30,000 hospital beds[58] but has not yet succeeded in overcoming strong public resistance to this move. Closure of small, local hospitals is underway. Ambulatory care is clearly designated as the preferred mode of hospital care whenever possible, but France does not seem ready to step away from its tradition of inpatient care.[59]

Public hospitals have specific obligations, such as ensuring the continuity of care, teaching, and training. The budgets they receive are largely based on history and on the number of patients they treat. Private for-profit hospitals concentrate on elective surgeries and obstetrics and rely financially on fee-for-service remuneration. Proprietary hospitals, which are typically smaller than public hospitals, have traditionally emphasized elective surgery and obstetrics, leaving more complex cases to the public sector. The proprietary sector has consolidated, and many proprietary hospitals have developed a strong capacity for cardiac surgery and radiation therapy. There is no significant difference in the quality of

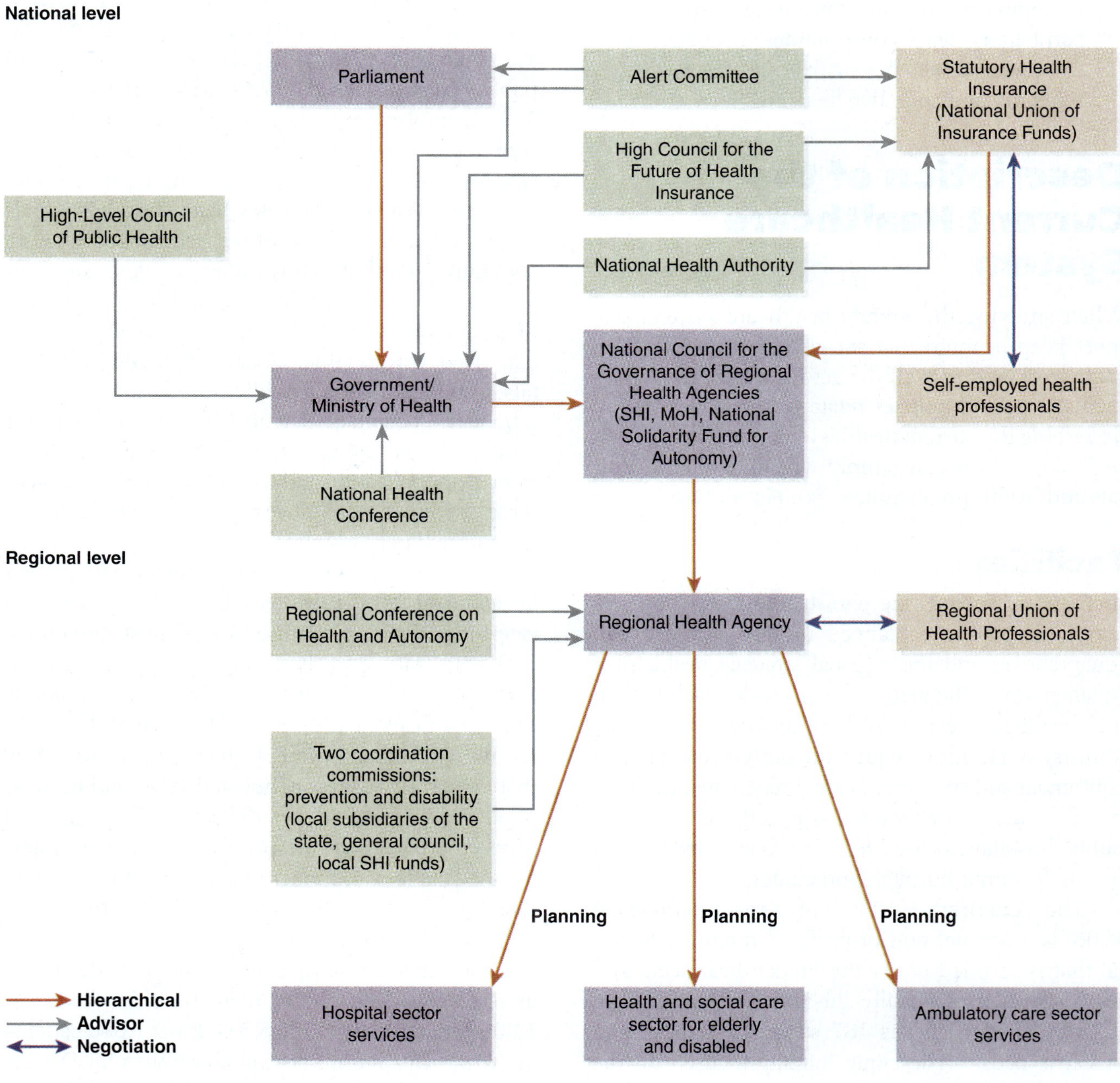

Figure 12-2 Healthcare System of France

Reproduced from Chevreul K, Durand-Zaleski I, Bahrami SB, et al. France: health system review. *Health Syst Transit.* 2010;12(6):xxi–xxii.

care offered by public versus private hospitals. All private and public establishments have switched to diagnosis-related group payment systems.

The number of nonphysician personnel per bed is higher in public hospitals than in private hospitals and overall lower than in U.S. hospitals. This difference in hospital staffing may reflect a more technical and intense level of service in U.S. hospitals. It also reflects differences between a national health insurance system and the U.S. health system, which is characterized by large numbers of administrative and clerical personnel whose main tasks focus on billing many hundreds of payers, documenting all medical procedures performed, and handling risk management and quality assurance activities.[60]

Hospitals are more labor intensive than the healthcare sector as a whole. Typically, as much as 60% to 70% of hospital spending is staff costs. In addition, service prices in hospitals are influenced by local as well as national wage levels. The structure of service provided, the market structure, and competition of both the payers and the providers can determine the price of services.[61]

Healthcare personnel and associated enterprises and organizations for ambulatory care are mostly in the private sector in France. Outpatient care is provided by generalists, specialists, and outpatient departments of hospitals. The trend has been for general practitioners (GPs) and specialists providing outpatient care to regroup in medical posts, conveniently located in industrialized and commercial areas with access to modern facilities and parking spaces. Other suppliers of medical support services, such as pharmacies and optical services, are often nearby. This geographic synergy provides efficiency and convenience for patients.

Workforce

Doctors and other healthcare professionals can work in both public hospitals and private practices, or they can choose to work in only one type of structure. They are mostly paid on a fee-for-service basis. A routine consultation costs between €25 and €55 ($27 and $60 USD, respectively), depending on the specialty of the doctor and treatment.[62] The state covers 70% of this cost for French residents.[62] Everyone in France is obligated to pay a token €1 ($1 USD) fee for doctor's appointments.[63] There are slightly more specialists than general practitioners in France. Of the 217,441 physicians in France in 2022, 175,054 were specialists, and 93,570 provided primary care.[64] Approximately 59% of physicians are self-employed on a full-time or part-time basis.[42] Private general practitioners in France still make home visits 24 hours a day, 7 days a week, 365 days a year; when contacted, a GP will arrive within the hour.[65] The majority of practicing medical doctors are concentrated in metropolitan France, and they operate essentially as independent practitioners. Concerns about "medical deserts" have grown and may be exacerbated in the future as a large proportion of GPs will retire in the next decade. The proportion of people living in a region with a density of GPs 20% lower than the national average increased from 1% in 2012 to 4% in 2021.[66]

French authorities launched several initiatives to address these concerns, including offering financial support for doctors to set up practices and various tax breaks.[66] Since 2007, the main policy to tackle this issue has been to create multidisciplinary medical centers, enabling GPs and other health professionals to work in the same location. In 2020, a total of 1,612 such centers were registered, 30% more than in 2017.[66] For physicians who work full-time in medical centers in underserved areas, the guaranteed salary is approximately €50,000 ($63,290 USD) per year.[42]

Providers receive full or partial payment from patients at the time of service, or they can be paid part of the fee directly by social security within 10 days. Experts set the relative weight of the procedures, and the prices are negotiated by physicians' unions and public health insurance funds.

Approximately 5.3% of the French population works in the healthcare sector.[66] Physicians play a key role in the healthcare system. Compared with 40 years ago, the number of physicians has tripled, but the number of physicians has remained relatively stable in France over the past decade.[66] Since 1971, the Ministry of Health has limited the number of medical students, which has resulted in a decrease in the number of physicians today and in the near future, since many currently active doctors will soon retire. As of 2020, there were 3.27 physicians per 1,000 people, even lower than in 2015, when there were 3.37 physicians per 1,000 people.[66] The number of nurses in France has increased from 7.9 per 1,000 population in 2008 to 11.1 in 2019—above the EU average of 8.4.[66] Following the COVID-19 pandemic, the government has taken some measures to increase the recruitment and retention of nurses in hospitals and other facilities.[66]

Since the creation of social security, the relationship between private-practice physicians and the state and public insurance funds has been strained.

Experts set the relative prices of procedures, which are then negotiated by physicians' unions and public health insurance funds. Almost all practitioners conform to the *Tarif de convention* (tariff references), which sets prices. Tariff references are the fixed rates to be used by doctors, and rates are set according to the national *convention* for all health services. A contract (*convention*) that sets the general regulatory framework and the remuneration of the profession is supposed to be signed every five years by physicians' unions. Subsequent *conventions* allowed some physicians to charge more than social security tariffs (1980), limited this right (1990), and implemented official medical practice guidelines (*Références médicales opposables*) in 1993. The negotiations between doctors' unions and the funds are usually strained. The root of the problem is that private-practice physicians are strongly opposed to caps on outpatient expenditures. They have always had a great deal of freedom over when they set up shop, how they practice, and what they prescribe (compared with their counterparts in other countries). Yet, the bulk of their income is paid by public funds. This contradiction has become more glaring as concerns about soaring health expenditures grow. Medical practitioners and clinics/hospitals that are not *conventions* (complying with the tariff references) must display their prices. In some situations, certain medical practitioners (such as surgeons with extra qualifications or experience) can charge more than the *Tarif de convention*. The extra fee is called a *dépassement*,[67] and it is not reimbursed by social security.

The most recent tariff *convention* of 2022 set a new standard for diagnostic-related groups (DRGs) and the relationship between physicians and the legal social insurance entities.[68] Fee-for-service remains the core of physician remuneration, but physicians can also get remuneration based on the Realization of Public Health Objectives (*Rémunération sur Objectifs de Santé Publique*). The objectives of DRGs are to create managed care bundled lump sums for providers and to improve the delivery of medical services.

French physicians earn substantially less than their American colleagues. On average, a physician earns approximately twice the average income of their fellow citizens. Once a year, the Ministry of Social Affairs, Health, and Women's Rights determines the maximum number of students who can be admitted to medical, dental, midwifery, and pharmacy schools, which are all public by law. Tuition fees are approximately €500 ($633 USD) per year.[42] Although medical school is inexpensive, competition is fierce—only 20,000 out of 60,000 students are selected after the first year. Attending an expensive and prestigious prep school before and during the first year of medical school has become the norm. Because malpractice suits are much less common in France, healthcare providers pay modest premiums for liability insurance.

Physicians continue to complete stressful administrative work that interferes with their clinical duties. The ever-growing administrative part of their daily workload makes the profession much less attractive for new generations. This has contributed to a shortage of GPs, who work extremely long hours. This is a bigger problem in remote parts of France that attract fewer physicians compared with those practicing in cities. French rural GPs tend to have a higher workload than urban GPs. Rural patients have more chronic conditions to be managed but are offered fewer preventive services during consultations. It is necessary to increase the GP workforce and develop cooperation with allied health professionals in rural areas.[69]

Technology and Equipment

Medical technology improves and saves lives every day. Data on the European medical technology industry show that in 2023, the medical technology market in Europe was projected to reach $163 billion in U.S. dollars.[70] France is the second-largest market in Europe for medical devices, accounting for 14.3% of this market.[71] In 2022, the average European expenditure on medical technology as a percentage of total expenditure in health care was estimated at around 7.6% (i.e., less than 1% of the GDP).[72] Expenditure on medical technology per capita in Europe was at around €284 ($310 USD).[72] The European medical technology industry employs more than 800,000 people.[72,73]

There are over 1,300 medical device firms in France. One-third of these firms are of foreign origin.[74] Foreign enterprises bring in two-thirds of the total turnover. American enterprises alone account for 22% of the total market.[74]

The medical device market size in France had an estimated turnover of €36.7 billion ($40.1 billion USD) in 2022.[74] The market turnover for medical devices exported from France was estimated at €9.4 billion ($10.3 billion USD), or 26% of the total market. The market is expected to see an annual growth of about 2% for the next several years.[74]

Compared with other European countries, France is the sixth-largest exporter of medical technology, exporting about €7.2 billion ($7.9 billion USD) in 2021.[75] France is the third-largest importer of medical technologies in Europe, with €11.7 billion ($12.8 billion USD), so there is a trade deficit.[75]

The French medical technology industry has a dynamic international profile due to its research and development sector.[76] Projects supported by the French national council for the promotion of research in industry (Oséo-ANVAR) concern breakthrough innovations (i.e., global or European firsts).

France has been a world leader in the science of immunology. The focus on infectious diseases, autoimmunity, and allergies originated with Louis Pasteur, a French chemist and microbiologist (1822–1895).[77] Pasteur founded the Alliance Française (along with his colleagues) as well as the *Institut Pasteur* (Pasteur Institute). He discovered the principles of vaccination, microbial fermentation, and pasteurization (named after him). His research in chemistry led to remarkable breakthroughs in the understanding of the causes and preventions of diseases (including vaccines for anthrax and rabies), which laid the foundations of hygiene, public health, and much of modern medicine.[77]

The Pasteur Institute is a French nonprofit private foundation dedicated to the study of biology, microorganisms, diseases, and vaccines.[78] For over a century, the Pasteur Institute has researched infectious diseases. It supports 133 research units in Paris and 32 institutes throughout the world, and has been associated with 10 Nobel Prizes. The Pasteur Institute is a research partner organization and a member of the Université Paris Cité community, a global partnership for research and education in the field of biology and health, which was formally established in June 2021.[78]

France's Sanofi-Aventis manufactures and markets prescription drugs across the globe,[79] with a focus on major therapeutic areas such as multiple sclerosis, cardiovascular, immunology, neurology, oncology, rare blood disorders, and diabetes. Sanofi operates through three Global Business Units: Specialty Care (neurology and immunology, rare diseases, rare blood disorders, and oncology), Vaccines and General Medicines (diabetes, cardiovascular, and established products), and Consumer Healthcare, a stand-alone unit.[79] Ipsen S.A., a pharmaceutical company headquartered in Boulogne-Billancourt, France,[79] is one of the world's top 15 biopharmaceutical companies in terms of oncology sales.

In France, 1,340 medical equipment and facilities providers generated €28 billion ($30.6 billion USD) in revenues and 85,000 jobs. France exports approximately €8 billion ($8.7 billion USD) in medical devices per year. France ranks within the top countries as the fifth largest market in the world and the second largest in Europe for human medicines.[80]

France is a leader in other medical fields. On December 8, 2013, the first artificial heart was implanted at the Georges Pompidou hospital in Paris. The technological innovation center of the Garches Hospital provides manufacturers with clinical expertise and evaluation protocols to help them develop new technical solutions for disabled persons (stair-climbing wheelchairs, puff-controlled alarm devices, etc.). Surgical robots coupled to 3-D simulators allow surgeons to practice and refine the most complex surgical procedures. ROSA, a robot manufactured by a company located in southern France, assists many surgeons worldwide.

France's commitment to advancing the healthcare industry—from regenerative medicine for neurodegenerative diseases to vaccines and vaccinotherapy—is noteworthy. Since 2005, France has established eight official innovation clusters that focus solely on biotechnology and health care. Projects within these clusters are selected for funding by the French government following a biannual request for project proposals.[81]

Evaluation of the Healthcare System

Cost

Existing data—whether coming from surveys or as by-products of the administrative system—consistently indicate that the French, compared with Americans, consult their doctors more often, are admitted to the hospital more often, and purchase more prescription drugs. Quality of care is good, although some indicators lag behind—including high rates of antibiotic prescribing.[82] Yet, health expenditures per capita are lower in France compared with the United States.[83] In 2020, the per capita administrative cost in France was $298 USD; in the United States, it was $1,055.[84] The cost of the technology created for an aging population, demand for higher standards, and the attitude that health care is public welfare all increase costs. Conversely, a decrease in state expenditures on welfare, plus controls to ensure more efficient use of medical facilities, act to reduce costs in France. Resources allocated for health care are above the OECD average.[82] A historical comparison among the OECD nations can be seen in **Figure 12-3**.

In 2020, France spent more on the health of its population, as a percentage of GDP, than most other OECD countries.

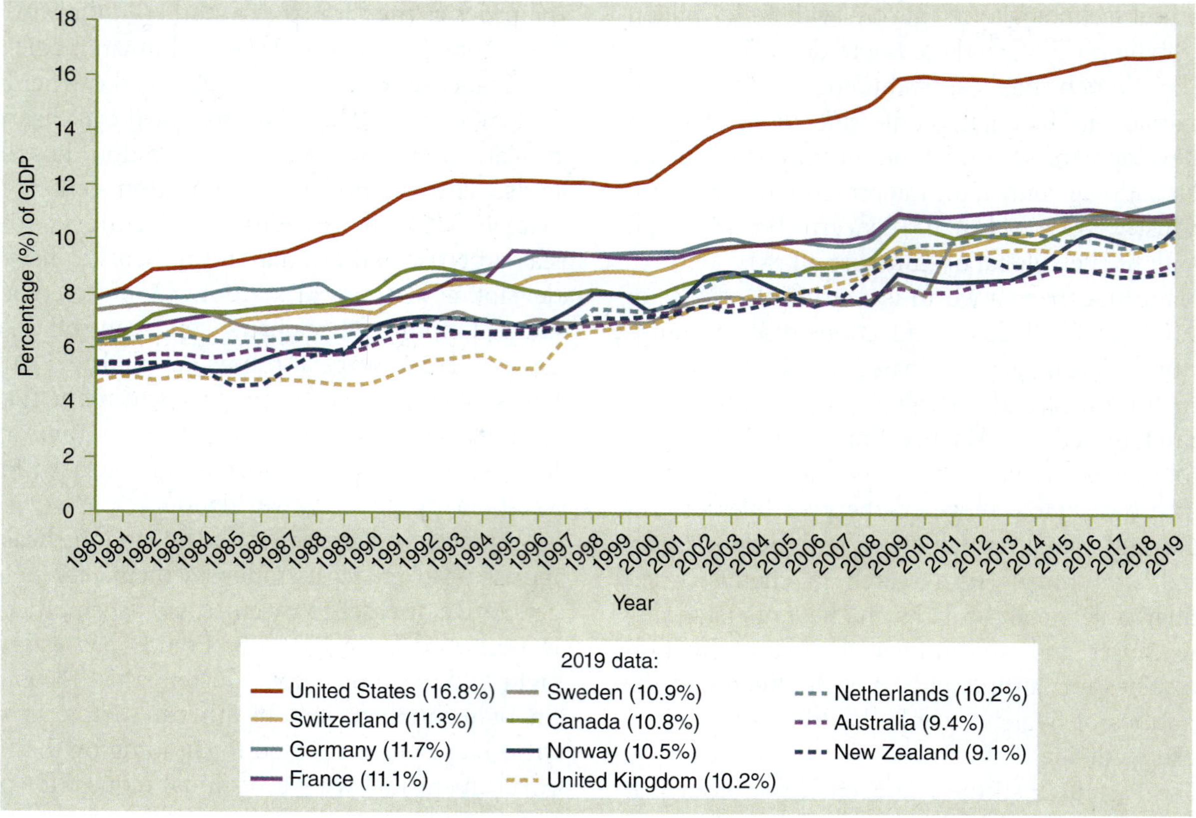

Figure 12-3 Healthcare Spending

Reproduced from The Commonwealth Fund. 2021. Mirror, mirror 2021: reflecting poorly—health care in the U.S. compared to other high-income countries. Accessed March 12, 2023. https://www.commonwealthfund.org/publications/fund-reports/2021/aug/mirror-mirror-2021-reflecting-poorly.

Prices in France for health-related goods and services are only slightly higher than in most European countries. On average, prescriptions and hospitalization times are the same in most European countries. However, French physicians and their patients have remarkable access to the latest chemotherapy, even experimental agents that may be unavailable to other EU patients.

France has a public health insurance plan called l'Assurance Maladie.[85] It is administered by the French social security office (la sécurité sociale), which manages social benefits related to medical care, retirement, family matters, and work-related accidents. Public health insurance is required for anyone who works or resides in France. It is based on three fundamental principles: equal access to care, a high quality of care, and mutual aid.

The French system is much more generous to its entire population than the United States is to its Medicare seniors.[86] There are no deductibles and French citizens have only modest copayments, which are dismissed for the chronically ill. In addition, most French people buy supplemental insurance to reduce any out-of-pocket expenses on eyeglasses, dental work, and private hospital rooms. Interestingly, in France, the sicker you get, the less you pay. Diabetes and other chronic diseases, as well as critical surgeries (e.g., coronary bypass), are reimbursed at 100%. Cancer patients are not charged for their treatment. Medication cost is also reduced for patients who are seriously ill.

France also excels in prenatal and early childhood care. Since 1945, there has been a widespread network of thousands of healthcare facilities, called Protection Maternelle et Infantile, to make sure that every mother and child receive basic preventive care. Mothers are paid for attending prenatal and postnatal appointments. Children are evaluated by a team of private-practice pediatricians, nurses, midwives, psychologists, and social workers. When parents fail to bring their children in for regular checkups, a social worker will make a visit to the family home.

The French government reimburses its doctors at a lower rate than U.S. physicians receive, in part, because medical schools in France are mostly paid for by the state. Malpractice insurance, a cost to French doctors as practice liability, is greatly diminished by a tort-adverse legal system.[87] Compared with American physicians, French physicians enter their careers with little, if any, debt and pay much lower malpractice insurance premiums. The average salary range for French physicians is between $107,000 and $205,000 USD,[88] whereas American physicians' average salary range is between $181,000 and $234,000 USD.[89] The French government pays two-thirds of the social security tax for most French physicians. This social security tax is typically 40% of the annual income.

The government's Assurance Maladie can control the healthcare system as France's largest buyer of medical services. Most GPs in France have an agreement with Assurance Maladie specifying what they can charge for a consultation. If a specialist has spent at least four years practicing in a hospital, that specialist is free to charge what they want. There is an unspoken and undefined limit to what physicians can charge.

France has been able to keep the cost burden for patients low through a combination of price controls and increased government spending, but the latter effort has led to higher taxes for both employers and workers. France runs a statutory health insurance (SHI) system providing universal coverage for its residents.[90] The system is financed through employee and employer contributions, and increasingly by earmarked taxes on a broad range of revenues. The SHI has a specific offering to the agricultural sector and another public offering with the same coverage and benefit policies. Funds are pooled at the national level. Voluntary, complementary private health insurance (VHI) also plays a large role. Almost 95% of the population has VHI, with means-tested subsidies available for 10.5% of the population and 8% of lower-income individuals being fully subsidized.[90]

The main players in the French health system are the SHI funds and the national government. Despite changes that gave power to regional health agencies, the central government has retained substantial control over the governance of the health system. Recently, France has moved in a new direction toward prevention, health promotion, and patient empowerment, which breaks from the previous more paternalistic system that focused on curative care.[90] SHI finances 83% of total health expenditure while private insurance and out-of-pocket payments account for the remaining 17%.[90] However, SHI does not cover some goods for financial reasons including, for example, dental and optical devices. While SHI covers over 90% of costs for hospital care, it covers only 44% of the costs for nonpharmaceutical medical goods in ambulatory (outpatient) care.[90]

The French government has attempted to reduce cost and has required patients to register with a general practitioner before visiting a specialist or else to agree to a lesser reimbursement, similar to many U.S. insurance plans. Reforms have focused on the following measures: developing ambulatory care to decrease the number of hospitalizations and to shift patients to outpatient facilities; encouraging the use of generic medicines; and decreasing the number of healthcare workers in the public sector, improving efficiency, and closing hospital beds that are not fully occupied. As a result of those actions, the 2010 general deficit of the *sécurité sociale* was lowered from €28 billion to €10.8 billion ($30.6 billion to $11.8 billion USD) in 2015. In 2018, it was reduced to €1.2 billion ($1.3 billion USD) before rebounding for 2019 and 2020 to around €5 billion ($5.5 billion USD).[91] With the COVID-19 pandemic in 2021, it climbed to €34.6 billion ($37.8 billion USD), with a forecast of €21.6 billion ($23.6 billion USD) in 2022.[91]

The French approach to reduce healthcare costs is a combination of four measures: (1) controlling the national habit of shopping around for treatment and medicines, (2) improving the health of the nation by routine preventive treatment, (3) enlisting the cooperation of the medical establishment and the health insurance industry in the management of the national health system, and (4) increasing the patient's participation in the cost of treatment.

Quality

In 2021, the Commonwealth Fund performed an assessment of healthcare system performance in Australia, Canada, France, Germany, the Netherlands, New Zealand, Norway, Sweden, Switzerland, the United Kingdom, and the United States.[92] This was done to compare the performance of healthcare systems of 11 high-income countries. The Commonwealth Fund used indicators available across five domains[92]: (1) access to care, (2) care process, (3) administrative efficiency, (4) equity, and (5) healthcare outcomes.

The top-performing countries overall were Norway, the Netherlands, and Australia. France came in eighth and the United States ranked last overall (11th).[92] France performed well on measures related to communication between primary care doctors and specialists.[92] Population coverage is high, with relatively few people reporting unmet needs. Also in 2021, the Foundation for Research on Equal Opportunity's (FREOPP) World Index of Healthcare Innovation ranked 31 national healthcare systems on quality, choice, science and technology, and fiscal sustainability. France's mostly government-run healthcare system ranked 25th overall, whereas the United States came in sixth and Switzerland was ranked number 1.[93]

According to FREOPP, France does best in the quality dimension (#12). France's healthcare infrastructure (#6) is solid, and the country holds its own in providing patient-centered customer service (#11). Although it ranks number 14 in measures of preventable disease, it scores particularly well on preventing hospitalizations and on cardiac and cancer survival rates. Despite these bright spots, France's overall quality rating is weighed down by poor performance in handling COVID-19 (#23).[93]

France ranks number 22 overall for choice. On the plus side, France ranks high in affordability of health insurance (#8). However, its overall choice ranking is weighed down by a low score in freedom to choose healthcare services (#26), in part because France's two-tier health insurance system—which helps eliminate out-of-pocket costs through supplemental insurance—weakens patient choice by making consumers less sensitive to the price of health care. In addition, there is virtually no choice in insurance carrier or plan design, with a single basic insurance choice determined by profession.[93]

France ranks number 14 in science and technology. It continues its tradition as a leader in scientific discoveries (#8), with the fourth highest score for Nobel laureates as well as a significant body of cited research. However, France lags behind in health digitization (#23).[93] France's fiscal sustainability ranking comes in at number 30, better only than Japan. In particular, its public health spending per capita is over 9% (#30), having grown by almost a full percentage point in the last 10 years. Without further cost-containment measures, the increasing public health spending threatens France's national solvency—which already ranks number 24 among countries in the Index.[93]

Access

The French enjoy free choice among a panoply of services in primary and secondary medical care. There is no limitation on doctors' or patients' freedom of choice and no GP gatekeeping role for hospital services. Healthcare consumption is highly concentrated among a small group of people, with a high level of medical care being consumed in the first year of life and beyond the age of 50. In addition, utilization differs significantly among social classes.

The accessibility of health services can be classified into two main categories: potential accessibility (ease of accessing services based on existing conditions) and revealed accessibility (actual use of healthcare services in a given location).[94] The French healthcare system is generally recognized as offering some of the world's best public healthcare services.

Basic treatment is free to all legal French residents, even those who are unemployed, thanks to mandatory public health insurance (social security).[46,94] Children in France are automatically eligible for healthcare coverage, regardless of nationality.[95] Preventive care is available for all, including free medical checkups every two years. Specialists are accessible without a doctor referral and getting an appointment at the doctor's office is easy.[46] Depending on the reason for seeing a doctor and the treatment needed, wait times for seeing a doctor in France can range up to 80 days, but on average, it is usually around six days. For certain specialist doctors, wait times are generally longer.[46]

The government has taken responsibility for the financial and operational management of health insurance. The Ministry of Social Affairs, Health, and Women's Rights is represented by the Regional Health Agencies, which are responsible for coordinating population health and health care, including prevention, care delivery, public health, and social care.[42] The supply of French hospitals and medical technologies is generally adequate. However, in rural areas, there are fewer hospitals and providers, and waiting for service is more common.

Social Disparity

Although French national health insurance has effectively eliminated significant financial barriers to medical care, and despite universal coverage, there remain wide disparities among social classes in patterns of medical care use. The distribution of health resources is also highly skewed in favor of urban areas and well-to-do regions. Well-to-do and educated French people rely on office-based private practice, particularly specialists and dentists. The more disadvantaged groups, including laborers, make greater use of GPs and public hospitals. These disparities are matched by disparities in life expectancy. Reducing disparities in social determinants of health and access to care is a national priority. There is a 6.3-year gap in life expectancy between males in the highest social category and those in the lowest, and poorer self-reported health among those with only state-sponsored insurance.[42]

The 2004 Public Health Act set targets for reducing geographic and financial inequities in access to services and inequities in preventive care related to obesity, cancer screening, and immunization. Financial incentives encourage physicians to practice in underserved areas. Furthermore, physician contracts under SHI prohibit physicians from denying care to beneficiaries of state-sponsored health insurance and put a cap on balance billing.[42] In France, inequalities in nutrition, physical activity, tobacco use, social class, type of employment, and participation in screening programs impact health outcomes. The medical system has been unable to compensate for inequalities in education, housing, working conditions, and access to medical care.[42]

The coordination of the various healthcare providers is clearly insufficient. The system encourages competition and discourages cooperation: There is friction between the public and private sectors, between outpatient facilities and hospitals, and between the many healthcare professions. Incentives have been initiated to increase the development of managed-care networks. Since mid-2005, patients have had control over which primary doctor they choose to see, but they need a GP to refer them to specialists to receive reimbursement. The patient first visits their *médecin traitant* (general practitioner)—that is, the physician who has been previously registered at the *caisse d'assurance maladie* as the one in charge of the coordination of care for the patient. The *médecin correspondant* (correspondent doctor) is the physician to whom the patient has been referred and is usually a specialist. With the authorization of the patient, this physician sends the relevant information to the *médecin traitant* in order to follow up and coordinate care. Several specialists have direct authorization for passing on information relevant to care, such as gynecologists, ophthalmologists, dentists, pediatricians, and psychiatrists, and their services are covered by the state without a referral by a *médecin traitant* (the patient does not have to go to their GP first). Patients visiting physicians and dentists pay full price and are later reimbursed for costs by public health insurance and complementary insurance. For other services, such as pharmaceutical costs, payment is made directly by *la sécurité sociale* and the complementary insurance to the provider through the use of the *carte vitale*. Patients are exempt from paying if they receive public assistance (CMU) or if they visit a procedure-oriented specialist. Patients who consult a specialist outside of the referring system see their reimbursement reduced.

In the French system, patients carry social security cards containing microchips that store basic information about the patient, and more importantly, information about their coverage by social security and the complementary insurance. Thus, the card allows patients to be almost immediately reimbursed for their medical care. The patient must present this *carte vitale*, which transmits all transactions to the *caisse d'assurance maladie* where they are registered. All medical procedures (hospitalization, laboratory tests, X-rays, etc.) have to take place in the locality of their *caisse d'assurance*. However, the patient can buy medicines anywhere in France through the *carte vitale*, and the pharmacy receives payment directly from the administration and the complementary insurance organizations. Administrative costs are significantly reduced by this nationwide system of electronic billing and payment. Originally, the *carte vitale* was designed to contain a patient's comprehensive medical information, allowing physicians immediate access to a patient's record. However, there has yet to be national use of the *carte vitale* as personal medical records storage.

To make consumers price sensitive, most patients pay the full cost of services out of pocket and request reimbursement from the statutory plan, except those requiring hospitalization and low-income beneficiaries under the Universal Health Care Act. Typically, patients receive only partial reimbursement and so, have a copayment for services. Patients without supplementary insurance typically receive a reimbursement rate of 70% for physician and dentist services and 60% for auxiliary and laboratory services. Reimbursements are, on average, 95% for major surgery, 80% for minor surgery, 95% to 100% for pregnancy and childbirth, and 70% for X-rays, routine dental care, and nursing care at home. Reimbursements for prescribed medicines depend on the type of medication, ranging from 15% to 65%. A patient can receive 100% coverage under certain conditions, such as having a chronic or acute medical condition (e.g., cancer, insulin-dependent diabetes, heart disease), requiring long-term care, having a long-standing condition, or requiring a hospital stay of more than 30 days.

Expanded Coverage

Although France provided nearly all residents with health insurance prior to 2000, the Universal Health Care Act (CMU) expanded coverage to all French residents. Single residents whose taxable income falls below a certain amount per year are entitled to free coverage. Key medical services covered by statutory health insurance in France include, but are not limited to, targeted preventive health services, inpatient care, outpatient care, prescription medication, and dental treatment.[96] Furthermore, people with major illnesses that require long-term care may be eligible to receive 100% reimbursement for their treatment costs. All medical costs associated with the delivery of a child are covered in full by the national health system. Some specialists, however, may impose additional charges.

In France, patients may choose to see their licensed practitioner at any time without limit. The French average five contacts with a general practitioner or a specialist each year, while Americans typically have four appointments, according to OECD in 2020.[97]

Current and Emerging Issues and Challenges

The French health system has a satisfactory level of access to care and service utilization, an abundant availability of choice without any significant waiting lists, and high life expectancy. Indeed, the *World Health Report 2000* ranked France as having the best healthcare system in the world. In 2023, the health system faced numerous challenges, many of which were common to neighboring countries.[98] The 2010–2012 Hospital, Patients, Health, Territories Bill (HPHTB), and the 2016 Loi Santé (currently in application) focused on some of these problems. These healthcare reforms were supposed to address the significant decrease in the number of doctors due to medical school quota systems. It should be noted that by 2040, it is projected that French physicians will comprise a younger population, who are more feminized, and more often salaried.[99]

The French government has also moved to control the growth of primary care spending. Hospice care, partial hospitalization, and day surgery care have become alternatives to inpatient hospitalization in France. However, there remains a shortage of long-term care.

Several major reforms were introduced in 2004: the Public Health Policy Act and the Health Insurance Reform Act, followed in 2005 and 2011 by new agreements between the national health insurance funds and medical trade unions on rules governing private practice. In 2006, a new strategic plan was also introduced to foster health workforce development. The main objectives of those reforms were to improve health system organization and management.

The Health Insurance Reform Act permits more flexibility and internal organizational freedom to public hospitals, despite relatively strict controls on hospital management. Hospital regulatory power was shifted, to some extent, from the central level to the regional level. The strategic plan for health workforce development promotes group practice and experiments with the transfer of tasks away from doctors to paramedic staff. The creation of a comprehensive electronic patient record, coupled with the preferred doctor system in primary care, was presented as a core component of the Health Insurance Reform Act, while quantitative targets and indicators were objectives of the Public Health Policy Act. However, these reforms did not fully answer many challenges, which led to the adoption of the 2010–2012 HPHTB.

The HPHTB aimed to emphasize medical awareness, prevention of addictions, and general education of the population in terms of health care. Given the excessively high rates of mortality in those under 65, there remains an urgent need to develop preventive actions within a coherent public health framework. Research shows that premature deaths of men and women could have been avoided with adequate primary prevention. These deaths are mostly linked to risky behaviors, such as smoking, drinking, and dangerous driving.

The Loi Santé (2016) is the logical extension of the 2010–2012 HPHTB. The goal is to go further than the HPHTB in terms of prevention of chronic diseases, which were the cause of more than 25% of deaths in France in 2016. The major challenge for the government remains the aging of the population and its many consequences. As the population of France ages, there are progressively fewer citizens of working age who pay into the national system. Meanwhile, health expenditures continue to increase, mainly due to technology advances and the aging of the population, leading to sizeable budget deficits for the social security fund. The deficit of *la sécurité sociale* still represents a major contributor to the country's public debt.

So far, measures taken have been directed toward the restriction of health services in the health plans and control of the diffusion of high technology. Ensuring equilibrium between various healthcare schemes has become a high priority in France. In a country with extremely high levels of taxation, new taxes cannot be the answer indefinitely, and reducing expenditures can only go to a certain point. In France, "free access to as much health care as you want" is considered an absolute right of the people, and measures like cost-sharing are highly unpopular. Therefore, raising cost participation can be just a small part of solving the problem.

The other solution the government has been working on since 2010 is reforming the age of retirement. In 2005, France was one of the countries with the lowest average retirement age: 58.5 years for men and 59.2 years for women.[100] As the population ages and as life expectancy increases, there will soon be more retired people to consume retirement and healthcare funds than active people to pay and provide those funds. Working people pay for their own health care through their salary taxes. The CSG tax (general social contribution used to partly finance health care) paid by workers is higher than that paid by retired people; the taxation rate applied is higher for workers, and the taxed revenues of working people are also usually more significant than pensions. Therefore, raising the retirement age should help contain, if not reduce, healthcare deficits by reducing the immediate number of nonpaying beneficiaries and increasing the amount of funds available for health care.

In 2010, President Sarkozy raised the retirement age by two years. Highly unpopular for this major step, he was not re-elected in 2012. The debate is sure to continue for future presidential candidates, and healthcare access and financing as well as retirement are likely to remain at the heart of reform proposals for some time. Presidential candidates have talked about universal access to comprehensive medical care, including full reimbursement for dental and eye care. All agree that the pension system must be saved, but there is much more at stake: the future of the healthcare system, so dear to the heart of the French.

In 2023, President Macron unilaterally decided that the pensionable age would be increased from 62 to 64 years primarily for economic reasons. This enraged the French populace. The fiscal struggle to reduce government debt is difficult to resolve, especially since French people already have one of the highest tax burdens in the OECD countries.

Evaluating Health Care During the Macron Presidency[101]

The French healthcare system had been in crisis well before COVID-19. The pandemic revealed many existing challenges, especially in emergency services. There are several key takeaways from Macron's current term in regard to health care:

- The *Ségur de la santé* (named after the avenue where the Health Ministry is located) refers to a council held between the government and various actors of the French healthcare system that took place during the summer of 2020, in response to the health crisis. This series of consultations led to the signing of the Ségur agreements, which are due to allocate €19.3 billion ($21.1 billion USD) to hospitals and nursing homes. The Ségur also includes a €2 billion ($2.2 billion USD) investment in health information systems, in order to improve interoperability and optimize the collection and analysis of health data.
- Telemedicine has experienced an unprecedented boom since the beginning of the COVID-19 crisis. In March 2021, 71% of the French reported having used an online platform to book their medical appointments.
- An online health portal, known as *Mon Espace Santé* ("My Health Space"), launched in 2022 to centralize all of a patient's medical data, to provide secure messaging between patients and health professionals, and to serve as a catalogue of digital health services.
- The Strategic Council for Health Industries (CSIS) has allocated a budget of €7 billion ($7.6 billion USD) to enable France to boost its innovation and medical autonomy. Priority has been given to cutting-edge advancements such as 5P Medicine (Personalized, Predictive, Preventive, Participatory, and Proof-Based), e-health and biotherapy. The government has also created the Health Innovation Agency.
- Psychiatry in France has been in a major crisis for years, due in part to a significant lack of means and personnel. GPs and primary care providers are to be given a greater role and more agency in the early detection and treatment of psychological disorders.
- There is significant need for improvement in the collection, management, and coordination of health data. The development and implementation of a Health Data Hub aims to support and promote innovation. Such an incentive is particularly relevant to prevention.
- Human capital and the training of healthcare professionals will target the development of new healthcare professions, reducing silos, a better delegation of tasks, training in digital technology, and management.

Sustainability and Resilience[102]

The challenges faced by health systems worldwide have been building over time with the rapid increase in costly new medical treatments and the growing prevalence of noncommunicable diseases in an aging population. Sustainability concerns the health system's ability to maintain key functions such as provision of services, financial protection, resource generation, and responsiveness to population needs, by withstanding internal and external stresses (economic, social, epidemiologic, and environmental challenges). Resilience refers to a health system's ability to prevent, absorb, adapt to, and rebound stronger from a crisis while minimizing negative impacts on population health, health services, and the wider economy.

A 2021 study by the Partnership for Health System Sustainability and Resilience (PHSSR)[102] evaluated the French health system's sustainability and resilience in the midst of the COVID-19 pandemic across five key domains: governance, health system financing, workforce, medicines and technology, and service delivery.[102]

COVID-19 Pandemic[35]

The COVID-19 pandemic had a major impact on population health and mortality in France. A broad set of containment measures were implemented to control the pandemic, though the success of these measures was mixed. The first cases of COVID-19 were identified in France at the end of January 2020. Within weeks, France instituted a series of measures to contain the spread and by mid-March 2020, a full lockdown was implemented, which resulted in a sharp drop in the number of cases. See **Figure 12-4**.

In 2020, life expectancy at birth in France was 82.3 years, which was almost two years higher than across the EU. It temporarily fell by 8 months in 2020 because of deaths due to COVID-19—the biggest reduction since 1945.[35] The measures taken to contain the pandemic led to a major contraction of the economy (French GDP fell by over 8% in 2020), rising unemployment rates, and poverty.[35]

During the first wave of the pandemic, France faced many issues with containing the transmission of the virus. There were few certified laboratories and a lack of necessary swabs and reagents, so mass

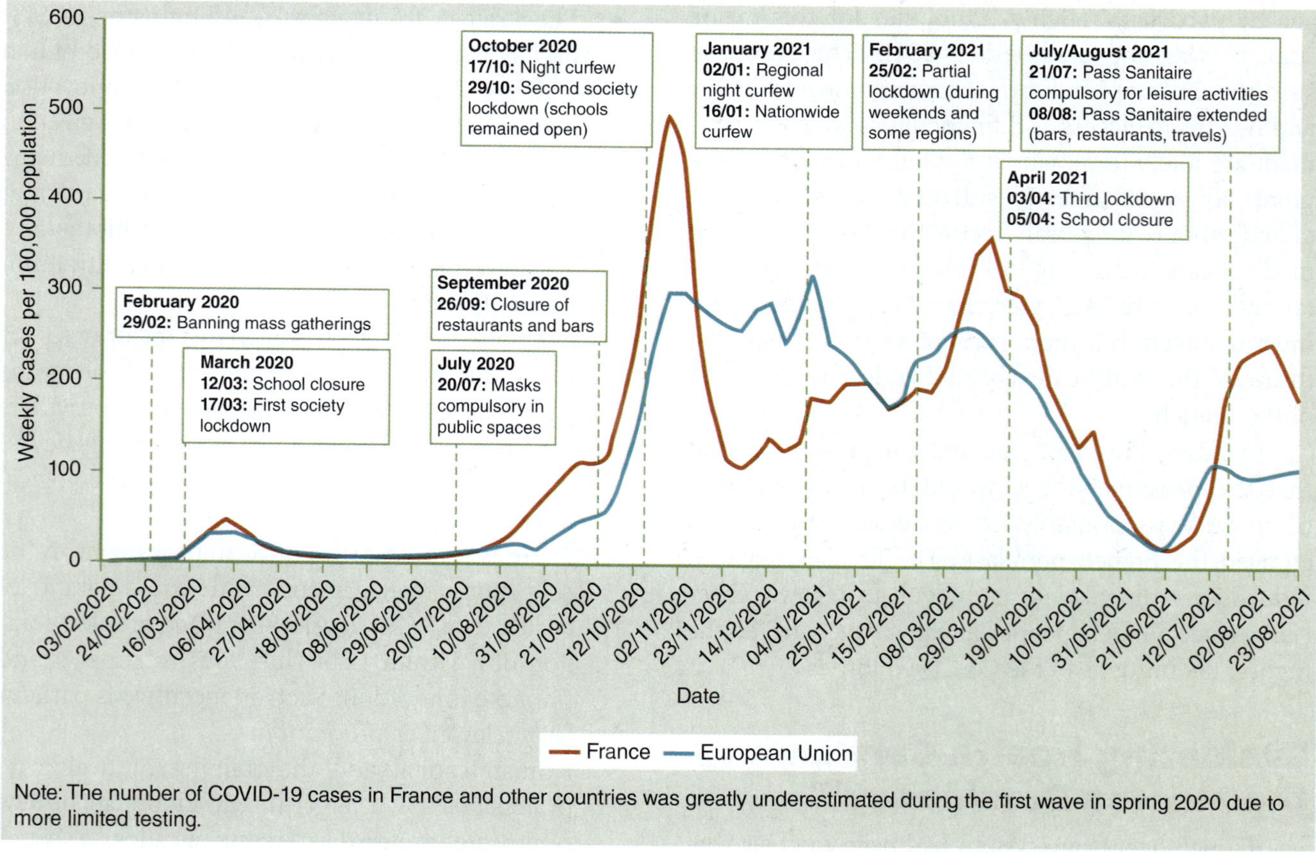

Figure 12-4 France Implemented Three Full Lockdowns in 2020 and 2021 to Contain Virus Transmission

Reproduced from ECDC for COVID-19 cases and review of government policies (https://www.gouvernement.fr/info-coronavirus/les-actions-du-gouvernement).

testing was limited mainly to people with COVID-19 symptoms seen in hospitals. Wearing masks in all shops and enclosed public places was made compulsory on July 20, 2020, in France for everyone over 11 years old.[35] Beginning in September 2020, France introduced new rules for patient prioritization in testing, established new testing centers, and promoted use of new rapid antigenic tests. These efforts were successful and by the end of 2020, France became one of the leading EU countries testing people.[35]

France also experienced difficulties administering and completing contact tracing. There was a limited number of professional contact tracers. Management of isolation and quarantine was not strictly applied and controlled throughout the pandemic. People with confirmed COVID-19 were asked to self-isolate at home. If self-isolation was not possible, people could isolate in dedicated hotels, but use of this plan remained very limited. To encourage greater compliance, the government simplified and extended sick-leave allowances in January 2021. The emergency hospital plan ("Segur de la Santé") was activated on March 13, 2020, to mobilize additional human resources and equipment to respond to the pandemic.

France used a national platform to recruit volunteers and students in medical and nursing education programs. Since a "health reserve" recruitment effort had been established in 2007 following the avian influenza epidemic, inactive and retired health professionals were available to join the team.

During the COVID-19 pandemic, France centralized policymaking at the national level through the National Defense and Security Council, a crisis management body established in 2008 composed of a selection of ministers and chaired by the president. While this process was highly centralized, policy implementation required the involvement and coordination of the many other people involved in the health system at the national, regional, and local levels.

Regional health agencies provided greater medical support to nursing homes, notably via additional health workers to increase testing and treatment, and by establishing a more integrated care network to support coordinated hospital admissions and proper follow-up after discharge. However, structural challenges such as the persistent lack of personnel and qualified medical staff, which was understood to occur because of the unattractive working conditions, continued to affect the quality and safety of long-term care (LTC) services. In response, the government provided bonuses for care workers to reward them for their exceptional efforts during the first wave of the pandemic.

Following the approval of the first COVID-19 vaccines in December 2020 and January 2021, the vaccination campaign started slowly in France. It then accelerated in February 2021 with the growing availability of doses. The target population groups were gradually widened, and several hundred immunization centers were set up to enable mass vaccination. In addition to physicians, pharmacists, nurses, and other health workers were allowed to administer vaccines.

At the start of the vaccination campaign in early 2021, vaccine hesitancy was high in France, with one in two French people reporting in mid-January 2021 that they were not willing to get vaccinated. The implementation of the Pass Sanitaire during the summer of 2021 provided a strong incentive for people who were not yet vaccinated to get their first and second doses. Vaccination became a requirement to access certain places and services.

By the end of August 2021, 59% of the population had received two doses (or the equivalent), a slightly higher proportion than the EU average. The government of France announced a mandatory COVID-19 vaccination for health and long-term care workers in mid-September 2021 to ensure greater protection for patients. While around two-thirds of health workers in hospitals and LTC facilities had already received two doses (or the equivalent) by the end of July 2021, only 43% of nursing aides and 42% of medical residents had received the recommended vaccination doses. Those health and long-term care workers not vaccinated by mid-September 2021 were no longer authorized to practice.

The government greatly increased public spending on health in 2020 in response to the crisis. In July 2020, the government adopted an ambitious plan to strengthen public hospitals and increase investment in the health workforce. The Recovery and Resilience Plan in France supported these investments. The proposed investments in health care, research, and cohesion amount to €7.7 billion ($8.4 billion USD), representing almost 20% of total grants for France under the EU Recovery and Resilience Fund. Priority areas include modernization of the health-care system, greater investment in elder-care facilities, wider implementation of technological health and e-health systems, and encouraging research and development, training, and scientific research.

References

1. Larousse. *Le Petit Larousse Illustré: France*. Paris, France: Editions Larousse; 2003.
2. *World History Encyclopedia*. France timeline. Accessed March 25, 2023. https://www.worldhistory.org/timeline/france/.
3. Escolona F. François Mitterrand gave French socialists power at the price of their soul. *Jacobin*. 2021. Accessed March 25, 2023. https://jacobin.com/2021/05/francois-mitterrand-french-socialism-parti-socialiste-40th-anniversary.
4. *BBC News*. Chirac: a life in French politics. 2019. Accessed March 25, 2023. https://www.bbc.com/news/world-europe-13299221.
5. Juritravail. Chiffres du chômage 2016 en France. Accessed May 23, 2016. http://www.juritravail.com/chiffres-et-indices/chiffres-chomage.html.
6. *Britannica*. Nicholas Sarkozy. 2023. Accessed March 25, 2023. https://www.britannica.com/summary/Nicolas-Sarkozy.
7. *BBC News*. French profile-timeline: modern France. 2023. Accessed March 25, 2023. https://www.bbc.com/news/world-europe-17299605.
8. *Britannica*. Emmanuel Macron: president of France. 2023. Accessed January 2, 2023. https://www.britannica.com/biography/Emmanuel-Macron.
9. Goar M. Pensions, inflation, climate: Macron is heading for a 2023 full of uncertainties. *Le Monde*. December 31, 2022. Accessed January 2, 2023. https://www.lemonde.fr/en/politics/article/2022/12/31/pensions-inflation-climate-macron-is-heading-for-a-2023-full-of-uncertainties_6009830_5.html.
10. *The World Factbook*. Central Intelligence Agency. Accessed May 23, 2016. https://www.cia.gov/library/publications/resources/the-world-factbook/geos/fr.html.
11. Vivid Maps. Maps of every country's Exclusive Economic Zone. Accessed December 18, 2022. https://vividmaps.com/exclusive-economic-zones-maps/.
12. Insee. Total population, on 1st January: Metropolitan France 000067670. 2022. Accessed December 18, 2022. https://www.insee.fr/en/statistiques/serie/000067670.
13. Insee. Total population, on 1st January: France (including Mayotte since 2014) 001641586. 2022. Accessed December 18, 2022. https://www.insee.fr/en/statistiques/serie/001641586.
14. Worldometer. Countries in the EU by population. 2024. Accessed August 9, 2024. https://www.worldometers.info/population/countries-in-the-eu-by-population/.
15. Worldometer. Europe population (live). 2023. Accessed March 17, 2023. https://www.worldometers.info/world-population/europe-population/.
16. Worldometer. France population (live). 2023. Accessed March 17, 2023. https://www.worldometers.info/world-population/france-population/.
17. Expatica. The French government and political system. 2023. Accessed March 25, 2023. https://www.expatica.com/fr/living/gov-law-admin/french-government-107814/.
18. Trading Economics. France GDP: Forecast. 2022. Accessed December 25, 2022. https://tradingeconomics.com/france/gdp.
19. Insee. Statistics and studies: in Q3 2022, the unemployment rate was virtually stable at 7.3%. 2022. Accessed March 17, 2023. https://www.insee.fr/en/statistiques/6659047.
20. World Population Review. Exports by country. 2022. Accessed December 24, 2022. https://worldpopulationreview.com/country-rankings/exports-by-country.
21. FocusEconomics. France economic outlook. May 31, 2022. https://www.focus-economics.com/countries/france.
22. Heritage Foundation. France. Accessed March 26, 2023. https://www.heritage.org/index/pdf/2023/countries/2023_IndexofEconomicFreedom-France.pdf.
23. World Bank Group. GDP per capital (current US$) – France. Accessed January 31, 2025. https://data.worldbank.org indicator/NY.GDP.PCAP.CD?locations=FR.
24. Institut national de la statistique et des etudes economiques (INSEE). In Q3 2024, the unemployment rate was virtually stable at 7.4%. Published November 13, 2024. Accessed January 31, 2025. https://www.insee.fr/en/statistiques/8283457.
25. Statista. Demographics in France: statistics & facts. 2022. Accessed March 17, 2023. https://www.statista.com/topics/5677/demography-in-france/#topicOverview.
26. Statista. Distribution of the population in France as of January 1, 2023, by age group. 2023. Accessed January 14, 2023. https://www.statista.com/statistics/464032/distribution-population-age-group-france/.
27. Insee. Statistics and studies: demographic balance sheet 2021. 2022. Accessed January 4, 2023. https://www.insee.fr/en/statistiques/6040011?sommaire=6323335.
28. Macrotrends. France fertility rate 1950–2023. 2023. Accessed January 4, 2023. https://www.macrotrends.net/countries/FRA/france/fertility-rate.
29. Sawe BE. Ethnic groups and demographics of France. *WorldAtlas*. July 18, 2019. Accessed January 28, 2024. https://www.worldatlas.com/articles/what-is-the-ethnic-composition-of-france.html.
30. Statista. Total number of Catholic baptisms in France between 2008 and 2019. 2022. Accessed January 15, 2023. https://www.statista.com/statistics/996904/number-catholic-baptisms-france/.
31. Statista. What religion do you feel bound to? 2022. Accessed January 15, 2023. https://www.statista.com/statistics/996244/feeling-belong-religion-france/.
32. Macrotrends. France infant mortality rate 1950–2023. 2023. Accessed January 17, 2023. https://www.macrotrends.net/countries/FRA/france/infant-mortality-rate#:~:text=The%20current%20infant%20mortality%20rate,a%202.52%25%20decline%20from%202021.
33. Federal Reserve Economic Data. Infant mortality rate for the European Union. 2023. Accessed January 17, 2023. https://fred.stlouisfed.org/series/SPDYNIMRTINEUU.
34. Cipan V. How many healthy life years do Europeans live? Viborc. 2022. Accessed January 19, 2023. https://viborc.com/how-many-healthy-life-years-at-birth-europeans-live/#:~:text=Show%20me%20the%20numbers%3A%20The,will%20have%20in%20good%20health.
35. OECD, World Health Organization. State of health in the EU: France: country health profile 2021. 2021. Accessed February 1, 2023. France-CountryHealthProfile2021.pdf.
36. Finnegan G. France measles outbreak: babies hit hardest. 2018. Accessed March 25, 2023. https://www.vaccinestoday.eu/stories/france-measles-outbreak-babies-hit-hardest/.
37. Statista. Vaccination coverage against measles, mumps, and rubella (MMR) in France among infants born from 2016 to 2019. 2022. Accessed March 25, 2023. https://www.statista.com/statistics/1318294/measles-mumps-and-rubella-mmr-vaccine-coverage-in-infants-in-france/.
38. Comiti VP. Que sais-je? *Histoire du droit sanitaire en France*. Paris, France: Presses Universitaires de France; 1994.

39. Schabloski AK. *Health Care Systems Around the World*. 2008. Accessed April 30, 2010. http://www.itup.org/Reports/Fresh%20Thinking/Health_Care_Systems_Around_World.pdf.
40. Couffinhal A. The French health care system: a brief overview. October 2001. Accessed April 30, 2010. http://www.irdes.fr/EspaceAnglais/DocumentationCentre/Documents/FrenchHealthCareSystem.pdf.
41. Insee. Population couverte par la CMU (assurés et ayants droits) au 30/12/2007. Accessed March 25, 2010. http://www.insee.fr/fr/themes/tableau.asp?reg_id=20&ref_id=revopte1032.
42. Tikkanen R, Osborn R, Mossialos E, et al. International health care system profiles: France. Commonwealth Fund. 2020. Accessed March 4, 2023. https://www.commonwealthfund.org/international-health-policy-center/countries/france.
43. Centre des Liaisons Europeennes et Internationales de Securite Sociale (CLEISS). The French Social Security System: Social Security and unemployment contribution rates. Accessed January 31, 2025. https://www.cleiss.fr/docs/regimes/regime_france/an_a2.html.
44. OECDiLibrary. State of health in the EU: France: country health profile 2021. 2021. Accessed February 6, 2023. https://www.oecd-ilibrary.org/docserver/7d668926-en.pdf?expires=1675725235&id=id&accname=guest&checksum=19411715A483B4EB5D2BE869B9AB7C1C.
45. GIP SPSI. Health and social protection: international expertise: the French health and social protection system, renowned expertise. Accessed February 6, 2023. Accessed March 25, 2010. http://www.gipspsi.org/GIP/layout/set/print/content/download/4971/55291/version/2/file/GIPSI_plaquette_savoir_faire_GB.pdf.
46. InterNations. Health insurance and healthcare in France explained. Accessed March 25, 2023. https://www.internations.org/france-expats/guide/healthcare.
47. Henry J. Kaiser Family Foundation. International health systems: France. Accessed April 30, 2010. http://www.kaiseredu.org/topics_im_ihs.asp?imID=4&parentID=61.
48. MediGlobus. American Hospital in Paris. 2023. Accessed March 13, 2023. https://mediglobus.com/clinic/american-hospital-of-paris/.
49. American Hospital of Paris. The Joint Commission renews its accreditation of the American Hospital of Paris. October 3, 2022. Accessed January 31, 2025. https://www.american-hospital.org/en/news-and-events/joint-commission-renews-its-accreditation-american-hospital-paris.
50. Statista. Number of hospitals in France from 2000 to 2020. 2023. Accessed March 4, 2023. https://www.statista.com/statistics/557012/hospitals-in-france/.
51. Insee. Etablissements de santé en 2013. Accessed May 25, 2016. http://www.insee.fr/fr/themes/tableau.asp?reg_id=0&ref_id=NATTEF06116.
52. Statista. Number of publicly owned hospitals in France from 2004 to 2020. 2022. Accessed March 4, 2023. https://www.statista.com/statistics/552182/publicly-owned-hospitals-in-france/.
53. Downward C. The French hospital landscape. 2022. Accessed March 11, 2023. https://info.idrmedical.com/blog/french-healthcare-system-and-hospital-landscape.
54. Statista. Number of non-profit private medical care facilities providing hospitalization capacities in France in 2020, by type. 2023. Accessed March 11, 2023. https://www.statista.com/statistics/759584/non-profit-health-care-facilities-hospitalization-capacities-type-france/.
55. Statista. Number of for-profit private medical care facilities providing hospitalization capacities in France in 2020, by type. 2023. Accessed March 11, 2023. https://www.statista.com/statistics/759578/for-profit-health-care-facilities-hospitalization-capacities-type-france/.
56. Organisation for Economic Co-operation and Development. Health statistics 2022: hospital beds, density per 1 000 population. Frequently requested data. Accessed March 18, 2023. https://www.oecd.org/health/OECD-Health-Statistics-2022-Frequently-Requested-Data.xls.
57. Eurostat. Healthcare expenditure statistics. 2022. Accessed March 11, 2023. https://ec.europa.eu/eurostat/statistics-explained/index.php?title=Healthcare_expenditure_statistics.
58. Statista. Number of hospital beds in France from 2010 to 2020. 2023. Accessed March 11, 2023. https://www.statista.com/statistics/557259/hospital-beds-in-france/.
59. Fargues L. La vérité sur la fermeture de lits d'hôpitaux. *Challenges*. February 8, 2015. Accessed May 26, 2016. http://www.challenges.fr/economie/20150205.CHA2834/pourquoi-la-france-n-arrive-pas-a-reduire-le-nombre-de-lits-d-hopitaux.html.
60. Rodwin VG. The healthcare system under French national health insurance: lessons for health reform in the United States. *Am J Public Health*. 2003;93(1):31-37. Accessed May 25, 2016. http://www.ncbi.nlm.nih.gov/pmc/articles/PMC1447687/.
61. Barber SL, Lorenzoni L, Ong P. Price setting and price regulation in health care: lessons for advancing universal health coverage. World Health Organization. 2019. Accessed March 25, 2023. https://apps.who.int/iris/bitstream/handle/10665/325547/9789241515924-eng.pdf.
62. Gawlik A. Finding a doctor in France. 2023. Accessed March 11, 2023. https://www.expatica.com/fr/healthcare/healthcare-services/doctors-in-france-101170/.
63. FrenchEntrée. The cost of going to the doctor in France. 2021. Accessed March 11, 2023. https://www.frenchentree.com/living-in-france/healthcare/the-cost-of-going-to-the-doctor/.
64. eurostat. Healthcare personnel statistics – physicians. Data extracted in December 2024. Accessed January 31, 2025. https://ec.europa.eu/eurostat/statistics-explained/index.php?title=Healthcare_personnel_statistics_-_physicians.
65. Hazelton Y. SOS medecins: French house calls 24/7. 2020. Accessed March 11, 2023. https://hipparis.com/2020/02/11/sos-medecins-french-house-calls-24-7/.
66. McVay D. France: health system personnel. 2022. Accessed March 11, 2023. https://healthsystemsfacts.org/france/france-health-system-personnel/.
67. Brunner S. The French healthcare system. *Medical News Today*. June 8, 2009. Accessed May 26, 2016. http://www.medicalnewstoday.com/articles/9994.php.
68. Med Tech Reimbursement Consulting. 2022 DRG tariffs published in France. 2022. Accessed March 11, 2023. https://mtrconsult.com/news/2022-drg-tariffs-published-france.
69. Lurquin B, Kellou N, Colin C, Letrilliart L. Comparison of rural and urban French GPs' activity: a cross-sectional study. *Rural Remote Health*. 2021;21(3):5865. doi: 10.22605/RRH5865. PMID: 34469693.
70. Statista. Medical technology: Europe. 2022. Accessed March 11, 2023. https://www.statista.com/outlook/hmo/medical-technology/europe.
71. MedTech Europe. The European medical technology in figures: market. 2022. Accessed March 11, 2023. https://www.medtecheurope.org/datahub/market/.

72. MedTech Europe. The European medical technology industry in figures: 2022. 2022. Accessed March 12, 2023. https://www.medtecheurope.org/wp-content/uploads/2022/09/the-european-medical-technology-industry-in-figures-2022.pdf.
73. Medtech Pulse. The European medtech industry directly employs more than 800,000 people. 2022. Accessed March 11, 2023. https://www.medtechpulse.com/article/infographic/medtech-europe-publishes-its-state-of-the-industry.
74. International Trade Administration. France: country commercial guide: medical devices. 2023. Accessed March 12, 2023. https://www.trade.gov/country-commercial-guides/france-medical-devices-med.
75. Statista. Exports of medical technology in Europe in 2021, by country (in million euros). 2022. Accessed March 12, 2023. https://www.statista.com/statistics/626804/medical-technology-exports-europe/.
76. Snitem. French medical technology industry the vanguard of innovation. FTPO North America product releases. April 28, 2006. Accessed May 4, 2010. http://www.infotechfrance.com/cgi-local/affichage_signet_secteur.pl?UNI_ID=13&RUB_ID=74&SS_ID=9163&SEC_ID=73.
77. Ligon BL. Biography: Louis Pasteur: a controversial figure in a debate on scientific ethics. *Semin Pediatr Infect Dis.* 2002;13(2):134-141. Accessed March 12, 2023. doi: 10.1053/spid.2002.125138. PMID 12122952. https://www.sciencedirect.com/science/article/pii/S1045187002500595?via%3Dihub.
78. Institut Pasteur. The Institut Pasteur in the world. 2023. Accessed March 12, 2023. https://www.pasteur.fr/en.
79. Macrotrends. Sanofi revenue 2010–2022 SNY. 2023. Accessed March 13, 2023. https://www.macrotrends.net/stocks/charts/SNY/sanofi/revenue#.
80. Omnia Health. France: a nation at the service of cutting-edge medicine. 2023. Accessed March 12, 2023. https://insights.omnia-health.com/reports/france-nation-service-cutting-edge-medicine.
81. Invest in France Agency. French's new stem cell research projects make opportunities for U.S. companies. FTPO North America product releases. November 19, 2009. Accessed May 4, 2010. http://www.infotechfrance.com/cgi-local/affichage_signet_secteur.pl?UNI_ID=13&RUB_ID=74&SS_ID=12650&SEC_ID=73.
82. OECD. Health at a glance 2021: OECD indicators: highlights for France. 2021. Accessed March 25, 2023. https://www.oecd.org/france/health-at-a-glance-France-EN.pdf.
83. Papanicolas I, Woskie LR, Jha AK. Health care spending in the United States and other high-income countries. *JAMA.* 2018;319(10):1024-1039. Accessed March 25, 2023. doi: 10.1001/jama.2018.1150. Erratum in: *JAMA.* 2018;319(17):1824. PMID: 29536101.
84. Statista. Per capita health administrative costs in select high-income countries 2020. 2022. Accessed March 25, 2023. https://www.statista.com/statistics/1264127/per-capita-health-administrative-costs-by-country/.
85. Inrae. Public health insurance. 2022. Accessed March 25, 2023. https://guide-for-international-scientists.inrae.fr/working-at-inrae/healthcare/public-health-insurance/.
86. Insee. Population par sexe et groupes d'âges quinquennaux au 1er janvier 2016. Accessed May 25, 2016. http://www.insee.fr/fr/themes/tableau.asp?reg_id=0&ref_id=NATnon02150.
87. Dutton PV. A primer on French health care. Accessed March 12, 2023. https://jan.ucc.nau.edu/pvd/Primer.htm.
88. Economic Research Institute. Physician salary in Paris, France. 2023. Accessed March 12, 2023. https://www.erieri.com/salary/job/physician/france/paris.
89. Leap Scholar. Salary of US doctors in 2023—most important guide on annual salaries in America. 2023. Accessed March 12, 2023. https://leapscholar.com/blog/doctor-salary-in-us/.
90. Chevreul K, Brigham KB, Durand-Zaleski I, Hernández-Quevedo C. France: health system review 2015. *Health Systems in Transition.* 2015;17(3). Accessed March 25, 2023. https://eurohealthobservatory.who.int/publications/i/france-health-system-review-2015.
91. Université de Montpellier. Debate: the "great social security," myth or reality? Accessed March 12, 2023. https://www.umontpellier.fr/en/articles/debat-la-grande-secu-mythe-ou-realite.
92. Commonwealth Fund. Mirror, mirror 2021: reflecting poorly: health care in the U.S. compared to other high-income countries. 2021. Accessed March 12, 2023. https://www.commonwealthfund.org/publications/fund-reports/2021/aug/mirror-mirror-2021-reflecting-poorly.
93. Girvan G. France: #25 in the 2021 World Index of Healthcare Innovation. 2021. Accessed March 12, 2023. https://freopp.org/france-freopp-world-index-of-healthcare-innovation-9b72dd8e551d.
94. Gao F, Kihal W, Le Meur N, Deguen S. Assessment of the spatial accessibility to health professionals at French census block level. *Intl J Equity Health.* 2016;15:125. Accessed March 16, 2023. https://doi.org/10.1186/s12939-016-0411-z.
95. Maunder S. Getting health insurance in France. *Expatica.* Accessed March 25, 2023. https://www.expatica.com/fr/healthcare/healthcare-basics/guide-to-health-insurance-in-france-108848/.
96. Pacific Prime. Private health insurance in France. Accessed March 19, 2023. https://www.pacificprime.com/country/europe/france-health-insurance/.
97. OECD. Health statistics 2022: doctors consultations, number per capita. Frequently requested data. Accessed March 19, 2023. https://www.oecd.org/health/OECD-Health-Statistics-2022-Frequently-Requested-Data.xls.
98. Cases C. French health system reform: recent implementation and future challenges. *Eurohealth.* 2006;12(3):10-11. Accessed April 30, 2010. http://www.Euro.who.int/Document/Obs/Eurohealth12_3.pdf.
99. Bachelet M, Anguis M. Doctors by 2040: a younger population, more feminized and more often salaried. *Studies and Results*, 1011. 2017. Accessed March 25, 2023. https://drees-solidarites--sante-gouv-fr.translate.goog/publications/etudes-et-resultats/les-medecins-dici-2040-une-population-plus-jeune-plus-feminisee-et?_x_tr_sl=auto&_x_tr_tl=en&_x_tr_hl=en&_x_tr_pto=wapp https://drees.solidarites-sante.gouv.fr/sites/default/files/2020-08/er1011.pdf.
100. Centre d'Analyse Stratégique. *L'Europe dans la mondialisation. Recueil de données.* Accessed May 31, 2016. http://www.strategie.gouv.fr/IMG/pdf/EuropedanslaMondialisation-RecueildedonneesCAS221107-FINAL.pdf.
101. Institut Montaigne. 5 years of Macron: zooming in on French healthcare. 2022. Accessed March 16, 2023. https://www.institutmontaigne.org/en/blog/5-years-macron-zooming-french-healthcare.
102. Or Z, Gandré C. Sustainability and resilience in the French health system. 2021. Accessed March 25, 2023. https://www3.weforum.org/docs/WEF_PHSSR_France_Report.pdf.

CHAPTER 13

Germany

Gerald (Jerry) Ledlow and Michael H. Kennedy

Country Description

Table 13-1 Germany

Nationality	Noun: German(s) Adjective: German
Ethnic groups	German 87.2%, Turkish 1.8%, Polish 1%, Syrian 1%, Romanian 1%, other/stateless/unspecified 9% (2024 est.)
Religions	Roman Catholic 24.8%, Protestant 22.6%, Muslim 3.7%, other 5.1%, none 43.8% (2022 est.)
Language	German (official); Danish, Frisian, Sorbian, and Romani are official minority languages; Low German, Danish, North Frisian, Sater Frisian, Lower Sorbian, Upper Sorbian, and Romani are recognized as regional languages under the European Charter for Regional or Minority Languages
Literacy	Definition: Age 15 and over and can read and write. Total population: 99% Male: 99% Female: 99% (2014 est.) There is no recent update regarding literacy.
Government type	Federal parliamentary republic
Date of independence	No independence day. Unification of eastern and western Germany, 1990.
Gross domestic product (GDP) per capita	52,745 USD (2023)
Unemployment rate	6.1% (2024)
Natural hazards	Flooding
Environment: current issues	Emissions from coal-burning utilities and industries contribute to air pollution; acid rain, resulting from sulfur dioxide emissions, is damaging forests; pollution in the Baltic Sea from raw sewage and industrial effluents from rivers in eastern Germany; hazardous waste disposal; government established a mechanism for ending the use of nuclear power by 2022; government working to meet EU commitment to identify nature preservation areas in line with the EU's flora, fauna, and habitat directive

(continues)

Table 13-1 Germany *(continued)*

Population	84,316,622 (2022 est.)
Age structure	0–14 years: 12.89% (male 5,302,850/female 5,025,863) 15–24 years: 9.81% (male 4,012,412/female 3,854,471) 25–54 years: 38.58% (male 15,553,328/female 15,370,417) 55–64 years: 15.74% (male 6,297,886/female 6,316,024) 65 years and over: 22.99% (male 8,148,873/female 10,277,538) (2020 est.)
Median age	Total: 47.8 years Male: 46.5 years Female: 49.1 years (2020 est.)
Population growth rate	–0.11% (2022 est.)
Birth rate	9.08 births/1,000 population (2022 est.)
Death rate	11.98 deaths/1,000 population (2022 est.)
Disease burden	Communicable disease deaths: 22/100,000 population Noncommunicable disease deaths: 365/100,000 population Injury deaths: 23/100,000 population (2016 est.)
Net migration rate	1.78 migrant(s)/1,000 population (2022 est.)
Gender ratio	At birth: 1.05 male/female 0–14 years: 1.04 male/female 15–24 years: 1.03 male/female 25–54 years: 1.05 male/female 55–64 years: 1 male/female 65 years and over: 0.7 male/female Total population: 0.98 male/female (2022 est.)
Infant mortality rate	Total: 3.19 deaths/1,000 live births Male: 3.56 deaths/1,000 live births Female: 2.8 deaths/1,000 live births (2022 est.)
Life expectancy at birth	Total population: 81.51 years Male: 79.15 years Female: 84 years (2022 est.)
Total fertility rate	1.57 children born/woman (2022 est.)
HIV/AIDS adult prevalence rate	0.10% (2021)
Number of people living with HIV/AIDS	96,700 (2023)
HIV/AIDS deaths	less than 500 (2021)

USD = U.S. dollars

Note: The German Empire unified on January 18, 1871. In 1945, after World War II, Germany was divided into four zones of occupation (the United Kingdom, the United States, the USSR, and later, France). The Federal Republic of Germany (West Germany) was proclaimed May 23, 1949, and included the former British, American, and French zones. The German Democratic Republic (East Germany) was proclaimed on October 7, 1949; it included the former USSR zone. Unification of West Germany and East Germany took place on October 3, 1990. All four powers formally relinquished rights on March 15, 1991.

Note: This is the International Labor Organization's estimated rate for international comparisons. Germany's Federal Employment Office estimated a seasonally adjusted rate of 10.1% for 2012.

Data from Akmatov MK, Hu E, Rüsenberg R, et al. Areas with high HIV prevalence: a spatial analysis of nationwide claims data in Germany. *HIV Med.* 2024 Apr;25(4):498-503. Accessed January 31, 2025. https://pubmed.ncbi.nlm.nih.gov/38072823/; Central Intelligence Agency. The World Fact Book, 2023: Germany. Accessed February 7, 2023, with estimates prior to 2017. Accessed April 19, 2016. https://www.cia.gov/the-world-factbook/countries/germany/; Robert Koch Institut. New key data and trends in HIV in Germany, 2022 and 2023. November 7, 2024. Accessed January 31, 2025. https://www.rki.de/EN/News/Newsroom/News/Archive/2024-07-11_HIV.html; Taylor E. Culture & diversity travel guide to Germany. BeGlobalii. August 12, 2024. Accessed January 31, 2025. https://beglobalii.com/articles/diversity-travel-guide-germany; Trading Economics. Germany unemployment rate. Accessed January 31, 2025. https://tradingeconomics.com/germany/unemployment-rate; World Bank Group. GDP per capital (current US$) – Germany. Accessed January 31, 2025. https://data.worldbank.org/indicator/NY.GDP.PCAP.CD?locations=DE; World Health Organization. Global Health Observatory Data Repository (European Union). Number of deaths due to HIV/AIDS. Estimates by country. Last updated July 11, 2023. Accessed January 31, 2025. https://apps.who.int/gho/data/view.main-eu.22600?lang=en.

History

The origin of what is known today as the Federal Republic of Germany lies not in the ancient Germanic forests but in the Holy Roman Empire, which at one point covered the entire midsection of the European continent. By the year 1400, several areas of this empire—including (although nominally) North Italy, Savoy, Burgundy, and the Swiss Confederations, along with Lorraine and Brabant—were considered *Teutsche Lande* (German Country).[1]

As a result of the Napoleonic war, the German Empire was replaced by the Confederation of the Rhine. Prussia and Austria remained outside of the Confederation. At the Vienna Congress in 1815, the German Confederation, a loose conglomerate of states in Germany that included Prussia and Austria, was founded. After the Prussian–Austrian War in 1867, the German Confederation was re-formed into the North German Confederation, without Austria and Bavaria.[1]

In 1862, Otto von Bismarck became prime minister (*ministerpräsident*) of Prussia. He ardently pursued German unity, not through "speeches and majority decisions" (*reden und majoritätsbeschlüsse*) but through "blood and iron" (*blut und eisen*).[2] In other words, Bismarck favored war over diplomacy. The foundation for the second German Empire was laid on January 18, 1871, when Wilhelm I was crowned emperor of the new constitutional monarchy, in the Room of Mirrors (Spiegelsaal) in the Palace of Versailles in Paris.[2] Only 5 years later, in 1876, the German Empire was created from above, with the merger of the German states, Austria not included. Under the chancellorship of Otto von Bismarck, Germany transitioned into a socially advanced state, with the stepwise introduction of a federal system of social insurance. Although the German political leadership loathed social democracy and sought to weaken social democratic movements by passing antisocialist laws, even Bismarck himself agreed that the social reforms he implemented—although he did so primarily to win workers for his political ideals—would not have been possible without social democracy.[2] Despite his fervent efforts to maintain a conservative empire, Bismarck was not able to find common ground with Wilhelm II, and he eventually resigned. Wilhelm followed a much more aggressive stance on foreign policy, and in the following decades, Germany played a central role in setting the stage for World Wars I and II.

The immediate trigger for World War I was the assassination of Archduke Francis Ferdinand of Austria-Hungary by a Serbian nationalist in 1914. Also known as the Great War, it was fought by two rival sets of powers—Germany and Austria-Hungary on one side, and Russia, France, Serbia, and Great Britain on the other—and ended in late 1918 as one of the deadliest conflicts in human history. What emerged in the aftermath became known as the Weimar Republic (Weimarer Republik), a "sort-of" democracy with a new constitution that had to contend with hyperinflation, political and paramilitaristic extremism, and a very contentious relationship with the victors of World War I. The continued tensions, in large part, allowed the rise of national socialism and Adolf Hitler; both held out the promise of a better social and political future.

Hitler and his Nazi party began to systematically eliminate all political opposition and to consolidate power, with the coordinated and methodical extermination of the Jewish race, via extermination camps or concentration camps (*Konzentrationslager*) as a central feature. In 1939, Hitler's army invaded Poland and thereby set off World War II, believed by many to be the single-most deadly conflict in human history. For example, the Battle of Stalingrad, fought between August 23, 1942, and February 2, 1943, resulted in 1.25 million casualties, although some estimates are as high as 1.8 million.[3] After the end of World War II in May 1945, Germany experienced a slow but steady rebuilding of its war-torn economy (more is discussed about this period in the chapter section on the history of the healthcare system). East and West Germany, two separate blocs since the end of World War II, were officially reunified in 1990, and Germany has since become a leader in the formation and advancement of the European Union.

Size and Geography

Today, the Federal Republic of Germany (*Bundesrepublik Deutschland*) is located in Central Europe and is bordered by the Netherlands, Belgium, Luxembourg, and France to the west; Switzerland and Austria to the south; the Czech Republic and Poland to the east; and Denmark to the north. The territory of Germany covers about 357,093 square kilometers (about 137,846 square miles),[4] making it slightly smaller than the state of Montana. The longest distance from north to south is 876 kilometers; from west to east, it is 640 kilometers. With a population of 84.316 million inhabitants at the end of 2022, it is the largest country by population in the European Union and the second largest in Europe after Russia.[4] The number actually reflects the highest population growth since 1992 and is the result of a high net immigration. At an average of 611.67 inhabitants per square mile, the population density in Germany is about 7 times higher than in the United States, which has an average of 90 inhabitants per square mile. However, only two German cities, Hamburg and the national capital of Berlin, had more than 1 million inhabitants in 2015, with 1.8 million and 3.5 million, respectively.[4]

Much like in the United States, Germany's population is not evenly distributed. More than three-quarters of inhabitants (76%) live in cities: 13% in small cities/towns, 28% in large cities, and 35% in medium-sized cities.[4] The largest proportion of Germany's total land area, approximately 53%, is used for agriculture; another 30% consists of forests. A much smaller land area, about 12%, is dedicated to settlements, including roads and railroads.[5]

Government and Political System

As its name implies, Germany is a federal republic that is composed of 16 federal states (*Bundesländer*) (see **Table 13-1** and **Figure 13-1**). The country's political system seeks to implement the republican, democratic, and socialist principles embodied in the federal constitution, known as the Basic Law (*Grundgesetz*). The Basic Law establishes Germany as a parliamentary democracy with separation of powers and three branches: executive, legislative, and judicial. Amendments to the Basic Law require a two-thirds majority in both houses of parliament. The constitutionally defined bodies, which have primarily legislative functions, are the lower and upper houses of parliament—namely, the Federal Assembly (Bundestag, lower house) and the Federal Council (Bundesrat, upper house). Simply put, the Federal Assembly represents the German people, while the Federal Council represents the 16 federal states.[6,7]

Members of both the Bundestag and the Bundesrat meet in the national capital of Germany, Berlin. The head of state is the federal president (*Bundespräsident*), who has mostly ceremonial duties. The second highest official in the German order of precedence is the president of the Bundestag, and the third-highest official is the federal chancellor (*Bundeskanzler*), who is the head of the government and handles day-to-day politics.[6] Each of the 16 federal states has a constitution that must also be consistent with the republican, democratic, and socialist principles embodied in the federal constitution. Each state is represented in the Bundesrat and, through this medium, participates in federal lawmaking.[8] In Germany, the highest judicial body is the supreme constitutional court, the Federal Constitutional Court (*Bundesverfassungsgericht*). Its sole purpose is to ensure that the Basic Law is respected and obeyed. Decisions of the Federal Constitutional Court are final, and all other legal and governmental bodies are required to follow its rulings.[9] In addition to ordinary law, Germany has four specialized jurisdictions: the Federal Administrative Court (*Bundesverwaltungsgericht*), the Federal Labor Court (*Bundesarbeitsgericht*), the Federal Social Court (*Bundessozialgericht*), and the Federal Tax Court (*Bundesfinanzhof*). A fifth specialized court is the Federal Patent Court (*Bundespatentgericht*).[10] Like the ordinary courts, these specialized courts are organized hierarchically, with the state court systems under a federal appeals court.

Germany in the European Union

In recent history, the most important characteristics of the German foreign policy have been its Western political orientation as well as its integration in Europe. In the period between 1945 and 1959, the European Union was formed by the six founding countries: Belgium, France, Germany, Italy, Luxembourg and the Netherlands. Its purpose was to unite European countries economically and politically in order to secure lasting peace. Today, the European Union has 28 member states.[11] Germany joined the North Atlantic Treaty Organization (NATO) in 1955, thereby laying the foundation for its Western political affiliation, and it signed the Treaty of Rome in 1957, which created the European Economic Communities. In addition to its membership in NATO, Germany is also a member of the United Nations, the Organization for Economic Cooperation and Development (OECD), the Organization for Security and Cooperation in Europe, and the Group of Seven, a governmental political forum that includes the United States, Canada, France, Germany, Great Britain, Italy, and Japan (although it has been suspended since 2014).

During the second half of the 20th century, Germany has become a leader in the European Union in its attempts to create a common, effective system of European foreign and security policy. Since then, two major events have prompted it to take a much more assertive role on the world stage. First, as a result of the September 11, 2001, attacks and the subsequent War on Terror, Germany, under the leadership of Angela Merkel (Germany's

Figure 13-1 Map of Germany

Bundeskanzler from 2005 to 2021) was one of the United States' strongest allies in the effort to combat terrorist and radical movements, although this alliance was not without discord. Second, with the emergence of the European refugee crisis in 2015, during which more than a million migrants and refugees crossed into Europe in that first year alone, a bitter controversy arose in the European Union about how best to cope with the influx of millions of people from the war-torn Middle East seeking asylum and holding hope for a better life elsewhere. In Germany, which received the highest number of new asylum applications in 2015 (almost 500,000), the crisis began to polarize society. While thousands of Germans have volunteered to help refugees, many have voiced their frustration over what they perceive to be an indifferent political leadership that does nothing to address their concerns about a slowly changing Germany.

Macroeconomics

Major Industries

Since Germany is comparatively poor in raw materials, the country's economy focuses on industrial manufacturing and on the service sector. Although only 2% to 3% of the population is employed in agriculture, approximately half of the total land area is used for agrarian purposes. With an estimated gross domestic product (GDP) of $3,355.77 trillion USD in 2015 and $4.424 trillion USD in 2021, the German economy represents over 5.41% of the world economy.[4] The German economy is heavily export-oriented; therefore, the country has been called the export champion of the world. Germany is the third largest exporter in the world, with $1.31 trillion USD in goods and services exported in 2015[12] and over $2 trillion USD in 2021 according to the CIA's *World Factbook*. Its top 10 exports are vehicles, machineries, chemical goods, electronic products, electrical equipment, pharmaceuticals, transport equipment, basic metals, food products, and rubber and plastics.[13]

Infrastructure, Transportation, Road Development, Airports, and Ports

The first paved roads in Germany were constructed during Roman times. The first large highways were built in the 18th century. With the invention of the automobile, the importance of road construction increased dramatically. The AVUS roadway in Berlin was the first motorway in the world when it was completed in 1921. During the economic recovery of the 1950s, roads replaced railways as the most important means of transportation. Today, Germany has one of the most dense road grids in the world, with about 650,000 kilometers of roads.[14] In 2013, the federal highway grid (autobahn) had almost 13,000 kilometers of highways, making it one of the longest systems in the world. At the same time, the grid also has almost 40,000 kilometers of federal roads (*Bundesstraßen*), 90,000 kilometers of state roads (*Landesstraßen*), 92,000 kilometers of country roads (*Kreisstraßen*), and more then 400,00 kilometers of local roads (*Ortsstraßen*).[14] The German railway system had approximately 43,468 kilometers of tracks in 2016,[13] down from 40,981 in 1990.[15] The network accommodates 27,196 passenger trains and 4,674 freight trains each day.[16]

Because of the extensive network of roads and railways, along with relatively short distances to be traveled, air travel is less popular in Germany. In fact, Germans like to walk: One in four trips is on foot. Nevertheless, 187 million Germans traveled by plane in 2014, with the majority of the trips (87.7%) being to destinations outside of Germany. The most important of the more than 100 civilian German airports is Frankfurt/Main, which is the hub for Lufthansa, the major German airline. Germany also has about 30 military airports.[14,17]

With its focus on foreign trade, Germany is also heavily dependent on maritime trade. In 2022, $1.6 trillion USD of exports were shipped overseas.[18] Although a number of modern seaports exists in Germany, a large portion of German trade is shipped overseas through ports in neighboring countries, especially the Netherlands. By far the most important German seaport is Hamburg. The most important Baltic seaport is Lübeck. In contrast, although Germany has a highly developed network of almost 7,000 kilometers of inland waterways,[17] inland water transportation has struggled since 2011 due to frequent low water levels that year. The most important inland waterway is the Rhine River (*Rhein*), which connects Germany with the major seaports of Antwerp, Rotterdam, and Amsterdam in the Netherlands, though the Rhine was closed for some time due to a major shipwreck.[19]

Demographics

Birth Rates

Like most industrialized countries in the 21st century, the Federal Republic of Germany has been experiencing low birth rates and an aging population. Although birth rates in the formerly divided West Germany and East Germany were similar up until the 1960s, they developed quite differently after the mid-1970s. In the former West Germany (Federal Republic of Germany), the birth rate fell to its lowest mark by the mid-1980s, when fewer than 1.30 children were born to each woman. In contrast, in the former East Germany (German Democratic Republic), spurred by government policy, the birth rate rose to 1.94 children per woman in the 1980s and then has declined somewhat since then. After the reunification in 1990, the decline first accelerated dramatically, when the overall birth rate fell from 1.52 children to 0.77 children per woman.[13] Since then, it has risen again slightly; in 2016, the total fertility rate in Germany was estimated to be 1.44 children per woman,[13] up slightly from 1.42 children per woman in 2013, and it increased to 1.57 in 2022.[20]

Nevertheless, Germany's birth rate continues to be the lowest in the world, with 8.2 babies born each year per 1,000 people, even lower than Japan's birth rate. By 2060, Germany's population could drop from about 84 million today to a possible low of 68 million. Such a precipitous change in the population may lead to a decline in the proportion of working-age Germans from 61% to 54% of the total population, resulting in fewer workers paying into Germany's social security system, which is expected to provide for the growing number of older Germans.[21] In fact, the old-age dependency ratio, the percentage of people ages 65 and older per 100 people in the labor force (i.e., people ages 15 to 64), which is assumed to be reflective of the economic burden due to rising health and pension expenditures, is currently hovering around 35%. It is expected to rise to over 50% by 2030—the highest ratio in Europe apart from the small Baltic state of Latvia.[22]

Life Expectancy and Age Distribution

Concurrent with the declining birth rate, life expectancy has been increasing, and consequently, the age distribution in Germany has been shifting upward. In 2050, male life expectancy at birth is projected to reach 83.5 years, while female life expectancy is projected to reach 88.0 years, an increase of 7.6 and 6.5 years, respectively, from 2003–2004.[4] In fact, by 2010, life expectancy at birth in Germany had reached 78.1 years for men and 83.1 years for women. However, although it has remained below the European average, the gender-based difference has been cut in half since 1990.[23] Today, Germany has more people aged 65 or older than people aged 15 years and younger. As Germany's 2022 population pyramid in **Figure 13-2** shows, more than one-third of the population is aged 55 years and older, and more than one-fifth is 65 years and older.[13]

Like most industrialized nations, Germany's population is almost evenly split between male and female residents, at 49.3% and 50.7%, respectively. In 2023, there were 41.3 million households. Of the 8.0 million families, 24.7% were headed by a single parent.[24]

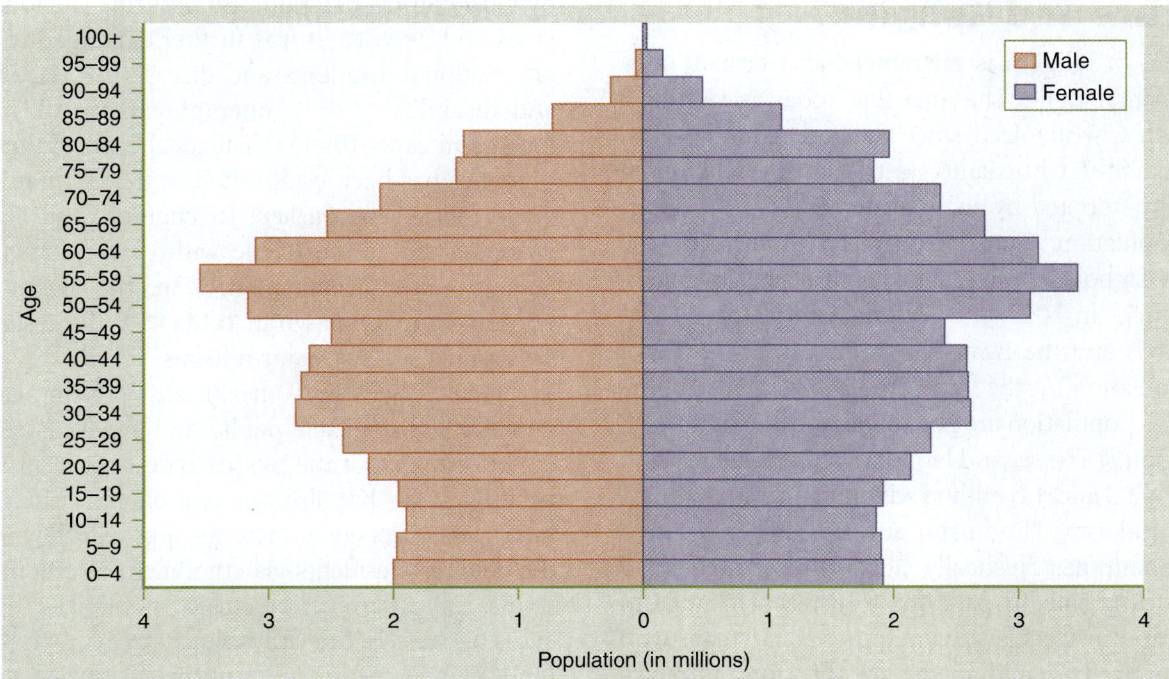

Figure 13-2 Germany Age Distribution, 2022

Reproduced from Central Intelligence Agency. The World Factbook, 2023: Germany. https://www.cia.gov/the-world-factbook/countries/germany/#people-and-society.

Educational System

In Germany, the 16 federal states are responsible for the organization of the educational system. Superordinate control, up to a certain degree, is provided via the nationwide Conferences of Ministers of Education (*Kultusministerkonferenzen*).[25] Pupils are required to attend school for 9 years to obtain a general education. Subsequently, they may choose to start vocational training or to continue their schooling to prepare them for higher education. Most federal states have a three-pronged school system beyond primary education: *Hauptschule* (lowest-level secondary school; up to 9th or 10th grade), *Realschule* (lower-level secondary school), and *Gymnasium* (equivalent to the American high school). Only a high school diploma from a *Gymnasium* affords pupils an opportunity to continue their studies at a traditional university. The general qualification required for university entrance is 12 or 13 years of schooling, depending on the state. Students graduating from *Hauptschule* usually continue on with vocational training. This form of training is typically a combination of practical skills training or work at a business or factory with theoretical instruction at a vocational school (*Berufsschule*). It usually lasts for 2 to 3 years. Institutions of higher education are divided into universities (103) and universities of applied sciences (176).[13] The latter are practice-oriented professional schools.

Culture and Religion

Freedom of religion is guaranteed in Germany as a fundamental right. The area that today is Germany has been Christianized since the early Middle Ages. Consequently, Christianity is the largest religion in Germany, adopted by an estimated 51% of the country's population. The two largest churches are the Roman Catholic Church and the Protestant Evangelical Church. In 2022, the Catholic Church accounted for 24.8% and the Evangelical Church for 22.6% of the population. At the same time, close to 50% of the country's population are not affiliated with any church or religion.[26] The second largest religion is Islam, with between 2.3 and 4.6 million adherents; smaller groups follow Judaism, Hinduism, and Buddhism. Church membership has drastically fallen in recent years and continues to fall. In part due to a recent change in the compulsory tax law that requires all Germans who were baptized as children and are, therefore, automatically members of the church and obliged to pay the tax, some 200,000 German Protestants renounced their church membership, while 178,000 Catholics renounced their membership in 2013.[27]

Mortality and Morbidity

In 2023, a little over one million people died in Germany. During the year, the number of deaths decreased from the year before.[28] The increase in life expectancy has coincided with an increase in the average age of death, up by nearly 2.0 years to 78.1 years in the last decade.[29] The five most common causes of death in Germany in 2023 were cardiovascular diseases (33.9%), followed by cancer (22.4%), illnesses of the respiratory system (7.1%), mental and behavioral issues (6.8%), and illnesses of the digestive system (4.4%).[30] The number of deaths for these five causes have steadily been increasing for adults in Germany.[29]

Brief History of the Healthcare System

The story of the German healthcare system is one of political compromise and of successful implementation of communitarian values. The system has remained relatively intact over time, even in the face of governmental change and recent reforms.[31] In fact, Germany is widely regarded as the first country to have introduced a national system of social and health insurance. As mentioned earlier, the first mandatory health insurance requirement was introduced by Otto von Bismarck in 1883; during the following years and decades, it was further expanded to cover occupational accidents and disease (1884), old age and disability (1889), unemployment (1927), and long-term care (1994).[23] The legal basis of these five branches has been established in the German Social Code (*Sozialgesetzbücher*) to guarantee all German citizens a minimum of life with dignity (*Menschenwürdiges Existenzminimum*).[32] In the past 50 to 60 years, and as shown in **Table 13-2**, the system has undergone several major reforms.[33,34]

Today, Germany's healthcare system can be described as a mixed public and private system. It is not only one of the world's oldest social insurance health systems but also one that offers near universal healthcare coverage. It includes approximately 95% of the country's residents via enrollment in one or more of the 120 government-regulated public health insurances (*Gesetzliche Krankenversicherung*, GKV, or sickness funds); or in one or more of the 40 private *substitutive* health insurances (*Private Krankenversicherung*) from a German or international insurance company;

Table 13-2 Selected Major Reforms in the German Healthcare System

Year	Reform
1977	▪ First law to address cost containment in health care (*Kostendämpfungsgesetz*) • Amended in 1982 (*Kostendämpfungs-Ergänzungsgesetz*)
Reunification	
1988	▪ Health Care Reform Act of 1989 (*Gesundheitsreformgesetz*)
1992	▪ Health Care Structure Act of 1993 (*Gesundheitsstrukturgesetz*)
1994	▪ Code of Social Law XI: Long-Term Care Insurance (social care) (*Sozialrecht—Sozial Pflegeversicherung*)
1996	▪ Health Insurance Contribution Rate Relief Act (*Beitragsentlastungsgesetz*)
1997	▪ First and Second Statutory Health Insurance (*Gesetzliche Krankenkenversicherung*, GKV) Restructuring Acts (*Neuordnungsgesetz*)
1998	▪ Act to Strengthen Solidarity in Statutory Health Insurance of 1999 (*Solidaritätsstärkungsgesetz*)
1999	▪ Statutory Health Insurance Reform Act of 2000 (*GKV Gesundheitsreform 2000*) • Act to Equalize Statutory Provisions in Statutory Health Insurance of 2000 (*Gesetz zur Rechtsangleichung in der Gestzlichen Krnakenversicherung*)
2000	▪ Infection Protection Act (*Infektionsschutzgesetz*)
2001	▪ Code of Social Law IX (rehabilitation and participation of disabled people) (*Rehabilitation und Teilhabe behinderter Menschen*) ▪ Reference Price Adjustment Act (*Festbetragsanpassungsgestz*) ▪ Act to Reform the Risk Structure Compensation Scheme in Statutory Health Insurance (*Gesetz zur Reform des Risikostrukturausgleichs in der GKV*) ▪ Act to Newly Regulate Choice of Sickness Funds (*Gesetz zur Neuregelung der Krankenkassenwahlrechte*) • Pharmaceutical Expenditure Limitation Act (*Arzneimittelbudget-Ablösungsgesetz*)
2002	▪ Pharmaceutical Expenditure Limitation Act (*Arzneimittelausgaben Begrenzungsgesetz*) ▪ Case Fees Act (*Fallpauschalengestz*) ▪ Long-Term Care Quality Assurance Act (*Pflegequalitätssicherungsgestz*)
2003	▪ Twelfth Social Codebook V Amendment Act (*12. Sozialgesetzbuch V Änderungsgesetz*) ▪ First Case Fees Amendment Act (*1. Fallpauschalenänderungsgesetz*) ▪ Statutory Health Insurance Modernization Act (*GKV Modernisierungsgesetz*)

(continues)

Table 13-2 Selected Major Reforms in the German Healthcare System *(continued)*

Year	Reform
2004	■ Act to Adjust the Financing of Dentures *(Gesetz zur Anpassung der Finanzierung von Zahnersatz)* ■ Second Case Fees Amendment Act *(2. Fallpauschalenänderungsgesetz)*
2006	■ Act to Improve Efficiency in Pharmaceutical Care *(Gesetz zur Verbesserung der Wirtschaftlichkeit in der Arzneimittelversorgung)*
2007	■ Act to Strengthen Competition in Statutory Health Insurance *(GKV Wettbewerbsstärkungsgesetz)*
2009	■ Hospital Financing Reform Act *(Krankenhausfinanzierungsreformgesetz)*
2010	■ Statutory Health Insurance Reform Act *(GKV Änderungsgesetz)* ■ GKV Reform Act *(GKV Finanzierungsgesetz)* ■ Pharmaceutical Market Reform Act *(Arzneimittelmarktneuordnungsgestz)*
2011	■ Statutory Health Insurance Care Structures Act *(GKV Versorgungsstrukturgesetz)*
2012	■ Long-Term Care Realignment Act *(Pflege-Neuausrichtungsgesetz)* ■ Act to Reimburse Psychiatric Care *(Psych-Entgeldgesetz)*
2013	■ Patient Rights Act *(Patientenrechtegestz)*
2015	■ Act to Strengthen SHI Health Care Provisions *(Gesetz zur Stärkung der Versorgung in der GKV)* ■ Act to Strengthen Health Promotion and Prevention *(Gesetz zur Stärkung der Gesundheitsförderung und Prävention)*
2016	■ Hospital Care Structure Reform Act *(Krankenhausstrukturgesetz)* ■ Transplant Registry Act, Third Strengthening Long-Term Care Act
2017–2019	■ Nursing Care Professions Act, Nursing Staff Empowerment Act, Increased Salaries for Nursing Professionals Act
2019	■ Digital Provision Act
2020	■ Intensive Care and Rehabilitation Strengthening Act, Patient Data Protection Act
2023	■ Act to Tackle Supply Shortages of Pharmaceuticals ■ Act to Accelerate the Digitization of the Healthcare System
2024	■ Cannabis Act ■ Hospital Care Improvement Act (adoption planned for late 2024)

Data from Blümel M, Spranger A, Achstetter K, et al. Germany: Health System Summary, 2024. Copenhagen: European Observatory on Health Systems and Policies, WHO Regional Office for Europe; 2024. Licence: CC BY-NC-SA 3.0 IGO. Accessed January 31, 2025. https://iris.who.int/bitstream/handle/10665/379914/9789289059954-eng.pdf?sequence=1; Busse R, Blümel M. Germany: health system review. *Health Syst Trans.* 2014;16(2):1-296; Bäcker G. Chronologie gesetzlicher Neuregelungen. Krankenversicherung und Gesundtheitswesen, 1998–2015. Institut Arbeit und Qualifikation der Universität Duisburg-Essen. Published April 2016. Accessed September 12, 2016. http://www.sozialpolitik-aktuell.de/tl_files/sozialpolitik-aktuell/_Politikfelder/Gesundheitswesen/Dokumente/Chronologie_GKVGesundheitssystem.pdf; Obermann K, Müller P, Müller HH, et al. Understanding the German health care system. Mannheim Institute of Public Health. Accessed September 15, 2016. http://miph.umm.uni-heidelberg.de/miph/cms/upload /pdf/GHCS_Kap._3.pdf.

or a combination of the two kinds. It is possible to combine both public and private health insurance. The system has been described as the most restriction-free and consumer-oriented healthcare system in Europe, one that permits patients to look for the best service provider of state health insurance or for the most suitable coverage from a private health insurer at a competitive rate.[31,34] Access to such high-quality comprehensive healthcare services is stipulated via the GKV, and the majority of Germans, about 71 to 72 million (85%), are insured that way. The GKV provides an organizational framework for the delivery of public health care that has shaped the roles of payers, sickness funds, and providers, physicians, and hospitals since major reforms in the system took place under Otto von Bismarck. At the time, the system was designed as statutory health insurance for low-income, blue-collar workers and certain government employees; over the next century, it was gradually expanded to cover virtually the entire population.[23]

The German healthcare system can be described as a mixed public and private system. As shown in **Table 13-3**, it has several key strengths and weaknesses: Although access to services is available to almost all German citizens and care is virtually free, the generous benefits and an ability to select providers freely have led to overconsumption and rising healthcare costs. Although the direct healthcare transaction cost is nearly free, the high tax rate and burden on the German population is significant; tax-based subsidies and support for the healthcare system contribute to the high individual tax rate, given that it is a socialist-leaning system. Membership is compulsory; contributions are based on income, and fees for the system have always been paid for almost entirely through the labor market. Perhaps the system's most significant strength is that its member contributions are based on a person's ability to pay, which essentially makes it a fund rather than an insurance (into which members pay risk-equivalent premiums).

The system is characterized by three fundamental principles: solidarity, subsidiarity, and corporatism.[34–36] Because of the principle of subsidiarity (i.e., decentralized governance, with implementation of policy by the smallest feasible political and administrative units in society), which has been written into the Basic Law, the German government neither finances nor pays for the provision of healthcare services, nor does it run the system per se. It has continued to subsidize costs for unemployed Germans and to partially reimburse costs for low-income workers; however, it primarily serves a legislative and regulatory role, much like the Health Care Financing Administration in the United States. Among other things, the government regulates drug prices, sets guidelines for private health insurances, and stipulates the rules under which employers are to provide coverage to their employees. In general, it does not involve itself in the daily management of the system, which results in greater flexibility, better understanding of local needs, and less bureaucracy.[23,36]

Historical Evolution of the German Healthcare System

The core component of the German healthcare system is the statutory sickness fund, whose precursor can be traced to the Middle Ages when guilds,

Table 13-3 Strengths and Weaknesses of the German Healthcare System

Strengths	Weaknesses
Ability to provide comprehensive, uniform, and universal coverage	Overconsumption of healthcare resources, due to generous benefit packages
Ability to cover almost every German citizen	Shifts escalating healthcare costs to employers and employees
Access to virtually cost-free outpatient, inpatient, and preventive care	Unresolved, ongoing tension between the forces of centralization and decentralization
Right to freely select a healthcare provider of choice or any physician within a given geographic area	Division of inpatient and outpatient care, leading to underutilization of outpatient care and significant inefficiencies
Simplified claims process	A dual financing system in which hospitals finance operational costs and state governments finance capital costs
An extremely patient-oriented healthcare system	Complex administrative system
Mandates that healthcare expenditures cannot rise faster than wages	Future demand for geriatric care will strain the sickness funds, as these funds are financed on a pay-as-you-go basis.

trade associations, industries, and mutual-aid societies established private relief funds to help pay for health care, funerals, and other related expenses. The earliest record of such a relief fund dates back probably to the year 1300, during the reign of King Wenceslas II of Bohemia. At the time, a few early miner society funds (*Knappschaftskassen*) maintained hospitals for members and townsfolk in mining communities, but most aimed to care for widows and orphans of members killed in accidents.[37] By the end of the 17th century, five distinct types of relief funds had emerged in different regions across Germany: relief funds for journeymen, relief funds for craftsmen modeled after the mutual support systems of the guilds, factory relief funds founded by socially oriented entrepreneurs, relief funds founded by local authorities for workers or trades people, and community relief funds for people who could not otherwise find insurance. Over the next 100 or so years, this patchwork of coverage was expanded, step by step, to include a variety of occupations, so that ultimately, no German would be without insurance. For example, farmers and forestry workers were enrolled in 1911, civil servants in 1914, unemployed people in 1918, housewives and daughters in 1919, all primary dependents in 1930, all retirees in 1941, people with physical disabilities in 1957, students in 1975, and artists in 1981.[23,38,39]

Throughout the 19th century, the emerging class of industrial workers continued the tradition of private and local assistance by establishing voluntary mutual-aid organizations specific to their various occupations. These organizations, along with similar mutual-aid schemes established by individual companies and local communities, augmented more formal assistance efforts given by municipalities and charitable institutions. By 1848, the German government had granted local municipalities the authority to recognize these voluntary funds and to make participation in them compulsory. For example, in Prussia—the largest of the German states—health insurance became compulsory for miners, and local communities could oblige employers and their employees to pay financial contributions toward health insurance.[37,38] In 1854, local authority was further expanded, allowing local communities to require that all uninsured local residents create insurance funds for mutual support. At the same time, a Prussian statute made membership compulsory and mandated employer contributions to be no less than half of that paid by workers. By 1876, over 850,000 citizens had insurance coverage through more than 5,000 sickness funds.[23,37–40] The private system developed around the turn of the 20th century, in tandem with the statutory system.[40]

By the end of the 19th century, it had become clear that the traditional systems of social support could no longer effectively address the social and health needs of a growing and industrialized citizenry. Even Pope Leo XIII raised the social question in a papal encyclical in 1891.[34] Just 15 years earlier, in 1876, the Ministry of Health (*Reichsgesundheitsamt*) was established, which laid the foundation for the modern system.[23] That same year, a formal law on relief funds (*Hilfskassengesetz*) was passed, stipulating that workers were to receive public financial support in case of illness or death. An imperial message (*Kaiserliche Botschaft*), delivered on November 17, 1881, by King Wilhelm I to parliament, recognized the importance of *material* protection (i.e., financial protection, *materielle Absicherung*) for all German citizens and announced pending laws regarding accidents, illness, disability, and retirement. It clearly announced the duty of the German government to ensure the welfare of the population, and it cleared the way for the creation of the modern German healthcare system. That is, with the passage of the Act on Health Insurance for Blue-Collar Workers (*Gesetz betreffend der Krankenversicherung der Arbeiter*) signed into law on June 15, 1883, the imperial message set the stage for the social health insurance system in place today.[23,34]

The subsequent evolution of that system can be best described according to five major periods in recent German history: German industrialization and the introduction of a mandatory health insurance requirement at the national level in 1883; social conflict and the strengthening of the medical profession during the time of the German Empire up to the Weimar Republic (1871–1919); Hitler's Third Reich and World War II (1933–1945); the immediate postwar period (1945–1949) with a divided Germany; and the period following German reunification in 1990.[23]

German Industrialization and the National Health Insurance Act of 1883

The German healthcare system, as it exists in its modern form today, is unanimously credited to Otto von Bismarck, the first German chancellor (*Bundeskanzler*), who began implementing his Bismarck System in the early 1880s with a series of social policies. Bismarck, known as the *iron chancellor* (*Eiserne Kanzler*), had recently overseen the unification of Germany, thereby establishing the German Empire under the rule of the Prussian King Wilhelm I. Shortly thereafter, Bismarck introduced legislation that resulted in the now famous Health Insurance Act of 1883, making Germany the first country in Europe to offer compulsory social health insurance. Bismarck's motive for doing so, at least primarily, was not to help those in need or to further social justice, but rather to deal a blow to the Social Democratic Party (*Sozialdemokratische Partei*, or SPD), which he considered a political threat. He also sought to maintain social order, and to win German workers over to the imperial regime.[38,39]

At the time, Germany's blue-collar workers were very poor with little public support, and Bismarck sought to *buy* their loyalty in exchange for economic security and material benefits. Indeed, his motivations were not purely altruistic; rather, they reflected his *sugarbread and whip* approach to politics (*Politik von Zuckerbrot und Peitsche*) in his attempt to separate the working class from the increasingly popular Social Democratic Party. In his quest to win over the working class and to weaken socialism, Bismarck continued his efforts to establish what has come to be known as the Bismarck System—one of the most advanced systems of social insurance in the world, in modified form still in existence in Germany today. For example, the law for work-related accidents (workers' compensation, *Unfallversicherung*) that was passed in 1884 included a mandate that employers must insure their employees against sickness; it also set up professional societies (*Berufsgenossenschaften*) and a disability pension (*Erwerbsunfähigkeits-rente*), the latter of which was to be paid for by employer contributions and federal subsidies.[23] Largely owing to his role in introducing social reform and despite his otherwise unwavering right-wing, nationalist views, Bismarck would later be called a socialist. Bismarck was not fazed; in his speech to Congress (*Reichstag*) during the 1881 debates, Bismarck remarked, "Call it socialism or whatever you like. It is the same to me." At the same time, he was quite frank about his political calculations. "Whoever has a pension for his old age," he said, "is far more content and far easier to handle than one who has no such prospect."[41]

In 1885, the Health Insurance Act covered only 26% of blue-collar workers (or 10% of the population); however, coverage through various sickness funds was subsequently expanded several more times to eventually include almost the entire German population. During the ensuing four decades, statutory health insurance (SHI) was gradually extended to cover 51% of the population in 1925. After World War II, in West Germany, the percentage rose to 88%, while in East Germany, almost everyone was covered from 1949 onward.[23] Between 2012 and 2015, approximately 70 million West Germans (85%) were covered through a sickness fund. In 2015, employed people (and other groups such as pensioners) earning less than €54,900 ($69,760 USD) per year were mandatorily covered by statutory insurance, while their non–wage-earning dependents were covered free of charge. Sickness funds continue to be funded by compulsory contributions levied as a percentage of gross wages. People whose gross wages exceed the annual threshold and those who are self-employed, civil servants, or working part-time and earning less than €450 per month can choose either to enroll in a sickness fund voluntarily—and 75% do—or to purchase substitutive public insurance. In 2015, 11% were covered through private schemes.[23,36] Since 2009, being uninsured has been illegal and all private health insurers have been required to offer a standard basic insurance policy (*Basistarif*) that can be purchased if specific requirements are met. As a result, virtually all Germans are covered by some form of healthcare insurance.

Social Conflict and the Strengthening of the Medical Profession

The success of the newly created healthcare system is evidenced by the longevity of the policies and programs first developed and implemented under Bismarck.[42] Even more remarkably, Bismarck was able to advance his political and social agendas with no input from individual physicians or medical organizations; in fact, the medical profession took scarcely any notice, and the new system was not even debated in professional journals until after it had already been adopted.[23,43] Bismarck was quite clever in introducing his system while at the same time avoiding the impression of making radical changes to the existing structure. In fact, the 1883 Health Insurance Act did not clearly define the relationship between sickness funds and physicians, nor did it address the qualification of healthcare professionals, leaving full authority to determine these matters to the sickness funds. By the 1890s, physicians had grown increasingly frustrated; they began to seek autonomy and to exert influence through several strikes and lobbying. In 1900, they formed a professional association, the Hartmann Union (*Hartmannbund*), and by 1910, 75% of all German physicians were members. Finally, in 1913, with intervention by the German government, sickness funds and physicians forged the Berlin Treaty (*Berliner Abkommen*), which significantly changed the relationship between physicians and sickness funds and established regular procedures for negotiating conflict; these procedures, in modified form, are still in practice today. For example, the treaty stipulated, for the first time, a physician-to-population ratio, thereby limiting the influence of the funds: At least one physician had to be available for every 1,350 insured.[34,43]

Hitler's Third Reich and World War II

The appointment of Adolf Hitler as chancellor on January 30, 1933, and the subsequent rise of the Third Reich marked the beginning of another, albeit not more progressive, phase in the German healthcare system. Soon after he was sworn in, Hitler began his stepwise process toward systematic and complete seizure of power and toward creating the absolute and totalitarian rule of his regime. At the time, Germany was beset by widespread unemployment, and the German people felt a general sense of insecurity and intimidation. At the same time, many saw Hitler as a new leader (führer) who could restore Germany to its former glory. For example, Hitler's autobiographical manifesto, *Mein Kampf*, published in 1925, quickly became a bestseller. Some municipalities even gave the book to newlywed couples after they exchanged vows, and by the end of World War II, approximately 13 million copies were in print.[44]

Hitler immediately set out to adopt a system of totalitarian control, to create a permanent state of emergency (*Ausnahmezustand*), and to implement *forcible coordination* (*Gleichschaltung*)—synchronization and tight, centralized management by means of an invasive police force—of all aspects of government, society, and commerce.[45,46] In 1934, the Hitler regime appointed a director for sickness funds and one for other insurance programs; both reported directly to the regime.[17] In fact, between 1933 and 1935, the funds, community health services, other nongovernmental organizations dealing with welfare and with health education, and health-related professional organizations came under centralized leadership in accordance with Hitler's leader principle (*Führerprinzip*). Just as the majority of Germans in general were, health professionals were swayed by Hitler's promises of a strong, stable, and unified Germany. In fact, after 1933, physicians joined the Nazi Party in greater numbers than any other profession. Between 1925 and 1944, the percentage of doctors in the party was almost three times as high as in the general population.[47,48]

One of Hitler's goals, and perhaps even his ultimate purpose, was to create a master race (*Herrenrasse*) of racially and ethnically pure Germans. One of the intended consequences was to expel German citizens of Jewish decent and other stigmatized minorities from membership in the sickness funds and to deny them access to healthcare services. Ultimately, Hitler sought to implement his *final solution* (*Endlösung*), which entailed the extermination of the Jewish people (and any other people deemed by the Nazi regime as impure or unwanted) in the concentration camps (*Konzentrationslager*) and extermination camps. Increasingly, but especially with the onset of World War II in 1939, public funds formerly intended for social care, welfare, and health education were diverted toward satisfying the political targets of racial hygiene, eugenics, and social control.[4] The notion of racial hygiene in particular became the basis for many health-related and other laws. One of the first Nazi laws, the Law for the Prevention of Progeny of Hereditary Disease (*Gesetz zur Verhütung erbkranken Nachwuchses*), passed on July 14, 1933, prohibited reproduction by people defined as genetically inferior. In 1935, an adjunct law allowed forcible abortions in such cases up to the sixth months of pregnancy. It also allowed the misuse of private health information to perform compulsory sterilizations, primarily on people with mental handicaps, because they were deemed likely to have defective children. A total of 300,000 to 400,000 people were sterilized, and approximately 5,000 (nearly all women) died as a result of these operations.[32,48]

Despite the strongly centralized, totalitarian rule under the Hitler regime, several improvements in social and health insurance coverage were made between 1933 and 1945, simply because they served the political agenda of the Nazi regime. In 1938, artisans came to be covered under compulsory social insurance, and in 1941, public health insurance coverage was extended to pensioners. In 1942, all wage earners, regardless of occupation, were covered by accident insurance, health care became unlimited, and maternity leave was extended to 12 fully paid weeks with job protection.[49] Swayed by Hitler's push for racial hygiene, Germany's medical community held the belief that curing patients was worthwhile; however, *healing* the nation was eminently more important. A majority of German physicians participated in the systematic exclusion of their Jewish colleagues from the practice of medicine; they also willingly adhered to and promoted the ideas of racial hygiene. To a large degree, the medical profession was not politicized but politics became medicalized.[50,51]

The Post-War Period and Two German States

At the end of World War II and after the surrender of Hitler's army on May 8, 1945, the four main Allied Forces (the United States, Great Britain, the Soviet Union, and France) took control of Germany, and the country was divided into two separate states. Correspondingly, virtually all sectors of German society, including health care, were divided into two separate systems, each with its own economic, administrative, political, and social structures. The American, British, and French controlled the western portion of the country that became the Western Federal Republic of Germany (*Bundesrepublik Deutschland*, or *West Deutschland*) and Russia controlled the eastern portion of the country that became the Eastern German Democratic Republic (*Deutsche Demokratische Republik*). In the years immediately following World War II, health care in Germany was characterized by ad hoc public health interventions aimed at controlling and/or preventing outbreaks of epidemics and at distributing meager and often inadequate resources for health care.[23]

While under Allied control, and then after the end of the Allied occupation on March 20, 1948, the healthcare systems in the two German states developed in a very different fashion, resulting in two different German health systems. East Germany gradually moved toward a national socialist, state-financed health system, with the option to purchase private health insurance for additional treatment. This system was one of strong, centralized state control; it established a single sickness fund, managed by the Free German Trade Union Federation (*Freier Deutscher Gewerkschaftsbund*), a federation of trade unions that was subordinate to the Socialist Unity Party of Germany (*Sozialistische Einheitspartei Deutschlands*).[52] Socialist state ideology ruled these institutions: Almost all hospitals were nationalized and independent physician practices were forced out of business. In West Germany, the pre–World War II system was reestablished. As before, it was supervised by the government but was not government run, and it further developed into a highly decentralized corporate system in the face of modest parliamentary control. Political authority extended to benefits, eligibility, compulsory membership, covered risks (physical, emotional, mental, curative, and preventive), income maintenance during temporary illness, employer–employee contributions to the GKV, and other central issues. Healthcare coverage was expanded considerably, codified by social law (*Sozialgesetzbuch*) and by the GKV. More than 1,000 autonomous statutory sickness funds arose, which led to the broadest coverage within the free market system.[53,54]

For West Deutschland, the new constitution, or Basic Law, was promulgated on May 23, 1949. In it, Germany was established as a democratic and social federal state (Article 20), in which *social rights* were defined by legislation. This legislation, with the exception of certain prescribed areas, came under the purview of state parliaments. When Germany was divided, West Germany consisted of 11 federal states (*Länder*); as is true today, each state had its own elected parliament (*Landtag*). Because health care is decentralized in Germany, its management is handled by three main bodies (see **Table 13-4**): the Federal Ministry of Health (*Bundesministerium für Gesundheit*, or BMG), established in 1961; the federal states; and the corporate bodies that comprise the sickness funds, the physicians associations, the hospital organizations, and patient representatives.[55] The BMG sets the legal framework of the system, with a primary focus on the drafting of bills, ordinances, and administrative regulations, including the principal benefits to be covered by the statutory health insurance system.[56] Within the legal framework set by the Ministry of Health, the Federal Joint Committee (*Gemeinsame Bundesausschuss*) functions as the central organ for self-administration; it has wide-ranging regulatory power to determine the services to be covered by sickness funds and to set quality measures for providers.[55,57]

Table 13-4 Number of Sickness Funds, by Type, 1993, 2014, and 2024

Type	1993	2014	2024
General regional sickness funds	269	11	10
Company-based sickness funds	744	107	71
Substitute sickness funds	15	6	6
Guild sickness funds	169	6	6
Sickness funds for agricultural workers	22	1	1
Sailors' sickness fund	1	—	—
Miners' sickness fund	1	1	1
Total	**1,221**	**132**	**95**

Data source Blümel M, Spranger A, Achstetter K, et al. Germany: Health System Summary, 2024. Copenhagen: European Observatory on Health Systems and Policies, WHO Regional Office for Europe; 2024. Licence: CC BY-NC-SA 3.0 IGO. Accessed January 31, 2025. https://iris.who.int/bitstream/handle/10665/379914/9789289059954-eng.pdf?sequence=1.

The federal states maintain the hospital infrastructure and supervise and monitor activities of public health personnel, goods, and diseases; undergraduate medical, dental, and pharmaceutical education; and regional physician and sickness fund organizations.[55] Today, all 16 states are also responsible for the implementation of federal health policy, but they have legislative power and considerable control in carrying out a wide range of tasks within their jurisdictions, as long as they do not violate federal mandate.[57]

The Fall of the Berlin Wall and a Reunified Germany

Twenty-eight years after construction began on the Berlin Wall on August 13, 1961, to formally demarcate the German Democratic Republic from the Federal Republic of Germany, German citizens from both states began scaling it and tearing it down on November 9, 1989. Eleven months later, on October 3, 1990, East Germany and West Germany were officially reunited. With the signing of the Treaty of Reunification (*Vereinigungsvertrag*), 17 million East German citizens became fully integrated into the system of the Federal Republic of Germany and thereby became the political, economic, and social responsibility of the West German government. Although the public was extremely critical of what was perceived to be a totalitarian regime created by the former East Germany's Socialist Unity Party (*Sozialistische Einheitspartei Deutschlands*), it regarded East Germany's social welfare, health care, and educational systems much more positively.[58] Therefore, early in the reunification process, East Germans argued that they had made considerable achievements in the field of health and social policy that deserved to be preserved; they were particularly proud of the exclusion of commercialization from health care as a historic achievement.[59] Yet, although some (minor) compromises were made in the way in which health care was to be financed and delivered, East Germany's national health insurance system was quickly transformed to adopt the pluralist system of West Germany. In the process, almost all ideas from the German Democratic Republic healthcare system (e.g., polyclinics and public health initiatives) fell out of favor; however, today, they are once again part of the debate on improving patient-centered care in the unified Germany.[34]

The extraordinary task of uniting and combining two formerly separate and distinct healthcare systems brought about unprecedented healthcare reforms in the late 20th century, which have continued into the 21st century. Over the course of the past 25 years since reunification, a large number of healthcare reforms have been introduced (see also Table 13-2). By the mid-1990s, healthcare benefits provided through the GKV were extensive and included, among other benefits, ambulatory care (care provided by office-based physicians), choice of office-based physicians, hospital care, full pay to mothers (from 6 weeks before to 8 weeks after childbirth), extensive home help, health checkups, sick leave to care for relatives, rehabilitation and physical therapy, medical appliances (such as artificial limbs), drugs, and stays of up to 1 month in health spas every two to five years. Particularly in the past two decades, reforms have included a focus on quality assurance, evidence-based medicine, and health technology assessment.[55] It is particularly noteworthy that the German healthcare system has embraced system-wide technologic advances, such the health insurance smart card that has a chip encoded with a beneficiary's insurance information and basic personal health data. This specific technology has been used since the 1990s.

By the turn of the 21st century, there was a general feeling that reform was needed. This reform movement was driven by increasing SHI contribution rates (from 13.5% of gross wages in 2001 to 14.3% in 2003) and perceived deficiencies in the quality of care.[23]

By 2004, there was considerable pressure to adopt a major reform, including integration of inpatient and ambulatory care, which traditionally had been completely separate services in Germany.[60] In 2009, employers and employees began to pay the sickness fund premiums as a uniform percentage of gross wages or of income across all sickness funds. Sickness funds then would immediately pass those premiums to a central national fund (*Gesundheitsfonds*). Additionally, every German has since been required to have health insurance coverage for the basic benefit package.[60]

Reform efforts have been ongoing. To aid in the process, the German federal minister of health (*Gesundheitsminister*), Herman Gröhe, issued an invitation to the ministers of health of six leading industrial nations—the United States, Great Britain, France, Italy, Japan, and Canada—to join Germany for a meeting on October 8–9, 2015. The leadership of this conference ultimately issued a declaration to address control of antimicrobial resistance and agreed to embrace responsibility for joint action toward ensuring global health.[61] On September 29, 2016, the Federal Ministry of Health passed amendments to the Second Long-Term Care Strengthening Act, which came into force on January 1, 2017. These amendments introduced a new vision for long-term care in Germany to support self-reliance of people in need of care.

To that end, regular benefits will be expanded by services for personal support and daily living assistance.[62]

At the time, reunification was not thought to cause significant problems. In fact, most Germans were initially very excited about the prospect of Germany being, once again, a unified nation. German citizens, in general, considered the West German welfare system to be one of the best and were eager to share it with their East German neighbors. However, in large part due to the seemingly never-ending reforms, attitudes about the social welfare system (and reunification itself) have since undergone a pronounced change. Because of the speed with which it occurred, the reunification process was culturally very disorienting for many East Germans, while it left many West Germans frustrated over what they perceived to be a lack of appreciation for the sacrifices they had made to help their "poor cousins in the land next door."[63] Not surprisingly, although 65% of East Germans rated the version social security system better than the version shortly after reunification, a short 5 years later, a whopping 92% favored their system, while only 3% preferred the Western system. Similarly, 65% of East Germans in 1990 thought that the healthcare system in West Germany was better than in the East; in 1995, 57% said the East German system was better.[64]

Solidarity and Subsidiarity: The Basis for the German Healthcare System

The modern German healthcare system has achieved a high degree of equity and justice, despite its fragmented federal organization: No single group is in a position to dictate the terms of service delivery, reimbursement, remuneration, quality of care, or any other important concerns. Access to health care is regarded as a right of all German citizens. That right reflects universality of coverage, comprehensive benefits, the principle of the healthy paying for the sick, and a redistributive element in the financing of health care. Healthcare provider reimbursement rates are negotiated with the federal government of Germany, health provider union organizations, and other stakeholder groups; this rate setting is done every few years. The structure of the German health insurance system is rooted in several assumptions about the nature of German society. First, it has been assumed that most Germans will have stable, long-standing connections to jobs, either through their own employment or through the employment of a spouse or parent. Second, it has been assumed that wage income would grow as quickly as the healthcare costs of the covered population. However, recent changes in German society have made these assumptions about the organizational structure of the German healthcare system much less valid.[65]

What does remain as two integral features of the system are the fundamental principles of solidarity and subsidiarity.[34,35,66] Both principles have been endorsed by the left, central, and right parties across the political spectrum and are secured in Germany's Basic Law of 1949. Solidarity refers to a shared commitment among members of society toward respect and mutual care; subsidiarity refers to their common understanding that social action should be transferred to the most appropriate level, with particular emphasis on the local and communal levels.[66] Both principles closely relate to the concept of generalized reciprocity, or the willingness to give to someone without expecting the person to return the benefit directly, but rather expecting that somehow, in some way, the benefit will be returned eventually. In the context of health care, it is the agreement among insured people to share health risks and to assess contributions commensurate with one's ability to pay,[67] while at the same time discharging the government from any functions that could be solved better, or at least equally as well, via private efforts and responsibility.[66] In Germany, the belief in generalized reciprocity ultimately provides the conceptual basis for the evolution of the modern health insurance system.[34] As of 2020, 12.8% of the country's GDP was devoted to health expenditures in Germany.[68]

The Current Healthcare System

Facilities

The current situation in the German healthcare system is marked by several recently implemented reform efforts. A central goal of such reforms by the German government has been to induce more competition in the healthcare marketplace, which in turn should lead to more efficiency. One result has been a steady decline, for years, in the number of general hospitals. In 2023, there were 1,874 hospitals with a total of 476,900 beds. It is important to note that hospitals and beds are declining every year.[69] Publicly owned hospitals reached an all-time low in 2023, with a total of 438 hospitals. Private hospitals accounted for 584 hospitals and not-for-profit hospitals were at 483.[70] It is important to note that the number of private for-profit hospitals has been growing in recent years and now account for around one-sixth of all hospital beds.[36] Although the total number of acute hospital beds has been reduced substantially in the last decade, Germany ranks highest.[71] The average length of stay in a German hospital in 2023 was 7.2 days on average. This statistic has been unchanged since 2018.[72] All hospitals are staffed principally by salaried doctors. They fall into four categories: basic service hospitals (usually up to 200 beds and two to three medical disciplines), regular service hospitals (up to 300 beds and four to five disciplines), central service hospitals (usually up to 500 beds and up to eight different disciplines), and maximum care hospitals (big institutions, usually more than 1,000 beds, mostly university hospitals with a comprehensive spectrum of medical specialties and services, responsible for research, training, and hospital treatment).[73]

One unique aspect of the German healthcare system is its well-developed rehabilitation sector. After patients have completed their stay in an acute care hospital, they often continue their treatment in a separate rehabilitation clinic to ensure, with the help of special procedures and facilities (e.g., physical therapy), the best possible outcome. This follow-up treatment must be booked separately, and the stay is determined by specialized post-acute care treatment plans depending on the patient's needs.[74]

The number of pharmacies has decreased since the early 2000s. In 2005, there were 20,248 pharmacies including their subsidiaries. During 2005, 326 new pharmacies opened; in 2023 there were only 62 new pharmacies opened in Germany.[75] For many years, German policymakers regulated public pharmacies in order to limit the increase in costs. However, they abandoned such restrictions in 2004 to encourage greater competition. Since then, it has been legal for individual pharmacists to own up to four pharmacies. In addition, mail-order pharmaceutical purchases became possible. The number of pharmacies has decreased. There were 17,571 in 2023 (including their subsidiaries).[75]

Workforce

The German healthcare system has significantly changed since the COVID-19 pandemic. There has been a steep decline in the number of healthcare personnel. **Figure 13-3** shows the proportion of physicians by specialty. Post-pandemic, the number of physicians in all sectors has declined, as has the number of nurses. There is a high demand for qualified medical staff today in the German medical sector.[76] In 2023, there were approximately 428,500 physicians employed in Germany. These physicians include those employed by the government sector as well as the private and non-profit sectors.[77] Foreign doctors are a staple in German medicine and the healthcare system. They made up 63,767 of the employed physicians in Germany in 2023.[78]

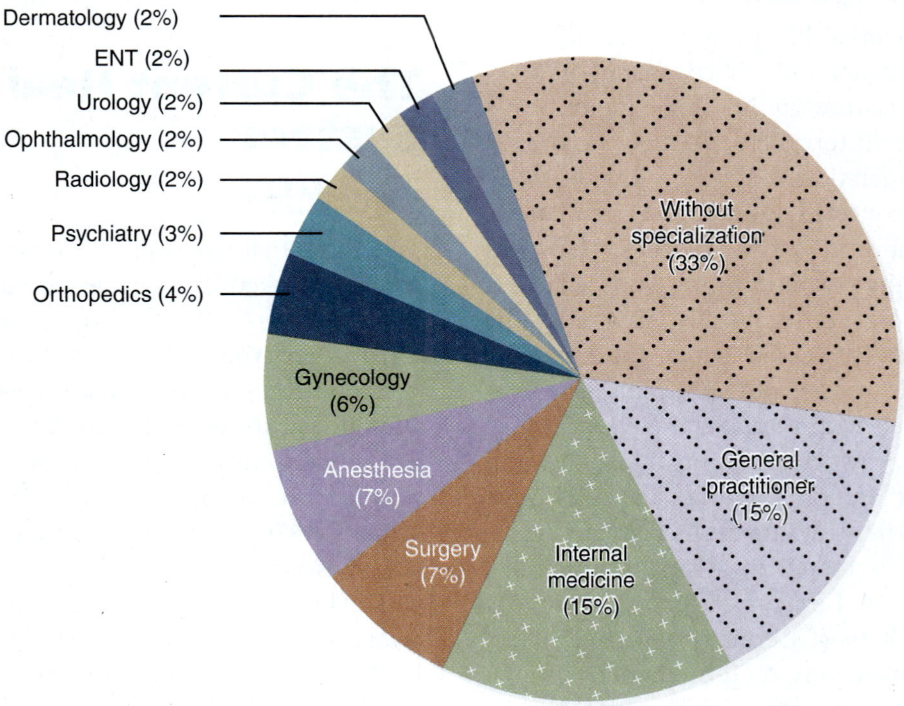

Figure 13-3 Proportions of Physicians, by Type

Reproduced from Obermann K, Müller P, Müller HH, Glazinski B. *The German Health Care System: Accessing the German Health Care Market*. 2nd ed. 2016. Used by permission of the publisher, medhochzwei, and the authors.

The number of nursing professionals greatly outnumber physicians in Germany. In 2021, there were 1 million nurses in Germany.[79] In contrast to nurses, who may work autonomously or in physician-led healthcare teams and assume responsibility for the planning, management, and execution of total patient care, nursing associate professionals carry out basic nursing and personal care tasks and generally work under the supervision of, and in support of, the healthcare team. In Germany, as well as in many other countries, ongoing concerns linger about the current (and projected to be lasting) nursing shortage, as do ongoing concerns about the challenges of caring effectively for a graying society (especially for the baby boom generation). Therefore, Germany, like many other countries, has undertaken efforts to increase the training of new nurses and to retain practicing nurses in the profession. As a result, there has been a large increase in the number of nurse graduates in recent years, related at least in part to a greater offering of registered nurse training programs in several German universities, in addition to the traditional vocational nursing school programs.[80]

Dentistry in Germany is ranked as one of the largest markets globally. In 2021 in Germany there were 71,297 practicing dentists. Germany has the largest amount of practicing dentists in the EU. These include stomatologists and maxillofacial surgeons.[81] In contrast, the number of physiotherapists was much higher in 2022, at 197,000.[82] Physiotherapists assess, plan, and implement rehabilitative programs that improve or restore human motor functions, maximize movement ability, relieve pain syndromes, and treat or prevent physical challenges associated with injuries, diseases, and other impairments.

Technology/Equipment

With the passage of the Statutory Health Insurance Reform Act of 2000, the newly created Federal Joint Committee was given the responsibility for assessing new health technologies. Such technologies include a wide range of healthcare products to diagnose, monitor, and treat diseases and medical conditions affecting humans. Revenue from these products has increased dramatically; in 2003, the German medical industry revenue was $19.0 billion USD. Within a decade, by 2013, the amount had more than doubled, to $42.4 billion USD. Germany is, with the United States and Japan, one of the largest manufacturers of medical technology worldwide. However, medical industry revenues in the United States continue to far exceed those elsewhere; in 2013, they totaled $216.2 billion USD, almost double the revenues of all European countries combined ($117.6 billion USD).[70] In Germany, as is true in other countries, the jump in medical industry revenues is directly related to the rapid proliferation of diagnostic technologies, such as computed tomography (CT) scanners and magnetic resonance imaging (MRI) units. For example, the number of MRI units increased from about 1 per million population in 1992 to 12.20 in 2000 and 18.30 in 2011. By 2021, there were 35.25 units per million residents in the country, although that number was still significantly below the number available in many other countries.[83] In the same year, there were 57.39 units per million residents in Japan, 37.99 units per million residents in the United States, 35.48 units per million residents in Korea, and 33.25 units per million residents in Italy.[83] The number of CT scanners in 2021 was much higher, with a total of 3,036, or 36.49 scanners per million residents.[84] But similar to the rate of MRI units, the rate of CT scanners in Germany was much lower than the rate of 115.7 scanners per million residents in Japan and 42.63 scanners per million residents in the United States.[85]

Evaluation of the Healthcare System

Cost

As is true in most of the Westernized countries, German citizens continue to pay relatively little out of pocket for their health care. With the German GDP reaching $3,355.77 billion USD in 2015, most SHI beneficiaries paid 0.9% of healthcare costs—the same as in previous years—and their out-of-pocket per capita spending was $649 USD. The remaining costs were assumed by social health insurance or by the government.[36] Yet, since the beginning of the new millennium, Germans have paid more than ever for their health care. In a deeply unpopular reform, those enrolled in the statutory insurance plan have been required to pay €10 (about $12–$13 USD) per quarter since January 2004 to see a general practitioner. Individuals covered by private health insurance as well as youths were exempted from these copayments. Beneficiaries now also must contribute toward the cost of, for example, prescription drugs, wound dressings, and bandages; they must assume 10% of the cost of prescriptions and of medical aids and supplies, with a €5 minimum and a €10 maximum (about $6–$13 USD). In addition, they must assume a share of the cost of inpatient preventive treatment and rehabilitation, outpatient rehabilitation, and inpatient hospital care (at €10 per day [about $12–$13 USD], for a maximum of 28 days annually). For dental prostheses, patients receive a lump-sum reimbursement, which on average covers 50% of actual costs.[52,86–88]

As mentioned earlier, healthcare coverage is universal for all legal residents of Germany. Employed citizens (and other groups such as pensioners) earning less than €54,900 ($69,760 USD) per year as of 2015 are mandatorily covered by SHI, and their nonearning dependents are covered free of charge. Individuals whose gross wages exceed the threshold and those who were already previously SHI-insured or are self-employed can remain in the publicly financed scheme on a voluntary basis. Through Chapter 3 of the Social Code Book V, the following types of benefits are currently legally included in the basic benefit package, usually in generic terms: preventive services, inpatient and outpatient hospital care, physician services, mental health care, dental care, prescription drugs, medical aids, rehabilitation, and sick leave compensation. SHI preventive services include regular dental checkups, child checkups, basic immunizations, checkups for chronic diseases, and cancer screening at certain ages.[36,88] Since 1995, long-term care has been covered by a separate insurance scheme, which is mandatory for the whole population. The contribution rate of 2.35% of gross salary is shared between employers and employees; people without children pay an additional 0.25%. Beneficiaries can choose between in-kind benefits and cash payments (around a quarter of long-term care insurance expenditure goes to these cash payments). Both home care and institutional care are provided almost exclusively by private not-for-profit and for-profit providers. Since 2013, family caregivers also have been receiving financial support through payments of up to 50% of what professional providers would have received for that care.[36]

Total Healthcare Spending and Health Dollars Spent Per Capita

Germany continues to spend a large amount of its wealth on health. Overall, healthcare expenditures have been steadily on the rise since the passage of the National Health Insurance Act in 1883. In 1985, they accounted for 8.8% of GDP; by 1995, they had risen to 10.1%; and since 2005, they have continued to hover between 10.0% and 11.0%, despite ongoing efforts to curb spending. In 2014, total expenditures were $492 billion USD; 58.5% were attributable to SHI spending.[4] By the latter part of the 20th century, and into the 21st century, dramatic increases in SHI spending occurred for physician services and ambulatory care; in contrast, and due to the strong ambulatory care sector, spending on acute hospital care has been relatively low.[23] SHI spending for pharmaceuticals has continued to fluctuate somewhat; it fell sharply between 1992 and 1994, rose slowly in 1996, fell in 1997, and then rose increasingly more quickly through 2003. By 2010, it had fallen again, largely due to manufacturers' rebates for prescription-only drugs and drugs without reference prices being raised from 6.0% to 16.0% in mid-2010.[23] Total spending, by type of expenditure, as of 2012, is shown in **Figure 13-4**. Similar to overall healthcare expenditures, per capita expenditures have also been on the rise in Germany. In 1970, per capita healthcare spending was $663 USD, accounting for 4.48% of the per capita GDP. By 2002, per capita spending had risen to $2,066 USD, in 2013, it was $4,819 USD, and in 2022, it was $6,191 USD.[89] The largest proportion of that amount was for public spending.[90,91] As of 2022, health expenditures amounted to 12.6% of German GDP.[92]

Multiparty Payer System and Third-Party Distribution

At first glance, healthcare financing in Germany appears to be a rather straightforward process because almost all German citizens belong to statutory sickness funds and the remainder belong to private insurance plans. Therefore, one might assume—incorrectly—that the system has purchasing agents on behalf of a government-run program with only two types of payers, or—because of the dominance of SHI, and again incorrectly—may go even further and classify it as a single-payer system. In fact, the German healthcare system is much more complex. In fact, in 2006, when Chancellor Angela Merkel proposed reforming the healthcare system by creating a centralized health fund (by shifting funding from payroll taxes to general revenues, trimming benefits, and increasing cost sharing), this proposal had to be quickly abandoned due to lack of public support and amidst political opposition.[93,94] Although the statutory sickness funds do represent the most important type of payer in Germany's healthcare system and are the country's version of a "public" healthcare system, there are actually a large number of these funds (see also Table 13-4). They make up a group of wholly private,

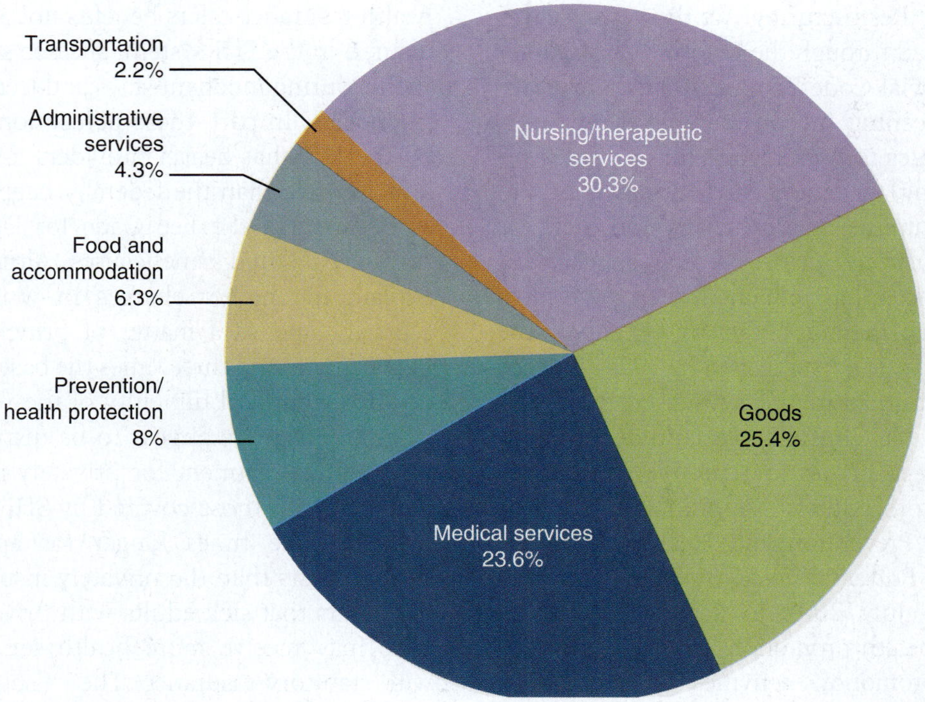

Figure 13-4 Total Healthcare Expenditures, by Type, 2022

Data from: Destatis. Health expenditure: Germany, years, types of service. Accessed February 18, 2025. https://www-genesis.destatis.de/datenbank/online/statistic/23611/table/23611-0002.

nonprofit insurers that are heavily regulated but function independently of the government.

Moreover, sickness funds only perform the function of purchasing agents on behalf of the government-run central health fund and their patients. Specifically, Germans pay their health insurance premiums into a national, government-run central health fund that effectively performs the risk-pooling function for the entire system. This health fund (*Gesundheitsfonds*) is administrated by the Federal Social Insurance Office (*Bundesgesundheitsamt*), which determines how much of the fund will be allocated to each sickness fund, based on specific criteria.[95] It is really much more accurate to describe the German healthcare system as multipayer, compulsory, employer-based, highly regulated, and fee-for-service.

Much like the German education system, the German public health system is decentralized to the states and localities, although the federal government holds legislative authority. Public health remains principally the responsibility of the 16 federal states and covers issues such as surveillance of communicable diseases and health promotion and education. As in the United States, the system is responsible for protecting public health, including water systems, sewer systems, other forms of environmental protection, food safety, and health promotion. The environmental protection measures have been quite successful in cleaning up major rivers and other forms of water pollution. Similarly, air quality has markedly improved over the past 35 years.[96]

Unfortunately, public health promotion efforts have received considerably less attention. Historically, the states have resisted the influence of the federal government on public health. Although some elements of public health have been included in SHI in recent decades (such as cancer screening) and other interventions have separate agreements (e.g., immunizations), there have not been overarching public health guidelines in place, like the U.S. Office of Disease Prevention and Health Promotion's *Healthy People 2030*. However, a decade ago, in September 2012, the 53 member states of the World Health Organization finally adopted a European health policy framework, *Health 2020*, that aims to "significantly improve the health and well-being of populations, reduce health inequalities, strengthen public health, and ensure people-centered health systems that are universal, equitable, sustainable, and of high quality."[97] A significant finding from *Health 2020* data indicated lower premature mortality and mortality from external causes, increased life expectancy, decreased infant mortality, and a decline in the overweight population. All indicators had improved.[98]

As a notable exception, from 1989 to 1996, health promotion measures were actually offered as a type of benefit by sickness funds directly to their members. This benefit was abandoned under the Second Social

Health Insurance Restructuring Act; however, it was partly reintroduced through the Reform Act of 2000.

While the Social Code Book regulates preventive services and screening in considerable detail (e.g., concerning diseases to be screened for and intervals between screening), it leaves further regulations to the Federal Committee of Physicians and Sickness Funds (*Bundesausschuss der Ärzte und Krankenkassen*). This committee has remained one of the most important decision-making bodies on benefits in the ambulatory care sector. Established in 1923, it is the oldest joint institution in the system of joint self-government and has considerable latitude in defining the benefits catalogue for curative, diagnostic, and therapeutic procedures.[23] Additionally, the German Forum for Prevention and Health Promotion (*Deutsches Forum Prävention und Gesundheitsförderung*) was founded in July 2002 to actively strengthen prevention and health promotion, primarily via concerted health promotion activities in preschools, schools, and workplaces. For the elderly, a comprehensive program to prevent cardiovascular diseases was initiated. In 2007, it merged with the *Deutsche Bundesvereinigung Prävention und Gesundheitsförderung*.

Quality

Infant Mortality

In 2023, Germany had an estimated 693,000 live births, which was a 6.2% decrease from 2022. This was the lowest number of births since 2013.[99] Due to the advanced and comprehensive nature of the German healthcare system, infant mortality has remained very low. In 2023, it was 2.13 per 1,000 live births; a 0.9% decline from 2022. The infant mortality rate in 2021 was 2.344 per 1,000 live births, a 8.26% decline from 2022.[100]

Mortality for children under 5 years has remained stable in recent years. It was 3.6 deaths per 1,000 live births in 2022.The rate was unchanged from 2021.[101] The main causes of deaths among children under 5 years of age appear to be unintentional; one of the leading causes is strangulation/choking.[102]

Total fertility rate, based on a 2022 estimate, is 1.57 children born per woman. Mothers' mean age at first birth is 29.9 years (2020 estimate).[103]

Two-Tiered Healthcare Systems (by Income)

Privately insured patients have long been perceived as receiving preferential treatment due to the higher reimbursement to physicians provided by the private health insurance system. In other words, private health insurance offers benefits not available to those insured in the SHI system, such as single-occupancy rooms during inpatient stays and treatment by senior physicians. In part, these perceptions may be fueled by the fact that health providers are able to charge a higher rate than the federally negotiated base rate, as outlined in the Fee Code for Doctors, for their privately insured beneficiaries. Although they must explain the higher charges in writing, physicians typically, and as a matter of principle, charge fees between one and three times the base rate, depending on the extent and difficulty of the work involved.[103] In addition, there appear to be disparate wait times for elective treatment for privately insured and SHI patients, with those covered by SHI waiting approximately three times longer for appointments for selected tests than the privately insured.[104] Similarly, it appears that sick adults with private health insurance may receive more health services than those with statutory insurance. They also tend to be more likely to see specialists, be admitted, and have nonemergency surgery.[105] At the same time, some evidence exists that the private health insurance system does not appear to have compromised the quality of or access in the SHI system. For example, in 2010, two-thirds of SHI patients received same-day or next-day appointments with a doctor or nurse when sick or in need of care.[106]

Vaccination Coverage

By 2015, vaccination rates for German children rose to an all-time high level and were much improved from even 15 years earlier. Mandatory vaccinations were abolished with reunification in 1990. Consequently, there are some regional fluctuations in vaccination coverage, with East German states showing higher coverage. In general, vaccination rates for almost all common childhood diseases reached a high in 2015, with rates between 85.0% and 99.0%. For example, while rates for diphtheria vaccinations were around 78.0% in 2000, they rose to 96.0% in 2016.[107] What remains of concern even today is the potential for measles outbreaks. For example, in 2011, although the measles vaccination rate was 96.1% for the East German state of Mecklenburg–Western Pomerania, it was only 89.8% in Bavaria.[108] However, measles outbreaks continue to be a problem. In 2019, there were 43 reported measles cases, leading to one death.[109] To date, Germany has not been able to meet the World Health Organization's progress indicator—less than one notified case per million. Like many EU member countries, Germany also recommends influenza vaccination for adults aged 65 and older.

In fact, Germany is one of four countries that recommends such vaccinations beginning at age 60 (the others are Greece, Iceland, and the Netherlands). In 2013, approximately 55.0% of the eligible population was immunized against influenza, in 2022, the rate was 43.3%.[110]

Quality Assurance

In Germany, quality assurance is addressed through a range of measures broadly defined by law, and in more detail by the Federal Joint Committee. In addition, in an advisory role, the Institute for Quality and Efficiency in Health Care, established in 2004, provides the committee with evidence-based evaluations of the benefits and cost benefits of health services and functions. Previously, quality assurance was carried out almost exclusively within one sector (in keeping with the deep divide between the hospital and ambulatory care sectors). Since 2007, with the passage of the Act to Strengthen Competition in SHI, multisector approaches to quality improvement have been encouraged. The law stipulates provisions for measuring quality of the following services:

- Services that are provided in at least two different healthcare settings, both with a significant contribution to the treatment outcome (multisector procedures)
- Services that can be provided in different sectors (procedures with sector equivalence)
- Services provided in one sector, with outcome quality measured in another sector (cross-sectoral follow-up procedures)[111]

In 2007, many of the previous regulations were combined to align quality requirements across all healthcare settings as much as possible. Further structural quality is assured by the requirement that providers have a quality management system, physicians continue their medical education, and health technology assessments are used for drugs and procedures. Although there is no revalidation requirement for physicians and hospital accreditation is voluntary,[36] hospitals participate in an external quality control process for acute care. This process is quite unique: For selected interventions (e.g., appendectomies), hospital treatment is documented for each patient based on a set of quality indicators specified in advance. Performance data are then transmitted to a central external agency (Institute for Applied Quality Improvement and Research in Health Care, or AQUA), as well as to the corresponding state offices for quality assurance where the data are evaluated.[111] The results are compiled in annual quality management reports that are discussed at regularly convened nationwide conferences on quality control, and they are incorporated into the day-to-day running of hospitals.

Patients' Rights

In 2004, Germany established a federal commissioner for patient issues in the health system (*Beauftragte der Bundesregierung für die Belange der Patientinnen und Patienten sowie Bevollmächtigter für Pflege*). The position is currently held by a political appointee; the commissioner is charged with ensuring that patient issues are considered at different levels in the health system. An analysis of the public inquiries received by the commissioner reveals that most complainants are older. Health insurance, especially medications, were a major topic, as were concerns over communication with healthcare providers. Older complainants were more likely to mention anxiety, uncertainty, and feelings of injustice, and the personal financial burden of health services was featured prominently.[112] Further expansion of patients' rights occurred in 2013, with the passage of the Patients' Rights Act (*Patientenrechtegesetz*). This general law on patients' rights bundles several existing jurisdictions and gives detailed regulations (e.g., for complaints). The act created the *treatment contract*, a special contract that by law now governs every interaction between a person administering medical treatment and the patient. Although the law is aimed primarily at physicians, its scope also encompasses other healthcare professionals.[23,113]

Access

Equity/Universality

As mentioned earlier, two of the main characteristics of the German healthcare system are free choice of providers and unrestricted access to all care levels. Such access is provided via near-universal insurance coverage, with the majority of the population either mandatorily or voluntarily insured by statutory health insurance and with approximately 10% of the population insured privately. In theory, insured people have free choice of physicians, psychotherapists (since 1999), dentists, pharmacists, and emergency room services; in reality, access to reimbursed care is available only upon referral by a physician.[23] In addition, there are differences in access between SHI-insured people and privately insured people, with the latter generally having better access (see the earlier discussion on the two-tiered nature of the system). In addition, inequities regarding access to health care exist for migrants, asylum seekers, and refugees. In theory, legal migrants are covered by the insurance system, asylum seekers can receive basic care as stipulated in the Asylum Seekers' Benefits Act (*Asylbewerberleistungsgesetz*), and undocumented immigrants who are ill are covered by social security.[36,114]

Uninsured Populations

Until the enactment of the U.S. Patient Protection and Affordable Care Act on March 23, 2010, by President Barack Obama, the number of uninsured people in Germany was far below that in the United States. And although that number had been increasing between 1999 and 2007, it has since declined drastically. Specifically, 145,000 people, or 0.2% of the population, were uninsured in 1999, and there were almost 200,000 people, or about 0.3%, uninsured during the first quarter of 2007, with some sources citing a number as high as 300,000. However, as a result of the 2007 Health Care Reform Act, the number of uninsured people dropped to 137,000 by 2011, a 30.0% decline.[23,115] In 2023, the data showed 61,000 inhabitants in Germany were uninsured.[116] The uninsured in Germany are mainly self-employed people who are unable or unwilling to pay the premiums after failed business ventures, self-employed people who take the risk of not buying coverage, privately insured people who are unable to continue to afford private coverage because of declining income or rising premiums, and long-term unemployed people who lost unemployment benefits (*Arbeitslosengeld II*) after introduction of the Hartz IV employment market reforms and, therefore, lost their entitlement for health insurance coverage. Low-income employees, divorced people, alien residents, university students, and people who did not graduate from school are also at risk.

Current and Emerging Issues and Challenges

Cost Containment

Rooted in the Bismarck System of social health insurance, the German healthcare system has always put more emphasis on free access and high numbers of providers and technological equipment than on cost-effectiveness or cost containment per se. Yet, by the turn of the millennium, the German government had become extremely concerned with the ever-rising cost of health care and undertook efforts to curb spending. In November 1999, the lower house of parliament passed the Reform 2000 bill, which was drafted to place severe limits on spending by physicians, dentists, and pharmacists and to impose heavy penalties on doctors who exceeded their budgets. The bill was rejected by the upper house of parliament only a month later. The era of cost containment had actually started much earlier, with the introduction of the Cost Containment Act of 1977, and it did not stop then. Politicians and lawmakers have continued to introduce a number of measures designed to contain costs, including sectoral budgets, rational prescribing, price reductions, and downsizing. Yet, over recent years, the revenues from contributions have increased more slowly than health expenditures and the GDP. Such low revenues have led to repeated deficits and increasing debts, although sickness funds have attempted to counteract the trend by increasing their contribution rates.[88]

More recent cost-containment strategies have been based on overall budgets for ambulatory physicians and hospitals, as well as on collective regional prescription caps for physicians. The Hospital Care Structure Reform Act of 2016 aimed not only to link hospital payments to good service quality but also to reduce payments for low quality.[36] The efforts and projects focused on cost containment continue today.

Integration of Care

Some 25 years ago, the challenge of achieving an integrated system of care arose directly from the need to combine the two healthcare systems in the two formerly separate German countries. At the time of reunification, the East German healthcare system could not have been more different from the West German system. It was a state-run system, with physicians as salaried state employees making an average of $10,000 USD annually. In contrast, physicians in the West were making an average of $100,000 USD annually.[93] Although the two systems roughly matched each other in numbers of physicians and hospital beds per capita, the characteristics and quality were quite different. Prior to reunification, East Germany had centralized, integrated, publicly financed, and provided health services. The great bulk of pharmaceutical, ambulatory medical care, and hospital services were organized under the state and were provided free of charge to patients. There was emphasis on ambulatory health centers ("polyclinics") and on occupational health services.

Services were funded by a mixture of payroll taxes and general taxes. Although patients could choose their doctor, the doctors themselves were salaried and were very much under the thumb of the state. There was only a very small private sector: Of the 20,840 active ambulatory care physicians, a mere 2% were in private practice.[59,117,118]

The major challenge of reunification of the two states along with the two healthcare systems can be summed up in one word: modernization. Many of the facilities in the former East Germany were old, substandard structures in great disrepair, and some were even obsolete. In a similar vein, health insurance coverage was provided primarily through company-based funds, in large part owing to the fact that many East German citizens were employees of state-run enterprises.[93] Shortly after reunification, the West German government set out to bring the Eastern system more in line with its Western counterpart and to reflect better the Western (i.e., modern) image. But rather than consider the strengths and weaknesses of both systems and pursue a more strategic merger emphasizing the former, the Western system was rapidly introduced into the East, even eliminating resources that had proven to be cost-effective, such as the policlinics with a defined referral system.[102] In hindsight, reunification had some positive consequences with respect to health. For example, life expectancy of East Germans rose dramatically. In 2015, it was identical for East and West German women, and it was nearly identical for East and West German men. In contrast, alcohol-related deaths remained much higher in East Germany. Notably, East Germans remained much more willing to be vaccinated.[119]

Today, integration and modernization refer to a very different challenge—namely, the urgent need to combine the traditionally strictly separate inpatient (stationäre), outpatient (ambulante), and rehabilitative sectors, thereby improving communication flow, economic efficiency, and quality of care. For the past 15 years, integration efforts, which aim to restructure and unify the health care Germans receive across these different sectors and providers, has taken center stage. In 2015, with the passage of the Health Care Strengthening Act, the German government took new steps toward integrating the delivery of healthcare services within the SHI system. Later, integrated care programs (ICPs) were introduced as an important element of the Health Care Reform Act of 2000. The basic premise of ICPs is that providers from various sectors form an integrated care network (ICN), and the network (or the individual providers) then creates an integrated care contract (ICC) with a payer (a sickness fund); at that point, the providers begin providing the negotiated services.[120] At least two health providers from two different sectors and/or at least two different specialties have to collaborate within a program to qualify as an ICN (e.g., inpatient and outpatient sectors, general practitioners and cardiologists).[121] In 2004, the Health Care Modernization Act removed existing barriers to developing and implementing ICPs and provided financial incentives for both sickness funds and providers to proceed. Specifically, the government provided start-up financing to ICPs of up to 1% of the entire compensation of physicians and hospitals, which amounted to about €680 million.[122] As a result, between 2004 and 2008, when government start-up funding ran out, a total of 6,400 ICPs with 1,661,283 enrollees were developed. Since then, the number of ICPs has dropped slightly and enrollment has slowed considerably. In 2011, a total of 6,339 ICPs with 1,926,133 enrollees existed.[120]

Although there clearly has been movement toward integration of care, much remains to be done. Germany has taken steps to create a more fertile environment for integrated healthcare approaches, yet it continues to lag behind other European countries. One issue is that evaluative information regarding the success (or lack thereof) of certain ICPs in terms of number of enrollees, degree of cooperation between providers, management capacity, and favorable/unfavorable outcomes is not publicly available. Mandatory reporting of a set of predefined and aligned quality indicators might improve the situation as integrated care efforts move ahead.[120]

The Aging Population

By 2050, one in three Germans will be older than 65.[123] The famous statement made in the 1950s by Chancellor Konrad Adenauer, who said that "people will always have children," could not have been more wrong. In increasing numbers, Germans have opted out of what is often referred to as a *generational contract*: Taken in a societal context, those of working age provide the economic resources both for the young, in terms of family support and schooling, and for the old, in terms of pension and healthcare financing. In Germany, the aging of the population and concomitant increasing prevalence of chronic diseases and need for greater healthcare resources will continue to put significant pressure on the political and healthcare systems. The latest projections by the Federal Statistical Agency (*Statistisches Bundesamt*) suggest an inevitable decrease in the German population, from 80.8 million in 2013 to somewhere between 68.0 million and 73.0 million by 2060. In particular, the working-age population will shrink tremendously; the number of people aged 20 to 64, 49.0 million in 2013, will drop to between 34.0 and 38.0 million by 2060. At the same time, the number of people aged 65 and older will continue to grow, with an expected increase to between 22.0 and 23.0 million by 2060. In 2013, every fifth person belonged to this age group (21%); it will be every third person in 2060.[123]

A parliamentary commission described the anticipated picture as follows: A decreasing population will lead to decreasing population density with great regional variations. The shift in the age structure of the population may also be greater than anticipated. Although immigration may soften the impact, it cannot reverse that shift; the average age of the population will increase considerably.[124] This trend is not limited to Germany but can be seen in most developed countries and has effects beyond the healthcare system. Because of a number of factors, Germany is rated by the European Union as at medium risk with regard to the sustainability of its public finances—aging of the population is prominent among the risk factors due to reforms of the pension system.[104]

The Refugee Crisis

In 2015, more than 1 million refugees crossed the borders into Europe, a massive movement of displaced people and families that has sparked political, economic, and social controversy. The largest number, more than 350,000, were Syrian refugees; the largest number of new asylum applications, more than 476,000, were in Germany.[125] One important aspect of the sudden and enormous influx of people in dire need of humanitarian aid into Germany has been the challenges to the German healthcare system. Many refugees arrive not only with infectious, communicable, noncommunicable, and/or chronic diseases but also with severe mental health needs due to stress and traumatic experiences.[126] According to the World Health Organization, effective response requires triage of refugees, followed by proper diagnosis and treatment, with full access to high-quality care for all refugees irrespective of their legal status. In the long term, national healthcare systems must ensure that they are adequately prepared.[127] In Germany, the current law restricts health care for current asylum seekers during the first 18 months of stay to "acute diseases of pain in which necessary medical or dental treatment has to be provided."[128] After 18 months, asylum seekers are entitled to the same social benefits to which German citizens are entitled.

To respond more effectively to the challenges of refugees and accepting asylum seekers, Chancellor Angela Merkel spearheaded the passage of a new integration law (*Integrationsgesetz, Artikel 8, Absatz 6*) in July 2016, which was designed to proactively regulate the support that refugees and asylum seekers will receive. Critics dubbed it the *dis-integration law* because of what they saw as demands and restrictions that make effective integration doubtful and that may, in fact, violate refugees' constitutional rights.[129] At the same time, the public's attitudes regarding how the German government should address the challenges have become much more divided, with many Germans now believing that the country cannot and should not welcome new refugees and should send those already there back home. In 2013, some frustrated Germans formed the Alternative for Germany party (*Alternative für Deutschland*), a right-wing populist party with extremist tendencies and a hardline stance on immigration; it has since been spreading anti-Islamic, anti-Semitic, and anti-minority rhetoric.[130]

Clearly, responding to the refugee crisis in an economically viable manner while reflecting humanitarian and social justice principles will require ongoing careful attention, not only in Germany but also globally. In September 2016, Germany joined 51 other countries and international organizations, at the invitation of President Barack Obama, at the Leaders' Summit on the Global Refugee Crisis, to develop renewed and significant new global commitments. Representatives agreed to (1) increase funding to humanitarian appeals and international organizations, (2) admit more refugees through resettlement or other legal pathways, and (3) increase refugees' self-reliance and inclusion through opportunities for education and legal work.[131]

COVID-19 Pandemic

Early in the pandemic, Germany used a strategy of mitigation including partial lockdowns, which contributed to relatively successful outcomes compared with its peers.[132,133] According to the World Health Organization, Germany had 38,413,078 confirmed cases of COVID-19 from January 3, 2020, through May 10, 2023. With 173,473 confirmed deaths, the mortality rate was 451.60 deaths per 100,000 confirmed cases. In comparison, the United States had 103,343,569 confirmed cases with 1,125,209 confirmed deaths, a mortality rate of 1,088.80 deaths per 100,000 confirmed cases.[134] The WHO Region (Europe) excluding Germany had 237,723,139 cumulative cases with 2,059,985 confirmed deaths, a mortality rate of

866.55 deaths per 100,000 confirmed cases. Thus, it appears that the German mortality experience was better than that of Europe as a whole.[135]

Of the 20 countries most affected by COVID-19 worldwide, Germany is ranked as 14th at 203.16 deaths per 100,000 population. This is somewhat better than the other listed European countries, such as Austria (13th, 243.94), France (12th, 254.68), Spain (11th, 255.54), Portugal (10th, 257.59), and Italy (6th, 311.47), and much better than the United States (2nd, 341.11).[136]

Final Thoughts

Today, great challenges remain for Germany, not just for the healthcare system but also for German politics. The idea of solidarity in financing and providing access to health irrespective of means to pay—which is fundamental to the German healthcare system—will be severely tested, as Germans are being asked to provide ever more funding. The heavy tax burden on German citizens, their ability to maintain a high standard of living and quality of life, and the push toward an equitable system of universal care may not be sustainable over the next decade without significant cost restructuring and reforms. The challenge for politicians and lawmakers is to make Germany's healthcare and social welfare systems sustainable. The first step is public debate. Fortunately, Germans seem to have gotten the message: Some 80% of the population believes that the system will become worse if nothing happens during the next 10 years. Revealingly, people between the ages of 33 and 54 are the most concerned, as they now have to pay for themselves and for their retired fellow Germans.[137] One step toward addressing the challenges ahead was the formation of a national forum, termed National Health Targets (*Nationale Gesundheitsziele*) in 2000, as an initiative between the federal government and the 16 federal states. Together, they formulated seven national health targets, with the goal of establishing a coordinated joint strategy to prepare Germany's decentralized and pluralistic health system for the challenges and health risks ahead.[23,138] Since then, additional health targets have been formulated, and the forum has been seeking to anchor itself as a permanent body and comprehensive cooperation platform for the main stakeholders in the German healthcare system. Against the backdrop of a national debt of over €2.1 trillion (about $2.625 trillion USD), with many federal states being heavily indebted and many municipalities being bankrupt, as well as the unabated refugee crisis during which Germany has been called upon to provide safe haven to migrants and refugees, it is clear that addressing the challenges will be both vital and incredibly complex for years to come. Germany's health system and infrastructure will be impacted over the next decade due to the demographic and socioeconomic changes as well as the aging of the population.[13]

References

1. Schulze H. *Kleine deutsche Geschichte. Erweiterte und aktualisierte Auflage*. München, Germany: C. H. Beck; 2007.
2. Kruse W. *Das deutsche Kaiserreich. Sozialdemokratie zwischen Ausnahmegestzen und Sozialreformen*. Bundeszentrale für politische Bildung. Published September 27, 2012. Accessed September 15, 2016. http://www.bpb.de/geschichte/deutsche-geschichte/kaiserreich/139650/sozialdemokratie-zwischen-ausnahmegesetzen-und-sozialreformen.
3. Military Education. 10 bloodiest battles of World War II. Published December 1, 2011. Accessed September 15, 2016. http://www.militaryeducation.org/10-bloodiest-battles-of-world-war-ii/.
4. Statistisches Bundesamt. Homepage. Facts and figures. Destatis Statistisches Bundesamt. Accessed September 5, 2016. https://www.destatis.de/EN/Homepage.html.
5. Statistisches Bundesamt. Land- ind Forstwirtschaft, Fischerei. Bodenfläche nach Art der tatsächlichen Nutzung. Published November, 25, 2015. Accessed September 5, 2016. https://www.destatis.de/DE/ZahlenFakten/Wirtschaftsbereiche/LandForstwirtschaftFischerei/Flaechennutzung/Flaechennutzung.html.
6. Deutscher Bundestag. Funktion und Aufgabe. Accessed September 8, 2016. http://www.bundestag.de/bundestag/aufgaben.
7. Bundesrat. Aufgaben des Bundesrates. Accessed September 8, 2016. http://www.bundesrat.de/DE/aufgaben/aufgaben-node.html.
8. Bundesverfassungsgericht. Das Gericht. Aufgaben. Accessed September 12, 2016.http://www.bundesverfassungsgericht.de/EN/Das-ericht/Aufgaben/aufgaben_node.html.
9. Der Bundesgerichtshof. Das Gericht. Stellung im Gerichtssystem. Accessed September 8, 2016. http://www.bundesgerichtshof.de/DE/DasGericht/StellungGerichtssystem/stellungGerichtssystem_node.html.
10. Rao S. German legal research guide: government and political structure. Law Library, University of Wisconsin, Madison. Updated September 2, 2016. Accessed September 8, 2016. http://law.wisc.libguides.com/c.php?g=125271&p=819917.
11. European Union. About the EU. History of the European Union. Updated September 15, 2016. Accessed September 15, 2016. https://europa.eu/european-union/about-eu/history/founding-fathers_en.

12. Statistisches Bundesamt. Foreign trade: ranking of Germany's trading partners in foreign trade. Published September 11, 2016. Accessed September 6, 2016. https://www.destatis.de/EN/FactsFigures/NationalEconomyEnvironment/ForeignTrade/TradingPartners/Tables/OrderRankGermanyTradingPartners.pdf?__blob=publicationFile.
13. *The World Factbook*. Washington, DC: Central Intelligence Agency. Accessed February 14, 2023. https://www.cia.gov/the-world-factbook/countries/germany/.
14. Statistisches Bundesamt. Verkehr auf einen Blick. Published April 2013. Accessed September 10, 2016. https://www.destatis.de/DE/Publikationen/Thematisch/TransportVerkehr/Querschnitt/BroschuereVerkehrBlick0080006139004.pdf?__blob=publicationFile.
15. The German Way. The Autobahn. Accessed September 3. 2016. http://www.german-way.com/travel-and-tourism/driving-in-europe/driving/autobahn/.
16. Deutsche Bahn. Facts and figures. Accessed September 6, 2016. http://www.deutschebahn.com/en/group/ataglance/facts_figures.html.
17. Statistisches Bundesamt. Fachserie 8, Serie 1.2. Verkehr im Überblick. Published February 1, 2014. Accessed September 8, 2016. https://www.destatis.de/DE/Publikationen/Thematisch/TransportVerkehr/Querschnitt/VerkehrUeberblick2080120147004.pdf?__blob=publicationFile.
18. Exports in December 2024: +2.9% on November 2024. Destatis. February 7, 2025. Accessed January 31, 2025. https://www.destatis.de/EN/Themes/Economy/Foreign-Trade/_node.html.
19. Warner MB. Traffic remains blocked after Rhine tanker accident. *Der Spiegel Online*. Published January 19, 2011. Accessed September 8, 2016. http://www.spiegel.de/international/germany/the-shipwreck-and-the-lorelei-traffic-remains-blocked-after-rhine-tanker-accident-a-740322.html.
20. Deutsche Welle. Demographics: Germany reports highest fertility rate since reunification. Published December 16, 2015. Accessed September 10, 2016. http://www.dw.com/en/germany-reports-highest-fertility-rate-since-reunification/a-18920557.
21. Chu H. For Germany, refugees are a demographic blessing, as well as a burden. *The Los Angeles Times*. Published September 10, 2015. Accessed September 9, 2016. http://www.latimes.com/world/europe/la-fg-germany-refugees-demographics-20150910-story.html.
22. The force assaulting the euro; free exchange. *The Economist*. June 6, 2015:70. *Biography in Context*. Accessed September 20, 2016. http://ic.galegroup.com/ic/bic1/MagazinesDetailsPage/MagazinesDetailsWindow?disableHighlighting=false&displayGroupName=Magazines&currPage=&scanId=&query=&prodId=BIC1&search_within_results=&p=BIC1&mode=view&catId=&limiter=&display-query=&displayGroups=&contentModules=&action=e&sortBy=&documentId=GALE%7CA416514580&windowstate=normal&activityType=&failOverType=&commentary=&source=Bookmark&u=usclibs&jsid=d0bbd7aa465a15a9986cbe961d7c6102.
23. Busse R, Blümel M. Germany: health system review. *Health Sys Transit. European Observatory on Health Systems and Policies*. 2014;16(2):1-296.
24. Households and families. Destatis. Accessed January 31, 2025. https://www.destatis.de/EN/Themes/Society-Environment/Population/Households-Families/_node.html#267584.
25. Kultusminister Konferenz. Aufgaben. Accessed September 15, 2016. https://www.kmk.org/kmk/aufgaben.html.
26. Taylor E. Culture & diversity travel guide to Germany. BeGlobalii. August 12, 2024. Accessed January 31, 2025. https://beglobalii.com/articles/diversity-travel-guide-germany.
27. *Ecumenical News*. German Protestants and Catholics flee churches after compulsory taxes imposed. Accessed September 11, 2016. http://www.ecumenicalnews.com/article/german-protestants-and-catholics-flee-churches-after-compulsory-taxes-imposed/28183.htm.
28. Population movement. Destatis. July 3, 2024. Accessed January 31, 2025. https://www.destatis.de/EN/Themes/Society-Environment/Population/Births/Tables/birth-deaths.html.
29. Statistisches Bundesamt. Fact and figures: press release: number of deaths down by 2.8% in 2014. Published December 15, 2015. Accessed September 16, 2016. https://www.destatis.de/EN/PressServices/Press/pr/2015/12/PE15_465_232.html.
30. Causes of death. Destatis. Accessed January 31, 2025. https://www.destatis.de/EN/Themes/Society-Environment/Health/Causes-Death/_node.html#267094.
31. Björnberg A. *Euro Health Consumer Index 2015*. Health Consumer Powerhouse Ltd; 2016. Published January 26, 2016. Accessed September 2, 2016. http://www.healthpowerhouse.com/files/EHCI_2015/EHCI_2015_report.pdf.
32. Bundesverfassungsgericht. Erlassungen. Leitsätze. Published February 9, 2010. Updated 2016. Accessed September 18, 2016. http://www.bundesverfassungsgericht.de/entscheidungen/ls20100209_1bvl000109.html.
33. Bäcker G. *Chronologie gesetzlicher Neuregelungen. Krankenversicherung und Gesundtheitswesen, 1998–2015*. Institut Arbeit und Qualifikation der Universität Duisburg-Essen. Published April, 2016. Accessed September 12, 2016. http://www.sozialpolitik-aktuell.de/tl_files/sozialpolitik-aktuell/_Politikfelder/Gesundheitswesen/Dokumente/Chronologie_GKV_Gesundheitssystem.pdf.
34. Obermann K, Müller P, Müller HH, et al. *Understanding the German healthcare system*. Mannheim Institute of Public Health. Accessed September 15, 2016. http://miph.umm.uni-heidelberg.de/miph/cms/upload/pdf/GHCS_Kap._3.pdf.
35. Green D, Irvine B, Clarke E, Bidgood E. *Health care systems: Germany*. Civitas. Updated January 2013. Accessed September 15, 2016. http://www.digitalezorg.nl/digitale/uploads/2015/03/germany.pdf.
36. Blümel M, Busse R, Osborn R, Sarnak D. The German healthcare system, 2015. In: Mossialos E, Wenzl M, eds. *2015 International Profiles of Health Care Systems*. New York, NY: Commonwealth Fund; January 2015:69-76.
37. Murray JE. Health insurance in developed countries: history of. *Encyclopedia of Health Economics*. 2014;1:365-372. doi:10.1016/B978-0-12-375678-7.00902-0.
38. Bump JP. The long road to universal health coverage: historical analysis of early decisions in Germany, the United Kingdom, and the United States. *Health Systems & Reform*. 2015;1(1):28-38.
39. Bärnighausen T, Suaerborn R. One hundred and eighteen years of the German health insurance system: are there any lessons for middle- and low-income countries? *Soc Sci Med*. 2002;54:1559-1587.
40. Porter ME, Guth C. *Redefining German Health Care: Moving to a Value-Based System*. Berlin, Germany: Springer Verlag; 2012.
41. Silber K. From Bismarck to Bush. ThinkAdvisor. *Research Magazine*. Published August 1, 2008. Accessed September 16, 2016. http://www.thinkadvisor.com/2008/08/01/from-bismarck-to-bush.

42. Starr P. *The Social Transformation of American Medicine: The Rise of a Sovereign Profession and the Making of a Vast Industry*. New York, NY: Basic Books; 1982.
43. Haffke D, ed. 100 Jahre Berliner Abkommen. *Niedersächsisches Ärzteblatt*. Updated January 15, 2014. Accessed September 16, 2016. http://www.haeverlag.de/nae/index.php?sheft=1&jgang=2014.
44. What the Führer means for Germans today. *The Economist*. Christmas Specials section. December 19, 2015. Accessed September 16, 2016. http://www.economist.com/news/christmas-specials/21683971-seventy-years-after-adolf-hitlers-death-how-germans-see-him-changing-what.
45. Evans R. *The Third Reich in Power, 1933–1939*. New York, NY: Penguin Press; 2006.
46. Jesse E. *Deutsche Geschichte: Vom Kaiserreich bis heute. Politik, Wirtschaft & Wissenschaft, Kunst & Kultur, Gesellschaft & Sport, Weltgeschichte*. München, Germany: Trautwein Lexikon Verlag; 2004.
47. Kater MH. *The Nazi Party: A Social Profile of Members and Leaders, 1919–1945*. Boston, MA: Harvard University Press; 1983. Dublin, Ireland: Albion Press Ltd; 2016.
48. Micozzi MS. National health care: medicine in Germany, 1918–1945. Foundation for Economic Education. Published November 1, 1993. Accessed September 16, 2016. https://fee.org/articles/national-health-care-medicine-in-germany-1918-1945/.
49. Solsten E. *Germany: A Country Study*. Collingdale, PA: DIANE Publishing; 1999.
50. Naas GE, Kretschmer R. Trauma nursing in the German healthcare system. *Intl J Trauma Nurs*. 2007;8(1):9-14.
51. Ernst E. Commentary: The Third Reich: German physicians between resistance and participation. *International Journal of Epidemiology*. 2001;30:37-42.
52. Ryu GC. Lessons from unified Germany and their implications for health care in the unification of the Korean peninsula. *J Prevent Med Pub Health*. 2013;46:127-133.
53. Arabin B, Raum E, Mohnhaupt A, Schwartz FW. Two types of health care systems and their influence on the introduction of perinatal care: an epidemiological twin model in Berlin from 1950 to 1990. *Matern Child Health J*. 1999;3(2):81-91.
54. Wahner-Roedler DL, Knuth P, Juchems RH. The German healthcare system. *Mayo Clin Proc*. 1997;72:1061-1068.
55. Perleth M, Gibis B, Göhlen B. A short history of health technology assessment in Germany. *Intl J Technol Assess Health Care*. 2009;25(suppl 1):112-119.
56. Bundesministerium für Gesundheit. Ministerium. Aufgaben und Organisation. Published 2016. Accessed October 6, 2016. http://www.bmg.bund.de/ministerium/aufgaben-und-organisation.html.
57. Braasch P. *Das Gesundheitswesen in Deutschland: Struktur, Leistungen, Weiterentwicklung*. 4th ed. Köln, Germany: Deutscher Ärzte Verlag; 2007.
58. Stockemer D, Elder G. Germans 25 years after reunification: how much do they know about the German Democratic Republic and what is their value judgment of the socialist regime? *Communist and Post-Communist Studies*. 2015;48:113-122.
59. Ryu GC. Lessons from unified Germany and their implications for healthcare in the unification of the Korean Peninsula. *J Prevent Med Pub Health*. 2013;46:127-133.
60. Cheng TM, Reinhardt UE. Shepherding major health systems reform: a conversation with German health minister Ulla Schmidt. *Health Aff (Millwood)*. 2008;27(3):204-213.
61. Bundesministerium für Gesundheit. Service. Publikationen. Shaping global health, taking joint action, embracing responsibility: the federal government's strategy paper. Published October 2013. Accessed October 6, 2016. https://www.bundesgesundheitsministerium.de/fileadmin/dateien/Publikationen/Gesundheit/Broschueren/Screen_Globale_Gesundheitspolitik_engl.pdf.
62. Bundesministerium für Gesundheit. Themen. Pflege. Pflegestärkungsgesetz. Fragen und Antworten zum PSGII. Published January 29, 2016. Accessed October 6, 2016. http://www.bmg.bund.de/themen/pflege/pflegestaerkungsgesetze/fragen-und-antworten-zum-psg-ii.html.
63. Dunbar RLM, Bresser RKF. Appreciating cultural differences: the case of German reunification. *Administration & Society*. 1997;29(4):440-470.
64. Dornberg J. Five years after reunification: Easterners discover themselves. *German Life*. December 1995/January 1996.
65. Amelung V, Glied S, Topan A. Health care and the labor market: learning from the German experience. *J Health Polit Policy Law*. 2003;28(4):693-714.
66. Schweigert FJ. Solidarity and subsidiarity: complementary principles of community development. *J Soc Philos*. 2002;33(1):33-44.
67. Maarse H, Paulus A. Has solidarity survived? A comparative analysis of the effect of social health insurance reform in four European countries. *J Health Polit, Policy Law*. 2003;28(4):585-614.
68. von Krause JW. What types of hospitals are there in Germany? Hospital treatment in Germany. Published January 23, 2005. Accessed October 6, 2016. http://www.english.german-hospital-service.com/2005/01/what-type-of-hospitals-are-there-in.html.
69. Statista. Number of hospitals in Germany from 2000 to 2023. Accessed February 1, 2025. https://www.statista.com/statistics/578444/number-of-hospitals-germany/.
70. Statista. Number of public general hospitals in Germany from 2005 to 2023. Accessed February 1, 2025. https://www.statista.com/statistics/578596/public-general-hospitals-germany/.
71. Eurostat. EU counted 2.3 million hospital beds in 2022. July 11, 2024. Accessed February 1, 2025. https://ec.europa.eu/eurostat/web/products-eurostat-news/w/ddn-20240711-2.
72. Statista. Average length of stay in hospitals in Germany from 1992 to 2023 (in days). Accessed February 1, 2025. https://www.statista.com/statistics/578489/hospital-length-of-stay-germany/.
73. Mau W. *Structures and Organization of Services for Medical Rehabilitation in Germany*. Presentation at the 9th World Congress of the International Society of Physical and Rehabilitation Medicine. Published June 23, 2015. Accessed October 6, 2016. http://www.dgrw-online.de/files/mau-german-rehab-isprm-2015.pdf.
74. Dialog Health. Rehabilitation and post-acute care in Germany. Accessed February 1, 2025. https://www.dialog-health.com/reha-germany#:~:text=During%20three%20days%20of%20intensive%20visits%2C%20the,the%20ZAR%20group%2C%20specialized%20in%20outpatient%20reha.
75. Bundesvereinigung Deutscher Apotekeverbände (ABDA). German pharmacies – figures, data, facts 2024. Accessed February 1, 2025. https://www.abda.de/fileadmin/user_upload/assets/ZDF/Zahlen-Daten-Fakten-24/ABDA_ZDF_2024_Brosch_english.pdf.

76. Can E, Konrad CM, Khan-Gökkaya S, et al. Foreign healthcare professionals in Germany: a questionnaire survey evaluating discrimination experiences and equal treatment at two large university hospitals. *Healthcare (Basel, Switzerland)*. 2022;10(12), 2339. Accessed February 1, 2025. https://pmc.ncbi.nlm.nih.gov/articles/PMC9777572/.
77. Statista. Number of practicing doctors in Germany between 1991 and 2022 (per 1,000 population). Accessed February 1, 2025. https://www.statista.com/statistics/236511/practicing-doctors-per-thousand-inhabitants-in-germany-since-1991/#:~:text=Other%20healthcare%20positions%20also%20increasing.%20Across%20the,to%20approximately%20one%20million%20nurses%20in%202021.
78. Statista. Number of employed foreign doctors in Germany from 1995 to 2023. Accessed February 1, 2025. https://www.statista.com/statistics/582146/foreign-doctors-germany/.
79. Statista. Number of practicing nurses employed in Germany from 2002 to 2021 (in 1,000s). Accessed February 1, 2025. https://www.statista.com/statistics/463429/practising-nurses-employment-in-germany/.
80. Cassier-Woidasky AK. *Nursing Education in Germany: Challenges and Obstacles in Professionalisation*. Stuttgart, Germany: DHBW; 2013.
81. Statista. Number of dentists employed in Germany from 2002 to 2021. Accessed February 1, 2025. https://www.statista.com/statistics/463509/dentists-employment-in-germany/.
82. Statista. Number of physiotherapists employed in Germany from 2000 to 2022 (in 1,000s). Accessed February 1, 2025. https://www.statista.com/statistics/550861/physiotherapists-employment-in-germany/.
83. Statista. Number of magnetic resonance imaging (MRI) units in selected countries as of 2021 (per million population). Accessed February 1, 2025. https://www.statista.com/statistics/282401/density-of-magnetic-resonance-imaging-units-by-country/.
84. Statista. Number of computed tomography (CT) scanners in Germany from 2008 to 2021. Accessed February 1, 2025. https://www.statista.com/statistics/961929/computed-tomography-scanners-in-germany/.
85. Statista. Number of computer tomography (CT) scanners in selected countries as of 2021 (per million population). Accessed February 1, 2025. https://www.statista.com/statistics/266539/distribution-of-equipment-for-computer-tomography/.
86. Ernst & Young. *Medical Technology Report 2015: Pulse on the Industry*. London, UK: Ernst & Young Global Ltd; 2015.
87. Böhm K. *The Transformation of the Social Right to Healthcare: Evidence from England and Germany*. New York, NY: Routledge; 2017.
88. Busse R. *Description of Health Care Systems: Germany and the Netherlands*. Commonwealth Fund. Accessed October 6, 2016. http://www.allhealth.org/briefingmaterials/CountryProfiles-FINAL-1163.pdf.
89. World Bank Group. Current health expenditure per capita (current US$) – European Union. World Health Organization Global Health Expenditure database. April 15, 2024. Accessed February 1, 2025. https://data.worldbank.org/indicator/SH.XPD.CHEX.PC.CD?locations=EU.
90. Organisation for Economic Co-operation and Development. *Health at a Glance 2015: OECD Indicators*. Paris, France: OECD Publishing; 2015.
91. Hagist C, Kotlikoff LJ. *Who's Going Broke? Comparing Healthcare Costs in Ten OECD Countries*. Paper #11833. Cambridge, MA: National Bureau of Economic Research; 2005.
92. Destatis. Germany has highest health expenditure in EU. Accessed February 1, 2025. https://www.destatis.de/Europa/EN/Topic/Population-Labour-Social-Issues/Health/HealthExpenditure.html.
93. Swami B. The German healthcare system. In: Thai KV, Wimberley ET, McManus SM, eds. *Handbook of International Health Care Systems*. New York, NY: Marcel Dekker; 2002: 333-358.
94. Shafrin J. Health care around the world: Germany. *Healthcare Economist*. Published April 24, 2008. Accessed October 6, 2016. http://healthcare-economist.com/2008/04/24/health-care-around-the-world-germany/.
95. Döring A, Paul F. The German health care system. *J Eur Assoc Predict Prevent Personal Med*. 2010;1:535-547.
96. Lassey ML, Lassey WR, Jinks MJ. *Health Care Systems Around the World: Characteristics, Issues, Reforms*. Upper Saddle River, NJ: Prentice-Hall; 1997.
97. World Health Organization. *Implementing Health 2020* [Brochure]. Accessed October 6, 2016. https://euro.sharefile.com/document/#preview/fi62ac19-2b98-89aa-42bb-f96cfcbfd7d5/s73db1a792664325a.
98. Zuidberg MRJ, Shriwise A, de Boer LM, Johansen AS. Assessing progress under Health 2020 in the European Region of the World Health Organization. *Eur J Public Health*. 2020;30(6):1072-1077. doi:10.1093/eurpub/ckaa091. Accessed February 1, 2025. https://academic.oup.com/eurpub/article/30/6/1072/5864950.
99. Destatis. Births. Accessed February 1, 2025. https://www.destatis.de/EN/Themes/Society-Environment/Population/Births/_node.html.
100. Macrotrends. Germany infant mortality rate 1950-2025. Accessed February 1, 2025. https://www.macrotrends.net/global-metrics/countries/DEU/germany/infant-mortality-rate.
101. Statista. Child mortality rate (under 5 years old) in Germany from 1825 to 2020. Accessed February 1, 2025. https://www.statista.com/statistics/1041718/germany-all-time-child-mortality-rate/.
102. European Child Safety Alliance. Child safety country profile 2012: Germany. Published June 2012. Accessed October 6, 2016. http://www.childsafetyeurope.org/reportcards/info/germany-country-profile.pdf.
103. EU-Patienten De. Treatment in Germany: planned treatment: after treatment: bills: questions about bills issued by healthcare providers. Updated June 24, 2016. Accessed October 6, 2016. http://www.eu-patienten.de/en/behandlung_deutschland/nach_der_behandlung/rechnungen/fragen_zu_rechnungen.jsp.
104. Lungen M, Stollenwerk B, Messner P, et al. Waiting times for elective treatments according to insurance status: a randomized empirical study in Germany. *Intl J Equity Health*. 2008;7:1.
105. Sawicki PT. Quality of health care in Germany: a six-country comparison. *Medizinische Klinik*. 2005;100(11):755-768.
106. Esmail N. *Health Care Lessons from Germany*. Lessons from Abroad: A Series on Healthcare Reform. Fraser Institute. Published May 2014. Accessed October 6, 2016. https://www.fraserinstitute.org/sites/default/files/health-care-lessons-from-germany.pdf.
107. World Health Organization. WHO vaccine-preventable diseases: monitoring system. 2016 global summary. Updated July 15, 2016. Accessed October 6, 2016. http://apps.who.int/immunization_monitoring/globalsummary/countries?countrycriteria%5Bcountry%5D%5B%5D=DEU.

108. Takla A, Wichmann O, Rieck T, Matysiak-Klose D. Measles incidence and reporting trends in Germany, 2007–2011. *Bull World Health Org*. 2014;92(10):697-772.
109. Hueppe K, Ortman J, Gauselmann H, Santibanez S, Mankertz A. Measles vaccination - An underestimated prevention measure: Analyzing a fatal case in Hildesheim, Germany. *Int J Med Microbiol*. 2024;314:151608. doi:10.1016/j.ijmm.2024.151608. Accessed February 1, 2025. https://www.sciencedirect.com/science/article/pii/S1438422124000122.
110. Shaheen H, König HH, Hajek A. Religious affiliation and flu vaccination in Germany: results of the German Ageing Survey. *Healthcare (Basel, Switzerland)*. 2022;10(10):2108. Accessed February 1, 2025. https://pmc.ncbi.nlm.nih.gov/articles/PMC9602020/.
111. Gemeinsamer Bundesausschuss. Special topics: quality assurance: quality assurance and quality improvement across healthcare settings. Accessed October 6, 2016. http://www.english.g-ba.de/special-topics/quality/.
112. Schneider N, Dierks LM, Seidel G, Schwartz FW. The federal government commissioner for patient issues in Germany: initial analysis of the user inquiries. *BMC Health Serv Res*. 2007;7:24.
113. Palmer E. Germany: patients' rights. *Global Legal Monitor*. Library of Congress. Published April 23, 2013. Accessed October 6, 2016. http://www.loc.gov/law/foreign-news/article/germany-patients-rights/.
114. Bundesamt für Migration und Flüchtlinge. Asyl und Flüchtlingsschutz. Ablauf des Asylverfahrens. Zuständige Aufnahmeeinrichtung. Published August 1, 2016. Accessed October 6, 2016. http://www.bamf.de/DE/Fluechtlingsschutz/AblaufAsylv/MeldungAE/meldung-aufnahmeeinrichtung-node.html.
115. Statistisches Bundesamt. Press release 285. Less people without health insurance. Published August 20, 2012. Accessed October 6, 2016. https://www.destatis.de/EN/PressServices/Press/pr/2012/08/PE12_285_122.html.
116. Stötzler M, Kaifie A. Healthcare for individuals without health insurance in Germany – a mixed methods approach to assess the situation and current challenges. *Int J Equity Health*. 2023 Jun 19;22(1):117. doi: 10.1186/s12939-023-01930-6.
117. Greß S, Walendzik A, Wasem J. *Persons Without Health Insurance in Germany: Who Are They and What Can Be Done*. Presentation at the Annual Meeting of the European Public Health Association (EUPHA), November 16–18, 2006; Montreux, Switzerland.
118. Hurst JW. Reform of health care in Germany. *Health Care Financ Rev*. 1991;12(3):73-86.
119. Frankfurter Allgemeine Zeitung. Politik. 25 Jahre Wiedervereinigung: Noch immer groβe Unterschiede zwischen Ost und West. Published July 22, 2015. Accessed October 6. 2016. http://www.faz.net/aktuell/politik/inland/ost-west-unterschiede-nach-wiedervereinigung-deutschlands-13715180.html.
120. Milstein R, Blankhart CR. The health care strengthening act: the next level of integrated care in Germany. *Health Pol*. 2016;120:445-451.
121. Milstein R, Blankart CR. Special care in Germany. Country background note: Germany. Office of Economic Collaboration and Development. Published February 2016. Accessed October 12, 2016. http://www. oecd.org/els/health-systems/Better-Ways-to-Pay-for-Health-Care-Background-Note-Germany.pdf.
122. Amelung V, Hildebrandt H, Wolf S. Integrated care in Germany: a stony but necessary road. *Intl J Integ Care*. 2012;12(27):1-8.
123. Statistisched Bundesamt. Press release 153. New projection of Germany's population by 2060. Published April 28, 2015. Accessed October 6, 2016. https://www.destatis.de/EN/PressServices/Press/pr/2015/04/PE15_153_12421.html.
124. Deutscher Bundestag. Schlussbericht der Enquête-Kommission Demographischer Wandel—Herausforderungen unserer älter werdenden Gesellschaft an den Einzelnen und die Politik (Drucksache 14/8800). Berlin, Germany: Deutscher Bundestag; March 28, 2002. Drucksache 14/8800.
125. British Broadcasting Corporation. Migrant crisis: migration to Europe explained in seven charts. Published March 4, 2016. Accessed October 12, 2016. http://www.bbc.com/news/world-europe-34131911.
126. Hunter P. Science and society: the refugee crisis challenges nations' health care systems. *EMBO reports*. 2016;17(4): 492-495.
127. World Health Organization, Regional Office for Europe. Migration and health: key issues. Accessed October 12, 2016. http://www.euro.who.int/en/health-topics/health-determinants/migration-and-health/migrant-health-in-the-european-region/migration-and-health-key-issues.
128. Fachinger T, Hoffmeyer-Zlotnik P, Stiller M. Country report: health care. Asylum Information Database. European Council of Refugees and Exiles. Updated October 7, 2024. Accessed February 2, 2025. https://asylumineurope.org/reports/country/germany/reception-conditions/health-care/.
129. Göpffart D, Bauhoff S. The public health dimension of Germany's refugee crisis. *Health Aff Blog*. Published October 22, 2015. Accessed October 12, 2016. http://healthaffairs.org/blog/2015/10/22/the-public-health-dimension-of-germanys-refugee-crisis/#one.
130. Deutsche Welle. Merkel presents new integration law as "mile stone." Published May 25, 2016. Accessed October 12, 2016. http://www.dw.com/en/merkel-presents-new-refugee-integration-law-as-milestone/a-19281722.
131. The White House. Office of the Press Secretary. Fact sheet on the Leaders' Summit on Refugees. Published September 20, 2016. Accessed October 12, 2016. https://www.whitehouse.gov/the-press-office/2016/09/20/fact-sheet-leaders-summit-refugees.
132. Müller O, Lu G, Jahn A, Razum O. COVID-19 control: can Germany learn from China? *Intl J Health Pol Manag*. 2020;9(10):432-435. doi: 10.34172/ijhpm.2020.78.
133. Lu G, Razum O, Jahn A, et al. COVID-19 in Germany and China: mitigation versus elimination strategy. *Glob Health Act*. 2021;14:1. doi: 10.1080/16549716.2021.1875601.
134. World Health Organization. Number of COVID-19 cases reported to WHO. Published 2024. Accessed May 13, 2023. https://covid19.who.int/region/euro/country/de.
135. World Health Organization. WHO COVID-19 dashboard. https://covid19.who.int/table. Accessed May 13, 2023.
136. Johns Hopkins University of Medicine. Mortality analyses. Published 2023. Accessed May 13, 2023. https://coronavirus.jhu.edu/data/mortality.
137. Disney H, Horn K, Hrobon P, et al. *Impatient for Change: European Attitudes to Healthcare Reform*. London, UK: Stockholm Network; 2004.
138. Gesellschaft für Versicherungswissenschaft und—gestaltung e.V. Gesundheitsziele.de. W17(4): assind Gesundheitsziele? Accessed October 6, 2016. http://gesundheitsziele.de/.

CHAPTER 14

Norway

Dan J. Vick, Joseph Adam Johnson, and Diluma M. Kariyawasam

Country Description

Table 14-1 Norway

Nationality	Noun: Norwegian(s) Adjective: Norwegian
Ethnic groups	Norwegian 81.5% (includes about 60,000 Sami), other European 8.9%, other 9.6%
Religions	Church of Norway (Evangelical Lutheran) 67.5%, Muslim 3.1%, Roman Catholic 3.1%, other Christian 3.8%, other 2.6%, unspecified 19.9% (2021 est.)
Language	Bokmal Norwegian (official), Nynorsk Norwegian (official), small Sami- and Finnish-speaking minorities. Note: Sami has three dialects: Lule, North Sami, and South Sami; Sami is an official language in nine municipalities in Norway's three northernmost counties: Finnmark, Nordland, and Troms.
Literacy	Total population: NA Male: NA Female: NA
Government type	Parliamentary constitutional monarchy
Date of independence	June 7, 1905 (union with Sweden declared dissolved); October 26, 1905 (Sweden agreed to the repeal of the union); notable earlier dates: ca. 872 (traditional unification of minor Norwegian kingdoms by Harald Fairhair); 1397 (Kalmar Union of Denmark, Norway, and Sweden); 1524 (Denmark–Norway); May 17, 1814 (Norwegian constitution adopted); November 4, 1814 (Sweden–Norway union confirmed)
Gross domestic product (GDP) per capita	67,500 USD (2022 est.)
Unemployment rate	4.99% (2021 est.)
Natural hazards	Rockslides, avalanches Volcanism: Beerenberg (2,227 m) on Jan Mayen Island in the Norwegian Sea is the country's only active volcano

Table 14-1 Norway

Environment: current issues	Water pollution; acid rain damaging forests and adversely affecting lakes, threatening fish stocks; air pollution from vehicle emissions
Population	5,597,924 (2023 est.)
Age structure	0–14 years: 17.83% (male 510,835/female 487,126) 15–64 years: 64% (male 1,842,794/female 1,739,688) 65 years and over: 18.18% (2023 est.) (male 474,878/female 542,603)
Median age	Total: 40.6 years Male: 39.9 years Female: 41.4 years (2023 est.)
Population growth rate	0.6% (2023 est.)
Birth rate	10.4 births/1,000 population (2023 est.)
Death rate	8.2 deaths/1,000 population (2023 est.)
Net migration rate	3.8 migrant(s)/1,000 population (2023 est.)
Gender ratio	At birth: 1.05 male/female 0–14 years: 1.05 male/female 15–64 years: 1.06 male/female 65 years and over: 0.88 male/female Total population: 1.02 male/female (2023 est.)
Infant mortality rate	Total: 1.8 deaths/1,000 live births Male: 2.1 deaths/1,000 live births Female: 1.5 deaths/1,000 live births (2023 est.)
Life expectancy at birth	Total population: 83 years Male: 81.4 years Female: 84.7 years (2023 est.)
Total fertility rate	1.57 children born/woman (2023 est.)

USD = U.S. dollars

Modified from Central Intelligence Agency. The World Factbook, 2023. Accessed March 21, 2024. https://www.cia.gov/the-world-factbook/countries/norway/.

History

The history of Norway dates back to prehistoric times, when the country was inhabited by various indigenous peoples. They included the Sami people, who have lived in the northern Sapmi region of Scandinavia for thousands of years and remain there to this day. These early inhabitants engaged in hunting, fishing, and gathering.

The Viking Age, which lasted from the 8th to the 11th centuries, played a significant role in shaping Norway's early history. Norwegian Vikings were renowned seafarers, explorers, and traders who established settlements across Europe. Norway's unification began in the 9th century under Harold Fairhair, who became the first king of a centralized Norwegian kingdom. Over the next several centuries, Norwegians slowly embraced Christianity, bringing the Viking Age to a close.

Significant political developments and alliances occurred during the medieval period when Norway, Sweden, and Denmark entered into the Kalmar Union, a political union that lasted until the 16th century. Norway's political power and standing diminished to a level of unimportance and Norway fell under Danish rule. Norway was proclaimed a Danish province and would remain so for the next several centuries. The Kalmar Union ended with Swedish independence in 1523, although Norway remained under the Danish crown[1] (**Table 14-1**).

In early 1814, Denmark ceded Norway to Sweden. Norway did not agree with this decision and on May 17, 1814, Norway declared independence and adopted a liberal constitution, which established limited self-rule. To avoid war, Norway entered into a limited union with Sweden that lasted until November 25, 1905, when Norway became an independent nation with the ascension of King Haakon VII.[2]

Following independence and with World War I on the horizon, Norway established a policy of neutrality. Norway had no difficulty remaining neutral militarily but was challenged because of trade agreements; both Britain and Germany were trading partners with Norway. Norway was dependent on British fuel and the economic partnerships during the war seemed to favor the Triple Entente over the Central Powers. The economic power that Britain held led Norway into a neutral alliance with Britain.[3]

Relations with Germany further deteriorated during World War II with the 5-year Nazi occupation of Norway. The occupation was met with constant resistance—including acts such as the destruction of railways, trading posts, and ships; the smuggling of people and goods; and the circulation of underground newspapers. A defining moment came when Norwegian resistance prevented Germany from obtaining heavy water from the Vemork water plant. Following Germany's defeat in 1945, Norway was liberated.[4,5]

After the war, Norway focused on rebuilding the country and its economy. The government implemented social democratic policies, establishing a welfare state, expanding public services, and nationalizing key industries. Norway also became a founding member of the United Nations (UN) in 1945 and joined NATO in 1949.

By the 1960s, oil reserves had been found in the North Sea, leading to an economic boom for the country. Revenue from oil exports played a significant role in Norway's economic growth and development. By the 1990s, Norway had become Europe's largest oil producer. Although Norway still relies on oil revenue, today the country is a global leader in renewable energy production, particularly hydroelectricity, and has made efforts to reduce greenhouse gas emissions. Norway is also known for its commitment to preserving its natural landscapes and supporting international initiatives like the Paris Agreement on climate change. Furthermore, Norway has been actively involved in peacekeeping efforts and diplomacy worldwide. It has played a key role in mediating conflicts, such as the Oslo Accords in the 1990s, which aimed to resolve the Israeli–Palestinian conflict.[1]

Norway has been committed to promoting human rights, sustainable development, and environmental protection. It consistently ranks highly in various global indicators, including human development, happiness, and quality of life. The country has a strong focus on environmental sustainability, renewable energy, and conservation. It has also embraced progressive social policies, such as gender equality and LGBTQ rights.

Size and Geography

Norway, officially known as the Kingdom of Norway, is a country located in Northern Europe on the Scandinavian Peninsula. It is bordered by the North Atlantic Ocean, the North Sea, and the Norwegian Sea, while sharing land borders with Sweden, Finland, and Russia (see **Figure 14-1**). The total area of Norway is 323,802 square kilometers, or 125,020 square miles (land: 304,282 sq, km, or 117,484 sq. miles, and water: 19,520 sq, km, or 7,536 sq. miles). The land mass of Norway is slightly larger than the state of New Mexico.

Norway is organized into 11 administrative divisions, or counties: Agder, Innlandet, Møre og Romsdal, Nordland, Oslo, Rogaland, Troms og Finnmark, Trøndelag, Vestfold og Telemark, Vestland, and Viken. Additionally, there are three dependent areas: Bouvet Island, Jan Mayen, and Svalbard.[6]

Government and Political System

Norway has a parliamentary constitutional monarchy. Power is divided between the legislative branch (Parliament or Storting), the executive branch or government, and the judicial branch. The current head of state is King Harald V. The capital city is Oslo. Norway's constitution was drafted in the spring of 1814 and adopted on May 16, 1814. It was signed by the Constituent Assembly on May 17, 1814. Amendments to the constitution begin as proposals that are submitted by members of Parliament or the government during the first 3 years of each 4-year parliamentary term. Passage occurs by a two-thirds majority vote during the next elected Parliament, in which there must be a two-thirds quorum. The constitution has been amended over 400 times since its adoption, the last time being in 2015.

The head of government is the prime minister. The leader of the majority party or coalition following parliamentary elections is appointed prime minister by the monarch with Parliament's approval. The Council of State is the cabinet and is appointed by the monarch, with parliamentary approval also required. The Parliament is Norway's sole legislative body. Its members are elected by proportional representation vote in multiseat constituencies. Members serve terms of 4 years and represent a number of political parties.

The judicial branch includes a Supreme Court consisting of a chief justice and 18 associate justices. Justices are appointed by the monarch based on recommendations by a Judicial Appointments Board. There are a number of subordinate courts, including

Figure 14-1 Map of Norway

Courts of Appeal, regional and district courts, Conciliation Boards, and ordinary and special courts.[7]

Local government consisted of 356 municipalities and 11 county authorities, as of 2021. Representatives are elected to both levels by their constituents. Municipalities and county authorities have the same administrative status. Their functions are overseen by Norway's central government and they are supervised by a county governor. County authorities have responsibility for regional planning and development; museums, libraries, and sports venues; county roads and public transport; environmental issues; cultural heritage; and upper secondary schools. Municipalities oversee nurseries, kindergartens, and primary and secondary schools; business development and culture; water supply, sanitation, and sewer; primary health care; social services and care for the disabled and the elderly; local roads and harbors; local planning; and agricultural and environmental issues.[8]

Macroeconomics

Norway chose not to join the European Union (EU). However, it is a member of the European Economic Area (EEA) and partially participates in the EU's single market. The country has a stable economy and abundant natural resources, including forests, fish, oil and gas, and minerals. It is the world's leading producer and second largest exporter of seafood. Norway is also a world leader in petroleum exports. The petroleum industry is responsible for 37% of the country's exports, 12% of the gross domestic product (GDP), 13% of the state's revenue, and 9% of jobs. Gas production has increased more than twofold since 2000 and oil production has been on the rise since that time as well. State revenue from the petroleum industry is placed in a sovereign wealth fund (the world's largest), which was valued at over $1 trillion USD in 2017. The federal budget is balanced each year by following a fiscal rule, which requires spending of petroleum and fund investment revenues to correspond to the fund's expected real rate of return.[9]

Norway's GDP showed solid growth from 2004 to 2007, followed by an economic slowdown in 2008 and contraction in 2009. Positive growth was seen from 2010 to 2017. The GDP is $485.5 billion USD, and GDP real growth rate is 0.5%.[10] The services sector makes up 50.1% of the GDP, industry accounts for 38.98%, and agriculture is responsible for the remaining 2.1%. The inflation rate is 2.4%. The labor force is 2.96 million people. Some 50.1% are employed in service occupations, with 19.34% in industrial jobs and 2.2% in agriculture. The unemployment rate is 4.2%.[11]

Demographics

Norway has a population of 5.6 million, of whom 49.5% are female and 50.5% are male (2023 est.). Approximately 84% of the total population live in urban areas. The two official languages of Norway are Norwegian and Sami; however, English is widely understood and spoken. Norwegian has two main dialects: Bokmal and Nynorsk. More than 82% of citizens belong to the Church of Norway (Evangelical Lutheran), while 3.9% are Pentecostals, Lutheran Free Church members, Jehovah's Witnesses, Methodists, or Baptists. Roman Catholics are 1.8% of the population, and Muslims make up 2.3%.[12]

The birth rate declined slightly in the 1990s, but the death rate also slowed as life expectancy increased. This resulted in a steady growth in the population at the end of the 20th century. A significant increase was seen in the proportion of the population aged 80 or older. As of 2020, 23.2% of the population was under the age of 19, 33.3% were 20 to 44 years old, 28% were 45 to 66 years old, 11.1% were 67 to 79 years old, and 4.4% were 80 years old or older.[10]

Brief History of the Healthcare System

Pre–World War II

The earliest healthcare institution in Norway was an infirmary founded at an Augustina monastery in Halsnoy around 1164. However, the Norwegian healthcare system had its genesis in July 1603, when a physician named Villads Nielsen was awarded a royal patent with a lifetime income to provide medical services in the town of Bergen. One hundred years later, a physician was appointed as *Provincial-medicus* in Kristiansand. Military hospitals and some local hospitals were established by the late 1700s. In 1812, a medical faculty was organized in Norway, followed by a school for midwifery in 1818 and a national teaching and research hospital around the same time. Leprosy and tuberculosis were very prevalent diseases in the 1800s and were responsible for the establishment of additional healthcare facilities.[13]

The Health Act of 1860 provided direction for the healthcare delivery model. This act established public health boards, which were chaired by a district medical officer (DMO) and composed of community members. The DMOs had vast responsibilities that were increased in the 1930s to include preventive medicine and hygiene. Additional legislation in 1912 expanded the state medical service by increasing the number of primary medical officers and establishing a role for county medical officers to serve as a link between the DMOs and the central government.[13]

Rapid hospital expansion occurred into the early 20th century and was influenced by local government. By the 1930s, private-sector ownership accounted for 21% of beds and local government owned 70% of beds. However, there was a growing disparity in terms of bed availability between urban and rural areas, which was heavily influenced by population and surplus wealth in the urban centers. This, in part, led to creation of state health policy in the 1930s, which included a national plan for hospital development.[13]

Post–World War II

Norway developed as a welfare state after World War II, with public health and the concept of state-financed health care for all being an integral component. Many of Norway's social welfare reforms derived from those occurring in Britain: Norwegian politicians had been exposed to, and influenced by, these ideologies while exiled in Britain during the war. Dr. Karl Evang, a Norwegian surgeon, was a strong proponent of this movement. His leadership as Norway's director of the Norwegian Directorate of Health (DOH) from 1938 to 1972 heavily influenced the development of Norway's healthcare system during the postwar period. Expansion of the public health service during the next 25 years included such components as school medical and dental services, universal sickness and social security benefits, and mental health and psychiatric care, among others. Both the private and public health sectors grew rapidly. Health care's share of the gross national product rose from 3.5% to 8% between 1950 and 1976, and the number of physicians and nurses doubled over the same period.[13,14]

The focus of healthcare reform during the 1970s was on equality and increased geographic access to healthcare services. As a result of rising healthcare costs, along with political and ideological changes occurring in Norway in the 1970s, the government passed legislation to regionalize the healthcare system. Act 66 in 1982 resulted in the transfer of most public healthcare services from the central government to the municipalities. Much of the focus of the healthcare system in the 1980s was on achieving cost containment and decentralization.[13,14]

Several challenges were present in the Norwegian healthcare system in the 1990s, the most significant being cost inefficiencies, long hospital wait lists, and access to health care in rural areas. Activity-based financing was implemented in 1997 and a diagnosis-related group (DRG) system was introduced in 1999 to address some of these issues. At the same time, healthcare costs continued to rise; between 1995 and 1999, healthcare budgets grew at twice the rate as the rest of the public sector. The importance of quality of care was affirmed by the passage of the Specialist Care Act in 1999. It mandated that patient safety and healthcare quality be a responsibility of all specialist care hospitals.

The 2000s were marked by structural changes in the organization and delivery of health care. The most significant was the 2002 hospital reform, which resulted in the transfer of ownership to the central state and management of hospitals shifting from counties to five newly established Regional Health Authorities (RHAs), two of which merged in 2007.[14] This change was a response to the rising costs of health care, the realization that counties were really not well suited for designing and governing hospitals, and the quest to achieve more equal distribution of healthcare resources. Provision of specialized services in a few large hospitals allowed for cost-savings through economies of scale and increased quality of care due to a higher volume of patients with complex conditions who are seen by specialists.

The 2010s led to more focus on coordination between healthcare providers and continued emphasis on patient safety and quality of care. The Municipal Health and Care Act (2011) was similar to the Specialist Care Act of 1999 but highlighted the role and responsibility of primary care in regard to patient safety and quality. In 2014, a quality-based financing (QBF) system was introduced to incentivize hospitals to improve in both of these areas.[13]

The Current Healthcare System

Norway has a semi-decentralized healthcare system that is overseen by the Ministry of Health and Care Services. Parliament is the national political decision-making body, which provides direction to the Ministry through legislation. The Ministry, in turn, sets national health policy and allocates healthcare funding. There are three levels of organization within the health system structure. The Ministry owns the four RHAs: Central Norway RHA, Northern Norway RHA, Southeastern Norway RHA, and Western Norway RHA. The RHAs control the hospital trusts and are responsible for specialty care.

Municipalities are responsible for primary care, organizing health services, nursing homes, care of individuals with developmental disabilities, and environmental health. Counties provide dental care and have some responsibilities for general public health. Mental health care and public health span various organizational levels. A further example of Norway's simultaneous centralization and decentralization is that, although the hospitals are owned by the RHAs (centralization), the day-to-day management of these facilities is the responsibility of a local general manager and executive board (decentralization). Regulation of the health system occurs through a number of acts and other legislation.[14]

The Norwegian healthcare system operates under a guiding principle of equal access for all inhabitants, regardless of socioeconomic status, age, gender, or location. In line with this, Norway has universal health coverage. Funding for the system is raised through taxes and payroll contributions. Every resident participates in the National Insurance Scheme (NIS), which is the primary third-party payer. Approximately 8.2% of income tax paid by resident employees is allocated to the NIS. Around 85% of total health expenditures are derived from public funds from the central and local governments. The NIS covers primary care, hospital care, mental health services, and ambulatory care. Certain outpatient prescription drugs are also covered. The other third-party payers are the private, for-profit providers of voluntary health insurance (VHI). Private financing accounts for 15% of health expenditures; most of this comes from out-of-pocket payments by inhabitants for general practitioner (GP) copayments, dental care, and pharmaceuticals. Approximately 10% of residents of Norway have private health insurance; 90% of these policies are employer-paid. The annual personal limit on expenditures is approximately NOK 2,460. Upon reaching this limit, individuals receive an exemption card entitling them to free health care for the remainder of the year.[15–17]

Healthcare financing is regulated by the National Insurance Act of 1997. This act also provides for entitlement to nonmedical benefits required due to illness, childbirth, disability, occupational injury, or rehabilitation. The healthcare budget is administered by the DOH.[14]

Facilities

There are approximately 16,000 healthcare facilities in Norway.[18] The four RHAs have responsibility for hospital care in Norway. There are 28 health trusts; of these, 20 are public hospital trusts, which are governed as publicly owned corporations and provide most of the acute care hospital services. Each RHA has at least one university hospital. The public hospital trusts had 11,000 beds in 2017 and covered 94% of all hospital stays. There are also nonprofit private hospitals, which have agreements with the RHAs and were responsible for 5% of hospital stays in 2017. A smaller number of for-profit hospitals accounted for 6.5% of daytime stays, primarily for outpatient surgeries. These hospitals do not provide acute care services.[17] The number of hospital beds in Norway had been steadily declining from 520 acute care beds per 100,000 people in 2004 until just prior to the COVID-19 pandemic, when there were 310 acute care beds per 100,000 people and 5.5 intensive care unit (ICU) beds per 100,0000 people, both of which were lower than the EU averages. However, the occupancy rate of acute care beds was among the highest in Europe, at 80%.[15,19] As of 2022, there were 18,272 hospital beds in Norway, a decrease from 18,387 the previous year.[20] Public funding covers 85% of hospital care. Except for emergencies, patients require a referral from a GP for acute care services.[17]

Most recipients of long-term care receive home care, 10% live in sheltered or assisted living facilities, and 20% reside in a facility with 24-hour staffing.[17] In 2021, there were 864 nursing and care institutions that were municipal-owned, offering 35,800 beds; 41 private nonprofit facilities, offering of 2,611 beds; and 17 private forprofit centers, with 763 beds.[21,22] However, home-based care is encouraged.

Other facilities consist of GP practices and specialty offices. Some multidisciplinary clinics have been established in the last few years. After-hours care is often provided through municipal contracts with GPs. Some cities also have walk-in centers staffed with physicians and nurses. Larger cities have a few private after-hours clinics as well.[17]

Workforce

In 2020, 452,000 healthcare workers were employed in Norway, which was an increase from 398,000 in 2015. Norway has higher numbers of both doctors and nurses than many countries in Europe, and most countries in the EU. There were approximately 2.9 physicians and 18.2 nurses and midwives per 1,000 people in 2018. However, there is a shortage of healthcare workers in rural areas.[18] The workforce attrition rate in general is high for nurses, particularly those employed in long-term care facilities.

The health system relies heavily on foreign-trained doctors and nurses; approximately 41% of doctors and 6% of nurses in the country receive their medical education outside of the country. Over half of these foreign-trained doctors are Norwegian citizens, and many of them study in Poland, Slovakia, and Hungary.[15]

Most GPs are self-employed; a typical practice has between one and six physicians. Municipalities contract with them to provide care. Although patients can choose their healthcare providers, the GPs act as gatekeepers to both specialists and hospital care. There are 2.8 specialists working in hospitals or outpatient practices for every primary care physician.[15,17]

Technology and Equipment

In 1998, the Norwegian Health Technology Assessment (HTA) Center, or SMM, was established by the Norwegian Ministry of Health and Social Affairs as a scientifically and professionally independent organization with a number of objectives, including the following: Identify needs for assessment and perform those assessments, including documentation of effects and cost-effectiveness; establish national expert groups; participate in the implementation and follow-up of the assessment results; and report to the relevant authorities the results of assessments. The SMM developed HTA reports as systematic reviews, overviews of international HTAs, and early warning reports. Among the many reports generated were a series on patient outcomes and treatment volumes, as well as a report highlighting the possible need for positron emission tomography (PET) as a diagnostic procedure in Norway. In its first 6 years, the SMM generated 31 reports that had a significant impact on the use of medical technologies in Norway.[23] In 2004, the SMM was reorganized and merged with two similar organizations to become the Norwegian Knowledge Centre for the Health Services (NOKC). The NOKC supports health service quality development by contributing to quality improvement, summarizing and promoting research results, and improving patient safety.[24] It also serves as the Secretariat for the Norwegian National Council for Priority Setting in Health Care. The Council's objectives include setting priorities for the allocation of healthcare resources and advising on the introduction of new health technologies.[23]

Every person in the healthcare system has an electronic medical record and a unique personal identification number. The eHealth Directorate oversees the national strategy for health information technology. The National Health Network provides electronic exchange of patient information as well as secure telecommunication for healthcare providers, including GPs, specialists, dentists, hospitals, and other facilities. Prescriptions are transmitted electronically and hospital discharge paperwork is sent to patients' GPs electronically. Laboratory and radiology orders and results are transmitted electronically between healthcare providers. Healthcare professionals can access patients' core medical records via a secure website. Patients also have online access to their core medical records and may request access to their complete medical records.[17]

The Norwegian Hospital Construction Agency oversees hospital planning and construction. This agency is under the control of the four RHAs. There is an emphasis on making health care more sustainable. Thus, green hospitals are currently being constructed according to standards to decrease energy use and heating costs, and to account for emissions. According to the Nasjonal Helse-og Sykehusplan 2020–2023, €9.3 billion ($10.2 billion USD or NOK 108.3 billion) will need to be invested for upgrading and updating current hospital buildings throughout the country. During this cycle, new hospitals were planned for Drammen and Stavanger, with a new children's hospital in Bergen.[18]

Evaluation of the Healthcare System

Cost

Healthcare expenditure accounted for 10.1% of Norway's gross domestic product (GDP) in 2021, a decrease from the all-time high of 11.4% in 2020. This amounted to $43 billion USD (NOK 456.6 billion) in total, for a per capita health care expenditure of $9,020 USD (NOK 95,787).[25,26] The country's high GDP per capita means that health expenditures per capita are higher than in most other European countries; indeed, they were the highest in Europe in 2019. This reflected a health expenditure growth rate of about 2.5% per year between 2015 and 2019.[15]

Norway spent approximately the same amounts (30%) on inpatient care, outpatient care, and long-term care in 2019. This proportion spent on long-term care was higher than in any EU country. By comparison, expenditures for medical devices and retail pharmaceuticals in 2019 accounted for slightly more than 10% of total healthcare spending, which was the lowest proportion among EU countries. Public spending, at 85%, accounts for the highest percentage of total healthcare expenditures of any EU country and has grown more rapidly than the GDP since 2000. The share of private spending decreased during that same time.[15]

The top five aggregate causes resulting in healthcare spending in Norway in 2019 were mental health and substance use disorders (20.7%), neurologic conditions (15.4%), cardiovascular diseases (10.1%), diabetes, kidney diseases, and urinary diseases (9.0%), and neoplasms (7.2%). Spending for these conditions increased with age. Dementias claimed the highest healthcare spending among individual conditions, accounting for 10.2% of total spending. Falls were second, at 4.6% of the total. Among individuals aged 15 to 49 years, mental health and substance use disorders accounted for 46.0% of total spending.[27]

The medical device market is expected to grow at 4.4% from 2021 to 2026, resulting in expenditures of $2.3 billion USD (NOK 19.2 billion). The country has one of the highest rates of spending for medical devices per capita, with a majority of these being imported from other countries, primarily the United States. The market for pharmaceuticals was projected to grow from $4.0 billion USD (NOK 34.6 billion) in 2021 to $4.2 billion USD (NOK 37.4 billion) in 2022. The market for generic drugs has grown in recent years and accounts for 49% of the market. A restrictive policy in setting prices and reimbursement, with a steep price scheme for generic drugs, has helped temper price increases.[25]

Quality

The Norwegian population is generally healthy, with a life expectancy that has steadily risen in the last 20 years to 83.3 years in 2020. This is the highest life expectancy in Europe and one of the highest in the world. The average lifespan for a woman is 84.9 years, compared with 81.6 years for men. Most of the improvement in life expectancy is a result of reductions in death rates from cardiovascular diseases; ischemic heart disease mortality declined by 73% from 1990 to 2015.[14] However, cardiovascular diseases are still the leading cause of death in Norway, followed by Alzheimer's disease and cancer. Ischemic heart disease, stroke, Alzheimer's disease, chronic obstructive pulmonary disease (COPD), and lung cancer are the most common causes of premature deaths.[18]

Norway's avoidable hospital admission rates for asthma and COPD were higher in 2019 than in most EU countries. Avoidable admission rates for heart failure and diabetes were among the lowest of these countries.[28] Mortality outcomes from acute myocardial infarction and stroke, both in hospital and within 30 days of hospitalization, are among the best in Europe. Much of the improvement in stroke survival is a result of quality initiatives that included more rapid access to care, along with development of a patient care pathway and increased public awareness regarding the early signs and symptoms of stroke.[14]

Pulmonary malignancies account for most cancer deaths, followed by colorectal cancer. The five-year survival rates for treatable cancers are higher than in most EU countries. This is a result of implementation of effective screening programs leading to more timely diagnosis, as well as improved treatment protocols and access. In an effort to improve care coordination, cancer patient pathways were introduced in 2015 for 28 different cancers.[14]

In 2019, approximately 75% of Norwegians reported being in good health, a percentage higher than that in most EU countries. Around 37% of inhabitants reported having at least one chronic condition. Income inequality was noted in this study, with 43% of persons in the lowest-income group self-reporting chronic conditions compared with 30% in the highest-income group.[15]

Behavioral risk factors are responsible for approximately one-third of deaths. The major risk factors are dietary and tobacco use. However, both are responsible for a smaller percentage of deaths than in the EU overall. Alcohol is also less of a contributing risk factor than in the rest of the EU. Obesity rates among Norwegian adults are below the EU average, reflecting a higher level of physical activity. However, the number of 15-year olds who are overweight or obese increased from 13% in 2013–2014 to 18% (close to the EU average for this age group) in 2018. In 2024, between 15% and 21% of adolescents aged 8–15 were considered to be overweight or obese.[29] Lower physical activity levels and fruit consumption rates, compared with EU averages, are thought to be contributory factors. Tobacco smoking has decreased in Norway, possibly related to robust tobacco control policies. However, the use of oral smokeless tobacco products has increased during the past 20 years, particularly among young people.[15]

Access

Norway's health system provides universal coverage to legal residents, offering a high level of social protection for the country's inhabitants. This same coverage is provided to the European Economic

Area (EEA) residents and Australians. Although coverage for inpatient and outpatient services is more extensive than the average coverage in the EU, pharmaceuticals and dental coverage is less than the average for the EU countries. As previously noted, public sources account for 85% of healthcare expenditures. Caps on out-of-pocket payments for copayments, pharmaceuticals, and dental care, in addition to some exemptions, afford protection from the financial pressures of health care. All of this is in line with the premise that access to health care is a basic social right in Norway.[14,15]

Surveys in 2021 showed a very small unmet need (1.1% of the population) for medical examinations in Norway, with most of this unmet need due to waiting time for appointments. This is much less than in most European countries. When segmented by income quintile, there is a gap between the lowest-income and highest-income households, with 2.4% of the lowest-income quintile individuals reporting delays in access to health care. Waiting times for elective care and procedures are long and pose a barrier to care access. Unmet needs for dental care are higher, averaging 5% in 2021. Among the poorest residents, 12% reported unmet dental needs compared with 1% of the richest residents.[30]

Although Norway has a higher ratio of doctors and nurses to inhabitants than most OECD countries, a disparity in the distribution of healthcare personnel has resulted in some geographic inequity. As a result, access to healthcare services is a challenge in rural and remote parts of the country. A 2019 study forecast an increase in demand for workers in the health and long-term care industry. Earlier studies had already predicted a shortage of doctors and nurses by 2035. Nursing homes and home care may be more strongly affected, as only a small percentage of new nurses choose to work in these settings. All of this, along with projected rising costs, will further challenge the Norwegian healthcare system and its financing.[14]

COVID-19 Pandemic

Norway's preparation for, and response to, the COVID-19 pandemic is described in James Johnson and Naomi Deshore's recent book *COVID-19 Global Pandemic: The World Responds*[31] and summarized here.

Norway has an established system of national preparedness based on legislation, including the 1950 Emergency Preparedness Act, the 1994 Act Relating to the Control of Communicable Diseases, and the 2000 Emergency Health Preparedness Act. The 1994 Act was amended several times during 2020. Planning, coordination, and response during a health emergency is guided by the National Health Preparedness Plan, the National Preparedness Plan for Outbreaks of Communicable Diseases, and the National Preparedness Plan for Pandemic Influenza.

In January 2020, the Ministry of Health formally delegated responsibility for coordinating the health system's response to COVID-19 to the DOH. The first case of COVID-19 in Norway was identified on February 26, 2020, involving a patient who had recently visited China.[32] The prime minister established a COVID Commission on March 11, 2020. Its purpose was to hold weekly discussions and facilitate rapid decision making and response to this health crisis. The first COVID-19–related death occurred in Norway on March 12, 2020. That same day, the DOH made the decision to shut down the country.[33] The Ministry of Justice assumed overall governance and the MOH and DOH coordinated the response of the health system to the pandemic. Norway invoked its national preparedness acts. The DOH, under a revision to the 1994 Act, mandated:

1. That everyone arriving in Norway after traveling outside the Nordic countries undergo quarantine (isolation) for 14 days after arrival.
2. That everyone arriving in Norway after traveling outside the Nordic countries undergo quarantine (isolation) in case of symptoms such as cold, fever, and/or shortness of breath. The isolation was to last for at least 7 days after symptom relief.[34]

Symptomatic travelers were required to isolate immediately and were banned from using public transportation.[34]

All schools from nursery to postsecondary levels were initially closed, although remote education was eventually permitted for primary, middle, and high schools, as well as universities. Social distancing recommendations were 2 meters (6.6 feet) indoors and 1 meter (3.3 feet) outdoors. Private gatherings were limited to groups of five or fewer.[33] Restaurants and bars were closed with the exception of those that could serve food while maintaining social distancing of 1 meter. Hair salons and other personal service businesses were shut down, as were fitness centers, swimming pools, and water parks. Cultural events and organized sports activities were canceled. An international travel ban was imposed. Cough etiquette and frequent hand hygiene were encouraged. A 20-day work furlough was implemented on March 20, 2020.[35] Additionally, the Norwegian Parliament passed the "Temporary Act to remedy the consequences of the outbreak of Covid-19, etc." (the "Corona Act") on March 27, 2020. This law was in effect until May 27, 2020, and allowed the government to implement additional specific restrictive and mitigating measures.[36]

Face masks were not mandated until June 10, 2020, and initially only for domestic flights. Later, the government advised cities with high incidence rates to mandate their use in situations where social distancing was not possible. Oslo recommended the use of face masks on public conveyances in August 2020, followed by a mask mandate in September 2020. However, the Norwegian Institute of Public Health (NIPH) did not recommend the use of face masks for children under 12 years of age.[33]

Norway did not engage in widespread testing for COVID-19. Rather, testing was reserved for symptomatic individuals, vulnerable populations, and healthcare workers and was performed by municipalities. During the summer of 2020, the DOH evaluated a testing methodology employing self-collected saliva samples. Beginning in August 2020, municipalities were directed to make testing available to any individuals with suspected infection without requiring referral from a doctor.[35,37] Contact tracing was conducted using manual and app-based methods.[37] Regional and local authorities had responsibility for this task, with assistance from the NIPH.

The country began easing restrictions in late April 2020. Kindergartens were reopened on April 20, 2020, followed by primary schools (pupils who were 6 to 10 years of age) a week later. Personal services, such as hair and beauty salons, also were reopened, and the recommendation for social distancing was reduced to 1 meter (3.3 feet) on April 30, 2020. Additional lifting of restrictions in May 2020 included allowing people to return to work outside of the home (as long as they did not require use of public transportation), permitting public gatherings for up to 50 people and private gatherings for up to 20 persons, and reopening high schools and postsecondary education institutions (with limitations) for in-person classes. In June 2020, pubs and bars reopened, travel restrictions to other Scandinavian countries were eased, and public gatherings of up to 200 persons were allowed. By the fall of 2020, restrictive measures differed by region and municipality based on local infection rates.[35]

Norway's efforts at restricting the early spread of COVID-19 appeared successful. Yarmol-Matusiak et al.[38] conducted a study of COVID-19 infection mortality data from February to July 2020. The cumulative testing rate per 1,000 population in Norway was 76.5, with a cumulative test-positivity rate of 2.3%. Compared with Sweden, where the absolute number of excess deaths (all-cause mortality rate) was 5% higher than expected during the study period, Norway showed a decrease in cumulative mortality of 5%. The authors attributed this to the strict government mandates that were implemented prior to observing high case numbers or deaths. Amiri[39] credited the reduction in Norway's infection and mortality rates to the track-and-trace system implemented by the government.

Although COVID-19 cases were well controlled during the summer of 2020, cases began to increase by late August, heralding a second wave. The peak in case incidence occurred in early January 2021.[40] A third wave began to appear later that winter and continued into the spring. Multiple viral variants had been identified by this time, including several named as variants of concern (VOC). One of these, the Alpha variant, was dominant during the third wave and was associated with a 1.9-fold risk of hospitalization.[41]

The NIPH developed a national plan for COVID vaccination that was published in October 2020.[33] This plan, along with a report published the following month by the NIPH on ethical considerations for vaccination and subsequent vaccine guidelines, shaped the government's vaccine program. The first dose of vaccine was administered in Norway on December 27, 2020.[40] Vaccines were administered either by municipalities or hospitals. Initial priority was given to high-risk groups, the elderly, and healthcare workers. During the early rollout phase, when the vaccine was in limited supply, municipalities with high incidence rates were given priority. The vaccine rollout coincided with the third wave of COVID-19 cases. The gradual decline in these cases during the spring of 2021 likely resulted from greater vaccination coverage and increased nonpharmaceutical interventions.[40]

About the same time that the third wave was ending, the Delta variant was identified in Norway in April 2021. It became the dominant variant by early July 2021, accounting for more than 90% of new cases. This coincided with a fourth wave of infections that commenced later that month, resulting in an increased number of hospitalizations.[41]

More worrisome was the emergence of the Omicron variant in late November 2021. The number of cases caused by this variant were doubling every 2 days in nearby Denmark and spreading much faster than the Delta variant. Seventy-five percent of the Omicron cases occurred in people who had been fully vaccinated, suggesting that the vaccine offered little protection from infection.[42] Although it was believed that the vaccine would still afford protection against significant disease and death, there was concern that the large number of cases, including those requiring hospitalization, would overwhelm the healthcare system. An outbreak at a Christmas party in Oslo on November 26, 2021, resulted in 80 of 111 attendees becoming infected. All were fully vaccinated and nearly all developed symptoms, although none were severe.[43]

As a result of the outbreak, the Norwegian government reintroduced some of its restrictions across the nation to help suppress the spread of the disease. These included a ban on serving alcohol in bars and restaurants, indoor mask mandates, and restrictions on social gatherings.[42] Fortunately, the vast majority of cases related to Omicron variant were mild and hospitalization rates did not increase commensurate with new cases. By late January 2022, the government believed that the pandemic was sufficiently under control. On February 12, 2022, the prime minister announced the end of nearly all COVID-19 requirements and recommendations.[44]

As of December 6, 2022, there had been 1,469,778 confirmed cases of COVID-19 in Norway, with 4,439 deaths (case fatality ratio = 0.30%). A total of 4,346,995 people have received at least one dose of vaccine (80.18% of the population).[45]

References

1. Nikel D. A brief history of Norway. *Life in Norway*. Accessed June 25, 2023. https://www.lifeinnorway.net/history-of-norway/.
2. McKay A. The Norway–Sweden union explained. *Life in Norway*. Accessed July 10, 2023. https://www.lifeinnorway.net/norway-sweden-union/.
3. McKay A. Norway in World War I: a neutral ally? *Life in Norway*. Accessed July 10, 2023. https://www.lifeinnorway.net/norway-in-world-war-one/.
4. *Life in Norway* Editorial Team. Norway in World War II. *Life in Norway*. Accessed July 11, 2023. https://www.lifeinnorway.net/norway-world-war-two/.
5. Kurtz B. The heavy water war. *Life in Norway*. Accessed July 5, 2023. https://www.lifeinnorway.net/the-heavy-water-war/.
6. Country Reports. Norway geography. Accessed July 15, 2023. https://www.countryreports.org/country/Norway/geography.htm.
7. *Country Reports*. Norway government. Accessed July 15, 2023. https://www.countryreports.org/country/Norway/government.htm.
8. European Commission. Norway: political, social, and economic background and trends: main executive and legislative bodies. Accessed July 15, 2023. https://eurydice.eacea.ec.europa.eu/national-education-systems/norway/main-executive-and-legislative-bodies#:~:text=Norway%20has%20a%20two%20tier,representatives%20responsible%20to%20their%20constituents.
9. *Country Reports*. Norway economy. Accessed July 16, 2023. https://www.countryreports.org/country/Norway/economy.htm.
10. World Bank Group. GDP per capital growth (annual %) – Norway. Accessed February 2, 2025. https://data.worldbank.org/indicator/NY.GDP.PCAP.KD.ZG?locations=NO.
11. Trading Economics. Norway labor force participation rate. Accessed February 2, 2025. https://tradingeconomics.com/norway/labor-force-participation-rate.
12. *Encyclopedia Britannica*. People of Norway. Accessed July 7, 2023. https://www.britannica.com/place/Norway/People.
13. Perera DA. The Norwegian health care system: a historical perspective. *Int J Rural Dev Environ Health Res*. 2021;5(4): 1-6. Accessed June 5, 2023. https://dx.doi.org/10.22161/ijreh.5.4.1.
14. Saunes IS, Karanikolos M, Sagan A. Norway: health system review 2020. *Health Syst Transit*. 2020;22(1):1-196. Accessed June 5, 2023. https://apps.who.int/iris/bitstream/handle/10665/331786/HiT-22-1-2020-eng.pdf?sequence=1&isAllowed=y.
15. World Health Organization. Norway: country health profile 2021. Accessed June 27, 2023. https://eurohealthobservatory.who.int/publications/m/norway-country-health-profile-2021.
16. Nikel D. Healthcare in Norway. *Life in Norway*. Accessed June 20, 2023. https://www.lifeinnorway.net/healthcare/.
14. Tikkanen R, Osborn R, Mossialos E, Djordjevic A, Wharton GA. International healthcare system profiles: Norway. Commonwealth Fund. Accessed June 27, 2023. https://www.commonwealthfund.org/international-health-policy-center/countries/norway#:~:text=Most%20hospital%20care%20is%20provided,governed%20as%20publicly%20owned%20corporations.
18. Netherlands Enterprise Agency. Norway: market study 2021. Accessed June 27, 2023. https://www.rvo.nl/sites/default/files/2021/11/Zorgsector%20Noorwegen%20marktrapport%202021.pdf.
19. World Bank. Hospital beds (per 1,000 people): Norway. Accessed June 28, 2023. https://data.worldbank.org/indicator/SH.MED.BEDS.ZS?locations=NO.
20. Statistik Sentralbyra Statistics Norway. Specialist health service. Accessed June 27, 2023. https://www.ssb.no/en/helse/helsetjenester/statistikk/spesialisthelsetjenesten.
21. Michas F. Number of nursing and care institutions in Norway in 2021, by ownership. Accessed June 27, 2023. *Statista*. https://www.statista.com/statistics/1022783/number-of-nursing-and-care-institutions-in-norway-by-ownership/#:~:text=Number%20of%20nursing%20and%20care%20institutions%20in%20Norway%202021%2C%20by%20ownership&text=Most%20nursing%20and%20care%20institutions,were%20under%20private%20commercial%20ownership.
22. Michas F. Number of beds in nursing and care institutions in Norway in 2021, by ownership. *Statista*. Accessed June 27, 2023. https://www.statista.com/statistics/1022806/number-of-beds-in-nursing-and-care-institutions-in-norway-by-ownership/.

23. Morland B. The history of health technology assessment in Norway. *Int J Technol Assess Health Care*. 2009;25(suppl 1): 148-155.
24. Norwegian Knowledge Center for the Health Services. About National Knowledge Center for the Health Services. Accessed July 5, 2023. http://www.adhophta.eu/partner/norwegian-knowledge-center-health-services-nokc.
25. International Trade Administration. Norway: country commercial guide: healthcare technologies. Accessed July 8, 2023. https://www.trade.gov/country-commercial-guides/norway-healthcare-technologies.
26. The Global Economy. Norway: health spending as percent of GDP. Accessed June 5, 2023. https://www.theglobaleconomy.com/Norway/health_spending_as_percent_of_gdp/.
27. Kinge JM, Dilelman JL, Karlstad O, et al. Disease-specific health spending by age, sex, and type of care in Norway: a national health registry study. *BMC Med.* 2023;21:201. Accessed July 8, 2023. https://bmcmedicine.biomedcentral.com/articles/10.1186/s12916-023-02896-6.
28. Organization for Economic Cooperation and Development. Health at a glance: Europe 2022: avoidable hospital admissions. Accessed July 9, 2023. https://www.oecd-ilibrary.org/social-issues-migration-health/health-at-a-glance-europe-2022_29d2934e-en.
29. Meyer HE. Overweight and obesity in Norway. NIPH. Published March 10, 2011. Updated June 19, 2024. Accessed February 2, 2025. https://www.fhi.no/en/he/hin/health-disease/overweight-and-obesity-in-norway---/?term=.
30. OECD/European Observatory on Health Systems and Policies. Norway: Country health profile 2021, State of health in the EU. OECD Publishing, Paris/European Observatory on Health Systems and Policies, Brussels. 2021. Accessed February 2, 2025. https://health.ec.europa.eu/system/files/2021-12/2021_chp_no_english.pdf.
31. Vick D, Kariyawasam DM. The response of Scandinavian countries to the COVID-19 pandemic. In: Johnson JA, DeShore NE, eds. *COVID-19 Global Pandemic: The World Responds*. Lakeway, TX: Sentia Publishing; 2023:167-171.
32. Norway: government confirms first case of COVID-19 February 26. February 26, 2020. Accessed November 14, 2022. https://crisis24.garda.com/alerts/2020/02/norway-government-confirms-first-case-of-covid-19-february-26.
33. Korseberg L, Saunes IS. Norway country snapshot: the role of public health agencies and services in the response to COVID-19. World Health Organization. April 7, 2022. Accessed November 14, 2022. https://eurohealthobservatory.who.int/news-room/articles/item/norway-country-snapshot-the-role-of-public-health-agencies-and-services-in-the-response-to-covid-19.
34. Norwegian Directorate of Health. Decision under the Act relating to control of communicable diseases, section 4-1, second paragraph, on quarantine (isolation) after travelling outside the Nordic region. March 12, 2020. Accessed November 14, 2022. https://www.helsedirektoratet.no/tema/beredskap-og-krisehandtering/koronavirus/anbefalinger-og-beslutninger/Decision%20under%20the%20Act%20relating%20to%20control%20of%20communicable%20diseases_section%204-1_second%20paragraph_on%20quarantine%20(isolation)%20after%20travelling%20outside%20the%20Nordic%20region.pdf/_/attachment/inline/9d809d07-7e4d-4b3b-8ca4-81cb924b7907:ba100772b4888f6d60ca39cf2963178cf11a9cdd/Decision%20under%20the%20Act%20relating%20to%20control%20of%20communicable%20diseases_section%204-1_second%20paragraph_on%20quarantine%20(isolation)%20after%20travelling%20outside%20the%20Nordic%20region.pdf.
35. Ursin G, Skjesol I, Tritter J. The COVID-19 pandemic in Norway: the dominance of social implications in framing the policy response. *Health Policy Technol.* 2020;9(4):663-672.
36. Norway. Coronavirus Legislation. May 7, 2020. Accessed November 15, 2022. https://www.coronavirus-legislation.com/home/norway.
37. Han E, Tan MM, Turk E, et al. Lessons learnt from easing COVID-19 restrictions: an analysis of countries and regions in Asia Pacific and Europe. *Health Policy*. 2020;396: 1525-1534.
38. Yarmol-Matusiak EA, Cipriano LE, Stranges SA. Comparison of COVID-19 epidemiological indicators in Sweden, Norway, Denmark, and Finland. *Scand J Public Health.* 2021;49:69-78.
39. Amiri A. Role of social distancing in tackling COVID-19 during the first wave of pandemic in Nordic region: evidence from daily deaths, infections and needed hospital resources. *Int J Nurs Sci.* 2021;8(2):145-151. doi: 10.1016/j.ijnss.2021.03.010.
40. Tunheim G, Ro GO, Trung T, et al. Trends in seroprevalence of SARS-CoV-2 and infection fatality rate in the Norwegian population through the first year of the COVID-19 pandemic. *Influenza Other Respir Viruses.* 2022;16(2):204-212.
41. Veneti L, Salamanca BV, Seppala E, et al. No difference in risk of hospitalization between reported cases of the SARS-CoV-2 Delta variant and Alpha variant in Norway. *Int J Infect Dis.* 2022;115:178-184.
42. Zimmer C, Anthes E. Denmark and Norway predict drastic spike in Omicron cases. *The New York Times.* December 13, 2021. Accessed November 20, 2022. https://www.nytimes.com/2021/12/13/health/omicron-cases-denmark-norway.html.
43. Preliminary findings from study after Christmas superspreader party in Oslo. December 9, 2021. Accessed November 20, 2022. https://medicalxpress.com/news/2021-12-preliminary-christmas-superspreader-party-oslo.html.
44. Nikel D. Coronavirus in Norway: the latest news on the COVID-19 outbreak. *Life in Norway.* February 12, 2022. Accessed November 20, 2022. https://www.lifeinnorway.net/coronavirus-in-norway/.
45. Johns Hopkins University & Medicine. Coronavirus Resource Center—Norway. December 6, 2022. Accessed December 6, 2022. https://coronavirus.jhu.edu/region/norway.

CHAPTER 15

Egypt

Ahmed Newera, Mohammed Al Faiomi, and Merette Khalil

Country Description

Table 15-1 Egypt

Ethnic groups	Egyptian 95%
Religion	Muslim (predominantly Sunni) 90%, Christian (majority Coptic Orthodox; other Christians include Armenian Apostolic, Catholic, Maronite, Orthodox, and Anglican) 10%
Languages	Arabic (official), English, and French widely understood by educated classes
Government type	Presidential republic
Real gross domestic product (GDP) per capita	11,600 USD (2021 est.) 11,400 USD (2020 est.) 11,200 USD (2019 est.)
Population	109,546,720 (2023 est.) Female: 1,209,001 Male: 1,150,608 (Population & Housing Census, 2022)
Top 10 causes of death	Ischemic heart disease, cirrhosis of the liver, stroke, liver cancer, neonatal conditions, kidney diseases, hypertensive heart disease, lower respiratory infections, diabetes mellitus, chronic obstructive pulmonary disease
Population growth rate	34% (2020 est.)
Infant mortality rate	16.23 deaths/1,000 live births (2022 est.)
Life expectancy at birth	Male: 69 years Female: 74 years (2021 est.)

Data from Central Intelligence Agency. The World Factbook, 2023: Egypt. https://www.cia.gov/the-world-factbook/countries/egypt/summaries/#economy; WorldAtlas. Major Ethnic Groups in Egypt. 2018. Accessed February 10, 2025. https://www.worldatlas.com/articles/what-is-the-ethnic-composition-of-egypt.html; World Health Organization. Egypt country profile, 2020. Accessed November 25, 2023. https://data.who.int/countries/818.

The history of Egypt extends over thousands of years. One of the oldest civilizations in the world, ancient Egypt was known for its famous temples and structures. Agriculture, animal husbandry, and pottery-making all advanced in prehistoric Egypt.[1] Under Pharaoh Narmer, Upper and Lower Egypt were united during the Early Dynastic Period, establishing a centralized kingdom and starting the pharaonic era.[1] Impressive pyramids were built during the Old Kingdom, a time of prosperity and stability, and government and administration were advanced.[2] The Middle Kingdom had a rise in strength, a widening of its realm, and amazing architectural accomplishments like the Temple of Karnak.[1] As well as the expansion of Egypt's dominion, the New Kingdom was distinguished by immense power, prosperity, and the construction of magnificent temples like those at Luxor and Abu Simbel. Due to invasions by outside forces, the growth of the Osiris cult, and the creation of the Book of the Dead, the Late Period saw collapse and instability.[2] Greek culture was introduced throughout the Greco-Roman Period, which was also the era of the famed Alexandrian library and the conquests of Alexander the Great and the Ptolemaic dynasty.[1] Egypt was incorporated into the Ottoman Empire during the Islamic Period, which began with the Arab invasion in 641 CE and ended with independence in 1922.[2] Islam grew and flourished during this time, and Islamic culture was also well developed. Notably, the rebellion led by Muhammad Naguib and Gamal Abdel Nasser in 1952 marked the beginning of the presidential era, which has since resulted in a number of political and social reforms that have shaped Egyptian history.[3] Recent political events in Egypt include the 2011 Egyptian Revolution, the Muslim Brotherhood's ascent, and the uprising in 2013, which led to the country's transformation into a presidential republic under President Abdel Fattah al-Sisi.[3]

Size and Geography

Egypt has a total area of 1,001,450 square kilometers (386,662 square miles), making it the 30th largest country in the world (**Table 15-1**). It is bordered by Libya to the west, Sudan to the south, the Occupied Palestinian Territory and the Gaza Strip to the northeast, and the Mediterranean Sea to the north. Egypt has a coastline along the Mediterranean Sea to the north and the Red Sea to the east, totaling approximately 2,450 kilometers (1,522 miles) in length. The country is predominantly desert, with the Sahara Desert covering much of it. The Western Desert, Eastern Desert, and Sinai Peninsula are all part of the Sahara. The Nile River is the most significant river in Egypt, running through the country from south to north and eventually emptying into the Mediterranean Sea. Egypt has several notable landforms, including the Nile River Valley and Delta, the Sinai Peninsula, the Western Desert, and the Eastern Desert.[4]

The following natural calamities are common in Egypt: earthquakes, dust and sandstorms, and flash floods. The earthquake in 1992 and the flash floods in Upper Egypt 2 years later were the two worst disasters in the last 30 years.[5]

Population Centers

Egypt is highly urbanized, with most of the population concentrated along the Nile Valley, in the Delta, and near the Suez Canal. Egyptian populations are divided demographically into those who live in the major urban centers, mostly Cairo, Alexandria, and Giza, and those who reside in rural villages. Cairo is the capital and the largest city in Egypt, with an estimated population of over 9 million people. It is located on the banks of the Nile River in northeastern Egypt and is the cultural, economic, and political center of the country. Alexandria follows as the second-largest city in Egypt. Located on the Mediterranean coast in northern Egypt, Alexandria is a major center for trade and industry. It has an estimated population of over 5 million people. Giza is a suburb of Cairo located on the west bank of the Nile River. It is home to several famous landmarks, including the Great Pyramid of Giza and the Sphinx. Shubra El-Kheima is a city located just north of Cairo with an estimated population of over 1 million people. It is a major transportation hub and industrial center.[6]

Government and Political System

Egypt is an Arabic, Islamic, and African country. Citizenship and the rule of law are the foundations of the democratic-republican system used in the Arab Republic of Egypt.[7]

The president of the country serves as the head of the republic and the executive authority and supreme commander of the armed forces. The prime minister is in charge of the cabinet, serves as the head of state, and has the power to make laws. The two-round election process elects the president with an absolute majority of the vote. The president appoints the prime minister, who is then approved by the Parliament.[7]

The constitution's declaration of political and party plurality describes the political system in Egypt, including the idea of peaceful power circulation, separation of powers and balance between them, relationship between powers and duties, and the respect for human rights and freedoms. A separate part of the government, the judicial system consists of both secular and religious courts.[7]

Egypt has a mixed legal structure based on Napoleonic civil and criminal law and Islamic religious law; the Supreme Constitutional Court adjudicates on the validity of laws.[8] The Supreme Administrative Court, Court of Cassation, and Supreme Constitutional Court are Egypt's three top courts. Disputes involving the legality of laws are decided only by the Supreme Constitutional Court. The highest court in the common law system is the Court of Cassation, whereas the highest court in the State Council's administrative court system is the Supreme Administrative Court.[8]

The Parliament passes laws, endorses country policies, oversees the work of the government, and has the authority to vote to remove the government and prime minister through a no-confidence vote or to impeach the president of the republic.[9]

In two rounds, the 176 Advisory Council members are chosen by absolute majority voting, while the president appoints the remaining 88 members. In addition, 166 members of the People's Assembly are chosen by absolute majority vote in a two-round process, and 332 are chosen using a closed-list proportional representation method.[9]

Macroeconomics

In 2021, Egypt was a low- and middle-income country according to the World Bank's world development indicators.[10] Between 2019 and 2021, Egypt's economic growth fell from 3.6% to 3.3%. On the supply side, the construction, communications, and agriculture industries performed better than expected. On the demand side, individual and public consumption as well as public investment drove economic expansion. The COVID-19 epidemic had a negative impact on manufacturing and tourism. Extreme poverty slightly decreased from 4.5% in 2019 to 4.4% in 2020, and in June 2021, the unemployment rate was 7.4%. In 2020, the public debt climbed from 87.9% of GDP to 92% of GDP, showing the fiscal reaction to the crisis.[11]

The new Country Partnership Framework (CPF) 2023–2027, which will direct the World Bank Group's operations and activities in Egypt, is currently being developed by the World Bank Group and the government of Egypt. The new CPF, which places "people" at the center of its strategy, focuses on boosting expansion of the private sector and job growth, enhancing human capital and inclusion outcomes, and enhancing resilience to climatic and macroeconomic shocks while incorporating governance, citizen engagement, and women's empowerment as cross-cutting themes. The World Bank Group will put the new CPF into action through its current and upcoming financing activities, as well as through technical assistance. The World Bank's active portfolio in Egypt as of September 2022 consisted of 14 operations with a net commitment of $6.83 billion USD. The portfolio's main emphasis was on environmental sustainability, improvements in service delivery to populations (particularly in rural and underserved areas), and human development.[12]

Major Industries, Ports and Airports, and Infrastructure and Transportation Development

Major Industries

Egypt has significant petroleum reserves and is one of the largest oil producers in Africa. The petroleum industry is a major contributor to the Egyptian economy.[13] The country is also known for its ancient historical sites, such as the Pyramids of Giza and the Sphinx, which attract millions of tourists every year. Tourism is a significant source of revenue for Egypt.[14] Moreover, Egypt has fertile agricultural land and is a major producer of crops such as cotton, rice, and wheat. Agriculture is also a significant sector of the Egyptian economy.[15]

Ports and Airports

In terms of ports, Egypt has two main ports (see **Figure 15-1**). The port of Alexandria, which is located on the Mediterranean coast, is considered the largest port in the country and the busiest one. The other main port is Port Said, which is located at the northern end of the Suez Canal and is an important port for trade between Europe and Asia. Cairo International Airport is the busiest airport in Egypt and one of the busiest in Africa. It serves as a hub for many international airlines and is a gateway to Egypt's tourism industry.[16]

Figure 15-1 Map of Egypt

Egypt map. Central Intelligence Agency; 1997. Library of Congress. Accessed May 10, 2023. https://www.loc.gov/item/2001628301/.

Infrastructure and Transportation Development

In 2015, Egypt completed a major expansion of the Suez Canal, which increased the canal's capacity and allowed for more ships to pass through it. This expansion is expected to boost Egypt's economy by increasing trade and creating jobs.[17]

Egypt is currently building a new administrative capital city, which is located to the east of Cairo and will serve as the country's new administrative center.[18]

The Cairo Metro is a rapid transit system that serves the Greater Cairo area. It is one of the busiest metro systems in Africa and the Middle East, with over 3 million passengers per day.[16]

Demographics

Age Distribution of the Population

In 2021, the Egyptian population was estimated to number 107,770,524. According to the United Nations Population Division, the age distribution of the Egyptian population is approximately 34% under the age of 15, 61% between the ages of 15 and 64, and 5% age 65 years or older. Egypt has the second-largest population in the Middle East and the third largest in the African continent.[19]

According to the World Bank, in 2020, the life expectancy of Egyptians at birth was 71 years, and the population's annual growth rate was 1.7% in 2021. Total unemployment of the Egyptian labor force reached 7.4% in 2021. Egypt's Human capital index (HCI) is 0.5 (on a scale of 0–1) and the Net Immigration is –32,370.[20]

In terms of its birth rate, Egypt was ranked 11th worldwide with 2.55 million births in 2021, equal to 6,985 births daily. The crude birth rate is 24.47 per 1,000 people. In terms of its death rate, the country was ranked 21st worldwide, with 0.6 million deaths in 2021 (1,634 deaths daily). The crude death rate is 5.73 per 1,000 people.

Urban regions are home to approximately 42.86% of the total population of Egypt. Egypt is ranked as the 177th most urbanized country in the world. The male population is 50.52% of the total, while the female population is 49.48%.[21]

Ethnic Groups

Many ethnic groups reside in Egypt, including Egyptians, Greeks, Abazas, Bedouins, and Berbers. Egyptians remain the country's biggest ethnic group (95%).[22]

Languages

The official language of Egypt is Arabic, and the majority of people speak Egyptian Arabic. The Siwa language is commonly used by Berbers, the Nubian language is spoken by Nubians, and English and French are widely used by certain locals in the country. As Christian people pray, meditate, and attend church services, they frequently speak in Coptic.[22]

Education Levels of the Population

According to the World Bank, the literacy rate in Egypt was approximately 75% in 2021, with higher rates among men (82%) than women (68%).[10] The net enrollment rate in primary education is approximately 94%, with slightly higher rates among boys (95%) than girls (94%). The net enrollment rate in secondary education is around 77%, with slightly higher rates among boys (79%) than girls (74%). For tertiary education, the gross enrollment rate is around 35%, with higher rates among men (40%) than women (29%).[21]

Major Religious Groups

Egypt is predominantly a Muslim country. Approximately 90% of the population is Sunni Muslim and 10% is Christian. Approximately 90% of Christians belong to the Coptic Orthodox Church. Other Christian communities together constitute less than 2% of the population.[23]

Brief History of the Healthcare System

In the 1990s, the Egyptian government introduced several reforms aimed at improving the efficiency and quality of healthcare services, including the introduction of cost-sharing measures and the decentralization of healthcare management. However, these reforms were not fully implemented, and the healthcare system continued to face challenges related to quality, availability, and access to services.[24]

After the 2011 revolution, Egypt experienced significant investments in the healthcare system, including the construction of new hospitals, and the renovation of existing ones, as well as the expansion of primary healthcare services and the introduction of universal health coverage. Despite these efforts, the healthcare system continues to face challenges, including shortages of medical staff, inadequate infrastructure, and disparities in access to services between urban and rural areas.[25]

The Current Healthcare System

Health Governance

Egypt has a wide range of public and private healthcare organizations, which currently manage, finance, and provide health care in the country. The Ministry of Health and Population (MOHP) is responsible for overseeing Egypt's health system. Additionally, it coordinates between the public and private sectors.[26]

The public sector comprises government and parastatal entities. "Parastatal" describes quasi-governmental institutions, such as the Teaching Hospitals and Institutes Organization (THO), the Curative Care Organization (CCO), and the Health Insurance Organization (HIO). The parastatal sector is subject to its own set of financial and operational standards, has its own budgets, and conducts daily operations with more autonomy. However, from a political perspective, the MOHP oversees most decisions made at parastatal institutions.[24] The HIO was initially established to offer health insurance and treatment to all Egyptians. The HIO offers basic coverage through its own hospitals and clinics, to four main categories of beneficiaries: all governmental employees, certain employees in the public and commercial sectors, retirees, and widows. Nevertheless, the HIO barely covers 60% of the population.[26] The Ministry of Higher Education (MOHE) provides healthcare services through the THO, representing 6.38% of the total health expenditure. Furthermore, the Ministry of Defense (MOD) and the Ministry of Interior (MOI) have their own facilities providing care for their employees, as well as civilians.[24]

The private sector presently controls the majority of health services delivered in Egypt and offers higher-quality treatment.[24] The private sector comprises traditional midwives, independent pharmacies, independent doctors, and independent hospitals (nonprofit and for-profit) of varied sizes. Many nongovernmental organizations (NGOs) provide health services via clinics with a religious affiliation and other charitable organizations, all of which are registered with the Ministry of Social Affairs (MOSA).[24] Private health insurance is hardly used, and most private services are paid for in cash.[27]

The government is encouraging the privatization of the health system. With government assistance, Egyptian citizens can purchase insurance coverage from private insurers. Via contracts with individuals and businesses, the CCO provides private inpatient and outpatient treatment.

MOHP Organizational Structure

In 1995, the "Ministry of Health" and the "Population Portfolio," previously separate ministries, amalgamated into the MOHP.[28] The MOHP is made up of two functional structures: the administrative structure and the service delivery structure (see **Figure 15-2**).

The MOPH administrative structure comprises the central headquarters and the governorate-level health directorates. The central headquarters primarily oversees, plans, and manages health programs. It has five administrative sectors: curative health services, population and family planning, basic and preventive health services, administration and finance, and central administration for the minister's office.[26,28]

There are 13 head office undersecretaries who answer to the minister. These undersecretaries are in charge of research and development, pharmaceuticals, dentistry, family planning, primary health care, endemic illnesses, curative care, preventive care, labs, and nursing. Under each sector area led by an undersecretary are typically 30 to 35 functional areas and specialized units, led by general directors and directors.[28]

Each governorate level replicates the sector-level paradigm. When it comes to technical issues, the governorate-level health directorates report to the MOHP; but, when it comes to administrative and day-to-day tasks, they answer to the governorate administration led by the governor. An undersecretary or general director oversees each governorate's health directorate. They answer to the minister, who, in turn, is in charge of the health district directors.[28]

There are 230 health districts that report to the governorate health directorates. There is a director for each district, who is occasionally also the district hospital director.[28,29]

The New Comprehensive Health Insurance System and Health System Reforming

The health system in Egypt has been suffering from many problems, including:

- Weak financial sustainability
- The inability of the health system to cover all segments of society, especially informal workers
- Dissatisfaction of the beneficiaries with the quality of the service provided
- Threats to the financial stability of many Egyptian families, as out-of-pocket payments account for approximately 60% of the total expenditures on health

In 2011–2012, the MOHP formed a committee of government and community representatives, which worked on preparing a new draft "health insurance" law in response to the Egyptian society's requirements for comprehensive health coverage.[30] The law is designed to achieve the strategic goals of the health axis of Egypt's 2030 Sustainable Development Plan:

1. Promoting the health of citizens within a framework of justice and fairness, while paying attention

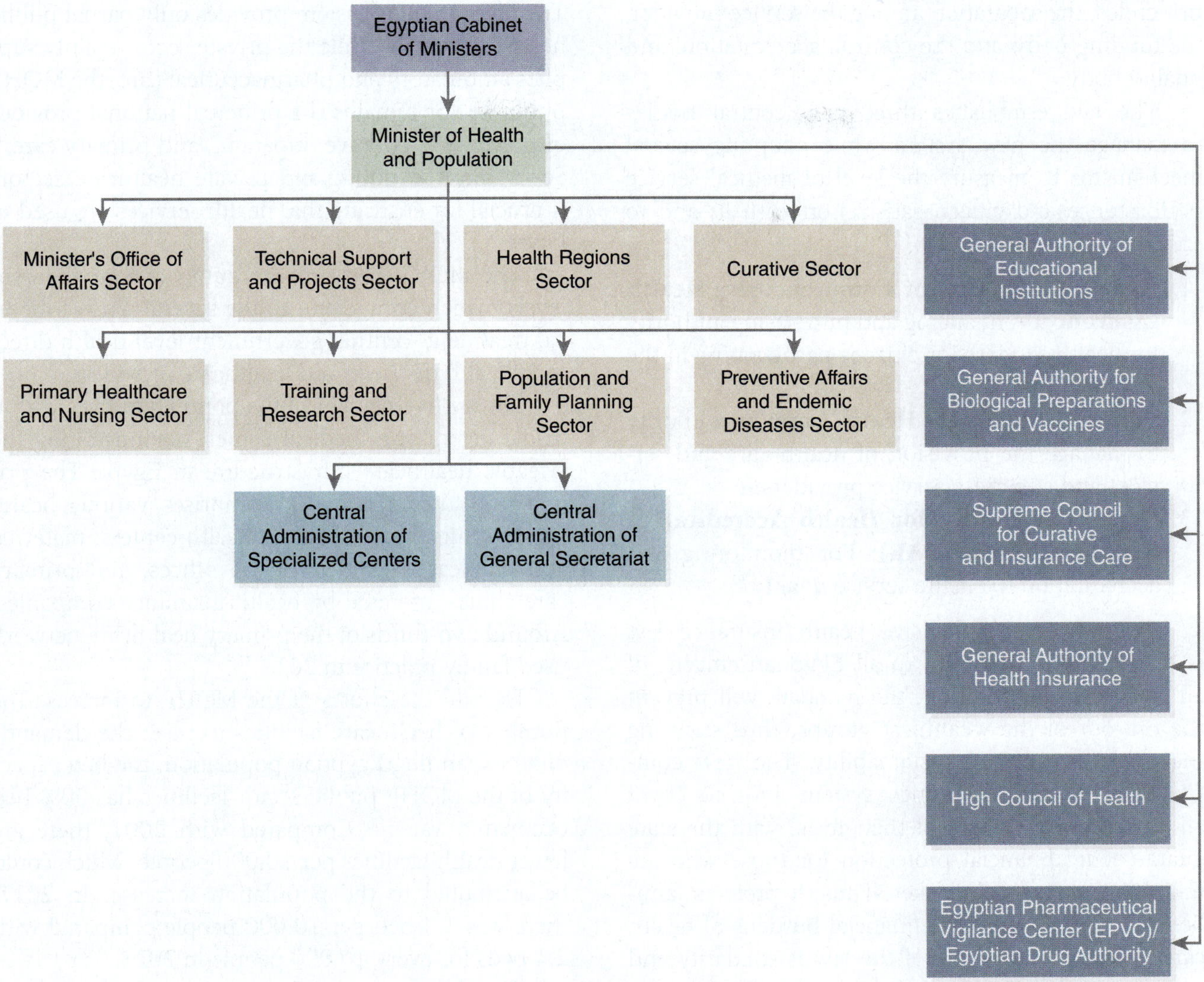

Figure 15-2 Organizational structure of the Egypt Ministry of Health and Population[24]

Data from Egypt Ministry of Health and Population. 2023. Accessed March 13, 2023. https://www.mohp.gov.eg/SectorServices.aspx?Deptcode=35&&SectorCode=5.

to all factors affecting the health of Egyptians in terms of social determinants, infrastructure, and public awareness
2. Encouraging the population to adopt a healthy lifestyle
3. Achieving comprehensive health coverage for all Egyptians, while ensuring the quality of the services provided, and paying attention to delivering high-quality curative and preventive services that are available to all Egyptians[30]

The objectives of the health axis of Egypt's 2030 Sustainable Development Plan were derived from Article 18 of the 2014 Egyptian Constitution, which states:

> Every citizen has the right to health and to integrated health care following quality standards, and the state guarantees the maintenance and support of public health service facilities, and the state is committed to allocating a percentage of government spending for health that is not less than 3% of the gross national product. The state is committed to establishing a comprehensive health insurance system for all Egyptians that covers all diseases. The state is committed to improving the conditions of doctors, nursing staff, and workers in the health sector. The state encourages the participation of the private and non-governmental sectors in healthcare services.[31]

The law represents an integrated framework for comprehensive health system reform; it is not just a law about providing health services to citizens. It addresses the shortcomings of the health system, in addition to being a substantial qualitative leap and a symbol of Egypt's ambition to reform the health system as a legislative tool through the following principles: the separation among the service provider, the funding body, and the control, accreditation, and quality body.[30]

The law establishes three new central bodies to manage the new system while adopting several mechanisms to measure the level of medical service performance and citizen satisfaction with it, and to ensure its quality:

1. **General Authority for Comprehensive Health Insurance:** A financing and purchasing authority for health services for citizens participating in the system.
2. **Public Authority for Health Care:** An authority to manage the provision of health care and services and supervise service providers.
3. **General Authority for Health Accreditation and Control (GAHAR):** For monitoring and accreditation to ensure service quality.[30]

The new comprehensive health insurance law is mandatory and applies to all Egyptian citizens of all categories. In addition, the mandate will prevent the opt-out of the wealthiest groups, thus ensuring the system's financial sustainability. The new comprehensive health insurance system aims to cover all citizens in all stages of their lives, with the state guaranteeing financial protection for those who are unable to pay out of pocket. Thus, it protects families and citizens from the financial burdens of health care. The basic principle of the law is solidarity and partnership between the different segments of society and the state.[31] The law was passed in late 2017, then approved by the House of Representatives, ratified by the President of the Republic in January 2018, and made ready for implementation. The new comprehensive health insurance law gradually replaces the laws currently in force through gradual stages (six stages), over a period ranging from 10 to 15 years.[32,33]

Health Services Delivery

The MOHP is the main institution in charge of the Egyptian health system and generally oversees the majority of healthcare facilities. Every Egyptian citizen is eligible for free medical care from the MOHP, including both inpatient and outpatient treatment, even though the country does not yet have 100% universal health coverage.

The quality of public health care in Egypt is considered low, due to constant underfunding of the public sector, low doctor bases, and income-based inequalities in service utilization, which moves suppliers and demand to the private healthcare sector.[34] The dichotomous system provides only partial public health coverage. While the private sector mainly supplies ambulatory and pharmaceutical care, the MOHP public sector remains the principal national provider of preventive, curative, inpatient, and primary care.[35] Separating the public and private healthcare sectors is crucial for ensuring that health services are used in Egypt.

The MOHP performs its duties at four different levels, which correspond to the several tiers of medical treatment: central, government-level health directors, health districts, and healthcare providers.[35]

Ninety-five percent of the population lives within 5 kilometers of a medical center, demonstrating the sizeable healthcare infrastructure in Egypt. The primary healthcare network comprises various health service units, such as family health centers, maternal and childcare facilities, health offices, and primary care clinics operated by health insurance companies. Around two-thirds of the primary healthcare network used family practice in 2014.[35]

Despite the efforts of the MOHP to increase the number of healthcare facilities to meet the demands of an expanding Egyptian population, the bed capacity of the MOHP public-sector facilities has 50% bed occupancy rates.[36] Compared with 2001, there are fewer health facilities per 10,000 people, which could be attributed to the population increase. In 2017, there was 1.4 bed per 10,000 people compared with 2.1 beds for every 10,000 people in 2021.[37]

The delivery of private health services is only loosely controlled. An estimated 50% of outpatient care is sought at private health facilities, 30% at pharmacies, and 20% only at public health facilities, with approximately two-thirds of childbirths occurring in private institutions. The health workforce is unequally distributed, with understaffing being particularly severe in rural and distant locations. At all levels of the health system, in both the public and private sectors, there is still room for improvement concerning the quality and safety of medical care.[35]

MOHP Public Health Programs

The MOHP has created a plan of action for maternal, newborn and child health, and mental health. The MOHP aims to incorporate mental health services into primary health care and promote awareness in schools and universities. There are a variety of public health programs, including those focusing on family planning and reproductive health; pandemic influenza; the Expanded Program of Immunization; hepatitis; maternal, newborn, and child health; and mental health. These programs have been successful in reducing sickness, disability, and mortality from illnesses such as diphtheria, tetanus, whooping cough, measles, and polio. The total fertility rate is 3 births per woman.[24]

Noncommunicable diseases (NCDs) are the main cause of mortality in Egypt. The MOHP is creating a multisectoral national action plan to reduce NCD risk and its underlying risk factors. Egypt has made significant strides in nutrition, violence, disability and injuries, and tobacco control, and it joined the WHO Framework Convention on Tobacco Control in 2005. Road management, infrastructure, vehicle safety, user behavior, road safety education, and postcrash reaction are part of the national plan to reduce road traffic accidents.[30]

Physical Resources

Table 15-2 shows the number of health units having beds, and the number of beds as per their distribution across different health sectors in Egypt. It demonstrates how specialized medical units are found in both the public and parastatal sectors. Seventy-two percent of Egypt's healthcare system beds are in the hands of governmental and quasi-governmental organizations. Despite controlling 63% of all hospitals, the private sector is significantly fragmented, with just 31 beds in each private facility compared with 96 in each government hospital and 209 in each parastatal facility. This creates an ideal opportunity for private-sector consolidation via mergers and acquisitions.[38] Notably, the number of beds per 10,000 population is 9.8 and 3.67 in the public and private sectors, respectively.[39]

The demand for physical and social infrastructure, including healthcare and education services, is increasing in Egypt. There were 1.3 beds per 1,000 population in 2019 (compared with 1.9 beds for the MENA Region). However, the healthcare sector lags in the provision of infrastructure and services. Egypt will need between 38,500 and 117,000 more beds by 2030, costing between $8 billion USD and $40 billion USD.[38]

Health Workforce

The 2020 annual report of the Central Agency for Public Mobilization and Statistics (CAPMAS) indicated that healthcare professionals in Egypt include 110,394 physicians, 30,566 dentists, 54,548 pharmacists, and 225,765 nurses.[40] **Table 15-3** shows the distribution of each cadre of the available health workforce per 10,000 population.

Many health professionals have refrained from practicing in Egypt's remote and rural areas. This has contributed to the unequal distribution of health professionals in those areas, resulting in inequity in healthcare access as well. In an attempt to promote better access in these areas, the government developed policies to encourage health professionals to work in rural and remote areas; however, that was met with resistance from the health workforce, and the government unfortunately failed to put these policies into action. Robust communication channels between the medical schools producing doctors and the policymaking authorities in the country are also lacking, which has exacerbated the problem of unequal distribution of health professionals countrywide.[41]

Table 15-2 Total Number of Units (with Beds) by Sector

Health Sector	Number of Units with Beds	Number of Beds
MOHP	400	37,822
Institutions affiliated with MOHP	145	25,109
Other government institutions	146	32,752
Private sector	1,377	35,648
Total	**2068**	**131,331**

Data from MOHP 2019. The annual statistics report: the central administration of the National Center for Population and Health Information, the General Administration of Information and Statistics Services: features of the health situation.

Table 15-3 Distribution of Health Workforce per 10,000 Population

Cadre	Distribution per 10,000 Population
Physicians	7.79
Nurses/midwives	14.7
Dentists	2.03
Pharmacists	4.6
Ancillaries	25.3

Data from World Health Organization, Regional Office for the Eastern Mediterranean. Health system country profile, 2018. Accessed April 10, 2023. https://rho.emro.who.int/sites/default/files/Profiles-briefs-files/EGY-Health-System-Profiles-2018.pdf.

Additionally, the rate of migration for health professionals has recently increased, as these individuals seek better salaries and postgraduate studies and training programs outside of the country. The Egyptian Medical Syndicate (EMS) raised a warning signal in March 2022, announcing that 65% of Egyptian doctors are working outside of Egypt, and the total number of doctors who have left the country since 2019 has reached approximately 11,536 doctors.[42]

Health Information System

Healthcare decision making in Egypt relies heavily on the health information system (HIS). Egypt has a robust information technology and communication network, which is used to collect data in accordance with international standards.[43] Egypt views the HIS as a priority to attain universal health coverage (UHC) through its new Universal Health Insurance System (UHIS), which will cover all Egyptian governorates by 2030. A robust HIS will be required to provide pertinent data and information that can be used in monitoring and evaluating the national health policies and plans.[43] The Digital Egypt Strategy also includes automation technology as an essential component of UHIS.[44] However, the current quality of data collection and unclear information flows continue to be problems. For instance, the Civil Registration and Vital Statistics (CRVS) system performs poorly when it comes to reporting the cause of death, yet performs well when it comes to registering deaths (up to 100%).[43]

WHO is supporting the reform of the present HIS by MOHP at both the macro and micro levels. With assistance from WHO, the CRVS is strengthening three key pillars: (1) resources, legal framework, and infrastructure; (2) procedures and recording; and (3) cause of death coding and certification.[43] The WHO country office has supported Egypt's efforts to achieve UHC and implement primary health care (PHC) and digitalization in Egypt by taking the following measures: establishing the system of clinical governance under the General Authority for Healthcare in the first-phase governorates of UHIS (i.e., Port Said, Luxor, and Ismailia); supporting digital management, monitoring, and costing of PHC services; supporting the development of electronic medical records and benefit plans; and establishing a clinical data dictionary.[45]

One success story for the establishment of HIS in Egypt is that of the MOHP—Family Planning Sector (FPS). It allows the flow of clinics' data from the health facility to the district, governorate, and then central level, and the development of reports quarterly and annually.[46]

Notably, hospitals in Egypt are also moving toward the use of electronic medical records (EMR). This is supported by high political will from the Egyptian government, which released and approved the electronic signature law, electronic payment law, and data privacy law. However, hospitals need further resources to implement HIS, which ensures continuity of care, patient safety, security, and confidentiality of information.[47] Implementation of information management systems and technologies in healthcare organizations will be monitored by the General Authority of Healthcare Accreditation and Regulation (GAHAR).[47]

In addition, health insurance companies are pursuing digitalization to ensure their market growth and progressively updating their online services and digital platforms to facilitate their customers' access. "There has been a move increasingly towards digital transformation, and insurance companies are making considerable efforts to prioritize the adoption of new technology," according to Mohammed Omran, the chairman of Egypt's Financial Regulatory Authority.[48]

Essential Medicines, Equipment, and Technology

Access to essential medicines is a key aspect of the healthcare system worldwide, including in Egypt. The government provides free access to essential medicines through public-sector healthcare facilities. Additionally, there are many private pharmacies that sell prescriptions and over-the-counter medicines. MOHP is responsible for ensuring the availability and quality of essential medicines in the country.[49] Despite the government's efforts, there are still challenges in terms of ensuring access to essential medicines. For example, there may be limited availability of certain medicines, especially in rural areas. In addition, the high cost of some medicines may make them inaccessible to some people, particularly those living in poverty.[50]

To address these challenges, the government has implemented several initiatives aimed at improving access to essential medicines. For example, the government has introduced a system of price controls for essential medicines, which helps to keep prices affordable. In addition, the government has implemented a program to increase the production of generic medicines, which are cheaper alternatives to brand-name medicines.[51]

Health Financing

For many years, Egypt has been suffering from a low public investment in health, with the public forced to provide large out-of-pocket payments that exceed

90% of the health expenditure.[52,53] Total health expenditure (THE) as a percentage of GDP has been almost stagnant in Egypt since the 2011 revolution, ranging from 3.0% (DHS, 2018) to 7.0% of GDP, while the governmental health expenditure (GHE) is approximately one-third of Egypt's GDP.[32]

MOHP is the primary government entity responsible for providing preventive and curative services at the primary, secondary, and tertiary levels. It provides subsidized services, such that almost 80% are free, and the rest require some user fees.[54,55] MOHP is a major and direct funder of parastatal organizations, including the Curative Care Organization (CCO) and the Teaching Hospitals and Institutes Organization (THIO).[55,56] Aside from Ministry of Finance (MoF) funding, MOHP directly collects funds from copayments and user fees. Donors are funding via grants and loans for vertical programs (specific programs that focus on certain health conditions).[54]

The MOHP budget ranged from 3.3% to 4.0% of the annual government budget[57–59] and accounted for 15% of health financing in Egypt.[60] Also equal to 57% of general government health expenditure, 28% of total spending by the MOHP was on medical goods in 2011–2012.[32] MoF is the primary funding source for the MOHP and other disparate ministries. It funds nearly one-third of the total health spending in Egypt, which finances 93% of the MOHP activities.[61]

The primary healthcare financing source is out-of-pocket payments, representing more than 60% of the total financing.[61] The CCO is a nonprofit governmental organization supervised by the MOHP that provides services for employees of companies with dedicated contracts. It has its own facilities and relies on multiple sources of funds such as copayments, general taxes, and user fees.[54,56] The HIO is an independent government organization providing compulsory insurance to most formal-sector employees, but allowing an opt-out strategy. The HIO coverage level exceeds 50% of Egyptians. In recent years, the HIO expenditure represented 8% of the THE and 19% of the governmental budget.[32] The primary sources of funds are premiums and employer contributions. Beneficiary payments through cost-sharing and copayments in some service areas accounted for 25% of the service fees. The remainder came from national taxes; payroll taxes; an earmarked tobacco tax; and government subsidies of some subgroups, such as school students, children under 7, and female, single-parent households.[32,54,60,62] By comparison, the percentage of the population covered by private insurance ranged from 1% to 10%.[32] Household out-of-pocket payments are considered the largest source of healthcare financing in Egypt, ranging from 41% to 72% of the total amount.[32] Private clinics consume the largest share at 38.4%, followed by pharmaceuticals at 33.1%. In regard to hospitalization services, private hospitals receive the lion's share of funding (8.2%), followed by MOHP hospitals (3.5%).[56]

One of the most significant issues in the Egyptian healthcare financing system is the huge proportion of funding provided by out-of-pocket payments, which puts families at a high financial risk of catastrophic expenditures and decreases the performance of the healthcare system. Thus, it was a pressing need for the Egyptian government to seek universal health insurance (UHI) to ensure available healthcare services to the whole population regardless of their income level. In 2018, the government issued its new health insurance scheme, which was aligned with the Sustainable Development Strategy for Egypt (Egypt Vision 2030).[32,63]

The Universal Health Insurance System (UHIS) is a new entity established to provide UHI services for all Egyptians. It is financed through several sources, including citizen-paid premiums, the state budget, government subsidization of the poor, a general tax, an earmarked tobacco tax, copayments (service fees), hospitals, medical clinics, treatment centers, pharmacies, and pharmaceutical companies that subscribe to the new health insurance system.[33,39] The cost of UHI for one citizen will range from EGP 1,300 to EGP 4,000, up from the mere EGP 112 paid in the current insurance system,[33] in line with Egypt's macroeconomic target to increase spending on health, education, and research and development to at least 10% of GDP.[63] Provision of the comprehensive basic package will be based on competition and choice among the different public and private service providers, under a single public health insurance fund (PHIF) using incentive-based and other provider payment mechanisms.[64]

Evaluation of the Healthcare System

The healthcare system in Egypt, including both the public and private sectors, is generally considered economical. However, out-of-pocket expenses continue to be significant, particularly for patients who use private healthcare providers, as discussed earlier.[65]

Quality

One of the strategic objectives for Egypt's Vision 2030 is the implementation of a clearly controlled, transparent, and fair regulatory system. To ensure the quality and safety of health services, it was established that the condition of accreditation is necessary for contracting with health facilities to provide services to citizens through the existence of an independent authority. The General Authority for Healthcare Accreditation & Regulation (GAHAR) was established under Law No. 2 for the year 2018 as an independent authority for accreditation of all health facilities that provide healthcare services to Egyptian citizens and as a contributor to the achievement of the UHI system in Egypt.[66] GAHAR is responsible for developing quality standards for health services and for monitoring health facilities and medical professionals to ensure compliance with these standards. GAHAR developed its standards for accreditation guided by the scientific literature and expert consensus, and these standards received international accreditation from the International Society for Quality in Health Care (ISQua). Different sets of accreditation standards have been developed to cover a wide range of health facilities and health services, including hospitals, PHC, clinical laboratories, physical therapy, ambulatory health care, diagnostic and therapeutic radiology, and mental health care.[67]

Access and Equity

Access to healthcare services in Egypt is limited, particularly for people living in rural and remote areas. The healthcare system is also characterized by long waiting times and overcrowding in public facilities, which exacerbate the unequal access to health services in the country.[68] Meanwhile, 95% of the population has access to a PHC facility within a radius of less than 5 km, demonstrating the broad geographic reach of PHC services. Availability and accessibility of child immunization, preventive interventions, some public health programs, and disease surveillance are robust in Egypt.[35]

However, there are significant inequities in healthcare access and outcomes in Egypt, with those living in poverty and rural areas experiencing poorer health outcomes than those in urban areas. In addition, women and girls often face significant barriers to accessing healthcare services, including cultural and social norms.[69]

Demand for maternal care and childcare facilities and services is expected to increase dramatically in Egypt, as the country expects to have an estimated 26 million newly born babies by 2030. With 15% of adults over age 20 having diabetes, 32% being obese, and 25% having hypertension, Egypt has one of the highest prevalence of lifestyle diseases worldwide.[69] Demand for services for older people will increase as the number of people age 60 and older is expected to more than double between 2020 and 2050, from 8.4 million to 22 million.[70] The majority of deaths in the country (82% of all deaths and 67% of premature deaths) are caused by noncommunicable diseases.[69]

Patient Satisfaction

Patient satisfaction with health care in Egypt is generally low, with complaints about the long waiting times, poor quality of care, unequal access to health services, and lack of transparency in the healthcare system.[71]

COVID-19 Pandemic

Like many countries around the world, Egypt has been significantly impacted by the COVID-19 pandemic. The pandemic put a strain on the country's healthcare system, with hospitals and healthcare facilities facing shortages of medical supplies and equipment, including ventilators and personal protective equipment (PPE). In addition, the pandemic highlighted existing inequalities in access to healthcare services in Egypt, with low-income families and those living in rural areas facing particular challenges in accessing these services during the pandemic.

Through a variety of focused measures, the "100 Million Healthy Lives" presidential initiative in Egypt seeks to improve the health results for Egyptians. MOPH is carrying out this effort, which was started by President Abdel Fattah El-Sisi in 2018 and is being implemented in partnership with other stakeholders. There are several key initiatives under the "100 Million Health" program.

The "Screening and Early Detection of Hepatitis C" initiative aims to screen all Egyptians over the age of 18 for hepatitis C, diabetes, and hypertension. As of 2021, over 61 million people had been screened and over 2 million individuals were receiving treatment for hepatitis C.[72]

Another "100 Million Healthy Lives" initiative focuses on promoting healthy lifestyles and preventing noncommunicable diseases such as obesity and cardiovascular diseases. This program has established health promotion units in all governorates of Egypt and has trained over 1.3 million health educators.[73]

The "Early Detection of Hearing Problems in Newborns" initiative aims to screen all newborns for hearing problems within the first 28 days of life. By 2021, over 2 million newborns had been screened, and around 8,000 were identified as having hearing problems and had received early intervention services.[74]

The "Women's Health Initiative" aims to improve women's health, focusing on reproductive health, family planning, breast cancer screening, and cervical cancer prevention. This program has established women's health clinics in all governorates of Egypt and has trained over 20,000 healthcare providers on women's health issues.[75]

The "Mother and Child" initiative aims to improve mothers' and children's health, focusing on health services including antenatal care, delivery services, and postnatal care. This program has established mother and child health units in all governorates of Egypt and has provided training for approximately 30,000 healthcare providers on maternal and child health issues.[75]

References

1. Mark JJ. Ancient Egypt. In: *World History Encyclopedia*. 2009. Accessed May 5, 2023, from https://www.ancient.eu/egypt/.
2. Baines JR, Bowman AK, Wente EF, et al. Ancient Egypt. In: *Encyclopedia Britannica*. 2023. Accessed May 5, 2023. https://www.britannica.com/place/ancient-Egypt.
3. State Information Service. *Egypt's History—Modern Era*. 2022. Accessed May 5, 2023. https://beta.sis.gov.eg/en/egypt/history/egypts-history/modern-era/.
4. Hopwood D, Little DP, Holt PM, et al. Egypt. In: *Encyclopedia Britannica*. 2023. Accessed May 12, 2023. https://www.britannica.com/place/Egypt.
5. UNISDR. *The Government of Egypt: National Report and Information on Disaster Reduction*. Presented at World Conference on Disaster Reduction—Kobe-Hyogo, Japan. 2005. Accessed May 10, 2023. https://www.unisdr.org/2005/mdgs-drr/national-reports/Egypt-report.pdf.
6. City Population. *Egypt—Arabic Republic of Egypt*. 2022. Accessed May 10, 2023. https://www.citypopulation.de/en/egypt/.
7. Arab Republic of Egypt Presidency. *The Fifteen Committee assigned by the Former Acting President of Egypt Adly Mansour. (2014). Constitution of the Arab Republic of Egypt 2014*. 2020. Accessed May 10, 2023. https://www.presidency.eg/ar/%D9%85%D8%B5%D8%B1/%D8%A7%D9%84%D8%AF%D8%B3%D8%AA%D9%88%D8%B1/%B1/.
8. Fahmy NS. *The Politics of Egypt: State–Society Relationship* (1st ed.). Routledge; 2002. Accessed May 10, 2023. https://doi.org/10.4324/9780203037485.
9. Ismael TY. *Government and Politics of the Contemporary Middle East: Continuity and Change* (2nd ed.). Routledge; 2018. Accessed May 10, 2023. https://doi.org/10.4324/9781315767239.
10. World Bank Group. World development indicator 2021 (WDI). 2021. Accessed March 18, 2023. https://databank.worldbank.org/source/world-development-indicators.
11. African Development Group Bank. Egypt economic outlook. 2023. Accessed March 18, 2023. https://www.afdb.org/en/countries/north-africa/egypt/egypt-economic-outlook.
12. World Bank Group. The World Bank in Egypt. 2023. Accessed March 20, 2023. https://www.worldbank.org/en/country/egypt/overview#2.
13. Dolson JC, Shann MV, Hammouda H, et al. The petroleum potential of Egypt. *AAPG Bull*. 1999;83(12). doi: https://doi.org/10.1306/E4FD46A7-1732-11D7-8645000102C1865D.
14. Khalifa G. Factors affecting tourism organization competitiveness: implications for the Egyptian tourism industry. *African J Hosp Tourism Leis*. 2020;9(3):116-130.
15. El-Enbaby H, Figueroa JL, El-Didi H, Breisinger C. The role of agriculture and the agro-processing industry for development in Egypt: an overview. 2016. https://ebrary.ifpri.org/digital/api/collection/p15738coll2/id/131007/download.
16. Hegazy M. Egypt transport policies 2014–2021. Arab Reform Initiative. 2022. Accessed April 10, 2023. https://www.arab-reform.net/publication/egypt-transport-policies-14-21/.
17. Zaazou ZA. Citizens' participation in financing national projects: an applied study on the enlargement of the Suez Canal of Egypt. *Rev Econ Pol Sci*. Ahead-of-print. https://doi.org/10.1108/REPS-10-2019-0131.
18. Ghalib H, El-Khorazaty MT, Serag Y. New capital cities as tools of development and nation-building: review of Astana and Egypt's new administrative capital city. *Ain Shams Engineer J*. 2021;12(3):3405-3409.
19. Central Intelligence Agency. Egypt. In: *The World Factbook*. 2023. Accessed April 13, 2023. https://www.cia.gov/the-world-factbook/countries/egypt/.
20. World Bank Group. Egypt, Arab Rep. 2020. Accessed April 13, 2023. https://data.worldbank.org/country/egypt-arab-rep.
21. United Nations, Department of Economic and Social Affairs Population Division. World population prospects 2022. 2022. Accessed March 22, 2023. https://population.un.org/wpp/Download/Standard/Population/.
22. *The World Atlas*. Major ethnic groups in Egypt. 2023. Accessed March 15, 2023. https://www.worldatlas.com/articles/what-is-the-ethnic-composition-of-egypt.html.
23. U.S. Embassy in Cairo. 2021 Report on international religious freedom: Egypt. 2021. Accessed March 2, 2023. https://eg.usembassy.gov/2021-report-on-international-religious-freedom/.
24. Ministry of Health and Population. Overview of health system in Egypt. In: *Egypt Service Provision Assessment Survey 2002*. Ministry of Health and Population/Egypt, El-Zanaty Associates/Egypt, ORC Macro, eds, Calverton, MD: Ministry of Health and Population/Egypt, El-Zanaty Associates/Egypt, and ORC Macro; 2003. Accessed March 2, 2023. http://dhsprogram.com/pubs/pdf/SPA5/SPA5.pdf.
25. Al Bahnasy RA, Mohamed OA, El-Shazly HA, et al. The successes and the challenges of Egyptian health sector

reform program. *Menoufia Med J.* 2016;29(4):979-983. doi: 10.4103/1110-2098.202500.

26. Gericke CA, Britain K, Elmahdawy M, Elsisi G. Health system in Egypt. In: van Ginneken E, Busse R, eds. *Health Care Systems and Policies.* New York, NY: Springer; 2018. doi: 10.1007/978-1-4614-6419-8_7-1.
27. Center for Global Health and Development. Egypt's health care system. 2018. Accessed March 4, 2023. https://www.cghd.org/index.php/global-health-partnerships-and-solutions/profiles/43-egypts-health-care-system.
28. Jurjus A. The health system in Egypt: an overview. *Hum Health J.* 2015;31:17-21. Accessed March 4, 2023. https://dhsprogram.com/pubs/pdf/SPA7/02Chapter02.pdf.
29. Fasseeh A, ElEzbawy B, Adly W, et al. Healthcare financing in Egypt: a systematic literature review. *J Egyptian Pub Health Assoc.* 2022;97(1):1.
30. Council of Ministers. *Healthcare Sector: 7 Years of Achievement.* Egypt Cabinet Information and Decision Support Center; January 22, 2022.
31. Mathauer I, Khalifa AY, Mataria A. *Implementing the Universal Health Insurance Law of Egypt: What Are the Key Issues on Strategic Purchasing and Its Governance Arrangements?* (No. WHO/UHC/HGF/HFCase Study/19.13). World Health Organization; 2019.
32. Fasseeh A, ElEzbawy B, Adly W, et al. Healthcare financing in Egypt: a systematic literature review. *J Egypt Public Health Assoc.* 2022;97(1):1. doi: 10.1186/s42506-021-00089-8.
33. Hamza M. Egypt's Universal Healthcare Act: a primer. 2017. Accessed March 13, 2023. https://enterprise.press/wp-content/uploads/2017/12/Egypts-Universal-Healthcare-Act-A-Primer.pdf.
34. Elgazzar H. Income and the use of health care: an empirical study of Egypt and Lebanon. *Health Econ Policy Law.* 2009;4(4):445-478.
35. World Health Organization, Regional Office for the Eastern Mediterranean. Egypt health profile. 2015. Accessed March 13, 2023. https://rho.emro.who.int/sites/default/files/Profiles-briefs-files/EMROPUB_EN_19264-EGY.pdf.
36. Radwan G, Adawy A. The Egyptian health map: a guide for evidence-based decision-making. *Eastern Mediterranean Health J.* 2019;25(5):350-361. https://doi.org/10.26719/emhj.18.048.
37. World Bank Group. The World Bank data 2023: hospital beds (per 1,000 people)—Egypt, Arab Rep. 2023. Accessed March 14, 2023. https://data.worldbank.org/indicator/SH.MED.BEDS.ZS?end=2017&locations=EG&start=2001.
38. Colliers Healthcare Advisory & Valuation Services. Egypt healthcare sector overview. 2021. Accessed April 10, 2023. https://www.colliers.com/en-eg/research/cairo/egypt-healthcare-overview.
39. World Bank Group. Egypt: transforming Egypt's healthcare system project. 2018. Accessed March 9, 2023. http://documents.worldbank.org/curated/en/796381530329773770/Egypt-Transforming-Egypts-Healthcare-System-Project.
40. CAPMAS 2020. Number of hospitals in private sector. Accessed April 25, 2023. https://www.capmas.gov.eg/Pages/IndicatorsPage.aspx?Ind_id=1066.
41. Jabbour S. Egypt in crisis: politics, health care reform, and social mobilization for health rights. In: *Public Health in the Arab World.* Cambridge, UK/New York, NY: Cambridge University Press; 2012:477-488.
42. Egyptian Medical Syndicate. 2022. Accessed 2023. ems.org.eg/ar/news/Committees/2430?fbclid=IwAR3rCqTgo7gwX8t9-ZwWDTvzxDZsn8tCA1wwHdfpIMDUWUXnR60rG48nuqM.
43. World Health Organization, Eastern Mediterranean Regional Office. *Health Systems Strengthening Towards Universal Health Coverage.* Cairo, Egypt: WHO EMRO; 2023. Accessed March 15, 2023. https://www.emro.who.int/egy/programmes/health-systems-strengthening.html#health-information-system.
44. Kadry A. Egypt to implement healthcare system nationwide within 10 years: finance minister. *Ahmed Kadry. Ahram Online*: Sunday July 24, 2022. Accessed March 17, 2023. https://english.ahram.org.eg/News/472012.aspx.
45. World Health Organization. How WHO is driving impact on the ground demonstrating greater accountability and transparency. 2021. Accessed March 17, 2023. https://www.who.int/about/accountability/results/who-results-report-2020-2021/country-profile/2021/egypt.
46. Mohamed NA, Abdel-Razik MS, Salem MR. Adjustment of Family Planning Service statistics reports to support decision-making at central and governorate level. *Egypt J Egypt Public Health Assoc.* 2022;97:4. https://doi.org/10.1186/s42506-021-00098-7.
47. GAHAR. *GAHAR Handbook for Hospital Standards.* February 2021. https://gahar.gov.eg/upload/gahar-handbook-for-hospital-standards--2021-english-version-.pdf.
48. Oxford Business Group. Covid-19 and Egyptian insurance: why are insurers cautiously optimistic about the future? 2020. Accessed April 20, 2023. https://oxfordbusinessgroup.com/articles-interviews/covid-19-and-egyptian-insurance-why-are-insurers-cautiously-optimistic-about-the-future.
49. Elsayed TM, Elsisi GH, Elmahdawy M. Pharmacy practice in Egypt. In: *Pharmacy Practice in Developing Countries.* Academic Press; 2016:291-317.
50. Wirtz VJ, Hogerzeil HV, Gray AL, et al. Essential medicines for universal health coverage. *Lancet.* 2017;389(10067):403-476.
51. World Health Organization. Health systems strengthening towards universal health coverage. 2022. Accessed March 9, 2023. https://www.emro.who.int/egy/programmes/health-systems-strengthening.html#health-financing.
52. Gericke CA. *Financing Health Care in Egypt: Current Issues and Options for Reform.* Diskussionspapier 2004/5. Berlin, Germany: Technische Universität Berlin, Fakultät Wirtschaft und Management; 2004. doi: 10.1007/s10389-005-0006-4.
53. Rashad AS, Sharaf MF. Who benefits from public healthcare subsidies in Egypt? *Soc Sci.* 2015;4(4):1162-1176. doi: 10.3390/socsci4041162.
54. Rizk R, Abou-Ali H. *Out of Pocket Health Expenditure and Household Budget: Evidence from Arab Countries.* Economic Research Forum; 2016. Accessed March 28, 2023. https://erf.org.eg/publications/out-of-pocket-health-expenditure-and-household-budgetevidence-from-arab-countries/.
55. Nakhimovsky S, Glandon D, Rafeh N, Hassan N. Egypt national health accounts: 2008/09. Health Systems 20/20 Project. 2011. Accessed March 28, 2023. https://www.hfgproject.org/egyptnational-health-accounts-200809/.
56. Saleh SS, Alameddine MS, Natafgi NM, et al. The path towards universal health coverage in the Arab uprising countries Tunisia, Egypt, Libya, and Yemen. *Lancet.* 2014;383(9914):368-381. doi: 10.1016/S0140-6736(13)62339-9.

57. Haley DR, Bég SA. The road to recovery: Egypt's healthcare reform. *Int J Health Plann Manage.* 2012;27(1):e83-e91. doi: 10.1002/hpm.1088.
58. Wanis H. Pharmaceutical pricing in Egypt. *Pharmaceutical Prices in the 21st Century*. 2015:59-78.
59. Ismail SA. The rocky road to universal health coverage in Egypt: a political economy of health insurance reform from 2005–15. *Int Soc Secur Rev.* 2018;71(2):79-101. doi: 10.1111/issr.12167.
60. Abbas Y, Abul-Magd E, Elmekkawy A, Abaza S. The evolution of private health insurance in Egypt within the implementation of universal health coverage. *Value Health.* 2016;19(3):A291. doi: 10.1016/j.jval.2016.03.833.
61. Zekri M. Egyptian initiative for personal rights. In: *Challenges Facing Health Expenditure in Egypt*. 1st ed. 2009. Accessed March 28, 2023. https://eipr.org/en/publications/challenges-facing-healthexpenditure-egypt.
62. Ministry of Finance. Egypt's five-year macroeconomic framework and strategy (FY14/15–FY18/19). Sharm Elsheikh. 2015. Accessed March 28, 2023. http://www.mof.gov.eg/MOFGallerySource/English/Strategy.pdf.
63. DHS Program. The health system and public health. *Health Communication Capacity: Collaborative Egypt*. 2018. Accessed March 5, 2023. https://dhsprogram.com/pubs/pdf/SPA5/02chapter02.pdf.
64. Ministry of Health and Population. Egypt health system review. 2019. Accessed March 23, 2023. http://apps.who.int/iris/bitstream/handle/10665/311544/9789290226872-eng.pdf.
65. GAHAR. Who we are. 2023. Accessed May 4, 2023. https://www.gahar.gov.eg/page/p/%D9%85%D9%86-%D9%86%D8%AD%D9%86.
66. GAHAR. Accreditation standards. 2023. Accessed May 4, 2023. https://www.gahar.gov.eg/page/p/%D9%85%D8%B9%D8%A7%D9%8A%D9%8A%D8%B1-%D8%A7%D8%B9%D8%AA%D9%85%D8%A7%D8%AF-%D8%A7%D9%84%D9%85%D8%B3%D8%AA%D8%B4%D9%81%D9%8A%D8%A7%D8%AA-1.
67. World Health Organization. Egypt: health equity profile. 2019. Accessed April 12, 2023. https://www.who.int/publications/i/item/egypt-health-equity-profile.
68. Ahmed M. Insight into Egypt's healthcare sector. Omnia Health. 2021. Accessed March 2, 2023. https://insights.omnia-health.com/management/insight-egypts-healthcare-sector.
69. Nabil NM, Elawady SS. Patient satisfaction with health care services provided at primary health care centers in Alexandria, Egypt. *J Educ Pract.* 2016;7(12):58-66. https://doi.org/10.7176/JEP.
70. UNFPA & HelpAge International. Country profile: the rights and wellbeing of older persons in Egypt. October 27, 2021. Accessed February 10, 2025. https://arabstates.unfpa.org/sites/default/files/pub-pdf/country_profile_-_egypt_27-10-2021_0.pdf.
71. Ministry of Health and Population. 100 Million Health Initiative. 2021. Accessed April 11, 2023. https://www.mohp.gov.eg/en/Initiatives/100-Million-Health-Initiative.
72. World Health Organization. Egypt launches the "100 Million Healthy Lives" initiative. 2021. Accessed April 11, 2023. https://www.who.int/emergencies/disease-outbreak-news/item/2021-DON280821.
73. Ministry of Health and Population. Early Detection of Hearing Problems in Newborns Initiative. 2021. Accessed April 11, 2023. https://www.mohp.gov.eg/en/Initiatives/Early-Detection-of-Hearing-Problems-in-Newborns-Initiative.
74. World Health Organization. Egypt launches Women's Health Initiative. 2021. Accessed April 11, 2023. https://www.emro.who.int/media/news/egypt-launches-womens-health-initiative.html.
75. Ministry of Health and Population. Mother and Child Health Initiative. 2021. Accessed April 11, 2023. https://www.mohp.gov.eg/en/Initiatives/Mother-and-Child-Health-Initiative.

CHAPTER 16

Israel

Carmen Stein

Country Description

As of April 25, 2023, Israel's population stood at 9,727,000. This is a more than 10-fold increase compared with when Israel was founded in 1948. **Table 16-1** contains significant details about Israel.

Table 16-1 **Israel***

Nationality	Noun: Israeli(s) Adjective: Israeli
Ethnic groups	Jewish 73.5% (Israel-born 79.7%, Europe/America/Oceania-born 14.3%, Africa-born 3.9%, Asia-born 2.1%), Arab 21.1%, other 5.4% (2022 est.)
Religions	Jewish 73.5%, Muslim 18.1%, Christian 1.9%, Druze 1.6%, other 4.9% (2022 est.)
Language	Hebrew (official), Arabic (special status under Israeli law), English (most commonly used foreign language)
Literacy	Definition: Age 15 and over and can read and write. Total population: 97.8% Male: 98.7% Female: 96.8% (2011 est.)
Government type	Parliamentary democracy
Date of independence	May 14, 1948 (from League of Nations mandate under British administration)
Gross domestic product (GDP) per capita	393.861 billion USD (2021 est.)
Unemployment rate	5.05% (2021 est.)
Natural hazards	Sandstorms may occur during spring and summer; droughts; minor earthquakes
Environment: current issues	Limited arable land and natural freshwater resources pose serious constraints; desertification; air pollution from industrial and vehicle emissions; groundwater pollution from industrial and domestic waste, chemical fertilizers, and pesticides

Table 16-1 Israel*

Population	9,043,387 (2023 est.)
Age structure	0–14 years: 25.96% (male 1,200,721/female 1,146,556) 15–64 years: 61.66% (male 2,839,124/female 2,737,054) 65 years and over: 12.38% (2023 est.) (male 506,536/female 613,396)
Median age	Total: 30.4 years (2020) Male: 29.8 years Female: 31 years
Population growth rate	1.43% (2023 est.)
Birth rate	17.3 births/1,000 population (2023 est.)
Death rate	5.05 deaths/1,000 population (2023 est.)
Net migration rate	1.99 migrant(s)/1,000 population (2023 est.)
Gender ratio	At birth: 1.05 male/female 0–14 years: 1.05 male/female 15–64 years: 1.04 male/female 65 years and over: 0.83 male/female Total population: 1.01 male/female (2023 est.)
Infant mortality rate	Total: 3.49 deaths/1,000 live births (2023 est.) Male: 3.75 deaths/1,000 live births Female: 3.22 deaths/1,000 live births
Life expectancy at birth	Total population: 83.54 years (2023 est.) Male: 81.65 years Female: 85.53 years
Total fertility rate	2.54 children born/woman (2023)

*The numbers in the table are from before the conflict in the Middle East began on October 7, 2023.

USD = U.S. dollars.

Population (includes populations of the Golan Heights or Golan Sub-District and also East Jerusalem, which was annexed by Israel after 1967). approximately 236,600 Israeli settlers live in East Jerusalem (2021); following the March 2019 U.S. recognition of the Golan Heights as being part of Israel, *The World Factbook* no longer includes the Israeli settler population of the Golan Heights (estimated at 23,400 in 2019) in its overall Israeli settler total.

Data from Central Intelligence Agency. The World Factbook, 2023: Israel. https://www.cia.gov/the-world-factbook/countries/israel/#introduction.

History

Background

Israel is an ancient land that has been inhabited by many different peoples, nations, and empires since the dawn of Western civilization. Although Jewish people have resided in Israel since approximately 1300 BCE, when Israelite communities started multiplying in the northern hills area of Canaan, the first unified nation was in the era of King David (1000 BCE). The Northern Israel kingdom was destroyed by the Assyrians in 710 BCE, and the Southern Kingdom of Judah was destroyed by the Babylonians in approximately 500 BCE. The Jews returned to Israel when Persian rule was crushed (538–516 BCE) and rebuilt what is known as the Second Temple, which had originally been built by King Solomon (960 BCE). In a revolt led by Judah Maccabee, Jewish independence from Macedonia (Greek rule) was reestablished in 166 BCE, which is commemorated by the holiday of Hanukkah. Under King Herod's Roman rule (64–63 BCE), King Solomon's Second Temple was declared a world wonder.[1] Visitors to Israel today can touch the Western Wall of the Second Temple and see its foundation in underground tunnels. The Roman Empire ended Jewish rule of Israel in approximately 70 CE. The Jewish Diaspora to the Iberian Peninsula and Europe followed, although a small population remained in Israel. Hundreds of years, the Inquisition, thousands of pogroms, and the Holocaust would mark the suffering of an exiled people longing to return to their homeland, Israel. The creation of the modern state of Israel was not dependent on the history of suffering, but surely anti-Semitism was a trigger for Zionism and the creation of a Jewish homeland in Israel.

In 1917, the Balfour Declaration by Great Britain validated the Jewish historical claim to Israel, endorsing the claim of the First Zionist Congress to establish a nation in what was then called Palestine under the British Mandate. At the end of World War II, on November 29, 1947, the United Nations General Assembly recommended partition of Palestine into a Jewish state and an Arab state; the recommendation was accepted by the Zionist leadership but was totally rejected by the Arab leadership.[1]

On May 14, 1948, David Ben-Gurion proclaimed the creation of Israel. In that proclamation, key values highlighted were liberty, democracy, justice, and peace with Arab neighbors.

Healthcare organizations are a bridge to peace. Bringing advanced medical care to all, regardless of race, ethnicity, or nationality, earned Hadassah's two hospitals in Jerusalem—Mount Scopus and Ein Kerem—a nomination for a Nobel Peace Prize in 2005. Notably, the three areas cited for the nomination included treating terrorists, having a diverse staff, and building bridges to peace through collaborating on medical activities with physicians.

Today's visitors to Israel will notice that the cultural orientation in Israel is *carpe diem*. One must seize the day because the threat to life is ubiquitous. Everyone has lost someone; Yom HaZichron, the Day of Remembrance, is marked nationwide by an early morning siren, during which Israelis stop whatever they are doing, including driving, and remember those who have fallen. But, after sunset, which is considered the next day according to Jewish tradition, Yom HaAtzmaut, Independence Day, is marked by public and private celebrations. In a land continually under siege, people know how to live life to the fullest.

Israel's history of accomplishments in its brief 68 years as a modern nation speaks to the industriousness and determination of the people to succeed and make significant, positive contributions to the modern world. In 2000, Israel invented the Pill Cam, an ingestible video camera used to noninvasively diagnose digestive diseases. Israel is known as the start-up nation; in *Start-Up Nation: The Story of Israel's Economic Miracle* (2009), the authors note: "Technology companies and global investors are beating a path to Israel and finding unique combinations of audacity, creativity, and drive everywhere they look. [That] may explain why, in addition to boasting the highest density of start-ups in the world (a total of 3,850 start-ups, one for every 1,844 Israelis)."[2] In January 2016, Dr. Dimitrios Karussis, of Hadassah Medical Organization, conducted the world's first clinical trial using patients' own bone marrow stem cells to treat amyotrophic lateral sclerosis (ALS, also known as Lou Gehrig's disease). Using identical protocols, the Mayo Clinic, Massachusetts General Hospital (a Harvard Medical School affiliate), and the University of Massachusetts Memorial Medical Center are conducting expanded stem cell trials in the United States. In modern Israel, medical care and world-class medical researchers continue to make significant contributions to the world.

Size and Geography

Slightly larger than New Jersey, Israel is located in the Middle East between Egypt and Lebanon and is surrounded by the Gaza Strip, Jordan, Syria, the West Bank, and the Mediterranean Sea. See **Figure 16-1**. Due to the geopolitics and hostile bordering countries, Israel is a nation constantly under siege, which impacts health care.

Israel is a land of geographic extremes, with the lowest point being 408 meters below sea level in the Dead Sea and the highest elevation being 1,208 meters on Har Hermon. One can ski on Har Hermon and swim in the Dead Sea, all on the same day in December, even as it might be raining in Haifa. The desert areas of the South and East are hot and dry. The *khamsin*, a hot, sandy wind, blows grit from the east onto streets, into houses, and into eyes and lungs. When the *khamsins* blow, those with respiratory illnesses, the elderly, and the very young are vulnerable. During the spring, in late February–April, the climate is mild, especially in the northern Upper Galilee, down through the coastal plains, and east to Jerusalem. During the hot, humid summers, one can often find cool relief in Jerusalem. Israel's very diverse population of 8 million people is spread over 20,700 square kilometers.[3,4]

Israel is not rich in natural resources; most of the timber was logged over 1,000 years ago. Today, Israeli homes and buildings are mainly stone, stucco, and concrete. Agriculture used to be Israel's prime income source; however, in the early 1980s, the agricultural income base transitioned to manufacturing, industry, technology, and medicine. The forests that do exist in Israel today are predominantly part of the Jewish National Fund forests; as such, they are forest reserves, not timberlands for harvest.

Lake Kinneret (sometimes known as the Sea of Galilee) is one of the main freshwater sources, as is the water table in Samaria. Water use and water rights were some of the primary underlying issues in the region. With a part Mediterranean and part desert climate, Israel has suffered water shortage and drought

Figure 16-1 Map of Israel

issues. However, since 2005, desalination plants—the largest of which can be seen along the Haifa–Tel Aviv highway—have significantly improved water issues in Israel, to the extent that some agronomists believe that water issues no longer exist. Says Shaul Ben-Dov, an agronomist at Ramat Rachel, "Now there is no problem of water. The price is higher, but we can live a normal life in a country that is half desert."[5] Even so, others argue that specific regions in Israel are at risk for water shortages; therefore, residents are constantly vigilant and conserving water.

Government and Political System

Israel is the only democracy in the Middle East. Citizens are exceptionally active in their democracy and vote on all levels: local, regional, and national. The voter percentage in Israel is extraordinarily high. In the 2013 election, 71.8% of the electorate voted.[6]

Like the United States, the Israeli government has executive, legislative, and judicial branches. Separation of powers is secured because the independence of the judicial branch is guaranteed by law and the executive branch is dependent on the confidence of the legislature.

The Israeli Congress (Knesset) is a parliamentary democracy, which means that political parties have historically been organized around political beliefs and world views. On a national level, citizens vote for party lists, members of whom then become Knesset members based on the percentage of votes their party receives. All citizens may vote, and each vote is counted equally. Citizens vote for the political party that most closely represents the citizen's values, although that seems to be in transition as Israelis debate both candidates and issues. In the 2015 elections, 26 parties submitted a list of candidates to the General Elections Committee.[4] The political parties are represented in the Knesset in proportion to how many votes the party receives. The prime minister is the person whose political party (1) gets the most votes and (2) can create a coalition in the Knesset.

Elections are usually held every 4 years, but they can be held earlier if the Knesset votes to dissolve before the end of the term, if it fails to pass a budget within 3 months, if the prime minister dissolves the Knesset because the Knesset members object to the coalition government, or if the prime minister fails to form a coalition government. Currently, the Likud party, with Benjamin Netanyahu as its head, has the controlling percentage of Knesset seats; therefore, Netanyahu is the prime minister of Israel. In the elections for the 24th Knesset (on March 23, 2021), the number of registered voters was 6,578,084 and the number of valid votes was 4,410,052, with an electoral threshold of 3.25 and 36,210 votes per seat.

Macroeconomics

Israel has a technologically advanced, mixed economy. Much of the economy is based on the free market. However, agriculture is heavily subsidized and food product prices are controlled. High-technology equipment and pharmaceuticals are among the country's leading exports. Its major imports include crude oil, grains, raw materials, and military equipment. Israel's trade deficits are offset by tourism and technology exports.[7] There is a significant inflow of foreign investment into Israel. The newest and upcoming Israeli industry is medical tourism. Israel is cited in the top three countries by the Medical Tourism Index.[8] Patients seek Israeli medical care for its services and top-quality patient care. The global medical tourism industry is expected to grow significantly from $11.20 billion USD in 2023 to $80.07 billion USD in 2032.[9]

Recently discovered natural gas fields off of Israel's coast promise a potential boost to the economy via energy independence. However, political and regulatory issues have delayed the development of one of the largest fields. Production from a smaller field yielded a "0.8% boost to Israel's GDP in 2013 and a 0.3% boost in 2014."[10]

Housing prices, income disparities, and a growing poverty rate are becoming major concerns in Israel. Most young Israelis seeking to purchase a home still rely on their parents to do so. In spite of a call for government reforms, the actual response has been slow and ineffective.

Recent changes in educational opportunities for the ultraorthodox and Arab Israeli communities are starting to result in a growing labor sector among these communities. For example, in Nazareth, the TRI/O Tech entrepreneurship hub provides education and services for Arab start-ups and participation in the technology sector. In Jerusalem, Hadassah Academic College provides gender-separate curricula for Jewish Orthodox men and women, without which those community members could not attend classes due to religious law.

Israelis have had to rely on brain power in the modern world to create a viable economic base. There was a time in Israel in the 1980s, when items on grocery store shelves did not have price tags. The price list was kept up at the cashier's stand. Daily inflation was well over 30%. Since 2016, agriculture has been almost entirely replaced by clean industry. Israel is a nation of innovation. Today, Israel's economic strengths lie in two areas, technology and medical research. The middle class is strong and growing.

Demographics

Israeli culture is as rich and diverse as its people. On Independence Day 2016, "Israel's population stood at a record 8,522,000."[4] Overall, the total population of Israel "experienced a growth rate of 2%,"[4] and by 2025, Israel is projected to have a population of 10 million. Israel is the 99th most populous country in the world, not counting the 250,000 refugees from Sudan and the illegal foreign workers. The ethnic breakdown in Israel roughly matches the breakdown in religions. According to the Israel Ministry of Foreign Affairs, the majority of the religious groups, which are also the ethnic groups, are those shown in **Table 16-2**.

In 2014, 75% of the population were sabras, native-born Israelis. However, "between Independence Day 2015 and 2016, 25% of the new immigrants arrived from France and 24% from Ukraine."[4] These data are not surprising, considering the terrorist activities in both of those countries. This recent immigration wave and increase in terrorism has impacted hospitals both in terms of additional patients needing services and in terms of patients and medical staff needing translators. In 2024, more than 60,000 Israelis emigrated from the country in the previous 2 years. Fears of terrorism, the war between Israel and Hamas, and a lack of security are the main reasons for leaving.[11]

Jewish people immigrated to Israel from many lands around the world: Europe, Russia, Latin America, and many Arab and North African countries. Jews are native to and have continued to reside on the same land for thousands of years. Arab Christians and Arab Muslims have also resided on this land and are now citizens in Israel. Tel Aviv, the economic center of Israel, received a top World Smart City Award in 2014 for taking advantage of the potential of technology to increase public engagement.[13] Jerusalem is a major spiritual center, with sites that are spiritually significant to Jews, Christians, and Muslims.

Table 16-2 Ethnic Groups in Israel[12]

Jews	75.0%
Muslims	17.5%
Christians	2.0%
Druze	1.6%
Not classified by religion	3.9%

Data from Rosen B, Waitzberg R, Merkur S. *Israel: Health System Review.* European Observatory on Health Systems and Policy; 2020.

Israel provides substantial benefits and services to women, including maternity leave and job protection. Under qualifying conditions, Israeli women can be paid 100% of their salary for 14 weeks of maternity leave and are granted significant extensions for multiple births.[14] In addition, a spouse may be eligible to receive the maternity leave benefits if the woman wishes to return earlier to work or in the case of multiple births or disabled children. The National Insurance Institute of Israel sets the policy and establishes salary payouts. Additionally, a woman who is in vocational training may receive maternity benefits. According to the CIA's *The World Factbook*, Israel's global healthy life expectancy ranked 11th out of 188 countries; its overall life expectancy is 82.4 years.[10]

About 25.2% of Israeli citizens are Arabs.[10] As citizens of Israel, they have full and equal voting rights. Furthermore, Israel is one of the few nations in the Middle East where women have full voting rights. Additionally, Arab Israelis have "their own political parties, serve on the Israeli Knesset, Cabinet, and Supreme Court."[15]

National Service and Security

Israel requires compulsory national service for all citizens, both men and women, commencing at 18 years old. Most serve in the Israel Defense Forces (IDF): Men are required to serve in the military for 3 years of active duty and women for 2 years of active duty. Men are also required to serve in the army reserves for a number of years after active duty; women are welcome to do so if they choose. Women also may be combatants and fighter pilots. Options for types of service are available; for example, based on their eligibility, some people may do community service. One area of controversy involves what kind of service certain ultra-Orthodox men must do. Currently, they are allowed to study in a yeshiva; however, bills are constantly proposed to the Knesset to change this option for required service. Druzes serve with distinction and can be officers in the IDF; however, Muslim Arab Israelis do not serve in Israel's military. This is a sensitive topic.

The IDF protects citizens and borders and serves in a defense capacity. Terrorist attacks occur inside Israel proper as well as in Judea and Samaria, often referred to by Western journalists as the West Bank. Both men and women serve in areas of high conflict.

Israeli citizens consider serving in the IDF not only an obligation to the nation but also an honor. When seniors graduate from high school and receive notification of their assignments, there are usually congratulations expressed and family gatherings to honor the inductees; after boot camp, family members attend the induction ceremonies at Masada or at the Western Wall in Jerusalem. IDF personnel make significant, crucial lifelong contacts that can result in important business connections, which often lead to start-up businesses and employment opportunities.

The Current Healthcare System

Although the nation of Israel was founded in 1948, it was not until 1995 that a National Health Insurance (NHI) program was put into place.[16] Since the start of the NHI, Israel has become a world-class example of how to provide highly effective health care to all citizens at a price significantly below that in the other OECD member nations.[17] According to 2013 data, Israel spent 7.5% of GDP on health services compared with the OECD average of 8.9%. In contrast, the United States spent 16.4% of GDP on health services. Life expectancy of those living in Israel was 82 years (81 for males and 84 for females). In contrast, life expectancy in the United States was 79 years (76 for males and 81 for females).[18] Life expectancy is but one measure of the overall success of the efforts throughout the healthcare system to keep people healthy and productive throughout their life spans.

Terrorism and mass casualties make Israeli medical personnel the world experts in mass casualty trauma care. Indeed, just prior to the terrorist incident at the April 2013 Boston Marathon, Hadassah's Dr. Avi Rivkind conducted a mass casualties workshop at Massachusetts General Hospital, the result of which enabled first responders and hospitals to save many lives after the attack.[3]

Before examining the organization, financing, and delivery of health services in Israel, it is useful to briefly explore how health services were delivered prior to the passage of the National Health Insurance Law in 1995. Prior to the founding of the nation, health services were delivered by a number of *sick funds* in addition to a number of nonprofit entities.[19] These sick funds ultimately morphed into the present payer groups. One of the more interesting organizations was the Hadassah Medical Organization—founded in 1912 by Henrietta Szold, an American—which established the Tipat Halav system (well-baby clinics, literally *drop-of-milk clinics*).[19] Today, Hadassah operates two hospitals in Jerusalem. Government hospitals provide more than half of all acute beds in Israel, along with most psychiatric facilities. A number of these hospitals are located in buildings abandoned by British Army camps, left over from the War of Independence in 1947–1948.[19]

As noted earlier, Israel is not a homogenous nation in any sense of the word. A healthcare system that proposes to provide coverage to all citizens must account for multiple religious and cultural norms. Israel is a diverse nation and all Israeli citizens and residents "have access to basic health care from the State, through their HMO."[20] Health indices suggest disparities between Arabs and Jews living in Israel. For example, differences exist in "infant mortality, at three per 1,000 live births for Jews and seven per 1,000 for Arabs; [and] a gap in life expectancy with Jews living longer, which increased from 2 years in 1998 to 3.7 years in 2008."[20]

Although a small nation in terms of both geographic size and population, and a young nation, having been established in 1948, Israel has succeeded in crafting a universal health system based on the principle of provision of health services to all people without discrimination.[21] Notably, Hadassah hospitals were nominated in 2005 for a Nobel Peace Prize because, by policy and deed, they serve all people, regardless of race, creed, religion, or ethnicity. To develop a clear understanding of health services in Israel, the remainder of this section will focus on the organization, financing, and delivery of health services.

Organization

Since 1995, health services in Israel have been organized under the National Health Insurance Law (NHI). The NHI is structured in a manner to provide health services to every citizen and permanent resident of the nation. Every eligible person elects to be part of one of four not-for-profit health insurance plans (Kupot Cholim): Clalit Health Services, Leumit Health Fund, Maccabi Healthcare Services, and Meuhedet Health Fund.[22] Israelis are free to choose one of these plans. The NHI system is primarily financed from public sources from general tax revenues.[19]

According to Dr. Bruce Rosen, the director of the Smokler Center for Health Policy Research at the Meyers-JDC-Brookdale Institute:

> Clalit was founded by the Labor Party–affiliated General Federation of Labor and, as such, historically had a decidedly Socialist orientation. Leumit was founded by the Nationalist Workers Association, which was affiliated with Israel's right wing parties; thus, while it did not share Clalit's Socialist origins, both approached health care as a service to be provided within the context of broader national goals. Maccabi and Meuhedet, in contrast, were founded by physicians with a liberal, free-market orientation.[21]

All four health plans have completely digitalized their operations; 100% of the physicians, and most of the other healthcare professionals, use an electronic medical record that is either connected online to, or an integral part of, the health plan's central medical record.[23]

Other significant differences among the plans include size; the mix of members in terms of age, income, and geographic location; the extent of reliance on salaried physicians (as opposed to independent physicans); the extent of reliance on group practices (as opposed to solo practitioners); and whether they own acute care hospitals.[24]

The Ministry of Health (MoH) requires that each of the health plans provide to its members a basic *basket of health services* that are available at either no cost or a heavily discounted rate. The elements of the basket include[21]:

- Clinic visits for consultation, diagnosis, and treatment by primary care and specialty physicians
- Prescription drugs
- Routine vaccinations
- Hospitalization and emergency room services
- Certain durable medical equipment
- Diagnostic services (including X-rays and imaging procedures)
- Mental health services
- Rehabilitation
- Fertility treatments (including genetic testing)
- Certain modalities of physical therapy
- Elective surgeries
- Organ transplants
- Critical cancer care
- Ambulatory services
- Dental care for children under 14 years old

Currently, dental services are not a covered benefit in the basic basket, with the exception of pediatric dental care up to age 14. However, the costs are significantly lower than they are in the United States. The basket of services is provided to all eligible citizens and permanent residents who live in Israel at least 183 days of the calendar year. Unlike in the preferred provider organizations (PPOs) in the United States, care from specialty physicians in Israel is available only with a referral from a primary care physician.

Supplemental health insurance (including long-term care insurance) is available for purchase through the four Kupot Cholim. While there are a number of supplemental health plans available, coverage through these plans includes[25]:

- Access to a broader range of medications
- Ability to choose surgeons and hospital locations
- Options for overseas treatment that may include innovative procedures not yet available in Israel
- Other components, such as new pioneering cancer management packages, critical illness coverage, and personal accident coverage

Without question, the most important stakeholder in the NHI system is the MoH, which has overall responsibility for the organization and functioning of the system. In addition to assuring the efficient operation of the overall system, the MoH is involved with technology assessment, prioritization of new technology, health plan regulation, quality monitoring of community-based care, and support for population health initiatives.[19]

In summary, the NHI system is organized in a way to assure all citizens and permanent residents of Israel a basic basket of services that are focused on primary and preventive care. Specialty care is available but requires a referral from the primary care provider. Hospitalization, pharmaceuticals, diagnostic testing, durable medical equipment, mental health, and rehabilitation services are all covered benefits. In addition, people can switch health plans annually if desired.[22]

Financing

According to data from the OECD, health spending in Israel accounted for 7.6% of GDP in 2022, below the average of 9.3% in other OECD countries.[26] In comparison, in the same year, the United States spent 17.3% of its GDP on health.[27] The public sector is the main source of health funding in nearly all OECD countries.[17] In Israel, 60% of health spending was

Table 16-3 Spending on Health Services in Israel as a Fraction of Total Health Expenditures, 2023

Outpatient/ambulatory physician services	36.6%[a]
Inpatient hospital care, including psychiatric and chronic care	32.7%
Pharmaceuticals, medical supplies, and medical equipment	13.8%
Outpatient/ambulatory dental services	7.7%
Health administration	4.4%
Fixed capital formation	3.1%
Health research and development	1.2%
Public health and prevention	0.4%

[a]OECD. Government at a glance 2023: Israel. https://www.oecd.org/en/publications/government-at-a-glance-2023_c4200b14-en/israel_cd0e2327-en.html.

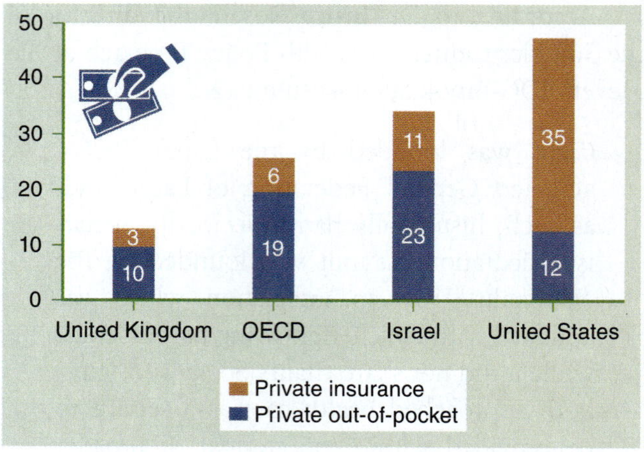

Figure 16-2 Private Health Spending as a Share of Health Expenditures, 2023

Reproduced from OECD. OECD health policy overview: health policy in Israel. 2023. Accessed November 1, 2023. http://www.oecd.org/health/bycountry/.

funded by public sources in 2023, well below the average of 72% in OECD countries.[28] In an international comparison, in 2023, Israel's per capita health expenditure was lower than most OECD countries, amounting to $3,803 USD.[28] **Table 16-3** shows spending on health services as a fraction of total health expenditures in Israel in 2012.

The overall NHI system is financed primarily by a health tax and general tax revenue. Over one-third of Israel's national health expenditures are covered by households, through a mix of out-of-pocket payments and supplemental insurance packages.

Payments by households cover copayments for certain services included in the NHI benefits package (such as visits to specialists and pharmaceuticals), as well as services not included in that package (such as dental and optometric care).[29] See **Figure 16-2**. The health tax is 3% of the gross monthly income for employees earning up to 60% of the average wage ($2,300 USD per month in 2023) ($1,965 USD) and 5% of the gross monthly income for those earning above the average wage.[20,30] Income above five times the average wage is not taxed for NHI purposes. Failure to pay the required health tax will result in government action to enforce payment but does not jeopardize the individual's right to NHI benefits. The tax is paid to the National Insurance Institute. Health taxes are supplemented by funds from the national budget that are also transferred to the NHI. Combined, these funds must equal the "cost of the basket of services" as defined by the National Health Insurance Law. They are distributed to the four health plans via a capitation formula based primarily on age, sex, and geographic region.[31] Since 1998, the Ministry of Finance has indexed inflationary increases for the basket of services to the standard national inflation rate and eliminated the previous practice of recognizing a separate and substantially higher inflation rate for the medical industry.[16]

According to the NHI, payment of health insurance premiums is mandatory for every person over 18 years of age. The level of payment is set on a progressive scale that varies according to income. People who work for an employer have their health insurance premiums deducted by their employer. Self-employed individuals or the unemployed must make arrangements directly with the National Insurance Institute. Certain categories of individuals are exempt from paying premiums or pay at a significantly reduced rate. These include married women who do not work outside of the home, soldiers in regular compulsory service, and recipients of specific types of National Insurance Institute allowances.[21]

Along with the low and decreasing public expenditure on health, there has been a constant increase in private spending. The voluntary health insurance (VHI) market is one of the largest in OECD countries, with about 87% of Israel's adult population being covered with a voluntary health plan and 53% being covered with commercial insurance. Household spending on VHI has increased over the past decade. Out-of-pocket expenditures are also high relative to many other countries (26% of total health expenditures, compared with a European Union average of 21%) and have increased somewhat over time. There are large differences in household expenditures on health by income quintile, which indicates the existence of inequalities.[19]

Hospital revenue is generated primarily through the provision of health services, with approximately 80% coming from the four health plans. Payment to public hospitals in Israel is based on a combination of fee-for-service, per diem fees, and case payments, which are subject to a revenue cap.[19] The revenue capping system's goal has been to eliminate incentives for hospitals to overprovide inpatient care and to constrain the growth in expenses, particularly those related to hospital services.

Despite the reimbursement mechanisms, the MoH subsidizes retrospectively almost all public hospitals. Subsidies have more than doubled from around €75 million in 2006 to €170 million ($79 million to $180 million USD) in 2012.[32] Nevertheless, both public and nonprofit hospitals have faced growing deficits in recent years. The extreme case of this was the near bankruptcy of the private nonprofit Hadassah Medical Center in 2014. The hospital did not dissolve because the MoH provided massive financial aid and increased the cap ceiling.[19] In addition, Hadassah, the Women's Zionist Organization, committed to a multimillion-dollar payment via fundraising efforts in order to retain ownership. From a symbolic perspective and considering its role in delivering inpatient hospital services, the closure of Hadassah Medical Center would have resulted in uncounted negative outcomes. In 2024, after at least 4 years without a stabilization budget and with increasing deficits looming, the MoH significantly increased the funds in the Health Services Basket to ensure that the funds can maintain strength and stability.[33]

In Israel, payment for physician services is the largest component of total health expenditures. Most physicians are paid employees of one of the four health plans or the public hospitals. As in the United States, physicians may choose to practice as an independent contractor and function as an independent business entity. A collective bargaining agreement between the Israel Medical Association and the major employers governs the payment terms for employed physicians in the health plans and hospitals. Physicians working independently are not covered by the agreement.[19] Physicians employed by the health plans are paid a combination of straight monthly salary plus a capitation fee for the panel of patients in the plan, depending on how the particular health plan operates.

It should be noted that physicians (both primary care and specialists) are well paid compared with their counterparts throughout other OECD countries. Although there are certainly differences in tax rates from one nation to the next, physicians in Israel appear to be fairly compensated for their work product.

In summary, financing of health services in Israel consists of a combination of public and private funds that serves as the foundation for a comprehensive set of services made available to all citizens and permanent residents. The majority of citizens pay an income-indexed health tax and are also responsible for an increasing level of out-of-pocket spending for copayments and health services not covered in the basic basket.

Delivery

This section examines the delivery of health services in Israel. Health services are divided between public health services and private health services, including hospitals and physicians. Delivery of health services to women and men on active duty in the military is not addressed because soldiers receive routine care through the IDF's Medical Corps.[34]

Public Health

Public health in Israel is coordinated through the Health Division within the MoH.[35] The Health Division is made up of six subordinate units:

- Department of Emergencies
- Medical Administration
- Medical Institute for Road Safety
- Medical Technologies and Infrastructure
- Public Health
- Quality, Service, and Safety Administration

Language from the MoH specific to public health services states:

> The Public Health Services concentrate on the healthy individual from the personal, community, and environmental preventive medicine perspectives through assimilation of the innovative concept of health promotion. The Public Health Services are committed to promoting health and disease prevention among the citizens of Israel, starting with family health stations, health services for school children, district health offices, through to the professional administrative staff.[35]

The range of public health services provided by the Health Division includes:

- Community genetics
- Community rehabilitation
- Employees' health

- Environmental health
- Epidemiology
- Health education and promotion
- Mother, child, and adolescent health
- National Food Service
- National Institute for Studying the Implications of Scalp Ringworm Treatment
- Nutrition
- Public health laboratories
- Public health nursing
- Tuberculosis and AIDS

Public health services are delivered through 18 health bureaus (roughly equivalent to local and county health departments) spread throughout the country.

Physicians

The Israeli Medical Association (IMA) allows post-graduate physicians, those who are in residency or beyond, to obtain a visiting physician license to volunteer in Israel. Israel has one of the most technologically advanced and highest-quality healthcare systems in the world. Hospitals in Israel are equipped with modern facilities and high-quality medical technology. Medical personnel are very well trained. Health Care in Israel is also delivered very efficiently. Access to physicians is made available through enrollment in one of the four health plans. Data from the World Bank enable comparison of the global ratio of 1.53 physicians to 1,000 people to Israel's 3.35 physicians per 1,000 people.[36] The PCPs work primarily in outpatient clinics throughout the nation, with higher concentrations of these clinics located in larger population centers. Access to primary care physicians is good, with most community clinics run by the health plans offering same-day visits.

Specialty care is provided through a network of over 17,000 board-certified specialty physicians. These specialty physicians are employed by the various hospitals or operate independently in community-based clinics. As might be expected, the four health plans are beginning to employ specialty physicians directly as a way of better controlling their expenses.[19] This effort by the health plans to bring more specialty care under their direct control has resulted in an increasing level of competition with hospitals and ambulatory clinics in the hospitals. Waiting times for specialists appear to be reasonable. In 2022–2023, wait times for most specialists decreased slightly.[28]

Specialty physicians employed by the hospitals are salaried members of the hospital staff and are prohibited from billing patients or health plans for additional services. This system of physician employment by hospitals is similar to what is currently in place in the United States, given the substantial growth of physician–hospital organizations (PHOs).[37] Generally speaking, patients in Israeli hospitals cannot select which specialist will care for them. They are assigned a physician according to the rotation schedule determined by department heads and their assistants. The exception is the private medical service in Jerusalem's nonprofit hospitals where, in return for an additional fee, the patient can choose a physician.[19]

Acute Care Hospitals

There are 28 acute care hospitals currently available in Israel.[38] The majority of hospitals in Israel have in excess of 100 beds each, and all are operated as not-for-profit organizations.[38] Hospital services are available across the country, with the largest concentration of hospitals being found in the major population centers. At the center of Israel, there are nine acute care hospitals, and Jerusalem is the home to three major hospitals. According to data from the OECD, Israel has one of the lowest ratios of acute care hospital beds to 1,000 people of any of the member states.

As is the case in the United States, hospitals in Israel are operated as public and private organizations. Public hospitals are required to accept payment from the four health plans, leaving patients with only their copayment. Private hospitals can accept payment from the health plans but can also bill separately for services. Among the largest hospitals in Israel as measured by number of beds are:

- Chaim Sheba–Academic Medical Center: 1,200 beds
- Hadassah Medical Organization: Ein Karem and Mount Scopus: 1,300 beds, 31 operating theaters, and nine special intensive care units, and runs five schools of medical professions
- Rabin Medical Center: 1,300 beds
- Shaare Zedek Medical Center: 1,000 beds
- Tel Aviv Sourasky Medical Center: 1,300 beds

Medical tourism is an important activity made available by most of the private hospitals in Israel. A wide variety of medical and surgical procedures are accessible through medical tourism, including oncology; orthopedics; cardiology; cardiac surgery; neurosurgery; neurology; ear, nose, and throat surgeries; endocrinology; gastroenterology; general surgery; pediatrics; urology; plastic and aesthetic surgery; ophthalmology; vascular surgery; bone marrow transplants;

pulmonology; fertility treatment (including IVF); and complex dental procedures.[39,40] The medical tourism was mainly from Russia in the past, but the financial crisis in Russia has resulted in a decrease in medical tourism. The advantage of offering medical tourism services is the ability to charge patients a predetermined rate without being concerned with reimbursement through one of the four health plans. For the patient, high-quality clinical care is available on demand at typically a lower cost than might be available in their home country.

Rehabilitation Services

Rehabilitation is included in the NHI benefits package and responsibility for its provision, therefore, lies with the health plans. Rehabilitation services are provided in the general hospitals, in designated rehabilitation hospitals, in geriatric hospitals, and in the community. Outpatient services include clinics for child development and rehabilitation, clinics for general rehabilitation, and daycare rehabilitation. All of these services are provided in community facilities of the health plans. All rehabilitation services incur a copayment.[19]

The current data on rehabilitation services in Israel consists of the services and facilities being used to care for soldiers who have been injured and continue to be injured from the war between Israel and Hamas that began in 2023. Of the 12,000 injured soldiers who have entered rehabilitation services since October 7, 2023, 66% are reservists, 93% are men, and 51% are between age 18 and 30.[41]

Long-Term Care Services

The vast majority of elderly people in Israel live or are cared for at home, with only 3.5% residing in any kind of institutional setting (with some 2.5% in a skilled nursing home). Even among the disabled elderly, nearly 80% still live in the community because of the extensive care provided by families and the development of formal services intended to reinforce this social support and to help families to cope with the burden of care.[19]

In addition to some 1,400 social clubs that provide a framework for activities and facilitate interpersonal contact and socialization for the elderly population who are in good health, a network of daycare centers for the disabled elderly has been developed. Daycare centers contribute significantly to the ability of the disabled elderly to remain in the community. The service also improves the quality of their lives and releases the family from caregiving duties during the day, freeing them to work and attend to other tasks.[19]

If institutional long-term care services are required, there are more than 400 care homes available across the country, providing a continuum of services similar to those in the United States, starting with senior housing and moving up to traditional nursing homes. Payment for skilled nursing services is also managed much as in the United States, in that residents and/or their family members are expected to pay a large monthly fee (approximately $3,000 USD per month). To help offset these costs, the MoH provides a subsidy that is pegged to the annual income of the elderly person and/or their family.[19]

Summary

The organization, financing, and delivery of health care in Israel are based on the principle of universal, comprehensive care for each and every citizen, regardless of religion, gender, or ethnicity. Despite being a small nation in a highly dangerous and volatile part of the world, the National Health Insurance Law established in 1995 has created a system in which the Iron Triangle[42] of health care—high quality, universal access, and (comparatively) low cost—has been achieved. While improvements are needed to help reduce health disparities—particularly among Arab Israelis and Palestinians living in Israel—and to help continue to manage costs and deal with discontent among physicians regarding their salaries, Israel serves as a beacon for nations around the world in making health care affordable and universally accessible.

Current and Emerging Issues and Challenges

The State of Israel was established in 1948, but the current healthcare system has been developing since the beginning of the 20th century with the establishment of the Clalit Sick Fund in 1911 for the treatment of workers. The system was built on the foundation of Otto Von Bismarck's principles of equality and social responsibility. Equality and social responsibility are the key values that have been preserved throughout the development of the Israeli healthcare system, and they remain its hallmarks.

Two other important players in the establishment of the healthcare systems were the generous Rothschild family and Hadassah, the Women's Zionist

Organization of America. Starting in 1912, Hadassah built and operated hospitals, medical clinics, pharmacies, and *drop-of-milk clinics* (mother and child welfare clinics that concentrated on child development and were responsible for vaccinations) across Israel, clinics that are still active today.

The population size of Israel in 1948 was 870,000. At the time, medical insurance was voluntary, and only 53% of the population was insured. With the immigration waves after World War II, the population of Israel doubled in 4 years. The Clalit Sick Fund became the main insurer and supplier for the majority of citizens.

"Israel has established one of the most enviable healthcare systems among OECD countries in the 15 years since it legislated mandatory health insurance," stated an OECD report published in 2012.[43]

The healthcare system is mainly public, with 28 general acute care hospitals. Ownership of the hospitals varies: 11 are government-owned, eight are owned by the Clalit Sick Fund, seven are privately owned public hospitals (e.g., Hadassah is owned by HWZOA), and two are private hospitals (one privately owned and one owned by the Maccabi Sick Fund).[44]

The primary care system in Israel is excellent, with a high level of clinical care, as seen in the national quality measures program, which takes advantage of the fully electronic medical records. There have been national quality measures for hospitals since 2012. Over 90% of Israelis are satisfied with the system.[45] The ability of Israel to contain the costs and to maintain some of the low-cost health expenditure is due to the following factors:

1. Tight regulation of both hospital beds and advanced expensive equipment, such as MRI and CT scans, to limit the supplier-induced demand phenomenon.
2. The simple and transparent reimbursement system. The tariff is published by the MoH after it is decided upon in a committee composed of all stakeholders (the ministers of finance and health as well as hospital and sick-fund stakeholders). There are annual discussions and updates about the tariff.
    a. There is only one bill per hospital admission. The basis is fee-for-service; surgeries and other procedures are reimbursed by diagnosis-related group (DRG), which means there is an all-inclusive payment; for other hospitalizations, such as pneumonia, when the patient is in the Internal Medicine department, the reimbursement is "per diem."
3. The capping system between hospitals and the sick funds. There is a defined amount of money (calculated based on the activity in the previous 3 years) above the capped amount, and the goal is to limit the hospital's incentive to increase activity.

Although Israeli health care is considered very good, the system is facing significant challenges.

Shortage of Resources

Financially, both the sick funds and the hospitals have deficient budgets. The sick funds are undercompensated for the rising costs of the basket of benefits and the salary increases that are part of national union agreements.

Hospitals are crowded because there is a bed shortage, with 3.1 beds per 1,000 inhabitants (compared with the average of 5.0 beds per 1,000 in OECD countries) including 1.9 acute care beds per 1,000 (higher only than Mexico's 1.6 beds per 1,000 inhabitants). The average occupancy rate `is 97% (usually much higher in the winter), compared with the OECD average of 75%. The length of stay of 4.3 days, on average, is shorter than the OECD average by 2.2 days.[46]

Without enough staff, quality of care can be diminished and patients and staff can experience frustration.

There is a shortage of advanced technology in remote rural areas—a limited number of MRI units and a severe shortage of radiotherapy—as part of the cost containment.

The shortage of health resources in Israel stabilized shortly after the COVID-19 pandemic but then quickly diminished once again due to the war between Israel and Hamas.[47] The chronic shortage is worsening. The per capita rate of physicians in Israel is lower than the OECD average in 2023.[47]

Public Versus Private Expenditure

There is significant use of private medicine services in Israel outside of the public hospitals (only a few hospitals have permission to practice both private and public medicine). Although there is physical separation of the private and public systems, there is some overlap, with physicians working in both systems and patients moving in both directions between the private and public systems. The physicians usually direct the less complicated cases to private medicine, thus retaining the more complicated patients in the public hospitals. This often presents a challenge in that if patients see a private physician who also works at a hospital, billing is often incorrect or confusing.

Comparatively speaking, the waiting times for office visits and surgeries are shorter in the private system. The private system is readily affordable due to the fact that 75% of the population carries complementary insurance; however, this also presents a challenge in that many citizens cannot afford the complementary insurance that the sick funds sell for about $100 USD per family per month.[45]

The benefits of these insurances are mainly the ability to be treated in a private hospital and the coverage of treatments that are not in the basket of benefits. The difficulty is that Israel's care system is part socialism and part capitalism, so access is a challenge.

In recent years, there has been a significant increase in the consumption of private medicine, with an increase in out-of-pocket payments. There is a significant ministerial effort to limit private medicine and bring patients back into the public system. The challenge is that this effort could result in a large tax increase to provide a revenue stream or, conversely, result in a reduction of private services, which would be unacceptable to most of the public.

Workforce

During the 1990s, there was a large wave of immigration from the former Soviet Union, which increased Israel's population size as well as its number of physicians. However, these physicians from Russia do not all speak Hebrew, nor do they have licenses to practice medicine in Israel. Sometimes, there was a knowledge gap, but the largest barrier was language, which was addressed in the *ulpan*, Hebrew language school. Partly due to the aging of these physicians who came in the Russian immigration wave, in future years, the shortage of physicians will be worse. In 2021, 2,024 new physician medical licenses were issued, which was 2.8 times greater than the number of licenses issued in 2010. Of the 2,2024 new licenses, 776 were issued to graduates of Israeli medical schools. The positive increase is still insufficient for the scale of health needs in the country.[47] In Israel, all hospital physicians are hospital employees.

The nursing situation is worse, with 6.53 nurses per 1,000 inhabitants, compared with the OECD average of 8.8.[48] Many factors contribute to the nursing shortage: overcrowded wards with inability to provide proper care, resignation during and after the COVID-19 pandemic, and comparatively low salaries, the stereotype that nursing is a feminine profession, the tendency for nurses to decrease their work hours or shift to less demanding nursing positions outside of hospitals, and early professional retirement.

Geographic Inequality

Although the National Health Insurance Law ensures that everyone has medical insurance, access to high-quality medical care differs geographically, with much better access available in urban centers compared with suburban or rural areas. In recent years, the inequality has improved due to significant financial incentives given to physicians working in the geographic periphery, but shortages and inequities still exist.

The Conflicting Roles of the Ministry of Health

The MoH is responsible for the whole healthcare system: for the licensing of institutions and health professionals, for the functionality of the sick funds and hospitals, and for the provision of directives and regulations. In addition, the MoH owns many hospitals—acute care, psychiatric care, and geriatric care. Thus, there are conflicting interests. This anomaly was recognized from the inception of the Israeli healthcare system, with many suggestions over the years for correction, but, practically speaking, the anomaly was not resolved.

Nursing Care

Long-term nursing care is currently not in the basket of benefits; there is limited financial assistance from the National Insurance Institute, but the bulk of the financial burden still falls on families. There have been recent suggestions to include nursing care in the basket of benefits in return for health tax increases.

An Integrated Healthcare System

I am an Israeli Arab, this is my country, I feel the same as Yochi (Doctor Schiffman) feels. It's my country and I'm doing my job, I try to do my best. This is the way I look at that. So, I don't wake up in the morning and start thinking "I'm an Arab not a Jew" and such things, I am focused on patient treatment, that's all.[49]

—Professor Ahmed Eid, Chief of the Department of Surgery, Hadassah Hospital, Mount Scopus

The Israeli healthcare system is well known in Israel for providing health care for the entire population, regardless of a patient's ability to pay, ethnicity, or religion. In contrast to other government institutions, such as public education, where separate, publicly funded schools may provide services to distinct, often segregated, populations, the Israeli healthcare system is a single integrated system where Arab and Jewish Israelis, religious and secular, all experience the same level of care and are treated by the same physicians regardless of their background. Despite years of conflict in the region between Arabs and Jews, in Israel, it is common to find Arab doctors and nurses treating Jewish patients, and vice versa, even in the context of ongoing violence between their two respective communities.[49–51] The Arab Israeli minority is well integrated at all levels of the Israeli healthcare system, and Arab Israelis run prominent academic medical departments at Israel's most prestigious hospitals in addition to serving as CEOs and medical directors for entire hospitals.[52–54] Indeed, one particular Israeli Arab community of Arraba in the lower Galilee has more than six doctors per 1,000 inhabitants, one of the highest ratios in the world.[55]

This remarkable success is no accident. Even before the founding of the State of Israel, health care was protected from the many divisions in Israeli society. Hadassah, the Women's Zionist Organization of America, which founded many of the hospitals and clinics in Israel many decades before the State of Israel was formally declared, has always had a mission to provide care to all, "regardless of race, ethnicity, or nationally."[56] The culture of medicine naturally serves such a humanitarian cause. The Abraham Fund Initiatives, a nonprofit organization with a mission to "promote coexistence and equality among Israel's Jewish and Arab-Palestinian citizens," found that Israeli healthcare employees state that a "patient's identity and cause of illness or injury are of no relevance in the ER or on the operating table, and the caretaker's identity or ethnic origin are similarly irrelevant."[54] This guiding ethos is formally stated in Israeli law. The Patient's Rights Act of 1996 includes a prohibition against discrimination, "no medical facility or clinician shall discriminate between patients on grounds of religion, race, sex, nationality, country of birth, or other such grounds."[57]

This close integration, which can go without notice or comment in a typical day at any Israeli hospital or clinic, can sometimes reveal itself in a dramatic fashion. One example, among many, occurred on August 4, 2014, when an Arab gunman on a motorbike opened fire on an Israeli soldier, Chen Schwartz. Schwartz was rushed to Hadassah's Mount Scopus hospital, where the chair of the surgery department, Professor Ahmed Eid, an Arab Israeli, saved the soldier's life. Asked later by the media about his role in the event, Professor Eid answered as almost any Israeli healthcare provider would, "I was doing my job. That's what I do.... We don't really think about who we are treating. We are focused on saving lives of patients. Preventing death."[49,50]

The Israeli humanitarian drive does not stop with Israeli citizens but extends to Palestinians from the West Bank and Gaza Strip. The Palestinian Ministry of Health, with the assistance of Israeli hospitals, has transferred many patients out of Gaza for advanced health treatments.[58] This kind of patient transfer is supported by various governmental and philanthropic agencies in Israel, the Palestinian Authority, and the international community. Perhaps most remarkable is the ongoing cooperation between the Palestinian Ministry of Health and the Israeli Ministry of Health in securing the safe medical transfer of thousands of Palestinians from the Gaza Strip, which has been controlled by Hamas since 2007. Hamas is a militant Islamic fundamentalist organization that openly calls for the destruction of the State of Israel by any means.[59] That thousands of Gazans depend on the State of Israel for advanced health care is an irony seemingly lost on Hamas leadership, who personally benefit from Israeli health care. Indeed, shortly following the 2014 war between Israel and Gaza, which cost over 2,000 lives, a daughter of Ismail Haniyeh, an important leader of Hamas in Gaza and a former prime minister, was urgently transferred to an Israeli hospital after suffering complications from a surgical procedure in Gaza.[60] Despite the well-documented integration of the Israeli and Palestinian healthcare system, a series of articles in 2009 on Palestinian health care published in the prominent British medical journal *The Lancet* failed to mention this cooperation at all, perhaps in part because it failed to include a single Israeli physician among its many authors and its steering committee.[61–65]

In a Middle East separated by ethnic and religious divisions that fuel violence, the cooperation in the Israeli healthcare system between Arabs and Jews, and between Palestinian physicians and Israeli physicians, is an inspiring and overlooked example of humanity and reason persevering in a region where humanity is too easily silenced in the name of religion, ethnicity, or nation state.

Israeli Leadership in Global Health

Despite its small size and relatively recent founding, Israel has had a disproportionately positive impact on health care in the Middle East and around the globe and is often among the first nations to respond to humanitarian crises. According to the Israel Ministry of Foreign Affairs, Israel has sent humanitarian teams to 140 nations around the world.[66] Both Israeli governmental and nongovernmental organizations have played decisive roles in providing emergency health care in humanitarian crises. Examples include the Israeli response to the devastating 2010 earthquake in Haiti and more long-term healthcare partnerships, such as infectious disease surveillance and healthcare capacity building in the Middle East and in Africa. This altruistic role predates the existence of the State of Israel and is in keeping with the priorities of the Zionist movement, which sought to create not only a Jewish state but also an exemplary moral state, in keeping with the biblical prophecy of Isaiah, to be "a light to the nations."[67] While its small size and many wars may at first glance seem to be a hindrance to Israel coming to the aid of other nations, it is these very challenges that give Israel the expertise to assist in a crisis. As the Israeli prime minister Golda Meir stated following her visit to postcolonial Africa, "We have been forced to find solutions to problems that large, wealthy, powerful states have never encountered."[68]

Remarkably, Israel's international development arm, MASHAV, began in 1958, a mere decade after the creation of the State of Israel and prior to the founding of the U.S. Agency for International Development in 1961. In the area of emergency medical response, Israel has an unrivaled track record. In partnership with IDF, MASHAV has quickly established field hospitals around the world in response to humanitarian crises. One notable example includes Israel's response to the Rwandan refugee crisis in 1994. A 120-bed field hospital with operating rooms and specialty care was established in Zaire, now the Democratic Republic of Congo. The decision was made on July 22 to establish the hospital, and the first patients were being treated on July 26—an incredibly rapid response. In the first 12 days, the hospital received 1,215 patients, of whom 723 required admission to the hospital and 16 required emergency surgery.[69] This experience was repeated following earthquakes in Turkey (1999) and in India (2001), as well as in humanitarian missions to Kosovo (1999).[70]

For Haiti's devastating earthquake in 2010 that killed an estimated 230,000 and injured approximately 250,000 people,[71] Israeli medical personnel were among the first on the ground. Within hours of the earthquake, Israel sent its initial response team, via one passenger plane and one cargo plane. The planes were in the air before Haiti's only international airport, which was damaged by the earthquake, was declared operational. As a result, only the passenger plane managed to land initially; the cargo plane, due to its larger size, was delayed for 8 hours, unable to land until the runway was declared safe.[72] Despite these logistical hurdles and the fact that Haiti is 6,500 miles away from Israel (in comparison, the distance from Miami to Port au Prince, Haiti's capital, is 700 miles), the Israeli field hospital was operational 89 hours after the earthquake, providing advanced care days before any other nation was able to accomplish this feat. During the 10 days that the hospital was operational, it treated 1,111 patients, of whom 737 required admission, and performed 244 operations on 203 patients.[71]

Critics of the Israeli government have maintained that such relief work, while commendable, is actually motivated by a cynical desire to "divert attention away from their behavior toward the Palestinians."[73] Such criticism is misleading because it ignores the extensive resources that Israel devotes to Palestinian health care, and indeed, to health care throughout the Middle East. Representatives of the Palestinian authority and even the militant terrorist group Hamas cooperate with Israel in order to ensure healthcare delivery to Palestinian civilians and combatants. Prior to the current conflict in progress at the time of this text (2025), there were monthly transfers of hundreds to thousands of Palestinian civilians out of the Gaza Strip and the West Bank to be treated in Israeli hospitals.[74] In the context of the ongoing violence between Hamas and Israel, this degree of cooperation is unprecedented in its scope and perseverance and provides needed inspiration in a seemingly intractable conflict.

Indeed, Israel's role in coordinating infectious disease surveillance and vaccine deployment extends to its current and former enemies, and it quietly predates the peace accords with Egypt and Jordan. Extensive polio monitoring and vaccine deployment, with the goal of eradication, began before the 1967 war in which Israel gained control of the Gaza Strip and the West Bank and continues despite the Hamas takeover of Gaza. This cooperation, even during conflict, ultimately resulted in the eradication of the disease from these territories.[75] Cooperation with Egyptian and Jordanian governments, expedited through the World

Health Organization, has enabled early detection of outbreaks and coordinated responses. Although understated and often under the radar, Israeli leadership in global health extends not just to nations thousands of miles away but also to its enemies, even those whose stated goal is the destruction of Israel.

Summary

The Israeli healthcare system, large, complex, and multifaceted, is currently undergoing changes that the MoH started implementing in 2015. According to the OECD Health Policy Overview, "While the Israel population enjoys good health outcomes and the health system performs fairly well, there are specific areas—health workforce and hospital care, in particular—where policy attention is needed."[63]

The Israeli government is in the process of standardizing the supplementary insurance packages across all of the four sick-fund organizations. Drugs not currently reimbursed in the supplementary insurance packages will be reimbursed under the new regulations. In addition, the government is exploring and planning to implement ways to pay the premiums for poor populations who cannot currently afford supplementary health insurance. The impact on pharmaceutical companies is unclear; however, if the government increases payment benefits on unreimbursed drugs, the pharmaceutical companies might experience financial gains. Additionally, a government increase in payments to accommodate the needs of the poor has the potential to increase the flow of funds into the four insurance systems.[64]

The good news for Israelis is that they need not travel abroad for world-class medical care. Israel's medical personnel, research facilities, and hospitals are among the best in the world. Additionally, patients benefit from Israel's translational (lab to bedside) medical practice, which quickly "brings the benefits of science back to the patient, with better technology to create improved infrastructure."[65] For example, in 2015 Hadassah received a $6.5 million USD grant to create the Wohl Centre for Translational Medicine, which will focus on cancers, ALS, Parkinson's disease, and other degenerative diseases.[65]

The Israeli healthcare system, with its cutting-edge research in Israel and its partnerships with many medical research centers throughout the world (for example, Massachusetts General Hospital in the United States and clinics in Kenya), serves not only Israeli citizens but also demonstrates its ability to improve the health and care for people around the world.

References

1. Moses J. My Jewish learning: Israel before the State. Accessed November 26, 2023. http://www.myjewishlearning.com/article/israel-before-the-state/.
2. Senor D, Singer S. *Start-Up Nation: The Story of Israel's Economic Miracle*. New York, NY: Twelve; 2009:18.
3. Werman M, Bell M. Israeli doctor paved the way for emergency response in Boston. Public Radio International. Accessed November 26, 2023. https://theworld.org/stories/2013-04-26/israeli-doctor-paved-way-emergency-response-boston.
4. Israel government and politics: how does the Israeli government work? Jewish Virtual Library. Accessed November 26, 2023. https://www.jewishvirtuallibrary.org/how-does-the-israeli-government-work.
5. Kershner I. Aided by the sea, Israel overcomes an old foe: drought. *The New York Times*. Accessed November 26, 2023. https://www.nytimes.com/2015/05/30/world/middleeast/water-revolution-in-israel-overcomes-any-threat-of-drought.html.
6. Final voter turnout at 71.8%, four percent more than 2013 election. *The Jerusalem Post*. Accessed November 26, 2023. https://www.jpost.com/israel-news/voter-turnout-at-10-am-higher-than-in-2013-election-394166.
7. The State: political structure. Ministry of Foreign Affairs. Accessed November 26, 2023. https://www.gov.il/en/Departments/General/the-state-political-structure.
8. Country ranking. Medical Tourism Index 2020–2021. Accessed November 26, 2023. https://www.medicaltourism.com/mti/home.
9. Polaris Market Research & Consulting. Medical tourism market is projected to be US $80.07 billion by 2032, at a CAGR of 24.7% from 2024 to 2032. Accessed February 11, 2025. https://pnr-files.pro1.gus.wdc.dianum.io/globenewswire/articles/2942837/en/medical-tourism-market-is-projected-to-be-us-80.pdf.
10. *The World Factbook*. Washington, DC: Central Intelligence Agency, 2023. Accessed November 26, 2023. https://www.cia.gov/the-world-factbook/countries/israel/#people-and-society.
11. Statista. Number of citizens who emigrated from Israel in the previous two-year period from June 2017 to May 2024. Accessed February 11, 2025. https://www.statista.com/statistics/1482469/israel-number-of-recent-emigrants/.
12. Facts about Israel: history. Israel Ministry of Foreign Affairs. Accessed November 26, 2023. https://embassies.gov.il/MFA/AboutIsrael/history/Pages/Facts%20about%20Israel-%20History.
13. Awards 2014. Smart City Expo World Congress. Accessed November 26, 2023. https://www.firabarcelona.com/en/press-release/uncategorized/smart-city-expo-world-congress-distinguishes-tel-aviv-as-best-smart-city-in-2014-2/.

14. Maternity allowance. National Insurance Institute of Israel. Accessed November 26, 2023. https://www.btl.gov.il/English%20Homepage/Benefits/Maternity%20Insurance/Maternity%20Allowance/Pages/default.aspx.
15. 10 facts about the Arab–Israeli conflict. Fact #2: one quarter of Israeli citizens are not Jewish. Accessed November 26, 2023. https://www.ajc.org/news/ten-basic-facts-about-the-israeli-palestinian-conflict.
16. Chinitz D. An overview of Israel's universal health care system. Accessed November 26, 2023. https://ldi.upenn.edu/our-work/research-updates/an-overview-of-israels-universal-health-care-system/.
17. Organisation for Economic Co-operation and Development. *Focus on Health Spending*. Accessed November 26, 2023. https://www.oecd.org/health/health-data.htm.
18. *World Health Statistics 2023*. Geneva, Switzerland: World Health Organization.
19. Rosen B, Waitzberg R, Merkur S. *Israel: Health System Review*. Copenhagen, Demark: European Observatory on Health Systems and Policy; 2015.
20. Southern J, Roizin H, Daana M, et al. Varied utilisation of health provisions by Arab and Jewish residents in Israel. *Int J Equity Health*. 2015;14(1). http://dx.doi.org/10.1186/s12939-015-0193-8.
21. Ministry of Aliyah and Immigrant Absorption. *Health Services in Israel*. Jerusalem, Israel: Publications Department; 2015.
22. Kupot Cholim. Nefesh B'Nefesh. Accessed November 26, 2023. https://www.nbn.org.il/life-in-israel/healthcare-in-israel/kupot-cholim/kupot-cholim/.
23. Telemedicine in Israel: Israel's health and care system organisation. *Momentum*. Accessed November 26, 2023. http://telemedicine-momentum.eu/israel/.
24. Rosen B. *How Health Plans in Israel Manage the Care Provided by Their Physicians*. Jerusalem, Israel: Myers-JDC-Brookdale Institute; 2011.
25. Goldfus Insurance and Investments. *Private Health Insurance*. 2016. Accessed November 26, 2023. http://www.goldfus-ins.co.il/logic_eng.asp?id=25.
26. International Trade Administration, U.S. Dept. of Commerce. Israel – country commercial guide, healthcare. Accessed February 11, 2025. https://www.trade.gov/country-commercial-guides/israel-healthcare.
27. National health expenditure data. Centers for Medicare and Medicaid Services. Accessed November 26, 2023. https://www.cms.gov/data-research/statistics-trends-and-reports/national-health-expenditure-data.
28. Taub Center for Social Policy Studies in Israel. The healthcare system in Israel, 2024: Between resilience and continued challenges. Accessed February 11, 2025. https://www.taubcenter.org.il/en/pr/health-system-2024/.
29. Rosen B, Kanel K. *Healthcare in the US and Israel: Comparative Overview*. Jerusalem, Israel: Brookdale Institute; 2010.
30. Statista. Average monthly wage in the human health sector in Israel from February 2022 to February 2023. Accessed February 12, 2025. https://www.statista.com/statistics/1306722/average-monthly-wage-in-the-human-health-sector-in-israel/.
31. Telemedicine in Israel: Israel's health and care system organisation. *Momentum*. Accessed November 26, 2023. http://telemedicine-momentum.eu/israel/.
32. Financial report 2012 for the governmental general. State of Israel Ministry of Health. Accessed November 26, 2023. http://www.health.gov.il/English/Pages/HomePage.aspx.
33. Siegel-Itzkovich J. Health funds to receive allocations at start of year as part of healthcare basket. *The Jerusalem Post*. Accessed February 12, 2025. https://www.jpost.com/health-and-wellness/article-779896.
34. *Israel Defense Forces: Medical Corps*. Jewish Virtual Library. Accessed November 26, 2023. https://www.jewishvirtuallibrary.org/idf-medical-corps.
35. Health Division. State of Israel Ministry of Health. Accessed November 19, 2023. http://www.health.gov.il/English/MinistryUnits/HealthDivision/Pages/Default.aspx.
36. World Bank. Physicians (per 1,000 people). Accessed November 19, 2023. http://beta.data.worldbank.org/indicator/SH.MED.PHYS.ZS?end=2011&start=2008.
37. Bader B. Clinically integrated physician–hospital organizations. *Great Boards*. Winter 2009. Baltimore, MD: Bader and Associates.
38. Hospitals and medical centers. Israel Science and Technology. Accessed November 19, 2023. http://www.science.co.il/Hospitals.asp.
39. Shirom A. Private medical services in acute-care hospitals in Israel. *Int J Health Plann Manage*. 2001;16(4):325-345.
40. *Medical Tourism to Israel*. Health-tourism.com. Accessed November 19, 2023. https://www.health-tourism.com/medical-tourism-israel/.
41. Jewish News Syndicate. 12,000 Israeli soldiers entered rehab since Oct. 7, 2023. Accessed February 12, 2025. https://www.jns.org/12000-israeli-soldiers-entered-rehab-since-oct-7-2003/.
42. Kissick W. *Medicine's Dilemmas*. New Haven, CT: Yale University Press; 1994.
43. Organisation for Economic Co-operation and Development. *OECD Reviews of Health Care Quality: Israel* 2012: *Raising Standards*. Paris, France: OECD Publishing; 2012. http://dx.doi.org/10.1787/9789264029941-en.
44. National Insurance Institute of Israel. Accessed November 19, 2023. https://www.btl.gov.il/English%20Homepage/Pages/default.aspx.
45. Israeli Ministry of Health. N Keidar & R Plotnik Planning & Strategy Division; May 2015. http://www.health.gov.il/PublicationsFiles/OECD_2012.pdf.
46. Organisation for Economic Co-operation and Development. *OECD Health Statistics 2014*. Paris, France: OECD Publishing; 2014.
47. Siegel-Itzkovich J. The challenges to Israel's healthcare system, pre- and post-October 7. Accessed February 13, 2025. *Jerusalem Post*. https://www.jpost.com/health-and-wellness/article-781511.
48. Savitsky B, Shvartsur R, Findling Y, et al. Components of professional satisfaction among novice nurses. *Isr J Health Policy Res*. 2023;12(35). https://doi.org/10.1186/s13584-023-00584-7. https://ijhpr.biomedcentral.com/articles/10.1186/s13584-023-00584-7.
49. Jerusalem doctors treat terrorists and victims alike, identities unknown. *Jerusalem Post*. Accessed November 19, 2023. http://www.jpost.com/Arab-Israeli-Conflict/Jerusalem-doctors-treat-terrorists-and-victims-alike-without-knowing-identities-431904.
50. Horovitz D. Arab doctor saves Jewish soldier hit by Arab bullets. No big deal? *The Times of Israel*. Accessed November 19, 2023. http://www.timesofisrael.com/arab-doctor-saves-jewish-soldier-hit-by-arab-bullets-no-big-deal/.
51. Mitnick J. For Israeli–Palestinian interaction, a new venue: the Arab doctor's office. *Christ Sci Monit*. Accessed

November 17, 2023. http://www.csmonitor.com/World/Middle-East/2016/0201/For-Israeli-Palestinian-interaction-a-new-venue-the-Arab-doctor-s-office.
52. Avraham R. Arab doctor to head emergency medicine at Hadassah. *United with Israel*. Published April 20, 2013. Accessed November 19, 2023. http://unitedwithisrael.org/arab-muslim-to-head-emergency-medicine-at-hadassah/.
53. Abraham Fund Initiatives. Research and publications. Accessed November 19, 2023. http://www.abrahamfund.org/10862.
54. Reznik R. *Integrating Israel's Arab Citizens in the Healthcare System: A Success Story?* Abraham Fund Initiatives. Accessed November 17, 2023. http://www.abrahamfund.org/webfiles/fck/Integration%20in%20the%20Healthcare%20System%20-%20English.pdf.
55. Press VS. The small Israeli village where everyone's a doctor. Israel21c. Accessed November 17, 2023. http://www.israel21c.org/the-small-israeli-village-where-everyones-a-doctor/.
56. History. Hadassah, the Women's Zionist Organization of America. Accessed November 19, 2023. http://www.hadassah.org/about/history.html.
57. Patient's Rights Act, 1996. Accessed November 19, 2023. http://waml.haifa.ac.il/index/reference/legislation/israel/israel1.htm.
58. United Nations. Health conditions in OPT and Golan – 68th World Health Assembly – Report of State of Palestine. Accessed February 12, 2025. https://www.un.org/unispal/document/auto-insert-201329/.
59. Avalon Project. Hamas covenant 1988: the covenant of the Islamic resistance movement. Lillian Goldman Law Library. Yale Law School. Accessed November 19, 2023. http://avalon.law.yale.edu/20th_century/hamas.asp.
60. Newman M, Associated Press. Hamas leader's daughter receives medical care in Israel. *The Times of Israel*. Accessed November 19, 2023. http://www.timesofisrael.com/hamas-leaders-daughter-said-to-receive-medical-care-in-israel/.
61. Horton R. The occupied Palestinian territory: peace, justice, and health. *Lancet*. 2009;373(9666):784-788. doi: 10.1016/S0140-6736(09)60100-8.
62. Chalmers I, Leaning J, Shannon HS, Zurayk H. *Lancet* Steering Group on the occupied Palestinian territory. *Lancet*. 2009;373(9666):788-790. doi:10.1016/S0140-6736(09)60102-1.
63. Organisation for Economic Co-operation and Development. Israel. In: *Health Policies and Data: Health Policy in Your Country*. Paris, France: OECD Publishing; April 2016. Accessed October 26, 2023. http://www.oecd.org/health.
64. IHS Markit. Israel to conduct major overhaul of health insurance system. Accessed October 26, 2023. https://www.ihs.com/country-industry-forecasting.html?ID=1065999186.
65. Hadassah receives $6.5 million grant to create Translational Medicine Institute. Hadassah, the Women's Zionist Organization of America. Accessed October 26, 2023. http://www.hadassah.org/news-stories/hadassah-receives-65.html?referrer=https://www.google.com/.
66. Israeli humanitarian relief operations: MASHAV: Israel's Agency for International Development Cooperation. Accessed August 18, 2023. http://mfa.gov.il/MFA/ForeignPolicy/Aid/Pages/Israeli%20Humanitarian%20Relief-%20MASHAV%20-%20the%20Israel%20F.aspx.
67. Jewish Values Online. Multiple Jewish perspectives on morals and ethics. Accessed August 18, 2023. http://www.jewishvaluesonline.org/665.
68. Africa's development needs: state of implementation of various commitments, challenges and the way forward. Address by Mr. Aaron Abramovich, Director-General of the Israel Ministry of Foreign Affairs, to the United Nations General Assembly High-Level Meeting on Development. Israel Ministry of Foreign Affairs. Accessed August 18, 2023. http://mfa.gov.il/MFA/InternatlOrgs/Speeches/Pages/MFA_Dir-Gen_Abramovich_Address_UN_General_Assembly_High-Level_Meeting_Development_22-Sep-2008.aspx.
69. Operation "Interns for Hope": Israeli medical aid for Rwandan refugees in Zaire. Israel Ministry of Foreign Affairs. Accessed August 18, 2023. http://mfa.gov.il/MFA/PressRoom/1994/Pages/ISRAELI%20MEDICAL%20AID%20FOR%20RWANDAN%20REFUGEES%20IN%20ZAIRE.aspx.
70. Summary of Israeli humanitarian relief operations: 1997–1999. Israel Ministry of Foreign Affairs. Accessed August 18, 2023. http://mfa.gov.il/MFA/MFA-Archive/1999/Pages/Summary%20of%20Israeli%20Humanitarian%20Relief%20Operations-.aspx.
71. Bar-On E, Abargel A, Peleg K, Kreiss Y. Coping with the challenges of early disaster response: 24 years of field hospital experience after earthquakes. *Disaster Med Public Health Prep*. 2013;7(5):491-498. doi: 10.1017/dmp.2013.94.
72. Israel's medical operation in Haiti. *Anderson Cooper 360*. CNN. Accessed November 26, 2023. https://www.cnn.com/audio/podcasts/anderson-cooper-360/episodes/847a2374-4c2d-11ee-b5d6-975cc2c5e0ba.
73. Freedman S. Israel's double standards over Haiti. *The Guardian*. Accessed November 26, 2023. https://www.theguardian.com/commentisfree/2010/jan/22/israel-haiti-relief-palestine.
74. World Health Organization. Regional Office for the Eastern Mediterranean. WHO monthly reports on referral of patients from the Gaza Strip. Accessed November 26, 2023. https://www.emro.who.int/opt/information-resources/monthly-report-on-health-access.html.
75. Tulchinsky TH, Ramlawi A, Abdeen Z, et al. Polio lessons 2013: Israel, the West Bank, and Gaza. *Lancet*. 2013;382(9905):1611-1612. doi: 10.1016/S0140-6736(13)62331-4.

CHAPTER 17

South Africa

Immaculate Sabelile Tenza and Yandisa Ngqangashe

Country Description

This chapter presents the health system of the Republic of South Africa. **Table 17-1** sets the scene by presenting an overview of the country. This is followed by a review of South Africa's historical background, geographic features, government and political systems, macroeconomics, transportation, demographics, education, and religious background of the population, to provide a context for in-depth discussions of the health system. We use the World Health Organization's (WHO's) framework of a health system to frame the discussion, focusing on the six building blocks of service delivery, health workforce, health information systems, access to essential medicines, financing, and leadership/governance. This is followed by a section on the COVID-19 pandemic in South Africa, which covers South Africa's response to the pandemic, and reflections on the effect of COVID-19 on South Africa's health system. This reflection also uses the six building blocks of the health system to frame the discussion.

Table 17-1 Descriptive Characteristics of South Africa

Nationality	South African
Ethnic groups	Black African 81.4%, Coloured 8.2%, White 7.3%, Indian/Asian 2.7% (2022 estimate)
Religions	Christianity, Islam, traditional African religion, Hinduism, Buddhism, Bahaism, Judaism, Atheism, and Agnosticism
Language	Official languages: English, isiZulu, isiXhosa, isiNdebele, Afrikaans, Siswati, Sepedi, Sesotho, Setswana, Tshivenda, and Xitsonga
Illiteracy	Definition: Age 20 years and over who cannot read and write Total population: 10% Male: 9.3% Female: 10.7%
Government type	Constitutional multiparty democracy, with three spheres: local, provincial, and national government
Date of becoming a democratic country	April 1994
Gross domestic product (GDP) per capita	6,962 USD (2021 estimate)

(continues)

Table 17-1 Descriptive Characteristics of South Africa *(continued)*

Unemployment rate	33.9% in the second quarter of 2022 (2022 estimate)
Natural hazards	Floods and landslides In April 2022, KwaZulu-Natal experienced devastating floods, leading to more than 400 deaths, and damage to over 17,000 houses.
Environment: current issues	The Office of Government Communications and Information Systems reported waste removal, littering, and land degradation as major problems of concern in 2019.
Population	60.60 million (2022 estimate)
Age structure	0–14 years: 28% (8,612,793 male/8,399,976 female) 15–24 years: 16% (4,918,471 male/4,862,229 female) 25–54 years: 40% (12,904,410 male/11,628,217 female) 55–64 years: 7% (1,776,953 male/2,329,306 female) 65 years and over: 6% (1,412,255 male/2,340,859 female) (2022 estimate)
Median age	Total: 28 years (2022 estimate)
Population growth rate	1.03% (2022 estimate)
Birth rate	19.5 births/1,000 population (2022 estimate)
Death rate	11.0 deaths/100,000 population (2022 estimate)
Disease burden	Communicable disease deaths: 30.7% Noncommunicable disease deaths: 57.8% Injury deaths: 11.5% (2017 estimate)
Net migration rate	1,979 migrants/1,000 population (2022 estimate)
Gender ratio	95.8 males/100 females (2024) Between 2018 and 2021, the gender ratio increased by 0.1%.
Infant mortality rate	Total: 24.3 deaths/1,000 live births Male: 28,401 deaths/1,000 live births Female: 24,357 deaths/1,000 live births (2021/2022 estimate)
Life expectancy at birth	Total population: 62.8 years Male: 61.5 years Female: 67.7 years (2022 estimate)
Total fertility rate	2.31 children born/woman (2022 estimate)
HIV/AIDS adult prevalence rate	13.5% (2022 estimate)
Number of people living with HIV/AIDS	8.45 million (2022 estimate)
HIV/AIDS deaths	85,796 (2022 estimate)

USD = U.S. dollars

Data from Bouchard J-P, Pretorius TB, Kramers-Olen AL, et al. Global warming and psychotraumatology of natural disasters: the case of the deadly rains and floods of April 2022 in South Africa. In: *Annales Médico-psychologiques, revue psychiatrique*. Elsevier; 2023:234-239; *Country Indicators: South Africa*. Focus Economics; 2023; GlobalData. The gender ratio of South Africa (2021–2029, males per 100 females). Accessed February 12, 2025. https://www.globaldata.com/data-insights/macroeconomic/the-gender-ratio-of-south-africa-325349/; Government Communications. *South Africa at a Glance: Official Guide to South Africa*. Pretoria, South Africa: Government communication and Information System. 2019; Khuluvhe M. Adult illiteracy in South Africa. In: *Pretoria: South African Department of Higher Education and Training*. 2021; Republic of South Africa. *The Constitution of the Republic of South Africa*. Pretoria, South Africa: Government Printer; 1996; Statistics SA. *Provinces of South Africa*. 2022; Statistics SA. *Quarterly Labour Force Survey*. STATS SA, 2022; Tsofa B, Goodman C, Gilson L, et al. Devolution and its effects on health workforce and commodities management: early implementation experiences in Kilifi County, Kenya. *Intl J Equity Health*. 2017;16:169. doi: 10.1186/s12939-017-0663-2; UNICEF. Key demographic indicators. Accessed March 15, 2023. https://www.unicef.org/reports/unicef-annual-report-2021; United Nations. *World Population Prospects*. 2022.

History

South Africa has a long and complex history that spans many centuries, and its discovery can be traced back to various events and processes over time.[1] Six phases of South African history are reported in the literature, as follows: the pre-1652 period; the period of Dutch rule at the Cape (1652–1795); the period of British rule and independent states (1806–1910); the Union of South Africa until apartheid (1910–1948); Apartheid (1948–1994); and the new South Africa (1994–today).[2] The early inhabitants are reported to have been ancestors of the Khoisan, who were hunter-gathers.[3] In 1652, the Dutch East India Company established a refreshment station at the Cape of Good Hope, marking the beginning of European colonization of the region.[2] Over the two centuries that followed, the Dutch and the British gradually extended their control over the territory, leading to the establishment of the Union of South Africa in 1910, which was a British Dominion comprising the former colonies of the Cape, Natal, the Orange Free State, and Transvaal. South Africa gained independence from Britain in 1961, and was officially declared a republic.[4] With the establishment of colonial rule, Western-style medicine and hospitals were introduced, primarily serving the White population.[5] The non-White population (Black, Colored, and Indian/Asian) was largely excluded from these facilities and services.[6]

Under apartheid, the healthcare system was racially divided, with the White population receiving far better access to care than the non-White population.[7] Since April 1994, South Africa has been established as a sovereign nation, with a constitutional democracy, and it held its first democratic elections under the interim Constitution.[4] Since the end of apartheid in 1994, the South African government has made substantial efforts to reform and improve the healthcare system.[5] The National Health Act of 2003 established a framework for a unified and equitable national health system, with a focus on improving access to care for underserved populations.[8] In 2011, the National Development Plan's (NDP's) 2030 vision was finalized; the NDP serves as a guide for targets and expectations from all government departments, including the National Department of Health (NDoH).[9] With regard to health, Chapter 10 of the NDP set goals such as increasing life expectancy to at least 70 years, reduction of the burden of diseases, and strengthening of the health system, to achieve long-term health for South Africans.[9]

The 20-year review postdemocracy reported that poverty, inequality, and unemployment remain huge challenges in the country.[10] With regard to the health system, challenges such as inadequate funding, a shortage of healthcare workers, and ongoing disparities in the quality and availability of services were reported.[7] Thus, the various phases of South African history have collectively influenced the current health system, which remains shaped by the remnants of colonialism and apartheid, and efforts toward equality and accessibility remain an ongoing struggle.[7]

A 2020 study focused on analyzing the influence of racial differences in the demand for public health care in South Africa, using the 2018 General Household Survey data.[11] The study revealed that race significantly explained the variance in demand for public health care, with the White population having the lowest probability of demand for public health care, compared with other races.[11] Other studies have reported that the major challenges prior to 1994 included policies that were structured to influence racial, gender, and age divisions. These policies influenced unequal access to basic resources such as health, income, education, and so on.[7] For example, access to quality health care was very limited in non-White population, and the apartheid education system deliberately aimed to ensure that the non-White population remained a source of unskilled labor, leading to struggles in finding jobs.[7] The struggle to find jobs led to migration across provinces and increased the influx into those provinces with mining industries. Due to the lack of proper accommodations, overcrowding and slums increased in the urban areas.[7] The racial tensions influenced lack of peace and contributed to dysfunctionality in families, including the abuse of children and women.[7]

Size and Geography

South Africa is located in the southern region of the African continent and is the southernmost country on the mainland of that continent.[12] It is bordered by Namibia to the northwest, Botswana to the north, Zimbabwe to the northeast, Mozambique to the east, Swaziland to the southeast, Lesotho in the south-central region, and the Indian and Atlantic Oceans to the south and southeast,[12] respectively. The size of South Africa is 1,219,602 km^2, making it the 25th largest country in the world.[13] As seen in **Figure 17-1**, there are nine provinces: Eastern Cape, Free State, KwaZulu-Natal, Limpopo, Gauteng, Mpumalanga, North West, Northern Cape, and Western Cape.[14]

- The Eastern Cape, at 168,966 km^2, is South Africa's second-largest province after the Northern

SOUTH AFRICA

Figure 17-1 Map of South Africa

Cape, taking up 13.9% of the total land area.[14] The province has a population of more than 6.6 million people, the majority of whom speak isiXhosa, followed by Afrikaans and English.

- The Free State has about 129,825 km^2 of land, with a population of over 2.9 million people in 2022, with the main languages spoken being Sesotho, Afrikaans, and isiXhosa.[14]
- KwaZulu-Natal is the second-most populous province in South Africa, with slightly fewer residents than Gauteng, the majority of whom speak IsiZulu (82.5%), followed by English (12.5%) and Afrikaans (1.0%).
- Limpopo is South Africa's most northernmost province and shares borders with Mozambique, Zimbabwe, and Botswana, making it a gateway to Africa. The most spoken languages are Sepedi (56.0%), Tshivenda (17.1%), Xitsonga (16.6%), and the population numbers approximately 5,941,439.[14]
- Gauteng has the largest share of the population with approximately 16.9 million people (26.3%), followed by KwaZulu-Natal, Western Cape, and Eastern Cape (mid-year estimates in 2022).[3] It is the business heart of South Africa, and the shopping mecca of Africa, with tourists from the rest of the continent citing shopping as their reason for visiting the province.[3] Financial and business services, logistics, manufacturing, property, telecommunications, and trade are some of the province's most important economic sectors.[3] As a result, interprovincial as well as international migration patterns significantly influence population numbers and structures in Gauteng.

- Mpumalanga province has 4 million people. With a surface area of only 76,495 km^2, it is the second smallest province after Gauteng, yet has the fourth-largest economy in South Africa.[3] The most spoken languages are Siswati, isiZulu, and IsiNdebele.
- The Northern Cape is South Africa's largest province, taking up almost a third of the country's total land area, at 372,889 km^2.[3] However, the province is sparsely populated, with only approximately 1.3 million people, about 68% of whom speak Afrikaans, though Setswana, isiXhosa, and English are also widely spoken.
- The North West province has a population of more than 4 million, who mainly speak Setswana (71.5%), Afrikaans (7.2%), and IsiXhosa (5.1%).[3]

Government and Political System

South Africa is a constitutional democracy with a three-tier system of government and an independent judiciary.[15] The national, provincial, and local levels of government all have legislative and executive authority in their own spheres and are defined in the Constitution of the Republic of South Africa as distinctive, interdependent, and interrelated.[15] The president is the head of state and government and is elected by the National Assembly (the lower house of Parliament).[16] The president appoints a Cabinet, which is responsible for running the country's affairs and implementing government policies.[16] The Parliament of South Africa consists of two houses: the National Assembly and the National Council of Provinces.[16] The National Assembly is responsible for making laws, while the National Council of Provinces represents the interests of the country's nine provinces.[16]

South Africa has several independent institutions tasked with promoting transparency and accountability in government. They include the Office of the Public Protector, which investigates complaints of government corruption and abuse of power, and the South African Human Rights Commission, which promotes and protects human rights.[17] The country is also known for its constitution, which is widely regarded as one of the most progressive in the world.[18] The constitution enshrines a wide range of rights and freedoms, including freedom of speech, religion, and assembly, as well as equality before the law.[15] The constitution provides the basis for all major health policies, such as the right to quality and safe health care, and patients' rights.[19]

Macroeconomics

Major Industries

South Africa has a diverse economy, with several key industries that contribute to its growth and development, such as mining, agriculture, manufacturing, tourism, and finance.[20] The mining industry produces minerals such as gold, platinum, and diamonds. Most of the country's mining activities are in the Gauteng, North West, and Free State provinces.[20] The agricultural sector produces wine, fruits and vegetables, livestock, and dairy products.[20] The country's agricultural industry is spread across various regions, including the Western Cape, Limpopo, and KwaZulu-Natal.[20] The manufacturing sector produces goods such as automobiles, textiles, and chemicals.

The country's main industrial centers are in Gauteng, the Western Cape, and KwaZulu-Natal.[20] South Africa is a popular tourist destination, attracting millions of visitors every year due to its attractive sites, cultural heritage, and adventure activities.[20] The country's tourism industry is centered in key cities such as Cape Town, Durban, and Johannesburg, as well as popular wildlife destinations such as the Kruger National Park.[20] The financial sector consists of a number of banks, insurance companies, and investment firms. The country's financial hub is in Sandton, a suburb of Johannesburg.[20]

The location of the major industries influences the health system, in the sense that there is an increased influx of migrants, mostly in the major cities, entering the country for a better livelihood. The cities also experience interprovincial migration, leading to challenges in management of the health services. For example, patients often struggle to reconnect with healthcare services to continue following up on their chronic treatment due to moving from one province to another, or from neighboring countries.

Infrastructure and Transportation

The Department of Transport is responsible for the legislation and policies for rail, pipelines, roads, airports, and ports and the intermodal operations of public transport and freight.[16] Different spheres of government take various responsibilities with regard to modes of transport and the associated infrastructure.[15]

The network of roads and highways has a total length of 750,000 km, corresponding to 12.63 meters for each of the country's 60 million inhabitants.[21] This puts South Africa in 41st place in the global ranking, reflecting the country's low population density of around 49 inhabitants per km²; it also means very long distances must be traveled to reach the most remote parts of the country.[21] Infrastructure and transportation in South Africa have been undergoing significant development and improvement in recent years, but there are challenges that remain to be addressed. In the rural parts of the country, the road network is not well developed, and patients still struggle to be transported to the nearest healthcare facilities, especially when weather conditions are unfavorable. The rail system that connects major cities has also been neglected and requires improvements.

Air transportation in South Africa is well developed, with several major airports and numerous smaller airports serving the country.[21] The main international airport is OR Tambo International Airport in Johannesburg.[21] The country has a national airline, South African Airways, which operates both domestic and international flights.[21]

South Africa has several major ports, which handle a significant amount of cargo and passenger traffic.[21] The Port of Durban is the busiest port in Africa, handling approximately 43% of the country's total trade.[22] In recent years, the government has launched several infrastructure projects aimed at improving transportation and connectivity in the country. These include the Gauteng Freeway Improvement Project, which aims to upgrade the highways in Gauteng, and the Integrated Rapid Transit system in Johannesburg, which will provide a more efficient public transportation system for commuters.[21] Despite these developments, there are still challenges in South Africa's transportation infrastructure.[21]

Many rural areas still lack adequate transportation infrastructure, which makes it difficult for people to access essential services and economic opportunities.[21]

Demographics

Age Distribution

As of 2022, South Africa's population of approximately 60.6 million included 22.12 million habitants aged 0 to 19 years, while 609,000 people were aged 80 years or older.[23] Children aged between 5 and 9 years made up the largest age group, and those aged up to 4 accounted for the second largest share of the population. Those above 60 years represented a small part of the population.[23]

In 2021, approximately 37% of the people in South Africa were aged 19 years or younger.[23] This means that there is a high demand for child and youth healthcare services in the South African health system. An additional challenge is an increased unemployment rate in the country, such that many children are being raised by unemployed parents.[23] For example, in 2018, 30% (5.9 million) children lived in households where no adults were working.[23] According to monthly surveys conducted in 2021 and 2022, more than 60% of South African youth experienced high unemployment rates.[23]

Education Levels

In 2020, only 5.9% (1.7 million) of South African adults had a degree as their highest level of education, and only 34% (3,034,719) had completed high school.[24] This indicates that the level of education in the country remains low. One contributor to this challenge is the large number of children who are not attending school.[24] In 2022, 919,817 children were not enrolled in school.[25] Contributing reasons for not attending school have included ill health, long walking distances to schools, disability, childminding, poor academic performance, working to support the family, and pregnancy.[24] It is, however, encouraging that despite the reported low levels of education, in 2019, the youth literacy was reported to be improving.[23] The youth literacy rate refers to the proportion of individuals between the ages of 15 and 24 years who can read and write as well as understand simple expressions about their daily lives; it reached 98.41% in 2019.[23] In 2021, there was a slight decrease in the youth literacy rate, which was 97%.[26] Even with the slight decrease, this could mean that the children who are not currently attending school may have dropped out after having learned to read and write, leading to increased youth literacy levels by definition.

The low education levels in South Africa have significant and far-reaching implications for health, since lower levels of education are associated with poor health literacy, which can lead to poor health outcomes.[27] For example, individuals with low health literacy may have difficulty understanding information about disease prevention and treatment, which can lead to delayed or inadequate care-seeking behavior.[27] In addition, low levels of education are associated with poverty, which is a major contributor to poor health in South Africa.[28] The high levels of poverty and limited access to basic services, such as clean water and sanitation, contribute to the high burden of infectious diseases such as tuberculosis and HIV/AIDS in the country.[29] Addressing this issue will require a multi-sectoral approach, including investments in education and poverty reduction.

Religion

Section 8(4) of the Constitution of the Republic of South Africa provides that everyone has the right to freedom of conscience, religion, thought, belief, and opinion.[15] Hence, South Africa is a multi-religious country with a diverse range of religious beliefs, including Christianity, Islam, traditional African religions, Hinduism, Buddhism, Bahaism, Judaism, atheism, and agnosticism.[30] The freedom of religion is beneficial for South Africans, but requires healthcare providers to be mindful of the religious influence on health decisions by patients, which include when to seek health care and how to deal with refusal of health services due to religious reasons. Like anywhere in the world, religious beliefs and practices can have a positive impact on health—for example, by providing social support, reducing stress, and promoting healthy behaviors.[31] Religious practices, such as prayer and meditation, have been shown to have a positive effect on mental health, reducing symptoms of anxiety and depression.[31] Religion plays an important role in the lives of many South Africans and has positive implications for health in the country.[32]

Brief History of the Healthcare System

The history of the healthcare system in South Africa is marked by inequalities and challenges, reflecting the country's broader political and social history.[7] Before democracy (1994), health care in South Africa was extremely fragmented, with a mix of private, public, and mission-run facilities.[7] There were significant disparities in access to care based on race, with non-White South Africans having limited access to healthcare services.[7] Non-White South Africans were confined to inadequate and poorly funded health facilities, while White South Africans had access to better-quality healthcare services. After the fall of apartheid, South Africa transitioned to a new democratic government, and significant efforts have been made to promote recovery of the health system from the legacy of apartheid. In 2003, the National Health Act was enacted to provide a framework for a comprehensive and equitable healthcare system.[8] Despite these efforts, South Africa still faces significant health challenges, including high rates of communicable and noncommunicable diseases, and ongoing disparities in access to care based on race and socioeconomic status.[33] The lasting impact of the unequal and segregated healthcare system during apartheid contributes to the ongoing disparities in health outcomes and access to care that persist today.[7]

The Current Healthcare System

The current healthcare system in South Africa is structured according to the different spheres of government: national, provincial, and local. The health system consists of the NDoH, nine Provincial Departments of Health, and 52 Health Districts. The NDoH establishes the policy framework that guides the implementation of programs at the provincial and local government levels. The Provincial Departments of Health are responsible for the actual delivery of health services, including the district health services and primary health care. The local government is primarily responsible for environmental health and, in some cases, provides clinic-based primary healthcare services.

This chapter uses the World Health Organization's building blocks of health systems as a framework to comprehensively discuss the South African health system. These six building blocks, or subdomains, which support delivering effective and safe health interventions to those who need them, are health service delivery, health workforce, health information systems, access to essential medicines, health financing, and leadership and governance.

Health Service Delivery

The domain of health service delivery entails the distribution of facilities, beds, service readiness, and services offered. For the purpose of this chapter, we focus on the decentralization and distribution of health services and the health services on offer. The South African health system is two-tiered, consisting of a public health sector, which serves 71% of the population, and the private sector, which serves a small proportion of the South African population.

The public sector is divided into tertiary hospitals, secondary hospitals, and primary healthcare (PHC) facilities. Tertiary hospitals are the highest level of care, are centralized, and are teaching hospitals that provide highly specialized services. They are often located in major cities. Secondary-level care consists of regional hospitals with general specialist services, such as surgery and medicine, as well as full hours of laboratory and radiography services on site. PHC facilities include the district hospitals and PHC centers; these are often the first point of access for patients but may offer limited services. District hospitals may have general doctors, some specialists, and emergency care, but will not have an after-hours laboratory and radiography. The PHC centers are mainly staffed by nurses, with visits by doctors.

While there are standards for each level of care, the availability of services varies across different regions and locations in South Africa. Overall, health services located in major cities are often better resourced compared with those in rural locations. In 2021, there were over 400 public hospitals and over 200 private hospitals in South Africa.[34] Large regional hospitals are managed by provincial health departments, and smaller hospitals and clinics are managed by local municipalities.

The ratio of hospitals is estimated to be 1 per 100,000 members of the population, but varies across the nine provinces of South Africa.[35] The Northern Cape, Free State, and Eastern Cape have ratios of 1.79, 1.65, and 1.31 hospitals per 100,000 population, respectively. The rest of the provinces have fewer than one hospital per 100,000 population.[35] In 2010, the distribution of hospital beds per capita was estimated at 2.3 beds per 1,000 persons.[36] A 2017 study estimated there were a total of 70,197 hospital beds, the majority of which were in district hospitals and regional hospitals.[35] Similarly, the distribution of facilities varies across the nine provinces, with the largest number of beds being available in KwaZulu-Natal, Gauteng, and the Eastern Cape.[35] With regard to the PHC level of care, there are over 3,500 clinics and community health centers in South Africa. Since the advent of democracy,[37] there has been an expansion of the PHC centers and clinics in the country. As a result, the number of visits per capita to PHC facilities increased from 1.6 in 1998 to 2.2 in 2015.[37] The number of visits to PHC facilities remained consistent until the COVID-19 pandemic in 2020, when a decline to an estimated 81.4 million visits was noted. In 2021, visits increased to 84.1 million.[38]

Despite the progress made to establish district health systems and expand PHC services in South Africa, poor infrastructure and a lack of facilities remain a huge challenge. The challenges with the lack of infrastructure are well documented both in academic research and in the news media. For example, there have been multiple reports of patients sleeping on hospital floors due to insufficient beds and oncology patients waiting for years to access treatment due to a lack of material resources.[39–41] A study conducted in 2021 found that poor infrastructure was one of the barriers to implementation of the National Health Insurance system (health financing reforms are discussed later in this chapter).[42] A systematic review of the challenges associated with working in South African public hospitals highlighted dilapidated infrastructure and the high number of litigation cases due to poor health service delivery.[43]

To address some of these challenges, the South African government has sought to improve the quality of care provided by health facilities across the country. In 2011, the NDoH published National Core Standards for Health Establishments in South Africa (NCS), which were to be overseen and enforced by the Office of Standards Compliance established by the National Health Amendment Act of 2013.[44] The NCS have seven domains that address different aspects of health service delivery: patient rights, patient safety, clinical governance and care, public health, leadership and care, operational management, and facilities and infrastructure.[44] The patient rights domain is concerned with how patients' rights are respected and upheld by the health system, while the domains of patient safety, clinical governance, and clinical care guide aspects such as the quality of clinical care and ethical practice by healthcare workers. The domain of clinical support services is concerned with the availability of medicines and provision of medical technology for diagnostic and therapeutic services. The public health domain covers multi-stakeholder collaborations by civil society, government, health facilities, and communities to promote health and prevent illness.[44] The management of health facilities, which includes senior management leadership, risk management, hospital boards, clinic committees, and quality improvement, falls under the leadership and governance domain.[44] The operational management domain is concerned with day-to-day running of health facilities, such as human resource management, finances, assets and consumables, and information and record management, while the facilities and infrastructure domain oversees the physical infrastructure of health facilities.[44]

Despite the existence of these standards, research shows that there are still challenges with health service delivery, as managers at the facility level are not able to implement the NCS effectively.[45] A study that investigated the compliance of public-sector PHC facilities with the NCS and the impact of health audits 3 years after baseline audits found no improvement in compliance after 3 years of implementation.[46] This is congruent with the findings of a literature review that showed quality improvement projects have not achieved much success.[43]

It is clear that while the South African government has taken major strides to transform health services and improve delivery, challenges exist across different parts of the health system.

Health Workforce

The health workforce entails the availability, distribution, and competency of healthcare professionals, and includes areas such as workforce planning, recruitment, training, retention, and regulation of healthcare professionals. In 2019, a total of 43 doctors, 30 allied health workers, and 282 nurses per 100,000 population made up the health workforce serving the public-sector population in South Africa.[47] Other skilled health professionals include rehabilitation professionals, pharmacists, dentists, and emergency workers.[51] Nurses, followed by doctors, account for the largest proportions of the South African health workforce, at 56% and 8.8%, respectively.[47]

Compared with other African countries, South Africa has a higher density of skilled health workforce.[47] However, disparities in distribution are a huge challenge: Urban provinces have significantly higher densities of skilled health professionals compared with rural provinces.[47] In 2019, the overall national density of medical specialists was estimated to be 16.5 per 100,000 persons; however, the majority are employed in the private sector, which serves only a very small proportion of the South African population.[47] Over and above the maldistribution, there are challenges related to emigration, shortage of specialists, inadequate training, and job satisfaction and staff morale. Although staff emigration was a major challenge in the late 1990s, statistics from the early 2000s show a decrease in the outward migration of health workers.[48] This is attributed to external factors, such as changes in demand for health workers, as well as internal factors, such as improvements in health policies and remuneration in South Africa.[48]

The emigration of skilled healthcare professionals, commonly known as the "brain drain", is a significant challenge in South Africa. Despite improvements in policies and remuneration, research shows that health workers in South Africa report significantly higher job dissatisfaction compared with their counterparts in other African countries with lower remuneration.[49] Job satisfaction among health workers in South Africa is related to factors such as supervision experience and career development, and low satisfaction with their compensation.[50] Furthermore, there are challenges with developing an adequate health workforce and certain specialists.

To address some of the challenges associated with the health workforce, South Africa's 2030 Human Resources for Health Strategy outlines a roadmap for human resources for health in South Africa.[47] This strategy prioritizes health workforce planning, health workforce management and investment, production of a skilled and multidisciplinary workforce, optimal governance, and environments that encourage a productive and motivated workforce.[47]

Health Information Systems

Health information systems (HIS) collect, store, manage, and transmit health data. HIS integrate the collation, processing, reporting, and utilization of information to improve the effectiveness and efficiency of the health system. These systems play a crucial role in monitoring public health, delivering effective health care, and addressing health challenges. The roadmap for improving HIS in South Africa is set out in the NDoH's e-Health Strategy, which outlines the vision, goals, and objectives for leveraging information and communication technology in the healthcare sector.[51] Since the democratic dispensation in 1994, South Africa has taken great strides to establish HIS, including the National Health Information System (NHIS), District Health Information System (DHIS), electronic health records (EHRs), health patient registration systems, and m-health initiatives.

First, the NHIS comprises a centralized database that integrates data from various HIS across the country. These data are managed and analyzed through the Health Information Management System (HIMS), which helps healthcare professionals and policymakers make informed decisions by providing accurate and timely information on health trends, resource allocation, and performance indicators.[52]

Second, the DHIS is the primary health information system used to collect data from health facilities, clinics, and hospitals at the district level, so as to provide real-time monitoring of key health indicators, such as disease prevalence, service delivery, and resource allocation.[52] The DHIS was established in 1996 and expanded across the whole country in 2001.[52] It focuses on data collection, collation, and analysis, which occurs in the facility and is analyzed by DHIS software. The DHIS covers hospital data, emergency medical services (EMS) data, environmental health system (EHS) data, client satisfaction surveys, core standards and measures of quality of care, survey data sets, and data sets related to infrastructure and populations. Since its inception, the number of patient encounters recorded and the number of DHIS uses has continuously increased.[52]

Third, South Africa has implemented EHRs—that is, digital systems that store and manage patients' health records, including medical history, progress notes, medications, immunizations, laboratory data, radiology reports, and administrative data.[53] South Africa has been implementing EHRs to improve access to patient information, enhance coordination of care, and reduce medical errors. The nine provinces in South Africa use different computer management systems for capturing data for their EHRs.[53]

South Africa has also adopted various m-health initiatives to support priority health programs in partnership with private health partners. Finally, it has established the Health Patient Registration System (HPRS), a national system that assigns unique identifiers to patients seeking healthcare services in order to keep track of patient records, manage appointments, and ensure continuity of care across different healthcare facilities.[54] Through this system, each patient is given a unique patient identifier that enables accurate identification and tracking of their health records. In addition, the system enables coordination and management of patients and continuity of care, as it allows healthcare providers to access patients' comprehensive health records.[55] As of 2020, the HPRS system had registered more than 44 million patients from over 3,000 clinics in South Africa.[56]

Over the past few years, there have also been developments in telemedicine and telehealth in South Africa. In line with this, the e-Health Strategy 2019–2024 outlines promotion of the use of telemedicine and telehealth solutions to bridge the gap between healthcare providers and patients, particularly in remote or underserved areas. This is often achieved by using software applications, which are accessed through smartphones. Telemedicine enables remote consultations, diagnosis, and treatment, while telehealth supports remote monitoring and health education. The use of telemedicine and telehealth grew greatly during the COVID-19 pandemic and was instrumental in providing remote consultations, monitoring patients, and reducing the burden on healthcare facilities.[57] Currently, South Africa has various telemedicine platforms, including the Connect Specialist Telemedicine* platform, which enables patients to access virtual consultations with specialists, who facilitate remote diagnosis and treatment. There is also Vula Mobile,** which connects PHC providers with specialists, enabling remote referrals and expert advice.

While major strides have been made in HIS in South Africa, there are still challenges. These include poor data quality and integrity, a lack of infrastructure and connectivity, lack of skilled personnel and training, challenges with privacy, and lack of financial resources to maintain systems.[58,59] In addition, while many South Africans have access to smartphones, studies on mobile health applications for malaria and tuberculosis adherence have found challenges with network disturbances.[57] Despite these challenges, efforts toward use of technology to improve health are progressing.

Access to Essential Medicines

This domain is concerned with equitable access to and availability of selected medicines that are deemed essential. In 1996, the National Drug Policy was instituted in South Africa, with the goal of ensuring the availability and accessibility of essential drugs to all South Africans; ensuring the safety, efficacy, and quality of drugs; ensuring good dispensing and prescribing; promoting the rational use of drugs by prescribers, dispensers, and patients through provision of training, education, and information; and promoting the concept of individual responsibility for health, preventive care, and informed decision making.[60] The National Drug Policy laid the foundation for the creation of the Essential Medicines List (EML) and the Standard Treatment Guidelines (STG) for health professionals at the PHC and district health levels.[61] The National Essential Medicines List Committee was created and given the responsibility of developing the EML for use in the public healthcare sector and preparing the STG for health professionals.[61] Creation of an EML is an internationally recognized cornerstone of better quality of care and efficient use of health resources. Ideally, the EML and STG should be adaptable and responsive to the health needs of the population, and ultimately improve the availability and use of essential drugs.[62] Since the STG and the EML were established, there have been 12 published editions for the two levels of health care, a PHC book, separate books for adult and pediatric hospital levels, and a tertiary-level EML for treatment of specific conditions. A study found that usage of the STG and EML ranged between 70% and 79% among nurses and doctors in South Africa, respectively.[63] It also found that there was limited training on the STG and EML, and that nurses had limited access to hard copies of the EML and STG.[63]

*https://www.connectspecialist.co.za

**https://www.vulamobile.com

Despite the existence of the EDL and STG, drug shortages and stockouts are a major problem and commonly reported occurrence in South Africa.[64,65] When there are stockouts, patients are sent home without the drugs they need or are given incomplete regimens. Drug stockouts are more prevalent in rural and poorer communities, which negatively affects health outcomes.[66] This is concerning, given that access to essential medicines is enshrined in universal health coverage (UHC).

Health Financing

Health financing entails functions of health systems concerned with the mobilization, accumulation, and allocation of financial resources to cover the needs of populations and individuals. The South African health system is financed through a combination of direct and indirect taxes, private insurance fund contributions, and direct out-of-pocket payments. South Africa has a two-tier system that comprises a public and a private healthcare sector. The public sector provides services to approximately 85% of the population, while the private sector covers approximately 15% of the population. South Africa spends about 9% of its GDP on health care,[67] and despite the fact that the public health sector provides services to the majority of the South African population, only 50% of total health expenditure is in the public health sector.[67] In contrast, the private sector is well funded and primarily caters to the upper-middle class, who can afford private medical insurance.[68] This creates health disparities in the quality of health services and ultimately in health outcomes.

After 1994, payment for health services in public-sector facilities was abolished for low-income households, to address barriers to accessing health services.[69] Following these reforms, the number of people who accessed and used preventive health services increased.[70] Abolition of payments for public health services means that out-of-pocket payments for services are much lower for low-income communities in South Africa compared with other low- to middle-income countries.[71] However, the underfinancing of public health services has not matched the increased utilization; consequently, public health facilities have limited specialty services and poor infrastructure. The low-income populations who rely on these services get substandard health care who subjects them to poorer health outcomes.

To address the disparities in accessing quality health services, in 2011, the National Ministry of Health announced the National Health Insurance (NHI) scheme. South Africa is pursuing universal health coverage, which is defined as a health system in which all people have access to quality promotive, preventive, curative, and rehabilitative health services without suffering financial hardship.[72] In 2016, an NHI White Paper was published for public consultation, and in 2017, it was revised and gazetted after approval by the Cabinet.[73] The NHI is a health financing system that will pool funds to provide quality, affordable health services for all South Africans, regardless of socioeconomic status, and prevent catastrophic financial losses due to spending on health services.[73] Its aims are to transform the financing of health services so as to provide financial risk protection to the South African public and improve the efficiency of collection, pooling, and allocation of money for funding health services.[73] This is to be achieved by providing comprehensive health care through accredited and contracted public and private providers.[73]

Health promotion and prevention at the community and household level—referred to as the reengineering of the PHC system—are the main focus of the NHI. The policy outlines how PHC services will be delivered through district-based clinical specialist support teams, school health services, and municipal ward-based PHC agents, as well as hospital-based benefits across different levels of care (district, regional, and specialized). There is also provision for delivery of health services through contracted, accredited private providers. The implementation of the NHI was to be done in phases, starting with phase 1 (2012–2017), which entailed the piloting of systems that would ensure implementation.[73] The second phase was scheduled for 2017–2022, and its focus was on creating systems and procedures to guarantee the efficient operation and administration of the NHI fund.[73] The third phase was planned for 2021–2025, and the focus is to introduce the NHI prepayments, contracting of private healthcare providers, and implementation of the NHI and the Medical Schemes Acts.[73]

While the ideas behind the NHI offer great promise, evaluations of the first phases show shortcomings and various barriers to the implementation of NHI. A 2022 study by Mukwena and Manyisa identified a lack of human resources, poor infrastructure, poor administration, and a lack of financial resources as problems.[74] A national evaluation of the implementation of the first phases of NHI found mixed successes across different districts. The conditions necessary for success during the first phase of implementation were political will, sufficient human and financial resources for implementation, good coordination and communication, and good monitoring systems being in place.[75] The barriers to implementation were inadequate planning, a lack of resources, inconsistent communication, a lack of coordination, and insufficient mechanisms to monitor progress and thereby ensure course correction.[75] Despite these challenges, there are reports of improvements in universal health coverage indicators in some districts.[75,76]

Leadership and Governance

The National Health Act No. 61 of 2003 provides for the roles and the responsibilities of different levels of government in the health system.[8] These roles include, but are not limited to, providing a system of cooperative governance and management of health services, ensuring that each province, municipality, and health district delivers quality healthcare services, establishment of decentralized management, and sound governance.[8] The National Health Council is the highest policymaking body; it includes the minister of health, Members of the Executive Council (MEC) for Health, and representatives of local government and the military.[8] The Provincial Health Council develops guidelines and terms of reference for health districts, and sets up consultative forums to share information on health issues. The District Health Council in every health district sets up health governance structures at the district level, promotes cooperative governance, and creates committees to advise on health matters, plan budgets, and monitor health services. Although these may seem to be clear roles and responsibilities, leadership- and governance-related challenges have been reported to include poor intergovernmental relations between spheres of government, insufficient communication, and poor financial management skills, including a lack of involvement of frontline leaders in decision making.[77,78]

COVID-19 Pandemic

There is growing development of knowledge on the COVID-19 pandemic since its inception in 2019. In this chapter, we split the discussion of the pandemic into two parts, which overlap. First, we focus on the actual response to the COVID-19 pandemic by the South African government, especially in terms of health. Second, we use the published scientific literature to reflect on the impact of COVID-19 on the health system. We frame these reflections within the building blocks of the health system framework.

Health System Response to the COVID-19 Pandemic: A National Multisectoral Response

The first case of COVID-19 in South Africa was diagnosed on March 5, 2020, and a little more than 2 weeks later, the number of cases had increased to 408.[79] In response to the increase in the number of cases, amendments to the Disaster Management Act of 2000 were promulgated to provide a legislative framework specific to the prevention and management of the COVID-19 pandemic in South Africa.[80] The South African government took a whole-of-government approach by establishing the National Command Council (NCC), which consisted of 20 national ministers and the directors-general from 20 government departments. This council was presided over by the president under the jurisdiction of the Ministry of Cooperative Governance and Traditional Affairs (COGTA).[80] All actions taken by the NDoH were subject to the governance and oversight of the NCC.

The initial response was presented in eight overlapping stages, which entailed actions for preparation, institution of lockdowns, and allocation of health resources to control the spread and prevent the health system from collapsing.[79] **Figure 17-2** outlines these stages. The actions taken during the initial stages of the pandemic delayed the peak in a number of cases, and prevented the health systems from being overwhelmed—at least during the first wave of the pandemic.

South Africa adopted the WHO strategies for containing and mitigating the spread of COVID-19, which outline priorities and/or pillars for managing pandemics as they progress. These pillars and priorities may change with context, availability of research, progression of disease, and availability of therapeutic interventions.[81] To describe the South African experience of the COVID-19 pandemic, we focus on:

- Leadership and governance
- Surveillance
- Risk communication and community engagement
- Infection control, prevention, and vaccination
- Health service readiness and management of infected patients

Leadership and Governance

The whole-of-government approach and coordination was considered a strength in South Africa's fight against the COVID-19 pandemic. Establishment of the NCC made expert advice available. The NDoH received strategic advice from this high-level advisory committee,

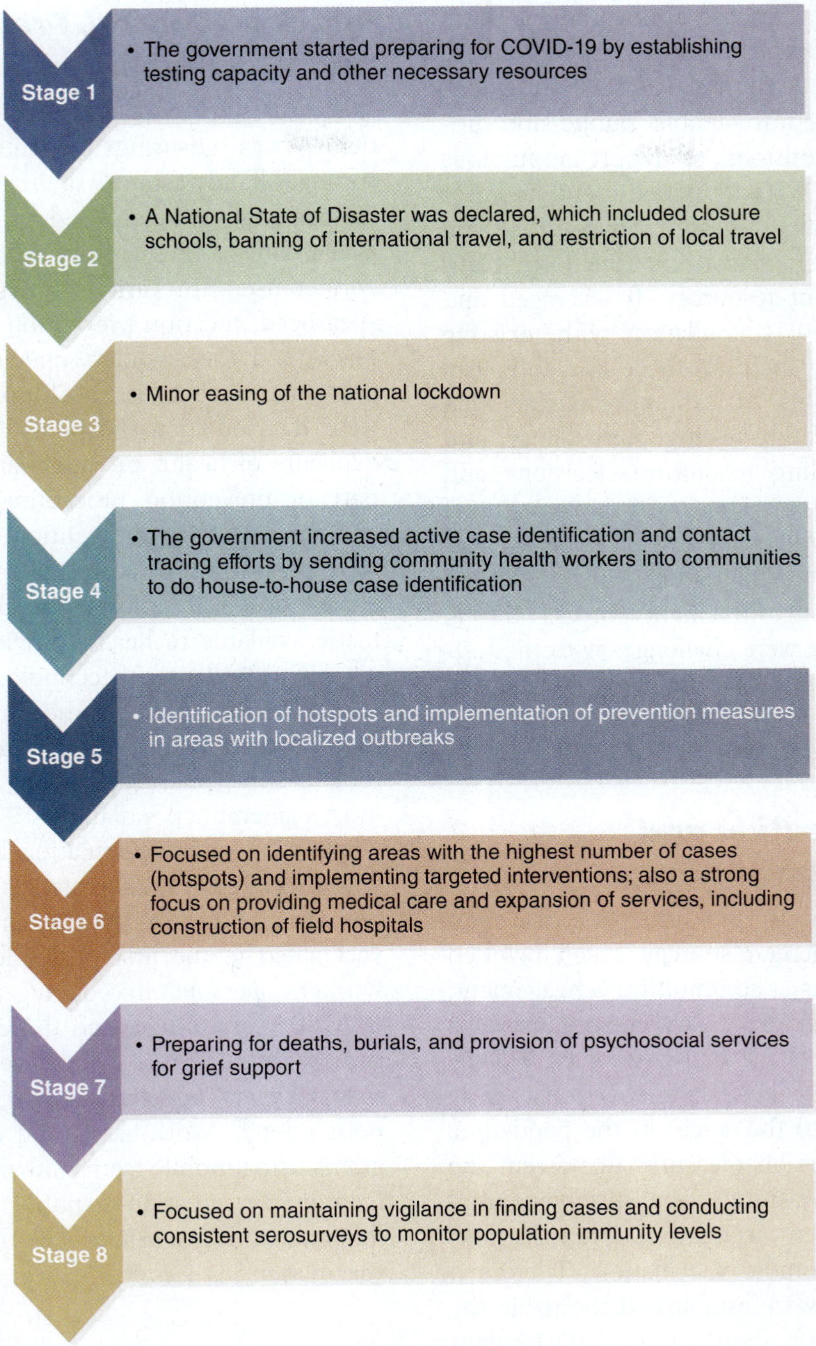

Figure 17-2 Steps taken in preparation for and response to the COVID-19 pandemic

Data from Ngqangashe Y, Heenan M, Pescud M. Regulating alcohol: strategies used by actors to influence COVID-19 related alcohol bans in South Africa. *Int J Environ Res Public Health.* 2021;18:11494.

which was composed of clinicians, virologists, epidemiologists, mathematical modelers, and public health practitioners to ensure evidence-based policy decisions.[79] National and provincial incident management teams were established to oversee key priorities.[82]

Screening, Testing, and Surveillance

COVID-19 was declared a notifiable disease, which meant that health authorities had to be notified of every diagnosis. As the number of imported cases and community cases increased, South Africa developed definitions for confirmed and suspected cases to enable disease notification.[83] The National Institute for Communicable Diseases, the public health institute responsible for surveillance, diagnosis, and management of outbreaks in South Africa, was responsible for the main laboratory for COVID-19 testing. However, as the number of cases increased, the National Health Laboratory Services and other private laboratories established capacity to perform COVID-19 testing.[83] A COVID-19 database was developed as a central disease notification platform for all COVID-19 cases. A national hospital surveillance system, called Data for COVID (DATCOV), was also implemented to enable public and private healthcare institutions to report admissions and diagnoses of COVID-19 patients and monitor the bed utilization rate.[83] In addition, South Africa developed a modeling consortium to inform planning and allocation of resources. It leveraged and integrated COVID-19 surveillance with existing surveillance systems such as those for influenza and pneumonia.[81] South Africa's approach included screening and community testing, surveillance, and epidemiologic modeling to inform decisions and distribution of resources. There was deployment of community health workers and use of digital applications tracing cases.[79,81] While South Africa displayed best practices regarding surveillance of COVID-19, at the beginning there were challenges with the testing capacity of laboratories, accuracy of information, and poor integration of the different data collection systems across the country.[84]

Risk Communication and Community Engagement

South Africa had a robust and systematic risk communication and engagement strategy, which included education campaigns, community engagement, and infodemic management. Awareness campaigns were started as soon as the first case of COVID-19 was diagnosed.[81,86] The messaging was consistently adapted in response to the stages of the pandemic. Initially, the focus was on measures to prevent the spread, such as handwashing, social distancing, and mask wearing.[81,85] When vaccination started, the messaging evolved to promote vaccination. Telephone and WhatsApp lines were established to enable the public to ask questions about the COVID-19 pandemic and what they needed to do in case of a positive test.[81,85] The government also actively engaged the community by providing daily press briefings on the number of new cases, deaths, pressures on the health facilities, and the steps that would be taken.[85] These messages were distributed through various social media channels as well. The government partnered with businesses, international multilateral organizations such as UNICEF, and nongovernmental organizations to develop an infodemic management strategy to identify misinformation, simplify COVID-19 messages, and amplify accurate and correct messaging.[86]

Infection Control, Prevention, and Vaccination

A crucial step in response to the COVID-19 pandemic was ensuring prevention of transmission through handwashing, sanitizing, and correct use of personal protective equipment. This required availability of these resources and training in their correct use.[77] In various provinces, committees to spearhead infection prevention training were put in place, and the standard operating procedures and guidelines for frontline health providers and patients were distributed to hospitals.[86] Policies to prevent exposure of health providers at high risk were also part of prevention procedures.[87] Vaccination was another important intervention, and health providers were prioritized for accessing vaccination as soon as it was available.[88] Information about vaccination was made available to health providers and the public, with increased use of technology to register people for vaccination, and most health establishments were used as vaccination sites. The rollout of the vaccine took a three-phase approach, beginning with the most vulnerable population.[87] The target was to vaccinate 67% of the population by the end of 2021, with this rate being estimated as necessary to achieve herd immunity. Frontline healthcare workers were vaccinated in the first phase, followed by essential workers, persons in congregate settings, persons over 60 years of age, and those over 18 years with comorbidities.[87] Phase 3 focused on persons older than 18 years, targeting 22,500,000 members of the population.[87] Work-based and outreach-based programs using mobile teams moving between facilities, including vaccination at public PHC facilities, were the main approaches to fast-track the COVID-19 vaccination services.[88]

Health Service Readiness and Management of COVID-19 Patients

It was evident that the normal capacity of the hospitals would not be able to handle the expected influx of COVID-19 patients.[89] Plans to increase capacity in terms of physical space and to rearrange existing structures to allow separation of COVID-19 patients and non-COVID-19 patients were put in place.[89] This included using of temporary structures such as tents in the hospitals. There was also a need to reshuffle staff allocation and intense prioritization of COVID services. Large venues in the country were converted into field hospitals, specifically earmarked for delivering care to COVID-19 patients. For example, the Cape Town International Convention Centre served to provide treatment to COVID-19 patients referred from existing acute-care hospitals, which provided initial management and stabilization of the acutely ill. Based on the admission criteria, patients could be admitted for further management in a field hospital for a maximum of 4 days.[89] **Figure 17-3** depicts the patient flow management approach at the field hospital at Cape Town International Convention Centre.

Reflections on the Effect of COVID-19 on the South African Health System

Despite the efforts put in place as described in previous sections, the scholarly literature has found that COVID-19 highlighted the existing weaknesses in the health system, some which have been discussed earlier of this chapter. In this section, we present the published literature on COVID-19 and South Africa's health system, organized according to the six building blocks of the health system.

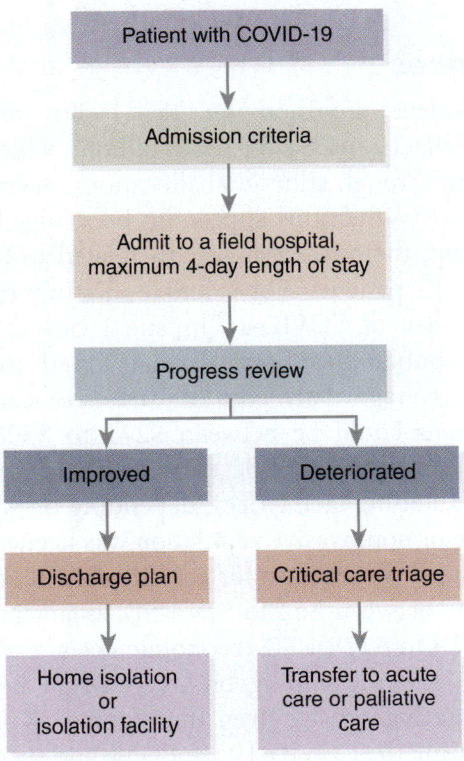

Figure 17-3 Patient flow through a field hospital at Cape Town International Convention Centre

Data from Bulajic B, Ekambaram K, Saunders C, et al. A COVID-19 field hospital in a conference centre: the Cape Town, South Africa experience. *Afr J Prim Health Care Fam Med.* 2021;13:3140. doi: 10.4102/phcfm.v13i1.3140.

Service Delivery

The ongoing delivery of health services amid the COVID-19 pandemic was one of the critical global goals, to ensure that health care was not compromised by the focus on COVID-19.[90] Ongole et al. assert that sustaining essential health care in South Africa during the COVID-19 pandemic became very important, yet challenging, as services needed to be essentialized to reduce the number of routine visits, and patients were controlled and reorganized to ensure patient safety through effective triage and infection control measures.[90] The reality is that the nature and scope of service delivery were different from the usual workflow. Some scholars suggest that there was a sudden shift of attention toward COVID-19 patients, with less focus on non-COVID-19 patients.[77] In addition, in an effort to increase capacity of resources, there was a need to postpone "nonurgent" health services, such as planned operative procedures.[91] One study focused on changes in hospital practice around surgical decision making, operating theaters, surgical services, and surgical trainees, and the potential long-term effect of these choices.[91] Some scholars reported reduced allocation of the health workforce to some services, suspension of services, reduced health-seeking behavior, and unavailability of supplies.[92] Several studies reported on the impact of COVID-19 on delivery of specific health programs originally designed to increase access to particular levels of care.[93–95]

A cross-cutting theme is the decline in utilization of health services, leading to disruption of essential services such as HIV and TB treatment. A 2022 study that examined the direct and indirect effects of the pandemic on access to HIV services found that lockdown restrictions coupled with reallocation of limited health resources used by adolescents living with HIV disrupted existing structures and established patent–provider relationships, leading to treatment failure and mental health conditions.[93] Another study reported a general sense of limited access to condoms in healthcare facilities during the COVID-19 pandemic,[94] which could be due to lack of prioritization on ordering of resources that were not related to COVID-19. Further declines were noted in TB treatment and HIV treatment; for example, numbers of antiretroviral treatment initiations declined sharply in all provinces in April through June 2020, compared with the same months in 2019, and remained low for the rest of 2020.[96] A systematic review to evaluate the impact of the pandemic on accessing HIV services at the PHC level in South Africa indicated a significant negative impact.[97] Another study reported decreased use of PHC services, evidenced by a decline in visits across provinces of nearly 500,000 after the lockdown period.[95] Family planning utilization—which is usually demand-driven—also declined during the lockdown.[99] Switching contraceptive methods to those with less effectiveness were noted as a trend during the COVID-19 pandemic. Year-over-year comparisons from April 2018 to April 2020 indicated a consistent decline in the use of injectable methods and increased use of oral contraceptive pills.[95]

Human Resources

By April 30, 2021, a total of 6,364 COVID-19 admissions (2.7% of all hospital admissions) were reported among healthcare workers across South Africa.[98] Health workers were infected and affected by COVID-19, and illness increased in general due to being directly infected with the illness or experiencing the deaths of family members, relatives, friends, or colleagues. These led to increased depression, anxiety, post-traumatic stress, and other mental health conditions noted among healthcare workers exposed to COVID-19.[99] Reflections from health providers indicate that they felt unheard, uncared for, and unsupported.[100] Rispel et al. assert that a shortage of staff was already a concern prior to the COVID-19 pandemic, with the pandemic adding to ongoing physical and mental exhaustion among healthcare providers.[77] In addition, some COVID-19 regulations mandated that all people above 60 years of age and those living with comorbidities should stay at home, putting an additional strain on the human resources available for health care, leading to a gap in terms of numbers and experience (increased age of healthcare workers is usually aligned with increased experience).[101] An additional frustration was lack of resources and, at times, lack of personal protective equipment, along with a general lack of managerial support.[102] Mahlangu et al. reported on resilience and commitment of frontline healthcare workers as driven by their faith and professional commitment, despite the stated challenges. Their study underscored the importance of prioritizing interventions to promote the mental wellness of frontline health providers during pandemics.[103] This recommendation was supported by Zungu et al., who assessed how South Africa prepared to protect its health workers from COVID-19 infection; these researchers found inconsistencies in occupational health and safety practices, including lack of a comprehensive occupational health and safety plan for health workers.[86]

Information

There are positive signs of information sharing leading to improved health literacy, specifically regarding COVID-19; this was due to frequent engagement by the government, and use of television and radio to broadcast COVID-19 updates.[104] The information sharing on COVID-19 has been applauded as one of the most effective health communication campaigns since the HIV epidemic, with South African citizens mastering application of knowledge on social distancing, handwashing, and alternative greeting practices.[105] This is an indication of the potential to engage communities in improving their knowledge on health-related matters and improve preventive care. Another study supports this notion, stating that communities showed increased COVID-19 knowledge, and their curiosity about the pandemic was evident in their use of web searches and social media regarding COVID-19; however, the authors warned that if not balanced with formal updates, a reliance on social media searches could potentially increase the spread of health misinformation.[106] This is an important lesson: Government officials are encouraged to increase their use of social media to reach communities with the correct health information, by addressing them through their social media sites of interest.

Finances

The budget provision for the health response to COVID-19 was over R20 billion, which was achieved through additional allocations and reprioritization.[107] While this appears to be a huge budget allocation, there was a high cost related to treating COVID-19 patients. For example, a study estimating the cost of COVID-19 inpatient care in South Africa's public healthcare system found that the highest average daily cost for intensive care unit admissions could be between $271 to $306 USD (financial costs) and $800 to $830 USD (economic costs, excluding facility fee), depending on whether invasive or noninvasive ventilation was needed.[108] In contrast, the lowest cost for general ward-based care could be between $62 to $79 USD (financial costs) and $119 to $278 USD (economic costs, excluding facility fees), depending on oxygenation needs.[108] These are high costs, given the number of patients seen during the COVID-19 pandemic and their need for lengthy stays as inpatients.

Additional resources were required to increase the pool of human resources at hospitals, including the extension of hospital sites. There was also a need for increasing resources to establish field hospitals.

Mismanagement of COVID-19 funds was identified in the report by a special investigation unit, which revealed a lack of integrity among the healthcare leaders.[109] Although the lockdown was applauded for having delayed the eventual peak of COVID-19 infections, there was insufficient consideration of the negative effect of the long lockdown on the economy and people's livelihoods. The economic implications of the lockdown included a reduction of future provincial health budget projections. This could have a negative effect on future spending needs for healthcare resources and maintenance of service delivery. We could not find studies reporting any financial benefits of COVID-19 for hospitals, even though there were several donations to hospitals and the COVID-19 fund was also used for hospital resources, nor could we find reports on how COVID-19 improved resource availability in hospitals. This could be an area for future research.

Medicines and Technology

Mash et al. reported on an initiative that was adopted to decongest facilities by sending community healthcare workers to do home delivery of medications to vulnerable patients.[110] This study attests to the challenges experienced by the community healthcare workers, including dealing with incorrect addresses and contact details, transporting parcels, communicating with patients, having a reliable audit trail, and handling out-of-area patients.[110] The report indicates that existing challenges in access to medications were further exacerbated by the COVID-19 pandemic. However, Mbunge et al. point to the positive and promising experience in which South Africa adopted digital technologies such as SMS-based solutions, mobile health applications, telemedicine and telehealth, WhatsApp-based systems, artificial intelligence, and chatbots and robotics to provide healthcare services during the pandemic.[111] Their study revealed use of innovative technologies for various purposes, such as screening for infectious and noninfectious diseases, disease surveillance and monitoring, medication and treatment compliance, and creating awareness and communication. The authors assigned names to various activities related to virtual delivery of healthcare services through digital health technologies during the COVID-19 pandemic in South Africa, saying that there was an increase in teleconsultation, ePrescription, telelaboratory, telepharmacy, tele-education and teletraining, teledermatology, teleradiology, telecardiology, teleophthalmology, teleneurology, telerehabilitation, teleoncology, and telepsychiatry.[111] These are areas for further research on how South Africa's health system can maximize on some of these innovations, which were initially coping mechanisms for COVID-19 but could possibly be opportunities for future adoption for efficient service delivery.

Leadership and Governance

Reflections on leadership and governance have shone a light on various challenges, including poor communication of stated guidelines; lack of a public health emergency operations center, which resulted in unclear commands and control; unclear linkages between the committees; delays in the hiring of additional health workforce members; and management of procurement services.[82] A study on Gauteng's response to COVID-19, using interviews with key informants, some of whom were implementers of COVID-19 regulations at coal mines, described communication of guidelines on managing the COVID-19 pandemic as overwhelming, fast-paced, and with frequent changes, leading to variations in interpretation and confusion.[77] Several studies alluded to disappointment at the numerous cases of corruption identified in the special investigating unit reports, which included inflation of costs and lack of compliance with procurement procedures.[109,112] Such practices point to poor leadership in the health sector, lack of servant leadership, and poor representation of the public interest.

Conclusion

Compared with the apartheid era, it seems that there has been positive progress in the health system in South Africa, although several challenges still need to be conquered. The reviewed literature reveals ongoing challenges, such as healthcare disparities, overcrowding and long waiting times, shortage of healthcare workers, limited access to technology and equipment, high cost of private health care, and limited funding for health care. There are several strengths, including the availability of good policies, including the constitution, the National Development Plan, National Health Act, and others, which serve as a good foundation to frame future implementation of better health systems.

The COVID-19 pandemic exaggerated existing health system challenges and highlighted practices that, while they were initially coping strategies for COVID-19, can be supported for possible acceptance in the health system. These practices include innovations such as those that improved information sharing with the public, increased the voice of public health to the community, and gave support to telemedicine. There is a need to find means to overhaul the current levels of corruption as experienced in the department of health during COVID-19 pandemic; that may restore the public trust. Most importantly, care and support to the health workforce requires prioritization to ensure recovery from trauma related to the COVID-19 pandemic and to enable capacity to deal with any pandemic that may arise in the future.

References

1. Nations Online. History of South Africa. Accessed October 12, 2023. https://www.nationsonline.org/oneworld/History/South-Africa-history.htm.
2. Fourie J. *An Inquiry into the Nature, Causes and Distribution of Wealth in the Cape Colony, 1652–1795*. Utrecht University; 2012.
3. Government Communications. *South Africa Year Book*. South Africa: Government Communications and Information System; 2022.
4. Republic of South Africa. South African government: history. Accessed March 15, 2023. https://www.gov.za/about-sa/history.
5. van den Heever AM. South Africa's universal health coverage reforms in the post-apartheid period. *Health Pol.* 2016;120:1420-1428.
6. Digby A. The medical history of South Africa: an overview. *History Compass.* 2008;6:1194-1210.
7. Coovadia H, Jewkes R, Barron P, et al. The health and health system of South Africa: historical roots of current public health challenges. *Lancet.* 2009;374:817-834. doi: 10.1016/S0140-6736(09)60951-X.
8. Republic of South Africa. *Government Gazette*. National Health Act No. 61 of 2003. Cape Town, South Africa: Government Printer; 2003.
9. National Planning Commission. National Development Plan 2030. *Our Future: Make It Work*. Pretoria, South Africa: Government Printer; 2012.
10. National Department of Health. *Twenty Year Review: South Africa*. South Africa: Government Printer; 2014.
11. Mhlanga D, Garidzirai R. The influence of racial differences in the demand for healthcare in South Africa: a case of public healthcare. *Intl J Environ Res Pub Health.* 2020;17:5043.
12. Republic of South Africa. Geography and climate. Accessed March 23, 2023. https://www.gov.za/about-sa/geography-and-climate.
13. Worldometer. Largest countries in the world. Accessed March 23, 2023. https://www.gov.za/about-government/government-system/structure-and-functions-south-african-government.
14. Statistics SA. *Provinces of South Africa*. 2022.
15. Republic of South Africa. *The Constitution of the Republic of South Africa*. Pretoria, South Africa: Government Printer; 1996.
16. Republic of South Africa. Structure and functions of the South African government. Accessed March 23, 2023. https://www.gov.za/about-government/government-system/structure-and-functions-south-african-government.
17. Republic of South Africa. *Government Communications Policy*. Pretoria, South Africa: Government Printer; 2018.
18. Department of Justice and Constitutional Development. The constitution. Accessed March 23, 2023. https://www.justice.gov.za/legislation/constitution/docs/2ndAnniversary.html.
19. National Department of Health. *National Health Insurance Policy: Towards Universal Health Coverage*. Pretoria, South Africa: National Department of Health; 2017.
20. Brand South Africa. SA's key economic sectors. Accessed March 23, 2023. https://brandsouthafrica.com/78205/economic-sectors-agricultural/.
21. Republic of South Africa. Transport. Accessed March 23, 2023. https://www.gov.za/about-sa/transport.
22. Republic of South Africa. *Comprehensive Maritime Transport Policy for South Africa*. Pretoria, South Africa: Department of Transport; 2017.
23. Galal S. Age distribution in South Africa. Accessed March 15, 2023. https://www.statista.com/statistics/1116077/total-population-of-south-africa-by-age-group/.
24. Khuluvhe M, Negogogo V. Fact sheet: the highest level of education attainment in South Africa. In: *Training*. Pretoria, South Africa: Department of Education; 2021.
25. Trading Economics. South Africa - Children out of school, primary. Accessed February 12, 2025. https://tradingeconomics.com/south-africa/children-out-of-school-primary-wb-data.html.
26. TheGlobalEconomy.com. South Africa: Youth literacy rate, ages 15-24. Accessed February 12, 2025. https://www.theglobaleconomy.com/South-Africa/Youth_literacy_rate_15_24/.
27. Coughlin SS, Vernon M, Hatzigeorgiou C, et al. Health literacy, social determinants of health, and disease prevention and control. *J Environ Health Sci.* 2020;6.
28. Moyo C, Mishi S, Ncwadi R. Human capital development, poverty and income inequality in the Eastern Cape province. *Dev Stud Res.* 2022;9:36-47.
29. Nguse S. Intersectionality in South African health care: what is to be done? *South African J Psychol.* 2022:00812463221141528.
30. Government Communications. *South Africa at a Glance: Official Guide to South Africa*. Pretoria, South Africa: Government communication and Information System; 2019.
31. Bosire EN, Cele L, Potelwa X, et al. God, church water and spirituality: perspectives on health and healing in Soweto, South Africa. *Glob Pub Health.* 2022;17:1172-1185. doi: 10.1080/17441692.2021.1919738.
32. Ishabiyi AO, Khan S. Religious associational life amongst Black African Christian students at Howard College Campus, University of KwaZulu-Natal. *J Stud Relig.* 2020;33(2):1-22.
33. Achoki T, Sartorius B, Watkins D, et al. Health trends, inequalities and opportunities in South Africa's provinces, 1990–2019: findings from the Global Burden of Disease 2019 study. *J Epidemiol Community Health.* 2022;76:471-481.
34. International Citizens Insurance. The healthcare system in South Africa. Accessed February 12, 2025. https://www.internationalinsurance.com/health/systems/south-africa.php.

35. Dell A, Kahn D. Geographical maldistribution of surgical resources in South Africa: a review of the number of hospitals, hospital beds and surgical beds. *S Afr Med J.* 2017;107:1099-1105.
36. World Bank. Hospital beds per 1000 persons—South Africa, Accessed June 10, 2023. https://data.worldbank.org/indicator/SH.MED.BEDS.ZS?locations=ZA.
37. World Health Organization. *Primary Health Care Systems (Primasys): Case Study from South Africa*. 2017.
38. Pillay Y, Museriri H, Barron P, Zondi T. Recovering from COVID lockdowns: routine public sector PHC services in South Africa, 2019–2021. *S Afr Med J.* 2022;113(1):17-23. doi:10.7196/SAMJ.2022.v113i1.16619.
39. Matlhabe G. Patients sleep on floor at Mamelodi hospital. *IOL*. 2017.
40. Pijoos I. Pregnant women forced to sleep on Joburg hospital floor, health ombud finds. *News24*. 2023.
41. Jojo LW, Nkutu NT. Experiences of patients on cancer treatment regarding decentralization of oncology services at a tertiary hospital in the Eastern Cape. *BMC Cancer.* 2023;23:1-9.
42. Passchier R. Exploring the barriers to implementing national health insurance in South Africa: the people's perspective. *S Afr Med J.* 2017;107:836-838.
43. Manyisa ZM, van Aswegen EJ. Factors affecting working conditions in public hospitals: a literature review. *Intl J Africa Nurs Sci.* 2017;6:28-38.
44. National Department of Health. *National Core Standards for Health Establishments in South Africa*. South Africa: National Department of Health; 2011.
45. Mogashoa MG, Pelser GPJ. An analysis of the implementation of the national core standards in public hospitals. *Africa Insight.* 2014;44:142-157.
46. Cloete BL. *Auditing Healthcare Facilities Against the National Core Standards for Occupational Health and Safety and Infection Prevention and Control: Compliance, Reliability and Impact*. University of Cape Town; 2016.
47. National Department of Health. *2030 Human Resources for Health*. South Africa: National Department of Health; 2020.
48. Labonté R, Sanders D, Mathole T, et al. Health worker migration from South Africa: causes, consequences and policy responses. *Human Res Health.* 2015;13:1-16.
49. Blaauw D, Ditlopo P, Maseko F, et al. Comparing the job satisfaction and intention to leave of different categories of health workers in Tanzania, Malawi, and South Africa. *Global Health Act.* 2013;6:19287.
50. Du Plessis Y, Tawana B, Barkhuizen NE. A comparative analysis of the antecedents and consequences of employee satisfaction for urban and rural healthcare workers in KwaZulu-Natal province, South Africa. *SA J Human Res Manag.* 2019;17:1-9.
51. National Department of Health. *National Digital Health Strategy for South Africa 2019–2024*. Pretoria, South Africa: Department of Health; 2019.
52. National Department of Health. *District Health Management Systems Policy*. South Africa: Department of Health; 2011.
53. Wright G, O'Mahony D, Cilliers L. Electronic health information systems for public health care in South Africa: a review of current operational systems. *J Health Inform Africa.* 2017;4.
54. Asah FN. Creating a "community of information practice" for improved routine health data management in resource constrained setting: the case of Mbingo Primary Healthcare facility, South Africa. *Elect J Inform Sys Devel Countries.* 2021;87:e12178.
55. Health Systems Trust. *Electronic Health Information Systems for Public Health Care in South Africa: A Review of Current Operational System*. South Africa: Health Systems Trust; 2011.
56. South Africa. 2020 State of the Nation address. Accessed February 14, 2025. https://www.gov.za/news/speeches/president-cyril-ramaphosa-2020-state-nation-address-13-feb-2020.
57. Mbunge E, Batani J, Gaobotse G, et al. Virtual healthcare services and digital health technologies deployed during coronavirus disease 2019 (COVID-19) pandemic in South Africa: a systematic review. *Glob Health J.* 2022;6(2):102-113. doi: 10.1016/j.glohj.2022.03.001.
58. Kekana M, Noe P, Mkhize B. The practice of telemedicine and challenges to the regulatory authorities. *South African J Bioeth Law.* 2010;3:33-37.
59. Dodoo JE, Al-Samarraie H, Alzahrani AI. Telemedicine use in sub-Saharan Africa: barriers and policy recommendations for Covid-19 and beyond. *Intl J Med Inform.* 2021;151:104467.
60. National Department of Health. *National Drug Policy for South Africa*. South Africa: National Department of Health; 1996.
61. Perumal-Pillay VA, Suleman F. Selection of essential medicines for South Africa: an analysis of in-depth interviews with national Essential Medicines List Committee members. *BMC Health Serv Res.* 2017;17:1-17.
62. Atif M, Malik I, Dawoud D, et al. Essential medicine list, policies, and the World Health Organization. *Encyclo Pharm Pract Clin Pharm.* 2019;1:239-249.
63. Govender T, Suleman F, Perumal-Pillay VA. Evaluating the implementation of the Standard Treatment Guidelines (STGs) and Essential Medicines List (EML) at a public South African tertiary institution and its associated primary health care (PHC) facilities. *J Pharma Pol Pract.* 2021;14:1-14.
64. Hwang B, Shroufi A, Gils T, et al. Stock-outs of antiretroviral and tuberculosis medicines in South Africa: a national cross-sectional survey. *PLoS One.* 2019;14:e0212405.
65. Hodes R, Price I, Bungane N, et al. How front-line healthcare workers respond to stock-outs of essential medicines in the Eastern Cape province of South Africa. *S Afr Med J.* 2017;107:738-740.
66. Koomen L, Burger R, Van Doorslaer E. Effects and determinants of tuberculosis drug stockouts in South Africa. *BMC Health Serv Res.* 2019;19:1-10.
67. World Bank. Current health expenditure (% of GDP): South Africa. Accessed June 10, 2023. https://data.worldbank.org/indicator/SH.XPD.CHEX.GD.ZS?locations=ZA.
68. Michel J, Tediosi F, Egger M, et al. Universal health coverage financing in South Africa: wishes vs reality. *J Glob Health Rep.* 2020;4:e2020061.
69. Brink AS, Koch SF. Did primary healthcare user fee abolition matter? Reconsidering South Africa's experience. *Devel Southern Africa.* 2015;32:170-192.
70. Wilkinson D, Gouws E, Sach M, et al. Effect of removing user fees on attendance for curative and preventive primary health care services in rural South Africa. *Bull World Health Organ.* 2001;79:665-671.
71. Koch SF, Setshegetso N. Catastrophic health expenditures arising from out-of-pocket payments: evidence from South African income and expenditure surveys. *PLoS One.* 2020;15:e0237217.
72. World Health Organization. *Universal Health Care*. Geneva, Switzerland: WHO; 2013.

73. South Africa. National Health Insurance. Accessed June 10, 2023. https://www.gov.za/about-government/government-programmes/national-health-insurance-0.
74. Mukwena NV, Manyisa ZM. Factors influencing the preparedness for the implementation of the national health insurance scheme at a selected hospital in Gauteng Province, South Africa. *BMC Health Serv Res.* 2022;22:1006.
75. National Department of Health. *Evaluation of the Phase 1 Implementation of the Interventions in the National Health Insurance Pilot Districts in South Africa.* South Africa: Department of Health; 2019.
76. Fusheini A, Eyles J. Achieving universal health coverage in South Africa through a district health system approach: conflicting ideologies of health care provision. *BMC Health Serv Res.* 2016;16:1-11.
77. Rispel LC, Marshall C, Matiwane B, et al. Innovations, contestations and fragilities of the health system response to COVID-19 in the Gauteng province of South Africa. *PloS One.* 2021;16:e0261339.
78. Muthathi IS, Rispel LC. Policy context, coherence and disjuncture in the implementation of the Ideal Clinic Realisation and Maintenance programme in the Gauteng and Mpumalanga provinces of South Africa. *Health Res Policy Syst.* 2020;18:1-15. doi: 10.1186/s12961-020-00567-z.
79. Abdool Karim SS. The South African response to the pandemic. *N Engl J Med.* 2020;382:e95.
80. Ngqangashe Y, Heenan M, Pescud M. Regulating alcohol: strategies used by actors to influence COVID-19 related alcohol bans in South Africa. *Intl J Envir Res Public Health.* 2021;18:11494.
81. Moonasar D, Pillay A, Leonard E, et al. COVID-19: lessons and experiences from South Africa's first surge. *BMJ Global Health.* 2021;6:e004393.
82. Ramkrishna W. *Republic of South Africa COVID-19 Experience and Multi-Sectoral Priorities for Future Pandemic Preparedness.* 2023. https://apps.who.int/gb/COVID-19/pdf_files/2023/30_03/Item3.pdf.
83. Silal S, Groome M, Govender N, et al. Leveraging epidemiology as a decision support tool during the COVID-19 epidemic in South Africa. *S Afr Med J.* 2022;112:361-365.
84. Modisenyane M, Madikezela L, Mngemane S, et al. COVID-19 response in South African communities: screening, testing, tracing and movement modelling. *S Afr Med J.* 2022;112:366-370. doi: 10.7196/SAMJ.2022.v112i5b.16072.
85. Adebisi YA, Rabe A, Lucero-Prisno DE III. Risk communication and community engagement strategies for COVID-19 in 13 African countries. *Health Prom Persp.* 2021;11:137.
86. Zungu M, Voyi K, Mlangeni N, et al. Organizational factors associated with health worker protection during the COVID-19 pandemic in four provinces of South Africa. *BMC Health Serv Res.* 2021;21:1080. doi: 10.1186/s12913-021-07077-w.
87. *COVID-19 Vaccine.* South Africa: National Department of Health; 2021.
88. National Institute for Communicable Disease. COVID-19 vaccine roll-out strategy. 2021. Accessed March 23, 2023. https://www.nicd.ac.za/south-africas-covid-19-vaccine-strategy-03-jan-2021/.
89. Bulajic B, Ekambaram K, Saunders C, et al. A COVID-19 field hospital in a conference centre: the Cape Town, South Africa experience. *Afr J Prim Health Care Fam Med.* 2021;13:3140. doi: 10.4102/phcfm.v13i1.3140.
90. Ongole J, Rossouw TM, Fourie PB, et al. Sustaining essential healthcare in Africa during the COVID-19 pandemic. *Int J Tuberc Lung Dis.* 2020;24(6):643-645.
91. Chu K, Smith M, Steyn E, et al. Changes in surgical practice in 85 South African hospitals during COVID-19 hard lockdown. *S Afr Med J.* 2020;110:916-919.
92. Nyasulu J, Pandya H. The effects of coronavirus disease 2019 pandemic on the South African health system: a call to maintain essential health services. *Afr J Prim Health Care Fam Med.* 2020;12:1-5.
93. van Staden Q, Laurenzi CA, Toska E. Two years after lockdown: reviewing the effects of COVID-19 on health services and support for adolescents living with HIV in South Africa. *J Int AIDS Soc.* 2022;25:e25904. doi: 10.1002/jia2.25904.
94. Bolarinwa OA. Factors associated with access to condoms and sources of condoms during the COVID-19 pandemic in South Africa. *Arch Pub Health.* 2021;79:186. doi: 10.1186/s13690-021-00701-5.
95. Adelekan T, Mihretu B, Mapanga W, et al. Early effects of the COVID-19 pandemic on family planning utilisation and termination of pregnancy services in Gauteng, South Africa: March–April 2020. *Wits J Clin Med.* 2020;2:145-152.
96. Benade M, Long L, Rosen S, et al. Reduction in initiations of HIV treatment in South Africa during the COVID pandemic. *BMC Health Serv Res.* 2022;22:428. doi: 10.1186/s12913-022-07714-y.
97. Jardim CGR, Zamani R, Akrami M. Evaluating the impact of the COVID-19 pandemic on accessing HIV services in South Africa: a systematic review. *Intl J Environ Res Public Health.* 2022;19:11899.
98. Tlotleng N, Cohen C, Made F, et al. COVID-19 hospital admissions and mortality among healthcare workers in South Africa, 2020–2021. *IJID Regions.* 2022;5:54-61. doi: https://doi.org/10.1016/j.ijregi.2022.08.014.
99. Robertson L, Maposa I, Somaroo H, et al. Mental health of healthcare workers during the COVID-19 outbreak: a rapid scoping review to inform provincial guidelines in South Africa. *S Afr Med J.* 2020;110:1010-1019.
100. Dawood B, Tomita A, Ramlall S. "Unheard," "uncared for" and "unsupported": The mental health impact of Covid-19 on healthcare workers in KwaZulu-Natal Province, South Africa. *PLoS One.* 2022;17:e0266008. doi: 10.1371/journal.pone.0266008.
101. Mbunge E. Effects of COVID-19 in South African health system and society: an explanatory study. *Diabet Metab Syn Clin Res Rev.* 2020;14:1809-1814.
102. Lewis S, Mulla F. Diagnostic radiographers' experience of COVID-19, Gauteng, South Africa. *Radiography.* 2021;27:346-351.
103. Mahlangu P, Sikweyiya Y, Gibbs A, et al. I carry the trauma and can vividly remember: Mental health impacts of the COVID-19 pandemic on frontline health care workers in South Africa. *Intl J Envi Res Pub Health.* 2023;20:2365.
104. Olaoye A, Onyenankeya K. Effectiveness of Mdantsane FM community radio in health information promotion among residents of eastern cape province, South Africa. *Inform Devel.* 2023. doi: 10.1177/02666669231187362.
105. Farao J. Digital health communication in South Africa during COVID-19. *Glob Health Innov.* 2020;3.
106. Fischer AE, Van Tonder T, Gumede SB, et al. Changes in perceptions and use of mobile technology and health

communication in South Africa during the COVID-19 lockdown: cross-sectional survey study. *JMIR Form Res*. 2021;5:e25273.

107. Blecher MS, Davén J, Meyer-Rath G, et al. The South African government's COVID-19 response: protecting lives and livelihoods. *South Afr Health Review*. 2021;2021:1-17.
108. Edoka I, Fraser H, Jamieson L, et al. Inpatient care costs of COVID-19 in South Africa's public healthcare system. *Int J Health Policy Manag*. 2022;11:1354-1361. doi: 10.34172/ijhpm.2021.24.
109. Mlambo VH, Masuku MM. Governance, corruption and COVID-19: the final nail in the coffin for South Africa's dwindling public finances. *J Public Admin*. 2020;55:549-565.
110. Mash RJ, Schouw D, Daviaud E, et al. Evaluating the implementation of home delivery of medication by community health workers during the COVID-19 pandemic in Cape Town, South Africa: a convergent mixed methods study. *BMC Health Serv Res*. 2022;22:1-11.
111. Mbunge E, Batani J, Gaobotse G, et al. Virtual healthcare services and digital health technologies deployed during coronavirus disease 2019 (COVID-19) pandemic in South Africa: a systematic review. *Glob Health J*. 2022;6:102-113. doi: https://doi.org/10.1016/j.glohj.2022.03.001.
112. Mmakwena M, Moses M. The nexus between corruption and opportunistic crimes during Covid-19 in South Africa. *Technium Soc Sci J*. 2022;27:980.

CHAPTER 18

Ghana

Umar Haruna, Anthony Mwinilanaa Tampah-Naah, and Musah A. Sugri

Country Description

Table 18-1 **Ghana**

Nationality	Noun: Ghanaian(s) Adjective: Ghanaian
Ethnic groups	Akan 47.5%, Mole-Dagbon 18.5%, Ewe 12.8%, Ga-Dangme 7.1%, Gurma 6.4%, Guan 3.2%, Grusi 2.7%, Mande-Busanga 2.0%, other 1.6% (2021 est.)
Religions	Christian 71.3% (Pentecostal/Charismatic 31.6%, Protestant 17.4%, Catholic 10%, other 12.3%), Muslim 19.9%, traditionalist 3.2%, other 4.5%, none 1.1% (2021 est.)
Language	Asante 16%, Ewe 14%, Fante 11.6%, Boron (Brong) 4.9%, Dagomba 4.4%, Dangme 4.2%, Dagarte (Dagaba) 3.9%, Kokomba 3.5%, Akyem 3.2%, Ga 3.1%, other 31.2%; English (official) (2010 est.)
Literacy	Definition: Age 15 and over and can read and write. Total population: 79% Male: 83.5% Female: 74.5%
Government type	Constitutional democracy
Date of independence	March 6,1957 (from the United Kingdom)
Gross domestic product (GDP) per capita	5,400 USD (2021 est.)
Unemployment rate	4.7% (2021 est.)
Natural hazards	Dry, dusty, northeastern harmattan winds occur from January to March; droughts
Environment: current issues	Recurrent drought in north severely affects agricultural activities; deforestation; overgrazing; soil erosion; poaching and habitat destruction threatens wildlife populations; water pollution by illegal mining; inadequate supplies of potable water
Population	33,846,114 (2023 est.)

Table 18-1 Ghana

Age structure	0–14 years: 37.44% (male 5,524,932/female 5,460,943) 15–24 years: 18.64% (male 2,717,481/female 2,752,601) 25–54 years: 34.27% (male 4,875,985/female 5,177,959) 55–64 years: 5.21% (male 743,757/female 784,517) 65 years and over: 4.44% (male 598,387/female 703,686)
Median age	Total: 21.4 years Male: 21 years Female: 21.9 years (2020 est.)
Population growth rate	2.19% (2023 est.)
Birth rate	28.04 births/1,000 population (2023 est.)
Death rate	5.99 deaths/1,000 population (2023 est.)
Disease burden	Communicable disease deaths: 476/100,000 population Noncommunicable disease deaths: 670/100,000 population Injury deaths: 76/100,000 population (2016 est.)
Net migration rate	−0.16 migrant(s)/1,000 population (2023 est.)
Gender ratio	At birth: 1.03 male/female 0–14 years: 1.02 male/female 15–64 years: 0.93 male/female 65 years and over: 0.81 male/female Total population: 0.95 male/female (2023 est.)
Infant mortality rate	Total: 31.87 deaths/1,000 live births Male: 35.25 deaths/1,000 live births Female: 28.38 deaths/1,000 live births (2023 est.)
Life expectancy at birth	Total population: 69.72 years Male: 68.06 years Female: 71.44 years (2023 est.)
Total fertility rate	3.61 children born/woman (2023 est.)
HIV/AIDS adult prevalence rate	1.7% (2019 est.)
Number of people living with HIV/AIDS	361,797 (2023 est.)
HIV/AIDS deaths	12,600 (2015 est.)

USD = U.S. dollars.

Data from Central Intelligence Agency. The World Factbook, 2024: Ghana. https://www.cia.gov/the-world-factbook/countries/ghana/.

History

The Republic of Ghana was named after the medieval Ghana Empire of West Africa in Ancient Ghana. Geographically, Ancient Ghana was approximately 500 miles (800 kilometers) north of the present Ghana and occupied the area between the rivers Ankobra and Volta. The actual name of the empire was Ouagadougou; Ghana was the title of the kings who ruled the kingdom. The word *ghana* means warrior king.[1] Ancient Ghana was controlled by Sundiata in 1240 CE and absorbed into the larger Mali Empire, which reached its peak of success under Mansa Musa in approximately 1307. Around 1235, a Muslim leader named Sundiata united warring tribes. He then brought neighboring states under his rule to create the Mali Empire. Its capital city was called Kumbi-Saleh. Ancient Ghana derived power and wealth from gold and the camel, introduced through trans-Saharan trade. The Islamic community at Kumbi-Saleh remained a separate community quite a distance away from the king's palace. It had its own mosques and schools, but the king retained traditional beliefs. He drew on the bookkeeping and literary skills of Muslim scholars to help run the administration of the territory.[2]

On March 6, 1957, when the leaders of the former British colony of the Gold Coast sought an appropriate name for their newly independent state, the first African nation to gain its independence from colonial rule, they named their new country after ancient Ghana. The choice was more than merely symbolic because modern Ghana, like its namesake, was equally famed for its wealth and trade in gold. The growth of trade stimulated the development of early Akan states located on the trade route to the gold fields in the forest zone of the south.[3]

The Europeans arrived on the Gold Coast in the late 15th century. The Portuguese were the first to arrive. By 1471, under the patronage of Prince Henry the Navigator, they had reached the area that is now known as the Gold Coast because Europeans knew the area as the source of gold that reached Muslim North Africa by way of trade routes across the Sahara.[4] The initial Portuguese interest in trading for gold, ivory, and pepper increased so much that in 1482, the Portuguese built their first permanent trading post on the western coast of present-day Ghana. This fortress, Elmina Castle, constructed to protect Portuguese trade from European competitors and hostile Africans, still stands. With the opening of European plantations in the New World during the 1500s, which suddenly expanded the demand for slaves in the Americas, trade in slaves soon overshadowed gold as the principal export of the area. During the 17th and 18th centuries, other European adventurers emerged on the Gold Coast. First Dutch traders, and later English, Danish, and Swedish traders, were granted licenses by their governments to trade overseas. On the Gold Coast, these European competitors built fortified trading stations and challenged the Portuguese. Sometimes, they were also drawn into conflicts with the local inhabitants, as Europeans developed commercial alliances with local chiefs.[5]

The principal early struggle was between the Dutch and the Portuguese. With the loss of Elmina in 1642 to the Dutch, the Portuguese left the Gold Coast permanently. The next 150 years saw drastic changes and uncertainty, marked by local conflicts and diplomatic maneuvers, during which various European powers struggled to establish or to maintain a position of dominance in the profitable slave trade. There were short-lived ventures by the Swedes and the Prussians.[6] The Danes remained until 1850, when they withdrew from the Gold Coast. The British gained possession of all Dutch coastal forts by the end of the 19th century, making them the dominant European power on the Gold Coast until March 6, 1957, when the new republic of Ghana was born with Osagyefo "liberator" Dr. Kwame Nkrumah as its first president. It was during the first republic that healthcare facilities were built to take care of the indigenous Ghanaian population.

Size and Geography

Until March 1957, Ghana was known to the world as the Gold Coast. See **Table 18-1**. The Portuguese who came to Ghana in the 15th century found so much gold between the rivers Ankobra and Volta that they named the place Mina, meaning mine. English colonists later adopted the name the Gold Coast.

The Republic of Ghana occupies an area of 239,460 square kilometers (92,440 square miles). It borders Côte d'Ivoire (also known as the Ivory Coast) to the west, Burkina Faso to the north, Togo to the east, and the Gulf of Guinea to the south. (Refer to **Figure 18-1**.)

Ghana is composed of 16 administrative regions and 216 administrative districts with a decentralized system of administration. Within this arrangement, the national level is responsible for policy and strategy development. The regional level is the intermediate level responsible for translating national policy into regional strategies and coordinating district actions. The district is the level at which all government policies are implemented. The district assemblies are the highest political and administrative authority at the local level. The district assemblies, through their subcommittees, harmonize and coordinate plans and activities of all decentralized ministries. They also facilitate grassroots participation and community involvement in socioeconomic development programs and activities. The district assemblies are generally supportive of decentralized departments. Undoubtedly, the district assemblies are very important in the implementation and sustainability of a multisectoral response to healthcare systems.[7]

Economy

Ghana's economy has been strengthened by a quarter century of relatively sound management, a competitive business environment, and sustained reductions in poverty levels. In late 2010, Ghana was recategorized as a lower middle-income country. Ghana is well endowed with natural resources. Agriculture accounts for roughly one-quarter of GDP and employs more than half of the workforce, mainly small landholders. The services sector accounts for 50% of GDP (see Table 18-1). Gold and cocoa production and individual remittances are major sources

GHANA

Figure 18-1 Map of Ghana

of foreign exchange. Oil production at Ghana's offshore Jubilee field began in mid-December 2010 and is producing close to target levels. Additional oil projects are being developed and are expected to come on line in a few years. Estimated oil reserves have jumped to almost 700 million barrels, and Ghana's growing oil industry is expected to boost economic growth as the country faces the consequences of years of loose fiscal policy, high budget and current account deficits, and depreciating currency.[8]

Demographics

Ghana has a population of 33.9 million, of whom 52% are female and 48% are male (2023 estimates). Ghana has a young age structure, with approximately 56% of the population under the age of 25 as of 2020. Life expectancy of the total population is 69.72 years, with males at 68.06 years and females at 71.44 years. The literacy rate is 79%. More than half of the population now live in urban settings. English is the official language of business and instruction. Local dialects include Akan (majority), Ga, and Ewe. The language distributions are as follows: Akan 47.5%, Mole-Dagbani 18.5%, Ewe 12.8%, Ga-Dangme 7.1%, Gurma 6.4%, Guan 3.7%, Grusi 3.2%, Mande-Busanga 2%, and other 1.6% (2021 census). The Christian population is 71.2%, with the following distributions by denomination: Pentecostal/Charismatic 28.3%, Protestant 18.4%, Catholic 13.1%, and other 11%. Other religions include Muslim (19.9%), traditional African religion (3.2%), other (0.7%), and none (3.3%) (2021 census).[9]

Brief History of the Healthcare System

Pre–World War II

Until October 19, 1923, when the Korle Bu Teaching Hospital (formerly known as the Gold Coast Hospital) was opened by the Gold Coast governor (Sir Gordon Guggisberg), health services were reserved solely for Europeans. The European physicians treated only the settlers. Most of the indigenous Ghanaian population relied on traditional African medicine. After the opening of the Gold Coast Hospital, the indigenous population of Accra was able to receive European health care at a minimal cost. Korle Bu Hospital had fewer than 200 beds and treated up to 200 patients daily.[10] At that time, Korle Bu Hospital was described as the finest hospital in Africa. This was on account of its impressive array of fine buildings and cadre of competent staff, who provided excellent medical services to the population of Ghana in general and the city of Accra in particular. Korle Bu Hospital, from its inception, has been used for the training of practical nurses, nurse anesthetists, dispensers, midwives, and other paramedical staff.

Post–World War II

In 1946, a nurses' training college was opened at Korle Bu to train a higher level of staff—registered nurses—for the hospital and for the entire country. In April 1963, the government made Korle Bu Hospital the teaching hospital for the University of Ghana Medical School.[11] After independence, medical services became free to all citizens of Ghana and were financed by the government. Under the leadership of Dr. Kwame Nkrumah, Ghana set up a national health service, which was fully financed from state revenues. During this time, because of the lack of facilities in rural areas, the quality of care received there was very poor. However, the concept during that time was concentrated on vaccine-preventable diseases, and all residents (including the populations in rural areas) had access to available vaccinations. It was the belief of the Nkrumah administration that "health before wealth" was more than just an old adage. The government developed programs that aimed to protect and improve the health of people as a measure to alleviate poverty.[12] The government was committed to the objective of health for all. Good health boosts labor productivity, educational attainment, and income and thus reduces poverty. A country's economic development is closely interrelated with the health status of its population, so an efficient and equitable healthcare system is an important instrument in breaking the vicious circle of poverty and ill health. Until 1983, Ghana's healthcare system was financed mainly out of the national budget.[13]

Ghana experienced a balance of payments crisis in the early 1980s, which soon generalized into an economic crisis that affected all sectors of the economy. The country not only experienced a general decline in agricultural productivity and exports, which included declining world prices for cocoa and gold, but also a shortfall in foreign exchange earnings, which negatively impacted import-dependent manufacturing firms. Furthermore, consumer goods shortages, inflationary pressures, and unemployment gradually built up and resulted in deficit financing via external borrowing, making the situation worse. During this period, the country's balance of payments was in disarray; budget deficits were ballooning and foreign investment flows had nearly dried up.[14]

In Ghana and across Africa, structural adjustments were foisted on one country after the other, and efforts were made to dismantle agricultural marketing boards; to privatize, commercialize, and liquidate state-owned enterprises; to deregulate various aspects of the economy; to reduce the size of the state bureaucracy through civil service retrenchments; to encourage the private sector; and to promote a free market. Structural adjusters were very concerned about balancing budgets and servicing public debt, both domestic and external. To do this, budget cuts were made to social spending, with education and health taking the heaviest brunt. Slowly but surely, in 1978, the government was forced to introduce cost recovery into the health system in Ghana.[15] This was popularly known as *cash-and-carry*. This system was a product of the structural adjustment program that the International Monetary Fund and the World Bank had prescribed and that Ghana readily adopted. It involved the wholesale withdrawal of government subsidies for health delivery. Under the *cash-and-carry* system, patients were asked to pay the full cost of medication and care. Because of economic crises and mismanagement, the government had to reduce spending on health and social affairs. Less money was available for health. The government was not able to finance the health system via general taxation. The Bamako Initiative, launched in 1987, also introduced user fees in government health facilities, the joint management of the resources generated by health staff and the community, and the decentralization of the health sector. The rationale behind full cost recovery was that there would be an increase in resources for healthcare facilities, which would allow them to expand and upgrade their services, improve access to health care, improve patient care, and achieve better efficiency because of the increased revenue from charges. Furthermore, there was the presumption that cost recovery would help reduce unnecessary visits by patients who were abusing the system because it was free. The evidence gathered suggests that none of these assumptions materialized. After its introduction, the *cash-and-carry* system appeared to have carried away health services from the people. The system could best be described as "stinking and dehumanizing" because patients who did not have the ability to pay for medical services were turned away from hospitals, only to die at home. The disabled, the poor, and accident victims were asked to pay on the spot before getting medical attention.[16] To make matters worse, cost recovery was introduced at a time when many people had been laid off from the public sector and income levels were extremely low. Many poor people were turned away from health centers for lack of funds.[17]

Unfortunately, the poor were simply priced out of hospital care, and a two-tier healthcare system came into operation with better facilities for those who could afford to pay. Once again, women and children bore the brunt of such harsh policies. The introduction of user fees further impoverished the majority of Ghanaians, and for a long time, it devastated their ability to sustain their livelihoods. Some people, especially those living below the poverty line, had to borrow money, take out loans, sell their animals or furniture, dissolve their little savings, cut down on buying food, and even stop sending their children to school in order to pay for health care. The process of borrowing money from extended family delayed treatment and, in many cases, caused deterioration of health and even death. In other cases, people did not seek medical treatment because they could not afford it, which often increased morbidity and mortality.[18]

It was welcome news when in 2004, the government rekindled social equity as a key part of healthcare policy by establishing the National Health Insurance Scheme (NHIS) to replace the *cash-and-carry* system.

The Current Healthcare System

There are four main categories of healthcare delivery systems in Ghana: public, private for-profit, private nonprofit, and traditional systems.[19] The public health system, centered around the Ministry of Health (MoH), has a hierarchical organizational structure, disseminating authority from the central headquarters in Accra to the regions, districts, and subdistricts. Services are delivered through a network of facilities, with health centers and district hospitals providing primary healthcare services, regional hospitals providing secondary health care, and five teaching hospitals—the Korle Bu Teaching Hospital (KBTH), the Komfo Anokye Teaching Hospital (KATH), the Tamale Teaching Hospital (TTH), the Cape Coast Teaching Hospital (CCTH), and the Ho Teaching Hospital (HTH)—at the apex providing tertiary services. However, there are concerns that this number falls short of the ratio of tertiary facilities needed to adequately provide quality health care to the over 30 million users in Ghana. In addition, having only one tertiary facility (TTH) serving the population in the whole of the northern part of the country contradicts an important equity objective of the national health policy.[19]

The five teaching hospitals play a key role in teaching and research, offering facilities for the training of doctors and other health professionals and for medical and public health research. KATH and TTH serve about half of the people of Ghana and also function as the main tertiary referral centers for neighboring Burkina Faso and Côte d'Ivoire.

Ghana's health system is composed of a variety of facilities and affiliations, ranging from government-owned to private facilities. Approximately one-third of Ghana's health facilities are operated under private ownership, and a 2008 McKinsey study indicated that more than 50% of health service provision in Ghana is delivered by the private sector.[20] However, consistently collected information on private-sector performance and delivery mechanisms is scanty. Data on private facility medical supplies, expenditures, and interventions are not routinely captured or included in Ghana's health information systems.[21] Thus, data on service delivery successes and challenges experienced by Ghana's private sector are not easily ascertained.[22]

Facilities

There are many different categories of hospitals in Ghana. Generally, more densely populated areas are served better than the rural areas. Rural areas have very limited access and archaic health institutions. This is why many people still rely on self-medication, especially in rural Ghana. Private facilities number around 1,294. Private hospitals usually provide better-quality treatment and have more modern equipment than public institutions. Public hospitals number around 1,818. They tend to be overcrowded and lacking in quality, especially compared with their counterparts in developed countries. Both public and private institutions are generally located in urban areas. Healthcare facilities sponsored by religious institutions, generally Christian and Muslim, number around 204. These are found predominantly in rural areas.[23]

Regional hospitals provide secondary health care, whereas the five teaching hospitals provide tertiary services. Health care is structured in a four-tier system. Level A is composed of health systems at the community level, including trained birth attendants and community health workers. Level B is composed of health posts and health centers at the subdistrict level. Level C is composed of hospitals that function as district referral units. Regional and teaching hospitals constitute level D and provide tertiary services at the national, regional, district, and subdistrict levels.

National Level

The national level is made up of the MoH, where health policy is formulated, the health system (see **Figure 18-2**) is monitored, and evaluation of progress in achieving targets is conducted. The second entity at the national level is Ghana Health Services, which is responsible for resource allocation and the creation of partnerships with the private sector.

Regional Level

There are 16 regional health administrations (previously they were 10 in number) that serve as links between the national and district levels and allocate resources within the region. Regional and district hospitals are set up as part of a national policy that is supposed to ensure that every region and district has a befitting health facility. However, not all regions and districts in the country have such facilities, especially now that new districts have been added in conformity with the decentralization policy. The regional hospitals depend on district hospitals for their patient load.

Most of the dentists in Ghana work in public regional hospitals. On site, there are usually a dentist,

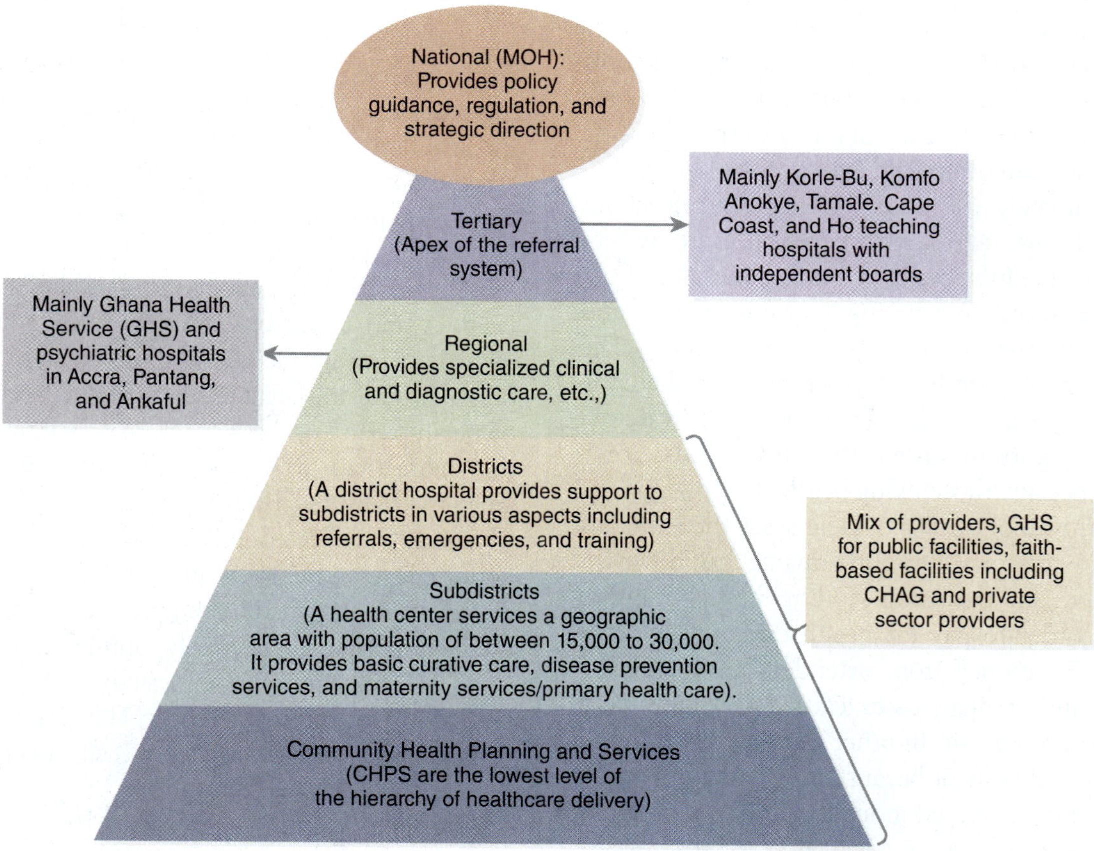

Figure 18-2 Structure of the health delivery system in Ghana

Reproduced from Sarkpoh F, Domapielle MK. Stakeholders' perspectives on facilitative supervision implementation in north-western Ghana: an exploration of adherence and quality of primary healthcare. *Prim Heath Care Res Dev.* 2022;23:e58. © The Author(s), 2022. Published by Cambridge University Press. doi: 10.1017/S1463423622000457.

two or three dental surgery assistants, and one or more dental laboratory technicians, depending on the size of the catchment area. The dentist works under the chief medical officer of the hospital. Unlike the medical profession, dentistry has no representation at the regional, district, or community levels.

District Level

The focal point of the healthcare system is the district level, where the implementation of the national healthcare strategy takes place. The district level is concerned with operational planning and implementation of service within the district. It is responsible for the construction of health facilities: hospital, health centers, and community health clinics. This is the key level of management of the primary healthcare system and provides leadership in district health care.

The attempt to provide middle, paradental personnel to provide oral health services in the district and rural areas, especially to school children, was defeated when 15 dental therapists trained overseas in the late 1970s ended up in schools within Accra, the capital.

Subdistrict Level

Community-Level Health Centers These centers provide outpatient services to relieve the district and regional hospitals of all but their most specialized functions. Health centers usually serve a catchment area of about 8 square kilometers and provide the first point of contact with health personnel from the MoH. There is no dental equivalent to the delivery system at this level, except for the odd outreach program by an already understaffed dental team from one of the regional hospitals.[24]

Health Centers, Health Posts, and Rural Clinics This is the smallest unit at the broad base of the three-tier system. Minor cases like cuts and wounds are treated in these facilities, and serious cases are referred to the health centers or the district hospitals. These stations are run by community clinic attendants and function as first-aid stations and health observational posts. There is no equivalent oral health delivery system at this level.

Community-Level Health Planning and Services This is a new system of healthcare delivery that was introduced in Ghana a few years ago based on research by the Navrongo Health Research Centre. It is similar to the primary healthcare concept, but a qualified health worker, called a community health officer, normally operates this program. Community health nurses have mostly been reoriented to assume this position, and it has been integrated into their training program. This system is operated on a zonal basis in a given subdistrict. The requirement for setting up the community-based health planning and services zone is similar to that for the health center. One distinct feature is that community-based health planning and services zones are normally established in remote areas composed of a number of communities with a total population of between 3,000 and 4,000. The emphasis is more on health promotion (preventive health) than on curative health.

Workforce

Ghana has five government-operated medical schools that are responsible for training physicians. They are the University of Ghana Medical School in Accra, Kwame Nkrumah University of Science and Technology Medical School in Kumasi, the University for Development Studies Medical School in Tamale, the University of Cape Coast School of Medical Sciences in Cape Coast, and the University of Health and Allied Sciences in Ho.

Besides these five teaching institutions, a number of other institutions with links to the MoH are located at Korle Bu and are involved in training the healthcare workforce in Ghana: Nurses Training School, Public Health Nurses Training School, Midwifery Training School, School of Hygiene, Disease Control Division of the MoH, Health Education Unit of the MoH, and Center for Health Statistics of the MoH. In addition, the University of Allied Health Sciences and the public nursing training colleges in the country have joined the public institutions tasked with training Ghana's health workforce. These institutions have been able to train an adequate workforce for the healthcare system. Hence, workforce training has not been an issue in Ghana; rather, the issue has been retention. The system's inability to craft adequate compensation and pay structures to retain the trained workforce has led to the migration of its healthcare workers to greener pastures in developed countries.[25]

A World Health Organization (WHO) report on international migration stated that by the end of 2005, Ghana had lost over 50% of its highly skilled labor. Of this number, 90% were healthcare professionals. Ghana was the only country to lose most of its professionals during the 1980s. However, Ghana's doctor–patient ratio and nurse–patient ratio have improved over the past years. According to the deputy minister of health, the doctor–patient ratio is one to 10,000, while the nurse–patient ratio is one to 1,251.[26]

Technology and Equipment

The provision of equitable, quality, and efficient health care requires an extraordinary array of properly balanced and managed resource inputs. Physical resources such as fixed assets and consumables, often described as healthcare technology, are among the principal types of these inputs. Technology is the platform on which the delivery of health care rests and is the basis for the provision of the majority of health interventions. Technology generation, acquisition, and utilization require massive investment, and related decisions must be made carefully to ensure the best match between the supply of technology and the health system needs, to ensure the appropriate balance of capital and recurrent costs, and to ensure the capacity to manage technology throughout its life. There is a large need for new medical equipment for the new facilities that are being built in Ghana and for the existing facilities that are being expanded and/or refurbished.

Due to the high incidence of various diseases, the government of Ghana has invested significant capital into the upgrading of the country's hospitals, removing obsolete equipment and replacing it with new and improved equipment. To meet its umbrella goal to improve healthcare services and make them more accessible to the population, medical imaging devices—particularly improved X-ray devices and ultrasound equipment—have been placed by the government in some selected public hospitals. In addition, the government is upgrading public laboratories—manual operations at labs are being automated, supporting sizeable growth in the analyzer market. The government's goal to have diagnostic capability easily accessible to the population is increasing the growth of this industry.

Much of the existing equipment is obsolete or broken and cannot be repaired locally because of a lack of spare parts or maintenance expertise. This need is expected to increase as more of the planned projects are started. Future demand will increase as there has been a recognized need to improve the health service in Ghana, and this is being addressed as funds become available.[27]

Doctors try to improve the information they have available on patients in various ways, but especially by prescribing tests. An ideal test is cheap, produces no adverse side effects, and is accurate in two senses: It always identifies pathology when present and it confirms the absence of pathology when not present. Even accurate and safe tests can be worthless—for instance, when no effective treatment is available. If resources dedicated to health care are limited, something has to be sacrificed (rationing). This is the case in Ghana when it comes to diagnostic or treatment procedures that require pieces of high-tech equipment that are either not available or scarce in the nation. Other nations have rationed health care for years by setting healthcare budgets or regulating fees, effectively controlling the number of hospitals or the amount of medical equipment or other devices.

The country depends on Ghanaians in the diaspora, nongovernmental organizations (NGOs), and bilateral and multilateral donors for donations of pieces of technological equipment in the medical field. The technological donations have been in the form of new, used, refurbished, and/or rehabilitated medical equipment and mobile medical services and equipment. For instance, on October 3, 2007, General Electric's vice president of corporate citizenship visited the KATH in Kumasi to donate essential health products. These included a fluoroscopy unit for radiology, ultrasounds, incubators, monitors, lighting, electrical distribution equipment, water purification, and Internet connectivity.[28] These items provide the much-needed infrastructure and technology for lifesaving healthcare facilities.

Evaluation of the Healthcare System

Cost

The costs of health service delivery can be divided into two basic categories: the capital cost and the recurrent cost. The capital cost is the hardware cost, which includes the provision of healthcare facilities—for example, the cost of building hospitals, maintaining healthcare facilities, and training health service providers. These costs had always been borne by the government under the previous health financing schemes. The health insurance system that is currently being implemented falls short of taking care of these costs.

The recurrent cost is the cost associated with consumables and other supplies such as medical supplies (disinfectants, surgical masks, syringes, etc.), drugs, laboratory inputs, ambulance fuel, and servicing of equipment. This is the cost, or more likely part of the cost, that users of health services are usually asked to pay. Notably, the cost passed on to the "ordinary Ghanaian" is usually not the full recurrent cost. The average cost of hospital admission varies tremendously from region to region and among districts.

According to the Ministry of Health, Ghana's health budget between 2019 and 2021 increased in all of the healthcare sectors. The financial allocation to the health sector increased from GH¢6,037.51 million to ¢8,852.33 million and then decreased marginally to ¢8,533.59 million in 2021. The increase in allocation in the year 2020 was due to more funding to support COVID-19 activities. To sustain the COVID-19 activities, the government in 2021 introduced a COVID-19 Health Levy of one percentage point increase in the National Health Insurance Levy and a one percentage point increase in the VAT Flat Rate. The government of Ghana is the main financier of these expenses, contributing more than half of the budgetary allocations needed to support the health system. Most of this cost appears to be based on increases in service and personnel expenditures. Regional referral hospitals and public hospitals spend the most among the various health facility types.

Across and within facility types, the average facility cost per patient visit varied substantially in 2017. An outpatient visit was generally the least expensive encounter for most facilities. The average facility cost per outpatient visit ranged widely, depending on facility location and type of visit. Maternity care visits had the highest cost.[29] All fees associated with delivery have been covered by NHIS since 2008, so the relatively high facility costs per birth have substantial financial implications for Ghana's nationwide insurance program.[28,30,31]

However, in comparison with Kenya, Uganda, and Zambia, the average facility cost per patient in Ghana in 2017 was generally higher, especially for average facility costs per birth. Ghana had slightly lower average costs per inpatient bed-day than those found in Kenya and Uganda.[30]

Finance

Identifying and quantifying the variety of health finance flows are challenging exercises. Where data are available, they are not collected or managed systematically because Ghana lacks a central entity responsible for carrying out these tasks. Accordingly, even the MoH acknowledges that its figures must be treated with care.[32] Often, and particularly in the case of flows that bypass the MoH's budget, data are simply not available. Rising allocations from the central government have allowed Ghana to reach the 2001 Abuja Declaration target of allocating 15% of the annual budget to improvements in the health sector. Derived mostly from national sources, these allocations are augmented by three foreign sources.

To begin, a number of donors (including the World Bank, the United Kingdom, the European Union, and the African Development Bank) have begun using general budget support as an aid modality through the Multi-Donor Budget Support initiative. Because budget support has generally not been tied to specific sectors, measuring the extent of its use for health is practically impossible. The share of health finance channeled through the central government is likely to increase in the future because several donors are currently considering a move to adopt budget support. Other sources of central government allocations to the health sector include commercial lending (15%) and debt relief (0.2%, from the Heavily Indebted Poor Country initiative).

The budget of the MoH distinguishes three sources of funding: allocations from central government (which accounted for 59.20% of its total budget of $435 million USD in 2005), support from bilateral and multilateral donors (27.20%), and internally generated funds from private households (13.60%). Similarly, in 2014, the total health expenditure was funded as follows: 40.00% was from central government allocations to public health, 30.00% from the National Health Insurance Fund, 17.00% from international donors, 11.00% from private households, and 1.06% from private employers. In 2015, of a total of GH¢4.456 billion, ¢1.34 billion came from the NHIS fund, ¢1.4 billion from the MoH's appropriations from parliament, ¢1 billion from internally generated funds, donor support of about ¢712.8 million, and loans of about ¢575 million.[33] The distinction between the three sources of health finance used in most government documents paints a simplified picture that does not adequately capture the various financing channels and actors in Ghana's health sector.

First, it is important to understand that funds from the central government are derived from different sources, including foreign ones. Second, donors use diverse channels to achieve health outcomes. Third, a large portion of the private financing bypasses the MoH's budget. Finally, new actors, such as foundations, global funds, and NGOs, have important roles to play in financing health. (Refer to **Figure 18-3**.)

Donors have an important stake in the healthcare sector in Ghana, providing between 25% and 35% of the MoH's budget.[34] Their support for health increased sixfold between 1999 and 2003, from $30.7 million to $192.5 million USD. The share of donor funding has been oscillating in recent years, from 13.38% to 14.87% and then to 10.3% in 2019, 2020, and 2021, respectively.[30] This can be seen as part of a larger global shift of official development assistance toward the social sectors, encouraged by the adoption of the Sustainable Development Goals and the Poverty Reduction Strategy Initiative of the

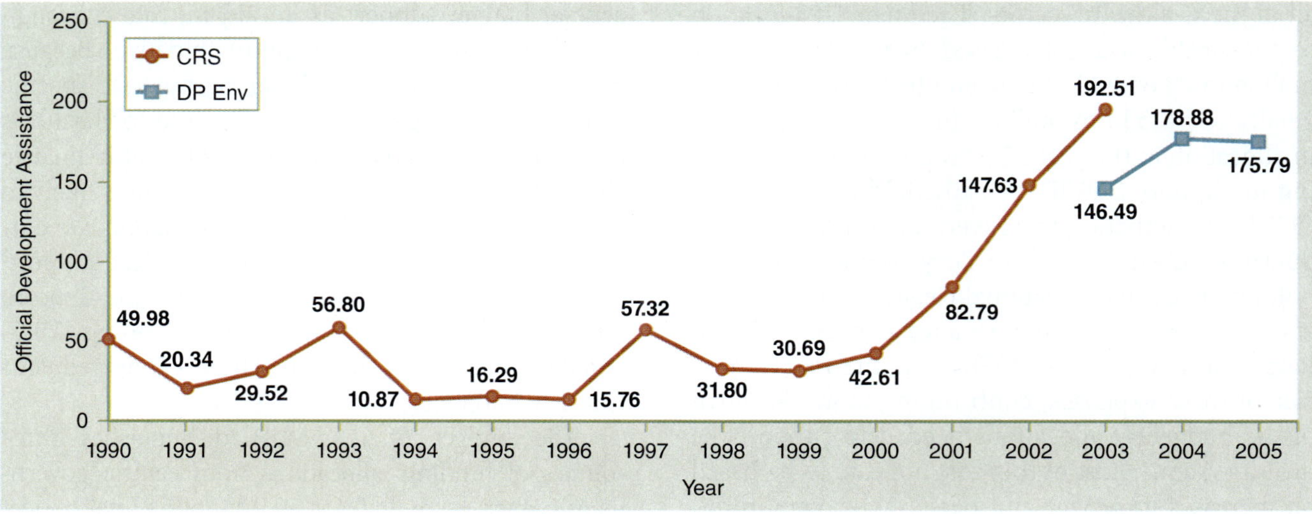

Figure 18-3 Official development assistance to Ghana's health sector

Author calculations based on data from DAC Creditor Reporting System (CRS) 2006 and Ghana Development Partner Envelope Overview (DP Env) 2006 on health in Ghana compared to the public sector's contribution of 35%.

World Bank. However, the volumes actually disbursed in Ghana may differ from those pledged and reported to the Development Assistance Committee.

Although the use of private capital inflows cannot be determined with certainty, evidence from Ghana suggests that remittances help households cover emergency expenses, for example, in the case of major illnesses.[33] New actors that have begun financing health in Ghana are NGOs, global funds, private donors, the pharmaceutical industry, and private foundations, as well as private commercial capital flows (see **Figure 18-4**).

Nongovernmental Organizations

According to the National Coalition of Health NGOs in 2015, 400 NGOs are active in the Ghanaian health sector, with a large majority acting as implementing agencies for donor-funded projects. This means that their self-generated financial contribution to the sector is minimal. Nevertheless, their proximity to local institutions and marginalized individuals, especially in remote areas, renders them a crucial part of the healthcare system. Faith-based NGOs, such as the Catholic Secretariat representing the Catholic Church and the Christian Health Association of Ghana, are particularly important in Ghana.

Global Funds

Global funds have had a tremendous impact on health sector finance in recent years. The two largest global funds in the Ghanaian health sector are the Global Fund and Gavi, the Vaccine Alliance. Between 2000 and 2015, the former disbursed $42 million of the $93.4 million USD pledged in its grant agreement with Ghana, directing funds to fight malaria (44%), HIV/AIDS (36%), and tuberculosis (20%). Gavi has disbursed around $20 million USD to Ghana since 2000, targeting hepatitis B (a total of $45 million USD pledged) and yellow fever ($4.5 million USD) in a multiyear vaccination plan (2002–2006) and providing cash support for vaccination services ($3.6 million USD) and injection safety ($855,000 USD).[35] In 2017, Gavi also provided $37.7 million USD to the government toward routine immunization and vaccines purchase.[36]

Private Donors

It is particularly difficult to determine an exact figure for private donations. They are neither recorded systematically nor captured by national statistics. According to the MoH, it administered a total of $176 million USD in financial and in-kind donations between 2004 and 2005. Although these numbers must be treated with caution, they show that private donations constitute a considerable inflow to the sector, especially bearing in mind that the MoH's total annual budget (excluding donations) amounted to only $435 million USD in 2005. Some private donors use informal financing channels, meaning that the magnitude of Ghana's total receipts is almost certainly even larger. The Catholic Secretariat, for example, reported donations of $160,000 USD in 2004. The Health Finance Coalition (HFC) and the International Finance Corporation (IFC) are private donors that have provided funds to improve health care in Ghana in recent years.[37]

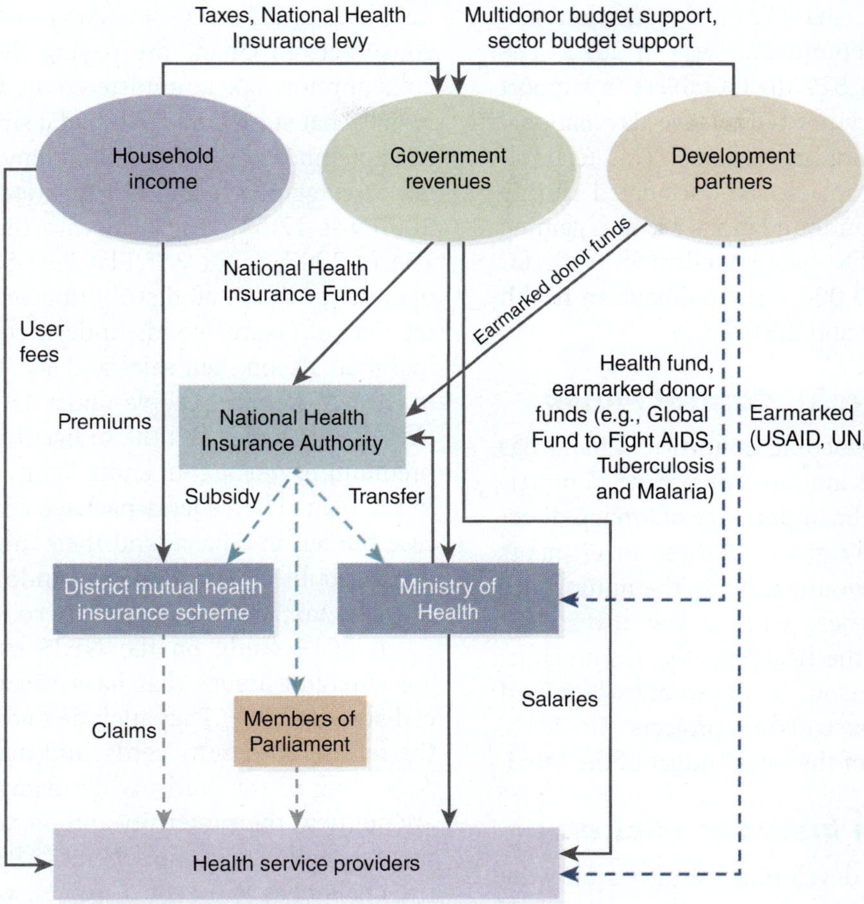

Figure 18-4 A complex picture of actors, channels, and flows

Data from Appiah-Denkyria, Nartey, and Enemark. 2005.

The Pharmaceutical Industry

Of the 14 pharmaceutical companies contacted, only one (Pfizer) provided details of program support through in-kind contributions. In 2005, the company delivered $1.6 million USD worth of Zithromax to fight trachoma (International Trachoma Initiative) and $320,000 USD worth of Diflucan to fight opportunistic infections—that is, infections that predominantly affect people with a poorly functioning or suppressed immune system (Diflucan Partnership Program).[38] Pfizer also engages in Ghana through the Pfizer Foundation, which provides grants for training and capacity—building activities in the health sector. In recent times, Pzifer Foundation donated $6.4 million USD for infectious disease control in Ghana and Nigeria.[39] Other pharmaceutical industry activities have been captured by the International Federation of Pharmaceutical Manufacturers and Associations (2004 and 2005).[40] For example, GlaxoSmithKline supports malaria prevention in Ghana through the African Malaria Partnership, and Merck & Co. has supported the dissemination of healthcare materials, together with the International Council of Nurses and Elsevier Science. Abbott Laboratories and Boehringer Ingelheim have donated Viramune within the framework of their joint initiative for the prevention of mother-to-child transmission of HIV. In 2015, GlaxoSmithKline supported the training of more than 9,000 health workers in Ghana, Kenya, and Nigeria.[41]

A more recent development is the initiative between Pfizer, its partners, and Ghana to strengthen the country's healthcare system. A medical drone delivery service is being used in remote areas of Ghana to deliver essential medical products, including medicines, blood, and vaccines.[42]

Private Foundations

Information on the activities of foundations in Ghana remains incomplete. Among the 11 foundations contacted, the Gates Foundation appears to be the largest sponsor of health-related projects. It granted $16.4 million USD between 2000 and 2005. The Rockefeller Foundation reported $3.4 million USD in grants to Ghana between 1999 and 2005, including projects by the MoH, the Forum of African Women, and the University of Ghana. The most recent donation from the Rockefeller Foundation was in 2022. The foundation provided 1,829 digital tablets to support the Ghana Health Service's (GHS) five-day national COVID-19 immunization campaign.[43] This technology allowed more people to be vaccinated during the campaign. European foundations are also gaining in importance. The U.K.-based Wellcome Trust, for example, granted $903,000 USD to Ghanaian health projects between 2000 and 2006.[44]

Private Commercial Capital Flows

Like many other low-income countries, Ghana has not yet attracted large amounts of private commercial capital. Although the importance of foreign direct investment is gradually growing, these investments have concentrated predominantly on the mining and manufacturing industries, with a few investment projects identified in the health sector. Commercial bank loans, by comparison, are important when used to finance health infrastructure projects. In 2015, they constituted 13% of the total budget of the MoH.

National Health Insurance Scheme

Households in many developing countries face the constant risk of having to finance the treatment of serious illnesses directly out of pocket. Health insurance systems, both public and private, based on prepayment and risk pooling, could help alleviate the exposure to these risks significantly.[45] In 2005, the Ghanaian government introduced the NHIS to replace the *cash-and-carry* system in the hope of easing the overall burden borne by private households. The law underpinning the NHIS makes membership in an insurance scheme compulsory, with households expected to make premium payments in line with their ability to pay.[46] Medical informatics would help create standards for the electronic exchange of financial and administrative data and also standards for unique identifiers, code sets, security, and privacy; however, this would require a tremendous investment in technology. This well-intended initiative is not founded on solid grounds, with doubts having been voiced regarding its financial sustainability.[47] Further information would allow the government to make a better distinction between those who could pay higher contributions for quality packages and those who must remain exempt from payments, which currently includes the poor Indigenous people and children with insured parents.

The National Health Insurance Levy was introduced on August 1, 2004, to provide seed money for the NHIS. The levy is a disguised value-added tax (VAT) of 2.5% on some goods and services; thus, consumers in Ghana are paying the levy. VAT is a consumption tax administered in Ghana. The tax regime that started in 1998 had a single tax rate, but in September 2007, Ghana implemented a multiple tax rate regime. The 1998 tax rate was 10%, and 2000 was 12.5%; however, with the passage of Act 734 of 2007, a 3% VAT Flat Rate Scheme began to operate for the retail distribution sector. This allows retailers of taxable goods under Act 546 to charge a marginal 3% on their sales and account for the same to the VAT service. People under 18 years old, those over 70 years old, and the indigent are exempt from premium payments. An entire family unit must enroll in the plan. The benefits package covers 95% of disease burden in Ghana, and there are no copayments or deductibles. The NHIS is funded by premiums, the sales tax, and social security contributions.

A 2014 study on the NHIS reveals that there are emerging issues that have threatened its financial sustainability. They include corruption, delay in the release of identity cards, and many other issues. According to the study, while many of these issues are not new, their intensity and impact pose a fundamental challenge to the scheme.[48] Prominent among the challenges is a lack of funds, which has led to persistent indebtedness to service providers by the National Health Insurance Authority (NHIA). The lack of funds has been blamed on escalating claims payments by the NHIA. Research shows that claims payment is the major cost driver of the scheme. Claims payments increased from GH¢7.60 million in 2005 to ¢549.77 million in 2011, representing 76.2% of the total expenditure of the NHIA.[44] This figure shot up to ¢787.24 million by the end of 2015.

A number of changes have been implemented to improve the NHIS. There are plans to roll out capitation payments to all providers of primary care; the electronic processing of claims is being extended countrywide; free-of-charge care available to NHIS members is being broadened to include all cancer services; and the NHIA is aiming to almost double NHIS membership, up from 33% to 60% of the population.

Quality

Effective health service delivery not only depends on being able to pay for drugs and other consumables but also requires state-of-the-art facilities that effectively promote diagnosis, treatment, and recovery from illness. It also requires well-qualified and motivated health personnel to use and manage those facilities. The ideal is to have an environment that shields people from falling ill, which means having the appropriate environment to reduce infections and other noncommunicable diseases. Ghana needs massive capital investments in its health and social service sectors to ensure such an ideal health environment. Ghanaians deserve good health facilities; indeed, all of the regional hospitals and district hospitals should be like those of Sunyani, Ho, and the Cape Coast hospitals. (These facilities are comparable to any standard hospital in the United States and Western Europe.) Because of the lack of diffusion of state-of-the-art technology in the country and because treatment of tertiary diseases does not meet the developing standard, the country's preventive care methods must be of top quality. There is an unequal distribution of healthcare delivery across the country, with severe disparities between regions and districts and between rural and urban areas in terms of both healthcare quality and access to services.

Access

Currently, Ghana lacks an adequate infrastructure to care for its citizens. There is also a disparity in the availability of healthcare facilities between rural and urban areas. As a result, access to health care in rural areas is difficult, and rural care fails to meet the standard of quality that Ghanaians deserve. With the introduction of NHIS advertising, more people are signing on to the concept of insurance that has open access to most people, including those who otherwise could not afford to visit the hospital.

The potential effects of insurance enrollment on access to health care and costs of health care have implications for the NHIS. One concern often raised in connection with prepayment schemes is whether the premiums will be affordable for the target population. The data from one study offer arguments for and against the premiums set by the government of Ghana for the NHIS. Although exemption policies and practices need to be flexible to respond to the needs of a given community, the NHIS premium structure and rates seem to be within reach of the majority of Ghanaians.[49]

Current and Emerging Issues and Challenges

In addition to significant disparities in service between north and south and between rich and poor, factors such as cultural and religious beliefs, poor physical infrastructure, and limited resources all work together to hamper the provision of equitable healthcare services. Malaria continues to be the major cause of high morbidity as well as mortality. Poor sanitation and the apparent unpreparedness of the healthcare system to prevent or manage potential epidemics create challenges for planners and policymakers.[50]

A major challenge for Ghana's health sector is the unequal distribution of healthcare delivery across the country. There are severe disparities between regions and districts and between rural and urban areas in terms of healthcare quality and access to services. In Ghana, there has long been a north–south divide, with those in the Northern, Savanna, North East, Upper East, and Upper West regions (an area containing approximately 17% of the population and covering around 40% of Ghana's land mass) having significantly less than those in the south. When compared with those in the south, the people living in the Northern, Savanna, North East, Upper East, and Upper West regions have very limited access to secondary healthcare facilities but are somewhat better served by community services. Perhaps as a reflection of the inequitable distribution of facilities, the northern regions are also poorly served in the number of clinical staff. For example, just 90 medical professionals covered the whole region in 2011.[51] Available data also show that 42% of the doctors are in Accra (the capital city), and up to 81.3% of all doctors are concentrated in just five regions—Greater Accra, Ashanti, Central, Northern, and Volta. The Teaching Hospitals in these five regions collectively have over 60% of all of the doctors in Ghana.[52] The number of doctors in Ghana has increased over time, but that number is still low compared to other countries in 2022.[53]

There are many ingrained cultural and religious practices traditionally undertaken by some Ghanaian groups and tribes that have an adverse impact on health, including early marriage of females and female genital mutilation. However, they are not widely practiced in the country. Some of these practices are against the law, but they continue to be practiced in more rural areas.

For instance, early marriage is common in some parts of the country. Although the legal age for girls to marry is 18, nearly 6% of girls between the ages of 12 and 17 are married. These practices are often related to gender discrimination. If women have the same rights to education, employment, and health care as men, they are better empowered to make decisions and to stand up for their rights. Ghana's achievements in this respect are measured against the fourth, fifth, and tenth Sustainable Development Goals (SDGs) on quality education, gender equality, and reduction of inequality, respectively. Although Ghana appears to be on track for achieving gender parity in its primary schools and junior high schools, female representation in parliament currently stands at 40 out of the 275 total member positions.

Ghana suffers from a chronic shortage of health workers and from inequities in the distribution and skills mix of workers; this severely restricts access to services and hampers the achievement of national health objectives. The country has just over 11 doctors, nurses, and midwives per 10,000 population, less than half the number (23 per 10,000) deemed necessary by the WHO for achievement of the health MDGs.[54] The health workforce shortage is not really caused by the lack of numbers since the various training institutions keep churning out a relatively skilled workforce. The problem has to do with refusal to accept postings and the recent freeze on employment in an attempt to curtail the ballooning wage bill, at the insistence of the International Monetary Fund. Many health workers have not been employed for years after completing their education.

Rural areas are particularly poorly served with access to health care. In 2009, for example, there was one doctor for every 5,103 people in Greater Accra, but in the Northern region, there was one doctor for every 50,751 people.[55] Some of the many reasons physicians give for preferring employment in urban areas are that rural facilities lack career development opportunities (no opportunity to specialize, seek mentoring support, or obtain study leave) and offer limited promotional opportunities. Others include longer working hours and a heavier workload; professional isolation; difficulties in referring patients who are often not prepared to travel; the requirement for physicians to be jacks of all trades, leading to concerns about quality of care; no opportunities to supplement income through local work; inadequate local housing; delayed insurance payments, which adversely affect supplies; and inadequate infrastructure/broken equipment.

The government has introduced a number of solutions to try to address this problem, including the Deprived Area Incentive Scheme, which offered an additional allowance of 20% to 35% of basic salary (this has been discontinued); the Health Staff Vehicle Hire Purchase Scheme; and various housing schemes. Unfortunately, none has proven particularly successful. The Single-Spine Pay Policy, aimed at rationalizing salaries of public-sector workers, has not solved the numerous agitations among the health workforce. Indeed, there appears to be a widening disparity in the pay structure of health workers, leading to numerous industry-wide actions by almost all categories of health workers.

As a result, diseases such as malaria are significantly more prevalent in rural areas than in urban areas. Malaria remains the main cause of mortality and morbidity in Ghana, accounting for approximately 21% of the under-5 mortality rate and 40% of outpatient morbidity. Over 60% of hospital admissions of children under the age of 5 and 8% of hospital admissions of pregnant women are related to malaria. As the disease particularly affects pregnant women and children, interventions such as promoting chemoprophylaxis for pregnant women and the use of insecticide-treated nets (ITNs) are often aimed at these groups.

Malaria is significant health problem in Ghana. The number of deaths has been reduced with increased efforts over the years, from 2,799 deaths in 2012 to 151 in 2022.[56] The government has been tackling this problem by making efforts to reduce the burden of malaria. It launched a Malaria Drug Policy in 2005 and, under its Intermittent Prevention Treatment strategy for malaria, adopted the amodiaquine–artesunate drug combination for prevention and treatment. In 2006, the Ghana Health Service changed the recommended dose of this drug combination after controversy over side effects also scaled up ITN distribution across the country. Over 5 million ITNs were procured for distribution, and ITN utilization increased by 40.5% for pregnant women and 31.0% for children under 5 years old in 2008. A target was set of achieving universal coverage of ITNs by 2015, with 80.0% of the population sleeping under a net. There were many challenges in achieving this target, however, including running out of stock, distribution problems, and cultural barriers.[57]

In Ghana, a lack of access to clean water and sanitation systems is a central public health concern, contributing to 70% of the disease burden. There is substantial variation in access to clean, affordable water and sanitation, depending on income, rural or urban area, and region. According to the Ghana Water Sector Restructuring Secretariat, in 2005, only 46% of the total population had access to piped water.[58] The figure fell to 22% for those classified as poor. Uninterrupted access to treated and piped water occurs only in some urban areas. Average urban access is 46%, whereas in rural areas, only 35% of the population has access. Access to proper sanitation is equally dismal. Similarly, according to the Water Sector Restructuring Secretariat, the percentage of the population with access to improved sanitation facilities is approximately 40% in urban areas and 35% in rural areas. This poor state of water and sanitation in both urban and rural areas has been one of the most significant causes of many diseases. For instance, the perennial deadly outbreaks of cholera, particularly in the Greater Accra region, have claimed many lives.

Related to this is the unpreparedness of the healthcare system in Ghana to prevent and or manage an outbreak of any potential disease. In October 2015, a strain of meningitis broke out in a remote area in the middle belt of the country. Health officials were severely challenged in controlling its spread. By February 2016, the Brong Ahafo had recorded the highest number of cases, 359, with 52 deaths; the Northern region had 62 cases with 15 deaths; the Upper East recorded 47 cases with two deaths; the Upper West had 44 cases with nine deaths; the Ashanti region recorded 18 cases with eight deaths; the Volta region had seven cases with one death; the Eastern region registered four cases with three deaths; and the Western region recorded two cases with one death. Indeed, only one region did not record a single incident of pneumococcal meningitis disease.[59]

Admittedly, Ghana lies in the meningitis belt of Africa, so such outbreaks are not uncommon. However, the spread rate and the mortality rate of this strain alarmed health workers and the citizenry at large. This called into question the preparedness of the health system to deal with public health concerns, bearing in mind the lurking threats of the Ebola and Zika viruses.

In response to the many health system challenges, the government over the past few years has attempted to resolve its infrastructure and equipment deficits. There are attempts to add 6,000 hospital beds to the existing 1,200. As such, a number of hospitals and health centers are under construction. The government has secured $100 million USD in start-up funding through the Ghana Investment Infrastructure Fund (GIIF) for the commencement of works on the "Agenda 111" district, which will comprise specialized and regional hospitals across the country. The Agenda 111 project includes 101 district hospitals, six regional hospitals in the newly created regions, two specialized hospitals in the middle and northern belts, as well as a regional hospital in the Western region and renovation of the Effia-Nkwanta Regional Hospital. The objective of the project, according to Oppong Nkrumah, is to significantly deepen delivery of quality health care at the district level and boost access to healthcare services for all citizens, thereby ensuring the attainment of the United Nations' SDG 3.[60]

There is also an attempt to re-equip various health facilities to make them more functional. The bottom line is that funding for the sector continues to dwindle, healthcare costs are increasing, and donor support continues to shrink. The NHIS has been strained to the point of distress, and the government must find a way to tackle all of these issues in a holistic and comprehensive manner.

The country also witnessed the introduction of medical drone delivery services, such as the Zipline program that was launched in 2019. To support the MoH in the distribution of COVID-19 vaccines requiring ultra-low storage temperatures, Zipline has procured three 700L Ultra low-temperature freezers to aid the country in the distribution of vaccines to hard-to-reach areas. Zipline currently has the capacity to store approximately 1 million Pfizer Bio NTech doses, 468,000 Moderna doses, and 1.7 million doses of either the AstraZeneca or Sputnik vaccines all at the same time.[30]

COVID-19 Pandemic

On March 12, 2020, the Ghana Ministry of Health reported the first two confirmed cases of the novel coronavirus disease known as COVID-19. The confirmation of the first two new cases triggered the government to introduce some restrictions to curb the disease. Ghana's territorial borders, including the land, sea, and air borders, were closed for human traffic on March 22, 2020, to prevent the inflow of persons who could be carrying COVID-19 into the country. A ban was also imposed on all nonessential public gatherings. As of March 10, 2021, there had been 86,737 confirmed COVID-19 cases and 656 COVID-19–related deaths in Ghana.[30] Ghana was the first country to receive COVID-19 vaccine doses under the COVAX program on February 24, 2021.

In response to the pandemic, guidelines on case management of COVID-19, antigen testing, and emergency preparedness and response were developed by the MoH with support from Ghana Health and the World Health Organization. These guidelines were adopted to guide the prevention, control, and management of the infection in Ghana.[60]

Additionally, to minimize infections in healthcare settings, the MoH recommended that healthcare workers apply standard and transmission-based infection prevention precautions consistently to all patients—symptomatic and asymptomatic alike—across all levels of health care. Concerning health system restructuring, the MoH directed medical care across all levels to make significant adaptations to routine procedures, the foremost being heightened hand and respiratory hygiene, triaging and source control, use of appropriate personal protective equipment, safe injection practices, decontamination of the environment and equipment, and safe corpse handling.[61]

About 600,000 doses of the AstraZeneca vaccines were shipped from India to Accra. Shortly after, a national COVID-19 vaccination program was rolled out, with the president of Ghana taking the first injection on live television.[62] This was done to encourage a large portion of the citizens to get vaccinated. However, this did not translate to massive uptake of the vaccine by the citizens. In addition, the country encountered challenges with accessibility, workforce, funding, and infrastructure as the major hindrances in fighting the pandemic.

Overall, there have been mixed reactions to the way the pandemic was handled. While members within the political cycles have repeatedly extolled the sterling handling of the pandemic, other commentators have raised concerns. Ghana's COVID-19 response was, however, constrained by limited resources and inadequate global cooperation to fight the pandemic, which are partly responsible for challenges in policy implementation. However, the gulf between planning and practice has been widened by an often reactionary stance from policymakers, limited data collection, inconsistent health system supplies, poor public examples, and an information vacuum created by poor risk communication.[63]

References

1. Jackson JG. *Introduction to African Civilizations*. 2nd ed. Chaleston, SC: Kensington Publishing, Citadel Press; 2001.
2. Stearns PN, Langer WL. *The Encyclopedia of World History: Ancient, Medieval, and Modern*. 6th ed. New York, NY: Houghton Mifflin; 2001.
3. Buah FK. *History of Ghana*. London, UK: Macmillan; 1980.
4. Nkrumah K. *Revolutionary Path*. New York, NY: International Publishers; 1973.
5. MacLean I. *Rational Choice and British Politics: An Analysis of Rhetoric and Manipulation from Peel to Blair*. Oxford, UK: Oxford University Press; 2001.
6. Ghana Information Services Department. *Ghana: A Brief Guide*. Accra, Ghana: GIS Publication; 1994.
7. Ghana Statistical Service (GSS), Ghana Health Service (GHS), and ICF International. *Ghana Demographic and Health Survey 2014*. Rockville, MD: GSS, GHS, and ICF International; 2015.
8. Ghana Statistical Service. 2010 population and housing census. Summary report of final results. Published 2012. Accessed February 13, 2013. http://www.statsghana.gov.gh/docfiles/2010phc/Census2010_Summary_report_of_final_results.pdf.
9. Ghana Statistical Service. *Ghana 2021 Population and Housing Census General Report*. 2021.
10. Twumasi PA. *Medical Systems in Ghana: A Study in Medical Sociology*. Accra, Ghana: Ghana Publishing; 1975.
11. Bossert TJ, Beauvais JC. Decentralization of health systems in Ghana, Zambia, Uganda and the Philippines: a comparative analysis of decision space. *Health Pol Plan*. 2002;17:14-31.
12. Agyapong IA. Reforming health service delivery at the district level in Ghana: the perspective of a district medical officer. *Health Pol Plan*. 1999;14:59-69.
13. Gaines K. *On Nkrumah Assassination by CIA: American Africans in Ghana, Black Expatriates and the Civil Rights Era*. Chapel Hill, NC: University of North Carolina Press; 2006.
14. Bonsi SK. *Studies on an Appropriate Mechanism for Exemptions from Charges for Drugs and Curative Care in Government Health Facilities in Ghana*. Accra, Ghana: Ghana Ministry of Health; 2001.
15. World Health Organization. Commission on Macroeconomics and Health. *Macroeconomics and Health: Investing in Health for Economic Development*. Geneva, Switzerland: World Health Organization; 2001.
16. Sikosana PL, Dlamini N, Issakov A. *Health Sector Reform in Sub-Saharan Africa: A Review of Experiences, Information Gaps and Research Needs*. Geneva, Switzerland: World Health Organization; 1997.
17. Asante AD, Zwi AB, Ho MT. Equity in resource allocation for health: a comparative study of the Ashanti and Northern regions of Ghana. *Health Pol*. 2006;78:135-148.
18. Reporters Without Borders. Worldwide Press Freedom Index 2006. Accessed November 3, 2016. https://rsf.org/en/worldwide-press-freedom-index-2006.
19. Sarkpoh F, Domapielle MK. Stakeholders' perspectives on facilitative supervision implementation in north-western Ghana: an exploration of adherence and quality of primary healthcare. *Prim Health Care Res Dev*. 2022;23:e5820.
20. Institute for Health Metrics and Evaluation. *Health Service Provision in Ghana: Assessing Facility Capacity and Costs of Care*. Seattle, WA: IHME; 2015.
21. Multiple Indicator Cluster Survey. *Ghana-Accra Multiple Indicator Survey in 5 High Density Populated Localities, 2010–2011*. Geneva, Switzerland: MICS/UNICEF; 2012.
22. Saleh K. *The Health Sector in Ghana: A Comprehensive Assessment*. Washington, DC: World Bank; 2012.
23. Quaicoe-Duho R. Ghana reports general improvement in doctor ratio. Published January 7, 2015. Accessed November 3, 2016. http://www.politicosl.com/articles/ghana-reports-general-improvement-doctor-ratio-0.
24. Dubbeldam R, Witter S, Silimperi D, et al. *Health Sector Five-Year Programme of Work: 2002–2006*. Accra, Ghana: Ghana Ministry of Health; 2007.
25. Adusei K, Akor SA, Oppong-Mensah D. *Ministry of Health Oral Health Policies and Medium Term Strategic Plan*. Accra, Ghana: Oral Health Unit, Ministry of Health; 2000.
26. Bampoe AV. *The State of Healthcare Delivery in Ghana*. Presentation. Atlanta, GA; 2014.
27. Adams O, Stilwell B. Health professionals and migration. *Bull World Health Organ*. 2004;82:550-558.
28. *Business Wire*. GE expands healthcare initiative to hospitals in Ghana: partner initiative to provide medical and infrastructure equipment across Africa. Published October 3, 2005. Accessed March 1, 2008. http://findarticles.com/p/articles/mi_m0EIN/is.
29. Dalaba MA, Welaga P, Matsurbara C. Cost of delivering health care services at primary health facilities in Ghana. *BMC Health Serv Res*. 2017;17(742). https://doi.org/10.1186/s12913-017-2676-3.
30. Ministry of Health Medium Term Expenditure Framework (MTEF): programme based budget estimates for 2022. 2022. https://mofep.gov.gh/sites/default/files/pbb-estimates/2022/2022-PBB-MoH.pdf.
31. Addae-Korankye A. Challenges of financing health care in Ghana: the case of National Health Insurance Scheme (NHIS). *Intl J Asian Soc Sci*. 2013;3(2):511-522.

32. Organisation for Economic Co-operation and Development. *Creditor Reporting System*. Paris, France: Development Assistance Center Report; 2006.
33. Anemana S. *Current Health Financing Issues in the Health Sector*. Presentation at GIMPA. Accessed May 23, 2016. http://www.moh.gov.gh/wp-content/uploads/2016/02/2015-Summit-Health-Financing-Strategy-Final-Presentation.pdf.
34. African Development Bank. African Development Report. Natural resources for sustainable development in Africa. Published 2007. Accessed March 12, 2008. http://www.afdb.org/en/documents/.
35. United States AID for International Development. *Private Remittances Flows to Ghana*. Washington, DC: Country Report; 2005.
36. UNICEF health budget brief. 2022. https://www.unicef.org/ghana/media/2296/file/Budget%20Brief%20-%20Health%20and%20Nutrition.pdf.
37. International Finance Corporation. IFC partners with Accra Medical Centre to expand access to affordable healthcare in Ghana. Published May 31, 2023. Accessed February 19, 2025. https://www.ifc.org/en/pressroom/2023/ifc-partners-with-accra-medical-centre-to-expand-access-to-affordable-healthcare-in-ghana.
38. Hudson Institute. *A Review of Pharmaceutical Company Contributions—HIV/AIDS, Tuberculosis, Malaria, and Other Infectious Diseases*. Washington, DC: Center for Science in Public Policy Report. Hudson Institute; 2004.
39. *Premium Times*. Pfizer Foundation donates $6.4 million to combat infectious. 2021. https://www.premiumtimesng.com/news/more-news/497778-pfizer-foundation-donates-6-4-million-for-infectious-disease-control-in-nigeria-ghana.html.
40. International Federation of Pharmaceutical Manufacturers Associations. *Building Healthier Societies through Partnerships*. Geneva: International Federation of Pharmaceutical Manufacturers Associations Report; 2005.
41. GlaxoSmithKline. GSK to support training of frontline health workers. 2022. https://www.gsk.com/en-gb/media/press-releases/gsk-to-support-training-of-frontline-health-workers-across-ghana-kenya-and-nigeria/.
42. AMR Industry Alliance. Pfizer helps deliver medical products by drone In Ghana. Accessed February 19, 2025. https://www.amrindustryalliance.org/case-study/pfizer-helps-deliver-medical-products-by-drone-in-ghana/.
43. The Rockefeller Foundation. The Rockefeller Foundation and USAID support Ghana Health Service's new national Covid-19 campaign. Published December 16, 2022. Accessed February 19, 2025. https://www.rockefellerfoundation.org/news/the-rockefeller-foundation-and-usaid-support-ghana-health-services-new-national-covid-19-campaign/.
44. World Health Organization. Commission on Macroeconomics and Health. *Macroeconomics and Health: Investing in Health for Economic Development*. Geneva, Switzerland: World Health Organization; 2001.
45. United Nations Development Program. *International Cooperation at a Crossroads: Aid, Trade and Security in an Unequal World*. New York, NY: United Nations Development Program Human Development Report; 2005.
46. Drechsler D, Jütting J. Is there a role for private health insurance in developing countries? *German Instit Econ Res*. 2005;15:123-138.
47. Dubbeldam R, Witter S, Silimperi D, et al. *Health Sector Five-Year Programme of Work: 2002–2006*. Accra, Ghana: Ghana Ministry of Health; 2007.
48. Owusu-Sekyere E, Bagah DA. Towards a sustainable health care financing in Ghana: is the national health insurance the solution? *Pub Health Res*. 2014;4(5):185-194. doi: 10.5923/j.phr.20140405.06.
49. Schieber G, Cashin C, Saleh K. Lavado R. *Health Financing in Ghana*. Washington, DC: World Bank; 2012. Accessed May 23, 2016. http://uhcforward.org/sites/uhcforward.org/files/718940PUB0PUBL067869B09780821395660.pdf.
50. Association of Chartered Certified Accountants. *Key Health Challenges in Ghana*. London, UK: ACCA; 2013.
51. Ghana Ministry of Health. The health sector in Ghana: facts and figures 2010. Published 2012. Accessed November 3, 2016. https://s3.amazonaws.com/ndpc-static/CACHES/NEWS/2015/07/14//2010±GHS±Facts±and±Figures.pdf.
52. World Health Organization. Stakeholders urged to take action to improve the distribution of doctors in Ghana. https://www.afro.who.int/countries/ghana/news/stakeholders-urged-take-action-improve-distribution-doctors-ghana 2022.
53. Mustard Insights. African countries with the highest number of doctors. Accessed February 19, 2025. https://blog.mustardinsights.com/in-africa/african-countries-with-the-highest-number-of-doctors-ednQo.
54. Parliament of Ghana. Members of Parliament. 2023. https://www.parliament.gh/mps?az&P=1e.
55. Government of Ghana, National Development Planning Commission, United Nations Development Programme. Ghana, 2010: Ghana Millennium Development Goals report. Published 2010. Accessed March 6, 2013. https://s3.amazonaws.com/ndpc-static/CACHES/NEWS/2015/07/11//Ghana±MDGs±Report±2008.pdf.
56. Ministry of Health/Ghana Health Service. National malaria elimination—strategic plan (NMESP) of Ghana: 2024-2028. Accessed February 19, 2025. https://ghs.gov.gh/wp-content/uploads/2023/12/NMEP-STRATEGIC%20PLAN%202024-2028.pdf.
57. International Organization for Migration. National profile of migration of health professionals—Ghana. Published 2011. Accessed March 7, 2013. http://www.mohprof.eu/LIVE/DATA/National_profiles/national_profile_Ghana.pdf.
58. Water and Sanitation Program. Economic impacts of poor sanitation in Africa: Ghana. Published 2012. Accessed March 7, 2013. http://siteresources.worldbank.org/INTGHANA/Resources/ghana-economic-impacts-of-poor-sanitation-in-africa.pdf.
59. Agbenyega P. 93 people die of meningitis in Ghana so far. *News Ghana*. Published February 16, 2016. Accessed May 27, 2016. https://www.newsghana.com.gh/93-people-die-of-meningitis-in-ghana-so-far/.
60. Ministry of Health. *COVID-19 Case Management Manual*. Accra, Ghana: Ghana Ministry of Health, Ghana Health Service, and World Health Organization; 2020.
61. Agbozo F, Albrecht J. COVID-19 in Ghana: challenges and countermeasures for maternal health service delivery in public health facilities. *Reprod Health* 2021;18(1):1-5.
62. Ministry of Health. Gov't secures US$100 million start-up fund for "Agenda 111" hospital project. 2023. https://www.moh.gov.gh/agenda-111-construction-of-largest-number-of-hospital-projects/.
63. Quakyi NK, Agyemang Asante NA, Nartey YA, et al. Ghana's COVID-19 response: the Black Star can do even better. *BMJ Global Health*. 2021;6:e005569. doi: 10.1136/bmjgh-2021-005569.

CHAPTER 19

India

Sudha Xirasagar, Puneet Misra, and Roy Daniel

Country Description

India is the world's second most populous country with an estimated 1.39 billion people in 2023, over four times the U.S. population, and a third of the U.S. land area.[1] Viewed from a global perspective, India has 17% of the world's population, 2.45% of the global land area, and 4% of fresh-water resources.[2] It has 22 officially recognized languages, spoken in 844 different dialects rooted in two ancient indigenous languages, Sanskrit and Tamil.[3] Elements of Persian, Arabic, and English were imbibed over the course of trade relations and armed conquests. **Table 19-1** presents some key descriptive information.

Table 19-1 **Country Profile—India**

Nationality	India, since independence on August 15, 1947 (Adjective: Indian)
Ethnic groups	Indo-Aryan 72%, Dravidian 25%, Mongoloid/other 3% (2007)[a]
Languages[b]	Official language of the Union: Hindi Official languages for governance communications: Central government: English and Hindi State governments: English and each state's official language (22 recognized languages)
Religion	Hindu 79%, Muslim 14%, Christian 2.3%, Sikh 1.7%, Buddhist 0.7%, Jain 0.4%, other 0.8%, unspecified 0.2%[c]
Government	Parliamentary democracy, constitutional republic, union of states
Natural hazards	Severe heat waves; droughts; catastrophic rainfall and flash flooding; drought prone (68% of cultivable area); monsoon flooding (12% of land area at risk); occasional moderate- to high-intensity earthquakes (58.6% of land area at risk); cyclones and tsunami (5,700 km at risk, out of total 7,516 km of coastline); and landslides in the north/northeastern mountainous/hilly areas[d]
Environmental challenges	Deforestation, soil erosion; overgrazing; air and ground water pollution from industrial effluents and vehicle emissions; scarcity of potable water in many areas of the country
Macroeconomic Indicators	
Gross domestic product (GDP)	3.39 trillion in 2022 (current USD)[e]
Per capita GDP	International PPP* 8,379 USD in 2022 versus 5,187 USD in 2014[f]

Table 19-1 Country Profile—India

Macroeconomic Indicators	
Poverty head count (<2.15 USD/day per person in household in 2017 PPP)	10% of population (2019[g] versus 18.5% in 2015)
Unemployment (total)	7.3% of total labor force in 2022[e] (modeled ILO estimate)
Labor force participation (usual principal activity)	(% of adults working, seeking, or available for work) 2019–2020[h] Female: rural 27.7%, urban 18.6%; Male: rural 57.1, urban 58.4
Demographic Indicators	
Population	1.392 billion (est. as of July 1, 2023)[i]
Median age	28.3 years (2023 est.)[i] Male: 28 years Female: 29.5 years (2020 GOINat PopCommPopProjections)
Total fertility rate	2.0 live births/woman (2019–2021)[j] versus (1.95 in 2022)[k]
Population growth rate (annual)	0.7% (2022 est.)[e]
Crude birth rate	19.5 births/1,000 population in 2020 (declined from 36.9 in 1971)[l]
Crude death rate	6 deaths/1,000 population (2020 est.)[l]
Net migration rate	0.12 migrant(s)/1,000 population (2022 est.)[m]
Sex ratio	946 females/1,000 males (2022 est., 943 in 2011)[i]

USD = U.S. dollars.
*PPP: Purchasing power parity (dollars).
[a]U.S. State Department. India (10/07). Accessed February 19, 2025. https://2009-2017.state.gov/outofdate/bgn/india/93310.htm.
[b]Government of India, Ministry of Home Affairs, Department of Official Language. Constitutional provisions. Accessed July 27, 2023. https://rajbhasha.gov.in/en/constitutional-provisions.
[c]Census of India 2011, National Population Register & Socioeconomic and Caste Census. Accessed July 31, 2023. https://censusindia.gov.in.
[d]Government of India, National Institute of Disaster Management. Disaster management in India. Accessed July 31, 2023. https://nidm.gov.in/PDF/pubs/DM%20in%20India.pdf.
[e]World Bank. 2023 country profile, India. Accessed July 28, 2023. https://databank.worldbank.org/views/reports/reportwidget.aspx?Report_Name=CountryProfile&Id=b450fd57&tbar=y&dd=y&inf=n&zm=n&country=IND.
[f]World Bank. 2023. GDP per capita, PPP (current international $)—India. Accessed July 28, 2023. https://data.worldbank.org/indicator/NY.GDP.PCAP.PP.CD?locations=IN.
[g]World Bank 2023. Country India. Accessed July 28, 2023. https://data.worldbank.org/country/india.
[h]Government of India Ministry of Statistics and Program Implementation. Annual report periodic labor force survey 2019–20. Accessed July 28, 2023. https://mospi.gov.in/sites/default/files/publication_reports/Annual_Report_PLFS_2019_20F1.pdf.
[i]Government of India, National Commission on Population. 2020 population projections for India and states, 2011–36. Report of the Technical Group on Population Projections. Accessed July 25, 2023. https://main.mohfw.gov.in/sites/default/files/Population%20Projection%20Report%202011-2036%20-%20upload_compressed_0.pdf.
[j]International Institute of Population Sciences. National Family Health Survey-5 in 2019–2021, Mumbai. 2023. (Survey interrupted in 2020 by COVID-19 pandemic.)
[k]Government of India, Department of Health and Family Welfare, Ministry of Health and Family Welfare. 2022–2023 annual report. Accessed July 19, 2023. https://main.mohfw.gov.in/sites/default/files/eng%201.pdf.
[l]Government of India, Registrar General and Census Commissioner. Sample Registration System (SRS)—2020. SRS Bull. 2022;55(1). Accessed July 28, 2023. https://censusindia.gov.in/nada/index.php/catalog/42687.
[m]Central Intelligence Agency. 2023. The World Factbook: India. Accessed July 27, 2023. https://www.cia.gov/the-world-factbook/countries/india/#people-and-society.

History

The Indo-Gangetic civilization of the Indian subcontinent is possibly the world's oldest, continually sustained culture to this day, dated as a mature and distinct civilization at about the 7th millennium BC.[4] Archaeological evidence of sewage systems and public baths is dated at about 4000 BC. The earliest Vedic treatises and scriptures transmitted in the oral tradition predate the archaeological evidence as per the dating of historical events based on astronomical configurations of the relative positions of the stars and planets. These treatises reflect a culture characterized by a strong hygiene orientation; a pastoral lifestyle; a predominantly lactovegetarian diet; locally practiced economic systems, including weights and measures; and the use of copper, iron, and barley.[4]

The Vedic culture laid the foundation of Hinduism's holistic approach to physical, mental, social, civic, and spiritual aspects of daily living, which continues to influence attitudes and lifestyle related to knowledge, health, fitness, illness, treatment, death, and dying. In addition, Hinduism birthed other ancient religious traditions: Buddhism, founded by Buddha (1887 to 1807 BC);[5] Jainism (mid first century BC); and more recently, Sikhism in the 16th century. These religions are together professed by approximately 2% of the population, per the Census of India.[6] These traditions share with Hinduism core doctrines of the sanctity of all life forms (therefore, a preference for vegetarianism), an introverted approach to living, pursuit of nirvana (enlightenment) as the goal of life through self-sacrifice and self-denial, belief in rebirth, karma, and a shared heritage of yoga and Ayurveda. Due to their shared philosophy and worldview, there has been a fluid interchange across these traditions, including intermarriage, conversions, and cross-identification with these religions. Some schools within Hinduism identify Buddha as humanity's 10th avatar (God taking human form).

Two major ancient traditions that are several millennia old and that evolved out of the cultural focus and life goals of seeking knowledge, truth, and spiritual enlightenment were yoga (union of body, mind, and soul) and Ayurveda (knowledge or science of life). Yoga, a spiritual, peace-affirming system of self-renewal in daily life, is widely practiced in India for its physical and mental/spiritual health-promoting effects. Yoga became a global phenomenon with the United Nations' adoption of June 21, the summer solstice, as World Yoga Day. Many nations have adopted yoga in their educational systems and curricula for developing physical, mental, and emotional resilience to cope with the multifaceted challenges of life and living in today's complex world. The surgical branch of Ayurveda gained momentum in the post-Buddha era,[5] in sync with the core emphasis of Buddhism on a practical approach to spirituality and compassionate problem solving in daily life (in contrast to Hinduism's emphasis on ritualized worship and lifestyle to attain enlightenment).

Together, yoga and Ayurveda prescribe a system of purposeful healthy living and physical–spiritual activities to preserve health, and the use of herbs and roots to treat disease. Many elements of yoga and Ayurveda are integrally woven into the culturally developed, routinely practiced, daily personal lifestyle, civic norms, and social traditions. Ayurveda, yoga, and Siddha (a south Indian system of medicine, several millennia old) provide the foundation of many indigenously evolved health and healing practices that continue in modern India, particularly among the rural population. In 2015, the government of India integrated these care modalities into the government public healthcare system, along with Unani (an Arabic tradition-influenced indigenous system) and homeopathy. These systems of medicine are offered through the AYUSH program (Ayurveda, yoga, Unani, Siddha, and homeopathy), through a subset of rural and urban health facilities, by trained doctors of these systems.[7] AYUSH facilities played a major role during the COVID-19 pandemic in providing care to patients with mild subacute COVID-19, as well as herbal/lifestyle advice to the public for protection against infection and mitigating severity.

The Indian subcontinent, known for its wealth from ancient times, experienced many invasions, beginning with Alexander of Macedon, successive Islamic invasions from the 8th century AD (up to the Persian invasion in the 15th century, followed by Moghul rule up to the 19th century), and finally British colonization (started in 1757, lasting up to 1947). These invasions triggered much religious and cultural diversity, particularly widespread conversions to Islam in the western and northern parts, and to Christianity in the south, as well as the birth of Sikhism. Christianity entered the subcontinent via the west coast during the 1st century, and significantly spread during British, Portuguese, and French colonial rule.

The British administration introduced many positive changes, starting with a transformation of the governance and civic administration mindset, from arbitrary rule of about 500 feudal/royal dynasties, to a rules-based governance system rooted in institutional structures that were charged with enforcing the rule of law. In parallel with these modernizing effects, colonialism also eroded and often actively destroyed centuries-old civic traditions, cottage industries, local art forms, crafts, valuable texts and treatises of Ayurveda and other indigenous medicinal systems, and local medicinal traditions and knowledge.[4,5]

Following World War II, freedom from British rule was achieved on August 15, 1947. The subcontinent was partitioned into two nation-states as per the provisions of the Indian Independence Act of 1947, consolidating the Muslim-majority regions into the Islamic Republic of Pakistan (east and west) subject to geographic contiguity and the choice of the princely states to politically accede to either country. India opted to be a secular state (explicit separation of religion from state) with a predominantly Hindu population along with a sizeable Muslim population and other religious minority populations, flanked by Pakistan on the west and east. (In 1971, East Pakistan gained independence from Pakistan to become the Islamic Republic of Bangladesh.) Following adoption of the Indian Constitution in January 1950, India formally became a sovereign, secular, democratic republic, governed by a parliamentary democracy.

The Indian Constitution[8] abolished untouchability and enacted stringent provisions to punish any form of discrimination against Dalits with prison time, designating the Dalit castes as Scheduled Castes and the Indigenous forest-dwelling tribal people as Scheduled Tribes. The constitution also enshrined guarantees of educational scholarships to these social groups, covering all levels of education, and reserved 22.5% of admissions in all public educational institutions (including professional programs) and jobs in the public/government sector for them. These measures have substantially elevated the socioeconomic status of these groups, which was also promoted by general social progress and modernization of the cultural ethos. In recent decades, social and civic equity has been further accelerated by mobile Internet penetration into every nook and corner of the country and cheap mobile phone and Internet service access, enabling viral dissemination of atrocities and immediate law enforcement action. Although caste-based injustice has largely been eliminated, occasional episodes occur from time to time fueled by local cultural tensions. Culturally, caste-based identity remains a powerful sociocultural force and framework of self-identification for much of the middle-aged and older adult population, particularly in rural areas and towns.

Size and Geography

India's land area is approximately 3.29 million square km, latitudes 8° 4' and 37° 6' north, longitudes 68° 7' and 97° 25', flanked by the Himalayan mountains to the north and northeast, and the Indian Ocean, Arabian Sea, and Bay of Bengal to the south, west, and east, respectively. It has a total coastline of 7,516 km, and a total of about 15,200 km of land borders with Pakistan, Bangladesh, and China (**Figure 19-1**).[9] The princely state of Jammu and Kashmir became politically integrated into India with the accession by the king to the Indian Union; however, it remains geographically divided between India (two-thirds of the state) and Pakistan/China (one-third) following the 1947 war over Pakistan's claim to the state on grounds of religious composition of the population.

Government and Political System

India is a union of 28 states (demarcated along linguistic dominance and tribal identity lines) and eight centrally administered union territories.[8] The states are divided into a total of 766 administrative units.[8] The political system is a multiparty, parliamentary democracy with a bicameral legislative structure at the national and state levels. At the national level, Parliament consists of Members of Parliament (MPs) who are directly elected by citizens (adults aged over 18 years) every 5 years to the Lok Sabha (People's Council, the Lower House equivalent to Britain's House of Commons), as well as MPs who are indirectly elected by specific constituents to the Rajya Sabha (literally, the Governing Council, similar to Britain's House of Lords). Similarly, state legislatures consist of Members of the Legislative Assembly and Members of the Legislative Council, who are elected directly and indirectly to these bodies, respectively.[8]

The Indian Constitution defined the roles of the legislature, the executive (the prime minister at the central level/the chief minister at the state level, and their council of ministers), and judiciary. Each state is governed by elected state legislature bodies along similar lines as the central government, with subject jurisdictions laid out between the central government (e.g., defense), state governments (e.g., education, health), or both.

Macroeconomics

The currency is the Indian rupee (exchange rate INR 82.4 = $1 USD in 2023). In 2021–2022, India's GDP of U.S. $3.39 trillion USD (per the World Bank) made it the world's fifth largest economy, advancing from the 10th position in 2014. Per capita GDP in purchasing power parity (PPP) dollars was estimated at PPP $8,319 in 2022 compared with PPP $5,187 in 2014 (per the World Bank). The estimated proportion of the population living in poverty (defined as daily average income less than $2.15 USD per person in the household) was 10%, nearly halved since 2015 (18.5%) (World Bank country data). The macroeconomic sectors, in order of contribution to GDP in 2021, were the primary sector, 21.8% (agriculture, forestry, fishing, and mining and quarrying); the secondary sector, 24.3% (manufacturing, power generation/gas/water/other utilities, and construction); and the tertiary or services sector, 53.9% (financial services, information technology/knowledge industry, tourism, etc.).[10]

Successive governments for over 40 years since independence have advocated for a mixed (public–private) economic policy, but heavily invested in public-sector industries, which were planned as the key engine of economic growth. Concurrently, the socialist-public sector dominated India's economy and produced pervasive negative impacts on governance and the polity.

Figure 19-1 Map of India

A major shift occurred with a serendipitous break in the stalemate triggered by the rise of a performance-tested, grassroots cadre-based political party to the national level in 2014. This party had, in one large drought-prone state, stewarded 13 uninterrupted years of macroeconomic and infrastructure progress on the backs of private industry and individual enterprises, as well as an inclusive model of socioeconomic development. Through the sheer dint of its transformative governance and economic/civic developmental results, by the next election cycle more political parties were attracted into its coalition, leading to its re-election to a second term in power with an overwhelming electoral mandate. This backing enabled the party to undertake more pervasive reforms in the macro- and micro-financial and economic realms, and to resolve many of the protracted political and ethnic rivalries that were retarding progress.

Nearly two completed political cycles (9 years) of a stewardship model of governance at the national level by the coalition government, coupled with visionary, yet pragmatic strategies to mitigate governance corruption in state governments, have transformed the central executive branch into a cohesive, development-focused team. The development philosophy has been to provide a fertile, fair, and frictionless platform for the private sector to innovate, create jobs, and fuel economic growth, and for people who are not employed in the formal sector, the wherewithal needed to rise out of poverty through self-started enterprises, however small. As a result of these policies, the proportion of the population living below the poverty line has been nearly halved in the last 8 years, from 18.5% in 2015 to 10% in 2022 on a larger population base (Table 19-1). The population proportion that is multidimensionally poor (United Nations' multidimensional poverty index, equally weighted on health, education, and standard of living with 12 indicators)[11] declined by 10 percentage points from 24.9% in 2015 to 2016 to 115% in 2023 (2023 GOI NITI Aayog MDI progress report).[12] The later section on health system performance presents granular facts supporting the transformative health impacts and infrastructure development impacts of specific programs at the household level, and the aggregate, national indicators of progress toward the United Nations' Sustainable Development Goals (SDGs) by 2030.[13]

Demographics

Population management was prioritized as a key determinant of economic growth beginning with the very first 5-Year Plan of 1951–1956.[7] In 1952, India became the first country in the world to officially incorporate family planning into its national development policy by implementing the National Family Planning (FP) program.[7] This program focused on mass education campaigns, motivating postpartum mothers/couples to consider adoption of modern family planning methods, and offering free family planning services to willing couples at government health facilities. Sustained efforts have led to achievement of replacement-level fertility (total fertility rate of 2.0 births per woman) in 2019, and then 1.95 by mid-2023.[7] Despite the fertility decline, the population is predicted to grow to approximately 1.5 billion in 2030, and stabilizing at 1.64 billion in 2050.[7] The continuing population increases reflect the birth–death rate differentials of the 1951–1981 period, which resulted in high population growth rates, peaking at 2.2% during 1971–1981. **Table 19-2** presents the demographic profile and vital statistical indicators for India.

According to India's National Commission on Population, the estimated population totaled 1.392 billion in 2023, with a population density of 421 people per square kilometer. The rural population has been largely stable in the last decade, and currently accounts for 65.1% of the total population (versus 68.8% in 2011, and 80% in 1951).The population distribution by age has changed substantially

Table 19-2 Demographic Profile and Vital Statistics

Indicator	Current Status
Population	1.392 billion (2023 est.)
Rural population	65.1% (est. mid-year 2022); slight decrease from 68.8% in 2011
Population density/sq. km	421; 10% increase from 382 in 2011
Age 0–14 years	26% in 2021 (29.5% in 2011)
Age >60 years	10.1% versus 8.4% in 2011
Age at effective marriage, female	Median: 19.2 years, 2019–2021 (17.2 in 2011)
Age dependency ratio	47 dependents per 100 working-age 18–64, 2022 (reduced from 53/100 in 2011–2015)
Literacy rate (% of population, 15+ years)	Total: 74% (2018 est.); Male: 82%, Female: 66%

(continues)

Table 19-2 Demographic Profile and Vital Statistics *(continued)*

Indicator	Current Status
Infant mortality rate	28/1,000 live births in 2020 (declined from 40 in 2013) 31/1,000 rural 19/1,000 urban
Maternal mortality ratio	97/100,000 births in 2021 (reduced from 167 in 2007–2009)
Life expectancy at birth (2015–2019)	Total: 69.7 years Male: 68.4 years (increased from 65.4 in 2008–2012) Female: 71.1 years (increased from 68.8 years)
Total fertility rate	2.0 births per woman (2019–2021, NFHS-5; 1.95 in 2022), declined from 2.4 in 2012

Data from Census of India 2011, National Population Register & Socioeconomic and Caste Census. Accessed July 31, 2023. https://censusindia.gov.in; Government of India, Department of Health and Family Welfare, Ministry of Health and Family Welfare. 2022–2023 annual report. Accessed July 19, 2023. https://main.mohfw.gov.in/sites/default/files/eng%201.pdf; Government of India, Ministry of Health and Family Welfare. Rural health statistics 2021–22. Accessed July 23, 2023. https://main.mohfw.gov.in/sites/default/files/RHS%202021-22_2.pdf; Government of India, National Commission on Population. 2020 population projections for India and states, 2011–36. Report of the Technical Group on Population Projections. Accessed July 25, 2023. https://main.mohfw.gov.in/sites/default/files/Population%20Projection%20Report%202011-2036%20-%20upload_compressed_0.pdf; Government of India, Registrar General and Census Commissioner. Sample Registration System (SRS)—2020. *SRS Bull.* 2022;55(1). Accessed July 28, 2023. https://censusindia.gov.in/nada/index.php/catalog/42687; Government of India, Registrar General. Sample Registration System. *SRS Bull.* 2014;49(1); International Institute of Population Sciences. National Family Health Survey-5 in 2019–2021, Mumbai. 2023. (Survey interrupted in 2020 by COVID-19 pandemic.); International Institute of Population Sciences. National Family Health Survey-4, 2015–2016. Mumbai, India: 2017; World Bank. 2023 country profile, India. Accessed July 28, 2023. https://databank.worldbank.org/views/reports/reportwidget.aspx?Report_Name=CountryProfile&Id=b450fd57&tbar=y&dd=y&inf=n&zm=n&country=IND; World Bank. Literacy rate, adult total, male and female–India. Accessed July 31, 2023. https://data.worldbank.org/indicator/SE.ADT.LITR.ZS?locations=IN.

in the last decade, with a decline in the child population aged 0 to 14 years and increase in the population older than age 60 years. The sex ratio has remained skewed toward males, with 945 females per 1,000 males in 2021 (943 in 2011). The age dependency ratio (dependents per 100 working-age population aged 18 to 64 years) remains favorable; it was 47 per 100 in 2022.

Literacy among the population aged 15 years or older was estimated at 74% in 2018, with most of the illiteracy accounted for by older adults. The gross enrollment ratio (GER), the ratio of enrolled students in elementary, middle, and high school to the population in the respective age-groups, has improved in recent years; it is 79.6% in secondary schools (9th and 10th grades) and 57.6% in the 11th and 12th grades in 2020–2021.[14]

The population health status indicators have improved substantially in recent years. Infant mortality declined from 40/1,000 live births in 2013 to 28 in 2020, and the urban–rural differential narrowed to 12 percentage points (31 versus 19). The maternal mortality ratio (deaths of mothers during pregnancy or within 28 days postpartum) declined from 167 in 2007 to 2009 to 97 in 2022. Life expectancy at birth has increased by about 3 years since 2008–2012 to 69.7 years in 2020 (SRS 2022 report), despite steep increases in noncommunicable disease prevalence. Fertility rates have fallen below replacement-level fertility.

Brief History of the Healthcare System

Pre–World War II

Before World War II, India's health system consisted primarily of hospitals in the major cities established for resident British officers and troops. Isolated institutions for public health also existed. To offer modern medicine and public health in rural areas, the first primary health centers (PHCs) were established in the 1920s by the Maharajah (king) of Mysore (in South India) to provide sanitation education, purification of wells, medical care, and small family promotion. These PHCs may be the earliest publicly financed public health facilities in the colonies set up with an integrated public health and primary care approach.

Traditional, Culturally Rooted Systems of Medicine

Ayurveda (first developed in north India) and Siddha (developed in the Tamil culture of South India) are two indigenous systems of medicine. They were well established before 1000 BC,[5] and constantly accrued new knowledge over time. Other alternatives to modern medicine (allopathy) are Unani (rooted in the Arabic culture) and homeopathy. Sushruta, placed between 600 and 1000 BC, was the founder of surgery in the Ayurvedic medical system,[5] and Charaka systematized Ayurveda into the earliest Ayurvedic pharmacopeia. The Ayurvedic system uses its pharmacopeia to guide the treatment of diseases and is particularly recognized for successful treatment of chronic diseases (e.g., allergies, rheumatoid arthritis).

Ayurveda and Siddha are practiced at both the household and professional levels. At the household level, common knowledge of herbs and practices passed on by word of mouth are part of people's routine response to prevent and treat certain illnesses. At the professional/institutional level, the traditional medicine care is offered at government-sponsored AYUSH centers (Ayurveda, Yoga, Unani, Siddha, and Homeopathy) headed by certified practitioners and available at selected Health and Wellness Centers (originally established as primary health centers and subcenters as described later in this section).[8] Ayurveda, Unani, Siddha, and homeopathy physicians' certification requires a formal college education of 4.5 years and 1 year of clinical internship (similar to the MBBS degree that qualifies physicians of modern medicine).

The historic 1978 Alma-Ata declaration of "Health for All by 2000" under the aegis of the World Health Organization called for the establishment of a population-wide, dispersed network of PHCs and subcenters in all populated regions to provide "essential health care to individuals, families, and communities (preventive and essential health care), in a culturally and socially acceptable manner, at a cost that the country and community could afford."[15] In India, PHCs were planned to reach a density of 1 per 30,000 population in rural areas and 1 per 20,000 population in remote tribal/hilly areas. They were to be staffed with one male and one female medical officer (trained physicians), male and female health workers to undertake public health program responsibilities, field supervisory staff, a basic delivery room (for institutional delivery with normal pregnancy), and a basic laboratory facility with microscopy facility for major communicable disease detection (malaria, tuberculosis, and leprosy). Each PHC was to have six subcenters dispersed among the covered villages, one per 5,000 rural population (3,000 in tribal areas), with one locally resident female health worker (auxiliary nurse midwife, ANM, trained in public health and midwifery) and one male health worker for field work of communicable disease programs. Health workers' responsibilities include active outreach to people's homes for screening and surveillance activities to detect communicable and noncommunicable diseases, refer them for treatment, and provide maintenance care, such as monitoring medication compliance, and maternal and child health follow-up.

For referral care (including surgical and obstetric), 30-bed CHCs were established in large villages or semiurban towns, with an internist, general surgeon, and obstetrician/gynecologist. Selected CHCs were designated as 24/7 delivery facilities and provided an anesthesiologist to provide caesarean delivery services. The next level of publicly funded curative facilities is the district level, with additional specialties, including ear/nose/throat (ENT), ophthalmology, psychiatry, and other specialties.

Despite establishment of the necessary infrastructure in rural and tribal areas, care utilization at PHCs and SCs remained low owing to the top-down, patronizing approach of providers in the government facilities. This prompted the National Rural Health Mission (NRHM) in 2005,[7] which marked a significant departure from the top-down, supplier-driven approach to demand generation. The NRHM provided for allocating part of the district health funds for disbursement to private health providers who offered antenatal care and institutional delivery services to rural mothers. Funding also covered the mother's transportation for institutional delivery by Accredited Social Health Activists (ASHAs), patient navigation, and decision-support services by the ASHA, and other outpatient and inpatient care for mothers and children. ASHAs (*asha* means "hope") are trained female health volunteers residing in the neighborhood who are compensated by a performance-linked incentive for services to facilitate MCH program service utilization at either public or private facilities. The success of the NRHM led to the National Urban Health Mission (NUHM) in 2013 to provide the urban poor with financial access to quality MCH care. The NUHM created community-based women's health committees (Mahila Arogya Samiti), one for every 50 to 100 households in low-income neighborhoods; one ASHA for every 1,000 to 2,500 population (200 to 500 households); one urban ANM for every 10,000 population; one urban PHC for every 50,000 population; and one urban CHC for every 250,000 population (per 500,000 in metropolitan cities).

The Current Healthcare System

Healthcare Infrastructure

The healthcare infrastructure consists of government, private for-profit, and nongovernment nonprofit facilities (NGOs). Government health facilities include primary healthcare facilities (offering public health services under public health programs and personal healthcare services) and referral care centers. Primary healthcare institutions include subcenters and PHCs, mostly located in rural and tribal areas. Referral care facilities for the rural population are primarily community health centers and district hospitals. Tertiary care facilities that offer free care to urban and rural populations include the government medical college hospitals, specialized government hospitals (e.g., cancer centers, mental hospitals), and the national/state institutes of excellence (e.g., All India Institutes of Medical Sciences). Private for-profit institutions include clinics and polyclinics run by private physicians (general practitioners, specialists) as well as hospitals. There are also not-for-profit, nongovernment service organizations engaged in providing primary health care in selected locations, along with nonprofit hospitals; the latter are dominated by Christian missionary hospitals dispersed all over the country.

Government Health Facilities

Government facilities are constructed with central government funding and transferred to the state government for administration and management, as health is a state subject. States fund the maintenance, personnel salaries, recurring supplies, and consumable costs, except for recurring expenditures under the priority national programs and missions. Care is provided free of charge for the general population. These facilities also offer amenities such as individual rooms and special amenities at a modest cost compared with the private sector to the better-off population that can pay for care or if they are state government employees or dependents (part of employee benefits).

As of 2022, 157,935 subcenters were available in rural areas (on average, 1/5,691 rural population, covering four villages, serving residents within 2.5 km radius). In addition, 25,308 PHCs were available (1/36,049 population covering 27 villages and 6.3 km radius), as well as 5,396 community health centers (1/164,027 people residing in 121 villages within a 13.4 km radius).[7,16] Additionally, there were 1,275 subdistrict hospitals in semi-urban towns. In tribal/hilly areas, the corresponding institutional availability in 2022 was one subcenter per 4,005 people (2.6 km radius), one PHC per 26,552 population (6.75 km radius), and one CHC per 105,893 population (13.5 km radius).

A total of 767 district hospitals and 315 medical college hospitals located in nonmetropolitan district headquarters towns were available to serve the referral care needs of the rural population.[16] Overall, the rural population had more than 10,000 government hospitals (including specialty hospitals such as cancer, TB, and mental hospitals) with 279,588 beds (i.e., one secondary/tertiary care bed per 3,020 people) accessible in a nearby town,[17] compared with one per 4,895 population in 2014.[18] In urban areas, there were 3,894 subcenters, 6,118 PHCs, 584 CHCs, and 3,188 other government hospitals, for a total of 3,772 urban hospitals with 431,173 beds, one bed per 1,088 urban population in the government sector.[17] Across the rural and urban populations, the average government facility bed availability was 1 per 1,953 population.[17]

AYUSH clinics with qualified doctors of the nonallopathic systems were available at 7,451 PHCs, 2811 CHCs, 487 district hospitals, and 4,022 rural, stand-alone AYUSH centers.[7]

Private and Nongovernment Health Facilities

A total of 25,628 private clinical establishments providing allopathic medicine services are centrally registered with the government of India's online portal.[7] With health being a state subject, state governments are responsible for regulating clinical establishments, but portal registration data are incomplete. Data on total bed capacity in the private and NGO sectors are not available.

Closed Network Health Infrastructure in the Employer-Sponsored Health Insurance Sector

All commercial entities with 10 or more employees are required to be registered with the state governments and participate in the Employees' State Insurance (ESI) Corporation scheme.[15] The ESI scheme is a nationwide closed network of outpatient clinics and hospitals exclusively serving private employees and their families. It is financed by the employer, the state government, and the central government each contributing a one-third share. A total of 130 million beneficiaries (about 9.7% of the population) avail themselves of free medical care from these facilities, which include 1,595 dispensaries (stand-alone outpatient clinics including multispecialty clinics) and 160 hospitals with 25,776 beds.[19] For inpatient care in areas without ESI hospitals, or for referral care, the ESI scheme covers the medical care costs at special amenity service rates in government hospitals.

Central government employees, retirees, and their families (3.9 million beneficiaries) are covered free of charge for all medical care by the Central Government Health Scheme (CGHS). Under this scheme, outpatient and preventive care are offered through 430 CGHS health and wellness centers, 19 polyclinics (multispecialty clinics) and 19 dental clinics. Secondary/tertiary care is accessed from 498 CGHS-empaneled public and private hospitals (with specified accreditations in place).[17]

The Indian Railways is a large employer covering employees, retirees, and their families (6.4 million beneficiaries) through its closed network of 661 clinics and 126 hospitals with 13,748 beds. Railway hospitals also provide care to victims of railway accidents and major disasters under specific authorization.[17]

Large enterprises (those with more than 1,000 employees) are required by law to provide exclusive in-house, closed-panel outpatient and inpatient facilities, supplemented by contracted services from tertiary care subspecialty hospitals. The large government-owned public sector industries together employ about 18.1 million people and cover a total of 72 million beneficiaries at each industry's on-site and local facilities. Privately owned enterprises in hazardous industries (e.g., mining, fire crackers manufacturing) are required to have on-site clinics (275 clinics in 2022) and, where appropriate, hospitals (575 hospitals).[17]

Workforce

India's medical education is modeled upon Britain's medical education system. Physicians of allopathic (modern) medicine are licensed by the National Medical Council (formerly Indian Medical Council). The general practitioner training is a 4.5-year academic program, followed by 1 year of internship rotations including rural primary care facility rotation. For specialty training, there are 3-year postgraduate programs (residency and additional academic preparation), leading to an MD (medical specialties) or MS (surgical specialties) degree, and for subspecialties, an additional 3 to 4 years of fellowship training.

The RN program is a 3.5-year program (including academic and practice hours). The bachelor's degree in nursing is earned after a 4-year program, including a clinical practice internship. Male and female health workers (the latter, trained as auxiliary nurse-midwives [ANMs]) are trained at Rural Health and Family Welfare Training Centers located in the various states. ANMs are trained in an 18-month program in midwifery and a broad range of community nursing skills oriented to the expectations and needs of rural and underserved populations. Their training includes antenatal and postpartum care of mothers, essential care skills for newborns and under-5 children (including growth monitoring and immunization), family planning promotion, provision of nonoperative contraceptive care services, and performance of other community/household-level public health tasks under the various public health programs. ANMs are primarily employed in government primary health facilities, subcenters, PHCs, and rural CHCs.

As of July 2021, there were 1,301,319 trained doctors of modern medicine, and 3.341 million nursing personnel (RN and bachelor's degree holders) and 839,863 trained midwives for hospital-based settings and the obstetric units of CHCs.[17] The availability of total nursing and midwifery personnel trained for hospital settings represents an 87% increase over the availability of 1,780,006 in 2014. Additionally, there were 943,951 ANMs available, almost all of them employed in the primary healthcare system and designated 24/7 obstetric care CHCs.

Altogether, the availability of modern allopathic-trained medical/nursing personnel amounted to 37.6 personnel per 10,000 population as of 2022.[7] A total of 1.052 million trained, locally resident ASHAs were available, serving as links between the population and government facilities.[7] ASHAs played a major role in containment of the COVID-19 epidemic in all phases (during lockdown, successive epidemic waves, and the vaccination program), performing the functions of community-based case detection, managing the logistics of quarantine, contact tracing, and facilitating vaccination coverage after vaccines became available.

There were also 56,854 lady health visitors in 2021—personnel who primarily focus on individual medical care of patients diagnosed with the priority communicable diseases (e.g., malaria, tuberculosis, leprosy). These personnel deliver and supervise drug consumption in intermittent treatment regimens or otherwise monitor compliance.[17] This cadre is now deprioritized in light of the changed public health strategies of the National Urban Health Mission and the emphasis on ASHAs.

There were 2,89,000 dentists in 2021 (66% increase from 154,436 in 2014), and 565,000 registered practitioners of AYUSH systems of medicine (graduates of medical colleges of the respective, recognized Indian systems of medicine and homeopathy).[7] Dentists complete a 4-year academic program and 6 months of clinical internship to earn the Bachelor of Dental Surgery degree. To practice specialized dentistry, those with a bachelor's degree must complete 2 years of fellowship training.

Health Workforce Training

As of September 2022, there were 648 medical colleges accredited by the National Medical Council with an annual intake of 98,013 medical students, increased by over 50% since 2014 (2022 National Health Profile). There were 318 dental colleges with an annual intake of 27,868 students, and 6,814 subspecialty dentists were in training each year, marginally increased over 2014 levels, by 3%. AYUSH medicine colleges, which total 789 with 63,477 annual admissions, are dominated by Ayurveda colleges (416 colleges, 34,119 admissions).[17] There were 3,313 nursing training institutions admitting 137,322 students to the general nursing program (RN) annually, 1,951 ANM schools graduating 137,322 ANMs annually, and 2,159 bachelor of nursing colleges with 110,760 annual admissions. There were 992 pharmacy colleges offering a bachelor's program with 62,540 annual admissions, 292 colleges offering doctor of pharmacy degrees admitting 8,760 students annually, and 1,275 institutions offering pharmacy diploma programs with 76,320 admissions; the last group of students are primarily qualified for medical dispensing at pharmacies.[17]

Social Health Insurance for Catastrophic Care Coverage of the Low-Income Population

Publicly funded social health insurance to reimburse providers for care provided to the low-income population started with the Rashtriya Swasthya Bima Yojana in 2008. It provided hospitalization coverage up to Rs 30,000 per person, for up to five family members, in low-income households earning less than $1.90 USD per day per person. In 2018, to address the inadequacy of financial risk coverage and the steep increase in noncommunicable disease prevalence among the poor, this program was revamped into the Prime Minister's Jan Arogya Yojana (PM-JAY).[17,20] The new program enables cashless access to hospital care including prehospitalization costs and post discharge care at any empaneled public or private hospital, covering up to Rs 500,000 per family per year ($6,000 USD), for 1,393 care procedures (including bone marrow transplants and cochlear implants, added in 2022). PM-JAY is currently on offer to the bottom 40% of the total population, with about 500 million people being eligible based on multiple criteria—poverty-level income, uncertain-wage/low-wage job, and deprivation of basic living infrastructure. Enrollment is about half of the estimated eligible population, primarily due to of a lack of awareness about the program among persons with limited education, and the challenges associated with personal identification documents such as Aadhar, due to poor accuracy of data across the identity documents needed for validation in the digital enrollment system. Costs of PM-JAY administration and care reimbursement are shared by the central and state governments.[20] In addition, several states have implemented supplementary insurance schemes to increase the risk coverage limits.

Functionality of the Government Health Infrastructure

Since the initiation of sweeping governance reforms to incentivize public personnel's accountability for their performance, the functioning of government health facilities has improved, enabling better access to these facilities, which are widely dispersed in most rural areas. Improvement in healthcare utilization has been particularly noteworthy in rural areas, where personal incomes and population density are too low to drive adequate market demand to sustain private health services. Despite these structural challenges, recent years have seen quite a rapid expansion of private-sector health facilities in some well-populated rural areas and subdistrict towns, largely buoyed by the PM-JAY social insurance program. Much increased functionality of public healthcare facilities was spurred by various programs and developments (outlined in the section on health system performance), improving the population's service utilization at the formerly nominally available healthcare facility buildings (subcenters, PHCs, CHCs, district hospitals). These facilities are now better equipped with providers, upgraded medical care equipment, drugs, and consumables.

Much of the expanded personnel availability and service utilization in rural healthcare facilities is attributable to the maternal health voucher program (Janani Suraksha Program) and the PM-JAY social health insurance program, which reimburses for services regardless of government or private facility. These programs offer incentives for providers to remain available and provide services and and enhance the quality of care and facility amenities so as to compete with the private sector for PM-JAY patients. Additionally, regular oversight and performance monitoring under various national health programs (**Table 19-3**) reinforce the accountability and availability of government health personnel to achieve program goals.

Table 19-3 Public Health Programs, Progress, and Related SDG Targets for 2030[a]

Program[a,b]	Key Strategies/Goals[a,b]	Program Performance[a,b]	Population-Based Outcomes[c,d] (Current and Comparator), Based on National Surveys/ Other Sources per Footnotes	Related SDG Target for 2030[b,d]
Overarching Benefit Programs				
-Aadhar program, universal legal identity card coverage, linked to all benefit schemes, critical for access	-Universal biometrics-based identity system to establish eligibility, prevent misuse, and prevent corrupt leakage of funds	-All legal citizens registered with identity cards -Birth certificate issue mandatory -Aadhar ID of 85% of Anganwadi-covered children registered -85% of all children are Aadhar-linked in immunization and other program records	-% population with Aadhar card: 90.2% (93% U, 90% R)* -% of all births registered (0–5 aged children): 89.1%*** (93.3% U, 87.5% R)	-Provide legal identity for all—universal birth registration
-Financial/banking inclusion: Jan Dhan Yojana (started 2016) -Issue BPL (below poverty line) cards to eligible beneficiaries to track benefit utilization	Universal coverage of women and men with cost-free bank accounts in banks or post office accounts if banks are not available (leakage-free direct cash transfer to beneficiaries of all programs)	-330.3 million new bank accounts of adults without banking access prior to 2014, including 275.3 million women; additional 165 million post office accounts for social security schemes	-% HH having bank or post office account: 95.7% (2019–2021)* -% HH having BPL card: 45.3% (31% U, 52% R)*	Ensure inclusive economic growth through universal access to finance and banking services

(continues)

Table 19-3 Public Health Programs, Progress, and Related SDG Targets for 2030[a] *(continued)*

Program[a,b]	Key Strategies/Goals[a,b]	Program Performance[a,b]	Population-Based Outcomes[c,d] (Current and Comparator), Based on National Surveys/ Other Sources per Footnotes	Related SDG Target for 2030[b,d]
Public Health Programs: Maternal and Reproductive Health				
-Maternal Health Program (Janani Suraksha Yojana, Janani Shishu Suraksha Yojana) -ASHAs, key workers for MCH navigation and grassroots implementation -High-risk pregnant women connected with specialist ob/gyn facilities -Maternal Death Surveillance and Response System (covering all public, private facilities, and home delivery to register and investigate every maternal death; entrusted to district health officers)	-Cash incentives by direct cash transfer to women's bank accounts for accessing care and nutrition in exchange for institutional delivery -Free care with zero incidental costs for delivery in public institutions (e.g., diet, transport), cesarean section (including hiring private gynecologist if not available at public facility) -ANC and delivery by specialist ob/gyn if high-risk pregnancy -Tracing/tracking monitoring portal for pregnant women -Integration of all schemes for women and child U-5 via pregnant women registration and Mother and Child Protection (MCP) card	-15.2 million births covered FY2021–2022 -600,000 high-risk pregnancies cared for -1.052 million trained ASHAs -ASHAs became the key link workers and contact tracing volunteers during the COVID-19 pandemic; also enabled achievement of over 2 billion doses of COVID-19 vaccine delivered to the population	-ANC visit in first trimester: 70% in 2019–2021* (2015–2016, 59%**) -Completed the recommended ≥4 ANC visits to skilled providers: 58%* (2015–2016, 51%**) -% births by skilled personnel: 84.4% in 2015–2016 -Institutional delivery: 89%* (2015–2016, 79%**; 2005–2006, 39%, NFHS-3) Rural: 87% Urban: 94% -Maternal mortality ratio: 97* (2015, 130)** -96% mothers with live birth received MCP card (2019–2021) -87% pregnant women received iron/folic acid pills (43% consumed)* -80% mothers knew high-risk pregnancy signs and if so, where to go*	-Reduce maternal mortality ratio to <70, with greatest focus on poorest performing regions (high declines seen in the worst, previously stagnant states) -Meet nutritional needs of pregnant and lactating women
Family Planning (FP) Program	-Free contraception care including terminal methods, abortion within 12 weeks gestation -IUD including postpartum IUD for birth spacing; injectable, oral, and emergency contraception -Beneficiary foregone wage compensation for surgical methods -Educate high-fertility subgroups on age at marriage, and FP (districts with TFR >3)	-3–3.5 million sterilizations annually (2018–2022) -5–6 million IUDs annually	-Total fertility rate: 2**** (2.3 in 2015–2016) -Unmet FP need: 9.4%**** (12.9% in 2015–2016) -Child spacing ≥3 years)=52.3 live births, 2020 (42.6%, 2012)*** -Modern contraception prevalence: 56.5% of couples 2019–2021 NFHS (47.7% in 2015–2016) -Women married by age 18: 23% 2019–2021 (27% NFHS-4)****	-Universal access to sexual and reproductive health and family planning education and services -Eliminate all harmful practices including early or child marriage of girls

Program[a,b]	Key Strategies/Goals[a,b]	Program Performance[a,b]	Population-Based Outcomes (Current and Comparator), Based on National Surveys/ Other Sources per Footnotes	Related SDG Target for 2030[b,d]
Child Health				
Facility-Based Newborn Care scale-up for high-risk newborns and sick neonates	-Special Newborn Care Units (SNCU) at district hospitals and medical colleges -Newborn Stabilization Units (NBSU) at First Referral Units (district hospitals) -Newborn Care Corner (NBCC) at 24/7 delivery centers (certain PHCs/CHCs)	-914 SNCUs -2,579 NBSUs -20,337 NBCCs (2022)	-Neonatal mortality rate: 20/1,000 live births (2020[b] versus 25 in 2015***)	-Reduce neonatal mortality to 12/1,000 live births
Universal Immunization Program, ASHA (accredited social health worker tracking and navigation to health care)	-11 vaccines free of charge, including the newer Rota, *H. influenzae*, and pneumococcal vaccines, provided over seven contacts with health facilities -Japanese encephalitis vaccine in endemic districts	Full immunization schedule with 11 vaccines completed by 1 year of age: 93% (2022), versus 62% fully immunization with BCG, DPT, polio, measles by 23 months, 2015–2016)	-Infant mortality rate: 28/1,000*** -Under-5 mortality: 32/1,000 (2020)***; declined by annual compounded rate of 6.2% (2008–2020) versus 3.3% in 1990–2007	-Reduce under-5 mortality to 25/1,000 live births
Anganwadi services -Under-5 children and maternal nutrition supplementation -Free early childhood education 2–6 years (under Integrated Child Development Scheme)	-Take-home nutritious food ration distribution (protein–energy–micronutrient supplementation) for pregnant and lactating mothers, children 6 months to 2 years -Hot cooked meal + protein supplement in preschool centers for children 6 months to 5 years -Extra protein and calorie take-home ration for underweight, stunted, and wasted children and underweight mothers	Served population: -73.5 million under-5 children in 2021–2022 -16.9 million pregnant/lactating mothers	-% under-5 underweight: 35.7% (2015–2016****) -% U-5 stunted: 38.4% (2015–2016****) -% under-5 wasted: 21% (2015–2016****) Anemia rates with capillary blood samples using WHO cutoffs have been shown to be invalid and, therefore, not reported (Sachdev 2021)	-End hunger/ all forms of malnutrition, meet targets of stunting, wasting in U-5 children by 2025 -Meet nutrition needs of pregnant & lactating women

(continues)

Table 19-3 Public Health Programs, Progress, and Related SDG Targets for 2030[a] *(continued)*

Program[a,b]	Key Strategies/Goals[a,b]	Program Performance[a,b]	Population-Based Outcomes (Current and Comparator), Based on National Surveys/ Other Sources per Footnotes	Related SDG Target for 2030[b,d]
Child Health				
-School Health and Wellness Program -School Mid-day Meal Program for primary and middle school (central and state government financing) -Cover all government and government-aided schools	-Health checkup, immunizations, annual deworming treatment -Weekly supervised iron–folic acid (IFA) supplement given to in-school and out-of-school adolescents through government and government-aided schools and preschool centers	-60 million children aged below 10 and 52 million adolescents covered for IFA tablets -300 million USD on mid-day meal program; 118 million children covered	-No data on health status of school-going children	Address nutritional needs of children and adolescent girls
National Comprehensive Adolescent and Teens Health Program (2014)	-Clinical care, counseling on reproductive and sexual health, substance use, and vaccinations at adolescent-friendly health clinics at health centers (AFHCs) and public hospitals	-14 million adolescent beneficiaries served during FY2022	-No data on program outcomes	Universal access to sexual and reproductive health and family planning education and services
Child Health Tracking	-Mother and Child Health Tracking system -ANM online (tablets for ANMs)			

Program[a,b]	Key Strategies/Goals[a,b]	Program Performance[a,b]	Population-Based Outcomes[c,d] (Current and Comparator), Based on National Surveys/ Other Sources per Footnotes	Related SDG Target for 2030[b,d]
National Communicable Disease Control Programs				
National Center for Vector-Borne Disease Control (malaria, dengue, Japanese encephalitis, Chikungunya, Kala azar, filariasis). Each is a state program, overseen and financially assisted by the National Center. International assistance from Global Fund against AIDS, TB and Malaria since 2005.	-Integrated vector control (targeted indoor residual spray, treated bed-nets in high-malaria-endemic areas, use of larvivarous fish, and source reduction) -Early case detection by surveillance and rapid public health response follow-up -Advocacy and behavior change communication to reduce mosquito breeding sources -Children 1-15 years vaccination against Japanese encephalitis in endemic districts in the Universal Immunization Program); adult vaccination completed in 316 endemic districts in 21 states -Annual mass drugs administration (MDA) against filariasis -Cash subsidy for housing for low-income people since 2015 -Awards to districts and states upon achieving milestones	-**Malaria:** 161,753 cases, with two-thirds PF cases (2021) (from 1.7 million cases 2015, >90% reduction).[e] Deaths: 46 (2022), from 384 (2015) -**Kala azar:** 1,357 cases (2021) reduced by 84.1% from 2015. Deaths increased in 2022 due to COVID-19 disruptions.[T] -**Lymphatic filariasis:** 705,928 cases (prevalence 2021; 20,872 new cases in 2019)[a,b] -**Dengue:** 192,245 cases (2021, nearly tripled since 2015). Deaths: 346. Case fatality rate 0.02%, steady since 2015 -**Chikungunya:** (debilitating, not fatal): 119,070 suspected cases in 2021, fourfold increase from 2015 -**Japanese encephalitis** (JE; high case fatality): 812 cases (2021), case fatality rate 9%–18%[T]	-**Malaria** set for elimination by 2030 (0 cases for 3 consecutive years. Incidence: 0.25/1,000 (from 0.92 in 2015[d]) (125 of 707 districts: 0 cases) -**Kala azar** (NTD) set for elimination by 2030 (<1/10,000 population); achieved in 98.7% of endemic blocks in four states. -Block level, filariasis and malaria targeted now for elimination after reaching near zero levels -**Filariasis** (NTD) set for elimination by mass use of DEC-fortified salt (MDA) in endemic districts, and mosquito control as indicated. -**Dengue** worsened since 2015, strategy underway -**JE** should be controlled soon with effective vaccine available and now indigenous vaccine ready for use	By 2030, end the epidemics of AIDS, tuberculosis, malaria, and neglected tropical diseases (NTD—kala azar (visceral leishmaniasis), filariasis, chikungunya), and combat hepatitis, waterborne diseases

(continues)

Table 19-3 Public Health Programs, Progress, and Related SDG Targets for 2030[a] *(continued)*

Program[a,b]	Key Strategies/Goals[a,b]	Program Performance[a,b]	Population-Based Outcomes (Current and Comparator), Based on National Surveys/ Other Sources per Footnotes	Related SDG Target for 2030[b,d]
National Communicable Disease Control Programs				
Leprosy Eradication Program Goals: Early case detection, and achieve Grade 2 disability (G2D) at diagnosis to zero	-Early case detection and free treatment -Reduce to zero G2D at diagnosis -Leprosy detection campaigns plus screening of adults aged >30 in HWCs -Stigma reduction	-Leprosy eliminated in 2005 (<1 case per 10,000 for 3 consecutive years, per WHO) -New case detection rate, 2022: 0.81/100,000[1]	-Prevalence reduced to 0.57/10,000[a] -G2D present at diagnosis of new cases reduced to 2.15% in 2021,[a] from 4.6 in 2015–2016[e]	
TB Elimination Program	-Molecular diagnosis expansion for case finding and drug resistance detection -Sputum testing continued -Expedite drug-resistant and multidrug-resistant TB detection and treatment -Prioritize TB screening for those with risky comorbidities (persons with HIV (PLHIV) diabetes, tobacco users, alcohol users) -Direct cash transfer for nutrition support -TB preventive treatment to household contacts of sputum-positive TB patients and PLHIV since 2021 -Strengthen district TB centers	-2.4 million new TB cases diagnosed, 2021 -%TB cases cured plus treatment completed: 65.3% (2017, HFWS2021–22)[b] ->96% of PLHIV attending ART centers screened for TB monthly in 2022 -8% of PLHIV diagnosed with TB -7 million TB patients provided cash benefit for nutrition improvement	-1.88/1,000 annual TB incidence (2021, versus 2.17 in 2015) (HFWStats 2019–2020 Rep) -2.59 million annual new cases -0.37 TB or TB-HIV death/1,000 population	

Program[a,b]	Key Strategies/Goals[a,b]	Program Performance[a,b]	Population-Based Outcomes[c,d] (Current and Comparator), Based on National Surveys/ Other Sources per Footnotes	Related SDG Target for 2030[b,d]
National Communicable Disease Control Programs				
AIDS Control Program Goal: Eliminate HIV-AIDS by: -Reducing new HIV infections and AIDS–related deaths -Universal access to free lifesaving first-line, second-line, and third-line ART, diagnostic and monitoring investigations for all PLHIV Target of 85% virally suppressed among those on ART -Prevent and treat opportunistic infections -Elimination of vertical transmission of HIV and syphilis (UNAIDS goals) -Control of all STIs and reproductive tract infections	-HIV education via 16 hours of sexual health school curricula (grades 8-12), via social media and venues of young people gatherings -Sentinel surveillance and periodic screenings via antenatal clinics, STI clinics, blood banks, targeted preventive efforts (peer link workers), referral to free treatment (TI) -Quarterly HIV screenings and STI screenings/early treatment among high-risk groups (HRG)—sex workers, MSM and transgender, IV drug users, migrant workers, and long-distance truckers -Monthly TB screenings among high-risk groups (HRG) -Needle exchange programs	-Targeted intervention coverage out of estimated total: Sex workers: 101% MSM: 103% IDU: 107% Migrants: 50% Truckers: 100% -30 million pregnant women screened for HIV/syphilis (2022) -0.03% new HIV cases detected -0.03% syphilis positive -Total new HIV cases detected in 2022: 62,970 total[a] Age 15–24: 15,080 %PLHIV know their HIV status: 77% (2021–2022 versus target 79% -Of estimated 20,410 HIV-positive pregnant women, 8,818 identified and enrolled in treatment (94% receiving free ART under NACP) -HIV-related deaths: 41,970[a] (down from 127,200 in 2013) -1.9% of high-risk groups screened were diagnosed with TB	-New HIV infections/1,000 uninfected population: 0.05 2015b -Adult HIV prevalence: 0.21 (2021, stable since 2015–2016) -HIV among pregnant women: 0.03 million in 2022–2023 (reduced from 0.72 million in 2006–2007) -% with comprehensive knowledge about HIV/AIDS= 87% women, 94% men (2019–2021, versus 22% and 32%, 2015–2016) -% PLHIV currently receiving ART: 82% (2019, 62% 2015)[2] -% PLHIV on ART who are virally suppressed: 85% -% pregnant women diagnosed with HIV on ART: 94% -% newborns of HIV-positive women provided ARV prophylaxis: 99%	-End epidemic of AIDS by 2030 -Access to safe affordable, essential medicines for all
Viral Hepatitis Control (2018) Goal: Eliminate hepatitis B and C by 2030 Reduce deaths due to liver cirrhosis and hepatic cancer -Reduce risk and morbidity due to hepatitis A and E	-Education on transmission risk factors -Target management of estimated 50 million people infected with hepatitis -Free treatment of hepatitis C in lower 2 quintiles of population, lifelong management of hepatitis B -Cross-linkage with HIV program	No data available on prevalence and progress		-Control viral hepatitis

(continues)

Table 19-3 Public Health Programs, Progress, and Related SDG Targets for 2030[a] *(continued)*

Program[a,b]	Key Strategies/Goals[a,b]	Program Performance[a,b]	Population-Based Outcomes[c,d] (Current and Comparator), Based on National Surveys/ Other Sources per Footnotes	Related SDG Target for 2030[b,d]
National Communicable Disease Control Programs				
Iodine-Deficiency Disorders (IDD) Control Program Goals: 100% of salt consumed to be iodized (15 ppm) Reduce prevalence of iodine deficiency disorder <5%	-IDD control cells in each state -100% centrally financed program -Monitor production and supply of iodized salt		-% population uses iodized salt: 94.3% (2019–2021)	
Noncommunicable Disease Control and Risk Mitigation				
National Program for Prevention/ Control of Cancer, Diabetes, Hypertension, CVD, and Stroke	- NCD screening at HWCs and referral to NCD clinics - NCD clinics in all government health facilities, cardiac care units in secondary/tertiary care facilities, daycare cancer centers - Strengthen state cancer institutes -Cancer treatment access through Cancer Care Cards for free care of BPL patients	NCD clinics: 707 district level 5,541 CHC level 268 daycare cancer centers Inpatient care: 193 new cardiac care units -51 million NCD screenings 2022–2023 versus 5.9 million in 2014–2015[a] -8 million wellness sessions (including yoga)	-Hypertension prevalence: men:14.8%, women: 11% (2015–2016)**** -% diabetics on treatment/took treatment: 81.3% women, 72.5% men (NFHS 4) -% women 15–49 had a cervical exam=22.3% -% consume alcohol: men: 19% (of them, 40% once or more weekly); women: 1% (35% once or more weekly) -Data not available on cancer deaths	Reduce premature mortality from NCDs (age <70 at death) by one-third
National Dialysis Program (2016)	-Public–private partnership model linking district hospitals and private dialysis centers -PM-JAY program coverage	-1,342 centers with 8,704 hemodialysis machines (all districts covered) -1.7 million patients with 18.4 million dialysis sessions covered by 2022		

Program[a,b]	Key Strategies/Goals[a,b]	Program Performance[a,b]	Population-Based Outcomes[c,d] (Current and Comparator), Based on National Surveys/ Other Sources per Footnotes	Related SDG Target for 2030[b,d]
Noncommunicable Disease Control and Risk Mitigation				
Tobacco Control Program	-Prohibit cigarette sales within 100 yards of educational institutions -Education via campaigns and opportunistic events	No data on tobacco control–related progress.	-% current tobacco users age 15–49: men: 42.4%, women: 14.2% (2015–2016, women up from 6.2% in 2015)**** -% adults 15–49 have asthma: men: 1.2%, women: 1.9% (2015–2016)****	-Reduce premature mortality from NCDs by one-third -Reduce deaths from hazardous airborne chemicals/air pollution
Mental Health Program	-Detection, management, treatment, counseling in schools/colleges, workplace stress management and awareness programs -Tele-mental health program via HWCs for specialist access	No data available on community-based mental health burden	Data not available	
Blindness and Visual Impairment Prevention/Control Target 2025: 0.25% -Cataract-free in all districts	-Detection via HWCs/other institutions and treatment, surgical or as appropriate -Covered in PM-JAY insurance	-6.5 million cataract surgeries annually -Campaign to clear COVID-19–related backlog of 2 years	-Prevalence: 0.36% per 2015–2019 survey[a] (reduced from 1% in 2007)	
Program for Health Care of Elderly (2010) Goal: To provide comprehensive health care to senior citizens at all health facilities -Prioritize women	-Clinics for elderly to build specialized care capacity for elderly needs and services -Counseling for healthy aging	-640 district hospitals with geriatric clinics -18 tertiary care geriatric centers operationalized		

(continues)

Table 19-3 Public Health Programs, Progress, and Related SDG Targets for 2030[a] *(continued)*

Program[a,b]	Key Strategies/Goals[a,b]	Program Performance[a,b]	Population-Based Outcomes[c,d] (Current and Comparator), Based on National Surveys/ Other Sources per Footnotes	Related SDG Target for 2030[b,d]
Emergency/Disaster Response				
Disaster Management Cell of Government of India, state disaster cells, Indian Red Cross Society (IRCS), and St John Ambulance India	-Disaster recognition and early warning systems fueled by scientific agencies of government -Training and certification of a pan-India brigade of volunteers in first aid, home nursing, hygiene and sanitation in disasters, etc. by IRCS for widespread, rapid deployment in disasters -Operational mitigation efforts by coordinated actions of central/state governments and IRCS and St John Ambulance, supplemented by army personnel	-All four major cyclonic storms (2022 and 2023) with accurate advance warnings, timely evacuations, quick response teams in flooding disasters, preventing many deaths and injuries -Quick response and containment of mpox and Zika outbreaks, avian flu outbreak, COVID-19 pandemic, minimizing deaths in India versus developed countries	-Zero to single-digit deaths in all major cyclones and floods as of 2022, compared with hundreds to thousands of deaths in prior events of similar or lower strength	Significantly reduce disaster-related deaths and limit affected people
Affordable Care Access for All for Catastrophic Care Needs				
Ayushman Bharat PM Jan Arogya Yojana (PM-JAY)—social health insurance scheme	-Social health insurance for bottom 2 quintiles of population (Rs 5 lakh coverage per family for inpatient, pre-inpatient, and follow-up care) -Empanel a dispersed network of authorized, good-quality hospitals (public and private) -Subsidize essential drugs at very low out-of-pocket copayments, dispensed at HWCs and public institutions -Administered digitally via secure information exchange systems	-214.9 million PM-JAY cards issued via outreach by health workers and ASHAs (target 500 million) -28,225 hospitals empaneled -447.7 million admissions at 15,512 hospitals; most common general medical and febrile illness, including dengue, dialysis	-% covered by any health insurance: 41% (31% U, 42% R)****	Universal care access including financial risk protection for catastrophic illness, and affordable essential drugs

Program[a,b]	Key Strategies/Goals[a,b]	Program Performance[a,b]	Population-Based Outcomes[c,d] (Current and Comparator), Based on National Surveys/ Other Sources per Footnotes	Related SDG Target for 2030[b,d]
Health System Strengthening and Infrastructure Program				
Accredited Social and Health Activists (ASHA) Program under National Health Mission (since 2006) Link workers between community and health system in every village, hamlet, and lower socioeconomic status neighborhoods of town/city; paid by performance-linked incentives, not salary	-Trained and certified health volunteers paid by performance-linked incentives for MCH, including navigation of pregnant women to HWCs and 24/7 delivery facilities for prenatal care, delivery, postpartum care, other primary care navigation, COVID-19 contact tracing	-1.05 million trained ASHAs provided basic drug kits, navigating and educating community members for care of all programs	-ASHAs available in every village and slums of every city and town	Achieve access to quality essential healthcare services
National Urban Health Mission (2013)	-Replicate rural primary care infrastructure, ASHA system, all other programs	-1,632 cities covered -4,698 HWCs staffed and functioning		
Ayushman Bharat (2018) Three components: -Universal access to health and wellness care facilities including 24/7 emergency and referral care access -E-Sanjeevini (telehealth for specialty care)	-Upgrade PHCs/SCs to health and wellness centers (HWC) -HWC nodal facility (24/7 HWC) for population-wide free care of all conditions, communicable, MCH, family planning, noncommunicable diseases -Telemedicine infrastructure at spokes and hubs	As of 2022, -154,070 HWCs operational -11,119 designated 24/7 HWCs at PHCs) -3,117 24/7 referral care centers for MCH -88.4 million specialist teleconsultations (via 112,137 spokes connected to 15,093 specialists (hubs)) -Essential drugs ensured		

(continues)

Table 19-3 Public Health Programs, Progress, and Related SDG Targets for 2030[a] *(continued)*

Program[a,b]	Key Strategies/Goals[a,b]	Program Performance[a,b]	Population-Based Outcomes[c,d] (Current and Comparator), Based on National Surveys/ Other Sources per Footnotes	Related SDG Target for 2030[b,d]
Ensuring Access to Quality Health Care				
National Quality Assurance Standards program for district hospitals (2013), National Quality Certification for PHC and CHCs (2021)[a]	-NQAS launched for district hospitals -Extended to all government public health facilities -Accreditation system per International Society for Quality in Health Care	-3,415 public health facilities achieved National Quality Certification, 2022 -304 district hospitals HQAS certified[a]	-Population-level outcomes not assessed	Access to quality essential healthcare services for all
LaQshya certification: Ensure quality standards in childbirth and post-delivery care in labor room and cesarean delivery care in high case load facilities (2017)[a]	-Targeted approach to strengthen key processes in care in labor rooms and maternity operating theaters with high case loads (medical college hospitals, district hospitals, and maternity care-designated CHCs)	-596 labor rooms certified by 2022 -474 maternity operating theaters certified[a]	-Population-level outcomes not measured	
Patient feedback portal (Mera-Aspatal: My Hospital), 2016 Goal: Promote people-centered service delivery, patient satisfaction with care quality	-All government healthcare facilities and district hospitals to be covered -Publicly available hospital quality data -Data monitored by state and central government to assess people-centeredness	-11,484 facilities integrated into portal for patient feedback by 2022	-No data on portal use and outcome measures	
PM Swasthya Suraksha Yojana (recent program)	Affordable tertiary medical care in underserved areas through new medical education and research facilities	-Tertiary care national medical institutes in underdeveloped regions in progress	-In progress	

Program[a,b]	Key Strategies/Goals[a,b]	Program Performance[a,b]	Population-Based Outcomes[c,d] (Current and Comparator), Based on National Surveys/ Other Sources per Footnotes	Related SDG Target for 2030[b,d]
Health-Impacting Living Infrastructure (Household (HH)-Targeted Programs)				
Household sanitary latrines (Swachh Bharat Mission) Goal: Open Defecation-free India (ODF) by October 2, 2019	-HH-level subsidy (Rs 12,000) to build toilets plus water storage facility for hygiene -Target: all households without toilet) -Implemented by states, panchayats	-109 million individual household latrines by 2020**** -All villages certified ODF-free by panchayats, October 2, 2019 (led to Jal Jeevan Mission).	-% households with own sanitary latrine: 69.3% (81% urban, 64% rural)* -% HH shared latrine: 8.4% (11% urban, 7% rural)* -% open defecation: 19.4%*	Universal access to hygienic sanitation for all; end open defecation
Jal Jeevan Mission Har Ghar Jal (launched August 2019) Goal: Universal access to improved/safe drinking water Goal: Piped water supply to every household by 2024	-Goal: Piped water to 190 million rural households by 2024 -Improve water supply source (tube well, public taps, or tanker supply in severe scarcity areas) for all	-50 million rural households newly provided tap connection by 2022[d] -0% rural HH given tap connection including those awaiting pumped water: 42.5%[d]	-% with improved safe water source: 96% (99% U, 95% R)* (60.3% by April 2023)[g] -% HH with inhouse tap water: 33% (54% U; 23% R)* -% accessing water from HH or public tap: 47%*	Universal and equitable access to safe and affordable drinking water
PM Awas Yoyana (Affordable robust, basic housing for all program)	-Provide subsidy or interest-free loan or combination, for improved house construction with basic amenities for all without a robust house in urban and rural areas	-11.8 million housing units approved and subsidy/credit disbursed (0.982 billion USD budgeted) -7.5 million houses completed	-% report living in improved housing: 94.1% (98% urban, 92% rural)*	End multidimensional poverty, one measure being resilient housing
Universal electricity access	-Expanding electricity networks and infrastructure, increased electricity generation to meet expanded need	-Every village connected to electricity infrastructure by 2021	-% households with electricity: 96.5% (99% urban, 95.3% rural)*	Universal access to electricity by 2030 (Goal 7)

(continues)

Table 19-3 Public Health Programs, Progress, and Related SDG Targets for 2030[a] *(continued)*

Program[a,b]	Key Strategies/Goals[a,b]	Program Performance[a,b]	Population-Based Outcomes[c,d] (Current and Comparator), Based on National Surveys/ Other Sources per Footnotes	Related SDG Target for 2030[b,d]
Health-Impacting Living Infrastructure (Household (HH)-Targeted Programs)				
Air pollution -Universal clean cooking fuel access -Phase out fossil fuel–generated electricity -Reduce population electricity needs	-Provide all households using fossil fuel sources for cooking, free natural gas cylinders and stoves -Subsidized recurring refills for poor -Renewable energy sources -Green fuels for vehicles -Free LED light bulbs for poor	-119 million households (595 million population) given cooking gas cylinders -44% of electricity generated nationally from non-fossil fuel sources -Target: 20% ethanol blended gasoline by end of 2023 (12% in 2022)	-% population using clean cooking fuels: 58.6% (89.7% urban, 43.2% rural)*	-Reduce substantially deaths and illnesses from air pollution -Affordable sustainable modern energy for all

ANC: antenatal care.

[a]Program information, performance data, and outcome data are extracted from the 2022–2023 Annual Report of the Department of Health and Family Welfare of the Government of India (unless otherwise stated). See Reference 11 for full citation.

[b]Government of India, Department of Health and Family Welfare. 2022: Health and Family Welfare Statistics 2021–2022.

[c]Annual Health Report 2021–2022, Ministry of Health and Family Welfare cited in National Health Profile, 2022. (See Reference 17).

[d]Government of India, Ministry of Statistics and Program Implementation, National Statistical Office. Sustainable Development Goals National Indicator Framework Progress Report 2020.

[e]World Health Organization. World Malaria Report 2022.

[f]Central Intelligence Agency. 2023. The World Factbook: India. Accessed July 27, 2023. https://www.cia.gov/the-world-factbook/countries/india/#people-and-society.

[g]Government of India, Jal Jeevan Mission. Jal Jeevan Mission dashboard. Accessed April 11, 2023. https://ejalshakti.gov.in/jjmreport/JJMIndia.aspx.

*National Family Health Survey-5 in 2019–2021, by International Institute of Population Sciences, Mumbai (interrupted in 2020 by COVID-19 lockdowns).

**National Family Health Survey-4 in 2015–2016.

***Registrar-General of India, Ministry of Home Affairs, cited in 2022–2023 Annual Report, Department of Health and Family Welfare, Ministry of Health and Family Welfare, Government of India.

****Data from three rounds of National Annual Rural Sanitation Survey, 2017–2018 to 2019–2020 by independent agency with World Bank support.

[i]Unless referenced otherwise, data on the programs and rates of vector-borne diseases are from Directorate of Vector-borne Disease Control Program, Directorate General of Health and Family Welfare, Government of India, as cited in the 2022–2023 Annual Report of the Department of Health and Family Welfare, or the Health and Family Welfare Statistics 2019–2020, Government of India;

Note: Deafness, fluorosis, oral health, trauma and burn injuries, organ transplant programs are not shown due to being recently launched programs or no population-based data available.

Health Expenditures

The estimated total per capita expenditure on health (public and private spending combined) in 2019 was $196 USD in India.[21] According to National Health Account estimates (based on the WHO-developed accounting framework using the internationally accepted system of health accounts), the total health expenditures amounted to 3.2% of GDP, with 1.35% being contributed by the government, (increased from 1.13% of GDP spent by the government on health in 2014–2015.[22] Government health expenditures as a proportion of total government expenditures also increased from 3.94% in 2014–2015 to 5.02% in 2019–2020. Furthermore, within the government health expenditure, the share of spending on primary healthcare services increased to 55.9%, up from 51.3% in 2014–2015, in a much-expanded health budget due to government spending on secondary-level health services under PM-JAY.

Out-of-pocket expenditures by households amounted to 47.1% of the total health expenditures in 2019–2020 compared with 62.6% in 2014–2015 and 69.5% in 2012, consistent with the large increase in risk coverage for the lowest two quintiles of the population via the PM-JAY program.[7,17,22] The share devoted to social health insurance–funded health expenditures out of the total healthcare expenditures (including government-funded health insurance, medical reimbursement to government employees, and industry/employer-funded health insurance programs increased) from 5.7% in 2014–2015 to 9.3% in 2019–2020. During this period, private-sector employer-funded care increased from 3.7% of total health expenditures in 2014–2015 to 7% in 2019–2020. Altogether, health insurance–funded expenditures (public insurance and employer-sponsored care) amounted to 16.3% of the total health expenditures, including public health program expenditures, infrastructure expenditures, and personal healthcare services.

These improvements in the population's burden of healthcare costs are reflected in the substantial reductions in self-reported financial burden for services in the National Family Health Survey 5 (2019–2021) compared with NFHS 4.[14,23,24] Another notable development is evidence of pulling away from a typical low-income country feature, the share of external/international donor funding: It accounted for 0.5% of the total health expenditures in 2019–2021, less than the reported 0.7% in 2015–2016.[22] Given the legal requirement that 1% of corporate profits of large corporations are to be spent on tangible community development and social causes (corporate social responsibility), 7.6% of India's 2019–2020 health expenditures were contributed by enterprises, nongovernment organizations, and domestic donors (6.9% in 2014–2015).[22]

Performance of the Healthcare System

Major Public Health Problems, Control Programs, and Progress Relative to Targets

Table 19-3 shows that all major communicable diseases except dengue and chikungunya fever have declined steeply in India. Malaria cases diagnosed declined to 160,000 cases in 2021 (compared with 880,000 in 2013), and malaria deaths decreased to 77 (from 440 in 2013).[7,25] This is attributable to aggressive malaria control and public health vigilance measures as well as accountability of personnel at the grassroots level owing to the growing political pressures of competitive electoral politics among the various political parties. These dynamics have been reinforced by a highly competitive mass-media environment in which the media seek out and showcase government failures in print and on web-based platforms to increase their customer base. A major extra-programmatic reason enabling achievement of malaria elimination status is the government's mission-driven programs to achieve last-mile, last-household outreach to provide subsidies for household infrastructure programs—for example, in-house sanitary latrines, piped water supply, and robust housing (see the section on health-impacting living infrastructure in Table 19-3). These programs interrupt human–vector contact opportunities and reduce disease transmission. In turn, these infrastructure programs have been successful because of the direct cash (subsidy) transfers to beneficiaries without middlemen, enabled by the Jan Dhan program (universal access to personal bank accounts regardless of education or residence status). Digital payments bypass the traditional routes of fund transfers through middlemen (local government officials and political leaders), which fueled massive corruption leakages of subsidy funds. Over 330 million new bank/post office savings accounts were established for the lowest-income segment of the Indian population.[26] This segment is the most targeted population for the household infrastructure programs. The collateral health benefits achieved through the control of vector-borne (predominantly), rural health problems, malaria, leishmaniasis (kala azar), and filariasis are noteworthy.

Tuberculosis and leprosy have also shown rapid declines. The current TB incidence, 172/100,000 population in 2022, represents a reduction by over half from the 2010 rate, 400/100,000 sputum-positive new cases diagnosed annually.[7,27,28] TB deaths have been drastically reduced to 37/100,000 diagnosed TB cases.[27] Leprosy cases have been reduced by half since 2014–2015, with 65,147 new cases detected during 2020–2021, and only 2.48% of new cases diagnosed with Grade II deformity or higher, a halving of the deformity rate since 2014–2015.[7] This indicates earlier diagnosis has been occurring in recent years—that is, before deformity sets in. The mechanism of achieving these population-based changes is borne out of program management changes over time. Since 1983, despite adoption of multidrug therapy for leprosy under the National Leprosy Eradication Program, the results had remained lackluster until the recent acceleration of implementation momentum by both the central and state governments. A key central government strategy has been to shine the light on poorly performing endemic districts (naming and shaming) at regular virtual meetings with state governments. Concomitantly, the government has invested in governance rigor, developing granular metrics of program implementation and holding state governments accountable for results. This strategy causes state officials to, in turn, follow through with field public health personnel. As a result, leprosy cases have rapidly declined, reflected in the child infection rate, deformity rate, and cumulative number of chronic cases, setting the stage for leprosy eradication.

Diarrheal disease among under-5 children has also declined, with 7.3% of households with an under-5 child reporting the child suffered from a diarrheal episode in the preceding 2 weeks, per the National Family Health Survey-5.[23] As with malaria control, diarrheal disease control owes as much to the diarrheal disease program efforts as to safe water, household sanitary latrines, and housing infrastructure program coverage of the poorest of urban and rural households.

Dengue fever is particularly prevalent in urban areas of India, and has now replaced malaria as the major communicable disease of concern. Dengue hemorrhagic fever carries a significant mortality risk, especially among children. Mosquito control is a far more difficult challenge in urban areas than in rural areas. The number of cases has shown regular seasonal surges with little sign of a decline. However, multiple programs operating in tandem have enabled a rapid decline in dengue deaths—the PM-JAY program (health insurance for low-income population), nationwide strengthening of the blood banking system, and active public health monitoring of detected dengue cases in the transmission season.

HIV control has been a success story, showing a stable, cumulative number of persons living with HIV (PLHIV), despite near doubling of the young adult population in the recent decade, and despite the addition of newly diagnosed cases to the large number of HIV-undetectable PLHIV accumulated from earlier infections due to the success of the ART program. The nationwide HIV-positivity rate is currently less than 0.2% among the 15–49 age group, and the cumulative number of PLHIV was estimated at 2.4 million in 2021.[7] The 2005–2006 NFHS survey had reported near universal awareness of the major routes of HIV transmission and prevention.[24]

Maternal and child health has also improved substantially in recent years. In the NFHS-5, 58% of mothers with a live birth had completed at least four antenatal visits. The Janani Suraksha Yojana (JSY; Mothers Protection Program) offers all pregnant women a Mother and Child Protection card. This card entitles pregnant women to personalized navigation to institutional antenatal care and delivery at a private or government health facility by designated ASHAs. As explained earlier, ASHAs are village- or neighborhood-level female auxiliary health volunteers who seek to enroll and retain pregnant women in antenatal care throughout pregnancy, connect every pregnant woman with a delivery facility (including navigation to specialized obstetric/newborn care facilities for high-risk pregnancies), personally arrange to transport the mother to the appropriate facility for delivery, and track the infant's well-baby visits to ensure receipt of all eligible services up to 5 years of age. Each rural mother who delivers at an institution is provided with cash assistance for her postpartum nutritional needs (remitted directly via digital funds transfer by the government to her bank or post office savings account). Private health facilities and both government and private doctors are reimbursed fixed service charges for providing care to women with the card, causing government and private providers to compete for clientele by providing high-quality care and culturally sensitive care.

The multifaceted components of JSY and the Mother and Child Tracking program have together resulted in rapid improvements in the MCH indicators as shown by population-based surveys in recent years. The rates of institutional deliveries and prenatal care had doubled in 2019–2021 compared with 2014–2015.[14,23] Heightened follow-up of newborns and infants for postnatal follow-up services through the ASHA program is reflected in several child health indicators, including timely immunization and mortality. The services are documented to have reached the most underserved sections of the population and the poorest states,[23] and the program success is reflected in population health outcomes. Immunization coverage for the full number of doses by the age of 12 to 23 months with all 11 recommended vaccines has increased to 83.8%,[23] compared with 61% coverage with the eight vaccines that were implemented in the national immunization program in 2009.[14] Contraception prevalence among age-eligible couples is also very high, at 66% (increased from 54% in 2013 before the JSY program).[7] Contraception prevalence is an information-rich indicator, reflecting confidence of families in the survival of their children, which in turn reflects the success of maternal, newborn, and child health programs. On another note, the high contraception prevalence reflects improvements in contraception rates among traditionally resistant population subgroups, as well as increased acceptability of child spacing methods among all subgroups. Consequently, total fertility declined from 2.4 per woman in 2013 to 2.0 in 2019–2020.[29] Maternal mortality has also declined rapidly since JSY program implementation. Maternal mortality was 540 deaths per 100,000 live births in the 1990s, 212 in 2007, and 167 in 2013 due to various government programs, notably the National Rural Health Mission and the ASHA program.[7] The maternal mortality rate was nearly halved to 97 in 2020 following implementation of the JSY program.

Nutritional deficiencies have been resistant to programmatic efforts thus far. Regarding protein-energy malnutrition, 35.5% of under-5 children were stunted in 2019–2021, and 19.3% showed wasting, similar to the 2015–2016 NFHS-4 survey rates.[7,14,23] Underweight status declined by about 25% (from 42.5% to 32.1%).[7] While survey data suggest that anemia prevalence rates have been largely stagnant since 2013, recent scientific studies have questioned the measurement validity of the benchmarks established many decades ago by the WHO; those benchmarks were based on studies of adult White males, who have since been shown to greatly vary from children and women in regard to the anemia thresholds.[30] Another complicating issue is the use of variations in blood sample drawing methods (venous blood versus pin-prick capillary blood). Experts question the validity of the observed "stable and high" anemia rates among under-5 children and women in India on these grounds. Anemia rates based on the finger prick method were reported as 67.1% among children 6 months to 5 years in 2019–2021 (per the NFHS-5), and 57.0% among women aged 15–49 years,[23] although interpretation of these rates remains uncertain in light of the measurement validity issues. The rate of severe anemia among women, 1.8%, has shown a decline.

Concurrently with the receding rates of communicable diseases, noncommunicable diseases have rapidly increased, requiring costly secondary and tertiary care. The key diseases of program focus are high blood pressure, cardiovascular disease, mental illness, diabetes, and cancer. Cardiovascular disease is a major silent killer, causing 25% of deaths among adults in the 30- to 50-year-old group. Bronchial asthma affects an estimated 15–20 million (about 1.5% of population). The estimated cancer burden for 2021 was 26.7 million disability-adjusted life-years (DALY) lost after adjusting mortality to the incidence rate (AMI) and is expected to increase to 29.8 million in 2025.[31] The highest cancer burden was in the northern states (2,408 DALYs AMI per 100,000) and northeastern states (2,177 DALYs AMI per 100,000), with this burden also being higher among males. More than 40% of the total cancer burden was due to seven cancers: lung (10.6%), breast (10.5%), esophagus (5.8%), mouth (5.7%), stomach (5.2%), liver (4.6%), and cervix uteri (4.3%). While population-based survey data on mental health are not available, the WHO estimates a mental health burden of 2,443 DALYs per 100,000 population, an age-adjusted suicide rate of 21.1 per 100,000, and a productivity loss of $1.03 trillion USD between 2012 and 2030 due to mental illness.[32]

Interconnectedness of Health and Infrastructure Programs

Based on key highlights of Table 19-3, this section summarizes the interconnectedness of several public health programs and the integrated service delivery approach, which together explain the rapid health improvements achieved in the past decade. Because many diseases and poor health status have multifactorial antecedents, integrating service delivery across programs improves program efficiencies as well as coverage (e.g., maternal and child health programs). Review of Table 19-3 suggests that success in certain programs cascades to multiple programs because of performance multiplier effects on related programs.

Control of communicable diseases has been significantly accelerated in the last decade. The multifaceted components of JSY, the Mother and Child

Table 19-4 Trends in Key Population Health Status Indicators

Indicator	1951 (Around Independence)	2001	2015	2020
Crude birth rate (per 1,000 population)	40.8	25.4	20.8	19.5
Crude death rate (per 1,000 population)	25.1	8.4	6.5	6.0
Total fertility rate (per woman)	6.0	3.1	2.3	2.0
Maternal mortality ratio (per 100,000 live births)	NA	301	130	97
Neonatal mortality rate (per 1,000 births)	NA	40	25	20
Under-5 mortality rate	NA	NA	43	32
Infant mortality rate (per 1,000 live births)	NA	68 (1998-1999, NFHS2)	40 (2013)	28.1
Life expectancy at birth	-	63.4	69	70 (2016–2020)

Data from Office of the Registrar-General of India, Ministry of Home Affairs, cited in 2022–2023 Annual Report, Department of Health and Family Welfare, Ministry of Health and Family Welfare, Government of India.

Tracking program, and community-based ASHAs carrying the benefits of MCH programs to the people, have together brought about rapid improvements in mothers' and children's health. Reductions in many communicable diseases can be tracked to rapid reductions in poverty and household infrastructure deprivations, as noted in the section on macroeconomics. Furthermore, the policies and investments to accelerate performance under the disease control programs, and to improve household living infrastructure, were complemented by improved performance in related areas. There was accelerated expansion of secondary- and tertiary-level healthcare facilities in rural and urban areas, as described in the section on the healthcare system's incentivization of mission-critical health personnel to remain available in rural areas via the PM-JAY program and the ASHA scheme under the National Rural Health Mission. These multifactorial improvements could rapidly reduce communicable disease incidence, in several cases, to the point of eradication or elimination phase. Concurrent expansion of financial access to acute inpatient care and chronic disease complications for the lower two socioeconomic status population quintiles, about 500 million people, via the PM-JAY program has instilled confidence in this population to seek care when they fall ill, and to feel confident about their health and future.

The convergence of programs that directly or indirectly seek to improve the population's health is reflected in substantial reductions in communicable disease deaths. In 2011–2012, 65% of all deaths were caused by communicable diseases and 35% by noncommunicable diseases. By 2023, the ratio was reversed: 65% of deaths were caused by NCDs and 35% by communicable diseases. Finally, confidence and access to child healthcare services has increased families' confidence about the survival and prospects of their children. **Table 19-4** shows considerable declines have occurred in the crude death rate since 2011–2012, neonatal mortality and under-5 mortality, and the total fertility rate.

Achieving the SDGs: What It Takes, the Lessons Learned

Given India's immense ethnic, religious, and socioeconomic diversity across over an enormous population (more than 1.25 billion) in 2014, and a political system that appeared doomed to a development stalemate due to political and governance dysfunction, the prospects for progress on the SDGs initially appeared grim. A core condition for SDG achievement is inclusive growth and health development. There were an estimated 407 million people living in multidimensional poverty in 2013, as defined by the United Nations' SDGs document.[33,34] Inclusivity of this magnitude of population was nowhere in sight, due to structurally ingrained dynamics of the political ecosystem—poor governance, pervasive corruption, the politician–bureaucrat–criminal nexus, and the near-absence of accountability and rule of law despite the multitude of laws on the books and the nominal presence of a legal justice system. The following analysis of programs and outcomes includes lessons learned on the how and why of the transformational changes described in Table 19-3, and highlights the innovative sequencing of strategies to maximize the last-mile, last-person reach of programs.

A Break in the Development Stalemate

Since 2014, a turnaround has been engineered by a performance-tested and democratically elected political coalition of parties with a strong parliamentary majority, reinforced by an executive branch with an unprecedented mission and vision orientation, along with the skills needed to use data-driven approaches to development. These developments enabled the country to rise from the rock bottom "fragile five countries of serious concern" in 2009–2013 to become the world's fifth-largest economy (rising from the 11th position, unseating the United Kingdom), with a GDP of $3.5 trillion USD in FY2022–2023, which has grown by more than 66% since 2013–2014.[35–37] Along the way, India has also overcome the crippling disruptions of the COVID-19 pandemic and the Russia–Ukraine war.

Inclusivity as a Strategic Tool of Macroeconomic Growth

Inclusivity has been a central part of the macroeconomic and health development story. Partly in response to limited international capital investment in the Indian economy early on, the administration opted to promote grassroots, individual enterprise as the engine of economic growth and employment generation. Policies were designed to facilitate and financially support the emergence and growth of medium, small, and micro enterprises (MSME). The rationale was that pending the establishment of new industries and the growth of large industries to employ the increasing youth population, suitable initiatives could enable large masses of the population to find their niche in the economy and become micro-engines of bottom-up growth. One of many programs was the Self-Help Group program launched in 2014 to provide bank credit linkage for small groups to start enterprises in rural and urban poor areas. By 2018–2019, 2.7 million Self Help Groups were formed and assisting individuals in setting up income-generating enterprises.[38] The credit and outstanding dues reports under this program indicate that these investments have stimulated microenterprise activity and success. The policy emphasis on MSME signified a fundamental shift in national growth. As a side effect, its success has deflated a key dysfunctional dynamic of competitive democratic politics—namely, the go-to strategy of political parties in which they wooed the electorate through fantasy promises of government job creation, cash handouts, and free services (e.g., electricity). In this dynamic, political parties groomed the population to adopt a passive and dependent mindset, expecting easy government jobs and handouts as their right, in exchange for votes.

In the new model, the government has focused on playing the role of a facilitator of the inherent enterprising spirit at the grassroots, by formulating and implementing policies to improve the ease of doing business, investing in public infrastructure (which generated jobs), and bridging logistical gaps to facilitate horizontal and vertical integration of production and marketing processes. Strategies included public infrastructure investments (highways, ports, railways, etc., and cross-linkages between these modalities), ease of access to enterprise financing and start-up capital for the poorest people, legislative action to remove legal hurdles and bureaucratic control systems that served to grease the wheels of corruption and frustrate individual entrepreneurship, and creation of new institutional support systems to facilitate the efficiency and productivity of micro-scale producers in all arenas of economic activity—ranging from farming and allied trades to fishing, street vending, and first-generation entrepreneurship. Underpinning these programs was the Jan Dhan Yojana program, which ensured financial and banking inclusivity for all segments of the population, including those who were illiterate. This program provided over 330 million hitherto excluded people with cost-free bank accounts, using outreach programs to actively recruit them and prioritizing women. Bank accounts and the resulting financial literacy empowered large segments of the deprived population to receive in full all government cash benefits under welfare programs, provided access to apply for and receive micro-loans, and fostered a "can-do" spirit of self-reliance and entrepreneurship. These strategies aggregated the impact of the individual enterprises started by hundreds of millions of newly empowered poor people to feed the macroeconomy, which fueled the funding for ambitious health programs.

Prerequisites for Accurate Targeting of Inclusive Social Benefit and Economic Programs

Targeting of benefits and minimizing corrupt diversion of funds has critically depended on the enforcement of a national citizens' identity system regardless of literacy status (the Aadhar unique identification system). This system is used to define the financial and civic identity of citizens, and is mandatory for participation in all economic activities. Another major pillar of growth has been transformation of the banking and benefit program ecosystem by migrating all transactions to digital platforms. This step has preempted politician-government officials from corrupt diversion of funds meant for beneficiaries. Digital banking and disbursement also increased the feasibility and permanence of the infrastructure financed under capital-intensive benefit programs, especially household infrastructure programs (sanitary latrines, household-level tap water connections, clean cooking fuel access, and subsidized housing). Because subsidies and credit for these programs (based on household income) were digitally devolved directly to beneficiaries' bank accounts, the funds were prudently used by beneficiaries and generated a sense of asset ownership of the created infrastructure, spurring them to create high-quality assets, and appropriately use and maintain the facilities constructed. This may explain why the government spending has translated into a commensurate reduction in multidimensional poverty and sustained progress on the population-level health indicators and SDG achievement (Table 19-3). Compared with prior decades' free government housing schemes and the government-constructed latrines and water facilities, the current round of household-driven infrastructure development appears to have created durable assets that are actually being used, per the National Family Health Survey 5.[23]

Resource Generation Reforms: Innovation and Digitization

Paralleling the gains in inclusivity, a critical success story is the generation of financial resources (tax resources) to fund these programs for India's billion-plus population. To this end, the government started its first administration stint with reforms to rid the taxation system and tax collection systems of legacy practices and legal mechanisms that promoted obfuscation, corruption, and cover for such practices. The key was to migrate all relevant government financial institutions and tax administration systems to digital platforms and to establish a system of trackable and traceable transactions to ensure public official accountability and a system-enforced fidelity to rules- and norm-driven decision making. Reforms to introduce digital governance and tax/tax collection reforms enabled more than tripling of the central government budget for 2023–2024 over 2013–2014,[39,40] and is reflected in better reach of government health facilities (8.2% increase in the number of subcenters, 7.3% increase in PHCs, and 64% increase in CHCs).[7] The functionality of preexisting health facility buildings also increased with funded personnel positions, new equipment, essential drugs, and consumables. Finally, spending on the PM-JAY program contributed to greater care productivity of these institutions by supporting healthcare purchasing power among the poorest quintiles through the social health insurance cards. The net outcome of reforms has been an increase of approximately 50% to 55% in the number of doctors and health workers at PHCs, CHCs, and subcenters from 2005 to 2022.[7]

Impacts of Inclusive Development and Resource Generation Reforms on the SDGs

The inclusive strategies implemented in both the systemic economic policies and the benefit programs for households are reflected in the population-reported indicators in population surveys. There has been a steady reduction in the number living in poverty—270 million lifted out of poverty by 2018–2019 (defined as living on less than $1.90 USD a day per capita at 2006–2015 prices), and an additional 135 million lifted by 2022, with the poverty achievements being sustained despite the massive disruptions of the COVID-19 pandemic and the Russia–Ukraine war.[33,41] Convergence of the inclusive social benefit programs, household infrastructure programs, and economic policies for the target population has produced grassroots change, as reflected in the aggregate, national multidimensional poverty index (MPI) score, rural–urban comparisons of the MPI decline, and rich–poor state comparisons.

The United Nations Development Program's composite measure of family-level multidimensional poverty incorporates several SDGs into the Multidimensional Poverty Index (MDPI) of deprivation based on the following criteria: access to sanitary latrines with associated water needs, household-level access to improved source of safe potable water, access to clean cooking fuel, social health insurance for referral hospital care, and improved (liveable) housing.[33] The MDPI accounts for deprivations based on household per capita income (below $1.90 USD), adverse living conditions (lack of access to clean and piped water, sanitation, and clean cooking fuel, and a dwelling that is unsafe/disease promoting), malnourished children in the household, and lack of primary education.

A household is defined as MDPI poor if its deprivation score exceeds the poverty cutoff of 33%.[38]

The prevalence of MDPI-poor fell from 32.6% in rural areas in 2015–2016 (based on NFHS-4)[14] to 19.3% in 2019–2021 (NFHS 5),[23] and in urban areas from 8.7% to 5.3%, with an estimated 135 million people exiting multidimensional poverty during this period.[38,42] Additionally, among the states, those with the highest sustained poverty rates since independence recorded the steepest decline.[38] Leading international economic experts and the UN agencies have noted the key role of political stability, visionary leadership, and a competent executive branch heading the central government in these achievements.

In summary, the serendipitous emergence of a robust political force with wide and deep roots of grassroots cadres of workers, led by a visionary and mission-driven competent leadership team, was able to overcome the dysfunctional dynamics of democratic systems that are pervasive in the developing world, to succeed at the task of inclusive development of a half-billion-strong left-behind population in India. These factors enabled large-scale implementation of innovative policies in all functional areas of governance, and helped a massive 400 million-plus population to rise to above the poverty level, 134 million to exit multidimensional poverty, and the country to achieve 66% of the SDG-2030 goal levels by 2022–2023.[38,43]

Future Prospects and Challenges to Sustain the Growth Momentum

The outlook for a continuing development trajectory and citizen-responsive governance remains generally favorable, even if unfavorable changes emerge in political leadership—an ever-present risk in a democracy. This is because many foundational reforms may not be reversible, such as the digital transformation of government business, the uniform national identity system based on biometric identification that underpins civic benefits, and a population (electorate) that has tasted transparency and accountability in governance and benefit administration. These transformations may minimize the likelihood of a return to the governance nadir seen in prior decades.

Certain structural challenges to health development have persisted. One challenge is the scarcity of doctors and nursing personnel in rural and tribal areas, which has defied solutions due to fundamental quality-of-life issues in rural areas. Another challenge that is being addressed gradually is the personal safety jeopardy of government personnel in violence-infested regions that are home to political anarchist forces such as violent and radical groups. Metropolitan areas and larger district headquarters towns continue to remain the star attraction for health and medical professionals. Current vacancy rates are 24% for PHC physician positions, 14% for female health workers/ANMs, and 40% for male health workers. Vacancy rates in rural CHCs for specialist positions are very high, ranging from 63% for ob/gyns to 72% for surgeons.

Other challenges include (1) inconsistent on-site availability of posted physicians and support personnel at PHCs and specialists at CHCs; (2) demands for informal payments in many government facilities, particularly in states having this long-standing practice; (3) private practice (moonlighting) by government doctors; (4) high rates of NCDs among all socioeconomic quintiles in light of increasing personal incomes; (5) challenges to NCD control due to the overwhelming role of risk factors involving personal lifestyle choices in these diseases; (6) uncertainties of political leadership continuity, especially in light of social media– and electronic news–driven misinformation that is eagerly harnessed by self-serving politicians chomping at the bit to return to power; and (7) politically driven polarization of the population for electoral ends due to the diminishing potential of economic development benefits to mobilize the electorate with increasing prosperity.

COVID-19 Pandemic

In India, a total of 4.4145 million confirmed COVID-19 cases had been documented as of January 3, 2023, with 530,707 deaths documented as COVID-19 deaths.[7] The volume of cases and deaths per million population and case fatality rate in India have been far lower than in other similarly affected countries, notably the United States and European countries. The COVID-19 trajectory, which was characterized by waves of ascending and declining rates up to July 2022, has since registered a sustained and significant decline that remains sustained to date. The potential for very high ravages in the population in the early months since March 2020 was greatly mitigated by the leadership's inspired total national lockdown of population movements (voluntarily complied with by most of the population) from March to June 2020, followed by gradual easing of lockdown, which resulted in a major first wave from July 2020 through November 2020. This was followed by focal lockdowns on and off until the end of 2021. The total death toll was disputed, with wildly varying estimates of deaths in various quarters, citing the lack of a universal coverage death registration system. A team of epidemiologists using assumptions based on anecdotal and media-driven reports projected a population-based estimate of 4.07 million COVID-19 deaths (95% CI 2.71–4.36) during 2020 and 2021.[44] Since this estimate was published, the Indian Registrar General's Sample Registration Scheme–based calculations have become available, based on the number of excess deaths in 2020 over 2019 (7.64 million total deaths in 2019 compared with 8.12 million in 2020). Comparison of estimated COVID-19 attributable deaths with the reported COVID-19 deaths by institutions verified the accuracy of the reported deaths.[45] Other programmatic factors support the validity of the number of reported COVID-19 deaths—severe morbidity and prolonged suffering of patients prior to death, which precludes patients staying home and dying without medical attention, and the central government's guarantee of reimbursement for care of all COVID-19 patients, which resulted in most cases with respiratory distress being hospitalized.

The COVID-19 pandemic was halted early on in India by mass vaccination with an indigenously developed effective vaccine provided at very low cost compared with Western country–developed vaccines. The earliest vaccinations commenced in January 2021, starting with healthcare workers including ASHAs and other public frontline responders, and then spread to the entire population, including booster doses offered free of cost. As of January 20, 2023, 2.213 billion doses had been administered, with coverage of 97% of the population older than 12 years with at least one dose, and 90% of the population covered with the required primary course of two doses.[7] Following vaccine coverage, COVID-19 cases and deaths declined precipitously, and there has been a minimal increase in cases and deaths following emergence of the omicron variant.

References

1. Government of India, National Commission on Population. 2020 population projections for India and states, 2011–36. Report of the Technical Group on Population Projections. Accessed July 25, 2023. https://main.mohfw.gov.in/sites/default/files/Population%20Projection%20Report%202011-2036%20-%20upload_compressed_0.pdf.
2. Central Intelligence Agency. 2023. The World Factbook India. Accessed July 27, 2023. https://www.cia.gov/the-world-factbook/countries/india/#people-and-society.
3. Government of India, Ministry of Home Affairs, Department of Official Language. Constitutional provisions. Accessed July 27, 2023. https://rajbhasha.gov.in/en/constitutional-provisions.
4. Lakshmikantham V. *The Origin of Human Past*. Mumbai, India: Bharatiya Vidya Bhavan Press; 1988.
5. Chari PS. Susruta and our heritage. *Indian J Plast Surg*. 2003;36:4-13.
6. Census of India 2011, National Population Register & Socio-economic and Caste Census. Accessed July 31, 2023. https://censusindia.gov.in.
7. Government of India, Department of Health and Family Welfare, Ministry of Health and Family Welfare. 2022–2023 annual report. Accessed July 19, 2023. https://main.mohfw.gov.in/sites/default/files/eng%201.pdf.
8. Government of India, Legislative Department. Constitution of India. Accessed July 15, 2023. https://legislative.gov.in/constitution-of-india/.
9. Government of India. 2020. Know India. Accessed August 1, 2023. https://knowindia.india.gov.in/profile/india-at-a-glance.php and https://knowindia.india.gov.in/states-uts/; https://knowindia.india.gov.in/districts/.
10. Government of India, Ministry of Statistics and Program Implementation. India GDP sector-wise 2021. *Statistics Times*. 2021. Accessed August 2, 2023. https://statisticstimes.com/economy/country/india-gdp-sectorwise.php.
11. United Nations Development Program. Multidimensional Poverty Index 2020: achieving the Sustainable Development Goals. 2023. Accessed July 10, 2023. https://reliefweb.int/report/world/multidimensional-poverty-index-2020-charting-pathways-out-multidimensional-poverty?gclid=EAIaIQobChMI9MGi1oOHgAMVzXxMCh3iaQv_EAAYAiAAEgIJwfD_BwE.
12. Government of India, Niti Aayog. National Multidimensional Poverty Index: 2023 final report. July 17, 2023. Accessed July 18, 2023. https://niti.gov.in/sites/default/files/2023-07/National-Multidimentional-Poverty-Index-2023-Final-17th-July.pdf.
13. United Nations. Transforming our world: the 2030 agenda for sustainable development. 2015. Accessed August 2, 2023. https://sdgs.un.org/2030agenda.
14. World Health Organization. 1978. Health for all by 2000. Accessed March 11, 2008. http://www.euro.who.int/AboutWHO/Policy/20010827_1.
15. Government of India, Department of School Education and Literacy. *Unified District Information System for Education Plus (UDISE+) 2021–22 on School Education in India and All India Survey on Higher Education (AISHE) 2021–2022*. 2022.
16. Government of India, Ministry of Health and Family Welfare. Rural health statistics 2021–22. Accessed July 23, 2023. https://main.mohfw.gov.in/sites/default/files/RHS%202021-22_2.pdf.
17. Government of India, Ministry of Health and Family Welfare. National health profile 2022. 2022. Accessed July 28, 2023. https://cbhidghs.mohfw.gov.in/WriteReadData/l892s/94203846761680514146.pdf.
18. Government of India, Ministry of Health and Family Welfare. *Rural Health Statistics 2014–2015*.

19. Government of India, Ministry of Labor and Employment, Employee's State Insurance Corporation coverage. Accessed July 15, 2023. https://www.esic.gov.in/coverage.
20. National Health Authority. Pradhan Mantri Jan Arogya Yojana (PM-JAY). Accessed March 15, 2023. https://pmjay.gov.in/about/pmjay.
21. World Bank IBRD. Current health expenditure per capita, PPP (current international $)—India. Accessed July 25, 2023. https://data.worldbank.org/indicator/SH.XPD.CHEX.PP.CD?locations=IN.
22. Government of India, Ministry of Health and Family Welfare. National health accounts estimates for India 2019–20. Press release. Accessed July 25, 2023. https://pib.gov.in/PressReleaseIframePage.aspx?PRID=1919582.
23. International Institute of Population Sciences. National Family Health Survey-5 in 2019–2021, Mumbai. 2023. (Survey interrupted in 2020 by COVID-19 pandemic.)
24. International Institute for Population Sciences and Macro International. National Family Health Survey—3, 2005–06: India: Volume I. Mumbai, India: IIPS. Accessed August 2, 2023. http://rchiips.org/nfhs/volume_1.shtml.
25. World Health Organization. World malaria report 2022. Accessed July 31, 2023. https://www.who.int/teams/global-malaria-programme/reports/world-malaria-report-2022.
26. Government of India, Department of Financial Services. Pradhan Mantri Jan Dhan Yojana progress report (financial and banking inclusivity program). Accessed July 25, 2023. https://www.pmjdy.gov.in/account.
27. Government of India, Ministry of Health and Family Welfare. India TB report 2023. Accessed August 1, 2023. https://tbcindia.gov.in/showfile.php?lid=3680.
28. Government of India, Ministry of Health and Family Welfare. *TB India 2015: Annual Status Report, Revised National Tuberculosis Control Programme, Central TB Division.*
29. Government of India, Department of Health and Family Welfare. *Health and Family Welfare Statistics 2021–22.* 2022.
30. Sachdev HS, Porwal A, Acharya R, et al. Haemoglobin thresholds to define anaemia in a national sample of healthy children and adolescents aged 1–19 years in India: a population-based study. *Lancet Glob Health.* 2021;9(6):e822-e831.
31. Kulothungan V, Sathishkumar K, Leburu S, et al. Burden of cancers in India - estimates of cancer crude incidence. YLLs, YLDs, and DALYs for 2021 and 2025 based on National Cancer Registry Program. *BMC Cancer.* 2022;22(527). doi:10.1186/s12885-022-09578-1.
32. World Health Organization. Mental health. Accessed March 28, 2023. https://www.who.int/india/health-topics/mental-health.
33. United Nations Development Program-OPHI. *The Global Multidimensional Poverty Index 2020: Charting Pathways out of Multidimensional Poverty.* Geneva, Switzerland: United Nations; 2020.
34. UN praises India's remarkable poverty reduction. *Times of India.* Accessed July 11, 2023. https://timesofindia.indiatimes.com/india/un-praises-indias-remarkable-poverty-reduction/articleshow/101670438.cms.
35. World Bank. 2023 country profile, India. Accessed July 28, 2023. https://databank.worldbank.org/views/reports/reportwidget.aspx?Report_Name=CountryProfile&Id=b450fd57&tbar=y&dd=y&inf=n&zm=n&country=IND.
36. World Bank. 2023. GDP per capita, PPP (current international $)—India. Accessed July 28, 2023. https://data.worldbank.org/indicator/NY.GDP.PCAP.PP.CD?locations=IN.
37. World Bank 2023. Country India. Accessed July 28, 2023. https://data.worldbank.org/country/india.
38. Government of India, Ministry of Statistics and Program Implementation. Sustainable Development Goals national indicator framework progress report 2020. Accessed July 28, 2023. https://mospi.gov.in/sites/default/files/main_menu/Sustainable_Development_Goals_National_Indicator_Framework_Progress_Report_2020_Version2.1.pdf.
39. GST collections for July rises 11% to Rs 1.65 lakh crore. *Times of India.* Accessed August 1, 2023. https://timesofindia.indiatimes.com/business/india-business/gst-collections-for-july-rises-11-to-rs-1-65-lakh-crore/articleshow/102308117.cms.
40. Reserve Bank of India. Annual report 2022–23: combined receipts and disbursements of the central and state governments. Accessed August 1, 2023. https://www.rbi.org.in/Scripts/AnnualReportPublications.aspx?year=2023 and https://www.rbi.org.in/Scripts/AnnualReportPublications.aspx?Id=1392 (comparing with prior reports up to 2014).
41. Government of India, Niti Aayog. Annual report 2022–23. Accessed July 28, 2023. https://www.niti.gov.in/sites/default/files/2023-02/Annual-Report-2022-2023-English_06022023_compressed.pdf.
42. Poverty intensity down: Niti Aayog. *Times of India.* 2023.
43. United Nations Development Program. The Sustainable Development Goals report 2023 special edition. Accessed August 1, 2023. https://unstats.un.org/sdgs/report/2023/The-Sustainable-Development-Goals-Report-2023.pdf.
44. COVID-19 Excess Mortality Collaborators. Estimating excess mortality due to the COVID-19 pandemic: a systematic analysis of COVID-19–related mortality, 2020–21. *Lancet.* 2022;399:1513-1536.
45. Deaths rose by 6.2% in pandemic year 2020. Registrar General of India report. *Times of India.* Accessed May 5, 2022. https://timesofindia.indiatimes.com/india/deaths-rose-by-6-2-in-pandemic-year-2020-registrar-general-of-india-report/articleshow/91294559.cms.

CHAPTER 20

China

Ning Lu, Kuo-Cherh Huang, and Ruiling Guo

Country Description

Table 20-1 China

Nationality	Noun: Chinese (singular and plural) Adjective: Chinese
Ethnic groups	Han Chinese 91.1%, ethnic minorities 8.9% (includes Zhang, Hui, Manchu, Uighur, Miao, Yi, Tujia, Tibetan, Mongol, Dong, Buyei, Yao, Bai, Korean, Hani, Li, Kazakh, Dai, and other nationalities) (2021 est.)*
Religions	China is officially atheist. Folk religion 21.9%, Buddhist 18.2%, Christian 5.1%, Muslim 1.8%, Hindu <0.1%, Jewish <0.1%, others 0.7% (include Daoist [Taoist]), unaffiliated 52.1% (2021 est.)
Language	Standard Chinese or Mandarin (Putonghua; based on the Beijing dialect), Yue (Cantonese), Wu (Shanghainese), Minbei (Fuzhou), Minnan (Hokkien-Taiwanese), Xiang, Gan, Hakka dialects, minority languages (see "Ethnic groups" row)**
Literacy	Definition: Age 15 and over and can read and write. Total population: 99.83% Male: 98% Female: 95% (2021 est.)
Government type	Communist state
Date of independence	January 1, 1912 (Qing Dynasty replaced by the Republic of China); October 1, 1949 (People's Republic of China established)
Gross domestic product (GDP) per capita	17,600 USD (2021 est.)
Unemployment rate	4.82% (2021 est.)***
Natural hazards	Frequent typhoons (approximately five per year along southern and eastern coasts); damaging floods; tsunamis; earthquakes; droughts; land subsidence; volcanism****
Environment: current issues	Air pollution (greenhouse gases, sulfur dioxide particulates), from reliance on coal, producing acid rain; water shortages, particularly in the north; water pollution from untreated wastes; deforestation; estimated loss of one-fifth of agricultural land since 1949 to soil erosion and economic development; desertification; trade in endangered species

Table 20-1 China

Population	1,413,142,846 (2023 est.)
Age structure	0–14 years: 16.48% (male 124,166,174/female 108,729,429) 15–64 years: 69.4% (male 504,637,819/female 476,146,909) 65 years and over: 14.11% (male 92,426,805/female 107,035,710) (2023 est.)
Median age	Total: 38.4 years Male: 37.5 years Female: 39.4 years (2020 est.)
Population growth rate	0.18% (2023 est.)
Birth rate	9.69 births/1,000 population (2023 est.)
Death rate	7.82 deaths/1,000 population (2023 est.)
Net migration rate	−0.11 migrant/1,000 population (2023 est.)
Gender ratio	At birth: 1.09 male/female 0–14 years: 1.14 male/female 15–64 years: 1.06 male/female 65 years and over: 0.86 male/female Total population: 1.04 male/female (2023 est.)
Infant mortality rate	Total: 6.49 deaths/1,000 live births Male: 6.93 deaths/1,000 live births Female: 6.01 deaths/1,000 live births (2023 est.)
Life expectancy at birth	Total population: 78.23 years Male: 75.5 years Female: 81.2 years (2023 est.)
Total fertility rate	1.45 children born/woman (2023 est.)
HIV/AIDS adult prevalence rate	4.27/100,000 (2021 est.)
Number of people living with HIV/AIDS	1.045 million (2020 est.)

USD = U.S. dollars.

*The Chinese government officially recognizes 56 ethnic groups.

**Zhuang is official in Guangxi Zhuang, Yue is official in Guangdong, Mongolian is official in Nei Mongol, Uighur is official in Xinjiang Uygur, Kyrgyz is official in Xinjiang Uygur, and Tibetan is official in Xizang (Tibet).

***Official data are for urban areas only; there is substantial unemployment and underemployment in rural areas.

****China contains some historically active volcanoes, including Changbaishan (also known as Baitoushan, Baegdu, or P'aektu-san), Hainan Dao, and Kunlun, although most have been relatively inactive in recent centuries.

Data from the Central Intelligence Agency. The World Factbook, 2022: China. Accessed March 17, 2023. https://www.cia.gov/the-world-factbook/countries/china/; GlobalData. Literacy rate in China (2018–2021, %). Accessed February 25, 2025. https://www.globaldata.com/data-insights/macroeconomic/literacy-rate-in-china/; Statista. AIDS incidence rate in China from 2015 to 2021. Accessed February 25, 2025. https://www.statista.com/statistics/860498/aids-incidence-rate-in-china/; Zhihui D, Luo Y, Yan Z, et al. Reported HIV/AIDS Cases—China, 2002–2021. *China CDC Weekly*. Accessed February 25, 2025. https://weekly.chinacdc.cn/fileCCDCW/journal/article/ccdcw/2023/42/PDF/CCDCW230249.pdf.

History

The People's Republic of China (hereinafter referred to as China) is one of the world's oldest civilizations (**Table 20-1**). The written records of China's history can be traced back to as early as 1500 BCE.[1] There are three distinct eras of Chinese history: the ancient era (2100–220 BCE), the imperial era (221 BCE–1911 CE), and the modern era (since 1912).

The earliest dynasties of the ancient era were Xia (2100–1600 BCE), Shang (1600–1046 BCE), and Zhou (1045–256 BCE), followed by the Warring States period (256–221 BCE). The imperial era began with the Qin Dynasty (221–206 BCE) after the Qin conquered all of the Warring States and unified China in 221 BCE. This period represented the first unified nation in Chinese history.[1]

Toward the end of the more than 2,000 years of the imperial dynasty, the Qing Empire was internally stagnant and externally threatened by Western powers. The Opium War (1839–1842), which ended in a victory for British colonists, plunged China into a semi-colonial and semifeudal society.[2] The revolutionary military uprising known as the Wuchang Uprising of October 1911 marked the end of the imperial era and the beginning of the Republican era, with the formation of the Republic of China in March 1912.[3] Sun Yat-Sen, who played an instrumental role in overthrowing the Qing Empire, was appointed the president of the Republic of China.

The Republican period (1912–1949) included several significant eras, including the warlord era (1915–1928), signified by the political and military power struggles of warlord generals, the Sino-Japanese war period (1937–1945), and the Chinese Civil War period (1927–1949).[3] Sun Yat-Sen, the leader of the Nationalist Party, or Kuomintang (KMT), resigned from his post as the president of the Republic of China 2 years after the overthrow of the Qing empire due to the pressure from the Beiyang Army, a Western-style imperial Chinese army founded by the Qing government in the late 19th century. The subsequent warlord factions known as the Beiyang cliques ushered in a period of regional divisions. With the help of the Soviet Union and the Chinese Communist Party (CCP), which had been founded in 1921, the KMT led by Chiang Kai-Shek launched the Northern Expedition in 1926 to bring the warlords under the control of the KMT, and they ended the warlord era in 1928.[3] By this time, the Chinese Civil War fought between the Nationalist Party and the CCP was already underway.

In October 1949, Mao Zedong declared the founding of the People's Republic of China. Following the Soviet Union's model, China was transformed into a socialist country. In 1978, after the death of Mao Zedong, Deng Xiaoping, who was considered the paramount leader of China, led the country through numerous market economy reforms. Since then, China has developed into one of the fastest-growing economies in the world.

Size and Geography

China, located in Southeast Asia, is the third-largest country in the world, with a coastline of 18,000 kilometers and an area of 9.6 million square kilometers. As shown in **Figure 20-1**, China is bordered by Russia and Mongolia to the north; Kazakhstan, Kyrgyzstan, Tajikistan, and Afghanistan to the west; Pakistan, Nepal, India, Myanmar, Laos, Thailand, and Vietnam to the south; and North Korea to the east. Southeastward, China is bordered by an arched coastline of 5,774 kilometers. The sea separates the country from Japan in the east and the Philippines, Malaysia, Brunei, Indonesia, and Singapore in the south.

The diverse geography of China encompasses high plateaus and mountains, such as Tibet and the Himalayas in the west, and basins and plains in the east. Plateaus, mountains, and hills jointly make up about 67% of the total land area. The Yangtze River and Yellow River are the two main eastward waterways. China's highest population densities are in the Yangtze River delta, Pearl River delta, Sichuan Basin, and Huang-Huai Plain.

Government and Political System

China is a socialist country led by a single party, the CCP. Shortly after the CCP founded the People's Republic of China in the mainland in 1949, socialism was instituted in the country and the new constitution was created. The Chinese government system is highly centralized, with a hierarchical structure of a central government and local governments at five levels: village, township, county, city, and province. In the centrally administered cities, the corresponding levels of government are municipal, district, subdistrict, and resident community.

The structure of the Chinese central government is similar to Western parliamentary systems, consisting of an executive branch, the State Council and 28 central ministries or commissions; the legislative branch, the National People's Congress (NPC); and the judicial branch, the Supreme People's Court and the Supreme People's Procuratorate.[4] The NPC is defined in the 1982 constitution as "the highest organ of state power." It has six permanent committees. Leaders of the NPC Standing Committee are invariably influential members of the CCP and leaders of major organizations. (See **Figure 20-2** for an illustration of the Chinese central government structure.)

The political system of China follows the framework of a socialist republic run by the CCP. Since the branches of the central government, and in fact, of all governments in China, are dominated by members of the CCP, checks and balances are difficult to achieve in practice. The NPC is the only legislative house in China. It is rare for the NPC to overthrow a proposal put before them, but the NPC has grown into a forum in which legislation is debated before being put to a vote. In the past, the president was elected by the NPC for up to two 5-year terms. However, in October 2022, Xi Jingping secured a third term as the president of China. The State Council consists of the heads of each governmental department and agency, is appointed by the NPC, and is chaired by the premier of China.

Figure 20-1 Map of China

The Chinese Communist Party is the founding and ruling political party in China. The National Congress of the Chinese Communist Party is held approximately once every 5 years. When the National Congress is not in session, the Central Committee is the highest body of the CCP. The CCP is the sole governing party in China. It is supplemented by the Chinese People's Political Consultative Conference, which consists of eight minority parties in political participation. These eight parties are the Revolutionary Committee of the Chinese Kuomintang, China Democratic League, China Democratic National Construction Association, China Association for Promoting Democracy, China Peasants and Workers' Democratic Party, China Zhigong Party, Jiu San Society, and Taiwan Democratic Self-Government League.[5]

The economic reforms in China since the late 1970s have pushed for political reform and a democratic system. In 1980, Deng Xiaoping suggested that three parallel central committees "mutually supervise and impose constraints on each other" and that "the work of the Party should be separated from the work of administrative organs, in enterprises and businesses, and enterprise management should be democratized."[6] Deng's political reforms would change the political system in China into a system with "checks and balances" between various political institutions. Although many policy reforms and organizational administrative reforms have occurred in China, they are mostly the changes made within the political system rather than the changes of the political system itself.[7]

Macroeconomics

In line with communist ideology and following the former Soviet Union's model, China's economy was highly centralized and planned without any private

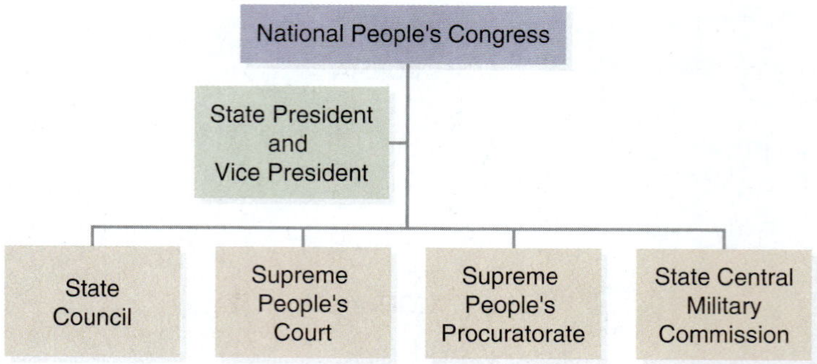

State Council Composition

Ministries			Commissions
• Agriculture	• Foreign Affairs	• Personnel	• National Development and Reform Commission
• Civil Affairs	• Information Industry	• Public Security	• Commission of Science, Technology and Industry for National Defense
• Commerce	• Justice	• Railways	• State Ethnic Affairs Commission
• Communications	• Labor and Social Security	• Science and Technology	• National Health and Family Planning Commission
• Construction	• Land and Resources	• State Security Supervision	• State Owned Assets Supervision and Administration Commission
• Culture	• National Defense	• Water Resources	
• Education			**Other**
• Finance			• People's Bank of China
			• National Audit Office

Figure 20-2 Central Government Structure

Data from China's State Organizational Structure. Accessed March 13, 2023. https://www.cecc.gov/chinas-state-organizational-structure.

entities from 1949 until 1978. All industries and enterprises were owned and controlled by the government. Workers were employees of government or state-owned enterprises (SOEs). In 1978, China launched economic reforms to convert the planned economic system to a market-based one. Since then, many policies that favor a market economy have been implemented. In rural areas, the household responsibility system replaced the communes. In urban areas, the SOEs were given autonomy and responsibilities for their profits and losses. Special economic zones in southern China were created with economic autonomy. Such economic autonomy was eventually extended to the rest of the country. These reforms have created market competition and consequently improved economic performance. Between 1979 and 2021, the national gross domestic product (GDP) had an average annual growth rate of 9.19%, with a per capita GDP of $18,721.6 USD in 2021. According to the World Bank, China's GDP at market prices reached $17.7 trillion USD in 2021 and was the world's second-largest economy after the United States ($23.0 trillion USD).[8] The breakdown of China's GDP in 2020 indicated that the agricultural, industrial, and service sectors accounted for 7.7%, 37.8%, and 54.5% of the economy, respectively.[9]

In the labor market, China has experienced a large-scale migration of workers from agriculture to the industrial and manufacturing sectors and from rural to urban areas. Major heavy industries include mining and ore processing, aluminum, coal, iron and steel, cement, machinery, automobiles, armaments, petroleum, chemicals, fertilizers, telecommunications, and transportation equipment such as ships, aircraft, locomotives, and rail cars. Light industries include textiles and apparel, food processing, and consumer products such as footwear, electronics, and toys. The information technology industry has rapidly developed and has become an essential component of the Chinese economy. Thanks to economic reforms and opening-up policies, more jobs have been created in the private sector. The registered urban unemployment rate was 4.2% by the end of 2020.[10]

As for international trade, total exports of goods and services from China equaled 20.0% of GDP in 2021, up from 4.3% in 1960, and total imports accounted for 17.4% of GDP in 2021, up from 4.4% in 1960.[11,12] In 2020, China imported $150 billion USD in crude petroleum (accounting for the highest percentage of its total imports) and became the largest importer of crude petroleum in the world, whereas broadcasting equipment accounted for the largest share of its export market (8.4%).[13] The Chinese economy, self-contained before 1978, now relies heavily on exports. Labor-intensive processing industries, such as electronic equipment, footwear, and clothing, are highly concentrated in coastal provinces and fuel the export of Chinese products. Major trade partners of China include the United States, Japan, South Korea, Russia, Taiwan, Singapore, and European Union countries, including Germany and the Netherlands. In addition, regional trade with other Asian countries has become an important economic driver for China. In recent years, due to the global economic recession caused by the coronavirus (COVID-19) pandemic, the demand for goods from China has declined significantly, adversely impacting the nation's economy.

Over the past 3 decades, China has experienced phenomenal growth in international trade and has maintained a high level of foreign exchange reserves due to the sustained favorable trade balance. To maintain the yuan's de facto pegging to the U.S. dollar and to prevent the yuan from appreciating, China keeps a substantial foreign exchange reserve of $3.3 trillion USD.[14] The government's preferential industrial development policies and its proximity to Hong Kong and Taiwan have made China an attractive destination for foreign direct investment (FDI), which has fueled economic growth over the past 3 decades. China is the second largest recipient of FDI, with more than $100 billion USD in recent years, compared with near zero in the early 1980s. In 2015, China attracted a total of $249.9 billion USD in FDI, according to the World Bank.[15]

China's sustained economic growth over the past few decades has significantly improved the living conditions in China and lifted millions of Chinese people out of poverty. Despite its rapid economic growth, China remains a developing country, with a per capita GDP of $7,924.7 USD in 2015 compared with a per capita GDP of $55,836.8 USD in the United States.[16]

Demographics

As of 2023, China was the most populous country in the world, with a population of over 1.4 billion. According to the World Bank,[17] the population aged 65 and above was 13% of the country's total population, and the population under 15 was 18% of the total in 2021. China's age dependency ratio (percentage of the working-age population) was 45% in 2021, compared with 77% in 1960. Although the number of children increased rapidly between the 1950s and the 1970s, it has declined significantly since the 1980s, partly due to China's one-child policy, which began to be formally phased out in 2015. In 2020, the population's natural growth rate was 1.45%, with a birth rate of 8.52% and a death rate of 7.07%.[9] In the next few decades, China is expected to experience serious economic and social challenges due to its aging population.

Buddhism is the most influential religion in China. Other major religions include Taoism, Confucianism, Islam, and Christianity. Buddhism, Confucianism, and Taoism have played significant roles historically in shaping Chinese culture. Some scholars prefer not to use the term "religion" in reference to Confucianism or Taoism, believing that they are "thought systems" or "philosophies."[18] According to China Family Panel Studies, approximately 74% of the population is unaffiliated with any religion, 16% follow Buddhism, 8% follow Taoism, and about 3% follow Protestantism, Islam, and Catholicism (among the officially recognized religions).[19]

Education

In July 2021, the State Council of China released a policy document detailing a set of reforms in the education sector aiming at nationalizing private schools.[20] China's education system includes preschool, primary school, secondary school, high school, college and university, and graduate school levels.[21] The 9-year compulsory education law covers primary school (6 years) and secondary school (3 years). High school education lasts 3 years for students who pass the high school entrance examination. Higher education at the undergraduate level includes 2- and 3-year colleges (also called short-cycle colleges) and 4-year colleges and universities (5 years for medical universities) leading to bachelor's degrees. Universities also offer graduate programs leading to master's and doctorate degrees. Admission to a university or college largely depends on the results of the highly competitive national higher education entrance examination (Gao Kao), which takes place in June. Approximately 11.93 million students took this examination in June 2022.[22]

Poverty

China is now an upper-middle-income country. Along with the rapid economic growth, living conditions in China have improved dramatically. The number of people living in poverty has decreased significantly, primarily due to economic growth and government-sponsored poverty intervention programs since the late 1970s. According to the World Bank, more than 800 million people were lifted out of poverty as China's poverty rate fell from 88% in 1981 to 15.80% in 2019.[23] Despite China's significant improvement in the poverty level, there were still 5.51 million rural residents living below the poverty line (defined by China as anyone in rural areas earning less than approximately $2.30 USD a day, adjusted for inflation) in 2019.[23] In addition, the income disparity between rural and urban areas has widened, resulting in rural–urban inequalities in access to and quality of healthcare services.

Brief History of the Healthcare System

China's health system has undergone three major phases since the founding of the People's Republic of China in 1949. Before 1949, China did not have an organized health system. Instead, most health care was provided by private healers, private clinics, and religious institutions. The first phase started with the founding of China and lasted until the early 1980s. During this phase, the government created a health system modeled on that of the Soviet Union, with the government owning, financing, and operating the health and healthcare sector. The government and state enterprises provided nearly 90% of the Chinese population with health insurance, and the health system offered free or near-free health services. The second phase began in 1978 with the initiation of the remarkable economic reforms in China. During this phase, the role of the government in health and the healthcare sector was reduced drastically as China converted to a free market economy. As a result, the health system was left mainly to the forces of the free market economy, which resulted in the vast majority of the Chinese population being without health insurance, created an inefficient healthcare delivery system, and bred public discontent toward the health system. Confronted with increasing healthcare problems and the severe acute respiratory syndrome (SARS) outbreak that spread from China to 37 countries worldwide in 2003,[24] the Chinese government launched the health reform that marked the beginning of the third phase. During this phase, the central government reasserted its role in the health and healthcare sector with unprecedented funding and a socialist ideology to promote equity and social stability. This resulted in universal health insurance coverage in 2012 and ongoing reform of its health delivery system. Today, 95% of the 1.4 billion Chinese population is covered through public health insurance programs.[25] Private insurance is less prevalent in China. It is purchased primarily by higher-income individuals or employers for their workers and covers deductibles, copayments, cost-sharing, and expensive services not covered by public insurance.[25]

Before 1949: Private and Unorganized Health Delivery

Although the practice of traditional Chinese medicine existed for several thousand years, China did not have an organized health or healthcare system until the mid-20th century. Most healthcare services were provided by private healers, small clinics, and religious and charity institutions. The earliest contemporary hospitals, run mainly by Western churches in the form of missionary hospitals, began to emerge in China in the mid-19th century. Before the establishment of the new China in 1949, there was little effort made to improve public health. Outbreaks of epidemics, such as typhoid, cholera, malaria, and tuberculosis, were frequent and rampant during the 19th century and the first half of the 20th century in China. During this period, China was one of the least healthy countries in the world.[26,27]

Phase I (1950–1978): A Government-Owned, -Funded, and -Operated Health System

After the Communist Party took control of China in 1949, the modern health system was developed under the planned economy of China. Private practices and private ownership of health facilities disappeared completely. The Ministry of Health, as an executive agency of the national government, was established in 1954 to coordinate health resources, ensure the accessibility of health services, monitor the quality of health services provided to the public, and establish and supervise health policies. The health system comprising hospitals, outpatient clinics, maternal and child care stations, and epidemic prevention centers was owned, funded, and run by the government at various administrative levels. The system was designed to provide affordable care to every member of the population, regardless of the ability to pay, by controlling and coordinating the distribution of financial resources, healthcare personnel, equipment, and technology.[27] All healthcare personnel—including physicians, nurses, pharmacists, and administrators—were government employees and were paid a fixed salary. The central government set and regulated the prices for all healthcare services, including medications.[27]

To provide universal coverage for healthcare services for all, China established three socialist health insurance schemes in rural and urban areas throughout China. In rural areas, the Rural Cooperative Medical System (RCMS) was implemented in the 1950s to cover health services for rural populations. The RCMS consisted of a three-tier healthcare delivery system and a community-based insurance scheme. The three-tier system was composed of village health clinics that provided basic health care by barefoot doctors (the first tier), township health centers consisting of outpatient clinics and small hospitals that provided care for the most common illnesses (the second tier), and county or higher-level hospitals that were used for treating severe illnesses (the third tier).[27] The township health centers played an essential role in providing health care for rural populations by supervising the care delivered at the village clinics and referring patients to the higher-level hospitals equipped with more advanced medical equipment and sophisticated technologies. In addition, township health centers were responsible for organizing and delivering preventive care in rural areas. The insurance scheme of RCMS was a prepayment pool consisting of individual contributions, a village collective welfare fund, and subsidies from the government. The RCMS members received health services free or at a reduced cost.[27]

In urban areas, two primary health insurance schemes covered urban populations for health services: the Labor Insurance Scheme (LIS) and the Government Employee Insurance Scheme (GIS), established in 1951 and 1952, respectively. The LIS covered healthcare costs for employees (and their dependents) of state-owned or collectively owned enterprises and their dependents. The GIS covered healthcare costs for government employees, government retirees, and college students.[27] Similar to the three-tier delivery system for the rural population, health care in urban areas was provided through public facilities at three levels: workplace or neighborhood clinics (the first level) that provided essential health services by mostly barefoot doctors; district hospitals (the second level) that provided primary care and treatment for common illnesses; and city hospitals (the third level) that treated patients with complicated illnesses. Both LIS and GIS provided open-ended healthcare coverage at no cost or very minimal cost (i.e., registration fee) to individuals. As a result, urban employees enjoyed essentially free outpatient and inpatient care, with little or no concerns about the cost.

Payment for health services was organized as fee-for-services, based on a predetermined fee schedule set by the government. To ensure that health care was affordable to all population members, the government set the prices for the medical services below their costs. By the end of 1975, the RCMS, LIS, and GIS insurance covered nearly 90% of the population, including almost all of the urban population and 85% of the rural population.[27,28]

To improve the nation's health, the Chinese government focused on controlling and preventing infectious diseases and rural health improvement.[29–31] This period in Chinese history saw remarkable achievements in improving population health and health services delivery in China. The life expectancy at birth increased from 35 years in 1952 to 68 years in 1985, and the infant mortality rate dropped from 250 to 34 per 1,000 live births over the same period.[32]

Phase II (1978–2002): Health System in the Era of Economic Reforms

Beginning in 1978, the government-owned health system started crumbling as the Chinese government introduced radical economic reforms that transformed China from a centrally planned economy into a market-oriented system. The private sector grew dramatically, accounting for nearly 70% of China's GDP by 2005.[31] These economic reforms profoundly affected China's health system, introducing substantial changes in the financing and delivery of health services.

In rural areas, the most remarkable economic reform was the introduction of the Household Production Responsibility System (HPRS). Before this economic reform, villages were called production brigades. A brigade was divided into several production teams, and the team leaders directed production and product distribution. The production teams recorded the farmers' work and other contributions as working points. The distribution of the products was based on the total working points and the number of heads in each household. After paying tax to the government in the form of agricultural products, the production teams would keep some for the Rural Cooperative Medical Fund (usually 30%–50%). The remainder was distributed to the households. Due to the implementation of HPRS as part of the economic reform in rural areas, the collective agriculture economy collapsed. Under HPRS, the arable land is distributed to individual households by capitation. The households assume the sole responsibility for their gains and losses. Every household pays a certain amount of the tax in the form of agricultural products to the government and keeps the remainder. Consequently, the villages no longer had collective funds for RCMS to finance the village clinics or provide income to barefoot doctors. Coupled with the decline in government funding to RCMS, most village clinics closed, and some transformed into private practices. Barefoot doctors became private providers or entered other professions. Most RCMS systems disappeared in rural areas.[33] Although various forms of voluntary health insurance programs were developed beginning in the mid-1980s, less than 1% of the rural population enrolled in them. By 1998, only 5% (down from 85% in 1975) of the rural population was covered by the RCMS, mostly in more developed and rich areas. As a result, approximately 900 million rural residents, including poor farmers in relatively richer rural localities, had to pay out of pocket for virtually all health services.[27]

In urban areas, alongside the privatization of state-owned industry, government funding of healthcare facilities declined considerably, forcing healthcare facilities and professionals to rely on user fees to support their operations. Many healthcare professionals who were state employees became private entrepreneurs.[27] At the same time, the moral hazard effect inherited in the GIS and LIS schemes started to emerge, such as overutilization of free health care, which drove up healthcare costs. As a result, healthcare costs rose four times faster than the government's fiscal income.[34] Neither GIS nor LIS could be financially sustained. Since the mid-1980s, both insurance schemes have been greatly altered. Significant copayment, co-insurance, deductible, and expenditure ceilings were introduced into both insurance schemes, with a substantial decline in their coverage and benefits. By 1989, direct patient payment through fee-for-service schemes accounted for 36% of the total health expenditure; the GIS, LIS, and RCMS health insurance schemes accounted for 44%; and the remaining 20% came from government funding.[35]

The decline of government funding to public health insurance coupled with the lack of private insurance left the vast majority of the Chinese population without health insurance coverage. By 1998, the health insurance rates fell to 36% and 5% in urban and rural areas, respectively.[36] The lack of access to health care and a shift in disease patterns to the increasingly costly illnesses of cancer, cerebrovascular, and cardiovascular diseases left the Chinese population largely at risk for medically caused financial catastrophe. Out-of-pocket payments increased to 18 times what they were in 1990. The average cost of a single hospitalization was more than double the average annual income of the lowest-income groups, who made up 20% of the population. More than 35% of rural households and 43% of urban households could not afford healthcare costs; many were left with no choice but to avoid care or became impoverished.[37]

From 1980 to 2000, the disparity in healthcare access and quality between rural and urban areas grew significantly due to several factors.[38–40] First, local government funding for health care through taxation was more than four times higher in urban areas than in rural areas.[41–44] Second, a disproportionately large amount of healthcare resources was concentrated on large urban hospitals, resulting in more than 80% of health expenditures being allocated to urban areas, despite 70% of the population living in rural areas.[45] Third, the rural–urban income gap grew wider. By 2005, the rural–urban income difference hit its highest point, with rural per capita income only 39% of urban per capita income.[46] As a result, the rural–urban inequality in healthcare delivery and utilization escalated. In 2003, the number of beds per 1,000 population in urban areas was 3.67 versus only 1.50 in rural areas, and the number of health professionals per 1,000 population was 4.84 in urban areas versus only 2.19 in rural areas.[47,48] According to the Third National Health Services Survey, conducted in China in 2003, healthcare utilization measured by hospitalization rate was 11% in urban areas and only 7% in rural areas.[47] Furthermore, the annual inpatient days per 1,000 population increased by 12.8% for urban residents, compared with a 10.3% decline for rural residents from 1985 to 1993. In 1993, nearly 40% of the rural population who did not seek necessary hospital care reported an inability to pay as the main reason, and 30% to 50% of poor rural households became impoverished due to illness, according to various estimates.[48] The provision of preventive care was also reduced significantly in rural areas. For example, in 1999, only 84% of rural children received recommended vaccinations compared with 96% of urban children. In 2000, the infant mortality rate per 1,000 live births was 37.0 in rural areas, compared with 11.8 in urban areas. The situation was even worse in rural areas of western China, a traditionally poor region, which had an infant mortality rate of as high as 52.3 per 1,000 live births.[49]

Due to the decline in government funding and the decentralization of the decision-making power of the central government, China's public health programs were severely weakened. Between 1978 and 1993, the financing of Epidemic Prevention Stations (EPSs) dropped from 0.11% of GDP to only 0.04% of GDP, forcing EPSs to cut back in providing and coordinating public health programs.[26] Public health workers and barefoot village doctors became independent practitioners charging for public health programs. For example, vaccinations against tuberculosis, diphtheria, pertussis, tetanus, polio, and measles required fees in many areas, creating major financial barriers for those rural and poor households who needed the services the most.

The decentralization of the public health system and the central government's fiscal system also resulted in diminished responsibility and ability of the Ministry of Health to organize and control its disease prevention and surveillance system. The infectious disease reporting and surveillance system was not updated regularly. For example, reporting was not required for SARS, and the information was not shared across health and healthcare organizations horizontally or vertically during the initial occurrence, which quickly turned into an epidemic in 2003.[50] Besides SARS, China had seen other emerging and reemerging infectious diseases, such as AIDS, gonorrhea, syphilis, and an alarming upward trend in tuberculosis, typically related to worsened living conditions and poverty in rural areas.

Phase III (2003–Ongoing): Rebuilding the Health System

The SARS outbreak in 2003 and other healthcare problems associated with the decentralization and marketization of China's health system have led to growing concerns and resentments of the general public toward the health system. The Chinese government, led by socialist ideology, realized that health is a sector that cannot simply be left to market forces,[26] and it started shifting its development strategy from prioritizing economic expansion to promoting equity and social stability. In 2003, within several months of the SARS outbreak, the Chinese government decided to reinstate its role in the health sector with a massive investment in public health programs, which marked a new era of health reform in China.[51–53]

Between 2003 and 2008, the government focused on health insurance reform by implementing three main public insurance schemes:

1. The New Rural Cooperative Medical Scheme (NRCMS) was launched in 2003 to cover the rural population.
2. The Urban Resident Basic Medical Insurance (URBMI) was introduced in 2007 to provide insurance coverage for children, students, and the unemployed in urban areas.
3. The Urban Employee Basic Medical Insurance (UEBMI), an employment-based insurance program, was launched in 1998.

The NRCMS is the successor of the RCMS, which had almost completely collapsed since the economic reforms in 1978. The initial coverage of NRCMS was quite shallow, with a goal to reduce the financial burden of inpatient costs for rural residents. The NRCMS is overseen by the Chinese National Health and Family Planning Commission (formerly the Ministry of Health) and is managed by the local governments, which are allowed to design and implement the NRCMS according to their local needs and condition, provided that three specific central government's guidelines are met: voluntary participation, coverage for catastrophic illnesses, and county-level administration.[34]

The financing of NRCMS comes from the central government, local government, and individual households. At its inception, the amount of financial contribution was equally split three ways among the central and local governments, and individual households. Gradually, the government increased its share. For example, in 2008, the annual contributions from the central and local governments each reached ¥80 (about $10.7 USD) per person, an 800% increase from 2003, and ¥20 (about $2.7 USD) from each participating household.[34] In order to encourage the local governments in poor areas to promote the NRCMS, the central government matches the contribution of the local government only when enrollment reaches 80% of the target population. In the meantime, governments subsidize 100% of the premiums for poor households who cannot afford health insurance through the Medical Financial Assistance (MFA) program, which was established in 2002.[54] Another unique feature of NRCMS financing is related to its household participation instead of individual participation, which is intended to avoid potential adverse selection and to generate a better risk pool. By 2008, in just a few years, NRCMS enrollment reached 90% of the rural population.[55]

Unlike its predecessor (RCMS), which provided basic and preventive care coverage, the NRCMS focused on covering expensive inpatient care. The reimbursement rate was between 30% and 60% for inpatient services in 2008, with higher reimbursement rates for services received from lower-level facilities. Deductibles and expenditure ceilings are commonly applied across all counties. In recent years, many NRCMS schemes have started to cover outpatient care. Currently, four main NRCMS coverage models exist: (1) covering both inpatient and outpatient care; (2) covering inpatient and high-cost outpatient care; (3) covering inpatient care only; and (4) covering inpatient care with pooled government contributions and covering outpatient care using household contributions as savings accounts.

The NRCMS, as one of the major public insurance programs, has made significant progress in improving access to health care for China's vast rural population. Yet, several challenges remain to be addressed. First, the benefit of the NRCMS has been narrow and shallow, focusing on inpatient costs. Thus its protection against a financial burden for enrollees is quite limited. Although the majority of rural residents have participated in the NRCMS, the utilization of the NRCMS has been low.[56,57] Only recently were general outpatient services added to the NRCMS with increased government funding.[58] Second, the portability of NRCMS has been restricted, and there are no cross-county subsidies. As a result, millions of migrant workers who have drifted from rural areas to work in urban areas have fallen through the insurance cracks. According to the National Bureau of Statistics of China, the number of rural workers in urban areas reached more than 225 million in 2008.[59] These migrant workers, although they work and live in urban areas, were still registered as rural residents in the Hukou system, a residence registration system that classifies residents according to their hometown locations. As a result, reimbursement for healthcare costs outside of an individual's registered county is seldom available, leaving millions of migrant workers without health insurance.

In urban areas, China launched two basic health insurance schemes, the UEBMI and the URBMI. The UEBMI is an employment-based insurance program that evolved from LIS and GIS, which were established in the 1950s during the planned economy era. The UEBMI was officially launched in 1998 to expand insurance coverage to private-sector employees. The financing of UEBMI comes from the contributions of employers and employees, who contribute 6% and 2% of employee wages, respectively.[60] Enrollment in UEBMI is mandatory, with risk pooled at the municipal level. The pooled funds are divided into two parts: socially pooled funds to pay for inpatient stays (with deductibles) and medical savings accounts to pay for outpatient visits.[61] Although the UEBMI is overseen by the national government's Ministry of Human Resources and Social Security (MOHRSS), municipal governments have the flexibility to determine the premium contributions for their UEBMI. For example, in more affluent areas, such as Shanghai, the premium contributions can be as high as 14% of employees' annual salaries. By the end of 2008, the enrollment of UEBMI rose to 81% of the total urban population from only 5% in 1998.[62,63] In 2015, the total enrollment was 96.5%.[64] In 2023, 96% of the total population was enrolled.[65]

URBMI mainly covers urban children, students, and residents without formal employment. Similar to the NRCMS, enrollment in URBMI is voluntary and at the household level. The program pools the premiums at the city level and is administered by the local governments and overseen by the MHRSS. The local governments develop and implement the URBMI according to their specific local needs. The financing of URBMI comes from individual contributions and subsidies from both local and central governments. On average, individual participants contribute a larger proportion of the funds. Governments provide certain predetermined and guaranteed subsidies required by the central government. For example, in 2007, the central government required an annual government subsidy of no less than ¥40 (about $7 USD) per year per enrollee. In 2023, the cost increased to ¥89 ($12.40 USD) per year per enrollee.[66] In 2023, the government increased the per-year subsidy to ¥89 ($12.40 USD) per enrollee.[66] For individuals with financial difficulties, the government provides an additional subsidy, of which 50% comes from the central government.[67]

The URBMI fund primarily covers inpatient costs and certain outpatient visits for chronic or critical diseases, such as diabetes and heart disease. Preventive services are not covered by the URBMI. The URBMI's reimbursement policy and premium level differ from city to city. As a result, the deductibles, copayments, and expenditure ceilings vary across cities.[67] In general, the reimbursement rate for healthcare expenses is higher for services received from lower-level facilities.[63]

URBMI has played a significant role in closing the health insurance gap by providing coverage to millions of Chinese who otherwise would have no financial access to healthcare services. Through URBMI,

UEBMI, and NRCMS, China has been making impressive progress toward providing universal insurance coverage for all of its citizens. In the meantime, many published studies suggest that to provide affordable health care for 1.3 billion people, the health insurance reform needs to go deeper, and the healthcare delivery system needs a fundamental transformation.[28,36,37,57]

In 2009, the Chinese government released a comprehensive health reform plan with unprecedented funding of ¥850 billion for 3 years (about $204 billion USD, adjusted for purchasing power parity) to improve five key areas with a goal of providing affordable basic health care for everyone by 2020: (1) expand health insurance to cover more than 90% of the total population; (2) establish a national essential drug system to ensure the safety, quality, access, and supply of essential medicines; (3) improve the primary care delivery system to enhance disease prevention and health promotion; (4) strengthen public health services; and (5) reform public hospitals.[53,68] The Chinese government formally reinstated its role in the health sector and abandoned market-based health reform. The year 2009 marked the beginning of comprehensive and historic health reform in China.[28]

By 2012, China had achieved near-universal health insurance coverage, with more than 95% of the 1.3 billion population covered by some form of health insurance, including rural migrant workers who could enroll in either the NRCMS in their hometowns or the URBMI where they work. Building up to that, to reduce excessive drug prescriptions and improve access to safe and effective essential medicines, the Ministry of Health published the "National Essential Drugs List" in late 2009, which consists of more than 300 Western and traditional Chinese medicines, with a policy of zero-markup national retail prices for drugs on the list. The list is for primary healthcare facilities and will be extended to hospitals to use.[69] In 2011, to strengthen public health and primary care, the government increased funding per person for primary care providers to deliver a predefined package of basic public health services. In addition, the government directed its funding to build the primary care infrastructure, focusing on improving the healthcare workforce distribution. The efforts include waiving tuition fees for medical graduates who agree to work at township health centers for at least 3 years. The reform of public hospitals has been challenging.[70–72] The main goal of public hospital reform is to make inpatient care affordable and cost-effective by prohibiting increases in drug prices, reducing medical test costs, and increasing prices for medical services, such as surgeries. The government has invested over $10 billion USD in pilot projects that were expected to expand to 200 cities. The result of public hospital reform, however, is less clear. Several recent studies have demonstrated that although medication costs have been reduced, total out-of-pocket spending has increased significantly.[69–73] In addition, many hospitals, mostly tertiary public hospitals, resisted the reform efforts. To counter the resistance, the government once again sought market forces by inviting private investors to own up to 20% of China's hospitals by 2015 in the hope of creating competition that would bring the public hospital sector in line with the health system.[28] In 2024, China's Ministry of Commerce, the National Health Commission, and the National Medical Products Administration announced the expansion of pilot programs for foreign investment in the healthcare sector.[74] These programs will bring money and improvements to the healthcare sector to China.

The Current Healthcare System

In March 2018, the State Council reorganized the central government's healthcare structure with various agencies responsible for national health legislation, policy, funding, and administration.[75] **Figure 20-3** illustrates the current organization of health administration in China.

Facilities

Health services in China are mainly provided by the public system, which consists of facilities that provide primary care, outpatient specialist care, inpatient care, and mental health care. Primary care is provided in village clinics, township, and community hospitals, and in secondary and tertiary hospitals. Outpatient specialist care is typically delivered in hospital outpatient settings. Patients can usually see outpatient specialists without a general practitioner referral. **Table 20-2** summarizes the types of facility and services provided.[76]

The health system in China is dominated by public hospitals that provide comprehensive healthcare services, including primary care, outpatient specialist care, and inpatient care. They also play a vital function in providing emergency services. The number of hospitals has increased significantly, with an annual average growth rate of 2.5% since the 1980s;

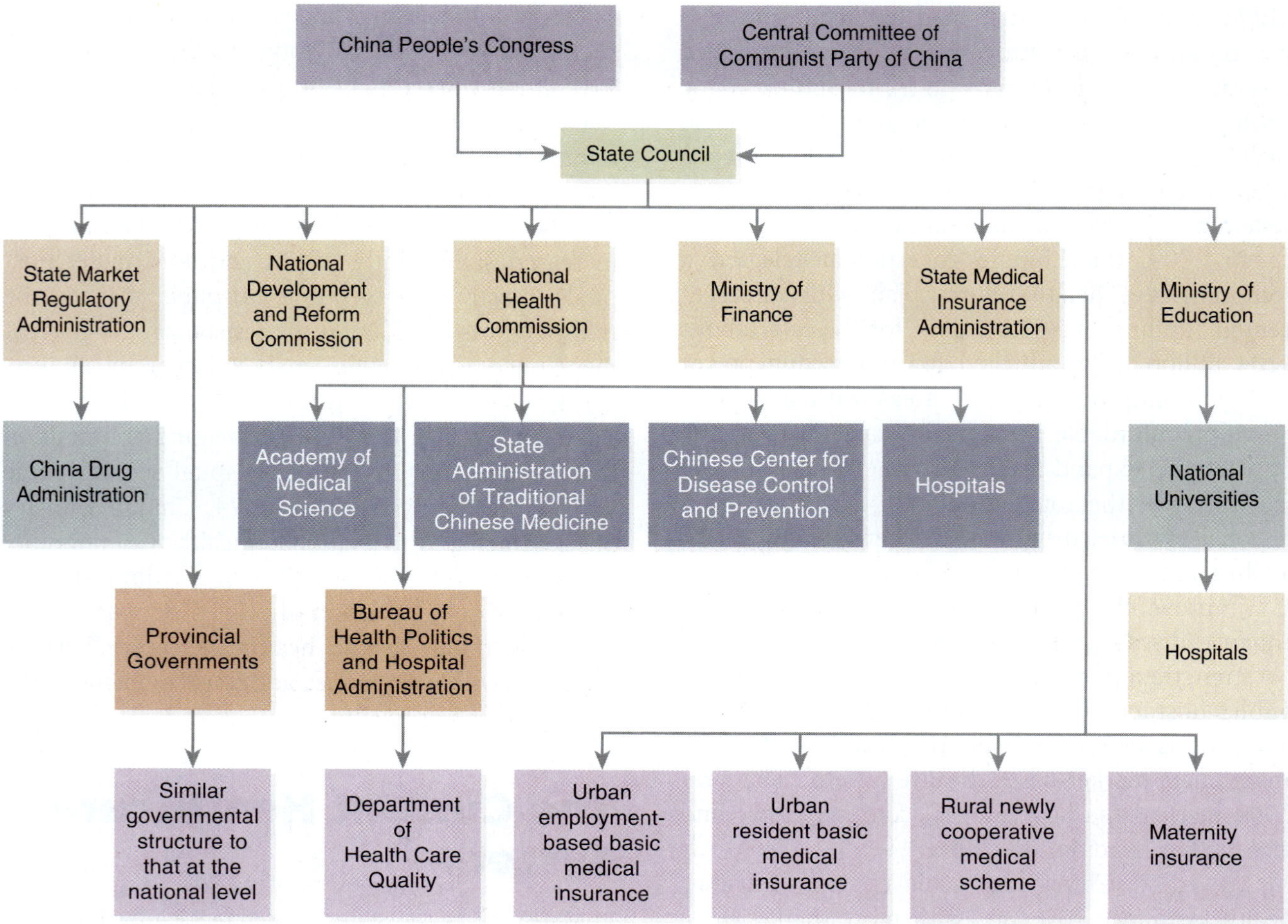

Figure 20-3 Organization of Health System in China

Reproduced from *2020 International Profiles of Health Care Systems*. The Commonwealth Fund; 2020.

Table 20-2 Healthcare Institutions (2021–2022)

Type of Facility	Number	Services Provided
Hospitals: 36,570		
General hospitals	20,307	General services including outpatient and inpatient, all kinds of physical examination and diagnosis, etc.
Hospitals specialized in traditional Chinese medicine	4,630	General traditional Chinese medicine services, including outpatient and inpatient, all kinds of physical examination and diagnosis, etc.
Specialized hospitals	9,699	Outpatient and inpatient; examination services; specialized in oral, eye, tumor, cardiovascular, pediatrics, mental health, ob/gyn, skin, infectious diseases
Outpatient Department: 321,000		
Grassroots Healthcare Facilities: 980,000		
Community health service centers	36,000	General diagnosis services and treatment of common diseases, acute care, rehabilitation, consultation, referrals, preventive care, hygiene, vaccination, health education, family planning, etc.
Township health service centers	34,000	Health services at township level in urban areas, including diagnosis and treatment of common diseases, acute care, rehabilitation, consultation, referrals, preventive care, hygiene, vaccination, health education, family planning, etc.
Village clinics[2]	588,000	Public health services including preventive care, maternal and child hygiene, and primary diagnosis and treatment of common diseases

Type of Facility	Number	Services Provided
Specialized Public Health Facilities		
Specialized public health institutions	13,000	Preventive health in oral diseases, mental health, skin diseases, sexually transmitted diseases, tuberculosis, occupational diseases, endemic diseases, schistosomiasis, drug rehabilitation, etc.
Center for Disease Control and Prevention (unit)	3,385	Disease prevention and control, public health emergency preparedness and response, behavior risk factor surveillance and intervention, clinical laboratory inspection and evaluation, health education and promotion, health service management, scientific research
Women and children care agencies	3,032	Basic health services, health promotion, health education, and preventive care for women and children
Health Inspection Institution (unit)	2,796	Enforcement of health law, inspection and supervision of food safety, public area sanitation, occupational health, and medical appliances, etc.

Data from National Bureau of Statistics of China, 2021–2022. Health care institutions 2021–2022. Accessed March 17, 2023. https://data.stats.gov.cn/english/easyquery.htm?cn=C01.

specialized hospitals have increased the fastest, at an annual rate of 9.4% since the 1980s.[9] In addition, hospitals are growing in size. Currently, 16 hospitals in China have more than 3,000 beds. The supersized hospitals are mostly university-affiliated and are located in the center of big cities, including Beijing, Shanghai, and Chengdu. The largest hospital in the world, with more than 7,000 beds, is in Henan province, one of the most populous provinces in China. As the number of hospitals has increased, the number of township health centers and village clinics has decreased.[9] **Figure 20-4** demonstrates the increase in the number of hospitals in the past 10 years,[77] and **Figure 20-5** demonstrates the decrease in the number of village clinics.[77]

In recent years, more private hospitals have entered the healthcare market. By the end of 2010, the percentage of private hospitals had increased from 33% to 17% in 2005. In 2021, two-thirds of the 36,570 hospitals were designated as private.[78] Despite the increase in the number of private hospitals, public hospitals still account for nearly 90% of total hospital beds and 92% of outpatient visits.[9] Traditional Chinese medicine is an integral part of healthcare services in China. Most hospitals have a department of traditional Chinese medicine. Public traditional Chinese medicine hospitals are arranged along four administrative levels.[77]

The number of acute care hospital beds per 1,000 population in China was the third highest (4.55), after

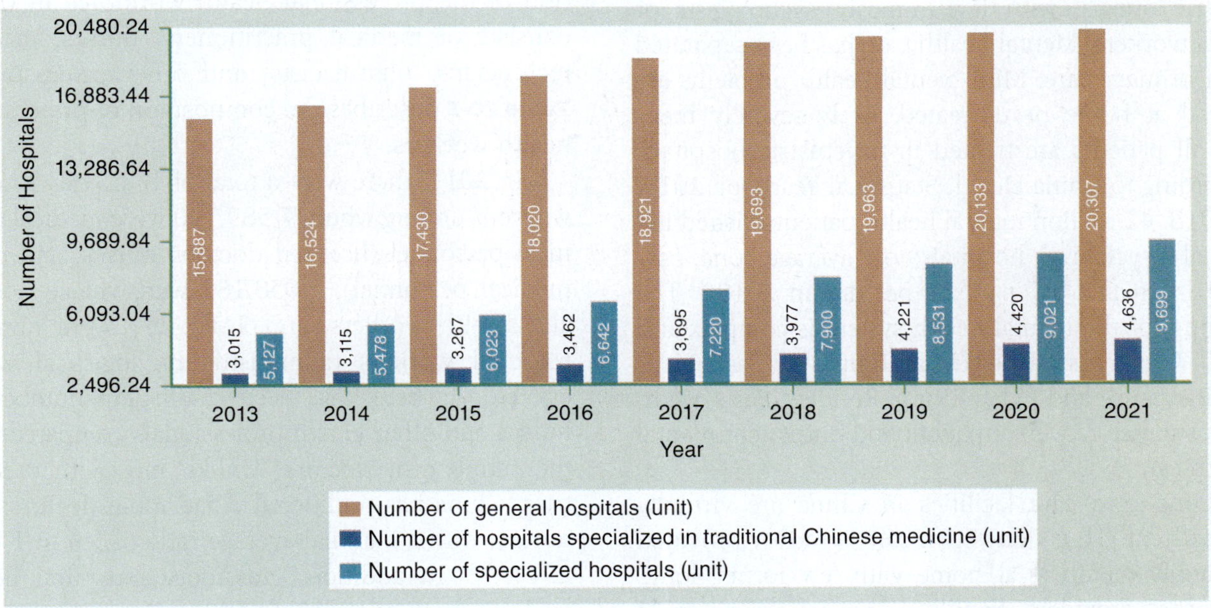

Figure 20-4 Number of Hospitals, 2013–2021

Data from National Bureau of Statistics of China, 2013–2021. Accessed March 17, 2023. https://data.stats.gov.cn/english/easyquery.htm?cn=C01.

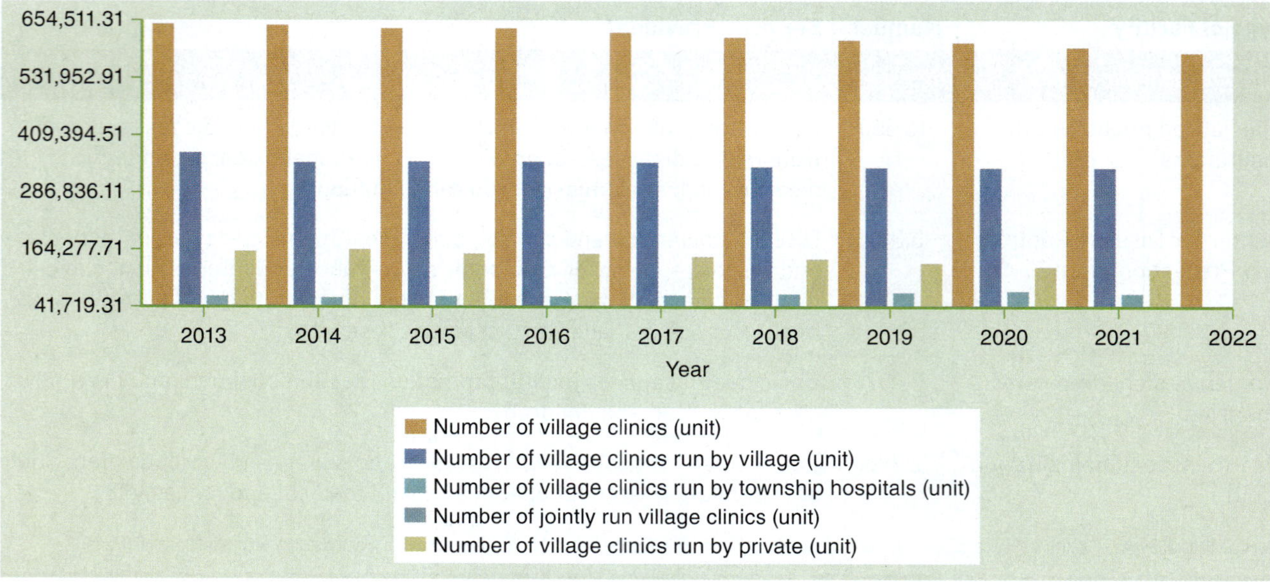

Figure 20-5 Number of Village Clinics, 2013–2022

Data from National Bureau of Statistics of China, 2013–2021. Accessed March 17, 2023. https://data.stats.gov.cn/english/easyquery.htm?cn=C01.

Japan (7.92) and Germany (5.34), in Organization for Economic Co-operation and Development countries in 2016.[79] China's health delivery system is typically centered on hospitals that are rewarded based on volume of services and sales of medicines and high-technology procedures. Therefore, the success of health delivery reform is largely depends on whether the government can reform public hospitals to build a primary-care–centered delivery system that provides high-quality and cost-effective health services.

Mental health service is primarily hospital based and is provided in special psychiatric hospitals or psychological departments of tertiary hospitals. Most mental health professionals are psychiatrists and psychiatric nurses, with few clinical psychologists or social workers. Mental health care has been separated from primary care. Mild mental health problems are treated at home or untreated. Only severely mentally ill patients are treated in psychiatric hospitals. According to China Health Statistical Yearbook 2019, in 2018, 42 million mental health patients visited the special psychiatric hospitals; on average, one psychiatrist treated 4.7 patients per day in 2018.[80] The funding for the mental health system is complex and small. Public insurance (Urban Employee Basic Medical Insurance and Urban–Rural Resident Basic Medical Insurance) covers inpatient and outpatient mental health care.[80,81]

Long-term care facilities in China are virtually nonexistent. Thus, long-term care is mostly provided by family members at home with few formal long-term care providers. Family caregivers are not paid formally, and long-term care insurance benefits are virtually absent from any health insurance scheme. There are some government efforts to develop a long-term care system, but there is no specific structure for delivering long-term care yet in place. In addition, formal long-term care facilities usually provide basic services, such as housekeeping, meals, and transportation. Health services are rarely provided by formal long-term care facilities.[75,82]

Workforce

There has been a significant growth in the quantity of health human resources in the past decade in China. Similar to most countries, the composition of the professional health workforce in China consists of medical practitioners, nurses, medical technicians, pharmacists, and other professionals. **Table 20-3** describes the composition of professional health workers.

In 2014, there were a total of 10,234,213 health workers, among whom 7,589,790 were medical technical personnel (licensed doctors, nurses, and other medical personnel), 1,058,182 were village doctors and health workers, and 1,586,241 were nonprofessional workers (administrators, logistical workers, etc.).[9] There have been insufficient numbers of nurses and other health professionals compared with the number of doctors. Unlike most other countries, China has traditionally had more doctors than nurses, with a national average ratio of 1.4 to 1 until 2014.[82–84] In addition, grassroots and rural health facilities, such as township hospitals and community health centers, have been experiencing shortages of

Table 20-3 Composition and Distribution of Health Workers in China (2021–2022)

Profession	Number
Medical personnel[a]	1,398.54 per 10,000 population
Medical technical personnel[a]	1,155.00 per 10,000 population
Licensed (assistant) doctors	440.00 per 10,000 population
Licensed doctors	359.08 per 10,000 population
Registered nurses	520.00 per 10,000 population
Pharmacists	52.09 per 10,000 population
Village doctors and assistants	69.67 per 10,000 population
Technical personnel	59.90 per 10,000 population
Administrative personnel	46.00 per 10,000 population
Logistics technical workers	98.54 per 10,000 population

[a]Data for medical personnel and medical technical personnel include sanitation supervisors and public servants.

Data from National Bureau of Statistics of China, 2013–2022. Accessed March 17, 2023. Accessed March 28, 2023. https://data.stats.gov.cn/english/easyquery.htm?cn=C01.

health professionals. Doctor density in urban areas is more than twice that in rural areas; nursing density is 3.3 times higher in urban areas than in rural areas.[9] The Chinese government has started to take measures to redistribute health human resources. Such measures include increasing the income of health professionals in the township and community health centers, waiving tuition for medical students who are willing to work in rural health facilities, and requiring regular staff exchanges between community health centers and hospitals.[84]

Higher education for professional health workers in China includes clinical medicine, preventive medicine, public health, traditional Chinese medicine, dentistry, medical laboratories, nursing, medical technology, and pharmacy programs. In 2018, China had 420 institutions that offered medical education, matriculating students in undergraduate, graduate, and postgraduate education, as well as in-service training.[85] The medical education system is complicated. In general, obtaining a medical doctorate in clinical medicine or medical technology requires 5 years of undergraduate study at a medical university, 2 to 3 years of master's degree study, and 3 years of postgraduate study consisting of 6 months at a medical university and 2.5 years of medical research, or 6 months of curriculum study and 1.5 years of clinical training in a hospital and 1 year of medical research.[85–87] To major in nursing or pharmacy, it usually takes 4 years of study for a bachelor's degree and 7 years for a master's degree.[85–87]

The educational background of Chinese medical graduates has been continuously improved. The number of higher clinical medicine graduates rose dramatically from 51,800 in 2002 to 182,900 in 2018, an annual growth rate of 8.2%.[85] Of the higher clinical medical graduates, 75% have a bachelor's degree or above. At the end of 2019, the national ratio of doctors to nurses was 1:1.15, amending the situation of more doctors than nurses before 2014 (see **Figure 20-6**).[85]

Technology

China's remarkable economic growth over the past 4 decades has led to the proliferation of health technology supporting specialized healthcare services in diagnosis and treatment in the country. High-technology medicine is a double-edged sword, however. It provides high-quality care but also drives up healthcare costs, in addition to its potential side effects. The unbalanced distribution of high technology is manifested in the growth of urban high-technology medicine at the expense of rural primary care. China has also become one of the top countries for biomedical technology development. Government policies favoring biomedical development combined with massive investments in health technology make China an emerging leader in the biomedical technology sector.[83]

In recent years, China has launched a series of aggressive campaigns to accelerate the adoption of health information technologies (HIT) to improve the quality of care, control costs, and enable regional and national information sharing for public health (e.g., disease outbreak surveillance) and other secondary-use purposes (e.g., research and policymaking). The 13th 5-Year Plan had identified "smarter health care" as a critical issue focusing on telemedicine, big data, electronic health records (EHRs), and health IT networks. To date, almost all healthcare providers have established EHR systems. However, due to the variations in EHR systems and the need for coordination, EHR systems can be operated only within an organization's own systems. The problem leads to low meaningful use of HIT for patients, diminishing the value of HIT for quality improvement and cost control purposes.[88]

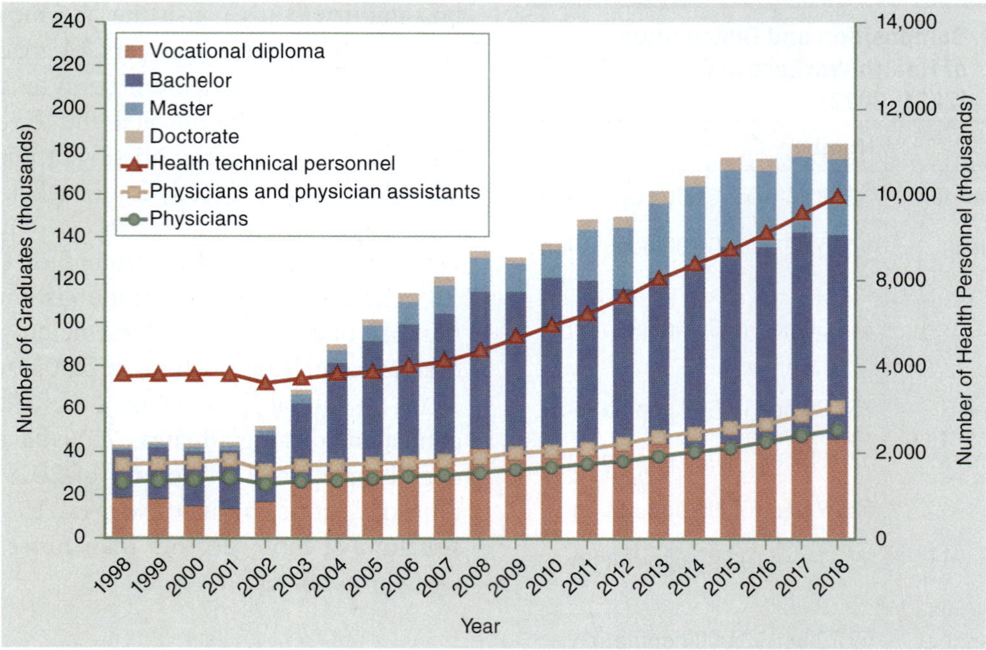

Figure 20-6 China's Health Technical Professionals and Clinical Medical Graduates by Education Level, 1998–2018

Reproduced from Wang, W. Medical education in China: progress in the past 70 years and a vision for the future. *BMC Med Educ.* 2021;21:453. doi: 10.1186/s12909-021-02875-6.

The most remarkable HIT achievement in China is perhaps the rapid establishment of a nationwide real-time, Internet-based notifiable disease reporting system, which is the world's largest: the China Information System for Disease Control and Prevention (CISDCP). Recognizing the importance of the timely collecting, processing, and reporting of epidemic information following the 2003 SARS crisis, the CHFPC mobilized tremendous resources within a very short period to create an integrated information-sharing network that links China's hospitals and clinics at all levels. The system, launched on January 1, 2004, covers 40 notifiable diseases (COVID-19 has been included since January 2020). The CISDCP has evolved to be implemented in 55,077 national health facilities in 397 cities and all 31 provinces in China.[80]

Another use of technology in China is digital health care and telemedicine, which have promoted growth in the number of distance healthcare cases in China. The use of telemedicine, digital health care, or eHealth can channel advanced health services available in large cities to grassroots rural areas.[89] Private investors have invested over $1 billion USD in digital health care, from e-commerce to online physician consultation services to health promotion and disease management applications. There are a number of challenges, though. For example, no clear regulation exists regarding eHealth or health technology applications, such as remote consultation—an issue the government must address. The quality, safety, and acceptance of using eHealth or digital health care are also unclear.[89,90]

Notably, artificial intelligence (AI) is being expanded in China's healthcare sector as part of the government's Made in China 2025 plan. There are artificial intelligence medical innovation systems (AIMIS) labs owned by Tencent in 10 hospitals across China.[91]

Evaluation of the Healthcare System

Cost

Health spending in China in recent decades has increased significantly, driven primarily by rapid economic growth, health insurance reforms, an aging population, health technology advancement, and a surge in noncommunicable diseases, such as cancer, diabetes, and heart disease. According to the National Bureau of Statistics of China, the country's health expenditure increased from ¥510 per capita in 2003 to ¥2,582 in 2014, and to ¥5,439 per capita in 2021.[91] Over the same period, government health spending as a percentage of total health expenditures rose from 17.8% to 30%. Health expenditures as a percentage of GDP rose from 4.8% to 5.6%.[91] It is projected that if the current hospital-centered delivery model that rewards volume and sales continues, health spending increases will average 8.4% per year. More than 60% of the projected growth in health spending will be due to increased hospital inpatient services.[92]

Some efforts have been made recently to control rising healthcare costs, such as the introduction of diagnosis-related groups (DRGs), global budgets, capitation to replace the fee-for-service provider payment system, and the release of the essential drugs list (zero markups for these drugs' retail price). In addition, the central government placed constraints on new hospital buildings, new hospital beds, and the purchase of high-technology equipment.[73] China needs further health system reform to meet the growing needs of the population and to control health costs, according to a 2-year study conducted jointly by the World Bank, the WHO, the Ministry of Finance, the National Health and Family Planning Commission, and the Ministry of Human Resources and Social Security of China.[92] This study pointed out that despite the remarkable achievements in universal health coverage from the government's 2009 health reforms, deeper health reform is needed for China to build a value-based health service delivery system that provides high-quality and cost-effective care.

Quality

In 2000, the World Health Organization conducted a study to measure the overall health system performance for 191 member countries using five key measures: disability-adjusted life expectancy; responsiveness of the health system, including speed of service; protection of privacy; quality of amenities; and fairness of financial contribution. China was ranked 144th.[93] Since then, China has instituted major health reforms and made significant progress toward improving health and healthcare quality. The health of the Chinese population has improved significantly, with life expectancy at birth increasing from 72 years in 2000 to 77.9 years in 2020.[93] The maternal mortality ratio decreased from 58 per 100,000 live births in 2000 to 16 per 100,000 live births in 2021.[93] The infant mortality rate dropped from 30.0 to 5.0 per 1,000 live births, and the under-5 mortality rate dropped from 37.0 to 7.1 per 1,000 live births from 2000 to 2021.[93] **Figure 20-7** shows that the child mortality rate has decreased since 2013 in China.

Despite the improvements in major health indicators, the profound rural–urban disparities in health and healthcare quality persist. In a study conducted in a province of China, neonatal mortality in rural areas was more than twice that in urban areas. The chances of neonatal death due to birth asphyxia, preterm low birth weight, and pneumonia were 2.2 to 2.6 higher for rural babies than urban babies. These differences largely reflect poor access to prenatal health services and poor quality of care provided in rural areas.[94] The authors of the study pointed out that most neonatal death in rural areas was caused by preventable or treatable conditions. In other words, those deaths could have been avoided if timely and appropriate health care had been provided.[94] **Figure 20-8** demonstrates the persistent rural–urban disparities in infant and child mortality rates in 2021.[93]

The quality of health workers, such as village doctors and facilities in rural areas, is generally low. Most village doctors are descended from barefoot doctors who were undertrained, had a low level of education, and had limited experience. In addition, there is no systematic strategy to monitor and evaluate

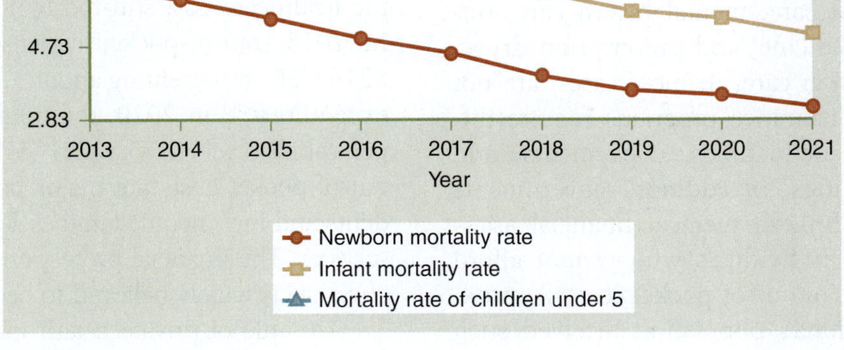

Figure 20-7 Mortality Rate, China, 2013–2021

Data from National Bureau of Statistics of China. Accessed March 28, 2023. https://data.stats.gov.cn/english/easyquery.htm?cn=C01.

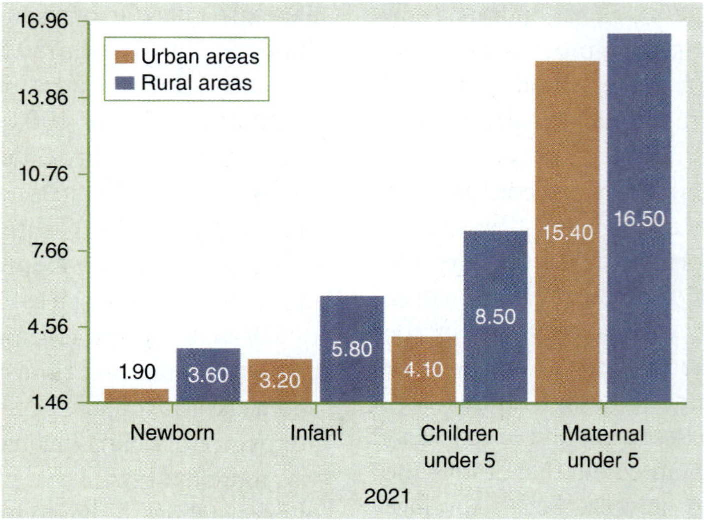

Figure 20-8 Infant and Child Mortality Rate: Urban Versus Rural in China, 2021

Data from Mortality rate, China, 2013–2021. National Bureau of Statistics of China, 2013–2022. Accessed March 28, 2023. https://data.stats.gov.cn/english/easyquery.htm?cn=C01.

village doctors.[95] A study of quality in rural areas of China concluded that the quality of care provided in rural clinics could be better.[96]

The central government has implemented some measures to improve the quality of health services in general and to reduce the rural–urban inequities in particular. For example, in 2009, the former Ministry of Health released clinical pathways that are now regulated nationally. Governments sponsor training for rural doctors in urban hospitals, provide financial incentives for new medical graduates to work in rural hospitals, and require new graduates to work as residents in rural health facilities.

Access

China achieved near-universal health coverage in 2012 with its three main publicly financed health insurance programs: NRCMS (for rural residents), UEBMI (for urban employed), and URBMI (for urban unemployed). The coverage rate reached more than 95% of the entire population of China.[53] All three programs cover primary care, specialist care, emergency care, hospital care, mental health care, traditional Chinese medicine, and prescription drugs. Dental care and vision care, in most cases, are not covered. All three insurance programs require different amounts of deductibles, copayments, and reimbursement ceilings. In addition, governments provide subsidies through medical financial assistance programs for individuals who cannot afford insurance premiums or out-of-pocket costs. Approximately 6.6% of China's population received such medical financial assistance for paying insurance premiums or health expenses.[80]

There is no limitation on a patient's choice and no general practitioner gatekeeping role for specialist or hospital services, although patients are encouraged to seek primary care in grassroots clinics and lower-level healthcare facilities. The reimbursement is usually higher for the services received from lower-level healthcare facilities.

The World Health Organization defines universal health coverage as "attained when people actually obtained the health services they need and benefit from financial risk protection" and universal access as "the opportunity or ability to do both of these things."[97] Despite China's universal health insurance coverage, two major problems of access to health care remain. One is the availability problem, with major urban hospitals (particularly tertiary hospitals) and academic health centers being crowded with long waiting lines, and rural areas suffering from poor quality of health providers and hospitals. The other is the financial burden of using health services. Out-of-pocket costs for copayments and deductibles, coupled with low reimbursement ceilings, make the healthcare cost still too high for many to afford. In 2013, out-of-pocket expenses per capita were $216 USD, representing about 34% of the total health expenditure.[80] In 2020, the total health expenditure per capita reached ¥5,112.3 ($701.49 USD).[98] High out-of-pocket costs are major barriers for rural residents and low-income families seeking needed health services. The financial protection offered by universal coverage is widely believed to be inadequate.

The role of private health insurance may include covering deductibles, copayments, and other cost-sharing, as well as providing coverage for expensive services not paid for by public insurance. Most private insurance purchasers are higher-income individuals and employers. In addition, private health insurance is mainly provided by for-profit commercial insurance companies. The Chinese government is encouraging the development of the private insurance market, and some foreign insurance companies have entered the market.

Innovation

When considering China's health system, a key question arises: How could China provide near-universal coverage (over 95% of the population is covered by the essential healthcare insurance system) for its enormous population of 1.4 billion in such a short time whereas the United States cannot?[81] Many factors fed into this achievement, including strong government financial and political commitment, rapid economic growth backing the Chinese government's ambitious move, strong public support of government intervention in the health sector, and socialist ideology endorsing health as a right of all.[53] Many of these factors are unique to China, and collectively they created the right timing and opportunity. But without one innovative strategy, universal coverage might not be realized in such a short time: First, provide shallow coverage for all; then gradually expand benefits to cover the specific needs of the population; then reduce out-of-pocket money as more government financing becomes available and involve private insurers to provide complementary coverage. This innovative strategy may provide a model for other countries that are pursuing universal health coverage. Another innovation in China's health sector is the focus on digital health developments, including telemedicine, which can bridge the rural–urban gap in health and health care.

Current and Emerging Issues and Challenges

China embarked on a systematic health reform to provide affordable basic health care for all of China's population by 2020. However, despite the impressive accomplishments of the ongoing health reform since 2009, such as successfully launching and implementing universal coverage for 1.3 billion Chinese people, China is facing a number of challenges. Some of these challenges are common to other countries, such as aging populations and an epidemiologic transition from infectious diseases to noncommunicable chronic diseases (NCDs); others reflect China's progress toward its goal of building a high-quality, value-based healthcare delivery system and becoming a wealthy and harmonious society.

Burden of Noncommunicable Chronic Diseases and an Aging Society

China is living through a rapid epidemiological transition from infectious diseases to NCDs.[97] NCDs, including heart disease, stroke, cancer, diabetes, and chronic lung disease, are collectively responsible for 74% of all deaths worldwide.[99] According to the Global Burden of Disease Study, NCDs accounted for 89.5% of all deaths in China.[100] The top causes of death have consistently been malignant tumors, cerebrovascular disease, heart disease, respiratory disease, trauma, and toxicosis; they accounted for 82.6% of deaths in 2000 and 86.49% of deaths in 2017 in urban areas, and 83.31% of deaths in 2000 and 88.34% of deaths in 2017 in rural areas.[101] The prevalence rates of most NCD risk factors are rising, challenging China's health system.[102]

The burden of NCDs is compounded by the aging population. The results of China's seventh population census show that China's 2020 population stood at 1.4118 billion, including 264 million people aged 60 and over and 191 million aged 65 and over, comprising 18.7% and 13.5% of the total population, respectively.[103] The unhealthy lifestyles associated with urbanization, such as smoking, excessive drinking, physical inactivity, and a diet high in fat, sugar, and salt are prevalent in China. For example, as many as 67% of Chinese men smoke, contributing to more than 1 million smoking-related deaths yearly. If the current trend continues, the number of smoking-related deaths will double to 2 million by 2030, making it the number one cause of preventable death.[104] To tackle the issue of NCDs, the General Office of the State Council of the People's Republic of China issued the "Medium-to-Long Term Plan of China for the Prevention and Treatment of Chronic Diseases (2017–2025)" in January 2017. This marked a milestone in the history of the prevention and treatment of chronic diseases in China.[105]

Inequity in Health and Health Care

The disparities and inequities in health and health care continue to be a crucial challenge for China. Significant variations in access to health care and healthcare outcomes exist between rural and urban areas, rural migrants and city dwellers, and geographic areas such as the eastern and western provinces in China.

China's 1.4 billion population lives in vastly diverse geographic areas with varying economic conditions. As a result, healthcare inequalities remain a serious problem.[106,107] Although the Chinese government has made efforts to tackle this problem, the inequity in health and health care continues to widen and most likely will worsen as society experiences substantial changes associated with the economic growth of the past 4 decades. Changes in living conditions, lifestyles, individual values, and consumer behaviors will confound the issues of inequities and disparities. One positive aspect is that the Healthy China Action (2019–2030) plan set a goal of achieving health equity by 2030.[108,109] It is hoped that the Chinese government and its people will accomplish this goal to reduce inequity in health and health care across the nation.

Air Pollution and Health

China is confronted with severe and extensive air pollution, with the highest concentrations in and near urban areas. The physical and psychological effects of air pollution have been recognized as having severe negative impacts on the health and well-being of people. Outdoor air pollution contributes to an estimated 1.6 million deaths in China annually.[104] About 38% of the Chinese population breathes air that would be rated unhealthy by U.S. standards. The most dangerous pollutants are fine airborne particles, less than 2.5 microns in diameter, which can be breathed deep into the lungs and absorbed into the bloodstream, where they cause various health problems, including asthma, strokes, lung cancer, and heart attacks.[110]

Air pollution of all types causes about 2 million deaths in China per year. Of those deaths, ambient air pollution alone causes more than 1 million deaths, while household air pollution from cooking with polluting fuels and technologies causes another million deaths.[111] Some studies have shown that general air pollution and haze episodes have resulted in a substantial disease burden in the form of an excess number of premature deaths, disability-adjusted life-years loss, and years of life lost.[112] Overall, the disease burden and health economic loss due to ambient air pollution in China are greater than those in the rest of the world.

Over the past decade, significant progress has been made in improving air quality in China.[113] This success has mainly been attributed to China's clean air policies and governmental funding to reduce the emissions of pollutants and alleviate the production of harmful aerosols. However, air pollution remains a significant risk factor that harms people's health and quality of life in China. The Chinese government announced it was allocating 405.3 billion yuan ($57.22 billion USD) for environmental protections in 2020. Out of this total, 25 billion yuan was to be used for air pollution prevention and control.[114]

Inefficient Healthcare Delivery

China faces the challenge of building an effective and efficient healthcare delivery system to serve its large and aging population.[115] Studies show that the reform in 2009 likely impacted the performance of the healthcare delivery system positively; however, low efficiency exists in China's healthcare delivery system, mainly attributed to the weakened primary healthcare system and inadequate quality of care.[116,117]

China's healthcare delivery model heavily centers on hospitals, which are used as one-stop shopping for all health services. Patients very often have difficulty accessing large hospitals for services that could be offered in a primary-care or ambulatory-care setting. Thus, establishing a tiered healthcare delivery system to coordinate primary and hospital health care is vital for delivering efficient and affordable health care.[118] China's healthcare reform can only be considered a complete success with the establishment of a tiered healthcare delivery system where general practitioners are empowered to provide needed and timely care and serve as gatekeepers. The Chinese government has prioritized primary health care in its Healthy China 2030 strategy as part of its effort to create such a healthcare delivery system.[118]

As China's health delivery model is shifting from expensive hospital-focused care to cost-effective, grassroots-based primary care, building a robust primary care infrastructure that is coordinated and integrated with tertiary care and referral systems is critical. However, such a transformation poses several challenges:

1. The quality of primary care providers at the grassroots level and health workforce distribution must be improved.
2. Provider payment mechanisms, including disconnecting financial incentives from service volumes and prescription drugs, must be established and reinforced.
3. Health resources need to be increased in the areas with the greatest needs.

4. The efficiency of hospitals must be improved.
5. Healthcare professionalism that puts patients' interests first must be developed.
6. A systematic strategy to monitor, evaluate, and control the quality of health services across the delivery system must be developed.

China still has a long way to go to deliver value-based and affordable quality care for all. Improving the efficiency of the healthcare system requires China to face and tackle these steep challenges.

COVID-19 Pandemic

The novel coronavirus (COVID-19) pandemic has been the greatest public health crisis in the 21st century across the world. As the world's most populous country, China was watched by the world for its countermeasures to control the COVID-19 spread. The pandemic's first outbreak was in Wuhan, Hubei Province, China. On December 31, 2019, Chinese health officials informed the WHO of unknown cases of pneumonia detected in Wuhan City.[119] Following the Chinese authorities' report, the virus spread quickly to over 100 countries, with more than 120,000 cases and over 4,000 deaths reported as of early March 2020.[120] Based on the alarming levels of the virus spread and severity, the WHO declared the COVID-19 outbreak a global pandemic on March 11, 2020.[121,122]

The mysterious, novel coronavirus was finally identified, and the newly confirmed cases increased exponentially in Hubei Province. The local government's initial response to the COVID-19 outbreak was slow in Wuhan City, which was the COVID-19 epicenter. The Chinese central government sent a medical expert team with officials to investigate the cause and the severity of the virus infection transmission in Wuhan City. As of April 24, 2020, 83,885 cases had been reported in China with 4,636 deaths, mostly (4,512) in Hubei Province.[123] To respond to this emerging health crisis, Chinese national authorities instituted extreme measures to contain the virus, putting Wuhan City in lockdown. Flights and trains were suspended, and roads were closed. The same strict measures of isolation were implemented around the country. Entertainment venues, schools, shopping markets, and workplaces were closed, and public gatherings were banned. With these highly aggressive measures, the number of newly confirmed cases was significantly reduced from thousands per day at the peak down to a couple of dozen since early March 2020.[123]

The extreme measures with well-organized planning and implementation, the effective dissemination of information, the support of Chinese medical professionals and scientists, and public compliance with the government's measures, such as reinforcing social distancing, using good hygiene, wearing face masks, and getting vaccinated resulted in significant success in China in controlling COVID-19 and saving lives.[123–125] As of December 29, 2022, 6,686,599 people had died of COVID-19 worldwide.[124] China has had far fewer deaths than any other large nation and one of the lowest deaths per capita in the world.

As the rest of the world relaxed its COVID policies and returned to normal life in late 2021 and early 2022, China continued its zero-case COVID policy with strict reporting, isolation, and lockdown measures. In late November 2022, however, the Chinese government faced a public outcry challenging the zero-case policy's value, efficiency, and practicality. An angry public in several big Chinese cities protested and demanded that the Chinese government lift its zero-case policy, stop the lockdowns, and open public facilities.[125] Global health experts and scholars predicted that China's zero-case policy could not be sustained and suggested changing or ending this policy.[125,126]

In early December 2022, Chinese national authorities lifted all restrictions, abolishing the zero-case policy overnight without any forewarning or planning of the public. Chinese people were eager to go back to everyday life after prolonged extreme measures. Following the abrupt and unprepared opening, China suffered a devastating surge in COVID-19 cases in December 2022. Hospitals were overflowing with individuals infected with the Omicron COVID-19 variant. The increased infections, coupled with an unprepared healthcare system, such as a lack of medications, medical supplies, and planned resources to meet the demands for a large, infected population, resulted in a significant increase in the death rate, especially in the elderly.[126] Although China's official COVID-19 death toll for the pandemic showed 83,150 deaths as of February 17, 2023, it is believed and estimated that the country's COVID-19 wave may have killed from 1 million to 1.5 million people, reversing the achievements of the 3-year extreme measures combined with the compliance of the public.[127]

We end this chapter with takeaways from China's experience. First, the strict prevention and control policies undoubtedly slowed the spread of COVID-19 and saved lives. Second, the 1.4 billion Chinese people of all genders, ages, and walks of life formed a united and resilient force led by the central government to fight the battle against the epidemic. Third, in addition to well-planned and well-organized efforts, the traditional Chinese collectivism culture and the social values revolving around what is best for the community and society endorsed the government's extreme measures to control the pandemic. Finally, the advanced use of digital technology in the fast and accurate tracking of new cases played a substantial role in preventing and stopping the spread. However, all of the success using the extreme measures, including the zero-case policy, came at a considerable cost that has long-term impacts on the Chinese economy and everyday life. We must ask if there is a balanced approach between saving lives and living life, or if other countries can or are willing to apply the Chinese model when preparing for the next pandemic.

References

1. Murphey R. *East Asia: A New History*. 5th ed. New York, NY: Longman-Pearson; 2009.
2. Ho PT. The significance of the Ch'ing Period in Chinese history. *J Asian Stud*. 1967;2(26):189-195.
3. Blunden C, Elvin M. *Cultural Atlas of China*. Revised ed. New York, NY: Checkmark Books; 1998.
4. China's state organizational structure. Accessed March 13, 2023. https://www.cecc.gov/chinas-state-organizational-structure.
5. National Committee of Chinese People's Political Consultative Conference. Accessed April 4, 2023. http://en.cppcc.gov.cn/structure.html.
6. Li C. *China's Leaders: The New Generation*. New York, NY: Rowman & Littlefield; 2001.
7. Hieyeon K, Campbell JR. The price of change: policy reform and leadership transitions in post 1978 Chinese politics with comparison to Gorbachev's Soviet Union. *J East Asian Aff*. 1994;8(1).
8. World Bank. GDP (current US$). World Bank national accounts data, and OECD National Accounts data files. Published 2022. Accessed November 28, 2022. https://data.worldbank.org/indicator/NY.GDP.MKTP.CD?view=chart.
9. National Bureau of Statistics of China. *China Statistical Yearbook 2021*. Beijing, China: National Bureau of Statistics of China; 2021.
10. National Bureau of Statistics of China. Statistical communique of the People's Republic of China on the 2020 national economic and social development. Published 2021. Accessed November 28, 2022. http://www.stats.gov.cn/english/PressRelease/202102/t20210228_1814177.html.
11. World Bank. Exports of goods and services (% of GDP). World Bank national accounts data, and OECD National Accounts data files. Published 2022. Accessed November 28, 2022. https://data.worldbank.org/indicator/NE.EXP.GNFS.ZS.
12. World Bank. Imports of goods and services (% of GDP). World Bank national accounts data, and OECD National Accounts data files. Accessed November 30, 2022. https://data.worldbank.org/indicator/NE.IMP.GNFS.ZS. 2022.
13. Observatory of Economic Complexity. China. Published 2022. Accessed November 29, 2022. https://oec.world/en/profile/country/chn.
14. China's State Administration of Foreign Exchange. The scale of China's foreign exchange reserves (1950–2015). Accessed July 14, 2016. http://www.safe.gov.cn/.
15. World Bank. Foreign direct investment, net inflows (BoP, current US $). International Monetary Fund, Balance of Payments database, supplemented by data from the United Nations Conference on Trade and Development and official national sources. Accessed March 18, 2023. http://data.worldbank.org/indicator/BX.KLT.DINV.CD.WD.
16. World Bank. GDP per capita (current US $). World Bank national accounts data, and OECD National Accounts data files. Accessed March 18, 2023. http://data.worldbank.org/indicator/NY.GDP.PCAP.CD.
17. World Bank. Age dependency ratio (% of working-age population). Accessed March 18, 2023. http://data.worldbank.org/indicator/SP.POP.DPND.
18. Taylor RL. Proposition and praxis: the dilemma of neo-Confucian syncretism. *Philos East West*. 1982;32(2).
19. Religion in China. Accessed March 16, 2023. https://en.wikipedia.org/wiki/.
20. Opinions on further reducing the burden on students in the compulsory education state from homework and extracurricular training. Published 2021. 'Accessed November 29, 2022. http://www.gov.cn/zhengce/2021-07/24/content_5627132.htm (original Chinese version). https://www.chinalawtranslate.com/en/two-burdens/ (unofficial translation).
21. Central People's Government of the People's Republic of China. China's education system. Published 2016. Accessed November 29, 2022. http://english1.english.gov.cn/2005-08/27/content_26661.htm.
22. China Education Center. Education in China. Published 2022. Accessed November 2022. https://www.chinaeducenter.com/en/cedu.php.
23. World Bank. The World Bank in China. Published 2022. Accessed November 29, 2022. https://www.worldbank.org/en/country/china/overview.
24. World Health Organization. Summary of probable SARS cases with onset of illness from 1 November 2002 to 31 July 2003. Accessed April 1, 2023. https://www.who.int/publications/m/item/summary-of-probable-sars-cases-with-onset-of-illness-from-1-november-2002-to-31-july-2003.
25. Zhang D. *The Social History of Disease in Modern China*. Shandong, China: Shandong Education Publishing House; 2006.
26. World Bank. *Financing Health Care: Issues and Options for China*. China 2020 Series. Washington, DC: World Bank; 1997.
27. Blumenthal D, Hsiao WW. Privatization and its discontents: the evolving Chinese health care system. *N Engl J Med*. 2005;353(11):1665-1670.
28. Blumenthal D, Hsiao W. Lessons from the East: China's rapidly evolving health care system. *N Engl J Med*. 2015;372(14):1165-1170.

29. Yuanli L. China's public health-care system: facing the challenges. *Bull World Health Organ*. 2004;82:532-538.
30. Zhang SN, Liu ZB, Gu ZW. Disease control and prevention in China in the 20th century and prospects. *Environ Health Prev Med*. 2002(7):132-137.
31. Ma J, Lu M, Quan H. From a national, centrally planned health system to a system based on the market: lessons from China. *Health Aff*. 2008;27(4):937-948.
32. World Bank. Life expectancy at birth, total (years). Accessed April 1, 2023. https://data.worldbank.org/indicator/SP.DYN.LE00.IN.
33. Liu G, Liu X, Meng Q. Privatization of the medical market in socialist China: a historical approach. *Health Policy*. 1994;27:157-174.
34. Barber SL, Lan Y. *Health Insurance Systems in China: A Briefing Note. World Health Report 2010: Background Paper*, No. 37. World Health Organization; 2010.
35. Hillier S, Shen J. Health care systems in transition: People's Republic of China. Part I: an overview of China's health care system. *J Public Health Med*. 1996;18(3):258-265.
36. Meng Q, Tang S. Universal health care coverage in China: challenges and opportunities. *Soc Behav Sci*. 2013;77:330-340.
37. Hu S, Tang S, Liu Y, et al. *Health System Reform in China 6*. World Health Organization. Published October 20, 2008. Accessed July 28, 2016. www.who.int/management/district/6.Financing.pdf.
38. Tao D, Hawkins L, Wang H, et al. *Fixing the Public Hospital System in China*. Washington, DC: World Bank; 2010.
39. Liu X, Liu Y, Chen N. The Chinese experience of hospital price regulation. *Health Policy Plan*. 2000;2(15):157-163.
40. Hesketh T, Zhu W. Health in China: the healthcare market. *BMJ*. 2004;314:1616-1618.
41. Daemmrich A. The political economy of healthcare reform in China: negotiating public and private. *SpringerPlus*. 2013;2(448):1-13.
42. Liu X, Mills A. The influence of bonus payments to doctors on hospital revenue: results of a quasi-experimental study. *Appl Health Econ Health Policy*. 2003;2(2):91-98.
43. *Healthcare in China: Toward Greater Access, Efficiency, and Quality*. IBM Institute for Business Value. Accessed April 1, 2023. https://www.yumpu.com/en/document/read/5584886/healthcare-in-china-ibm-business-consulting-services.
44. Shi L. Health care in China: a rural–urban comparison after the socioeconomic reforms. *Bulletin of the World Health Organization*. 1993;71(6):723-736.
45. Shi G, Gong S. Analysis about China's health investment since market open and reform. *China Dev Rev*. 2005.
46. Park A. *Rural–Urban Inequality in China*. World Bank; 2010.
47. Liu M, Zhang Q, Lu M, Kwon CS, Quan H. Rural and urban disparity in health services utilization in China. *Med Care*. 2007;45(8):767-774.
48. Liu Y, Hsiao WC, Eggleston K. Equity in health and health care: the Chinese experience. *Soc Sci Med*. 1999;49:1349-1356.
49. Hsiao WC. Disparity in health: the underbelly of China's economic development. *Harvard School of Public Health*. 2004;1(5):64-70.
50. Liu Y. China's public health-care system: facing the challenges. *Bull World Health Organ*. 2004;82(7):532-538.
51. Jiang Y, Jin S. *Social Economic Burden Attributed to Smoking in China*. Paper presented at National Conference on Policy Development of Tobacco Control in China in the 21st Century, Beijing, China, 2000.
52. Ma J, Lu M, Quan H. From a national, centrally planned health system to a system based on the market: lessons from China. *Health Aff*. 2008;27(4):937-948.
53. Yu H. Universal health insurance coverage for 1.3 billion people: what accounts for China's success. *Health Policy*. 2015;119:1145-1152.
54. Ma X, Zhang J, Meessen B, et al. Social health assistance schemes: the case of medical financial assistance for the rural poor in four counties of China. *Int J Equity Health*. 2011;10(44):1-13.
55. Yip WCM, Hsiao WC, Chen W, et al. Early appraisal of China's huge and complex health-care reforms. *Lancet*. 2012;379:833-841.
56. Li C, Hou Y, Sun M, Lu J. An evaluation of China's new rural cooperative medical system: achievements and inadequacies from policy goals. *BMC Public Health*. 2015;15(1079):1-9.
57. Long Q, Xu L, Bekedam H, Tang S. Changes in health expenditures in China in 2000s: has the health system reform improved affordability. *Int J Equity Health*. 2013;12(40):1-8.
58. You X, Kobayashi Y. The new cooperative medical scheme in China. *Health Policy*. 2009;91:1-1.
59. China National Bureau of Statistics. Statistical communiqué of the People's Republic of China on the 2010 national economic and social. Accessed April 6, 2023. http://www.stats.gov.cn/english/NewsEvents/201102/t20110228_26426.html.
60. Guo B. China's urban health care system. *Asian Survey*. 2003;43(2):385-403.
61. Liu Y. Reforming China's urban health insurance system. *Health Policy*. 2002(2):133-150.
62. James CA. Reform plans promise significant change, but what does that mean for foreign healthcare players? *China Business Rev*. 2009.
63. Dong K. Medical insurance system evolution in China. *China Econ Rev*. 2009;20(4):591-597.
64. UNICEF China. Basic medical insurance for children in China. August 2023;3. Accessed February 25, 2025. https://www.unicef.cn/media/25331/file/BASIC%20MEDICAL%20INSURANCE%20FOR%20CHILDREN%20IN%20CHINA.pdf.
65. Si W. Public health insurance and the labor market: Evidence from China's urban resident basic medical insurance. October 23, 2020. Accessed February 25, 2025. https://weisi.website/wp-content/uploads/2020/12/full_paper_urbmi_he_r2.pdf.
66. National Medical Products Administration. China raises government subsidies for basic public health services. 2023. Accessed February 25, 2025. https://english.nmpa.gov.cn/2023-07/13/c_902761.htm.
67. Lin W, Liu GG, Gang C. The urban resident basic medical insurance: a landmark reform towards universal coverage in China. *Health Econ*. 2009;18(suppl 2):S83-S96.
68. Zhu C. Launch of the health-care reform plan in China. *Lancet*. 2009;373:1322-1324.
69. Ministry of Health. National essential medicines list for primary health institutions. Central People's Government of People's Republic of China. [In Chinese.] Accessed April 6, 2023. http://www.gov.cn/gzdt/2009-08/18/content_1395524.htm.
70. Cheng TM. Early results of China's historical health reforms: the view from Minister Chen Zhu. *Health Aff*. 2012;31(11):2536-2544.

71. Zhang Y, Ma Q, Chen Y, Gao H. Effects of public hospital reform on inpatient expenditures in rural China. *Health Econ*. 2016. doi: 10.1002/hec.3320.
72. Guan X, Qi L, Liu L. Controversy in public hospital reforms in China. *Lancet Global Health*. 2016;4(4 e420):1.
73. Zhang Y, Ma Q, Chen Y, Gao H. Effects of public hospital reform on inpatient expenditures in rural China. *Health Econ*. 2016. doi: 10.1002/hec.3320.
74. Lu Y, Wang, Z. China expands pilot program for foreign investment in the healthcare sector. Accessed February 25, 2025. https://www.lexology.com/library/detail.aspx?g=b66e2f33-a22b-4719-9012-d43109029011.
75. *International Profiles of Health Care Systems*. Commonwealth Fund; 2020. Accessed March 17, 2023. https://www.commonwealthfund.org/international-health-policy-center/countries/china.
76. Health care institutions (2021–2022). National Bureau of Statistics of China. 2021–2022. Accessed March 17, 2023. https://data.stats.gov.cn/english/easyquery.htm?cn=C01.
77. National Bureau of Statistics of China, 2013–2021. Accessed March 17, 2023. https://data.stats.gov.cn/english/easyquery.htm?cn=C01.
78. Zhang, W. Number of public and private hospitals in China from 2014 to 2021. February 1, 2023. Accessed February 25, 2025. https://www.statista.com/statistics/624593/china-hospital-number-by-ownerships.
79. Kahler C. China's healthcare reform: how far has it come? *China Business Review*. 2011.
80. National Health Commission. *China Health Statistical Yearbook 2019*. Accessed April 6, 2023. http://www.stats.gov.cn/sj/ndsj/2019/indexeh.htm.
81. Liu J, Ma H, He YL, et al. Mental health system in China: history, recent service reform and future challenges. *World Psychiatry*. 2011;10(3):210-216.
82. Du P. *Long-Term Care for Older Persons in China. Working paper*. United Nations Economic and Social Commission for Asia and the Pacific; 2015.
83. National Bureau of Statistics of China, 2013–2022. Accessed March 17, 2023. https://data.stats.gov.cn/english/easyquery.htm?cn=C01.
84. Anand S, Fan V, Zhang J, et al. China's human resources for health: quantity, quality, and distribution. *Lancet*. 2008;372(9651):1774-1781.
85. Wang W. Medical education in China: progress in the past 70 years and a vision for the future. *BMC Med Educ*. 2021;21:453. https://doi.org/10.1186/s12909-021-02875-6.
86. Xu D, Sun B, Wan X, Ke Y. Reformation of medical education in China. *Lancet*. 2010;375(10):1502-1504.
87. Lijuan W, Wang Y, Peng X, et al. Development of a medical academic degree system in China. *Med Educ Online*. 2014;19:1-7.
88. Chen Y, He Y, Chi X, et al. Development of health technology assessment in China: new challenges. *Biosci Trends*. 2018;12(2):102-108. doi: 10.5582/bst.2018.01038.
89. Zhao N, Wu B, Samples C, Shaw RJ. Mobile technology for health care in rural China. *Intl J Nurs Sci*. 2014;1:323-324.
90. Chaua PY, Hu PJH. Investigating healthcare professionals' decisions to accept telemedicine technology: an empirical test of competing theories. *Inform Manag*. 2002;39:297-311.
91. Lee C, Rao E, Tong A, Wang M. *Tech in China: The Future of Chinese Healthcare*. Accessed December 27, 2022. https://www.coresponsibility.com/wp-content/uploads/2018/09/Technology-China-Future-Chinese-Healthcare.pdf.pdf 2018.
92. World Bank Group, World Health Organization, Ministry of Finance, National Health and Family Planning Commission, Ministry of Human Resources and Social Security. *Healthy China: Deepening Health Reform in China, Building High-Quality and Value-Based Service Delivery*. World Bank Group; 2016.
93. Mortality rate, China, 2013–2021. National Bureau of Statistics of China, 2013–2022. Accessed March 28, 2023. https://data.stats.gov.cn/english/easyquery.htm?cn=C01.
94. Yi B, Wu L, Liu H, et al. Rural–urban differences of neonatal mortality in a poorly developed province of China. *BMC Public Health*. 2011;11(477):1-7.
95. Tang S, Ehiri J, Longcorrespo Q. China's biggest, most neglected health challenge: non-communicable diseases. *Infect Dis Poverty*. 2013;2(1):7.
96. Sylvia S, Shi Y, Xue H, et al. Survey using incognito standardized patients shows poor quality care in China's rural clinics. *Health Pol Plan*. 2015;30(3):322-333. doi: 10.1093/heapol/czu014.
97. Evans D, Hsu J, Boerma T. Universal health coverage and universal access. *Bull World Health Organ*. 2013;91:546-546A. doi: http://dx.doi.org/10.2471/BLT.13.125450.
98. Wang N. The temporal and spatial interpretation of China's health financing: what do Chinese' government 'do' in new healthcare reform? *Health Econ Rev*. 2024;14(76). Accessed February 25, 2025. https://healtheconomicsreview.biomedcentral.com/articles/10.1186/s13561-024-00551-1.
99. World Health Organization. Noncommunicable diseases. Accessed February 23, 2023. https://www.who.int/health-topics/noncommunicable-diseases#tab=tab_1.
100. Yang G, Kong L, Zhao W, et al. Emergence of chronic non-communicable disease in China. *Lancet*. 2008;372(9650):1679-1705.
101. Collaborators GBDM. Global, regional, and national age-sex-specific mortality and life expectancy, 1950-2017: a systematic analysis for the Global Burden of Disease Study 2017. *Lancet*. 2018;392:1684-1685. doi:10.1016/S0140-6736(18)31891-9.
102. Zou H, Li Z, Tian X, Ren Y. The top 5 causes of death in China from 2000 to 2017. *Sci Rep*. 2022;12(1):8119. doi: 10.1038/s41598-022-12256-8.
103. Tu WJ, Zeng X, Liu Q. Aging tsunami coming: the main finding from China's seventh national population census. *Aging Clin Exp Res*. 2022;34(5):1159-1163. doi: 10.1007/s40520-021-02017-4.
104. Koplan J, Eriksen M. Smoking cessation for Chinese men and prevention for women. *Lancet*. 2015;386:1422-1423.
105. Kong LZ. China's medium-to-long term plan for the prevention and treatment of chronic diseases (2017–2025) under the Healthy China initiative. *Chronic Dis Transl Med*. 2017;3(3):135-137. doi: 10.1016/j.cdtm.2017.06.004.
106. Wang T, Zeng R. Addressing inequalities in China's health service. *Lancet*. 2015;386(10002):1441. doi:10.1016/S0140-6736(15)00402-X.
107. Guo B, Xie X, Wu Q, et al. Inequality in the health services utilization in rural and urban China: a horizonal inequality analysis. *Medicine*. 2020. doi: 10.1097/MD.0000000000018625.
108. People's Republic of China. Healthy China Action (2019–2030). Accessed February 19, 2023. http://www.gov.cn/xinwen/2019-07/15/content_5409694.htm.
109. Wang Z, Yang G, Guo Y. Harnessing the opportunity to achieve health equity in China. *Lancet Public Health*.

2021;6(12):e867-e868. doi: 10.1016/S2468-2667(21)00211-5.

110. Rohde R, Muller R. Air pollution in China: mapping of concentrations and sources. *PLoS One*. 2015;10(8):e0135749. http://dx.doi.org/10.1371/journal.pone.0135749.

111. World Health Organization. Air pollution in China. Accessed February 19, 2023. https://www.who.int/china/health-topics/air-pollution.

112. Niu Y, Chen R, Kan H. Air pollution, disease burden, and health economic loss in China. *Adv Exp Med Biol*. 2017;1017:233-242. doi: 10.1007/978-981-10-5657-4_10.

113. Yin P, Brauer M, Cohen AJ, et al. The effect of air pollution on deaths, disease burden, and life expectancy across China and its provinces, 1990–2017: an analysis for the Global Burden of Disease Study 2017. *Lancet Planet Health*. 2020;4(9):e386-e398. doi: 10.1016/S2542-5196(20)30161-3.

114. Reuters. China to allocate $57 billion to environment protection. Published May 21, 2020. Accessed February 20. https://www.reuters.com/article/us-china-environment-budget-idUSKBN22Y0BU.

115. Mattke S, Liu H, Hunter LE, et al. The role of health care transformation for the Chinese dream: powering economic growth, promoting a harmonious society. *Rand Health Qtrly*. 2014;4(3):4.

116. Wang C, Rao K, Wu S, Liu Q. Health care in China: improvement, challenges, and reform. *Chest*. 2013;143(2):524-531. doi: 10.1378/chest.12-1839.

117. Zhang L, Cheng G, Song S, et al. Efficiency performance of China's health care delivery system. *Int J Health Plann Manage*. 2017;32(3):254-263. doi: 10.1002/hpm.2425.

118. A tiered health-care delivery system for China. *Lancet*. 2019;393(10177):1178. doi: 10.1016/S0140-6736(19)30730-5.

119. World Health Organization. Pneumonia of unknown cause—China. Published 2020. Accessed December 20, 2022. https://www.who.int/emergencies/disease-outbreak-news/item/2020-DON229.

120. Mahase E. Covid-19: WHO declares pandemic because of "alarming levels" of spread, severity, and inaction. *BMJ*. 2020;368:m1036. doi: 10.1136/bmj.m1036. PMID: 32165426.

121. Cucinotta D, Vanelli M. WHO declares COVID-19 a pandemic. *Acta Biomed*. 2020;91(1):157-160. doi: 10.23750/abm.v91i1.9397.

122. World Health Organization. Coronavirus disease (COVID-19) pandemic, 2020. Accessed December 20, 2022. https://covid19.who.int/.

123. Lu N, Cheng KW, Qamar N, et al. Weathering COVID-19 storm: successful control measures of five Asian countries. *Am J Infect Control*. 2020;48(7):851-852. doi: 10.1016/j.ajic.2020.04.021.

124. Johns Hopkins University & Medicine Coronavirus Resource Center. Accessed December 29, 2022. https://coronavirus.jhu.edu/map.html.

125. Chen JM, Chen YQ. China can prepare to end its zero-COVID policy. *Nat Med*. 2022;28(6):1104-1105. doi: 10.1038/s41591-022-01794-3.

126. Mallapaty S. China is relaxing its zero-COVID policy: here's what scientists think. *Nature*. 2022;612(7940):383-384. doi: 10.1038/d41586-022-04382-0.

127. Glanz J, Chang A, Hvistendahl M. How deadly was China's COVID wave? *The Seattle Times*. Accessed February 23, 2023. https://www.seattletimes.com/nation-world/how-deadly-was-chinas-covid-wave/.

CHAPTER 21

Japan

Takuya Aoki and Leiyu Shi

Country Description

Table 21-1 Japan

Nationality	Noun: Japanese (singular and plural) Adjective: Japanese
Ethnic groups	Japanese 97.9%, Chinese 0.6%, Korean 0.4%, other 1.1% (2017 est.)*
Religions	Shintoism 70.5%, Buddhism 67.2%, Christianity 1.5%, other 5.9% (2019 est.)**
Language	Japanese
Government type	Parliamentary constitutional monarchy
Date of independence	660 BCE (traditional founding by Emperor Jimmu)
Gross domestic product (GDP) per capita	33,834 USD (2023 est.)
Unemployment rate	2.58% (2023 est.)
Natural hazards	Many dormant and some active volcanoes; approximately 1,500 seismic occurrences (mostly tremors but occasional severe earthquakes) every year; tsunamis; typhoons; volcanism***
Environment: current issues	Japan is one of the largest consumers of fish and tropical timber, contributing to the depletion of these resources in Asia and elsewhere. Following the 2011 Fukushima nuclear disaster, Japan originally planned to phase out nuclear power, but it has now implemented a new policy of seeking to restart nuclear power plants that meet strict, new safety standards.
Population	124,214,766 (2022 est.)
Age structure	0–14 years: 12.49% (male 8,047,183/female 7,623,767) 15–24 years: 9.47% (male 6,254,352/female 5,635,377) 25–54 years: 36.80% (male 22,867,385/female 23,317,140) 55–64 years: 12.06% (male 7,564,067/female 7,570,732) 65 years and over: 29.18% (male 16,034,973/female 20,592,496) (2020 est.)

Table 21-1 Japan

Median age	Total: 48.6 years Male: 47.2 years Female: 50.0 years (2020 est.)
Population growth rate	−0.39% (2022 est.)
Birth rate	6.95 births/1,000 population (2022 est.)
Death rate	11.59 deaths/1,000 population (2022 est.)
Net migration rate	0.74 migrant/1,000 population (2022 est.)
Gender ratio	At birth: 1.06 male/female 0–14 years: 1.06 male/female 15–24 years: 1.09 male/female 25–54 years: 1 male/female 55–64 years: 1 male/female 65 years and over: 0.65 male/female Total population: 0.95 male/female (2022 est.)
Infant mortality rate	Total: 1.9 deaths/1,000 live births Male: two deaths/1,000 live births Female: 1.79 deaths/1,000 live births (2022 est.)
Life expectancy at birth	Total population: 84.83 years Male: 81.92 years Female: 87.90 years (2022 est.)
Total fertility rate	1.38 children born/woman (2022 est.)

USD = U.S. dollars.

*Up to 230,000 Brazilians of Japanese origin migrated to Japan in the 1990s to work in industries; some have returned to Brazil (2004).

**The total of adherents exceeds 100% because many people practice both Shintoism and Buddhism.

***Unzen (elevation 1,500 meters) and Sakurajima (elevation 1,117 meters) are decade volcanoes with explosive history and close proximity to human populations; other historically active volcanoes include Asama (the most active volcano on Honshu Island), Aso, Bandai, Fuji, Iwo-Jima, Kikai, Kirishima, Koma-ga-take, Oshima, Suwanosejima, Tokachi, Yake-dake, and Usu.

Data from Central Intelligence Agency. The World Fact Book: Japan. Accessed December 26, 2022. https://www.cia.gov/the-world-factbook/countries/japan/; Statistica Japan. Accessed February 12, 2025. https://www.statista.com/statistics/263700/unemployment-rate-in-japan/; and World Bank Group. Accessed on February 12, 2025. https://www.worldbank.org/en/search?q=gdp%20per%20capita%20japan.

History

Archaeological evidence indicates that the current inhabitants of Japan may have been there continuously for the last 30,000 years. The first period of Japanese prehistory is from approximately 10,000 BCE to 300 BCE, which is known as the Jomon era. The name *Jomon* is derived from design patterns found on clay vessels that are created by pressing a rope. It is assumed that Jomon people lived a simple nomadic life consisting of hunting, fishing, and picking edibles. The Yayoi era began at approximately 300 BCE. During this period, residents of Japan developed a more sophisticated lifestyle. They adopted wet-field or water-irrigated rice cultivation, which ensured them a steady food supply. This adoption of agriculture made it possible for the early Japanese to stop being nomadic and to form permanent communities.[1]

For over 1,000 years from the Yamato era to the Azuchi-Momoyama era, Japan's history has been characterized by continuous civil wars. It was not until the Edo era that began in the early 17th century that Japan became a peaceful country. It was at this time that the Dutch began to visit Japan for trading. Being afraid of strong foreign influences, especially of the spread of Christianity, the Japanese government promulgated Sakoku-rei (an isolationist policy) in the mid-17th century, which protected Japan from being Westernized by an influx of foreign influences. This isolationist policy prohibited any interactions with foreign countries except China and the Netherlands. Trading with the Dutch was allowed only in Dejima, a human-made island in Nagasaki. This arrangement continued for nearly 230 years.[2]

It was during the Meiji era (1868–1912) that Japan passionately adopted Western technology to establish a modernized and militaristic nation. At the end of the 19th century, Japan used its military force to gain new territories, including Korea and part of China. Japan's military invasions continued into the mid-20th century. This eventually led to a war against the United States initiated with a surprise attack by Japanese aircraft on the U.S. Pacific Fleet in Pearl Harbor, Hawaii, on December 7, 1941. Japan's militaristic ambition was finally forced to end in August 1945 when the United States detonated two atomic bombs in Japan, the first on Hiroshima on August 6, 1945, and the second on Nagasaki 3 days later. The U.S. occupation that followed immediately after Japan's unconditional surrender and lasted until 1952 immensely impacted the construction of modern Japan in various areas from the economy to politics. During this period of U.S. occupation, a framework for a democratic government was established. Based on the British model, Japan established a parliamentary system and an independent judiciary. The emperor was retained as a symbol of the state (see **Table 21-1**).[1]

The current educational system was also restructured during this period by adopting the American system of a 6-year elementary school, a 3-year junior high school, and a 3-year high school.[1] The Japanese are nearly 100% literate, and their level of educational attainment is high.[3]

Size and Geography

Japan, the nation of the rising sun, lies off the coast of the Eurasian continent in the Far East, or in the western end of the northern Pacific Ocean. The Japanese Archipelago consists of four large islands and several thousand small islands that stretch 1,200 miles from northeast to southwest. The four main islands are, from north to south, Hokkaido, Honshu, Shikoku, and Kyushu. Honshu is the largest. It is narrow and long in shape, and the widest point is only 160 miles. Unlike many other islands and continents, Japan did not break off from the Eurasian continent. Instead, the Japanese islands were formed as a result of volcanic eruptions.[4]

The total land area of Japan is approximately 146,000 square miles, which is larger than Great Britain or Italy. Because the great majority of its land area is extremely mountainous, nearly all of the population inhabits approximately one-sixth of its total land area. Japan is, therefore, more crowded than the population density per square mile indicates.[1] See **Figure 21-1**.

Government and Political System

The foundation of Japan's current democratic government was laid during the U.S. occupation. The present constitution was written and adopted in 1947; it provides for universal suffrage for both genders and for an independent judicial system. The National Diet consists of two houses. The upper house, or House of Councilors, has 248 members who are elected for 6-year terms. The lower house, or House of Representatives, has 465 members who serve 4-year terms. Terms in the lower house can be shortened, however, if opposing parties call for a new election because of a no-confidence vote. Whenever the election takes place, the prime minister must be elected again.

A great deal of political power remains in the lower house, because a bill, once defeated by the upper house, can still be passed and become law if the lower house passes it for a second time with a two-thirds majority.[1] The prime minister is elected by the House of Representatives from among its members; therefore, the support of the majority party becomes essential in the selection of the prime minister, who, in turn, appoints the members of his cabinet.[3] The cabinet members are composed of heads of ministries and other government agencies.[1]

The Japanese political world includes multiple parties: the majority leading party and several minority opposition parties. The Liberal Democratic Party (LDP), which is conservative and pro-business, was the majority leading party for most of the second half of the 20th century, during which time Japan strived for and achieved its goal of becoming an economic giant. Structural change within Japanese political dynamics took place in the mid-1990s when the Japanese economy faced a serious economic crisis. With the burst of the bubble economy, the LDP was no longer able to maintain the majority; however, the LDP maintained its control by forming a coalition with other minority parties. At this time, the LDP has successfully regained its members and currently holds the majority on its own.

Macroeconomics

Japan experienced rapid and acute economic growth during the 1960s and 1970s, during which time Japan was reconstructed as a modernized nation. Its economy slowed down in the 1980s, and the growth rate of the gross domestic product (GDP) decreased. Japan's economy suffered severely during the 1990s as a result of the abrupt ending of the bubble economy.

Figure 21-1 Map of Japan

Japan's real GDP in recent years, when compared globally, maintained second place, following the United States, until 2009. However, it fell to third place, following the United States and China, in 2010. In early 2024, Japan dropped to number four among the world's largest economies, behind the United States, China, and Germany.[5]

Demographics

Japan's population as of June 2022 was estimated to be approximately 125.1 million, consisting of slightly more females (over 3.5 million more) than males; this gap had increased slightly since 2008. The population aged 15 to 64 years makes up slightly less than two-thirds (59.4%) of the total population. The population aged 65 and over constitutes approximately 29.0% of the total population, which is a considerable increase from 26.0% in 2016. Conversely, the current young population (aged 0–14 years) declined to 11.7% from 12.8% in 2016. As these statistics indicate, an aging population has become a persistent concern for today's Japan.[6]

Statistics indicate that Japan is relatively safe society compared with many of its counterparts in the world. The rates of violent crime, theft, and drug abuse in Japan are among the lowest in the world. A statistical comparison between Japan and the United States revealed that despite the fact that Japan has one-third as many police per capita as the United States, it has only 37 prisoners for every 100,000 people, 7% of the number of prison inmates (519) per 100,000 in the United States.[1] The reasons for Japan's low crime rate include the fact that the country is composed of a single culture and ethnic group, and the informal social norms regarding crime prevention that have traditionally existed due to the national character.

Poverty

Poverty has become an urgent concern for the Japanese in recent years. According to a report by the Organisation for Economic Co-operation and Development (OECD), the relative poverty rate, which is defined as earning less than one-half of the median household disposable income, was 15.7% in Japan in 2019. This was higher than the OECD average of 11.7%.[7] In fact, Japan is the sole OECD country in which the lowest income decile has faced an absolute decline in their real income and the poverty level has kept rising since the mid-1980s. Furthermore, the coronavirus disease 2019 (COVID-19) pandemic spurred a new problem of poverty in Japan, especially among women who want to work but have long been out of regular employment.[8] According to the government's 2019 Comprehensive Survey of Living Conditions, relative poverty rates by household structure among men and women between the ages of 20 and 64 were highest among single-mother households, at 25.2%, followed by single-woman households, at 24.5%.[9] This is also damaging children's educational environment.

Religion

The two major religions in Japan are Shintoism and Buddhism (sometimes referred to as a philosophy). Shinto is an indigenous, shamanic religion of Japan that venerates kami (superior beings) whose spirits are believed to inhabit objects or plants temporarily. The central tenets of Shinto are thought to have originated in the Yayoi era (300 BCE to 300 CE). It was not until the 7th century; however, that these beliefs became recognized as a coherent religion called Shinto, primarily in order to differentiate these existing beliefs from those of Buddhism, the newly introduced religion.[2] Shinto is a nonexclusive religion that has no founder, doctrines, or texts. The kami (often translated as "deity") are numerous and frequently applied to objects such as mountains, big trees, and large rocks, which is very dissimilar to the transcendent deities of Western religions.[10]

Since the 7th century, Buddhism has constantly been supported by the Japanese government and has come to be the major religion, along with Shinto.[11] Both Shinto shrines and Buddhist temples are found throughout Japan and are visited by people on numerous occasions every year. Although approximately 90% of Japanese report that they are Buddhists, they also visit Shinto shrines.[1] Religion to the Japanese, whether it is Shinto or Buddhism, is an important aspect of their traditional lifestyle and is qualitatively different from what it means to be religious for Christians, Muslims, Hindus, or Jews. Many Japanese marry and christen babies at Shinto shrines and gather for funerals at Buddhist temples. At the same time, more young people are choosing Christian churches as the place to get married. It is perhaps more accurate to conclude that most Japanese are much more secular than their American counterparts.[1]

It has long been debated whether Confucianism is a religion or a philosophy. There is no doubt that it has profoundly influenced northeast Asian nations, including Japan. Although Confucian teachings have long been influential, their influence was enhanced when Confucianism was incorporated into the nation's legal system more than 300 years ago. Teachings of Confucius are deeply integrated into Japanese life. These teachings emphasize appropriate virtue and conduct in this world, such as hard work, education, obligation, and reciprocity. Japanese society is status conscious, one of the characteristics of the Confucian influence. Vertical relationships are clearly structured, and superiors and subordinates owe each other certain obligations, including protection, loyalty, and good teamwork. Many Japanese, however, do not connect these values imbedded in Japanese culture with Confucianism.[1]

Brief History of the Healthcare System

Pre–World War II

Foreign influences on Japanese health care and medicine began in the 6th century when traditional Chinese medicine was introduced, the treatment of which featured the use of acupuncture and herbal medicines. Both are still popular in Japan.[11] A thousand years after the Chinese influence, the Japanese were exposed to Western medical practices by Portuguese missionaries. This influence was minimal, however, because of the isolation policy the Tokugawa government issued in the 17th century, effectively barring the Portuguese from Japan. Besides the Chinese, only the Dutch were allowed to trade with Japan during the centuries of this isolation period. Because of this, the influence of Dutch medical care practices, which emphasized the importance of anatomy, physiology, and pathology, on the development of Japan's healthcare system has been profound.[12]

During the Meiji era that began in the late 19th century, the Japanese were willing to open themselves up to a variety of Western influences.[11] Although the Japanese accepted various Western concepts and technologies for the modernization of their nation, they expressed a particular interest in the German healthcare system, which was regarded as the best in Europe at that time.[13] The Japanese built their national health insurance system by relying heavily on the German model, which originated as a system to address labor issues and the labor movements.[11]

Japan's health insurance system improved gradually from the 1920s to the 1960s. The Health Insurance Law enacted in 1922 was designed to direct employers to provide health insurance coverage mainly for their blue-collar workers, such as factory workers and miners.[14] In 1938, the Ministry of Public Health and Social Welfare was established, and the National Health Insurance Law was enacted, which required local governments to offer health insurance coverage to those who were not subject to the 1922 law, such as those engaged in fishing, farming, and forestry.[15] Even so, as many as one-third of the citizens were uninsured in 1955. It was not until 1961 that health insurance coverage was extended to every citizen.[15]

In 1931, when the population was 64.5 million, Japan had 3,710 hospitals. By 1940, that number had increased to 4,732 with an approximate ratio of one doctor and two nurses per 1,000 Japanese. These conditions worsened, however, during the early 1940s when Japan was at war and the number of hospitals and clinics as well as doctors, nurses, and beds per 1,000 decreased sharply. In 1945, when World War II ended, all of these conditions began to improve again.[15]

Post–World War II

One of the most important public health issues during the U.S. occupation immediately after the end of World War II was infectious diseases such as smallpox, cholera, and diphtheria. The most feared disease was smallpox. Some 17,000 cases were reported during the first year of the occupation. Immediate measures were taken that included production and inoculation of sufficient vaccines for the total population, as a result of which the epidemic subsided. Tuberculosis was also a major threat to the Japanese during the 1930s and 1940s. It had been the leading cause of death, and in the year 1945 alone, more Japanese died from tuberculosis than by all the fire raids and bombings, including the two atomic bombs. When the U.S. occupation first took place, it was estimated that there were 1 to 2 million clinical cases of tuberculosis. The Public Health and Welfare officials, concluding that vaccination was the best approach, developed a dried BCG vaccine and successfully vaccinated 30 million people under 30 years old. Although vaccination contributed to the drop in mortality and morbidity, it was not until 1960 that streptomycin became available to treat those who were already infected and that tuberculosis stopped being the number one cause of death in Japan.[15]

Another challenge in reestablishing Japan's healthcare systems after World War II was rebuilding the physical infrastructure of costly healthcare facilities. At this point, because of the successful reduction of the rates of infectious disease, hospital resources could be reallocated for other purposes. The quality of care provided by these hospitals, however, was in need of improvement. To cope with issues related to quality care, a model hospital was set up in each prefecture that was to serve as a benchmark for cleanliness and efficient management. A legal step was taken in 1948 to improve healthcare quality by reinspecting and classifying hospitals. Small hospitals that had fewer than 10 beds were downgraded to clinics and were limited in patient care as they lacked sufficient operating rooms and laboratory services. Although the number of doctors in Japan was adequate, their quality was questioned, as more than 60% of the 77,000 doctors were graduates of second-class medical schools that required only 4 years of medical education beyond high school. Based on the new standards established, all of the medical schools were inspected, and schools not meeting the standards were closed. By the early 1950s, the quality of doctors in Japan had improved significantly. The quality of nursing was also improved in a similar fashion during this period.[15] Currently, all physicians, dentists, and pharmacists must attend 6 years of college beyond high school and pass the national exam to be certified. This allows Japanese professionals to practice medicine at a younger age than their American counterparts.

The number of physicians in relation to the population steadily increased, and by the end of 1992, there were approximately 220,000 physicians (1.77 physician per 1,000 population). More than 95% of these physicians were in medical practice. Approximately 27% of them were owners of medical care facilities such as hospitals or clinics, whereas the rest were employed in medical care facilities.[16]

The Current Healthcare System

Facilities

As of October 1, 2020, the number of healthcare facilities in operation in Japan was 178,724, down by 692 from the previous year. Of these facilities,

8,238 (4.6%) were hospitals (20 or more beds), 102,612 (57.4%) were clinics (19 or fewer beds), and 67,874 (38.0%) were dental clinics.[17]

Whereas 87.1% (7,179) of hospitals were general hospitals in 2020, the rest were psychiatric hospitals (1,059). When these hospitals were classified according to sponsorship, 5,687 (69.0%) were medical corporations, followed by 1,199 (14.6%) hospitals run by public (governmental) medical organizations. Of the 102,612 clinics, 93.9% (96,309) were clinics with no beds. As for the sponsorship of these clinics, 39.3% (40,310) were individually owned, and most of the others were owned by medical corporations (44,219).[17]

In 2020, the total number of hospital beds was 1,593,633. More than one-half of these beds (887,920) were general beds. There were 1,195.1 beds per 100,000 inhabitants. A little more than one-half (703.9 beds per 100,000) were for general patients, whereas approximately a quarter (257.2 per 100,000) were psychiatric beds and another quarter (229.2 per 100,000) were for long-term care.[17] Considering Japan's fast-growing elderly population, demands for beds, especially long-term care beds, are expected to increase.[17]

Workforce

By 2020, the number of physicians was 339,623; 77.2% were males and nearly two-thirds (216,474) worked in hospitals. The average age of these physicians was 50.1 years. The number of physicians per 100,000 population was 269.2, a slight improvement from 258.8 in 2018.[18] The number of dentists by 2020 was 107,443, more than three-quarters (75.0%) of whom were males; their average age was 52.4 years. A great majority (85.4%) of these dentists were engaged in clinics. The number of dentists per 100,000 population was 85.2, a slight improvement from 83.0 in 2018.[18]

The number of pharmacists was 321,982 by 2020; 58.7% (188,982) were engaged in pharmacies and 19.1% (61,603) in hospitals and clinics, and 12.1% (39,044) worked for pharmaceutical corporations. Unlike physicians and dentists, the majority (61.4%) of pharmacists were females. The average age of the pharmacists was 46.6 years. The number of pharmacists per 100,000 population was 255.2, a slight improvement from 246.2 in 2018.[18] Six years of education beyond high school are required to become a pharmacist.

There were 1,280,911 nurses and 284,589 assistant nurses working in Japan in 2020. The number of nurses has increased significantly (34.4% increase) since 2010, whereas the number of assistant nurses has decreased from 368,148 in 2010.[19] Also, there were 55,595 public health nurses and 37,940 midwives. There were 1,015.4 nurses, 225.6 assistant nurses, 44.1 public health nurses, and 30.1 midwives per 100,000 population.[19]

Disparities in the distribution of these medical professionals from prefecture to prefecture are readily apparent. For instance, compared with the 338.4 physicians in Tokushima and the 332.6 in Kyoto per 100,000 population, only 177.8 physicians per 100,000 population were available in Saitama. Similarly, the number of dentists per 100,000 population in Tokyo (118.4) was twice as high as in some other prefectures, such as Aomori (56.5) and Shimane (58.1).[18] The number of nurses per 100,000 population also showed a disparity, varying from 1,623.4 in Kochi to 736.9 in Saitama; the number of assistant nurses ranged from 540.6 per 100,000 population in Miyazaki to 85.9 in Tokyo. Distribution disparities are equally extreme for public health nurses, varying from 82.6 per 100,000 population in Nagano to 26.9 in Kanagawa, but is less apparent for midwives, varying from 50.7 per 100,000 population in Shimane to 24.0 in Hiroshima.[19]

Technology and Equipment

Computed tomography (CT; also called computed axial tomography [CAT]) scanners, magnetic resonance imaging (MRI) units, mammography, and radiation therapy equipment are major modern medical technologies. CT scanners and MRI units are both used to produce cross-sectional views of the inside of the patient's scanned body, which can assist physicians in making a prompt diagnosis. There were 115.7 CT scanners per 1 million population in Japan in 2020, which was by far the highest number among the OECD countries. There were 57.4 MRI units per 1 million population in Japan, far less than the number of CT scanners. However, that was also the highest number among all the OECD countries.[20] See **Table 21-2**.

Table 21-2 Medical Technologies in OECD Countries, Number per Million Population, 2021 (or Latest Available)

Rank	CT Scanners		MRI Units	
	Country	Per Million	Country	Per Million
1	Japan	115.7	Japan	57.4
2	Australia	69.4	United States	38.0

Rank	CT Scanners		MRI Units	
	Country	Per Million	Country	Per Million
3	Iceland	46.4	Germany	34.5
4	New Zealand	45.0	Korea	34.2
5	Greece	43.7	Italy	34.2
6	Denmark	43.7	Greece	33.6
7	United States	42.6	Norway	31.2
8	Korea	40.6	Finland	30.9
9	Italy	40.1	Austria	25.4
10	Switzerland	39.6	Iceland	19.1
11	Latvia	37.4	Spain	18.2
12	Germany	35.3	Luxembourg	17.3
13	Norway	30.1	New Zealand	16.6
14	Lithuania	29.3	France	16.3
15	Austria	28.5	Ireland	16.0
16	Brazil	28.0	Latvia	15.8
17	Belgium	24.6	Estonia	15.0
18	Chile	24.2	Australia	15.0
19	Luxembourg	22.1	Brazil	14.5
20	Ireland	20.4	Lithuania	14.3
21	Estonia	20.3	Netherlands	13.4
22	Poland	20.1	Slovenia	13.3
23	Spain	20.0	Chile	12.3
24	Slovak Republic	19.1	Belgium	11.4
25	Slovenia	19.0	Türkiye	11.3
26	France	18.9	Czech Republic	11.0
27	Finland	17.0	Poland	10.5
28	Czech Republic	16.3	Canada	10.1
29	Türkiye	15.0	Slovak Republic	9.9
30	Netherlands	14.7	Israel	5.3
31	Canada	14.6	Russia	5.1
32	Russia	13.9	Hungary	4.9
33	Israel	9.8	Mexico	2.6
34	Hungary	9.6	Colombia	0.2
35	Mexico	6.7		
36	Colombia	5.9		

Data from Organisation for Economic Co-operation and Development. OECD health statistics 2022. Accessed December 26, 2022. https://www.oecd.org/health/health-data.htm.

Evaluation of the Healthcare System

Cost

Japan is the first nation in Asia to have introduced a comprehensive social insurance program. Its program features universal coverage achieved by mandating that everyone join the plan, at either a place of employment or a place of residence. It is mandatory for all companies employing five or more workers to contribute to a health insurance plan for their employees. Those not covered by their employers join the National Health Insurance (NHI) program administered by municipal governments and NHI associations.[12] Both the Employee's Health Insurance (EHI) and NHI plans cover dependent family members in the same household. Premiums for the EHI plan are determined based on the employee's monthly income, which is adjusted periodically according to the medical expenditure. The employer is required to contribute 50% of the cost. While the premiums vary from union to union as well as from location to location, in 2016, the monthly payment for the EHI plan was approximately 10% of the employee's monthly income for those who were under 40 years of age; those who were 40 years old and older paid slightly more per month due to added responsibility to cover long-term care insurance.

The average income over a 3-month period (April–June) is calculated to determine the EHI payment, which is applied for the coming year starting on September 1. This includes every form of income, such as overtime pay and commuting expenses covered by the employer. For example, for a 39-year-old man employed in the Tokyo district with an average income for the 3-month period of ¥300,000 (approximately $2,205 USD, based on the December 19, 2022, exchange rate of ¥136.01 to the dollar), the EHI payment will be ¥29,430 ($216 USD) per month (¥300,000 × 9.81%), half of which (¥14,715 = $108 USD) is covered by the employer and the rest (¥14,715) by the employee. The EHI premium is adjusted annually. A 40-year-old person in the same condition will also be required to pay long-term care insurance, which is 1.64%; therefore, their monthly payment will be ¥17,175 (¥300,000 × 11.45% [9.81% + 1.64%]/2). Retired people who are no longer eligible for the EHI plans switch to the NHI plans or become dependents of other family members, such as their adult children who are covered by the EHI plans.

Monthly payment for the NHI plan also depends on the resident's income. Because the NHI is administered by local governments and each government uses its own system in calculating the cost, the figure varies widely, depending on residence. The difference could be more than double between two neighboring cities. It is likely to be around 5% to 10% of the resident's income. The maximum amount of premium per year per household for the NHI is ¥650,000 ($5,000 USD). Because the employer does not cover any of the premiums, individuals insured by the NHI may pay more than those insured by the EHI. Individuals insured by both NHI and EHI are responsible for 30% of their medical expenses, as the NHI covers 70%. Therefore, if a doctor's visit costs $100 USD, the NHI covers $70 USD and the patient is responsible for $30 USD. Individuals insured by the EHI also share 30% of the cost. Individuals aged 70 to 74 are responsible for 20% and those aged 75 and older are responsible for 10% of their medical expenses. However, high-income individuals aged 70 and older are responsible for 30% of their expenses.[21]

The nation's medical expenditure has gradually increased over the past decade, as has the ratio of the nation's medical expenditure to its gross domestic product (GDP). In 2012, the medical expenditure per capita was $3,970.80 USD, accounting for 10.7% of GDP; it increased to $4,610.80 USD, 11.0% of GDP in 2019.[20] According to the latest OECD data available, Japan's health expenditure per capita is $4,666 USD, ranking 17th out of 46 OECD nations. This is slightly higher than the OECD average of $4,087 USD and less than one-half of the highest ranked expenditure, that of the United States ($12,318 USD).[20,22] Japan's health expenditure as a share of GDP is 11.1%, ranking 11th out of 46 OECD nations, which is considerably higher than the OECD average of 8.8%.[20,22] Japan's annual average growth rate in its per capita health expenditure from 2015 to 2019 was 1.3%, which was lower than the OECD average (2.7%).[22]

Quality

Detailed licensing regulations for hospitals, including the structure, equipment, and number of staff, are provided by the Medical Service Law, which contributes to the quality of health care available to citizens. All hospitals must meet these standards before they are given permission from the prefectural governor to operate. The prefectural government sends medical inspectors periodically to ensure that all hospitals are continuing to abide by the regulations.

Because the number of medical schools is limited and only so many seats are available each year, it is very competitive to become a physician in Japan.

There are only 82 medical schools throughout Japan, 43 of which are national schools and eight of which are public schools (e.g., prefectural schools). Those who wish to be admitted to medical school study very hard throughout their high school years. Many of the students who fail to be admitted to medical school spend 1 or more years just studying for the following year's entrance exam. Although it is not very costly to attend public medical school, it is much more costly to attend private medical school. After successfully completing 6 years of medical school education, all medical school students must pass the national medical examination administered by the Ministry of Health, Labour and Welfare before they are licensed to practice medicine. While it had been customary for new physicians to be engaged in residency training for at least 2 years in the medical school hospitals or in those hospitals designated by the Ministry of Health, Labour and Welfare, this 2-year residency training was formally mandated in 2004.[23] This law should increase confidence in the ability to practice in novice physicians, which, in turn, contributes to the quality of medical care made available.

Assessment of healthcare quality is by no means simple and easy, as many elements are intertwined. One way of assessing healthcare quality is to examine current health status, including life expectancy and other outcomes, such as the mortality rate and the survival rate following cardiac arrest. Life expectancy at birth for the Japanese in 2022 was 84.5 years, ranked at the top of OECD nations.[24] This is a remarkable accomplishment considering that the life expectancy in 1960 was 67.8 years, ranked 1 of the bottom 5. Focusing on the gender difference, women live longer than men in every OECD country: While the life expectancy at birth of Japanese women is 87.4 years, the top in the OECD nations, that of men is 81.4 years, ranking fourth. This gender difference is due partially to the greater tendency among men to engage in risky behaviors such as tobacco and alcohol use.[22]

Life expectancy at age 65 is 20.1 years for Japanese men and 24.9 years for Japanese women, ranked at the top among the OECD nations. This gain of nearly 8 years since 1970 is the highest among OECD countries. Life expectancy at age 65 also highly correlates with that at age 80. Based on 2020 data, for women in Japan, life expectancy at age 80 was the highest; they can expect to live an additional 12.3 years.[20]

Cardiovascular diseases remain the leading cause of mortality among OECD countries, accounting for a third (30%) of deaths in 2019. While cardiovascular diseases include a wide range of circulatory-related illnesses, ischemic heart disease (IHD), commonly known as heart attack, accounted for 11% and stroke accounted for 7% of mortality in 2019.[22] Japan's mortality from IHD is the second lowest in the OECD countries. Mortality from cancer remains high, accounting for 24% of all deaths in 2019; cancer is the second leading cause of deaths in OECD countries following cardiovascular diseases. Japan's age-standardized rate per 100,000 population for cancer mortality in 2019 was 164.0, ranked the seventh lowest of OECD countries.[22]

In addition to mortality, the 30-day acute myocardial infarction (AMI) case-fatality rate—deaths occurring in the same hospital within 30 days of admission for AMI—is a good indicator of care quality, which includes effective medical interventions as well as timely transport of patients. Among OECD countries, Iceland has the lowest rate at 2.0% (age-sex standardized rate per 100 admissions). By comparison, Mexico's AMI case-fatality rate is the highest at 27.5%, indicating that AMI patients do not have access to timely recommended care. Japan's AMI case-fatality rate is 9.7%, more than four times greater than that of Iceland. While the Japanese people are less likely to die from heart disease, when compared with other OECD countries, they are more likely to die once hospitalized for AMI. See **Table 21-3**. One possible reason for this can be attributed to the patients' severe AMI

Table 21-3 In-Hospital Case Fatality Rates Within 30 Days of Admission for AMI, 2019

Country	Age-Gender Standardized Rate
Iceland	2.0
Netherlands	2.9
Norway	3.2
Australia	3.2
Sweden	3.5
Turkiye	3.9
Slovenia	4.2
New Zealand	4.3
Denmark	4.5
Canada	4.6
Poland	4.7

(continues)

Table 21-3 In-Hospital Case Fatality Rates Within 30 Days of Admission for AMI, 2019 *(continued)*

Country	Age-Gender Standardized Rate
Ireland	4.7
United States	4.9
Switzerland	5.1
Austria	5.2
Israel	5.3
Italy	5.4
France	5.6
Colombia	5.6
Slovak Republic	6.3
Belgium	6.4
Spain	6.5
United Kingdom	6.6
Finland	6.8
Czech Republic	7.0
Chile	7.2
Portugal	7.3
Germany	8.3
Luxembourg	8.5
Korea	8.9
Estonia	9.2
Lithuania	9.3
Japan	9.7
Hungary	—
Latvia	14.4
Mexico	27.5
OECD	**6.6**

Data from Organisation for Economic Co-operation and Development. Health at a glance 2021: OECD indicators. Accessed December 26, 2022. https://www.oecd.org/health/health-at-a-glance/.

conditions at the time of hospital admission. Japan's case-fatality rate within 30 days of admission for ischemic stroke, however, is 3.0%, the second lowest among OECD countries.[22] See **Table 21-4**.

Vaccination rates are a reliable indicator for assessing quality of care for communicable diseases. Although influenza is a common infectious disease that affects individuals of all ages, the elderly and those with chronic medical conditions are at higher risk for complications, including death. Effective vaccination is a recommended way to prevent illness, hospitalization, and mortality among this at-risk population. Based on the latest OECD available data (2019 or nearest, depending on the nation), Japan's influenza vaccination rate in people aged 65 years and over is not very high. While more than 70% of the elderly received the influenza vaccination in Mexico, Korea, the United Kingdom, and the United States, only 48% of Japanese elderly people were vaccinated. This is not much different from the vaccination rate in 2005, an indication that more efforts are needed to promote vaccination.[22]

Table 21-4 In-Hospital Case Fatality Rates Within 30 Days of Admission for Ischemic Stroke, 2019

Country	Age-Gender Standardized Rate
Costa Rica	2.8
Japan	3.0
Korea	3.5
Norway	3.8
Iceland	3.9
United States	4.1
Denmark	4.8
Netherlands	5.0
Sweden	5.4
Switzerland	5.4
Australia	5.4
Israel	5.8
Austria	6.1
Colombia	6.1
Germany	6.2
Italy	6.3
New Zealand	6.5
Ireland	6.7
France	7.1
Turkiye	7.5
Luxembourg	7.5
Canada	7.5

Country	Age-Gender Standardized Rate
Belgium	7.9
Estonia	8.2
Chile	8.3
Finland	8.4
Slovak Republic	8.6
United Kingdom	9.0
Spain	9.3
Hungary	—
Portugal	9.8
Czech Republic	10.3
Slovenia	10.8
Poland	11.8
Lithuania	12.4
Latvia	19.6
Mexico	21.1
OECD	**7.7**

Data from Organisation for Economic Co-operation and Development. Health at a glance 2021: OECD indicators. Accessed December 26, 2022. https://www.oecd.org/health/health-at-a-glance/.

Children are also vulnerable to communicable diseases. Appropriate vaccination is one of the most cost-effective health policy interventions. Effective vaccination successfully eradicated polio and diphtheria across OECD countries. Vaccination against measles and diphtheria, tetanus, and pertussis (DTP) has also been promoted; as a result, vaccination rates for these diseases reached beyond 90% in most OECD countries, so that the OECD average is now 95% for DTP and measles. Based on 2020 data, Japan's vaccination rate for DTP was 96.2% and that for measles was 98.5%. Vaccination against hepatitis B has also been promoted in many OECD countries, resulting in the vaccination rate reaching higher than 90% in OECD countries. In 2020, Japan's vaccination rate for hepatitis B was 92.3%.[20]

The majority of patients in Japan, both inpatients and outpatients, were satisfied with the overall hospital care they received in 2020. For example, 61.3% of the outpatients and 67.0% of inpatients were satisfied with their communication with doctors. The major dissatisfaction outpatients express is the long waiting time. Dissatisfactions expressed by inpatients focus on the content of meals and the quality of facilities such as hospital rooms and bathrooms.[25]

Patient-reported experience measures are also used in many OECD countries to assess the quality of medical care. In regard to doctors providing easy-to-understand explanations and giving an opportunity to ask questions or raise concerns, the majority of outpatients report positive experiences across countries. A great majority of patients in Japan (94.2%) report that doctors provide easy-to-understand explanations, ranking fourth in 18 OECD countries in 2020. However, in regard to doctors spending enough time with a patient during consultation, only 42.1% of Japanese patients reported positive experiences, ranking 19th across 19 OECD countries. Japan has a particularly low rating for patient perceptions of the time spent with a doctor; this is likely to be associated with the high number of consultations per doctor.[22]

Access

One factor that influences patients' access to high-quality medical care is the supply of well-trained and geographically well-distributed health professionals such as physicians and nurses. This can be assessed by examining physician density (the number of practicing doctors per capita). In 2020, there were 2.6 physicians per 1,000 inhabitants in Japan, which ranked 30th of 38 OECD nations.[20] It is common in many countries to have a greater density of physicians in urban areas than in rural regions, which reflects the concentration of specialized services, including surgery. This gap in distribution of physicians between urban and rural areas is much smaller in Japan than in many other OECD countries.[22] However, access to medical care in Japan varies, depending on residence, due to an apparent disparity in physician density across prefectures. For instance, in 2020, there were 338.4 physicians per 100,000 population in Tokushima prefecture and 332.6 per 100,000 in Kyoto prefecture, while there were only 177.8 per 100,000 in Saitama, one of Tokyo's neighboring prefectures.[18] Disparity in dentist density was also apparent across prefectures. There were 85.2 dentists per 100,000 in Japan but 118.4 dentists per 100,000 in Tokyo; however, this number dropped to 56.5, less than half of the Tokyo density, in Aomori.[18] Nurse shortages have become an issue for some countries, and it is expected to continue to be an issue, especially in aging countries such as Japan. In 2019, the number of practicing nurses per 1,000 population in Japan was 12.0, ranking ninth out of OECD countries; this was higher than the OECD average of 8.8.[22] Disparities in nurses were equally apparent across prefectures; while there were 1,623.4 nurses per 100,000 in Kochi prefecture, there were only 736.9 in Saitama prefecture.[19]

In addition to the overall number of doctors, the age and gender composition of the doctors influences the supply of medical services. The higher age of Japan's doctors raises concerns that there may be a shortage of doctors in the near future due to a lack of new recruits to replace those who retire. The increase in the number of female doctors may affect the availability of doctors, as they are likely to work shorter hours than male doctors. In Japan in 2019, 38% of doctors were 55 years and older, ranking 13th in the 35 OECD countries. With regard to gender, only 22% of doctors were females; this was the smallest share of female doctors across 37 OECD countries. This may create an access issue for patients who prefer female doctors.[22]

Another important element in assessing quality of care, especially in aging countries like Japan, is access to long-term care beds in hospitals and nursing homes—that is, beds that are mostly used to care for the elderly with chronic illness or disability. Japan's number of long-term care beds ranked 26th out of 33 OECD nations in 2019. There were 35.1 long-term care beds per 1,000 people aged 65 years and over in Japan, which was far fewer than the OECD average of 45.6, and less than one-half of the rate in Luxembourg. It is preferred by most OECD countries to have more long-term care beds in nursing homes where services are more care oriented than treatment oriented and also less costly than in hospitals; however, only three-fourths of the long-term care beds in Japan belonged to nursing institutions. This was fewer than in most OECD countries.[22]

Access to emergency medical care in Japan varies across disciplines. Although 49.7% of facilities specializing in internal medicine accepted emergency patients during night hours in 2020, only 17.4% of those specializing in pediatrics were available for night-time emergencies, while 11.6% of obstetricians were available, and 14.1% of psychiatric care services were available.[17]

Because medical cost is an issue for most individuals, one factor that influences access to healthcare services is health insurance coverage. Lack of coverage frequently discourages many people from having access to appropriate medical care in a prompt manner. Lack of coverage also restricts those in need from having access to innovative treatments, as well as preventive services such as screening and vaccination. As in the majority of the OECD nations, 100% of Japanese have public health insurance coverage for a core set of services. One advantage of the Japanese health insurance system is that practically every clinic and hospital accepts any type of health insurance. All one has to do is to present an insurance card at the window at the time of the first visit.

In Japan, the distinction between primary and secondary care may not always be clear. Individuals can select any medical facility of their choice (free access system). However, patients must pay additional costs to receive care directly at higher-level hospitals instead of through a primary care physician. Japanese primary care services are generally provided in clinics and outpatient departments of small-sized and medium-sized hospitals that are predominantly privately owned. The Ministry of Health, Labour and Welfare has recommended that all individuals should have a primary care physician, called a "kakaritsukei" in Japanese, voluntarily, and former surveys have reported that approximately half of the Japanese adult residents had a primary care physician.[26] Access to high-quality primary care, however, may depend on each individual's attention to their local doctor's reputation for high quality.[14]

Current and Emerging Issues and Challenges

Care for the Elderly Population

Japan is one of the world's most rapidly aging societies, with 28.4% of the population aged 65 years and over in 2019, the highest proportion across all OECD countries (the OECD average was 17.3% and the U.S. proportion was 16.5%). It is projected that in Japan, this proportion will increase to 37.7% by 2050, while that in the United States will be 22.0%. The percentage of adults aged 80 years and over in Japan reached 8.9% in 2019, also ranked the highest across all OECD countries. This is projected to increase to 15.8% by 2050.[22] It is not only the increased proportion of the population made up of elderly persons in Japan that requires attention, but also the rapid speed with which this demographic change is occurring. The projected population shares accounted for by adults aged 65 years and over and aged 80 years and over in Japan are the greatest across OECD countries. This trend of increased population proportions made up of elderly adults is expected to rapidly accelerate in the coming decades.

Furthermore, while Japan's longevity ranks the highest, its fertility rate is one of the lowest in OECD countries.[27] These trends clearly indicate the importance of healthcare services for the elderly population in Japan. The number of elderly people in need of medical care has increased over the past few decades. In 2010, of the 7,137,500 outpatients per day, 3,618,800 were 65 years or older, indicating that nearly one-half of all outpatients were 65 or older. Of all the inpatients per day in Japan, more than 70% of all inpatients were elderly.[28]

National medical care expenditures are continually increasing, and now consume more than 10% of the national income. Japan's national medical care expenditure per capita constantly increases with age, and the higher the age, the more apparent the increase is. Because of continuously increasing medical costs, the premiums for each insured individual, as well as patients' share of their medical cost, have increased. To cope with the extra medical expenditure related to nursing home care for the elderly, everyone aged 40 to 64 years pays an additional premium. This system is intended to lighten the financial burden of those who are in need of long-term care; however, for this system to efficiently support those in need, many remaining issues must be dealt with, such as accessibility and a sufficient number of providers.

Traditionally, Japanese families formed extended families consisting of three generations. The family's eldest son would keep living with his parents after marriage, and his wife was expected to take care of her husband's aging parents; therefore, each family was expected to be self-sufficient in caring for the elderly in the family. However, this type of family structure is no longer common even in conservative rural areas. Frequently, adult children of elderly adults are not able to live close enough to their parents to make regular visits, or to be available for their aging parents when help is needed. Many Japanese women are hesitant to marry if there is a possibility that they will have to live with their husband's parents in the future.

To address the healthcare needs of an ever-increasing elderly population in Japan, an innovative healthcare system must be quickly developed to ensure an adequate number of facilities and workforce, effective methods of delivering nursing care, and sufficient funds for the system to be smoothly sustained.

Dementia Care

More than 21 million people in OECD countries were estimated to have dementia in 2021; with population aging and a lack of effective preventive measures, this number is expected to keep rising, as is the cost associated with dementia. Because dementia is strongly associated with the elderly, countries with a greater share of older adults, including Japan, are likely to be greatly affected by dementia. In 2021, it was estimated that 26.7 Japanese people per 1,000 were affected by dementia, ranking first out of all OECD nations. This number is projected to rise to 44.7 per 1,000 in Japan by 2050; these figures indicate that dementia care and treatment are one of the most serious and pressing health and medical issues in Japan.[22]

The number of people over 65 years old with dementia in Japan is estimated to be about 6 million (as of 2020), and it is predicted that about 7 million people (about 1 in 5 elderly people) will have dementia by 2025. To cope with the increasing prevalence of dementia, in 2019, the Japanese cabinet issued the Framework for Promoting Dementia Care, in which prevention and the opportunity for persons with dementia to age in place were set as the main goals. With accelerated population aging, all of these measures against dementia are bound to be critically important in improving quality of late life for the elderly in Japan.[29]

Antismoking Campaigns

In the arena of public health, smoking continues to be an issue in Japan. Smoking is known to be the single largest preventable cause of disease and premature death. It has been documented that smoking can lead to heart disease, stroke, lung disease, and cancer of many types. Tobacco causes almost 6 million deaths each year; sadly, more than 600,000 of such victims are nonsmokers exposed to secondhand smoke. Furthermore, smoking during pregnancy leads to low birth weight and illness among infants. Smoking is still the largest avoidable health risk factor worldwide.[22]

Although the number of smokers in Japan has decreased by more than 30% in the past 2 decades, it remains high among developed countries. In 2019, 16.5% of Japanese adults were daily smokers; this is close to the OECD average of 16.5%. Only 7.6% of Japanese women are daily smokers, ranking the 8th lowest among 37 OECD countries. However, 27.1% of Japanese men remain daily smokers, ranking the 13th highest across 37 OECD countries.[22]

According to the World Health Organization, Japan's antitobacco laws are weaker than in other developed nations. In 2018, the Health Promotion Law was amended and for the first time in Japan, smoking was prohibited indoors in principle. However, there are still a number of gaps and further efforts are required. For example, smoking is allowed in existing restaurants with a seating area of 100 square meters or less and operated by individuals or by small and medium-sized enterprises with capitalization of 50 million yen or fewer.[30]

Diabetes Prevention

As in many other nations, diabetes has become one of the most important public health concerns in Japan. It is estimated that over 463 million people were affected worldwide in 2019, and the number is projected to increase to almost 700 million by 2045.[22] Diabetes can lead to blindness, renal failure, cardiovascular diseases, and cerebrovascular diseases. While it is difficult to accurately estimate the number of people with diabetes, it is estimated that 8.4% of male adults and 5.0% of female adults in Japan have diabetes.[31]

The higher the age, the higher the risk of developing diabetes is. For both men and women, the incidence rate greatly increases for those aged 50 years and over. In 2019, for men, 17.8% of those aged 50 to 59 years, 25.3% of those aged 60 to 69 years, and 26.4% of those aged 70 years and over had diabetes; for women, 5.9% of those aged 50 to 59 years, 10.7% of those aged 60 to 69 years, and 19.6% of those aged 70 and over had diabetes.[32] To improve health quality, as well as to lighten the financial burden of the nation, effective preventive approaches, including promotion of physical activity and proper diet, must be promptly implemented.

Suicide Prevention

High suicide rates are another very serious issue in Japan. Numerous factors are associated with attempting and committing suicide, including low income, alcohol and drug abuse, unemployment, social isolation, and psychiatric disorders, such as severe depression, bipolar disorder, and schizophrenia. The OECD average age-standardized suicide rate declined from 16.2 per 100,000 in 1990 to 11.0 per 100,000 in 2019; however, Japan's has remained high, only declining slightly in the past few years, to 14.7 per 100,000 in 2019. This was the fifth highest in all OECD countries.[22] According to statistics published in 2019 by the Ministry of Health, Labour and Welfare, suicide is the leading cause of death for individuals aged 15 to 39 years in Japan and the second leading cause for those aged 10 to 14 years and 40 to 49 years. See **Table 21-5**. Some gender differences are observed. Among men, suicide is the leading cause of death for those aged 15 to 44 years, the second for those aged 10 to 14 years, the third for those aged 45 to 54 years, the fourth for those aged 55 to 59 years, and the fifth for those aged 60 to 64 years. Among women, suicide is the leading cause of death for those aged 10 to 29 years, the second for those aged 30 to 49 years, and the fourth for those aged 50 to 64 years.[33] It is a disturbing fact that suicide remains a leading cause of death for teenagers. Furthermore,

Table 21-5 Leading Causes of Deaths by Age, Japan, 2019

Age, Years	First	Second	Third
Total	Malignant neoplasms	Heart diseases	Senility
0	Congenital malformations	Respiratory and cardiovascular disorders	Accidents
1–4	Congenital malformations	Accidents	Malignant neoplasms
5–9	Malignant neoplasms	Accidents	Congenital malformations
10–14	Malignant neoplasms	Suicide	Accidents
15–19	Suicide	Accidents	Malignant neoplasms
20–24	Suicide	Accidents	Malignant neoplasms
25–29	Suicide	Malignant neoplasms	Accidents
30–34	Suicide	Malignant neoplasms	Accidents
35–39	Suicide	Malignant neoplasms	Heart diseases
40–44	Malignant neoplasms	Suicide	Heart diseases
45–49	Malignant neoplasms	Suicide	Heart diseases
50–54	Malignant neoplasms	Heart diseases	Suicide
55–59	Malignant neoplasms	Heart diseases	Cerebrovascular diseases

Age, Years	First	Second	Third
60–64	Malignant neoplasms	Heart diseases	Cerebrovascular diseases
65–69	Malignant neoplasms	Heart diseases	Cerebrovascular diseases
70–74	Malignant neoplasms	Heart diseases	Cerebrovascular diseases
75–79	Malignant neoplasms	Heart diseases	Cerebrovascular diseases
80–84	Malignant neoplasms	Heart diseases	Cerebrovascular diseases
85–89	Malignant neoplasms	Heart diseases	Senility
90–94	Heart diseases	Senility	Malignant neoplasms
95–99	Senility	Heart diseases	Pneumonia
100–	Senility	Heart diseases	Pneumonia

Data from Vital Statistics of Japan, 2019, p. 32. https://www.mhlw.go.jp/english/database/db-hw/dl/81-1a2en.pdf.

the COVID-19 crisis has had a significant and negative impact on population mental health. In Japan, the prevalence of depression more than doubled to 17% in early 2020, compared with the previous year.[22] Stigmas related to mental illness must also be dealt with more effectively, and mental healthcare services must be made more accessible. More attention has been paid to mental health in recent years, and campaigns are carried out that focus on mental health; however, considering that suicide is the number one cause of death for people of varying ages, both men and women, continuous and consistent efforts are needed to enhance the mental health of the nation.

COVID-19 Pandemic

The COVID-19 pandemic dealt serious blows to the health system globally. In Japan, approximately 25 million COVID-19 infections and about 50,000 deaths from the virus had been recorded as of December 1, 2022.[34] The seventh wave, which began in June 2022, was the largest ever in Japan, with more than 200,000 new cases occurring daily. Eighty percent of the Japanese population has completed the initial COVID-19 vaccination protocol; however, the vaccination rate of the Omicron-targeting booster was sluggish at 34% (as of December 26, 2022).[35]

During the pandemic, primary-care capabilities played pivotal roles, including the prevention of hospitalization.[36] In Japan, as in other countries, the primary-care sector performed the initial assessment, including testing for COVID-19, and triaged patients to determine those in need of hospitalization. The government notified the public that they should first visit their primary care physician, called a "kakaritsukei," if they have symptoms suspected to be infection. However, restricted access to outpatient care owing to some kakaritsukeis' refusal to see patients with suspected COVID-19 was reported. Thus, the Japanese government has begun to reform the primary-care systems.[37] First, the government is considering a system for reporting and disclosing the primary-care functions of each medical institution.[38] Primary-care specialists, newly certified by the Japanese Medical Specialty Board starting in 2018, are also expected to play a role.[39] Further effective measures are required to strengthen Japan's primary care system and address infectious diseases and complex health issues such as multimorbidity.

References

1. Ellington L. *Japan: A Global Studies Handbook*. Santa Barbara, CA: ABC-CLIO; 2002.
2. Frederic L. *Japan: Encyclopedia*. Cambridge, MA: Harvard University Press; 2002.
3. Richie D. *Introducing Japan*. New York, NY: Kodansha International; 1996.
4. Woolley PJ. *Geography and Japan's Strategic Choices: From Seclusion to Internationalization*. Washington, DC: Potomac Books; 2005.
5. Jie HL. Japan is no longer the world's third-largest economy as it slips into recession. CNBC. Accessed February 12, 2025. https://www.cnbc.com/2024/02/15/japan-loses-spot-as

-worlds-third-largest-economy-to-germany.html#:~:text=Japan%20is%20no%20longer%20the%20world%27s%20third%2Dlargest,exchange%20rate%20that%20year%2C%20official%20data%20showed.

6. Statistics Bureau. Statistics: result of the population estimates. Japanese Ministry of Internal Affairs and Communications. Accessed December 26, 2022. https://www.stat.go.jp/english/data/jinsui/tsuki/index.html.
7. Organisation for Economic Co-operation and Development. OECD economic surveys: Japan. December 2021 overview. Accessed December 26, 2022. https://www.oecd.org/economy/surveys/Japan-2021-OECD-economic-survey-overview.pdf.
8. Women frozen out of Japanese workforce amid pandemic facing poverty. *The Mainichi*. Published October 28, 2021. Accessed December 26, 2022. https://mainichi.jp/english/articles/20211028/p2a/00m/0na/028000c.
9. Single women in Japan struggling to maintain "wholesome and cultured" lives: study. *The Mainichi*. Published April 2, 2022. Accessed December 26, 2022. https://mainichi.jp/english/articles/20220402/p2a/00m/0na/034000c.
10. Richie D. *Introducing Japan*. New York, NY: Kodansha International; 1996.
11. Graig LA. *Health of Nations: An International Perspective on U.S. health care reform*. 3rd ed. Washington, DC: Congressional Quarterly; 1999.
12. Iglehart JK. Japan's medical care system. *N Engl J Med*. 1988;319:807-812.
13. Hashimoto M. Health services in Japan. In: Raffel MW, ed. *Comparative Health Systems*. University Park, PA: Pennsylvania State University Press; 1984.
14. Steslicke WE. Development of health insurance policy in Japan. *J Health Polit Policy Law*. 1982;7:197-226.
15. Jones SG, Hilborne LH, Anthony RC, et al. *Securing Health: Lessons from Nation-Building Missions*. Santa Monica, CA: RAND Corp.; 2006.
16. Nakahara T. The health system of Japan. In: Raffel MW, ed. *Health Care and Reform in Industrialized Countries*. University Park, PA: Pennsylvania State University Press; 1997:105-133.
17. Japanese Ministry of Health, Labour and Welfare. Summary of static/dynamic surveys of medical institutions and hospital report 2020. [In Japanese.] https://www.mhlw.go.jp/toukei/saikin/hw/iryosd/20/index.html.
18. Japanese Ministry of Health, Labour and Welfare. Statistics of physicians, dentists and pharmacists 2020. [In Japanese.] Accessed December 26, 2022. https://www.mhlw.go.jp/toukei/saikin/hw/ishi/20/index.html.
19. Japanese Ministry of Health, Labour and Welfare. Report on public health administration and services 2020. [In Japanese.] Accessed December 26, 2022. https://www.mhlw.go.jp/toukei/saikin/hw/eisei/20/.
20. Organisation for Economic Co-operation and Development. OECD health statistics 2022. Accessed December 26, 2022. https://www.oecd.org/health/health-data.htm.
21. Japanese Ministry of Health, Labour and Welfare. Co-payment or medical expenses. [In Japanese.] Accessed December 26, 2022. https://www.mhlw.go.jp/bunya/shakaihosho/iryouseido01/info02d-37.html.
22. Organisation for Economic Co-operation and Development. Health at a glance 2021: OECD indicators. Accessed December 26, 2022. https://www.oecd.org/health/health-at-a-glance/.
23. Japanese Ministry of Health, Labour and Welfare. Outline of clinical training system for medical practitioners. Accessed December 26, 2022. https://www.mhlw.go.jp/english/policy/health-medical/medical-care/dl/150407-03.pdf.
24. World Health Organization. Japan Life Expectancy Data. Accessed February 12, 2025. https://data.who.int/countries/392#:~:text=In%20Japan%2C%20life%20expectancy%20at%20birth%20(years),84.5%20[84.5%20%2D%2084.5]%20years%20in%202021.&text=In%20Japan%2C%20healthy%20life%20expectancy%20at%20birth,73.4%20[72.7%20%2D%2074.1]%20years%20in%202021.
25. Japanese Ministry of Health, Labour and Welfare. Patient's Behavior Survey 2020. [In Japanese.] Accessed December 26, 2022. https://www.mhlw.go.jp/toukei/saikin/hw/jyuryo/20/kakutei.html.
26. Aoki T, Matsushima M. Factors associated with the status of usual source of care during the COVID-19 pandemic: a nationwide survey in Japan. *BMC Prim Care*. 2023; 24(1):193.
27. Organisation for Economic Co-operation and Development. Society at a glance 2019: OECD social indicators. Accessed December 26, 2022. https://www.oecd.org/social/society-at-a-glance-19991290.htm.
28. Japanese Ministry of Health, Labour and Welfare. Patient Survey 2020. [In Japanese.] Accessed December 26, 2022. https://www.mhlw.go.jp/toukei/saikin/hw/kanja/20/index.html.
29. Japanese Ministry of Health, Labour and Welfare. Framework for promoting dementia care. [In Japanese.] Accessed December 26, 2022. https://www.mhlw.go.jp/stf/seisakunitsuite/bunya/0000076236_00002.html.
30. Japanese Ministry of Health, Labour and Welfare. Measures against passive smoking. [In Japanese.] Accessed December 26, 2022. https://www.mhlw.go.jp/stf/seisakunitsuite/bunya/0000189195.html.
31. Organisation for Economic Co-operation and Development. Health at a glance: Asia/Pacific 2022. Accessed December 26, 2022. https://www.oecd.org/health/health-at-a-glance-asia-pacific-23054964.htm.
32. Japanese Ministry of Health, Labour and Welfare. National Health and Nutrition Survey. [In Japanese.] Accessed December 26, 2022. https://www.mhlw.go.jp/bunya/kenkou/kenkou_eiyou_chousa.html.
33. Japanese Ministry of Health, Labour and Welfare. Vital statistics of Japan 2019. Accessed December, 2022. https://www.mhlw.go.jp/english/database/db-hw/dl/81-1a2en.pdf.
34. Our World in Data. Coronavirus pandemic. Accessed December 26, 2022. https://ourworldindata.org/coronavirus.
35. Cabinet Public Affairs Office. COVID-19 vaccines. Accessed December 26, 2022. https://japan.kantei.go.jp/ongoingtopics/vaccine.html.
36. Aoki T, Sugiyama Y, Mutai R, Matsushima M. Impact of primary care attributes on hospitalization during the COVID-19 pandemic: a nationwide prospective cohort study in Japan. *Ann Fam Med*. 2023;21(1):27-32.
37. Aoki T, Fujinuma Y, Matsushima M. Patient experience of residents with restricted primary care access during the COVID-19 pandemic. *Fam Med Community Health*. 2022;10:e001667.
38. Cabinet Secretariat. Report of the conference on building an all-generational social security system. [In Japanese.] Accessed December 26, 2022. https://www.cas.go.jp/jp/seisaku/zensedai_hosyo/pdf/20221216houkokusyo.pdf.
39. Japanese Medical Specialty Board. Sougoushinryou-senmoni. [In Japanese.] Accessed December 26, 2022. https://jbgm.org.

CHAPTER 22

Korea

Eunkyung Han and Leiyu Shi

Country Description

Table 22-1 Korea (South)

Nationality	Noun: Korean(s) Adjective: Korean
Ethnic groups	Homogenous
Religions	Protestant 17%, Buddhist 16%, Catholic 6%, none 60% (2021 est.) Note: Many people also carry on at least some Confucian traditions and practices
Language	Korean Note: English widely taught in junior high and high school
Literacy	Definition: Age 15 and over and can read and write Total population: 98.8% Male: 99.2% Female: 98.4%
Government type	Republic
Date of independence	August 15, 1945 (from Japan)
Real gross domestic product (GDP) per capita	50,600 USD (2023 est.) 49,900 USD (2022 est.) 48,600 USD (2021 est.) Note: Data are in 2021 USD
Unemployment rate	2.64% (2023 est.)
Natural hazards	Occasional typhoons with high winds and floods; low-level seismic activity common in the southwest
Environment: current issues	Air pollution in large cities, acid rain, water pollution from the discharge of sewage and industrial effluents, drift net fishing; solid waste disposal; transboundary air pollution from China
Population	51,966,948 (2023 est.)

(continues)

Table 22-1 Korea (South) *(continued)*

Age structure	0–14 years: 11.53% (male 3,072,352/female 2,916,984) 15–64 years: 70.1% (male 18,788,714/female 17,639,714) 65 years and over: 18.38% (male 4,196,789/female 5,352,395) (2023 est.)
Median age	Total: 43.2 years Male: 41.6 years Female: 45 years (2020 est.)
Population growth rate	0.23% (2023 est.)
Birth rate	6.92 births/1,000 population (2022 est.)
Death rate	7.28 deaths/1,000 population (2023 est.)
Disease burden	Communicable disease deaths: 34/100,000 population Noncommunicable disease deaths: 302/100,000 population Injury deaths: 53/100,000 population (2016 est.)
Net migration rate	2.61 migrant/1,000 population (2023 est.)
Gender ratio	At birth: 1.07 male/female Under 15 years: 1.07 male/female 15–24 years: 1.12 male/female 25–54 years: 1.06 male/female 55–64 years: 0.98 male/female 65 years and over: 0.71 male/female Total population: 0.73 male/female (2016 est.)
Infant mortality rate	Total: 2.83 deaths/1,000 live births Male: 3.04 deaths/1,000 live births Female: 2.6 deaths/1,000 live births (2023 est.)
Life expectancy at birth	Total population: 83.17 years Male: 81.2 years Female: 87.2 years (2023 est.)
Total fertility rate	1.11 children born/woman (2023 est.)

USD = U.S. dollars.

Data from Central Intelligence Agency. The World Factbook: Korea (South). Accessed April 29, 2023. https://www.cia.gov/the-world-factbook/countries/korea-south.
Statistica. Estimated life expectancy at birth in South Korea from 1950 to 2023 with forecasts up to 2100, by gender. Accessed February 13, 2025. https://www.statista.com/statistics/959606/south-korea-life-expectancy-at-birth-by-gender/#:~:text=In%202023%2C%20the%20average%20life%20expectancy%20at,to%2015%20years%20behind%20women%20for%20decades.

Owing to continuous economic growth and social progress, the healthcare system in Korea has undergone many important developments and reforms, and has experienced rapid improvement in health outcomes over the past decades. Korea achieved universal health coverage through the National Health Insurance (NHI) system in 1989, in a record 12 years of rapid coverage expansion. This was quite unique in the history of countries' transitions to universal coverage. Korea started to adopt a single-payer approach in 2000, with government-run health insurance financing, claims processing, quality controlling, and fee negotiation. Korea's single-payer system, while quite similar to other countries' single-payer systems in many respects, has not been able to control the rate of growth in health spending as well. Among Organization for Economic Co-operation and Development (OECD) countries, Korea has been the country with the highest rate of health spending growth. In contrast to public health financing, healthcare delivery in Korea is characterized by the dominance of private providers, with approximately 90% of total medical institutions being private facilities. Moreover, the wide use of traditional, complementary, and integrative medicine (TCIM) makes the Korean healthcare system unique. In recent years, the rapid increase in the aged population has been the major challenge facing the Korean healthcare system. The implementation of Korea's long-term care insurance scheme is aimed at improving access for elderly people to long-term care and reducing their socioeconomic burden. However, the coordination among long-term care facilities and hospitals remains a crucial issue in Korea. Moreover, the role of primary care in gatekeeping is relatively weak. Policies to increase efficiency across the continuum of care may be a priority for future reforms.

The main objective of this chapter is to provide a general overview of Korea as a nation and its healthcare delivery system. We will also describe the content, process, and implementation of healthcare policies and will highlight areas and challenges that require more in-depth reforms.

History

Korea is located in eastern Asia and has one of the oldest histories in the world. Throughout the establishment and collapse of many dynasties over 5,000 years of history, Korea developed its own distinctive culture. Under the last dynasty, Joseon, before modernization, Korea became known as the Land of Morning Calm because the name *Joseon* in Korean means "morning calm." With Confucianism and Buddhism in its long history, Korea is also known as the country of courtesy in the East.

From 1910 to 1945, Korea was under Japanese rule. During this period, many different groups inside and outside of Korea fought for independence. The Korean Provisional Government was established at that time to fight for independence. It declared war on Japan and provided close cooperation with Allied powers during World War II. In 1945, Japan surrendered to the Allies, ending war in the Pacific, and withdrew from the Korean Peninsula.

Soon after, Korea was divided into two parts along the 38th parallel, South and North Korea, because of ideological conflicts among various groups. A communist form of government came into power in North Korea (Democratic People's Republic of Korea), and the United States turned its authority over to South Korea (Republic of Korea). On Sunday morning, June 25, 1950, North Korea invaded South Korea (Korea hereafter) without a declaration of war. It was the beginning of the Korean War, which lasted for about three years. With military support from the United Nations, the Korean War ended with an armistice on July 27, 1953.

The war destroyed the country and yielded many economic, political, and social problems. In the aftermath, the Korean government focused on rebuilding the country. In 1960s, Korea achieved dramatic economic growth. During the Park administration period, the economy began to grow at an annual rate of 9.2%. The per capita gross domestic product (GDP) increased from a mere US $87 USD in 1962 to $1,503 USD in 1980, and exports rose by 32.8% per year from $56.7 million USD in 1962 to $17.5 billion USD in 1980.[1] With continuous efforts, Korea has accomplished noteworthy success by merging speedy economic advancement with substantial reductions in poverty. In 1996, Korea joined the OECD, marking its advancement into the ranks of developed nations. As of 2023, the GDP of Korea was $1.71 trillion USD, and GDP per capita was $33,190 USD.[2]

In the presidential election of 2013, Geun-hye Park, the daughter of former president Jeong-Hee Park, was elected. She was the first woman to be elected as president in Korea. President Park was impeached during her tenure for reasons such as manipulation of state affairs, and President Jae-In Moon took office in 2017. President Moon's health initiative was once known as the "Moon Care" program; it sought to enhance public health spending in an attempt to expand health insurance coverage. In 2022, following the conclusion of President Moon's term, President Yoon Suk-yeol assumed office and introduced a healthcare policy that embraced a more market-oriented approach and increased private-sector involvement. This marked a departure from his predecessor's focus on public health spending.

Size and Geography

Figure 22-1 shows a map of the Korean Peninsula. The Korean Peninsula lies in East Asia, adjacent to China and Japan. Because of the long north–south stretch and topographic character, Korea has several distinct regions with significantly different climates, although it is a geographically small country. The total area of the Korean Peninsula, including South Korea (Korea) and North Korea, is approximately 223,600 square kilometers, and it includes 3,300 scattered islands. The total land area of Korea, which occupies approximately 45% of the Korean Peninsula, is 100,364 square kilometers, with a population of 51.9 million as of 2023.[3] The area of Seoul, the capital city of Korea, is 605 square kilometers. The distance between South Korea's two major cities, Seoul and Busan, one in the very northwest and the other in the very southeast, is only 202 miles.

Rapid industrialization and urbanization in the 1960s and 1970s were accompanied by continuing migration of rural residents into the cities, particularly Seoul. The administrative divisions of Korea consist of nine provinces, six metropolitan cities, and one special city (Seoul), and one special self-governing city (Sejong). In 2015, more than 83% of the entire population lived in metropolitan areas.[1] In recent years, however, an increasing number of people have been moving to suburban areas.

Figure 22-1 Map of Korea

Government and Political System

Korea has a democratic form of government based on the separation of powers. Its constitution was first adopted in 1948 when the Republic was established, and it has been revised nine times as the country has struggled to make democracy work effectively. Among other things, the most recent revision of the constitution provided for the direct election of the president for a single 5-year term and for the institution of a system of local autonomy for the first time in 30 years. These two provisions are keys to the strengthening of democratic institutions in the Republic. The revision also reinstated the right of the National Assembly to inspect all aspects of state affairs on a regular basis, as a check on the power of the executive branch. Finally, it charged the government with seeking to reunify the nation.

The political system of Korea is based on a republic form of government, with the president as chief of the state and the prime minister as the head of government. The government consists of three branches: (1) the legislature, in the form of a unicameral National Assembly; (2) the judiciary, consisting of district and appellate courts and the Supreme Court; and (3) the executive, headed by the president. The president is also commander-in-chief of the armed forces, and the president is assisted by the prime minister and the State Council.

Macroeconomics

Korea has achieved exponential economic growth since the mid-20th century. Over several decades, Korea enjoyed an average of 5.0% in GDP growth per year. Referred to as the "Miracle of the Han River," the economy of Korea grew dramatically, and it ranked 11th in the world in terms of GDP in 2015. More recently, economic factors have shifted and Korea is now ranked number 14 as of 2023.[4]

In the 1970s and 1980s, the Korean economy emphasized heavy industry and the automotive industry. Hyundai, Samsung, LG, and POSCO are Korean-based global companies that have a strong reputation across the world. In the 1980s, the Korean economy started to divert into the service industry. Since then, service industries have grown to represent 57% of the GDP, whereas manufacturing accounts for 37% of the GDP.[1,5] In the 1990s, Korea entered into the information technology business, starting this information technology project with strong government support. Within a few years, Korea became a world leader in information technology.

In 1998, the Korean economy, like other Asian countries, faced a financial crisis. All industries and citizens suffered from the crisis. With well-planned government strategies and financial support from the International Monetary Fund, Korea overcame the financial difficulty and bounced back in a few years. After the crisis, the government attempted financial reform to restore economic stability. The economic growth rate again reached 9% in 2000, and by 2006, the unemployment rate started to decline from 6.0% to 3.5%.[1] In the 2007–2008 global economic downturn, Korea's export-focused economy experienced decreases, but it rebounded rapidly with over 6% growth in 2010. Since 2011, however, the economy has experienced slow growth, mostly ranging between 2% and 3% per year, primarily due to sluggish domestic consumption and investment as well as the demographic transition to an aging society. This recent slowdown was further exacerbated by the COVID-19 pandemic. Despite these challenges, statistics showed a growth rate of 4.1% for Korea in 2021.[6]

A well-developed infrastructure, including transportation, roads, and communication, facilitated expansion of industries. Rapid improvement in transportation and road systems increased mobility. Because of the topographic characteristics of Korea, most industries are located in the northwest or southeast of the country. Services and manufacturing are located in the northwest, whereas heavy industry is located in the southeast.

Koreans believe that education is a critical key to success; thus, much energy is put into learning. Learning a second language, particularly English and Chinese, is believed to be a stepping stone for future success given the trend of globalization. For this reason, English is taught as a required subject starting in elementary school. Many people, especially in the business sectors, are voluntarily learning Chinese as well. The five countries with the largest number of Korean high school and college-level students studying abroad have been the United States, China, Australia, Japan, and Canada.[7] According to U.S. statistics, 40,000 Korean students were studying in the United States in 2023. Korea ranked third in terms of the number of active students in the United States from abroad.[8]

Demographics

According to data from the Economically Active Population Survey, administered by Statistics Korea (KOSTAT; formerly named the National Statistical Office of Korea), the population in Korea was estimated in July 2016 to be 50.9 million. Of that number, 43.4 million (85.3%) were age 15 years and older. Almost 27.6 million were economically active. Among them, 26.6 million were employed, and the labor participation rate in economic activities was 63.5% in July 2016. Because of a low birth rate and the aging society, however, KOSTAT projected that the number of economically active people would decrease from 2016 and the total population would start to decline in 2019.[9] By age group, the number of those less than 15 years old has steadily decreased since 1970, whereas the population that is aged 65 years and over is increasing. The population growth rate in Korea was 0.48 in the years between 2010 and 2015.[10]

One problem in the population structure of Korea is the population density in city areas. In 2015, 50.3% of the total population lived in the Seoul metropolitan area, including Incheon and Gyeonggi provinces. Seoul, by itself, had more than 10 million people (19.4%) living in it. The population density in Seoul was 16,700 people per square kilometer.[1] This unequal population distribution creates many problems, such as housing shortages, high prices of commodities, pollution, unequal education opportunities, and even lack of availability of medical services.

In 2023, each Korean household had an average of 2.2 people.[11] Average annual income per house was $47,715 USD. Among people aged 25 to 34 in 2022, 70% had a college degree.[12]

Religion

The major religious groups in Korea include Protestant, Buddhist, and Catholic. According to the Korean National Statistical Office, 56.0% of Koreans report that they do not hold religious beliefs.[9] Because of influences from China during the history of Korea, Buddhism and Confucianism were dominant religious groups until the late 19th century. Buddhism remains one of the major religions in Korea, and it is estimated that 16% of Koreans are Buddhists.[5] With the beginning of modernization and industrialization, however, Confucianism rapidly declined, and only 0.2% of Koreans report that they hold Confucianism as a religious belief. Because of the influence of Buddhism and Confucianism, Koreans still place a high value on family, relationships, respect, and cooperation.

Arriving Catholic and Protestant missionaries in Korea in the 19th century changed many people's religious affiliation in Korea. Christianity and Catholicism spread rapidly, and a significant number of Koreans converted. Currently, it is estimated that approximately 17% of the population in Korea is Protestant and 6% is Catholic.[5]

Brief History of the Healthcare System

Pre–World War II

Throughout the long history of Korea, Koreans have used traditional Korean medicine and remedies, including acupuncture and herbal medicine. Korean medicine focuses on prevention as well as treatment of diseases. People often visit traditional medicine clinics to promote their health or to cure sickness. This long-held tradition was almost destroyed when Japan annexed Korea in the early 20th century.

During the period of occupation, the Japanese prohibited Koreans from using traditional medicine. Instead, the Japanese put their own healthcare system in Korea, which included Westernized medicine.

Post–World War II

National liberation in 1945 brought back these revered Korean traditional medicine practices. Since then, both Westernized medicine and traditional medicine have coexisted in Korea. After World War II, Korea experienced Western culture and medicine at an accelerating pace. Rapid development of the economy in the 1960s pushed the Korean government to more strongly consider the welfare and health of its citizens.

In 1963, the Korean government enacted the Medical Insurance Law, permitting voluntary health insurance. After this first step, however, development of a healthcare system was slow because of the government's devotion to economic expansion. Health insurance corporations, such as Busan Blue Cross Plan, offered individual policies, but they did not become a major source of health insurance coverage because of the very low participation from citizens.[13]

In 1977, the government passed a law mandating that employers with more than 500 employees provide health insurance to their employees and families. This requirement of health insurance coverage has been gradually increased over time. In 1979, all companies with 300 or more employees were required to provide health insurance. The same year, the government expanded mandatory health insurance coverage to government employees and private school teachers. It was expanded again in 1981 to companies with more than 100 workers and to the self-employed. In addition, the government started demonstration programs in some rural areas to provide health insurance coverage. These step-by-step expansions finally achieved universal coverage in 1989.[14] A year before, the Korean government mandated health insurance coverage for all residents in rural areas, and in 1989, the government mandated coverage for all residents in urban areas, no matter what their employment status was. At that time, the government controlled three different medical insurance societies: (1) the medical insurance society for employees, (2) a regional medical society of the self-employed, and (3) a society for government employees and private school employees.

Next, the Korean government implemented two major reforms: integration reform in 1998 and separation reform in 2000. In October 1998, the first integration reform integrated two medical insurance societies into one. With the establishment of the National Health Insurance Corporation (NHIC) in 2000, the second initiative of integration was implemented, where all medical insurance societies were integrated under the control of the NHIC.[15,16]

The separation reform in July 2000 was for specialization and quality improvement. Before this reform, both physicians and pharmacists could prescribe and dispense drugs for outpatient services. The reform separated the functions of prescribing and dispensing drugs between doctors and pharmacists in an attempt to prevent the overuse and misuse of drugs.

In 2000, the Health Insurance Review and Assessment (HIRA) Service was established to assess the effectiveness and efficiency of clinical services in order to improve quality of care. Moreover, the Hospital Service Evaluation Program was launched in 2004 to ensure high quality of services.

The Current Healthcare System

Facilities

In 2021, the total number of hospitals and clinics in Korea was 71,422. There were 23,724 pharmacies and 2,587 public health center–related facilities.

Table 22-2 indicates the total number of hospitals and clinics. Total numbers have been gradually increasing over time, though the ratio of each type of facility has held steady. From 2018 to 2021, the increase in long-term hospitals slowed slightly compared with the previous period, in contrast to the increase observed in Korean medicine hospitals. As of 2022, dental facilities accounted for 26.3% of the total and Korean medicine facilities accounted for 21.1% of the total.[6]

In terms of specialized hospitals and clinics, long-term care hospitals (acute hospitals for long-term care) have markedly increased over the past decades, mainly due to the increasing needs and demands of an aging society. With relatively few regulations during the first phase of a growing, hypercompetitive market, many healthcare providers diverted into long-term care as a niche market for their business. In July 2008, the country's long-term care insurance scheme was launched with the aim of controlling healthcare expenditures, which were high due to using acute hospitals for long-term care. Although some studies report a positive effect of reducing total medical costs after the implementation of long-term care, competition between publicly assisted long-term care facilities (such as nursing homes) and acute care services for long-term care also emerged. Altogether, the expansion of long-term care facilities has been a consistent trend in past years. The number of midwifery facilities significantly decreased due to more women going to hospital maternity wards to deliver their babies.

Table 22-3 shows the number of inpatient care beds in Korea, by type of institution. Since 2000, the number of beds has greatly increased in Korea (+164%), with a significant number of these being dedicated to long-term care; by comparison, the number of beds per capita has decreased in nearly all OECD countries.[16] According to OECD health data published in 2022, the number of beds per 1,000 population in Korea was 12.7, which was the highest ratio among other OECD countries, followed by Japan (12.6 beds/1,000 population). The growing demand for and supply of dental surgeries, such as for dental implants, also led to an increase in the number of beds available in dental hospitals/clinics.[6]

Most healthcare facilities in Korea are owned and operated by the private sector. All citizens have freedom in the selection of healthcare providers. Insurance beneficiaries, however, are required to receive their initial treatments from first-level healthcare providers. All providers in Korea, except specialized hospitals, are endowed as first-level providers. When patients need to have specialized care, they can be referred to the second-level providers. This two-level provider system was intended to ensure efficient use of the limited medical resources but also curtails patients' tendency of preferring general hospitals. The first-level hospitals or clinics, therefore, play the role of gatekeeper for health services. However, gatekeeping is weak in reality due to the competition between hospitals and clinics.[17]

Table 22-2 Number of Hospitals and Clinics by Type, 2018–2021

Year	Total	Hospital and Clinic				Specialized Hospital			Dental Facility		Korean Medicine Facility		Dispensary	Midwifery
		General Hospital	Long-Term Care Hospital	Hospital	Clinic	Tuberculosis Hospital	Leprosy Hospital	Mental Hospital	Dental Hospital	Dental Clinic	KM Hospital	KM Clinic		
2018	67,847	353	1,448	1,462	31,672	2	1	114	237	17,664	307	14,329	237	21
2019	69,118	356	1,468	1,487	32,441	2	1	114	239	17,955	353	14,442	241	19
2020	70,151	361	1,471	1,513	33,032	2	1	112	235	18,253	411	14,487	255	18
2021	71,422	365	1,467	1,394	33,818	2	1	250	234	18,582	479	14,557	257	16

Data from South Korean Ministry of Health and Welfare. *Yearbook of Health and Welfare Statistics, 2022.*

Table 22-3 Number of Beds by Type of Institutions, 2018–2021

Year	Total	Hospital and Clinic				Specialized Hospital			Dental Facility		Korean Medicine Facility		Dispensary	Midwifery
		General Hospital	Long-Term Care Hospital	Hospital	Clinic	Tuberculosis Hospital	Leprosy Hospital	Mental Hospital	Dental Hospital	Dental Clinic	KM Hospital	KM Clinic		
2018	708,372	152,104	272,469	163,608	62,763	994	700	31,695	262	95	20,038	3,368	238	38
2019	705,079	152,977	273,284	160,929	57,140	988	700	31,316	452	103	22,794	4,119	247	30
2020	716,752	155,210	277,035	164,072	55,256	972	677	31,111	256	94	26,555	5,227	253	34
2021	722,813	156,783	276,654	132,060	54,141	558	677	63,467	252	97	30,484	7,359	250	31

Data from South Korean Ministry of Health and Welfare. *Yearbook of Health and Welfare Statistics, 2022.*

Table 22-4 Healthcare Facilities Located in Rural Area, 2018–2021

	2018	2019	2020	2021
Rural hospitals, clinics, and midwiferies	7,853	7,962	8,030	8,090
% (Total hospitals, clinics, and midwiferies)	11.5	11.5	11.4	11.3

Data from South Korean Ministry of Health and Welfare. *Yearbook of Health and Welfare Statistics, 2022.*

Because the majority of healthcare facilities are owned and managed by the private sector, many medical service providers target mass markets. In 2021, 89.7% of hospitals, clinics, and midwiferies were concentrated in urban areas. This unequal distribution of medical services has created a problem in accessibility. Citizens living in rural areas have difficulty accessing medical services, especially specialty and emergency care, compared to those in urban areas. With a great safety net system, however, accessibility to primary care has been supplemented. **Table 22-4** shows healthcare facilities by geographic locations, and **Table 22-5** indicates the number of safety net providers available in Korea.

Public health centers, public subhealth centers, and primary healthcare posts are mostly located in rural areas in Korea. As safety net providers, these public facilities mainly provide primary care services to citizens in rural areas and those who cannot afford the high cost of care in hospitals or clinics.

In 2021, a total of 3,587 facilities were classified as public health centers, public subhealth centers, or primary healthcare posts. Public subhealth centers and primary healthcare posts are considered branches of public health centers that supervise these facilities. These providers also act as gatekeepers in primary care. When patients need complex care, they refer these patients to a higher level of medical institution or to specialty physicians.[18]

Table 22-5 Public Health Centers, Public Subhealth Centers, and Primary Healthcare Posts, 2018–2021

Year	Public Health Center	Public Subhealth Center	Primary Healthcare Post	Community Health Promotion Center
2018	254	1,338	1,904	57
2019	256	1,340	1,904	64
2020	256	1,337	1,901	77
2021	258	1,342	1,904	83

Data from South Korean Ministry of Health and Welfare. *Yearbook of Health and Welfare Statistics, 2022.*

Emergency medical facilities in Korea include central, regional, and local organizations. In 2021, among 16 major cities/provinces, Seoul, Gyunggi, and Incheon (metropolitan area) had 33.6% of total emergency care infrastructures. **Table 22-6** indicates the number of emergency medical centers and institutions.

Workforce

Tables 22-7 and **22-8** indicate the number of licensed healthcare professionals and qualified medical specialists, respectively. The number of licensed healthcare professionals in Korea has grown rapidly over the last decades. From 2020 to 2022, the average overall growth rate for healthcare professionals was approximately 5.3%.[19] The number of nurse assistants increased the most over the 10-year period of 2010–2020, growing by 222,052. In spite of this fast-growing workforce, the number of practicing physicians per 1,000 population in Korea was 2.5 in 2022, which ranked 32 out of 34 among OECD countries.

Table 22-6 Number of Emergency Medical Centers and Institutions, 2018–2021

Year	Total	Central Emergency Medical Center	Regional Emergency Medical Center	Local Emergency Medical Center	Local Emergency Medical Institution
2018	402	1	36	117	248
2019	402	1	38	123	240
2020	403	1	38	128	236
2021	404	1	38	127	238

Data from Korean Government. Ministry of Health and Welfare. *Health and Welfare Statistical Yearbook, 2022.*

Table 22-7 Number of Licensed Healthcare Professionals, 2018–2021

Year	Medical Doctor	Dentist	Doctor of Korean Medicine	Pharmacist	Nurse
2018	123,173	30,918	24,885	69,347	394,627
2019	126,795	31,640	25,592	70,904	414,983
2020	129,294	32,340	26,115	72,530	436,340
2021	132,065	33,036	26,807	73,948	457,849

Data from Korean Government. Ministry of Health and Welfare. *Health and Welfare Statistical Yearbook, 2022.*

Table 22-8 Number of Qualified Medical Specialists by Type of Specialty, 2018–2021

Year	2018	2019	2020	2021
Total	97,271	100,161	103,379	106,011
Internal medicine	17,307	17,797	18,814	19,326
Surgery	7,113	7,202	7,326	7,438
Orthopedics	6,869	7,090	7,277	7,464
Neurosurgery	3,057	3,137	3,205	3,281
Cardiothoracic surgery	1,267	1,286	1,306	1,322
Plastic/cosmetic surgery	2,379	2,460	2,532	2,598
Anesthesiology	5,258	5,493	5,694	5,883
Obstetrics and gynecology	6,841	6,969	7,069	7,173
Pediatrics	6,912	7,127	7,298	7,492
Ophthalmology	3,713	3,805	3,900	3,991
Otolaryngology	4,234	4,346	4,450	4,542
Dermatology	2,467	2,543	2,609	2,680
Urology	2,783	2,816	2,833	2,853
Pathology	1,078	1,108	1,139	1,169
Laboratory medicine	1,057	1,087	1,111	1,147
Tuberculosis	170	166	164	160
Rehabilitation	2,232	2,342	2,458	2,566
Preventive medicine	713	718	721	729
Diagnostic radiology	3,876	4,016	4,157	4,292
Radiation oncology	482	497	505	511
Neurology	2,106	2,181	2,267	2,342
Psychiatry	3,789	3,932	4,048	4,179
Family medicine	8,146	8,427	8,682	8,882

Year	2018	2019	2020	2021
Occupational and environmental medicine	753	788	814	846
Nuclear medicine	357	366	375	381
Emergency medicine	1,830	1,986	2,154	2,302
Neuropsychiatry	262	261	257	254
Radiology	220	215	214	208

Data from South Korean Ministry of Health and Welfare. *Yearbook of Health and Welfare Statistics, 2022.*

Similarly, the ratio of practicing nurses per 1,000 population was 4.8. This ratio ranked 29 out of 34 among OECD countries. The average number of practicing nurses per 1,000 population in OECD countries was 7.9 in 2019.[16] Like other countries, Korea faces a nursing shortage. In 2023, the number of registered nurses had increased by 64% since 2013.[6,20–22]

Table 22-9 shows the number of healthcare professionals in health centers, subhealth centers, and primary healthcare posts. To increase accessibility and counter the unequal distribution of services, the Korean government forced medical college/university graduates to serve in rural areas. By serving in rural areas as public health doctors, they can waive service in the army, which is mandatory for all Korean males. Most medical college graduates take this option as a replacement of military service.

Technology and Equipment

In terms of medical technology and equipment, Korea is a country with rapid adoption of new medical technology. According to the OECD, the number of computed tomography scanners per million population in Korea increased rapidly from 12.2 in 1990 to 41 in 2020,[23] which makes Korea a leader on this criterion among the OECD member countries. Similarly, the number of magnetic resonance imaging machines per million population dramatically increased, from 1.4 in 1990 to 34.2 in 2020. Again, Korea is a leader among OECD member countries concerning this medical technology.[20,21]

Table 22-9 Healthcare Professionals in Public Health Centers, Public Subhealth Centers, and Primary Healthcare Posts, 2018–2021

Year	Medical Doctors*	Dentists*	Korean Medicine Doctors*	Nurses
2018	2,092	491	1,013	7,855
2019	2,066	498	1,024	8,982
2020	2,032	502	1,007	9,986
2021	1,993	507	930	11,216

*Includes medical officers and public health doctors.

Data from South Korean Ministry of Health and Welfare. *Yearbook of Health and Welfare Statistics, 2022.*

Evaluation of the Healthcare System

Cost

Over the decades, Korea has experienced fast economic growth and rapid industrialization. As a result of its rapidly developing economy, Korea joined the OECD in 1996, becoming the 29th member country and the second member country in Asia.[24] Economic development has dramatically improved the health of the Korean population, particularly with the inception of national health insurance.

National health insurance was introduced in Korea in 1977. Through the gradual coverage of additional population groups, Korea was able to provide universal health coverage to all of its citizens by 1989, only 12 years after its first introduction. Since then, healthcare expenditures have increased rapidly.[25]

Healthcare expenditures in Korea accounted for 8.4% of its GDP in 2020, which was 1.3% lower than the OECD average. Medical spending per capita in Korea was $3,582 USD in the same year, below the OECD average of $4,000 USD.[16] The rate of growth in health spending was higher (6.9%) than the average of the OECD countries in last decade (3.3%) as the result of the increase in public spending. The proportion of medical expenses (direct household burden) borne by households gradually decreased to 34.0% in 2010, 33.7% in 2015, and 27.8% in 2020.[20] Another factor affecting the rise of health spending is pharmaceutical spending. Although the growth of pharmaceutical spending has slowed, it still comprises a large part of the healthcare expenditure. Spending on pharmaceuticals in 2020 was $760.9 USD, which was higher than the OECD average of $547.2 USD.[24]

Korea's NHIC provides health coverage to citizens based on their employment status. Two medical insurance societies for industrial workers and the self-employed are under the Korean National Health Insurance (NHI) program, which covers approximately 97% of citizens. The Medical Aid program, which is under local government control, provides health coverage to low-income and indigent people. **Table 22-10** shows the enrollment in the NHI and Medical Aid programs, which cover all citizens. In 2021, more than 51 million (97.1%) were insured with NHI, and the remaining 1.4 million (2.9%) were covered by Medical Aid.[26]

Financing of health care comes from three sources: the mandatory health insurance contribution (premium), government subsidies, and patients' out-of-pocket payments.[27] The mandatory health insurance contribution is set by and includes a contribution from both the employer and employee. The contribution rate for industrial workers is based on income and their personal property. Employers are responsible for paying 50% of the contribution of their employees. As of 2022, the contribution rate was about 6.99% of salaried income.[28] Although this rate is one of the lowest among OECD countries, many Koreans feel that it is a heavy financial burden for them. According to a national survey in 2016, only 19% said that the contribution rate was appropriate for the offered benefits.[9,18] For the self-employed, the contribution is set by economic activity, income, and property.

The government subsidy accounts for a small portion of total financing. The government's share, however, has been increasing since 2002, to give financial relief to the NHI. The subsidy comes from tax revenue, both general taxation and a cigarette tax in accordance with the Special Act for Financial Stabilization. This act was legislated to solve the NHI's financial crisis, as its stability has rapidly deteriorated since 1999.[14,25]

One of the distinct features of the Korean healthcare system is the dominance of the private sector in healthcare delivery and even in healthcare financing. The relatively high private share (about 42%) of healthcare financing is related to substantial out-of-pocket payments.[29,30] Private providers supply the majority of healthcare services, with public providers playing a residual role. More than 90% of hospitals and clinics are privately owned. In most cases, therefore, physicians both own and manage the facilities. Physician clinics have inpatient facilities, and most hospitals operate large outpatient centers, which promotes competition among hospitals and clinics. All pharmacies are owned and operated by individual pharmacists as well.

Cost sharing is controlled by one insurer, the NHIC of Korea. The insurance allowance is also controlled, with strong government intervention; however, it is difficult to control the costs for services that are not covered by NHI. Since adoption of the NHI system, administration costs have been managed with strong governmental regulation. With expansion of benefit coverage and increasing demands from customers, however, it has been rapidly increasing in recent years.

The reimbursement mechanism in Korea is traditional fee-for-service, which calculates medicine, material, and treatment costs separately and

Table 22-10 People Covered by Health Insurance, by Category of Insured (Unit: 1,000 Population, Percentage), 2017–2021

Year	Total*,**	Health Insurance for Industrial Workers**,***	Health Insurance for Self-Employed**	Health Insurance for Medical Aid**
2018	52,557 (100)	36,990 (70.4)	14,082 (26.8)	1,485 (2.8)
2019	52,880 (100)	37,227 (70.4)	14,164 (26.8)	1,489 (2.8)
2020	52,871 (100)	37,150 (70.3)	14,195 (26.8)	1,526 (2.9)
2021	52,929 (100)	37,180 (70.2)	14,232 (26.9)	1,517 (2.9)

*All numbers include dependents.

**Numbers in parentheses are proportion of enrollments.

***Industrial workers include government employees and private school teachers.

Data from HIRA, Health Insurance Review & Assessment. https://opendata.hira.or.kr/op/opc/selectStcPblc.do?sno=13600&odPblcTpCd=002&searchCnd=&searchWrd=&pageIndex=1.

reimburses under a predetermined fee schedule.[14] Many medical examinations and treatments are done competitively under fee-for-service. To create demand and to secure more patients, providers excessively purchase new and advanced technologies. Providers induce demand by prescribing more drugs, requiring that patients have more visits for care, and encouraging treatments that are not included in the NHI's benefit package. This results in increases in customers' out-of-pocket costs and total healthcare expenditures.

For medical services, patients are responsible for paying some portion of the medical cost, in the form of either a deductible or coinsurance. Deductibles and coinsurance are predetermined by the NHIC in annual negotiations with organizations representing providers, such as the Korean Medical Association, the Korean Dental Association, and the Association of Korean Medicine. Deductibles are applied only to people in the Medical Aid programs. Depending on the patient's income level, a patient can use medical services either at no cost or for a small charge (about $1–2 USD).

Coinsurance rates vary by type of service (inpatient or outpatient care) and type of healthcare facility (clinic, hospital, or general hospital). For outpatient services in clinics, patients are responsible for 30% of the total charges. The rate is 50% for services in hospitals and 55% in general hospitals. For inpatients, the coinsurance is 20% of total medical charges.[14,18]

Other than deductibles and coinsurance, some patients pay an extra fee for outpatient services from certain physicians. When patients want services from certain doctors who have more experience and an exceptional reputation, they are required to pay this special fee on top of the regular medical charges. Typically, senior medical staff in general hospitals are in this category.

To control increasing healthcare expenditures, the NHIC introduced diagnosis-related groups in 1997 as a pilot program. It was planned to apply to all providers after 3 years. Because of strong opposition from providers, however, only a few providers voluntarily participate in this system, which is currently applied to eight selected procedures. In 2001, a Resources-Based Relative Value Scale payment system was implemented in Korea. The payments to providers increased, but without a mechanism to control the volume and expenditure.[25]

The flow of medical claims is important to understand. After providers supply medical services to insurance beneficiaries, they send medical claims to both the NHIC and the HIRA. The HIRA reviews claims submitted by providers for appropriateness of medical procedures supplied and the claim costs. After the HIRA evaluates claims, the NHIC makes payments to providers in accordance with the review results.[14]

For certain chronic diseases and serious illnesses (e.g., diabetes and cancer), the NHI cuts patients' out-of-pocket costs for the elderly. The benefit package of the NHI has been expanded over time.

Even with separation of dispensing authority from medical practices, antibiotics are still overused because of the practice patterns of physicians. Most primary care and preventive services, which are critical for public health, are still not included in the NHI's benefit package. Complaints from customers regarding preventive services are growing.

Overutilization, low reimbursement rates, addition of preventive services in the benefit package, and duplication of medical shopping services are issues to be solved by the Korean government. These factors yield high administrative costs and eventually will increase the country's healthcare expenditures.

Quality

The rapid economic development in Korea was paralleled by unprecedented achievements in the health of the population. Dramatic improvements have been attained in life expectancy, and infant mortality rates have been steadily reduced. Mortality and morbidity patterns have changed from communicable diseases to chronic and lifestyle-related diseases. The infant mortality rate per 1,000 live births decreased to 2.83 in 2023 from 45.0 in 1970, whereas life expectancy at birth for males reached 81.2 years and for females, 87.2 years.[5,31] For comparison, the average for OECD countries is 77.9 and 83.3 years, respectively.[6,20]

One factor in the improvement of population health is the regulated healthcare system in Korea. Because the fee-for-service system in Korea is strongly regulated, healthcare providers do not compete on price. Instead, to secure more patients, providers compete on quality of service. Providers realize that patient-centered care, high quality achieved with advanced medical technologies, and friendly services are essential for success in their businesses. This phenomenon in a hypercompetitive market contributes to continuous improvements in the quality of health services. However, unchecked provider-induced demand in some areas yields overutilization. In addition, the areas with lower-income populations still have limited access and poor quality of care because of risk pooling.

Table 22-11 Level of Satisfaction for Medical Services, by Type of Healthcare Facility

Facility Type	% Very Satisfied	% Moderately Satisfied	% Acceptable	% Moderately Dissatisfied	% Very Dissatisfied
General hospital	18.8	35.7	33.4	10.8	1.4
Hospital/clinic	11.7	36.2	44.8	6.8	0.5
Public health center	29.4	38.9	27.7	3.6	0.4

Data from Statistics Korea (KOSTAT). http://kostat.go.kr/portal/eng/pressReleases/11/5/index.board.

For the year 2021, the 10 leading causes of death in Korea were ischemic heart disease, stroke, lower respiratory infections, trachea and lung cancers, self-harm, Alzheimer disease and other dementias, kidney diseases, liver cancer, colon and rectum cancers, and stomach cancer.[32] The leading cause of death in people aged 10 to 39 years was suicide. The rate has significantly increased over the past few years. Suicide accounted for more than half of all death among people in their twenties The leading cause of death of those 40 and older was cancer.[33]

According to results of Social Survey, which was done by KOSTAT in 2014, the majority of people who used medical services responded that they were satisfied with those medical services. **Table 22-11** shows the level of satisfaction for medical services by type of healthcare facility.[6,18] An updated Social Survey by KOSTAT in 2020 found similar findings in some categories. Most questions from the 2014 survey were left out of the 2020 survey. Overall findings and outcomes from the 2020 survey were limited and not included in this text.[34] For those who were dissatisfied with medical services, the most common reasons for that dissatisfaction were high medical charges (24.7%), unsatisfactory treatment (20.7%), and long waiting times (20.2%).

Healthcare expenditure depends not only on price but also on the volume of services provided. Under the fee-for-service system, which strictly regulates fees, there is a concern that medical providers may increase the frequency of office visits and hospital admissions, as well as the intensity of services.

Obesity is a growing health issue in many countries. As shown in **Table 22-12**, the prevalence of obesity among those age 20 years and older in Korea was 31.5% in 2014, which was the lowest rate among the OECD countries. This prevalence has increased over recent decades. Since 2001, however, the growth has slowed.[1,6] Interestingly, the increase of overweight in the male population was a driver of the overall increase of overweight/obesity in the whole population, whereas the prevalence of obesity in women declined slightly during the same time.[1,6]

Access

The Korean NHI achieved a goal to cover all citizens for medical care. With freedom of choice, citizens can access medical services at any time of the year and from any provider they want. When NHI was introduced in Korea, it initially allowed citizens to use medical services for only 180 days per year, but by 2006, this service limitation was removed. According to OECD health data, the number of physician visits per citizen in Korea was 15.65 in 2022, exceeding the average number of visits in OECD member countries.[35] In addition, length of stay in hospitals in Korea was 16.5 days as compared with the OECD average of 8.1 days. This is mainly because the Korean NHI does not have a prospective payment system that could help to contain costs. Moreover, many hospitals tend to increase capacity for the same reason. Korea is the only country among the OECD countries that has experienced an increasing number of beds over time.[6,20,36]

Accessibility to medical care in Korea is considered high overall, but as in many countries, accessibility can be problematic in rural areas. The distribution

Table 22-12 Prevalence of Obesity Among Those 20 Years and Older, in Selected Years

Classification	2001	2005	2010	2014	2021
Total	30.6	31.8	31.4	31.5	38.4
Men	32.4	35.2	36.5	37.7	49.2
Women	29.4	28.3	26.4	25.3	27.8

Obesity is defined as a body mass index equal to or greater than 25.0.

Data from *Journal of Obesity and Metabolic Syndrome*. Accessed February 22, 2025. https://www.jomes.org/journal/view.html?doi=10.7570/jomes24012; Ministry of Health and Welfare, Health Investment Planning Team. http://www.medicalkorea.or.kr/content.do?method=getContent&gcd=G1001&cmscd=CM9015; and http://kosis.kr/eng/statisticsList/statisticsList_01List.jsp?vwcd=MT_ETITLE&parmTabId=M_01_01#SubCont.

of medical services is not even. Because most of the healthcare facilities are privately owned, they tend to be concentrated in cities where there are many customers and where the desired lifestyle for healthcare providers' families can be realized. The limited availability of healthcare services in rural areas with small populations is a problem for Korea.

Current and Emerging Issues and Challenges

Along with a rapid expansion of the economy, health care in Korea improved remarkably in a short period. Every citizen has had healthcare coverage since the introduction of NHI. With strong government regulation, NHI has been successful in both cost containment and quality improvement. Some statistics, however, indicate that healthcare expenditures in terms of GDP in Korea are still below the OECD average, although the growth of healthcare expenditures in Korea is fast and above the average for OECD countries. For example, Korea spent 33.9% of its GDP on public expenditures in 2019, below the OECD average of 46.6%. Social protection expenditures were 6.9% of GDP, around half of the OECD average of 13.3%.[37]

Moreover, factors contributing to the rapidly changing environment, such as increasing demand, seeking high quality of care, and hypercompetitive healthcare markets, have put more burdens on the national insurer (NHIC), providers, and even citizens. The recent financial constraints on the NHI service can be attributed to a decrease in health insurance premium income resulting from changes in the health insurance imposition system, as well as an increase in medical expenses due to the country's aging population. Moreover, the COVID-19 pandemic led to a surge in medical demand, contributing to the financial strains on the system since 2020. The government may need to implement payment reform based on a prospective payment mechanism and expand the role of public hospitals to reduce the disparities in health care and health outcomes.

Furthermore, it is imperative to address the rapid aging trend and avoid solutions in silos within the healthcare delivery system. The focus is largely on strengthening primary care and effectively integrating medical care with long-term care when discussing potential solutions. Since 2003, the number of long-term care providers has been growing, and the number of long-term care facilities has dramatically increased. In July 2008, the long-term care insurance scheme was launched with the aim of controlling healthcare expenditures on acute hospitals for long-term care. Since then, the expansion of long-term care facilities has been ongoing. The implementation of the long-term care insurance scheme is intended to improve access for elderly people to long-term care and to reduce the socioeconomic burden. However, the coordination among long-term care facilities and hospitals remains an unresolved issue in Korea.[36] Expanding public long-term care benefits and enhancing financial sustainability for the long-term care insurance system are still challenges a decade after this system's implementation. In 2023, the Ministry of Health and Welfare announced plans to increase home-based primary care centers and LTC home health centers. At the time of this writing, pilot projects are being implemented with the plan coming to fruition in 2027.[38]

Additionally, the structure of the healthcare industry in Korea is changing. One distinct characteristic in Korea is that the private sector, particularly small hospitals and clinics, dominates the healthcare market. Either horizontal or vertical integration activities through networking, franchising, or partnerships among providers are becoming prevalent in Korea's healthcare market.

In December 2006, the Korean government announced Service Industry Development Plans for the healthcare sector. The government proposed to (1) encourage providers to adopt practice guidelines and clinical pathways in order to improve quality of care; (2) allow the establishment of management service organizations (MSO) to provide management services for healthcare providers; (3) consider having for-profit hospitals in the healthcare market, which are still illegal in Korea; (4) introduce private health insurance for healthcare services; and (5) give governmental support to providers to attract customers from abroad (medical tourism).

After the government's plans were announced, several MSOs were established to provide management services to healthcare providers. Typically, hospitals/clinics in Korea are owned and managed by physicians. By contracting with MSOs, physicians at hospitals and clinics can focus more on delivering care and can gain efficient management; nevertheless, private health insurance and for-profit hospitals are controversial. These proposed changes will face strong opposition from stakeholders.

COVID-19 Pandemic

The COVID-19 pandemic brought a significant change in the South Korean health system. During the pandemic, telemedicine was temporarily allowed in Korea for medical providers to treat patients via phone or video. This had not been allowed previously, except for consultations between medical providers. During this period, the telehealth service market and investment growth dramatically increased. In contrast to the private-sector demands, as of 2023, multiple bills were proposed to expand telehealth between medical professionals and patients, which are still on table.

Summary

Like many developed countries, Korea must face the challenge of growing healthcare costs, as the portion of GDP going to healthcare continues to increase. Because healthcare spending exceeds economic growth, there is cause for concern in the long run. However, this problem is not unique to Korea. The government may be considering moving to a prospective payment system or to global budgeting to control use. It may be that Korea must revisit its benefit package and include more preventive care services.

Continuous quality improvement will remain a challenge. The government will make every effort to improve and monitor quality of care, especially for long-term care. There is no systemized control system to monitor and evaluate long-term care services. The government should strengthen the accreditation process for long-term care facilities.

An appropriate method to incentivize providers, especially in the wake of COVID-19 pandemic, should be considered, as this event raised various questions about the best means of allocating health-related resources. These are resources that could be better used elsewhere in the system. Future reforms of incentive structures for providers should focus on healthcare quality and efficiency, such as implementing the pay-for-performance scheme to reward providers for achieving specified performance targets.

The NHI's main considerations include maintaining its financial status in balance. Since the beginning of the 2000s, the NHI has suffered from financial difficulty and huge deficits. Consideration might be given to raising contribution rates and tight cost control, especially to cope with emergencies like COVID-19. The contribution rate (premium) from citizens is relatively low compared with other countries, even though Koreans enjoy high-quality and technology-driven medical services. Although the NHIC could face opposition from citizens, it is noted that the NHI contribution rates have been gradually increasing. One of the mechanisms being used effectively now is an electronic data interchange (EDI) system to ensure more stable resource collection.

Finally, the NHI in Korea has been remarkably successful in the past. Since the 2010s began, however, the NHIC has been facing not only financial burdens but also complaints from both providers and citizens. Reestablishing trust in the NHI system and reinforcing the NHIC's accountability will be another challenge. The Korean government should improve public relations and be more responsive to the increasing demands of its citizens.

It will be crucial to build a transparent policy process for greater trust in the government's decision making. Stakeholder discussions and raising public awareness can play influential roles in convincing citizens that there is a need for reforms. Consistent and continuous efforts to reach a consensus, to contain costs, and to build social solidarity around the objectives of equity, efficiency, and quality will be the ultimate task for future growth of the Korean healthcare system.

References

1. Korea National Statistical Office. Korean statistical services. Accessed April 18, 2016. http://kosis.kr/eng/.
2. International Monetary Fund. IMF Datamapper. Accessed April 3, 2024. https://www.imf.org/external/datamapper/profile/KOR.
3. Korean Government. About Korea: geography. Accessed April 18, 2016. http://www.korea.net/AboutKoreaSociety/South-Korea-Summary.
4. WorldBank. All Countries and Economies. Accessed February 12, 2025. https://data.worldbank.org/indicator/NY.GDP.MKTP.CD?most_recent_value_desc=true.
5. Central Intelligence Agency. Korea (South). In: *The World Factbook*. Accessed April 29, 2023. https://www.cia.gov/the-world-factbook/countries/korea-south.
6. Korean Government. *Ministry of Health and Welfare. Health and Welfare Statistical Yearbook, 2022*. Seoul, Korea: Ministry of Health and Welfare.
7. Statistics of Korean students studying abroad by Ministry of Education. 2022. Accessed July 28, 2023. https://www.moe.go.kr/boardCnts/viewRenew.do?boardID=350&lev=0&statusYN=W&s=moe&m=0309&opType=N&boardSeq=93468.
8. StudyGroup. Spotlight on South Korea: U.S. education recruitment trends. Accessed February 12, 2025. https://www.studygroup.com/blog/spotlight-on-south-korea.
9. Korea National Statistical Office. Economically Active Population Survey. Accessed January 31, 2024. https://kosis.kr/statHtml/statHtml.do?orgId=101&tblId=DT_1PM1502&conn_path=I2.

10. United Nations, Department of Economic and Social Affairs. Population Division, *World Population Prospects*. 2015 revision. Accessed April 18, 2016. http://esa.un.org/unpd/wpp/Download/Standard/Population/.
11. Statistica. Distribution of households in South Korea in 2023, by number of members. Accessed February 12, 2025. https://www.statista.com/statistics/995644/south-korea-household-distribution-by-number-of-members/.
12. Statistica. Higher education in South Korea- statistics & facts. Accessed February 12, 2025. https://www.statista.com/topics/4707/tertiary-education-in-south-korea/#editorsPicks.
13. Anderson GF. Universal health care coverage in Korea. *Health Aff*. 1989;8(2):24-34.
14. Korean National Health Insurance Corporation. *National Health Insurance Program in Korea*. Seoul, Korea: National Health Insurance Corporation; 2004.
15. Kwon SM. *Changing Health Policy Process: Politics of Health Care Reform in Korea*. Accessed April 19, 2016. https://cdn1.sph.harvard.edu/wp-content/uploads/sites/114/2012/10/RP206.pdf.
16. Lee JC. Health care reform in South Korea: success or failure? *Am J Public Health*. 2003;93(1):48-51.
17. Kwon S, Lee TJ, Kim CY. Republic of Korea: health system review. *Health Systems in Transition*. 2015;5(4):1-102.
18. Korean Government. Ministry of Health and Welfare. *The White Paper on Health and Welfare 2006*. [In Korean.] Seoul, Korea: Ministry of Health and Welfare; July 2007.
19. Korean National Health Insurance Corporation, Health Insurance Review and Assessment Service. *2013 National Health Insurance Statistical Yearbook*. Seoul, Korea: NHIC and HIRA; December 2014.
20. Organisation for Economic Co-operation and Development. *OECD Health Data 2022*. Paris, France: OECD; 2022.
21. Bae SI, Kim YS, Tae YH, Lee CJ. *The Current Condition and Prospect of Health Care in Korea: View from International Statistics*. [In Korean.] Research Paper Series. Korea: National Health Insurance Corporation; December 2007: 2007-2027.
22. Statistica. Annual number of licensed nurses in South Korea from 2013 to 2023. Accessed February 13, 2025. https://www.statista.com/statistics/1315473/south-korea-yearly-number-of-nurses/.
23. Organisation for Economic Co-operation and Development. Computed tomography (CT) scanners. https://data.oecd.org/healtheqt/computed-tomography-ct-scanners.htm.
24. Organisation for Economic Co-operation and Development. How does Korea compare? *OECD Health Statistics 2014*. Accessed April 20, 2016. http://www.oecd.org/els/health-systems/Briefing-Note-KOREA-2014.pdf.
25. Kwon SM. Payment system reform for health care providers in Korea. *Health Policy Plan*. 2003;18(1):84-92.
26. HIRA, NHIS. *National Health Insurance Statistical Yearbook 2021*. https://opendata.hira.or.kr/op/opc/selectStcPblc.do?sno=13600&odPblcTpCd=002&searchCnd=&searchWrd=&pageIndex=1.
27. Mathauer I, Xu K, Garrin G, Evans DB. An analysis of the health financing system of the Republic of Korea and options to strengthen health financing performance. Published September 2009. Accessed April 20, 2016. http://www.who.int/health_financing/documents/hsfr_e_09-korea.pdf.
28. World Health Organization, Korea Ministry of Health and Welfare. *Health Service Delivery Profile: Republic of Korea 2012*. Accessed April 20, 2016. http://www.wpro.who.int/health_services/service_delivery_profile_republic_of_korea.pdf.
29. Shin Y. Health care systems in transition II. Korea, part I: an overview of health care systems in Korea. *J Public Health Med*. 1998;20(1):41-46.
30. Yang BM. The role of health insurance in the growth of the private health sector in Korea. *Int J Health Plan Manage*. 1996;11(3):231-251.
31. Statistica. Estimated life expectancy at birth in South Korea from 1950 to 2023 with forecasts up to 2100, by gender. Accessed February 13, 2025. https://www.statista.com/statistics/959606/south-korea-life-expectancy-at-birth-by-gender/#:~:text=In%202023%2C%20the%20average%20life%20expectancy%20at,to%2015%20years%20behind%20women%20for%20decades.
32. World Health Organization Data. Republic of South Korea top causes of death. Accessed February 12, 2025. https://data.who.int/countries/410.
33. Statistica. Main causes of death in South Korea in 2023, by age group. Accessed February 12, 2025. https://www.statista.com/statistics/1267450/south-korea-main-causes-of-death-by-age/#:~:text=In%202023%2C%20the%20leading%20cause%20of%20death,death%20among%20people%20over%2040%20was%20cancer.
34. Statistics Korea. 2020 Social Survey. Accessed February 12, 2025. https://www.kostat.go.kr/board.es?mid=a20111050000&bid=11761&act=view&list_no=386681.
35. Statistica. Number of doctors' consultations in-person per year per capita in selected countries as of 2022. Accessed February 12, 2025. https://www.statista.com/statistics/236589/number-of-doctor-visits-per-capita-by-country/.
36. Anderson GF, Poullier JP. Health spending, access, and outcomes: trends in industrialized countries. *Health Aff*. 1999;18(3):178-192.
37. Organisation for Economic Co-operation and Development. Health at a glance 2021: OECD indicators. https://doi.org/10.1787/ae3016b9-en.
38. Ga H. The Korean long-term care system: 2024 update. *Ann Geriatr Med Res*. 2024;28(3):235-237. doi:10.4235/agmr.24.0132.

CHAPTER 23

Taiwan

Shin-Yi Tsai and Leiyu Shi

Country Description

Table 23-1 Taiwan**

Nationality	Noun: Taiwan (singular and plural) Adjective: Taiwan (or Taiwanese)
Ethnic groups	Han Chinese, more than 95% Indigenous Malayo-Polynesian peoples 2.3%*
Religions	Traditional folk religions 27.9% Buddhism 19.8% Taoism 18.7% Nonbelievers 23.9% Protestants 5.5% I-Kuan Tao 2.2% Catholics 1.4% (2021 est.)[1]
Language	Mandarin (official), Min Nan, Hakka dialects, approximately 16 indigenous languages
Literacy	Total population: 99.2% Male: 99.9% Female: 98.5% (2022 est.)[2]
Government type	Democratic republic
Gross domestic product (GDP) per capita	Int$ 72,485.43 (2023 est.)[3]
Unemployment rate	3.33% (2023 est.)[4]
Natural hazards	Earthquakes, typhoons, volcanism
Environment: current issues	Air pollution; water pollution from industrial emissions, raw sewage; contamination of drinking water supplies; trade in endangered species; low-level radioactive waste disposal
Population	23,420,422 (2023.12 est.)[5]

Table 23-1 Taiwan**

Age structure	0-14 years: 11.93% (male 1,447,138/female 1,346,275) 15-64 years: 69.73% (male 8,164,037/female 8,166,007) 65 years and over: 18.35% (male 1,942,002/female 2,354,893) (2023 est.)[5]
Median age	Total: 44.43 years Male: 43.29 years Female: 45.53 years (2023 est.)[6]
Population growth rate	0.03% (2023 est.)
Birth rate	5.82 births/1,000 population (2023 est.)[7]
Death rate	7.9 deaths/1,000 population (2023 est.)[7]
Net migration rate	0.96 migrant/1,000 population (2023 est.)
Gender ratio	At birth: 1.06 male/female 0–14 years: 1.06 male/female 15–64 years: 1 male/female 65 years and over: 0.82 male/female Total population: 0.97 male/female (2023 est.)
Infant mortality rate	Total: 3.59 deaths/1,000 live births Male: 4.2 deaths/1,000 live births Female: 3.6 deaths/1,000 live births (2023 est.)
Life expectancy at birth	Total population: 81.4 years Male: 78.4 years Female: 84.54 years (2023 est.)
Total fertility rate	1.09 children born/woman (2023 est.)
HIV/AIDS prevalence rate	35,566/23,420,422 (0.15%)
Number of people living with HIV/AIDS	35,566 (2023 est.)[8]
HIV/AIDS deaths	8,510 (2023)[8]

Int$ = International dollars.

**Although not definitive, the majority of current genetic, archeological, and linguistic data support the theory that Taiwan is the ultimate source for the spread of humans across the Pacific to Polynesia.

*There are 16 officially recognized indigenous groups. Amis, Paiwan, and Atayal are the largest and account for roughly 70% of the indigenous population.

Data from Central Intelligence Agency. *The World Factbook: Taiwan.* https://www.cia.gov/the-world-factbook/countries/taiwan/.

Table 23-1 presents a comprehensive demographic and economic snapshot of Taiwan, reflecting the latest statistics up to 2023. It includes details on ethnic composition, religious affiliations, literacy rates, economic indicators like GDP per capita and the unemployment rate, and other critical measures such as birth and death rates, median age, and the burden of HIV/AIDS. This information is vital for understanding the social and economic fabric of Taiwan and provides an essential reference for researchers and policymakers alike.

History

In the 1500s during the age of discovery, European explorers sailed past Taiwan, an island in the Orient, and dubbed it "Ilha Formosa," or beautiful island in Portuguese. Taiwan had been home to Austronesian people for millennia before that. The Dutch and Spanish adventurers established bases in southwestern and northern Taiwan, respectively, in the 17th century. The Dutch banished the Spanish in 1642. The Dutch were later conquered in 1662 by Zheng Chenggong–led Ming dynasty loyalists, who were then vanquished by the Qing dynasty in 1683. The Qing dynasty possessed full control of Taiwan until the government ceded Taiwan to Japan in 1895 after being defeated in war. With the surrender of Japan in World War II in 1945, Taiwan was restored to the Republic of China (ROC), which overthrew the Qing dynasty in 1911. As the Chinese civil war ran rampant between the Kuomintang (KMT), the ruling party since the birth of ROC governed by Chiang Kai-shek, and the Chinese Communist Party (CCP), commanded by Mao Zedong, the Temporary Provisions Effective During the Period of National Mobilization for Suppression of the Communist Rebellion order was enacted.[9] It superseded the ROC constitution, expanded presidential powers, and limited political freedom until the provisions were repealed in 1991.

Following a crushing defeat in 1949, the ROC, together with 2 million people, retreated to Taiwan, while the CCP established the People's Republic of China (PRC) with total control of mainland China. Both the ROC and the PRC claiming to be the legitimate government for mainland China and Taiwan, a political and military standoff across the Taiwan Strait was established, and no armistice or peace treaty has been signed to date. In 1971, the PRC replaced the ROC as the sole legitimate representative of China in the United Nations (UN) to the globe and the ROC withdrew from the UN. Rapid development in democratization in the 1980s brought about the founding of the Democratic Progressive Party (DPP), the first opposition party in Taiwan, in 1986. Martial law was lifted in the following year. Taiwan held its first direct presidential election ever in 1996, and underwent peaceful transfers of power in 2000, 2008, and 2016, with Tsai Ing-wen being the first-ever female president in Taiwan.[10,11] At the time of this writing, the president of Taiwan is Lai Ching-te.

Size and Geography

Taiwan is located off the southeast coast of the Asian continent, separated by the Taiwan Strait, at the western edge of the Pacific Ocean, adjacent to Japan, the Philippines, and China. The South China Sea lies to the southwest, East China Sea to the north, and Philippine Sea to the east. Including the Pescadores, Matzu, and Kinmen islands, Taiwan covers an area of 35,980 square kilometers, as shown in **Figure 23-1**. The eastern two-thirds is covered with rugged mountains with the peak reaching 3,952 meters; the majority of the population of approximately 23 million resides on the north and west coasts. The tropical marine climate brings Taiwan abundant rain, sometimes with the assistance of typhoons. Taipei, the capital, sits in northern Taiwan.[11–13]

Government and Political System

Taiwan is a democratic republic. Instead of the typical separation of powers into three branches (a legislature, an executive, and a judiciary), two additional branches, or yuans, were included based on the revolutionary leader Sun Yat-sen's theory: Examination Yuan, which manages the civil service system, and Control Yuan, which impeaches, supervises, and censures officials and audits government agencies. The ROC Constitution was promulgated on January 1, 1947, but did not start to serve its full purpose as the foundation for democracy until martial law was lifted. It has been revised seven times to fit Taiwan's ongoing condition. The president, who is directly elected every 4 years in general, is the head of state and the chief executive of the armed forces and foreign relations. Likewise, members of the Legislative Yuan are directly elected and serve 4-year terms. The president is authorized to appoint heads of the four yuans aside from the legislature, though all except the head of the Executive Yuan, or the premier, must be confirmed by the Legislative Yuan.[14]

Since its relocation to Taiwan in 1949, cross-strait relations with China have been one of the major, if not the greatest, concerns of the government. Civil exchanges with and travel to China were banned initially; however, relaxation of the restrictions came into effect with Taiwan's democratization. Over the years, China has set prerequisites for cross-strait exchanges, unilaterally suspended official communications, and unceasingly exerted political suppression and military intimidation in Taiwan, seeking to breach the status quo. Facing China's increasing aggression, Taiwan's basic principles are targeted at simultaneously maintaining peace while defending democracy. In addition, Taiwan is dedicated to improving the welfare of the people and participating in the world community to contribute wherever possible. As proclaimed in the ROC Constitution, the country endeavors to "cultivate good-neighborliness with other nations, and respect treaties . . . promote international cooperation, protect international justice and ensure world peace."[15]

Economy

Taiwan, which practices mixed capitalism, plays a crucial role in the global economy, mainly through industrial manufacturing and exports of electronics, machinery, and petrochemicals. According to the World Trade Organization (WTO), Taiwan was the 15th largest exporter ($447.7 billion USD) and 17th largest importer ($382.1 billion USD) of merchandise in 2021, both just behind Singapore. It was also one of the largest holders of reserves of foreign exchanges and gold. In 2021, Taiwan's nominal gross domestic product (GDP) per capita

Figure 23-1 Map of Taiwan[13]

reached $28,371 USD.[16] Its GDP per capita of (Int$) $72,485.33 positioned Taiwan as the world's 12th richest economy in 2023.[3]

After the end of World War II, the Taiwanese economy was blighted by poverty, a lack of resources, and unemployment, all of which contributed to extreme hyperinflation in the late 1940s. Prices rose at a 5-fold rate annually and even skyrocketed to about a 30-fold increase in 1949. Despite substantial fluctuation in the inflation rate with the oil crises in the 1970s, successful stabilization was carried out in the 1960s and again in the 1980s. Not long after the country's early years, which were primarily focused on post-war reconstruction, the government adopted a strategy geared toward export promotion, which has greatly contributed to the successful development of Taiwan's economy. In the beginning, food processing was the most prominent industry in exports, but it was replaced by textiles by the 1960s. The electrical machinery industry boomed in the 1960s with rapid industrialization, which absorbed labor, both the newcomers and the formerly unemployed. In the 1970s, import substitution and further expansion in exports, joined with the previous efforts, helped establish Taiwan as a newly industrializing country. Gross national product (GNP) per capita rose from less than $100 USD in 1952 to $2,344 USD in 1980, achieving in 30 years what had taken the industrialized countries nearly 200 years to accomplish. The growth rate of real GDP per capita averaged more than 8% from 1950 to 2000. Whereas Britain was able to rely on rich natural resources for its success, Taiwan, along with Korea, Singapore, Hong Kong, and Japan, demonstrated such extraordinary or, some would say, miraculous, economic progress that it drew academic attention. Eventually, the benefits from industrialization decelerated, accompanied by a few financial crises, and a transition became necessary. Its heavy dependence on foreign trade makes Taiwan susceptible to fluctuations in global supply and demand. To avoid its previous reliance on the United States, Japan, and China, Taiwan signed an economic cooperation agreement with New Zealand in July 2013 and an economic partnership accord with Singapore in November of the same year. President Tsai promoted economic integration with South and Southeast Asia through the New Southbound Policy initiative from 2016 and also expressed interest in participating in regional economic integration blocs such as bilateral trade deals with partners such as the United States and the Comprehensive and Progressive Agreement for Trans-Pacific Partnership and Regional Comprehensive Economic Partnership. In fact, Taiwan and the United States launched the Taiwan–U.S. Economic Prosperity Partnership Dialogue in November 2020 and resumed talks on the Trade and Investment Framework Agreement in June 2021.[11,17–22]

Demographics

In December 2023, the population in Taiwan was 23,420,442, with a sex ratio around 0.97 male/female (11,553,267/11,867,175). In this population, 11.93% were aged 14 or younger, and 18.35% were 65 or above. In 2023, the crude birth rate was 5.82 per 1,000 people, and the crude death rate was 7.9 per 1,000 people.[7] Life expectancy at birth was 81.4 years, with females and males living, on average, 84.54 years and 78.4 years, respectively.

The net migration rate was estimated to be 0.96 immigrant per 1,000 population in 2023, mostly from China and Southeast Asia, and primarily through marriage. Besides the more than 95% of the population claiming Han ancestry, including Holo, Hakka, and others originated in China, 16 officially recognized indigenous tribes make up a little more than 2.3% of the population.

The urban population was 79.7% of total population, with an annual rate of urbanization at 0.65%. Major urban areas include Taipei, New Taipei, Taoyuan, Taichung, Tainan, and Kaohsiung, all of which are situated in the north and west coast. The literacy rate was 99.09% in 2021 and 99.2% in 2022.[23] The labor force in Taiwan was roughly 11.841 million in October 2022,[24] 3.33% of whom were unemployed. Of the labor force, 59.2% work in the tertiary sector of the economy and 35.9% work in the secondary sector, leaving only 4.9% practicing agriculture.[11,25]

Religion

Taiwan is highly diversified in terms of religious belief, with Christianity, Buddhism, Taoism, Mormonism, Yiguandao, the Unification Church, Catholicism, Islam, Eastern Orthodoxy, Judaism, Hinduism, and many other religions being practiced. The country not only respects traditional religious thoughts but also opens its arms to other types of faiths from the outside. Buddhism, Taoism, and folk religions have commonly been believed to be the most popular. Nevertheless, the majority of the island's places of worship for different religions actually combine all three traditions.[26]

Brief History of the Healthcare System

Chinese medicine used to be the primary healthcare delivery in Taiwan before the 20th century. The government played an essential role in healthcare delivery and financing; therefore, there were formal school education and licensing systems for Chinese medicine. The arrival of several Western missionaries, including the earliest, Dr. James Laidlaw Maxwell in 1864; later, Dr. George L. MacKay in 1871; and Dr. David Landsborough in 1895; helped the practices of Western medicine in Taiwan. Their goodwill and devotion to Taiwan earned the gratitude and admiration of the Taiwanese people,[27] even to the present. The hospitals they founded still save millions of lives, although their impact was geographically limited initially. Government action did not take place until Japanese colonization started. During this period, epidemics were prevalent in Taiwan due to humidity and poor hygiene. To some extent, realizing that inferior public health might indeed hold back their rule in Taiwan, the Japanese colonial government prioritized laying a sustainable foundation for Taiwan's public health system, including instituting schools and erecting hospitals with well-trained faculty, and constructing a formal licensure system. In addition, Chinese medicine was massively suppressed during that period. Finally, the few highly educated professional medical doctors in that period were deemed elites at the top of the society, a social perception that has remained relevant to the present day. During World War II, medical facilities were severely crippled, and epidemics were prevalent then. The government focused on widely establishing health stations; eradicating malaria, plague, and cholera; implementing universal vaccination; improving women's and children's health; and enhancing family planning.

Since the 1950s, the mortality rate has declined remarkably among all ages. Infant mortality decreased from 83.102% in 1952 to 3.9% in 2023.[28] The leading causes of death transitioned from infectious diseases, such as pneumonia, chronic lower respiratory tract diseases, and bronchitis, to noninfectious diseases, including malignant neoplasms, heart diseases, cerebrovascular diseases, diabetes mellitus, accidents and adverse effects, chronic lower respiratory tract diseases, nephritis/nephrotic syndrome/nephrosis, and chronic liver diseases and cirrhosis, by the 21st century.[29]

The Department of Health (DOH) was organized in 1971, marking the beginning of the advanced era, and actively leading to the government's healthcare reforms.[30] In 1986, the government officially announced that the National Health Insurance (NHI) scheme would be implemented,[31] directed at pursuing a generally affordable universal health insurance. The DOH then set up the NHI Planning Team in 1991 and established a Provisional Office in 1993. The NHI Act was established in 1994. The Bureau of National Health Insurance (BNHI) was established on January 1, 1995. Two months later, the NHI program was launched; its important features included mandatory enrollment, a single-payer system, and premium financing. On January 1, 2004, the BNHI replaced the NHI paper-based card with the NHI Smart Card, which can serve as a key to the information network between patients, healthcare providers, and the BNHI. On January 1, 2013, the second-generation NHI was officially implemented, and supplementary premiums were levied. The systems were integrated into a single ministry and the DOH was transformed into the Ministry of Health and Welfare (MOHW) for implementing further health policies. The BNHI was renamed the National Health Insurance Administration and became the agency responsible for planning and implementing relevant policies.[31] Before the NHI era, around 57% of the population was covered by a variety of separate insurance schemes, including labor insurance, governmental employee insurance, farmers' health insurance, and fishermen's health insurance. Still, there was a high level of out-of-pocket payments for patients, not to mention those who were uninsured. By the end of 1995, the year the NHI was implemented, 92% of the population was enrolled.[32–34] The NHI has covered over 99.9% of the civilians in recent years.

The Current Healthcare System

The NHI

The NHI provides a complete package of benefits, including inpatient, outpatient, and dental care; traditional Chinese medicine; renal dialysis; prescription drugs; prenatal care; physical rehabilitation; home nursing care; chronic mental illness care; and preventive services such as pediatric and adult health examinations and cancer screening. In addition to offering comprehensiveness, health care is readily obtained. Patients enjoy easy access to specialists from all fields and rarely face long wait times. When patients

Table 23-2 Basic Copayments for Outpatient Visits Under NHI System (NT$)

Institution Class	Basic Copayments					
	Western Medicine Outpatient Care		Emergency Care ER Examination			
Types of Institution	With Referral	Without Referral	Levels 1, 2	Levels 3–5	Dental Care	Traditional Chinese Medicine
Medical centers	170	420	450	550	50	50
Regional hospitals	100	240	300	300	50	50
District hospitals	50	80	150	150	50	50
Clinics	50	50	150	150	50	50

NT$ = New Taiwan dollar.

Modified from National Health Insurance Administration, Ministry of Health and Welfare. *Strengthening the Referral System and Adjustments to National Health Insurance Co-Payments for Outpatient and Emergency Visits.* 2017. https://www.nhi.gov.tw/en/cp-271-196ce-8-2.html.

covered under the NHI program visit a doctor, with their NHI IC card, the hospitals will claim the related charges from the government. The copayment is not intended for profit but for reminding the insured that medical resources are used to help those in need and should not be wasted under any circumstance. **Table 23-2** shows an example. There are copayment exemptions for 30 catastrophic illnesses or conditions; prenatal care and delivery; preventive health services; medical services in remote, mountainous areas and on offshore islands; and low-income households, veterans, and children under age 3. Whenever a doctor wants to recommend a course of treatment that is not covered under the NHI, the patient's approval must be obtained first before proceeding. The premiums of the NHI, which covers most of the medical expenses, are paid by the insured, the employers, and the government itself. Currently, Taiwan's healthcare delivery system is a mixture of private nonprofit and government-owned hospitals, private clinics, and other healthcare facilities. For-profit hospitals are prohibited.[34–36]

Facilities

In 2021, the total numbers of hospitals and clinics in Taiwan were 478 and 22,800, respectively. **Table 23-3** indicates the total numbers of hospitals and clinics, including public and nonpublic, and Western, dental, and Chinese medicine, from 2017 to 2021. Total numbers have been gradually increasing, though the ratio claimed by each category has been steady. Clinics in all three categories—Western medicine, dental, and Chinese medicine—have been on the rise, however.

As **Table 23-4** shows, the greater part of healthcare facilities in Taiwan are owned and operated by

Table 23-3 Number of Hospitals and Clinics by Category, 2017–2022

	Western Medicine		Dental		Chinese Medicine	
Year	Hospital	Clinic	Hospital	Clinic	Hospital	Clinic
2017	478	11,499	0	6,791	5	3,836
2018	478	11,580	0	6,836	5	3,917
2019	476	11,663	0	6,874	4	3,975
2020	475	11,724	0	6,893	4	4,036
2021	473	11,835	1	6,922	4	4,043
2022	475	11,998	1	6,969	4	4,131

Data from Ministry of Health and Welfare. Statistics of medical care institution & hospital utilization 2022. 2023. Accessed April 2, 2024. https://www.mohw.gov.tw/lp-6614-2.html.

Table 23-4 Number of Hospitals and Clinics by Ownership, 2017–2021

Year	Hospital		Clinic	
	Public	Nonpublic	Public	Nonpublic
2017	80	403	436	21,693
2018	81	402	429	21,904
2019	82	398	428	22,084
2020	82	397	426	22,227
2021	81	397	423	22,377
2022	82	398	421	22,677

Data from Ministry of Health and Welfare. Statistics of medical care institution & hospital utilization 2022. 2023. Accessed April 2, 2024. https://www.mohw.gov.tw/lp-6614-2.html.

Table 23-5 Beds in Hospitals and Clinics, 2017–2022

Year	Hospital	Clinic
2017	97,748	30,456
2018	98,828	32,025
2019	98,477	33,009
2020	99,747	32,751
2021	100,813	32,268
2022	101,460	32,654

Data from Ministry of Health and Welfare. Statistics of medical care institution & hospital utilization 2022. 2023. Accessed April 2, 2024. https://www.mohw.gov.tw/lp-6614-2.html.

the private sector, including medical-care foundations, medical-care corporations, religious organizations, private medical colleges, and others. The public hospitals are operated by the municipalities, cities, counties, public medical colleges, military, veterans, or other public agencies. Of the 478 hospitals in 2021, 21 were medical centers, 3 were regional hospitals/medical centers, 72 were regional hospitals, 309 were district hospitals, 43 were psychiatric hospitals, 4 were children's hospitals, and 28 were hospitals without accreditation.[37]

As shown in **Table 23-5**, the number of beds in hospitals and clinics has demonstrated an upward trend, revealing a growing supply and demand. The number of beds in Table 23-5 includes general beds and special beds, such as ICU beds, burn center beds, and palliative care beds. There were 7.1 beds in hospitals and clinics per 1,000 population in Taiwan in 2018, considerably fewer compared with Japan (13.0) and South Korea (12.4).[37,38]

Workforce

Table 23-6 shows the number of registered health professionals working in hospitals and clinics. Like beds, the number of healthcare professionals is gradually increasing. Despite the increase, the numbers of practicing physicians and nurses per 1,000 population in Taiwan in 2018, 2.0 and 5.3, respectively, are lagging on the world stage.

Medical Benefits

In Taiwan, the total medical points are the unit of measure used to calculate the reimbursement for medical services rendered by healthcare providers, and essentially a quantifiable measure that reflects the value of medical services provided under Taiwan's NHI system. In 2022, they amounted to 823 billion points, a 0.5% increase from 2021. Of this amount, the total requested points accounted for 823 billion, and copayments represented 39 billion points. The total outpatient medical points amounted to 581 billion,

Table 23-6 Registered Health Professionals in Hospitals and Clinics, 2017–2022

Year	Western Medicine Physician	Doctor of Chinese Medicine	Dentist	Pharmacist	Nurse
2017	46,311	6,685	14,379	14,695	122,063
2018	47,426	6,873	14,717	14,823	125,746
2019	49,493	7,094	15,127	15,126	130,371
2020	50,999	7,300	15,429	15,474	134,587
2021	52,124	7,467	15,741	15,479	138,190
2022	53,104	7,670	15,966	15,438	140,514

Data from Ministry of Health and Welfare. Statistics of medical care institution & hospital utilization 2022. 2023. Accessed April 2, 2024. https://www.mohw.gov.tw/lp-6614-2.html.[37,39,40]

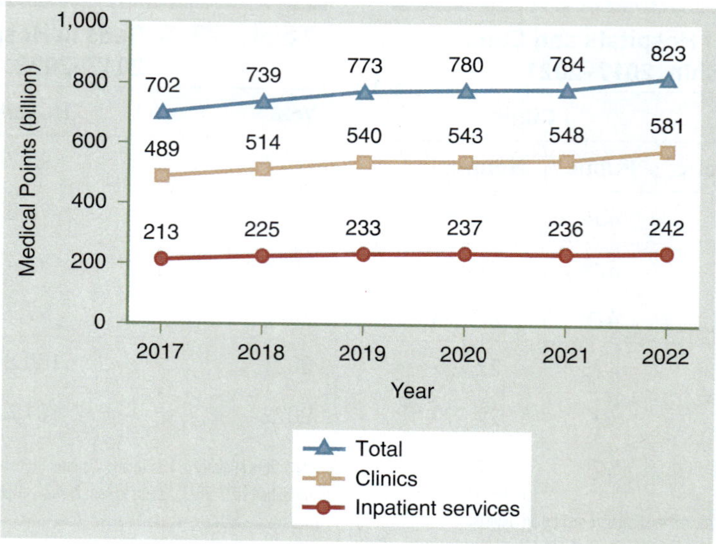

Figure 23-2 Medical points of clinics in 2017-2022[41]

Data from World Bank. Hospital beds (per 1,000 people). 2019. Accessed November 2, 2022. https://data.worldbank.org/indicator/SH.MED.BEDS.ZS.

a 6.1% increase from 2021. Of these, requested points accounted for 550 billion, and copayments 31 billion. The total inpatient medical points amounted to 242 billion, a 2.2% increase from 2021. Of these, the requested points amounted to 231 billion and copayments represented 10 billion points. A total of 339 million outpatient cases were documented in 2022, an increase of 8.0% from 2021. By comparison, 3 million inpatient cases were recorded, 0.1% more than in 2021. The average medical points per case amounted to 1,715 for outpatient services and 77,421 for inpatient services. The average length of stay was 9.42 days.[41] Refer to **Figure 23-2**.

In terms of facility categories, clinics had the most medical points for outpatient services in 2022, at 224 billion points (38.6%), while medical centers had the most medical points for inpatient services, at 103 billion points (42.9%). The average medical points per outpatient case were 4,305 for medical centers and 972 for clinics. The average medical points per inpatient case were 97,192 for medical centers and 30,052 for clinics.[41] Refer to **Figures 23-3** and **23-4**.

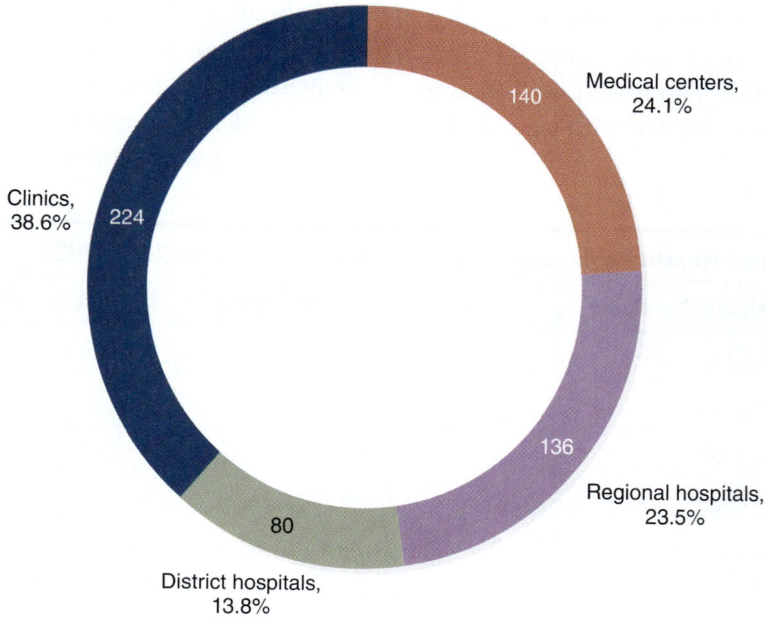

Figure 23-3 Medical points for clinics in 2022[41]

Data from World Bank. Hospital beds (per 1,000 people). 2019. Accessed November 2, 2022. https://data.worldbank.org/indicator/SH.MED.BEDS.ZS.

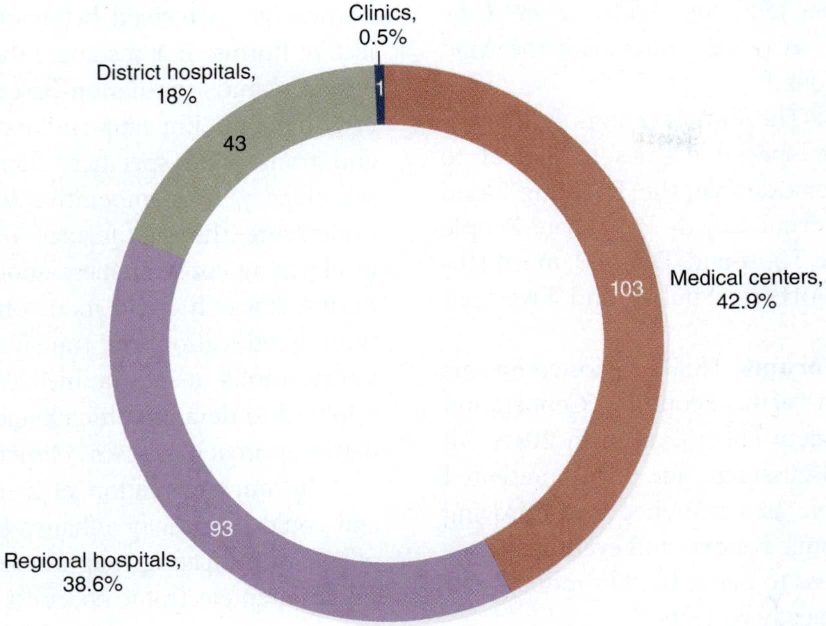

Figure 23-4 Medical points for inpatient services in 2022[41]

Data from World Bank. Hospital beds (per 1,000 people). 2019. Accessed November 2, 2022. https://data.worldbank.org/indicator/SH.MED.BEDS.ZS.

Cancer Burden

Cancer has been the leading cause of death in Taiwan since 1982 and has been getting worse. In 2019, the number of diagnoses and the incidence rate per 100,000 population were 121,254 and 513.72, respectively. In that same year, 50,232 people died of cancer, accounting for 28.63% of total mortality.[42] Cancers of the female breast; colon, rectum, rectosigmoid junction, and anus; trachea, bronchus, and lung; prostate gland; and liver and intrahepatic bile duct are the top five in terms of incidence rate. Cancers of the trachea, bronchus, and lung; liver and intrahepatic bile duct; colon, rectum, rectosigmoid junction and anus; female breast; and oral cavity, oropharynx, and hypopharynx are the most lethal, in descending order.[43]

Infectious Diseases

Infectious diseases in Taiwan have been greatly diminished with improved hygiene, modernized health care, and large-scale immunization since the latter half of the 20th century. Currently, the NHI covers for all newborn vaccinations for hepatitis A and B, BCG, diphtheria, tetanus, pertussis, *Haemophilus influenzae* type b, polio, *Pneumococcus*, varicella zoster, measles, mumps, rubella, Japanese encephalitis, and influenza. HPV vaccination is promoted as well.

In 2023, there were 944 reported new HIV infections, including 908 cases in males, 25.2 times as many cases as in females. As for AIDS, 586 new cases were reported in the same year. Collectively, 76.28% of reported new HIV infection and AIDS cases in 2023 were in people between the ages of 25 and 49 years.[8] By the end of 2023, the cumulative HIV infection and AIDS cases stood at 44,263 and 21,585 people, respectively.[8] Also in 2023, 26,703 cases of dengue fever were confirmed.[44] The same year, 6,415 people were diagnosed with tuberculosis.[45]

Patient Blood Management and Blood Supply Chain

Blood products are in high demand due to population aging and the increasing prevalence of cancers. Taiwan has the highest blood donation rate in the world. The Taiwan Blood Services Foundation (TBSF) has implemented several initiatives to promote blood donation.

1. **Educational Books:** The *Handbook of Precise and Practical Blood Transfusion* has been distributed to hospitals since June 2020 to help integrate the "Patient Blood Management (PBM)" guideline into their services.[46] The second edition of this guideline was officially published in May 2022 after the content was revised in 2021.[47] This guideline is mainly based on indications, supplemented by evidence-based medicine. It provides clinicians and transfusion practitioners with a more comprehensive blood transfusion protocol.[46] In 2023, TBSF created Taiwan's first tailored blood knowledge book for adolescents,

Easy Blood Lessons for Young Adults, to help the younger generation better understand the need for blood donations.[48]

2. **Special Events:** The donor centers hold various events with special themes to appeal to more donors. For example, the Taichung Blood Center held an event called "Passionate People in Changhua: A Thousand Donors" in collaboration with KuoHsing Poultry and Livestock Feeds Co.[49]
3. **Speeches and Forums:** TBSF has hosted forums such as the Asia-Pacific Economic Cooperation (APEC) Blood Safety Policy Forum in 2018. All the speeches, discussions, and ideas presented at the forum serve as a reference for improving health and economic benefits and eventually providing equal access to better blood products and medical care for needy patients.[50]

As for the blood donation rate, as of 2023, Taiwan had a blood donation rate of 7.55%, which is higher than the average of 4% to 5% in other countries.[51] This achievement, the highest blood donation rate in the world,[52] is a testament to the effectiveness of TBSF's initiatives. In addition, some other global organizations contribute significantly to this cause. For instance, the International Federation of Blood Donor Organizations (IFBDO) has been organizing International Blood Donor Day since 1995.[53] The International Federation of Red Cross and Red Crescent Societies supports 191 Red Cross and Red Crescent Societies to deliver and promote safe and sustainable blood programs around the world.[54]

In 2016, the Taiwan Haemovigilance System was established by the TBSF and the Taiwan Society of Blood Transfusion to improve blood transfusion safety.[47] Since 2017, some hospitals have demonstrated how to send notifications, and by 2022, 70 hospitals had qualified for notification.[47] The aim is to expand the system to all hospitals in Taiwan to collect and analyze blood data from patients, provide better blood transfusion strategies, and improve blood transfusion safety.[47] The collective efforts across the globe are crucial in ensuring a safe and adequate blood supply for all. The ultimate goal is to work internationally to promote blood donation and PBM.

After evaluations of the determinants that influence physicians' propensity to prescribe transfusions, guided by the theory of planned behavior, several PBM strategies have been recommended. These strategies encompass the establishment of a comprehensive, real-world-based transfusion education program, which can concurrently enhance knowledge, perceived behavioral control, and subjective norms. For instance, the integration of conferences and simulation-based clinical rehearsals can augment clinicians' understanding of guidelines and transfusion specifics, thereby bolstering their self-efficacy. It is imperative for national policy to underscore the significance of medical education in elevating consciousness about blood transfusion. Future research could focus on the efficacy of continuing education on transfusion and behavioral interventions, using the metric of learning hours as opposed to demographic characteristics, as an alternative approach to assess clinicians' behaviors.[55]

The implementation of a decision support system could potentially enhance patient outcomes and safety by mitigating inappropriate transfusions. For instance, an electronic checklist could serve as a tool to evaluate the necessity for blood transfusion. Given the rapid advancement of artificial intelligence, the exploration of electronic decision support systems is a promising avenue.[55]

Evaluation of the Healthcare System

Quality

The quality of healthcare professionals, including physicians, nurses, pharmacists, and many others, are assured by required official board examinations held by the Ministry of Examination or healthcare authorities. Individuals should have graduated from medical colleges or medical schools with appropriate years of internship after passing corresponding examinations and joining the associations of clinical practitioners. Licenses must be renewed regularly with continuing medical education.

A hospital accreditation system has been in force since 1978, based on the quality of personnel, facilities, hospital management, community services, and the quality of medical care. Clinics, in contrast, must apply to the local health station for an operating license.[56]

Data show that public satisfaction with the National Health Insurance System hit an all-time high of 89.7% in 2019.[57] Life expectancy at birth of females and males, respectively, increased from 77.74 and 71.85 years in 1995 to 84.25 and 77.67 years in 2021,[58] not too far away from Japan at 88.09 and 81.91 years.[59] Taiwan's health care ranks among the best in the world.[60]

Equity

The NHI has adopted and implemented various strategies to achieve universal enrollment. By the end of 2021, coverage reached 99.9%.[61]

In terms of finance, annual growth in expenditures typically surpassed revenues in the NHI's early years. At that time, the NHI's revenue was primarily derived from payroll-based premiums, yet payroll represented just 60% of total national income. This gave rise to the second-generation NHI reform, building a supplemental premium base, in 2013. Six additional sources of non-regular-payroll income were designated, yielding a total premium base covering 90% of Taiwan's total national income.[62]

Geographically, health care is unevenly distributed across Taiwan. People living in remote areas or outlying islands have a much harder time accessing health care compared with those living in cities. Measures have been carried out to remove the geographic barriers, such as payment incentives to healthcare providers.[60]

Access

Taiwanese citizens can see a doctor of any specialty or visit a hospital of any level freely and directly without a referral. There is generally short to no waiting times unless the physician is very popular. The cost is usually incredibly cheap, if covered by the NHI. The global budget is set every year to keep costs low. There is also a panel review system that cuts payments for tests, medications, and procedures considered inappropriate or unnecessary.[36]

Efficiency

Taiwan's national health expenditure (NHE) has shown an upward trend, increasing from 216 billion NT$ (New Taiwan dollar) in 1991 to 1.3 trillion NT$ in 2020. Nevertheless, the NHE as a percentage of the GDP has remained only slightly above 6% since 2004,[63] higher than that of China and Singapore and lower than that of Japan and Korea.[64] The average annual number of physician visits per capita was 17.6 in 2019, markedly higher than that in many other countries (e.g., United States, 2.6; England, 2.8; Japan, 2.43; Singapore, 2.3; China, 2.01).[65] For physicians, it is not uncommon to see over 50 patients in the morning, a pace that seriously cuts into the consultation time that a patient receives. The hospital occupancy rate has hovered around 70% since 2002, and the average length of a hospital stay has been lingering around 8 to 9 days.[37] Additionally, due to the absence of a referral system, patients can freely choose their preferred physicians and health facilities. Consequently, many opt for larger medical institutions, which often incur higher costs."[36,60]

Current and Emerging Issues and Challenges

Aging Population

Taiwan became an aging society in 1993 and turned into an aged society in 2018.[66] In 2021, the proportion of the population over age 65 was 16.85%, relatively younger than the population of Japan (28.86%), the United States (16.83%), Germany (22.09%), and many other developed countries. However, with people living longer and fewer children being born, the rate of aging is accelerating, and Taiwan is expected to grow into a super-aged society by 2025.[67] Aging is a major driving force of the increasing prevalence of noncommunicable diseases (NCDs). The cost of medical care for the elderly will, therefore, become more of a concern with the acceleration of aging.[62]

In the face of this aging of the population, Executive Yuan with the Ministry of Health and Welfare and Social and Family Affairs Administration promoted and implemented countermeasures to rejuvenate Taiwan. To address the low birth rates, emphasis is placed on family values, including increasing marriage opportunities, and strengthening gender and marital education. Health care for pregnant women and children is made as friendly as possible, such as providing pregnant women with prenatal care services as well as infertility prevention and education, and working on ways to prevent a sex ratio imbalance. Moreover, pay spent on children is exempt or deducted from taxes. Affordable, high-quality, diverse, and accessible childcare services are offered. Those in need are granted financial support.

For the elderly, long-term care services and home-based and community-based resources were developed. In addition, the Taiwan Association of Gerontology and Geriatrics was founded in 1982 to improve the health of older adults in Taiwan by advancing the study of gerontology, geriatrics, and allied specialties.[68,69]

Finance

The NHI of Taiwan is committed to ensuring universal access to comprehensive medical services, particularly for the most vulnerable groups. The National Health Insurance Administration (NHIA) has implemented policies to waive all copayments and coinsurances for individuals affected by one or more of 30 identified catastrophic illnesses and for residents of remote mountainous regions and offshore islands. Additional exemptions are extended to pregnant women and those in postnatal care, children under the age of 3, veterans and their dependents, and low-income households. These measures effectively remove financial barriers to health care for these populations, significantly enhancing their access to necessary medical services.

Despite the clear benefits of these policies, the long-term sustainability of such comprehensive copayment exemptions—and indeed the broader framework of this benevolent insurance system—raises concerns. Between 2017 and 2020, the NHI reported budget deficits, marking a concerning shift from previous financial surpluses. This downturn can be attributed to several factors:

1. **Increased Medical Demand:** As the demographic landscape of Taiwan shifts toward an aging population, the demand for medical services has escalated, naturally leading to higher healthcare expenditures.
2. **Advancements in Medical Technology:** Integrating new and often costlier medical technologies and treatments into the health coverage system has further increased expenses.
3. **Generous Copayment Exemptions:** While these policies alleviate the financial load on specific groups, such as the elderly, children, or those with chronic conditions, they concurrently reduce the inflow of copayment revenues, thereby straining the financial viability of the healthcare system.

These dynamics suggest that the current fiscal policies of the NHI, though initially successful, may require reevaluation to ensure their sustainability in the face of evolving economic and demographic challenges.

Personnel Shortages

As mentioned earlier, the number of practicing physicians and nurses per 1,000 population in Taiwan is lower than that in most other developed countries, especially considering Taiwan's high utilization of healthcare services. Furthermore, there have been growing concerns over doctor shortages in certain specialties, including internal medicine, surgery, obstetrics and gynecology, pediatrics, and emergency medicine,[70] probably owing to the threat of malpractice suits, long working hours, and low profit. Moreover, despite adequate qualified and licensed nurses, the practice rate has been just below 60% over the years.[71] The lack of willingness to practice probably stems from heavy workloads, irregular shifts, low salaries, underappreciation, and abusive seniors.[72,73] Improving nursing staff should be attended to enhance the quality of care and patient safety.[62] Also, the shortage of medical technologists has been of huge concern. In 2021, 1,125 students in this field graduated, but only 24% of examinees passed the examination. Of the 23,480 licensed medical technologists, only 10,207 (43.5%) completed their registrations.[74]

Clinical Decision Support Systems

The Ministry of Health and Welfare established a Health and Welfare Data Center (HWDC), a data repository site that centralizes the National Health Insurance Research Database (NHIRD), and approximately 70 other health-related databases for data management and analyses.[75] NHIRD covers a highly representative sample of Taiwan's general population because the reimbursement policy is universal and operated by a single buyer—namely, the Taiwanese government. All insurance claims are scrutinized and coded by medical reimbursement specialists and peer reviewed according to the standard criteria for diagnoses in the studies. Moreover, incorrect diagnoses or coding mistakes result in considerable penalties for physicians. The reliability and validity of the NHI research database for epidemiologic investigations have been reported in the past.

Considering that ethnic and geographic discrepancies exist in different populations, we investigated the NHIRD to illustrate Taiwan's prevalence of specific diseases, such as chronic fatigue syndrome (CFS), antiphospholipid syndrome,[76] and the risks that CFS caused following infections,[77–79] and to demonstrate the treatment pattern[79,80] and the effects of different interventions,[81] as well as the clinical implications in a variety of diseases.[81–93]

In terms of the applications of artificial intelligence to smart health, recruiting participants for longitudinal follow-up makes it easier to determine causal relationships and apply the findings in the real world. By investigating the association between genotyping data (e.g., circadian genes) and phenotyping data (e.g., metabolic syndromes in the Taiwanese population), we built several machine learning models to predict the risk of metabolic syndrome based on circadian gene data using a Taiwan Biobank.[94] We used circadian-related single-nucleotide polymorphisms (SNPs) in our prediction models but found a small sample size cohort including healthy and aware participants, raising the main challenge to the setting of a robust clinical decision support system (CDSS).

After using genetic and phenotypic data to develop predictive models for metabolic syndrome, our findings underscored the necessity for rigorous validation and expansion of the initial findings. Our initial study utilized genotypic data, specifically SNPs in circadian genes, and phenotypic data on metabolic syndromes from the Taiwanese population, sourced from the Taiwan Biobank. We developed machine learning models to predict the risk of metabolic syndrome, leveraging this genetic information.

While innovative, the predictive models were based on a relatively small sample size, including healthy individuals and those at risk for metabolic syndrome. This limited sample size poses a significant challenge in setting up a robust CDSS due to potential biases and the limited generalizability of the findings. Thus, replicating and validating our findings across diverse populations is crucial to enhance our models' robustness and applicability. This would involve coordinating with international researchers to access a more comprehensive array of genetic and phenotypic data. Partnering with international investigators to address this essential syndrome will allow the recruitment of participants from different genetic backgrounds and environments, providing a more comprehensive data set. By incorporating more variables into our models, we can address more nuanced aspects of metabolic syndrome risk that a broader range of genetic and environmental factors may influence. Furthermore, high dimensionality, where the number of variables in the model significantly exceeds the number of observations, can lead to overfitting and model inaccuracy. Utilizing dimensionality reduction techniques or more sophisticated algorithms can help mitigate this issue.

Ultimately, to enhance the model's accuracy and generalizability, a multidimensional approach is essential. This includes the expansion of the dataset, collaboration with a diverse range of scientists, and advanced data analysis techniques. These steps will better equip us to develop a CDSS that can effectively utilize genetic data for predicting metabolic syndrome globally. By aligning our approach with scientific rigor, we not only enhance the potential clinical implications of our research but also provide a clear pathway toward improving healthcare outcomes through precision medicine.

COVID-19 Pandemic

At the end of 2019, a novel coronavirus was identified as the cause of a cluster of pneumonia cases in Wuhan, Hubei, China. It spread rapidly throughout China, and then to the rest of the world. In February 2020, the WHO designated the disease as COVID-19. The pathogen was labeled as SARS-CoV-2.[95] Since then, the virus has killed over 7 million people (as of January 2024) out of the 774 million it infected around the globe and changed the lives of all humanity.[96] Taiwan, a neighbor of China, despite being able to withstand the early days of the pandemic, could not escape the inevitable. Up to September 7, 2023, Taiwan had recorded 10,241,523 COVID-19 cases, and the total number of confirmed COVID-19 fatalities was 17,668.[97]

With experience with the SARS outbreak in 2003, the National Health Command Center (NHCC) acted rapidly. On January 20, 2020, to curb the disseminating and worsening epidemic, Taiwan's Centers for Disease Control (CDC) established the Central Epidemic Command Center (CECC). The next day, the CECC confirmed Taiwan's first imported COVID-19 case, a female who entered by airplane from Wuhan. In March 2022, the pandemic wreaked havoc in Europe, especially in Italy. The United States, after Europe, saw an escalation of the number of confirmed cases and even surpassed China for the highest confirmed number of cases. In 2020, while the vast majority of the world was in shambles, the pandemic had a relatively minor impact on Taiwan. As of December 24, 2020, there had been 58,712,326 confirmed cases of COVID-19, including 1,388,528 deaths worldwide.[98] Meanwhile, Taiwan had 618 confirmed cases with 7 deaths reported. From April 12 to November 21, there was no locally transmitted case for 222 consecutive days, though 148 imported cases were reported.[99] Taiwan's effectiveness in containing the outbreak drew attention from health authorities around the world. Experts summarized the approaches to management: stringent quarantine of all travelers and returning residents to Taiwan; rigorous contact tracing and enforced quarantine of all close contacts; and community-based enforcement of social distancing, hand washing, and mandatory use of face masks.[99]

Since the outbreak of COVID-19, extensive research has been conducted by scientists all over the planet to combat the disease. As vaccines were developed, clinical treatment guidelines were revised, and diagnostic methods were refined, the coronavirus was also evolving, continually mutating into new variants. Initially, Taiwan procured vaccines from AstraZeneca and Moderna, and the first batch of 117,000 doses arrived in Taiwan on March 5, 2021, with many to come afterward. Furthermore, Taiwan's own vaccine was in progress. However, people showed little interest in receiving injections due to previously low case numbers. In May, an upsurge in cases from Taipei and New Taipei City were reported. In response, multiple measures were implemented: School courses were replaced with home online learning; border control was reinforced; most indoor activities were restricted; and hospital policies were adjusted repeatedly. With the arrival of subsequent vaccine doses, donations from Japan, the United States, Lithuania, Czech, Slovakia, and Poland; donation of the Pfizer–BioNTech vaccine from TSMC (Taiwan Semiconductor Manufacturing Company Limited), Hon Hai Yonglin, and Tzu Chi; and approval of Medigen, Taiwan's domestic vaccine, full-scale immunization kicked off. On October 27, 2021, Taiwan's first-dose coverage reached 70%, and the second-dose coverage reached 30%. To date, 73.8% of the population has received their third dose. As case numbers seesawed, regulations were tightened and loosened accordingly. In 2022, the oral antivirals Paxlovid and molnupiravir became available. Beginning in late April 2022, case numbers spiked to tens of thousands daily. With time, the impact of the pandemic dwindled, and the CECC began to ease control measures gradually.[100–103]

Taiwan's economy faced disruptions due to its heavy reliance on global supply chains, and industries such as tourism suffered significant losses.[104] The COVID-19 pandemic demonstrated the importance of economic resilience, such as diversifying the economy, strengthening supply chains, and providing support for small businesses and workers.[105] It also highlighted the need for Taiwan to continue its efforts in disease prevention and control, to invest in medical technology and research, and to improve collaboration and communication with international organizations and countries.[106]

Key lessons from Taiwan's response to the COVID-19 pandemic include the importance of early detection and response, rapid implementation of effective containment measures, the value of transparency and open communication, and the need for collaboration and partnerships across sectors.[106] Furthermore, technology played a significant role in Taiwan's response to the COVID-19 pandemic, such as in developing contact tracing apps, using telemedicine and telecommunication services, and promoting online learning and work.[107]

Regarding Taiwan's economy, the economy showed a sharp drop in GDP growth, which plummeted to 0.62% in Q2 2020 from 2.99% growth registered in the same period in 2019.[108] The unemployment rate showed a sharp growth from May to June of 2021, from 4.11% to 4.80%. This likely reflected the Novotel hotel cluster and the outbreak at Wanhua Teahouse during that period. By comparison, the unemployment rate was 3.33% in March 2023.[4] Even though the COVID-19 pandemic had a significant impact on Taiwan's economy and industries, with a decline in exports and tourism, increased demand for medical supplies and technology, and shifts in consumer behavior,[109] the Taiwanese government was able to implement practical measures to control the spread of COVID-19, such as border controls, quarantine measures, contact tracing, and providing access to testing and treatment.[106] Furthermore, the Taiwanese government proactively provided supports for citizens and businesses during the pandemic through various measures, such as income subsidies, loan guarantees, tax relief, and support for job creation.[107] It provided a stimulus package to support businesses and individuals affected by the pandemic. For instance, Triple and Quintuple Stimulus Vouchers were issued and significantly increased the private consumption expenditure. Additionally, Taiwan's technology sector and the electronics industry continued to perform well, driving the country's economic recovery.

The COVID-19 pandemic led to changes in social behavior, shifts in social norms, and new cultural practices in Taiwan, particularly with regard to the use of digital technology for remote communication and telework,[106] and virtual events, social distancing measures, and greater awareness and adherence to public health guidelines and hygiene practices.[107] Taiwan's healthcare system faced several challenges during the pandemic, including shortages of personal protective equipment (PPE) in the early stages of the pandemic, and difficulties in contact tracing due to privacy concerns. The increased demand for healthcare services; the need for rapid expansion of testing capacity and hospital capacity, as well as enhanced infection prevention and control measures; and a massive surge in demand for medical facilities, supplies, and services for COVID-19 patients,[106] exposed areas in need of improvement, such as the need for more comprehensive disease surveillance.[109] Specific COVID-19 policy reforms were also proposed to strengthen public health, such as investing in and expanding the capacity of the healthcare system, establishing a robust public health workforce, implementing pandemic preparedness plans, increasing funding for research and development of vaccines and treatments, and providing equitable access to healthcare services.[110–112] Taiwan effectively curbed the spread of COVID-19 by taking early actions and using sustainable public health infrastructures. Additionally, there was an increase in telemedicine and virtual consultations, which minimized in-person contacts and reduced the risk of infections.

Going forward, Taiwan can take various measures to mitigate future pandemic-related impacts, such as increasing investment in technology and digital infrastructure to promote remote work, online learning, or telemedicine; strengthening its disease surveillance and early warning systems; improving the affordability and accessibility of health care; enhancing the capacity of healthcare workers; and developing pandemic-specific protocols and plans. It can also focus on developing a reliable and modern transportation network to ensure smooth flow of goods and people, even during a pandemic; using an integrative platform to maintain and distribute more PPE stockpiles, including critical infection-control equipment, to reduce iatrogenic infection exposure appropriately[113]; building more resilient supply chains by diversifying sources of raw materials and reducing reliance on a single supplier and dependence on global supply chains; encouraging innovation and entrepreneurship to spur growth and create new economic opportunities; providing financial support and resources to businesses and individuals affected by the pandemic; enhancing healthcare facilities and infrastructure to handle future pandemics effectively; and strengthening collaboration with international partners to facilitate trade and investment and maintain a stable supply chain. Through these changes, Taiwan can foster adaptability in the face of future pandemic crises.

References

1. Taiwan 2022. *International Religious Freedom Report*. 2022. https://www.state.gov/wp-content/uploads/2023/05/441219-TAIWAN-2022-INTERNATIONAL-RELIGIOUS-FREEDOM-REPORT.pdf.
2. Literacy. https://www.gender.ey.gov.tw/gecdb/Stat_Statistics_DetailData.aspx?sn=cC3K6vUAfeUlTCcfbr03CQ%40%40.
3. International Monetary Fund. World Economic Outlook database: October 2023. Accessed October 10, 2023. https://www.imf.org/en/Publications/WEO/weo-database/2023/October/weo-report?a=1&c=001,998,&s=NGDPD,PPPGDP,PPPPC,&sy=2021&ey=2028&ssm=0&scsm=1&scc=0&ssd=1&ssc=0&sic=0&sort=country&ds=.&br=1.
4. Unemployment rate. https://www.stat.gov.tw/News_Content.aspx?n=2706&s=232930.
5. Population, age structure. https://www.ris.gov.tw/app/portal/346.
6. Median age. https://pop-proj.ndc.gov.tw/main_en/.
7. Minister of the Interior. https://www.moi.gov.tw/News_Content.aspx?n=9&s=312388.
8. Number of people living with HIV/AIDS. https://www.cdc.gov.tw/File/Get/g0cZnRJEKX9isE3vcN-scQ.
9. Appendix 8: Temporary Provisions Effective During the Period of the Communist Rebellion (1948). https://andyreiter.com/wp-content/uploads/military-justice/tw/Laws%20and%20Decrees/Taiwan%20-%201948%20-%20Temporary%20Provisions%20to%20Supress%20the%20Communist%20Rebellion.pdf.
10. Ministry of Foreign Affairs (Taiwan). History of Taiwan. 2022. Accessed November 13, 2022. https://www.taiwan.gov.tw/content_3.php.
11. Central Intelligence Agency. *The World Factbook: Taiwan*. 2024. https://www.cia.gov/the-world-factbook/countries/taiwan/.
12. Tourism Bureau (Taiwan). General information. 2021. Accessed November 13, 2022. https://eng.taiwan.net.tw/m1.aspx?sNo=0002004.
13. Map of Taiwan. https://www.nationsonline.org/oneworld/taiwan.htm.
14. Political system. https://www.taiwan.gov.tw/content_4.php.
15. Ministry of Foreign Affairs (Taiwan). Politics and diplomacy of Taiwan. 2022. Accessed November 13, 2022. https://www.taiwan.gov.tw/politics.php.
16. Taiwan National Statistics. Macro database. 2022. Accessed November 23, 2022. https://nstatdb.dgbas.gov.tw/dgbasall/webMain.aspx?sys=100&funid=qryouteng&funid2=E018101010&outmode=8&cycle=4&outkind=11&compmode=0&ratenm=Value&fldlst=11111111111111&compmode=0&ymf=10800&ymt=11000&rdm=R76919&eng=1.
17. Ministry of Foreign Affairs (Taiwan). Economy of Taiwan. 2022. Accessed November 20, 2022. https://www.taiwan.gov.tw/content_7.php.
18. World Trade Organization. Merchandise trade of 2021. 2022. Accessed November 20, 2022. https://stats.wto.org/dashboard/merchandise_en.html.
19. World Bank. Total reserves. 2022. Accessed November 20, 2022. https://data.worldbank.org/indicator/FI.RES.TOTL.CD?most_recent_value_desc=true.
20. Central Bank of the Republic of China (Taiwan). Foreign exchange reserves as of the end of December 2021. 2022. Accessed November 20, 2022. https://www.cbc.gov.tw/en/cp-448-145254-8d7b6-2.html.
21. Kuo SW. *The Taiwan Economy in Transition*. Routledge; 2019.
22. Mai Z, Shi J. *Taiwan's Economic Success since 1980*. Edward Elgar Publishing; 2001.

23. Gender Equality Committee of the Executive Yuan. *Population of 15 Years and over by Educational Attainment*. Gender Equality Committee of the Executive Yuan; 2022.
24. Ministry of Labor (Taiwan). Labor force by age. 2022. Accessed November 23, 2022. https://statdb.mol.gov.tw/statis/jspProxy.aspx?sys=220&ym=10910&ymt=11110&kind=21&type=1&funid=q02023&cycle=41&outmode=0&compmode=0&outkind=11&fldspc=0,5,&rdm=R112516.
25. Ministry of Foreign Affairs (Taiwan). People of Taiwan. 2022. Accessed November 20, 2022. https://www.taiwan.gov.tw/content_2.php.
26. Tourism Bureau (Taiwan). Religion in Taiwan. 2021. Accessed November 20, 2022. https://eng.taiwan.net.tw/m1.aspx?sNo=0029044.
27. Wu HY. *The Missionary Gaze: The Social Biography and Archiving of Dr. David Landsborough IV's Photographic Collection*. https://ianthro.ioe.sinica.edu.tw/wp-content/uploads/2017/07/ettja010-2-001-1.pdf.
28. United Nations. World population prospects. https://population.un.org/wpp/Download/Standard/MostUsed/.
29. Cause of death statistics. https://www.mohw.gov.tw/np-128-2.html.
30. Lu J-F, Chang T-L. Evolution of Taiwan's health care system. *Health Econ Pol Law*. 2011;6(1):85-107.
31. Tikkanen R, Osborn R, Mossialos E, Djordjevic A, Wharton GA. International health care system profiles: Taiwan. https://www.commonwealthfund.org/international-health-policy-center/countries/taiwan.
32. Lu J-F, Chiang T-L. Evolution of Taiwan's health care system. *Health Econ Pol Law*. 2011;6(1):85-107.
33. National Health Insurance Administration. Ministry of Health and Welfare. Development of the healthcare system in Taiwan. 2022. Accessed November 20, 2022. https://www.nhi.gov.tw/english/Content_List.aspx?n=1EC853AA62EE6D76&topn=ED4A30E51A609E49.
34. Cheng TM. Reflections on the 20th anniversary of Taiwan's single-payer National Health Insurance System. *Health Aff (Millwood)*. 2015;34(3):502-510.
35. National Health Insurance Administration. Copayments. 2021. Accessed November 21, 2022. https://www.nhi.gov.tw/English/Content_List.aspx?n=E5509C8FE29950EA&topn=1D1ECC54F86E9050.
36. Wu TY, Majeed A, Kuo KN. An overview of the healthcare system in Taiwan. *London J Prim Care (Abingdon)*. 2010;3(2):115-119.
37. Ministry of Health and Welfare. Statistics of medical care institution & hospital utilization 2022. 2022. https://www.mohw.gov.tw/cp-6614-75351-2.html.
38. World Bank. Hospital beds (per 1,000 people). 2019. Accessed November 21, 2022. https://data.worldbank.org/indicator/SH.MED.BEDS.ZS.
39. World Bank. Physicians (per 1,000 people). 2019. Accessed November 21, 2022. https://data.worldbank.org/indicator/SH.MED.PHYS.ZS?most_recent_value_desc=true.
40. World Bank. Nurses and midwives (per 1,000 population). 2019. Accessed November 21, 2022. https://data.worldbank.org/indicator/SH.MED.NUMW.P3?most_recent_value_desc=true.
41. The National Health Insurance statistics, 2017–2022. https://www.nhi.gov.tw/en/np-44-2.html.
42. Formosa Cancer Foundation. https://www.canceraway.org.tw/pagelist.php?keyid=130.
43. Health Promotion Administration, Ministry of Health and Welfare (Taiwan). *Cancer Registry Annual Report, 2019 Taiwan*. Health Promotion Administration, Ministry of Health and Welfare; 2021.
44. Center for Diseases Control, Ministry of Health and Welfare. Dengue daily confirmed cases in latest 12 months. https://data.cdc.gov.tw/en/dataset/dengue-daily-determined-cases-latest-12m.
45. Infectious Disease Query System. https://nidss.cdc.gov.tw/nndss/disease?id=010.
46. Wang L-M, Chen Y-Y, Wun W-C, et al. *Lean Blood Transfusion Manual*. 2022.
47. Transfusion Society and Blood Foundation join forces to establish transfusion reaction notification system. 2015. https://www.blood.org.tw/Internet/main/docDetail.aspx?uid=6383&pid=9&docid=35974.
48. Taiwan's first tailored blood knowledge book for adolescents, "Easy Blood Lessons for Young Adults," is born in 2023! 2023. https://www.blood.org.tw/Internet/english/docDetail.aspx?uid=7935&pid=7679&docid=52526.
49. Taichung Blood Center. https://www.blood.org.tw/Internet/english/docDetail.aspx?uid=7741&pid=7681&docid=37135.
50. *Taiwan Hosted its first APEC Blood Safety Policy Forum in 2018*. https://www.blood.org.tw/Internet/english/docDetail.aspx?uid=7935&pid=7679&docid=45963.
51. Chung J. Foundation aims to raise age cap for blood donors. 2019. https://www.taipeitimes.com/News/taiwan/archives/2019/10/04/2003723368.
52. Everington K. *Taiwan has highest blood donation rate in world: WHO*. 2018. https://www.taiwannews.com.tw/en/news/3458192.
53. 14 June is World Blood Donor Day. https://www.who.int/campaigns/world-blood-donor-day.
54. CIFRC. https://www.ifrc.org/our-work/health-and-care/community-health/blood-donation.
55. Liao Y-H, Tang K-P, Chou C-Y, Kuo C-F, Tsai S-Y. Assessment of factors influencing physicians' intention to prescribe transfusion using the theory of planned behavior. *BMC Health Serv Res*. 2023;23(1):973.
56. Hospital accreditation and certification. https://www.jct.org.tw/cp-1127-8352-44faf-2.html.
57. National Health Insurance Administration, Ministry of Health and Welfare. News. 2019. Accessed November 25, 2022. https://www.nhi.gov.tw/English/News_Content.aspx?n=996D1B4B5DC48343&sms=F0EAFEB716DE7FFA&s=B8D5EE50036E8B4D.
58. Ministry of the Interior. *Life Expectancy since 1957*. 2022.
59. Worldometer. Life expectancy by country and in the world. 2022. Accessed November 28, 2022. https://www.worldometers.info/demographics/life-expectancy/.
60. Ho Chan WS. Taiwan's Healthcare Report 2010. *Epma J*. 2010;1(4):563-585.
61. Executive Yuan. National Health Insurance. 2022. Accessed November 25, 2022. https://www.ey.gov.tw/state/A01F61B9E9A9758D/fa06e0d2-413f-401e-b694-20c2db86f404.
62. Cheng T-M. Taiwan's health care system: the next 20 years. *Taiwan–US Qtly Analy*. 2015;17.
63. Ministry of Health and Welfare. *2020 NHE Statistical Tables*. 2022.
64. World Bank. *Current health expenditure (% of GDP)*. 2022. Accessed November 23, 2022. https://data.worldbank.org/indicator/SH.XPD.CHEX.GD.ZS.

65. Commonwealth Fund. Average annual number of physician visits per capita. 2019. Accessed November 23, 2022. https://www.commonwealthfund.org/international-health-policy-center/system-stats/annual-physician-visits-per-capita.
66. Government of Taiwan. *Number of Population by Age of 0–14, 15–64, 65+, Dependency Ratio, Index of Aging and Dependency Ratio*. Department of Household Registration; 2022.
67. National Development Council. Data query. 2022. Accessed November 27, 2022. https://pop-proj.ndc.gov.tw/main_en/dataSearch.aspx?uid=78&pid=78.
68. Chien HJ, Chen YF. Rejuvenate Taiwan: time to act now: strategies of fewer children and population aging in Taiwan. *J Formos Med Assoc*. 2017;116(3):137-138.
69. Lin Y-Y, Huang CS. Aging in Taiwan: building a society for active aging and aging in place. *Gerontologist*. 2015;56(2): 176-183.
70. How can Taiwan fix its doctor shortage? https://english.cw.com.tw/article/article.action?id=3198.
71. Taiwan Union of Nurses Association. *Taiwan Nursing Workforce Statistics in Year 2021*. 2022.
72. Lin C-F, Huang C-I, Kao C-C, Lu M-S, Hu LZ. The nursing shortage and nursing retention strategies in Taiwan. *Hu Li Za Zhi*. 2013;60(3):88.
73. Teng S-W. Nursing manpower and solutions in Taiwan. *Hu Li Za Zhi*. 2014:61(2):5.
74. Taiwan Association of Medical Technologists. Statistics. 2022. Accessed November 28, 2022. https://www.mt.org.tw/wholecountry/laws.php?uid=68&searchkey=&x=12&y=16.
75. Hsieh CY, Su C-C, Shao S-C, et al. Taiwan's National Health Insurance Research Database: past and future. *Clin Epidemiol*. 2019;11:349-358.
76. Yao W-C, Leong K-H, Chiu L-T, et al. The trends in the incidence and thrombosis-related comorbidities of antiphospholipid syndrome: a 14-year nationwide population-based study. *Thrombos J*. 2022.
77. Chang H, Kuo C-F, Yu T-S, et al. Increased risk of chronic fatigue syndrome following infection: a 17-year population-based cohort study. *J Transl Med*. 2023;21(1):804.
78. Hsu H-J, Chang H, Lin C-L, et al. Increased risk of chronic fatigue syndrome following pneumonia: a population-based cohort study. *J Infect Public Health*. 2024;17(8):102495.
79. Chen C, Yip H-T, Leong K-H, et al. Presence of depression and anxiety with distinct patterns of pharmacological treatments before the diagnosis of chronic fatigue syndrome: a population-based study in Taiwan. *J Transl Med*. 2023.
80. Leong KH, Yip H-T, Kuo C-F, Tsai S-Y. Treatments of chronic fatigue syndrome and its debilitating comorbidities: a 12-year population-based study. *J Transl Med*. 2022;20(1):268.
81. Yao WC, Chen H-J, Leong K-H, et al. The risk of fibromyalgia in patients with iron deficiency anemia: a nationwide population-based cohort study. *Sci Rep*. 2021;11(1):10496.
82. Tsai SY, Lin C-L, Wong Y-C, et al. Increased risk of herpes zoster following dermatomyositis and polymyositis: a nationwide population-based cohort study. *Medicine (Baltimore)*. 2015;94(28):e1138.
83. Yang TY, Kuo H-T, Chen H-J, et al. Increased risk of chronic fatigue syndrome following atopy: a population-based study. *Medicine (Baltimore)*. 201594(29):e1211.
84. Tsai S-Y, Chen H-J, Lio C-F, et al. Increased risk of herpes zoster in patients with psoriasis: a population-based retrospective cohort study. *PLoS One*. 2017;12(8):e0179447.
85. Tsai S-Y, Lin C-L, Shih S-C, et al. Increased risk of chronic fatigue syndrome following burn injuries. *J Transl Med*. 2018;16(1):342.
86. Tsai S-Y, Chen H-J, Chen C, et al. Increased risk of chronic fatigue syndrome following psoriasis: a nationwide population-based cohort study. *J Transl Med*. 2019;17(1):154.
87. Tsai S-Y, Chen H-J, Lio C-F, et al. Increased risk of chronic fatigue syndrome in patients with inflammatory bowel disease: a population-based retrospective cohort study. *J Transl Med*. 2019;17(1):55.
88. Kuo C-F, Shi L, Lin C-L, et al. How peptic ulcer disease could potentially lead to the lifelong, debilitating effects of chronic fatigue syndrome: an insight. *Sci Rep*. 2021;11(1):7520.
89. Shi L, Lin C-L, Su C-H, et al. The risk of developing osteoporosis in hemolytic anemia: what aggravates the bone loss? *J Clin Med*. 2021;10(15).
90. Yang T-Y, Lin C-L, Yao W-C, et al. How *Mycobacterium tuberculosis* infection could lead to the increasing risks of chronic fatigue syndrome and the potential immunological effects: a population-based retrospective cohort study. *J Transl Med*. 2022;20(1):99.
91. Yao WC, Leong K-H, Chiu L-T, et al. The trends in the incidence and thrombosis-related comorbidities of antiphospholipid syndrome: a 14-year nationwide population-based study. *Thromb J*. 2022;20(1):50.
92. Chen C, Yip H-T, Leong K-H, et al. Presence of depression and anxiety with distinct patterns of pharmacological treatments before the diagnosis of chronic fatigue syndrome: a population-based study in Taiwan. *J Transl Med*. 2023;21(1):98.
93. Chang H, Kuo C-F, Yu T-S, et al. Increased risk of chronic fatigue syndrome following infection: a 17-year population-based cohort study. *J Transl Med*. 2023;21(1):804.
94. Hsu N-W, Chou K-C, Wang Y-T, et al. Building a model for predicting metabolic syndrome using artificial intelligence based on an investigation of whole-genome sequencing. *J Transl Med*. 2022;20(1):190.
95. World Health Organization. WHO-convened global study of origins of SARS-CoV-2: China part. 2021. https://www.who.int/publications/i/item/who-convened-global-study-of-origins-of-sars-cov-2-china-part.
96. World Health Organization. WHO COVID-19 dashboard. 2024. Accessed January 31, 2024. https://data.who.int/dashboards/covid19/cases.
97. Centers for Disease Control. *Taiwan pandemic report*. 2024. https://covid-19.nchc.org.tw/.
98. Novel corona virus (COVID-19) update. https://ethiopia.un.org/sites/default/files/2020-11/20201124_COVID-19_SitRep%20228.pdf.
99. Dai CY, Dai T-H, Sheng W-H, Ho C-K. 222 days without COVID in Taiwan: what are the reasons for this success? *J Travel Med*. 2021;28(2).
100. COVID-19 dashboard: Taiwan epidemic report. National Center for High Performance Computing. Updated September 7, 2023. Accessed February 13, 2025. https://covid-19.nchc.org.tw/index.php.
101. Ministry of Health and Welfare. Crucial policies for combating COVID-19. 2022. Accessed November 23, 2022. https://covid19.mohw.gov.tw/en/sp-timeline0-206.html.
102. McIntosh MK. COVID-19: epidemiology, virology, and prevention. 2022. Accessed November 23, 2022. https://www.uptodate.com/contents/covid-19-epidemiology-virology-and-prevention?search=covid&source=covid19_landing&usage_type=main_section#H3116389471.

103. Taiwan Centers for Disease Control. COVID-19 (SARS-CoV-2 infection). 2022. Accessed November 23, 2022. https://sites.google.com/cdc.gov.tw/2019-ncov/.
104. Chang M-L, Lin K-L. Challenges and policy recommendations of Taiwan's economy in the COVID-19 pandemic era. *Asia Pac J Manag*. 2020.
105. Baldwin R, Weder di Mauro B. *Economics in the Time of COVID-19*. CEPR Press; 2020.
106. Lin Y-H, Tu Y-M, Lai F, et al. Online work and its influence on work and personal life as the COVID-19 pandemic spreads: the case of Taiwan. *Sustainability*. 2020.
107. Lai YH, Shih TF, Lin HJ. An analysis of the effectiveness of social media during the COVID-19 crisis in Taiwan. *BMC Public Health*. 2020.
108. Ministry of Economic Affairs. Economy growth rate. https://dmz26.moea.gov.tw/GA/common/Common.aspx?code=A&no=4u.
109. Chen YM, Chen KH. The impact of COVID-19 pandemic on international trade: an empirical analysis. *Intl Environ Res Pub Health*. 2020;6522.
110. Fauci AS, Lane HC, Redfield RR. Covid-19: navigating the uncharted. *N Engl J Med*. 2020;382(13):1268-1269.
111. Kavanagh MM, Erondu NA, Tomori O, et al. Access to lifesaving medical resources for African countries: COVID-19 testing and response, ethics, and politics. *Lancet*. 2020; 395(10238):1735-1738.
112. Gross domestic product rate: private consumption expenditure. https://dmz26.moea.gov.tw/GA/common/Common.aspx?code=A&no=4.
113. Ma KS, Tsai SY. Big Data-driven personal protective equipment stockpiling framework under universal healthcare for disease control and prevention in the COVID-19 era. *Intl J Surg*. 2020;79:290-291.

CHAPTER 24

Singapore

Robin Choo and Leiyu Shi

Country Description

Table 24-1 Singapore

Nationality	Singaporean(s)
Ethnic groups	Chinese: 74.1% (2022 est.) Malay: 13.6% Indian: 9.0% Others: 3.3%
Religions	Buddhism (31.1%) Christianity (18.9%) Islam (15.6%) Taoism and other Chinese religions (8.8%) Hinduism (5%) No religion (20%)
Language	Official languages are English, Malay, Mandarin, and Tamil. English is the most commonly used language in business, education, and government.
Literacy	97.5%
Government type	Parliamentary republic with unicameral parliament and a president as head of state
Date of independence	1964
Gross domestic product per capita	108,000 USD (2022 est)
Unemployment rate	2.3%
Natural hazards	Haze
Population	Total population: 5.637 million ■ Singapore citizens: 3,553 million ■ Permanent residents: 0.519 million ■ Others: 1.563 million

(continues)

Table 24-1 Singapore *(continued)*

Age structure	65 and above: 18.4%
Median age	42.8
Population growth rate	3.4%
Birth rate	1.12 per female 8.6 per 1,000 residents
Death rate	5.6 per 1,000 residents
Disease burden	Disease burden relatively low compared with other countries. Common noncommunicable diseases: cancer, cardiovascular diseases, and diabetes Common communicable diseases: dengue fever and influenza
Net migration rate	11.2 migrants per 1,000 population
Gender ratio	0.955 male/female
Infant mortality rate	1.8 per 1,000 resident live births
Life expectancy at birth	Average: 83.5 Males: 81.1 Females: 85.9
Total fertility rate	1.12
HIV/AIDS adult prevalence rate	0.2%
People living with HIV/AIDS	8,200 people
HIV/AIDS death rate	0.1 death per 1,000 population

**Population in Brief 2022.* National Population and Talent Division, Strategy Group, Prime Minister Office, Singapore; 2022.

Data from Central Intelligence Agency. The World Factbook: Singapore. Accessed April 4, 2024. https://www.cia.gov/the-world-factbook/countries/singapore/.

Since the founding of Singapore in 1965, the healthcare system in the country has been built from the ground up. Today, it ranks as one of the best healthcare systems in the world, according to several global ranking organizations. According to the World Health Organization, the Singapore healthcare system achieved top levels of universal healthcare coverage by international standards, despite very low government expenditure on healthcare spending as a percentage of GDP compared with other OECD countries. See **Table 24-1** for more details on Singapore.

The excellent performance of the Singapore healthcare system is due to its good governance, well-planned healthcare policies, an emphasis on individual responsibility in healthcare services utilization, excellent healthcare facilities, and a strong healthcare workforce.

This chapter aims to give an overview of the Singapore healthcare system, how it evolved over the years, how its healthcare delivery is organized, and how its financing is done. The current status of Singapore health care will be evaluated, and future challenges will be described.

History

Singapore is a small island nation located at the southern tip of the Malay Peninsula in Southeast Asia. The history of Singapore dates back to the 14th century, when the island was known as Temasek. It was a small trading port, and several different empires ruled it, including the Majapahit Empire of Java and the Sultanate of Malacca.

In 1819, Sir Stamford Raffles, a British East India Company representative, arrived in Singapore and negotiated with the local ruler to establish a trading post on the island. The British recognized Singapore's strategic location as a vital trading port, and it quickly grew into a major commercial hub for the region. During this period, Singapore's population proliferated as immigrants from China, India, and other parts of Southeast Asia came to the island seeking work. However, during World War II, Singapore was occupied by the Japanese, and it suffered greatly during the war, with many buildings destroyed and thousands of civilians killed.

After the war, Singapore returned to British control, but there was growing discontent among the local population, demanding greater political autonomy. In 1959, Singapore became a self-governing state within the British Commonwealth, with Lee Kuan Yew becoming its first prime minister. Under Lee's leadership, Singapore underwent a period of rapid modernization and economic growth, with a focus on manufacturing and exports. The government also implemented strict laws and regulations to maintain social order and cleanliness.

In 1963, Singapore joined the Federation of Malaysia, but the union was short-lived, and Singapore declared independence in 1965. The country faced many challenges in its early years as an independent nation, including high unemployment and a need for more natural resources.

Despite these challenges, Singapore continued to grow and prosper, becoming Southeast Asia's major financial and commercial center. The government implemented several policies to attract foreign investment, and Singapore became known for its highly educated workforce, efficient infrastructure, and low levels of corruption.

Today, Singapore is a highly developed, modern city-state with a thriving economy and a diverse population. It is home to many multinational corporations and a popular tourist destination known for its world-class shopping, dining, and entertainment options.

Size and Geography

Singapore is a small island city-state located in Southeast Asia, at the southern tip of the Malaysian Peninsula. It has a total land area of 728.3 square kilometers and a population of close to 6 million. This makes Singapore one of the most densely populated countries in the world.

Government and Political System

Singapore is a parliamentary republic, with a president as the head of state and a prime minister as the head of government. The government operates under a framework of representative democracy, where citizens elect representatives to make decisions on their behalf. The current president is Tharman Shanmugaratnam, and the current prime minister is Lawrence Wong.

The president of Singapore is elected by popular vote for a term of 6 years and serves as the ceremonial head of state. The president has limited powers, including the power to approve appointments to key government positions, veto certain legislative bills, and grant pardons. The president appoints the prime minister of Singapore from among the members of parliament who had won seats in the general election. The prime minister is the head of government and has executive authority to manage the affairs of the state. The prime minister selects other cabinet members responsible for various government administration aspects, such as the Ministry of Health.

The parliament of Singapore consists of a single chamber, the House of Representatives, also known as the parliament. The parliament has 93 members, of whom 89 are elected by popular vote; the other four are appointed as nonconstituency members of parliament. The members of parliament serve a term of 5 years and are responsible for making laws, approving the government's budget, and holding the government accountable.

The ruling party in Singapore is the People's Action Party (PAP), which has been in power since the country gained independence in 1965. The PAP has a strong mandate and enjoys a significant majority in the parliament, with only a few opposition members elected in each general election.

Singapore's political system has a unique feature called the group representation constituency (GRC) system. This system was introduced in 1988 to ensure that each constituency in the parliament has at least one member from a minority race. Under this system, a group of candidates from the same political party run together as a team in a constituency, and the team with the most votes wins the seat. At least one member of the team must be from a minority race. This policy is designed to increase social cohesion among different races in Singapore.

Another important feature of Singapore's political system is the use of the Non-Constituency Member of Parliament (NCMP) scheme. This scheme allows up to nine candidates who lost in the general election to be appointed as nonvoting members of parliament. This ensures that there is still a voice for the opposition in the parliament, even if the PAP wins a significant majority.

The government of Singapore is known for its efficiency and effectiveness in implementing policies. It strongly focuses on economic development and has implemented several policies to attract foreign investment and promote entrepreneurship. The country is also known for its strict laws and regulations, including harsh punishments for crimes such as drug trafficking and corruption.

Singapore's political system has played a significant role in the country's success and stability. The parliamentary republic, with a president as the head of state and a prime minister as the head of government, has ensured a smooth transition of power and a focus on economic development. Using the GRC system and NCMP scheme has ensured a voice for minorities and the opposition in the parliament. The government's efficiency and effectiveness in implementing policies have contributed to Singapore's success as a global economic powerhouse.

Macroeconomics

Singapore is an open economy that has experienced significant economic growth and development over the past 60 years. The country has a highly diversified economy with a strong emphasis on international trade and services.

Singapore has a high GDP per capita, approximately $65,233 USD in 2020. Its gross primary productivity (GPP) is driven by the service sector, which accounts for around 70% of its economy. Manufacturing also plays a vital role in the economy, particularly in producing electronics and pharmaceuticals.

Singapore had a low unemployment rate of around 2.9% in 2020. This is primarily due to its highly educated workflow and the government's various policies to support job creation and training.

Singapore relies heavily on international trade, with exports accounting for around 170% of its GDP. The country had a strong presence in the global shipping and logistics industry. Singapore is also a major international financial center in the Asia Pacific.

The fiscal position of Singapore is very strong, with a budget surplus of 2.1% of GDP in 2020. During the COVID-19 pandemic, the government implemented various measures to support businesses and individuals, such as cash payouts and tax rebates.

The Monetary Authority of Singapore uses a targeted approach to monetary policy, focusing on the exchange rate as its primary policy tool. Its goal is to keep inflation under control while supporting economic growth.

Singapore's macro economy is characterized by solid growth, low inflation, low unemployment, and a high reliance on international trade and services. The government actively maintains a stable and prosperous economy through targeted fiscal and monetary policies.

Brief History of the Healthcare System

The Founding of Singapore in 1965

Since the founding of Singapore in 1965, its healthcare system has evolved into one of the best in the world, with Singaporeans having one of the highest life expectancies globally.[1] However, such achievements were not always the case throughout Singapore's history.

In the 1960s, the Singapore healthcare system was largely undeveloped, with inadequate healthcare facilities and a shortage of medical professionals. According to records from the World Health Organization, in 1966, there were only 3.3 hospital beds per 1,000 population in Singapore, compared with the global average of 4.5 beds per 1,000 population.

The Singapore government's focus on healthcare started in the 1970s with the establishment of the Ministry of Health in 1970. It played a crucial role in formulating policies and regulations to ensure the accessibility and affordability of health care for all Singaporeans.

National Health Plan, 1983

On February 2, 1983, the Singapore government published the National Health Plan, which was a 20-year plan to overhaul Singapore's health system. The plan aimed to maintain a high standard of health care within Singapore's limited resources while trying to meet rising demands for the increasingly health-conscious, affluent, and aging Singapore population. Fast forward to today, and this healthcare blue paper continues to form the guiding principles of the Singapore healthcare system.

The first part of the plan proposed in the 1983 plan included:

1. Building community hospitals in Singapore's new towns to cater to essential healthcare treatment needs of patients who do not require specialized care

2. Building communal clinics (also known as polyclinics) in every major Housing Development Board (HDB) new town to provide essential outpatient services
3. Designing a means-testing mechanism for admissions to subsidized wards (Class C wards) in hospitals based on family income and creating more high-end wards (Class A and Class B) to substitute for Class C wards and cater to patient demands
   a. Class C wards are typically basic wards with lower fees and between four and six beds in a room.
   b. Class B wards offer more amenities and privacy and have two to four beds per room.
   c. Class A wards are the most expensive ones with one to two beds per room and access to a private bathroom.

The second part of the 1983 health plan, and perhaps the more well-known reform globally, proposed a compulsory national contribution scheme called Medisave. The system was designed to enable individuals to pay for their medical expenses through their savings, thereby providing citizens with personal responsibility for their health and healthcare spending. A monthly deduction from Singaporeans' Central Provident Fund was put into a personal savings account to pay for their hospitalization expenses. The government opted for this self-financing mechanism, rejecting social insurance for healthcare financing, to balance the supply and demand for healthcare services while keeping healthcare costs in check.

The 1980s also saw the start of the corporatization of public-sector hospitals to improve their operating efficiency. Full autonomy in strategic and operational matters was granted to these corporatized public hospitals to compete for paying patients. The National University Hospital became the first privately run, government-owned hospital in 1985. Later, in 1989, the Singapore General Hospital was corporatized. By the end of the 1980s, hospital beds had increased to 6.7 beds per 1,000 population.

In the 1990s, the government continued to improve the healthcare system by introducing the MediShield scheme in 1990 as a supplement to Medisave, which provided basic health insurance coverage for all Singaporeans. Soon after, the Medifund plan was presented as a safety net for patients who cannot pay for their medical expenses despite the availability of Medisave and Rebreak: MediShield schemes. Medifund accounts for only a tiny share of the total healthcare expenditure, as Singaporeans must pass a very stringent means test to receive benefits.

The Health Promotion Board (HPB) was established in 2001 as a platform to promote health and disease prevention programs. Some programs include a smoking control program, workplace health promotion program, healthy dining program, cancer screening program, school health screening services, and school dental service.

Healthcare 2020 Masterplan

In 2012, the Singapore Ministry of Health issued a strategic blueprint that outlined the country's healthcare goals, called Healthcare 2020.[2] This plan aims to ensure that Singaporeans can access affordable, high-quality health care that meets their changing needs. It sets out three key strategies:

1. Enhancing the accessibility and affordability of healthcare services
2. Building a strong and sustainable healthcare system
3. Fostering a culture of healthy living

To achieve these strategies, the Healthcare 2020 Masterplan outlines a series of initiatives and targets in areas such as healthcare financing, infrastructure, workforce development, and technology. Some of the key initiatives include:

1. Increasing the capacity and capabilities of community care services to support aging in place and reduce hospital admissions
2. Implementing a national electronic health record system to improve care coordination and patient outcomes
3. Expanding the use of telemedicine to provide more convenient and accessible care for patients
4. Increasing the number of healthcare professionals and enhancing their skills and competencies
5. Encouraging healthier lifestyles through public education and targeted interventions

Overall, the Healthcare 2020 Masterplan is a comprehensive and ambitious plan that seeks to ensure that Singapore's healthcare system remains world-class and able to meet the evolving needs of its population.

HealthierSG 2022

In 2017, the Ministry of Health issued HealthierSG 2022 (HS2022), the current healthcare master plan for Singapore. This plan builds upon the achievements of the Healthcare 2020 Masterplan and aims to further enhance Singapore's healthcare system by focusing on three key areas:

- **Keeping Singaporeans healthy:** HS2022 aims to promote healthy living and disease prevention through initiatives such as healthy eating, physical activity, and early detection of illnesses.
- **Improving the healthcare system:** The plan focuses on improving the quality of care and patient outcomes through integrating care, enhanced health IT infrastructure, and strengthened partnerships with the private sector.
- **Making health care affordable:** HS2022 aims to ensure that health care remains affordable and accessible for all Singaporeans by implementing cost-effective measures and leveraging technology to reduce costs.

While the Healthcare 2020 Masterplan and HS2022 share similar goals of improving the healthcare system in Singapore, HS2022 places a greater emphasis on disease prevention, healthcare integration, and leveraging technology to enhance the quality of care and affordability.

Singapore's healthcare system has evolved tremendously since its founding in 1965. The average life expectancy in this country has increased by 20 years, from 63 years (in 1965) to 83 years (in 2022).[3] Infant mortality rates have improved from 34.9 per 1,000 live births (in 1965) to 1.8 per 1,000 live births (in 2022), one of the world's lowest. Singapore has the second highest healthy life expectancy in the world,[4] and Bloomberg ranks the Singapore healthcare system as one of the most efficient in the world.

The Current Healthcare System

Organization

Singapore provides universal healthcare coverage for all of its citizens via heavily subsidized medical costs and policy controls. The government uses several policy tools to manage the health sector: (1) an organization tool, (2) a fiscal tool, (3) a regulation tool, and (4) an information tool.[5]

The mission of the Singapore Ministry of Health is to promote good health and reduce illness, ensure access to excellent and affordable health care, and pursue medical excellence.[6] Through the Ministry of Health, the Singapore government manages the public healthcare system to ensure that good and affordable basic healthcare services are available to all citizens by providing subsidized medical services while promoting individual responsibility for the costs of healthcare services.

The Ministry of Health organization is designed to have certain centralized functions to achieve better control and economies of scale. A unique feature of this organization is the creation of the Ministry of Health Holdings, as shown in **Figure 24-1**.

Healthcare Delivery

Singapore has a dual healthcare delivery system consisting of public and private healthcare providers. Approximately 80% of the primary healthcare services are provided by private clinics, while public polyclinics provide the remaining 20%. The ratio is reversed for tertiary care, which is more complex and costly: The public sector provides 80% of hospital care.

The Singapore public healthcare system consists of three clusters. The Ministry of Health Holdings (MOHH) is the holding company for Singapore's public healthcare clusters: (1) National University of Health System (NUHS), (2) National Healthcare Group (NHG), and (3) Singapore Health Services (Singhealth) . See **Table 24-2**. MOHH aims to enhance public healthcare performance by unlocking synergies and economies of scale.

Each health cluster covers a region of Singapore with the original six clusters being merged into three, as shown in Table 24-2: Central Region (NHG), Eastern Region (Singhealth), and Western Region (NUHS). This scheme allows for more patient-centric care deeper into the community as part of the HealthierSG master plan.

There are currently 19 acute care hospitals, one psychiatric hospital, and nine community hospitals in Singapore. The number of healthcare facilities and beds are shown in **Table 24-3**. Of the 19 acute care hospitals, 42% are private hospitals, and 58% are public and not-for-profit hospitals. However, these public hospitals cover 85.8% of the hospital beds in Singapore. Public hospitals also offer excellent subsidized basic and tertiary healthcare services, but some patients choose private hospitals for reduced waiting time and more comfort in inpatient settings.

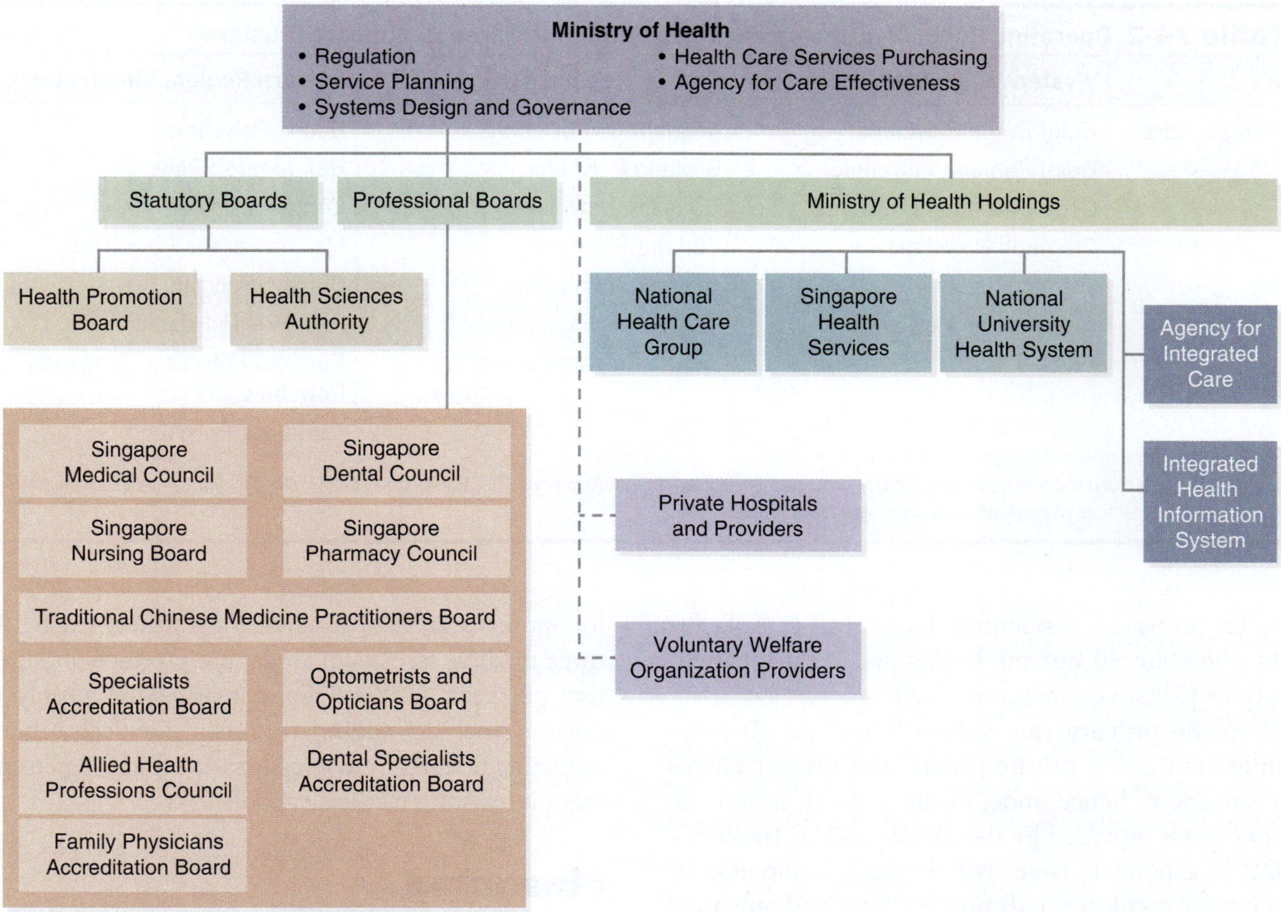

Figure 24-1 Organization of the health system in Singapore

Reproduced from Tikkanen R, Osborn R, Mossialos E, Djordjevic A, Wharton GA. Singapore. Commonwealth Fund, June 5, 2020. [Online]. Accessed April 4, 2024. https://www.commonwealthfund.org/international-health-policy-center/countries/singapore.

Table 24-2 Operating Public Healthcare Facilities Within the Three Healthcare Clusters

	Western Region: NUHS	Central Region: NHG	Eastern Region: SingHealth
Tertiary care	National University Hospital Alexandra Hospital Ng Teng Fong General Hospital Jurong Community Hospital	Khoo Teck Puat Hospital Tan Tock Seng Hospital Institute of Mental Health Woodlands General Hospital Yishun Community Hospital Woodlands Community Hospital	Bright Vision Community Hospital Changi General Hospital KK Women and Children's Hospital Outram Community Hospital Sengkang Community Sengkang General Hospital Singapore General Hospital
National specialty centers	National University Cancer Institute National University Centre for Oral Health National University Heart Centre Jurong Medical Centre	National Centre for Infectious Diseases National Skin Centre	National Cancer Centre National Dental Centre National Neuroscience Institute Singapore National Eye Centre

(continues)

Table 24-2 Operating Public Healthcare Facilities Within the Three Healthcare Clusters *(continued)*

	Western Region: NUHS	Central Region: NHG	Eastern Region: SingHealth
Primary care	Bukit Batok Polyclinic Bukit Panjang Polyclinic Choa Chu Kang Polyclinic Clementi Polyclinic Jurong Polyclinic Queenstown Polyclinic Pioneer Polyclinic	Ang Mo Kio Polyclinic Geylang Polyclinic Hougang Polyclinic Kallang Polyclinic Toa Payoh Polyclinic Woodlands Polyclinic Yishun Polyclinic	Bedok Polyclinic Bukit Merah Polyclinic Eunos Polyclinic Marine Parade Polyclinic Outram Polyclinic Pasir Ris Polyclinic Punggol Polyclinic Sengkang Polyclinic Tampines Polyclinic

Data from Ng KG. Three-cluster healthcare system should not be further reviewed: Ong Ye Kung. *The Straits Times*, May 31, 2021. [Online]. Accessed April 4, 2024. https://www.straitstimes.com/singapore/health/three-cluster-healthcare-system-should-not-be-further-reviewed-ong-ye-kung.

In terms of residential long-term care facilities, there are 80 nursing homes and eight inpatient hospice palliative care service facilities.[7]

In the primary care sphere, there are 20 polyclinics and 2,410 private general practitioner clinics in Singapore; hence, most of the primary healthcare services are provided by the private sector. Traditionally, Singaporeans have had the basic awareness to seek basic medical care from GP clinics and only turn to hospitals when more specialized care is required. Therefore, the primary and tertiary care sectors seemed to operate like separate independent systems. Recently, MOHH did a great job of getting most of the private clinics to enroll in the nationwide electronic health IT system, and the implementation of CHAS allowed healthcare subsidies to reach the primary care sector. As part of the HealthierSG 2022 initiative, the Singapore government is pushing forward with a plan to have all Singaporeans enrolled with a family doctor, which is challenging given that the GP sector is mainly private and fragmented.

Workforce

There are a large number of qualified healthcare personnel working in the Singapore healthcare sector. In 2021, there were 75,745 professionals in healthcare services, including 15,423 medical doctors, as shown in **Table 24-4**. This is an increase of 60% more medical doctors than a decade ago (2011–2021), as shown in **Figure 24-2**.

The number of medical doctors per 1,000 population is 2.7, similar to the United States, United Kingdom, Japan, and South Korea ratios. However, with the number of senior citizens set to increase in the next decade, experts believe that there is a need for more medical doctors in the future.[8] Currently, three medical schools in Singapore produce 500 doctors per year. Options for increasing the supply of doctors include adding a fourth medical school, attracting doctors from overseas, or expanding enrollment in existing medical schools.

Financing

The Singapore government keeps healthcare affordable by using government subsidies for healthcare expenditure, supplemented by the Medisave, MediShield, MediFund, and the ElderShield programs.

Medisave

Medisave is a mandatory national savings account. Individuals contribute a portion of their annual income into their Medisave account for medical expenses such as hospitalization, day surgeries, or some outpatient services. Immediate family members can also use the Medisave accounts of family members if their accounts are inadequate. Depending on their age group, individuals contribute between 6.5% and 10% of their annual income into the Medisave account. Medisave can cover daily ward charges, doctors' fees, surgical fees, and other inpatient charges that the government heavily subsidizes. There is a cap for Medisave expenses, depending on different medical procedures, even though the amount in the account was contributed by and belongs to each individual. The system is designed so that Singaporeans will not deplete their Medisave funds on certain medical procedures when they are younger and adequate amounts can be set aside for future medical expenses.

Table 24-3 Beds in Inpatient Facilities and in Non-Residential Long-Term Care Facilities

Hospitals Beds	2021	2022	2023
Acute Hospitals	**11,704**	**11,830**	**12,025**
Public	9,762	9,820	9,956
Not-for-profit	270	273	347
Private	1,672	1,737	1,722
Psychiatric Hospitals	**1,950**	**1,950**	**1,950**
Public	1,950	1,950	1,950
Not-for-profit	-	-	-
Private	-	-	-
Community Hospitals	**2,079**	**2,194**	**2,303**
Public	1,180	1,226	1,331
Not-for-profit	899	968	972
Private	-	-	-
Residential Long-Term Care Facility Beds	**2021**	**2022**	**2023**
Nursing Homes	**17,064**	**18,157**	**19,201**
Public	7,099	8,087	8,573
Not-for-profit	6,060	6,138	6,154
Private	3,905	3,932	4,474
Inpatient Hospice Palliative Care Service (IHPCS)	**264**	**264**	**264**
Public	64	64	64
Not-for-profit	200	200	220
Private	-	-	-

Data from Ministry of Health Singapore. Beds in inpatient facilities and places in non-residential long-term care facilities. July 25, 2024. Accessed October 12, 2024. https://www.moh.gov.sg/resources-statistics/singapore-health-facts/beds-in-inpatient-facilities-and-places-in-non-residential-long-term-care-facilities.

Individual cash payments, private insurance, or MediShield finance the remaining amounts outside of the use of Medisave. Even so, the amounts are generally affordable as the government already heavily subsidizes medical expenses.

The combination of government subsidies and Medisave use reduces the copayments to affordable levels, which is the goal of the Singapore government's healthcare financing system. The Singapore government has reiterated many times that it would never consider having copayments go to zero, as having some form of copayment ensures personal responsibility and minimizes moral hazard due to overuse of healthcare services.

Table 24-4 Number of Medical Doctors in Singapore, 2021–2023

	2021	2022	2023
Total Number of Doctors	**15,423**	**16,009**	**16,753**
Public	9,844	10,146	10,586
Non-public	4,601	4,682	4,869
Not in active practice	978	1,181	1,298
Doctor-to-population ratio	1:369	1:354	1:353
Doctor per 1,000 population	2.8	2.8	2.8
Specialists	**6,431**	**6,699**	**6,956**
Public	4,267	4,474	4,599
Non-public	1,776	1,800	1,882
Not in active practice	388	425	475
Non-Specialists	**8,992**	**9,310**	**9,797**
Public	5,577	5,672	5,987
Non-public	2,825	2,882	2,987
Not in active practice	590	756	823

Data from Ministry of Health Singapore-Health manpower. August 21, 2024. Accessed October 12, 2024. https://www.moh.gov.sg/resources-statistics/singapore-health-facts/health-manpower.

MediShield

MediShield is a nationwide catastrophic medical insurance that helps Medisave account holders and dependents meet the cost of treatment for severe or prolonged illnesses at basic ward levels. Singaporeans can use their Medisave accounts to pay for the premiums of MediShield or other private insurance.

MediShield aims to provide an insurance scheme to pay for large medical bills beyond the patient's deductibles in cash or use of Medisave. Depending on the size of the bill, MediShield can cover approximately 80% to 90% of the remaining amount beyond the deductibles. It is an opt-out scheme; hence, individuals are automatically enrolled into the plan unless they opt out for reasons such as adequate personal procured private insurance or being self-insured.

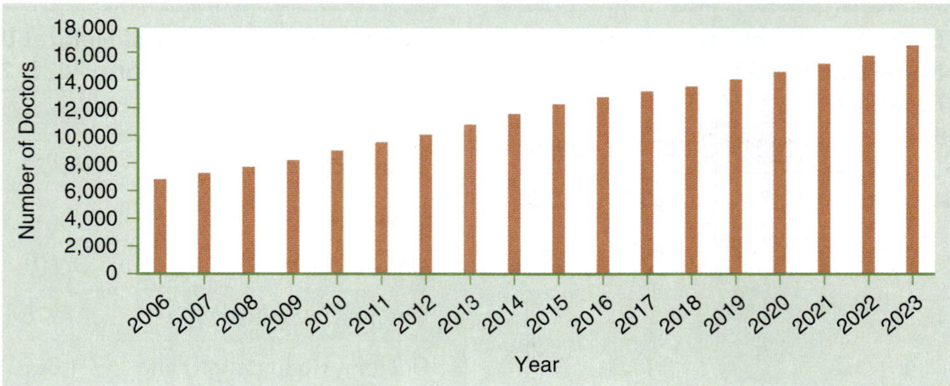

Figure 24-2 Number of doctors in Singapore from 2006 to 2023

Data from SingStat, Registered health personnel (end of period). Department of Statistics Singapore July 18, 2024. Accessed October 12, 2024. https://tablebuilder.singstat.gov.sg/table/TS/M870011.

MediFund

MediFund is an endowment fund set up by the Singapore government as a safety net for needy Singaporeans who cannot pay for their heavily subsidized medical expenses. Currently, the size of the endowment is SGD 1.5 billion. Only profits earned from the endowment (managed by Ministry of Health) can be used, and the responsibility for how much to use and on which patients to use MediFund is controlled by each approved hospital's MediFund committee.

Evaluation of the Healthcare System

In 2022, the World Health Organization published a framework to assess the performance of health system, as shown in **Figure 24-3**. This section evaluates the Singapore healthcare system using this framework.

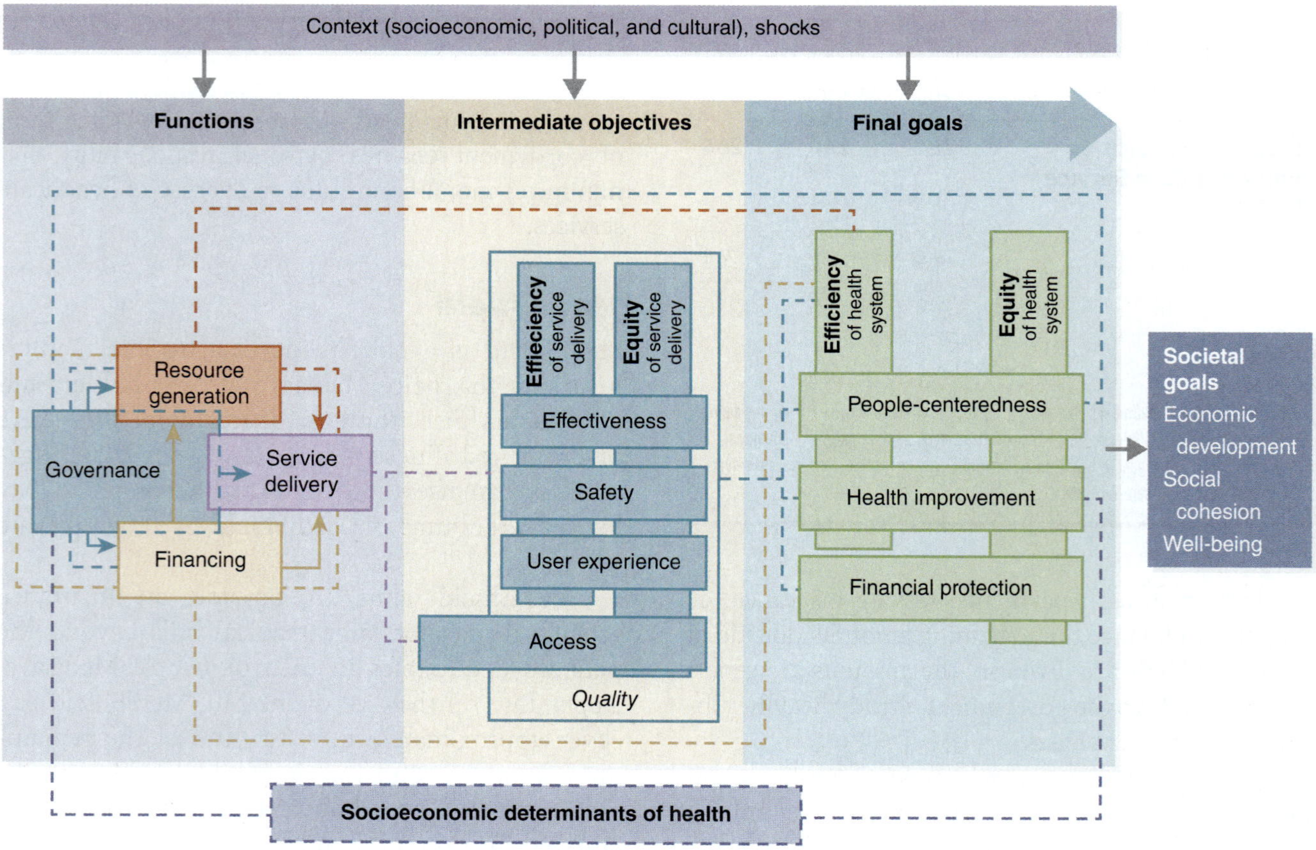

Figure 24-3 Health system performance assessment (HSPA) framework for universal health care: an overview

Reproduced from Papanicolas I, Rajan D, Karanikolos M, Soucat A, Figueras J. *Health System Performance Assessment: A Framework for Policy Analysis.* World Health Organization; 2022.

Governance

The mission statement of the Ministry of Health in Singapore calls for this agency to (1) promote good health and reduce illness, (2) ensure access to excellent and affordable health care, and (3) pursue medical excellence. It has primarily performed according to the missions laid out and achieved good health outcomes for Singaporeans via good governance and policymaking.

The Ministry of Health works through three main groups: the Policy and Corporate Group, Operational Groups, and Professional Cluster. The Ministry publishes guidelines for healthcare professionals and formulates legislation to regulate the healthcare sector, both public and private.[9] This includes the Private Hospital and Medical Clinics Act,[10] which governs the minimal quality to which private medical institutions must adhere. During the COVID-19 pandemic, the Ministry of Health took the lead in providing timely communication and regulations to safeguard Singaporeans' health.

In terms of management, the Ministry of Health has organized the public healthcare sector into three health clusters to achieve economies of scale while catering to local demand for healthcare services. These health clusters include both tertiary hospitals and primary care clinics. The chief executives of these health clusters are appointed only with approval by the Ministry of Health. The CEOs of the individual hospitals report to the cluster group CEO but still enjoy a fair degree of operational autonomy.[11]

The Ministry of Health also publishes timely white papers to communicate the various healthcare strategic initiatives to Singaporeans, resulting in strong trust between the government and its people. In addition, total hospital bill sizes and healthcare spending budgets are published on the Ministry's website to promote transparency between the Ministry and the citizens it serves. The healthcare budget is also debated in parliamentary sessions every year. The Ministry has also implemented a performance measurement framework (Public Hospital Scorecard) to review the performance of the public acute care hospitals under its management.

The Ministry of Health created additional organizations to support the different health clusters. The Ministry of Health Holdings (MOHH) was created to manage human resources/talents, conduct centralized procurement, and plan and set up new healthcare facilities. MOHH created the Integrated Health Information Systems (IHiS) to manage all IT systems across the public health clusters while at the same time allowing private healthcare facilities to access the National Electronic Health Record depository. The Agency for Integrated Care (AIC) was created to integrate primary care, long-term care, and mental health care.

Overall, the governance of healthcare services in Singapore is excellent and plays a strong role in building a successful healthcare system. The critical values in its governance are transparency, efficiency, and accountability, which have resulted in much trust from Singaporeans.

Resource Generation

As Singapore's population ages and more medical services are needed, the size of the health workforce has increased substantially. The number of doctors increased by 50% from 10,200 in 2012 to more than 15,000 today. The number of nurses increased by 20% during the same period from around 34,500 in 2012 to about 43,000 today. This increment in the healthcare workforce was made possible by increased availability of healthcare-related education at tertiary institutions and a third medical school being established in Singapore.

The healthcare facilities in Singapore are world-class. The Singapore General Hospital is ranked by *Newsweek* as the ninth best hospital in the world,[12] and many national institutions, such as the Singapore National Eye Center, are among the largest in the Asia Pacific region. Careful planning by the Singapore government has ensured acute care hospitals and community clinics are distributed across the island nation and managed via its three healthcare clusters. These hospitals are all equipped with state-of-the-art medical equipment. The quality of medical care in Singapore is further evident by the large influx of international patients from around the region, mainly seeking treatment from the world-class private hospitals in Singapore. Primary care clinics are easily accessible by patients and distributed across Singapore; they include more than 2,000 private GP clinics and 20 public polyclinics.

Electronic health record systems are well established in the tertiary care setting but need to improve in the primary care sector due to the latter's fragmented nature. However, the government has established an initiative for a National Electronic Health Record system that allows patient data to be recorded and archived in a national depository. Many primary care clinics have signed up for the program, but participation has yet to reach 100%.

Overall, healthcare resources in Singapore are excellent, and more initiatives are being put forward for future improvements.

Financing

Healthcare financing is one of the core strengths of the Singapore healthcare system. The previous sections described the 3M model—Medisave, MediShield, and MediFund—which has been extensively studied globally. This scheme results in relatively low government expenditures for healthcare services compared with other OECD countries, as the bulk of healthcare expenses are borne by individuals via their Medisave account or out-of-pocket expenses.

While the 3M model performs well for acute care and inpatient services, primary care expenditures are paid for mainly out of pocket, which can be difficult for low-income families. The government has sought to reduce the burden on low-income families by introducing the Community Health Assist (CHAS) scheme, which allows subsidies to be used in private GP clinics. In addition, older-generation patients are eligible for other schemes that can further subsidize their primary care expenditure, such as those covering chronic illness management.

The government health expenditure in 2020 was S$15.2 billion, or 3% of GDP.[13] The total Medisave balance (individual savings account for medical services) stands at S$110 billion; roughly S$1 billion is withdrawn annually (year 2020 actuals). The average balance per Medisave account is around S$29,600. Although these numbers are relatively healthy, there is a trend toward increasing healthcare expenditures, and the Ministry of Health is introducing strategies to slow down healthcare expenditure growth.

Overall, healthcare financing in Singapore is well funded and can handle the needs of most of its citizens. However, the system is designed based on personal responsibility (via mandatory savings) and requires out-of-pocket expenses, which may burden low-income households. The Ministry of Health recognizes these challenges and constantly seeks ways to help low-income families and other priority groups dealing with chronic illnesses requiring long-term healthcare spending.

Service Delivery

In the three sectors of public health, primary care, and tertiary care, Singapore performed well in all three areas, but especially in public health and tertiary care. Healthcare services are easily accessible, and the system is fair toward its citizens. The government emphasizes smoking cessation programs, vaccination campaigns, and health promotion.

Healthcare service delivery in the public sector is organized into three clusters that provide care for patients in those clusters. Each cluster includes its own acute care hospitals and primary care polyclinics for better patient access. In addition, many private GP clinics supplement the essential medical services their patients need. Currently, the private sector provides 80% of primary care services in Singapore, while the public sector provides 80% of the acute care services in Singapore.

However, primary care in Singapore can be improved by helping patients develop the habit of seeking a continuum of care from one family doctor. To encourage this behavior, the government started strategic initiatives to better integrate primary care clinics with the public sector via IT systems. Also, it launched programs for every citizen to be enrolled with a family doctor. Its plans are highlighted in the HealthierSG 2022 master plan, where the government emphasizes disease prevention and management of chronic illness more strongly than in the past.

Other Factors Affecting Health in Singapore

The World Health Organization defines the social determinants of health as "the non-medical factors that influence health outcomes."[14] It provides examples such as income protection, education, job security, work-life conditions, childhood development, housing, etc. These are the conditions in which people are born, grow, work, live, and age that shape their lives and health outcomes. WHO suggests that social determinants of health account for 30% to 55% of health outcomes.

Housing Policy

The unique housing policy in Singapore is one area where it differs from many other parts of the world and has contributed to its population's health outcomes. Singapore has one of the highest home ownership rates in the world: 90% of its population owns their homes today, compared with 9% in 1959.[15] In addition, more than 80% of its citizens live in public housing. In comparison, places with notable public housing policies, such as Hong Kong, Sweden, the Netherlands, and Austria, have public housing rates ranging between 25% and 30%.

The Housing and Development Board (HDB) is a government agency in Singapore responsible for public housing. The HDB was established in 1960 to provide affordable and quality housing for the people of Singapore. In the 1970s, the HDB introduced the Home Ownership Scheme (HOS), enabling Singaporeans to buy their homes at subsidized prices. This policy helped create a homeownership culture in Singapore, and today, over 80% of Singapore's population lives in public housing provided by the HDB.

In the 1980s and 1990s, the HDB shifted its focus toward improving the quality of public housing and upgrading older estates. This included initiatives such as the Home Improvement Program (HIP), which provided subsidies for residents to renovate their homes, and the Main Upgrading Program (MUP), which aimed at improving older estates' physical and social infrastructure. During this time, the Ethnic Integration Policy was introduced, whereby ethnic quotas were implemented for each HDB estate, thereby increasing social integration as children of different races would be neighbors and attend school together. This policy, while draconian (the ethnic quotas are imposed by the government against the free will of the market and its people) to a certain extent, allows for multiple ethnic groups to live together, thereby increasing social inclusion and nondiscrimination, another aspect of social determinants of health described by WHO.

Mwoka et al. (2021) collected evidence from Singapore, the United Kingdom, and Kenya. By comparing the three nations, they provided evidence showing that a sound housing policy was instrumental in good health outcomes.[16] Compared with the United Kingdom and Kenya, Singapore's affordable housing and convenient financing tools reduced the mental illness and stress that comes with the inability to meet housing goals (in the case of the United Kingdom). Meanwhile, its built environment reduced infant mortality rates compared with housing settlements in Kenya, which lack adequate access to safe water and sanitation where 61% of all Kenyan households reside.

Education

The Singapore education system is widely recognized for its outstanding achievements and is often regarded as one of the world's best. This system plays a crucial role in shaping Singaporean society, and its impact on the social determinants of health is noteworthy.

The education system is characterized by its strong emphasis on academic excellence, discipline, and rigorous standards. It follows a meritocratic approach that aims to identify and nurture the talents of every student. The Ministry of Education oversees the system and ensures quality education for all at a negligible cost to Singaporeans.

The system's success is evident through its exceptional performance in global education rankings. Singaporean students consistently achieve top scores in international assessments, such as the Programme for International Student Assessment (PISA) and Trends in International Mathematics and Science Study (TIMSS). This demonstrates the system's effectiveness in providing students with the necessary knowledge and skills to compete globally.

One of the strengths of the system lies in its high-quality teaching force. Singaporean teachers undergo rigorous training and professional development, ensuring they are well equipped to deliver effective and engaging lessons. The student–teacher ratio is kept low, allowing for personalized attention and support for every student.

Regarding social determinants of health, the Singapore education system plays a crucial role in promoting health equity. Its strong emphasis on equal opportunities for all students, regardless of their socioeconomic background, helps reduce disparities in access to education. The system supports students from disadvantaged backgrounds, ensuring they have equal opportunities to succeed academically.

Moreover, the Singapore education system promotes the importance of a healthy lifestyle and physical well-being. Physical education is mandatory, and schools often organize various sports and fitness programs. Health education is also integrated into the curriculum, promoting nutrition, hygiene, and mental health awareness. Schools also provide dental services and free vaccinations to students. Every student has a "health booklet" to allow parents to follow the child's developmental milestones.

Environmental Public Health Act

The Environmental Public Health Act (EPHA) was enacted in Singapore in 1969 to ensure public health and sanitation. It standardized the code governing public health–related matters such as hygiene standards of eating places, markets, and public areas and creating public cleaning services. It was modeled after similar initiatives in the United Kingdom, New Zealand, and New York. One example of the actions taken by the act was the requirement for food stall handlers to undergo regular medical examinations and immunization.

Since then, the EPHA has undergone several revisions to address emerging public health concerns and to keep up with changing societal and technological trends.

Here is a timeline of the significant revisions and amendments made to the EPHA in Singapore:

- **1977:** The EPHA was amended to give the authorities more power to control the use and disposal of hazardous substances. The law was also extended to cover hazardous substances' import, export, and transit.
- **1984:** The EPHA was amended to incorporate new regulations for food hygiene, food establishment licensing, and food safety standards enforcement.
- **1990:** The EPHA was amended to regulate toxic industrial waste disposal and set up a licensing system for toxic waste disposal facilities.
- **1997:** The EPHA was amended to provide for the licensing of public swimming pools and establish water quality and safety standards.
- **2008:** The EPHA was amended to introduce new provisions for controlling smoking in public places, including the prohibition of smoking in all air-conditioned public areas, such as shopping malls, offices, and restaurants.
- **2014:** The EPHA was amended to enhance food safety standards and to establish a risk-based approach to food safety regulation.

Overall, the EPHA has evolved to address emerging public health concerns and keep up with changing societal and technological trends in Singapore. The government has demonstrated a commitment to ensuring the health and well-being of its citizens through implementing these regulatory measures.

Current and Emerging Issues and Challenges

According to a white paper released by the Singapore Ministry of Health ("White Paper on Healthier SG"), Singapore faces several healthcare challenges. These include:

1. Aging of the population
2. Rising impact of chronic diseases

In 2022, 18.4% of Singaporean citizens were aged 65 and above, an increase from 11.1% 10 years ago. Over the same span, the number of citizens aged 80 and above increased by more than 70%, and this group makes up 3.7% of the population today. By 2030, approximately a quarter of the country's citizens, or 23.8%, will be 65 years and above.[17] This creates more financial pressure on Singaporeans and the government to provide better care for its aging population.

Equally worrying for Singapore is the rising prevalence of chronic diseases such as hypertension and hyperlipidemia, which affect 32% and 37% of the Singaporean population, respectively. Between 2009 and 2019, cardiovascular diseases accounted for one-third of the deaths in Singapore every year.[18]

HealthierSG

To address these healthcare challenges, the Singapore Ministry of Health released a HealthierSG white paper to initiate actions that could have future benefits for Singaporeans' health. There are five features highlighted in this white paper: (1) using family doctors to deliver preventive care for residents; (2) developing health plans that include lifestyle adjustments, regular health screenings, and appropriate vaccinations; (3) activating community partners to support residents in leading healthier lifestyles; (4) national enrollment of family doctor scheme; and (5) setting up necessary enablers such as IT systems, manpower development plan, and financing policies to make HealthierSG work.

Unmet Primary Care Needs

Singapore's current primary care system is optimized for episodic visits and primarily based on a fee-for-service model,[19] albeit supplemented by some government subsidies. This is ill suited for the expected increase in noncommunicable disease management, where quality and consistency are essential. Therefore, there will be a need to develop longitudinal family doctor–patient relationships, and the government is pushing to get everyone enrolled with a family doctor in the future. In addition, connections should be built within and beyond primary care, such as links to hospitals, long-term care services, or community activities to encourage the maintenance of healthier lifestyles.

Healthcare Financing

Minister of Health, Ong Ye Kung, in a parliamentary speech in May 2023, acknowledged that Singapore had done well to "deliver good health outcomes given what we are spending," which was 4% of the GDP. However, he also noted that the government only covered 43% of healthcare costs in 2019, much lower than the average of 75% for OECD countries.[20] This meant that out-of-pocket healthcare expenses were high, approximately 40% of Singapore's total healthcare expenditure as estimated in 2015.[21,22]

With the population aging rapidly and getting sicker, healthcare expenditures have quickly increased. Hence, there is a need to rethink the financing model because the existing 3M model is mainly designed for inpatient services, and costs for long-term outpatient care are expected to increase. The government has taken steps to provide more subsidies in the future for private GP services and long-term care facilities, which would be welcome, especially for lower-income families who could not afford the out-of-pocket healthcare expenses.

COVID-19 Pandemic

Singapore's management of the COVID-19 pandemic has been widely praised for its effectiveness and proactive approach. Through its multidisciplinary task force, the Singaporean government implemented a series of measures and strategies to curb the spread of the virus and protect its population. This section provides an overview of the various phases of Singapore's COVID-19 management, focusing on crucial government task force press releases. The chronology illustration of the pandemic response is shown in **Figure 24-4**.

Phase 0: Pre-Crisis Background

Before the COVID-19 pandemic, Singapore experienced a similar outbreak during the SARS incident in 2003. Back then, 238 patients were infected, resulting in 33 deaths. Singapore introduced several pandemic management capabilities after SARS. The Disease Outbreak Response System Condition (DORSCON) framework was established. The framework serves as the foundation for the national response to any outbreaks. It is separated into four levels of incremental severity (Green, Yellow, Orange, and Red) based on the disease's risk and public health impact. In addition, the National Centre of Infectious Diseases (NCID) was built and became operational in 2019, right before the outbreak of COVID-19. The professional workforce and training of healthcare workers related to outbreak response was expanded, with the number of infectious physicians rising from 11 in 2003 to 73 in 2020.[23]

Phase 1: Containment and Contact Tracing

On January 23, 2020, Singapore confirmed the first case of COVID-19 in a tourist from Wuhan who had arrived on January 20, 2020. The government quickly formed a "Multi-Ministry Taskforce on Wuhan Coronavirus" comprising several cabinet appointment holders from different ministries and co-chaired by the then Minister of Health, Gan Kim Yong, and Minister of National Development, Heng Swee Keat. The goal of the task force was to (1) direct the national whole-of-government response to the novel coronavirus outbreak, (2) coordinate the community response to protect Singaporeans and stay vigilant against the spread of the disease, and (3) work with the international community to respond to the outbreak.

The task force maintained a communication channel with the public, using media tools such as WhatsApp, telegram, Facebook, and television to disseminate information quickly and transparently, thus reducing the amount of fake news circulated on Singapore social media. Such fake news included rumors spread via social media that Singapore was running out of face masks, train stations were closed for disinfection, and schools were closed due to the widespread of COVID-19 infections.

At this time, Singapore focused on containment and contact tracing. The government swiftly implemented strict border control measures, enforced quarantine for incoming travelers, and conducted extensive contact tracing to identify and isolate potential cases. A ban on entry and transit by visitors from mainland China was imposed to stop or slow down the spread of the disease. Researchers lauded Singapore's early efforts in identifying the number of COVID-19 cases from visitors as the gold standard.

On February 7, 2020, the government raised its national risk assessment level, DORSCON, from "yellow" to "orange" to alert the public of the possibility of a local pandemic. On March 4, the travel ban was expanded to South Korea, Iran, and northern Italy, before extending to the whole of Italy, France, Spain, and Germany from March 15, 2020, onward.

The first two local COVID-related deaths occurred on March 21, 2020, and the government began to struggle to contain the spread of the virus. Initiatives to reopen schools on March 23 were stopped, and the government put in more stringent measures to deny entry to all visitors and banned all public events and all mass gathering.

Singaporeans with respiratory symptoms were encouraged to seek treatment at Public Health Preparedness Clinics (PHPCs), a network of over 800 primary health clinics (mostly private clinics) that provided subsidized care and medical leave. This

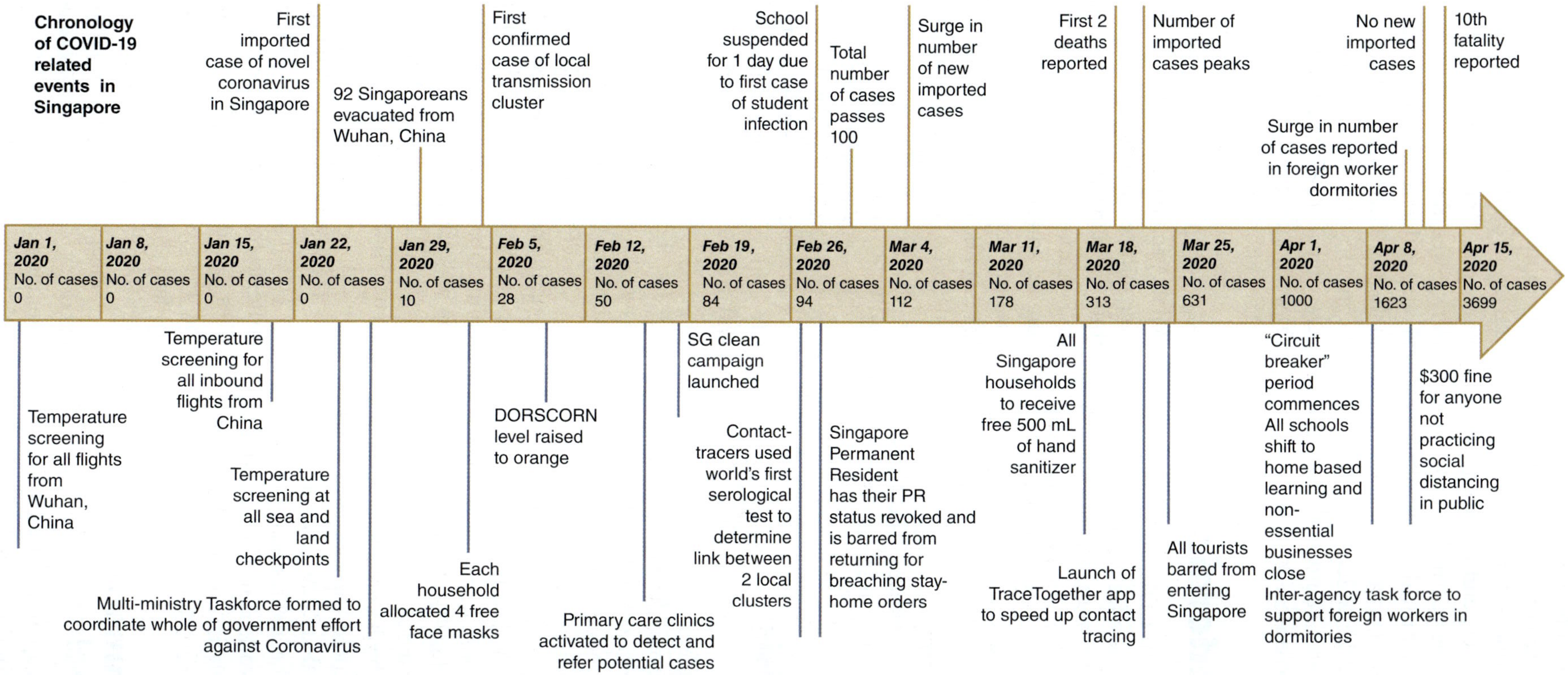

Figure 24-4 Timeline of coronavirus actions taken in Singapore, January–April 2020

Reproduced from Ansah JP, Matchar DB, Shao Wei SL, et al. The effectiveness of public health interventions against COVID-19: lessons from the Singapore experience. *PLoS One.* 2021;16:e0248742. https://journals.plos.org/plosone/article?id=10.1371/journal.pone.0248742.

allowed patients with possible mild cases of COVID-19 to rest at home and reduce community transmission. Patients requiring more care were sent to NCID for more specialized treatment.

Before April 3, 2020, the government had discouraged citizens from wearing face masks unless they were unwell. However, on this day, the government reversed course and said that it would no longer discourage people who were well from wearing masks.[24]

Phase 2: Circuit Breaker Measures

As the number of COVID-19 cases increased in April 2020, Singapore entered the "Circuit Breaker" phase; it began on April 7 and lasted until May 4, 2020. The government announced a series of stringent measures to curb the spread of the virus, including the closure of nonessential businesses, remote work arrangements, and restrictions on social gatherings. The Ministry of Health and the Task Force issued regular press releases to update the public on the evolving situation, the rationale behind the measures, and the importance of collective responsibility.

During this period, while local transmission rates remained low, there were many COVID-related cases among the foreign workers. These workers are housed in packed dormitories with less-than-ideal living conditions. As the short- and long-term effects of COVID-19 were not well understood during that time, Singaporeans were worried about the thousands of new cases discovered and the impact it could have on them if locals outside of dormitories started getting infected. The Singapore government's response was quick and assertive in dealing with the problem: It performed intensive testing of these migrant workers and temporarily isolated the dormitories for migrant workers.

On April 14, 2020, the government mandated all citizens to wear masks when leaving home. COVID-19 testing was used as a tool to reduce the rate of infection within the population. Such tests were conducted systematically in all healthcare facilities for patients showing symptoms of respiratory infections or those with travel histories and their close contacts. Individuals who tested positive were immediately isolated and interviewed for contact tracing. Contact tracing operations were led by the Ministry of Health and aided by teams from hospitals, the Singapore Armed Forces, Certis security offices, the Government Technology Agency, and the Singapore Police Force.[25]

Phase 3: Gradual Reopening and Safe Management Measures

In June 2020, Singapore transitioned into the third phase, which focused on gradually reopening the economy while maintaining strict safe management measures. The government introduced a risk-based approach, allowing certain industries to resume operations under specific conditions.

Between June 2 and 19, 2020, people from the same household were allowed to visit their parents or grandparents in groups of two. Later, the group size was expanded to five as part of the reopening measures, and families could receive five visitors at any time.

In early 2021, there was a rise in cases related to the Delta variant. The policy was changed so that each household could host only eight unique visitors a day, rather than at any time. This group size was later reduced to five people, and then to two people in May 2021 as cases increased.

During this period, COVID-19 vaccinations started to roll out for Singaporeans. By February 2021, all 20 polyclinics nationwide began offering COVID-19 vaccinations, with another 40 vaccination centers ready to be set up with a capacity of around 120,000 vaccinations per day for this country of 5 million people. The first set of vaccines were by Sinovac. Subsequently, all other vaccines (e.g., Moderna, Pfizer-BioNTech, Noravax) were used in Singapore once they were available. The government launched a national vaccination program, prioritizing older citizens who were at higher risk for COVID-19–related complications and essential workers such as healthcare workers, financial service professionals, and public transport workers. Press releases from the Ministry of Health highlighted the importance of vaccination, provided vaccine supply updates, and addressed vaccine safety and efficacy concerns. Vaccination was free, and the vaccination campaign was very successful due to the willingness of Singaporeans to be vaccinated and the ready stockpile of vaccines procured by the Singapore government. By the end of 2021, around 83% of the population had been vaccinated against COVID-19.

The Task Force regularly communicated updates on the various reopening process, guidelines for businesses, and public health advisories to ensure a smooth transition.

Phase 4: Living with COVID-19

With the availability of vaccines, Singapore entered Phase 4 of its COVID-19 management strategy. The Task Force also emphasized the need to adapt to the new normal and continue practicing safe management measures despite the vaccination campaign.

On April 22, 2022, Singapore announced major easing of COVID-19 rules, signaling the start of Singapore's decision to "co-exist with COVID-19."[26] All group size restrictions for social gatherings were removed, and mask wearing was no longer mandatory outdoors though still required indoors. All workers were allowed to return to work, up from the limit of 75% of those who could work from home. Fully vaccinated travelers to Singapore were no longer required a pre-departure PCR test, a change from the requirement to take a test within 48 hours of departure for Singapore. Safe management tools such as TraceTogether and SafeEntry (for vaccine status monitoring) were no longer required to enter restaurants and other public places. This also meant that contact tracing activities were stopped. In addition, COVID-19 vaccination centers were reduced and eventually ceased their operations.

By the end of 2022, all COVID-19–related measures were eliminated.

Conclusion for Singapore COVID-19 Management

Between 2020 and the end of 2022, a total of 2.202 million Singaporeans were infected with COVID-19, from which 2.196 million Singaporeans recovered and 1,711 patients died. That translates to a mortality rate of 0.07%. According to the Johns Hopkins Coronavirus Resource Center, Singapore had the second lowest COVID-19 case-fatality rate globally, behind Bhutan.[27] This success can be attributed to several factors. During the early stages of the COVID-19 pandemic (January–December 2020), strict social distancing measures and intensive contact tracing plus testing were taken to reduce the rate of increase of infections. Upon the rollout of the vaccination campaign in early 2021, more than 83% of its population became vaccinated by the end of 2021, which reduced the number of patients with severe complications from COVID-19. Patients with mild symptoms were encouraged to stay home so as not to overwhelm the hospital system, and only patients with acute or serious symptoms were hospitalized. This way, proper medical care could be used for patients with severe disease, which further reduced the mortality rate of COVID-19. Collectively, these factors contributed to Singapore's successful management of the COVID-19 pandemic.

A proactive and systematic approach marked Singapore's response to the COVID-19 pandemic. The government's task force, through regular press releases, played a crucial role in keeping the public informed about the evolving situation, the rationale behind various measures, and the importance of collective responsibility.

Conclusion

The Singapore healthcare system has achieved good outcomes at relatively low costs since its founding in 1965. The results were a combination of good governance, excellent policymaking, and other factors such as great education and housing policy, including a population that was relatively young in its short history. As the population ages rapidly, Singapore would need to reinvent its healthcare system to meet future challenges, a task its team of policymakers and healthcare workers have accomplished many times in the past.

References

1. World Health Organization. *World Health Statistics 2022: Monitoring Health for the SDGs, Sustainable Development Goals*. Geneva, Switzerland: World Health Organization; 2022.
2. Ministry of Health Singapore, MOH 2012 Committee of Supply Speech. *Healthcare 2020: Improving Accessibility, Quality and Affordability for Tomorrow's Challenges*. 2012. Accessed July 2, 2023. https://www.moh.gov.sg/news-highlights/details/moh-2012-committee-of-supply-speech-healthcare-2020-improving-accessibility-quality-and-affordability-for-tomorrow-s-challenges-(part-2-of-2).
3. Singapore Department of Statistics. Death and life expectancy. Accessed July 2, 2023. https://www.singstat.gov.sg/find-data/search-by-theme/population/death-and-life-expectancy/latest-data.
4. World Health Organization. *World Health Statistics 2023: Monitoring Health for the SDGs, Sustainable Development Goals*. Geneva, Switzerland: World Health Organization; 2023.
5. Ramesh M, Bali AS. The healthcare system in Singapore. Accessed April 4, 2024. https://lkyspp.nus.edu.sg/docs/default-source/gia-documents/the-healthcare-system-in-singapore-with-graphics.pdf?sfvrsn=f0446c0a_2.

6. Ministry of Health. About us. Accessed March 23, 2023. https://www.moh.gov.sg/about-moh.
7. Ministry of Health Singapore. Health facilities. 2022. Accessed March 23, 2023. https://www.moh.gov.sg/resources-statistics/singapore-health-facts/health-facilities.
8. Lee B, Lim J. Commentary: Singapore needs more doctors, but setting up a fourth medical school isn't the answer. *CNA*. 2022. Accessed March 23, 2023. https://www.channelnewsasia.com/commentary/singapore-doctor-get-medical-school-healthcare-system-3138696.
9. Ministry of Health Singapore. Legislation. Accessed July 2, 2023. https://www.moh.gov.sg/policies-and-legislation.
10. Ministry of Health of Singapore. Guidelines under the Private Hospitals and Medical Clinics Act. 2007. Accessed July 2, 2023. https://www.moh.gov.sg/docs/librariesprovider5/licensing-terms-and-conditions/guidelines-under-the-private-hospitals-and-medical-clinics-act-2007-(supercedes-year-1993's-edition).pdf.
11. Quah E, Neo BS. Evolving the governance of public healthcare institutions: a continuous improvement journey. In: *Singapore's Health Care System: What 50 Years Have Achieved*. Singapore: World Scientific; 2016:57-73.
12. The world's best hospitals. *Newsweek*, 2023. Accessed July 2, 2023. https://www.newsweek.com/rankings/worlds-best-hospitals-2023.
13. Ministry of Health Singapore. Government health expenditure and healthcare financing. Accessed July 2, 2023. https://www.moh.gov.sg/resources-statistics/singapore-health-facts/government-health-expenditure-and-healthcare-financing.
14. World Health Organization. Social determinants of health. Accessed March 20, 2023. https://www.who.int/health-topics/social-determinants-of-health#tab=tab_1.
15. Jha A. But what about Singapore? Lessons from the best public housing program in the world. World Bank. Accessed March 20, 2023. https://blogs.worldbank.org/sustainablecities/what-about-singapore-lessons-best-public-housing-program-world.
16. Mwoka M, Biermann O, Ettman CK, et al. Housing as a social determinant of health: evidence from Singapore, the UK, and the Kenya: the 3-D Commission. *J Urban Health*. 2021;98:S15-S30.
17. Chin SF. S'pore's population ageing rapidly: nearly 1 in 5 citizens is 65 years and older. *The Straits Times*, 28 Sep 2022. Accessed April 4, 2024. https://www.straitstimes.com/singapore/singapores-population-ageing-rapidly-184-of-citizens-are-65-years-and-older.
18. Ministry of Health. Principal causes of death. 2021. Accessed March 20, 2023. https://www.moh.gov.sg/resources-statistics/singapore-health-facts/principal-causes-of-death.
19. Yong SE, Lee CE, How CH. Population health for Singapore: does primary care need strengthening. *Singapore Med J*. 2023:1-2.
20. Ng A. Singapore must ensure healthcare fiscal burden does not spiral out of control: Ong Ye Kung. *Channel News Asia*, May 10, 2023. Accessed July 2, 2023. https://www.channelnewsasia.com/singapore/ong-ye-kung-health-ministry-healthcare-costs-spending-3478476.
21. Tan CC, Lam CS, Matchar DB, et al. Singapore's health-care system: key features, challenges, and shifts," *Lancet*. 2021;398:1091-1104.
22. Ministry of Health Singapore. Healthcare services and facilities. Accessed March 23, 2023. https://www.moh.gov.sg/home/our-healthcare-system/healthcare-services-and-facilities.
23. Lin JR, Lee TH, Chien BL. From SARS to COVID-19: the Singapore journey. *Med J Austr.* 2020;11(1):497-502.
24. Goh T. New Covid-19 rules kick in: timeline of S'pore's measures over the last 2 years. *The Straits Times*. 2022. Accessed July 2, 2023. https://www.straitstimes.com/singapore/two-years-of-twists-and-turns-a-timeline-of-singapores-covid-19-measures.
25. Lai HS, Tang QY, Kurup A, Thevendran G. The experience of contract tracing in Singapore in the control of COVID-19: highlighting the use of digital technology. *Intl Orthopaed.* 2021;45:65-69.
26. Goh YH. Singapore announces major easing of Covid-19 rules from April 26: what you need to know. *The Straits Times*. 2022. Accessed July 2, 2023. https://www.straitstimes.com/singapore/singapore-announces-major-easing-of-covid-19-rules-from-april-26-what-you-need-to-know.
27. Johns Hopkins Coronavirus Resource Center. Mortality analyses. 2023. Accessed July 2, 2023. https://coronavirus.jhu.edu/data/mortality.

CHAPTER 25

Australia

Gary E. Day

Country Description

Table 25-1 Australia

Nationality	Noun: Australian(s) Adjective: Australian
Ethnic groups	English 33%, Australian 29.9%, Irish 9.5%, Scottish 8.6%, Italian 4.4%, German 4%, Indian 3.1%, Australian Aboriginal 2.9%, Greek 1.7%, unspecified 4.7% (2021 est.)
Religions	Roman Catholic 20%, Protestant 18.1% (Anglican 9.8%, Uniting Church 2.6%, Presbyterian and Reformed 1.6%, Baptist 1.4%, Pentecostal 1%, other Protestant 1.7%), other Christian 3.5%, Muslim 3.2%, Hindu 2.7%, Buddhist 2.4%, Orthodox 2.3% (Eastern Orthodox, 2.1%, Oriental Orthodox 0.2%), other 2.1%, none 38.4%, unspecified 7.3% (2021 est.)
Language	English 72%, Mandarin 2.7%, Arabic 1.4%, Vietnamese. 1.3%, Cantonese 1.2%, other 15.7%, unspecified 5.7% (2021 est.)
Literacy[#]	Below Level 1: 3.7% Level 1: 10% Level 2: 30% Level 3: 38% Level 4: 14% Level 5: 1.2%
Government type	Federal parliamentary democracy
Date of independence	January 1, 1901 (federation of U.K. colonies)
Gross domestic product (GDP) per capita	64,9600 USD (2023 est.)
[*]Unemployment rate	3.6% (2023 est.)
Natural hazards	Cyclones along the coast; severe droughts; forest fires

Table 25-1 **Australia**

Environment: current issues	Soil erosion from overgrazing, industrial development, urbanization, and poor farming practices; soil salinity rising because of the use of poor-quality water; desertification; clearing for agricultural purposes threatens the natural habitat of many unique animal and plant species; the Great Barrier Reef off the northeast coast, the largest coral reef in the world, is threatened by increased shipping and its popularity as a tourist site; limited natural freshwater resources
Population	26,461,166 (2023 est.)
Age structure	0–14 years: 18.43% (male 2,515,636/female 2,359,859) 15–64 years: 64.89% (male 8,602,204/female 8,568,004) 65 years and over: 16.69% (male 2,034,383/female 2,381,080) (2023 est.)
Median age	Total: 37.5 years Male: 36.5 years Female: 38.5 years (2020 est.)
Population growth rate	1.19% (2023 est.)
Birth rate	12.23 births/1,000 population (2023 est.)
Death rate	6.76 deaths/1,000 population (2023 est.)
Net migration rate	6.39 migrants/1,000 population (2023 est.)
Sex ratio	At birth: 1.06 male/female 0–14 years: 1.07 male/female 15–64 years: 1.00 male/female 65 years and over: 0.85 male/female Total population: 0.99 male/female (2023 est.)
Infant mortality rate	Total: 2.96 deaths/1,000 live births Male: 3.2 deaths/1,000 live births Female: 2.71 deaths/1,000 live births (2023 est.)
Life expectancy at birth	Total population: 3.28 years Male: 81.14 years Female: 85.54 (2023 est.)
Total fertility rate	1.73 children born/woman (2023 est.)
HIV/AIDS adult prevalence rate[++]	0.12% (2022 est.)
Number of people living with HIV/AIDS[+++]	29,090 (2020 est.)
HIV/AIDS deaths[**]	Less than 100 (2021 est.)

USD = U.S. dollar.

Data from Australia. *The World Factbook*. 2023 ed. Central Intelligence Agency. Accessed June 5, 2023. https://www.cia.gov/the-world-factbook/countries/australia/.

*Australian Bureau of Statistics. Labour force, Australia. Accessed June 5, 2023. https://www.abs.gov.au/statistics/labour/employment-and-unemployment#:~:text=Labour%20Force%2C%20Australia,employment%20increased%20to%2013%2C878%2C900.

#Australian Bureau of Statistics. Programme for the international assessment of adult competencies, Australia, 2011–2012. Catalogue No. 4228.0. September 10, 2013. Accessed June 5, 2023. http://www.abs.gov.au/ausstats/abs@.nsf/Lookup/4228.

[0]Main+Features202011-12

^International Monetary Fund. GDP per capital, current prices. Accessed June 5, 2023. https://www.imf.org/external/datamapper/NGDPDPC@WEO/OEMDC/ADVEC/AUS.

++Trading Economics. Australia: prevalence of HIV, total (% of population ages 15–49). Accessed June 5, 2023. https://tradingeconomics.com/australia/prevalence-of-hiv-total-percent-of-population-ages-15-49-wb-data.html.

+++Multicultural HIV and Hepatitis Service. HIV in Australia (2021). Accessed June 5, 2023. https://mhahs.org.au/index.php/en/media-page/statistics/hiv-statistics.

**World Data Atlas. Australia: AIDS estimated deaths. Accessed June 5, 2023. https://knoema.com/atlas/Australia/topics/Health/Risk-factors/AIDS-estimated-deaths.

History

Australia is a vast, ancient island continent. It was first settled more than 50,000 years ago by migrating tribes making the short trip across from Southeast Asia to the northern parts of the continent. These Aboriginal and Torres Strait Islander peoples spread across the land, including the island of Tasmania to the south, and are thought to have numbered around 350,000 at the time of the first European contact in the 17th century.[1]

After a period of exploration by Dutch, French, and English explorers, the eastern parts of Australia were claimed in 1770 by Captain James Cook in the name of Great Britain. Initial settlement quickly followed. The first fleet of 11 ships carrying 700 convicts and 400 guards and officials arrived in January 1788 to establish the penal colony of New South Wales. Five more self-governing British crown colonies were then established during the early part of the 19th century. On January 1, 1901, after a countrywide referendum, the six colonies federated, and the Commonwealth of Australia was formed.

Australia's history since British settlement in 1788 has been marked by several important events. The discovery of gold in the early 1850s brought many immigrants to Australia from Britain, Ireland, Europe, North America, and China. This and subsequent gold discoveries heralded a period of considerable prosperity, population growth, and spread. Involvement in two world wars and in other major conflicts of the 20th century, notably in Korea and Vietnam, while creating a large loss of life (mainly young men) and a strain on national resources, helped create a sense of national unity and identity.

Colonization, however, severely disrupted Aboriginal society and economy. Epidemic disease caused an immediate loss of life, and the occupation of land by settlers and the restriction of Aboriginal and Torres Strait Islanders to reserves disrupted their ability to support themselves. This combination of factors had such an impact that by the 1930s, only an estimated 80,000 of this population remained in Australia.[1]

A massive program of European immigration after World War II—some 2 million people arriving between 1948 and 1975—saw Australia's population grow substantially, helping to fuel a lengthy period of economic prosperity and growth. Discovery and exploitation of the country's natural and mineral resources have underpinned Australia's development and wealth and encouraged rapid development of the agricultural, mining, and manufacturing industries up until 2009.

Most recently, a downturn in global commodities has seen sharp falls in the export earnings from Australia's natural resources, putting pressure on the revenues that underpin the national economy. Similarly, Australia is at a nexus in terms of large-scale manufacturing due to the relatively small size of the Australian market and cost of local salaries and wages compared with less expensive imports. With large-scale industries, such as motor vehicle manufacturing, ceasing in 2017, Australia is looking to redefine its economy with new markets and approaches to manufacturing and exports.

Size and Geography

Australia has a land area of some 7.7 million square kilometers. This is about twice the size of the European Union and is close to the size of the United States (excluding Alaska). Situated in the southern hemisphere between the Indian and Pacific oceans, a large proportion of the continent (around 40%) lies within the tropics (see the map in **Figure 25-1**). Distances are huge, some 4,000 kilometers from west (Steep Point in Western Australia) to east (Byron Bay in New South Wales) and 3,680 kilometers from north (Cape York in Queensland) to south (Wilson's Promontory in Victoria).

Beyond its continental shores, Australia has jurisdiction over a large number of islands, most notably the island of Tasmania, but also many others such as Melville Island (off the Northern Territory), Kangaroo Island (South Australia), King and Flinders Islands (Tasmania), the Torres Strait Islands (Queensland), and more distant islands including Macquarie Island (well south of Tasmania), Christmas Island (off Western Australia), and Lord Howe Island (off New South Wales).

Government and Political System

Since achieving nationhood in 1901, Australia has had a federal system of government whereby power is divided among the Commonwealth Government and the governments in each of Australia's six states and two territories. The form of government reflects the country's British heritage, a constitutional monarchy with the British sovereign as head of state (currently King Charles III). The monarch is represented federally by the governor-general and at state levels by state governors.

Figure 25-1 Map of Australia

Separation of powers—legislative, executive, and judicial—is embedded in the system of government. This is well described by Healy et al.[2]

The parliament makes the laws, the government implements and supervises, and the courts interpret them. The legislative power of the Commonwealth is vested in the Federal Parliament. The executive power is vested in the king and is exercisable by the governor-general as the king's representative. Judicial power is exercised by the High Court of Australia and the Federal Court of Australia, and other state courts exercising federal jurisdiction.

The Commonwealth Parliament, located in the nation's capital, Canberra (in the Australian Capital Territory), is bicameral. Elections for the two chambers, the House of Representatives (the lower house) and the Senate (the upper house), take place every 3 years. Electorates in the 150-seat lower house are allocated by population size, and members are elected for 3 years with a preferential voting system. Senators in the upper house are allocated equally across the states. Each state is represented by 12 senators and each territory by two, elected for 6 years by proportional representation. Through a system of rotation, half of the Senate retires every 3 years and is replaced (or re-elected) at the time of a general election for House of Representatives members.[3]

The political party that wins the majority of seats in the lower house is empowered to form a government. Since 1944, when the Liberal Party was formed by Robert Menzies, successive Commonwealth Governments have been formed by the Australian Labor Party and by a coalition of the Liberal and National parties. Over the last 27 years, there has been a succession of prime ministers and changes of government from Liberal/National (conservative) to Labor (progressive). Over this time, Australia has seen multiple changes of prime minister: 1996–2007, John Howard (Liberal/National); 2007–2010, Kevin Rudd (Labor); 2010–2013, Julia Gillard (Labor); 2013, Kevin Rudd (Labor); 2013–2015, Tony Abbott (Liberal/National); 2015–2018, Malcolm Turnbull (Liberal/National); 2018–2022, Scott Morrison (Liberal/National); since 2022, Anthony Albanese (Labor). As it stands in 2024, the current federal government is led by the Labor Party. From a state government perspective, only Tasmania is led by a Liberal/National government, while the remaining six states and the Australian Capital Territory are ruled by the Labor Party, with the Northern Territory ruled by the Country Liberal Party.

Australia has a compulsory voting system for all enrolled citizens aged 18 years and over, in each local, state, territory, and federal election.

Changes to the Australian Constitution to enshrine an Aboriginal voice in the federal parliament were proposed and went to a national referendum in late 2023. Across Australia, over 66% of the population voted against the change to the constitution, and the amendment was rejected.

Macroeconomics

During the 1990s and early 2000s, Australia's economy performed particularly well, boasting one of the Organisation for Economic Co-operation and Development's (OECD) fastest-growing economies during that period. Significant reforms since the 1980s, including financial deregulation, floating the exchange rate, free trade agreements, stronger trade ties with Asia, lowering of tariffs, and changes to the tax system, have helped to produce a diversified and internationally competitive economy with a per capita gross domestic product (GDP) (A$60,443/41,387 USD in 2021) on a par with several major European economies, such as the United Kingdom, Germany, and Canada.

An abundance of natural resources has enabled Australia to become a major exporter of agricultural products, minerals, metals, and fossil fuels. Much of Australia's economic focus has been on the economies of the Asia Pacific region. The boom in mining exports in recent years, driven largely by China's rapid growth, has now slowed substantially, placing pressure on natural resource revenues and national balance of payment emergence as an economic force in the world economy. The COVID-19 pandemic of 2020–2022 caused significant disruption to trade, inflation, and interest rates, both in Australia and internationally.

A short summary of Australia's most recent economic statistics reveals that (1) annual inflation dropped to 7% in Q1 of 2023 (down from a 30-year high of 7.8% in the previous quarter); (2) unemployment has been steady at 3.5% (February 2023); (3) the exchange rate has been around A$1.00 to 0.68 USD; and (4) in an effort to curb rising inflation, exacerbated by the pandemic, the Reserve Bank of Australia increased cash rates from a historic low of 0.1% (April 2022), to 4.1% (June 2023). The Reserve Bank of Australia has tightened monetary policy by increasing interest rates in an attempt to rein in inflation and a burgeoning housing market.[4] As to the future, the Australian economy is entering a phase of significant international uncertainty. The global economy, and in particular, the Asian economies (China, Japan) that Australia trades with, is slowing, and this is substantially affecting all Australians with borrowings. As a result, Australia's strong economic footing will be at risk. Australia's economic growth has slowed considerably over the last 10 years, and with the government carrying larger burdens of national debt, there will be pressure on its national credit ratings.

Demographics

Australia's population was 26,268,359 in December 2022,[5] a 1.0% increase over the previous year. Around half of this increase is due to natural increase (births less deaths) and half to net overseas migration. In the last 50 years, Australia's population has almost doubled, with an average annual growth rate of 1.4%.[6] The majority of Australians are of European descent, a reflection of early settlement from the British Isles during the colonial era and of postfederation immigration from Europe. More recently, an increasing number of immigrants to Australia are from Asia and Oceania. Australia has one of the largest proportions of immigrant populations in the world. Nearly 30% of Australians were born overseas[7] (see **Table 25-1**).

The Aboriginal and Torres Strait Islander population was 984,000 (3.8% of the total population) in 2021.[8] There has been an increase of 185,000 Aboriginal and Torres Strait Islanders (23.3%) since June 2016. Over one-third (33.1%) of the Aboriginal and Torres Strait Islander population is under 15 years of age.[8] Australia's population is highly urbanized, with two-thirds living in major cities around the coastal fringe. The state capitals are all coastal: Sydney, Melbourne, Brisbane, Adelaide, Perth, and Hobart. The exception is the nation's capital, Canberra, which is inland from Sydney but still within 100 kilometers from the coast.

Although Australia has no official state religion, the 2011 national census provides a snapshot of the religious beliefs of the population. In the census, 43.9% of Australians called themselves Christian. Followers of non-Christian religions (Buddhism, Islam, Hinduism, Judaism) accounted for 78.3% of the population, and nearly 39% were categorized as having "no religion" (which includes nontheistic beliefs, such as humanism, atheism, agnosticism, and rationalism).[9]

Brief History of the Healthcare System

Pre–World War II

A range of influences have shaped the complex system of health care now in place in Australia. From its early beginnings as a convict settlement in the colony of New South Wales in 1788, health services in Australia have evolved into a mix of public and private delivery, based largely on British and American models and shaped inevitably by unique political, economic, and social events.

The first 100 or so years of European settlement were characterized by a somewhat haphazard mix of private medical services and government-funded hospitals for convicts, paupers, and the impoverished. Support for health costs was also forthcoming from a range of benevolent and charitable organizations and friendly societies. During the 19th century, colonial governments across the country also assumed responsibility for the maintenance of public health, such as sanitation and the control of infectious diseases, through the passage of comprehensive public health acts modeled on British legislation of the time.[10]

The coming of nationhood in 1901 brought with it a federal system of government under which responsibility for the provision of health services was shared among the Commonwealth Government and the governments of the six states and two territories.

Post–World War II

Initially, the Commonwealth's health responsibilities were restricted to quarantine matters only, but an amendment to the constitution in 1946 enabled the Commonwealth to make laws with respect to (among other things) "pharmaceutical, sickness and hospital benefits, medical and dental services, but not so as to authorize any form of civil conscription." This latter clause was inserted into the amendment following pressure from the medical profession—no doubt as a response to the perceived threat of a British-style National Health Service being introduced in Australia.

Prohibition of civil conscription, interpreted to mean that medical practitioners could not be compelled to work for the government, not only helped to entrench the predominant fee-for-service payment system for medical services but also played a part in delaying the introduction of the Commonwealth-funded prescription insurance system under which all Australians have access to subsidized life-saving medicines. As a result, the Pharmaceutical Benefits Scheme (PBS), as it is known, first proposed in 1945, was not fully implemented until the Pharmaceutical Benefits Act passed through Federal Parliament in 1948. Passage of this act was not easy. It was passed twice and overturned once; it was the subject of a national referendum, constitutional change, and fierce public debate on the powers of the Commonwealth Government.

The 1946 constitutional amendment also enabled the Commonwealth Government to enter into funding agreements with the states for the provision of free public hospital care for patients in public wards. This arrangement, intended to protect patients from the high cost of hospital care, has remained the basis of hospital financing agreements between the Commonwealth and the states ever since.

The other main features of the health system (given effect through the 1953 National Health Act) were the pensioner medical services arrangements and the medical benefits scheme. The former ensured the provision of free health services to aged and invalid pensioners through agreements with the Australian Medical Association, whereas the latter subsidized medical costs for members of nonprofit health insurance schemes.

These four pillars of Australia's health system—(1) subsidized medicines, (2) Commonwealth funding for state hospitals, (3) subsidized health care for pensioners, and (4) subsidized private health insurance—remained in place largely unaltered for the next 20 years, until the introduction of a national health insurance scheme known as Medibank in 1975. Not surprisingly, the move from a system funded predominantly through subsidized private insurance to one funded predominantly by government was met with strident opposition from vested interests and political opponents alike. After rejection of the necessary legislation by the opposition-controlled

Senate in 1973 and 1974, dissolution of both houses of Parliament, and a subsequent general election, Medibank was finally enacted in July 1974 and came into operation a year later. The major elements of the new scheme were subsidized medical services for patients and free access to public hospital care through hospital cost-sharing arrangements among the Commonwealth and the state and territory governments.

From 1975, a period of conservative government ensued (the Fraser-led Liberal-National Coalition), during which several changes were made to Medibank, which saw a gradual return to greater reliance on private health insurance for medical services.[10] Election of a Labor Party government in 1983 then heralded the return of a universal tax-funded national health insurance scheme known as Medicare. The subsequent change of government in 1996 did not materially affect these arrangements, which now enjoy bipartisan political support and widespread public support.

The Current Healthcare System

The Australian healthcare system is complex, with numerous providers of services, funding arrangements, and regulatory mechanisms. The overall aim of the system is to provide all Australians with ready access to healthcare services at low cost or no cost at all. Service providers include medical practitioners (physicians), various health professionals, private and public hospitals, and government and nongovernment agencies. Responsibility for funding is shared among all levels of government and the nongovernment sector, such as private health insurers and individual consumers.

The Commonwealth Government is responsible for funding the provision of medical services, pharmaceutical benefits, residential care services for the older population, and disability services, as well as public health, research, and national information management. The state and territory governments are responsible for delivery and management of a range of health services, such as public hospital services, mental health programs, community support programs, and women's and children's services.

Facilities

Medicare is the centerpiece of Australia's health system. It is a universal, publicly funded health insurance system that allows all Australians to access affordable, high-quality health care. In place in its present form since 1984, Medicare is financed by general taxation revenue and a Medicare levy based on taxable income. Medicare provides free or subsidized treatment by medical practitioners (physicians) and grants to the states and territories to assist with the cost of running public hospitals.

The Commonwealth jointly funds public hospitals with the states so that these services are provided free of charge to patients. In 2020–2021, there were 1,354 acute care hospitals throughout Australia, of which 697 were public hospitals containing a total of 63,333 beds.[11] Available public beds represent 2.5 beds per 1,000 population. In that same year, there were 657 private hospitals in Australia, with a total of 32,000 beds.[11] Of the 13,098 available specialized mental health beds, 10,674 beds were available in specialized mental health hospital services (7,097 in public services and 3,577 in private services), and 2,424 beds in residential mental health services (1,683 public beds and 741 private beds).[12]

In 2021, there were 2,704 residential care facilities for the older population across Australia, providing over 219,105 beds.[13]

Workforce

In common with many other countries around the world, Australia is experiencing significant shortages of health professionals across the spectrum of occupations. This issue was particularly highlighted during, and following, the COVID-19 pandemic of 2020–2022. There were more than 642,000 health practitioners working in their registered professions in Australia in 2020, including 105,300 medical practitioners, 350,000 nurses and midwives, 21,500 dental practitioners, and 166,000 allied health professionals.[14] Between 2015 and 2020, the Australian registered health workforce increased by more than 110,500 professionals. The number of full-time equivalent (FTE) health professionals per 100,000 population (FTE rate) rose steadily for each professional group between 2015 and 2020.[14] **Table 25-2** shows the total numbers employed in selected health occupations, as well as FTEs per 100,000 population. Australia has a similar number of practicing medical practitioners per capita as the OECD average and a higher per capita number of practicing nurses.[15]

While the health workforce grew by over 20% from 2015 to 2020, workforce shortages will continue into the future due in part to an aging population and lower numbers coming into the health workforce due to falling fertility rates in the 1980s and 1990s. The

Table 25-2 Australia's Health Workforce, Selected Occupation, 2022

Occupation	2015 (Number of Practitioners)	2020 (Number of Practitioners)	% Change	Full Time Equivalent (FTE) per 100,000 Population (2020)
Nurses and midwives	306,487	349,589	14.1	1,191
Medical practitioners	87,999	105,293	19.7	420
Allied health	118,418	166,048	40.2	594
Dental practitioners	19,051	21,549	13.1	76

Data from Australian Institute of Health and Welfare. Health workforce. 2022. https://www.aihw.gov.au/reports/workforce/health-workforce#overview.

average age of the medical workforce in 2016 was 45.9 years. The average age of male workers was 48.3, with 33.7% of the male workforce aged 55 years and over and 14.1% aged 65 years and over. The average age of female workers was 42.5, with 17.8% of the female workforce aged 55 years and over and 4.1% aged 65 years and over.[15] In 2019, the average age of the nursing and midwifery workforce was 43.6 years.[16]

Technology and Equipment

Australia's fortunate status as a wealthy developed nation has enabled it to build and foster a health system with access to advanced, up-to-date medical and surgical technologies and health facilities. Although direct measures of the stock and spread of these technologies and equipment are not available, it is possible to identify technologies—new pharmaceutical listings, for example—and to measure their impact on health costs and (in some instances) health outcomes.

The scale of the medical technology industry in Australia is immense. In 2017, it was estimated that the total market (market size equals the total local production and imports minus exports) for medical devices in Australia was valued at $4.6 billion USD. In 2021, the amount rose to $5.5 billion USD.[17] Given these figures, regulation and monitoring have been necessary to keep health expenditures in check and to ensure that only the most effective and efficient technologies are approved for use. An earlier study by the Productivity Commission (a Commonwealth Government agency) into the impacts of advances in medical technology in Australia[18] concluded that (1) advances in medical technology in Australia have brought large benefits but have also been a major driver of increased health spending in recent years and (2) overall, advances in medical technology have provided value for money, particularly as people highly value improvements in the quality and length of life.

The predominance of public funding in Australia's health system brings with it various rationing and gatekeeping mechanisms aimed at controlling the cost impact of new technologies. The underlying philosophy of these mechanisms is to provide evidence-based health care. New drugs and medical procedures, for example, must be assessed as cost-effective before they can be subsidized for listing on the PBS or the Medicare Benefits Schedule. Indeed, Australia was the first country in the world to require drug manufacturers seeking to have a new drug listed on the PBS to demonstrate its cost-effectiveness.

Another feature of Australia's system is the drive to increase the diffusion and use of information technology at all levels of health care. There is a high-level commitment from all levels of government to encourage the uptake of information technology to improve clinical and medical practice. Most physician practices are computerized both for clinical and administrative purposes, and the introduction of a national electronic medical record is currently being implemented, albeit with a slow uptake. This is due mainly to an opt-in system for patients. This national electronic medical record is intended to reduce errors, adverse events, and duplication of services; reduce the incidence of inappropriate treatments; and allow for access across Australia. There remains considerable scope for progress.

Evaluation of the Healthcare System

Over the last decade, there has been an awareness of and emphasis on health system performance in Australia. An indication of this was the establishment in 2011 of the National Health Performance Authority (NHPA). The NHPA was responsible for monitoring, reporting, and benchmarking hospital performance and a range of other health performance measures, including national reporting on *MyHospital* and *MyHealthyCommunities*. In 2016, the NHPA ceased operations, and its role and functions were taken up by the Australian Institute of Health and Welfare and the Australian Commission on Safety and Quality in Health Care.[19] The performance criteria cover a wide range of indicators, including equity, effectiveness, appropriateness, efficiency, responsiveness, accessibility, safety, continuity, capability, and sustainability. Also high on the list in any evaluation of health system performance are measures of health status and health outcomes.

Cost

Health spending (on health goods and services) in Australia totaled nearly A$221 billion (149 billion USD) in 2020–2021 or A$8,617 (5,824 USD) per person.[20] This represents 10.7% of Australia's GDP, which puts Australia around the average in comparison with other OECD countries, including Norway, Finland, and Greece; below countries, such as the United States, Canada, Japan, and New Zealand; and above the United Kingdom. **Table 25-3** shows how spending on health services in Australia has progressed in the past decade.

In 2020–2021, health spending accounted for 10.7% of the gross domestic product (GDP) in Australia, 0.5 percentage point higher than in 2019–2020. In this reporting period, Australia spent an estimated A$220.9 billion (148.3 billion USD) on health. In real terms, this represented a 7.1% growth in spending from 2019–2020, equating to an additional A$14.6 billion (9.81 billion USD). The real growth in spending in 2020–2021 (7.1%) was higher than the average over the decade from 2010–2011 (3.4%); however, the 2020–2021 value was broadly consistent with the longer-term trend.

Funding and responsibility for Australia's health system comprise a complex blend of purchasers and providers. The system is funded predominantly from taxation sources managed by the federal, state, and territory governments. In 2020–2021, governments funded A$156.0 billion (104.7 billion USD) of the total health expenditure (70%), with nongovernment sources funding the remaining A$64.9 billion (43.6 billion USD) (29%). Of the total government funding in 2020–2021, the Australian Government contributed A$94.4 billion (63.4 billion USD), with state and territory governments contributing A$61.6 billion (41.38 billion USD). In 2020–2021, health spending by nongovernment entities (including individuals, private health insurers, injury compensation insurers, and other private sources) increased by 6.4% in real terms compared with 2019–2020.

Spending by individuals was the largest source of growth in nongovernment spending at A$33.2 billion (22.3 billion USD) (9.3% more than in 2019–2020), likely associated with the easing of pandemic restrictions.[20]

Nongovernment funding is drawn mainly from out-of-pocket payments by individuals and health insurance funds, which help to cover the cost of treatment in private hospitals and a range of other medical and ancillary health services.

In recent times, funding for health has become a topic of heated debate among the Commonwealth and the states and territories. There has been strong disagreement about the adequacy of health funding from the Commonwealth, particularly in a time where the economy is shrinking and the population is aging. Attempts to curb the growth in health funding in recent years have been largely unsuccessful. (refer to **Figure 25-2**).

The public share of health spending has varied markedly over the years, reflecting the major policy

Table 25-3 Trends in Health Spending in Australia, 2013–2021

	2013–2014	2015–2016	2017–2018	2020–2021
Total health expenditure, current prices (A$ billion) (USD billion)	 154 82.6	 187 125.5	 196.7 132	 221 148.3
Total health expenditure as a percentage of GDP	9.78%	10%	10.1%	10.7%
Total per capita health expenditure, current prices (A$) (USD)	 6,639 3,990	 7,000 4,697	 7,772 5,215	 8,617 5,782

A$ = Australian dollar.

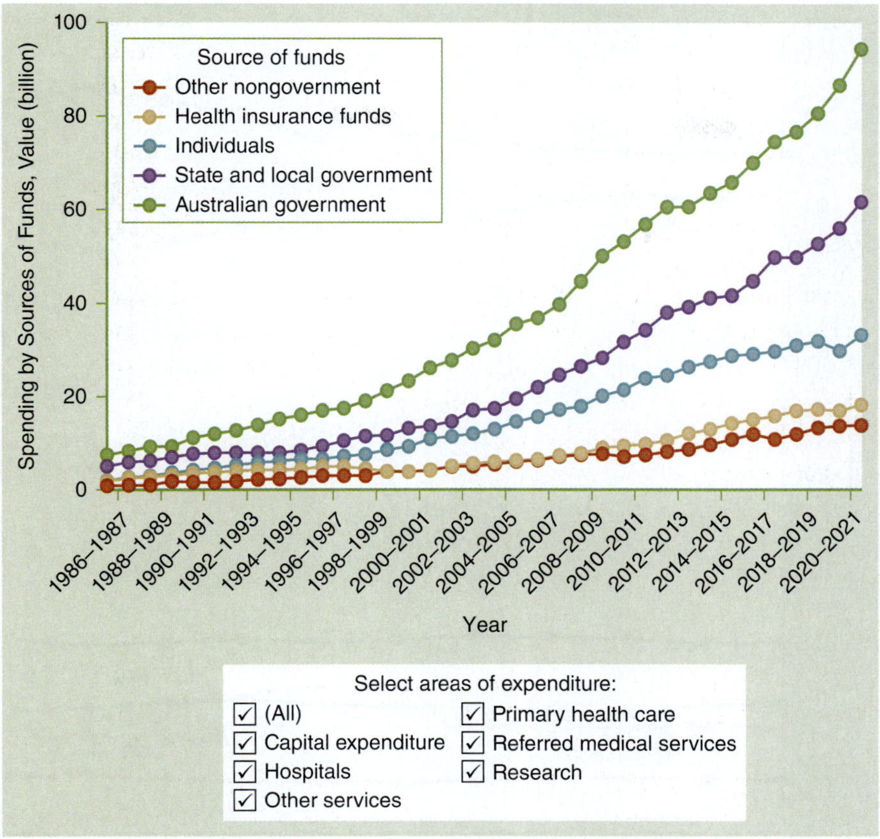

Figure 25-2 Proportion of total health spending by source of funds, current prices, 1986–1987 to 2020–2021

Reproduced from Australian Institute of Health and Welfare. Health expenditure 2020–21. https://www.aihw.gov.au/reports/health-welfare-expenditure/health-expenditure-australia-2020-21/contents/main-visualisations/sources-and-areas.

changes of the federal government. The introduction of Medibank in 1975 saw the public share jump from 57.0% to 73.0%; this share then declined to 63.0% in the late 1970s with the gradual dismantling of Medibank by the Fraser coalition government. The public share of health spending jumped to 72% after the introduction of Medicare by Hawke's Labor Party government in 1984. In 2013–2014, the public share of health funding was 67.8%, with the nongovernment sector (insurance funds, individuals, and other) accounting for 32.2% of funding.[21] By 2021–2022, the public share of health funding was 71%, with the nongovernment sector accounting for 29%.[20]

Figure 25-3 shows that the greatest proportion of health funding in 2020–2021 was spent on hospitals, followed by primary health care and other recurrent costs. Component costs, public hospitals, medications, and medical services were the single largest contributors to health expenditure.[20]

Under Medicare, patients are entitled to access public hospital care at no charge. This includes free medical and surgical care from physicians and surgeons, accommodation, meals, and other health services while in the hospital if they are admitted as public patients.

In addition to having a publicly funded social health insurance scheme (Medicare), Australians can subscribe to private health insurance. If privately insured patients choose to be admitted as private patients, additional fees and charges are likely. In these instances, the patient can choose their own physician/surgeon. When in private hospitals, patients are charged fees for accommodation, nursing care, and other hospital care. They are also charged separately for any medical and surgical treatment. Private health insurance is available to cover such expenses (and ancillaries, such as optical, dental, and allied health) if people wish to subscribe. Any premiums are additional to the Medicare levy (2% of income, with some reductions and exclusions), which all Australian taxpayers are obligated to pay.[22] In recent years, the government has introduced several policies to reduce the pressure on the public health system by penalizing higher-earning taxpayers with an additional Medicare surcharge if they do not take out private insurance.

Under Medicare, the government pays a flat rate per physician consultation. A physician can choose to charge the patient either that amount or more. A patient pays any difference. Other services funded through

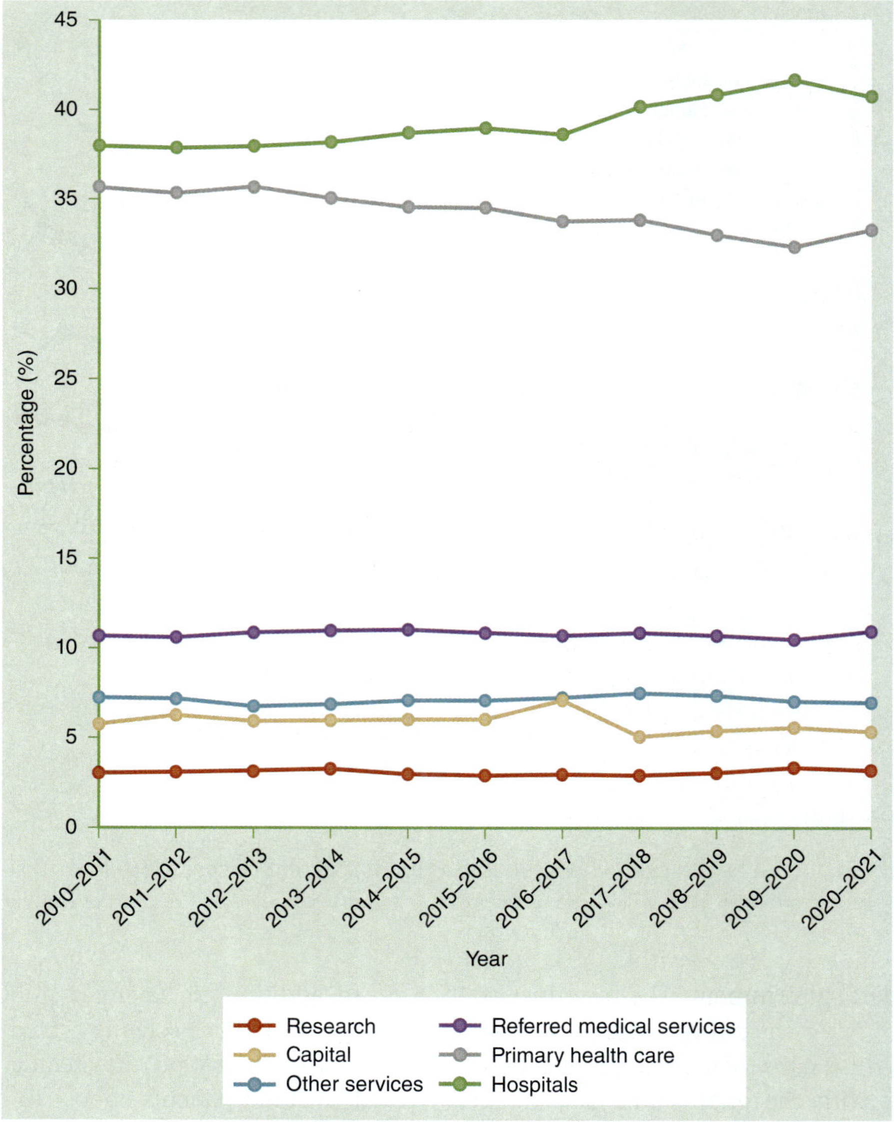

Figure 25-3 Proportion of total health spending, by area of expenditure, current prices, 2010–2011 to 2020–2021

Reproduced from Australian Institute of Health and Welfare. Health expenditure 2020–21. https://www.aihw.gov.au/reports/health-welfare-expenditure/health-expenditure-australia-2020-21/contents/spending-trends-by-sources.

Medicare include services from participating optometrists, services delivered by a practice nurse on behalf of a general practitioner, and certain services from eligible dentists and allied health practitioners. Claims can be made by post or over the counter at Medicare offices, or the physician can "bulk bill" patients. In this case, physicians send accounts directly to Medicare and accept the Medicare rebate as full payment for the service. There is no cost to the patient. Just over eight of 10 physicians "bulk billed" the government for their patient consultations in 2022–2023.[23]

In 2023 (YTD), there were 339.4 million Medicare services delivered, at a total cost of A$20.4 billion (13.6 billion USD).[23] The main services were general practitioner consultations, followed by pathology tests, diagnostic imaging, and specialist physician attendances.

Like Medicare, the PBS is a central and unique feature of Australia's health system. Since its inception in 1948, the PBS has consistently provided reliable, timely, and affordable access to important medicines for all Australians. In so doing, the PBS has proven itself to be one of the best systems in the world. Medicines on the Australian market are not only of high quality but are also less costly than in most other countries. Under this scheme, consumers can access more than 2,300 brands of prescription medicines that they are assured have been rigorously tested and found to be cost-effective. These medicines are available from a network of 5,000 independently owned community pharmacies spread across all parts of Australia.

Currently, most of the population (general consumers) pay a maximum of A$30.00 (20.03 USD) for any one prescription item. Concessional patients and pensioners pay only A$7.30 (4.87 USD) per item. There are two safety net thresholds—one for general patients and the other for concessional patients. From January 1, 2016, the general patient safety net threshold was A$1,563.50 (1,044.00 USD). When patients and/or their families reach this amount, they can apply for a Safety Net Concession Card and pay only A$7.30 (4.87 USD) per prescription for the rest of the calendar year. The concessional safety net threshold is A$262.80 (175.50 USD). Once patients and/or their families reach this amount, they can apply for a Safety Net Entitlement Card and receive items free of charge for the rest of the calendar year.[24]

The cost of the PBS scheme has risen significantly over the years. In 2005, its first year of operation, around 300,000 prescriptions for PBS medicines were dispensed, at a cost to the Commonwealth Government of A$150,000 (113,000 USD). By 2021–2022, total PBS government expense for the supply of medicines under Section 85 and Section 100 on an accrual accounting basis was A$14.7 billion (excluding revenue) (9.6 billion USD), compared with A$13.8 billion (9.2 billion USD) for the previous year. This was an increase of 6.7%. Total 2021–2022 PBS subsidized prescription volume increased by 0.7% to a total of 215 million, compared with 213.6 million for the 2020–2021 financial year.

The majority of government expenditures in 2021–2022 on PBS Section 85 and Section 100 prescriptions were directed toward concessional card holders (A$9.3 billion, 6.2 billion USD, 64.4% of the total), compared with concessional card holders expenditure for 2020–2021 (A$9 billion, 6.1 billion USD), 66.3% of the total). The average dispensed price (patient payment plus government benefit) per prescription of PBS subsidized medicines increased to A$74.63 (49.84 USD) in 2021–2022, compared with A$70.65 (47.18 USD) in 2020–2021.

There were 925 different medicines in 5,178 brands listed on the PBS as of June 30, 2022.[25]

There are several reasons for this increasing cost. First, the number of available medicines continues to grow. As new drugs come onto the market and get approved, they are added to the list of subsidized medications. Second, the new-generation drugs listed on the PBS are more costly and doctors tend to prescribe the newer, more potent, and more effective products. Thus, the mix of drugs being prescribed by doctors is increasing in cost. Third, Australia's aging population and chronic disease profile are driving the use of more medications. The number of prescriptions dispensed per person increases with age, as medicines play an important role in improving the quality and longevity of people's lives. Finally, the number of people eligible for concessional and pensioner pharmaceutical benefits is increasing, which in turn adds to the cost for the PBS.

Quality of Life

Quality of life is but one of several factors, in addition to socioeconomic, environmental, behavioral, biomedical, and genetic factors, that help to determine the health and well-being of the population. Quality is difficult to define and even more difficult to measure. It can be subjective, such as an individual patient's view of the quality of a particular encounter with the health system or the wider public's view of the performance of their local hospital or ambulance service.

A key biennial government publication, *Australia's Health*, outlines the health improvement of the nation over time. Since *Australia's Health* was first published over 30 years ago, Australia's ranking among comparable countries has improved on most measures: (1) Australia's life expectancy at birth (81.2 years for females and 85.3 years for males in 2020) placed Australia among the top six nations in the world.[26] (2) Marked improvements in ranking are evident for mortality rates from coronary heart disease, stroke, lung cancer, and transport accidents. (3) Rates of smoking continue to fall, moving Australia into the "best third" of OECD countries on this measure. (4) Australia also scores well and has improved rankings on self-rated health, dental health, various mortality measures, and lower alcohol consumption.

On the downside, Australia's ranking has fallen on measures of mortality from suicide, diabetes, respiratory diseases, and infant mortality. The ranking for obesity has not changed, with 67% of Australians classified as overweight or obese.[27] Australia is among the "worst third" group of OECD countries on this measure.

Australia's health system has also been compared with other developed health systems worldwide. Australia had mixed results when compared internationally:

- Australia's life expectancy at birth was 83.0 years—above the OECD average of 80.6 years, and the sixth highest among OECD countries. The highest life expectancy was in Japan, where people could expect to live 84.4 years at birth.
- Infant mortality rate (with no minimum threshold of gestation period or birth weight) was 3.3 deaths

per 1,000 live births—below the OECD average of 4.2 deaths per 1,000 live births. Iceland experienced the lowest rate of infant mortality (1.1 deaths per 1,000 live births).

- Among those aged 15 and over, Canadians were most likely to perceive their health as "good/very good" (89%), followed by those living in the United States (88%), New Zealand (87%), and Australia (85%). Those living in Korea (34%) and Japan (37%) were least likely to rate their health as "good/very good."
- Australia had the second highest rate of cancer (all malignant neoplasms [C00–C97]) among OECD countries (323 cases per 100,000 population), while Denmark had the highest rate (338 per 100,000 population).
- Australia had the eighth lowest proportion of daily smokers among people aged 15 and over (11.2%), with Turkey ranking highest at 28%.
- Australia was above the OECD average for liters per capita of pure alcohol consumed by people aged 15 and over, at 9.5 liters compared with 8.7 liters per capita. The highest amount of alcohol consumed was in Latvia (12.9 liters per capita), while the lowest was in Turkey (1.3 liters per capita).
- Australia had the eighth highest proportion of people aged 15 and over who are overweight and obese (65%), out of the 22 countries that reported measured height and weight data. This was higher than the OECD average of 59%.[28]

Access

Equity of access to health services is one of the main objectives of Australia's health system. In particular, it is one of the underpinning principles of the universal taxpayer-funded Medicare and pharmaceutical benefits (PBS) systems. Both are funded through general taxation as well as by a 2% Medicare levy on income. Patients also contribute through a system of structured copayments for prescription medicines. For physician services, patients pay any gap between the amount that the physician charges and the Medicare rebate for the service.

Access to public hospital services is available for Australian citizens, who can elect to have free accommodation, medical and nursing care, and necessary medicines as public patients. Patients can also choose, if they wish, to be treated in a private hospital, or as a private patient in a public hospital. They are then required to meet the associated medical, surgical, and accommodation costs with the assistance of private health insurance and some assistance from Medicare.

Access to a wide range of prescription medicines is made possible through the PBS. As described earlier, patients are required to contribute to the cost of their medicines through a system of copayments. In addition, a safety net is in place that provides further protection for individuals and families against the financial burden associated with high use of medicines. Access to pharmaceutical services is also facilitated through a set of regulations that govern where Australia's nearly 5,700 community pharmacies are located. This is particularly important in rural and remote parts of Australia, where population density is low and communities are few and far between.

In 2013, the federal government commenced the centrally funded National Disability Insurance Scheme (NDIS). Currently under trial in multiple sites across Australia, this scheme will provide all Australians under the age of 65 (who have a permanent, significant disability) with reasonable and necessary supports to be as active as possible in the community. More than 10 years after its launch, there are now approximately 520,000 active participants having accessed the scheme.

Current and Emerging Issues and Challenges

Australia is fortunate to have a health system that features a sophisticated infrastructure, advanced medical technologies, and highly trained health professionals, all of which have helped to deliver high levels of health across most sectors of the population. Several challenges and emerging issues are apparent in the early years of the 21st century. This section focuses on four of these: (1) the challenges of an aging population, (2) the inequality of Aboriginal and Torres Strait Islander health, (3) the twin health challenges of increasing levels of obesity and diabetes, and (4) the organizational and structural challenges that the government faces with a publicly funded healthcare system.

An Aging Population

"Demography shapes destiny" was one of the catch phrases of former Australian treasurer Peter Costello, referring to the inevitability of the aging of the population in the country. This process has been described elsewhere as "a quiet transformation, because it is gradual, but also unremitting and ultimately pervasive."[28] Falling fertility, the aging of the baby-boomer generation, declining mortality, and increased life expectancy are combining to increase the number and proportion of the population that is older—that is, those aged 65 years or more. Australia's population has grown older, with the median age increasing from 32.7 years from June 30, 1992, to 38.5 years in June 30, 2022. The percentage of the population aged 65 and over increased from 11% to 17% over the same period. The number of deaths grew faster than the number of births over this period, reflecting the declining fertility rate and aging of the population.[29]

The 2021 Australian Census reported a growing shift of the population aged 40 and above (48.3% of the population), This finding is in line with other developed-country populations (see **Figure 25-4**).

The implications of an aging population for healthcare costs have been the focus of much analysis and commentary in the past two decades. The upward pressure on health costs applied by an aging population results from the fact that older people tend to have a greater need for health services and that they use those services more often than other age groups. The other major drivers of rising health costs are the increasing cost and availability of new health technology, as well as burgeoning consumer demands and expectations. Consumers increasingly expect and demand the latest and best, whether it is the latest medical/surgical advance or the latest "miracle" drug.

Growing older is accompanied by an increasing incidence of nonfatal diseases of aging and chronic degenerative diseases. These include arthritis, diabetes, heart disease, cancer, and dementia. Such diseases can severely impact the quality of life and independence of older people. They also bring with them markedly increased utilization of health services, such as medications, doctor consultations, and hospital admissions.

Although there are many who believe an aging population is a crisis in the making, the prevailing view is not so pessimistic. Population aging is gradual. Governments, health planners, and administrators have plenty of time to develop new policy approaches to address the challenges ahead. The Productivity Commission, for example, points out[30] that future productivity growth will ensure that Australians are much richer and are better able to afford the costs associated with aging. Moreover, although people are living longer, they are generally healthier than previous generations. In the last few years, more discussion has focused on healthy aging and contributing to the workforce in later life.

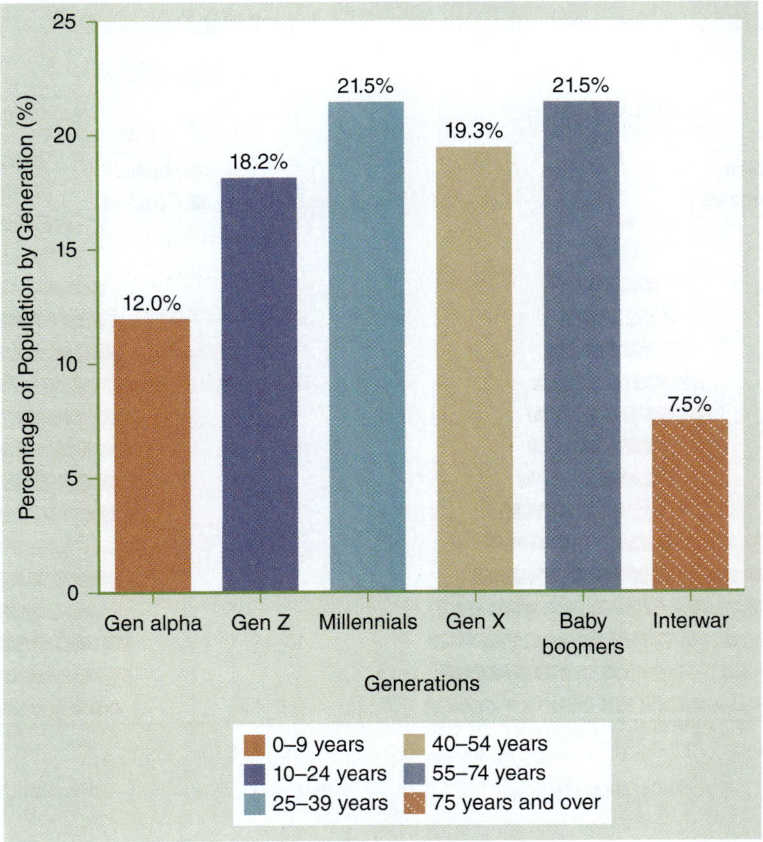

Figure 25-4 Population by generation in Australia, 2021

Reproduced from Australian Bureau of Statistics. Population: census. 2021. Accessed May 27, 2024. https://www.abs.gov.au/statistics/people/population/population-census/latest-release.

The government's *Intergenerational Report*[31] concluded that Australians will live longer and continue to have one of the longest life expectancies in the world. For 2054–2055, life expectancy at birth is projected to be 95.1 years for men and 96.6 years for women.

> Not only will Australians live longer, but improvements in health mean they are more likely to remain active for longer. "Active ageing" presents great opportunities for older Australians to keep participating in the workforce and community for longer, and to look forward to more active and engaged retirement years. There will be fewer people of traditional working age compared with the very young and the elderly. This trend is already visible, with the number of people aged between 15 and 64 for every person aged 65 and over having fallen from 7.3 people in 1974–1975 to an estimated 4.5 people today. By 2054–2055, this is projected to nearly halve again to 2.7 people.[31]

Aboriginal and Torres Strait Islander Health

One of the major challenges for all levels of government, but particularly the federal government, is the state of health of Australia's Aboriginal and Torres Strait Islanders. In Australia, there are approximately 250 mobs or nations that make up the Aboriginal and Torres Strait Islander population.[32] While each of these nations has its own customs, traditions, and language, for the purposes of data collection and reporting, governments aggregate the data for anyone self-identifying as a First Nations person.[33]

This population (there were approximately 798,400 in Australia in 2019) dies, on average, 8 years earlier (8.6 years for males and 7.8 years for females) than other Australians.[34]

The population profile of the Aboriginal and Torres Strait population in Australia is quite different from that of the non-Indigenous population. While the Aboriginal and Torres Strait population accounts for approximately 3.3% of the total Australian population, its age profile creates additional considerations for health policy in Australia (**Figure 25-5**).

Although the life expectancy gap has decreased over the last decade, by any measure, it is still unacceptable. On almost every measure of health, the gap between Indigenous and non-Indigenous people in Australia is significant. In terms of health disparity:

- The rate of disease burden among Aboriginal and Torres Strait Islander people was more than double (2.3 times) that of non-Indigenous Australians in 2018.[34]

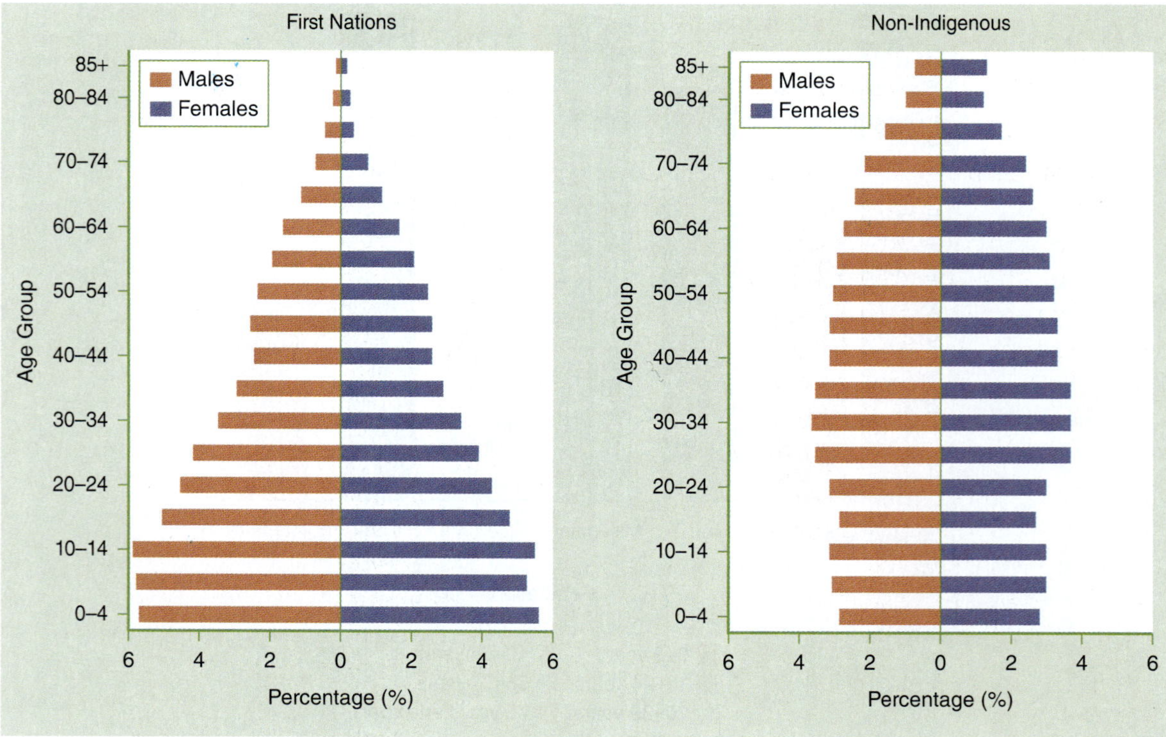

Figure 25-5 Age profile for the Indigenous and Nonindigenous population of Australia, 2021

Reproduced from Australian Institute of Health and Welfare. *Aboriginal and Torres Strait Islander Health Performance Framework Summary Report 2023.* Accessed April 4, 2024. https://www.indigenoushpf.gov.au/report-overview/overview/summary-report/2-demographic-and-social-context#:~:text=In%202021%2C%20one%2Dhalf%20of,Indigenous%20Australians%20aged%20under%2015.

- The age-standardized death rate for endocrine, nutritional, and metabolic diseases for Indigenous Australians was 3.7 times as high as for non-Indigenous Australians.[34]
- Injury, poisoning, and respiratory disease rates were twice as high for Indigenous Australians as for non-Indigenous Australians.[34]
- For chronic obstructive pulmonary disease, the age-standardized death rate for Indigenous Australians was almost three times higher than for non-Indigenous Australians.[34]
- After adjusting for differences between the age structures of the two populations, Indigenous Australians were hospitalized for intentional self-harm at nearly three times the rate of non-Indigenous Australians.[34]
- Death rates from diabetes remain relatively high for Indigenous Australians compared with non-Indigenous Australians, with Indigenous Australians dying from diabetes at about 4.7 times the rate (age-standardized) of non-Indigenous Australians.[34]
- In the 3-year period from 2015 to 2017, 950 Indigenous Australians began kidney replacement therapy for kidney failure, an incidence rate of 64 per 100,000 (age-standardized). In comparison, the age-standardized incidence rate of kidney failure with replacement therapy for non-Indigenous Australians was 9.2 per 100,000.[34]
- In 2018–2019, 43% of Indigenous Australians aged 18 and over were current smokers (down from 54.5% in 1994), compared with 15.1% of the non-Indigenous population.[35]

Much of this disparity in health status is due to a range of social conditions that affect health, including inadequate and overcrowded living conditions, inadequate education, poor access to suitable employment, and partaking in risky health behaviors (tobacco, alcohol, drugs, and other substances).[36]

In 2015–2016, the average health expenditure per person for Indigenous Australians was estimated to be A$8,949 (5,979 USD), which was 1.3 times the amount for non-Indigenous Australians (A$6,657; 4,447 USD). Almost half of this spending was on hospital services (A$4,436; 2,963 USD), followed by medical services (A$1,332; 890 USD) and community health services (A$998; 667 USD).[37]

A much higher proportion of health dollars for Indigenous peoples is spent on hospital services, and proportionately much less on primary health care, particularly on Medicare and the PBS. Average Medicare and PBS spending for each Indigenous Australian in 2011 was around 20% to 30% less than for other Australians.[38] Average spending per Indigenous person on dental, private hospital, and other professional health services was also much lower than for other Australians.

Obesity and Diabetes

Two significant and related health challenges for Australia in the early years of the 21st century have been obesity and diabetes. In common with many other developed nations, Australia has been experiencing an increasing prevalence of obesity in recent years, largely due to changes in dietary and exercise practices. Described by the World Health Organization as a global epidemic, obesity (or excess body fat) is associated with an increased risk of type 2 diabetes, cardiovascular disease, high blood pressure, certain cancers, sleep apnea, osteoarthritis, psychological disorders, and social problems.[39]

The latest statistics on the prevalence of overweight and obesity in Australia show that:

- Two of three people (67%) are living with overweight or obesity. This is approximately 12.5 million adults.
- Thirty-six percent are living with overweight but not obesity.
- Thirty-one percent are living with obesity.
- Twelve percent are living with severe obesity, which is defined in this report as having a BMI of 35 or more.[40]

The proportion of adults with overweight or obesity differs by age and sex, as shown in **Figure 25-6**.

These rates of adult obesity in Australia are well above the OECD averages. Australia ranked ninth out of 21 countries with available data for the proportion of people aged 15 and over who were living with overweight or obesity (65%)—this was greater than the OECD average of 60%. When comparing the proportion of obesity in men and women across OECD countries, Australia had the fourth highest proportion of men living with obesity (32%), behind New Zealand (33%), Hungary (36%) and the United States (44%). The proportion of obesity in women in Australia was ninth highest out of 21 countries (29%)—higher than the OECD average of 26% for women.[40] The Department of Health estimates that in 2018, obesity cost the Australian community A$11.8 billion (7.93 billion USD), and if it continues to go unchecked, obesity may cost upward of A$87.7 billion (58.9 billion USD) by 2032.[41]

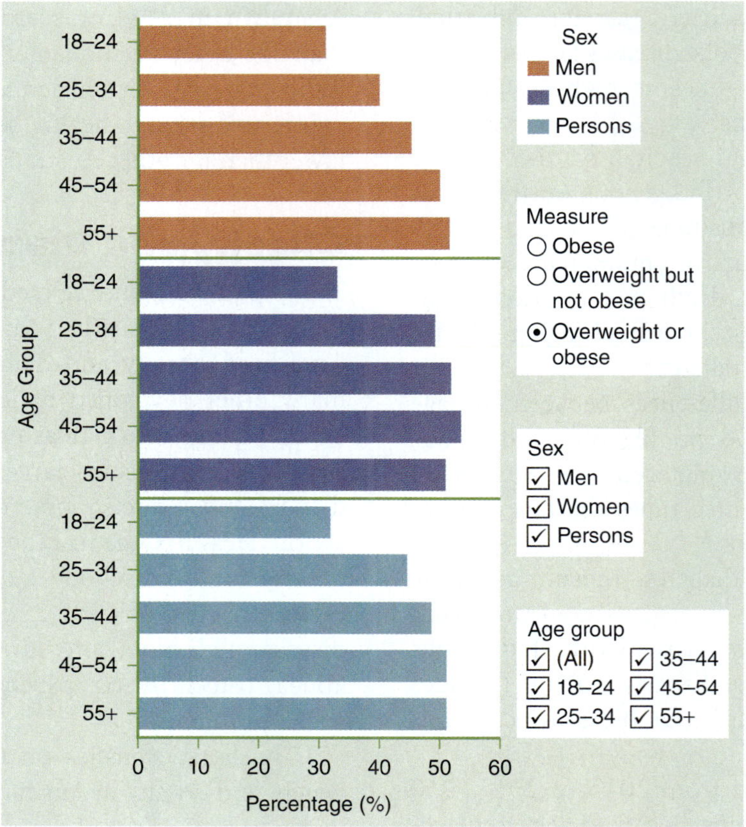

Figure 25-6 Proportion of adults living with overweight and obesity, by age and sex, 2018–2019

Reproduced from Australian Institute of Health and Welfare. Overweight and obesity. 2023. Accessed April 4, 2024. https://www.aihw.gov.au/reports/overweight-obesity/overweight-and-obesity/contents/overweight-and-obesity.

Policy options abound, but successful outcomes are few and far between. Imposing a tax on those food products considered likely to contribute to obesity is not widely favored, as it targets food products consumed by obese and nonobese persons alike. While a sugar tax on soft drinks has been adopted overseas, it has yet to gain traction among Australian law makers. It also cannot be assumed that higher tax on certain foods will necessarily shift consumption away from them toward healthier alternatives. Pressure on the government to impose advertising restrictions, such as bans on food advertisements for children, has also been rejected to date. Instead, there is a voluntary code of practice in place for advertising to children that aims to not encourage or promote an inactive lifestyle combined with unhealthy eating or drinking habits.[42] While much of the focus to date has been on self-control or government regulation of the food industry, the government's preferred approach in recent times has been to fund awareness, health promotion, and prevention campaigns.

Diabetes is a significant and growing chronic disease in Australia. The latest statistics show that:

- In 2020, an estimated one in 20 (almost 1.3 million) Australians were living with diabetes (prevalence). This includes people with type 1 diabetes, type 2 diabetes, and other diabetes, but excludes gestational diabetes.
- In 2020, the prevalence of diabetes increased with age, with almost one in five Australians aged 80 to 84 living with diabetes—almost 30 times as high as for those aged under 40 (0.7%). Diabetes was more common in males (4.8%) than females (3.8%), after controlling for age.
- After accounting for differences in the age structure of the population, the age-standardized prevalence rate of diabetes increased from 2.4% in 2000 to 4.3% in 2020.
- Almost 1.3 million hospitalizations were associated with diabetes in 2020–2021, with 4.7% recording diabetes as the principal diagnosis and around 95% recording diabetes as an additional diagnosis. This represents 11% of all hospitalizations in Australia.
- Diabetes was among the 10 leading causes of death of Australians in 2020.
- After adjusting for differences in the age structure of the populations, diabetes death rates were five times higher among Indigenous Australians than for non-Indigenous Australians.[43]

Diabetes can cause diseases of the eyes, kidneys, nerves, and cardiovascular system, which can lead to a reduced quality of life and premature death. Type 2 diabetes, the most common form, has increased in prevalence in Australia since the 1980s, and further increases in obesity and physically inactive lifestyles and increases in the aging of the population have the potential to continue this increase. Diabetes has been among conditions of concern for Australia's health ministers (federal, state, and territory) for some time and continues to be a focus of the Council of Australian Governments' broader commitment to reducing the prevalence of avoidable chronic diseases and their risk factors.

There is also much concern about the financial burden of diabetes. A study conducted in 2013 showed annual direct per-person costs ranged from A$1,898 (1,273 USD) for those with normal glucose tolerance to A$4,390 (2,974 USD) for those with known diabetes. The total annual cost of diabetes in 2005 for Australians aged 30 years or older was A$10.6 billion (7.12 billion USD), which equates to A$14.6 billion (9.8 billion USD) in 2010 dollars.[44] Annual direct costs for people with diabetes complications are more than twice those for people without complications: A$9,600 (7,328 USD) compared with A$3,500 (2,672 USD).[45]

Structural and Organizational Issues

International comparisons suggest that Australia has a health system that produces high levels of health at a reasonable cost (close to the OECD average). The predominantly publicly funded system provides universal access to high-quality health and hospital services, ensuring that Australians are ahead of most other comparable countries on most measures of health. Despite these successes, Australia's historic, political, and societal characteristics, in particular the complexities associated with its federal/state structure, have given rise to some fundamental and somewhat intractable fiscal and organizational problems. Five-year Health Reform Agreements between the Commonwealth and state/territory governments determine the amount of federal funding to be allocated to the states and territories to help cover the costs of running public hospitals. Funding for the current agreement (from 2020 to 2025) is likely to exceed A$149.8 billion (100.6 billion USD).[46] Tensions inevitably arise between federal and state governments concerning the adequacy and distribution of this funding. Accusations of cost shifting among different levels of government, of inefficiencies, of systems growth, and of overlap and duplication of services are commonplace and make for ongoing public controversy and debate.

Over 15 years ago, Australia's Labor Party government was determined to address these problems, to improve the way health care was delivered, and to make it sustainable for the future. To this end, the National Health and Hospitals Reform Commission was established and charged with developing "a blueprint for tackling future challenges in Australia's health system, including: (1) the rapidly increasing burden of chronic disease; (2) the aging of the population; (3) rising health costs; and (4) inefficiencies exacerbated by cost shifting and the blame game."[47] Following the release of the National Health and Hospitals Reform Commission Report in 2009, the Commission was disbanded. Since that time, successive governments have implemented and later disbanded bodies charged with reviewing, advising, and monitoring current health performance. This role has now been largely taken up by the Australian Institute of Health and Welfare and the Australian Commission on Safety and Quality in Health Care.

Similarly, successive governments in recent years have taken approaches to addressing primary healthcare needs across Australia. With an emphasis on regional general practice, chronic disease management, community mental health services, nurse primary care, and after-hours medical services, Rudd's Labor Party government established Medicare Locals in 2010. These were disbanded by Abbott's Liberal-National coalition government in 2015 and replaced by Primary Health Networks (PHNs). The primary distinction between the Medicare Local approach and PHNs is that the role of the general practitioner was strengthened and there was an emphasis on coordinating and purchasing services, rather than being a healthcare provider that competes with other local healthcare services. It is currently too early to assess the success of this change in approach in terms of patient outcomes, particularly in regional and rural areas.

The Australian healthcare system is large and complex, approaching A$221 billion (148 billion USD) in cost and close to 11% of GDP. Despite the relatively favorable health outcomes and life expectancies of Australians, there will be much political and philosophical debate about the sustainability, efficiency, and equity of the system going forward. With pressures on the national budget due to a changing economy and an aging population, the future funding and subsidization of the health system will continue to be a source of discussion. Future governments will need to carefully consider the funding of health care as it takes up an increasingly larger proportion of the overall national budget, albeit on a smaller taxation base.

COVID-19 Pandemic

Australia's response to the COVID-19 pandemic emphasized protecting the right to life and health of people in Australia.[48] Australian governments implemented significant restrictions on movement, especially when and how people could visit friends or relatives in aged and disability care facilities and access to detention facilities. For example, the Australian governments introduced the following restrictions on movement and association:

- Closing overseas and interstate borders
- Restricting when people were permitted to leave their homes, including by way of curfew in Victoria
- Restricting the number of people who were allowed to gather in private residences, restaurants, and businesses
- Restricting the number of attendees at funerals and weddings
- Restricting access to family members living in aged care facilities
- Limiting the size of public gatherings

In addition, the Australian Government introduced measures to provide financial support to Australian citizens and permanent residents during the COVID-19 pandemic, including the following:

- The JobKeeper Payment, which supported businesses so they could continue to pay their employees some or all of their regular wages if a number of criteria were met
- A temporary COVID-19 supplement to the JobSeeker (formerly "Newstart") Payment, Youth Allowance JobSeeker Payment, Parenting Payment, Farm Household Allowance, Special Benefit and the Abstudy, Austudy and Youth Allowance for Payments for full-time students
- One-off stimulus payments for veteran income support recipients and eligible concession card holders

References

1. Smith L. *The Aboriginal Population of Australia*. Canberra, Australia: Australian National University Press; 1980.
2. Healy J, Sharman E, Lokuge B. Australia: health system review. *Health Systems in Transition*. 2006;8:9.
3. Parliament of Australia. About the Senate. Canberra, Australia. Accessed July 6, 2016. http://www.aph.gov.au/About_Parliament/Senate/About_the_Senate.
4. Reserve Bank of Australia. Cash rate target. Published November 2, 2016. Accessed June 19, 2023. https://www.rba.gov.au/statistics/cash-rate/snapshots/economy-snapshot/.
5. Australian Bureau of Statistics. Population. Accessed June 19, 2023. https://www.abs.gov.au/statistics/people/population.
6. Australian Bureau of Statistics. 50 years of estimated resident population. December 16, 2021. Accessed June 19, 2023. https://www.abs.gov.au/articles/50-years-estimated-resident-population.
7. Australian Bureau of Statistics. Migration, Australia. 2019–2020. Accessed June 19, 2023. https://www.abs.gov.au/statistics/people/population/migration-australia/latest-release.
8. Australian Bureau of Statistics. Estimates of Aboriginal and Torres Strait Islander Australians. 2021. Accessed June 19, 2023. https://www.abs.gov.au/statistics/people/aboriginal-and-torres-strait-islander-peoples/estimates-aboriginal-and-torres-strait-islander-australians/jun-2021.
9. Australian Bureau of Statistics. Religious affiliation in Australia. 2022. Accessed June 19, 2023. https://www.abs.gov.au/articles/religious-affiliation-australia.
10. Sax S. *A Strife of Interests*. Sydney, Australia: Allen & Unwin; 1984.
11. Australian Institute of Health and Welfare. Australia's hospitals at a glance. 2022. Accessed June 22, 2023. https://www.aihw.gov.au/reports/hospitals/australias-hospitals-at-a-glance/contents/access-to-hospitals.
12. Australian Institute of Health and Welfare. Mental health. 2022. Accessed June 22, 2023. https://www.aihw.gov.au/mental-health/topic-areas/facilities#Specialised%20beds.
13. Australian Institute of Health and Welfare. Aged care data snapshot. 2021. Accessed June 22, 2023. https://www.gen-agedcaredata.gov.au/Resources/Access-data/2021/October/Aged-care-data-snapshot%E2%80%942021.
14. Australian Institute of Health and Welfare. Health workforce. 2022. Accessed June 22, 2023. https://www.aihw.gov.au/reports/workforce/health-workforce#overview.
15. Department of Health. Medical workforce 2016 fact sheet. Accessed June 22, 2023. https://hwd.health.gov.au/webapi/customer/documents/factsheets/2016/Medical%20workforce%20factsheet%202016.pdf#:~:text=The%20average%20age%20of%20the%20medical%20workforce%20in,and%204.1%20per%20cent%20aged%2065%20and%20over.
16. National Health Workforce Dataset. Nurses and midwives 2016–2019. Accessed June 23, 2023. https://hwd.health.gov.au/resources/publications/factsheet-nrmw-2019.pdf.
17. MTPConnect. Medical Technology, Biotechnology & Pharmaceutical Sector Competitiveness Plan. Accessed

February 13, 2025. https://www.mtpconnect.org.au/images/2020%20MTPConnect%20Sector%20Competitiveness%20Plan.pdf.
18. Australian Government, Productivity Commission. *Impacts of Advances in Medical Technology in Australia*. Research report. Melbourne, Australia: Productivity Commission; 2005.
19. National Health Performance Authority. Published April 2016. Accessed July 24, 2016. http://www.nhpa.gov.au/internet/nhpa/publishing.nsf/Content/home-1.
20. Australian Institute of Health and Welfare. *Health Expenditure 2020–21*. Accessed June 22, 2023. https://www.aihw.gov.au/reports/health-welfare-expenditure/health-expenditure.
21. Australian Institute of Health and Welfare. *Health Expenditure 2013–14*. Health and Welfare Expenditure series. Canberra, Australia: AIHW.54 (Cat. HWE 63); 2015.
22. Australian Taxation Office. Medicare levy. Accessed July 7, 2016. https://www.ato.gov.au/Individuals/Medicare-levy/.
23. Australian Government. Department of Health. Annual Medicare statistics. Accessed June 26, 2023. https://www.health.gov.au/sites/default/files/2023-05/medicare-annual-statistics-year-to-date-dashboard-july-to-march-2022-23.pdf.
24. Services Australia. PBS Safety Net Thresholds. Accessed June 26, 2023. https://www.servicesaustralia.gov.au/pbs-safety-net-thresholds?context=22016#:~:text=Once%20you%20or%20your%20family%20spend%20a%20certain,were%20updated%20to%3A%20%24262.80%20for%20concession%20card%20holders.
25. Department of Health and Aged Care. *PBS Expenditure and Prescriptions Report 1 July 2021 to 30 June 2022*. Accessed June 26, 2023. https://www.pbs.gov.au/info/statistics/expenditure-prescriptions/pbs-expenditure-and-prescriptions-report-1-july-2021-to-30-june-2022.
26. Australian Institute of Health and Welfare. *Deaths in Australia*. 2022. Accessed June 26, 2023. https://www.aihw.gov.au/reports/life-expectancy-death/deaths-in-australia/contents/life-expectancy#International%20Comparisons%20of%20Life%20Expectancy.
27. Australian Institute of Health and Welfare. *Overweight and Obesity*. 2022. Accessed June 26, 2023. https://www.aihw.gov.au/reports/overweight-obesity/overweight-and-obesity/contents/summary.
28. Australian Institute of Health and Welfare. *International Health Data Comparisons*. 2022. Accessed June 26, 2023. https://www.aihw.gov.au/reports/international-comparisons/international-health-data-comparisons#Risk.
29. Australian Institute of Health and Welfare. *Profile of Australia's Population*. 2023. Accessed June 27, 2023. https://www.aihw.gov.au/reports/australias-health/profile-of-australias-population.
30. Australian Government. *Economic Implications of an Ageing Australia*. Research Report. Canberra, Australia: Productivity Commission; 2005.
31. Australian Government, Treasury. *2015 Intergenerational Report: Australia in 2055*. Published March 5, 2015. Accessed July 21, 2016. http://www.treasury.gov.au/PublicationsAndMedia/Publications/2015/2015-Intergenerational-Report.
32. *Aboriginal People*. Deadly stories. Accessed January 27, 2024. https://deadlystory.com/page/culture/articles/World_s_Indigenous_Peoples_Day/Aboriginal_people#:~:text=Aboriginal%20people%20belong%20to%20Mobs,have%20upwards%20of%207%20clans.
33. Australian Institute of Health and Welfare. *Profile of First Nations People*. Accessed January 26, 2024. https://www.aihw.gov.au/reports/australias-welfare/profile-of-indigenous-australians.
34. Australian Institute of Health and Welfare. *Aboriginal and Torres Strait Islander Health Performance Framework Summary Report 2023*. Accessed April 4, 2024. https://www.indigenoushpf.gov.au/report-overview/overview/summary-report/2-demographic-and-social-context#:~:text=In%202021%2C%20one%2Dhalf%20of,Indigenous%20Australians%20aged%20under%2015.
35. Australian Institute of Health and Welfare. *Alcohol, Tobacco & Other Drugs in Australia* 2023. Accessed June 27, 2023. https://www.aihw.gov.au/reports/alcohol/alcohol-tobacco-other-drugs-australia/contents/priority-populations/aboriginal-and-torres-strait-islander-people.
36. Australian Institute of Health and Welfare. Aboriginal and Torres Strait Islander health performance framework. Accessed January 26, 2024. https://www.indigenoushpf.gov.au/measures#tier2.
37. Australian Institute of Health and Welfare. Expenditure on Aboriginal and Torres Strait Islander health compared to need. Accessed June 27, 2023. https://www.indigenoushpf.gov.au/measures/3-21-expenditure-atsi-compared-need.
38. Australian Institute of Health and Welfare. The health and welfare of Australia's Aboriginal and Torres Strait Islander peoples 2015. 2015. Accessed July 10, 2016. http://www.aihw.gov.au/WorkArea/DownloadAsset.aspx?id=60129551281.
39. World Health Organization. *Obesity: Preventing and Managing the Global Epidemic*. Report of a WHO Consultation. WHO Technical Report Series 894. Geneva, Switzerland: WHO; 2000.
40. Australian Institute of Health and Welfare. *Overweight and Obesity*. 2023. Accessed April 4, 2024. https://www.aihw.gov.au/reports/overweight-obesity/overweight-and-obesity/contents/overweight-and-obesity.
41. Commonwealth of Australia 2022. The National Obesity Strategy 2022–2032: at a glance. Health Ministers Meeting. Accessed June 27, 2023. https://www.health.gov.au/sites/default/files/documents/2022/03/national-obesity-strategy-2022-2032-at-a-glance-summary-with-a-logic-framework_0.pdf.
42. Barr E, Magliano DJ, Zimmet PZ, et al. *The Australian Diabetes, Obesity and Lifestyle Study*. Melbourne, Australia: International Diabetes Institute; 2006.
43. Australian Institute of Health and Welfare. Diabetes: Australian fact sheet. 2023. Accessed June 27, 2023. https://www.aihw.gov.au/reports/diabetes/diabetes-australian-facts/contents/summary.
44. Lee CM, Colagiuri R, Magliano DJ, et al. The cost of diabetes in adults in Australia. *Diabetes Res Clin Pract*. 2013;99(3):385-390. doi:10.1016/j.diabres.2012.12.002. https://pubmed.ncbi.nlm.nih.gov/23298663/.
45. Australian Government. *Nation's Largest Diabetes Conversation*. Media release. Canberra, Australia: Minister for Health and Minister for Sport; April 15, 2015.
46. Department of Health and Aged Care. Record investment in the future of Australia's health system. 2022. Accessed June 27,

2023. https://www.health.gov.au/ministers/the-hon-greg-hunt-mp/media/record-investment-in-the-future-of-australias-health-system#:~:text=%24149.8%20billion%20over%205%20years%20to%20continue%20our,in%202022%E2%80%9323%20growing%20to%20%2432.7%20billion%20in%202025%E2%80%9326.

47. Australian Government. National Health and Hospitals Reform Commission. Accessed July 9, 2016. http://www.health.gov.au/internet/nhhrc/publishing.nsf/Content/home-1.

48. Australia Human Rights Commission. Australia's response to the COVID-19 pandemic. Australia's third UPI, 2021. Accessed November 2023. https://humanrights.gov.au/sites/default/files/2020-10/australias_response_to_the_covid-19_pandemic_-_australias_third_upr_2021.pdf.

PART III

Challenges, Innovations, and Opportunities

CHAPTER 26

Health Systems During Crisis and Disaster

Caren C. Rossow, James A. Johnson, and Beth Taylor

Introduction

Health systems in all countries face challenges that occur within, adjacent to, or external to the geographic areas in which the system operates. These events can be in the form of threats, disasters, conflicts, environmental events, epidemics/pandemics, or terrorism. Additionally, occurrences such as an economic crisis can introduce powerful dynamics that significantly impact health system function.[1] Any of these events is likely to create direct disruptions in a health system's ability to meet its principal mission as well as provide services effectively to meet the needs of those people affected by the event. Damage to health facility physical plants, workforce availability, and the supply chain, as well as social disturbances arising from the stresses of the disaster or crisis, may all impact the function of the system. Changes in the short-, intermediate-, and/or long-term healthcare needs of a population may be greatly affected, thus altering the health systems' routine operations and requiring an agile redistribution of financial and human resources.

Given the fact that no country or geography is immune to disruptive events, it becomes imperative for leaders to position their organizations and communities to anticipate the varied needs of multiple populations and to optimize health and outcomes not only through the immediate event, but also through the challenges that may present subsequently. This requires awareness and study of previous events, evaluation of the effectiveness of preparation and response, and a continuous improvement approach to planning. In this chapter, to demonstrate the incredible range of events and locales that can be affected, we profile several countries that are included in other chapters of this book, including Japan, Haiti, Botswana, Brazil, the western Africa region, Canada, China, Turkiye, and the United States. Furthermore, we provide a brief discussion of the COVID-19 pandemic and a few of the lessons learned by the global health community as well as a general overview of considerations for health systems in facing future challenges.

Natural Disasters

The International Committee of the Red Cross and Red Crescent (ICRC) defines natural disasters as naturally occurring phenomena, physical in nature, caused by geophysical, hydrologic, climatologic, meteorologic, and biologic reasons. Geophysical natural disasters are best described as earthquakes, landslides, tsunamis, and volcanic activity; hydrologic—floods and avalanches; climatologic—weather extremes (hot and cold), drought, and wildfires; meteorologic—severe storms, cyclones, and wave surges; and biologic—epidemics and plagues. In addition, technological or human-generated hazards due to conflicts, famine, displaced populations, and industrial and large transport accidents are events usually close to communities. Other critical factors include climate change, population growth, unplanned urbanization, uncontrolled building on flood plains, poverty and threats associated with pandemics, and increased human vulnerability to complexity and severity of disasters.

According to the United Nations Office for Disaster Risk Reduction (UNDRR), in the last 20 years, 7,348 total disasters (excluding biologic and technological) were recorded, contributing to 1.23 million lives lost, with impacts to over 4 billion people and $2.97 trillion USD in economic losses worldwide.[2] This represents a significant increase in events, deaths, and economic impact as compared with the previous 20-year period. UNDRR requires that one of the following four criteria must be present to designate an event a disaster:

- 10 or more people killed
- 100 or more people affected
- Declaration of a state of emergency
- Call for international assistance

Hazards are defined as naturally occurring events (floods, heatwaves, etc.) and can transition to disaster if one of the above criteria is met.[2]

In March 2015, the Sendai Declaration and Framework for Disaster and Risk Reduction 2015–2030 was adopted at the third UN World Conference in Sendai, Japan.[3] This plan outlines seven targets (see **Figure 26-1**) to prevent new disasters and reduce existing disaster risks. As of this writing, over 100 states have indicated their support for this approach.

Preliminary assessments of pieces of the framework have emerged and show some promise,[4] but evaluation of the impact of this international agreement will continue for many years to come.

Geophysical Disasters

Japan: Earthquake and Tsunami

On March 11, 2011, the Great East Japan Earthquake struck off the coast of Japan. The 9.0 magnitude double earthquake, centered 130 kilometers off shore under the city of Sendai on the eastern coast of Honshu Island, triggered a horrendous tsunami, the largest in Japan's history. The large tsunami waves hit the eastern coast and peaked at 37.9 meters (124.27 feet), flooding an area of 560 square kilometers, causing severe damage to coastal towns, and destroying over a million buildings. Approximately 130,927 individuals were displaced, and the infrastructure of 2,126 roads, 56 bridges, and 26 railways was damaged or destroyed.[5]

According to the World Nuclear Association, at the time of the quake, 11 reactors at four nuclear power plants were in operation, and all shut down when the quake hit.[6] Initial inspection of the nuclear power plants led to the conclusion that there was no significant damage to the reactors. However, Tokyo Electric Power Company's Fukushima-Daiichi nuclear power

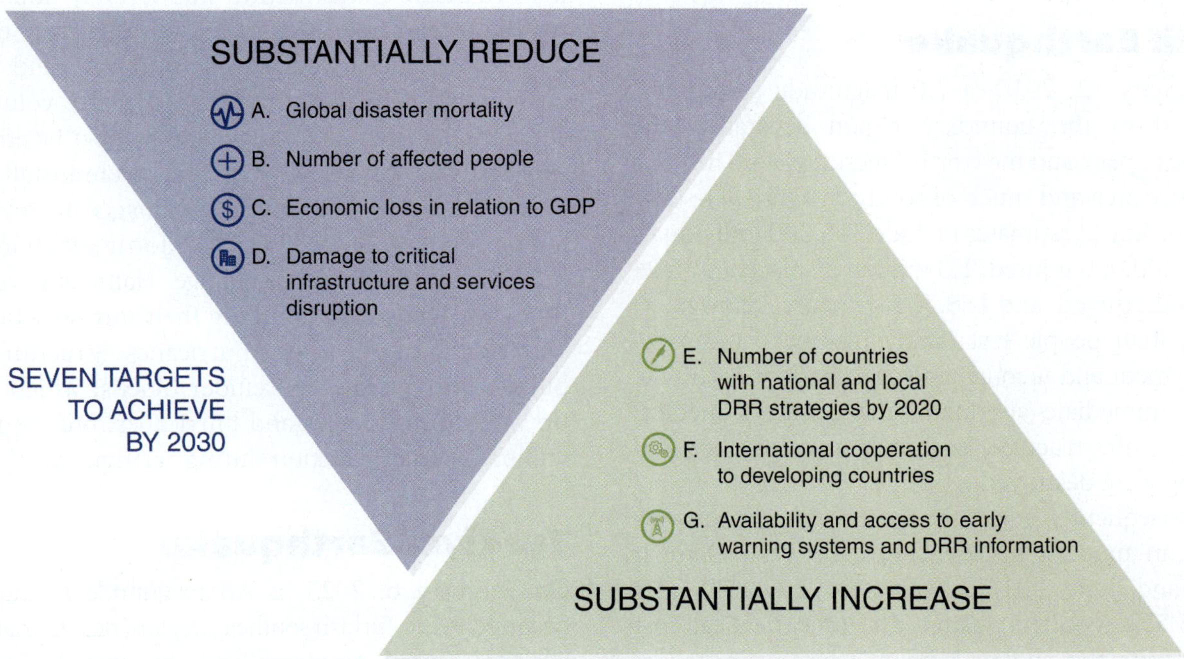

Figure 26-1 The Sendai Framework for Disaster and Risk Reduction

Reproduced from United Nations Office for Disaster and Risk Reduction. https://www.undrr.org/publication/sendai-framework-disaster-risk-reduction-2015-2030.

plant lost power an hour after the quake when the entire site was flooded by 15-meter tsunami waves. This rendered the backup generators useless, resulting in a situation in which four of the nuclear reactors had no workable instrumentation to regulate reactor cooling. Three of the reactors quickly heated up due to reactor decay, leading to a series of explosions, causing radiologic contamination to spread into areas of the environment, as described by the International Atomic Energy Agency.[6] This led to radioactive contamination of large areas of farmland, inhabited areas, and forest.

Six months after the earthquake and tsunami, nearly 20,000 people were dead and 4,041 remained missing.[6,7] In the immediate aftermath, the primary health focus was on survivor evacuation to safety. Due to the damage to water and sewer infrastructure, basic sanitation was a key concern and outbreaks of acute respiratory infections and gastroenteritis were noted.[8] The number of people (54,429) living in close quarters in almost 400 evacuation centers allowed for easier spread of these diseases. Mental health issues were also prevalent in survivors, with females more likely to exhibit symptoms,[9] and addressing these issues proved challenging given the living situation. The Japanese Red Cross Society (JRCS) published its final report[10] on March 31, 2021. It indicated that at the time of the report's publication, 41,000 people remained displaced from their homes, the majority due to the radiologic contamination as a result of the nuclear power plant damage. The long-term health effects are yet to be fully captured.

Haiti: Earthquake

On January 12, 2010, a 7.0 magnitude earthquake occurred in the boundary region separating the Caribbean plate and the North America plate. The Port-au-Prince area and much of southern Haiti were devastated. Official estimates include 316,000 individuals killed, 300,000 injured, 1.3 million displaced, 97,294 houses destroyed, and 188,383 structures damaged.[11] The Haitian people lost family members, means of employment and income, and their basic ways of life. In the immediate aftermath, the country's medical capacity, infrastructure, economic sustainability, and housing were destroyed.

Consequently, one of the most severe cholera outbreaks in modern history began. Between October 2010 and June 2014, there were 705,207 cases with 8,559 reported deaths. The total medical cost to eradicate the cholera epidemic was estimated at $82 million USD, plus another $310 million USD to cover the cost of health and water sanitation through 2017, according to the World Bank. Despite humanitarian efforts from around the world, Haiti remains one of the poorest countries in the western hemisphere, with $846 USD GDP per capita, ranking 163 out of the 188 countries covered by the United Nations' Human Development Index.[12]

Reconstruction programs focused on repairing and/or building safer housing, allowing 1.4 million individuals who were living in camps to relocate to permanent housing. Over the 10 years after the earthquake, extreme poverty dropped from 31% to 24% in urban areas and foremost in Port-au-Prince.[13] Quality education remains a challenge; however, access and participation from school-age children has risen to 90%.

Although considerable challenges remain, Haiti has seen positive developments since the earthquake. Community-based mental health services were established or strengthened in some areas through planning and partnerships.[14] Immediately after the earthquake, there was a considerable international response, including the establishment of multiple foreign field hospitals (FFH)[15] as well as the deployment of the United States Navy Ship (USNS) *Comfort*, a 1,000-bed hospital ship,[16] as Haiti was completely dependent on external support efforts for trauma care.

Since 2010, Haiti has experienced a number of earthquakes. The most severe, a 7.2 magnitude (stronger than the earthquake in 2010) on August 16, 2021, killed over 2,200 individuals, led to 12,700 injuries (80% of them orthopedic), and left over 675,000 people in need of humanitarian aid.[17] Once again, the healthcare infrastructure was severely impacted, with approximately 55% of the infrastructure either damaged or destroyed across southern Haiti.[18] To ensure access to the continuum of care, volunteer surgeons, anesthesiologists, and other healthcare professionals were deployed. Tents were installed in 28 facilities that were severely damaged to serve as temporary health facilities.[19] Unfortunately, in the near future, this may not change. Haitians have traditionally focused on building their infrastructure to withstand a bigger threat, hurricanes. Structures are built from concrete and cinder blocks, which hold up well during storms and hurricanes, but are more vulnerable to destruction during earthquakes.[17]

Turkiye: Earthquake

On February 6, 2023, a 7.8 magnitude earthquake occurred in the Turkish southeast region, near Gaziantep, affecting several provinces and the broader Central Mediterranean region. In addition to the human toll, hundreds of buildings either collapsed or sustained damage. Hundreds of families were displaced and moved into temporary shelters in the form of tents. Search-and-rescue teams from Turkiye's health and interior ministries rescued many people from the rubble. While critical life-saving operations were underway, the World Health Organization (WHO) and health partners initiated the next steps for recovery. These included watching for communicable diseases, particularly in any overcrowded areas; providing mental health and psychosocial support; and ensuring that any chronic conditions continued to be treated.[20] As described by Cinar and colleagues in the *British Medical Journal*, the immediate- and long-term effects of this and subsequent earthquakes on the health system will be widespread.[21] Responding to the direct health needs of the population, including physical injuries and psychological trauma, as well as recovering from the disruption caused to routine services will place an extraordinary demand on the remaining health infrastructure.[21] In fact, Sean Kivlehan with the Emergency Health Systems Program at the Harvard Humanitarian Initiative (HHI), has stated, "What is almost invisible at first is the interruption to daily health services. We'll see the effects later in upticks of vaccine-preventable diseases and in the noncommunicable diseases that turn into acute problems because care was interrupted."[22] Furthermore, the HHI points out, this crisis is particularly complicated and catastrophic in northwest Syria, which has been experiencing a large-scale humanitarian crisis for over a decade. There were already several million people who were fully dependent on humanitarian aid due to conflict in Syria and limited cross-border transport of supplies.[22]

Biological Events

Botswana: HIV

Human immunodeficiency virus (HIV) attacks the immune system and diminishes the body's defense system—that is, its ability to fight infections and some cancers. As the process continues, the body gradually becomes immune deficient (measured by CD4 cell or T cells), leaving the individual susceptible to infections and diseases. Once these opportunistic infections and/or diseases occur, the individual is diagnosed with acquired immune deficiency syndrome (AIDS).

The origin of the virus is unknown, but scientists believe that the chimpanzee version of the virus (*simian immunodeficiency virus*, or SIV) was most likely the cause. Transmitted from chimpanzees to humans, it mutated into HIV when humans hunted for their meat and came in contact with the chimpanzees' infected blood.[23] Research suggests that this may have occurred as early as the late 1800s. Transmission of HIV in humans is through body fluids from infected individuals: blood, semen, vaginal secretions, and breast milk.

As reported by the WHO, in 2021, there were an estimated 38.4 million people worldwide diagnosed with HIV, with just slightly more women than men (51%) being affected.[24] According to the U.S. Centers for Disease Control and Prevention (CDC), Botswana is one of a few countries where the HIV epidemic has passed "the tipping point." According to the United Nations Children's Fund (UNICEF) Botswana,[25] this country is ranked among the top four countries in the world most affected by HIV and AIDS, behind South Africa, Eswatini, and Lesotho. Approximately 370,000 people were living with HIV in Botswana in 2018; 29,500 were aged 15 to 24 years, and females are more likely than males to be infected (64% to 47%, respectively). Given that 30% of all new infections in 2018 occurred in the 15- to 24-year age group, the strategies to mitigate transmission are shifting to focus on this subpopulation.

Although health organizations have a long way to go to eliminate HIV, the battle to conquer the global HIV epidemic and support health improvement has continued with evidence of its positive impact. A collaboration between the CDC, Harvard University, and government of Botswana was established to oversee the Ya Tsie study between 2013 and 2018. This community-focused approach to universal testing and antiretroviral treatment (ART) found a 30% reduction of HIV incidence in the intervention communities.[26] The UNAIDS Global AIDS Monitoring Botswana Country Progress Report indicates that this country is the first high-HIV-burden country to achieve indicators that demonstrate progress toward eliminating vertical transmission of the disease.[27] Specifically, 95% of pregnant women in Botswana received ART and the vertical transmission rate dropped from 9.0% to 2.2% in the decade starting in 2010.[27]

UNAIDS has published an approach to ending the AIDS epidemic worldwide by 2030 that focuses on three principal strategic tracks: universal testing and enhanced access to treatment, decreasing new infections, and elimination of discrimination.[27] Attention to enhancing facilitators and minimizing barriers to achieving the aggressive 2030 targets will continue to challenge public health leaders. Support and education from health providers is important for increasing the acceptance of ART. It is also important to understand that HIV-positive patients may consider HIV care as basic or fundamental and, therefore, feel stigmatized if they must visit a special clinic or separately designated area to receive their care and treatment.[28] The concern about up-front cost is a debatably weak argument against universal testing and treatment. Health leader considerations of cost/benefit should be weighed against the future burden of disease and lives lost.[29] Testing and treatment as a strong health promotion and disease prevention strategy is seen as fundamental to the UNAIDS plan.

Brazil: Zika Virus

Zika virus is a mosquito-borne flavivirus that was first detected in a rhesus monkey in the Zika forest of Uganda in 1947. In 1952, Zika virus was identified in humans in Uganda and Tanzania. Periodic outbreaks during the latter half of the 20th century have been confirmed in Africa, the Americas, Asia, and the Pacific. Those infected with the disease usually report only mild symptoms, including mild fever, skin rash, conjunctivitis, muscle and joint pain, malaise, and headache; symptoms typically last 2 to 7 days. In February 2015, Brazil reported a cluster of individuals in the northeastern part of the country complaining of febrile rash related to the virus. Then, in October 2015, Bahia, a single state in northeast Brazil, reported 56,318 suspected cases.[30]

Brazil reported in July 2015 an association between Zika virus infection and Guillain-Barré syndrome (GBS), and in October 2015 an association between the virus and microcephaly.[31] Guillain-Barré syndrome is a rare condition in which the body's immune system attacks part of the peripheral nervous system, which may result in muscle weakness and loss of sensation. Complications can cause permanent paralysis that affects breathing, requiring mechanical ventilation. Microcephaly is an uncommon birth defect in which a newborn's head circumference and brain are significantly smaller than expected for the age and weight. According to the CDC, congenital Zika syndrome is a unique pattern of birth defects and disabilities that may include microcephaly as well as a specific pattern of brain damage, scarring of the back of the eye, joints with limited range of motion, and muscle tone issues that restrict body movements.[31] Children affected by these symptoms have difficulty sitting independently, feeding, and sleeping, and may exhibit hearing and visual irregularities as well as seizures. The care and health cost burden for the lifespan of these children is not insignificant.

Initially, authorities in Brazil estimated that between 497,593 and 1,482,701 cases of Zika virus infection had occurred since the outbreak began. Once established in Brazil, the virus spread rapidly within the country and then throughout Latin America and the Caribbean. Within a year, the virus had been detected in nearly every country or territory infested with *Aedes aegypti*, the principal mosquito species that transmits Zika. Since 2015, 65 countries and territories have documented cases of the vector-borne illness, and the virus was considered a public health emergency of international concern.

The official end of the Brazil Public Health Emergency of International Concern period occurred in November 2016.[32] However, since then, over 100,000 cases have been reported, including hotspots of sustained transmission in some municipalities having more than 40 cases reported per 100,000 population consistently each year. An estimated 8,476 cases in Brazil were forecasted for 2021–2022, with the northeast and southeast regions experiencing the highest infections. Intense vector control is essential to decrease the burden of transmission.[32]

Brazil's Zika Strategic Response Plan was revised and published in June 2016; key actions focus on detection, prevention, care and support, and research.[33] Although there are no approved treatments currently available as of this writing, vaccines in various stages of clinical trial are in process and some appear to have promise.[34] The primary method of control and prevention of Zika and similar viruses remains vector control. The social and economic impacts on affected families may be long lasting and require continued support from the health system; likewise, the health burden from GBS and congenital Zika syndrome warrant prophylactic expenditures for virus control and prevention.[35] There is much yet to be learned about the epidemiology and virology of Zika, and closing the gaps in understanding will be imperative to ensure better management of outbreaks for future generations.[36]

Guinea, Liberia, and Sierra Leone: Ebola

Ebola virus disease (EVD), formerly known as Ebola hemorrhagic fever, is a severe and often fatal disease in humans, with a case mortality rate of approximately 50%. EVD can be found in humans and nonhumans. According to the CDC, there are five identified Ebola virus species: *Zaire ebolavirus*; *Sudan ebolavirus*; *Taï Forest ebolavirus*, formerly *Côte d'Ivoire ebolavirus*; *Bundibugyo ebolavirus*; and *Reston ebolavirus*. Four are known to cause disease in humans, and one causes disease in nonhumans. The natural reservoir host of

Ebola virus remains unknown. However, researchers suspect that the virus is animal-borne and that bats are the most likely reservoir.

Humans can get EVD through direct contact (through broken skin and membranes, eyes, and oral cavities) with contaminated blood, body fluids (possibly including semen from an infected male), needles and syringes, and contact with infected fruit bats and primates. Signs and symptoms may appear anywhere from 2 to 21 days after exposure and include fever, severe headache, muscle pain and weakness, fatigue, diarrhea, vomiting, abdominal pain, and unexplained hemorrhaging.

The first EVD cases appeared in 1976 with two outbreaks, one near the Ebola River in the Democratic Republic of the Congo and the other in South Sudan. Since its discovery, periodic outbreaks have ensued. In March 2014, the largest and most complex Ebola outbreak occurred, causing more deaths than all other outbreaks combined.[37]

The most severely affected countries—Guinea, Liberia, and Sierra Leone—have very weak healthcare systems. Liberia has only one academic referral hospital, which was severely damaged during the years of civil war. The hospital suffers from frequent floods and electrical fires. As in Sierra Leone, some of Liberia's healthcare workers who strived to heal the sick, while working in minimally equipped hospitals, became infected with EVD themselves and died. During the peak of the epidemic in Liberia, the overwhelmed healthcare systems had diminished capacity to deliver basic care, treatment, or emergency services. In some facilities, desperate families and their ill loved ones were turned away in large numbers. In addition, years of conflict and instability in the region have diminished infrastructure and human resources. Although they were rebuilding prior to the epidemic, businesses shut down, impacting the availability of food and fuel, which added to the plight of patients and their families. The Ebola outbreak required getting essential health services reestablished and addressing the weaknesses of the health system.

On August 8, 2014, the WHO declared the epidemic to be an international public health emergency. Supported by the WHO, United Nations, World Food Programme, CDC, USAID, and other humanitarian agencies, Liberia received aid in the form of Ebola clinics (stationary and mobile) to provide supportive care, laboratories for diagnosis, medical supplies, healthcare workers, and food. Several countries sent physicians, nurses, and other essential healthcare personnel.

On March 29, 2016, the WHO inspector director-general declared the end of the public health emergency of international concern in West Africa. A total of 28,616 confirmed, probable, and suspected cases had been reported in Guinea, Liberia, and Sierra Leone, with 11,325 deaths and over 10,000 survivors of Ebola.[37]

The scale and duration of this Ebola outbreak, with multi-continent spread, provided an opportunity to study evidence-based protocols and approaches such as fluid and electrolyte treatment. Although the initial international response to the outbreak was slow and lacking, extraordinary collaboration was ultimately realized. Healthcare utilization declined sharply in the affected geographic areas during the early and peak phases in West Africa due to concern about potential exposure,[38] and the impact of this change is unknown for the non-Ebola diseases and health concerns.

On December 19, 2019, the CDC announced the first approved vaccine for Ebola.[39] Health systems support of manufacturing, availability, and distribution of the vaccine to vulnerable populations may eventually eliminate future outbreaks.

Canada: SARS

Severe acute respiratory syndrome (SARS) emerged in Guangdong, China, in November 2002 with outbreaks occurring in early 2003 in Hong Kong, Hanoi, Toronto, and Singapore.[40] Overall, 30 countries were affected and 8,098 probable cases were reported, with 774 deaths occurring during the outbreak.[41] SARS is a viral respiratory illness caused by a coronavirus, called SARS-associated coronavirus (SARS-CoV). Typically, SARS begins with a fever greater than 100.4°F (38°C), headache, body aches, and general feelings of discomfort. Mild respiratory symptoms occur at the onset, with a dry cough that usually develops into pneumonia.

SARS was first found in Toronto, Canada, in a woman who returned from Hong Kong on February 23, 2003.[42] Transmission to other individuals occurred, resulting in an outbreak among 257 individuals in several Greater Toronto area hospitals (according to Public Health Agency of Canada). SARS continued to spread in Toronto among patients, staff, and visitors at one local hospital, forcing the hospital to close its emergency and intensive care services and to divert new admissions and potential transfers to other facilities. The local healthcare sector was in crisis. Strict public health isolation measures were implemented to lessen the transmission of the disease. The government designated SARS as a reportable, communicable, and virulent disease under the Health Protection and Promotion Act of March 25, 2003, allowing authorities to restrict individuals from engaging in activities that allowed for the spread of the disease, including isolation and quarantine. Anyone who had visited local hospitals was asked to adhere to a 10-day home quarantine.

On March 26, the Ontario Ministry of Health declared a medical state of emergency in the province.[43] The state of emergency was lifted on May 17 when the outbreak was thought to be over. Seven days later, several more cases of SARS were discovered in four of the local hospitals in Toronto. Again, intensive protective measures were implemented throughout the healthcare sector. On July 2, 2003, the state of emergency ended, with a total of 250 people diagnosed and 38 dead from the outbreak. The healthcare sector was radically impacted by the outbreak. Approximately 40% of the SARS cases in the Toronto outbreak were in healthcare workers. Of them, two nurses and one family physician died.

COVID-19 Pandemic

Severe acute respiratory syndrome coronavirus (SARS-CoV), Middle East respiratory syndrome coronavirus (MERS-CoV), and SARS-CoV-2 (COVID-19) have all infected humans over the past few decades. SARS-CoV and MERS-CoV, two highly pathogenic human coronaviruses, emerged early in the 21st century, which resulted in global epidemics.

The first case of COVID-19 occurred in China in the last 60 days of 2019 and was reported to the WHO shortly afterward.[44] The WHO officially announced a cluster of pneumonia cases in Wuhan, Hubei Provence, on December 31, 2019, and a novel coronavirus was subsequently identified. Two weeks later, China shared the genetic sequence for the virus and the first case outside of China was identified in Thailand. Due to the alarming rate of viral spread and the severity of the disease, the WHO announced that COVID-19 could be defined as a pandemic on March 11, 2020.[45]

Globally, the focus has been on individual countries, government leadership, and healthcare systems' (public and private) response and ability to care for those infected with COVID-19 virus. How did health systems respond in this time of crisis? How were they supported by their government? The following subsections examine some of the great success stories from the onset of the China epidemic to the global pandemic.

China

This section is based on Rossow's (2023) chapter in Johnson and DeShore, *COVID-19 Global Pandemic: The World Responds.*[46]

On December 31, 2019, the Wuhan Municipal Health Commission reported a cluster of pneumonia cases (of unknown etiology) detected in Wuhan City, Hubei Province, in China. The virus quickly spread and on January 3, 2020, 44 cases were reported. Of these cases, 11 were severely ill, showing fever, difficulty breathing, and, on chest radiographs, invasive lesions of the lungs. The remaining 33 were in stable condition. All were isolated and received treatment in Wuhan medical facilities. The genomic sequence of the virus was identified and released on January 10, 2020.[46]

With the new public health threat, a leadership system—the Epidemic Prevention and Control Headquarters System—was initiated at all levels, enabling a whole-of-government response and whole-of-society measures. The Chinese government initiated several public health measures to reduce the spread of COVID-19. Wuhan was placed under an extreme lockdown for 76 days, which soon spread to the entire Hubei province. Extreme public health containment efforts included regional lockdowns of more than 53 million people, severe travel restrictions, closure of schools, and forced quarantines. Throughout China, 14,000 health checkpoints were established at public transport hubs. Individuals with COVID-19 were treated only in designated hospitals. Wuhan built two new hospitals and a total of 16 shelter hospitals. Large public venues were used to facilitate the shelter (Fangcang) hospitals to treat and isolate less acutely ill patients not requiring intensive care services.[20] Initially, the local healthcare system was completely overwhelmed. Over 40,00 medical staff were deployed across China to ensure safe treatment.[46]

China's containment of COVID-19 was achieved and sustained by a whole-government and whole-people plan focusing on actively finding and managing patients (treatment and isolation); rapid expansion of polymerase chain reaction (PCR) testing (within 6 hours); ensuring isolation and treatment (designated hospitals); contract tracing and quarantine; mass screening, when necessary; lockdown to achieve initial containment; border control; and precision lockdowns and movement restrictions as indicated.[46]

Germany

Germany's response to COVID-19 is described by Rossow (2023), *The COVID-19 Pandemic: Health System Preparedness and Impact to Countries*, in the text *COVID-19 Global Pandemic: The World Responds* by Johnson and Deshore.[46]

Germany's pandemic preparedness existed at a federal and 16-state level. In preparation for a COVID-19 outbreak, Germany's Public Health Institute (the Robert Koch Institute), along with scientists from other institutions, analyzed data and other information to help inform and prepare Germany's COVID-19 response plan. By January 16, 2020, Germany's public health system issued a preparedness strategy, including procedures for risk assessment, testing guidelines, contract tracing, hygiene, and disease management. Measures also included surge capacity plans that included increasing the workforce (overtime, reallocation of staff, recruitment of student workers, retirees, and volunteers), canceling elective procedures, and using alternative facilities for care. Each state's preparedness plan varied considerably regarding strategies. However, this effort provided early success with an emphasis on prevention, detection, containment, and treatment. In early January 2020, PCR testing was developed at Charite Hospital, was made publicly available, and is currently used throughout the world.

On January 27, 2020, the first reported case of COVID-19 was identified in the southern Bavarian town of Starnsberg. Germany's public health system was able to provide a rapid response. One month later, on February 27, 2020, there were a total of 26 confirmed cases. The government then initiated an interministerial national crisis management group and soon required travelers entering from high-risk countries to provide information on potential exposure/contact. At the beginning of March 2020, mass gatherings and travel restrictions were imposed. Shortly thereafter, schools and some businesses started to close. On March 22, 2020, Germany's government announced a federal states/national "contact ban" that prohibited public gatherings of more than two people (except family) and required physical distancing of 5 feet. This plan worked effectively for the first phase of the pandemic as infection rates decreased. On May 4, 2020, the country's first lockdown was lifted, only to have restrictions imposed again to a strict lockdown with additional waves of the virus. In June 2020, the government issued a unique "Corona-Warn-App" allowing users with smartphones to know when they had tested positive for COVID-19.

During the first phase, due to planning and restrictions, hospital capacity, especially intensive care unit (ICU) beds, was adequate. In fact, German hospitals actually accepted patients from other countries. However, as the pandemic expanded, hospitals experienced shortages of personal protective equipment (PPE) and ICU beds primarily due to a lack of trained ICU nurses. Although challenging and difficult at times, Germany's strong primary care system adapted quickly, continuing to care for patients with COVID-19.

Aotearoa (New Zealand)

This section is based on Rossow's (2023) chapter in the text *COVID-19 Global Pandemic: The World Responds* by Johnson and Deshore.[46]

New Zealand's response to COVID-19 was described by government officials as "Hard and Early." Taking a proactive approach, the government evacuated all New Zealanders from affected regions of China. Initially, the New Zealand healthcare system was not well equipped to manage an epidemic of the magnitude of COVID-19. Public health was fragmented and underfunded, and hospital ICU beds, ventilators, and PPE were limited. On March 17, 2020, funding of NZ$500 million was approved for public health (contract tracing), primary care (community testing centers and telehealth), and hospitals (ICU beds, ventilators, equipment, and PPE).

Initially, there were 153 ICU beds, with the potential to surge to 560. The health system believed it had sufficient staffing to manage the patient load once hospitals made the decision to postpone elective services, reallocating and cross-training staff to care for patients with COVID-19. In addition, the government called for extra health professionals to return to the workforce, with a large response occurring from retired health professionals and those on maternity leave.

Early on in the pandemic, there were so few patients that some caseloads remained at zero with no reported staffing concerns. However, primary care and outpatient services were negatively impacted as volumes decreased dramatically (especially during lockdowns). Practitioners turned to using telehealth to deliver services. In August 2021, total cumulative cases of COVID-19 remained relatively low (under 3,000) until variants arrived in New Zealand, causing the number of cases to rise to a high of over 16,000 within 6 months.

In March 2022, a major outbreak involving the Omicron variant spread rapidly throughout the country. Hospitalizations quickly grew with increasing numbers of COVID-19–infected patients.

Hospital wards became understaffed as the number of infected healthcare workers increased. To keep the healthcare system running, mildly infected healthcare workers were encouraged to help out on understaffed COVID-19 wards. Overall, due to high vaccination rates, deaths were minimized.

Republic of Korea (South Korea)

The following discussion is based on Rossow's (2023) chapter in the text *COVID-19 Global Pandemic: The World Responds* by Johnson and Deshore.[46]

South Korea was relatively successful in preventing the spread of COVID-19 due to its experience with prior outbreaks, including the 2015 MERS outbreak. The first reported case of COVID-19 in South Korea was on January 20, 2020. As part of its attempts to combat the virus, the federal government sought to implement public health initiatives based on early response, speed, transparency, public–private partnerships, and national organization. This included a strong, early public health response and an almost immediate response after the first case; placing a premium on moving with speed as quickly as possible in setting up a testing regimen; transparent communication; real-time and frequent information dissemination to the public; and enlisting companies with needed resources in a private–public sector in the response. Innovative drive-through testing centers, wearing masks, social distancing, cancellation of social events, restriction on public transportation, and suspension of schools also helped to decrease the spread. In early 2022, due to public concerns, mitigation rules for public health and social measures were relaxed during the initial phase of the highly virulent Omicron variant. On March 16, 2022, the number of COVID-19 infections increased dramatically, to a single-day high of approximately 600,000 cases; it was the highest worldwide number since the start of the pandemic. In spite of this surge, the confirmed death rate remained low due to South Koreans' high vaccination rate, identification of high-risk individuals, preventive treatment, and early hospitalization.[46]

United States

The CDC confirmed the first laboratory-verified case of COVID-19 in the United States on January 18, 2020, in Washington State, with community transmission occurring by late February. The U.S. federal government provided a slow response, communicating inconsistent messages, which only complicated the situation. The lack of a national policy forced the individual states to come up with their own plans, which varied widely on how to manage the pandemic crisis. Initially, there were no standardized approaches to treatment, infection-control measures, use of PPE, and even lockdowns.

Rossow (2023) described the U.S. situation in Johnson and DeShore, *COVID-19 Global Pandemic: The World Responds.*[46]

Virtually all of the healthcare systems in the United States faced stiff challenges. The dominant health system concern was addressing the immediate needs of individuals (patients and staff) infected with the virus. Shortages of PPE (masks, N95 respirators, gloves, gowns) as well as patient equipment (ventilators, oxygen, beds, and even rooms) made the delivery of care challenging and at times almost impossible. Shortages in some healthcare systems led to compromises in safety. Some clinicians were forced to provide care with no PPE or limited to a single mask for an entire shift or multiple days, and some were told to provide their own. The Strategic National Stockpile, a source of emergency equipment for deployment during crisis situations, fell far short. Initially, the total number of stockpiled N95s was 13 million. Yet, statistics from the Census Bureau's 2019 American Community Survey state that 22 million clinicians were employed in the healthcare fight against COVID-19. COVID-19 placed extreme demands on an already stretched health system workforce. Long hours, extra shifts, significant stress, and inadequate resources were the norm during the pandemic. Staffing shortages of nurses and physicians nationwide led to emotional and physical exhaustion, manifesting in increased rates of depression, anxiety, insomnia, and post-traumatic stress disorder. As a result of the pandemic, approximately 66% of nurses have considered leaving the profession.[46]

According to the WHO, over 766 million cases of COVID-19 have been confirmed worldwide, with the death toll approaching 7 million, and over 13 billion vaccine doses administered.[47] The total economic impact of the pandemic has been estimated at up to $16 trillion USD for the United States alone.[48] Many weaknesses of the health systems throughout the world were laid bare during the pandemic. The special needs related to vulnerable populations, infrastructure, and communications are but a few, and highlight the need for a more cohesive approach of the world health community going forward.

Climate Events

India: Cyclones, Droughts, and Floods

India is extremely susceptible to a variety of significant natural disasters. A nation with varied climate and elevations, India's land is especially susceptible to drought (69%), earthquake (60%), flood (12%), and cyclone (8%).[49] Approximately 85% of the land mass is vulnerable to natural hazards, with 22 states designated as hazard prone. Research suggests that natural disaster losses in India are equal to 2% of the country's GDP and up to 12% of the federal government's revenues. Approximately 50 million people are affected yearly through destruction of personal belongings, damage to property, human suffering, and loss of life.

Population growth and urbanization have resulted in individuals living on marginal lands or in overpopulated cities that are at great disaster risk. Millions of people are affected on India's coastline (5,700 kilometers), which is subject to severe cyclones, and approximately 40% of India's population lives within 100 kilometers of the coastline. These natural disasters impact India's economy as well as the infrastructure, food and water supply, sanitation, public health, and agriculture.

In 2010, the government of India and the World Bank initiated the National Cyclone and Risk Mitigation Program to reduce the vulnerability of coastal communities to cyclone and other hydro-meteorological hazards. Initial goals include development of an Early Warning Dissemination System (EWDS) and shelters for coastal communities. On October 12, 2013, this system was tested when the severe cyclone Phailin reached the coast. The cyclone resulted in 44 deaths, damaged about 256,600 homes, and impacted 13.2 million people in over 18,370 villages.[50] Damages were due to high winds of up to 220 kilometers per hour, followed by flooding from torrential rains. The storm surge was up to approximately 3.5 meters above normal. Casualties were minimized due to preparedness planning and evacuation of nearly 1 million individuals and rescue teams. From this experience, an improvement plan for disaster risk reduction and management capabilities has been devised.

The National Cyclone Risk Mitigation Program was approved in May 2015 and the Implementation Completion and Results Report was published in August 2019.[51] This report included five key recommendations for cyclone mitigation based on the experience with the plan:

- Local community capacity building regarding infrastructure maintenance
- Climate-resilient infrastructure asset management systems
- Comprehensive procurement planning and investments, good governance
- Reinvestigation and review of the best available technology
- Effective and reliable emergency communications

Preparedness planning has helped to mitigate loss of life in India. Community members, health leaders, government organizations, academic and research institutions, the armed forces, and nongovernmental organizations have joined forces to contribute to disaster preparedness and management in India.

United States: Hurricane Katrina

Hurricane Katrina was one of the costliest and most devastating natural disasters in the history of the United States; it was responsible for 1,833 deaths and approximately $108 billion USD in damages. On August 23, 2005, tropical storm Katrina formed off the coast of the southeast Bahamas. Tracking west, the storm intensified, and on August 25, it reached landfall along the southeast Florida coast as a Category 1 hurricane (80 mph) on the Saffir–Simpson Hurricane Wind Scale. Moving southwest across the Gulf of Mexico, the hurricane strengthened significantly, with its winds reaching 175 mph, which classified it as a Category 5 hurricane. Katrina turned northwest, diminishing in strength to a Category 3 hurricane with 125 mph winds, and made landfall on August 29 near Buras, Louisiana.

Although the hurricane was destructive, the devastation in New Orleans was not directly from the hurricane but rather from the breaching of the levee system used to restrict the flow of waters from rivers, estuaries, and, most importantly, Lake Ponchatrain.[52] The intense storm surge overflowed the levee system in Orleans and St. Bernard parishes, leading to extensive levee failures and flooding of the parishes. Flooding of 80% of the city of New Orleans ensued at depths up to 20 feet.[53] In its wake, the storm left a trail of devastation and destroyed homes, businesses, and city infrastructure. Those who could afford to had evacuated before the storm hit, but those who stayed waited for days for rescue. Approximately 1 million individuals were displaced.[54]

Several of the healthcare facilities sustained primary damage from the storm. Hospitals were evacuated, and the remaining healthcare system was overwhelmed while attempting to care for patients with chronic conditions as well as those with immediate injuries. Patients with preexisting health conditions worsened as they were cut off from access to essential medications and treatments, such as oxygen, insulin, and kidney dialysis. Hospitals that did not evacuate prior to the storm found themselves and their patients under dismal circumstances when the rising floodwaters made it difficult, with shortages of medical supplies, to maintain standards of care. Communications with the outside world were minimal to nonexistent in the hard-hit areas. When possible, critically ill patients were evacuated to triage centers, which then became overwhelmed. Patients were sent for treatment to various permanent and temporary healthcare facilities across the south-central United States, separating them from family and loved ones. Public health emergencies were declared in nine parishes, and nearby states became hosts to large numbers of evacuees needing health care.

Basic needs of fresh water, food, and sewage handling were concerns. Public health challenges included keeping responders and victims safe, preventing diseases in temporary shelters, safely storing food supplies, and controlling mosquitoes. The short- and long-term behavioral health needs of victims, first responders, and healthcare providers had to be addressed.[54] Psychological problems—including acute stress disorder, post-traumatic stress disorder, depression, substance abuse, and anxiety—are some of the behavioral health problems that can result from exposure to natural disasters. Federal, state, and local governments, the community at large, the faith community, and volunteers worked tirelessly to provide relief to Katrina's victims. Evidence suggests that a decade after this event, one in six still exhibited symptoms indicating possible post-traumatic stress disorder.[55]

Studies show that some of those survivors, wherever they ultimately ended up, proved more resilient than others. "One household or family manages to recover," says David Abramson, a public health researcher who studies disasters at New York University.[55] "The other remains dysfunctional." His team has been surveying people affected by Katrina every few years since the storm. Poor, minority families in lower-lying areas faced disproportionate damage from Katrina and a more challenging path to recovery. But with the passage of years, the paths of survivors have diverged in complex, hard-to-predict ways. Abramson is one of three social scientists who led a project called Katrina@10 that looked for long-term predictors of resilience—factors that can cushion the shock of disaster and set the course for recovery. In their three long-running studies, the researchers have found a range of factors that seem to help, such as financial resources, social and cultural ties, and access to stable housing after the event. The 20th anniversary of Hurricane Katrina is quickly approaching, and 20 years after the devastating hurricane, there is much to learn from the longitudinal studies of Katrina@10. Survivors of the hurricane indicate that a sense of community and a feeling of belonging were huge factors in recovery efforts. Being back in the community where there is a shared emotional connection has soothed angst and hurt. Mental health conditions and poverty are staggering in the directly affected areas.[56–58]

Health System Response

As the previous sections have illustrated, many types of local, regional, or global crises and disasters have occurred over the past two decades. For the events that undoubtedly lie ahead, health systems and policy leaders have a responsibility to ensure the health systems' infrastructure has the capacity and capability to respond to the immediate and subsequent health needs of the population they serve. In addition, leaders must not only assist organizations in preparing for local events that are limited to a defined population (tornados, fires, mass-casualty events), but also anticipate the potential operational challenges of events that have a much broader impact (earthquakes, nuclear disaster, hurricanes, epidemics/pandemics) and affect a much larger population. As we have seen in a couple of the previous examples, developing partnerships and collaborative agreements with other organizations and agencies will be crucial to support the health needs of regional or global communities for optimizing coordination and efficacy of the response. The evaluation of response adequacy and effectiveness is essential after the conclusion of each event so lessons learned may be identified and iterative improvements in plans, communication, and training can be made. Ideally, studying mistakes or miscalculations as well as successful interventions made in response plans and their execution will assist health leaders in developing stronger and more comprehensive, effective, and proactive plans, ultimately saving many more lives than was previously possible.

In disaster situations, a quick response must be achieved. Damage can be considerably minimized with adequate disaster planning and preparedness. The four phases of emergency management can be used by national, state, and local governments as well as business organizations. Cyclical in nature, they include mitigation, preparedness, response, and recovery.[59]

Mitigation is the cornerstone of disaster management and includes activities to decrease the potential loss of life and property by lessening the impact of disasters.[60] Mitigation should start early, long before a disaster occurs, and involve all key stakeholders.

The focus of preparedness is to enhance the capacity to respond to an incident. Planners must take steps to ensure who, what, where, when, and how people and resources are available before an event occurs. Preparedness involves development of training programs for the community, public awareness, logistical support, and communications, early warning systems, and ongoing monitoring.

Response is the implementation of the time-critical plan to take action—that is, to save lives and prevent further damage. The recovery phase incorporates actions necessary to maintain and/or return the community to normal after the disaster. It may include repairing buildings, streets, railways, and other infrastructure damaged during the disaster.

From a healthcare perspective, recovery can include plans for addressing delayed care, assistance with the ongoing mental health needs of a community, or supporting care needs resulting from the sequela of the crisis or disaster.

Several critical success factors for all communities should be considered. As described by Johnson and Johnson,[61] critical success factors on the local level include training and education; mitigation of confusion, fear, and panic; time management; building response capacity; and economic empowerment. Health systems and public health leaders need to take responsibility for addressing concerns about the possibility of any of the disruptors described in this chapter. Clear roles and responsibilities as well as clarity and consistency of messaging are pivotal. Leaders should inform all of their key stakeholders that preventive and response policies and programs are under way. This may take place in the form of briefings, in-service workshops, simulations and mock exercises, security enhancements, and coordination with local health facilities. Health systems will want to develop disaster plans and crisis management initiatives that help victims and their families remain in the information loop or, in some cases, to evacuate affected areas. Additionally, the private sector will need to have contingency plans and backup systems to deal with business downtime. A robust communication plan for the public will also be essential. There are several critical success factors for a health system to consider, including the following:

1. Health system workforce training
2. Mitigation of confusion
3. Time management (time is critical)
4. Building a response capacity
5. Economic constraints
6. Coordination with local health agencies
7. Mitigation of fear and panic

Training

Training is essential for all health personnel. This could take the form of awareness enhancement or actual training in disease detection and early intervention. Additionally, the training of disaster coordinators is important. These individuals can serve as resource people, advisors, counselors, and/or organizers. They also could have the responsibility for staying informed and maintaining contact networks with local health agencies. Ideally, these coordinators would receive continuing education and periodic updates on the skills and knowledge needed to be effective in this role.

Mitigation of Confusion

Mitigation of confusion is a critical success factor in managing any crisis. The natural tendency of humans in a state of confusion is to panic. If this occurs, more harm can result. Training, preparedness, and prior discussion of the range of possibilities and response scenarios can all help to mitigate confusion. Fast, clear communication to all personnel is essential. Some organized protocols for testing and prophylaxis will help provide much-needed reassurance that the organization cares for its people and is taking appropriate steps. Finally, a key to avoiding confusion is the development of roles and responsibilities that are clearly understood and communicated widely.

Time Management

Time is critical in all matters pertaining to infectious disease. Early signs, early diagnosis, early warning to the noninfected, and early intervention all have positive implications for the decreased spread and eventual decreased impact of the disease.

Response Capacity

Response capacity may be in the form of trained personnel, along with needed equipment and proper training. It also includes working with local health agencies to develop quick response to a crisis. Financial considerations, such as cost of training, supplies, equipment, and downtime, should be part of the capacity building within the organization. Some might even consider a "health crisis reserve" for contingency planning.

Mitigation of Fear and Panic

There is no better way to decrease stress and anxiety in anticipation of a possible disruptive event, and likewise, no better way to control for panic, than putting in the requisite time and resources to properly train the workforce and larger community. This should include the design of a disaster-control command center where all communications originate. When just a few people direct the response, it tends to minimize panic and maximize effective distribution of information. Also, the importance of a regular cadence of communication cannot be overemphasized.

Importance of Planning

All health systems, regardless of size and geographic location, should have a disaster plan or crisis management plan for the populations they serve. See **Box 26-1** for a generic overview of the key elements for consideration in plan development and implementation. There will be wide variation in the plans according to local culture, political structure, and economics.

Conclusion

Health systems and societies everywhere will continue to be challenged by disasters and crises of many types. As profiled in the examples in this chapter, there is every indication that there will be no two events that are completely the same.[62] However, health systems and the communities they serve can prepare for likely events, and by working with international agencies, such as the WHO, we can better anticipate the unexpected. One example of this is the Global Health Security Agenda, a 30-plus nation initiative to promote global health security by strengthening countries' ability to prevent, detect, and respond to health threats.[63] Furthermore, if we are to achieve the Sustainable Development Goals[64] being promulgated by the United Nations, we will certainly have to develop and maintain robust health systems that have the capacity to effectively manage crises. With adequate planning and surveillance, events and disasters can—one hopes—become less disruptive to health systems and less deadly to affected populations.

Box 26-1 A General Preparedness Plan for Health Systems

Address the following areas in the plan:

- A collaboration plan, including area health care; public health; veterinary, physician, and medical group practices; and law enforcement with specific preparation action steps (training, stockpiling appropriate levels of material, etc.) and with the local hospital(s)
- Reporting of incidents and possible incidents and how they can be handled
- Infection control practices, procedures, and decontamination procedures
- A postexposure management plan for employees (prophylactics, vaccines, and a plan to prevent secondary infections)
- An offsite contingency operation plan
- An education plan (prospective and concurrent to an attack) and a public relations plan

Components of an Effective Response

- Establish protocols
- Establish a response command and control structure with which critical decisions can be made (should be community-based)
- Develop and implement a training and awareness program with local healthcare, public health, and law enforcement officials
- Ensure surveillance systems are in place

Cost Considerations (consider when preparing a budget)

- Cost of detection devices
- Cost of personal protection devices, such as masks and body covering
- Cost of vaccines and prophylaxis (antibiotics, etc.)
- Cost of training: training professionals, resources, and personnel hours
- Cost of constructing evacuation avenues, decontamination sites, and "safe rooms"
- Cost of temporary or permanent loss of business and government functionality
- Cost of securing substitute personnel in case of temporary or permanent loss of regular personnel

References

1. Pereira PL, Casanova AP, Sanz-Barbero B. A "before and after" in the use of emergency services in Spain? The impact of the economic crisis. *Intl J Health Serv*. 2016;46(3):430-447. doi: 10.1177/0020731416636591.
2. United Nations Office for Disaster and Risk Reduction. Human cost of disasters: an overview of the last 20 years. Accessed May 30, 2023. https://www.undrr.org/media/48008/download.
3. United Nations Office for Disaster and Risk Reduction. Accessed May 30, 2023. https://www.undrr.org/publication/sendai-framework-disaster-risk-reduction-2015-2030.
4. United Nations Office for Disaster and Risk Reduction. Accessed May 30, 2023. https://www.undrr.org/event/undrr-roac-caribbean-regional-workshop-measuring-effectiveness-early-warning-systems-through.
5. Nakahara S, Ichikawa M. Mortality in the 2011 tsunami in Japan. *J Epidemiol*. 2013;23(1):70-73. doi: 10.2188/jea.je20120114.
6. World Nuclear Association. Fukushima accident. 2016. Accessed May 30, 2023. https://world-nuclear.org/information-library/safety-and-security/safety-of-plants/fukushima-daiichi-accident.aspx.
7. National Oceanic and Atmospheric Administration. National Center for Environmental Information. https://www.ngdc.noaa.gov/hazel/view/hazards/tsunami/event-more-info/5413.
8. Kawano T, Hasegawa K, Watase H, et al. Infectious disease frequency among evacuees at shelters after the Great Eastern Japan Earthquake and Tsunami: a retrospective study. *Disaster Med Pub Health Prepared*. 2014;8(1):58-64. doi: 10.1017/dmp.2014.15.
9. Yokoyama Y, Otsuka Y, Kawakami N, et al. Mental health and related factors after the Great East Japan Earthquake and Tsunami. July 24, 2011. https://doi.org/10.1371/journal.pone.0102497.
10. Japanese Red Cross Society. *Japan: Earthquake and Tsunami. Final Report*. Glide Number EQ-2011-000028-JPN. March 2021.
11. U.S. Geological Survey. The MW 7.0 Haiti earthquake of January 12, 2010: USGS/EERI Advance Reconnaissance Team Report. Accessed May 30, 2023. https://pubs.usgs.gov/of/2010/1048/.
12. United Nations Development Programme. Human Development Index. Published 2015. Accessed May 30, 2023. http://hdr.undp.org/en/content/human-development-index-hdi.
13. World Bank Group. *Clean Water, Improved Sanitation, Better Health*. Haiti Conference, Washington, DC. Published October 2014. https://www.worldbank.org/content/dam/Worldbank/document/book_haiti_6oct_print.pdf.
14. Raviola G, Rose A, Fils-Aimé J, et al. Development of a comprehensive, sustained community mental health system in post-earthquake Haiti, 2010–2019. *Glob Ment Health*. 2020;7:E6. doi: 10.1017/gmh.2019.33.
15. Gerdin M, Wladis A, von Schreeb J. Foreign field hospitals after the 2010 Haiti earthquake: how good were we? *Emer Med J*. 2013;30:e8.
16. Amundson D, Dadekian G, Etienne M, et al. Practicing internal medicine onboard the USNS *Comfort* in the aftermath of the Haitian earthquake. *Ann Intern Med*. 2010. https://doi.org/10.7326/0003-4819-152-11-201006010-00215.
17. Diaz J. Why earthquakes in Haiti are so catastrophic. *NPR Environment*. Accessed May 26, 2023. https://www.npr.org/2021/08/16/1027990749/haiti-earthquake-why-deadly-explaine.
18. Health Equity International. Our work. Disaster response. 2021 earthquake response. Accessed May 26, 2023. https://healthequityintl.org/our-work/disaster-response/2021-earthquake-response.
19. Crickx J. Securing health in Haiti when the earthquake ruined hospitals. Published September 13, 2021. Accessed May 26, 2023. https://www.unicef.org/lac/en/stories/securing-health-haiti-when-earthquake-ruined-hospitals.
20. World Health Organization. Turkey and Syria earthquake. Accessed May 29, 2023. https://www.who.int/europe/emergencies/situations/turkiye-and-syria-earthquakes.
21. Cinar EN, Abbara A, Yilmaz E. Earthquakes in Turkey and Syria: collaboration needed to mitigate longer term risks to health. *BMJ*. 2023;380:559.
22. Kivlehan S. The Turkey–Syria earthquake's humanitarian challenges. 2023. Accessed May 29, 2023. https://www.hsph.harvard.edu/news/features/turkey-syria-earthquake/.
23. Sharp PM, Hahn BH. Origins of HIV and the AIDS pandemic. *Cold Spring Harb Perspect Med*. 2011;1(1):a006841. doi: 10.1101/cshperspect.a006841.
24. World Health Organization. Global Health Observatory: HIV/AIDS. https://www.who.int/data/gho/data/themes/hiv-aids.
25. United Nations Children's Fund (UNICEF) Botswana. https://www.unicef.org/botswana/hiv#:~:text=Botswana%20is%20ranked%20among%20the,female%20(64%20per%20cent).
26. Lockman S, Holme MP, Makhema J, et al. Implementation of universal HIV testing and treatment to reduce HIV incidence in Botswana: the Ya Tsie Study. *Curr HIV/AIDS Rep*. 2020;17:478-486. https://doi.org/10.1007/s11904-020-00523-0.
27. UNAIDS. Botswana leads the way for high HIV burden country certification on the path to eliminate vertical HIV transmission. Published July 2022. Accessed May 30, 2023. https://www.unaids.org/en/resources/presscentre/featurestories/2022/july/20220727_botswana-leads-way-eliminate-vertical-HIV-transmission.
28. Kebaabetswe P, Manyake K, Kadima E, et al. Barriers and facilitators to linkage to care and ART initiation in the setting of high ART coverage in Botswana, *AIDS Care*. 2020;32(6):722-728. doi: 10.1080/09540121.2019.1640843.
29. Havlir D, Lockman S, Ayles H, et al. What do the universal test and treat trials tell us about the path to HIV epidemic control? *J Int AIDS Soc*. 2020;23(2):e25455.
30. World Health Organization. The history of Zika virus. Published February 7, 2016. Accessed May 30, 2023. https://www.who.int/news-room/feature-stories/detail/the-history-of-zika-virus.
31. Centers for Disease Control and Prevention. Zika virus: microcephaly & other birth defects. Accessed May 30, 2023. https://www.cdc.gov/zika/healtheffects/birth_defects.html.
32. Yakob L. Zika virus after the Public Health Emergency of International Concern period, Brazil. *Emerg Infect Dis*. 2022. Accessed May, 27, 2023. https://doi.org/10.3201/eid2804.211949.
33. World Health Organization. Strategic response plan revised. June 2016. Accessed May 30, 2023. https://www.who.int/publications/i/item/zika-strategic-response-plan---revised-for-july-2016-december-2017.

34. Pattnaik A, Sahoo BR, Pattnaik AK. Current status of Zika virus vaccines: successes and challenges. *Vaccines.* 2020;8(2):266. https://doi.org/10.3390/vaccines8020266.
35. Alfaro-Murillo JA, Parpia AS, Fitzpatrick MC, et al. A cost-effectiveness tool for informing policies on Zika virus control. *PLoS Negl Trop Dis.* 2016;10(5):e0004743. https://doi.org/10.1371/journal.pntd.0004743.
36. Lowe R, Barcellos C, Brasil P, et al. The Zika virus epidemic in Brazil: from discovery to future implications. *Il J Environ Res Pub Health.* 2018;15(1):96. https://doi.org/10.3390/ijerph15010096.
37. World Health Organization. Ebola, West Africa, March 2014–2016. Accessed May 30, 2023. https://www.who.int/emergencies/situations/ebola-outbreak-2014-2016-West-Africa.
38. Wilhelm JA, Helleringer S. Utilization of non-Ebola health care services during Ebola outbreaks: a systematic review and meta-analysis. *J Glob Health.* 2019;9(1):010406. doi: 10.7189/jogh.09.010406.
39. Centers for Disease Control and Prevention. Ebola vaccine: information about ERVEBO®. Accessed May 30, 2023. https://www.cdc.gov/vhf/ebola/clinicians/vaccine/index.html.
40. Haagmans BL, Osterhaus A. SARS: from zoonosis to pandemic threat. In: Lashley FR, Durham JD, eds., *Emerging Infectious Diseases*. 2nd ed. New York, NY: Springer; 2016.
41. Centers for Disease Control and Prevention. SARS basics fact sheet. Accessed May 30, 2023. http://www.cdc.gov/sars/about/fs/-sars.html.
42. Varia M, Wilson S, Sarwal S, et al. Investigation of a nosocomial outbreak of severe acute respiratory syndrome. *Can Med Assoc J.* 2003;169(4):285-292.
43. Silverman A, Simor A, Loutfy, ML. Toronto emergency medical services and SARS. *Emerg Infect Dis.* 2004;10(9). doi: 10.3201/eid1009.040170.
44. Allam Z. The first 50 days of COVID-19: a detailed chronological timeline and extensive review of literature documenting the pandemic. In: *Surveying the Covid-19 Pandemic and Its Implications: Urban Health, Data Technology and Political Economy*. Elsevier; 2020:1-7. doi: 10.1016/B978-0-12-824313-8.00001-2.
45. World Health Organization. WHO coronavirus disease interactive timeline. https://www.who.int/emergencies/diseases/novel-coronavirus-2019/interactive-timeline#!
46. Rossow CC. The Covid-19 pandemic: health system preparedness and impact to countries. In: Johnson JA, DeShore NE, eds. *The Covid-19 Pandemic: Health System Preparedness and Impact to Countries*. Sentia Publishing; 2023:56-79.
47. World Health Organization. WHO coronavirus disease (COVID-19) dashboard. Accessed May 30, 2023. https://covid19.who.int.
48. Cutler DM, Summers LH. The COVID-19 pandemic and the $16 trillion virus. *JAMA.* 2020;324(15):1495-1496. doi: 10.1001/jama.2020.19759.
49. Sharma VK, Ashtutosh DK. Natural disaster management in India. *Yojana.* 2012;30-36. Accessed May 30, 2023. https://www.insightsonindia.com/wp-content/uploads/2013/09/natural-disaster-management-in-india.pdf.
50. World Bank. India averts devastation from cyclone Phailin. Published April 10, 2014. Accessed May 30, 2023. https://www.worldbank.org/en/results/2014/04/10/india-averts-cyclone-phailin-devastation.
51. World Bank. Implementation completion and results report. Accessed May 30, 2023. https://documents1.worldbank.org/curated/en/482381567532199583/pdf/India-First-National-Cyclone-Risk-Mitigation-Project.pdf.
52. Graumann A, Houston T, Lawrimore J, et al. *Hurricane Katrina: A Climatological Perspective.* National Oceanic and Atmospheric Administration. August 2006. Accessed May 30, 2023. https://repository.library.noaa.gov/view/noaa/13833.
53. Johnson JA. *Health Organizations: Theory, Behavior, and Development*. Sudbury, MA: Jones and Bartlett Publishers; 2009.
54. Lister SA. *Hurricane Katrina: The Public Health and Medical Response*. Library of Congress, Congressional Research Service; 2005.
55. Raker EJ, Lowe SR, Arcaya MC, et al. Twelve years later: the long-term mental health consequences of Hurricane Katrina. *Soc Sci Med.* 2019;242. https://doi.org/10.1016/j.socscimed.2019.112610.
56. Servick S. More than 12 years after Hurricane Katrina, scientists are learning what makes some survivors more resilient than others. *Science*. Published February 27, 2018. Accessed May 30, 2023. https://www.science.org/content/article/more-12-years-after-hurricane-katrina-scientists-are-learning-what-makes-some-survivors.
57. Tulane University. CSDP: Katrina@10. Demographic and health disparities in recovery from Hurricane Katrina. Accessed May 30, 2023. https://sph.tulane.edu/katrina10.
58. Abramson DM, VanLandingham MJ, Waters MC (eds.). Disaster recovery and population health. *Int J of Environ Res Public Health*. 2023; special issue. Accessed March 03, 2025. https://www.mdpi.com/journal/ijerph/special_issues/Disaster_Recovery_Population_Health#info.
59. Martin JR. Disaster phases and earthquake policies. Accessed May 30, 2023. https://training.fema.gov/emiweb/downloads/earthquakeem/session%2008/session%208%20-%20disaster%20phases%20final_01.pdf.
60. Federal Emergency Management Agency (FEMA). Hazard mitigation planning. Accessed May 30, 2023. https://www.fema.gov/emergency-managers/risk-management/hazard-mitigation-planning.
61. Johnson JA, Johnson A. Community preparedness and response. *Natl Soc Sci Perspect J.* 2006;33(1):27-30.
62. Dowell SF, Tappero JW, Frieden TR. Public health in Haiti: challenges and progress. *N Engl J Med.* 2011:300-301. http://www.nejm.org/doi/pdf/10.1056/NEJMp1100118.
63. Kanji L. Hidden dangers: the implications of the global security agenda. *Harvard Intl Rev.* 2016;37(2):8-12.
64. Rosenbaum B. Making the Millennium Development Goals sustainable: the transition from MDG's to SDG's. *Harvard Intl Rev.* 2015;37(1):58-62.

CHAPTER 27

The Business of Health Care

Steven W. Howard, Morgan House, and Danny House

Introduction

Health systems around the world often function based on a mix of public and private funding in the provision of care for their populations. These systems focus on the value of care for patients in terms of their ability to access care and the care of elderly patients. This chapter discusses value-based care and long-term care as it relates to the business of health care.

The Business of Health Care

Introduction and Origins of Value-Based Health Care and Alternative Payment Models

Value-based health care (VBHC or VBC) is typically defined as a system of providing (and paying for) healthcare services that promotes results that are valuable to patients (and payers), including better health outcomes and patient experiences, reduced unnecessary utilization, improved health equity, and reducing cost of care.[1-3] Skyrocketing healthcare inflation has been a key driver for VBC reforms, particularly in countries like the United States, where population health metrics have been poor. Many researchers and practitioners over the past decades have proposed that the root of the problem is the fee-for-service healthcare payment system, which pays providers for each service provided without regard for outcomes or quality. The term "perverse incentives" arose to describe this phenomenon of providers increasing the volumes of services beyond what was necessary or in the interest of patients (but increasing provider incomes). Policymakers, as well as payers, employers, and citizens, recognized the problem and sought solutions for better aligning their interests with those of providers. The result has been a plethora of policy experiments aiming at value-based health care.

There are many ways "value" can be promoted in healthcare systems around the world. Some of the better-known tools include accountable care organizations (ACOs), episode-based payments, bundled payments, and other alternative payment models (APMs). All of these aim to provide explicit financial incentives for providers or provider organizations (or confederations of provider organizations) to reduce the costs of care and thereby improve their own financial margins. However, most ACO or APM arrangements also require the providers to achieve specified measures for quality of care, efficiency, effectiveness of care, safety, equity, timeliness, appropriate utilization, and/or patient experience.[4] While interest in VBHC is growing worldwide, the leaders in value-based care innovations are the United States and the Netherlands.[3,4] As described elsewhere in this text, both countries have relatively market-oriented healthcare models with private healthcare providers and private health insurance companies.

Both countries allow payers and providers to independently contract with one another, including allowing flexible payment terms. Germany has also launched some ACO-like APM pilots, although they required special government waivers and had less ability to experiment than is permitted in the Netherlands and in the United States.[4] Following are overviews of the U.S. Medicare ACO model and some other APM models in multiple countries.

Accountable Care Organizations

The 2010 Affordable Care Act was the most significant health reform legislation in the United States in 45 years. Most of its provisions pertained to health insurance, but the most impactful element directly affecting healthcare providers was the creation of the U.S. federal government's Medicare Shared Savings Program (MSSP) Accountable Care Organization (ACO) provision.[5] An ACO needed to be large enough to serve at least 5,000 Medicare patients in a defined geographic area and had to be able to meet all of their healthcare needs. While some provider organizations were large enough to provide the entire continuum of medical care from hospital services through primary care, other providers needed to form joint ventures with other providers to create an ACO entity that was able to do so. The resulting ACO entity contracted with Medicare to provide services in the designated area. Any patients receiving the "plurality of care"—that is, most of their primary care and/or specialty care visits—from a given ACO's providers would be "attributed" to that ACO, and it would be responsible for the patient's health metrics and spending.[6,7]

Providers could volunteer to participate in the program, and if they met quality metrics, they would share in the savings they helped produce for Medicare (compared to a 3-year rolling average of the most recent historical spending). Quality metrics included healthcare process measures aimed at improving health outcomes for chronic disease patients, such as getting recommended screenings for patients with diabetes and hypertension or recommended maintenance medications for patients with heart failure or coronary artery disease. Other quality metrics were aimed at overall prevention, such as ensuring that most of a provider's Medicare patients received annual wellness exams, promotion of smoking-cessation program(s), cancer screenings, and recommended vaccines for illnesses that are particularly dangerous for elders, like flu and pneumonia.[8] When provider organizations met these targets and reduced spending versus their 3-year rolling average costs, the providers would share in the savings produced (the percentage of savings paid to the provider varied by year and by the degree of financial risk they agreed to accept from Medicare).

ACO-like APMs have arisen in other countries as well. Multiple models have been implemented by OptiMedis in Germany, beginning with the pioneering Gesundes Kinzigtal model in the Black Forest area of southwest Germany in 2005, and subsequently in Eschwege, Hessen, and the Horn and Billstedt areas of east Hamburg.[4] Other models that bear similarities to Medicare-style ACOs have arisen in the Netherlands, including arrangements between primary care providers and multiple payers that hold the providers accountable for quality metrics (but with greater emphasis on outcome measures than process measures), and with the provider organization sharing in any savings produced (although in some cases, providers may be "capitated").[4]

Capitation

Except for employers, hospitals, or governments paying simple salaries to individual physicians, capitation is probably one of the oldest forms of alternative payment in health care.[9] In capitation, the physician or provider organization receives a fixed payment per patient, or "per member per month" (PMPM or PPPM). This is the opposite end of the payment spectrum from fee-for-service, as payment has no connection to volume of services provided. Multiple U.S. states' Medicaid programs began to experiment with this model in the 1970s by paying PMPM to managed care organization (MCO) insurance companies, which contracted with provider groups to provide the care.[9] While there is no requirement for MCOs to in turn pay individual providers or clinics by capitation, this is sometimes done in practice, particularly with larger provider organizations that have many patients and would be less affected if one patient has very high healthcare needs during a given period. In the United Kingdom, the National Health Service (NHS) general practitioners (GPs) receive a capitated payment of approximately £163.65 (214.33 USD) per patient per year to cover all needed primary care visits.[10] In addition to capitation, the NHS uses pay-for-performance incentives with its contracted primary care physicians.

Pay-for-Performance (P4P)

Pay for performance (P4P) is a common component of many APM models. Whereas the shared-savings ACO model allows providers to share in the savings produced if they achieve performance metrics, P4P is simply an additional payment to providers for hitting certain metrics. As with the ACO models, those metrics could be associated with health outcomes, healthcare processes, equity, efficiency, or spending targets.

Bundled Payments

Bundled payments are one of the most prevalent and increasingly popular forms of APM. While the bundle is still somewhat volume-based, it is typically designed to include a major type of procedure and the multiple related provider visits, diagnostic imaging, lab tests, and even prescription drugs provided within a time frame logically related to the episode of care. The earliest forms of bundled payment include the diagnosis-related group (DRG) payment model for hospitals, which began in the U.S. Medicare program in 1982.[11] The DRG includes all or nearly all of the inpatient care for a patient's hospitalization related to a given hospital stay for a given diagnosis. Paying hospitals a single, predetermined amount for a hospital stay shifted incentives away from longer lengths of stay and less efficient hospital care. After implementing the DRG model, hospital lengths of stay were reduced as hospitals discharged patients to home or rehabilitation centers more quickly than before. The newer evolutions in bundled payment take the DRG idea a step further by including "upstream" and "downstream" services provided over time. Examples include hip or knee replacement surgeries, maternity care bundles, and cancer treatment. In those bundles, the pre-procedure clinician visits, labs, and imaging, along with post-procedure follow-up visits, labs, and imaging, may all be included under a single payment to the provider. This incentivizes better coordination and communication between clinicians and departments within a health system and introduces financial incentives to reduce waste (such as redundant imaging or labs) and avoidable or unnecessary office visits. APMs like bundled payments also create financial incentives for innovation.[4] Because the fixed payment has already been received, there is little or no incentive to perform additional services solely for the added revenue. Instead, the door is opened to providing necessary care in more efficient, economical ways, including using nonphysician allied health providers (personnel who were able to be billed via the fee-for-service approach in the past) or remote patient care (previously uncompensated or lower paid than in-person care).

Future Directions for Value-Based Health Care and Alternative Payment Models

With healthcare costs continuing to rise, healthcare workforce shortages becoming increasingly acute, and governments seeking new approaches to getting more and better health care for their money, the pursuit of value and experimentation with APMs will only accelerate.[4] We expect to see increasingly more budget-constrained and risk-averse governmental and private payers continuing to seek means to push more risk onto providers. Healthcare services can be provided more effectively and efficiently, but not when payment model "perverse incentivizes" promote waste and inattention to quality and patient experiences. The COVID-19 pandemic forced healthcare providers and the global population to learn new approaches to interacting and communicating. As payment models recognize these changes in societal norms, we anticipate many of these forced adaptations will remain and become an integral part of health care.[1,4]

The Aging Population and Long-Term Care

Introduction

The population of people aged 65 will nearly double between now and 2050, from 48 million to 88 million, and 70% of these individuals will require some form of long-term care support services.[12] Because of this surge, there will be an increased need for paid caregivers who serve this population, many of whom will reside in long-term or residential living. Long-term care is an extended type of care used over long periods, with only respite periods as breaks, and generally continuing throughout the patient's remaining life. While many different and interchangeable names are associated with long-term care, these services are typically received after acute healthcare services. Long-term care is a continuum of care. Put simply, people who benefit from long-term care are not ill enough to require continued hospital care and are not well enough to receive only minimal healthcare services at home.

Long-term care facilities provide various services and residential living options for individuals who cannot live independently. Long-term care facilities may be classified as assisted living facilities and/or skilled nursing facilities. Assisted living facilities provide services to individuals who do not need skilled nursing care. Individuals may receive help with activities of daily living, including housekeeping, laundry service, meal preparation, and transportation to and from social outings and medical appointments. Skilled nursing facilities provide these same items plus 24-hour skilled nursing services.

Long-Term Care in the United States: How and Why It Came to Be

The long-term care of today, as we know it, looked very different in the United States long ago. It is difficult for us to imagine a country without some form of long-term care, but not so long ago, relatively speaking, the United States had no long-term care. In a formal institutionalized environment, there was no mechanism to provide care or assistance to the aging population.

When the United States was in its infancy, most of the population lived in a rural setting. As people aged and required assistance with their activities of daily living, they depended primarily on family members to provide that assistance within the home. It was not until the mid- to late 1800s that the shift from rural to urban living started to blossom. In the latter part of the 1800s, in the increasingly urban society, many families were unable to care for loved ones due to lack of space or because all family members, including children, were employed 6 days per week, 12 hours a day.[13] At the turn of the 20th century, many members of the aged population lived in community housing due to busy working families. This type of housing was substandard at best, and often unkempt, and the living conditions were atrocious. As a result, the country started trending away from this type of long-term care with the addition of in-home nurses; this was the first introduction of what we now know as home health nurses. These nurses delivered much-needed care to the aged population in the home setting, which improved outcomes and allowed people to live at home until death.

As this industry started to emerge, many initiatives were undertaken that aimed to increase the care provided to elderly Americans. Those initiatives came from both the private and governmental sectors. Between the 1930s and 1960s, two landmark programs aimed at assisting with older adults' care, housing, and funding were established: Social Security and Medicare/Medicaid. The Social Security Act aimed to provide retirement assistance to older adults and allowed for a nursing home stipend; this caused many in the private sector to begin building nursing homes all across America. Social Security has seen many amendments, such as those creating Medicare and Medicaid, which allow people at a certain age to receive short-term rehabilitation and long-term care, respectively. Combined, they ignited the long-term care industry as a whole.

Public policy and healthcare reform have been at the forefront for many decades. While access to health care is not delineated in the U.S. Constitution, the Bill of Rights, or other federal statutes, it has become a de facto "right" in the minds of most Americans.[14] Vast challenges exist in creating an agreed-upon system that is accessible and affordable. The United States has the highest healthcare costs, measured as a percentage of the gross domestic product (GDP), of any developed nation in the world, yet was 11th of 25 on quality indicators.[14]

Today's long-term care looks quite different than it did during its inception. The Omnibus Budget Reconciliation Act (OBRA) of 1987 brought about much-needed, long-term care reform—specifically, nursing home reform. OBRA ensured that nursing homes played by the same rules, bringing about changes centered on patient treatment and accountability. OBRA placed long-term care providers in an arena that promoted patient safety, patient dignity, and respect; ensured the patient would be involved in their care and care delivery; and ensured nursing homes maintained a comfortable and clean environment, free from abuse and neglect. However, there have been amendments made to OBRA, and nursing homes still have to maintain the same level of care and accountability that OBRA provides.

Long-Term Care Issues

The long-term care industry is the most highly regulated industry in the United States. Today, nursing facilities are required to maintain a high level of patient care, while caring for today's most ill and elderly population. The industry has seen many changes and challenges throughout the last 50 to 60 years. The past 20 years or so have been especially challenging. The industry has not only been subjected to cuts in reimbursement rates, but has also had to shift to a more performance-based or outcome-driven approach to providing care. Nursing homes, more specifically, have had to change their approach to care delivery and focus more intensely on results and improved patient outcomes rather than maintaining patients' current level of function. Nursing homes now gear their care toward returning patients to a prior level of function. In the skilled arena, they focus on quality over quantity, meaning they have a shorter window in which to rehabilitate individuals back to a functional level at which they might not have functioned in quite some time. As a result, nursing homes are no longer paid according to what outcome they plan to produce, but based on the outcomes they actually achieve; this is called paid-for-performance.

Payment Methods

During the first two decades of the 20th century, there was very little government in long-term care, happening only when private resources could not be found.[14] Historically, facilities were built on the outskirts of town to help residents avoid, or perhaps protect, those receiving the care. The Great Depression created many hardships and prevented individuals from being able to provide for themselves; it also limited resource sharing to care for the aged or chronically ill. The passage of the Social Security Act of 1935 and other related welfare programs, however, caused the federal government to become deeply involved in long-term care. This has been identified as the beginning of the formal, private nursing home industry, where many forms of long-term care have developed and evolved.[15]

The most regulated healthcare sector in the United States is the nursing home or long-term care industry.[16] Yet, the ever-changing personal needs, increased life expectancy, and chronic conditions of patients posit the need for flexibility within the industry. Even so, third-party payers have become restrictive and rigid regarding allowable services and reimbursement; long-term care providers must operate efficiently and cost-effectively.

How Long-Term Care Is Financed

The vast majority of people aged 65 and over will need some form of long-term care for at least a year before their death. The cost of care at a nursing home or assisted living facility could be $100,000 USD or more, depending on the state. This cost could prove to be more than most people could afford, such that individuals often spend down their entire life savings on care services. Individuals pay for long-term care services in several ways: Medicare, Medicaid, private pay, managed care (Medicare replacement), private insurance, and/or long-term care insurance. All payer types come with limitations. Medicare, for example, will pay for room and board and some specialized services such as therapy. Medicaid, which pays for more than half of the U.S. long-term care services, will pay for most or all services a person needs monthly, but qualifications are limited to those who show limited available income and assets. People with small end-of-life savings usually spend those savings on a long-term care facility to qualify for Medicaid. Most states have individualized qualification criteria, and each state varies somewhat as to which services are provided to an individual on Medicaid.

The long-term care industry is a multi-billion-dollar industry but has had to operate on a minimal budget. The COVID-19 pandemic forced an already dismal budget to be tightened, producing even more significant challenges for care providers. Labor markets changed drastically; a labor shortage that had only recently recovered from the 1994 shortage experienced even worse impacts. The American Health Care Association and National Center for Assisted Living (AHCA/NCAL), representing 14,000 nursing homes and assisted-living communities, conducted a study released in February 2023 that analyzed the pandemic's effects on the long-term care labor shortage. During the pandemic, more than 210,000 nursing home sector jobs were lost, and the nursing home workforce declined by more than 13%. Currently, 84% of nursing homes face moderate to high staffing shortages, posing a significant limitation on the quality of care these nursing homes can provide.[17] It felt as though this shortage was met with increased staffing mandates when there were few to no staff to be found.

Following the pandemic, staff recruitment was at all-time lows, staff retention was becoming an issue, and the workforce—or at least the workforce that is certified or licensed for delivery of care—was not entering the job market or at least did not have the desire to enter the long-term care sector of the job market. As a result, long-term care providers had to think outside the box and create ways to attract employees. Many of them had to increase new-hire wages, adding to the burden of inflation and the cost of goods and services. Many providers want to offer higher salaries and better benefits to attract and retain employees but lack the necessary funds to do so. For years, nursing homes have faced low Medicaid reimbursement rates that do not adequately cover the cost of care. These low rates, coupled with additional expenses from the pandemic, have left many facilities in financial turmoil. As staff challenges grew, providers were left without the means to hire new workers or keep their current ones.[18] Nursing homes were forced to enter into agreements with staffing agencies and often had to prove to state and federal legislators that those contracts were in place should there be a need. Facility owners and operators began offering sign-on bonuses often higher than industry averages; they also offered extra shift bonuses to current staff to cover vacant shifts, in addition to mandated overtime. These changes made it hard for companies in the long-term care business to remain open, and many subsequently had to close. Because these facilities are often considered significant employers in many communities, their closure may impact many families and communities.

Triple Aim

The Triple Aim is a framework developed in 2007 by the Institute for Healthcare Improvement (IHI) that describes an approach to optimizing health system performance. IHI believes that new designs must be established to simultaneously pursue three dimensions, or the "Triple Aim": improving the patient experience of care (including quality and satisfaction), improving the health of populations, and reducing the per capita cost of health care.[19] Seven years later, a fourth Aim was added to acknowledge widespread burnout—namely, improving the satisfaction of physicians and healthcare professionals. Since then, the Triple and Quadruple Aims have been widely adopted as a guide for healthcare improvement.[20] However, improving healthcare quality without a focus on equity will not create a favorable situation because individuals without access to care disproportionately come from socially marginalized groups. These quality improvement efforts, a staple in healthcare innovation and improvement efforts, risk exacerbating health disparities.[20]

Hardships

The AHCA/NCAL study showed that 55% of nursing homes are operating at a loss, and if the economic strain continues, 52% may have to close within a year. The loss of COVID-19 aid, including Provider Relief Funds, Medicaid-enhanced FMAP, and American Rescue Plan state funding, will exacerbate this financial strain.[17] It is a difficult and slow process to recover from such a shortage. Given the current staffing issues, it's estimated that nursing homes will not return to their prepandemic workforce levels until 2027.[17]

The long-term care industry has never before had a hardship like it experienced with the COVID-19 pandemic. The pandemic changed the entire landscape of what long-term care looked like. The industry basically "shut the doors"; patients were not allowed to leave, and visitors were not allowed to enter. This concept went against everything those in the business had lived and had been taught. Nursing homes suddenly become almost prison-like. Nursing homes that once would be cited for not allowing visitors would now be cited for accepting visitors, even though the regulation for receiving visitors had not changed. Facilities had to become creative in how they balanced regulation versus pandemic mandates. Visitation, for example, was not allowed, yet nursing facilities were still mandated to enable some visitation. They achieved this through some degree of window visits, outdoor visits, and visits via Zoom, FaceTime, Skype, or other means that allowed for resident-to-family interaction, keeping the industry in good graces with federal regulation.

References

1. Commonwealth Fund. Health care delivery system reform. 2023. Accessed August 21, 2023. https://www.commonwealthfund.org/programs/health-care-delivery-system-reform.
2. Commonwealth Fund. Value-based care: what it is, and why it's needed. 2023. Accessed August 21, 2023. https://www.commonwealthfund.org/publications/explainer/2023/feb/value-based-care-what-it-is-why-its-needed.
3. BCG. How Dutch hospitals make value-based health care work. 2018. Accessed August 21, 2023. https://www.bcg.com/publications/2018/how-dutch-hospitals-make-value-based-health-care-work.
4. Howard S, Bradford N, Henning M, et al. Building alternative payment models in health care: a subject-matter expert analysis. *Eur J Manag.* 2023.
5. Kaiser Family Foundation. Summary of the Affordable Care Act. 2018. Accessed August 21, 2023. https://www.kff.org/health-reform/fact-sheet/summary-of-the-affordable-care-act/.
6. MedPac. Medicare Accountable Care Organization models: recent performance and long-term issues. Accessed June 11, 2023. https://www.medpac.gov/wp-content/uploads/import_data/scrape_files/docs/default-source/reports/jun18_ch8_medpacreport_sec.pdf.
7. Chartspan.com. 2023. Accessed June 11, 2023. https://www.chartspan.com/blog/improve-your-patient-attribution-rates-and-your-aco-performance/.
8. Centers for Medicare and Medicaid Services. CMS.gov and/or CMS.gov/Downloads. Accessed June 11, 2023. https://www.cms.gov/medicare/medicare-fee-for-service-payment/sharedsavingsprogram/program-guidance-and-specifications and/or https://www.cms.gov/files/document/py-2022-apm-performance-pathway-cms-web-interface-measure-benchmarks-acos.pdf; https://www.cms.gov/medicare/medicare-fee-for-service-payment/sharedsavingsprogram/downloads/aco-shared-savings-program-quality-measures.pdf.
9. MacPac (Medicaid and CHIP Payment and Access Commission). Medicaid managed care capitation rate setting. 2022. Accessed August 21, 2023. https://www.macpac

.gov/wp-content/uploads/2022/03/Managed-care-capitation-issue-brief.pdf.

10. Lind S. GP practices received an average £4.04 more per registered patient in 2021/22. *Pulse Today.* 2022. https://www.pulsetoday.co.uk/news/practice-personal-finance/gp-practices-received-an-average-4-04-more-per-registered-patient-in-2021-22/.
11. Centers for Medicare and Medicaid Services. Design and development of the diagnosis related group. https://www.cms.gov/icd10m/version37-fullcode-cms/fullcode_cms/Design_and_development_of_the_Diagnosis_Related_Group_(DRGs).pdf.
12. He W, Goodkind D, Kowal P. *An Aging World: 2015*. U.S. Census Bureau, International Population Reports, P95/16-1. Washington, DC: U.S. Government Publishing Office; 2016.
13. NCPC. The evolution of long-term care services. March 20, 2109. Accessed April 27, 2023. https://www.longtermcarelink.net/articles/The-Evolution-of-Long-Term-Care-Services.htm.
14. Chies S, Pratt JR. *Pratt's Long-Term Care: Managing Across the Continuum*. Burlington, MA: Jones & Bartlett Learning; 2022.
15. Goldsmith SB. *Essentials of Long-Term Care Administration*. Aspen; 1994.
16. Pratt J. *Long-Term Care: Managing Across the Continuum*, 4th ed. Burlington, MA: Jones & Bartlett Learning; 2016.
17. Cerulli P. AHCA State of the Nursing Home Sector Fact Sheet reveals key industry findings. I Advance Senior Care; 2023. Accessed April 28, 2023. https://www.iadvanceseniorcare.com/ahca-state-of-the-nursing-home-sector-fact-sheet-reveals-key-industry-findings/.
18. American Health Care Association. Staffing challenges in long term care facilities continue to threaten access to care for residents. 2021. https://www.ahcancal.org/News-and-Communications/Press-Releases/Pages/Staffing-Challenges-In-Long-Term-Care-Facilities-Continue-To-Threaten-Access-to-Care-for-Residents.aspx.
19. Institute for Healthcare Improvement. The IHI triple aim. Accessed April 27, 2023. https://www.ihi.org/Engage/Initiatives/TripleAim/Pages/default.aspx.
20. Nundy S. Healthcare needs the Quintuple Aim. *MedCity News*. 2022. Accessed April 27, 2023. https://medcitynews.com/2022/11/healthcare-needs-the-quintuple-aim/.

CHAPTER 28

Comparative Global Challenges and Opportunities

Kimberly S. Davey and Richard G. Greenhill

Introduction

Health systems in the 21st century are facing many new challenges as they seek to provide health care for growing populations with increasingly complex medical conditions. There is a global labor shortage of skilled professionals, especially nurses and physicians. Many facilities need repair or upgrading; improvements in efficiency, effectiveness, and equity remain elusive in many cases; and financial resources are often in short supply. Advancements in technology include a host of opportunities and threats for healthcare leaders across the globe to consider.

As described in previous chapters of this book, there are many aspirations and opportunities for improving the scope and effectiveness of health systems within the overall agenda for global health. The United Nations (UN) has approved goals that will help achieve this. These Sustainable Development Goals (SDGs) are designed to support well-being at all levels of society.[1] However, one, SDG 3, is specifically focused on health. SDG 3 has 13 targets, which are summarized here[2]:

- By 2030, reduce the global maternal mortality ratio to less than 70 per 100,000 live births.
- By 2030, end preventable deaths of newborns and children under 5 years of age, with all countries aiming to reduce neonatal mortality to at least as low as 12 per 1,000 live births and under-five mortality to at least as low as 25 per 1,000 live births.
- By 2030, end the epidemics of AIDS, tuberculosis, malaria, and neglected tropical diseases and combat hepatitis, waterborne diseases, and other communicable diseases.
- By 2030, reduce by one-third premature mortality from noncommunicable diseases through prevention and treatment and promote mental health and well-being.
- Strengthen the prevention and treatment of substance abuse, including narcotic drug abuse and harmful use of alcohol.
- By 2020, halve the number of global deaths and injuries from road traffic accidents.
- By 2030, ensure universal access to sexual and reproductive healthcare services, including for family planning, information and education, and the integration of reproductive health into national strategies and programs.
- Achieve universal health coverage, including financial risk protection, access to quality essential healthcare services, and access to safe, effective, quality, and affordable essential medicines and vaccines for all.

- By 2030, substantially reduce the number of deaths and illnesses from hazardous chemicals and air, water, and soil pollution and contamination.
- Strengthen the implementation of the World Health Organization (WHO) Framework Convention on Tobacco Control in all countries.
- Support the research and development of vaccines and medicines for the communicable and noncommunicable diseases that primarily affect developing countries and provide access to affordable essential medicines and vaccines.
- Substantially increase health financing and the recruitment, development, training, and retention of the health workforce in developing countries, especially in the least developed countries and small island developing states.
- Strengthen the capacity of all countries for early warning, risk reduction, and management of national and global health risks.

Concurrent with these aspirations and the requisite work that will be done to achieve the goals and meet targets, there are other opportunities, as described in the remainder of this chapter. Sustainability has not only touched national governments but also caught the attention of business leaders. This is evidenced by the increasing discussion and strategy focused on environment, social, and governance (ESG) issues. These point to the need to focus more broadly on the ecosystem of business rather than the narrower scope of profit and expansion of enterprises. There are also challenges and perhaps a few barriers, which will require robust health systems and strong leadership to overcome.

International Health Policy, Globalization, and Privatization

It is the policy of most international funding organizations, such as the World Bank and the International Monetary Fund (IMF), to encourage developing countries to move to privatization of their healthcare systems.[3] The World Bank advances this agenda by having privatization as an objective of many of its funded projects in developing countries, through the funding priorities of the International Funding Corporation (IFC), and by providing investment guarantees through the Multilateral Investment Guarantee Agency (MIGA).[4,5] The IFC invests only in the private sector and is targeting areas such as water, transportation systems, education, health care, and the environment.[4] The Trade-Related Aspects of Intellectual Property Rights (TRIP) group works actively on a global scale to ensure that pharmaceutical companies and their patents are protected in developing countries, keeping the cost of drugs high worldwide, contributing to the profits of those countries, and preventing countries from making their own drugs and providing them at cost to their own citizens.[6] The IMF has as its policy the privatization of public services, including healthcare systems, as a condition for obtaining its loans.

Second, multinational corporations are marketing to developing countries. The World Trade Organization (WTO) has spent a decade promoting the privatization of healthcare systems as well. Through the General Agreement on Trade in Service, privatization is promoted as a core principle of the WTO.[7] Adding to this trend is the role that the United States–Mexico–Canada Agreement (USMCA) and the European Union (EU) are playing. Both work to open the markets of developing countries to private companies of the developed world. These groups are seen as treating health care worldwide as a marketing opportunity. What is being promoted in developing countries is an expansion of their sales for diagnostic and therapy services, such as dialysis, blood products, and magnetic resonance imaging scans. Also, these treaties work to open markets to health maintenance organizations (HMOs) and other insurers to operate in developing countries.

The policies of the organizations outlined previously are consistent with that of creating competition in economies and consistent with their push for free trade across countries. These policies are also consistent with the belief that competition provides the best product or service at the lowest price. In addition, competition creates an environment conducive to innovation in which services are provided and how they are delivered. Regarding healthcare organizations, a privately financed healthcare system would rely on a third-party payer and health insurance premiums paid by individuals or paid in conjunction with employers. When services are delivered, the healthcare practitioner will be reimbursed for their services by the health insurance plan. There have been some attempts by U.S. groups to move their financing and delivery services for health care into other countries, but so far, this effort has been weak. Also, U.S. hospitals have not been successful in expanding into other countries. What has been successful is the expansion and privatization of such healthcare services as cleaning, laundry, and food service. However, as we move further into the 21st century, it is believed that multinational companies and their subsidiaries will try to continue their expansion. They hope that as more free trade agreements emerge, profitable opportunities will grow.

There are several problems with privatization and competition in healthcare services. First, most people do not want to purchase this service. Second, people purchasing health care do so with serious information inequality (or information asymmetry) regarding the services they are purchasing. How does a patient know whether they have purchased the best appendectomy? Comparison shopping is not easily done for most healthcare services, especially emergency services. Third, where individual healthcare services are concerned, no one wants a bargain. Everyone wants premium services, whereas with other services, the purchaser may not actually buy the most expensive product for a variety of rational reasons. Consumers are irrational when it comes to purchasing health services. Fourth, other services are not bought through a third-party payer, a situation that removes the individual from the purchasing process. Finally, outcomes are difficult to measure. Health is often intangible from both the consumers' and producers' perspectives, which results in unpredictable and hard-to-define outputs.[8]

Although it is understandable that governments want and need employers to assist in paying for healthcare services, this type of system can lead to inequities in healthcare access and services and to a two-tier system of care—those with insurance and those without. Health equity is difficult to achieve, if not elusive, for many populations. Population segments around the world experience health disparities and discrimination due to structural barriers to well-being.[9] In some countries described in this book, such as Russia and Turkiye, patients without health insurance partially paid by an employer are left to access a public healthcare system that often has limited resources and substandard government facilities. Not only are these systems poorly funded, but their healthcare practitioners also tend to migrate to the private systems that serve the privately insured, as the potential for increased incomes is much greater, especially in high-technology, specialized medicine. This leaves only a few practitioners, who often are not specialized, to care for "the other half of society" in public systems with limited equipment and administrative support, poor infrastructure, limited resources such as laboratories and pharmacies, and reduced nursing care. Thus, creating a government network that is available to patients without employment-based insurance often forces the most vulnerable (the elderly and the poor) to use only safety net providers and gives them little access to higher-quality care.[10]

Barriers to privatization of healthcare systems in developing countries include installation and maintenance of advanced information systems and technology. Privatization with a role for insurance companies or HMOs requires that health information is collected on patients, access and utilization information is captured, billing information can be made available, and financing can be tracked. There are also issues of dealing with unionized workers in countries where unions have been a tradition; understanding local and culture-specific healthcare needs and marketing to those groups; providing high-technology equipment and maintaining it while making a profit; and providing pharmaceuticals at a price that can be afforded in these markets.

One solution to this problem can be seen when people who are not working have their health insurance premiums paid by the government. This places these vulnerable populations in the health insurance risk pool with the entire population and gives them access to the same quality of health services that the working population has. It also allows for privatization. This approach reduces the probability of creating a two-tier system and promotes the concept of a true risk pool, where risk is spread across the entire population. South Korea is a country that engages in this type of health insurance coverage for all of its population.[8]

Decentralization

Most countries are attempting to decentralize their healthcare systems. *Decentralization* shifts decision-making authority from national to subnational levels. Subnational refers to local governments, civil society, and the private sector. There are three types of decentralization—political, administrative, and fiscal (or financial).[11] The level of decentralization used in healthcare systems is a continuous issue of concern.

Decentralization is praised as an instrument for improving efficiency and quality. Theoretically, when decisions are made locally, people who have more knowledge of local conditions will have better input regarding the services needed, can give more immediate feedback on the quality of care, and are more attuned to what healthcare services actually cost. This approach is advantageous from the perspective that those making decisions are closer to the problems in their jurisdiction. Local administrators and politicians do tend to have a better understanding of local problems and populations and, therefore, should be able to use resources in the most efficient manner for that locale. Local officials can be held accountable for poor quality by the people who live in their communities.

The downside of decentralization is that the needed funding and other resources do not necessarily accompany the responsibility or mandate for providing appropriate health care in local areas. Rather, a noticeable trend is for central governments to put demands on local governments to provide part of the funding for the healthcare system, something that many are not prepared to do. The local governments now have the responsibility but not the resources. A lack of financial resources is widely cited as a limitation of local governments. They have the authority to raise money but a population who cannot afford to be further taxed. The health systems in some countries have given much responsibility to regional and local governments for the provision of health care but without providing the means to do so. The local governments are unable to raise the money from their poor populations to provide quality health care, so the demand for health care goes unmet.

Some of the other issues that are raised in relation to decentralization, especially in developing countries, are information asymmetry, local politics, capability of local officials, a poor local tax base, keeping the same values between the central and local administrations (congruence), and difficulty in coordinating services. Perhaps the biggest hurdle to successful decentralization is ensuring that local leaders, especially healthcare leaders, have the training necessary to carry out the complex activities of finding resources, deciding on their use, and providing a range of health services while meeting the hugely diverse needs of the population being served. Should resources be spent on preventive care, primary care, or care of elderly people? A major difference seen between the United States and some other developed countries and less-developed countries is the use of specially trained healthcare management professionals who are educated specifically in business. To be successful at all levels of healthcare system management, the people doing the administering must understand financing, work design, information systems, policy, and human resources, to name a few topics, as well as basics of medicine and science. The melding of the skills of business managers, politicians, and medical practitioners is not easy to achieve at any level, but especially not in small, local arenas.

The quality of decision making at these lower levels of the healthcare system may not be very good. The complexities of providing health care at a local level often result in healthcare systems that are ineffective and wasteful. The person making the healthcare decisions must work within the framework of local politics. Local politicians may have their own reasons for providing certain types of healthcare services, such as ownership of hospitals or long-term care facilities. Local healthcare administrators may work for the politicians. Unfortunately, in developing countries, funds that are put into the hands of local administrators or officials are not always used for the intended purpose. The problem of graft in developing countries among government officials at all levels seriously contributes to ongoing poverty.

Health Care as an Increasing Portion of GDP

Nearly all countries have reported that their healthcare expenditures are continuing to increase as a percentage of GDP.[12,13] The question is how high can these percentages go before the opportunity costs are too high? Although this trend is seen virtually everywhere, it is a problem primarily for the many developed countries, where the percentage of GDP consumed by healthcare expenditures is inching over 10%.[12,14] Countries including Japan, South Korea, Germany, Switzerland, the United Kingdom, and the United States are struggling to control their healthcare expenditures, as the percentage of GDP that they represent continues to creep upward. In the United States, healthcare costs as a percentage of GDP now exceed 18%.[15] The crucial question is, what could we be spending our money on instead? Could it be infrastructure, education, or manufacturing? Would some of this money be better directed toward eliminating, or at least addressing, poverty, inequity, and social injustices?

Is there such a thing as too much health care? Of course, the healthcare industry itself is very desirable for many communities. In the United States, for example, small hospitals in rural areas are often the major employers in that community. Most jobs in healthcare systems are well paid, and for those that are not (food service, custodial care), there are good employment benefits. Healthcare workers as a group perhaps form the most educated industry overall. The jobs are often highly technical and highly credentialed and require a fair amount of education, even in supporting roles such as administrative positions. These healthcare workers have higher salaries, pay more taxes, own more homes, purchase more, and make major contributions to their communities. The future appears to promise continuing increases in healthcare expenditures, especially in developed countries.

Injuries and Violence

There has been an increase in injuries, trauma, and death caused by violence globally.[16] Violence is defined as "the intentional use of physical force or power, threatened or actual, against oneself, another person, or against a group or community that either results in or has a high likelihood of resulting in injury, death, psychological harm, maldevelopment or deprivation."[17] Although vital statistics and surveillance are inadequate in many areas of the world, there is still evidence of increases in injuries and violence. Injuries increase as more people in developing countries purchase automobiles while safety laws lag. Inadequate preparation of new drivers, poorly maintained vehicles, and a lack of traffic signs and laws make roads in many parts of the world unsafe. Second, there are areas where violence from cartels, smuggling, and gangs is common (Latin America), and other areas of the world that are experiencing violence caused by wars and political/tribal unrest (sub-Saharan Africa and the Middle Eastern crescent). The chapters on Mexico and Nigeria highlight these concerns.

In addition to deaths from motor vehicle accidents, crime, and war, there is a tremendous amount of violence that does not end in death but instead results in extensive injury and disability. Included in this category are spousal and child abuse, neglect by caregivers, elder abuse, sexual violence, self-directed abuse, and collective violence.

Acts of violence and their consequences put considerable strain on healthcare systems and divert resources from other pressing healthcare needs. Incidents of violence often have long-term consequences, not only physically but also for mental health. In fact, psychological violence can cause extensive disruption to individuals, families, and communities. Another type of violence is deprivation, in which individuals are deprived of basic needs, such as shelter, food, and water, or deprived of emotional support. Violence is often enabled by the presence of alcohol and drugs, availability of firearms, and social and economic inequities or injustices. Consequences of violence include behavioral problems, depression, suicide, and/or anxiety, drug and alcohol abuse; increased risk of cardiovascular disease and other chronic and infectious diseases; and reproductive health problems.[18] Causes of violence can be categorized into four levels: (1) personal/biological factors, (2) close relationships, (3) community, and (4) broad societal factors.[19] The health effects of violence can be cumulative, and people can experience multiple levels and forms of violence.[18]

In response to violence, countries provide adequate and appropriate services to the victims of violence, engage in legislative reform, perform better data collection and research on the causes of violence and successful interventions, and have organizations responsible for monitoring violence. Most needed to carry out these activities are a commitment to funding nationally, community empowerment so that individuals feel ownership of the behavior in their communities, and a global commitment to reducing wars and conflicts.

Mental Health

Necessary to health and well-being is good mental health. The global burden of mental illness continues to steadily increase and result in premature death. The global number of DALYs due to mental disorders increased from 80.8 million to 125.3 million from 1990 to 2019. The most prevalent mental illnesses are depression and anxiety disorders.[20] Substance abuse and eating disorders also impact populations around the world. The importance of mental health is closely associated with a variety of physical diseases, both chronic and communicable, as well as increased injury. Depression is of special concern as social and economic conditions worsen, such as with overcrowding, increased war and refugees, decreased access to food and water due to climate change, competition for fuel, and greater disparity between the world's rich and poor.[20-22]

The challenge for the future is for healthcare providers, insurers, and policymakers to put mental health on a par with physical illnesses in terms of early diagnosis and correct diagnosis, as well as treatment. More importantly, the causes of mental illness, in particular the causes of depression and substance abuse, must be recognized and addressed. Once again, the conversation turns to social determinants of health status, especially those associated with mental illness. Such factors as socioeconomic development, educational attainment, technological advances, environmental hazards, and how they are distributed in populations continue to be major contributors to morbidity and mortality.[21]

Globally, resources for mental health are well below those provided for other types of illness, in both developed and developing countries. The least developed countries put the fewest resources in mental health, and the care that is available is usually institutionally based. Coupled with the negative cultural views of people with behavioral health conditions prevalent in many populations, services are poorly funded and provided and not considered a priority.

Most countries lack qualified health practitioners in numbers adequate to diagnose, treat, and care for their residents with mental illness or behavioral conditions. The inability to address mental illness will impact the treatment of other illnesses. Given that today many mental illnesses are treatable, this is difficult to witness. Even in developed countries, where identification and treatment of mental illness are more advanced, there is inequity in access, treatment, and outcomes among varying groups in these populations.[13] Furthermore, people who are mentally ill often face many difficulties in their communities, where mental illness may be associated with "bad spirits" or the supernatural, or viewed as an embarrassment to family and friends and the entire community.[23]

Aging Population

All developed countries, and to a lesser extent developing countries, are facing the issues of an aging population because people are living longer. These issues include (1) increasing healthcare costs/fewer young people to spread the risk, (2) an inability to replace older adults in the workforce, (3) inadequate planning for long-term care solutions/facilities, (4) challenges in financing health care and pensions, and (5) end-of-life costs. The older population is generally defined as people aged 60 and older. The world is experiencing a significant demographic shift in which the number of older adults will eventually outnumber children under 5. The proportion of the world's population that is elderly is forecast to almost double from 12% in 2015 to 22% in 2050. This will mean that by 2025, approximately 67% of the world's population will be over 60 years of age. Estimates also indicate that 80% of older adults will live in low- and middle-income countries. In addition, those in the 60-and-older category are aging, and more people are living to age 80 and older. Between 2020 and 2050, the number of 80-year-old people is expected to triple. Europe and North America currently lead in the percentage of older people in their populations, but all countries, including developing countries, are experiencing population aging.[24]

Although in some areas of the world aging is not occurring as fast, it is nevertheless occurring. As populations age, the need for healthcare services increases. Moreover, the services needed by the older population are often different from those provided to the younger part of the population, such as chronic disease management versus vaccinations and infectious disease management. Aging also puts more strain on other types of services provided by caregivers, case managers, and other groups that support adequate shelter, food, protection, and support/social networks for older people.

A second problem that arises with an increase in the share of the total population accounted for by the older population is that there are fewer individuals in the workforce to support pensions, to share in the risk pool of health insurance, and to provide a tax base for all government functions. Fertility has declined worldwide, even in developing countries, which exacerbates the problem created by the aging of the population. At the same time, those who reach age 60 now have a longer predicted life span than ever before. This is especially true in developed countries where modern medicine and improvements in lifestyle have fostered the highest proportions of older people. As less developed countries continue to move forward in the world economy, the life expectancy of their older people will lengthen as well. The the elderly population is growing at a rate of 2.6% per year, whereas the overall population is growing at a rate of 1.1% per year. In developing countries, the fastest growth among those 60 years and older is being seen among those in the lowest socioeconomic groups, who are already vulnerable due to many other factors. All of these demographic changes have consequences on many levels, and much work is needed to ensure that those 65 years and older have quality health care, adequate pensions, affordable housing and food, social networks and support, and good quality of life and well-being.[25,26]

Environment and Climate Change

As climate change proceeds, there is considerable evidence that the world is getting warmer and drier. This has resulted in an increase in droughts in North America, Africa, and China. In general, climate change contributes to food scarcity and political destabilization. Unfortunately, despite the efforts of many international groups and the high-profile work of people like Nobel Laureate Al Gore, there still is no grand consensus on how to best deal with an impending global crisis. Some countries, such as Germany, have worked hard to reduce carbon emissions; others, like the United States, have applied a mixed approach. The 2008 and 2022 Olympics in China underscored the need for China and other rapidly developing countries to control air and water pollution better. An increasing incidence of respiratory

Box 28-1 Sustainability in Health Systems

Dr. George Velez

Sustainability uses the *triple bottom line* of financial viability, social responsiveness, and environmental responsibility and applies systems thinking to the strategic development of sustainability efforts. This is a critical component for health systems to integrate holistic strategic processes to support sustainability efforts of initiatives, services, and the mission of the organization as a whole. A healthcare organization is a micro-community living within a larger community. Hence, the sense of culture and community, stewardship, and neighborliness are essential components of most healthcare system sustainability strategies. Healthcare systems in the near future will confront several critical issues on multiple levels. These issues are not unique to health care but certainly will drive urgencies and opportunities in the years to come. Some examples of these critical issues are significant changes in the aging of the population, in family structure, and in employment patterns that will influence reimbursement schemes and change traditional healthcare benefits. In view of these challenges, health systems cannot be sustained without addressing the trade-off between restricted resources (financial, people, environmental) and reaching overall health policy goals within the context of community and environmental stewardship. It will be crucial to generate new strategies for controlling the complex mechanisms that affect expenditures and performance of healthcare sustainability while striving for the achievement of core objectives of healthcare policies, such as universal access, high-quality standards, efficiency and effectiveness, adequate funding, and satisfaction of patients.

disorders furthers the urgency of addressing this problem. Furthermore, the Intergovernmental Panel on Climate Change (established by the United Nations and the World Meteorological Society) issued a report in 2007 concluding that without a dramatic reduction in human-induced carbon dioxide emissions, climate change may bring "abrupt or irreversible" effects on air, oceans, glaciers, land, coastlines, and species.[16] Climate change also contributes to an increase in infectious disease because the range of disease vectors increases with the warming of various regions of the world. Climate change has also been associated with changes in weather patterns that have resulted in increases in storms and floods. Hurricane Katrina in the United States provided a glaring example of how ill prepared even the wealthy nations are in dealing with such disasters. As we have seen, health systems are often vulnerable during times of disaster, leaving people unserved at a time of greatest need. Many health systems are already functioning on limited budgets and are currently understaffed. The extra stressors brought by a natural disaster are often enough to cause a serious disruption in even the most basic services.

There is a slow but vibrant movement to create sustainable health systems (**Boxes 28-1**, **28-2**, and **28-3**) that can generate their own electricity and be independent of local power grids. Others have ongoing disaster training exercises and contingency plans to address the challenges of natural disasters.

Box 28-2 Community Health Centers

Dr. Neil Steven Gardner

The community health center (CHC) movement in the United States began in the mid-1960s, as an outgrowth of the neighborhood health clinics that were part of the early social programs of that period. The CHC model reflects the pioneering work done in South Africa in the 1940s by Drs. Sidney and Emily Kark. The early centers in the United States were sometimes established more on social/political considerations than with the objective of delivering primary health care. This was also the case with the Community Health Program (CHP) centers established in South Australia. The current CHC model in the United States, more specifically the Federally Qualified Health Centers, provides primary healthcare services to people who otherwise would not have access to such services. Many CHCs are housed in state-of-the-art clinical facilities providing professional and pleasant family-oriented health care. In the case of South Australia, the CHP centers have been used as part of a national program to provide universal access to health care. The Australian model was initially supported by the Commonwealth Government, but with subsequent revisions to the program, the centers became the responsibility of the Australian states.

India has a three-tier system of public healthcare delivery that includes community health centers. In that nation, the CHCs receive cases from the basic primary health centers, which are the foundation of health services serving some 25,000 in the rural areas of India. The CHCs refer cases to the 30-bed hospitals and higher-level hospitals at the district level as necessary.

In the United States, there is collaboration between the federal government and the communities that are being served. The federal funding to a CHC never represents the total budget. There is the expectation for the CHC to leverage the federal dollars through enhanced Medicaid reimbursement, additional sources of funding, and private insurance reimbursements, as well as self-payment by users of the center based on a sliding fee scale that determines an individual's ability to pay.

In both the United States and Australia, there has been an emphasis on community involvement; an aspect that may be a factor contributing to the sustainability of the CHC model. This community involvement includes a U.S. requirement of 51% user representation on the governing board of the center.

In addition to well visits, specialty care services are often available in community health centers in the United States or through paid referral for services. The model has emphasized wellness and prevention. Under the current models, no one is denied access to care. After care is sought, there is the opportunity to promote wellness and prevention through the services offered by the center. Although most of the current users in the United States have incomes below 200% of the federal poverty level and are without health coverage, there are a number of center users who have private commercial health insurance coverage. In the United States, especially in rural areas where there are no other healthcare facilities available, insured and self-paying users make up a significant portion of the patient mix of the CHC. This is also the case in centers that are established around a culturally specific community, with the attraction being culturally sensitive care.

Box 28-3 Health System Designs for the 21st Century

Dr. Glenn A. Croxton

A series of papers related to the design of hospitals for the 21st century were presented by the Center for Health Design and Health Care Without Harm at a conference sponsored by the Robert Wood Johnson Foundation in September 2006. The Center for Health Design is a nonprofit research and advocacy organization. Its mission is to transform healthcare settings into healing environments. The healing environment is seen as a vital part of therapeutic treatment, where the design of healthcare setting contributes to health rather than adding to the burden of stress.

Health Care Without Harm is an international coalition of 440 groups in 55 countries working to transform the healthcare industry so that it is ecologically sustainable and no longer of harm to people and the environment.

First, Do No Harm

Gary Cohen discussed how healthcare institutions that support the Hippocratic Oath have a special responsibility to ensure that their operations are not major sources of chemical exposure and environmental harm. Until recently, healthcare professionals and hospital administrators were unaware of their contributions to chemical contaminants and broader societal disease burdens, according to Cohen.

Chronic diseases and disabilities now affect more than 90 million men, women, and children in the United States alone. In spite of much advancement in medical practice, the best available data show an increase in the incidence of asthma, autism, birth defects, childhood brain cancer, acute lymphocytic leukemia, endometriosis, Parkinson's disease, and infertility. The economic costs of these diseases by 2020 were expected to exceed $1 trillion USD yearly in healthcare cost and lost productivity.

The field of environmental health is attempting to link each of these diseases and disorders to exposure to toxic chemicals. The old way of looking at chemical risk and safety would have missed these links, as they are not as simple as a single cause and a single effect. Through the new lens of science, we have learned that exposure to toxic chemicals, at levels thought to have been safe, is increasing the chronic disease burden of millions of Americans.

Green Hospitals

The second paper, "Values-Driven Design and Construction: Enriching Community Benefits through Green Hospitals," was presented by Robin Guenther, Gail Vittori, and Cynthia Atwood. They discussed how many hospitals are successfully reaching beyond measures that have economic payback and are achieving community benefits beyond their four walls. Healthcare leaders recognize the high costs of inaction on matters of the environment—such as climate change and chemical contamination on the health of our families, neighbors, and communities at hand and globally. By embedding sustainable design in a broader vision of leadership and mission, these projects and organizations are succeeding in delivering the first generations of sustainable healthcare projects.

(continues)

Box 28-3 Health System Designs for the 21st Century *(continued)*

Ted Schettler, MD, MPH, identified three tiers of operational environmental performance evolving in hospitals.

- Tier 1: minimum local, state, and national environmental performance
- Tier 2: beyond compliance to measures that save money
- Tier 3: informed by an inextricable link between environment and human health and moving beyond both compliance and monetary savings with a long-term plan to reduce environmental footprints

He contended that applying a *triple bottom line* approaches to pollution-prevention initiatives—that is, measuring economic, social, and environment benefits—would deliver significant benefits for healthcare organizations and the communities they serve. Early tier 3 hospitals supported this notion. Named one of the state's top four recyclers, the University of Michigan Health System described its program's social benefit as an institution-wide initiative that engages everyone.

As building initiatives accelerate, it is clear that we can apply the same system-tiered performance to organizations engaged in sustainable building. Tier 1 organizations will not undertake green building until they are mandated to do so through legislative policy initiatives. They will not make the link or the organizational leap between the health of their facilities and the patients they serve.

Creating Safe and Healthy Spaces: Selecting Materials That Support Healing

Mark Rossi, PhD, and Tom Lent outlined the relationship of the materials and products used in healthcare facilities to the chemicals to which our communities are exposed. Rossi and Lent further described the opportunities available to healthcare organizations to help society break from its dependence on toxic materials and define the path to healthier, sustainable materials that benefit patients, communities, nature, and the organizational bottom line.

Kaiser Permanente, for example, framed its environmental goals for building design in terms of community health in March 2002 in the Kaiser Permanente Position Statement on Green Buildings.

> Kaiser Permanente's mission is to improve the health of the communities served. In recognition of the critical linkages between environmental health and public health, it is Kaiser's desire to limit adverse impacts upon the environment resulting from the siting, design, construction, and operation of our health facilities. We will address the life cycle impacts of facilities through design and construction standards, selection of material and equipment, and maintenance practices. Additionally, KP will require architects, engineers, and contractors to specify commercially available, cost-competitive materials, products, technologies, and processes—where appropriate—that have positive impact or that limit negative impact on environmental quality and human health.

Preventive Medicine for the Environment: Developing and Implementing Environmental Programs that Work

Laura Brannen suggested moving from the theoretical aspects of why healthcare facilities should adopt green principles to how to do it. According to Brannen, healthcare facilities generate a tremendous variety and quantity of wastes—at least 2 million tons of waste per year—that may represent real occupational and environmental health threats. Healthcare facilities are the fourth-largest consumer of energy, spending $6.5 billion USD on energy cost alone and accounting for 11% of all commercial energy use. Water consumption and discharges to public sewer systems are excessive. Wastewater contains toxic laboratory and cleaning chemicals and pharmaceutical compounds, many of which are not broken down in sewage treatment plants and are disposed of in landfills, resulting in sewage sludge applied to farmland and released in rivers and streams.

Finally, Brannen sees healthcare facilities of the future as high-performance buildings that use less energy and less water, require fewer chemicals to maintain, and are designed for maximum operational waste management systems: where materials are purchased with health and environmental considerations, where materials are used efficiently and staff take responsibility for and participate in waste minimization programs, where end-of-life considerations are maximized, and where reuse and recycling are effective.

Redefining Healthy Food: An Ecological Health Approach to Food Production, Distribution, and Procurement

The fifth paper in this series was presented by Jamie Harvie, who discussed the ecological health approach to food production. According to Harvie, food production, distribution, and procurement intersect with a wide variety of issues. Economics, immigration policy, spirituality, agriculture and trade, culture, environment, and nutrition are but several of the myriad concerns associated with the food we grow and eat. There is perhaps no issue that has such a wide depth of actively involved interests. The complexity of these interests requires a system, or ecological, approach. Such an approach is challenging because it is not linear and requires observation of the whole context while seeking to understand the connections between the parts.

Hospital food is big business. In 2004 alone, the top healthcare group purchasing organizations purchased approximately $2.75 billion USD worth of food. Although patient food receives considerable attention in the media, it is cafeteria and catered food that make up the largest percentage of the food budget, accounting for approximately 55% to 70% of hospital volume.

Hospital and health systems are not only changing procurement practices to support healthy food systems, but also explicitly identifying the link between healthy food systems and healthy patients, communities, and the planet in their policies and programs. These systems are pioneers of the ecological approach to preventive medicine.

Toward an Ecological View of Health: An Imperative for the 21st Century

The final paper presented at the conference was by Ted Schettler, MD, MPH. Schettler began by discussing the relationship between human and environmental health. In 2005, the United Nations released the largest assessment ever undertaken of the health of the earth's ecosystems. More than 1,000 experts from 95 countries prepared the report, which was then reviewed by a large independent board of editors and commented on by hundreds of experts and governments before being released.

The Green Building Council of Australia's environmental rating system, Green Star, has now developed tools to assess buildings in the education, retail, and healthcare sectors. The Green Star—Healthcare rating tool, in particular, aims to address the unique qualities, constraints, and opportunities within hospitals and other medical facilities.

However, it remains much harder to measure the true value of a green hospital because the productivity and operation have different measures and often different management. The majority of hospitals will look at patient recovery time, bed turnover, and staff retention to estimate their attributes and performance. The truly green hospital can look at benefits in all of these areas and more, but the situation requires true, holistic investment in people's health.

Changi General Hospital is Singapore's first purpose-built, multidisciplinary regional hospital, providing healthcare services to approximately 750,000 people in the eastern and northeastern parts of Singapore. Changi General Hospital instilled several green practices within these grounds. Some of these were waste composting from water conservation (the first hospital to use NewWater), increased energy efficiency of the hospital building and installations, waste-minimization methods to control the generation of unnecessary waste in both the administration and day-to-day running of the hospital, and participation in community grassroots education and staff enrichment programs.

Refugees, Displaced People, and Humanitarian Crises

The number of people who are displaced forcibly has never been higher. The United Nations High Commission on Refugees estimates that over 100 million people have been forcibly displaced worldwide due to war and violence, sustained droughts, earthquakes, and severe weather events. The reality of this is that 1 in 78 people on Earth has been forced to flee. This number is more than double since a decade ago, when 42.7 million people were forcibly displaced.[27] Ten million people are considered stateless, which means that they have "been denied a nationality and access to basic human rights that include education, health care, employment, and freedom of movement."[28] According to the World Health Organization, "A refugee is someone who fears being persecuted for reasons of race, religion, nationality, membership of a particular social group, or political opinion. A refugee is outside the country of his or her nationality, and is unable to, or unwilling to be protected by that country."[29] The majority (82%) of refuges originate from 10 countries. This means 8 of every 10 displaced people are from one of these 10 countries. The majority of the refugees comes from just three countries: Syria (6.7 million), Venezuela (4 million), and Afghanistan (2.6 million). Turkiye and Germany have received a large proportion of refugees.[27]

The medical challenges of refugees include many common problems, but with a higher incidence and prevalence. The most prevalent are accidental injuries, hypothermia, burns, cardiovascular events, pregnancy and delivery complications, diabetes, and hypertension. Women experience problems related to maternal, newborn, and child health; sexual and reproductive health; and violence. Refugee children have high rates of respiratory infections, diarrhea, and skin infections due to poor hygiene.[29]

The poor health status of refugees occurs for a variety of reasons. Most importantly is lack of hygiene facilities (adequate toilets, sewage disposal, and bathing areas) and clean water supplies, which contribute to diarrhea and skin infections. Furthermore, refugees experience an increase in psychosocial disorders associated with the complete disruption in their lives, which increases the rates of alcohol and drug abuse and can lead to increased violence. Refugees lose all continuity in their health care, especially among those with chronic diseases. Notably, the incidences of heart disease, diabetes, and hypertension are greatly increased among refugees due to disruption in their care and medications. Many of these chronic health issues are made worse by the stress and conditions endured by people who find themselves in the most untenable situations. Although health care may be available, it is generally not enough care, the right care, or provided in a timely manner. The refugee healthcare "system" is dependent on donors and the ability of the host nation to provide healthcare services. Food supplies are uncertain for most refugees, both in camps and during the process of fleeing their countries, resulting in a higher incidence of malnutrition, especially among children. Finally, refugees, who are already compromised in so many ways, sometimes fall victim to violence by those who view these situations as opportunities for crime. The health of refugees creates health challenges and crises that health systems in host countries, international health agencies, and nongovernmental organizations (NGOs) must work to meet. The challenges are daunting.[27,29]

At any given time, many healthcare systems in countries worldwide are challenged by humanitarian crises and require humanitarian assistance from outside their borders. It is incumbent on donor nations, international agencies, and NGOs to meet these challenges. Some humanitarian crises go on for years, and others are episodic. It is the challenge of the 21st century to be prepared to react swiftly and in unison to meet the basic needs of people in terms of water, food, shelter, safety, and health care.

Many humanitarian crises are the result of violence. Many nations are under siege of violence, creating conditions that require immediate humanitarian assistance. These situations are the impetus for people migrating and adding to the problems associated with displaced people and refugees. Other nations are experiencing humanitarian crises of a different nature that deserve and need the attention of the international community. Climate change is creating and exacerbating a number of humanitarian crises around the world. Heatwaves, droughts, tropical storms, and acute floods are creating dire conditions around the world. Hunger is on the rise around the world. Conflict is having devasting impacts. As a result of humanitarian crises, forced displacement is at record levels; infectious and communicable diseases are threating the well-being of millions; health systems, services, and healthcare workforces are experiencing unprecedented strain; economic conditions are fragile; schools and education are experiencing interruptions due to crises; inequities are increasing; and more resources are being mobilized from the private sector to response to emergencies.[30]

The need for humanitarian aid is varied and unrelenting. Currently, the coordination of international relief and health services is, at best, piecemeal and has little coordination. A challenge of the future is to be able to better respond to the crises as they begin. There is a need for quick assessment, movement of appropriate materials and personnel, protection, and the expertise to build and rebuild infrastructure, maintain health services and public health systems, and mitigate damage.

Responding to the challenges of the 21st century and recognizing the need to respond to emergencies quickly, the WHO is building a new Health Emergencies Program. This program will be available to member states and is designed to help nations build their capacities to manage health emergency risks, assist when national capacities are overwhelmed, and lead and coordinate the international health response in collaboration to contain outbreaks, provide effective relief, and assist in recovery. WHO will "work with countries and partners to prepare for, prevent, respond to, and recover from all hazards that create health emergencies, including disasters, disease outbreaks, and conflicts."[31] The new Health Emergencies Program will change the way WHO handles emergencies worldwide. It will not be primarily a technical and normative organization, but rather will be an agency of its own, with a common structure across the organization, its own budget and planning mechanism, a single workforce, and its own standards and processes. Accountability will be clearly defined. Its goals are to plan for and rapidly deploy expertise and materials to respond to health emergencies worldwide effectively and predictably.[31]

While health systems will continue to be challenged, they will also adapt and continue to move toward greater sustainability.

In conclusion, health systems around the globe will be challenged in the future in ways never before considered. The governments and private sectors in these countries will have to work in partnership to ensure the sustainability of vital health services. Additionally, health systems will need to realize their interconnectedness with the rest of the world as we face global pandemics and macro problems, such as climate change. Likewise, at the micro level, health systems will need to reduce bureaucracy by streamlining management, increasing cost-effectiveness, improving efficiency through reorganized services, decentralizing services, and allocating resources to better address the needs of the population.

References

1. United Nations. The sustainable development agenda. Accessed May 11, 2023. https://www.un.org/sustainable development/development-agenda/.
2. United Nations. Goal 3: ensure healthy lives and promote well-being for all at all ages. Accessed May 11, 2023. https://www.un.org/sustainabledevelopment/health/.
3. International Monetary Fund. What is the IMF? Published 2022. Accessed May 11, 2023. https://www.imf.org/en/About/Factsheets/IMF-at-a-Glance.
4. International Finance Corporation. About IFC. Published 2023. Accessed May 11, 2023. https://www.ifc.org/wps/wcm/connect/corp_ext_content/ifc_external_corporate_site/about+ifc_new.
5. Multilateral Investment Guarantee Agency. About us. Published 2023. Accessed May 11, 2023. https://www.miga.org/about-us.
6. World Trade Organization. TRIPS: trade-related aspects of intellectual property rights. Accessed May 11, 2023. https://www.wto.org/english/tratop_e/trips_e/trips_e.htm.
7. World Trade Organization. The General Agreement on Trade in Services (GATS). Accessed May 11, 2023. https://www.wto.org/english/tratop_e/serv_e/gatsintr_e.htm.
8. Hicks L. *Economics of Health and Medical Care*. 7th ed. Jones & Barlett Learning; 2021.
9. Deloitte. 2023 global health care outlook. Published 2022. Accessed May 11, 2023. https://www.deloitte.com/global/en/Industries/life-sciences-health-care/analysis/global-health-care-outlook.html.
10. Commonwealth Fund. *When Costs Are a Barrier to Getting Health Care: Reports from Older Adults in the United States and Other High-Income Countries*. Published 2021. Accessed May 11, 2023. https://www.commonwealthfund.org/publications/surveys/2021/oct/when-costs-are-barrier-getting-health-care-older-adults-survey.
11. World Bank. Decentralization. Published 2013. Accessed May 11, 2023. https://www.worldbank.org/en/topic/community drivendevelopment/brief/Decentralization.
12. World Health Organization. Global health expenditure database. Published 2023. Accessed May 11, 2023. https://apps.who.int/nha/database.
13. World Health Organization. Global expenditure on health: Rising to the pandemics challenges. Published 2022. Accessed May 11, 2023. https://apps.who.int/iris/bitstream/handle/10665/365133/9789240064911-eng.pdf.
14. Commonwealth Fund. *Mirror, Mirror 2021: Reflecting Poorly*. Accessed May 11, 2023. https://www.commonwealthfund.org/publications/fund-reports/2021/aug/mirror-mirror-2021-reflecting-poorly.
15. Centers for Medicare and Medicaid Services. NHE fact sheet. Published 2023. Accessed May 11, 2023. https://www.cms.gov/research-statistics-data-and-systems/statistics-trends-and-reports/nationalhealthexpenddata/nhe-fact-sheet.
16. United Nations. A new era of conflict and violence. Accessed May 11, 2023. https://www.un.org/en/un75/new-era-conflict-and-violence.
17. Krug EG, Dahlberg LL, Mercey JA, et al. *World Report on Violence and Health*. 2002. Accessed May 11, 2023. https://apps.who.int/iris/bitstream/handle/10665/42495/9241545615_eng.pdf.
18. Rivara F, Adhia A, Lyons V, et al. The effects of violence on health. *Health Aff*. 2019;38(10). doi:10.1377/hlthaff.2019.00480.
19. Centers for Disease Control and Prevention. The social-ecological model: a framework for prevention. Published 2022. Accessed May 11, 2023. https://www.cdc.gov/violence prevention/about/social-ecologicalmodel.html.
20. GBD 2019 Mental Disorders Collaborators. Global, regional, and national burden of 12 mental disorders in 204 countries and territories, 1990–2019: a systematic analysis for the Global Burden of Disease Study 2019. *Lancet Psychiatry*. 2022;9(2):137-150. doi:10.1016/S2215-0366(21)00395-3.
21. Patel V, Saxena S, Lund C, et al. The Lancet Commission on global mental health and sustainable development. *Lancet*. 2018;392(10157):1553-1598. https://www.thelancet.com/journals/lancet/article/PIIS0140-6736(18)31612-X/fulltext?amp;utm_source=twitter&.
22. Arias D, Saxena S, Verguet S. Quantifying the global burden of mental disorders and their economic value. *eClinical Med*. 2022;54. doi:10.1016/j.eclinm.2022.101675.
23. World Health Organization. Mental health workers. Accessed May 11, 2023. https://www.who.int/data/gho/data/themes/topics/indicator-groups/indicator-group-details/GHO/mental-health-workers.
24. World Health Organization. Ageing and health. Accessed May 11, 2023. https://www.who.int/news-room/fact-sheets/detail/ageing-and-health#:~:text=By 2030%2C 1 in 6, will double (2.1 billion).
25. World Bank. Societal aging. Accessed May 11, 2023. https://www.worldbank.org/en/topic/pensions/brief/societal-aging.
26. International Monetary Fund. Aging is the real population bomb. Published 2022. Accessed May 11, 2023. https://www.imf.org/en/Publications/fandd/issues/Series/Analytical-Series/aging-is-the-real-population-bomb-bloom-zucker.
27. United Nations Refugee Agency. Global trends. Published 2022. Accessed May 11, 2023. https://www.unhcr.org/media/global-trends-forced-displacement-2020.
28. United National Refugee Agency. About statelessness. Accessed May 11, 2023. https://www.unhcr.org/ibelong/about-statelessness/.
29. World Health Organization. Refugee and migrant health. Accessed May 11, 2023. https://www.who.int/news-room/fact-sheets/detail/refugee-and-migrant-health.
30. United Nations Office for the Coordination of Humanitarian Affairs. Global humanitarian overview 2022. Published 2022. Accessed May 11, 2023. https://2022.gho.unocha.org/.
31. World Health Organization. WHO Health Emergencies Programme. Accessed May 11, 2023. https://www.who.int/westernpacific/about/how-we-work/programmes/who-health-emergencies-programme.

Glossary of Health Systems Terms[1]

A

Access An individual's ability to obtain appropriate healthcare services. Barriers can be financial (insufficient monetary resources), geographic (distance to providers), organizational (lack of available providers), or sociological (e.g., discrimination, language barriers). Efforts to improve access often focus on providing/improving health coverage.

Accreditation A process whereby a program of study or an institution is recognized by an external body as meeting certain predetermined standards. For facilities, these standards are usually defined in terms of physical plant, governing body, administration, and medical and other staff. This recognition process is often carried out by organizations created to assure the public of the quality of the institution or program. The state or federal government can grant this recognition in lieu of, or as the basis for, licensure or other mandatory approvals. Public or private payment programs often require such recognition as a condition of payment for covered services. This recognition may be permanent or may be given for a specified period of time.

Activities of daily living (ADL) An index or scale that measures a patient's degree of independence in bathing, dressing, using the toilet, eating, and moving from one place to another.

Acute care Medical treatment rendered to individuals whose illnesses or health problems are of a short-term or episodic nature. Providers of this treatment are hospitals that mainly serve people with short-term health problems.

Acute disease A disease that is characterized by a single episode of a relatively short duration from which the patient returns to their normal or previous level of activity. Although these diseases are frequently distinguished from chronic diseases, there is no standard definition or distinction. It is worth noting that a short, severe episode of a chronic disease (e.g., an episode of diabetic coma in a patient with diabetes) is often treated as acute disease.

Advanced practice nursing (APN)[9] A category of nurses that includes nurse practitioners, clinical nurse specialists, nurse anesthetists, and nurse midwives, all of whom will play a pivotal role in the future of health care.

Adverse event In a medical context, an injury resulting from a medical intervention.

Adverse selection A tendency for utilization of health services in a population group to be higher than average. From an insurance perspective, this tendency occurs when people with poorer than average health status apply for, or continue, insurance coverage to a greater extent than do people with average or better health expectations.

Affiliation An agreement (usually formal) between two or more otherwise independent entities or individuals that defines how they will relate to each other. These agreements between hospitals may specify procedures for referring or transferring patients from one facility to another, joint faculty and/or medical staff appointments, teaching relationships, sharing of records or services, or provision of consultation between programs.

Affordable Care Act of 2010 Often referred to as Obamacare; this U.S. legislation was a major reform of the healthcare system that sought to improve access, improve quality of care, and reduce costs. Under this legislation, 20 million uninsured people were able to get healthcare insurance.

Agency for Healthcare Research and Quality (AHRQ) An agency created in December 1989 as the Agency for Healthcare Policy and Research (AHCPR), a public health service agency within the U.S. Department of Health and Human Services. This agency was reauthorized in December 1999 under the new name. Its mission is to support research designed to improve the outcomes and quality of health care, reduce its costs, address patient safety and medical errors, and broaden access to effective services. The research sponsored, conducted, and disseminated by this agency provides information that helps people make better decisions about health care.

All patient diagnosis-related groups (APDRG) An enhancement of the original DRGs designed to apply to a population broader than that of Medicare beneficiaries, who are predominately older individuals. The APDRG set includes groupings for pediatric and maternity cases as well as services for HIV-related conditions and other special cases.

All-payer system A system in which prices for health services and payment methods are the same, regardless of who is paying. For instance, in this system, federal or state government, a private insurer, a self-insured employer plan, an individual, or any other payer could pay the same rates. The uniform fee bars healthcare providers from shifting costs from one payer to another (see *cost-shifting*).

Allied health personnel Specially trained and licensed (when necessary) health workers other than physicians, dentists, optometrists, chiropractors, podiatrists, and nurses. The term has no constant or agreed-upon detailed meaning. It is sometimes used synonymously with paramedical personnel, sometimes meaning all health workers who perform tasks that must otherwise be performed by a physician, and at other times referring to health workers who do not usually engage in independent practice.

Allowable costs Items or elements of an institution's costs that are reimbursable under a payment formula. Both Medicare and Medicaid reimburse hospitals on the basis of only certain costs. These reimbursements may exclude, for example, luxury accommodations and costs that are not reasonable expenditures or that are unnecessary for the efficient delivery of health services to people covered under the program in question.

Ambulatory care All kinds of health services that are provided on an outpatient basis, in contrast to services provided in the home or to people who are inpatients. Although many inpatients have traveled for care, this term usually implies that the patient must travel to a location to receive services that do not require an overnight stay (see also *ambulatory setting* and *outpatient*).

Ambulatory care setting A kind of institutional, organized health setting in which health services are provided on an outpatient basis. This kind of setting may be either mobile (when the facility is capable of being moved to different locations) or fixed (when the person seeking care must travel to a fixed service site).

Ambulatory payment classification (APC) The basis for payment for care in the outpatient prospective payment system. This classification is used similarly to the way diagnosis-related groups (DRGs) are used for payment for inpatients. Both are intended to represent groups of patients who are similar clinically and who also have roughly the same resource consumption. The significant difference between them is that this classification depends on the procedures performed, whereas DRGs depend on the diagnoses treated.

American Association of Health Plans (AAHP) An association, located in Washington, D.C., that represents more than 1,000 HMOs, PPOs, and other network-based plans. Together they care for close to 140 million Americans nationwide. This association was created by the merger of the Group Health Association of America (GHAA) and the American Managed Care and Review Association (AMCRA). The merger of the two groups created a new organization that delivers a unified message about the modern style of healthcare delivery pioneered by HMOs, PPOs, and similar health plans.

Ancillary services Supplemental services, including laboratory, radiology, physical therapy, and inhalation therapy, that are provided in conjunction with medical or hospital care.

Antiretroviral therapy (ART) Treatment for HIV, which consists of a combination of medicines.

Antitrust A legal term encompassing a variety of efforts on the part of the government to ensure that sellers do not conspire to restrain trade or fix prices for their goods or services in the market.

Any willing provider laws Laws that require managed care plans to contract with all healthcare providers that meet their terms and conditions.

Apartheid[10] A system of institutionalized racial segregation that existed in South Africa and South West Africa from 1948 to the early 1990s.

Appropriateness Appropriate health care is care for which the expected health benefit exceeds the expected negative consequences by a wide enough margin to justify treatment.

Assignment A process in which a Medicare beneficiary agrees to have Medicare's share of the cost of a service paid directly to a doctor or other provider and the provider agrees to accept the Medicare-approved charge as payment in full. For most services, Medicare pays 80% of the cost and the beneficiary pays 20%.

Assisted living A broad range of residential care services that includes some assistance with activities of daily living and instrumental activities of daily living but does not include nursing services, such as administration of medication. Assisted-living facilities and in-home assisted-living care stress independence and generally provide less intensive care than that delivered in nursing homes and other long-term care institutions.

Association A term signifying a relationship between two or more events or variables. Events are said to be associated when they occur more frequently together than one would expect by chance. This term does not necessarily imply a causal relationship. Statistical significance testing enables a researcher to determine the likelihood of observing the sample relationship by chance if in fact no association exists in the population that was sampled. This term is often used interchangeably with "relationship."

Average wholesale price (AWP) of prescription drugs Relates to the price that wholesalers charge pharmacies and is often used by pharmacists to price prescriptions. Drug manufacturers and labelers commonly publish suggested wholesale prices for their products. Price surveys of wholesalers are also available.

Avoidable hospital admission A hospitalization due to ambulatory care-sensitive conditions (ACSCs), such as hypertension and pneumonia, that should be largely prevented if ambulatory care is provided adequately and in a timely manner.

B

Bad debts Income lost to a provider because of failure of patients to pay amounts owed. This lost income may sometimes be recovered by increasing charges to paying patients.

Some cost-based reimbursement programs reimburse for certain lost income. The impact of the loss of revenue may be partially offset for proprietary institutions by the fact that income tax is not payable on income not received.

Balance billing In Medicare and private fee-for-service health insurance, the practice of billing patients for charges that exceed the amount that the health plan will pay. Under Medicare, the excess amount cannot be more than 15% above the approved charge.

Behavioral health An umbrella term that includes mental health and substance abuse and frequently is used to distinguish this aspect of health from "physical" health. Healthcare services provided for depression or alcoholism would be considered this kind of care, whereas setting a broken leg would be physical health.

Behavioral Risk Factor Surveillance System (BRFSS) The world's largest telephone survey. This system tracks risk behaviors related to chronic diseases, injuries, and death in the United States. Administered and supported by the Division of Adult and Community Health, National Center for Chronic Disease Prevention and Health Promotion, and Centers for Disease Control and Prevention, this system is an ongoing data collection program. By 1994, all states, the District of Columbia, and three territories were participating in this system.

Benchmark A level of care set as a goal to be attained. This kind of internal goal is derived from similar processes or services within an organization. Competitive goals of this kind are comparisons with the best external competitors in the field. Generic goals of this kind are drawn from the best performance of similar processes in other industries.

Beneficiary An individual who receives benefits from, or is covered by, an insurance policy or other healthcare financing program.

Biased selection The market imperfection that results from the uneven grouping of risks among competing subscribers. It includes favorable selection (attracting good risks and repelling bad ones) as well as adverse selection (the reverse). This can occur naturally, according to historical or accidental patterns, or strategically, according to conscious choices by either subscribers or insurers.

Biotechnology Technology that utilizes biological systems or parts of living organisms to develop new products.

Bioterrorism The unlawful use, or threatened use, of microorganisms or toxins derived from living organisms to produce death or disease in humans, animals, or plants. The act is intended to create fear and/or intimidate governments or societies in the pursuit of political, religious, or ideologic goals.

Bismarck model Also referred as the social health insurance model; a healthcare system in which people pay a fee to a fund that in turn pays for their healthcare services, which are provided by either public or private institutions.

Board certified Status granted to a medical specialist who completes a required course of training and experience (residency) and passes an examination in their specialty. Individuals who have met all requirements except examination are referred to as *board eligible*.

Buddhism One of the world's largest religions originating 2,500 years ago in India. Buddhists believe that the human life is one of suffering, and that meditation, spiritual and physical labor, and good behavior are the ways to achieve enlightenment, or nirvana.

C

Capital Fixed or durable nonlabor inputs or factors used in the production of goods and services, the value of such factors, or the money specifically allocated for their acquisition or development. Such costs include, for example, the buildings, beds, and equipment used in the provision of hospital services. Such assets are usually thought of as permanent and durable as distinguished from consumables, such as supplies.

Capital costs Expenditures for land, facilities, and major equipment. They are distinguished from operating costs, which include such items as labor, supplies, and administrative expenses.

Capital expenditure An expenditure for the acquisition, replacement, modernization, or expansion of facilities or equipment that, under generally accepted accounting principles, is not properly chargeable as an expense of operation and maintenance.

Capitation A method of payment for health services in which an individual or institutional provider is paid a fixed amount for each person served, without regard to the actual number or nature of services provided to each person in a set period of time. This is the characteristic payment method in certain health maintenance organizations. It also refers to a method of federal support of health professional schools. Under these authorizations, each eligible school receives a fixed payment, called a *capitation grant*, from the federal government for each student enrolled.

Carrier A private organization, usually an insurance company, that finances health care.

Carve out Regarding health insurance, an arrangement whereby an employer eliminates coverage for a specific category of services (e.g., vision care, mental health/psychological services, and prescription drugs) and contracts with a separate set of providers for those services according to a predetermined fee schedule or capitation arrangement. This term may also refer to a method of coordinating dual coverage for an individual.

Case based Refers to a single patient or case.

Case management The monitoring and coordination of treatment rendered to patients with specific diagnoses or requiring high-cost or extensive services.

Case mix A measure of the various kinds of patients being treated by a particular healthcare provider that is intended to reflect the patients' different needs for resources. This measure is generally established by estimating the relative frequency of various types of patients seen by the provider in question during a given time period, and may be measured by factors such as diagnosis, severity of illness, utilization of services, and provider characteristics.

Case severity A measure of intensity or gravity of a given condition or diagnosis for a patient.

Catastrophic health insurance Health insurance that provides protection against the high cost of treating severe or lengthy illnesses or disability. Generally, such policies cover all, or a specified percentage of, medical expenses above an amount that is the responsibility of another insurance policy up to a maximum limit of liability.

Catchment area A geographic area defined and served by a health program or institution, such as a hospital or community mental health center, that is delineated on the basis of such factors as population distribution, natural geographic boundaries, or transportation accessibility. By definition, all residents of the area needing the services of the program are usually eligible for them, although eligibility may also depend on additional criteria.

Causality Relating causes to the effects they produce. Most of epidemiology concerns this relationship, and several types of causes can be distinguished. A cause is termed *necessary* when a particular variable must always precede an effect. This effect need not be the sole result of the one variable. A cause is termed *sufficient* when a particular variable inevitably initiates or produces an effect. Any given cause may be necessary, sufficient, neither, or both.

Centers for Disease Control and Prevention (CDC) The agency, based in Atlanta, Georgia, that is charged with protecting U.S. public health by providing direction in the prevention and control of communicable and other diseases and responding to public health emergencies. Within the U.S. Public Health Service, this is the agency that led efforts to prevent such diseases as malaria, polio, smallpox, toxic shock syndrome, Legionnaire's disease, and, more recently, acquired immunodeficiency syndrome (AIDS), tuberculosis, and COVID-19. This agency's responsibilities evolve as the agency addresses contemporary threats to health, such as injury, environmental, and occupational hazards, behavioral risks, and chronic diseases.

Centers for Medicare and Medicaid Services (CMS) The government agency within the Department of Health and Human Services that directs the Medicare and Medicaid programs (Titles XVIII and XIX of the Social Security Act) and conducts research to support those programs. It was formerly the Health Care Financing Administration (HCFA).

Charity care Physician and hospital services provided to people who are unable to pay for the cost of services, especially those who are low income, uninsured, and underinsured. A high proportion of the costs of this care relate to services for children and pregnant women (e.g., neonatal intensive care).

Chronic care Care and treatment rendered to individuals whose health problems are of a long-term and continuing nature. Rehabilitation facilities, nursing homes, and mental hospitals provide this kind of care.

Chronic disease A disease that has one or more of the following characteristics: is permanent; leaves residual disability; is caused by nonreversible pathological alternation; requires special training of the patient for rehabilitation; or may be expected to require a long period of supervision, observation, or care.

Clinic A facility, or part of one, devoted to diagnosis and treatment of outpatients. "Clinic" is irregularly defined. It may either include or exclude physicians' offices, may be limited to facilities that serve poor or public patients, and may be limited to facilities in which graduate or undergraduate medical education is done.

Clinical condition A diagnosis (e.g., cerebrovascular hemorrhage) or a patient state that may be associated with more than one diagnosis (e.g., paraplegia) or that may not be diagnosed yet (e.g., low back pain).

Clinical event Services provided to patients (items of history taking, physical examination, preventive care, tests, procedures, drugs, advice) or information on clinical condition or on patient state used as a patient outcome.

Clinical performance measures Instruments that estimate the extent to which a healthcare provider delivers clinical services that are appropriate for each patient's condition; provides them safely, competently, and in an appropriate time frame; and achieves desired outcomes in terms of those aspects of patient health and patient satisfaction that can be affected by clinical services.

Clinical practice guidelines Systematically developed statements to assist practitioners and patients' decisions about health care to be provided for specific clinical circumstances.

Coinsurance A cost-sharing requirement under a health insurance policy. It provides that the insured party will assume a portion or percentage of the costs of covered services. The health insurance policy provides that the insurer will reimburse a specified percentage of all, or certain specified, covered medical expenses in excess of any deductible amounts payable by the insured. The insured is then liable for the remainder of the costs until their maximum liability is reached.

Community-based care The blend of health and social services provided to an individual or family in their place of residence for the purpose of promoting, maintaining, or restoring health or minimizing the effects of illness and disability.

Community rating A method of calculating health plan premiums using the average cost of actual or anticipated health services for all subscribers within a specific geographic area. The premium does not vary for different groups or subgroups of subscribers to reflect their specific claims experience or health status. Under a *modified* rating (the most common form), rates may vary based on subscribers' specific demographic characteristics (such as age and gender), but rate variation based on individuals' health status, claims experience, or policy duration is prohibited. Under a *pure* rating, variation based on demographic as well as health factors is prohibited, and all subscribers in an area pay the same rate.

Community rating by class (CRC, class rating) For Federally Qualified HMOs, the adjustment of community-rated premiums on the basis of such factors as age, family size, and tobacco use. These health plan premiums reflect the experience of all enrollees of a given class within a specific geographic area, rather than the experience of any one employer group.

Comorbidities Conditions that exist at the same time as the primary condition in the same patient (e.g., hypertension exists at the same time as diabetes, ischemic heart disease, and end-stage renal disease).

Competition A characteristic of market economics in which buyers choose from among alternative goods and services made available in the market by two or more sellers. In a classic competitive market, there are many buyers and many sellers.

Complementary and alternative medicine Medical products and practices that are not part of standard (i.e., Western) medical care.

Consumer A person who purchases or receives goods or services for personal needs or use and not for resale.

Continuum of care Clinical services provided during a single inpatient hospitalization or for multiple conditions over a lifetime. It provides a basis for evaluating quality, cost, and utilization over the long term.

Contractual allowance The difference between what hospitals bill and what they receive in payment from third-party payers, most commonly government programs. Also known as contractual adjustment.

Coordination of benefits (COB) Procedures used by insurers to avoid duplicate payment for losses insured under more than one insurance policy. A coordination of benefits clause, or nonduplication clause, in either policy prevents double payment by making one insurer the primary payer and assuring that not more than 100% of the cost is covered. Standard rules determine which of two or more plans, each having COB provisions, pays its benefits in full and which becomes the supplementary payer on a claim.

Copayment A fixed amount of money paid by a health plan enrollee (beneficiary) at the time of service. For example, the enrollee may pay a $10 copayment at every physician office visit and $5 for each drug prescription filled. The health plan pays the remainder of the charge directly to the provider. This method of cost-sharing between the enrollee and the plan serves as an incentive for the enrollee to use healthcare resources wisely. An enrollee might be offered a lower price benefit package in return for a higher copayment.

Cost Expenses incurred in the provision of services or goods. Many different kinds of expenses are defined and used. The charge—that is, the price of a service or amount billed to an individual or third party—may or may not be equal to the service cost.

Cost-based reimbursement Payment made by a health plan or payer to healthcare providers based on the actual costs incurred in the delivery of care and services to plan beneficiaries. This method of paying providers is still used by some plans; however, it is being replaced by prospective payment and other payment mechanisms.

Cost–benefit analysis An analytic method in which a program's cost is compared with the program's benefits for a period of time, and is expressed in dollars, as an aid in determining the best investment of resources. For example, the cost of establishing a vaccination service might be compared with the total cost of medical care and lost productivity that will be eliminated as a result of more people being vaccinated. This method can also be applied to specific medical tests and treatments.

Cost center An accounting device whereby all related costs attributable to some *financial center* within an institution, such as a department or program, are segregated for accounting or reimbursement purposes.

Cost–effectiveness analysis A form of analysis that seeks to determine the costs and effectiveness of a medical intervention compared with similar alternative interventions to determine the relative degree to which they will lead to the desired health outcome(s). This analysis can be applied to any of a number of standards, such as median life expectancy or quality of life after an intervention.

Cost of illness analysis An assessment of the economic impact of an illness or condition, including treatment costs.

Cost sharing Any provision of a health insurance policy that requires the insured individual to pay some portion of medical expenses. The general term includes deductibles, copayments, and coinsurance.

Cost-shifting Recouping the cost of providing uncompensated care by increasing revenues from some payers to offset losses and lower net payments from other payers.

Coverage The guarantee against specific losses provided under the terms of an insurance policy. This term is sometimes used interchangeably with *benefits* or *protection* and is also used to mean *insurance* or *insurance contract*.

Covered entity Any of the three kinds of entities that must comply with federal health information privacy regulations (i.e., HIPAA Privacy Rule): healthcare providers, health plans, and healthcare clearinghouses. For these purposes, healthcare providers include hospitals, physicians, and other caregivers, as well as researchers, who provide health care and receive, access, or generate individually identifiable healthcare information.

Covered services Healthcare services covered by an insurance plan.

COVID-19 Coronavirus disease 2019; an infectious disease caused by the SARS-CoV-2 virus.

Credentialing The recognition of professional or technical competence. This process may include registration, certification, licensure, professional association membership, or the award of a degree in the field. Certification and licensure affect the supply of health personnel by controlling entry into practice, and they influence the stability of the labor force by affecting geographic distribution, mobility, and retention of workers. This process also determines the quality of personnel by providing standards for evaluating competence and by defining the scope of functions and how personnel may be used.

Critical access hospital (CAH) A rural hospital designation established by the Medicare Rural Hospital Flexibility Program (MRHFP) enacted as part of the 1997 Balanced Budget Act. Rural hospitals meeting criteria established by their state may apply for this status. Designated hospitals are reimbursed based on cost (rather than prospective payment), must comply with federal and state regulations for this status, and are exempt from certain hospital staffing requirements.

Crowd out A phenomenon whereby new public programs or expansions of existing public programs designed to extend coverage to the uninsured prompt some privately insured people to drop their private coverage and take advantage of the expanded public subsidy.

Cultural competence A practitioner's or institution's understanding of and sensitivity to the cultural background and primary language of patients in any component of service delivery, including patient education materials, questionnaires, office or healthcare organization setting, direct patient care, and public health campaigns.

Current Population Survey (CPS) A national survey conducted annually by the U.S. Department of Commerce's Census Bureau to gather information on the noninstitutionalized population of the United States. This survey is the most commonly reported source for the number of people without health insurance and other information about this population.

Current Procedural Terminology (CPT) A manual that assigns five-digit codes to medical services and procedures to standardize claims processing and data analysis.

Customary charge One of the factors determining a physician's payment for a service under Medicare; calculated as the physician's median charge for that service over a prior 12-month period.

D

Debt service Required payments for interest on and retirement of a debt. The amount needed, supplied, or accrued for meeting such payments during any given accounting period. A budget or operating statement heading for such items.

Decentralization The transfer of control from central or top-level government to local levels rather than one single one.

Deductible The amount of loss or expense that must be incurred by an insured or otherwise covered individual before an insurer will assume any liability for all or part of the remaining cost of covered services. This loss or expense may be either a fixed-dollar amount or the value of specified services (such as two days of hospital care or one physician visit). This loss or expense is usually tied to some reference period over which it must be incurred—for example, $100 per calendar year, benefit period, or spell of illness.

Defined benefit Funding mechanisms for pension plans that can also be applied to health benefits. Typical pension approaches include pegging benefits to a percentage of an employee's average compensation over their entire service or over a particular number of years; calculation of a flat monthly payment; and setting benefits based on a definite amount for each year of service, either as a percentage of compensation for each year of service or as a flat dollar amount for each year of service.

Deidentification A process whereby information that could identify the clinician, the reporter, the healthcare institution, or another organization involved in a medical error is removed from an error report after it is received. This process is used to maintain records of factors that could cause errors, but it assures those who report errors that their reports will not be used in civil lawsuits against them.

Deinstitutionalization Policy that calls for the provision of supportive care and treatment for medically and socially dependent individuals in the community rather than in an institutional setting.

Demand In health economics, the amount of a good or service consumers are willing and able to buy at varying prices, given constant income and other factors. This amount should be distinguished from utilization (the amount of services actually used) and need (which has a normative connotation and relates to the amount of goods or services that should be consumed based on professional value judgments).

Denominator For a performance measure, the sample of cases that will be observed (e.g., the number of patients discharged alive with a confirmed diagnosis of acute myocardial infarction, excluding patients with bleeding or other specified conditions).

Deprivation[n] The severe lack of material benefits considered to be basic necessities in a society.

Diagnosis-related groups (DRGs) Groupings of diagnostic categories drawn from the International Classification of Diseases and modified by the presence of a surgical procedure, patient age, presence or absence of significant comorbidities or complications, and other relevant criteria. These groupings are the case-mix measure used in Medicare's prospective payment system.

Direct cost A cost that is identifiable directly with a particular activity, service, or product of the program experiencing the costs. These costs do not include the allocation of costs to a cost center that are not specifically attributable to that cost center.

Direct patient care Any activities by a health professional involving direct interaction, treatment, administration of medications, or other therapy or involvement with a patient.

Disability Any limitation of physical, mental, or social activity of an individual compared with other individuals of similar age, gender, and occupation. Frequently refers to limitation of a person's usual or major activities, most commonly vocational. There are varying kinds (functional, vocational, learning), degrees (partial, total), and durations (temporary, permanent) of limitation. Public programs often provide benefits for specific limitations, such as total and permanent.

Discharge The release of a patient from a provider's care, usually referring to the date when a patient checks out of a hospital.

Disease A failure of the adaptive mechanisms of an organism to counteract adequately, normally, or appropriately the stimuli and stresses to which it is subjected, resulting in a disturbance in the function or structure of some part of the organism. This definition emphasizes that the failure is multifactorial and may be prevented or treated by changing any or a combination of the factors. This term is a very elusive and difficult concept to define, as it is largely socially defined. Thus, criminality and drug dependence are presently seen by some as diseases, whereas they were previously considered to be moral or legal problems.

Disease burden The amount, or level, of disease in a specific population. It is quantified using morbidity rates for specific diseases, various mortality rates, injury rates, and nutritional status. Disease burden is important for planning and operating healthcare systems.

Disease management The process of identifying and delivering within selected patient populations (e.g., patients with asthma or diabetes) the most efficient, effective combination of resources, interventions, or pharmaceuticals for the treatment or prevention of a disease. This process could include team-based care where physicians and/or other health professionals participate in the delivery and management of care. It also includes the appropriate use of pharmaceuticals.

Drug risk-sharing arrangements Healthcare provider organizations may be at partial, full, or no risk for drug costs. Provider groups at partial risk share in a proportion of savings and/or cost overruns. The group can share in savings if it prescribes less than the budgeted amount (*upside risk*), but may also share in any over-expenditures (*downside risk*). Groups at full risk realize all of the savings or absorb all of the losses. Groups at no risk absorb none of the losses and profits (typically, risks are absorbed by the HMO or other managed care organization).

Drug utilization review (DUR) A formal program for assessing drug prescription and use patterns. This program typically examines patterns of drug misuse, monitors current therapies, and intervenes when prescribing or utilization patterns fall outside pre-established standards. This program is usually retrospective but can also be performed before drugs are dispensed. Such programs were established by the Omnibus Budget Reconciliation Act (OBRA) in 1990 and are required for Medicaid programs.

E

Electronic claim A digital representation of a medical bill generated by a provider or by the provider's billing agent for submission using telecommunications to a health insurance payer.

Emergency medical services (EMS) Services used in responding to the perceived individual need for immediate treatment for medical, physiological, or psychological illness or injury.

Epidemic A group of cases of a specific disease or illness clearly in excess of what one would normally expect in a particular geographic area. There is no absolute criterion for using the term—as standards and expectations change, and based on the specific disease, so might the definition (e.g., of violence).

Epidemiology The study of the patterns of determinants and antecedents of disease in human populations. This study uses biology, clinical medicine, and statistics in an effort to understand the etiology (causes) of illness and/or disease. The ultimate goal of an epidemiologist is not merely to identify underlying causes of a disease, but to apply findings to disease prevention and health promotion.

Etiology Cause; a term is used by epidemiologists.

Evidence-based decision making In a health policy context, the application of the best available scientific evidence to policy decisions about specific medical treatments or changes in the delivery system. The goals are to improve the quality of care, increase the efficiency of care delivery, and improve the allocation of healthcare resources.

Evidence-based medicine The conscientious, explicit, and judicious use of current best evidence in making decisions about the care of individual patients. This approach must balance the best external evidence with the desires of the patient and the clinical expertise of healthcare providers.

Exclusive provider arrangement (EPA) All indemnity or service plans that provide benefits only if care is rendered by the institutional and professional providers with which they contract (with some exceptions for emergency and out-of-area services).

Experience rating A method of adjusting health plan premiums based on the historical utilization data and distinguishing characteristics of a specific subscriber group.

F

Family practice A form of specialty practice in which physicians provide continuing, comprehensive primary care within the context of the family unit.

Favorable selection A tendency for utilization of health services in a population group to be lower than expected or estimated.

Federal poverty level (FPL) The amount of income determined by the U.S. Department of Health and Human Services to provide a bare minimum for food, clothing, transportation, shelter, and other necessities; reported annually and varies according to family size. Public assistance programs usually define income limits in relation to this threshold.

Fee-for-service Method of billing for health services under which a physician or other practitioner charges separately for each patient encounter or service rendered. It is the method of billing used by the majority of U.S. physicians. Under this kind of payment system, expenditures increase if the fees themselves increase, if more units of service are provided, or if more expensive services are substituted for less expensive ones. This system contrasts with salary, per capita, or other prepayment systems where the payment to the physician is not changed with the number of services actually used.

Fee schedule An exhaustive list of physician services in which each entry is associated with a specific monetary amount that represents the approved payment level for a given insurance plan.

Financial feasibility The projected ability of a provider to pay the capital and operating costs associated with the delivery of a proposed healthcare service.

Formulary A list of drugs, usually by their generic names, and indications for their use; intended to include a sufficient range of medicines to enable physicians, dentists, and, as appropriate, other healthcare practitioners to prescribe all medically appropriate treatment for all reasonably common illnesses. An *open* formulary allows coverage for almost all drugs, whereas a *closed* formulary provides coverage for a limited set of drugs. A *managed* formulary includes a list of preferred drugs that the health plan prefers to use because they cost less or are more effective or for other reasons. A *tiered* formulary financially rewards patients for using generic and formulary drugs by requiring the patient to pay progressively higher copayments for brand-name and nonformulary drugs.

G

Gatekeeper The primary care practitioner in managed care organizations who determines whether the presenting patient needs to see a specialist or requires other nonroutine services. The goal is to guide the patient to appropriate services while avoiding unnecessary and costly referrals to specialists.

General practice A form of practice in which physicians without specialty training provide a wide range of primary healthcare services to patients.

Generic drug A prescription drug that has the same active-ingredient formula as a brand-name drug but usually costs significantly less than the brand-name drug.

Generic substitution In cases in which the patent on a specific pharmaceutical product expires and drug manufacturers produce generic versions of the original branded product, the generic version of the drug (which is theorized to be identical to the product manufactured by a different firm) is dispensed even though the original product is prescribed. Some managed care organizations and Medicaid programs mandate generic substitution because of the generally lower cost of generic products. There are state and federal regulations regarding generic substitutions.

Genomics The study of genomes, which includes gene mapping, gene sequencing, and gene function.

Global budgeting A method of hospital cost-containment in which participating hospitals must share a prospectively set budget. Methods for allocating funds among hospitals may vary, but the key is that the participating hospitals agree to an aggregate cap on revenues that they will receive each year. This method may also be mandated under a universal health insurance system.

Global fee A total charge for a specific set of services, such as obstetric services that encompass prenatal, delivery, and postnatal care.

Global Health Security Agenda (GHSA) An international effort launched by the United States for partnerships on health incidents related to the spread of infectious disease.

Globalization[2,3] The process whereby national and international policymakers promote domestic deregulation and external liberalization; the removal of barriers to international trade, foreign direct investments, and short-term financial flows. Globalization impacts health in many ways as world markets are opened. Access to world markets affects national economies and politics, which in turn affect the health-related sectors of the economy. These changes then affect each country's healthcare system, population-level health, and individual risks. Globalization also has an impact on the economies of countries and the economies of households. In turn, the wealth of individuals and countries is highly correlated with the health status of populations.

Graduate medical education (GME) Medical education after receipt of the Doctor of Medicine (MD) or equivalent degree, including the education received as an intern, resident (which involves training in a specialty), or fellow, as well as continuing medical education. The Centers for Medicare and Medicaid Services partly finances this education through direct and indirect Medicare payments.

Gross domestic product (GDP) The market value of all goods and services produced by labor and property within a single country during a particular period of time. Income from overseas operations of a domestic corporation would not be included in this value, but activities carried out within a country's borders by a foreign company would be. This value measures how the country's economy is doing.

Group practice A formal association of three or more physicians or other health professionals providing health services. Income from the practice is pooled and redistributed to the members of the group according to some prearranged plan (often, but not necessarily, through partnership). Groups vary a great deal in size, composition, and financial arrangements.

Guaranteed issue Requirement that insurance carriers offer coverage to groups and/or individuals during some period each year. HIPAA states that insurance carriers, for all products to small groups (2–50), must meet this requirement. Some state laws exceed HIPAA's minimum standards and require carriers to guarantee issue to additional groups and individuals.

Guaranteed renewal HIPAA requirement that insurance carriers renew existing coverage for all products to all groups and/or individuals.

H

Handicapped As defined by Section 504 of the Rehabilitation Act of 1973, any person who has a physical or mental impairment that substantially limits one or more major life activity, has a record of such impairment, or is regarded as having such an impairment.

Health The state of complete physical, mental, and social well-being and not merely the absence of disease or infirmity. This state has many dimensions (anatomic, physiologic, and mental) and is largely culturally defined. The relative importance of various disabilities will differ, depending on the cultural milieu and the role of the affected individual in that culture. Most attempts at measurement have been assessed in terms or morbidity and mortality.

Health consumer One who may receive or is receiving health services. Although all people at times use health services, a consumer, as the term is used in health legislation and programs, is usually someone who is not associated in any direct or indirect way with the provision of health services.

Health education Any combination of learning opportunities designed to facilitate voluntary adaptations of behavior (in individuals, groups, or communities) conducive to health.

Health facilities Collectively, all physical establishments used in the provision of health services—usually limited to establishments that were built for the purpose of providing health care, such as hospitals and nursing homes. An office building that includes a physician's office would not be included. Classifications include hospitals (both general and specialty), long-term care establishments, kidney dialysis treatment centers, and ambulatory surgical establishments.

Health insurance Financial protection against healthcare costs arising from disease or accidental bodily injury. Such protection usually covers all or part of the costs of treating the disease or injury. Financial protection may be obtained on either an individual or a group basis. Although the term is often used by policymakers to refer to comprehensive coverage, insurers and regulators also use it to refer to other forms of coverage such as long-term care, supplemental, specific disease, and accidental death and dismemberment.

Health maintenance organization (HMO) An entity with four essential attributes: (1) an organized system that provides health care in a geographic area and that accepts the responsibility to provide or otherwise assure the delivery of (2) an agreed-upon set of basic and supplemental health maintenance and treatment services to (3) a voluntarily enrolled group of people and (4) for which services the entity is reimbursed through a predetermined fixed, periodic prepayment made by, or on behalf of, each person or family unit enrolled. The payment is fixed without regard to the amounts of actual services provided to an individual enrollee. Individual practice associations involving groups or independent physicians can be included under the definition.

Health manpower shortage area (HMSA) An area or group that the U.S. Department of Health and Human Services designates as having an inadequate supply of healthcare providers. This may be an urban or rural geographic area; a population for which access barriers prevent individuals from using local providers; or medium- or maximum-security correctional institutions and public or nonprofit, private residential facilities.

Health personnel Collectively, all people working in the provision of health services, whether as individual practitioners or employees of health institutions and programs. They may be professionally trained or not, and may be subject to public regulation or not.

Health plan An organization that provides a defined set of benefits. This term usually refers to an HMO-like entity, as opposed to an indemnity insurer.

Health planning Planning concerned with improving health, whether undertaken comprehensively for a whole community or for a particular population, kind of health service, institution, or health program. The components include data assembly and analysis, goal determination, action recommendation, and implementation strategy.

Health policy An insurance contract consisting of a defined set of benefits.

Health promotion Any combination of health education and related organizational, political, and economic interventions designed to facilitate behavioral and environmental adaptations that will improve or protect health.

Health-related quality of life (HRQL) In public health and in medicine, a person or group's perceived physical and mental health over time. Physicians have often used such indicators to measure the effects of chronic illness in their patients to better understand how an illness interferes with a person's day-to-day life. Similarly, public health professionals use such indicators to measure the effects of numerous disorders, short- and long-term disabilities, and diseases in different populations. Tracking these indicators in different populations can identify subgroups with poor physical or mental health and can help guide policies or interventions to improve their health.

Health risk factors Chemical, psychological, physiologic, or genetic factors and conditions that predispose an individual to the development of a disease.

Health service area Geographic area designated on the basis of such factors as geography, political boundaries, population, and health resources for the effective planning and development of health services.

Health services research The multidisciplinary field of scientific investigation that studies how social factors, financing systems, organizational structures and processes, health technologies, and personal behaviors affect access to health care, the quality and cost of health care, and ultimately health and well-being. Its research domains are individuals, families, organizations, institutions, communities, and populations.

Health status The state of health of a specified individual, group, or population. It may be measured by obtaining proxies such as people's subjective assessments of their health; by one or more indicators of mortality and morbidity in the population, such as longevity or maternal and infant mortality; or by using the incidence or prevalence of major diseases (communicable, chronic, or nutritional). Conceptually, this is the proper outcome measure for the effectiveness of a specific population's medical care system, although attempts to relate effects of available medical care to variations in health status have proved difficult.

Healthcare cost and utilization project quality indicators (HCUP QIs) A set of 33 clinical performance measures that inform hospitals' self-assessments of inpatient quality of care as well as state and community assessments of access to primary care. Developed by the Agency for Healthcare Research and Quality (AHRQ) as quick and easy-to-use screening tools, these measures are intended as starting points in identifying clinical areas appropriate for further, more in-depth study and analysis. These measures span three dimensions of care: potentially avoidable adverse hospital outcomes, potentially inappropriate utilization of hospital procedures, and potentially avoidable hospital admissions.

Healthcare paraprofessionals Home health aides, certified nurse's aides, and personal care attendants who provide direct care and personal support services in hospitals, nursing homes, and other institutions, as well as home-based care to disabled, elderly, and infirm individuals.

High-risk pool A subsidized health insurance pool organized by some states as an alternative for individuals who have been denied health insurance because of a medical condition or whose premiums are rated significantly higher than the average because of health status or claims experience; commonly operated through an association composed of all health insurers in a state. HIPAA allows states to use these pools as an *acceptable alternative mechanism* that satisfies the statutory requirements for ensuring access to health insurance coverage for certain individuals.

HIV/AIDS Human immunodeficiency virus/acquired immunodeficiency syndrome. AIDS is a chronic health condition caused by the human immunodeficiency virus.

Holism The integration of mind, body, and spirit of a person; emphasizes the importance of perceiving the individual (regarding physical symptoms) in a *whole* sense. This integration teaches that the healthcare system must extend its focus beyond solely the physical aspects of disease and consider the whole person and the inter-relationships between the emotional, social, spiritual, and physical elements of disease and health.

Home- and community-based services (HCBS) Any care or services provided in a patient's place of residence or in a noninstitutional setting located in the immediate community. These services may include home health care, adult day care or day treatment, medical equipment services, or other interventions provided for the purpose of allowing a patient to receive care at home or in the community.

Home health care Health services rendered in the home to elderly, disabled, sick, or convalescent individuals who do not need institutional care. The services may be provided by a visiting nurse association (VNA), home health agency, county public health department, hospital, or other organized community group, and may be specialized or comprehensive. The most common kinds of nursing services are speech, physical, occupational, and rehabilitation therapy; homemaker services; and social services.

Horizontal integration Merging of two or more firms at the same level of production in some formal, legal relationship (see *vertical integration*).

Hospice A program that provides palliative and supportive care for terminally ill patients and their families, either directly or on a consulting basis with the patient's physician or another community agency. Originally a medieval name for a way station for crusaders where they could be replenished, refreshed, and cared for; now used for an organized program of care for people going through life's "last station." The entire family is considered the unit of care, and care extends through their period of mourning.

Hospital An institution whose primary function is to provide inpatient diagnostic and therapeutic services for a variety of medical conditions, both surgical and nonsurgical.

In addition, most of these institutions provide some outpatient services, particularly emergency care. These institutions may be classified by length of stay (short- or long-term), as teaching or nonteaching, by major type of service (general, psychiatric, tuberculosis, and other specialties such as maternity, pediatric, or ear, nose, and throat), and by type of ownership or control (federal, state, or local government; for-profit and nonprofit). Such short-term, general, nonprofit community institutions are often called voluntary and dominate the sector.

Human Development Index (HDI) A composite measure for assessing long-term progress in three basic dimensions of human development: a long and healthy life, access to knowledge, and a decent standard of living.

Hydrotherapy A branch of alternative medicine that involves the use of water for pain relief and treatment.

I

Iatrogenic Caused by medical treatment, such as a drug side effect or a postoperative infection.

Incidence In epidemiology, the number of cases of disease, infection, or some other event having their onset during a prescribed period of time in relation to the unit of population in which they occur; measures morbidity or other events as they happen over a period of time. Examples include the number of accidents occurring in a manufacturing plant during a year in relationship to the number of employees in the plant, or the number of cases of mumps occurring in a school during a month in relation to the number of pupils enrolled in the school. It refers only to the number of new cases.

Incurred but not reported (IBNR) Claims that have not been reported to the insurer as of some specific date for services that have been provided. The estimated value of these claims is a component of an insurance company's current liabilities.

Indemnity Health insurance benefits provided in the form of cash payments rather than services. Such a contract usually defines the maximum amounts that will be paid for covered services.

Independent practice association (IPA) An organized form of prepaid medical practice in which participating physicians remain in their independent office settings, seeing both enrollees in this form of organization and private-pay patients. Participating physicians may be reimbursed by the organization on a fee-for-service basis or a capitation basis.

Indicator A quantitative or statistical measure or gauge for monitoring clinical care.

Indigent care Health services provided to the poor or those unable to pay. Because many of these patients are not eligible for federal or state programs, the costs that are covered by Medicaid are generally recorded separately from these care costs.

Indirect cost A cost that cannot be identified directly with a particular activity, service, or product of the entity incurring the cost. These costs are usually apportioned among an entity's services in proportion to each service's share of direct costs.

Individually identifiable health information A subset of health information that includes demographic information collected from an individual and that is created or received by a healthcare provider, health plan, employer, or healthcare clearinghouse; relates to the past, present, or future physical or mental health or condition of an individual, the provision of health care to an individual, or the past, present, or future payment for the provision of health care to an individual.

Infant mortality The death of a baby between the time it is born and 1 year of age.

Infectious disease An illness resulting from the presence of a pathogenic biological agent in a host, human, or animal. The pathogen may or may not be able to be transmitted to other humans or animals.[4]

Inpatient A person who has been admitted at least overnight to a hospital or other health facility (which is, therefore, responsible for their room and board) for the purpose of receiving diagnostic treatment or other health services.

Institutional health services Services delivered on an inpatient basis in hospitals, nursing homes, or other inpatient institutions. May also refer to services delivered on an outpatient basis by departments or other organizational units of, or sponsored by, such institutions.

Instrumental activities of daily living (IADL) An index or scale that measures a patient's degree of independence in aspects of cognitive and social functioning, including shopping, cooking, doing housework, managing money, and using the telephone.

Integrated services network (ISN) A network of organizations, usually including hospitals and physician groups, that provides or arranges to provide a coordinated continuum of services to a defined population and is held both clinically and fiscally accountable for the outcomes of the populations served.

Intermediate care facility (ICF) An institution that is licensed under state law to provide, on a regular basis, health-related care and services to individuals who do not require the degree of care or treatment that a hospital or skilled nursing facility is designed to provide. Public institutions for care of developmentally disabled individuals or people with related conditions are also included in the definition. The distinction between *health-related care and services* and *room and board* has often proved difficult to make but is important because these institutions are subject to quite different regulations and coverage requirements than institutions that do not provide health-related care and services.

International Classification of Diseases (ICD) A publication of the World Health Organization (WHO), which is revised periodically. The full title is *International Statistical*

Classification of Diseases and Related Health Problems. This classification, which originated for use with deaths, is used worldwide for that purpose. In addition, it has been used widely in the United States for hospital diagnosis classification since about 1955, with various adaptations and modifications.

International Health Regulations (IHR) The legal framework adopted by the international community, which defines each ratifying nation's rights and responsibilities in managing a public health emergency.

International medical graduate (IMG) A physician who graduated from a medical school outside of the United States, usually Canada. U.S. citizens who go to medical school abroad are classified as international medical graduates, as are foreign-born people who are not trained in medical school in the United States. U.S. citizens represent only a small portion of nondomestic medical school students.

Internist A physician who focuses their practice on the care of critically ill and injured patients. After initial training in internal medicine, anesthesiology, or surgery, additional training in critical care is required to become board certified.

Intervention strategy A generic term used in public health to describe a program or policy designed to have an impact on an illness or disease. For example, a mandatory seat belt law is designed to reduce automobile-related fatalities.

Inventory A detailed description of quantities and locations of different kinds of facilities, major equipment, and personnel that are available in a geographic area and the amount, type, and distribution of services these resources can support.

J

Joint Commission on Accreditation of Healthcare Organizations (JCAHO) A national private, nonprofit organization whose purpose is to encourage the attainment of uniformly high standards of institutional medical care; establishes guidelines for the operation of hospitals and other health facilities and conducts survey and accreditation programs.

L

LGBTQ+ An acronym for lesbian, gay, bisexual, transgender, queer or questioning, intersex, asexual, and more.

License/licensure A permission granted to an individual or organization by a competent authority, usually public, to engage lawfully in a practice, occupation, or activity; the process by which the permission is granted. It is usually granted on the basis of examination and/or proof of education rather than on measures of performance. This permission is usually permanent but may be conditioned on annual payment of a fee, proof of continuing education, or proof of competence.

Long-term care A set of healthcare, personal care, and social services required by people who have lost, or never have acquired, some degree of functional capacity (e.g., chronically ill, elderly, disabled, or developmentally disabled people) in an institution or at home for a long time. The term is often used more narrowly to refer only to ongoing institutional care, such as that provided in nursing homes, homes for developmentally disabled individuals, and mental hospitals. Ambulatory services such as home health care and assisted living, which can also be provided on a long-term basis, are seen as alternatives.

M

Macroeconomics A field focused on the performance of economies—changes in economic output, inflation, interest and foreign exchange rates, and the balance of payments.

Magnetic resonance imaging (MRI) A form of diagnostic radiology; a method of imaging body tissues that uses the response or resonance of the nuclei of the atoms of one of the bodily elements, typically hydrogen or phosphorus, to externally applied magnetic fields.

Malpractice Professional misconduct or failure to apply ordinary skills in the performance of a professional act. A practitioner is liable for damages or injuries caused by this kind of misconduct or failure. For some professions, such as medicine, insurance can cover the costs of defending lawsuits instituted against the professional and/or any damages assessed by the court, usually up to a maximum limit; a patient must demonstrate some injury and must prove that the injury was caused by the professional's negligence.

Managed behavioral health organization An organization that assumes the responsibility for managing the behavioral health benefit for an employer or payer organization under a *carve-out* arrangement. The management may include utilization management services through its own organization or provider network. Reimbursement may be on a fee-for-service, shared risk, or full-risk basis. This is a specialty managed care organization (MCO).

Managed care The body of clinical, financial, and organizational activities designed to ensure the provision of appropriate healthcare services in a cost-efficient manner. Its techniques are most often practiced by organizations and professionals that assume risk for a defined population (e.g., health maintenance organizations).

Management services organization (MSO) An organization that provides administrative and practice management services to physicians; typically owned by a hospital, hospitals, or investors. Large group practices may also establish this kind of organization to sell management services to other physician groups.

Mandatory reporting A system under which physicians or other health professionals are required by law to inform health authorities when a specified event occurs (e.g., a medical error or the diagnosis of a certain disease).

Maximum allowable actual charge (MAAC) A limitation on billed charges for Medicare services provided by nonparticipating physicians. For physicians with charges exceeding 115% of the prevailing charge for nonparticipating physicians, this limit increases in actual charges to 1% per year. For physicians whose charges are less than 115% of the prevailing charge, the limit on actual charge increases so they may not charge more than 115%.

Measure set A collection of measures with a common purpose and developer (see *clinical performance measures*).

Medicaid (Title XIX) A U.S. federally aided, state-operated and -administered program that provides medical benefits for certain indigent or low-income people in need of health and medical care. The program, authorized by Title XIX of the Social Security Act, is basically for the poor. It does not cover all of the poor—only people who meet specified eligibility criteria. Subject to broad federal guidelines, states determine the benefits covered, program eligibility, rates of payment for providers, and methods of administering the program.

Medical audit Detailed retrospective review and evaluation of selected medical records by qualified professional staff; used in some hospitals, group practices, and occasion ally in private, independent practices for evaluating professional performance by comparing it with accepted criteria, standards, and current professional judgment; usually concerned with the care of a given illness and undertaken to identify deficiencies in that care in anticipation of educational programs to improve it.

Medical error An error or omission in the medical care provided to a patient; can occur in diagnosis, treatment, preventive monitoring, or in the failure of a piece of medical equipment or other component of the medical system; often, but not always, results in adverse events, such as injury or death.

Medical informatics The systematic study, or science, of the identification, collection, storage, communication, retrieval, and analysis of data about medical care services that can be used to improve decisions made by physicians and managers of healthcare organizations.

Medical internationalism After the 1959 Cuban Revolution, Cuba established a health program that sends its medical personnel overseas, particularly to developing countries in Latin America, Africa, and Oceania as a gesture of providing overseas assistance.

Medically indigent People who cannot afford needed health care because of insufficient income and/or lack of adequate health insurance.

Medical management information system (MMIS) A data system that allows payers and purchasers to track healthcare expenditure and utilization patterns.

Medical review criteria Systematically developed statements that can be used to assess the appropriateness of specific healthcare decisions, services, and outcomes.

Medical savings account (MSA) An account in which individuals can accumulate contributions to pay for medical care or insurance. Some states give tax-preferred status to contributions to this kind of account, but such contributions are still subject to federal income taxation. This kind of account differs from medical reimbursement accounts, sometimes called flexible benefits or Section 115 accounts, in that it does not need to be associated with an employer. It is not currently recognized in any federal statute.

Medical tourism Traveling to another country for medical care.

Medically necessary A treatment or service that is appropriate and consistent with a patient's diagnosis and that, in accordance with locally accepted standards of practice, cannot be omitted without adversely affecting the patient's condition or the quality of care.

Medically needy People who are categorically eligible for Medicaid and whose income, less the accumulated medical bills, is below state income limits for the Medicaid program.

Medically underserved population A population group experiencing a shortage of personal health services. This group may or may not reside in a particularly medically underserved area or be defined by its place of residence. Thus, migrants, American Indians, prison inmates, or mental hospital residents may constitute such a population. The term is defined and used to give priority for federal assistance (e.g., the National Health Service Corps).

Medicare (Title XVIII) A U.S. health insurance program for people aged 65 and over, for people eligible for Social Security disability payments for 2 years or longer, and for certain workers and their dependents who need kidney transplantation or dialysis. Monies from payroll taxes and premiums from beneficiaries are deposited in special trust funds for use in meeting the expenses incurred by the insured. It consists of two separate but coordinated programs: hospital insurance (Part A) and supplementary medical insurance (Part B).

Medicare+Choice A Medicare program created by the 1997 Balanced Budget Act; allows the Centers for Medicare and Medicaid Services to contract with a variety of different managed care and fee-for-service entities offering greater flexibility to Medicare participants. People eligible for Medicare parts A and B are also eligible for this program (Medicare Part C).

Medicare Payment Advisory Commission (MedPAC) An independent federal body that advises the U.S. Congress on issues affecting the Medicare program. It was established by the Balanced Budget Act of 1997 (P.L. 105-33), which merged the Prospective Payment Assessment Commission (ProPAC) and the Physician Payment Review Commission (PPRC).

Medicare Rural Hospital Flexibility Program (MRHFP) A limited service hospital program created by the Balanced Budget Act of 1997 and modified by the

Balanced Budget Refinement Act in 1999. Under this program, rural hospitals meeting criteria specified by their state can apply to become critical access hospitals. This program provides regulatory relief and a cost-based payment option for smaller, low-volume facilities that lack the resources needed to meet hospital staffing and other requirements under Medicare.

Medigap policy A private health insurance policy offered to Medicare beneficiaries to cover expenses not paid by Medicare. This policy is strictly regulated by federal rules. It is also known as Medicare supplemental insurance.

Mental health The state of being of an individual with respect to emotional, social, and behavioral maturity. Although the term is often used to mean *good mental health*, it is a relative state, varying from time to time in the individual, with some people being more healthy than others in this regard.

Morbidity The extent of illness, injury, or disability in a defined population. It is usually expressed in general or specific rates of incidence or prevalence.

Mortality Death. This term is used to describe the relation of deaths to the population in which they occur. This rate of death expresses the number of deaths in a quantified population within a prescribed time and may be expressed as a *crude death rate* (e.g., total deaths in relation to total population during a year) or as death rates for specific diseases and sometimes for age, gender, or other attributes (e.g., number of deaths from cancer in White males in relation to the White male population during a given year).

Multi-sectoral approach (MSA) An integrated, collaborative process whereby different actors come together to address complex health challenges.

N

National Committee for Quality Assurance (NCQA) A national organization founded in 1979, composed of 14 directors representing consumers, purchasers, and providers of managed health care. It accredits quality assurance programs in prepaid managed healthcare organizations and develops and coordinates programs for assessing the quality of care and service in the managed care industry.

National Health Service Corps (NHSC) A program administered by the U.S. Public Health Service that places physicians and other providers in health profession shortage areas by providing scholarship and loan repayment incentives. Since 1970, NHSC members have worked in community health centers, migrant centers, Indian health facilities, and in other sites targeting underserved populations.

National Pharmaceutical Stockpile (NPS) Program A program, in conjunction with the Centers for Disease Control and Prevention, that is intended to ensure the availability and rapid deployment of lifesaving pharmaceuticals, antidotes, and other medical supplies and equipment necessary to counter the effects of nerve agents, biological pathogens, and chemical agents. This program stands ready for immediate deployment to any U.S. location in the event of a terrorist attack using a biological toxin or chemical agent directed against a civilian population.

Neoplasms Abnormal growth of tissue in part of the body, especially as a characteristic of cancer.

Network An affiliation of providers through formal and informal contracts and agreements. Networks may contract externally to obtain administrative and financial services.

Noncommunicable disease (NCD) A non-transmissible disease, often of long duration.

Numerator For a performance measure, the cases in the denominator group that experience events specified in a medical review criterion (e.g., the number of patients discharged alive with a confirmed diagnosis of acute myocardial infarction, excluding patients with bleeding or other specified conditions, who were discharged on aspirin) (see *denominator*).

Nurse An individual trained to care for the sick, the elderly, or the injured; can be defined as a professional qualified by education and authorized by law to practice nursing. There are many different types, specialties, and grades within this profession.

Nurse practitioner A registered nurse qualified and specially trained to provide primary care, including primary health care in homes and in ambulatory care facilities, long-term care facilities, and other healthcare institutions. These professionals generally function under the supervision of a physician but not necessarily in their presence. They are usually salaried rather than reimbursed on a fee-for-service basis, although the supervising physician may receive fee-for-service reimbursement for their services.

Nursing home Any of a wide range of institutions that provide various levels of maintenance and personal or nursing care to people who are unable to care for themselves and who have health problems that range from minimal to very serious. The term includes free-standing institutions or identifiable components of other health facilities that provide nursing care and related services, personal care, and residential care. It includes skilled nursing facilities and extended-care facilities but not boarding homes.

O

Occupancy rate A measure of inpatient health facility use, determined by dividing available bed-days by patient-days. It measures the average percentage of a hospital's beds occupied and may be institution-wide or specific for one department or service.

Occupational health services Health services concerned with the physical, mental, and social well-being of an individual in relation to their working environment and with the adjustment of individuals to their work. The term applies to more than the safety of the workplace and includes health and job satisfaction. In the United

States, the principal statute concerned with this field is the Occupational Safety and Health Act administered by the Occupational Safety and Health Administration (OSHA) and the National Institute of Occupational Safety and Health (NIOSH).

OECD The Organisation for Economic Co-operation and Development; an international organization of 38 countries committed to democracy and the market economy.

Office of Public Health Preparedness (OPHP) Directs the Department of Health and Human Services' (DHHS) efforts to prepare for, protect against, respond to, and recover from all acts of bioterrorism and other public health emergencies that affect the civilian population, and serves as the focal point within DHHS for these activities. This office is headed by a director, who reports directly to the DHHS secretary, and serves as the secretary's principal advisor on DHHS activities related to protecting the civilian population from acts of bioterrorism and other public health emergencies. This office was created in January 2002.

One Health The study of the relationships among humans, animals, and ecosystems, and how the interconnectedness of these three impact human health; the health of all living things.[4]

Open enrollment A method for making sure that insurance plans, especially prepaid plans, do not exclusively select good risks. With this requirement, a plan must accept all people who apply during a specific period each year.

Operating cost Necessary expenses to operate an activity that provides health services. These expenses normally include personnel, materials, overhead, depreciation, and interest.

Operating margin Revenues from sales minus current cost of goods sold. A measure of operating efficiency that is independent of the cost flow assumption for inventory. Sometimes called *current (gross) margin*.

Opportunity cost The cost of foregone outcomes that could have been achieved through alternative investments.

Outcome The finding of a given diagnostic procedure. It may also refer to the cure of the patient, restoration of function, or extension of life. When used for populations or the healthcare system, it typically refers to changes in birth or death rates, or some similar global measure.

Outcomes research Research on measures of changes in patient treatment results—that is, patient health status and satisfaction resulting from specific medical and health interventions. Attributing changes in results to medical care requires distinguishing the effects of care from the effects of the many other factors that influence patients' health and satisfaction.

Outpatient A patient who is receiving ambulatory care at a hospital or other facility without being admitted to the facility. Usually, it does not mean people receiving services from a physician's office or other program that also does not provide inpatient care.

Overhead The general costs of operating an entity that is allocated to all of the revenue-producing operations of the entity but that are not directly attributable to a single activity. For a hospital, these costs normally include facility maintenance, occupancy costs, housekeeping, administration, and other factors.

P

Palliative care Specialized medical care for people living with a serious illness, such as cancer or heart failure.

Pandemic Influenza Preparedness (PIP) Framework A global approach approved by the world between national health ministries and the World Health Organization to facilitate pandemic preparedness and response.

Parity Equality or comparability between two things. Associated legislation, usually applicable to mental health conditions, such as depression or schizophrenia, requires that health insurers adhere to a principle of equal treatment when making decisions regarding mental health benefits compared with other kinds of medical benefits. *Data parity* is a term used by researchers to describe the degree to which different data measures are equivalent.

Parliamentary republic[12] Republic that operates under a parliamentary system of government, where the executive branch (the government) derives its legitimacy from and is accountable to the legislature (the parliament).

Participating physician A physician who agrees by contractual arrangement to accept the rules, terms, and fee schedule of a given health plan or provider network. In Medicare, a physician who signs an agreement to accept assignment on all Medicare claims for one year (see *assignment*).

Pathological Indicative of or caused by a disease or condition.

Patient safety[13] The prevention of harm to patients. Emphasis is placed on the system of care delivery that (1) prevents errors; (2) learns from the errors that do occur; and (3) is built on a culture of safety that involves healthcare professionals, organizations, and patients.

Peer review Generally, the evaluation by practicing physicians or other professionals of the effectiveness and efficiency of services ordered or performed by other members of the profession. Frequently, this term refers to review of research by other researchers.

Per member per month (PMPM) A unit of measure referring to health plan costs, revenues, hospital days, or patient visits.

Performance measures Methods or instruments to estimate or monitor the extent to which the actions of a healthcare practitioner or provider conform to practice guidelines, medical review criteria, or standards of quality.

Personal protective equipment (PPE)[14] Equipment worn to minimize exposure to a variety of hazards, such as gloves, foot and eye protection, protective hearing devices (earplugs, muffs), hard hats, respirators, and full-body suits.

Pharmaceutical assistance program A public program to provide pharmaceutical coverage to those who cannot afford or have difficulty obtaining prescription drugs. Several states operate such state-funded programs primarily to provide benefits to low-income elderly people or people with disabilities who do not qualify for Medicaid.

Pharmaceutical care system A strategy that attempts to use drug therapy more efficiently to achieve definite outcomes that improve a patient's quality of life. This kind of system requires a reorientation of physicians, pharmacists, and nurses toward effective drug therapy outcomes. It is a set of relationships and decisions through which pharmacists, physicians, nurses, and patients work together to design, implement, and monitor a therapeutic plan that will produce specific therapeutic outcomes.

Pharmacoeconomics The study of the costs and benefits associated with various pharmaceutical treatments.

Pharmacy benefit manager (PBM) Many insurance companies, HMOs, and self-insured employers contract with these managers to manage drug benefit coverage for employees and health plan members. Common tools employed by these managers for drug benefits include management of pharmacy networks, implementation of generic substitution and mail-order programs, negotiation of rebates with drug manufacturers, formulary management, and clinical programs such as for disease management.

Physician assistant (PA) Also known as a physician extender; a specially trained and licensed or otherwise credentialed individual who performs tasks that might otherwise be performed by a physician, under the direction of a supervising physician.

Physician–hospital organization (PHO) A legal entity formed by a hospital and a group of physicians to further their mutual interests and to achieve market objectives; generally combines physicians and a hospital into a single organization for the purpose of obtaining payer contracts. Doctors maintain ownership of their practices and agree to accept managed care patients according to the terms of a professional services agreement with the entity. The entity serves as a collective negotiating and contracting unit. It is typically owned and governed jointly by a hospital and shareholder physicians.

Point of service A health insurance benefits program in which subscribers can select between different delivery systems (i.e., HMO, PPO, and fee-for-service) when in need of healthcare services, rather than making the selection between delivery systems at the time of open enrollment at the place of employment. Typically, the costs associated with receiving care from HMO providers are less than when care is rendered by PPO or noncontracting providers.

Population A set of individual people, objects, or items from which samples are taken for statistical measurement—for example, all of the patients with a disease or condition that are of interest for a particular study, such as all of the cases of myocardial infarction occurring within a given year.

Population-based services Health services targeted at populations of patients with specific diseases or disorders (e.g., patients with asthma or diabetes). The concept that health care can be better administered if patients are examined as populations as well as specific cases is one basis for disease management and managed care.

Portability Requirement that health plans guarantee continuous coverage without waiting periods for people moving between plans.

Postacute care Also called *subacute care* or *transitional care*; a kind of short-term care provided by many long-term care facilities and hospitals that may include rehabilitation services, specialized care for certain conditions (such as stroke and diabetes), and/or postsurgical care and other services associated with the transition between the hospital and home. Residents on these units often have been hospitalized recently and typically have more complicated medical needs. The goal is to discharge residents to their homes or to a lower level of care.

Potentially preventable adverse outcomes Complications of a condition that may be modified or prevented with appropriate treatment (e.g., permanent hearing loss as an outcome of otitis media with effusion).

Practice guidelines/parameters Standards used to guide providers based on accepted clinical treatment protocols for typical cases.

Preadmission certification A process under which admission to a health institution is reviewed in advance to determine need and appropriateness and to authorize a length of stay consistent with norms for the evaluation.

Preexisting condition A medical condition developed prior to issuance of a health insurance policy. Some policies exclude coverage of such conditions for a period of time or indefinitely.

Preferred drug list (or drug formulary) A list of prescription drugs that are covered by a health plan (or other payer; e.g., Medicaid). Some drugs may be subject to a prior authorization mechanism, whereby the physician or other prescriber must justify why the patient would need a particular brand-name product (see *prior authorization*).

Preferred provider arrangement (PPA) Selective contracting with a limited number of healthcare providers, often at reduced or prenegotiated rates of payment.

Preferred provider organization (PPO) Formally organized entity generally consisting of hospital and physician providers. The entity provides healthcare services to purchasers, usually at discounted rates, in return for expedited claims payment and a somewhat predictable market share. In this model, consumers have a choice of using providers in network or out of network; however, financial incentives are built into benefit structures to encourage utilization of in-network providers.

Premium The amount an individual pays each year to keep their insurance policy active.

Prepayment Any payment to a provider for anticipated services (such as an expectant mother paying in advance for maternity care). Sometimes this kind of payment is distinguished from insurance; that is, it refers to payments to organizations that, unlike insurance companies, take responsibility for arranging for and providing needed services as well as paying for them (such as health maintenance organizations, prepaid group practices, and medical foundations).

Prevailing charge One of the factors determining a physician's payment for a service under Medicare, set at a percentile of customary charges of all physicians in the locality.

Prevalence The number of cases of disease, infected people, or people with some other attribute, present at a particular time and in relation to the size of the population from which drawn. It can be a measurement of morbidity at a moment in time (e.g., the number of cases of hemophilia in the country as of the first day of the year).

Preventive medicine Care that has the aim of preventing disease or its consequences. It includes healthcare programs aimed at warding off illnesses (e.g., vaccinations), early detection of disease (e.g., Pap smears), and inhibiting further deterioration of the body (e.g., exercise or prophylactic surgery). This kind of care was developed after the discovery of bacterial diseases and was concerned in its early history with specific medical control measures taken against the agents of infectious diseases. It is also concerned with general preventive measures aimed at improving the healthfulness of the environment. In particular, the promotion of health through altering behavior, especially using health education, is gaining prominence as a component of preventive care.

Primary care Basic or general health care focused on the point at which a patient ideally first seeks assistance from the medical care system. This kind of care is considered comprehensive when the primary provider takes responsibility for the overall coordination of the care of the patient's health problems, be they biological, behavioral, or social. The appropriate use of consultants and community resources is an important part of effective care. Such care is generally provided by physicians but is increasingly provided by other personnel, such as nurse practitioners or physician assistants.

Primary care case management (PCCM) The use of a primary care physician to manage the use of medical or surgical care. This kind of program usually pays for all care on a fee-for-service basis.

Primary care provider (PCP) A generalist physician (family practice, general internal medicine, general pediatrics, and sometimes obstetrics/gynecology for female patients) who provides primary care services.

Primary payer The insurer obligated to pay losses before any liability is assumed by other, secondary insurers. Medicare, for instance, is a primary payer with respect to Medicaid.

Prior authorization A formal process requiring a provider to obtain approval to provide particular services or procedures before they are done. This is usually required for nonemergency services that are expensive or likely to be abused or overused. A managed care organization will identify those services and procedures that require this process, without which the provider may not be compensated.

Probability (*P* value) The likelihood that an event will occur. When looking at differences between data samples, statistical techniques are used to determine whether the differences are likely to reflect real differences in the whole group from which the sample is drawn or whether they are simply the result of random variation in the samples.

Proprietary Owned and operated for the purpose of making a profit, whether or not one is actually made.

Prospective payment Any method of paying hospitals or other health programs in which amounts or rates of payment are established in advance for a defined period (usually a year). Institutions are paid these amounts regardless of the costs they actually incur. These systems of payment are designed to introduce a degree of constraint on charge or cost increases by setting limits on amounts paid during a future period. In some cases, such systems provide incentives for improved efficiency by sharing savings with institutions that perform at lower than anticipated costs. This kind of payment contrasts with the method of payment originally used under Medicare and Medicaid (as well as other insurance programs) where institutions were reimbursed for actual expenses incurred.

Provider Hospital or licensed healthcare professional or group of hospitals or healthcare professionals that provide healthcare services to patients. May also refer to medical supply firms and vendors of durable medical equipment.

Public good A good or service whose benefits may be provided to a group at no more cost than that required to provide it for one person. The benefits of the good are indivisible and individuals cannot be excluded. For example, a public health measure that eradicates smallpox protects all members of the population, not just those paying for the vaccination.

Public health The science dealing with the protection and improvement of community health by organized community effort. Such activities are generally those that are less amenable to being undertaken by individuals or are less effective when undertaken on an individual basis and do not typically include direct personal health services. Such activities include administering vaccinations; sanitation; preventive medicine, quarantine, and other disease-control activities; occupational health and safety programs; assurance of the healthfulness of air, water, and food; health education; and epidemiology.

Q

Quality-adjusted life years (QALYs) Years of life saved by a medical technology or service, adjusted according to the quality of those years (as determined by some evaluative measure); the most commonly used unit to express the results in some types of cost-effectiveness analysis.

Quality improvement The sum of all of the activities that created a desired change in quality. In the healthcare setting, this kind of improvement requires a feedback loop that involves the identification of patterns of care for patients (or of the performance of other systems involved in care), the analysis of those patterns to identify opportunities for improvement (or instances of departure from standards of care), and then action to improve the quality of care for future patients.

Quality of care The degree to which delivered health services meet established professional standards and judgments of value to the consumer; may also be seen as the degree to which actions taken or not taken maximize the probability of beneficial health outcomes and minimize risk and other outcomes, given the existing state of medical science and art. It is frequently described as having three dimensions: quality of the input resources (certification and/or training of providers), quality of the process of service delivery (the use of appropriate procedures for a given condition), and quality of the outcome of service use (actual improvement in condition or reduction of harmful effects).

R

Rate A measure of the intensity of the occurrence of an event. For example, for mortality, this measure equals the number of people who die in one year divided by the number at risk of dying. This measure is usually expressed using a standard denominator, such as 1,000 or 10,000 people. It may also be expressed as a percentage.

Rate band The allowable variation in insurance premiums as defined in state regulations. The acceptable variation may be expressed as a ratio from highest to lowest, or as a percentage of the index rate (e.g., ±20%). It is used to limit variation for individual factors (such as age, gender, occupation, or geographic region) or to limit variation for all of these factors together (composite).

Rate review Evaluation by a government or private agency of a hospital's budget and financial data, performed for the purpose of determining the reasonableness of the hospital's charges and proposed increases of them.

Rate setting A method of paying healthcare providers in which the federal or state government establishes payment rates for all payers for various categories of health services.

Reference-based drug pricing A scheme adopted both within Canada (in British Columbia and Nova Scotia) and in other countries (including the United Kingdom, Australia, New Zealand, and Germany) as a means of limiting expenditures for drug subsidy and insurance programs; limits reimbursement for a group of drugs with similar therapeutic application but different active ingredients to the price of the lowest-cost drug within the group (the reference standard). Patients have the option of purchasing drugs that are partially subsidized, in which case they pay the difference between the retail price and the reference price.

Referral The process of sending a patient from one practitioner to another for healthcare services. Health plans may require that designated primary care providers authorize coverage of specialty services.

Rehabilitation The combined and coordinated use of medical, social, educational, and vocational measures for training or retraining individuals disabled by disease or injury to the highest possible level of functional ability. Several different types of training are distinguished: vocational, social, psychological, medical, and educational.

Reimbursement The process by which healthcare providers receive payment for their services. Because of the nature of the healthcare environment, providers are often paid by third parties that insure and represent patients.

Reinsurance The resale of insurance products to a secondary market, thereby spreading the costs associated with underwriting.

Relative risk The rate of disease in one group exposed to a particular factor (e.g., a toxic spill) divided by the rate in another group that is not exposed; indicates whether the two groups have the same rate of disease.

Reliability The extent to which a measurement can be replicated with low levels of random error in measurement.

Respite care Care given to a hospice patient by another caregiver so that the usual caregiver can rest.

Retrospective reimbursement Payment made after-the-fact for services rendered on the basis of costs incurred by the facility (see also *prospective payment*).

Revenue The gross amount of earnings received by an entity for the operation of a specific activity. It does not include any deductions for such items as expenses, bad debts, or contractual allowances.

Risk A term used by epidemiologists to quantify the likelihood that something will occur. Responsibility for paying for or otherwise providing a level of healthcare services based on an unpredictable need for these services.

Risk adjustment A process by which premium dollars are shifted from a plan with relatively healthy enrollees to another with sicker members. It is intended to minimize any financial incentives that health plans may have to select healthier-than-average enrollees. In this process, health plans that attract higher-risk providers and members would be compensated for any differences in the proportion of their members who require high levels of care compared with other plans.

Risk-based capital formula A method of establishing the minimum amount of capital appropriate for an insurance company to support its overall business operations in consideration of its size, structure, and risk profile. It is used to assess a managed care organization's financial viability and help prevent insolvency.

Risk-bearing entity An organization that assumes financial responsibility for the provision of a defined set of benefits by accepting prepayment for some or all of the cost of care; may be an insurer, a health plan or self-funded employer, or a physician–hospital organization or other form of professional services network.

Risk factor Something that either increases or decreases an individual's chance of developing a disease; however, it does not mean that, if exposed, an individual will definitely contract a particular disease.

Risk selection Occurs when a disproportionate share of high or low users of care join a health plan.

Risk sharing The distribution of financial risk among parties furnishing a service. For example, if a hospital and a group of physicians from a corporation provide health care at a fixed price, this kind of arrangement would entail both the hospital and the group being held liable if expenses exceed revenues.

Root-cause analysis A process for identifying the basic or causal factor(s) that underlies variations in performance, including the occurrence or possible occurrence of an error.

S

Safety net The network of providers and institutions that provide low-cost or free medical care to medically needy, low-income, or uninsured populations. This network can include (but is not limited to) individual practitioners, public and private hospitals, academic medical centers, and smaller clinics or ambulatory care facilities.

Safety net providers Providers that historically have had large Medicaid and indigent care caseloads relative to other providers and are willing to provide services regardless of the patient's ability to pay.

Sample In a statistical analysis, a finite subset of a statistical population whose properties are studied to gain information about the whole population or universe.

Screening The use of quick procedures to differentiate apparently well people who have a disease or a high risk of disease from those who probably do not have the disease. It is used to identify high-risk individuals for more definitive study or follow-up. *Multiple screening* is the combination of a battery of tests for various diseases performed by technicians under medical direction and applied to large groups of apparently well people.

Secondary care Services provided by medical specialists who generally do not have first contact with patients (e.g., cardiologists, urologists, dermatologists). In the United States, there has been a trend toward self-referral by patients for these services, rather than referral by primary care providers. This is quite different from the practice in England, for example, where all patients must first seek care from primary care providers and are then referred to secondary and/or tertiary providers, as needed.

Secondary payer An insurer obligated to pay losses above or beyond losses that are assumed by a primary payer.

Secondary prevention Early diagnosis, treatment, and follow-up. These activities start with the assumption that illness is already present and that primary prevention was not successful. The goal is to diminish the impact of disease or illness through early detection, diagnosis, and treatment (e.g., blood pressure screening, treatment, and follow-up programs).

Self-funding, self-insurance A scheme in which an employer or group of employers sets aside funds to cover the cost of health benefits for their employees. Benefits may be administered by the employer(s) or handled through an administrative service-only agreement with an insurance carrier or third-party administrator. Under this arrangement, it is generally possible to purchase stop-loss insurance that covers expenditures above a certain aggregate claim level and/or covers catastrophic illness or injury when individual claims reach a certain dollar threshold.

Semasko system A single-payer system that allows health care to be free for everyone. The state pays for all financial and coverage aspects of the healthcare system for its citizens through taxation.

Sensitivity A high rate of detection of *true positives* (e.g., the fraction of patients who actually received good care who are classified as recipients of good care).

Sentinel event An unexpected occurrence or variation involving death or serious physical or psychological injury, or the risk thereof. Serious injury specifically includes loss of limb or function. The event sends a signal or sounds a warning that requires immediate attention—hence the term.

Service period Period of employment that may be required before an employee is eligible to participate in an employer-sponsored health plan, most commonly 1 to 3 months.

Severity of illness A risk prediction system to correlate the seriousness of a disease in a particular patient with the statistically expected outcome (e.g., mortality, morbidity, efficiency of care). Most effectively, the seriousness is measured at or soon after admission, before therapy is initiated, giving a measure of pretreatment risk.

SF-12 A shorter version of the SF-36 (one-page, 2-minute) survey form, which has been shown to yield summary physical and mental health outcome scores that are interchangeable with those from the SF-36 in both general and specific populations. This shorter version of the SF-36 was published in early 1995 and is one of the most widely used surveys of health status.

SF-36 A comprehensive short-form health status questionnaire with only 36 questions that yields an eight-scale health profile as well as summary measures of health-related quality of life. As documented in more than 750 publications, this questionnaire has proved useful in monitoring general and specific populations, comparing the burden of different diseases, differentiating the health benefits produced by different treatments, and screening individual patients. This questionnaire is a standard measure of healthcare quality used by health service researchers and others who monitor quality of care. The survey is produced by Quality Metric, Inc.

Skilled nursing facility (SNF) A nursing care facility participating in the Medicaid and Medicare programs that meet specified requirements for services, staffing, and safety.

Social solidarity A principle of universal coverage that every insured person has the right to healthcare services under the same conditions.

Solo practice Lawful practice of a health occupation as a self-employed individual; by definition, a private practice but not necessarily a general practice or fee-for-service practice (this kind of practice may be paid by capitation, although fee-for-service is more common); common among physicians, dentists, podiatrists, optometrists, and pharmacists.

Specialist A physician, dentist, or other health professional who is specially trained in a certain branch of medicine or dentistry related to specific services or procedures (e.g., surgery, radiology, pathology), certain age categories of patients (e.g., geriatrics), certain body systems (e.g., dermatology, orthopedics, cardiology), or certain types of diseases (e.g., allergy, periodontics). These health professionals usually have advanced education and training related to their specialties.

Specificity A high rate of detection of *true negatives* (e.g., the fraction of patients who actually received bad care who are classified as recipients of bad care).

Spend down The amount of expenditures for healthcare services, relative to income, that qualifies an individual for Medicaid in states that cover categorically eligible, medically indigent individuals. Eligibility is determined on a case-by-case basis.

Standard error In statistics, the standard deviation of an estimate. That is, multiple measurements of a given value will generally group around the mean (or average) value in a normal distribution. The shape of this distribution is known by this term.

State Children's Health Insurance Program (SCHIP) A program enacted as part of the Balanced Budget Act of 1997, which established Title XXI of the Social Security Act to provide states with $24 billion in federal funds for 1998–2002, and targets children in families with incomes up to 200% of the federal poverty level.

Substance Abuse and Mental Health Services Administration (SAMHSA) The mission of this agency is to provide, through the U.S. Public Health Service, a national focus for the federal effort to promote effective prevention and treatment of addictive and mental disorders. It is primarily a grant-making organization, promoting knowledge and scientific state-of-the-art practice. It strives to reduce barriers to high-quality, effective programs and services for individuals who suffer from or are at risk for these disorders, as well as for their families and communities.

Supply In health economics, the quantity of services provided or personnel in a given area.

Survey An investigation in which information is systematically collected. For a population, this may be conducted by face-to-face inquiry, by self-completed questionnaires, by telephone, by postal service, or in some other way. Each method has its advantages and disadvantages. The generalizability of results depends on the extent to which those surveyed are representative of the entire population.

Swing-bed hospital A hospital participating in the Medicare program that allows rural hospitals with fewer than 100 beds to provide skilled postacute care services in acute care beds.

Systems approach A school of thought evolving from earlier systems analysis theory, which asserts that virtually all outcomes are the result of systems rather than individuals. In practice, this school of thought is characterized by attempts to improve the quality and/or efficiency of a process through improvements to the system.

Systems error An error that is not the result of an individual's actions, but the predictable outcome of a series of actions and factors that constitute a diagnostic or treatment process.

T

Taoism[15] Philosophy that holds humans and animals should live in balance with the Tao, or the universe. Taoists believe in spiritual immortality, where the spirit of the body joins the universe after death.

Technology assessment A comprehensive form of policy research that examines the technical, economic, and social consequences of technological applications. It is especially concerned with unintended, indirect, or delayed social impacts. In health policy, the term has come to mean any form of policy analysis concerned with medical technology, especially the evaluation of efficacy and safety.

Telehealth The use of telecommunications technologies and electronic information to support long-distance clinical health care, patient and professional health-related education, or public health and health administration.

Telemedicine The use of telecommunications (i.e., wire, radio, optical, or electromagnetic channels transmitting voice, data, and video) to facilitate medical diagnosis, patient care, and/or distance learning.

Tertiary care Services provided by highly specialized providers (e.g., neurologists, neurosurgeons, thoracic surgeons, and intensive care units). Such services frequently require highly sophisticated equipment and support facilities. The development of these services has largely been a function of diagnostic and therapeutic advances attained through basic and clinical biomedical research.

Tertiary prevention Prevention activities that focus on the individual after a disease or illness has manifested itself. The goal is to reduce long-term effects and to help individuals cope better with symptoms.

Third-party administrator (TPA) A fiscal intermediary (a person or an organization) that serves as another's financial agent. This intermediary processes claims, provides services, and issues payments on behalf of certain private, federal, and state health benefit programs or other insurance organizations.

Third-party payer Any organization, public or private, that pays or insures health or medical expenses on behalf of beneficiaries or recipients. An individual pays a premium for such coverage in all private and in some public programs; the payer organization then pays bills on the individual's behalf. These payments are distinguished by the separation among the individual receiving the service (the first party), the individual or institution providing it (the second party), and the organization paying for it (third party).

Title XIX (Medicaid) The title of the part of the Social Security Act that contains the principal legislative authority for the Medicaid program and, therefore, a common name for the program.

Title XVIII (Medicare) The title of the part of the Social Security Act that contains the principal legislative authority for the Medicare program and, therefore, a common name for the program.

U

Uncompensated care Services provided by physicians and hospitals for which no payment is received from the patient or from third-party payers. Some costs for these services may be covered through cost-shifting. Not all uncompensated care results from charity care. It also includes bad debts from people who are not classified as charity cases but who are unable or unwilling to pay their bill.

Underinsured People with public or private insurance policies that do not cover all necessary healthcare services, resulting in out-of-pocket expenses that exceed their ability to pay.

Underwriting In insurance, the process of selecting, classifying, evaluating, and assuming risks according to their insurability. Its purpose is to make sure that the group or individual insured has the same probability of loss and probable amount of loss, within reasonable limits, as the universe on which premium rates were based. Because premium rates are based on an expectation of loss, the underwriting process must classify risks into groups with about the same expectation of loss.

Uninsurables High-risk people who do not have healthcare coverage through private insurance and who fall outside the parameters of risks of standard health underwriting practices.

Uninsured People who lack public or private health insurance.

Unit (of analysis) The unit to which a performance measure is applied (e.g., patients, clinician, group of clinicians, institution).

Usual, customary, and reasonable (UCR) fees The use of fee screens to determine the lowest value of physician reimbursement based on the physician's usual charge for a given procedure, the amount customarily charged for the service by other physicians in the area (often defined as a specific percentile of all charges in the community), and the reasonable cost of services for a given patient after medical review of the case.

Utilization Use; commonly examined in terms of patterns or rates of use of a single service or type of service (e.g., hospital care, physician visits, prescription drugs). Use is also expressed in rates per unit of population at risk for a given period.

Utilization review Evaluation of the necessity, appropriateness, and efficiency of the use of healthcare services, procedures, and facilities. In a hospital, this includes review of the appropriateness of admissions, services ordered and provided, length of a stay, and discharge practices, both on a concurrent and a retrospective basis. This evaluation can be done by a peer review group or a public agency.

V

Validity The ability of a performance measure to capture what it purports to measure (e.g., a particular aspect of clinical care).

Vertical integration Organization of production whereby one business entity controls or owns all stages of the production and distribution of goods or services.

Vital statistics Statistics relating to births (natality), deaths (mortality), marriages, health, and disease (morbidity). For the United States, these are published by the National Center for Health Statistics.

Voluntary reporting A medical error reporting system where the reporter chooses to report an error to prevent similar errors from occurring in the future. One theory of this kind of system is that they allow reporters to focus on a set of errors broader than just those that cause serious harm and that they help to detect system weaknesses before the occurrence of serious harm.

W

Wellness A dynamic state of physical, mental, and social well-being. A way of life that equips the individual to realize the full potential of their capabilities and to overcome and compensate for weaknesses. A lifestyle that recognizes the importance of nutrition, physical fitness, stress reduction, and self-responsibility. Wellness has been viewed as the result of four key factors over which an individual has varying degrees of control: human biology, environment, healthcare organization (system), and lifestyle.

Withhold A form of compensation whereby a health plan does not pay a provider until the end of a value-based purchasing period, at which time the plan distributes any remaining funds based on provider performance. Provider performance can include measures such as the number and appropriateness of referrals to specialists, or the number of patients who receive preventive screenings (i.e., measures of cost-efficiency and/or quality of care). Value-based purchasing brings together information on the quality of health care, such as patient outcomes and health status, with data on the dollar outlays going toward health. It focuses on managing the use of the healthcare system to reduce inappropriate care and to identify and reward the best-performing providers. This strategy can be contrasted with more limited efforts to negotiate price discounts, which reduce costs but do little to ensure that quality of care is improved.

Working capital The sum of an institution's short-term or current assets, including cash, marketable (short-term) securities, accounts receivable, and inventories. Net working capital is defined as the excess of total current assets over total current liabilities.

World Bank[5,6] An organization that is a vital source of financial and technical assistance to developing countries around the world. Its primary focus is on helping the poorest people and countries. Two unique development institutions owned by 185 member countries—the International Bank for Reconstruction and Development (IBRD) and the International Development Association (IDA)—make up this organization. The IBRD focuses on middle-income and creditworthy poor countries, whereas IDA focuses on the poorest countries in the world. This organization provides low-interest loans and interest-free credit and grants to developing countries for education, health, infrastructure, communications, and many other purposes.

World Health Organization (WHO)[7] The organization that is the directing and coordinating authority for health within the United Nations system. Established in 1948, it has grown to have 193 member countries. It is responsible for providing leadership on global health matters, shaping the health research agenda, setting norms and standards, articulating evidence-based policy options, providing technical support to countries, and monitoring and assessing health trends.

World Trade Organization (WTO)[8] The only global international organization that deals with the rules of trade among nations. Led by the General Agreement on Tariffs and Trade (GATT), this organization was created on January 1, 1995. At the heart of the system, known as the multilateral trading system, are the organization's agreements, negotiated and signed by a large majority of the world's trading nations and ratified in their parliaments. These agreements are the legal ground rules for international commerce and cover trade in services and in traded inventions, creations, and designs (intellectual property). The goal is to help producers of goods and services, exporters, and importers conduct their business and thereby improve the welfare of the peoples of the member countries.

References

1. All terms, unless otherwise indicated, are from *Glossary of Terms Commonly Used in Health Care*, 2004 edition, published by AcademyHealth. A more expansive glossary is available on its website, www.academyhealth.org.
2. Cornia GA. Globalization and health: results and options. *Bull World Health Organ*. 2001;79(9):834-841.
3. Woodward D, Drager N, Beaglehole R, Lipson D. Globalization and health: a framework for analysis and action. *Bull World Health Organ*. 2001;79(9):875-881.
4. Riegelman R, Kirkwood B. *One Health: From AIDS to Zika*. Burlington, MA: Jones & Bartlett Learning; 2018.
5. World Bank. About the World Bank. Available from http://web.worldbank.org/WBSITE/EXTERNAL/EXTABOUTUS/0,pagePK:50004410~piPK:36602~theSitePK:29708,00.html.
6. World Bank. *World Bank Group: Working for a World Free of Poverty*. http://siteresources.worldbank.org/EXTABOUTUS/Resources/wbgroupbrochure-en07.pdf.
7. World Health Organization. About WHO. Accessed December 4, 2016. http://www.who.int/about/en/.
8. World Trade Organization. *The World Trade Organization*. Published in 2014. Accessed December 4, 2016. http://www.wto.org/english/res_e/doload_e/inbr_e.pdf.
9. American Nurses Association, American Nurses Credentialing Center, American Nurses Foundation. Advanced Practice Registered Nurse. https://www.nursingworld.org/practice-policy/workforce/what-is-nursing/aprn/#:~:text=APRNs%20include%20nurse%20practitioners%2C%20clinical,care%20services%20to%20the%20public.
10. McCallaghan S. Work-place diversity climate: its association with racial microaggressions and employee work-place well-being. *J Psychol Africa*. 2022;32(6):560-568. doi: 10.1080/14330237.2022.2121476.

11. Brainly. Definition of Deprivation. https://brainly.in/question/55721887.
12. Wikipedia, Definition of Parliamentary republic. https://en.wikipedia.org/wiki/Parliamentary_republic#:~:text=A%20parliamentary%20republic%20is%20a,the%20legislature%20(the%20parliament).
13. Mitchell PH. Chapter 1. Defining patient safety and quality care. In: Hughes RG, ed. Patient Safety and Quality: An Evidence-Based Handbook for Nurses. Agency for Healthcare Research and Quality (US); 2008. https://www.ncbi.nlm.nih.gov/books/NBK2681/
14. U.S. Department of Labor Occupational Safety and Health Administration, Personal Protective Equipment. https://www.osha.gov/sites/default/files/publications/OSHA3151.pdf.
15. National Geographic Society, ENCYCLOPEDIC ENTRY: Taoism. https://education.nationalgeographic.org/resource/taoism/.

Index

Note: Page numbers followed by *b*, *f*, or *t* indicate material in boxes, figures, or tables, respectively.

D

E

F

G

H

I

J

K

L

M

N

O

P

R

U

V

W

Z